SOFTWARE INFORMATION!

for

Macintosh®
COMPUTERS

TABLE OF CONTENTS

ABOUT MENU® PUBLISHING

Since 1979, MENU® has been building

a database of information about

software for *any* system and

publishing this information in

directories and special-interest books.

The information is also available on

disk, through on-line services such as

DIALOG® and AppleLink®, and will

soon be available on CD-ROM.

As the premiere software

information broker, MENU® is

dedicated to helping consumers make

educated software-buying decisions.

Each MENU® book is carefully

researched for accuracy and includes

helpful indexes.

HOW TO USE THIS DIRECTORY

In each directory ...
We list vital information for thousands of software packages — price, publisher name, system and memory requirements, and a short description.

Find what you need fast ...
MENU® directories are easy to use. We've grouped software listings into over 140 subject categories, and we've included three indexes to help you quickly locate a particular subject, package, or publisher. The Publisher Directory includes publishers' addresses; phone, fax, and telex numbers.

Special requirements ...
Some software is available in lab packs or school versions, or may have special requirements. You'll find this information in the "Requires" section of each listing.

To arrange a purchase ...
Use the Publisher Directory to locate a publisher's phone number — and then call! Or call your favorite software store.

Need more information?
Call MENU® at (412) 746-MENU®. For $3.50 per package, we'll compile and mail you an ISPN® Print — an in-depth description of a package's features, functions, and benefits.

If you have any questions ...
Just give us a call at (412) 746-MENU®.

SUBJECT CATEGORY INDEX

CONTINUED

700 PROFESSIONS/SERVICES

800 SYSTEMS

101 PRODUCTIVITY/ ACCOUNTING – FIXED ASSET

SBT CORP.
SBT DASSETS-COMPILED (VER. 6.20)

Provides a computerized system for maintaining records of assets and calculating depreciation.
System: MAC, II, PLUS, SE, XL
Minimum Memory: 512K
Medium: 3 1/2-inch disk
ISPN: 68057-051   **Price: $295.00**

SBT CORP.
SBT DASSETS-STANDARD (VER. 6.20)

Provides a computerized system for maintaining records of assets and calculating depreciation.
System: MAC, II, PLUS, SE, XL
Minimum Memory: 512K
Medium: 3 1/2-inch disk
ISPN: 68057-050   **Price: $395.00**

103 PRODUCTIVITY/ ACCOUNTING – GENERAL LEDGER

LAKE AVE. SOFTWARE
ASSISTANT CONTROLLER SERIES-GENERAL LEDGER

Offers double-entry bookkeeping with a complete audit trail. Includes advanced error-checking routines.
System: MAC, II, PLUS, SE, XL
Minimum Memory: 512K
Medium: 3 1/2-inch disk
ISPN: 43418-310   **Price: $495.00**

SATORI SOFTWARE
COMPONENTS GENERAL LEDGER (VER. 1.0)

Includes flexible set-up, unlimited custom journals such as cash disbursements and cash receipts, and forms oriented output.
System: MAC, II, PLUS, SE, XL
Minimum Memory: 1024K
Requires: 800K disk drive.
Medium: 3 1/2-inch disk
ISPN: 68024-110   **Price: $595.00**

FLEXWARE, INC.
FLEXWARE GENERAL LEDGER

Accommodates small or large companies and includes audit trails and up-to-the-minute analysis.
System: MAC
Minimum Memory: 256K
Requires: 20 MB hard disk.
Medium: 3 1/2-inch disk
ISPN: 52468-150   **Price: $795.00**

COMPUTER ASSOCIATES/MICRO PRODUCTS DIVISION
GENERAL ACCOUNTING FOR THE MACINTOSH

Provides an enhanced general ledger with subsidiary ledgers for payroll with data export capabilities included.
System: MAC
Minimum Memory: 512K
Medium: 3 1/2-inch disk
ISPN: 74700-780   **Price: $89.00**

JAMES RIVER GROUP, INC.
GENERAL LEDGER

Standard double entry accounting for firms with under $2,000,000 per year in sales. Interfaces with other modules.
System: MAC, II, PLUS, SE, XL
Minimum Memory: 512K
Medium: 3 1/2-inch disk
ISPN: 41412-100   **Price: $125.00**

BLACK BANANA, INC.
GENERAL LEDGER

Provides unlimited chart of accounts with categories and types, amortization and depreciation option, and system defined accounts.
System: MAC, II, PLUS, SE, XL
Minimum Memory: 512K
Requires: Two 800k disk drives or hard disk drive.
Medium: 3 1/2-inch disk
ISPN: 07838-200   **Price: $250.00**

EXCEIVER CORP.
GENERAL LEDGER

Contains the modifiable core module of a basic integrated accounting system, written in the Omnis 3 Plus database manager.
System: MAC, II, PLUS, SE, XL
Minimum Memory: 512K
Medium: 3 1/2-inch disk
ISPN: 91574-251   **Price: $295.00**

CHAMPION BUSINESS SYSTEMS
GENERAL LEDGER

Allows for automatic update of cash receipts journal, cash disbursements journal, general journal and general ledger.
System: MAC, II, PLUS, SE, XL
Minimum Memory: 1024K
Requires: 800K hard disk.
Medium: 3 1/2-inch disk
ISPN: 12175-400   **Price: $395.00**

GREAT PLAINS SOFTWARE
GREAT PLAINS ACCOUNTING SERIES-GENERAL LEDGER 5.0

Can handle 2000 accounts, 99 cross accounts, 36 locations and 999 departments. Retains financial detail for a full fiscal year.
System: MAC, II, PLUS, SE, XL
Minimum Memory: 512K
Requires: 20 MB hard disk, 132 column printer, or 80 column printer with condensed print.
Medium: 3 1/2-inch disk
ISPN: 33475-075   **Price: $795.00**

LAYERED, INC.
INSIGHT EXPERT GENERAL LEDGER (VER. 2.10)

Includes flexible reporting formats and provides graphical analysis with textual explanation and recommendations for management action.
System: MAC, II, PLUS, SE, XL
Minimum Memory: 1024K
Requires: Hard disk.
Medium: 3 1/2-inch disk
ISPN: 43760-650   **Price: $695.00**

LAKE AVE. SOFTWARE
MULTI COMPANY-GENERAL LEDGER

Offers double-entry bookkeeping with a complete audit trail, also includes advanced error-checking routines.
System: MAC, II, PLUS, SE, XL
Minimum Memory: 512K
Medium: 3 1/2-inch disk
ISPN: 43418-682   **Price: $695.00**

CHANG LABORATORIES, INC.
RAGS TO RICHES-GENERAL LEDGER (VER. 3.0)

Double entry general ledger module which is used as the 'core' of an integrated accounting system.
System: MAC, II, PLUS, SE, XL
Minimum Memory: 128K
Medium: 3 1/2-inch disk
ISPN: 12200-770   **Price: $199.95**

SBT CORP.
SBT DLEDGER-COMPILED (VER. 6.20)

Provides complete general ledger and financial reporting capabilities. Allows user-defined ledger accounts.
System: MAC, II, PLUS, SE, XL
Minimum Memory: 512K
Medium: 3 1/2-inch disk
ISPN: 68057-201   **Price: $295.00**

SBT CORP.
SBT DLEDGER-STANDARD (VER. 6.20)

Provides complete general ledger and financial reporting capabilities and allows user-defined ledger accounts.
System: MAC, II, PLUS, SE, XL
Minimum Memory: 512K
Medium: 3 1/2-inch disk
ISPN: 68057-200   **Price: $395.00**

FUTURE DESIGN SOFTWARE
STRICTLY BUSINESS MODULE I-GEN LEDGER (VER. 1.91)

Provides complete up-to-the-minute records and reports: multiple profit centers, chart of accounts, systems reports and more.

System: MAC, II, PLUS, SE, XL
Minimum Memory: 512K
Medium: 3 1/2-inch disk
ISPN: 91864-750　　　**Price: $395.00**

107 PRODUCTIVITY/ ACCOUNTING – INTEGRATED SYSTEMS

SOFTSYNC, INC.
ACCOUNTANT, INC. (VER. 2.11)

Includes Accounts Receivable, Accounts Payable, Inventory Control, and General Ledger Modules, fully integrated, on one disk.

System: MAC, II, PLUS, SE, XL
Minimum Memory: 512K
Requires: 800k disk drive, ImageWriter printer.
Medium: 3 1/2-inch disk
ISPN: 72240-050　　　**Price: $299.95**

SOFTSYNC, INC.
ACCOUNTANT, INC. PROFESSIONAL (VER. 1.0)

Includes General Ledger, Accounts Payable, Accounts Receivable, Payroll, Inventory, Job Costing and Reporting functions.

System: MAC, II, PLUS, SE, XL
Minimum Memory: 1024K
Requires: 800K disk drive.
Medium: 3 1/2-inch disk
ISPN: 72240-055　　　**Price: $595.00**

JAMES RIVER GROUP, INC.
ACCOUNTING FOR MICROS

Contains general ledger, accounts receivable, accounts payable and inventory or payroll.

System: MAC, II, PLUS, SE, XL
Minimum Memory: 512K
Medium: 3 1/2-inch disk
ISPN: 41412-050　　　**Price: $395.00**

S & J ENTERPRISES
AR/AP/INVENTORY (VER. 3.2)

Provides for an open item Accounts Payable and Accounts Receivable, with inventory control and password protection.

System: MAC, II, PLUS, SE, XL
Minimum Memory: 512K
Requires: Hard disk and ImageWriter printer.
Medium: 3 1/2-inch disk
ISPN: 67356-100　　　**Price: $250.00**

LAKE AVE. SOFTWARE
ASSISTANT CONTROLLER SERIES-BANK RECONCILIATION

Works together with general ledger, accounts receivable/payable and payroll to reconcile various cash accounts.

System: MAC, II, PLUS, SE, XL
Minimum Memory: 512K
Medium: 3 1/2-inch disk
ISPN: 43418-100　　　**Price: $125.00**

PEACHTREE SOFTWARE, INC.
BACK TO BASICS: PRO (4 PAK) GL/AP/AR/INVOICING

A double-entry accrual accounting system consisting of accounts payable, accounts receivable, invoicing and general ledger options.

System: MAC, II, PLUS, SE, XL
Minimum Memory: 512K
Requires: Two disk drives, 80 column printer.
Medium: 3 1/2-inch disk
ISPN: 60150-226　　　**Price: $199.00**

BAKER GRAPHICS
BAKERFORMS PACKAGE

Contains four separate programs, Accounts Receivable, Purchasing, Payroll and Accounts payable.

System: MAC, II, PLUS, SE, XL
Minimum Memory: 512K
Requires: Microsoft Works (ISPN 53150-740) and ImageWriter printer.
Medium: 3 1/2-inch disk
ISPN: 06712-150　　　**Price: $169.00**

BEDFORD SOFTWARE
BEDFORD INTEGRATED ACCOUNTING SYSTEM

Contains an integrated system for small business that does not require user to have extensive accounting or computer experience.

System: MAC, II, PLUS, SE, XL
Minimum Memory: 512K
Medium: 3 1/2-inch disk
ISPN: 07243-100　　　**Price: $349.00**

MONOGRAM SOFTWARE, INC.
BUSINESS SENSE (VER. 1.2)

Contains integrated General Ledger, Accounts Receivable, Accounts Payable, Payroll, Invoicing and Budgeting.

System: MAC, II, PLUS, SE, XL
Minimum Memory: 512K
Requires: Two 800k disk drives or hard disk.
Medium: 3 1/2-inch disk
ISPN: 55240-100　　　**Price: $495.00**

WORKING COMPUTER
CLIENTS AND PROFITS FOR ADVERTISING AGENCIES

Builds job tickets and manages progress to the completed invoice.

System: MAC, II, PLUS, SE, XL
Minimum Memory: 1024K
Requires: Hard disk.
Medium: 3 1/2-inch disk
ISPN: 96949-127　　　**Price: $2495.00**

WORKING COMPUTER
CLIENTS AND PROFITS FOR ADVERTISING AGENCIES

Builds job tickets and manages progress to the completed invoice.

System: MAC, II, PLUS, SE, XL
Minimum Memory: 1024K
Requires: Multi-user. Hard disk and network server software.
Medium: 3 1/2-inch disk
ISPN: 96949-127　　　**Price: $3795.00**

UNICOM SOFTWARE DEVELOPMENT GROUP
DBJOBS

Provides a job management system that integrates with accounting modules from SBT Corporation for job costing.

System: PLUS, SE
Minimum Memory: 1024K
Requires: 10 MB hard disk.
Medium: 3 1/2-inch disk
ISPN: 83550-410　　　**Price: $895.00**

EQUAL PLUS
FINANCIAL PLUS

Provides general ledger, accounts payable and receivable, and payroll programs on one disk.

System: MAC, II, PLUS, SE, XL
Minimum Memory: 512K
Medium: 3 1/2-inch disk
ISPN: 29584-300　　　**Price: $295.00**

NILES AND ASSOCIATES
GRANT MANAGER

An accounting program used to track grant expenditures.

System: MAC, II, PLUS, SE, XL
Minimum Memory: 512K
Medium: 3 1/2-inch disk
ISPN: 56952-300　　　**Price: $425.00**

GREAT PLAINS SOFTWARE
GREAT PLAINS ACCT SERIES-NETWORK MANAGER 4.1

Provides a multi-user solution on a LAN for modules in the Great Plains Accounting Series (4.2 or higher).

System: MAC, II, PLUS, SE, XL
Minimum Memory: 1024K
Requires: Great Plains Accounting Series modules, 20 MB hard disk, dedicated file server, 132 column printer.
Medium: 3 1/2-inch disk
ISPN: 33475-600　　　**Price: $795.00**

BLACK BANANA, INC.
IC & GL

A complete accounting system for small businesses which contains Inventory Control and General Ledger packages.

System: MAC, II, PLUS, SE, XL
Minimum Memory: 512K
Medium: 3 1/2-inch disk
ISPN: 07838-100　　　**Price: $400.00**

MIGENT SOFTWARE CORP.
IN-HOUSE ACCOUNTANT FOR MACINTOSH (VER. 1.04)

Performs accounts receivable, payables, a general ledger, invoicing, billing, inventory and ATF Payroll functions.

System: MAC, II, PLUS, SE, XL
Minimum Memory: 512K
Requires: 800K drive or two 400K drives.
Medium: 3 1/2-inch disk
ISPN: 87037-380 **Price: $199.00**

LAYERED, INC.
INSIGHT ONEWRITE (VER. 1.00)

Contains three systems used in small businesses which include cash disbursement, accounts receivable and general ledger.

System: MAC, II, PLUS, SE, XL
Minimum Memory: 1024K
Medium: 3 1/2-inch disk
ISPN: 43760-660 **Price: $299.00**

CHECKMARK SOFTWARE, INC.
MULTILEDGER (VER. 1.1)

Integrates general ledger, accounts payable, accounts receivable and inventory tracking.

System: MAC, II, PLUS, SE, XL
Minimum Memory: 512K
Medium: 3 1/2-inch disk
ISPN: 04612-500 **Price: $395.00**

CIRCO BUSINESS SOLUTIONS
MULTIUSER DESKTOP ACCOUNTING

A multi-user, multi-functional accounting package that organizes businesses and offers procedures to run a competitive company.

System: MAC, II, PLUS, SE, XL
Minimum Memory:
Medium: 3 1/2-inch disk
ISPN: 12676-500 **Price: $2495.00**

ABACOUNT, INC.
NOVACOUNT (VER. 1.0)

A totally integrated job costing, invoicing and accounting system for businesses which bill their clients for labor and materials.

System: MAC, II, PLUS, SE, XL
Minimum Memory: 2048K
Medium: 3 1/2-inch disk
ISPN: 00293-200 **Price: $4000.00**

JANAC ENTERPRISES
OMNIBOOKS (VER. 1.0)

Contains General Ledger, Accounts Receivable with invoicing, and Accounts Payable with check writing.

System: MAC, II, PLUS, SE, XL
Minimum Memory: 512K
Requires: 800K disk drive, hard disk, Omnis 3 Plus/Express (ISPN 58775-515), or Omnis 3 Plus Runtime.
Medium: 3 1/2-inch disk
ISPN: 41438-050 **Price: $139.95**

JAMES RIVER GROUP, INC.
OPEN FOR BUSINESS I (VER. 1.1)

Provides the user with three modules including accounts receivable, cash disbursements and general ledger.

System: MAC, II, PLUS, SE, XL
Minimum Memory: 512K
Medium: 3 1/2-inch disk
ISPN: 41412-780 **Price: $595.00**

JAMES RIVER GROUP, INC.
OPEN FOR BUSINESS II (VER. 1.1)

Allows the user to perform the following accounting functions: accounts receivable and payable, general ledger and inventory.

System: MAC, II, PLUS, SE, XL
Minimum Memory: 512K
Requires: Hard disk.
Medium: 3 1/2-inch disk
ISPN: 41412-790 **Price: $995.00**

GREAT PLAINS SOFTWARE
PLAINS & SIMPLE

AR, AP and GL in familiar One-Write format with Cashflow Calendar, sample charts of accounts, on-line help and two dozen reports.

System: MAC, II, PLUS, SE, XL
Minimum Memory: 512K
Requires: Two disk drives or hard disk. ImageWriter or compatible printer.
Medium: 3 1/2-inch disk
ISPN: 33475-850 **Price: $395.00**

CHANG LABORATORIES, INC.
RAGS TO RICHES GENERAL BUSINESS 3-PAK (VER. 3.0)

Includes General Ledger, Accounts Payable, and Accounts Receivable.

System: MAC, II, PLUS, SE, XL
Minimum Memory: 512K
Medium: 3 1/2-inch disk
ISPN: 12200-745 **Price: $499.95**

WORKING COMPUTER
S.B.A. SMALL BUSINESS ACCOUNTING

Integrates receivables, payables, invoicing, purchase orders, inventory, publishers and customers for Omnis 3 Plus/Express.

System: MAC, II, PLUS, SE, XL
Minimum Memory: 1024K
Requires: Hard disk, ImageWriter, Omnis 3 Plus/Express (ISPN 58775-320).
Medium: 3 1/2-inch disk
ISPN: 96949-300 **Price: $995.00**

SBT CORP.
SBT DMAINTENANCE-COMPILED (VER. 6.10)

Tracks maintenance, service contracts, and lease payments on a wide variety of equipment categories.

System: MAC, II, PLUS, SE, XL
Minimum Memory: 512K
Medium: 3 1/2-inch disk
ISPN: 68057-950 **Price: $295.00**

SBT CORP.
SBT DMAINTENANCE-STANDARD (VER. 6.10)

Tracks maintenance, service contracts, and lease payments on a wide variety of equipment categories.

System: MAC, II, PLUS, SE, XL
Minimum Memory: 512K
Medium: 3 1/2-inch disk
ISPN: 68057-900 **Price: $395.00**

CIRCO BUSINESS SOLUTIONS
SINGLEUSER DESKTOP ACCOUNTING

An integrated accounting package that will fit any business need.

System: MAC, II, PLUS, SE, XL
Minimum Memory: 512K
Medium: 3 1/2-inch disk
ISPN: 12676-600 **Price: $1795.00**

COLLIER SOFTWARE
TIME IS MONEY-ARCHITECTS AND ENGINEERS (VER. 1.1)

A complete billing and management program for architects and engineers.

System: MAC, II, PLUS, SE, XL
Minimum Memory: 512K
Requires: Reflex Plus (ISPN 08225-086), two 800K disk drives or a hard disk.
Medium: 3 1/2-inch disk
ISPN: 13456-705 **Price: $399.00**

COLLIER SOFTWARE
TIME IS MONEY-BASIC PROFESSIONAL (VER. 1.1)

A complete billing and management program for design or service professionals.

System: MAC, II, PLUS, SE, XL
Minimum Memory: 512K
Requires: Reflex Plus (ISPN 08225-086), two 800K disk drives or a hard disk.
Medium: 3 1/2-inch disk
ISPN: 13456-700 **Price: $265.00**

WOS DATA SYSTEMS, INC.
WOS FUND ACCOUNTING SYSTEM

Includes general ledger, payroll, accounts receivable, purchase order and voucher, and revenue and expenditure.

System: MAC, II, PLUS, SE, XL
Minimum Memory: 512K
Medium: 3 1/2-inch disk
ISPN: 96946-151 **Price: $4995.00**

109 PRODUCTIVITY/ ACCOUNTS PAYABLE/ CHECKWRITING

CHAMPION BUSINESS SYSTEMS
ACCOUNTS PAYABLE

Provides check printing with automatic updates to other programs, several reports and automatic computation of payroll taxes.

System: MAC, II, PLUS, SE, XL
Minimum Memory: 1024K
Requires: 800K hard disk.
Medium: 3 1/2-inch disk
ISPN: 12175-105   **Price: $395.00**

EXCEIVER CORP.
ACCOUNTS PAYABLE

Provides one part of a complete accounting system that can stand alone or be integrated with other accounting modules.

System: MAC, II, PLUS, SE, XL
Minimum Memory: 512K
Requires: Omnis 3 Plus/Express (ISPN 58775-515), 800K disk drive.
Medium: 3 1/2-inch disk
ISPN: 91574-280   **Price: $295.00**

LAKE AVE. SOFTWARE
ASSISTANT CONTROLLER SERIES-ACCOUNTS PAYABLE

Keeps track of cash disbursements and projecting cash requirements. Also prints checks.

System: MAC, II, PLUS, SE, XL
Minimum Memory: 512K
Medium: 3 1/2-inch disk
ISPN: 43418-062   **Price: $495.00**

BAKER GRAPHICS
BAKERFORMS FOR ACCOUNTS PAYABLE

Allows user to keep accurate records and process pin-feed accounts payable checks.

System: MAC, II, PLUS, SE, XL
Minimum Memory: 512K
Requires: Microsoft Works (ISPN 53150-740) and ImageWriter printer.
Medium: 3 1/2-inch disk
ISPN: 06712-200   **Price: $49.95**

HEIZER SOFTWARE
BUSINESS CHECK PRINTER

Includes payee, check amount in both numbers and text, date, sequential check number, memo, additional notes and date.

System: MAC, II, PLUS, SE, XL
Minimum Memory: 512K
Requires: Microsoft Excel (ISPN 53150-270).
Medium: 3 1/2-inch disk
ISPN: 35175-005   **Price: $20.00**

FLEXWARE, INC.
FLEXWARE ACCOUNTS PAYABLE (VER. 5.0)

Helps user increase profits through reduced labor, cash flow forecasting and automatic payments.

System: MAC, II, PLUS, SE, XL
Minimum Memory: 256K
Medium: 3 1/2-inch disk
ISPN: 52468-050   **Price: $795.00**

GREAT PLAINS SOFTWARE
GREAT PLAINS ACCOUNTING SERIES-ACCOUNTS PAY 4.1

Efficiently handles 3000 publishers with complete publisher history.

System: MAC, II, PLUS, SE, XL
Minimum Memory: 512K
Requires: 20 MB hard disk, 800K disk drive, 132 column printer or 80 column with condensed print.
Medium: 3 1/2-inch disk
ISPN: 33475-025   **Price: $795.00**

LAYERED, INC.
INSIGHT EXPERT ACCOUNTS PAYABLE (VER. 2.02)

A full-featured program which supports either the cash or accrual methods of accounting.

System: MAC, II, PLUS, SE, XL
Minimum Memory: 1024K
Requires: Hard disk.
Medium: 3 1/2-inch disk
ISPN: 43760-600   **Price: $695.00**

LAKE AVE. SOFTWARE
MULTI COMPANY-ACCOUNTS PAYABLE

Keeps track of cash disbursements and projection cash requirements.

System: MAC, II, PLUS, SE, XL
Minimum Memory: 512K
Medium: 3 1/2-inch disk
ISPN: 43418-558   **Price: $695.00**

ORION COMPUTER TRAINING SYSTEMS
ORION FINANCIAL MANAGER I

Includes multiple checking accounts, auto pay, check printing, auto deposit, bank statement reconciliation and auto balance.

System: MAC, II, PLUS, SE, XL
Minimum Memory: 1024K
Medium: 3 1/2-inch disk
ISPN: 58862-520   **Price: $69.95**

ORION COMPUTER TRAINING SYSTEMS
ORION FINANCIAL MANAGER II

Includes multiple checking accounts, auto pay, check printing, auto deposits, bank statement reconciliation, and auto balance.

System: MAC, II, PLUS, SE, XL
Minimum Memory: 1024K
Requires: Omnis 3 Plus/Express (ISPN 58775-515).
Medium: 3 1/2-inch disk
ISPN: 58862-530   **Price: $199.95**

EXCEIVER CORP.
PAYROLL

A complete package for payroll needs.

System: MAC, II, PLUS, SE, XL
Minimum Memory: 512K
Requires: Omnis 3 Plus/Express (ISPN 58775-515), 800K disk drive.
Medium: 3 1/2-inch disk
ISPN: 91574-275   **Price: $295.00**

ANAMATRIX, INC.
POS-IM

A point-of-sale inventory management system.

System: MAC, II, PLUS, SE, XL
Minimum Memory: 1024K
Requires: 20MB hard disk, ImageWriter printer.
Medium: 3 1/2-inch disk
ISPN: 03468-100   **Price: $2495.00**

ANAMATRIX, INC.
POS-IM

A point-of-sale inventory management system.

System: MAC, II, PLUS, SE, XL
Minimum Memory: 1024K
Requires: 20MB hard disk, ImageWriter printer.
Medium: 3 1/2-inch disk
ISPN: 03468-100   **Price: $3995.00**

CHANG LABORATORIES, INC.
RAGS TO RICHES-ACCOUNTS PAYABLE (VER. 3.0)

Tracks all outstanding accounts payable. Invoices may be aged according to length from date of receipt.

System: MAC, II, PLUS, SE, XL
Minimum Memory: 512K
Medium: 3 1/2-inch disk
ISPN: 12200-750   **Price: $199.95**

SBT CORP.
SBT DPAYABLES-COMPILED (VER. 6.20)

Provides an accounts payable system including check register and checks, aged cash requirements and distribution of payment to G/L.

System: MAC, II, PLUS, SE, XL
Minimum Memory: 512K
Medium: 3 1/2-inch disk
ISPN: 68057-301   **Price: $295.00**

SBT CORP.
SBT DPAYABLES-STANDARD (VER. 6.20)

Provides an accounts payable system including check register and checks, aged cash requirements and distribution of payment to G/L.

System: MAC, II, PLUS, SE, XL
Minimum Memory: 512K
Medium: 3 1/2-inch disk
ISPN: 68057-300   **Price: $395.00**

112 PRODUCTIVITY/ ACCOUNTS RECEIVABLE

JAMES RIVER GROUP, INC.
ACCOUNTS RECEIVABLE

Contains a standard double-entry accounting module providing on-screen prompting and error checking.

System: MAC, II, PLUS, SE, XL
Minimum Memory: 512K
Medium: 3 1/2-inch disk
ISPN: 41412-300 **Price: $125.00**

CHAMPION BUSINESS SYSTEMS
ACCOUNTS RECEIVABLE

Provides both point-of-sale invoicing and invoicing from sales orders.

System: MAC, II, PLUS, SE, XL
Minimum Memory: 1024K
Requires: 800K hard disk.
Medium: 3 1/2-inch disk
ISPN: 12175-100 **Price: $395.00**

EXCEIVER CORP.
ACCOUNTS RECEIVABLE

Provides custom entry screens and reports, and can be used as a stand-alone or integrated with other modules.

System: MAC, II, PLUS, SE, XL
Minimum Memory: 512K
Requires: Omnis 3 Plus/Express (ISPN 58775-515), 800K disk drive.
Medium: 3 1/2-inch disk
ISPN: 91574-270 **Price: $295.00**

LAKE AVE. SOFTWARE
ASSISTANT CONTROLLER SERIES-ACCOUNTS RECEIVABLE

Provides quick, up-to-date reports of accounts receivable balances.

System: MAC, II, PLUS, SE, XL
Minimum Memory: 512K
Medium: 3 1/2-inch disk
ISPN: 43418-186 **Price: $495.00**

BAKER GRAPHICS
BAKERFORMS FOR ACCOUNTS RECEIVABLE

Allows user to keep accurate records and process pin-feed invoices and statements.

System: MAC, II, PLUS, SE, XL
Minimum Memory: 512K
Requires: Microsoft Works (ISPN 53150-740) and ImageWriter printer.
Medium: 3 1/2-inch disk
ISPN: 06712-220 **Price: $49.95**

SHOPKEEPER SOFTWARE
BILL-IT (VER. 1.09)

Consists of Accounts Receivable, Billing, Inventory list, Invoicing and Sales. Each part may operate separately.

System: MAC, II, PLUS, SE, XL
Minimum Memory: 512K
Requires: ImageWriter II or compatible, two 800K disk drives or hard disk.
Medium: 3 1/2-inch disk
ISPN: 69805-200 **Price: $159.00**

FLEXWARE, INC.
FLEXWARE ACCOUNTS RECEIVABLE (VER. 5.30)

Designed for manual use or for interface with the order processing program for automatic invoicing and general ledger update.

System: MAC, II, PLUS, SE, XL
Minimum Memory: 256K
Medium: 3 1/2-inch disk
ISPN: 52468-100 **Price: $795.00**

GREAT PLAINS SOFTWARE
GREAT PLAINS ACCOUNTING SERIES-ACCOUNTS REC. 4.1

Handles 3000 customers, balance forward or open item.

System: MAC, II, PLUS, SE, XL
Minimum Memory: 512K
Requires: 800K disk drive, 10 MB hard disk, 132 column printer or 80 column printer with condensed print.
Medium: 3 1/2-inch disk
ISPN: 33475-026 **Price: $795.00**

LAYERED, INC.
INSIGHT EXPERT ACCTS. REC. & BILLING (VER. 2.1)

Offers full billing functions, which include generating multiple types of invoices and statements.

System: MAC, II, PLUS, SE, XL
Minimum Memory: 1024K
Requires: 800K disk drive, AppleTalk, and LaserWriter.
Medium: 3 1/2-inch disk
ISPN: 43760-610 **Price: $695.00**

LAKE AVE. SOFTWARE
MULTI COMPANY-ACCOUNTS RECEIVABLE

Includes option to account for receivables on an open item or a balance forward method.

System: MAC, II, PLUS, SE, XL
Minimum Memory: 512K
Medium: 3 1/2-inch disk
ISPN: 43418-620 **Price: $695.00**

CHANG LABORATORIES, INC.
RAGS TO RICHES-ACCOUNTS RECEIVABLE (VER. 3.0)

Tracks all information pertaining to outstanding customer balances.

System: MAC, II, PLUS, SE, XL
Minimum Memory: 512K
Medium: 3 1/2-inch disk
ISPN: 12200-760 **Price: $199.95**

SBT CORP.
SBT DSTATEMENTS-COMPILED

Provides an accounts receivable system which includes open receivables aging and cash receipts register.

System: MAC, II, PLUS, SE, XL
Minimum Memory: 512K
Medium: 3 1/2-inch disk
ISPN: 68057-501 **Price: $70.00**

SBT CORP.
SBT DSTATEMENTS-STANDARD (VER. 6.20)

Provides an accounts receivable system that includes open receivables aging and cash receipts register.

System: MAC, II, PLUS, SE, XL
Minimum Memory: 512K
Medium: 3 1/2-inch disk
ISPN: 68057-500 **Price: $100.00**

SHOPKEEPER SOFTWARE
SHOPKEEPER-4 (VER. 1.58)

Includes accounts receivable, billing, inventory, invoicing, customer files and point of sale.

System: MAC, II, PLUS, SE, XL
Minimum Memory: 512K
Requires: 800K disk drive, hard disk, printer.
Medium: 3 1/2-inch disk
ISPN: 69805-700 **Price: $395.00**

HEIZER SOFTWARE
SMALL BUSINESS WORKS

Contains 12 programs to automate tracking from sales/receivable through records to a balance sheet for the small business.

System: MAC, II, PLUS, SE, XL
Minimum Memory: 512K
Requires: Microsoft Works (ISPN 53150-740).
Medium: 3 1/2-inch disk
ISPN: 35175-720 **Price: $50.00**

114 PRODUCTIVITY/ BUSINESS FORMS

1ST DESK SYSTEMS, INC.
1STSCAN (VER. 4.0)

Forms generator with database interface.

System: MAC, II, PLUS, SE, XL
Minimum Memory: 512K
Medium: 3 1/2-inch disk
ISPN: 81083-630 **Price: $295.00**

HABA/ARRAYS SYSTEMS, INC.
BUSINESS FORMS

Creates customized business forms.

System: MAC, II, PLUS, SE, XL
Minimum Memory: 512K
Medium: 3 1/2-inch disk
ISPN: 33987-010 **Price: $29.95**

TRONSOFT, INC.
BUSINESS POWER OF ATTORNEY (VER. 1.0)

A sophisticated document processor integrated with an extensive library of legal forms.

System: MAC, II, PLUS, SE, XL
Minimum Memory: 1024K
Requires: 800K disk drive.
Medium: 3 1/2-inch disk
ISPN: 82788-110 **Price: $1495.00**

DATAPAK SOFTWARE, INC.
COMPUFORM

Contains twenty five forms including invoices, calendars, etc.

System: MAC, II, PLUS, SE, XL
Minimum Memory: 128K
Medium: 3 1/2-inch disk
ISPN: 23762-010   **Price: $29.95**

DATA MANAGEMENT ASSOCIATES
DRAW FORMS (VER. 2.0)

A disk of MacDraw business forms and form constructions kits.

System: MAC, II, PLUS, SE, XL
Minimum Memory: 512K
Requires: MacDraw (ISPN 12784-505).
Medium: 3 1/2-inch disk
ISPN: 17245-200   **Price: $59.95**

DESKTOP GRAPHICS
DRAWFORMS (VER. 2.0)

Popular business forms with reduced layout for easy input, locked templates, laser capability, click data cell entry.

System: MAC, II, PLUS, SE, XL
Minimum Memory: 128K
Requires: MacDraw (ISPN 12784-500).
Medium: 3 1/2-inch disk
ISPN: 23555-300   **Price: $59.00**

DATAPAK SOFTWARE, INC.
EXECUFORMS

Contains a selection of more than 20 Executive Office templates for invoices, billing, statements, product cost calculations and more.

System: MAC, II, PLUS, SE, XL
Minimum Memory: 512K
Requires: Executive Office (ISPN 23762-100).
Medium: 3 1/2-inch disk
ISPN: 23762-095   **Price: $29.95**

POWER UP SOFTWARE CORP.
FAST FORMS

A forms management system that allows you to create, fill and print professional forms.

System: MAC, II, PLUS, SE, XL
Minimum Memory: 512K
Requires: System File (Ver. 3.2 or later).
Medium: 3 1/2-inch disk
ISPN: 61687-250   **Price: $149.95**

SHANA CORP.
FAST FORMS (VER. 1.2)

A forms drafting application that includes a desk accessory allowing easy retrieval and data entry of forms.

System: MAC, II, PLUS, SE, XL
Minimum Memory: 512K
Medium: 3 1/2-inch disk
ISPN: 69475-200   **Price: $149.00**

ANTIC PUBLISHING, INC.
FLEXFORM BUSINESS TEMPLATES (VOL. 1)

A library of professionally-created electronic forms to use for billing, collecting, delivery, sales, production and stock keeping.

System: MAC, II, PLUS, SE, XL
Minimum Memory: 512K
Requires: SmartForm Designer (ISPN 12784-600).
Medium: 3 1/2-inch disk
ISPN: 03735-227   **Price: $89.95**

ANTIC PUBLISHING, INC.
FLEXFORM BUSINESS TEMPLATES (VOL. 2)

A library of professionally-created electronic forms to use for accounting, disbursing, payroll and purchasing.

System: MAC, II, PLUS, SE, XL
Minimum Memory: 512K
Requires: SmartForm Designer (ISPN 12784-600).
Medium: 3 1/2-inch disk
ISPN: 03735-228   **Price: $89.95**

LAYERED, INC.
INSIGHT FORMS DESIGN (VER. 1.00)

Works with Insight Expert Accounts Receivable and Billing to design customized invoices, or use existing invoice formats.

System: MAC, II, PLUS, SE, XL
Minimum Memory: 1024K
Requires: Insight Expert Accounts Receivable & Billing (ISPN 43760-610).
Medium: 3 1/2-inch disk
ISPN: 43760-450   **Price: $149.00**

DESKTOP GRAPHICS
MACFORMS (VER. 2.0)

One hundred different business forms for production of ready made business letters. Includes 4 disks.

System: MAC, II, PLUS, SE, XL
Minimum Memory: 128K
Requires: MacPaint (ISPN 12784-510).
Medium: 3 1/2-inch disk
ISPN: 23555-500   **Price: $79.95**

GRAPHIC ENHANCEMENTS, INC.
MACMEDFORM

An AMA Universal Claims form on-screen for inputting information. Users can output to a LaserWriter or ImageWriter.

System: MAC, II, PLUS, SE, XL
Minimum Memory: 512K
Requires: 800K disk drive, printer.
Medium: 3 1/2-inch disk
ISPN: 33419-500   **Price: $50.00**

SOFTWARE DISCOVERIES INC
MERGEWRITE

Used with MacWrite and other data managers as a mail merger to create form letters or as a stand-alone program.

System: MAC, II, PLUS, SE, XL
Minimum Memory: 512K
Medium: 3 1/2-inch disk
ISPN: 72775-500   **Price: $49.95**

TRONSOFT, INC.
REAL ESTATE POWER OF ATTORNEY (VER. 1.0)

A document processor integrated with an extensive library of legal forms. Includes customizable real estate forms.

System: MAC, II, PLUS, SE, XL
Minimum Memory: 1024K
Medium: 3 1/2-inch disk
ISPN: 82788-600   **Price: $1495.00**

CLARIS CORP.
SMARTFORM ASSISTANT

Facilitates quick completion of electronic forms created with SmartForm Designer (ISPN 12784-600).

System: MAC, II, PLUS, SE, XL
Minimum Memory: 1024K
Requires: Two 800K disk drives, printer.
Medium: 3 1/2-inch disk
ISPN: 12784-700   **Price: $49.00**

CLARIS CORP.
SMARTFORM DESIGNER

Provides an object-oriented drawing program optimized for forms creation.

System: MAC, II, PLUS, SE, XL
Minimum Memory: 1024K
Requires: Two 800K disk drives, printer.
Medium: 3 1/2-inch disk
ISPN: 12784-600   **Price: $399.00**

ARTSCI, INC.
SOFTFORMS

A collection of commonly used business and personal forms that have been created as MacPaint data files.

System: MAC, II, PLUS, SE, XL
Minimum Memory: 512K
Requires: MacPaint (ISPN 12784-510) or FullPaint (ISPN 90343-475).
Medium: 3 1/2-inch disk
ISPN: 05425-700   **Price: $39.95**

ARTSCI, INC.
SOFTLETTERS

Provides 50 form letters for use in business situations including sales, thank you, and condolences.

System: MAC, II, PLUS, SE, XL
Minimum Memory: 512K
Requires: MacWrite (ISPN 12784-530).
Medium: 3 1/2-inch disk
ISPN: 05425-720   **Price: $19.95**

115 PRODUCTIVITY/ COMPUTER TUTORIALS

HEIZER SOFTWARE
ADVANCED CHART TUTORIAL I

Covers the concept of dynamic labeling in Excel charts.

System: MAC, II, PLUS, SE, XL
Minimum Memory: 512K
Requires: Microsoft Excel (ISPN 53150-270).
Medium: 3 1/2-inch disk
ISPN: 35175-335　　　　　**Price: $15.00**

HEIZER SOFTWARE
ADVANCED CHART TUTORIAL II

Covers a numbering concept which allows numbers to be put in chart labels, using the Excel program.

System: MAC, II, PLUS, SE, XL
Minimum Memory: 512K
Requires: Microsoft Excel (ISPN 53150-270).
Medium: 3 1/2-inch disk
ISPN: 35175-336　　　　　**Price: $15.00**

HEIZER SOFTWARE
ADVANCED CHART TUTORIAL SET

Covers labeling, dynamic numbering and scatter chart plotting techniques for the Excel program.

System: MAC, II, PLUS, SE, XL
Minimum Memory: 512K
Requires: Microsoft Excel (ISPN 53150-270).
Medium: 3 1/2-inch disk
ISPN: 35175-334　　　　　**Price: $36.00**

HEIZER SOFTWARE
ADVANCED TUTORIALS (VER. 1.0)

Contains ten templates and tutorials covering advanced Microsoft Excel topics including Macros, functions, and the Macro Recorder.

System: MAC, II, PLUS, SE, XL
Minimum Memory: 512K
Requires: Microsoft Excel (ISPN 53150-270).
Medium: 3 1/2-inch disk
ISPN: 35175-050　　　　　**Price: $49.00**

HEIZER SOFTWARE
ANIMATION TUTORIAL

A tutorial to show how to create animated stacks.

System: MAC, II, PLUS, SE, XL
Minimum Memory: 1024K
Requires: HyperCard (ISPN 3900-300).
Medium: 3 1/2-inch disk
ISPN: 35175-079　　　　　**Price: $8.00**

HEIZER SOFTWARE
ARRAY TUTORIAL

Tutors on how to build and use the arrays feature included in the Microsoft Excel spreadsheet.

System: MAC, II, PLUS, SE, XL
Minimum Memory: 512K
Requires: Microsoft Excel (ISPN 53150-270), HyperCard (ISPN 03900-300).
Medium: 3 1/2-inch disk
ISPN: 35175-913　　　　　**Price: $15.00**

HEIZER SOFTWARE
BEYOND HELP

Consists of an index of over 1400 words contained in HyperCard's Help stack.

System: MAC, II, PLUS, SE, XL
Minimum Memory: 512K
Requires: HyperCard (ISPN 03900-300).
Medium: 3 1/2-inch disk
ISPN: 35175-916　　　　　**Price: $6.00**

HEIZER SOFTWARE
CALCULATED FIELDS TUTORIAL

Teaches users how to perform calculations in HyperCard. Learn how to reference numbers and store the results in a separate field.

System: MAC, II, PLUS, SE, XL
Minimum Memory: 1024K
Requires: HyperCard (ISPN 3900-300).
Medium: 3 1/2-inch disk
ISPN: 35175-083　　　　　**Price: $8.00**

HEIZER SOFTWARE
CHART TUTORIAL

A series of lessons which cover Excel's basic through intermediate charting techniques.

System: MAC, II, PLUS, SE, XL
Minimum Memory: 512K
Requires: Microsoft Excel (ISPN 53150-270) or Microsoft Works (ISPN 53150-740).
Medium: 3 1/2-inch disk
ISPN: 35175-305　　　　　**Price: $15.00**

HEIZER SOFTWARE
COMMAND MACRO TUTORIAL

Contains between one and ten working examples of over 120 functions available in Excel's command macro language.

System: MAC, II, PLUS, SE, XL
Minimum Memory: 512K
Requires: Microsoft Excel (ISPN 53150-270).
Medium: 3 1/2-inch disk
ISPN: 35175-330　　　　　**Price: $25.00**

HEIZER SOFTWARE
COMMUNICATIONS

A basic introduction to the use of Microsoft Works' communications program.

System: MAC, II, PLUS, SE, XL
Minimum Memory: 512K
Requires: Microsoft Works (ISPN 53150-740).
Medium: 3 1/2-inch disk
ISPN: 35175-896　　　　　**Price: $9.00**

HEIZER SOFTWARE
CUSTOM MENU TUTORIAL

A tutorial which discusses all features of Microsoft's Excel, from start to finish.

System: MAC, II, PLUS, SE, XL
Minimum Memory: 512K
Requires: Microsoft Excel (ISPN 53150-270) (Ver. 1.5 or higher).
Medium: 3 1/2-inch disk
ISPN: 35175-926　　　　　**Price: $15.00**

HEIZER SOFTWARE
DATABASE TUTORIAL

An interactive step-by-step tutorial on how to set up and use an Excel database.

System: MAC, II, PLUS, SE, XL
Minimum Memory: 512K
Requires: Microsoft Excel (ISPN 53150-270) or Microsoft Works (ISPN 53150-740).
Medium: 3 1/2-inch disk
ISPN: 35175-304　　　　　**Price: $15.00**

HEIZER SOFTWARE
DATE/TIME/CALENDAR FUNCTION TUTORIAL

Provides examples of Excel's date, time and calendar functions.

System: MAC, II, PLUS, SE, XL
Minimum Memory: 512K
Requires: Microsoft Excel (ISPN 53150-270).
Medium: 3 1/2-inch disk
ISPN: 35175-310　　　　　**Price: $8.00**

HEIZER SOFTWARE
DIALOG BOX TUTORIAL

Provides instructions on how to build custom dialog boxes using buttons, text, list boxes, and icons.

System: MAC, II, PLUS, SE, XL
Minimum Memory: 512K
Requires: Microsoft Excel (ISPN 53150-270) (Ver. 1.5 or higher), HyperCard (ISPN 03900-300).
Medium: 3 1/2-inch disk
ISPN: 35175-929　　　　　**Price: $15.00**

HEIZER SOFTWARE
DRAW TUTORIAL

Gives instructions on how the Microsoft Works word processing program deals with graphics.

System: MAC, II, PLUS, SE, XL
Minimum Memory: 512K
Requires: Microsoft Works (ISPN 53150-740).
Medium: 3 1/2-inch disk
ISPN: 35175-890　　　　　**Price: $5.00**

PERSONAL TRAINING SYSTEMS
EXCELLERATE TRAINING SERIES

Eight audio and disk-based tutorials providing hands-on, self-paced training for Microsoft Excel.

System: MAC, II, PLUS, SE, XL
Minimum Memory: 512K
Medium: 3 1/2-inch disk
ISPN: 94817-400　　　　　**Price: $39.95**

HEIZER SOFTWARE
FILE IMPORT AND EXPORT

Illustrates use of the import and export features of the Microsoft Works program.

System: MAC, II, PLUS, SE, XL
Minimum Memory: 512K
Requires: Microsoft Works (ISPN 53150-740).
Medium: 3 1/2-inch disk
ISPN: 35175-897　　　　　**Price: $7.00**

HEIZER SOFTWARE
FINANCIAL FUNCTION TUTORIAL

Demonstrates the use of Excel's financial functions for forecasting and analysis.

System: MAC, II, PLUS, SE, XL
Minimum Memory: 512K
Requires: Microsoft Excel (ISPN 53150-270) or Microsoft Works (ISPN 53150-740).
Medium: 3 1/2-inch disk
ISPN: 35175-306   **Price: $8.00**

HEIZER SOFTWARE
FORMAT NUMBER TUTORIAL

Provides 176 examples of 64 different number formats for the Excel program.

System: MAC, II, PLUS, SE, XL
Minimum Memory: 512K
Requires: Microsoft Excel (ISPN 53150-270).
Medium: 3 1/2-inch disk
ISPN: 35175-300   **Price: $6.00**

HEIZER SOFTWARE
FUNCTION MACRO TUTORIAL

Instructs the user on how to write and use function macros in the Excel program.

System: MAC, II, PLUS, SE, XL
Minimum Memory: 512K
Requires: Microsoft Excel (ISPN 53150-270).
Medium: 3 1/2-inch disk
ISPN: 35175-331   **Price: $15.00**

HEIZER SOFTWARE
GUIDED TOUR OF EXCEL

Guides the user through every menu bar option available in the Excel program.

System: MAC, II, PLUS, SE, XL
Minimum Memory: 512K
Requires: Microsoft Excel (ISPN 53150-270).
Medium: 3 1/2-inch disk
ISPN: 35175-301   **Price: $15.00**

HEIZER SOFTWARE
GUIDED TOUR OF HYPERCARD

A HyperCard tutorial which introduces the Home stack, user levels, and the painting tools.

System: MAC, II, PLUS, SE, XL
Minimum Memory: 512K
Requires: HyperCard (ISPN 03900-300).
Medium: 3 1/2-inch disk
ISPN: 35175-944   **Price: $15.00**

BANTAM ELECTRONIC PUBLISHING
HARD DISK MANAGEMENT FOR THE MACINTOSH

A book/disk program that covers the selection and installation of a hard disk system and exploring the powerful features it offers.

System: MAC, II, PLUS, SE, XL
Minimum Memory: 512K
Medium: 3 1/2-inch disk
ISPN: 06781-334   **Price: $34.95**

PERSONAL TRAINING SYSTEMS
HYPEREASY TRAINING SERIES

Four audio and disk-based tutorials providing hands-on, self-paced training for HyperCard.

System: MAC, II, PLUS, SE, XL
Minimum Memory: 1024K
Medium: 3 1/2-inch disk
ISPN: 94817-500   **Price: $49.95**

INDIVIDUAL SOFTWARE, INC.
INDIVIDUAL TRAINING FOR PAGEMAKER

Provides interactive training for PageMaker 2.0 and 3.0 with hands-on exercises, quizzes, and tips for experienced users.

System: MAC, II, PLUS, SE, XL
Minimum Memory: 1024K
Medium: 3 1/2-inch disk
ISPN: 37275-070   **Price: $69.95**

HEIZER SOFTWARE
INTEGRATING WORKS

Shows how to move information from document to document within the Microsoft Works program.

System: MAC, II, PLUS, SE, XL
Minimum Memory: 512K
Requires: Microsoft Works (ISPN 53150-740).
Medium: 3 1/2-inch disk
ISPN: 35175-901   **Price: $10.00**

HEIZER SOFTWARE
INTRODUCTORY TUTORIALS FOR EXCEL

Contains tutorials and templates which cover the basics of Excel with self-guided, disk-based programs.

System: MAC, II, PLUS, SE, XL
Minimum Memory: 512K
Requires: Microsoft Excel (ISPN 53150-270).
Medium: 3 1/2-inch disk
ISPN: 35175-650   **Price: $49.00**

PERSONAL TRAINING SYSTEMS
LEARN 88 TRAINING SERIES

Four audio and disk-based tutorials providing hands-on, self-paced training for Adobe Illustrator 88.

System: MAC, II, PLUS, SE, XL
Minimum Memory: 1024K
Medium: 3 1/2-inch disk
ISPN: 94817-800   **Price: $49.95**

PERSONAL TRAINING SYSTEMS
LEARNMORE TRAINING SERIES

Three audio and disk-based tutorials providing hands-on, self-paced training for MORE.

System: MAC, II, PLUS, SE, XL
Minimum Memory: 1024K
Medium: 3 1/2-inch disk
ISPN: 94817-300   **Price: $49.95**

PERSONAL TRAINING SYSTEMS
LEARNWORD TRAINING SERIES

Three audio and disk-based tutorials providing hands-on, self-paced training for Microsoft Word.

System: MAC, II, PLUS, SE, XL
Minimum Memory: 512K
Medium: 3 1/2-inch disk
ISPN: 94817-200   **Price: $49.95**

HEIZER SOFTWARE
LINKING TUTORIAL

Teaches the mechanics of setting up references to linked sheets and changing file names when sheets are linked, using Microsoft Excel.

System: MAC, II, PLUS, SE, XL
Minimum Memory: 512K
Requires: Microsoft Excel (ISPN 53150-270).
Medium: 3 1/2-inch disk
ISPN: 35175-955   **Price: $10.00**

HEIZER SOFTWARE
LOOKUP TABLE TUTORIAL

Cover the many forms and uses of the lookup functions contained in the Microsoft Excel spreadsheet.

System: MAC, II, PLUS, SE, XL
Minimum Memory: 512K
Requires: Microsoft Excel (ISPN 53150-270).
Medium: 3 1/2-inch disk
ISPN: 35175-956   **Price: $9.00**

HEIZER SOFTWARE
MACRO RECORDER TUTORIAL

A tutorial on the use of Excel's macro recorder.

System: MAC, II, PLUS, SE, XL
Minimum Memory: 512K
Requires: Microsoft Excel (ISPN 53150-270).
Medium: 3 1/2-inch disk
ISPN: 35175-332   **Price: $9.00**

PERSONAL TRAINING SYSTEMS
MACTEACH TRAINING SERIES

Two audio and disk-based tutorials providing hands-on, self-paced training for the Macintosh.

System: MAC, II, PLUS, SE, XL
Minimum Memory: 1024K
Medium: 3 1/2-inch disk
ISPN: 94817-100   **Price: $49.95**

PERSONAL TRAINING SYSTEMS
MASTERWORKS TRAINING SERIES

Three audio and disk-based tutorials providing hands-on, self-paced training for Microsoft Works.

System: MAC, II, PLUS, SE, XL
Minimum Memory: 512K
Medium: 3 1/2-inch disk
ISPN: 94817-700   **Price: $49.95**

GRAPHSOFT, INC.
MIKE MEYER'S HYPERCARD TUTORIAL FOR MINICAD +

A seven disk HyperCard-based tutorial that provides detailed training in MiniCad, including the version 4.0 features.

System: MAC, II, PLUS, SE, XL
Minimum Memory: 1024K
Requires: HyperCard (ISPN 03900-300), MiniCad (ISPN 25184-500).
Medium: 3 1/2-inch disk
ISPN: 25184-510   **Price: $89.00**

LAYERED, INC.
NOTES FOR MICROSOFT WORD

Instructs how to use every feature of Microsoft Word and includes over twenty-one template with a collection of clip art.

System: MAC, II, PLUS, SE, XL
Minimum Memory: 512K
Requires: Microsoft Word (ISPN 53150-732).
Medium: 3 1/2-inch disk
ISPN: 43760-720   **Price: $79.00**

LAYERED, INC.
NOTES FOR READY, SET, GO!

Explains all functions and commands for the Ready, Set, Go! program and includes over twenty templates.

System: MAC, II, PLUS, SE, XL
Minimum Memory: 512K
Requires: Ready, Set, Go! (ISPN 44293-600).
Medium: 3 1/2-inch disk
ISPN: 43760-740   **Price: $79.00**

PERSONAL TRAINING SYSTEMS
PAGETUTOR TRAINING SERIES

Four audio and disk-based tutorials providing hands-on, self-paced training for PageMaker 3.0.

System: MAC, II, PLUS, SE, XL
Minimum Memory: 1024K
Medium: 3 1/2-inch disk
ISPN: 94817-600   **Price: $49.95**

HEIZER SOFTWARE
PRINTING WORKS

Shows how to integrate the features of Microsoft Works for adding further dimension to printed reports.

System: MAC, II, PLUS, SE, XL
Minimum Memory: 512K
Requires: Microsoft Works (ISPN 53150-740).
Medium: 3 1/2-inch disk
ISPN: 35175-898   **Price: $6.00**

HEIZER SOFTWARE
SPECIAL-PURPOSE FUNCTION TUTORIAL

Provides detailed examples of Excel's fifteen special-purpose functions.

System: MAC, II, PLUS, SE, XL
Minimum Memory: 512K
Requires: Microsoft Excel (ISPN 53150-270).
Medium: 3 1/2-inch disk
ISPN: 35175-308   **Price: $15.00**

HEIZER SOFTWARE
SPREADSHEET DESIGN

A step-by-step guide for setting up a simple spreadsheet, using the Microsoft Works program.

System: MAC, II, PLUS, SE, XL
Minimum Memory: 512K
Requires: Microsoft Works (ISPN 53150-740).
Medium: 3 1/2-inch disk
ISPN: 35175-892   **Price: $10.00**

HEIZER SOFTWARE
SPREADSHEET GUIDED TOUR

A guide through the menu functions associated with Microsoft Works spreadsheet and graphics program.

System: MAC, II, PLUS, SE, XL
Minimum Memory: 512K
Requires: Microsoft Works (ISPN 53150-740).
Medium: 3 1/2-inch disk
ISPN: 35175-891   **Price: $9.00**

HEIZER SOFTWARE
STATISTICAL FUNCTION TUTORIAL

Demonstrates Excel's built-in statistical functions for data analysis.

System: MAC, II, PLUS, SE, XL
Minimum Memory: 512K
Requires: Microsoft Excel (ISPN 53150-270) or Microsoft Works (ISPN 53150-740).
Medium: 3 1/2-inch disk
ISPN: 35175-307   **Price: $8.00**

HEIZER SOFTWARE
SURFACE CHARTS

Discusses the use of Excel's charting techniques by the author of the Solar Position Chart.

System: MAC, II, PLUS, SE, XL
Minimum Memory: 512K
Requires: Microsoft Excel (ISPN 53150-270).
Medium: 3 1/2-inch disk
ISPN: 35175-333   **Price: $25.00**

HEIZER SOFTWARE
TABLE TUTORIAL

A macro-guided tour of how to set up both one-way and two-way tables, using the features of Microsoft's Excel.

System: MAC, II, PLUS, SE, XL
Minimum Memory: 512K
Requires: Microsoft Excel (ISPN 53150-270).
Medium: 3 1/2-inch disk
ISPN: 35175-992   **Price: $10.00**

AMERICAN TRAINING INT'L. (ATI)
TEACH YOURSELF EXCEL

A two-disk training program that teaches you how to set up a worksheet, enter data and formulas, prepare memos, and graphs.

System: MAC, II, PLUS, SE, XL
Minimum Memory: 512K
Requires: Microsoft Excel (ISPN 53150-270)
Medium: 3 1/2-inch disk
ISPN: 03156-070   **Price: $75.00**

AMERICAN TRAINING INT'L. (ATI)
TEACH YOURSELF JAZZ

Interactive software simulation that guides the user step-by-step to understand and operate Jazz.

System: MAC, II, PLUS, SE, XL
Minimum Memory: 512K
Requires: Jazz (ISPN 45525-025).
Medium: 3 1/2-inch disk
ISPN: 03156-075   **Price: $75.00**

AMERICAN TRAINING INT'L. (ATI)
TEACH YOURSELF MULTIPLAN

Enables user to start-up Multiplan, set up a worksheet, enter numbers and formulas, save a worksheet, load an existing worksheet.

System: MAC, II, PLUS, SE, XL
Minimum Memory: 512K
Requires: Microsoft Multiplan (ISPN 53150-550).
Medium: 3 1/2-inch disk
ISPN: 03156-089   **Price: $75.00**

SOLAR SYSTEMS SOFTWARE
TEMPLATES OF DOOM

Teaches the user how to use spreadsheet programs and is written in an interactive game format.

System: MAC, II, PLUS, SE, XL
Minimum Memory: 512K
Medium: 3 1/2-inch disk
ISPN: 74212-800   **Price: $69.95**

HEIZER SOFTWARE
TEXT STRING TUTORIAL

A series of examples for text handling and combining text with numbers in the Excel program.

System: MAC, II, PLUS, SE, XL
Minimum Memory: 512K
Requires: Microsoft Excel (ISPN 53150-270).
Medium: 3 1/2-inch disk
ISPN: 35175-309   **Price: $7.00**

HEIZER SOFTWARE
TOP TEN EXCEL QUESTIONS

Discusses each of the top ten questions asked by Excel users.

System: MAC, II, PLUS, SE, XL
Minimum Memory: 512K
Requires: Microsoft Excel (ISPN 53150-270).
Medium: 3 1/2-inch disk
ISPN: 35175-302   **Price: $8.00**

HEIZER SOFTWARE
TUTORIAL WORKS

Demonstrates how Microsoft Works graphics, words and numbers can be integrated.

System: MAC, II, PLUS, SE, XL
Minimum Memory: 512K
Requires: Microsoft Works (ISPN 53150-740).
Medium: 3 1/2-inch disk
ISPN: 35175-710   **Price: $50.00**

HEIZER SOFTWARE
WORD PROCESSING TOUR

A guide through each of the features of the Microsoft Works word processing program.

System: MAC, II, PLUS, SE, XL
Minimum Memory: 512K
Requires: Microsoft Works (ISPN 53150-740).
Medium: 3 1/2-inch disk
ISPN: 35175-889   **Price: $6.00**

HEIZER SOFTWARE
WORD TUTORIAL SET

Ten lessons for Microsoft Word 3.01 which include spell checking, math functions, columns, glossary, formulas, and style sheets.

System: MAC, II, PLUS, SE, XL
Minimum Memory: 512K
Requires: Microsoft Word (ISPN 53150-732).
Medium: 3 1/2-inch disk
ISPN: 35175-500   **Price: $40.00**

HEIZER SOFTWARE
WORKSHEET FUNCTION TUTORIAL

Contains working examples of all eighty-plus Excel worksheet functions.

System: MAC, II, PLUS, SE, XL
Minimum Memory: 512K
Requires: Microsoft Excel (ISPN 53150-270).
Medium: 3 1/2-inch disk
ISPN: 35175-303   **Price: $15.00**

HEIZER SOFTWARE
WORKSXCHANGE SAMPLE DISK

Offers a free 'program of the month' and up to fifteen demonstration disks of the manufacturer's choice.

System: MAC, II, PLUS, SE, XL
Minimum Memory: 512K
Requires: Microsoft Works (ISPN 53150-740).
Medium: 3 1/2-inch disk
ISPN: 35175-888   **Price: $4.00**

118 PRODUCTIVITY/ FINANCIAL

LAKE AVE. SOFTWARE
ASSISTANT CONTROLLER SERIES-FINANCIAL REPORTING

Provides enhanced financial management reporting. Including comparative analysis.

System: MAC, II, PLUS, SE, XL
Minimum Memory: 512K
Medium: 3 1/2-inch disk
ISPN: 43418-248   **Price: $495.00**

ILAR SYSTEMS, INC.
BOTTOMLINE-V (VER. 3.0)

Generates all the financial reports necessary to manage a business through six models and four budget/cashflow programs.

System: MAC, II, PLUS, SE, XL
Minimum Memory: 512K
Requires: Printer.
Medium: 3 1/2-inch disk
ISPN: 37131-200   **Price: $595.00**

TRONSOFT, INC.
CAPITAL IDEAS (VER. 1.0)

Lists hundreds of venture capitalists and provides information on what type of funding they specializes in.

System: MAC, II, PLUS, SE, XL
Minimum Memory: 1024K
Requires: HyperCard (ISPN 03900-300).
Medium: 3 1/2-inch disk
ISPN: 82788-120   **Price: $295.00**

PROFESSIONAL AUTOMATION RESOURCES
EA$Y CHECK$ (VER. 2.0)

Automates process of checkbook management. Has user defined check formats and editing.Configured as a desk accessory.

System: MAC, II, PLUS, SE, XL
Minimum Memory: 512K
Medium: 3 1/2-inch disk
ISPN: 59723-305   **Price: $99.95**

STRATEGIC PLANNING SYSTEMS
FINANCIAL MASTER

A financial planning and client/office management system built around Omnis 3 Plus and Microsoft Excel.

System: MAC, II, PLUS, SE, XL
Minimum Memory: 512K
Requires: 20MB hard disk.
Medium: 3 1/2-inch disk
ISPN: 76493-500   **Price: $4000.00**

TRONSOFT, INC.
FRANCHISE FINDER (VER. 1.0)

Allows users to hunt for franchises based on industry, cash to invest, and locality.

System: MAC, II, PLUS, SE, XL
Minimum Memory: 1024K
Requires: HyperCard (ISPN 03900-300).
Medium: 3 1/2-inch disk
ISPN: 82788-250   **Price: $99.00**

HEIZER SOFTWARE
INCOME STATEMENT/BALANCE SHEET-CORPORATION

Income statement, balance sheet and financial ratio for the current period, previous period and new year-to-date.

System: MAC, II, PLUS, SE, XL
Minimum Memory: 512K
Requires: Microsoft Excel (ISPN 53150-270) or Microsoft Works (ISPN 53150-740).
Medium: 3 1/2-inch disk
ISPN: 35175-002   **Price: $15.00**

HEIZER SOFTWARE
INCOME STATEMENT/BALANCE SHEET-PARTNERSHIP

Income statement, balance sheet and financial ratio for the current period, previous period and new year-to-date.

System: MAC, II, PLUS, SE, XL
Minimum Memory: 512K
Requires: Microsoft Excel (ISPN 53150-270) or Microsoft Works (ISPN 53150-740).
Medium: 3 1/2-inch disk
ISPN: 35175-003   **Price: $15.00**

HEIZER SOFTWARE
INCOME STATEMENT/BALANCE SHEET-PROPRIETORSHIP

Income statement, balance sheet and financial ratio for the current period, previous period and new year-to-date.

System: MAC, II, PLUS, SE, XL
Minimum Memory: 512K
Requires: Microsoft Excel (ISPN 53150-270) or Microsoft Works (ISPN 53150-740).
Medium: 3 1/2-inch disk
ISPN: 35175-004   **Price: $15.00**

LAKE AVE. SOFTWARE
MULTI COMPANY-FINANCIAL REPORTING

Provides management reports for individual companies, locations, or consolidated companies.

System: MAC, II, PLUS, SE, XL
Minimum Memory: 512K
Medium: 3 1/2-inch disk
ISPN: 43418-496   **Price: $495.00**

TRONSOFT, INC.
PROFIT CENTER (THE) (VER. 1.0)

A cash flow evaluation program that works as a modeling tool for start-up and existing businesses.

System: MAC, II, PLUS, SE, XL
Minimum Memory: 1024K
Medium: 3 1/2-inch disk
ISPN: 82788-540   **Price: $695.00**

121 PRODUCTIVITY/ FINANCIAL FORECASTING/ MODELLING

HEIZER SOFTWARE
ABC'S OF BORROWING

Teaches the fundamentals of borrowing, including the considerations of a lending institution when reviewing a loan application.

System: MAC, II, PLUS, SE, XL
Minimum Memory: 512K
Requires: HyperCard (ISPN 03900-300).
Medium: 3 1/2-inch disk
ISPN: 35175-909   **Price: $7.00**

HEIZER SOFTWARE

ADDED PAYMENT MORTGAGE

Provides a visual effect of paying off a mortgage using a 'what-if' analysis.

System: MAC, II, PLUS, SE, XL
Minimum Memory: 512K
Requires: Microsoft Excel (ISPN 53150-270) or Microsoft Works (ISPN 53150-740).
Medium: 3 1/2-inch disk
ISPN: 35175-688   **Price: $15.00**

HEIZER SOFTWARE

ALL-PURPOSE MORTGAGE CALCULATOR

Calculates a monthly mortgage amortization when any three of four key loan variables are known.

System: MAC, II, PLUS, SE, XL
Minimum Memory: 512K
Requires: Microsoft Excel (ISPN 53150-270) or Microsoft Works (ISPN 53150-740).
Medium: 3 1/2-inch disk
ISPN: 35175-686   **Price: $20.00**

SOFTFLAIR, INC.

AM PACK PLUS

Prepares loan amortization schedules, calculating the unknown variable, given three of four variables.

System: MAC, II, PLUS, SE, XL
Minimum Memory: 512K
Medium: 3 1/2-inch disk
ISPN: 95747-100   **Price: $89.95**

HEIZER SOFTWARE

BOND PRICING

Calculates the current yield and the yield to maturity from standard bond price, coupon and maturity data.

System: MAC, II, PLUS, SE, XL
Minimum Memory: 512K
Requires: Microsoft Excel (ISPN 53150-270) or Microsoft Works (ISPN 53150-740).
Medium: 3 1/2-inch disk
ISPN: 35175-296   **Price: $8.00**

HEIZER SOFTWARE

BREAKEVEN ANALYSIS

Users enter appropriate data and obtain a breakeven analysis.

System: MAC, II, PLUS, SE, XL
Minimum Memory: 1024K
Requires: HyperCard (ISPN 3900-300).
Medium: 3 1/2-inch disk
ISPN: 35175-072   **Price: $10.00**

HEIZER SOFTWARE

BUSINESS PLAN-MANUFACTURING-FIVE YEAR

Covers income and expense categories, profit and loss and cash flow projections.

System: MAC, II, PLUS, SE, XL
Minimum Memory: 512K
Requires: Microsoft Excel (ISPN 53150-270) or Microsoft Works (ISPN 53150-740).
Medium: 3 1/2-inch disk
ISPN: 35175-157   **Price: $15.00**

HEIZER SOFTWARE

BUSINESS PLAN-MANUFACTURING-TWELVE MONTH

Covers income and expense categories, profit and loss and cash flow projections.

System: MAC, II, PLUS, SE, XL
Minimum Memory: 512K
Requires: Microsoft Excel (ISPN 53150-270) or Microsoft Works (ISPN 53150-740).
Medium: 3 1/2-inch disk
ISPN: 35175-156   **Price: $15.00**

HEIZER SOFTWARE

BUSINESS PLAN-PROFESSIONAL SERVICE-12 MO.

Covers income and expense categories, profit and loss and cash flow projections.

System: MAC, II, PLUS, SE, XL
Minimum Memory: 512K
Requires: Microsoft Excel (ISPN 53150-270) or Microsoft Works (ISPN 53150-740).
Medium: 3 1/2-inch disk
ISPN: 35175-158   **Price: $15.00**

HEIZER SOFTWARE

BUSINESS PLAN-PROFESSIONAL SERVICE-5 YEAR

A model plan for professionals which covers income and expense, profit and loss, and cash flow projections for a five-year period.

System: MAC, II, PLUS, SE, XL
Minimum Memory: 512K
Requires: Microsoft Works (ISPN 53150-740) or Microsoft Excel (ISPN 53150-270).
Medium: 3 1/2-inch disk
ISPN: 35175-042   **Price: $15.00**

HEIZER SOFTWARE

BUSINESS PLAN-RETAIL-FIVE YEAR

Covers income and expense categories, profit and loss, and cash flow projections.

System: MAC, II, PLUS, SE, XL
Minimum Memory: 512K
Requires: Microsoft Excel (ISPN 53150-270) or Microsoft Works (ISPN 53150-740).
Medium: 3 1/2-inch disk
ISPN: 35175-155   **Price: $15.00**

HEIZER SOFTWARE

BUSINESS PLAN-RETAIL-TWELVE MONTH

Covers income and expense categories, profit and loss, and cash flow projections.

System: MAC, II, PLUS, SE, XL
Minimum Memory: 512K
Requires: Microsoft Excel (ISPN 53150-270) or Microsoft Works (ISPN 53150-740).
Medium: 3 1/2-inch disk
ISPN: 35175-007   **Price: $15.00**

ICONIX SOFTWARE ENGINEERING, INC.

COCOPRO

A software cost modelling program that uses the CoCoMo (TRW Constructive Cost Modelling) technique.

System: MAC, II, PLUS, SE, XL
Minimum Memory: 1024K
Medium: 3 1/2-inch disk
ISPN: 37012-175   **Price: $495.00**

MARKET ENGINEERING CORP.

CRYSTAL BALL

A forecasting and risk management program that uses the power of simulation to clarify decisions.

System: MAC, II, PLUS, SE, XL
Minimum Memory: 1024K
Requires: 800K disk drive, Microsoft Excel (ISPN 53150-270, Microsoft Works (ISPN 53150-740) or Multiplan (ISPN 53150-550).
Medium: 3 1/2-inch disk
ISPN: 47365-100   **Price: $395.00**

HEIZER SOFTWARE

CURRENCY CONVERTER

Calculates widely traded currencies in terms of each other, based on exchange rates to the dollar.

System: MAC, II, PLUS, SE, XL
Minimum Memory: 512K
Requires: Microsoft Excel (ISPN 53150-270), Microsoft Works (ISPN 53150-740) or HyperCard (ISPN 03900-300).
Medium: 3 1/2-inch disk
ISPN: 35175-375   **Price: $6.00**

HEIZER SOFTWARE

DEBT AMORTIZATION SCHEDULE

Calculates a five-year amortization schedule, which shows interest, principal, and the principal balance of each loan for the year.

System: MAC, II, PLUS, SE, XL
Minimum Memory: 512K
Requires: Microsoft Excel (ISPN 53150-270).
Medium: 3 1/2-inch disk
ISPN: 35175-928   **Price: $20.00**

HEIZER SOFTWARE

DEPRECIATION POWER PAC

Performs multiple assets vintage depreciation, straight line, sum of the years digits and declining balance.

System: MAC, II, PLUS, SE, XL
Minimum Memory: 512K
Requires: Microsoft Excel (ISPN 53150-270).
Medium: 3 1/2-inch disk
ISPN: 35175-293   **Price: $20.00**

HEIZER SOFTWARE
DEPRECIATION TEMPLATE
Methods of depreciation include straight line, declining balance, sum of the year's digits and with or without investment tax credit.
System: MAC, II, PLUS, SE, XL
Minimum Memory: 512K
Requires: Microsoft Excel (ISPN 53150-270) or Microsoft Works (ISPN 53150-740).
Medium: 3 1/2-inch disk
ISPN: 35175-292   **Price: $8.00**

HEIZER SOFTWARE
FHA QUALIFICATION
Evaluates an individual's ability to qualify for a Federal Housing Administration loan.
System: MAC, II, PLUS, SE, XL
Minimum Memory: 512K
Requires: Microsoft Works (ISPN 53150-740).
Medium: 3 1/2-inch disk
ISPN: 35175-868   **Price: $20.00**

PALO ALTO SOFTWARE
FINANCIAL FORECASTING TOOLKIT (VER. 1.0)
Explains and illustrates ProForma statements and financial planning.
System: MAC, II, PLUS, SE, XL
Minimum Memory: 512K
Requires: Microsoft Excel (ISPN 53150-270), Multiplan (ISPN 53150-550), or Appleworks (ISPN 12784-100).
Medium: 3 1/2-inch disk
ISPN: 37443-237   **Price: $69.95**

HEIZER SOFTWARE
FINANCIAL MODELS
A set of seven financial decision-making models which demonstrate the power of Excel to the corporate business world.
System: MAC, II, PLUS, SE, XL
Minimum Memory: 512K
Requires: Microsoft Excel (ISPN 53150-270).
Medium: 3 1/2-inch disk
ISPN: 35175-290   **Price: $9.00**

HEIZER SOFTWARE
FINANCIAL RATIO ANALYSIS
Calculates eleven standard financial ratios from the annual report data of firms entered for analysis.
System: MAC, II, PLUS, SE, XL
Minimum Memory: 512K
Requires: Microsoft Excel (ISPN 53150-270), Microsoft Works (ISPN 53150-740) or HyperCard (ISPN 03900-300).
Medium: 3 1/2-inch disk
ISPN: 35175-291   **Price: $15.00**

HEIZER SOFTWARE
FIRST AND SECOND MORTGAGE AMORTIZATION
Calculates both a first and second mortgage amortization schedule, side-by-side.
System: MAC, II, PLUS, SE, XL
Minimum Memory: 512K
Requires: Microsoft Works (ISPN 53150-740).
Medium: 3 1/2-inch disk
ISPN: 35175-862   **Price: $8.00**

HEIZER SOFTWARE
FIRST/SECOND MORTGAGE AMORTIZATION
Calculates both a first and second mortgage amortization schedule for user-defined specifics.
System: MAC, II, PLUS, SE, XL
Minimum Memory: 512K
Requires: Microsoft Excel (ISPN 53150-270) or Microsoft Works (ISPN 53150-740).
Medium: 3 1/2-inch disk
ISPN: 35175-690   **Price: $8.00**

PALO ALTO SOFTWARE
FORECASTER
Allows you to use the mouse to draw your business forecasts as lines on a graph. Program then converts lines to numbers.
System: MAC, II, PLUS, SE, XL
Minimum Memory: 512K
Requires: 800K disk drive.
Medium: 3 1/2-inch disk
ISPN: 37443-300   **Price: $69.95**

HEIZER SOFTWARE
HOME REFINANCE ANALYSIS
Compares a current mortgage with three refinancing alternatives.
System: MAC, II, PLUS, SE, XL
Minimum Memory: 512K
Requires: Microsoft Excel (ISPN 53150-270) or Microsoft Works (ISPN 53150-740).
Medium: 3 1/2-inch disk
ISPN: 35175-685   **Price: $9.00**

GOOD SOFTWARE CORP.
INVESTOR 3000
Assists user in sound investment decisions and analysis, fractional ownership reports and participation loans.
System: MAC, II, PLUS, SE, XL
Minimum Memory: 512K
Medium: 3 1/2-inch disk
ISPN: 33278-201   **Price: $795.00**

HEIZER SOFTWARE
MAXIMUM HOME PRICE
Calculates the maximum home price for which a borrower qualifies.
System: MAC, II, PLUS, SE, XL
Minimum Memory: 512K
Requires: Microsoft Works (ISPN 53150-740).
Medium: 3 1/2-inch disk
ISPN: 35175-867   **Price: $12.00**

HEIZER SOFTWARE
MAXMORTGAGE
Determines the maximum mortgage at different interest rates, based on income, installment debt and key payment-to-income ratios.
System: MAC, II, PLUS, SE, XL
Minimum Memory: 512K
Requires: Microsoft Excel (ISPN 53150-270) or Microsoft Works (ISPN 53150-740).
Medium: 3 1/2-inch disk
ISPN: 35175-683   **Price: $12.00**

HEIZER SOFTWARE
MODIFIED TIME-WEIGHTED INTERNAL RATE OF RETURN
Calculates the modified internal rate of return for uneven periods.
System: MAC, II, PLUS, SE, XL
Minimum Memory: 512K
Requires: Microsoft Excel (ISPN 53150-270).
Medium: 3 1/2-inch disk
ISPN: 35175-298   **Price: $12.00**

HEIZER SOFTWARE
MONTHLY LOAN MACROS
Designs a monthly loan form on a worksheet, and uses the specified loan data to set up and calculate the loan amortization schedule.
System: MAC, II, PLUS, SE, XL
Minimum Memory: 512K
Requires: Microsoft Excel (ISPN 53150-270).
Medium: 3 1/2-inch disk
ISPN: 35175-295   **Price: $9.00**

HEIZER SOFTWARE
MORTGAGE AMORTIZATION
Calculates a mortgage amortization schedule based on known amount, interest rate and term.
System: MAC, II, PLUS, SE, XL
Minimum Memory: 512K
Requires: Microsoft Excel (ISPN 53150-270) or Microsoft Works (ISPN 53150-740).
Medium: 3 1/2-inch disk
ISPN: 35175-687   **Price: $6.00**

HEIZER SOFTWARE
MORTGAGE RATE COMPARISON
A database for maintaining and sorting mortgage data from lenders, based on points, percent, term and Annual Percentage Rate (APR).
System: MAC, II, PLUS, SE, XL
Minimum Memory: 512K
Requires: Microsoft Works (ISPN 53150-740).
Medium: 3 1/2-inch disk
ISPN: 35175-866   **Price: $25.00**

HEIZER SOFTWARE
PORTFOLIO I
Records buy and sell dates and prices, commissions, dividends and overall portfolio performance statistics.
System: MAC, II, PLUS, SE, XL
Minimum Memory: 512K
Requires: Microsoft Excel (ISPN 53150-270).
Medium: 3 1/2-inch disk
ISPN: 35175-351   **Price: $15.00**

SDG DECISION SYSTEMS
PROFESSIONAL SUPERTREE (VER. 5.3)
Performs deterministic sensitivity analysis on spreadsheet models and probabilistic analysis of complex decision trees,
System: MAC, II, PLUS, SE, XL
Minimum Memory: 512K
Medium: 3 1/2-inch disk
ISPN: 76475-800   **Price: $1500.00**

DOANE INFORMATION SERVICES, DIV. OF CONTROL DATA

PROFIT PROJECTOR-BREAKEVEN ANALYSIS

Enter costs and the program returns profit projections plus the break-even point. Chart expenses or graph profit potentials.

System: MAC, II, PLUS, SE, XL
Minimum Memory: 512K
Medium: 3 1/2-inch disk
ISPN: 34425-700　　　　　**Price: $95.00**

GOOD SOFTWARE CORP.

REMS FINANCIER 2000

Provides video or presentation-ready reports on over sixteen different loan types for calendar or fiscal year schedules.

System: MAC, II, PLUS, SE, XL
Minimum Memory: 192K
Medium: 3 1/2-inch disk
ISPN: 33278-321　　　　　**Price: $395.00**

GOOD SOFTWARE CORP.

REMS INVESTOR 2000

Assists user in making sound investment decisions by analyzing the financial information entered.

System: MAC, II, PLUS, SE, XL
Minimum Memory: 512K
Medium: 3 1/2-inch disk
ISPN: 33278-151　　　　　**Price: $395.00**

GOOD SOFTWARE CORP.

REMS INVESTOR 3000

Analyzes financial information and forecasts cash flows resulting from the acquisition and sale of properties.

System: MAC, II, PLUS, SE, XL
Minimum Memory: 512K
Medium: 3 1/2-inch disk
ISPN: 33278-153　　　　　**Price: $795.00**

HEIZER SOFTWARE

SBA FORM 1100

Calculates cash flow and repayment schedule in a Small Business Administration format.

System: MAC, II, PLUS, SE, XL
Minimum Memory: 512K
Requires: Microsoft Excel (ISPN 53150-270).
Medium: 3 1/2-inch disk
ISPN: 35175-173　　　　　**Price: $10.00**

HEIZER SOFTWARE

SIMPLE INTEREST LOAN

Calculates interest and principal for simple interest loans with payments of unequal amounts and periods.

System: MAC, II, PLUS, SE, XL
Minimum Memory: 512K
Requires: Microsoft Excel (ISPN 53150-270) or Microsoft Works (ISPN 53150-740).
Medium: 3 1/2-inch disk
ISPN: 35175-294　　　　　**Price: $12.00**

LIONHEART PRESS

SIMULATIONS (VER. 5.0)

Provides Monte Carlo simulations for inventory management, queues and financial risk management.

System: MAC, II, PLUS, SE, XL
Minimum Memory: 512K
Medium: 3 1/2-inch disk
ISPN: 44900-867　　　　　**Price: $95.00**

L & L PRODUCTS, INC.

SPREAD (VER. 3.1)

An interactive financial modeling language designed to aid business planners in decision making.

System: MAC, II, PLUS, SE, XL
Minimum Memory: 512K
Medium: 3 1/2-inch disk
ISPN: 43306-100　　　　　**Price: $500.00**

HEIZER SOFTWARE

STACK MONEY

A HyperCard stack consisting of seven cards, each of which performs a different financial function.

System: MAC, II, PLUS, SE, XL
Minimum Memory: 512K
Requires: HyperCard (ISPN 03900-300).
Medium: 3 1/2-inch disk
ISPN: 35175-988　　　　　**Price: $20.00**

HEIZER SOFTWARE

TIME-WEIGHTED INTERNAL RATE OF RETURN

Calculates the internal rate of return for uneven periods and amounts.

System: MAC, II, PLUS, SE, XL
Minimum Memory: 512K
Requires: Microsoft Excel (ISPN 53150-270).
Medium: 3 1/2-inch disk
ISPN: 35175-297　　　　　**Price: $12.00**

HEIZER SOFTWARE

USER-DEFINED MORTGAGE PAYMENT

Calculates a mortgage amortization schedule when the monthly payment is set first rather than the mortgage period.

System: MAC, II, PLUS, SE, XL
Minimum Memory: 512K
Requires: Microsoft Excel (ISPN 53150-270) or Microsoft Works (ISPN 53150-740).
Medium: 3 1/2-inch disk
ISPN: 35175-689　　　　　**Price: $10.00**

HEIZER SOFTWARE

VA QUALIFICATION

Evaluates an individual's ability to qualify for a Veteran Administration loan.

System: MAC, II, PLUS, SE, XL
Minimum Memory: 512K
Requires: Microsoft Works (ISPN 53150-740).
Medium: 3 1/2-inch disk
ISPN: 35175-906　　　　　**Price: $20.00**

HEIZER SOFTWARE

VARIABLE COMPOUNDING COMBINATION

Shows the effect of different compounding periods on a lump sum investment and calculates the effects on an amortized loan.

System: MAC, II, PLUS, SE, XL
Minimum Memory: 512K
Requires: Microsoft Excel (ISPN 53150-270) or Microsoft Works (ISPN 53150-740).
Medium: 3 1/2-inch disk
ISPN: 35175-299　　　　　**Price: $10.00**

HEIZER SOFTWARE

VARIABLE COMPOUNDING OF A LOAN

Calculates the effects of different compounding periods on an amortized loan.

System: MAC, II, PLUS, SE, XL
Minimum Memory: 512K
Requires: Microsoft Excel (ISPN 53150-270) or Microsoft Works (ISPN 53150-740).
Medium: 3 1/2-inch disk
ISPN: 35175-289　　　　　**Price: $7.00**

HEIZER SOFTWARE

VARIABLE COMPOUNDING OF INVESTMENT

Shows the effect of different compounding periods on a lump sum investment.

System: MAC, II, PLUS, SE, XL
Minimum Memory: 512K
Requires: Microsoft Excel (ISPN 53150-270), Microsoft Works (ISPN 53150-740) or HyperCard (ISPN 03900-300).
Medium: 3 1/2-inch disk
ISPN: 35175-288　　　　　**Price: $7.00**

HEIZER SOFTWARE

VARIABLE COMPOUNDING OF LOAN

Demonstrates the effects of different compounding periods on an amortized loan.

System: MAC, II, PLUS, SE, XL
Minimum Memory: 512K
Requires: Microsoft Works (ISPN 53150-740) or HyperCard (ISPN 03900-300).
Medium: 3 1/2-inch disk
ISPN: 35175-783　　　　　**Price: $7.00**

HEIZER SOFTWARE

YEARLY MORTGAGE AMORTIZATION

Calculates the interest and principal of a mortgage for each year, based on a monthly payment.

System: MAC, II, PLUS, SE, XL
Minimum Memory: 512K
Requires: Microsoft Works (ISPN 53150-740).
Medium: 3 1/2-inch disk
ISPN: 35175-872　　　　　**Price: $15.00**

---

123 PRODUCTIVITY/ FONTS/IMAGES

EMDASH

18 POSTSCRIPT FONTS

Provides Architext, UpStart, Caspian, Briar, ArrowDynamic and BulletsNStuff PostScript fonts in several font styles.

System: MAC, II, PLUS, SE, XL
Minimum Memory: 512K
Requires: PostScript printer.
Medium: 3 1/2-inch disk
ISPN: 28901-200   **Price: $63.00**

ADOBE SYSTEMS, INC.

AACHEN/REVUE/UNIV. ROMAN/ FREESTYLE SCRIPT

Contains four variations of the Aachen/ Revue/Univ.Roman/Freestyle script font suitable for use with any PostScript printer.

System: MAC, II, PLUS, SE, XL
Minimum Memory: 512K
Requires: PostScript printer.
Medium: 3 1/2-inch disk
ISPN: 01012-105   **Price: $185.00**

FREEMYERS DESIGN

AD/ART/PLUS (VOL 2) 'BORDERS'

Designs of complete borders (1/4, 1/2, 1/3, 2/3 and full page). Use for page layout, desk top publishing, business, personal, school.

System: MAC, II, PLUS, SE, XL
Minimum Memory: 512K
Requires: MacPaint (ISPN 12784-510) or compatible paint software.
Medium: 3 1/2-inch disk
ISPN: 31415-300   **Price: $49.95**

FREEMYERS DESIGN

AD/ART/PLUS LASERART/ BORDERS (VER. 1.0)

Contains designs of complete borders and a selection of designs which may be resized.

System: MAC, II, PLUS, SE, XL
Minimum Memory: 128K
Requires: MacDraw (ISPN 12784-505) or any program that reads PICT files, ImageWriter or LaserWriter.
Medium: 3 1/2-inch disk
ISPN: 31415-500   **Price: $49.95**

ADOBE SYSTEMS, INC.

ADOBE COLLECTOR'S EDITION 1

Contains 100 borders, 300 dingbats and two medium weight typeface outlines (a serif and a sans serif).

System: MAC, II, PLUS, SE, XL
Minimum Memory: 512K
Requires: Adobe Illustrator (ISPN 01012-050) or Adobe Illustrator 88 (ISPN 01012-060).
Medium: 3 1/2-inch disk
ISPN: 01012-040   **Price: $125.00**

STORM KING TECHNOLOGY

AIRART

MacPaint clip-art of aerospace subjects including spacecraft, U.S and foreign aircraft, and insignia.

System: MAC, II, PLUS, SE, XL
Minimum Memory: 128K
Requires: MacPaint (ISPN 12784-510) or compatible program.
Medium: 3 1/2-inch disk
ISPN: 76406-100   **Price: $69.95**

STORM KING TECHNOLOGY

AIRART

MacPaint clip-art of aerospace subjects including spacecraft, U.S and foreign aircraft, and insignia.

System: XL
Minimum Memory: 512K
Requires: MacPaint (ISPN 12784-510) or compatible program.
Medium: 3 1/2-inch disk
ISPN: 76406-100   **Price: $69.95**

KINGSLEY/ATF SOFTWARE DIVISION

AMERICANA

Contains four downloadable PostScript fonts including Americana Roman, Americana Italic, Americana Bold and Americana Extra Bold.

System: MAC, II, PLUS, SE, XL
Minimum Memory: 512K
Requires: PostScript printer.
Medium: 3 1/2-inch disk
ISPN: 43012-100   **Price: $195.00**

GOLDMIND PUBLISHING

ANIMALS (VOL. 2)

A collection of large format Fullpaint files for illustrating desk top publishing documents. Up to 2470 dots per inch resolution.

System: MAC, II, PLUS, SE, XL
Minimum Memory: 512K
Requires: 800K disk drive.
Medium: 3 1/2-inch disk
ISPN: 33256-030   **Price: $39.95**

IMAGE WORLD, INC.

APPLES OF OUR EYE

Delicate images of children from old children's books, school books, music sheets, early advertising art, etc.

System: MAC, II, PLUS, SE, XL
Minimum Memory: 128K
Requires: PictureBase (ISPN 77437-550). MacPaint (ISPN 12784-510).
Medium: 3 1/2-inch disk
ISPN: 37181-075   **Price: $30.00**

EMDASH

ARCHITEXT

Provides a PostScript downloadable font in condensed, bold, bold condensed and regular font style.

System: MAC, II, PLUS, SE, XL
Minimum Memory: 512K
Requires: PostScript printer.
Medium: 3 1/2-inch disk
ISPN: 28901-100   **Price: $43.00**

STORM KING TECHNOLOGY

ARMYART

MacPaint and PICT clip art of military subjects including modern and historic combat equipment, soldiers and insignia.

System: MAC, II, PLUS, SE, XL
Minimum Memory: 128K
Requires: MacPaint (ISPN 12784-510) or compatible program.
Medium: 3 1/2-inch disk
ISPN: 76406-150   **Price: $69.95**

STORM KING TECHNOLOGY

ARMYART

MacPaint and PICT clip art of military subjects including modern and historic combat equipment, soldiers and insignia.

System: XL
Minimum Memory: 512K
Requires: MacPaint (ISPN 12784-510) or compatible program.
Medium: 3 1/2-inch disk
ISPN: 76406-150   **Price: $69.95**

EMDASH

ARROWDYNAMIC

Provides a downloadable PostScript font in regular, bold, and heavy weights.

System: MAC, II, PLUS, SE, XL
Minimum Memory: 512K
Requires: PostScript printer.
Medium: 3 1/2-inch disk
ISPN: 28901-110   **Price: $43.00**

SPRINGBOARD SOFTWARE, INC.

ART A LA MAC (VOL. 1)-PEOPLE AND PLACES

Features people in a variety of amusing, unpredictable situations. Places include U.S. Capitol, Taj Mahal and more.

System: MAC, II, PLUS, SE, XL
Minimum Memory: 512K
Medium: 3 1/2-inch disk
ISPN: 75309-010   **Price: $39.95**

SPRINGBOARD SOFTWARE, INC.

ART A LA MAC (VOL. 2)- VARIETY PACK

Contains over 600 pieces of common images such as music, plants, vehicles, astrology, outerspace and more.

System: MAC, II, PLUS, SE, XL
Minimum Memory: 512K
Medium: 3 1/2-inch disk
ISPN: 75309-011   **Price: $39.95**

DV FRANKS

ART DISK I

Contains clip-art drawings of buildings, landscapes, and objects of decor in a bit-mapped format.

System: MAC, II, PLUS, SE, XL
Minimum Memory: 128K
Requires: Paint program that can read MacPaint format.
Medium: 3 1/2-inch disk
ISPN: 26925-100   **Price: $39.95**

DV FRANKS

ART DISK II

Contains clip-art drawings of people, animals, and birds in a bit-mapped format.

System: MAC, II, PLUS, SE, XL
Minimum Memory: 128K
Requires: Paint program that can read MacPaint format.
Medium: 3 1/2-inch disk
ISPN: 26925-110   **Price: $39.95**

DV FRANKS

ART DISK III

Contains clip-art drawings of lawyers, doctors, food and drink, business and home.

System: MAC, II, PLUS, SE, XL
Minimum Memory: 128K
Requires: Paint program that can read MacPaint format.
Medium: 3 1/2-inch disk
ISPN: 26925-120   **Price: $39.95**

IMAGE WORLD, INC.

ART NOVEAU

Floral and structural images by the famous artists of the memorable Art Noveau period.

System: MAC, II, PLUS, SE, XL
Minimum Memory: 128K
Medium: 3 1/2-inch disk
ISPN: 37181-135   **Price: $30.00**

DEVONIAN INT'L. SOFTWARE CO.

ARTAGENIX-PLANES OF FAME (VER. 1.0)

Contains bit-mapped images of modern military aircraft.

System: MAC, II, PLUS, SE, XL
Minimum Memory: 512K
Requires: 800K disk drive, a program that can read MacPaint (ISPN 12784-510) files.
Medium: 3 1/2-inch disk
ISPN: 24987-100   **Price: $39.50**

OLDUVAI CORP.

ARTCLIP

Includes 70 high resolution abstract graphic images including icons, logos,and graphics for use with a PostScript printer.

System: MAC, II, PLUS, SE, XL
Minimum Memory: 512K
Requires: Cricket Draw (ISPN 35512-020).
Medium: 3 1/2-inch disk
ISPN: 57812-605   **Price: $99.00**

OLDUVAI CORP.

ARTFONTS (VER. 1.0)

A collection of downloadable PostScript fonts from J. Ciccone's graphic design studio.

System: MAC, II, PLUS, SE, XL
Minimum Memory: 512K
Medium: 3 1/2-inch disk
ISPN: 57812-050   **Price: $99.00**

ARTWARE SYSTEMS, INC.

ASSORTMENT I (S1D1.0)

Includes thirty business, presentation, and commercial PostScript images, designed with Adobe Illustrator.

System: MAC, II, PLUS, SE, XL
Minimum Memory: 512K
Requires: PostScript printer.
Medium: 3 1/2-inch disk
ISPN: 05432-100   **Price: $69.95**

IMAGE WORLD, INC.

ATTENTION GRABBERS

Standouts for attracting attention. Silhouettes, pointers, arrows, characters, comic figures, symbols, and decorations.

System: MAC, II, PLUS, SE, XL
Minimum Memory: 128K
Medium: 3 1/2-inch disk
ISPN: 37181-195   **Price: $30.00**

BITSTREAM, INC.

BASKERVILLE MACFONTWARE LIBRARY

Contains four weights of one typeface, including Baskerville, Italic, Bold and Bold Italic.

System: MAC, II, PLUS, SE, XL
Minimum Memory: 512K
Requires: LaserWriter, LaserWriter IISC or ImageWriter printer.
Medium: 3 1/2-inch disk
ISPN: 07836-200   **Price: $195.00**

BEDE TECH

BEDE TECH BUSINESS CLIP ART (VOL. 1)

Contains MacPaint style illustrations of art for business .

System: MAC, II, PLUS, SE, XL
Minimum Memory: 128K
Requires: MacPaint (ISPN 12784-510) or other program that can read MacPaint documents.
Medium: 3 1/2-inch disk
ISPN: 07237-150   **Price: $14.95**

BEDE TECH

BEDE TECH CHRISTMAS CLIP ART (VOL. 1)

Contains drawings in MacPaint format that deal with the Christmas season.

System: MAC, II, PLUS, SE, XL
Minimum Memory: 128K
Requires: MacPaint (ISPN 12784-510) or other program that can read MacPaint documents.
Medium: 3 1/2-inch disk
ISPN: 07237-170   **Price: $14.95**

BEDE TECH

BEDE TECH EASTER CLIP ART (VOL. 1)

Contains MacPaint style drawings dealing with the Easter season.

System: MAC, II, PLUS, SE, XL
Minimum Memory: 128K
Requires: MacPaint (ISPN 12784-510) or other program that can read MacPaint documents.
Medium: 3 1/2-inch disk
ISPN: 07237-160   **Price: $14.95**

ADOBE SYSTEMS, INC.

BELWE

Contains four variations of the Belwe downloadable font for use with any PostScript printer.

System: MAC, II, PLUS, SE, XL
Minimum Memory: 512K
Requires: PostScript printer.
Medium: 3 1/2-inch disk
ISPN: 01012-106   **Price: $185.00**

ADH SOFTWARE

BEVERLY HILLS

A high-quality font which provides professional output on the ImageWriter printer.

System: MAC, II, PLUS, SE, XL
Minimum Memory: 512K
Requires: ImageWriter printer.
Medium: 3 1/2-inch disk
ISPN: 00915-100   **Price: $15.00**

BITSTREAM, INC.

BITSTREAM CHARTER MACFONTWARE TYPEFACE LIBRARY

Contains four weights of one typeface, including Bitstream Charter, Italic, Black and Black Italic.

System: MAC, II, PLUS, SE, XL
Minimum Memory: 512K
Requires: LaserWriter, LaserWriter IISC or ImageWriter printer.
Medium: 3 1/2-inch disk
ISPN: 07836-201   **Price: $195.00**

ADOBE SYSTEMS, INC.

BODONI

Contains four variations of the Bodoni font for use with a PostScript printer.

System: MAC, II, PLUS, SE, XL
Minimum Memory: 512K
Requires: PostScript printer.
Medium: 3 1/2-inch disk
ISPN: 01012-110   **Price: $185.00**

KINGSLEY/ATF SOFTWARE DIVISION

BODONI

Contains four downloadable PostScript fonts including Bodoni Roman, Bodoni Italic, Ultra Bodoni and Ultra Bodoni Italic.

System: MAC, II, PLUS, SE, XL
Minimum Memory: 512K
Requires: PostScript printer.
Medium: 3 1/2-inch disk
ISPN: 43012-110   **Price: $195.00**

JAPANESE LANGUAGE SERVICES

BORDER SCROLLS

Contains a collection of MacPaint drawn clip-art garnered from 18th and 19th century Japanese publications.

System: MAC, II, PLUS, SE, XL
Minimum Memory: 128K
Medium: 3 1/2-inch disk
ISPN: 20012-200   **Price: $99.95**

IMAGE WORLD, INC.
BORDERS & FRAMES-MACMEMORIES SERIES BLUE RIBBON

Graphics from the Turn-of-the-Century-borders, frames and signs of all varieties and descriptions to use as-is or modify to need.

System: MAC, II, PLUS, SE, XL
Minimum Memory: 128K
Medium: 3 1/2-inch disk
ISPN: 37181-250   **Price: $30.00**

DECISION SCIENCE SOFTWARE
BORDERS (VOL. 1)

A collection of 160 different borders for use in graphic design applications.

System: MAC, II, PLUS, SE, XL
Minimum Memory: 512K
Medium: 3 1/2-inch disk
ISPN: 24325-910   **Price: $35.00**

ARTWARE SYSTEMS, INC.
BORDERS I (S1D1.5-1.7)

Provides forty PostScript images of assorted border artwork designed with Adobe Illustrator.

System: MAC, II, PLUS, SE, XL
Minimum Memory: 512K
Requires: PostScript printer.
Medium: 3 1/2-inch disk
ISPN: 05432-150   **Price: $129.95**

EMDASH
BRIAR

Provides a downloadable PostScript font in book, bold, and heavy weights.

System: MAC, II, PLUS, SE, XL
Minimum Memory: 512K
Requires: PostScript printer.
Medium: 3 1/2-inch disk
ISPN: 28901-150   **Price: $43.00**

CASEYS PAGE MILL
BULLETS AND BOXES (VER. 1.4)

Macintosh PostScript font that contains bullets, boxes, triangles arrows, diamonds, octagons and fractional slashes and bullets.

System: MAC, II, PLUS, SE, XL
Minimum Memory: 512K
Medium: 3 1/2-inch disk
ISPN: 11563-100   **Price: $89.00**

IMAGE WORLD, INC.
BUSINESS ILLUSTRATIONS

Contains Turn-of-the-Century clip-art fonts illustrating commerce, business meetings and discussions.

System: MAC, II, PLUS, SE, XL
Minimum Memory: 128K
Medium: 3 1/2-inch disk
ISPN: 37181-257   **Price: $30.00**

TRONSOFT, INC.
BUSINESS IMAGE (VER. 1.0)

A HyperCard based database of hundreds of nationally recognized, copyrighted company and agency logos and trademarks.

System: MAC, II, PLUS, SE, XL
Minimum Memory: 1024K
Requires: HyperCard (ISPN 03900-300).
Medium: 3 1/2-inch disk
ISPN: 82788-100   **Price: $225.00**

IMAGE WORLD, INC.
BUTCHER, BAKER AND CANDLESTICK MAKER

Early development of trades and professions gives humorous, quaint, satirical and serious memories of the ways people used to work.

System: MAC, II, PLUS, SE, XL
Minimum Memory: 128K
Medium: 3 1/2-inch disk
ISPN: 37181-255   **Price: $30.00**

AAH COMPUTER GRAPHIC PRODUCTIONS
BYTES OF FRIGHT

A carefully crafted collection of supernatural horror images.

System: MAC, II, PLUS, SE, XL
Minimum Memory: 128K
Requires: MacPaint (ISPN 12784-510) or Paint-compatible program.
Medium: 3 1/2-inch disk
ISPN: 00181-100   **Price: $29.95**

GOLDMIND PUBLISHING
CARICATURES (VOL. 8)

A collection of large format full paint files for illustrating desktop publishing documents. Up to 2470 dots per inch resolution.

System: MAC, II, PLUS, SE, XL
Minimum Memory: 512K
Requires: 800k disk drive.
Medium: 3 1/2-inch disk
ISPN: 33256-065   **Price: $39.95**

ADOBE SYSTEMS, INC.
CARTA

Contains the downloadable carta type font for use with PostScript printers.

System: MAC, II, PLUS, SE, XL
Minimum Memory: 512K
Requires: PostScript printer.
Medium: 3 1/2-inch disk
ISPN: 01012-115   **Price: $95.00**

ADOBE SYSTEMS, INC.
CASLON

Contains two variations of the Caslon 3 and two variations of the Caslon 540 downloadable font for use with any PostScript printer.

System: MAC, II, PLUS, SE, XL
Minimum Memory: 512K
Requires: PostScript printer.
Medium: 3 1/2-inch disk
ISPN: 01012-116   **Price: $185.00**

EMDASH
CASPIAN

Provides a downloadable PostScript font in book, condensed, bold, and bold condensed formats.

System: MAC, II, PLUS, SE, XL
Minimum Memory: 512K
Requires: PostScript printer.
Medium: 3 1/2-inch disk
ISPN: 28901-175   **Price: $43.00**

ADOBE SYSTEMS, INC.
CENTURY OLD STYLE

Contains three variations of the Century Old Style font for use with any PostScript compatible printer.

System: MAC, II, PLUS, SE, XL
Minimum Memory: 512K
Requires: PostScript printer.
Medium: 3 1/2-inch disk
ISPN: 01012-120   **Price: $145.00**

KINGSLEY/ATF SOFTWARE DIVISION
CENTURY SCHOOLBOOK

Contains four downloadable PostScript fonts including Century Schoolbook Roman, Italic, Bold, and Bold Italic.

System: MAC, II, PLUS, SE, XL
Minimum Memory: 512K
Requires: PostScript printer.
Medium: 3 1/2-inch disk
ISPN: 43012-130   **Price: $195.00**

SPRINGBOARD SOFTWARE, INC.
CERTIFICATE LIBRARY (VOL. 1)

Provides 100 certificates to be used with the Certificate Maker program.

System: MAC, II, PLUS, SE, XL
Minimum Memory: 512K
Requires: Certificate Maker (ISPN 75309-025).
Medium: 3 1/2-inch disk
ISPN: 75309-020   **Price: $29.95**

SPRINGBOARD SOFTWARE, INC.
CERTIFICATE MAKER

Enables the user to create and print 200 professionally designed certificates from strictly official to fun and witty.

System: MAC, II, PLUS, SE, XL
Minimum Memory: 512K
Medium: 3 1/2-inch disk
ISPN: 75309-025   **Price: $39.95**

COMPUGRAPHICS CORP.
CG TYPE FONTS (VOL. 1) GARTH GRAPHIC

Provides the Garth Graphic font in a screen font, a downloadable PostScript printer font, and a Font metric file.

System: MAC, II, PLUS, SE, XL
Minimum Memory: 512K
Requires: PostScript printer.
Medium: 3 1/2-inch disk
ISPN: 15303-100   **Price: $149.00**

COMPUGRAPHICS CORP.

CG TYPE FONTS (VOL. 10) CG SYMPHONY

Provides the CG Symphony font in a screen font, a downloadable PostScript printer font, and a font metric file.

System: MAC, II, PLUS, SE, XL
Minimum Memory: 512K
Requires: PostScript printer.
Medium: 3 1/2-inch disk
ISPN: 15303-145   **Price: $149.00**

COMPUGRAPHICS CORP.

CG TYPE FONTS (VOL. 11) CG TRIUMVIRATE

Provides the CG Triumvirate font in a screen font, a downloadable PostScript printer font, and a font metric file.

System: MAC, II, PLUS, SE, XL
Minimum Memory: 512K
Requires: PostScript printer.
Medium: 3 1/2-inch disk
ISPN: 15303-150   **Price: $149.00**

COMPUGRAPHICS CORP.

CG TYPE FONTS (VOL. 12) GOUDY

Provides the Goudy font in a screen font, a downloadable PostScript printer font, and a font metric file.

System: MAC, II, PLUS, SE, XL
Minimum Memory: 512K
Requires: PostScript printer.
Medium: 3 1/2-inch disk
ISPN: 15303-155   **Price: $149.00**

COMPUGRAPHICS CORP.

CG TYPE FONTS (VOL. 13)

Provides Branding Iron, Isabella, McCullough, and Raphael fonts in a screen font, a downloadable PostScript font and a metric file.

System: MAC, II, PLUS, SE, XL
Minimum Memory: 512K
Requires: PostScript printer.
Medium: 3 1/2-inch disk
ISPN: 15303-160   **Price: $149.00**

COMPUGRAPHICS CORP.

CG TYPE FONTS (VOL. 2) ANTIQUE OLIVE

Provides the Antique Olive font in a screen font, a downloadable PostScript font, and a font metric file.

System: MAC, II, PLUS, SE, XL
Minimum Memory: 512K
Requires: PostScript printer.
Medium: 3 1/2-inch disk
ISPN: 15303-105   **Price: $149.00**

COMPUGRAPHICS CORP.

CG TYPE FONTS (VOL. 3) CG COLLAGE

Provides the CG Collage font in a screen font, a downloadable PostScript print font, and a font metric file.

System: MAC, II, PLUS, SE, XL
Minimum Memory: 512K
Requires: PostScript printer.
Medium: 3 1/2-inch disk
ISPN: 15303-110   **Price: $149.00**

COMPUGRAPHICS CORP.

CG TYPE FONTS (VOL. 4) CG TRUMP MEDIAEVAL

Provides the CG Trump Mediaeval font in a screen font, a downloadable PostScript printer font and a font metric tool.

System: MAC, II, PLUS, SE, XL
Minimum Memory: 512K
Requires: PostScript printer.
Medium: 3 1/2-inch disk
ISPN: 15303-115   **Price: $149.00**

COMPUGRAPHICS CORP.

CG TYPE FONTS (VOL. 5) GARAMOND

Contains the Garamond Antiqua, Kursiv, Halbfett, and Kursiv Halbfet font in a screen font, and a downloadable PostScript font.

System: MAC, II, PLUS, SE, XL
Minimum Memory: 512K
Requires: PostScript printer.
Medium: 3 1/2-inch disk
ISPN: 15303-120   **Price: $149.00**

COMPUGRAPHICS CORP.

CG TYPE FONTS (VOL. 6) CG NASHVILLE MEDIUM

Provides the CG Nashville Medium font in a screen font, a downloadable PostScript font and a font metric tool.

System: MAC, II, PLUS, SE, XL
Minimum Memory: 512K
Requires: PostScript printer.
Medium: 3 1/2-inch disk
ISPN: 15303-125   **Price: $149.00**

COMPUGRAPHICS CORP.

CG TYPE FONTS (VOL. 7) ITC NOVARESE BOOK

Provides the ITC Novarese Book font in a screen font, a downloadable PostScript printer font and a font metric tool.

System: MAC, II, PLUS, SE, XL
Minimum Memory: 512K
Requires: PostScript printer.
Medium: 3 1/2-inch disk
ISPN: 15303-130   **Price: $149.00**

COMPUGRAPHICS CORP.

CG TYPE FONTS (VOL. 8) SCHNEIDLER

Provides the Schneidler font in a screen font, a downloadable PostScript font and a font metric file.

System: MAC, II, PLUS, SE, XL
Minimum Memory: 512K
Requires: PostScript printer.
Medium: 3 1/2-inch disk
ISPN: 15303-135   **Price: $149.00**

COMPUGRAPHICS CORP.

CG TYPE FONTS (VOL. 9) SHANNON BOOK

Provides the Shannon Book font in a screen font, a downloadable PostScript printer font and a font metric tool.

System: MAC, II, PLUS, SE, XL
Minimum Memory: 512K
Requires: PostScript printer.
Medium: 3 1/2-inch disk
ISPN: 15303-140   **Price: $149.00**

IMAGE WORLD, INC.

CHRISTMAS AND WINTER

Delightful fun with happy snow scenes, snow fun, angels, old time santas, religious and other symbols and pictures of the season.

System: MAC, II, PLUS, SE, XL
Minimum Memory: 128K
Requires: MacPaint (ISPN 12784-510), MacDraw (ISPN 12784-500) or MacDraft (ISPN 37053-400).
Medium: 3 1/2-inch disk
ISPN: 37181-270   **Price: $30.00**

ARTWARE SYSTEMS, INC.

CHRISTMAS IMAGES (S1D1.9,1.10)

Provides thirty-seven PostScript images pertaining to Christmas designed with Adobe Illustrator.

System: MAC, II, PLUS, SE, XL
Minimum Memory: 512K
Requires: PostScript printer.
Medium: 3 1/2-inch disk
ISPN: 05432-170   **Price: $89.95**

AAH COMPUTER GRAPHIC PRODUCTIONS

CLASSIC CLIPS FROM AAH

Presents popular images of twentieth century life in the United States.

System: MAC, II, PLUS, SE, XL
Minimum Memory: 128K
Requires: MacPaint (ISPN 12784-510) or compatible paint program.
Medium: 3 1/2-inch disk
ISPN: 00181-120   **Price: $29.95**

AAH COMPUTER GRAPHIC PRODUCTIONS

CLASSIC SCIENCE FICTION

Carefully crafted collection of classic science fiction images.

System: MAC, II, PLUS, SE, XL
Minimum Memory: 128K
Requires: MacPaint (ISPN 12784-510) or Paint-compatible program.
Medium: 3 1/2-inch disk
ISPN: 00181-125   **Price: $29.95**

T/MAKER CO.
CLICKART-BOMBAY LASERLETTERS

Contains downloadable PostScript fonts in gray, bold, italic, underline, outline, and shadow styles. Includes foreign characters.
System: MAC, II, PLUS, SE, XL
Minimum Memory: 512K
Requires: PostScript printer.
Medium: 3 1/2-inch disk
ISPN: 79465-031   **Price: $79.95**

T/MAKER CO.
CLICKART-BUSINESS IMAGES

A portfolio of over 1000 business-oriented images for enhancing and illustrating overhead slides, reports, charts, and newsletters.
System: MAC, II, PLUS, SE, XL
Minimum Memory: 128K
Medium: 3 1/2-inch disk
ISPN: 79465-030   **Price: $49.95**

T/MAKER CO.
CLICKART-CHRISTIAN IMAGES

Contains a portfolio of Christian-oriented religious images for enhancing and illustrating church-related publications.
System: MAC, II, PLUS, SE, XL
Minimum Memory: 128K
Medium: 3 1/2-inch disk
ISPN: 79465-020   **Price: $59.95**

T/MAKER CO.
CLICKART-EPS BUSINESS ART

Contains over 200 business-oriented encapsulated postscript images for use in enhancing all types of business-related documents.
System: MAC, II, PLUS, SE, XL
Minimum Memory: 512K
Requires: Program that can read encapsulated postscript format (EPS) and a postscript compatible printer.
Medium: 3 1/2-inch disk
ISPN: 79465-046   **Price: $129.95**

T/MAKER CO.
CLICKART-EPS ILLUSTRATIONS

Contains 180 encapsulated PostScript images for use in enhancing newsletters, reports, and other forms of desktop publishing.
System: MAC, II, PLUS, SE, XL
Minimum Memory: 512K
Requires: Program that can read EPS format, PostScript compatible printer.
Medium: 3 1/2-inch disk
ISPN: 79465-045   **Price: $129.95**

T/MAKER CO.
CLICKART-HOLIDAYS

Contains images of Christmas and Hanukkah, and art for Thanksgiving, Fourth of July, Easter, and Valentine's Day.
System: MAC, II, PLUS, SE, XL
Minimum Memory: 128K
Requires: 1024K required if using with HyperCard (ISPN 3900-300).
Medium: 3 1/2-inch disk
ISPN: 79465-055   **Price: $49.95**

T/MAKER CO.
CLICKART-LETTERS I

A high quality lettering system which consists of 24 large alphabet styles, for creating flyers and posters.
System: MAC, II, PLUS, SE, XL
Minimum Memory: 128K
Medium: 3 1/2-inch disk
ISPN: 79465-066   **Price: $49.95**

T/MAKER CO.
CLICKART-LETTERS II

A collection of bitmapped fonts and typefaces ranging in size from 24 to 72 points.
System: MAC, II, PLUS, SE, XL
Minimum Memory: 128K
Medium: 3 1/2-inch disk
ISPN: 79465-067   **Price: $49.95**

T/MAKER CO.
CLICKART-PERSONAL GRAPHICS

A collection of 100 professionally drawn images that can be used decorate letters, invitations or programs.
System: MAC, II, PLUS, SE, XL
Minimum Memory: 128K
Medium: 3 1/2-inch disk
ISPN: 79465-050   **Price: $49.95**

T/MAKER CO.
CLICKART-PLYMOUTH LASERLETTERS

Contains downloadable PostScript fonts in grey, bold, italic, underline, outline and shadow styles. Includes foreign characters.
System: MAC, II, PLUS, SE, XL
Minimum Memory: 512K
Requires: PostScript printer.
Medium: 3 1/2-inch disk
ISPN: 79465-032   **Price: $79.95**

T/MAKER CO.
CLICKART-SEVILLE LASERLETTERS

Provides downloadable PostScript fonts in gray, bold, italic, underline, outline and shadow styles. Includes foreign characters.
System: MAC, II, PLUS, SE, XL
Minimum Memory: 512K
Requires: PostScript printer.
Medium: 3 1/2-inch disk
ISPN: 79465-033   **Price: $79.95**

GENERIC SOFTWARE, INC.
CLIP ART

Contains 100 symbols which can be used for creating greeting cards, banners and posters.
System: MAC, II, PLUS, SE, XL
Minimum Memory: 512K
Requires: Program that can read bit-mapped images.
Medium: 3 1/2-inch disk
ISPN: 32537-100   **Price: $24.95**

DECISION SCIENCE SOFTWARE
CLIP ART (VOL. 1)

A collection of almost 300 images and paint patterns for use in graphics.
System: MAC, II, PLUS, SE, XL
Minimum Memory: 512K
Medium: 3 1/2-inch disk
ISPN: 24325-920   **Price: $35.00**

HEIZER SOFTWARE
CLIP ART COLLECTION I

Offers 150 public domain and digitized clip art images in a HyperCard stack.
System: MAC, II, PLUS, SE, XL
Minimum Memory: 1024K
Requires: HyperCard (ISPN 03900-300).
Medium: 3 1/2-inch disk
ISPN: 35175-440   **Price: $20.00**

ENABLING TECHNOLOGIES, INC.
CLIP3D ACCENTS

Includes 200 predrawn, full-color three-dimensional images of accents. Includes Clip3D, a program to manipulate the artwork.
System: MAC, II, PLUS, SE, XL
Minimum Memory: 512K
Medium: 3 1/2-inch disk
ISPN: 29051-150   **Price: $99.99**

ENABLING TECHNOLOGIES, INC.
CLIP3D BUSINESS

Includes 100 predrawn, full-color three-dimensional images dealing with business. Includes Clip3D, a program to manipulate the art.
System: MAC, II, PLUS, SE, XL
Minimum Memory: 512K
Medium: 3 1/2-inch disk
ISPN: 29051-155   **Price: $99.99**

ENABLING TECHNOLOGIES, INC.
CLIP3D FONTS

Includes five full-color, three-dimensional fonts with over 400 characters. Includes Clip3D, a program to manipulate the artwork.
System: MAC, II, PLUS, SE, XL
Minimum Memory: 512K
Medium: 3 1/2-inch disk
ISPN: 29051-160   **Price: $99.99**

ENABLING TECHNOLOGIES, INC.
CLIP3D GEOGRAPHY

Includes 250 predrawn, full-color three-dimensional geography images. Includes Clip3D, a program to manipulate the artwork.
System: MAC, II, PLUS, SE, XL
Minimum Memory: 512K
Medium: 3 1/2-inch disk
ISPN: 29051-165   **Price: $99.99**

FOR MORE DETAILED INFORMATION, CALL (412) 746-MENU

ENABLING TECHNOLOGIES, INC.
CLIP3D LIFESTYLE

Includes 140 predrawn, full-color, three-dimensional images of life styles. Includes Clip3D, a program to manipulate the artwork.

System: MAC, II, PLUS, SE, XL
Minimum Memory: 512K
Medium: 3 1/2-inch disk
ISPN: 29051-170 **Price: $99.99**

ENABLING TECHNOLOGIES, INC.
CLIP3D MESSAGES

Includes 40 predrawn, full-color, three-dimensional images of messages. Includes Clip3D, a program to manipulate the artwork.

System: MAC, II, PLUS, SE, XL
Minimum Memory: 512K
Medium: 3 1/2-inch disk
ISPN: 29051-175 **Price: $99.99**

ENABLING TECHNOLOGIES, INC.
CLIP3D PEOPLE

Includes predrawn, full-color, three-dimensional images of people. Includes Clip3D, a program to manipulate the artwork.

System: MAC, II, PLUS, SE, XL
Minimum Memory: 512K
Medium: 3 1/2-inch disk
ISPN: 29051-180 **Price: $99.99**

ENABLING TECHNOLOGIES, INC.
CLIP3D RECREATION

Includes 100 predrawn color, three-dimensional images dealing with recreation. Includes Clip3D, a program to manipulate the artwork.

System: MAC, II, PLUS, SE, XL
Minimum Memory: 512K
Medium: 3 1/2-inch disk
ISPN: 29051-185 **Price: $99.99**

DREAM MAKER SOFTWARE
CLIPTURES (VOL. 1) BUSINESS IMAGES

Encapsulated PostScript business images of people, cartoons, objects, symbols, and graphics.

System: MAC, II, PLUS, SE, XL
Minimum Memory: 1024K
Requires: 800K disk drive. Graphics program that accepts Encapsulated PostScript (EPS) files.
Medium: 3 1/2-inch disk
ISPN: 91255-100 **Price: $129.95**

DREAM MAKER SOFTWARE
CLIPTURES (VOL. 2) BUSINESS IMAGES 2

Encapsulated PostScript (EPS) graphics for for desktop publishing and presentations. Includes people, computers, aircraft and more.

System: MAC, II, PLUS, SE, XL
Minimum Memory: 1024K
Requires: 800K disk drive. Graphics program that accepts Encapsulated PostScript (EPS) files.
Medium: 3 1/2-inch disk
ISPN: 91255-102 **Price: $129.95**

BEDE TECH
COLORING BOOK SOFTWARE (VOL. 1)

Contains full page illustrations of dinosaurs, dogs, cats and horses in MacPaint format for children to color with crayons.

System: MAC, II, PLUS, SE, XL
Minimum Memory: 128K
Requires: MacPaint (ISPN 12784-510) or other program that can read MacPaint documents.
Medium: 3 1/2-inch disk
ISPN: 07237-100 **Price: $12.95**

BEDE TECH
COLORING BOOK SOFTWARE (VOL. 2)

Contains full-page illustrations of more dinosaurs, dogs, cats and horses in MacPaint format for children's coloring activities.

System: MAC, II, PLUS, SE, XL
Minimum Memory: 128K
Requires: MacPaint (ISPN 12784-510) or other program that can read MacPaint documents.
Medium: 3 1/2-inch disk
ISPN: 07237-110 **Price: $12.95**

BEDE TECH
COLORING BOOK SOFTWARE (VOL. 3)

Contains full-page illustrations of more dinosaurs, small animals, oceanic fish, and birds of America in MacPaint format.

System: MAC, II, PLUS, SE, XL
Minimum Memory: 128K
Requires: MacPaint (ISPN 12784-510) or other program that can read MacPaint documents.
Medium: 3 1/2-inch disk
ISPN: 07237-120 **Price: $12.95**

BEDE TECH
COLORING BOOK SOFTWARE (VOL. 4)

Contains full-page illustrations of tropical fish, birds, plants, and wild flowers in MacPaint format for children's coloring.

System: MAC, II, PLUS, SE, XL
Minimum Memory: 128K
Requires: MacPaint (ISPN 12784-510) or other program that can read MacPaint documents.
Medium: 3 1/2-inch disk
ISPN: 07237-130 **Price: $12.95**

BEDE TECH
COLORING BOOK SOFTWARE (VOLS. 1-4)

Contains all four volumes of the Coloring Book Software series in a MacPaint format for children's coloring activities.

System: MAC, II, PLUS, SE, XL
Minimum Memory: 128K
Requires: MacPaint (ISPN 12784-510) or other program that can read MacPaint documents.
Medium: 3 1/2-inch disk
ISPN: 07237-140 **Price: $39.95**

SOFTSTYLE, INC.
COLORMATE ART

Clip art with over 130 pre-colored images for creating business, professional and educational presentations.

System: MAC, II, PLUS, SE, XL
Minimum Memory: 512K
Medium: 3 1/2-inch disk
ISPN: 72235-015 **Price: $45.00**

FOUNDATION PUBLISHING
COMIC PEOPLE (VOL. 1)

Contains thousands of clip-art drawings suitable for use with Comic Strip Factory.

System: MAC, II, PLUS, SE, XL
Minimum Memory: 128K
Requires: Comic Strip Factory (ISPN 42743-200).
Medium: 3 1/2-inch disk
ISPN: 42743-205 **Price: $39.95**

ARTWARE SYSTEMS, INC.
COMPUTERS & COMMUNICATIONS

A collection of images related to computers and communications in business, such as hardware components and communication devices.

System: MAC, II, PLUS, SE, XL
Minimum Memory: 512K
Requires: PostScript printer.
Medium: 3 1/2-inch disk
ISPN: 05432-160 **Price: $89.95**

ARTFACTORY
CONTEMPORARY BACKGROUNDS (VOL. 1)

A collection of 12 encapsulated PostScript illustrations which can be used in page layout programs that support PostScript.

System: MAC, II, PLUS, SE, XL
Minimum Memory: 1024K
Requires: Page layout program that imports Encapsulated PostScript images.
Medium: 3 1/2-inch disk
ISPN: 90358-100 **Price: $89.95**

KINGSLEY/ATF SOFTWARE DIVISION
COOPER

Contains three downloadable PostScript fonts including Cooper Black Roman, Cooper Black Italic and Cooper Hilite.

System: MAC, II, PLUS, SE, XL
Minimum Memory: 512K
Requires: PostScript printer.
Medium: 3 1/2-inch disk
ISPN: 43012-140 **Price: $195.00**

ADOBE SYSTEMS, INC.
COOPER BLACK

Contains two variations of the Cooper Black downloadable font for use with any postscript printer.

System: MAC, II, PLUS, SE, XL
Minimum Memory: 512K
Requires: PostScript printer.
Medium: 3 1/2-inch disk
ISPN: 01012-125 **Price: $145.00**

ADOBE SYSTEMS, INC.
CORONA
Contains Corona, Corona Italic and Corona Bold PostScript fonts.
System: MAC, II, PLUS, SE, XL
Minimum Memory: 512K
Requires: PostScript printer.
Medium: 3 1/2-inch disk
ISPN: 01012-127   **Price: $145.00**

ALLOTYPE TYPOGRAPHICS
CZASY
Specialized downloadable LaserWriter font of four styles of serif Polish fonts.
System: MAC, II, PLUS, SE, XL
Minimum Memory: 512K
Medium: 3 1/2-inch disk
ISPN: 90338-140   **Price: $85.00**

ALLOTYPE TYPOGRAPHICS
CZASY-SMALL CAPS
Small caps set for Polish typesetting. Available in Roman, italic bold, and bold-italic styles.
System: MAC, II, PLUS, SE, XL
Minimum Memory: 512K
Medium: 3 1/2-inch disk
ISPN: 90338-145   **Price: $40.00**

DAVKA CORP.
DAVKAGRAPHICS III
Judaic clip art applicable for all seasons and occasions.
System: MAC, II, PLUS, SE, XL
Minimum Memory: 512K
Medium: 3 1/2-inch disk
ISPN: 91205-205   **Price: $34.95**

ALLOTYPE TYPOGRAPHICS
DEMOTIKI
A complete character set for typesetting in modern Greek.
System: MAC, II, PLUS, SE, XL
Minimum Memory: 512K
Medium: 3 1/2-inch disk
ISPN: 90338-160   **Price: $85.00**

BOSTON PUBLISHING SYSTEMS
DESIGNS FOR MACPUBLISHING
Designs pictures, fonts and graphics.
System: MAC, II, PLUS, SE, XL
Minimum Memory: 512K
Requires: MacPaint (ISPN 12784-510)
Medium: 3 1/2-inch disk
ISPN: 08268-050   **Price: $39.95**

DYNAMIC GRAPHICS, INC. (IL)
DESKTOP ART-ARTFOLIO I
A selection of 200 pictograms, seasonal symbols and design elements of all kinds.
System: MAC, II, PLUS, SE, XL
Minimum Memory: 512K
Requires: MacPaint (ISPN 12784-510), FullPaint (ISPN 05500-195) or MacPaint II.
Medium: 3 1/2-inch disk
ISPN: 27181-210   **Price: $74.95**

DYNAMIC GRAPHICS, INC. (IL)
DESKTOP ART-BORDERS & MORTICES I
A selection of 200 border designs for ad, coupon and certificate production.
System: MAC, II, PLUS, SE, XL
Minimum Memory: 512K
Requires: MacPaint (ISPN 12784-510), MacDraw (ISPN 12784-500), FullPaint (ISPN 05500-195), MacDraw II (ISPN 12784-505) or MacPaint II.
Medium: 3 1/2-inch disk
ISPN: 27181-260   **Price: $74.95**

DYNAMIC GRAPHICS, INC. (IL)
DESKTOP ART-BUSINESS I
A selection of 200 illustrations for business and industrial desktop publishing applications.
System: MAC, II, PLUS, SE, XL
Minimum Memory: 512K
Requires: MacPaint (ISPN 12784-510), MacDraw (ISPN 12784-500), FullPaint (ISPN 05500-195), MacDraw II (ISPN 12784-505) or MacPaint II.
Medium: 3 1/2-inch disk
ISPN: 27181-250   **Price: $74.95**

DYNAMIC GRAPHICS, INC. (IL)
DESKTOP ART-EDUCATION I
A selection of 200 contemporary illustrations of school and educational themes, from kindergarten through college.
System: MAC, II, PLUS, SE, XL
Minimum Memory: 512K
Requires: MacPaint (ISPN 12784-510), MacDraw (ISPN 12784-500), FullPaint (ISPN 05500-195), MacDraw II (ISPN 12784-505) or MacPaint II.
Medium: 3 1/2-inch disk
ISPN: 27181-230   **Price: $74.95**

DYNAMIC GRAPHICS, INC. (IL)
DESKTOP ART-FOUR SEASONS I
A collection of 200 illustrations and symbols for every season and major holiday.
System: MAC, II, PLUS, SE, XL
Minimum Memory: 512K
Requires: MacPaint (ISPN 12784-510), MacDraw (ISPN 12784-500), FullPaint (ISPN 05500-195), MacDraw II (ISPN 12784-505) or MacPaint II.
Medium: 3 1/2-inch disk
ISPN: 27181-220   **Price: $74.95**

DYNAMIC GRAPHICS, INC. (IL)
DESKTOP ART-GRAPHICS & SYMBOLS I
A selection of 200 pictograms, seasonal symbols and design elements.
System: MAC, II, PLUS, SE, XL
Minimum Memory: 512K
Requires: MacPaint (ISPN 12784-510), FullPaint (ISPN 05500-195) or MacPaint II.
Medium: 3 1/2-inch disk
ISPN: 27181-270   **Price: $74.95**

DYNAMIC GRAPHICS, INC. (IL)
DESKTOP ART-HEALTH CARE I
A selection of 200 scenes and symbols for hospitals, medical schools, clinics, fitness and nutrition centers.
System: MAC, II, PLUS, SE, XL
Minimum Memory: 512K
Requires: MacPaint (ISPN 12784-510), MacDraw (ISPN 12784-500), FullPaint (ISPN 05500-195), MacDraw II (ISPN 12784-505) or MacPaint II.
Medium: 3 1/2-inch disk
ISPN: 27181-200   **Price: $74.95**

DYNAMIC GRAPHICS, INC. (IL)
DESKTOP ART-SPORTS I
A selection of 200 action graphics for every sport and season, and many recreational activities.
System: MAC, II, PLUS, SE, XL
Minimum Memory: 512K
Requires: MacPaint (ISPN 12784-510), MacDraw (ISPN 12784-500), FullPaint (ISPN 05500-195), MacDraw II (ISPN 12784-505) or MacPaint II.
Medium: 3 1/2-inch disk
ISPN: 27181-240   **Price: $74.95**

DYNAMIC GRAPHICS, INC. (IL)
DESKTOP ART/EPS-ATHLETICS I
A collection of graphic images in Encapsulated PostScript to print at the resolution of the printer whether reduced or enlarged.
System: MAC, II, PLUS, SE, XL
Minimum Memory: 1024K
Requires: Pagemaker (ISPN 02226-700), QuarkExpress (ISPN 64285-800), Ready,Set,Go! (ISPN 44293-600) or other page layout program.
Medium: 3 1/2-inch disk
ISPN: 27181-340   **Price: $74.95**

DYNAMIC GRAPHICS, INC. (IL)
DESKTOP ART/EPS-COMMERCE I
A collection of graphic images in Encapsulated PostScript to print at the resolution of the printer whether reduced or enlarged.
System: MAC, II, PLUS, SE, XL
Minimum Memory: 1024K
Requires: Pagemaker (ISPN 02226-700), QuarkExpress (ISPN 64285-800), Ready,Set,Go! (ISPN 44293-600) or other page layout program.
Medium: 3 1/2-inch disk
ISPN: 27181-310   **Price: $74.95**

DYNAMIC GRAPHICS, INC. (IL)
DESKTOP ART/EPS-DESIGN ELEMENTS I
A collection of graphic images in Encapsulated PostScript to print at the resolution of the printer whether reduced or enlarged.
System: MAC, II, PLUS, SE, XL
Minimum Memory: 1024K
Requires: Pagemaker (ISPN 02226-700), QuarkExpress (ISPN 64285-800), Ready,Set,Go! (ISPN 44293-600) or other page layout program.
Medium: 3 1/2-inch disk
ISPN: 27181-330   **Price: $74.95**

FOR MORE DETAILED INFORMATION, CALL (412) 746-MENU

DYNAMIC GRAPHICS, INC. (IL)
DESKTOP ART/EPS-PEOPLE I

A collection of graphic images in Encapsulated PostScript to print at the resolution of the printer whether reduced or enlarged

System: MAC, II, PLUS, SE, XL
Minimum Memory: 1024K
Requires: Pagemaker (ISPN 02226-700), QuarkExpress (ISPN 64285-800), Ready,Set,Go! (ISPN 44293-600) or other page layout program.
Medium: 3 1/2-inch disk
ISPN: 27181-350   **Price: $74.95**

DYNAMIC GRAPHICS, INC. (IL)
DESKTOP ART/EPS-POTPOURRI I

A collection of graphic images in Encapsulated PostScript to print at the resolution of the printer whether reduced or enlarged.

System: MAC, II, PLUS, SE, XL
Minimum Memory: 1024K
Requires: Pagemaker (ISPN 02226-700), QuarkExpress (ISPN 64285-800), Ready,Set,Go! (ISPN 44293-600) or other page layout program.
Medium: 3 1/2-inch disk
ISPN: 27181-300   **Price: $74.95**

DYNAMIC GRAPHICS, INC. (IL)
DESKTOP ART/EPS-SEASONAL I

A collection of graphic images in Encapsulated PostScript to print at the resolution of the printer whether reduced or enlarged.

System: MAC, II, PLUS, SE, XL
Minimum Memory: 1024K
Requires: Pagemaker (ISPN 02226-700), QuarkExpress (ISPN 64285-800), Ready,Set,Go! (ISPN 44293-600) or other page layout program.
Medium: 3 1/2-inch disk
ISPN: 27181-320   **Price: $74.95**

IMAGE CLUB GRAPHICS
DIGIT-ART LASER GRAPHICS (VOL. 1)

Three-disk set of PostScript graphics including decorative fonts, graphics, forms, borders and symbols in MacDraw format.

System: MAC, II, PLUS, SE, XL
Minimum Memory: 512K
Requires: MacDraw (ISPN 12784-500) or Cricket Draw (ISPN 35512-020).
Medium: 3 1/2-inch disk
ISPN: 37146-200   **Price: $99.00**

IMAGE CLUB GRAPHICS
DIGIT-ART LASER GRAPHICS (VOL. 2)

This is a three-disk set of PostScript graphics consisting of fonts, graphics, pictures, forms, borders and symbols.

System: MAC, II, PLUS, SE, XL
Minimum Memory: 312K
Requires: MacDraw (ISPN 12784-500) or Cricket Draw (ISPN 35512-020).
Medium: 3 1/2-inch disk
ISPN: 37146-205   **Price: $99.00**

IMAGE CLUB GRAPHICS
DIGIT-ART LASER GRAPHICS (VOL. 3)

Contains a five-disk set of PostScript graphics clip art that includes people, business, food, travel and decorative borders.

System: MAC, II, PLUS, SE, XL
Minimum Memory: 512K
Requires: MacDraw (ISPN 12784-500) or Cricket Draw (ISPN 35512-020).
Medium: 3 1/2-inch disk
ISPN: 37146-210   **Price: $150.00**

IMAGE CLUB GRAPHICS
DIGIT-ART LASER GRAPHICS SUPER SET

Combines Volumes 1 and 2 in a six-disk set consisting of decorative fonts, graphics, pictures, forms, borders and symbols.

System: MAC, II, PLUS, SE, XL
Minimum Memory: 312K
Medium: 3 1/2-inch disk
ISPN: 37146-700   **Price: $168.00**

IMAGE WORLD, INC.
DIVINE IMAGES, WE ARE ONE

Graphics from the Turn-of-the-Century including the spiritual essence of Christian and other religious works.

System: MAC, II, PLUS, SE, XL
Minimum Memory: 128K
Requires: MacPaint (ISPN 12784-510), MacDraw (ISPN 12784-500) or MacDraft (ISPN 37053-400).
Medium: 3 1/2-inch disk
ISPN: 37181-290   **Price: $30.00**

ALTSYS CORP.
DOUG MILES FONTS

A collection of eight complete bitmap fonts. All are completely editable with Fontastic or preferably, Fontastic Plus.

System: MAC, II, PLUS, SE, XL
Minimum Memory: 512K
Requires: Fontastic Plus (ISPN 2675-125).
Medium: 3 1/2-inch disk
ISPN: 02675-075   **Price: $19.95**

DESKTOP GRAPHICS
DRAWART (VOL. 1)

A collection of graphic images created using MacDraw.

System: MAC, II, PLUS, SE, XL
Minimum Memory: 512K
Requires: MacDraw (ISPN 12784-500).
Medium: 3 1/2-inch disk
ISPN: 23555-250   **Price: $49.95**

MODERN GRAPHICS
DRAWSTRUCTURES

Contains a chemical structure library with hundreds of drawings in PICT format.

System: MAC, II, PLUS, SE, XL
Minimum Memory: 512K
Requires: PICT formatted drawing program.
Medium: 3 1/2-inch disk
ISPN: 54925-300   **Price: $79.95**

ARTWARE SYSTEMS, INC.
EQUESTRIAN I (S1D1.8,1.11)

Provides an assortment of twenty seven PostScript images of equestrian art designed with Adobe Illustrator.

System: MAC, II, PLUS, SE, XL
Minimum Memory: 512K
Requires: PostScript printer.
Medium: 3 1/2-inch disk
ISPN: 05432-200   **Price: $89.95**

ADOBE SYSTEMS, INC.
EUROSTILE

Contains six variations of the Eurostile PostScript font.

System: MAC, II, PLUS, SE, XL
Minimum Memory: 512K
Requires: PostScript printer.
Medium: 3 1/2-inch disk
ISPN: 01012-128   **Price: $275.00**

ADOBE SYSTEMS, INC.
EXCELSIOR

Contains Excelsior, Excelsior Italic and Excelsior Bold PostScript fonts.

System: MAC, II, PLUS, SE, XL
Minimum Memory: 512K
Requires: PostScript printer.
Medium: 3 1/2-inch disk
ISPN: 01012-129   **Price: $145.00**

ALLAN BONADIO ASSOCIATES
EXPRESSIONIST (VER. 2.0)

Generates typeset quality equations with a word processor and layout such as MacWrite, Microsoft Word, Write Now, and PageMaker.

System: MAC, II, PLUS, SE, XL
Minimum Memory: 512K
Requires: 800K disk drive.
Medium: 3 1/2-inch disk
ISPN: 08168-200   **Price: $129.95**

GDT SOFTWORKS, INC.
EXPRESSIVE FONTS (VER. 1.0)

Includes 22 scalable fonts from seven families for the JetLink Express Macintosh printer driver.

System: MAC, II, PLUS, SE, XL
Minimum Memory: 1024K
Requires: Hard disk.
Medium: 3 1/2-inch disk
ISPN: 92112-100   **Price: $198.00**

ALTSYS CORP.
FACES

Postscript fonts for Apple's LaserWriter and other postscript printers.

System: MAC, II, PLUS, SE, XL
Minimum Memory: 512K
Medium: 3 1/2-inch disk
ISPN: 02675-300   **Price: $59.95**

DESKTOP VIDEO PRODUCTIONS

FACES

Includes a range of faces both in size and style, including two full pages of small male and female Roman profiles.

System: MAC
Minimum Memory: 512K
Medium: 3 1/2-inch disk
ISPN: 46012-515 **Price: $39.95**

GENNY SOFTWARE

FANCY FONTS 'BIZ-PAC' (BUSINESS PACKAGE)

A three-disk package providing 50 fonts, a total of 50 programs each designed to create calendars, graphs, charts, more.

System: MAC, II, PLUS, SE, XL
Minimum Memory: 128K
Medium: 3 1/2-inch disk
ISPN: 32612-200 **Price: $49.95**

GOLDMIND PUBLISHING

FANCY LETTERS (VOL. 11)

A collection of large format FullPaint files for illustrating desktop publishing documents. Up to 2470 dots per inch resolution.

System: MAC, II, PLUS, SE, XL
Minimum Memory: 512K
Requires: 800K disk drive, FullPaint (ISPN 05500-195).
Medium: 3 1/2-inch disk
ISPN: 33256-033 **Price: $39.95**

AAH COMPUTER GRAPHIC PRODUCTIONS

FANTASY REALMS (VER. 1.0)

A collection of MacPaint images that is devoted entirely to fantasy themes.

System: MAC, II, PLUS, SE, XL
Minimum Memory: 128K
Requires: MacPaint (ISPN 12784-510) or program that can read MacPaint files.
Medium: 3 1/2-inch disk
ISPN: 00181-300 **Price: $29.95**

IMAGE WORLD, INC.

FISH, FUR AND FOWL

Old engravings and etchings of the Animal Kingdom from children's books, encyclopedias, and dictionaries.

System: MAC, II, PLUS, SE, XL
Minimum Memory: 128K
Medium: 3 1/2-inch disk
ISPN: 37181-315 **Price: $30.00**

CASADY & GREENE, INC.

FLUENT FONTS (VER. 2.0)

Includes 60 plus font styles to add to any program with font menu. Text, decorative, scientific symbols, electrical symbols and more.

System: MAC, II, PLUS, SE, XL
Minimum Memory: 128K
Medium: 3 1/2-inch disk
ISPN: 11556-300 **Price: $49.95**

CASADY & GREENE, INC.

FLUENT LASER FONTS (VOL. 1)-BODONI FAMILY

Provides bit-map and PostScript Bodoni fonts.

System: MAC, II, PLUS, SE, XL
Minimum Memory: 512K
Medium: 3 1/2-inch disk
ISPN: 11556-355 **Price: $89.95**

CASADY & GREENE, INC.

FLUENT LASER FONTS (VOL. 10)-BODONI ULTRA FAMILY

Contains bit-map and PostScript Bodoni Ultra fonts.

System: MAC, II, PLUS, SE, XL
Minimum Memory: 512K
Medium: 3 1/2-inch disk
ISPN: 11556-400 **Price: $89.95**

CASADY & GREENE, INC.

FLUENT LASER FONTS (VOL. 11)-SANS SERIF BOLD

Contains bit-map and PostScript Sans Serif Bold fonts.

System: MAC, II, PLUS, SE, XL
Minimum Memory: 512K
Medium: 3 1/2-inch disk
ISPN: 11556-405 **Price: $89.95**

CASADY & GREENE, INC.

FLUENT LASER FONTS (VOL. 12)-SANS SERIF EXTRA BOLD

Contains bit-map and PostScript Sans Serif Extra Bold fonts.

System: MAC, II, PLUS, SE, XL
Minimum Memory: 512K
Medium: 3 1/2-inch disk
ISPN: 11556-410 **Price: $89.95**

CASADY & GREENE, INC.

FLUENT LASER FONTS (VOL. 13)-GATSBY FAMILY

Contains bit-map and PostScript Gatsby, a classic deco font.

System: MAC, II, PLUS, SE, XL
Minimum Memory: 512K
Medium: 3 1/2-inch disk
ISPN: 11556-415 **Price: $89.95**

CASADY & GREENE, INC.

FLUENT LASER FONTS (VOL. 14)-MICRO FAMILY

Consists of bit-map and PostScript Micro Family fonts.

System: MAC, II, PLUS, SE, XL
Minimum Memory: 512K
Medium: 3 1/2-inch disk
ISPN: 11556-420 **Price: $89.95**

CASADY & GREENE, INC.

FLUENT LASER FONTS (VOL. 15)-MICRO EXTENDED FAMILY

Consists of bit-map and PostScript Micro Extended family fonts.

System: MAC, II, PLUS, SE, XL
Minimum Memory: 512K
Medium: 3 1/2-inch disk
ISPN: 11556-425 **Price: $89.95**

CASADY & GREENE, INC.

FLUENT LASER FONTS (VOL. 16)-GALILEO ROMAN

Contains four PostScript compatible fonts, Galileo Roman, Galileo Roman Bold, Galileo Roman Italic and Galileo Roman Bold Italic.

System: MAC, II, PLUS, SE, XL
Minimum Memory: 512K
Requires: PostScript printer.
Medium: 3 1/2-inch disk
ISPN: 11556-430 **Price: $89.95**

CASADY & GREENE, INC.

FLUENT LASER FONTS (VOL. 17)-CAMPANILE/GIOTTO

Contains three PostScript compatible fonts, Campanile, Giotto and Giotto Bold.

System: MAC, II, PLUS, SE, XL
Minimum Memory: 512K
Requires: PostScript printer.
Medium: 3 1/2-inch disk
ISPN: 11556-435 **Price: $89.95**

CASADY & GREENE, INC.

FLUENT LASER FONTS (VOL. 18)-ALEXANDRIA

Contains four PostScript compatible fonts, Alexandria, Alexandria Bold, Alexandria Italic and Alexandria Bold Italic.

System: MAC, II, PLUS, SE, XL
Minimum Memory: 512K
Requires: PostScript printer.
Medium: 3 1/2-inch disk
ISPN: 11556-440 **Price: $89.95**

CASADY & GREENE, INC.

FLUENT LASER FONTS (VOL. 19)-JOTT CASUAL

Contains bit-map and PostScript Jott Casual fonts.

System: MAC, II, PLUS, SE, XL
Minimum Memory: 512K
Requires: PostScript printer.
Medium: 3 1/2-inch disk
ISPN: 11556-445 **Price: $89.95**

CASADY & GREENE, INC.

FLUENT LASER FONTS (VOL. 2)-SANS SERIF FAMILY

Consists of bit-map and PostScript Sans Serif fonts.

System: MAC, II, PLUS, SE, XL
Minimum Memory: 512K
Medium: 3 1/2-inch disk
ISPN: 11556-360 **Price: $89.95**

FOR MORE DETAILED INFORMATION, CALL (412) 746-MENU

CASADY & GREENE, INC.

FLUENT LASER FONTS (VOL. 20)-GAZELLE/KELLS MEATH

Contains bit-map and PostScript Gazelle, Kells Meath fonts.

System: MAC, II, PLUS, SE, XL
Minimum Memory: 512K
Requires: PostScript printer.
Medium: 3 1/2-inch disk
ISPN: 11556-450 **Price: $89.95**

CASADY & GREENE, INC.

FLUENT LASER FONTS (VOL. 21)-PALADIN/ABILENE

Consists of bit-mapped and PostScript Paladin and Abilene fonts.

System: MAC, II, PLUS, SE, XL
Minimum Memory: 512K
Requires: PostScript printer.
Medium: 3 1/2-inch disk
ISPN: 11556-455 **Price: $89.95**

CASADY & GREENE, INC.

FLUENT LASER FONTS (VOL. 22)-COLLEGIATE BLACK

Contains bit-mapped and PostScript Collegiate Black fonts.

System: MAC, II, PLUS, SE, XL
Minimum Memory: 512K
Requires: PostScript printer.
Medium: 3 1/2-inch disk
ISPN: 11556-460 **Price: $89.95**

CASADY & GREENE, INC.

FLUENT LASER FONTS (VOL. 3)-RITZ/RIGHT BANK

Consists of bit-map and PostScript Ritz and Right Bank fonts.

System: MAC, II, PLUS, SE, XL
Minimum Memory: 512K
Medium: 3 1/2-inch disk
ISPN: 11556-365 **Price: $89.95**

CASADY & GREENE, INC.

FLUENT LASER FONTS (VOL. 4)-MONTEREY FAMILY

The Monterey family is an unique text or headline font.

System: MAC, II, PLUS, SE, XL
Minimum Memory: 512K
Medium: 3 1/2-inch disk
ISPN: 11556-370 **Price: $89.95**

CASADY & GREENE, INC.

FLUENT LASER FONTS (VOL. 5)-CALLIGRAPHY/REGENCY

Consists of bit-map and PostScript Calligraphy and Regency Script decorative fonts.

System: MAC, II, PLUS, SE, XL
Minimum Memory: 512K
Medium: 3 1/2-inch disk
ISPN: 11556-375 **Price: $89.95**

CASADY & GREENE, INC.

FLUENT LASER FONTS (VOL. 6)-PRELUDE SCRIPT FAMILY

Consists of bit-map and PostScript Prelude Script fonts.

System: MAC, II, PLUS, SE, XL
Minimum Memory: 512K
Medium: 3 1/2-inch disk
ISPN: 11556-380 **Price: $89.95**

CASADY & GREENE, INC.

FLUENT LASER FONTS (VOL. 7)-COVENTRY SCRIPT/ZEPHYR

The Coventry Script is an elegant, decorative PostScript font and Zephyr is a modern informal PostScript font.

System: MAC, II, PLUS, SE, XL
Minimum Memory: 512K
Medium: 3 1/2-inch disk
ISPN: 11556-385 **Price: $89.95**

CASADY & GREENE, INC.

FLUENT LASER FONTS (VOL. 8)-GREGORIAN/DOROVAR

Gregorian is an Old English style decorative typeface and Dorovar is similar to uncial lettering. Has PostScript and bitmap fonts.

System: MAC, II, PLUS, SE, XL
Minimum Memory: 512K
Medium: 3 1/2-inch disk
ISPN: 11556-390 **Price: $89.95**

CASADY & GREENE, INC.

FLUENT LASER FONTS (VOL. 9)-KUPURRUUA

Consists of Russian, Ukranian, Bulgarian and Serbian PostScript fonts.

System: MAC, II, PLUS, SE, XL
Minimum Memory: 512K
Medium: 3 1/2-inch disk
ISPN: 11556-395 **Price: $89.95**

VIKING TECHNOLOGIES

FONT TIME

Fifteen new fonts: Basel, Broadway, Camelot, Fallingwater, Future, Lineal, Ottowa, Palo Alto, Pica, plus more. Plus a Font Tester.

System: MAC, II, PLUS, SE, XL
Minimum Memory: 512K
Medium: 3 1/2-inch disk
ISPN: 85231-200 **Price: $19.95**

DEVONIAN INT'L. SOFTWARE CO.

FONTAGENIX FOURPAK

A collection of all the fonts contained in Fontagenix I, II, III and IV.

System: MAC, II, PLUS, SE, XL
Minimum Memory: 512K
Requires: Dot matrix printer.
Medium: 3 1/2-inch disk
ISPN: 24987-250 **Price: $139.50**

DEVONIAN INT'L. SOFTWARE CO.

FONTAGENIX I

A collection of 11 fonts containing many different styles.

System: MAC, II, PLUS, SE, XL
Minimum Memory: 512K
Requires: Dot matrix printer.
Medium: 3 1/2-inch disk
ISPN: 24987-275 **Price: $39.50**

DEVONIAN INT'L. SOFTWARE CO.

FONTAGENIX II

A collection of 11 fonts containing many different styles.

System: MAC, II, PLUS, SE, XL
Minimum Memory: 512K
Requires: Dot matrix printer.
Medium: 3 1/2-inch disk
ISPN: 24987-276 **Price: $39.50**

DEVONIAN INT'L. SOFTWARE CO.

FONTAGENIX III

A collection of 12 fonts for graphic artists to give a greater range of styles for headlines.

System: MAC, II, PLUS, SE, XL
Minimum Memory: 512K
Requires: Dot matrix printer.
Medium: 3 1/2 inch disk
ISPN: 24987-277 **Price: $39.50**

DEVONIAN INT'L. SOFTWARE CO.

FONTAGENIX IV

A collection of graphic fonts and font utilities containing many styles.

System: MAC, II, PLUS, SE, XL
Minimum Memory: 512K
Requires: Dot matrix printer.
Medium: 3 1/2-inch disk
ISPN: 24987-325 **Price: $39.50**

DEVONIAN INT'L. SOFTWARE CO.

FONTAGENIX SERIES

A collection of all the fonts contained in Fontagenix I, II, and III.

System: MAC, II, PLUS, SE, XL
Minimum Memory: 512K
Requires: Dot Matrix Printer.
Medium: 3 1/2-inch disk
ISPN: 24987-280 **Price: $99.50**

ALTSYS CORP.

FONTASTIC FONTS-FOREIGN LANGUAGE PACKAGE

Consists of eight foreign language fonts including Volga, Ararat, Shenute, Saloniki, Mesrob, Eznik, Pskov, and Vladimir.

System: MAC, II, PLUS, SE, XL
Minimum Memory: 512K
Medium: 3 1/2-inch disk
ISPN: 02675-110 **Price: $29.95**

ALTSYS CORP.

FONTASTIC FONTS-MATH & SPECIAL SYMBOLS

Consists of four unique and specialized fonts which are useful when using mathematical and scientific notations.

System: MAC, II, PLUS, SE, XL
Minimum Memory: 512K
Medium: 3 1/2-inch disk
ISPN: 02675-115　　　　　　　**Price: $19.95**

ALTSYS CORP.

FONTASTIC PLUS (VER. 2.0)

Enhanced version of Fontastic with multi-windowing, curting pairs, fractional character spacing and new edit tools.

System: MAC, II, PLUS, SE, XL
Minimum Memory: 512K
Medium: 3 1/2-inch disk
ISPN: 02675-125　　　　　　　**Price: $79.95**

ALTSYS CORP.

FONTOGRAPHER (VER. 2.4)

Professional outline font editor for the Macintosh computer and postscript printers.

System: MAC, II, PLUS, SE, XL
Minimum Memory: 512K
Medium: 3 1/2-inch disk
ISPN: 02675-200　　　　　　　**Price: $395.00**

ALTSYS CORP.

FONTOGRAPHER FONTS-BORDERS I

A collaboration between Richard Mitchell and Richard Beatty who created screen fonts and added some extra characters.

System: MAC, II, PLUS, SE, XL
Minimum Memory: 512K
Medium: 3 1/2-inch disk
ISPN: 02675-126　　　　　　　**Price: $59.95**

ALTSYS CORP.

FONTOGRAPHER FONTS-BORDERS II

A fine collection of borders and decoratives, created by Richard Beatty. Contains editable Fontographer-format files.

System: MAC, II, PLUS, SE, XL
Minimum Memory: 512K
Medium: 3 1/2-inch disk
ISPN: 02675-127　　　　　　　**Price: $59.95**

ALTSYS CORP.

FONTOGRAPHER FONTS-BORDERS III

Collection of holiday and festive borders and icons, although some are more general purpose.

System: MAC, II, PLUS, SE, XL
Minimum Memory: 512K
Medium: 3 1/2-inch disk
ISPN: 02675-128　　　　　　　**Price: $59.95**

ALTSYS CORP.

FONTOGRAPHER FONTS-BORDERS IV

A collection of borders and icons, created by Richard Beatty. Printed on the LaserWriter instead of the Linotronic 300.

System: MAC, II, PLUS, SE, XL
Minimum Memory: 512K
Medium: 3 1/2-inch disk
ISPN: 02675-129　　　　　　　**Price: $59.95**

ALTSYS CORP.

FONTOGRAPHER FONTS-COOPER

Type styles that work well in display and can also be used for text.

System: MAC, II, PLUS, SE, XL
Minimum Memory: 512K
Medium: 3 1/2-inch disk
ISPN: 02675-130　　　　　　　**Price: $59.95**

ALTSYS CORP.

FONTOGRAPHER FONTS-COOPEROLDSTYLE

Includes short lowercase letters with long ascenders in the tradition of early type design.

System: MAC, II, PLUS, SE, XL
Minimum Memory: 512K
Medium: 3 1/2-inch disk
ISPN: 02675-131　　　　　　　**Price: $59.95**

ALTSYS CORP.

FONTOGRAPHER FONTS-COOPERXTRA

Supplies special alternate designs that augment the standard versions.

System: MAC, II, PLUS, SE, XL
Minimum Memory: 512K
Medium: 3 1/2-inch disk
ISPN: 02675-132　　　　　　　**Price: $59.95**

ALTSYS CORP.

FONTOGRAPHER FONTS-GOUDY NEWSTYLE

Provides literary matrix keyboard mapping.

System: MAC, II, PLUS, SE, XL
Minimum Memory: 512K
Medium: 3 1/2-inch disk
ISPN: 02675-150　　　　　　　**Price: $59.95**

ALTSYS CORP.

FONTOGRAPHER FONTS-VENEZIA

Produces a very sophisticated face that would feel very comfortable in the Modern style of the 1920's and does again in the 1980's.

System: MAC, II, PLUS, SE, XL
Minimum Memory: 512K
Medium: 3 1/2-inch disk
ISPN: 02675-185　　　　　　　**Price: $59.95**

DECISION SCIENCE SOFTWARE

FONTS (VOL. 1)

A collection of 18 new and different fonts. Exciting fonts for artwork, presentations, bold displays, formal writings, and fun.

System: MAC, II, PLUS, SE, XL
Minimum Memory: 512K
Medium: 3 1/2-inch disk
ISPN: 24325-930　　　　　　　**Price: $35.00**

DECISION SCIENCE SOFTWARE

FONTS (VOL. 2)

A collection of 25 fonts for artwork presentations, bold displays, and formal writing.

System: MAC, II, PLUS, SE, XL
Minimum Memory: 512K
Medium: 3 1/2-inch disk
ISPN: 24325-935　　　　　　　**Price: $35.00**

IMAGE WORLD, INC.

FOOD & FEASTING

Includes serious and funny festive food fixins, menu frames and scenes of feasting and drinking gaiety.

System: MAC, II, PLUS, SE, XL
Minimum Memory: 128K
Requires: MacPaint (ISPN 12784-510), MacDraw (ISPN 12784-500) or MacDraft (ISPN 37053-400).
Medium: 3 1/2-inch disk
ISPN: 37181-325　　　　　　　**Price: $30.00**

GOLDMIND PUBLISHING

FOOD AND BEVERAGES (VOL. 5)

A collection of large format full paint files for illustrating desktop publishing documents. Up to 2470 dots per inch resolution.

System: MAC, II, PLUS, SE, XL
Minimum Memory: 512K
Requires: 800k disk drive.
Medium: 3 1/2-inch disk
ISPN: 33256-050　　　　　　　**Price: $39.95**

DEVONIAN INT'L. SOFTWARE CO.

FOREIGN FONTS EDITION

A collection of 22 fonts that include numerical systems and alphabet of many foreign languages.

System: MAC, II, PLUS, SE, XL
Minimum Memory: 128K
Requires: Dot matrix printer.
Medium: 3 1/2-inch disk
ISPN: 24987-285　　　　　　　**Price: $69.50**

GOLDMIND PUBLISHING

FRAMES AND BORDERS (VOL. 12)

A collection of large format full paint files for illustrating desk top publishing documents. Up to 2470 dpi resolution.

System: MAC, II, PLUS, SE, XL
Minimum Memory: 512K
Requires: 800k disk drive.
Medium: 3 1/2-inch disk
ISPN: 33256-068　　　　　　　**Price: $39.95**

DATA MANAGEMENT ASSOCIATES
FRAMEWORK FONTS (VER. 1.2)

Contains PostScript laser fonts that are used to provide frames and borders for PostScript documents.

System: MAC, II, PLUS, SE, XL
Minimum Memory: 512K
Requires: PostScript printer.
Medium: 3 1/2-inch disk
ISPN: 17245-250   **Price: $79.95**

KINGSLEY/ATF SOFTWARE DIVISION
FRANKLIN GOTHIC

Contains four downloadable PostScript fonts including Franklin Gothic Roman, Italic, Wide, and Extra Condensed.

System: MAC, II, PLUS, SE, XL
Minimum Memory: 512K
Requires: PostScript printer.
Medium: 3 1/2-inch disk
ISPN: 43012-200   **Price: $195.00**

ADOBE SYSTEMS, INC.
FUTURA

Contains six variations of the Futura font for use with any PostScript compatible printer.

System: MAC, II, PLUS, SE, XL
Minimum Memory: 512K
Requires: PostScript printer.
Medium: 3 1/2-inch disk
ISPN: 01012-132   **Price: $275.00**

ADOBE SYSTEMS, INC.
FUTURA CONDENSED

Contains eight variations of the Futura Condensed font for use with any PostScript compatible printer.

System: MAC, II, PLUS, SE, XL
Minimum Memory: 512K
Requires: PostScript printer.
Medium: 3 1/2-inch disk
ISPN: 01012-133   **Price: $370.00**

ADOBE SYSTEMS, INC.
FUTURA LIGHT

Contains six variations of the Futura Light downloadable font for use with any PostScript compatible printer.

System: MAC, II, PLUS, SE, XL
Minimum Memory: 512K
Requires: PostScript printer.
Medium: 3 1/2-inch disk
ISPN: 01012-130   **Price: $275.00**

BITSTREAM, INC.
FUTURA MEDIUM MACFONTWARE TYPEFACE LIBRARY

Contains four weights of one typeface, including Futura Medium, Medium Italic, Bold and Bold Italic.

System: MAC, II, PLUS, SE, XL
Minimum Memory: 512K
Requires: LaserWriter, LaserWriter IISC or ImageWriter printer.
Medium: 3 1/2-inch disk
ISPN: 07836-202   **Price: $195.00**

ADOBE SYSTEMS, INC.
GLYPHA

Variations of the Glypha font.

System: MAC, II, PLUS, SE, XL
Minimum Memory: 512K
Requires: PostScript printer.
Medium: 3 1/2-inch disk
ISPN: 01012-135   **Price: $185.00**

MACTOGRAPHY
GOTHICA

A downloadable PostScript Gothica font for use with any PostScript compatible printer.

System: MAC, II, PLUS, SE, XL
Minimum Memory: 512K
Requires: PostScript printer.
Medium: 3 1/2-inch disk
ISPN: 00031-300   **Price: $44.95**

ADOBE SYSTEMS, INC.
GOUDY EXTRA BOLD AND HEAVYFACE

Contains the Goudy Extra Bold, Goudy Heavyface and Goudy Heavyface Italic fonts.

System: MAC, II, PLUS, SE, XL
Minimum Memory: 512K
Requires: PostScript printer.
Medium: 3 1/2-inch disk
ISPN: 01012-142   **Price: $145.00**

ADOBE SYSTEMS, INC.
GOUDY OLD STYLE

Contains four variations of the Goudy Old Style downloadable font for use with any postscript compatible printer.

System: MAC, II, PLUS, SE, XL
Minimum Memory: 512K
Requires: PostScript printer.
Medium: 3 1/2-inch disk
ISPN: 01012-140   **Price: $185.00**

MINDSCAPE, INC.
GRAPHICWORKS (VER. 1.1)

A desktop publishing tool that fully integrates graphics, text and page layout with features such as paint, design, write and print.

System: MAC, II, PLUS, SE, XL
Minimum Memory: 512K
Medium: 3 1/2-inch disk
ISPN: 54375-076   **Price: $149.95**

IMAGE WORLD, INC.
GUTENBERG SET

Combines five disks with images and scenes from the turn of the century nostalgic clip-art of famous artists and illustrators.

System: MAC, II, PLUS, SE, XL
Minimum Memory: 512K
Requires: MacPaint (ISPN 12784-510) or PictureBase (ISPN 77437-550).
Medium: 3 1/2-inch disk
ISPN: 37181-800   **Price: $130.00**

ALLOTYPE TYPOGRAPHICS
HABER AND THOMSON

Specialized downloadable LaserWriter sans-serif and serif fonts for scientific texts with standard characters and symbols in one font.

System: MAC, II, PLUS, SE, XL
Minimum Memory: 512K
Medium: 3 1/2-inch disk
ISPN: 90338-120   **Price: $75.00**

ALLOTYPE TYPOGRAPHICS
HABER AND THOMSON/ STRUCTURE

Specialized downloadable LaserWriter fonts including sans-serif and serif fonts for scientific texts and 100 chemical structures.

System: MAC, II, PLUS, SE, XL
Minimum Memory: 512K
Medium: 3 1/2-inch disk
ISPN: 90338-105   **Price: $160.00**

IMAGE WORLD, INC.
HEAD AND TAIL PIECES

Provides a full range of topical head and tail pieces including headers,indexes, contents, finis and exLibris.

System: MAC, II, PLUS, SE, XL
Minimum Memory: 128K
Medium: 3 1/2-inch disk
ISPN: 37181-328   **Price: $30.00**

BITSTREAM, INC.
HEADLINES 1 MACFONTWARE TYPEFACE LIBRARY

Includes four individual display typefaces, including Bitstream Cooper Black, University Roman, Cloister Black and Broadway.

System: MAC, II, PLUS, SE, XL
Minimum Memory: 512K
Requires: LaserWriter, LaserWriter IISC or ImageWriter printer.
Medium: 3 1/2-inch disk
ISPN: 07836-205   **Price: $195.00**

BITSTREAM, INC.
HEADLINES 2 MACFONTWARE TYPEFACE LIBRARY

Contains four individual display typefaces, including Brush Script, Blippo Black, Hobo and Windsor.

System: MAC, II, PLUS, SE, XL
Minimum Memory: 512K
Requires: LaserWriter, LaserWriter IISC or ImageWriter printer.
Medium: 3 1/2-inch disk
ISPN: 07836-206   **Price: $195.00**

ARTWARE SYSTEMS, INC.
HEALTH & MEDICINE

A two-disk set of images relating to the medical field including medical staff and equipment. Graphics are Encapsulated PostScript.

System: MAC, II, PLUS, SE, XL
Minimum Memory: 512K
Requires: PostScript printer.
Medium: 3 1/2-inch disk
ISPN: 05432-240   **Price: $89.95**

MACTOGRAPHY
HELHEAVY

Consists of PostScript Helheavy downloadable fonts.

System: MAC, II, PLUS, SE, XL
Minimum Memory: 512K
Requires: PostScript printer.
Medium: 3 1/2-inch disk
ISPN: 00031-310   **Price: $44.95**

ADOBE SYSTEMS, INC.
HELVETICA

Variations of the Helvetica font.

System: MAC, II, PLUS, SE, XL
Minimum Memory: 512K
Requires: PostScript printer.
Medium: 3 1/2-inch disk
ISPN: 01012-145   **Price: $185.00**

ADOBE SYSTEMS, INC.
HELVETICA COMPRESSED

Contains Helvetica Compressed, Helvetica Extra Compressed, and Helvetica Ultra Compressed fonts for use with PostScript printers.

System: MAC, II, PLUS, SE, XL
Minimum Memory: 512K
Requires: PostScript printer.
Medium: 3 1/2-inch disk
ISPN: 01012-242   **Price: $145.00**

ADOBE SYSTEMS, INC.
HELVETICA CONDENSED

This system contains eight variations of the Helvetica condensed downloadable font for use with a PostScript compatible printer.

System: MAC, II, PLUS, SE, XL
Minimum Memory: 512K
Requires: PostScript printer.
Medium: 3 1/2-inch disk
ISPN: 01012-200   **Price: $370.00**

PLEASANT GRAPHIC WARE
HERALDRY

Provides clip-art and text that explains and illustrates the origin and basic design requirements of coats-of-arms.

System: MAC, II, PLUS, SE, XL
Minimum Memory: 128K
Requires: Program capable of reading MacPaint format files.
Medium: 3 1/2-inch disk
ISPN: 61360-300   **Price: $42.95**

PLEASANT GRAPHIC WARE
HERALDRY II

Provides clip-art illustrations on coats of arms to supplement Heraldry (ISPN 63160-300) in MacPaint format on a 400K disk.

System: MAC, II, PLUS, SE, XL
Minimum Memory: 128K
Requires: Program capable of reading MacPaint format files.
Medium: 3 1/2-inch disk
ISPN: 61360-305   **Price: $42.95**

PLEASANT GRAPHIC WARE
HERALDRY III

Contains clip-art illustrations on medieval coats of arms found in Heraldry (ISPN 61360-300) and Heraldry II (ISPN 61360-305)

System: MAC, II, PLUS, SE, XL
Minimum Memory: 128K
Requires: Program capable of reading MacPaint format files.
Medium: 3 1/2-inch disk
ISPN: 61360-310   **Price: $82.95**

ARTFACTORY
HI-TECH BACKGROUNDS (VOL. 1)

Twelve full-page Encapsulated PostScript background illustrations which can be used in page layout programs that support PostScript.

System: MAC, II, PLUS, SE, XL
Minimum Memory: 1024K
Requires: Page layout program that imports Encapsulated PostScript images.
Medium: 3 1/2-inch disk
ISPN: 90358-300   **Price: $89.95**

BITMAP, INC.
HOLIDAY CLIP ART

One hundred sixty clip art illustrations for use with publishing packages.

System: MAC, II, PLUS, SE, XL
Minimum Memory: 128K
Medium: 3 1/2-inch disk
ISPN: 07834-400   **Price: $39.95**

VISATEX CORP.
HOLLYWOOD GREATS CLIP ART (VER. 1.0)

Contains clip art portrait drawings of great Hollywood stars. Available in MacPaint or PCX format.

System: MAC, II, PLUS, SE, XL
Minimum Memory: 512K
Requires: MacPaint (ISPN 12784-510) or compatible program.
Medium: 3 1/2-inch disk
ISPN: 85340-350   **Price: $35.00**

AAH COMPUTER GRAPHIC PRODUCTIONS
HORROR/FANTASY COLLECTION I

A carefully crafted collection of fantastic images. A sampler of science fiction, fantasy and horror graphics.

System: MAC, II, PLUS, SE, XL
Minimum Memory: 128K
Requires: MacPaint (12784-510) or Paint-compatible package.
Medium: 3 1/2-inch disk
ISPN: 00181-050   **Price: $29.95**

HYPERPRESS PUBLISHING CORP
ICON FACTORY

Provides an Icon editor and Icon art library for HyperCard.

System: MAC, II, PLUS, SE, XL
Minimum Memory: 512K
Requires: HyperCard (ISPN 03900-300)
Medium: 3 1/2-inch disk
ISPN: 36737-300   **Price: $49.95**

IMAGE WORLD, INC.
ILLUMINATED LETTERS

Interesting, humorous and eyecatching old letters from the illuminated text of Punch of the 1800's.

System: MAC, II, PLUS, SE, XL
Minimum Memory: 128K
Medium: 3 1/2-inch disk
ISPN: 37181-330   **Price: $30.00**

3G GRAPHICS
IMAGES WITH IMPACT! BUSINESS 1

A collection of business-related illustrations and symbols with categories such as computers, communications, aerospace and money.

System: MAC, II, PLUS, SE, XL
Minimum Memory: 1024K
Medium: 3 1/2-inch disk
ISPN: 00062-200   **Price: $129.95**

3G GRAPHICS
IMAGES WITH IMPACT! GRAPHICS & SYMBOLS I

Consists of illustrations designed in an Encapsulated PostScript format (EPS).

System: MAC, II, PLUS, SE, XL
Minimum Memory: 1024K
Medium: 3 1/2-inch disk
ISPN: 00062-400   **Price: $99.95**

PAUL RAPOPORT
INTERNATIONAL FONTS

Contains four ImageWriter I and II international fonts that include Roman, Greek, Cyrillic and Phonetic in 12 and 24 point size.

System: MAC, II, PLUS, SE, XL
Minimum Memory: 128K
Requires: ImageWriter I or II.
Medium: 3 1/2-inch disk
ISPN: 95403-300   **Price: $21.75**

ADOBE SYSTEMS, INC.
ITALIA

Contains three variations of the Italia downloadable font for use with any PostScript printer.

System: MAC, II, PLUS, SE, XL
Minimum Memory: 512K
Requires: PostScript printer.
Medium: 3 1/2-inch disk
ISPN: 01012-146   **Price: $145.00**

ADOBE SYSTEMS, INC.

ITC AMERICAN TYPEWRITER/ ITC MACHINE

Contains three downloadable PostScript fonts including ITC American Typewriter Medium, American Typewriter Bold and ITC Machine.

System: MAC, II, PLUS, SE, XL
Minimum Memory: 512K
Requires: PostScript printer.
Medium: 3 1/2-inch disk
ISPN: 01012-150　　　　**Price: $145.00**

ADOBE SYSTEMS, INC.

ITC AVANT GARDE

Variations of the ITC Avant Garde Gothic font.

System: MAC, II, PLUS, SE, XL
Minimum Memory: 512K
Requires: PostScript printer.
Medium: 3 1/2-inch disk
ISPN: 01012-170　　　　**Price: $185.00**

MACTOGRAPHY

ITC AVANT GARDE

Consists of the ITC Avant Garde PostScript font.

System: MAC, II, PLUS, SE, XL
Minimum Memory: 512K
Requires: PostScript printer.
Medium: 3 1/2-inch disk
ISPN: 00031-320　　　　**Price: $44.95**

ADOBE SYSTEMS, INC.

ITC BENGUIAT/ITC FRIZ QUADRATA

Variations of two ITC fonts.

System: MAC, II, PLUS, SE, XL
Minimum Memory: 512K
Requires: PostScript printer.
Medium: 3 1/2-inch disk
ISPN: 01012-155　　　　**Price: $185.00**

ADOBE SYSTEMS, INC.

ITC BOOKMAN

Contains ITC Bookman Light, Italic, Demi and Demi Italic PostScript downloadable fonts.

System: MAC, II, PLUS, SE, XL
Minimum Memory: 512K
Requires: PostScript printer.
Medium: 3 1/2-inch disk
ISPN: 01012-165　　　　**Price: $185.00**

ADOBE SYSTEMS, INC.

ITC CHELTENHAM

Contains ITC Cheltenham Book PostScript downloadable fonts including Regular, Italic, Bold and Bold Italic.

System: MAC, II, PLUS, SE, XL
Minimum Memory: 512K
Requires: PostScript printer.
Medium: 3 1/2-inch disk
ISPN: 01012-160　　　　**Price: $185.00**

MACTOGRAPHY

ITC ERAS

Consists of the ITC Eras PostScript font.

System: MAC, II, PLUS, SE, XL
Minimum Memory: 512K
Requires: PostScript printer.
Medium: 3 1/2-inch disk
ISPN: 00031-330　　　　**Price: $44.95**

ADOBE SYSTEMS, INC.

ITC ERAS

Contains six variations of the ITC Eras downloadable font for use with PostScript printers.

System: MAC, II, PLUS, SE, XL
Minimum Memory: 512K
Requires: PostScript printer.
Medium: 3 1/2-inch disk
ISPN: 01012-171　　　　**Price: $275.00**

ADOBE SYSTEMS, INC.

ITC FRANKLIN GOTHIC

Contains six ITC Franklin Gothic PostScript downloadable fonts Book, Book Oblique, Demi, Demi Oblique, Heavy, Heavy Oblique.

System: MAC, II, PLUS, SE, XL
Minimum Memory: 512K
Requires: PostScript printer.
Medium: 3 1/2-inch disk
ISPN: 01012-175　　　　**Price: $275.00**

ADOBE SYSTEMS, INC.

ITC GALLIARD

Contains four ITC Galliard PostScript downloadable fonts including Roman, Italic, Bold, and Bold Italic.

System: MAC, II, PLUS, SE, XL
Minimum Memory: 512K
Requires: PostScript printer.
Medium: 3 1/2-inch disk
ISPN: 01012-180　　　　**Price: $185.00**

BITSTREAM, INC.

ITC GALLIARD MACFONTWARE TYPEFACE LIBRARY

Contains four weights of one typeface, including ITC Galliard, Italic, Bold and Bold Italic.

System: MAC, II, PLUS, SE, XL
Minimum Memory: 512K
Requires: LaserWriter, LaserWriter IISC or ImageWriter printer.
Medium: 3 1/2-inch disk
ISPN: 07836-203　　　　**Price: $195.00**

ADOBE SYSTEMS, INC.

ITC GARAMOND

Variations of the ITC Garamond font.

System: MAC, II, PLUS, SE, XL
Minimum Memory: 512K
Requires: PostScript printer.
Medium: 3 1/2-inch disk
ISPN: 01012-185　　　　**Price: $185.00**

BITSTREAM, INC.

ITC GARAMOND BOOK MACFONTWARE TYPEFACE LIBRARY

Contains four weights of one typeface, including ITC Garamond Book, Book Italic, Bold and Bold Italic.

System: MAC, II, PLUS, SE, XL
Minimum Memory: 512K
Requires: LaserWriter, LaserWriter IISC or ImageWriter printer.
Medium: 3 1/2-inch disk
ISPN: 07836-204　　　　**Price: $195.00**

MACTOGRAPHY

ITC KABEL

ITC Kabel typefaces are downloadable PostScript fonts for use with any PostScript compatible printer.

System: MAC, II, PLUS, SE, XL
Minimum Memory: 512K
Requires: PostScript printer.
Medium: 3 1/2-inch disk
ISPN: 00031-340　　　　**Price: $44.95**

ADOBE SYSTEMS, INC.

ITC KORINNA

Contains four ITC Korinna PostScript downloadable fonts that include Regular, Kursiv Regular, Bold and Kursiv Bold.

System: MAC, II, PLUS, SE, XL
Minimum Memory: 512K
Requires: PostScript printer.
Medium: 3 1/2-inch disk
ISPN: 01012-195　　　　**Price: $185.00**

ADOBE SYSTEMS, INC.

ITC LUBALIN GRAPH

Variations of the ITC Lubalin Graph font.

System: MAC, II, PLUS, SE, XL
Minimum Memory: 512K
Requires: PostScript printer.
Medium: 3 1/2-inch disk
ISPN: 01012-205　　　　**Price: $185.00**

ADOBE SYSTEMS, INC.

ITC NEW BASKERVILLE

Contains four ITC New Baskerville PostScript downloadable fonts including Roman, Italic, Bold and Bold Italic.

System: MAC, II, PLUS, SE, XL
Minimum Memory: 512K
Requires: PostScript printer.
Medium: 3 1/2-inch disk
ISPN: 01012-210　　　　**Price: $185.00**

ADOBE SYSTEMS, INC.

ITC SOUVENIR

Variations of the ITC Souvenir font.

System: MAC, II, PLUS, SE, XL
Minimum Memory: 512K
Requires: PostScript printer.
Medium: 3 1/2-inch disk
ISPN: 01012-215　　　　**Price: $185.00**

BITSTREAM, INC.
ITC SOUVENIR LIGHT MACFONTWARE TYPEFACE LIBRARY

Contains four weights of one typeface, including ITC Souvenir Light, Light Italic, Demi and Demi Italic.

System: MAC, II, PLUS, SE, XL
Minimum Memory: 512K
Requires: LaserWriter, LaserWriter IISC or ImageWriter printer.
Medium: 3 1/2-inch disk
ISPN: 07836-209   **Price: $195.00**

ADOBE SYSTEMS, INC.
ITC TIFFANY

Contains six ITC Tiffany PostScript downloadable fonts including Regular, Italic, Demi, Demi Italic, Heavy and Heavy Italic.

System: MAC, II, PLUS, SE, XL
Minimum Memory: 512K
Requires: PostScript printer.
Medium: 3 1/2-inch disk
ISPN: 01012-220   **Price: $275.00**

ADOBE SYSTEMS, INC.
ITC ZAPF CHANCERY/ITC ZAPF DINGBATS

Variations of ITC Zapf fonts.

System: MAC, II, PLUS, SE, XL
Minimum Memory: 512K
Requires: PostScript printer.
Medium: 3 1/2-inch disk
ISPN: 01012-240   **Price: $145.00**

ADOBE SYSTEMS, INC.
JANSON

Contains variations of Janson Text downloadable fonts for use with any PostScript printers.

System: MAC, II, PLUS, SE, XL
Minimum Memory: 512K
Requires: PostScript printer.
Medium: 3 1/2-inch disk
ISPN: 01012-221   **Price: $185.00**

JAPANESE LANGUAGE SERVICES
JAPANESE CLIP ART SCROLL I (HEAVEN)

Provides electronic clip art images of traditional Japanese religious and secular images and symbols in MacPaint format.

System: MAC, II, PLUS, SE, XL
Minimum Memory: 128K
Medium: 3 1/2-inch disk
ISPN: 20012-400   **Price: $150.00**

JAPANESE LANGUAGE SERVICES
JAPANESE CLIP ART SCROLL II (EARTH)

Provides electronic clip-art images of images gamered from Japanese paintings, woodblock prints and kanji calligraphy.

System: MAC, II, PLUS, SE, XL
Minimum Memory: 128K
Medium: 3 1/2-inch disk
ISPN: 20012-410   **Price: $150.00**

ALLOTYPE TYPOGRAPHICS
KADMOS

Classical Greek downloadable LaserWriter font.

System: MAC, II, PLUS, SE, XL
Minimum Memory: 512K
Requires: PostScript printer. Specify SMK Greekkeys or Colophon format.
Medium: 3 1/2-inch disk
ISPN: 90338-110   **Price: $85.00**

PAPERBACK SOFTWARE INT'L.
KEYCAP FONTS

Expand your graphic capabilities.

System: MAC, II, PLUS, SE, XL
Minimum Memory: 512K
Requires: PostScript printer.
Medium: 3 1/2-inch disk
ISPN: 59721-101   **Price: $149.95**

ALTSYS CORP.
KEYMASTER

Generates a PostScript font from imported artwork. Creates screen fonts that can be edited with a built-in font editor.

System: MAC, II, PLUS, SE, XL
Minimum Memory: 1024K
Medium: 3 1/2-inch disk
ISPN: 02675-250   **Price: $99.95**

DESKTOP VIDEO PRODUCTIONS
LANDSCAPES (VER. 1.0)

Contains a range of full page pictures that can be used alone or with other images. Art data disks for MacPaint on Macintosh.

System: MAC, II, PLUS, SE, XL
Minimum Memory: 512K
Requires: MacPaint (ISPN 12784-510).
Medium: 3 1/2-inch disk
ISPN: 46012-505   **Price: $39.95**

LINGUIST'S SOFTWARE, INC.
LASER CYRILLIC (VER. 2.4)

Includes Soviet, Russian-Ukrainian and transliterated PostScript fonts for LaserWriter printers.

System: MAC, II, PLUS, SE, XL
Minimum Memory: 512K
Requires: PostScript printer.
Medium: 3 1/2-inch disk
ISPN: 44825-025   **Price: $149.95**

LINGUIST'S SOFTWARE, INC.
LASER FRENCH GERMAN SPANISH (VER. 3.0)

Two postscript and ImageWriter fonts in 82 languages, including all Roman-based European languages. Includes a time based font.

System: MAC, II, PLUS, SE, XL
Minimum Memory: 512K
Requires: Any word processing program.
Medium: 3 1/2-inch disk
ISPN: 44825-125   **Price: $99.95**

POSTCRAFT INT'L., INC.
LASER FX (VER. 1.6)

A desktop publishing program that customizes PostScript fonts into millions of possible special effect combinations.

System: MAC, II, PLUS, SE, XL
Minimum Memory: 512K
Medium: 3 1/2-inch disk
ISPN: 81203-400   **Price: $195.00**

NEOSCRIBE INT'L.
LASER PERFECT AMBO (VER. 1.0)

Contains a PostScript downloadable font in a classic bookface and includes roman small caps and italic.

System: MAC, II, PLUS, SE, XL
Minimum Memory: 512K
Requires: PostScript printer.
Medium: 3 1/2-inch disk
ISPN: 56537-080   **Price: $75.00**

NEOSCRIBE INT'L.
LASER PERFECT ANTIQUE AND NEULAND (VER. 1.0)

Contains two downloadable display typefaces for PostScript laser printers, Antique and Neuland.

System: MAC, II, PLUS, SE, XL
Minimum Memory: 512K
Requires: PostScript printer.
Medium: 3 1/2-inch disk
ISPN: 56537-100   **Price: $55.00**

NEOSCRIBE INT'L.
LASER PERFECT ARABIC (VER. 1.0)

Contains an Arabic language PostScript font.

System: MAC, II, PLUS, SE, XL
Minimum Memory: 512K
Requires: PostScript printer.
Medium: 3 1/2-inch disk
ISPN: 56537-125   **Price: $125.00**

NEOSCRIBE INT'L.
LASER PERFECT ATHINA (VER. 1.0)

A modern and classical Greek downloadable PostScript font.

System: MAC, II, PLUS, SE, XL
Minimum Memory: 512K
Requires: PostScript printer.
Medium: 3 1/2-inch disk
ISPN: 56537-422   **Price: $75.00**

NEOSCRIBE INT'L.
LASER PERFECT BENARES (VER. 1.0)

Provides a Devanagari font for PostScript laser printers.

System: MAC, II, PLUS, SE, XL
Minimum Memory: 512K
Requires: PostScript printer.
Medium: 3 1/2-inch disk
ISPN: 56537-150   **Price: $125.00**

FOR MORE DETAILED INFORMATION, CALL (412) 746-MENU

NEOSCRIBE INT'L.
LASER PERFECT BEOGRAD (VER. 1.0)
Contains a Beograd PostScript downloadable font.
System: MAC, II, PLUS, SE, XL
Minimum Memory: 512K
Requires: PostScript printer.
Medium: 3 1/2-inch disk
ISPN: 56537-130 **Price: $55.00**

NEOSCRIBE INT'L.
LASER PERFECT CYRILLIC (VER. 1.0)
Provides a downloadable Cyrillic PostScript laser font.
System: MAC, II, PLUS, SE, XL
Minimum Memory: 512K
Requires: PostScript printer.
Medium: 3 1/2-inch disk
ISPN: 56537-175 **Price: $125.00**

NEOSCRIBE INT'L.
LASER PERFECT DIACRITIC TIMES (VER. 1.0)
Provides a downloadable PostScript laser font that supports Diacritic marks.
System: MAC, II, PLUS, SE, XL
Minimum Memory: 512K
Requires: PostScript printer.
Medium: 3 1/2-inch disk
ISPN: 56537 200 **Price: $75.00**

NEOSCRIBE INT'L.
LASER PERFECT DIGITAL AND OCR-A & BARCODE(VER.1.0)
Provides downloadable Postscript laser fonts that provide for OCR-A characters and digital characters used in LCD displays.
System: MAC, II, PLUS, SE, XL
Minimum Memory: 512K
Requires: PostScript printer.
Medium: 3 1/2-inch disk
ISPN: 56537-225 **Price: $55.00**

NEOSCRIBE INT'L.
LASER PERFECT FINE TYPOGRAPHY LIBRARY
Contains eleven Laser Perfect PostScript fonts and the LaserStatus desk accessory utility.
System: MAC, II, PLUS, SE, XL
Minimum Memory: 512K
Requires: PostScript printer.
Medium: 3 1/2-inch disk
ISPN: 56537-230 **Price: $745.00**

NEOSCRIBE INT'L.
LASER PERFECT FRACTIONS (VER. 1.0)
A downloadable PostScript font for fractions.
System: MAC, II, PLUS, SE, XL
Minimum Memory: 512K
Requires: PostScript printer.
Medium: 3 1/2-inch disk
ISPN: 56537-240 **Price: $55.00**

NEOSCRIBE INT'L.
LASER PERFECT GARAJON (VER. 1.0)
Provides the classic Renaissance typeface originally drawn by Robert Garajon in a downloadable PostScript font.
System: MAC, II, PLUS, SE, XL
Minimum Memory: 512K
Requires: PostScript printer.
Medium: 3 1/2-inch disk
ISPN: 56537-250 **Price: $75.00**

NEOSCRIBE INT'L.
LASER PERFECT HEBREW (VER. 1.4)
A downloadable PostScript compatible font that includes the regular set of consonants, vowels, diacritics and punctuation of Hebrew.
System: MAC, II, PLUS, SE, XL
Minimum Memory: 512K
Requires: PostScript printer.
Medium: 3 1/2-inch disk
ISPN: 56537-350 **Price: $125.00**

NEOSCRIBE INT'L.
LASER PERFECT KANGAROO AND TSCHICHOLD (VER. 1.0)
Provides two downloadable PostScript laser fonts, Kangaroo, a form of architectural handwriting, and Tschichold.
System: MAC, II, PLUS, SE, XL
Minimum Memory: 512K
Requires: PostScript printer.
Medium: 3 1/2-inch disk
ISPN: 56537-275 **Price: $55.00**

NEOSCRIBE INT'L.
LASER PERFECT LIBRARY PACKAGES
Contains all eighteen Laser Perfect font packages and the LaserStatus desk accessory utility.
System: MAC, II, PLUS, SE, XL
Minimum Memory: 512K
Requires: PostScript printer.
Medium: 3 1/2-inch disk
ISPN: 56537-280 **Price: $1430.00**

NEOSCRIBE INT'L.
LASER PERFECT MACSLAB
A book-weight, square-serif typeface designed with the LaserWriter printer in mind.
System: MAC, II, PLUS, SE, XL
Minimum Memory: 512K
Requires: PostScript printer.
Medium: 3 1/2-inch disk
ISPN: 56537-415 **Price: $75.00**

NEOSCRIBE INT'L.
LASER PERFECT NORFOLK (VER. 1.0)
Displays sans-serif typeface, bold and extremely condensed, ideal for creating posters.
System: MAC, II, PLUS, SE, XL
Minimum Memory: 512K
Requires: PostScript printer.
Medium: 3 1/2-inch disk
ISPN: 56537-360 **Price: $55.00**

NEOSCRIBE INT'L.
LASER PERFECT OLDSTYLE & MACANGELO (VER. 1.0)
Includes PostScript oldstyle figures for four fonts with a display of capitals.
System: MAC, II, PLUS, SE, XL
Minimum Memory: 512K
Requires: PostScript printer.
Medium: 3 1/2-inch disk
ISPN: 56537-290 **Price: $55.00**

NEOSCRIBE INT'L.
LASER PERFECT PHONETIQUE (VER. 1.0)
Provides a downloadable PostScript laser font, containing International Phonetic Association (IPA) symbols.
System: MAC, II, PLUS, SE, XL
Minimum Memory: 512K
Requires: PostScript printer.
Medium: 3 1/2-inch disk
ISPN: 56537-300 **Price: $75.00**

NEOSCRIBE INT'L.
LASER PERFECT RAILWAY (VER. 1.0)
Provides a downloadable laser Postscript font adapted from a design by British typographer Eric Gill.
System: MAC, II, PLUS, SE, XL
Minimum Memory: 512K
Requires: PostScript printer.
Medium: 3 1/2-inch disk
ISPN: 56537-325 **Price: $95.00**

LINGUIST'S SOFTWARE, INC.
LASER TECH (VER. 1.5)
Four PostScript LaserWriter and ImageWriter fonts in 10, 12, 20 and 24 point size for technical, scientific and mathematical equations.
System: MAC, II, PLUS, SE, XL
Minimum Memory: 512K
Requires: Any word processing program.
Medium: 3 1/2-inch disk
ISPN: 44825-060 **Price: $99.95**

LINGUIST'S SOFTWARE, INC.
LASER TIBETAN (VER. 1.0)
2 PostScript Tibetan fonts with corresponding ImageWriter bit map fonts in 12, 18, 24, 36, 48, 60 and 72 point size.
System: MAC, II, PLUS, SE, XL
Minimum Memory: 512K
Requires: Printer.
Medium: 3 1/2-inch disk
ISPN: 44825-065 **Price: $149.95**

LINGUIST'S SOFTWARE, INC.
LASER TRANSLITERATOR (VER. 3.1)
PostScript and ImageWriter fonts which contain all Roman-based European character sets plus African and American Indian languages.
System: MAC, II, PLUS, SE, XL
Minimum Memory: 512K
Requires: Any word processing program.
Medium: 3 1/2-inch disk
ISPN: 44825-075 **Price: $99.95**

MACTOGRAPHY

LASERFONTS-COLUMBIA

Provides a downloadable PostScript compatible font used to highlighted information in advertisements, reports and more.

System: MAC, II, PLUS, SE, XL
Minimum Memory: 512K
Requires: PostScript printer.
Medium: 3 1/2-inch disk
ISPN: 00031-455   **Price: $34.95**

MACTOGRAPHY

LASERFONTS-CONGO

Fonts work with LaserWriter printer. Used to highlight information in advertisements, reports, and more.

System: MAC, II, PLUS, SE, XL
Minimum Memory: 512K
Requires: PostScript printer.
Medium: 3 1/2-inch disk
ISPN: 00031-460   **Price: $34.95**

MACTOGRAPHY

LASERFONTS-CUMBERLAND

Fonts work with LaserWriter printer. Used to highlight information in advertisements, reports and more.

System: MAC, II, PLUS, SE, XL
Minimum Memory: 512K
Requires: PostScript printer.
Medium: 3 1/2-inch disk
ISPN: 00031-461   **Price: $34.95**

MACTOGRAPHY

LASERFONTS-DEVOLL

Fonts work with LaserWriter printer. Used to highlight information in advertisements, reports and more.

System: MAC, II, PLUS, SE, XL
Minimum Memory: 512K
Requires: PostScript printer.
Medium: 3 1/2-inch disk
ISPN: 00031-462   **Price: $34.95**

MACTOGRAPHY

LASERFONTS-MANISTEE

Will work with any program that uses the standard Apple LaserWriter and LaserPrep files and also PageMaker.

System: MAC, II, PLUS, SE, XL
Minimum Memory: 512K
Requires: PostScript printer.
Medium: 3 1/2-inch disk
ISPN: 00031-465   **Price: $34.95**

MACTOGRAPHY

LASERFONTS-MICROFONTS PLUS

Allows the LaserWriter's built-in fonts to be printed in sizes below nine point from programs like MacWrite.

System: MAC, II, PLUS, SE, XL
Minimum Memory: 512K
Requires: PostScript printer.
Medium: 3 1/2-inch disk
ISPN: 00031-470   **Price: $34.95**

MACTOGRAPHY

LASERFONTS-NEOSHO

Font works with LaserWriter printer. Used to highlight information in advertisements, reports, and more.

System: MAC, II, PLUS, SE, XL
Minimum Memory: 512K
Requires: PostScript printer.
Medium: 3 1/2-inch disk
ISPN: 00031-477   **Price: $34.95**

MACTOGRAPHY

LASERFONTS-SHADOW EFFECTS

Special effect fonts for the LaserWriter printer.

System: MAC, II, PLUS, SE, XL
Minimum Memory: 512K
Requires: PostScript printer.
Medium: 3 1/2-inch disk
ISPN: 00031-471   **Price: $34.95**

MACTOGRAPHY

LASERFONTS-SPOKANE

Font works with LaserWriter printer. Used to highlight information in advertisements, reports and more.

System: MAC, II, PLUS, SE, XL
Minimum Memory: 512K
Requires: PostScript printer.
Medium: 3 1/2-inch disk
ISPN: 00031-473   **Price: $34.95**

MACTOGRAPHY

LASERFONTS-STYX

Takes your laserWriter into the 21st Century.

System: MAC, II, PLUS, SE, XL
Minimum Memory: 512K
Requires: PostScript printer.
Medium: 3 1/2-inch disk
ISPN: 00031-472   **Price: $34.95**

MACTOGRAPHY

LASERFONTS-THAMES

Great for informal text and headlines. Is designed to resemble loosely the traditional calligraphic forms of the Middle Ages.

System: MAC, II, PLUS, SE, XL
Minimum Memory: 512K
Requires: PostScript printer.
Medium: 3 1/2-inch disk
ISPN: 00031-474   **Price: $34.95**

MACTOGRAPHY

LASERFONTS-TRENT

Fonts work with LaserWriter printer. Used to highlight information in advertisements, reports, and more.

System: MAC, II, PLUS, SE, XL
Minimum Memory: 512K
Requires: PostScript printer.
Medium: 3 1/2-inch disk
ISPN: 00031-476   **Price: $34.95**

MACTOGRAPHY

LASERFONTS-WILLAMETTE

Comes in several weights and widths. The fonts have been configured to make the Macintosh and LaserWriter operate like a typesetter.

System: MAC, II, PLUS, SE, XL
Minimum Memory: 512K
Requires: PostScript printer.
Medium: 3 1/2-inch disk
ISPN: 00031-475   **Price: $34.95**

DEVONIAN INT'L. SOFTWARE CO.

LASERGENIX-FONTANA (VER. 1.0)

Provides the Bold Sans-Serif downloadable PostScript font.

System: MAC, II, PLUS, SE, XL
Minimum Memory: 512K
Requires: PostScript printer.
Medium: 3 1/2-inch disk
ISPN: 24987-310   **Price: $39.50**

DEVONIAN INT'L. SOFTWARE CO.

LASERGENIX-FRACTIONAL (VER. 1.0)

Provides the Sans-Serif downloadable laser font for fractions.

System: MAC, II, PLUS, SE, XL
Minimum Memory: 512K
Requires: PostScript printer.
Medium: 3 1/2-inch disk
ISPN: 24987-320   **Price: $39.50**

DEVONIAN INT'L. SOFTWARE CO.

LASERGENIX-IPA (VER. 1.0)

Provides a downloadable PostScript compatible IPA Serif font.

System: MAC, II, PLUS, SE, XL
Minimum Memory: 512K
Requires: PostScript compatible printer
Medium: 3 1/2-inch disk
ISPN: 24987-290   **Price: $39.50**

DEVONIAN INT'L. SOFTWARE CO.

LASERGENIX-NEWPORT NEWS (VER. 1.0)

Provides a PostScript downloadable Serif display font.

System: MAC, II, PLUS, SE, XL
Minimum Memory: 512K
Requires: PostScript printer.
Medium: 3 1/2-inch disk
ISPN: 24987-300   **Price: $39.50**

DEVONIAN INT'L. SOFTWARE CO.

LASERGENIX-RIVERSIDE

Provides a downloadable PostScript font in the Riverside format.

System: MAC, II, PLUS, SE, XL
Minimum Memory: 512K
Requires: PostScript printer.
Medium: 3 1/2-inch disk
ISPN: 24987-350   **Price: $39.50**

FOR MORE DETAILED INFORMATION, CALL (412) 746-MENU

DEVONIAN INT'L. SOFTWARE CO.

LASERGENIX-SVERDLOVSK

Provides the Extended Cyrillic Laser font for use with PostScript printers.

System: MAC, II, PLUS, SE, XL
Minimum Memory: 512K
Requires: PostScript printer.
Medium: 3 1/2-inch disk
ISPN: 24987-255						**Price: $39.50**

LINGUIST'S SOFTWARE, INC.

LASERGREEK (VER. 4.1)

Three PostScript SuperGreek fonts for LaserWriter and ImageWriter Greek printing in MacWrite and Microsoft Word.

System: MAC, II, PLUS, SE, XL
Minimum Memory: 512K
Requires: Any word processing program.
Medium: 3 1/2-inch disk
ISPN: 44825-050						**Price: $99.95**

LINGUIST'S SOFTWARE, INC.

LASERHEBREW (VER. 2.4)

Five postscript and screen fonts. Superhebrew with all the Hebrew vowel points and accents of Biblia Hebraica (Old Testament).

System: MAC, II, PLUS, SE, XL
Minimum Memory: 512K
Requires: Any word processing program.
Medium: 3 1/2-inch disk
ISPN: 44825-035						**Price: $119.95**

LINGUIST'S SOFTWARE, INC.

LASERIPA (VER. 2.2)

Contains IPATimes and LaserIPAplus, two International Phonetic Alphabet PostScript fonts with corresponding bit map fonts.

System: MAC, II, PLUS, SE, XL
Minimum Memory: 512K
Requires: Any word processing program.
Medium: 3 1/2-inch disk
ISPN: 44825-055						**Price: $99.95**

LINGUIST'S SOFTWARE, INC.

LASERKOREAN (VER. 1.3)

Contains five PostScript and ImageWriter fonts including NewSeoul, NewJeju, HiInchon, NewHiPusan and HiGwangju.

System: MAC, II, PLUS, SE, XL
Minimum Memory: 512K
Requires: PostScript printer.
Medium: 3 1/2-inch disk
ISPN: 44825-080						**Price: $119.95**

LINGUIST'S SOFTWARE, INC.

LASERTHAI (VER. 2.9)

A set of 13 distinctive Thai language PostScript and ImageWriter fonts, including Thai Key Caps.

System: MAC, II, PLUS, SE, XL
Minimum Memory: 512K
Requires: Any word processing program.
Medium: 3 1/2-inch disk
ISPN: 44825-090						**Price: $149.95**

ADOBE SYSTEMS, INC.

LETTER GOTHIC

Contains four Letter Gothic PostScript downloadable fonts including Regular, Slanted, Bold and Bold Slanted.

System: MAC, II, PLUS, SE, XL
Minimum Memory: 512K
Requires: PostScript printer.
Medium: 3 1/2-inch disk
ISPN: 01012-230						**Price: $185.00**

BITSTREAM, INC.

LETTER GOTHIC MACFONTWARE TYPEFACE LIBRARY

Contains four weights of one typeface, including Letter Gothic (12 pitch), Italic, Bold and Bold Italic.

System: MAC, II, PLUS, SE, XL
Minimum Memory: 512K
Requires: LaserWriter, LaserWriter IISC or ImageWriter printer.
Medium: 3 1/2-inch disk
ISPN: 07836-207						**Price: $195.00**

ADOBE SYSTEMS, INC.

LUCIDA

Contains four Lucida PostScript downloadable fonts including Roman, Italic, Bold and Bold Italic.

System: MAC, II, PLUS, SE, XL
Minimum Memory: 512K
Requires: PostScript printer.
Medium: 3 1/2-inch disk
ISPN: 01012-225						**Price: $185.00**

ADOBE SYSTEMS, INC.

LUCIDA SANS

Contains Lucida Sans, Lucida Sans Italic, Lucida Sans Bold, and Lucida Sans Bold Italic fonts for use with any PostScript printer.

System: MAC, II, PLUS, SE, XL
Minimum Memory: 512K
Requires: PostScript printer.
Medium: 3 1/2-inch disk
ISPN: 01012-226						**Price: $185.00**

ALPHABETS, INC.

M/A PROSPERA

Provides a downloadable PostScript font that includes Roman and Oblique with screen bit-map fonts from 10 to 36 point size.

System: MAC, II, PLUS, SE, XL
Minimum Memory: 512K
Requires: PostScript printer.
Medium: 3 1/2-inch disk
ISPN: 02406-600						**Price: $74.95**

MILES COMPUTING, INC.

MAC THE KNIFE (VOL. 3) (MAC THE RIPPER)

Hundreds of clip-art images for special occasions like birthdays, Christmas, Hanukkah, New Years and more.

System: MAC, II, PLUS, SE, XL
Minimum Memory: 128K
Medium: 3 1/2-inch disk
ISPN: 54075-201						**Price: $49.95**

MILES COMPUTING, INC.

MAC THE KNIFE (VOL. 4) (ORCHESTRA OF FONTS)

A two disk set of 30 ImageWriter fonts varying in five sizes for a total of 150 in sizes ranging from nine to 24 points.

System: MAC, II, PLUS, SE, XL
Minimum Memory: 128K
Medium: 3 1/2-inch disk
ISPN: 54075-500						**Price: $49.95**

MILES COMPUTING, INC.

MAC THE KNIFE (VOL. 5) (PEOPLE, PLACES & THINGS)

Contains two disk selection of art that ranges from classic to modern drawn with MacPaint.

System: MAC, II, PLUS, SE, XL
Minimum Memory: 128K
Medium: 3 1/2-inch disk
ISPN: 54075-505						**Price: $49.95**

MEGATHERIUM ENTERPRISES

MAC THE LINGUIST 2- PHONETIC FONTS FOR THE MAC

Set of fonts designed for use by linguists and others who make use of phonetic transcription systems.

System: MAC, II, PLUS, SE, XL
Minimum Memory: 512K
Medium: 3 1/2-inch disk
ISPN: 48961-100						**Price: $40.00**

COMPUCRAFT (CO)

MAC-ART LIBRARY (ANIMALS) (VER. 1.1)

Collection of MacPaint art files illustrating animals, insects, reptiles, birds, sea life. Used to illustrate ideas.

System: MAC, II, PLUS, SE, XL
Minimum Memory: 128K
Requires: A graphics software program that can read MacPaint format files.
Medium: 3 1/2-inch disk
ISPN: 15178-500						**Price: $39.95**

COMPUCRAFT (CO)

MAC-ART LIBRARY (BUILDINGS) (VER. 1.1)

A collection of MacPaint art files depicting buildings, houses and furnishings.

System: MAC, II, PLUS, SE, XL
Minimum Memory: 128K
Requires: Graphics software that can read MacPaint format files.
Medium: 3 1/2-inch disk
ISPN: 15178-452						**Price: $39.95**

COMPUCRAFT (CO)

MAC-ART LIBRARY (FLOWERS, TREES, PLANTS) (VER. 1.1)

Collection of MacPaint art files illustrating flowers, trees, and plants. Use to illustrate ideas.

System: MAC, II, PLUS, SE, XL
Minimum Memory: 128K
Requires: Graphics software capable of reading MacPaint format files.
Medium: 3 1/2-inch disk
ISPN: 15178-475						**Price: $39.95**

COMPUCRAFT (CO)

MAC-ART LIBRARY (GEOGRAPHY) (VER. 1.1)

Illustrates maps and famous landmarks.

System: MAC, II, PLUS, SE, XL
Minimum Memory: 128K
Requires: Graphics software that can read MacPaint format files.
Medium: 3 1/2-inch disk
ISPN: 15178-477   **Price: $39.95**

COMPUCRAFT (CO)

MAC-ART LIBRARY (GREETING CARD ART) (VER. 1.1)

MacPaint art files addressing holidays, and other greeting card occasions. Used to create your own cards.

System: MAC, II, PLUS, SE, XL
Minimum Memory: 128K
Requires: Graphics software that can read MacPaint format files.
Medium: 3 1/2-inch disk
ISPN: 15178-478   **Price: $39.95**

COMPUCRAFT (CO)

MAC-ART LIBRARY (IN THE KITCHEN) (VER. 1.1)

Illustrates things normally found in the kitchen. Useful in illustrating ideas.

System: MAC, II, PLUS, SE, XL
Minimum Memory: 128K
Requires: Graphics software that can read MacPaint format files.
Medium: 3 1/2-inch disk
ISPN: 15178-485   **Price: $39.95**

COMPUCRAFT (CO)

MAC-ART LIBRARY (ON THE FARM) (VER. 1.1)

Illustrates those things normally found on the farm.

System: MAC, II, PLUS, SE, XL
Minimum Memory: 128K
Requires: Graphics software that can read MacPaint format files.
Medium: 3 1/2-inch disk
ISPN: 15178-495   **Price: $39.95**

COMPUCRAFT (CO)

MAC-ART LIBRARY (PEOPLE) (VER. 1.0)

Collection of MacPaint art files on disk illustrating people at work, at home, and at play. Use to illustrate ideas.

System: MAC, II, PLUS, SE, XL
Minimum Memory: 128K
Requires: Graphics software that can read MacPaint format files.
Medium: 3 1/2-inch disk
ISPN: 15178-505   **Price: $39.95**

COMPUCRAFT (CO)

MAC-ART LIBRARY (PICTUREBASE FORMAT)

Collection of 12 disks of electronic clip-art, in picturebase format, illustrating a wide variety of subjects.

System: MAC, II, PLUS, SE, XL
Minimum Memory: 128K
Requires: Picturebase (ISPN 77437-550).
Medium: 3 1/2-inch disk
ISPN: 15178-507   **Price: $275.00**

COMPUCRAFT (CO)

MAC-ART LIBRARY (SIGNS, SYMBOLS, BORDERS)

Illustrates a variety of signs, common symbols, and borders. Useful in illustrating ideas.

System: MAC, II, PLUS, SE, XL
Minimum Memory: 128K
Requires: Graphics software that can read MacPaint format files.
Medium: 3 1/2-inch disk
ISPN: 15178-510   **Price: $39.95**

COMPUCRAFT (CO)

MAC-ART LIBRARY (SPORTS) (VER. 1.1)

Illustrates athletes and athletic equipment. Useful in illustrating ideas.

System: MAC, II, PLUS, SE, XL
Minimum Memory: 128K
Requires: Graphic software capable of reading MacPaint format files.
Medium: 3 1/2-inch disk
ISPN: 15178-513   **Price: $39.95**

COMPUCRAFT (CO)

MAC-ART LIBRARY (TOOLS) (VER. 1.1)

Illustrates tools used by a wide range of trades and professions. To illustrate ideas.

System: MAC, II, PLUS, SE, XL
Minimum Memory: 128K
Requires: Graphics software that can read MacPaint format files.
Medium: 3 1/2-inch disk
ISPN: 15178-515   **Price: $39.95**

COMPUCRAFT (CO)

MAC-ART LIBRARY (TRANSPORTATION) (VER. 1.1)

A collection of MacPaint art files on disk depicting old and new modes of transportation.

System: MAC, II, PLUS, SE, XL
Minimum Memory: 128K
Requires: Graphics software that can read MacPaint format files.
Medium: 3 1/2-inch disk
ISPN: 15178-520   **Price: $39.95**

COMPUCRAFT (CO)

MAC-ART LIBRARY (VARIETY PAK) (VER. 1.1)

A sample of all the Mac-Art library disks that includes animals, buildings, sports, tools, geography, kitchen, and more.

System: MAC, II, PLUS, SE, XL
Minimum Memory: 128K
Requires: Graphics software that can read MacPaint format files.
Medium: 3 1/2-inch disk
ISPN: 15178-525   **Price: $49.95**

COMPUCRAFT (CO)

MAC-ART LIBRARY (VER. 1.1) COMPLETE

Collection of twelve disks of MacPaint images illustrating a wide variety of subjects.

System: MAC, II, PLUS, SE, XL
Minimum Memory: 128K
Requires: Graphics software that can read MacPaint format files.
Medium: 3 1/2-inch disk
ISPN: 15178-470   **Price: $250.00**

LINGUIST'S SOFTWARE, INC.

MACAKKADIAN (VER. 1.2)

Contains over 740 basic Non-Assyrian Akkadian signs in six fonts. Fonts are in both 12 and 24 point.

System: MAC, II, PLUS, SE, XL
Minimum Memory:
Medium: 3 1/2-inch disk
ISPN: 44825-150   **Price: $79.95**

LINGUIST'S SOFTWARE, INC.

MACARABIC & FARSI (VER. 2.5)

A bidirectional word processing facility which includes Arabic and Farsi fonts. Includes a system switcher for use with a hard disk.

System: MAC, II, PLUS, SE, XL
Minimum Memory: 512K
Medium: 3 1/2-inch disk
ISPN: 44825-100   **Price: $79.95**

LINGUIST'S SOFTWARE, INC.

MACARMENIAN (VER. 1.1)

Provides 12 and 24 point Selagir and Boloragir fonts, and a font that transliterates any MacArmenian document.

System: MAC, II, PLUS, SE, XL
Minimum Memory: 512K
Requires: Any word processing program.
Medium: 3 1/2-inch disk
ISPN: 44825-155   **Price: $79.95**

MICROMAPS SOFTWARE, INC.

MACATLAS-PAINT (VER. 2.0)

Provides a set of United States and World maps in MacPaint format.

System: MAC, II, PLUS, SE, XL
Minimum Memory: 512K
Requires: MacPaint (ISPN 12784-510) or any other paint program.
Medium: 3 1/2-inch disk
ISPN: 50675-510   **Price: $79.00**

MICROMAPS SOFTWARE, INC.

MACATLAS-PROFESSIONAL VERSION

Contains maps of the USA, seven continents and all 50 states in MacDraw (PICT) format.

System: MAC, II, PLUS, SE, XL
Minimum Memory: 512K
Requires: MacDraw (ISPN 12784-500), an external disk drive, or any other draw program that accepts PICT images.
Medium: 3 1/2-inch disk
ISPN: 50675-475   **Price: $199.00**

MACPOINT PUBLICATIONS

MACBITS

A three-disk set of MacPaint images generated directly from native Macintosh icons.

System: MAC, II, PLUS, SE, XL
Minimum Memory: 128K
Medium: 3 1/2-inch disk
ISPN: 45902-300   **Price: $50.00**

CODY COMPUTERS

MACBORDERS

Contains 32 border patterns, implemented as a font, that can be used in Macpaint, Macwrite or other applications.

System: MAC, II, PLUS, SE, XL
Minimum Memory: 128K
Medium: 3 1/2-inch disk
ISPN: 13340-500   **Price: $27.95**

LINGUIST'S SOFTWARE, INC.

MACBURMESE (VER. 1.0)

Contains 12 and 24-point bitmap screen and ImageWriter fonts for Burmese.

System: MAC, II, PLUS, SE, XL
Minimum Memory: 128K
Medium: 3 1/2-inch disk
ISPN: 44825-151   **Price: $79.95**

LINGUIST'S SOFTWARE, INC.

MACCHEROKEE (VER. 1.0)

12 and 24 point Cherokee fonts with user's manual and laminated keyboard layout chart.

System: MAC, II, PLUS, SE, XL
Minimum Memory: 512K
Medium: 3 1/2-inch disk
ISPN: 44825-156   **Price: $79.95**

LINGUIST'S SOFTWARE, INC.

MACCHINESE (VER. 2.0)

Includes over 6000 characters and 2600 traditional characters for word processing in Microsoft Word (Ver. 3.02) or (Ver. 3.01).

System: MAC, II, PLUS, SE, XL
Minimum Memory: 512K
Requires: Microsoft Word (ISPN 53150-732), Mandarin or Cantonese. 800K disk drive.
Medium: 3 1/2-inch disk
ISPN: 44825-160   **Price: $114.95**

LINGUIST'S SOFTWARE, INC.

MACCHINESE (VER. 2.0)

Includes over 6000 characters and 2600 traditional characters for word processing in Microsoft Word (Ver. 3.02) or (Ver. 3.01).

System: MAC, II, PLUS, SE, XL
Minimum Memory: 512K
Requires: Microsoft Word (ISPN 53150-732), 800K disk drive.
Medium: 3 1/2-inch disk
ISPN: 44825-160   **Price: $99.95**

LINGUIST'S SOFTWARE, INC.

MACCHINESE SUPPLEMENT-CANTONESE (VER. 2.0)

Contains 2010 traditional Chinese Cantonese characters in ten fonts.

System: MAC, II, PLUS, SE, XL
Minimum Memory: 512K
Requires: MacChinese (ISPN 44825-160).
Medium: 3 1/2-inch disk
ISPN: 44825-162   **Price: $49.95**

LINGUIST'S SOFTWARE, INC.

MACCHINESE SUPPLEMENT-MANDARIN (VER. 2.0)

Includes 2010 traditional Chinese Mandarin characters in 10 fonts.

System: MAC, II, PLUS, SE, XL
Minimum Memory: 512K
Requires: MacChinese (ISPN 44825-160).
Medium: 3 1/2-inch disk
ISPN: 44825-161   **Price: $49.95**

LINGUIST'S SOFTWARE, INC.

MACCYRILLIC (VER. 2.4)

Includes Soviet, Russian-Ukrainian and transliterated layouts, plus extra symbols for eight languages including Serbian and Bulgarian.

System: MAC, II, PLUS, SE, XL
Minimum Memory: 512K
Requires: Any word processing program.
Medium: 3 1/2-inch disk
ISPN: 44825-175   **Price: $79.95**

LINGUIST'S SOFTWARE, INC.

MACCYRILLIC LQ SC (VER. 1.0)

Contains 12, 24, 36, 48 and 96 point CyrillicNuTransliterated fonts for ImageWriter LQ and LaserWriter II SC printers.

System: MAC, II, PLUS, SE, XL
Minimum Memory: 128K
Requires: ImageWriter LQ or LaserWriter II SC printer.
Medium: 3 1/2-inch disk
ISPN: 44825-152   **Price: $79.95**

SUNCOM, INC.

MACFONT I

Collection of new Macintosh typefaces, ranging from Lilliput 9 (very small) to Pasadena (pen-like).

System: MAC
Minimum Memory:
Medium: 3 1/2-inch disk
ISPN: 95763-450   **Price: $19.99**

DREAM MAKER SOFTWARE

MACGALLERY-HYPERCARD FORMAT

A HyperCard collection of 400 pieces of artwork including pictures for holidays, sports, business, food, borders and teddy bears.

System: MAC, II, PLUS, SE, XL
Minimum Memory: 1024K
Requires: HyperCard (ISPN 03900-300).
Medium: 3 1/2-inch disk
ISPN: 91255-505   **Price: $49.95**

DREAM MAKER SOFTWARE

MACGALLERY-MACPAINT FORMAT

A collection of 400 pieces of artwork including pictures for holidays, sports, business, food, borders, and teddy bears.

System: MAC, II, PLUS, SE, XL
Minimum Memory: 128K
Requires: MacPaint (ISPN 12784-510) or program that can read MacPaint format.
Medium: 3 1/2-inch disk
ISPN: 91255-500   **Price: $49.95**

LINGUIST'S SOFTWARE, INC.

MACGEORGIAN (VER. 1.0)

Contains 12 and 24 point styles of the Mxedruli alphabet and a font that transliterates any MacGeorgian document.

System: MAC, II, PLUS, SE, XL
Minimum Memory: 512K
Requires: Any word processing program.
Medium: 3 1/2-inch disk
ISPN: 44825-500   **Price: $79.95**

GOLDMIND PUBLISHING

MACGRAPHICS FOR MACINTOSH (VER. 2.0)

A collection of large format full paint files for illustrating desk top publishing documents. Up to 2470 dots per inch resolution.

System: MAC, II, PLUS, SE, XL
Minimum Memory: 512K
Requires: 800K disk drive.
Medium: 3 1/2-inch disk
ISPN: 33256-080   **Price: $225.00**

LINGUIST'S SOFTWARE, INC.

MACGREEK (VER. 2.9)

Contains 10, 12, 20, and 24 point Greek, TLG, and text critic fonts.

System: MAC, II, PLUS, SE, XL
Minimum Memory: 512K
Requires: Any word processing program.
Medium: 3 1/2-inch disk
ISPN: 44825-580   **Price: $79.95**

LINGUIST'S SOFTWARE, INC.
MACGREEK, HEBREW AND PHONETICS (VER. 4.0)
Contains all vowel points, dages, punctuation, marks, accent marks, and cantillation marks used in BHS, GREEK, IPS and SIL.
System: MAC, II, PLUS, SE, XL
Minimum Memory: 512K
Requires: Any word processing program.
Medium: 3 1/2-inch disk
ISPN: 44825-590 **Price: $129.95**

LINGUIST'S SOFTWARE, INC.
MACHEBREW (VER. 2.2)
Contains all vowel points, dages, punctuation marks, accent symbols, and cantillation marks used in Kittel or Stuttgartensia.
System: MAC, II, PLUS, SE, XL
Minimum Memory: 512K
Requires: Compatible word processor.
Medium: 3 1/2-inch disk
ISPN: 44825-350 **Price: $99.95**

LINGUIST'S SOFTWARE, INC.
MACHIEROGLYPHICS (VER. 3.0)
One thousand fifty characters in 8 fonts, with Cartouche development capabilities and 235 overstrike keys.
System: MAC, II, PLUS, SE, XL
Minimum Memory: 512K
Requires: Any word processing program.
Medium: 3 1/2-inch disk
ISPN: 44825-355 **Price: $79.95**

LINGUIST'S SOFTWARE, INC.
MACHINDI SANSKRIT (AJMER) (VER. 1.4)
Twelve and twenty-four point fonts for high quality printing. Includes complete Hindi and Sanskrit characters with Vedic accents.
System: MAC, II, PLUS, SE, XL
Minimum Memory: 512K
Requires: Compatible word processor
Medium: 3 1/2-inch disk
ISPN: 44825-365 **Price: $79.95**

LINGUIST'S SOFTWARE, INC.
MACKANA & BASIC JAPANESE KANJI (VER. 1.5)
Provides Hiragana, Katakana, punctuation and 70 Kanji fonts for English systems.
System: MAC, II, PLUS, SE, XL
Minimum Memory: 512K
Requires: Any word processing program.
Medium: 3 1/2-inch disk
ISPN: 44825-400 **Price: $49.95**

LINGUIST'S SOFTWARE, INC.
MACKOREAN (VER. 3.8)
Transforms the keyboard from English to Korean, with Korean appearing on the Macintosh monitor.
System: MAC, II, PLUS, SE, XL
Minimum Memory: 512K
Requires: Any word processing program.
Medium: 3 1/2-inch disk
ISPN: 44825-450 **Price: $79.95**

STRATEGIC LOCATIONS PLANNING
MACMAP COUNTRIES OF THE WORLD
Constructs maps and displays data for a wide variety of geographic areas.
System: MAC, II, PLUS, SE, XL
Minimum Memory: 128K
Requires: Filevision (ISPN 81077-040) or Business Filevision (81077-045).
Medium: 3 1/2-inch disk
ISPN: 76481-548 **Price: $75.00**

STRATEGIC LOCATIONS PLANNING
MACMAP COUNTY BY STATE (SPECIFY STATE)
Constructs maps and displays data for a wide variety of geographic areas.
System: MAC, II, PLUS, SE, XL
Minimum Memory: 128K
Medium: 3 1/2-inch disk
ISPN: 76481-546 **Price: $75.00**

STRATEGIC LOCATIONS PLANNING
MACMAP THREE DIGIT ZIP FOR REGION (SPECIFY
Constructs maps and displays data for a wide variety of geographic areas.
System: MAC, II, PLUS, SE, XL
Minimum Memory: 128K
Requires: Filevision (ISPN 81077-040) or Business Filevision (81077-045).
Medium: 3 1/2-inch disk
ISPN: 76481-550 **Price: $75.00**

ELECTRONIC PUBLISHER, INC.
MACMATBOOK (VOL. 1-3)
Professional quality graphic images in PictureBase format that can be copied to MacWrite, MacDraw, Pagemaker and others.
System: MAC, II, PLUS, SE, XL
Minimum Memory: 512K
Requires: PictureBase (ISPN 77437-550).
Medium: 3 1/2-inch disk
ISPN: 28553-504 **Price: $99.95**

ELECTRONIC PUBLISHER, INC.
MACMATBOOK (VOL. 1-6)
Contains hundreds of professional quality graphic images that can be copied to MacWrite, MacDraw, PageMaker and others.
System: MAC, II, PLUS, SE, XL
Minimum Memory: 512K
Medium: 3 1/2-inch disk
ISPN: 28553-500 **Price: $179.95**

ELECTRONIC PUBLISHER, INC.
MACMATBOOK (VOL. 4-6)
Professional quality graphic images in PictureBase format that can be copied to MacWrite, MacDraw, PageMaker and others.
System: MAC, II, PLUS, SE, XL
Minimum Memory: 512K
Requires: PictureBase (ISPN 77437-550).
Medium: 3 1/2-inch disk
ISPN: 28553-505 **Price: $99.95**

IMAGE WORLD, INC.
MACMEMORIES BLUE RIBBON SET
Five award-winning graphic disks bringing works of artists and illustrators of the past into partnership with user's creativity.
System: MAC, II, PLUS, SE, XL
Minimum Memory: 128K
Medium: 3 1/2-inch disk
ISPN: 37181-350 **Price: $130.00**

IMAGE WORLD, INC.
MACMEMORIES MEDALLION SET
Includes 13 disks of turn of the century images from artists and illustrators of the past.
System: MAC, II, PLUS, SE, XL
Minimum Memory: 512K
Medium: 3 1/2-inch disk
ISPN: 37181-500 **Price: $340.00**

IMAGE WORLD, INC.
MACMEMORIES-CATALOGUE DISK
Graphics featuring turn of the century images of all kinds.
System: MAC, II, PLUS, SE, XL
Minimum Memory: 128K
Medium: 3 1/2-inch disk
ISPN: 37181-375 **Price: $30.00**

IMAGE WORLD, INC.
MACMEMORIES-WORLD CLASS COMBO
Eighteen award-winning graphic disks bringing works of artists and illustrators of past into partnership with user's creativity.
System: MAC, II, PLUS, SE, XL
Minimum Memory: 128K
Medium: 3 1/2-inch disk
ISPN: 37181-380 **Price: $450.00**

LINGUIST'S SOFTWARE, INC.
MACPHONETICS (VER. 2.6)
International Phonetic Alphabet with diacritics, pronunciation symbols, accent and stress signs, SIL and MacTransliterator.
System: MAC, II, PLUS, SE, XL
Minimum Memory: 512K
Requires: Any word processing program.
Medium: 3 1/2-inch disk
ISPN: 44825-515 **Price: $79.95**

LINGUIST'S SOFTWARE, INC.
MACPUNJABI (VER. 1.0)
12 and 24-point, high quality printing fonts in the Gurmukhi script.
System: MAC, II, PLUS, SE, XL
Minimum Memory: 512K
Medium: 3 1/2-inch disk
ISPN: 44825-516 **Price: $79.95**

LINGUIST'S SOFTWARE, INC.
MACSEMITIC COPTIC DEVANAGRI (VER. 2.7)

Includes overstrike accents and diacritical marks, such as Syriac, Jacobite, Nestorian, Estrangela, Coptic, and DeVanagri.

System: MAC, II, PLUS, SE, XL
Minimum Memory: 512K
Requires: Any word processing program.
Medium: 3 1/2-inch disk
ISPN: 44825-520   **Price: $79.95**

ALPHABETS, INC.
MACSTAMP DIGITAL IMAGE LIBRARIES-DISK I

Provides bit-map 'click-art' images licensed from the rubberstamp designs of Letters Stamps of Chicago.

System: MAC, II, PLUS, SE, XL
Minimum Memory: 512K
Medium: 3 1/2-inch disk
ISPN: 02406-610   **Price: $34.95**

ALPHABETS, INC.
MACSTAMP DIGITAL IMAGE LIBRARIES-DISK II

Provides bit-map 'click-art' full page images from assorted sources for laser-reduction.

System: MAC, II, PLUS, SE, XL
Minimum Memory: 512K
Medium: 3 1/2-inch disk
ISPN: 02406-620   **Price: $34.95**

LINGUIST'S SOFTWARE, INC.
MACTAMIL (VER. 1.0)

12 and 24-point size printing fonts in the Tamil sylabary.

System: MAC, II, PLUS, SE, XL
Minimum Memory: 128K
Medium: 3 1/2-inch disk
ISPN: 44825-185   **Price: $79.95**

LINGUIST'S SOFTWARE, INC.
MACTHAI (VER. 1.1)

Contains fonts for printing Thai language documents on ImageWriter printers.

System: MAC, II, PLUS, SE, XL
Minimum Memory: 512K
Requires: MacWrite(ISPN 12784-530), Microsoft Word (ISPN 53150-732) or compatible word processing program.
Medium: 3 1/2-inch disk
ISPN: 44825-180   **Price: $79.95**

DUBL-CLICK SOFTWARE, INC.
MACTUT/PROGLYPH

A bundled pack of both MacTut and ProGlyph, collections of Egyptian hieroglyphics and clip art.

System: MAC, II, PLUS, SE, XL
Minimum Memory: 512K
Requires: 800K disk drive
Medium: 3 1/2-inch disk
ISPN: 26806-350   **Price: $49.95**

MAGNUM SOFTWARE
MCPIC! (VOL. 1)

Contains 150 pictures which can be used as is or changed, combined, cloned or customized in many different ways.

System: MAC, II, PLUS, SE, XL
Minimum Memory: 512K
Requires: Any paint program, such as MacPaint (ISPN 12784-510).
Medium: 3 1/2-inch disk
ISPN: 46032-100   **Price: $49.95**

MAGNUM SOFTWARE
MCPIC! (VOL. 2)

Contains 150 pictures which can be used as is or changed, combined, cloned or customized. Also contains a People Maker.

System: MAC, II, PLUS, SE, XL
Minimum Memory: 512K
Requires: Any paint program, such as MacPaint (ISPN 12784-510).
Medium: 3 1/2-inch disk
ISPN: 46032-105   **Price: $49.95**

ADOBE SYSTEMS, INC.
MELIOR

Contains four Melior PostScript downloadable fonts including Regular, Italic, Bold and Bold Italic.

System: MAC, II, PLUS, SE, XL
Minimum Memory: 512K
Requires: PostScript printer.
Medium: 3 1/2-inch disk
ISPN: 01012-235   **Price: $185.00**

IMAGE WORLD, INC.
MEMORY LANE

Love, comfort, tenderness, wonder and excitement are seen in these renditions by the great artists and early illustrators.

System: MAC, II, PLUS, SE, XL
Minimum Memory: 128K
Medium: 3 1/2-inch disk
ISPN: 37181-390   **Price: $30.00**

ADOBE SYSTEMS, INC.
MEMPHIS

Contains seven variations of the Memphis font for use with any PostScript compatible printer.

System: MAC, II, PLUS, SE, XL
Minimum Memory: 512K
Requires: PostScript printer.
Medium: 3 1/2-inch disk
ISPN: 01012-236   **Price: $370.00**

BEYOND, INC.
MENUFONTS 2 (VER. 2.01)

Allows display of actual font style in the fonts menu of applications.

System: MAC, II, PLUS, SE, XL
Minimum Memory: 512K
Medium: 3 1/2-inch disk
ISPN: 90615-500   **Price: $49.95**

MACTOGRAPHY
MICRON

Provides the Micron/Demi downloadable PostScript font.

System: MAC, II, PLUS, SE, XL
Minimum Memory: 512K
Medium: 3 1/2-inch disk
ISPN: 00031-350   **Price: $44.95**

MACTOGRAPHY
MISSIVE

A cursive type of font for the Macintosh and Laserwriter.

System: MAC, II, PLUS, SE, XL
Minimum Memory: 512K
Requires: PostScript printer.
Medium: 3 1/2-inch disk
ISPN: 00031-360   **Price: $44.95**

IMAGE WORLD, INC.
MUSIC & DANCE

Add a little music to your holidays and other celebrations with age old images of dancing, singing, musical instruments and more.

System: MAC, II, PLUS, SE, XL
Minimum Memory: 512K
Requires: MacPaint (ISPN 12784-510), MacDraw (ISPN 12784-500) or MacDraft (ISPN 37053-400)
Medium: 3 1/2-inch disk
ISPN: 37181-400   **Price: $30.00**

STORM KING TECHNOLOGY
NAVYART

MacPaint clip-art of naval and Marine Corps subjects including ships, equipment and insignia.

System: MAC, II, PLUS, SE, XL
Minimum Memory: 128K
Requires: MacPaint (ISPN 12784-510) or compatible program.
Medium: 3 1/2-inch disk
ISPN: 76406-500   **Price: $69.95**

STORM KING TECHNOLOGY
NAVYART

MacPaint clip-art of naval and Marine Corps subjects including ships, equipment and insignia.

System: XL
Minimum Memory: 512K
Requires: MacPaint (ISPN 12784-510) or compatible program.
Medium: 3 1/2-inch disk
ISPN: 76406-500   **Price: $69.95**

ADOBE SYSTEMS, INC.
NEW CENTURY SCHOOLBOOK

Variations of the New Century Schoolbook font.

System: MAC, II, PLUS, SE, XL
Minimum Memory: 512K
Requires: PostScript printer.
Medium: 3 1/2-inch disk
ISPN: 01012-245   **Price: $185.00**

ADOBE SYSTEMS, INC.
NEWS GOTHIC

Contains four News Gothic PostScript downloadable fonts including Regular, Oblique, Bold and Bold Oblique.

System: MAC, II, PLUS, SE, XL
Minimum Memory: 512K
Requires: PostScript printer.
Medium: 3 1/2-inch disk
ISPN: 01012-250   **Price: $185.00**

BITSTREAM, INC.
NEWS GOTHIC MACFONTWARE TYPEFACE LIBRARY

Contains four weights of one typeface, including News Gothic, Italic, Bold and Bold Italic.

System: MAC, II, PLUS, SE, XL
Minimum Memory: 512K
Requires: LaserWriter, LaserWriter IISC or ImageWriter printer.
Medium: 3 1/2-inch disk
ISPN: 07836-208   **Price: $195.00**

GOLDMIND PUBLISHING
OCCUPATIONS (VOL. 7)

A collection of large format full paint files for illustrating desktop publishing documents. Up to 2470 dots per inch resolution.

System: MAC, II, PLUS, SE, XL
Minimum Memory: 512K
Requires: 800K disk drive.
Medium: 3 1/2-inch disk
ISPN: 33256-060   **Price: $39.95**

ARTBASE COMPUTER GRAPHIC SERVICES
OPTICAL ILLUSIONS (VER. 1.2)

Essentially a MacPaint template but can also be used as a Mac-art source for desktop publishing.

System: MAC, II, PLUS, SE, XL
Minimum Memory: 512K
Requires: MacPaint (ISPN 12784-510), or FullPaint (ISPN 90343-375).
Medium: 3 1/2-inch disk
ISPN: 05324-560   **Price: $39.95**

ADOBE SYSTEMS, INC.
OPTIMA

Variations of the Optima font.

System: MAC, II, PLUS, SE, XL
Minimum Memory: 512K
Requires: PostScript printer.
Medium: 3 1/2-inch disk
ISPN: 01012-255   **Price: $185.00**

MACTOGRAPHY
OPTION

An Option font that consists of PostScript text files that stay on your systems disks.

System: MAC, II, PLUS, SE, XL
Minimum Memory: 512K
Requires: PostScript printer.
Medium: 3 1/2-inch disk
ISPN: 00031-370   **Price: $44.95**

ADOBE SYSTEMS, INC.
ORATOR

Contains Orator and Orator Slanted Postscript downloadable fonts.

System: MAC, II, PLUS, SE, XL
Minimum Memory: 512K
Requires: PostScript printer.
Medium: 3 1/2-inch disk
ISPN: 01012-260   **Price: $145.00**

ADOBE SYSTEMS, INC.
PALATINO

Contains four Palatino Postscript downloadable fonts including Regular, Italic, Bold and Bold Italic.

System: MAC, II, PLUS, SE, XL
Minimum Memory: 512K
Requires: PostScript printer.
Medium: 3 1/2-inch disk
ISPN: 01012-265   **Price: $185.00**

ADOBE SYSTEMS, INC.
PARK AVENUE

Contains the Park Avenue PostScript downloadable font.

System: MAC, II, PLUS, SE, XL
Minimum Memory: 512K
Requires: PostScript printer.
Medium: 3 1/2-inch disk
ISPN: 01012-270   **Price: $95.00**

GOLDMIND PUBLISHING
PEOPLE (VOL. 6)

A collection of large format full paint files for illustrating desktop publishing documents. Up to 2470 dots per inch resolution.

System: MAC, II, PLUS, SE, XL
Minimum Memory: 512K
Requires: 800K disk drive.
Medium: 3 1/2-inch disk
ISPN: 33256-055   **Price: $39.95**

PAGE STUDIO GRAPHICS
PIXYMBOLS ONE-PICTORIAL SYMBOLS

Provides PostScript based pictorial symbol fonts displaying illustrative devices relating to in-house newsletter topics.

System: MAC, II, PLUS, SE, XL
Minimum Memory: 1024K
Requires: 800K disk drive, PostScript printer.
Medium: 3 1/2-inch disk
ISPN: 59575-600   **Price: $50.00**

PAGE STUDIO GRAPHICS
PIXYMBOLS TWO-REFERENCE

Provides PostScript based pictorial symbol fonts displaying illustrative devices relating to business applications.

System: MAC, II, PLUS, SE, XL
Minimum Memory: 1024K
Requires: 800K disk drive, PostScript printer.
Medium: 3 1/2-inch disk
ISPN: 59575-605   **Price: $50.00**

PAGE STUDIO GRAPHICS
PIXYMBOLS-CUBIX DISPLAY FONT

Provides a PostScript font based on an old graphic specialty display typeface reminiscent of the art deco style.

System: MAC, II, PLUS, SE, XL
Minimum Memory: 1024K
Requires: 800K disk drive, PostScript printer.
Medium: 3 1/2-inch disk
ISPN: 59575-635   **Price: $25.00**

PAGE STUDIO GRAPHICS
PIXYMBOLS-ICONS REFERENCE

Provides PostScript based pictorial symbol fonts that display Macintosh Icons and include several new icons.

System: MAC, II, PLUS, SE, XL
Minimum Memory: 1024K
Requires: 800K disk drive, PostScript printer.
Medium: 3 1/2-inch disk
ISPN: 59575-630   **Price: $25.00**

PAGE STUDIO GRAPHICS
PIXYMBOLS-US MAPS AND MAP SYMBOLS

Provides PostScript based graphic fonts which generate outline U.S. and state maps as well as standard map symbols.

System: MAC, II, PLUS, SE, XL
Minimum Memory: 1024K
Requires: 800K disk drive, PostScript printer.
Medium: 3 1/2-inch disk
ISPN: 59575-625   **Price: $50.00**

PAGE STUDIO GRAPHICS
PIXYMBOLSCMDKEYS-PICTORIAL SYMBOLS

Provides PostScript based pictorial symbol fonts displaying the command keys for both Macintosh and IBM PC keyboards.

System: MAC, II, PLUS, SE, XL
Minimum Memory: 1024K
Requires: 800K disk drive, PostScript printer.
Medium: 3 1/2-inch disk
ISPN: 59575-620   **Price: $50.00**

PAGE STUDIO GRAPHICS
PIXYMBOLSKEYS-PICTORAL SYMBOLS

Provides PostScript based symbol fonts that graphically represent the key or combination of keyboard keys needed to execute a command

System: MAC, II, PLUS, SE, XL
Minimum Memory: 1024K
Requires: 800K disk drive, PostScript printer.
Medium: 3 1/2-inch disk
ISPN: 59575-610   **Price: $50.00**

PAGE STUDIO GRAPHICS
PIXYMBOLSPCKEYS-PICTORIAL SYMBOLS

Provides a downloadable PostScript and bit-mapped font for the key legends for the IBM PC, AT, and PS/2 keyboards.

System: MAC, II, PLUS, SE, XL
Minimum Memory: 1024K
Requires: 800K disk drive, PostScript printer.
Medium: 3 1/2-inch disk
ISPN: 59575-615   **Price: $50.00**

FOR MORE DETAILED INFORMATION, CALL (412) 746-MENU

DESKTOP VIDEO PRODUCTIONS
PORTRAIT OF THE 49ERS

Graphics of the 1985 Super Bowl
Champions, The San Francisco 49ers.

System: MAC, II, PLUS, SE, XL
Minimum Memory: 128K
Medium: 3 1/2-inch disk
ISPN: 46012-100   **Price: $39.95**

OLDUVAI CORP.
POST-ART

Includes 34 full-size, highly-detailed
illustrations by Jose Antonio Ciccone
designed to support PostScript printers.

System: MAC, II, PLUS, SE, XL
Minimum Memory: 512K
Medium: 3 1/2-inch disk
ISPN: 57812-600   **Price: $69.95**

STRIDER SOFTWARE
POSTERMAKER TEMPLATES (VOL. 1)

Eye-catching designs perfect for handbills,
flyers, posters or banners. Intended for
use with Postermaker.

System: MAC, II, PLUS, SE, XL
Minimum Memory: 128K
Requires: PosterMaker Plus (ISPN 76569-551),
   ImageWriter or LaserWriter printer.
Medium: 3 1/2-inch disk
ISPN: 76569-555   **Price: $20.00**

STRIDER SOFTWARE
POSTERMAKER TEMPLATES VOL 2

Second clip art companion to Postermaker
graphics scaling program. twenty digitized
poster designs.

System: MAC, II, PLUS, SE, XL
Minimum Memory: 128K
Requires: PosterMaker Plus (ISPN 76569-551),
   ImageWriter or LaserWriter printer.
Medium: 3 1/2-inch disk
ISPN: 76569-556   **Price: $20.00**

ADOBE SYSTEMS, INC.
PRESTIGE ELITE

Contains four Prestige Elite PostScript
downloadable fonts including Elite, Elite
Slanted, Elite Bold and Elite Bold
Slanted.

System: MAC, II, PLUS, SE, XL
Minimum Memory: 512K
Requires: PostScript printer.
Medium: 3 1/2-inch disk
ISPN: 01012-275   **Price: $185.00**

DESKTOP VIDEO PRODUCTIONS
PRINCE

Includes graphics of the rock star Prince.

System: MAC, II, PLUS, SE, XL
Minimum Memory: 128K
Medium: 3 1/2-inch disk
ISPN: 46012-475   **Price: $39.95**

BEAR ROCK SOFTWARE CO., INC.
PRINTBAR (VER. 1.0)

Bar code fonts in code 39, UPC and EAN
for the Macintosh; BitMap and Postscript
fonts for ImageWriter and LaserWriter.

System: MAC, II, PLUS, SE, XL
Minimum Memory: 20K
Medium: 3 1/2-inch disk
ISPN: 07196-600   **Price: $225.00**

MGI
PUBLISHER'S PICTURE PAK-EXECUTIVE/MGT ED-MACPAINT

An executive and management edition of
vector-based electronic art files in a
MacPaint format.

System: MAC, II, PLUS, SE, XL
Minimum Memory:
Requires: MacPaint (ISPN 12784-510) or
   compatible desktop publishing program.
Medium: 3 1/2-inch disk
ISPN: 49362-705   **Price: $99.95**

MGI
PUBLISHER'S PICTURE PAK-EXECUTIVE/MGT. ED-EPS

An executive and management edition of
vector based, Encapsulated PostScript
electronic art files in a Macintosh format.

System: MAC, II, PLUS, SE, XL
Minimum Memory: 512K
Requires: PostScript compatible desktop
   publishing program.
Medium: 3 1/2-inch disk
ISPN: 49362-685   **Price: $99.95**

MGI
PUBLISHER'S PICTURE PAK-EYE OPENER SERIES-.EPS

Provides three libraries of vector based,
Encapsulated PostScript electronic art files
in a Macintosh format.

System: MAC, II, PLUS, SE, XL
Minimum Memory: 512K
Requires: PostScript compatible desktop
   publishing program.
Medium: 3 1/2-inch disk
ISPN: 49362-700   **Price: $250.00**

MGI
PUBLISHER'S PICTURE PAK-EYE OPENER SERIES-MACPAINT

Includes three editions of the Publisher's
Picture Pak series in a MacPaint format.

System: MAC, II, PLUS, SE, XL
Minimum Memory: 512K
Requires: MacPaint (ISPN 12784-510) or
   compatible program.
Medium: 3 1/2-inch disk
ISPN: 49362-720   **Price: $250.00**

MGI
PUBLISHER'S PICTURE PAK-FINANCE/ADMIN ED-.EPS

A financial and administrative edition
vector based, Encapsulated PostScript
electronic art files in a Macintosh format.

System: MAC, II, PLUS, SE, XL
Minimum Memory: 512K
Requires: PostScript compatible desktop
   publishing Program.
Medium: 3 1/2-inch disk
ISPN: 49362-690   **Price: $99.95**

MGI
PUBLISHER'S PICTURE PAK-FINANCE/ADMIN ED-MACPAINT

A finance and administrative edition of
raster based electronic art files in a
MacPaint format.

System: MAC, II, PLUS, SE, XL
Minimum Memory: 512K
Requires: MacPaint (ISPN 12784-510) or
   compatible desktop publishing program.
Medium: 3 1/2-inch disk
ISPN: 49362-710   **Price: $99.95**

MGI
PUBLISHER'S PICTURE PAK-SALES/MKTG ED-.EPS

A sales and marketing edition of vector
based, Encapsulated PostScript electronic
art files in a Macintosh format.

System: MAC, II, PLUS, SE, XL
Minimum Memory: 512K
Requires: PostScript compatible desktop
   publishing program.
Medium: 3 1/2-inch disk
ISPN: 49362-695   **Price: $99.95**

MGI
PUBLISHER'S PICTURE PAK-SALES/MKTG ED-MACPAINT

A Sales and Marketing edition of raster-
based electronic art files in a MacPaint
format.

System: MAC, II, PLUS, SE, XL
Minimum Memory: 512K
Requires: MacPaint (ISPN 12784-510) or
   compatible program.
Medium: 3 1/2-inch disk
ISPN: 49362-715   **Price: $99.95**

QUEUE
Q-ART

Consists of more than 200 original
pictures created with MacPaint. Also
includes a variety of other objects and
scenes.

System: MAC, II, PLUS, SE, XL
Minimum Memory: 128K
Medium: 3 1/2-inch disk
ISPN: 64387-690   **Price: $34.95**

MICROMAPS SOFTWARE, INC.

QUICKMAP

A geographic analysis tool that allows users to represent data on a map and analyze and map data on the 50 states.

System: MAC, II, PLUS, SE, XL
Minimum Memory: 512K
Requires: Hypercard (ISPN 03900-300).
Medium: 3 1/2-inch disk
ISPN: 50675-400   **Price: $99.00**

ALTSYS CORP.

RICHARD ROBERTS-DISK I

Includes Arboreal 72, Illustro 72, Picto 72, Star 72, Rockwell Kent A-R 72, Rockwell Kent S-Z 72, Brickwall 72, Candy Strip 72 fonts.

System: MAC, II, PLUS, SE, XL
Minimum Memory: 512K
Medium: 3 1/2-inch disk
ISPN: 02675-400   **Price: $29.95**

ALTSYS CORP.

RICHARD ROBERTS-DISK II

Includes Fantasia, 3-DPoster, Ivy Leaf Font, Portraito, Soft Poster A-R and S-Z, Black Picto A-S and T-Z, and Bold Poster fonts.

System: MAC, II, PLUS, SE, XL
Minimum Memory: 512K
Medium: 3 1/2-inch disk
ISPN: 02675-410   **Price: $29.95**

ALTSYS CORP.

RICHARD ROBERTS-DISK III

Includes Imagination, Rockwell Decor, Fantasy, Hollow Lean Bean, Wedge, Lean Bean, Imaginative, and Black Fantasy in 48 point size.

System: MAC, II, PLUS, SE, XL
Minimum Memory: 512K
Medium: 3 1/2-inch disk
ISPN: 02675-420   **Price: $29.95**

ALTSYS CORP.

RICHARD ROBERTS-DISK IV

Contains 35 different font faces including Georgrid, Rockwell, Robert's and Dagger font.

System: MAC, II, PLUS, SE, XL
Minimum Memory: 512K
Medium: 3 1/2-inch disk
ISPN: 02675-430   **Price: $29.95**

ALTSYS CORP.

RICHARD ROBERTS-DISK V

A collection of incredibly magnificent bitmap borders.

System: MAC, II, PLUS, SE, XL
Minimum Memory: 512K
Medium: 3 1/2-inch disk
ISPN: 02675-440   **Price: $29.95**

ALTSYS CORP.

RICHARD ROBERTS-DISK VI

Contains unbelievably fantastic borders and artwork.

System: MAC, II, PLUS, SE, XL
Minimum Memory: 512K
Medium: 3 1/2-inch disk
ISPN: 02675-450   **Price: $29.95**

DESKTOP VIDEO PRODUCTIONS

ROMANTIC IMAGES (VER. 1.0)

Art data disks for use with MacPaint. Described by their titles: 'Awakening Her', 'Falling For Her', 'Kiss', 'Embrace', and more.

System: MAC, II, PLUS, SE, XL
Minimum Memory: 512K
Requires: MacPaint (ISPN 12784-510).
Medium: 3 1/2-inch disk
ISPN: 46012-485   **Price: $39.95**

DESKTOP VIDEO PRODUCTIONS

SAMPLER (VER. 1.0)

Includes one to three samples from: Erotica, Faces, Hands, The Beatles, Portraits of Prince, Landscapes, Romantic images and more.

System: MAC, II, PLUS, SE, XL
Minimum Memory: 512K
Requires: MaePaint (ISPN 12784-510).
Medium: 3 1/2-inch disk
ISPN: 46012-525   **Price: $39.95**

P PRODUCTIONS

SCHOOLART (VER. 2.0)

A HyperCard based collection of 175 paint images on academics, computers, library, math, office and sports.

System: MAC, II, PLUS, SE, XL
Minimum Memory: 1024K
Requires: HyperCard (ISPN 03900-300).
Medium: 3 1/2-inch disk
ISPN: 59187-700   **Price: $39.00**

P PRODUCTIONS

SCHOOLART (VER. 2.0)

A HyperCard based collection of 175 paint images on academics, computers, library, math, office and sports.

System: MAC, II, PLUS, SE, XL
Minimum Memory: 1024K
Requires: Large school district license. HyperCard (ISPN 03900-300).
Medium: 3 1/2-inch disk
ISPN: 59187-700   **Price: $249.00**

P PRODUCTIONS

SCHOOLART (VER. 2.0)

A HyperCard based collection of 175 paint images on academics, computers, library, math, office and sports.

System: MAC, II, PLUS, SE, XL
Minimum Memory: 1024K
Requires: Small school district license (under 5,000 students). HyperCard (ISPN 03900-300).
Medium: 3 1/2-inch disk
ISPN: 59187-700   **Price: $99.00**

PROBABILTY DISTRIBUTION

SCIENTIFIC SYMBOLS FONT

Contains all the characters in IBM's Selectric symbols ball and more.

System: MAC
Minimum Memory: 256K
Medium: 3 1/2-inch disk
ISPN: 65993-725   **Price: $40.00**

PARAGON CONCEPTS, INC.

SCIFONTS

A full regular alpha numeric set of characters together with the full Greek alphabet and all the mathematical symbols.

System: MAC, II, PLUS, SE, XL
Minimum Memory: 512K
Medium: 3 1/2-inch disk
ISPN: 59740-600   **Price: $50.00**

IMAGE WORLD, INC.

SEASONS AND HOLIDAYS

Symbols and images to highlight the change of the seasons and accent favorite holidays.

System: MAC, II, PLUS, SE, XL
Minimum Memory: 128K
Requires: MacPaint (ISPN 12784-510).
Medium: 3 1/2-inch disk
ISPN: 37181-435   **Price: $30.00**

IMAGE WORLD, INC.

SEASONS AND HOLIDAYS

Symbols and images to highlight the change of the seasons and accent favorite holidays.

System: MAC, II, PLUS, SE, XL
Minimum Memory: 512K
Requires: Picturebase (ISPN 77437-550).
Medium: 3 1/2-inch disk
ISPN: 37181-435   **Price: $30.00**

MACTOGRAPHY

SHADOW EFFECT II

Contains letters made up from patterns of circles, grids, triangles, diamonds, random dots and more.

System: MAC, II, PLUS, SE, XL
Minimum Memory:
Medium: 3 1/2-inch disk
ISPN: 00031-380   **Price: $34.95**

MACPOINT PUBLICATIONS

SHAREWARE COLLECTION (VER. 1.0)

Collects utilities to enhance use of Database, spreadsheet and products. Includes a science/math font for publication use,

System: MAC, II, PLUS, SE, XL
Minimum Memory: 512K
Medium: 3 1/2-inch disk
ISPN: 45902-350   **Price: $10.00**

FOR MORE DETAILED INFORMATION, CALL (412) 746-MENU

GOLDMIND PUBLISHING

SIGNS AND SYMBOLS-VOL. 10

A collection of large format full paint files for illustrating desktop publishing documents. Up to 2470 dpi resolution.

System: MAC, II, PLUS, SE, XL
Minimum Memory: 512K
Requires: 800k disk drive.
Medium: 3 1/2-inch disk
ISPN: 33256-075 **Price: $39.95**

PLEASANT GRAPHIC WARE

SMART BORDERS-BRAVE NEW BORDERS

Contains 94 clip-art borders in MacPaint format that shows objects such as tools, foods, wrought iron, and toys on a 400K disk.

System: MAC, II, PLUS, SE, XL
Minimum Memory: 128K
Requires: MacPaint (ISPN 12784-510) or compatible program.
Medium: 3 1/2-inch disk
ISPN: 61360-700 **Price: $42.95**

PLEASANT GRAPHIC WARE

SMART FAMILY-SMART FOODS

Provides Smart Family and Smart Foods clip-art on one 800K disk in MacPaint format.

System: MAC, II, PLUS, SE, XL
Minimum Memory: 128K
Requires: MacPaint (ISPN 12784-510) or compatible program.
Medium: 3 1/2-inch disk
ISPN: 61360-715 **Price: $82.95**

PLEASANT GRAPHIC WARE

SMART FAMILY-THE GOOD LIFE

Contains clip-art of adults and children, singles and groups, in various activities of life in a MacPaint format on a 400K disk.

System: MAC, II, PLUS, SE, XL
Minimum Memory: 128K
Requires: MacPaint (ISPN 12784-510) or compatible program.
Medium: 3 1/2-inch disk
ISPN: 61360-705 **Price: $42.95**

PLEASANT GRAPHIC WARE

SMART FOODS-WHAT'S COOKIN'?

Provides clip-art images of vegetables, fruits, nuts, proteins, staples, utensils and more in a MacPaint format on a 400K disk.

System: MAC, II, PLUS, SE, XL
Minimum Memory: 128K
Requires: MacPaint (ISPN 12784-510) or compatible program.
Medium: 3 1/2-inch disk
ISPN: 61360-710 **Price: $42.95**

PLEASANT GRAPHIC WARE

SMART MOUSE

Provides clip-art graphics of animals, birds, dancers, warriors, celebrities, flowers, buildings, holiday images on a 400K disk.

System: MAC, II, PLUS, SE, XL
Minimum Memory: 128K
Requires: MacPaint (ISPN 12784-510) or compatible program.
Medium: 3 1/2-inch disk
ISPN: 61360-720 **Price: $42.95**

SMK

SMK ATTIKA (VER. 1.3)

Classical, biblical and modern Greek laser font for postscript devices.

System: MAC, II, PLUS, SE, XL
Minimum Memory: 512K
Requires: PostScript printer.
Medium: 3 1/2-inch disk
ISPN: 95739-090 **Price: $40.00**

SMK

SMK GREEK KEYS (VER. 4.0)

Displays and prints in several fonts in classical greek.

System: MAC, II, PLUS, SE, XL
Minimum Memory: 128K
Requires: Hard disk.
Medium: 3 1/2-inch disk
ISPN: 95739-100 **Price: $30.00**

BITSTREAM, INC.

SOFTFONTS FOR THE MAC-B10

A collection of ten solid typefaces well suited for use in books, manuals, newsletters, directories and reports.

System: MAC, II, PLUS, SE, XL
Minimum Memory: 512K
Requires: LaserWriter or ImageWriter printer.
Medium: 3 1/2-inch disk
ISPN: 07836-221 **Price: $345.00**

BITSTREAM, INC.

SOFTFONTS FOR THE MAC-B12

A collection of twelve typefaces well suited to the variety of documents found in any office.

System: MAC, II, PLUS, SE, XL
Minimum Memory: 512K
Requires: LaserWriter or ImageWriter printer.
Medium: 3 1/2-inch disk
ISPN: 07836-222 **Price: $395.00**

BITSTREAM, INC.

SOFTFONTS FOR THE MAC-B13

Contains a combination of typefaces well suited for virtually all word processing and spreadsheet applications.

System: MAC, II, PLUS, SE, XL
Minimum Memory: 512K
Requires: LaserWriter or ImageWriter printer.
Medium: 3 1/2-inch disk
ISPN: 07836-220 **Price: $195.00**

BITSTREAM, INC.

SOFTFONTS FOR THE MAC-B22

A collection of 22 typefaces which can be used in virtually any word processing document, database project or spreadsheet need.

System: MAC, II, PLUS, SE, XL
Minimum Memory: 512K
Requires: LaserWriter or ImageWriter printer.
Medium: 3 1/2-inch disk
ISPN: 07836-223 **Price: $595.00**

BITSTREAM, INC.

SOFTFONTS FOR THE MAC-B35

A collection of 35 typefaces ranging from Dutch to ITC Chancery. Well suited to the variety of documents found in any office.

System: MAC, II, PLUS, SE, XL
Minimum Memory: 512K
Requires: LaserWriter or ImageWriter printer.
Medium: 3 1/2-inch disk
ISPN: 07836-224 **Price: $695.00**

ADOBE SYSTEMS, INC.

SONATA

Downloadable fonts that support music notation suitable for any PostScript compatible printer.

System: MAC, II, PLUS, SE, XL
Minimum Memory: 512K
Requires: PostScript printer.
Medium: 3 1/2-inch disk
ISPN: 01012-300 **Price: $95.00**

KINGSLEY/ATF SOFTWARE DIVISION

SPARTAN

Contains four downloadable PostScript fonts including Spartan Medium, Medium Italic, Black, and Black Italic.

System: MAC, II, PLUS, SE, XL
Minimum Memory: 512K
Requires: PostScript printer.
Medium: 3 1/2-inch disk
ISPN: 43012-700 **Price: $195.00**

GOLDMIND PUBLISHING

SPECIAL OCCASIONS (VOL. 9)

A collection of large format full paint files for illustrating desktop publishing documents. Up to 2470 dots per inch resolution.

System: MAC, II, PLUS, SE, XL
Minimum Memory: 512K
Requires: 800K disk drive.
Medium: 3 1/2-inch disk
ISPN: 33256-077 **Price: $39.95**

HYPERFORMANCE

STATE-SMART CLIP ART

Provides 150 full screen paint state maps-50 with 1200 cities, 50 topographical maps and 50 map templates.

System: MAC, II, PLUS, SE, XL
Minimum Memory: 128K
Requires: 800K disk drive. Paint program.
Medium: 3 1/2-inch disk
ISPN: 36732-710 **Price: $49.95**

ADOBE SYSTEMS, INC.

STENCIL/HOBO/BRUSHSCRIPT

Contains Stencil, Hobo and Brushscript PostScript downloadable fonts.

System: MAC, II, PLUS, SE, XL
Minimum Memory: 512K
Requires: PostScript printer.
Medium: 3 1/2-inch disk
ISPN: 01012-280   **Price: $145.00**

ADOBE SYSTEMS, INC.

STONE INFORMAL

Contains six Stone Informal Postscript downloadable fonts including Regular, Italic, Semibold, Semibold Italic, Bold and Bold Italic.

System: MAC, II, PLUS, SE, XL
Minimum Memory: 512K
Requires: PostScript printer.
Medium: 3 1/2-inch disk
ISPN: 01012-285   **Price: $275.00**

ADOBE SYSTEMS, INC.

STONE SANS

Contains six Stone Sans Postscript downloadable fonts including Regular, Italic, Semibold, Semibold Italic, Bold and Bold Italic.

System: MAC, II, PLUS, SE, XL
Minimum Memory: 512K
Requires: PostScript printer.
Medium: 3 1/2-inch disk
ISPN: 01012-290   **Price: $275.00**

ADOBE SYSTEMS, INC.

STONE SERIF

Contains six Stone Serif PostScript downloadable fonts including Regular, Italic, Semibold, Semibold Italic, Bold and Bold Italic.

System: MAC, II, PLUS, SE, XL
Minimum Memory: 512K
Requires: PostScript printer.
Medium: 3 1/2-inch disk
ISPN: 01012-295   **Price: $275.00**

ALLOTYPE TYPOGRAPHICS

STRUCTURE

Specialized downloadable LaserWriter font of over 100 chemical structures.

System: MAC, II, PLUS, SE, XL
Minimum Memory: 512K
Requires: PostScript printer.
Medium: 3 1/2-inch disk
ISPN: 90338-100   **Price: $125.00**

KINGSLEY/ATF SOFTWARE DIVISION

STYMIE

Contains four downloadable PostScript fonts including Stymie Light, Stymie Medium, Stymie Bold, and Stymie Bold Italic.

System: MAC, II, PLUS, SE, XL
Minimum Memory: 512K
Requires: PostScript printer.
Medium: 3 1/2-inch disk
ISPN: 43012-750   **Price: $195.00**

LINGUIST'S SOFTWARE, INC.

SUPER FRENCH GERMAN SPANISH (VER. 2.3)

Fonts for French, German, Spanish and the complete character sets of over 80 other languages. Contains point sizes 10, 12, 20, 24.

System: MAC, II, PLUS, SE, XL
Minimum Memory: 512K
Requires: Any word processing program.
Medium: 3 1/2-inch disk
ISPN: 44825-575   **Price: $49.95**

SOFTWARE APPLE CATIONS

SUPERFONTS (VER. 1.5)

Contains 23 fonts ranging in size from 9 to 36 points.

System: MAC, II, PLUS, SE, XL
Minimum Memory: 512K
Medium: 3 1/2-inch disk
ISPN: 72325-700   **Price: $29.95**

ARTWARE SYSTEMS, INC.

SYMBOLS 1

Contains 50 images for assisting desktop publishers in generating publications of all types.

System: MAC, II, PLUS, SE, XL
Minimum Memory: 512K
Requires: PostScript printer.
Medium: 3 1/2-inch disk
ISPN: 05432-650   **Price: $69.95**

GENERIC SOFTWARE, INC.

SYMBOLS LIBRARY-COMMERCIAL/RESIDENTIAL FURNISHINGS

Contains over 90 predrawn symbols for interior decorating and professional office space planning.

System: MAC, II, PLUS, SE, XL
Minimum Memory: 1024K
Requires: Generic Cadd (ISPN 32537-330, or 340), Two 800K disk drives or a hard disk.
Medium: 3 1/2-inch disk
ISPN: 32537-710   **Price: $49.95**

GENERIC SOFTWARE, INC.

SYMBOLS LIBRARY-ELECTRONIC I-IEEE

Contains over 100 logic symbols, diodes, IC transistors and resistors and more. Most symbols conform to IEEE standards.

System: MAC, II, PLUS, SE, XL
Minimum Memory: 1024K
Requires: Generic Cadd (ISPN 32537-330 or 340), two 800K disk drives or a hard disk.
Medium: 3 1/2-inch disk
ISPN: 32537-720   **Price: $24.95**

GENERIC SOFTWARE, INC.

SYMBOLS LIBRARY-FLOW CHARTS & SCHEDULES

Contains over 90 predrawn symbols for use in professional flow charts and program schedules.

System: MAC, II, PLUS, SE, XL
Minimum Memory: 1024K
Requires: Generic Cadd (ISPN 32537-330 or 340), two 800K disk drives or a hard disk.
Medium: 3 1/2-inch disk
ISPN: 32537-730   **Price: $24.95**

GENERIC SOFTWARE, INC.

SYMBOLS LIBRARY-HEATING, VENTILATION & AIR CONDIT

Contains over 130 pre-drawn symbols, all conforming to current mechanical system standards.

System: MAC, II, PLUS, SE, XL
Minimum Memory: 1024K
Requires: Generic Cadd (ISPN 32537-330 or 340), two 800K disk drives or hard disk.
Medium: 3 1/2-inch disk
ISPN: 32537-740   **Price: $49.95**

GENERIC SOFTWARE, INC.

SYMBOLS LIBRARY-HOME LANDSCAPING

Contains over 90 symbols in both plan and elevation views. Includes symbols for trees and shrubs in different seasons.

System: MAC, II, PLUS, SE, XL
Minimum Memory: 1024K
Requires: Generic Cadd (ISPN 32537-330 or 340), two 800K disk drives or a hard disk.
Medium: 3 1/2-inch disk
ISPN: 32537-810   **Price: $24.95**

GENERIC SOFTWARE, INC.

SYMBOLS LIBRARY-INDUSTRIAL PIPE FITTINGS

Contains over 160 pre-drawn symbols, all conforming to ANSI standards.

System: MAC, II, PLUS, SE, XL
Minimum Memory: 1024K
Requires: Generic Cadd (ISPN 32537-330 or 340), two 800K disk drives or a hard disk.
Medium: 3 1/2-inch disk
ISPN: 32537-760   **Price: $69.95**

GENERIC SOFTWARE, INC.

SYMBOLS LIBRARY-KITCHEN DESIGN

Provides over 500 symbols for the kitchen. Includes both plan and elevation views.

System: MAC, II, PLUS, SE, XL
Minimum Memory: 1024K
Requires: Generic Cadd (ISPN 32537-330 or 340), two 800K disk drives or a hard disk.
Medium: 3 1/2-inch disk
ISPN: 32537-770   **Price: $74.95**

GENERIC SOFTWARE, INC.
SYMBOLS LIBRARY-LANDSCAPE ARCHITECTURE

Contains 150 symbols for common plants, trees, and landscaping components. Includes two disks.

System: MAC, II, PLUS, SE, XL
Minimum Memory: 1024K
Requires: Generic Cadd (ISPN 32537-330 or 340), two 800K disk drives or a hard disk.
Medium: 3 1/2-inch disk
ISPN: 32537-800 **Price: $74.95**

ALLOTYPE TYPOGRAPHICS
SZWAJCARSKIE

Sans-serif character set for Polish. Fonts work with almost every program.

System: MAC, II, PLUS, SE, XL
Minimum Memory: 512K
Medium: 3 1/2-inch disk
ISPN: 90338-500 **Price: $85.00**

LINGUIST'S SOFTWARE, INC.
TECH (VER. 2.6)

For technical, scientific and mathematical equations. Includes 9, 10, 12, 18, 20, 24, 36, and 48 point size fonts.

System: MAC, II, PLUS, SE, XL
Minimum Memory: 512K
Requires: Any word processing program.
Medium: 3 1/2-inch disk
ISPN: 44825-600 **Price: $79.95**

ALLOTYPE TYPOGRAPHICS
TEMPORA

A downloadable LaserWriter font: Serif small caps, all standard alphanumeric characters and all European accented characters.

System: MAC, II, PLUS, SE, XL
Minimum Memory: 512K
Medium: 3 1/2-inch disk
ISPN: 90338-875 **Price: $40.00**

MACTOGRAPHY
TERRA

A downloadable Terra PostScript typefaces for use with any Macintosh and LaserWriter.

System: MAC, II, PLUS, SE, XL
Minimum Memory: 512K
Requires: PostScript printer.
Medium: 3 1/2-inch disk
ISPN: 00031-390 **Price: $44.95**

ARTFACTORY
TEXTURED BACKGROUNDS

Encapsulated PostScript background illustrations which can be used in page layout programs that support PostScript.

System: MAC, II, PLUS, SE, XL
Minimum Memory: 1024K
Requires: Page layout program that imports Encapsulated PostScript images.
Medium: 3 1/2-inch disk
ISPN: 90358-400 **Price: $89.95**

EASTERN LANGUAGE SYSTEMS
THE ORIENTALIST SERIES

Provides the Islamic Images Clip Art Collection.

System: MAC, II, PLUS, SE, XL
Minimum Memory: 128K
Requires: MacPaint (ISPN 12784-510) or SuperPaint (ISPN 70237-020).
Medium: 3 1/2-inch disk
ISPN: 04837-550 **Price: $29.95**

IMAGE WORLD, INC.
TOOLS, MACHINES AND MERCHANDISE

A fond remembrance and tribute to the changes and developments in the tools, machines and merchandise of yesteryear.

System: MAC, II, PLUS, SE, XL
Minimum Memory: 128K
Medium: 3 1/2-inch disk
ISPN: 37181-599 **Price: $30.00**

GOLDMIND PUBLISHING
TRANSPORTATION (VOL. 1)

A collection of large format FullPaint files for illustrating desktop publishing documents. Up to 2470 dots per inch resolution.

System: MAC, II, PLUS, SE, XL
Minimum Memory: 512K
Requires: 800K disk drive.
Medium: 3 1/2-inch disk
ISPN: 33256-025 **Price: $39.95**

GOLDMIND PUBLISHING
TREES (VOL. 3)

A collection of large format full paint files for illustrating desktop publishing documents. Up to 2470 dots per inch resolution.

System: MAC, II, PLUS, SE, XL
Minimum Memory: 512K
Requires: 800K disk drive.
Medium: 3 1/2-inch disk
ISPN: 33256-035 **Price: $39.95**

ADOBE SYSTEMS, INC.
TRUMP MEDIAEVAL

Variations of the Trump Mediaeval font.

System: MAC, II, PLUS, SE, XL
Minimum Memory: 512K
Requires: PostScript printer.
Medium: 3 1/2-inch disk
ISPN: 01012-305 **Price: $185.00**

IMAGE WORLD, INC.
TWIG, LEAF, ROOT AND FLOWER

Early sensitive and decorative renditions of flowers, plants and trees illustrate Mother Nature at her best.

System: MAC, II, PLUS, SE, XL
Minimum Memory: 128K
Medium: 3 1/2-inch disk
ISPN: 37181-698 **Price: $30.00**

VISATEX CORP.
U.S. PRESIDENT'S CLIP ART (VER. 1.0)

Contains clip-art portrait drawings of all the presidents in a MacPaint compatible bit-mapped or PCX format.

System: MAC, II, PLUS, SE, XL
Minimum Memory: 128K
Requires: MacPaint (ISPN 12784-510) or compatible program.
Medium: 3 1/2-inch disk
ISPN: 85340-600 **Price: $35.00**

MACTOGRAPHY
ULTRA FONTS DELUXE

Includes both Ultrafonts and Technical and Business set, packaged together.

System: MAC, II, PLUS, SE, XL
Minimum Memory: 512K
Medium: 3 1/2-inch disk
ISPN: 00031-825 **Price: $49.95**

MACTOGRAPHY
ULTRAFONTS EDITION TWO

Includes 21 fonts (19 of them text), sizes range from 6 points to 36 points, 2 specialty font – borders and symbols.

System: MAC, PLUS, SE, XL
Minimum Memory: 512K
Requires: Requires System 4.2 or earlier version.
Medium: 3 1/2-inch disk
ISPN: 00031-800 **Price: $29.95**

ADOBE SYSTEMS, INC.
UNIVERS

Contains eight Univers PostScript downloadable fonts.

System: MAC, II, PLUS, SE, XL
Minimum Memory: 512K
Requires: PostScript printer.
Medium: 3 1/2-inch disk
ISPN: 01012-315 **Price: $370.00**

ADOBE SYSTEMS, INC.
UNIVERS CONDENSED

Contains six Univers Condensed PostScript downloadable fonts.

System: MAC, II, PLUS, SE, XL
Minimum Memory: 512K
Requires: PostScript printer.
Medium: 3 1/2-inch disk
ISPN: 01012-320 **Price: $275.00**

TPS ELECTRONICS
UPC POSTSCRIPT FONT FOR THE MACINTOSH

Allows users to create UPC bar code symbols for retail packaging using word processing and page layout programs.

System: MAC, II, PLUS, SE, XL
Minimum Memory: 128K
Medium: 3 1/2-inch disk
ISPN: 82421-700 **Price: $219.00**

EMDASH

UPSTART

Provides a downloadable PostScript font in regular, condensed and extended font styles.

System: MAC, II, PLUS, SE, XL
Minimum Memory: 512K
Requires: PostScript printer.
Medium: 3 1/2-inch disk
ISPN: 28901-700   **Price: $43.00**

DUBL-CLICK SOFTWARE, INC.

WETPAINT (VOL. 1-2) CLASSIC CLIP

Over 2000 clip art borders, symbols and more for home or business use.

System: MAC, II, PLUS, SE, XL
Minimum Memory: 512K
Requires: Two 800K disk drives, MacPaint (ISPN 12784-510) or compatible program.
Medium: 3 1/2-inch disk
ISPN: 26806-450   **Price: $79.95**

DUBL-CLICK SOFTWARE, INC.

WETPAINT (VOL. 11-12) INDUSTRIAL REVOLUTION

A collection of 2000 turn of the century clip art images showing the development of tools and machines.

System: MAC, II, PLUS, SE, XL
Minimum Memory: 512K
Requires: Two 800K disk drives, MacPaint (ISPN 12784-510) or compatible program.
Medium: 3 1/2-inch disk
ISPN: 26806-455   **Price: $79.95**

DUBL-CLICK SOFTWARE, INC.

WETPAINT (VOL. 13-14) OLD EARTH ALMANAC

A collection of over 2000 clip art images of animals, romance characters, borders and more.

System: MAC, II, PLUS, SE, XL
Minimum Memory: 512K
Requires: Two 800K disk drives, MacPaint (ISPN 12784-510) or compatible program.
Medium: 3 1/2-inch disk
ISPN: 26806-456   **Price: $79.95**

DUBL-CLICK SOFTWARE, INC.

WETPAINT (VOL. 15-16) ISLAND LIFE

A collection of over 2000 clip art images of palm trees, dolphins, birds, the surf and other things related to the beach.

System: MAC, II, PLUS, SE, XL
Minimum Memory: 512K
Requires: Two 800K disk drives, MacPaint (ISPN 12784-510) or compatible program.
Medium: 3 1/2-inch disk
ISPN: 26806-457   **Price: $79.95**

DUBL-CLICK SOFTWARE, INC.

WETPAINT (VOL. 17-18) PEOPLE

A collection of over 2000 clip art images of people for home or business use.

System: MAC, II, PLUS, SE, XL
Minimum Memory: 512K
Requires: Two 800K disk drives, MacPaint (ISPN 12784-510) or compatible program.
Medium: 3 1/2-inch disk
ISPN: 26806-458   **Price: $79.95**

DUBL-CLICK SOFTWARE, INC.

WETPAINT (VOL. 3-4) FOR PUBLISHING

A collection of over 2000 general clip art and larger images for home or business use.

System: MAC, II, PLUS, SE, XL
Minimum Memory: 512K
Requires: Two 800K disk drives, MacPaint (ISPN 12784-510) or compatible program.
Medium: 3 1/2-inch disk
ISPN: 26806-451   **Price: $79.95**

DUBL-CLICK SOFTWARE, INC.

WETPAINT (VOL. 5-6) ANIMAL KINGDOM

A collection of over 200 clip art images featuring all kinds of animals and outdoor gear.

System: MAC, II, PLUS, SE, XL
Minimum Memory: 512K
Requires: Two 800K disk drives, MacPaint (ISPN 12784-510) or compatible program.
Medium: 3 1/2-inch disk
ISPN: 26806-452   **Price: $79.95**

DUBL-CLICK SOFTWARE, INC.

WETPAINT (VOL. 7-8) SPECIAL OCCASIONS

A collection of over 2000 clip art images for holidays, parties and other special occasions.

System: MAC, II, PLUS, SE, XL
Minimum Memory: 512K
Requires: Two 800K disk drives, MacPaint (ISPN 12784-510) or compatible program.
Medium: 3 1/2-inch disk
ISPN: 26806-453   **Price: $79.95**

DUBL-CLICK SOFTWARE, INC.

WETPAINT (VOL. 9-10) PRINTER'S HELPER

A collection of over 2000 clip art images from popular 1890's to 1920's books and magazines.

System: MAC, II, PLUS, SE, XL
Minimum Memory: 512K
Requires: Two 800K disk drives, MacPaint (ISPN 12784-510) or compatible program.
Medium: 3 1/2-inch disk
ISPN: 26806-454   **Price: $79.95**

IMAGE WORLD, INC.

WHEELS, HULLS, RAILS AND WINGS

The history and commemoration of transportation in images.

System: MAC, II, PLUS, SE, XL
Minimum Memory: 128K
Medium: 3 1/2-inch disk
ISPN: 37181-797   **Price: $30.00**

IMAGE WORLD, INC.

WILD WILD WEST

Rough and ready images of the early West with cowboys, indians, dance hall girls and the rugged life.

System: MAC, II, PLUS, SE, XL
Minimum Memory: 128K
Medium: 3 1/2-inch disk
ISPN: 37181-896   **Price: $30.00**

SPRINGBOARD SOFTWARE, INC.

WORKS OF ART-ASSORTMENT SERIES SAMPLER

Contains 500 clip-art items covering topics such as business, farming, celebrations, holidays and more.

System: MAC, PLUS, SE, XL
Minimum Memory: 512K
Requires: MacPaint (ISPN 12784-510) or HyperCard (ISPN 03900-300). Note: 1 MB of RAM needed if used with HyperCard.
Medium: 3 1/2-inch disk
ISPN: 75309-015   **Price: $49.95**

SPRINGBOARD SOFTWARE, INC.

WORKS OF ART-EDUCATION SERIES SAMPLER

Contains 500 clip-art items covering educational subjects, maps, kids, animals, plants, astronomy and more.

System: MAC, II, PLUS, SE, XL
Minimum Memory: 512K
Requires: MacPaint (ISPN 12784-510) or HyperCard (ISPN 03900-300). Note: 1 MB of RAM needed if used with HyperCard.
Medium: 3 1/2-inch disk
ISPN: 75309-175   **Price: $49.95**

SPRINGBOARD SOFTWARE, INC.

WORKS OF ART-HOLIDAY SERIES SAMPLER

Contains 500 clip-art items covering all major holidays, special days and famous people.

System: MAC, II, PLUS, SE, XL
Minimum Memory: 512K
Requires: MacPaint (ISPN 12784-510) or HyperCard (ISPN 03900-300). Note: 1 MB of RAM needed if used with HyperCard.
Medium: 3 1/2-inch disk
ISPN: 75309-300   **Price: $49.95**

DUBL-CLICK SOFTWARE, INC.

WORLD CLASS FONTS (VOL. 1-2) THE ORIGINALS

Contains Montreal, Venice, Chicago and many other typefaces.

System: MAC, II, PLUS, SE, XL
Minimum Memory: 512K
Requires: 800K disk drive.
Medium: 3 1/2-inch disk
ISPN: 26806-600 **Price: $79.95**

DUBL-CLICK SOFTWARE, INC.

WORLD CLASS FONTS (VOL. 3-4) THE STYLISH

Contains Ann Arbor, Assisi, Drafty City and many other typefaces.

System: MAC, II, PLUS, SE, XL
Minimum Memory: 512K
Requires: 800K disk drive.
Medium: 3 1/2-inch disk
ISPN: 26806-610 **Price: $79.95**

DUBL-CLICK SOFTWARE, INC.

WORLD CLASS FONTS (VOL. 5-6) THE GIANTS

Contains Cupertino, Postal City , Chicago and many other typefaces.

System: MAC, II, PLUS, SE, XL
Minimum Memory: 512K
Requires: 800K disk drive.
Medium: 3 1/2-inch disk
ISPN: 26806-620 **Price: $79.95**

DUBL-CLICK SOFTWARE, INC.

WORLD CLASS FONTS (VOL. 7-8) THE TRIPLES

Contains Geneva, Berkeley, Monaco, Chicago and many other typefaces.

System: MAC, II, PLUS, SE, XL
Minimum Memory: 512K
Requires: 800K disk drive.
Medium: 3 1/2-inch disk
ISPN: 26806-630 **Price: $79.95**

DUBL-CLICK SOFTWARE, INC.

WORLD CLASS LASER FONTS (VOL. 1)

A collection of PostScript typefaces including Aukland, Calais, Calais Bold, and Metropolitan.

System: MAC, II, PLUS, SE, XL
Minimum Memory: 512K
Requires: 800K disk drive, laser printer.
Medium: 3 1/2-inch disk
ISPN: 26806-800 **Price: $79.95**

DUBL-CLICK SOFTWARE, INC.

WORLD CLASS LASER FONTS (VOL. 2)

A collection of PostScript typefaces including Ixtapa, Ixtapa Bold, Hobokin and Saigon.

System: MAC, II, PLUS, SE, XL
Minimum Memory: 512K
Requires: 800K disk drive, laser printer.
Medium: 3 1/2-inch disk
ISPN: 26806-801 **Price: $79.95**

DUBL-CLICK SOFTWARE, INC.

WORLD CLASS LASER FONTS (VOL. 3)

A collection of PostScript typefaces including Versailles, Versailles Bold, Versailles Sans and Versailles Sans Bold.

System: MAC, II, PLUS, SE, XL
Minimum Memory: 512K
Requires: 800K disk drive, laser printer.
Medium: 3 1/2-inch disk
ISPN: 26806-802 **Price: $79.95**

DUBL-CLICK SOFTWARE, INC.

WORLD CLASS LASER FONTS (VOL. 4)

A collection of PostScript typefaces including El Paso, Tiajuana, and Borders

System: MAC, II, PLUS, SE, XL
Minimum Memory: 512K
Requires: 800K disk drive, laser printer.
Medium: 3 1/2-inch disk
ISPN: 26806-803 **Price: $79.95**

DUBL-CLICK SOFTWARE, INC.

WORLD CLASS LASER FONTS (VOL. 5)

A collection of PostScript typefaces including Hancock Park, Hancock Park Light and Hancock Park Bold.

System: MAC, II, PLUS, SE, XL
Minimum Memory: 128K
Requires: 800K disk drive, laser printer.
Medium: 3 1/2-inch disk
ISPN: 26806-804 **Price: $59.95**

DUBL-CLICK SOFTWARE, INC.

WORLD CLASS LASER FONTS (VOL. 6)

A collection of PostScript fonts with Symbols Galore and Math Whiz.

System: MAC, II, PLUS, SE, XL
Minimum Memory: 512K
Requires: 800K disk drive, laser printer.
Medium: 3 1/2-inch disk
ISPN: 26806-805 **Price: $79.95**

JAPANESE LANGUAGE SERVICES

YEAR OF THE DRAGON 88

Contains a collection of dragons from all over the world in MacPaint files.

System: MAC, II, PLUS, SE, XL
Minimum Memory: 128K
Medium: 3 1/2-inch disk
ISPN: 20012-800 **Price: $29.95**

---

127 PRODUCTIVITY/ GRAPHICS

ABVENT

ACTION!

Collects screen images from a program, compresses the screens, and plays back a 'film' of the screens you've collected.

System: MAC, II, PLUS, SE, XL
Minimum Memory: 1024K
Medium: 3 1/2-inch disk
ISPN: 00437-075 **Price: $149.00**

ADOBE SYSTEMS, INC.

ADOBE ILLUSTRATOR

Powerful art production tool for producing high quality line art and illustrations.

System: MAC, II, PLUS, SE, XL
Minimum Memory: 512K
Medium: 3 1/2-inch disk
ISPN: 01012-050 **Price: $495.00**

ADOBE SYSTEMS, INC.

ADOBE ILLUSTRATOR 88

Assists artists in producing high quality illustrations with a PostScript drawing tool.

System: MAC, II, PLUS, SE, XL
Minimum Memory: 1024K
Requires: PostScript or QMS ColorScript 100 printer.
Medium: 3 1/2-inch disk
ISPN: 01012-060 **Price: $495.00**

AEGIS DEVELOPMENT, INC.

AEGIS SHOWCASE F/X

A presentation and animation system for text and graphics. Adds new dimensions to business presentations and video productions.

System: MAC, II, PLUS, SE, XL
Minimum Memory: 2048K
Requires: Hard disk or two floppy disks.
Medium: 3 1/2-inch disk
ISPN: 01718-120 **Price: $395.00**

ALDUS CORP.

ALDUS FREEHAND

Provides drawing tools with color support, special effects and text handling capability that outputs to PostScript printers.

System: MAC, II, PLUS, SE, XL
Minimum Memory: 1024K
Requires: Two 800K disk drives or a hard disk, and a PostScript printer.
Medium: 3 1/2-inch disk
ISPN: 02226-100 **Price: $495.00**

VIKING TECHNOLOGIES

ARISTO DA

Cut pictures from MacPaint or FullPaint into any other application almost instantly.

System: MAC, II, PLUS, SE, XL
Minimum Memory:
Medium: 3 1/2-inch disk
ISPN: 85231-100 **Price: $19.95**

HEIZER SOFTWARE
ARTISTO + DESK ACCESSORY

Opens and copies all or a portion of any Paint or PICT type document to the clipboard without leaving the current application.

System: MAC, II, PLUS, SE, XL
Minimum Memory: 512K
Medium: 3 1/2-inch disk
ISPN: 35175-020   **Price: $9.00**

INTRACORP, INC.
BUSINESS CARD MAKER (VER. 2.0)

Includes a drawing and font program which allows the user to design and develop business cards.

System: MAC, PLUS, SE, XL
Minimum Memory: 512K
Medium: 3 1/2-inch disk
ISPN: 40531-600   **Price: $39.95**

INTRACORP, INC.
BUTTON AND BADGE MAKER

Design and print button and badge inserts for education, entertainment or business use.

System: MAC, II, PLUS, SE, XL
Minimum Memory: 512K
Medium: 3 1/2-inch disk
ISPN: 40531-275   **Price: $59.95**

DENEBA SOFTWARE
CANVAS (VER. 2.0)

Integrates object oriented graphics with Bitmap graphics of any resolution and PostScript in one document.

System: MAC, II, PLUS, SE, XL
Minimum Memory: 512K
Requires: 800K disk drive.
Medium: 3 1/2-inch disk
ISPN: 24765-100   **Price: $299.95**

MACRO MIND PUBLISHING
CLIP CHARTS

Contains templates for creating 30 styles of animated bar, pie, line and bullet charts.

System: MAC, II, PLUS, SE, XL
Minimum Memory: 512K
Requires: VideoWorks II (ISPN 45904-440), two disk drives or one disk drive and a hard disk.
Medium: 3 1/2-inch disk
ISPN: 45904-105   **Price: $59.95**

PALOMAR SOFTWARE, INC.
COLORIZER (VER. 1.1)

Allows user to custom-color menus, color and save screen images and files.

System: II
Minimum Memory: 1024K
Requires: High resolution RGB monitor, hard disk, Finder 5.5 or later.
Medium: 3 1/2-inch disk
ISPN: 59684-200   **Price: $49.95**

CRICKET SOFTWARE
CRICKET PAINT (VER. 1.0)

A monochrome paint program featuring FreshPaint which offers control of PICT drawings with the precision of bitmap painting.

System: MAC, PLUS, SE, XL
Minimum Memory: 1024K
Medium: 3 1/2-inch disk
ISPN: 35512-065   **Price: $195.00**

CRICKET SOFTWARE
CRICKET PICT-O-GRAPH

Designed for the creation of presentation quality color pictograms complete with integrated text.

System: MAC, II, PLUS, SE, XL
Minimum Memory: 512K
Medium: 3 1/2-inch disk
ISPN: 35512-060   **Price: $175.00**

CRICKET SOFTWARE
CRICKET PRESENTS

Designed for the creation of high quality full-color or black and white presentations.

System: MAC, II, PLUS, SE, XL
Minimum Memory: 512K
Medium: 3 1/2-inch disk
ISPN: 35512-070   **Price: $495.00**

ROCKWARE, INC.
D.C. RESISTIVITY

Allows the user to model resistivity data acquired, fast-paced trial and error forward-modeling session.

System: MAC, II, PLUS, SE, XL
Minimum Memory: 512K
Requires: ImageWriter
Medium: 3 1/2-inch disk
ISPN: 66643-201   **Price: $100.00**

DAVKA CORP.
DAVKAGRAPHICS II (VER. 1.0)

Clip Art Disk with Judaic Symbols, Holiday Scenes and Israeli Pictures.

System: MAC, II, PLUS, SE, XL
Minimum Memory: 128K
Medium: 3 1/2-inch disk
ISPN: 91205-201   **Price: $34.95**

UNICOM SOFTWARE DEVELOPMENT GROUP
DBMEDIA (VER. 1.0)

Provides microcomputer based cataloging of films following the R. R. Bowker format.

System: MAC, II, PLUS, SE, XL
Minimum Memory: 800K
Medium: 3 1/2-inch disk
ISPN: 83550-500   **Price: $1995.00**

ZEDCOR, INC.
DESKPAINT (VER. 2.01) WITH DESKDRAW (VER. 1.3)

A pair of graphics editors that allow creation and modification of PICT, TIFF and MacPaint images.

System: MAC, II, PLUS, SE, XL
Minimum Memory: 512K
Requires: 800K disk drive.
Medium: 3 1/2-inch disk
ISPN: 70625-100   **Price: $129.95**

BRODERBUND SOFTWARE, INC.
DRAWING TABLE

Provides object-oriented drawing tools with automatic control, and the ability to mix PostScript art with PICT and paint graphics.

System: MAC, II, PLUS, SE, XL
Minimum Memory: 512K
Medium: 3 1/2-inch disk
ISPN: 08850-220   **Price: $129.95**

KINKOS ACADEMIC COURSEWARE EXCHANGE
ESCHER-SKETCH (VER. 1.0)

Transforms a motif created by the user according to one of 17 different symmetry schemes to produce a wallpaper-type pattern.

System: MAC, II, PLUS, SE, XL
Minimum Memory: 512K
Requires: 800K disk, Finder (Ver. 5.5 or later).
Medium: 3 1/2-inch disk
ISPN: 43025-110   **Price: $24.50**

INVENTION SOFTWARE CORP. (MI)
EXTENDER GRAFPAK (VER. 2.1) (LSP, MPW P)

Contains object code libraries for creating high quality, completely customizable graphs and plots.

System: MAC, PLUS, SE, XL
Minimum Memory: 512K
Requires: 800K disk drive.
Medium: 3 1/2-inch disk
ISPN: 38337-500   **Price: $89.95**

BRIDGEPORT MACHINES
EZ-CAM

Contains 2D cross sections, positioning curves in space, editing curve links, completed part surface and more.

System: MAC, II, PLUS, SE, XL
Minimum Memory: 1024K
Requires: 800K disk drive, 20MB hard disk, math co-processor.
Medium: 3 1/2-inch disk
ISPN: 90656-200   **Price: $2500.00**

ASHTON-TATE
FULLPAINT

Provides four document full screen painting with the ability to paint at laser resolution and then print from 25% to 400% size.

System: MAC, II, PLUS, SE, XL
Minimum Memory: 512K
Medium: 3 1/2-inch disk
ISPN: 05500-195   **Price: $99.95**

FOR MORE DETAILED INFORMATION, CALL (412) 746-MENU

POLARWARE PENGUIN SOFTWARE
GRAPHICS MAGICIAN PICTURE PAINTER

An image storage and recall system for designing multi-colored adventure games, educational software and more.

System: MAC, II, PLUS, SE, XL
Minimum Memory: 512K
Medium: 3 1/2-inch disk
ISPN: 60425-106   **Price: $49.95**

LIPA SOFTWARE
GRAPHPACK (VER. 3.1)

Microsoft/Absoft Subroutine Library for scientific and technical graphs. Drawing can be output to screen Laserwriter, Imagewriter.

System: MAC, II, PLUS, SE, XL
Minimum Memory: 512K
Requires: Microsoft Fortran 2.1 or 2.2.
Medium: 3 1/2-inch disk
ISPN: 44925-150   **Price: $69.95**

LASERWARE, INC.
LASER PAINT COLOR II (VER. 1.9)

An integrated color graphics workshop supporting PostScript graphics and text environment in eight or 24 bit color.

System: II
Minimum Memory: 2048K
Requires: Expanded color board and color monitor.
Medium: 3 1/2-inch disk
ISPN: 27734-600   **Price: $595.00**

LASERWARE, INC.
LASERPAINT (VER. 1.9)

Integrated graphics workshop. PostScript graphics and text environment for creation of camera ready artwork.

System: MAC, II, PLUS, SE, XL
Minimum Memory: 1024K
Medium: 3 1/2-inch disk
ISPN: 27734-500   **Price: $495.00**

DAVKA CORP.
MAC KTAV (VER. 1.0)

Contains a bilingual, bidirectional Hebrew/English page layout program based on Ready, Set, Go! (ISPN 44293-600).

System: MAC, PLUS, SE, XL
Minimum Memory: 512K
Medium: 3 1/2-inch disk
ISPN: 91205-510   **Price: $595.00**

MICROMAPS SOFTWARE, INC.
MACATLAS PRESENTATION PACK (VER. 1.0)

Maps of the USA, US States and World Regions in PICT format. Designed for use with presentation software applications.

System: MAC, II, PLUS, SE, XL
Minimum Memory: 1024K
Requires: Presentation software application, 800K disk drive.
Medium: 3 1/2-inch disk
ISPN: 50675-500   **Price: $199.00**

FGM, INC.
MACBRIEFER

Builds presentations and displays different images on multiple monitors or projectors at once.

System: II
Minimum Memory: 1024K
Medium: 3 1/2-inch disk
ISPN: 30774-500   **Price: $495.00**

JAPANESE LANGUAGE SERVICES
MACCALLIGRAPHY (VER. 2.0)

Enables the user to create calligraphic and oriental brush painting effects.

System: MAC, II, PLUS, SE, XL
Minimum Memory: 128K
Medium: 3 1/2-inch disk
ISPN: 20012-500   **Price: $175.00**

CLARIS CORP.
MACDRAW (VER. 1.9)

Create drawings from symbols to maps for reports and presentations.

System: MAC, II, PLUS, SE, XL
Minimum Memory: 512K
Medium: 3 1/2-inch disk
ISPN: 12784-500   **Price: $195.00**

CLARIS CORP.
MACDRAW II (VER. 1.1)

The fast, flexible and precise drawing tool for business, design and engineering.

System: MAC, II, PLUS, SE, XL
Minimum Memory: 512K
Medium: 3 1/2-inch disk
ISPN: 12784-505   **Price: $399.00**

MAINSTAY
MACFLOW (VER. 3.0)

A visual power tool for logic and project flow. Allows user to resize graphic elements for quick changes and quality output.

System: MAC, II, PLUS, SE, XL
Minimum Memory: 1024K
Medium: 3 1/2-inch disk
ISPN: 46041-555   **Price: $195.00**

CREATIVE SOLUTIONS, INC.
MACFORTH 3-D LIBRARY

A set of three-dimensional graphics to the MacForth language that allow users to quickly build their own graphics applications.

System: MAC, II, PLUS, SE, XL
Minimum Memory: 512K
Requires: MacForth (ISPN 20700-590).
Medium: 3 1/2-inch disk
ISPN: 20700-300   **Price: $25.00**

CLARIS CORP.
MACPAINT (VER. 2.0)

The standard free-form graphics tool for painting, sketching or illustrating in bit-map form.

System: MAC, II, PLUS, SE, XL
Minimum Memory: 512K
Medium: 3 1/2-inch disk
ISPN: 12784-510   **Price: $125.00**

SELECT MICRO SYSTEMS, INC.
MAPMAKER (VER. 3.0)

Creates maps of United states by individual state, group of states, or county or by the entire country. Also the world by country.

System: MAC, II, PLUS, SE, XL
Minimum Memory: 512K
Medium: 3 1/2-inch disk
ISPN: 69106-500   **Price: $349.00**

APPLIED SYSTEMS & TECHNOLOGIES, INC.
MAXPAGE (VER. 1.2)

A page make-up program for creating newsletters, reports, manuals, brochures, programs, menus, presentations, papers and letters.

System: MAC, II, PLUS, SE, XL
Minimum Memory: 512K
Requires: 800K disk, MacWorks Plus (ISPN 77034-500).
Medium: 3 1/2-inch disk
ISPN: 04768-300   **Price: $89.00**

SOFTWARE FOR RECOGNITION TECHNOLOGIES
MINIDRAW (VER. 2.0)

A desk accessory which allows user to create drawings and paste them into an application.

System: MAC, II, PLUS, SE, XL
Minimum Memory: 512K
Requires: 800K disk drive.
Medium: 3 1/2-inch disk
ISPN: 72943-200   **Price: $44.95**

COMPUTER FRIENDS
MODERN ARTIST (VER. 2.0)

Allows users to create sketches and designs, paint and illustrate in color, and make four-color separations of artwork.

System: II
Minimum Memory: 2048K
Requires: Color monitor
Medium: 3 1/2-inch disk
ISPN: 16839-600   **Price: $495.00**

NUEQUATION, INC.
NUPAINT (VER. 1.04)

A bit-mapped paint program with high resolution editing and printing capabilities including 300 dpi on Laser printers.

System: MAC, II, PLUS, SE, XL
Minimum Memory: 512K
Requires: 800K disk drive.
Medium: 3 1/2-inch disk
ISPN: 57416-500   **Price: $139.95**

HEIZER SOFTWARE
PAINT DOTTED LINES

Allows user to draw a dotted or dashed line in HyperCard, using twenty-one different styles.

System: MAC, II, PLUS, SE, XL
Minimum Memory: 512K
Requires: HyperCard (ISPN 03900-300).
Medium: 3 1/2-inch disk
ISPN: 35175-973   **Price: $6.00**

HEIZER SOFTWARE
PAINTING ASSISTANT

Uses three buttons to paint a circular arc through three points, paint a smooth curve through four points, and a Bezier curve.

System: MAC, II, PLUS, SE, XL
Minimum Memory: 512K
Requires: HyperCard (ISPN 03900-300).
Medium: 3 1/2-inch disk
ISPN: 35175-975   **Price: $10.00**

CHRIS TIGGES
PASSAGE (VER. B.1)

A professional x,y graphics and numerical analysis program producing publication quality graphics.

System: MAC, II, PLUS, SE, XL
Minimum Memory: 1024K
Requires: Printer.
Medium: 3 1/2-inch disk
ISPN: 81781-600   **Price: $100.00**

DYNACOMP, INC.
PC PLOT HIGH RESOLUTION GRAPHICS

Makes pixel-resolution screen and printer graphs.

System: MAC, II, PLUS, SE, XL
Minimum Memory: 512K
Medium: 3 1/2-inch disk
ISPN: 27050-164   **Price: $89.95**

BV ENGINEERING
PCPLOT

A graphics package that allows graphing, making pixel resolution, screens and printer graphs for scientific and financial users.

System: MAC, II, PLUS, SE, XL
Minimum Memory: 512K
Medium: 3 1/2-inch disk
ISPN: 09875-195   **Price: $125.00**

DYNACOMP, INC.
PDP PEN PLOTTER DRIVER

Makes multi-color scientific and financial graphs on pen plotters.

System: MAC, II, PLUS, SE, XL
Minimum Memory: 512K
Medium: 3 1/2-inch disk
ISPN: 27050-176   **Price: $89.95**

MICROILLUSIONS
PHOTON PAINT

A full-featured paint program with extensive manipulation operations, such as 3D mapping, light source shading, and twisting.

System: II, SE
Minimum Memory: 1024K
Requires: Orchid card, color monitor.
Medium: 3 1/2-inch disk
ISPN: 50425-600   **Price: $299.99**

SUPERMAC SOFTWARE
PIXEL PAINT (VER. 2.0)

Creates and enhance color and gray-scale images either from scratch or by importing them from other programs for coloring.

System: II
Minimum Memory: 1024K
Medium: 3 1/2-inch disk
ISPN: 77125-600   **Price: $395.00**

BRODERBUND SOFTWARE, INC.
POSTERMAKER PLUS

Provides a desktop publishing layout and special effects font tool.

System: MAC, II, PLUS, SE, XL
Minimum Memory: 512K
Medium: 3 1/2-inch disk
ISPN: 08850-120   **Price: $59.95**

MICROSOFT CORP.
POWERPOINT (VER. 2.0)

Design presentation visuals, arrange and organize a presentation and develop audience handouts.

System: MAC, II, PLUS, SE, XL
Minimum Memory: 512K
Requires: Two 800K disk drives or a hard disk. Apple-supported impact and laser printers.
Medium: 3 1/2-inch disk
ISPN: 53150-540   **Price: $395.00**

BRODERBUND SOFTWARE, INC.
PRINT SHOP

Grades K-12: School-age children can create their own greeting cards, stationery and banners.

System: MAC, II, PLUS, SE, XL
Minimum Memory: 512K
Requires: School edition.
Medium: 3 1/2-inch disk
ISPN: 08850-125   **Price: $69.95**

BRODERBUND SOFTWARE, INC.
PRINT SHOP

Grades K-12: School-age children can create their own greeting cards, stationery and banners.

System: MAC, II, PLUS, SE, XL
Minimum Memory: 512K
Requires: Printer.
Medium: 3 1/2-inch disk
ISPN: 08850-125   **Price: $59.95**

INVENTION SOFTWARE CORP. (MI)
PROFESSIONAL EXTENDER GRAFPAK (VER. 2.1)

A full source code version of Extender Grafpak, containing object code libraries to create high-quality, customized graphs and plots.

System: MAC, II, PLUS, SE, XL
Minimum Memory: 512K
Medium: 3 1/2-inch disk
ISPN: 38337-666   **Price: $159.95**

QUARK, INC.
QUARKXPRESS (VER. 2.0)

A professional electronic publishing system that integrates word processing with page layout, typesetting and graphics.

System: MAC, II, PLUS, SE, XL
Minimum Memory: 1024K
Requires: PostScript or Imagewriter printer, hard disk.
Medium: 3 1/2-inch disk
ISPN: 64285-800   **Price: $795.00**

DESKTOP ENGINEERING
QUICKPLOT (VER. 1.23)

Easy-to-use plotting program reads data from text file or clipboard and creates line, scatter plots: 1000+ pts, splines and zooming.

System: MAC, II, PLUS, SE, XL
Minimum Memory: 256K
Medium: 3 1/2-inch disk
ISPN: 24943-600   **Price: $49.95**

HEIZER SOFTWARE
RANDOM DRAW

A HyperCard stack which allows users to create graphic designs, with tools chosen from a palette of over fifty tools.

System: MAC, II, PLUS, SE, XL
Minimum Memory: 512K
Requires: HyperCard (ISPN 03900-300).
Medium: 3 1/2-inch disk
ISPN: 35175-981   **Price: $12.00**

MICROTEK LAB, INC.
READRIGHT

A high-resolution painting, editing and scanning program.

System: MAC, II, PLUS, SE, XL
Minimum Memory: 512K
Requires: Scanner.
Medium: 3 1/2-inch disk
ISPN: 53662-800   **Price: $24.95**

LETRASET
READY,SET,GO! (VER. 4.5)

Creates any document from office memos to full-length novels and includes graphics capability.

System: MAC, II, PLUS, SE, XL
Minimum Memory: 512K
Medium: 3 1/2-inch disk
ISPN: 44293-600   **Price: $495.00**

FOR MORE DETAILED INFORMATION, CALL (412) 746-MENU

LETRASET
READYSETSHOW/STANDOUT

Create color transparencies and slides with integrated charting capabilities including pie, scatter, line, bar and column charts.

System: MAC, II, PLUS, SE, XL
Minimum Memory: 1024K
Medium: 3 1/2-inch disk
ISPN: 44293-610　　　　　　**Price: $395.00**

ROCKWARE, INC.
SHAPE (VER. 3.0)

Allow the user to input the crystal class, the unit-call parameters and the Miller indices of one face of each form.

System: PLUS
Minimum Memory: 512K
Requires: Imagewriter or Laserwriter.
Medium: 3 1/2-inch disk
ISPN: 66643-701　　　　　　**Price: $99.00**

HEIZER SOFTWARE
SLIDE SHOW MAKER

Creates self-running presentations or slide shows when graphics and information are entered on a card.

System: MAC, II, PLUS, SE, XL
Minimum Memory: 1024K
Requires: HyperCard (ISPN 3900-300).
Medium: 3 1/2-inch disk
ISPN: 35175-056　　　　　　**Price: $10.00**

SOLUTIONS INT'L.
SMART SCRAP & THE CLIPPER (VER. 2.01)

A pair of graphic desk accessories that is used to store and size graphics. Smartscrap is an improvement on the old scrapbook.

System: MAC, II, PLUS, SE, XL
Minimum Memory: 1024K
Requires: 800K disk drive.
Medium: 3 1/2-inch disk
ISPN: 74437-110　　　　　　**Price: $89.95**

SPRINGBOARD SOFTWARE, INC.
SPRINGBOARD PUBLISHER (VER. 2.0)

A desktop publishing program with text and graphics.

System: MAC, II, PLUS, SE, XL
Minimum Memory: 512K
Medium: 3 1/2-inch disk
ISPN: 75309-900　　　　　　**Price: $199.95**

SOLUTIONS INT'L.
SUPERGLUE (VER. 1.05)

Allows the transfer of full and multi-page documents between most Macintosh programs. Provides a 'print to disk' facility.

System: MAC, II, PLUS, SE, XL
Minimum Memory: 512K
Medium: 3 1/2-inch disk
ISPN: 74437-105　　　　　　**Price: $89.95**

SOLUTIONS INT'L.
SUPERGLUE II WITH GLUENOTES

Captures data that normally goes to a printer and saves it on disk. Allows attachment of electronic notes or graphics.

System: MAC, II, PLUS, SE, XL
Minimum Memory: 512K
Medium: 3 1/2-inch disk
ISPN: 74437-700　　　　　　**Price: $119.95**

SILICON BEACH SOFTWARE
SUPERPAINT (VER. 2.0)

Combines features of MacPaint and MacDraw with 300 dots per inch editing. Supports LaserWriter fonts.

System: MAC, II, PLUS, SE, XL
Minimum Memory: 512K
Medium: 3 1/2-inch disk
ISPN: 70237-020　　　　　　**Price: $199.00**

IMAGE WORLD, INC.
SYMBOLS, SIGNS & FANCY LETTERS

Includes graphic images of symbols, signs and fancy letter for use in desktop publishing.

System: MAC, II, PLUS, SE, XL
Minimum Memory:
Medium: 3 1/2-inch disk
ISPN: 37181-801　　　　　　**Price: $30.00**

ROCKWARE, INC.
TERNARY PLOT (VER. 3.0)

Graphic plotting package that normalizes and plots three values on a triangular diagram.

System: MAC, II, PLUS, SE, XL
Minimum Memory: 512K
Requires: Imagewriter or Laserwriter.
Medium: 3 1/2-inch disk
ISPN: 66643-703　　　　　　**Price: $150.00**

ROCKWARE, INC.
TERRAMOBILIS (VER. 2.0)

Allows the user to move continents around the globe.

System: MAC, II, PLUS, SE, XL
Minimum Memory: 512K
Medium: 3 1/2-inch disk
ISPN: 66643-705　　　　　　**Price: $795.00**

ROCKWARE, INC.
TERRAMOBILIS (VER. 2.0)

Allows the user to move continents around the globe.

System: MAC, II, PLUS, SE, XL
Minimum Memory: 512K
Requires: For non-profit institutions.
Medium: 3 1/2-inch disk
ISPN: 66643-705　　　　　　**Price: $295.00**

BRODERBUND SOFTWARE, INC.
TYPESTYLER

Enables you to manipulate type to produce special effects. You can bend, twist, stretch, rotate and flip type.

System: MAC, II, PLUS, SE, XL
Minimum Memory: 512K
Medium: 3 1/2-inch disk
ISPN: 08850-155　　　　　　**Price: $149.95**

MICROSERVE, INC.
WANT ADS COMPOSER (VER. 3.46)

Database for tracking and typesetting classified ads, sales ads, directories and other applications.

System: MAC, II, PLUS, SE, XL
Minimum Memory: 512K
Medium: 3 1/2-inch disk
ISPN: 53112-850　　　　　　**Price: $995.00**

---

130 PRODUCTIVITY/ GRAPHICS (COMMERCIAL ART)

FREEMYERS DESIGN
AD/ART/PLUS (VOL. 1) 'VARIETY' FOR MACPAINT

Produces high quality drawings and images for creating logo's and advertisements for desktop publishing, school and personal use.

System: MAC, II, PLUS, SE, XL
Minimum Memory: 128K
Medium: 3 1/2-inch disk
ISPN: 31415-100　　　　　　**Price: $49.95**

FREEMYERS DESIGN
AD/ART/PLUS-ARCHITECTURAL GRAPHICS (VER. 1.0)

Contains graphic drawings and symbols for creating architectural drawings, plans and landscape design in PICT format.

System: MAC, II, PLUS, SE, XL
Minimum Memory: 512K
Requires: MacDraw (ISPN 12784-500) or any program that reads PICT format.
Medium: 3 1/2-inch disk
ISPN: 31415-140　　　　　　**Price: $49.95**

FREEMYERS DESIGN
AD/ART/PLUS-CARTOON DESIGNER (VER. 1.0)

Contains files of graphic cartoon clip art templates, expressions and features for designing and constructing user defined characters

System: MAC, II, PLUS, SE, XL
Minimum Memory: 512K
Requires: MacDraw (ISPN 12784-500) or any program that reads PICT format.
Medium: 3 1/2-inch disk
ISPN: 31415-150　　　　　　**Price: $49.95**

GOLDMIND PUBLISHING

ADVERTISING GRAPHICS (VOL. 4)

A collection of large format full paint files for illustrating desktop publishing documents. Up to 2470 dots per inch resolution.

System: MAC, II, PLUS, SE, XL
Minimum Memory: 512K
Requires: 800K disk drive.
Medium: 3 1/2-inch disk
ISPN: 33256-020   **Price: $39.95**

FREEMYERS DESIGN

ART EPS BORDERS 1 (VER. 1.0)

A collection of PostScript Border designs created in Adobe Illustrator 88.

System: MAC, II, PLUS, SE, XL
Minimum Memory: 128K
Requires: Any Draw, Illustration or Page Layout program that accepts PostScript format files.
Medium: 3 1/2-inch disk
ISPN: 31415-070   **Price: $49.95**

FREEMYERS DESIGN

ART EPS HOLIDAY (CHRISTMAS) (VER. 1.0)

A collection of PostScript illustrations of Christmas subjects created in Adobe Illustrator 88.

System: MAC, II, PLUS, SE, XL
Minimum Memory: 128K
Requires: Any Draw, Illustration or Page Layout program that accepts PostScript format files.
Medium: 3 1/2-inch disk
ISPN: 31415-050   **Price: $49.95**

FREEMYERS DESIGN

ART EPS SYMBOLS 1 (VER. 1.0)

A collection of 42 PostScript international sign symbol designs created in Adobe Illustrator.

System: MAC, II, PLUS, SE, XL
Minimum Memory: 128K
Requires: Any Draw, Illustration or Page Layout program that accepts PostScript format files.
Medium: 3 1/2-inch disk
ISPN: 31415-060   **Price: $49.95**

BAUDVILLE

AWARD MAKER PLUS

Creates awards, certificates, licenses, coupons, or other documents of the users' design.

System: MAC, II, PLUS, SE, XL
Minimum Memory: 512K
Medium: 3 1/2-inch disk
ISPN: 07087-060   **Price: $49.95**

ARTSCI, INC.

CARD SHOP

Allows users to create customized greeting cards.

System: MAC, II, PLUS, SE, XL
Minimum Memory: 512K
Requires: MacPaint (ISPN 12784-510) or FullPaint (ISPN 90343-375).
Medium: 3 1/2-inch disk
ISPN: 05425-020   **Price: $39.95**

FOUNDATION PUBLISHING

COMIC STRIP FACTORY

A comic strip production tool specifically for writers and producers for professional-looking comic strips. Manual included.

System: MAC, II, PLUS, SE, XL
Minimum Memory: 512K
Medium: 3 1/2-inch disk
ISPN: 42743-200   **Price: $89.95**

CRICKET SOFTWARE

CRICKET DRAW (VER. 1.1)

An object-oriented drawing program for the Macintosh that has been designed to get the most from PostScript printers.

System: MAC, II, PLUS, SE, XL
Minimum Memory: 512K
Medium: 3 1/2-inch disk
ISPN: 35512-020   **Price: $295.00**

GREAT WAVE SOFTWARE

CRYSTAL PAINT (VER. 1.0)

Provides a symmetry drawing tool which can be used independently or in conjunction with other write, paint or layout programs.

System: MAC, II, PLUS, SE, XL
Minimum Memory: 512K
Medium: 3 1/2-inch disk
ISPN: 33476-100   **Price: $49.95**

SOLUTIONS INT'L.

CURATOR (THE) (VER. 1.05)

Contains an art manager and integrator for the desktop publisher and graphics professional.

System: MAC, II, PLUS, SE, XL
Minimum Memory: 512K
Medium: 3 1/2-inch disk
ISPN: 74437-115   **Price: $139.95**

HEIZER SOFTWARE

DISK LABEL TEMPLATE

A template and full instructions for making professional-quality disk labels.

System: MAC, II, PLUS, SE, XL
Minimum Memory: 512K
Requires: Microsoft Excel (ISPN 53150-270).
Medium: 3 1/2-inch disk
ISPN: 35175-539   **Price: $5.00**

DESKTOP GRAPHICS

DRAWART (VOL. 2)

Collection of over 300 different graphic images created in MacDraw specifically designed for the professional desktop publisher.

System: MAC, II, PLUS, SE, XL
Minimum Memory: 512K
Requires: MacDraw (ISPN 12784-500).
Medium: 3 1/2-inch disk
ISPN: 23555-275   **Price: $79.95**

PUBLISHING INT'L.

HOMETOWN, U.S.A.

Provides a series of plans for model buildings (house, store, church, railway station, etc.) from a typical small American town.

System: MAC, II, PLUS, SE, XL
Minimum Memory: 512K
Medium: 3 1/2-inch disk
ISPN: 63743-100   **Price: $29.95**

NIKROM TECHNICAL PRODUCTS, INC.

LASEROPTICS (MAC) (VER. 2.1)

Provides special lettering effects for PostScript printers.

System: MAC, II, PLUS, SE, XL
Minimum Memory: 1024K
Medium: 3 1/2-inch disk
ISPN: 56950-150   **Price: $1595.00**

NIKROM TECHNICAL PRODUCTS, INC.

LETTEREFFECTS (MAC) (VER. 1.0)

Provides special optical lettering effects for PostScript printers.

System: MAC, II, PLUS, SE, XL
Minimum Memory: 1024K
Medium: 3 1/2-inch disk
ISPN: 56950-250   **Price: $395.00**

CE SOFTWARE

MACBILLBOARD (VER. 4.01)

Create and modify standard Paint files. Make posters, certificates, T-shirts, banners, coupons and greeting cards.

System: MAC, II, PLUS, SE, XL
Minimum Memory: 512K
Requires: ImageWriter, ImageWriter II, or LaserWriter printer.
Medium: 3 1/2-inch disk
ISPN: 11725-205   **Price: $35.00**

AVALON DEVELOPMENT GROUP

PHOTOMAC

A 24-bit color image-processing and separation software package for the Macintosh II.

System: II
Minimum Memory: 2048K
Requires: 40 MB hard disk, color monitor, video expansion card.
Medium: 3 1/2-inch disk
ISPN: 06337-600   **Price: $695.00**

---

133 PRODUCTIVITY/ GRAPHICS SUPPORT

REAS NABLE SOFTWARE
4PAINT (VER. 1.0)
Graphics utility for making full-page MacPaint documents out of line drawings.
System: MAC, II, PLUS, SE, XL
Minimum Memory: 512K
Requires: MacPaint (ISPN 12784-510).
Medium: 3 1/2-inch disk
ISPN: 65634-050   **Price: $39.95**

FINGERTIP SOFTWARE
500 MENU PATTERNS FOR MACPAINT (VER. 1.0)
Gives the user access to 500 extra menu patterns in addition to the 38 that come standard with MacPaint.
System: MAC, II, PLUS, SE, XL
Minimum Memory: 128K
Medium: 3 1/2-inch disk
ISPN: 30831-100   **Price: $29.95**

BAUDVILLE
AWARD MAKER-CARTOONS SPORTS LIBRARY
Offers forty six professionally drawn cartoons illustrating your favorite sports and activities.
System: MAC, II, PLUS, SE, XL
Minimum Memory: 512K
Requires: Award Maker Plus (ISPN 07087-060).
Medium: 3 1/2-inch disk
ISPN: 07087-063   **Price: $19.95**

BAUDVILLE
AWARD MAKER-EDUCATION AWARD LIBRARY
Includes awards, diplomas, coupons, invitations, scholarships and licenses for educators, students, parents, volunteers and speakers.
System: MAC, II, PLUS, SE, XL
Minimum Memory: 512K
Requires: Award Maker Plus (ISPN 07087-060).
Medium: 3 1/2-inch disk
ISPN: 07087-062   **Price: $29.95**

BAUDVILLE
AWARD MAKER-SPORTS AWARD LIBRARY
Includes ten new border styles, four new text fonts and hundreds of style options for both male and female sports awards.
System: MAC, II, PLUS, SE, XL
Minimum Memory: 512K
Requires: Award Maker Plus (ISPN 07087-060).
Medium: 3 1/2-inch disk
ISPN: 07087-061   **Price: $29.95**

T/MAKER CO.
CLICKART-PUBLICATIONS
Contains a portfolio of 300 images for use in enhancing and illustrating newsletters and other types of publications.
System: MAC, II, PLUS, SE, XL
Minimum Memory: 512K
Requires: 1024K required if used with HyperCard (ISPN 3900-300).
Medium: 3 1/2-inch disk
ISPN: 79465-082   **Price: $49.95**

DESKTOP VIDEO PRODUCTIONS
CLIP ANIMATION SAMPLER (VER. 1.0)
Contains several animated clip sequences on business and industry, sales and marketing, borders and symbols.
System: MAC, II, PLUS, SE, XL
Minimum Memory: 512K
Requires: Videoworks II (ISPN 45904-440) or Videoworks Professional (ISPN 45904-460), 800K disk drive.
Medium: 3 1/2-inch disk
ISPN: 46012-104   **Price: $59.95**

HEIZER SOFTWARE
CLIP-ART VIEWER
Catalog's clip-art with buttons which can select and copy art to the clipboard and import art from the scrapbook.
System: MAC, II, PLUS, SE, XL
Minimum Memory: 1024K
Requires: HyperCard (ISPN 03900-300).
Medium: 3 1/2-inch disk
ISPN: 35175-439   **Price: $10.00**

COMPLAN SOFTWARE SYSTEM, INC.
CONTRACT OFFICE PLANNING
A symbols library compatible with MacDraw or MacDraft.
System: MAC, II, PLUS, SE, XL
Minimum Memory: 512K
Requires: MacDraw (ISPN 12784-500) or MacDraft (ISPN 37053-400).
Medium: 3 1/2-inch disk
ISPN: 14587-150   **Price: $499.95**

SILICON BEACH SOFTWARE
DIGITAL DARKROOM (VER. 1.0)
A computerized darkroom that enhances and composes scanned images such as photographs.
System: MAC, II, PLUS, SE, XL
Minimum Memory: 1024K
Requires: 800K disk drive.
Medium: 3 1/2-inch disk
ISPN: 70237-150   **Price: $395.00**

POSTCRAFT INT'L., INC.
FX-PAK I
Contains ten PostScript font special effects and five background screens for use with Laser FX.
System: MAC, II, PLUS, SE, XL
Minimum Memory: 512K
Requires: Laser FX (ISPN 81203-400), PostScript printer.
Medium: 3 1/2-inch disk
ISPN: 81203-300   **Price: $49.00**

POSTCRAFT INT'L., INC.
FX-PAK II
Contains ten PostScript font special effects which include Marble, Candy Cane, Fun House, Alcatraz, Old Wallpaper, and Rail Tracks.
System: MAC, II, PLUS, SE, XL
Minimum Memory: 512K
Requires: Laser FX (ISPN 81203-400), PostScript printer.
Medium: 3 1/2-inch disk
ISPN: 81203-310   **Price: $49.00**

POSTCRAFT INT'L., INC.
FX-PAK III
Contains ten PostScript font special effects which include Bi Line, Climbing, Crash, Fade Back, Guardrail, Horizon and Letter Shade.
System: MAC, II, PLUS, SE, XL
Minimum Memory: 512K
Requires: Laser FX (ISPN 81203-400), PostScript printer.
Medium: 3 1/2-inch disk
ISPN: 81203-320   **Price: $49.00**

POSTCRAFT INT'L., INC.
FX-PAK IV
Contains ten PostScript font special effects which include Filler, Film, Fireworks, Focus, Music, Pyramid, Zoom Along, and Zoom Out.
System: MAC, II, PLUS, SE, XL
Minimum Memory: 512K
Requires: Laser FX (ISPN 81203-400), PostScript printer.
Medium: 3 1/2-inch disk
ISPN: 81203-330   **Price: $49.00**

POSTCRAFT INT'L., INC.
FX-PAK V
Contains ten PostScript font special effects which include Cloud, Cracked, Fence, Fire, Hot Dog, Hypnotic, Piano, and Vibrate.
System: MAC, II, PLUS, SE, XL
Minimum Memory: 512K
Requires: Laser FX (ISPN 81203-400), PostScript printer.
Medium: 3 1/2-inch disk
ISPN: 81203-340   **Price: $49.00**

POSTCRAFT INT'L., INC.
FX-PAK VI
Contains ten PostScript font special effects which include Bunker, Balloons, Black Box, Dee-Three, Embossed, Split, and Twin Screen.
System: MAC, II, PLUS, SE, XL
Minimum Memory: 512K
Requires: Laser FX (ISPN 81203-400), PostScript printer.
Medium: 3 1/2-inch disk
ISPN: 81203-350   **Price: $49.00**

BRAINPOWER, INC.
GRAPHIDEX
Indexes and retrieves graphics from inside any standard application.
System: MAC, II, PLUS, SE, XL
Minimum Memory: 512K
Medium: 3 1/2-inch disk
ISPN: 08413-250   **Price: $124.95**

FOLKSTONE DESIGN, INC.
GRIDMAKER
Used to create a variety of three dimensional perspective grids that can be used as a guide for rendering drawings.
System: MAC, II, PLUS, SE, XL
Minimum Memory: 512K
Medium: 3 1/2-inch disk
ISPN: 31108-300   **Price: $49.00**

FOLKSTONE DESIGN, INC.
GRIDMAKER SAMPLER

Provides a collection of three-dimensional perspective grids created with Gridmaker.

System: MAC, II, PLUS, SE, XL
Minimum Memory: 512K
Requires: MacDraw (ISPN 12784-500) or MacDraft (ISPN 37053-400).
Medium: 3 1/2-inch disk
ISPN: 31108-350 **Price: $15.00**

LETRASET
IMAGESTUDIO (VER. 1.5)

Edits and processes continuous tone images that have been digitized and produces camera ready halftones.

System: MAC, II, PLUS, SE, XL
Minimum Memory: 1024K
Requires: Two disk drives or a hard disk.
Medium: 3 1/2-inch disk
ISPN: 44293-300 **Price: $495.00**

AMERICAN INTELLIWARE CORP.
INTERACTIVE TEACHER

Sequence images, time the duration of images, replaces slideshow presentations. Compatible with MacPaint and other bit-map programs.

System: MAC, II, PLUS, SE, XL
Minimum Memory: 512K
Medium: 3 1/2-inch disk
ISPN: 02896-300 **Price: $295.00**

LETRASET
LETRASTUDIO (VER. 1.0)

Allows you access to the Letraset Type Library, thereby providing a significant choice in selecting display type for printed material.

System: MAC, II, PLUS, SE, XL
Minimum Memory: 1024K
Requires: LetraFonts software, two disk drives or hard disk.
Medium: 3 1/2-inch disk
ISPN: 44293-400 **Price: $495.00**

ADVANCED GEOGRAPHIC SYSTEMS
MAC NEST (VER. 2.1)

A electronic storage tray that lets you pull information using a straight forward filing system.

System: MAC, II, PLUS, SE, XL
Minimum Memory: 128K
Medium: 3 1/2-inch disk
ISPN: 31215-500 **Price: $49.00**

ENGINEERED SOFTWARE
MACPLOTS II-BUSINESS

Enables MacDraw documents to be color-plotted in extremely high resolution.

System: MAC, II, PLUS, SE, XL
Minimum Memory: 512K
Medium: 3 1/2-inch disk
ISPN: 17509-490 **Price: $150.00**

ENGINEERED SOFTWARE
MACPLOTS II-DRAFTING

Enables MacDraw documents to be color-plotted in extremely high resolution.

System: MAC, II, PLUS, SE, XL
Minimum Memory: 512K
Medium: 3 1/2-inch disk
ISPN: 17509-500 **Price: $250.00**

MACTRONICS
PHOTOSCAN (VER. 1.1)

Video digitizer using camara attached to mouse, riding in track over photograph.

System: MAC, II, PLUS, SE, XL
Minimum Memory: 512K
Requires: 400K disk drive.
Medium: 3 1/2-inch disk
ISPN: 93904-600 **Price: $120.00**

ENTERSET
QUICKPAINT (VER. 2.0)

A clip art utility for browsing entire volumes of MacPaint minutes. Includes over 400 pictures.

System: MAC, II, PLUS, SE, XL
Minimum Memory: 128K
Medium: 3 1/2-inch disk
ISPN: 29481-690 **Price: $49.00**

SPRINGBOARD SOFTWARE, INC.
SPRINGBOARD PUBLISHER STYLE SHEETS-NEWSLETTERS

Contains over 3 dozen style sheets, ranging from a 1-column layout to more sophisticated 5-column formats.

System: MAC, II, PLUS, SE, XL
Minimum Memory: 512K
Requires: Springboard Publisher (ISPN 75309-900).
Medium: 3 1/2-inch disk
ISPN: 75309-910 **Price: $29.95**

137 PRODUCTIVITY/ HUMAN RESOURCE MANAGEMENT

ABRA MACDABRA SOFTWARE
ABRA 2000

A human resource management system. Allows you to quickly respond to management, employee and government requests.

System: MAC, II, PLUS, SE, XL
Minimum Memory: 1024K
Requires: 800K hard disk.
Medium: 3 1/2-inch disk
ISPN: 90306-100 **Price: $995.00**

LAKE AVE. SOFTWARE
ASSISTANT CONTROLLER STAFF SCHEDULING (VER. 5.0)

Schedules staff by days and hours and presents various management reports.

System: MAC, II, PLUS, SE, XL
Minimum Memory: 256K
Medium: 3 1/2-inch disk
ISPN: 43418-380 **Price: $695.00**

SOFTOUCH SOFTWARE, INC.
CONTINUITY PLANNING SYSTEM (CPS) II (VER. 2.0)

Integrates human resource appraisal and planning to support continuity and development within an organization.

System: MAC, II, PLUS, SE, XL
Minimum Memory: 512K
Requires: Excel (ISPN 53150-270).
Medium: 3 1/2-inch disk
ISPN: 72162-150 **Price: $495.00**

LIONHEART PRESS
DECISION ANALYSIS TECHNIQUES

Helps users develop an understanding of various routines to improve management skills.

System: MAC, II, PLUS, SE, XL
Minimum Memory: 512K
Medium: 3 1/2-inch disk
ISPN: 44900-200 **Price: $145.00**

LEGALWARE, INC.
DOCUMENT MODELER

Assists the user to build a document template and then uses those templates to prompt the user for specifics.

System: MAC, II, PLUS, SE, XL
Minimum Memory: 512K
Requires: MacWrite (ISPN 12784-530) or Microsoft Word (ISPN 53150-732).
Medium: 3 1/2-inch disk
ISPN: 44063-220 **Price: $599.00**

ALLIED COMPUTER SERVICE
INTELLIGENT RECRUITMENT SYSTEM

Handles all employee and applicant data such as resume, skills and areas of expertise. Program is artificial intelligence based.

System: MAC, II, PLUS, SE, XL
Minimum Memory:
Requires: Hard disk, printer.
Medium: 3 1/2-inch disk
ISPN: 90337-310 **Price: $795.00**

MAGIC SOFTWARE, INC.
SALARY MAGIC (VER. 1.01)

A salary negotiations and office management system which aids administrators in projecting future employee costs.

System: MAC, II, PLUS, SE, XL
Minimum Memory: 512K
Medium: 3 1/2-inch disk
ISPN: 45962-100 **Price: $495.00**

CRAIG MANAGEMENT, INC.

SCHEDULE MAKER

Provides personnel scheduling and labor management functions to assist the user in tracking and cutting labor service costs.

System: MAC, II, PLUS, SE, XL
Minimum Memory: 512K
Medium: 3 1/2-inch disk
ISPN: 20309-700 **Price: $295.00**

139 PRODUCTIVITY/ INTEGRATED PRODUCTIVITY

SYMMETRY CORP.

ACTA ADVANTAGE (VER. 1.01)

An outliner, organizer and planner in a stand-alone and desk accessory. Saves in various text formats.

System: MAC, II, PLUS, SE, XL
Minimum Memory: 512K
Requires: 800K disk drive.
Medium: 3 1/2-inch disk
ISPN: 77437-120 **Price: $129.00**

RH COMMUNICATIONS, INC.

ADVANCED PUBLISHERS BUSINESS SYSTEM (VER. 5.0)

Processes orders, billings, backorders, royalties and commissions. Performs sales analysis and inventory control.

System: MAC, II, PLUS, SE, XL
Minimum Memory: 1024K
Requires: System 4.2 or higher, Finder 6.0 or higher.
Medium: 3 1/2-inch disk
ISPN: 66287-100 **Price: $1695.00**

AFFINITY MICROSYSTEMS LIMITED

AFFINIFILE

Contains a desk accessory that gives fast access to notes and graphics.

System: MAC, II, PLUS, SE, XL
Minimum Memory: 512K
Medium: 3 1/2-inch disk
ISPN: 90318-500 **Price: $79.95**

PERSONAL SOFTWARE, INC.

AS & M PHONE (VER. 1.0.1)

Provides E-Mail and file transfer capability between any two Macintosh on an AppleTalk network.

System: MAC, II, PLUS, SE, XL
Minimum Memory: 1024K
Requires: Single user license. AppleTalk network.
Medium: 3 1/2-inch disk
ISPN: 05440-100 **Price: $50.00**

PERSONAL SOFTWARE, INC.

AS & M PHONE (VER. 1.0.1)

Provides E-Mail and file transfer capability between any two Macintosh on an AppleTalk network.

System: MAC, II, PLUS, SE, XL
Minimum Memory: 1024K
Requires: Zone license. AppleTalk network.
Medium: 3 1/2-inch disk
ISPN: 05440-100 **Price: $300.00**

BEYOND, INC.

AUTOPILOT (VER. 1.0)

Builds sequences or batchfiles, which allows users to run several applications one after another without quitting to Finder.

System: MAC, II, PLUS, SE, XL
Minimum Memory: 512K
Requires: 800K disk drive.
Medium: 3 1/2-inch disk
ISPN: 90615-200 **Price: $99.95**

HEIZER SOFTWARE

BBS LOG

A HyperCard stack which keeps track of telecommunications sessions and stores phone numbers for Bulletin Board systems.

System: MAC, II, PLUS, SE, XL
Minimum Memory: 512K
Requires: HyperCard (Ver. 1.2) (ISPN 03900-300).
Medium: 3 1/2-inch disk
ISPN: 35175-914 **Price: $7.00**

DENEBA SOFTWARE

COMMENT (VER. 2.0)

Can be used to keep appointments, post reminders, create telephone directories, and replace note pad and scrapbook.

System: MAC, II, PLUS, SE, XL
Minimum Memory: 512K
Requires: 800K disk drive.
Medium: 3 1/2-inch disk
ISPN: 24765-050 **Price: $99.95**

HELP SOFTWARE, INC.

DESKTOP HELP (VER. 2.1)

Creates text and graphics on-line help files, with index, table of contents, context sensitive help and more.

System: MAC, II, PLUS, SE, XL
Minimum Memory: 1024K
Requires: 800K disk drive.
Medium: 3 1/2-inch disk
ISPN: 35212-300 **Price: $395.00**

HARVARD ASSOCIATES, INC.

DESKTOPPERS (VER. 3.0)

Set of five desk accessories-calendar, doodle pad, little black book, music maker and scrapbook library.

System: MAC, II, PLUS, SE, XL
Minimum Memory: 512K
Medium: 3 1/2-inch disk
ISPN: 34579-050 **Price: $19.95**

GRAHAM SOFTWARE (CO)

DISK RANGER (VER. 3.1)

Catalog disks, make disk labels and find files on hard disks and floppy disks.

System: MAC, II, PLUS, SE
Minimum Memory: 512K
Medium: 3 1/2-inch disk
ISPN: 33406-200 **Price: $34.95**

ELECTRONIC ARTS

DISK TOOLS PLUS

A full-featured 'finder' type utility which allows complete file management within any application and is MultiFinder compatible.

System: MAC, II, PLUS, SE, XL
Minimum Memory: 512K
Medium: 3 1/2-inch disk
ISPN: 28512-004 **Price: $49.95**

CE SOFTWARE

DISKTOP (VER. 3.0.4)

Consists of DiskTop and Laser Status, two desk accessory programs, and Widget, an application program.

System: MAC, II, PLUS, SE, XL
Minimum Memory: 512K
Requires: Hard disk, ImageWriter, ImageWriter II, or LaserWriter printer.
Medium: 3 1/2-inch disk
ISPN: 11725-100 **Price: $49.95**

KEVIN J. DOYLE, COMPUTER SYSTEMS CONSULTANT

ESP-EXECUTIVE SEARCH AND PLACEMENT

Provides executive search and placement capabilities for management recruiters.

System: MAC, II, PLUS, SE, XL
Minimum Memory: 1024K
Requires: 20MB hard disk.
Medium: 3 1/2-inch disk
ISPN: 26752-200 **Price: $1795.00**

KEVIN J. DOYLE, COMPUTER SYSTEMS CONSULTANT

ESP-EXECUTIVE SEARCH AND PLACEMENT

Provides executive search and placement capabilities for management recruiters.

System: MAC, II, PLUS, SE, XL
Minimum Memory: 1024K
Requires: Office Master version. 20MB hard disk.
Medium: 3 1/2-inch disk
ISPN: 26752-200 **Price: $2495.00**

KEVIN J. DOYLE, COMPUTER SYSTEMS CONSULTANT

ESP-EXECUTIVE SEARCH AND PLACEMENT

Provides executive search and placement capabilities for management recruiters.

System: MAC, II, PLUS, SE, XL
Minimum Memory: 1024K
Requires: Multi-user version. 20MB hard disk.
Medium: 3 1/2-inch disk
ISPN: 26752-200 **Price: $5995.00**

NEW WEST SOFTWARE
EXECUTIVE LIFE (VER. 1.1)

Provides professional task/time management in a HyperCard stack format.

System: MAC, II, PLUS, SE, XL
Minimum Memory: 1024K
Requires: HyperCard (ISPN 03900-300).
Medium: 3 1/2-inch disk
ISPN: 94216-300   **Price: $79.95**

MEDIAGENIC/TENPOINT0
FOCAL POINT II

An intelligent personal information manager that organizes schedules, tasks and communications for the busy professional.

System: MAC, II, PLUS, SE, XL
Minimum Memory: 1024K
Requires: Hypercard (ISPN 03900-300).
Medium: 3 1/2-inch disk
ISPN: 48702-200   **Price: $199.95**

ASHTON-TATE
FULL IMPACT

Combines spreadsheet sophistication with the presentation quality of desktop publishing.

System: MAC, II, PLUS, SE, XL
Minimum Memory: 1024K
Requires: Two 800K disk drives or one 800K disk drive and a hard disk.
Medium: 3 1/2-inch disk
ISPN: 05500-205   **Price: $395.00**

ASHTON-TATE
FULLWRITE PROFESSIONAL

Combines word processing features, desktop publishing capabilities and a built-in MacDraw style environment.

System: MAC, II, PLUS, SE, XL
Minimum Memory: 1024K
Medium: 3 1/2-inch disk
ISPN: 05500-200   **Price: $395.00**

HEIZER SOFTWARE
GREAT IDEAS!

A HyperCard stack which organizes ideas, and indexes them by topic, keyword, and the description.

System: MAC, II, PLUS, SE, XL
Minimum Memory: 512K
Requires: HyperCard (ISPN 03900-300) Ver-1.2.
Medium: 3 1/2-inch disk
ISPN: 35175-943   **Price: $15.00**

HABA/ARRAYS SYSTEMS, INC.
HABA/DEX (WITH COMMUNICATION) (VER. 2.1)

Database manager with phone directory and dialer, monthly calendar, appointment book and prints labels, letters and lists.

System: MAC, II, PLUS, SE, XL
Minimum Memory: 512K
Medium: 3 1/2-inch disk
ISPN: 33987-081   **Price: $99.95**

HABA/ARRAYS SYSTEMS, INC.
HABA/DEX (WITH COMMUNICATION) (VER. 2.1)

Database manager with phone directory and dialer, monthly calendar, appointment book and prints labels, letters and lists.

System: PLUS
Minimum Memory:
Medium: 3 1/2-inch disk
ISPN: 33987-081   **Price: $99.95**

ELECTRONIC ARTS
HOMEPAK

Integrates word processing, information management and a 'smart' telecommunications terminal.

System: MAC, II, PLUS, SE, XL
Minimum Memory: 512K
Medium: 3 1/2-inch disk
ISPN: 28512-022   **Price: $19.95**

SYMMETRY CORP.
HYPERDA (VER. 1.1)

A desk accessory that allows user to open and browse a HyperCard stack without having to use the HyperCard program.

System: MAC, II, PLUS, SE, XL
Minimum Memory: 512K
Medium: 3 1/2-inch disk
ISPN: 77437-500   **Price: $69.00**

HEIZER SOFTWARE
HYPERDRAFT

An organizer of fully expressed or 'chunky' ideas for authors and writers.

System: MAC, II, PLUS, SE, XL
Minimum Memory: 1024K
Requires: HyperCard (ISPN 03900-300).
Medium: 3 1/2-inch disk
ISPN: 35175-430   **Price: $25.00**

HEIZER SOFTWARE
HYPERFINDER

A HyperCard stack which allows buttons to be added or removed from the Home stack with a few mouse clicks.

System: MAC, II, PLUS, SE, XL
Minimum Memory: 512K
Requires: HyperCard (ISPN 03900-300).
Medium: 3 1/2-inch disk
ISPN: 35175-950   **Price: $10.00**

LAYERED, INC.
INSIGHT EXPORT (VER. 3.00)

Allows user to create analyses with several variables and reformat reports using graphical forms, type styles and design elements.

System: MAC, II, PLUS, SE, XL
Minimum Memory: 1024K
Medium: 3 1/2-inch disk
ISPN: 43760-620   **Price: $149.00**

INTERLEAF, INC.
INTERLEAF PUBLISHER (VER. 3.5)

Allows user to manage long documents, produce graphs, size and copy photographs, and has integrated word processing capabilities.

System: II
Minimum Memory: 5120K
Requires: 40MB hard disk, AppleTalk.
Medium: 3 1/2-inch disk
ISPN: 39678-300   **Price: $2495.00**

LOTUS DEVELOPMENT CORP.
JAZZ (VER. 1A)

Integrated package combines database management, word processing, work sheets, communications and graphics.

System: MAC, II, PLUS, SE, XL
Minimum Memory: 512K
Requires: Two disk drives.
Medium: 3 1/2-inch disk
ISPN: 45525-025   **Price: $395.00**

PERIPHERALS COMPUTERS SUPPLIES, INC.
KALEIDAGRAPH (VER. 1.1)

Provides data analysis using graphing tools, statistical functions, and user defined macros.

System: MAC, II, PLUS, SE, XL
Minimum Memory: 512K
Medium: 3 1/2-inch disk
ISPN: 60539-500   **Price: $179.00**

HEIZER SOFTWARE
LAUNCHER

A HyperCard stack which provides access to frequently-used applications outside of HyperCard, with a click of the mouse.

System: MAC, II, PLUS, SE, XL
Minimum Memory: 512K
Requires: HyperCard (ISPN 03900-300).
Medium: 3 1/2-inch disk
ISPN: 35175-951   **Price: $8.00**

HEIZER SOFTWARE
MESSAGE BROWSER

A HyperCard stack for downloading messages. And automatically establishes links between identification numbers and replies.

System: MAC, II, PLUS, SE, XL
Minimum Memory: 512K
Requires: HyperCard (ISPN 03900-300).
Medium: 3 1/2-inch disk
ISPN: 35175-961   **Price: $15.00**

FINDER AIDS
MFS FOLDERMAKER

A desk accessory which names or renames files and moves files and folders on the desktop level.

System: MAC
Minimum Memory: 128K
Requires: 400K disk drive.
Medium: 3 1/2-inch disk
ISPN: 91837-500   **Price: $79.00**

CASHMASTER BUSINESS SYSTEMS, INC.
MICROSOFT EXCEL BUSINESS SOURCEBOOK

A book that covers over 100 business applications and a set of five disks which contain all spreadsheets discussed in the book.
System: MAC, II, PLUS, SE, XL
Minimum Memory: 512K
Requires: Microsoft Excel (ISPN 53150-270). Includes book and 5 disks.
Medium: 3 1/2-inch disk
ISPN: 90903-523 **Price: $100.00**

MICROSOFT CORP.
MICROSOFT WORKS (VER. 2.0)

An integrated business productivity tool containing a spreadsheet with graphics, word processor, database, and communications.
System: MAC, II, PLUS, SE, XL
Minimum Memory: 512K
Requires: ImageWriter or LaserWriter printer.
Medium: 3 1/2-inch disk
ISPN: 53150-740 **Price: $295.00**

CE SOFTWARE
MOCKPACKAGE PLUS (VER. 4.4)

A professional desk accessories set which includes MockTerminal, MockWrite, MockPrint, MockChart and EZ-Menu.
System: MAC, II, PLUS, SE, XL
Minimum Memory: 128K
Requires: ImageWriter, ImageWriter II, or LaserWriter printer.
Medium: 3 1/2-inch disk
ISPN: 11725-250 **Price: $35.00**

OLDUVAI CORP.
MULTICLIP (VER. 1.0)

A multiple, editable clipboards, allowing for repetitive cut, copy and paste actions without loss of information.
System: MAC, II, PLUS, SE, XL
Minimum Memory: 512K
Medium: 3 1/2-inch disk
ISPN: 57812-510 **Price: $69.00**

DATAPAK SOFTWARE, INC.
MY EXECUTIVE OFFICE (VER. 4.7) NCP

An office management system with desktop design tools, flat file management, word processing, mail merge and electronic worksheets.
System: MAC, II, PLUS, SE, XL
Minimum Memory: 512K
Medium: 3 1/2-inch disk
ISPN: 23762-100 **Price: $195.00**

DATAPAK SOFTWARE, INC.
MY OFFICE

Creates stationary, invoices, memos, letters, graphics, files. Will also sort and list.
System: MAC, II, PLUS, SE, XL
Minimum Memory: 128K
Medium: 3 1/2-inch disk
ISPN: 23762-575 **Price: $99.00**

HEIZER SOFTWARE
NETWORK

A client message, memorandum and contact tracking system that records and stores notes from phone conversations.
System: MAC, II, PLUS, SE, XL
Minimum Memory: 1024K
Requires: HyperCard (ISPN 03900-300).
Medium: 3 1/2-inch disk
ISPN: 35175-433 **Price: $25.00**

DAZZL
ORGANIZER+ (VER. 1.5)

Keeps track of names, addresses, appointments, 'to do' lists, notes, phonelogs and projects in a set of HyperCard stacks.
System: MAC, II, PLUS, SE, XL
Minimum Memory: 1024K
Requires: HyperCard (ISPN 3900-300), hard disk.
Medium: 3 1/2-inch disk
ISPN: 91213-500 **Price: $79.95**

IMAGINE SOFTWARE
PERFECT TIMING

A multi-user network calendar system that runs as a desk accessory which is available from within any application.
System: MAC, II, PLUS, SE, XL
Minimum Memory: 512K
Requires: Starter Kit (1-3 users). AppleTalk compatible network.
Medium: 3 1/2-inch disk
ISPN: 41387-600 **Price: $295.00**

IMAGINE SOFTWARE
PERFECT TIMING

A multi-user network calendar system that runs as a desk accessory which is available from within any application.
System: MAC, II, PLUS, SE, XL
Minimum Memory: 512K
Requires: Node Kit (for 3 additional users). AppleTalk compatible network.
Medium: 3 1/2-inch disk
ISPN: 41387-600 **Price: $150.00**

FARALLON COMPUTING
PHONENET CHECKNET – MULTI-USER LICENSE

A desk accessory used to search an AppleTalk local area network for AppleTalk devices, displaying information on that device.
System: MAC, II, PLUS, SE, XL
Minimum Memory: 512K
Requires: AppleTalk network.
Medium: 3 1/2-inch disk
ISPN: 91809-610 **Price: $95.00**

FIFTH GENERATION SYSTEMS, INC.
POWERSTATION (VER. 2.5)

Provides arrangement of software tools on up to 16 'pages' for immediate access to any of hundreds of applications or documents.
System: MAC, II, PLUS, SE, XL
Minimum Memory: 512K
Requires: 800K disk drive.
Medium: 3 1/2-inch disk
ISPN: 30787-400 **Price: $59.95**

HABA/ARRAYS SYSTEMS, INC.
QUARTET

Handles simultaneous operation of spreadsheet, graphics, data base and text editing.
System: MAC, II, PLUS, SE, XL
Minimum Memory: 512K
Medium: 3 1/2-inch disk
ISPN: 33987-700 **Price: $49.95**

PARAGON CONCEPTS, INC.
QUED/M MACRO EDITOR

A macro editor with features which also make it a text data base, appointment book and recipe book.
System: MAC, II, PLUS, SE, XL
Minimum Memory: 512K
Medium: 3 1/2-inch disk
ISPN: 59740-574 **Price: $119.00**

ENTERSET
QUICKSET (VER. 2.0)

Combines calendar, cardex, note filer, encryptor calculator, phone dialer, and print spooler under one desk accessory menu.
System: MAC, II, PLUS, SE, XL
Minimum Memory: 512K
Medium: 3 1/2-inch disk
ISPN: 29481-700 **Price: $49.00**

BORLAND INT'L.
SIDEKICK-THE MACINTOSH OFFICE MANAGER (VER-2.0)

Contains an Organizer integrated with ten desk accessories, word processing, and XModem file transfer communications protocol.
System: MAC, II, PLUS, SE, XL
Minimum Memory: 512K
Requires: Modem.
Medium: 3 1/2-inch disk
ISPN: 08225-087 **Price: $99.95**

HEIZER SOFTWARE
SPORTSLOG

Logs fitness training and calculates average speed when running, walking, cycling or swimming.
System: MAC, II, PLUS, SE, XL
Minimum Memory: 1024K
Requires: HyperCard (ISPN 03900-300).
Medium: 3 1/2-inch disk
ISPN: 35175-447 **Price: $10.00**

FIFTH GENERATION SYSTEMS, INC.
SUITCASE II (VER. 1.22)

Makes desk accessories and fonts always available without having to install them in your system file.
System: MAC, II, PLUS, SE, XL
Minimum Memory: 512K
Requires: 800K disk drive.
Medium: 3 1/2-inch disk
ISPN: 30787-300 **Price: $79.00**

MLT SOFTWARE

SUN CLOCK (VER. 1.4)

A desk accessory that displays the areas of day and night with the current date and time, or any other date and time, on a world map.

System: MAC, II, PLUS, SE, XL
Minimum Memory: 128K
Medium: 3 1/2-inch disk
ISPN: 54834-700   **Price: $17.00**

ACCESS TECHNOLOGY, INC.
ACCESS/MINDWORK DIVISION

TRAPEZE (VER. 2.1)

Blends the capabilities of a spreadsheet with those of a desktop presentation tool to create the presentation worksheet.

System: MAC, II, PLUS, SE, XL
Minimum Memory: 512K
Medium: 3 1/2-inch disk
ISPN: 00506-600   **Price: $295.00**

HABA/ARRAYS SYSTEMS, INC.

WINDOWDIALER WITH HABADIALER

Hardware and software phone directory and dialing package with a look over list of names, addresses and phone numbers.

System: MAC, II, PLUS, SE, XL
Minimum Memory: 512K
Medium: 3 1/2-inch disk
ISPN: 33987-087   **Price: $79.95**

HEIZER SOFTWARE

WORLD TIMES

Displays current time and date for over 30 major cities around the world.

System: MAC, II, PLUS, SE, XL
Minimum Memory: 1024K
Requires: HyperCard (ISPN 03900-300).
Medium: 3 1/2-inch disk
ISPN: 35175-451   **Price: $7.00**

---

142 PRODUCTIVITY/ INVESTMENT MANAGEMENT

HEIZER SOFTWARE

ANNUITY DISTRIBUTION OPTIONS

Calculates the value of annuity distribution options to facilitate making decisions on the best available option.

System: MAC, II, PLUS, SE, XL
Minimum Memory: 512K
Requires: Microsoft Excel (ISPN 53150-270).
Medium: 3 1/2-inch disk
ISPN: 35175-910   **Price: $20.00**

HEIZER SOFTWARE

ASSET ALLOCATION

Calculates tables which summarize an investors position using the viewpoints of liquidity, composition, diversification and risk.

System: MAC, II, PLUS, SE, XL
Minimum Memory: 512K
Requires: Microsoft Excel (ISPN 53150-270) or Microsoft Works (ISPN 53150-740).
Medium: 3 1/2-inch disk
ISPN: 35175-391   **Price: $12.00**

HEIZER SOFTWARE

BENEFIT PLAN CONTRIBUTION ANALYSIS

Provides an analytical method for determining the economic benefits of sheltering business income via profit-sharing contributions.

System: MAC, II, PLUS, SE, XL
Minimum Memory: 512K
Requires: Microsoft Excel (ISPN 53150-270).
Medium: 3 1/2-inch disk
ISPN: 35175-915   **Price: $12.00**

HEIZER SOFTWARE

BROKERAGE COMMISSIONS

Figures the commissions for trading stocks, bonds or options.

System: MAC, II, PLUS, SE, XL
Minimum Memory: 512K
Requires: Microsoft Excel (ISPN 53150-270) or Microsoft Works (ISPN 53150-740).
Medium: 3 1/2-inch disk
ISPN: 35175-390   **Price: $15.00**

LARRY ROSEN CO.

COMPLETE BOND ANALYZER (VER. 1.20)

Performs bond calculations, including yield to maturity, yield to call, duration and spot analysis.

System: MAC, II, PLUS, SE, XL
Minimum Memory: 128K
Medium: 3 1/2-inch disk
ISPN: 66987-200   **Price: $89.00**

COMPUTRAC

COMPUTRAC/M

A set of technical analysis tools that determines the trend and momentum of price movements on stocks, equities and commodities.

System: MAC, II, PLUS, SE, XL
Minimum Memory: 512K
Requires: 800K disk drive.
Medium: 3 1/2-inch disk
ISPN: 18537-100   **Price: $695.00**

HEIZER SOFTWARE

CURRENCIES DATABASE

A database indicating weekly prices for the Yen, Pound Sterling Deutsche Mark, and the Swiss Franc.

System: MAC, II, PLUS, SE, XL
Minimum Memory: 512K
Requires: Microsoft Excel (ISPN 53150-270) or Microsoft Works (ISPN 53150-740).
Medium: 3 1/2-inch disk
ISPN: 35175-923   **Price: $20.00**

HEIZER SOFTWARE

DISCOUNT STOCK DATABASE

A database of eighty-eight firms offering stock at approximately five percent with reinvestment of dividends.

System: MAC, II, PLUS, SE, XL
Minimum Memory: 512K
Requires: Microsoft Excel (ISPN 53150-270), Microsoft Works (ISPN 53150-740) or HyperCard (ISPN 03900-300).
Medium: 3 1/2-inch disk
ISPN: 35175-374   **Price: $10.00**

HEIZER SOFTWARE

DOW INDUSTRIALS 1951-1987 MONTHLY

A database format using the Dow industrial average for over thirty-five years.

System: MAC, II, PLUS, SE, XL
Minimum Memory: 512K
Requires: Microsoft Excel (ISPN 53150-270), Microsoft Works (ISPN 53150-740) or HyperCard (ISPN 03900-300).
Medium: 3 1/2-inch disk
ISPN: 35175-384   **Price: $12.00**

DOW JONES & CO., INC.

DOW JONES MARKET ANALYZER

Performs technical analyses with historical stock data which is automatically retrieved from Dow Jones News/Retrieval.

System: MAC, II, PLUS, SE, XL
Minimum Memory: 512K
Requires: Modem.
Medium: 3 1/2-inch disk
ISPN: 26725-100   **Price: $299.00**

DOW JONES & CO., INC.

DOW JONES MARKET MANAGER PLUS (VER. 1.0)

Accommodates 256 portfolios. Tracks stocks, bonds, options, mutual funds and treasury issues through Dow Jones News and Retrieval.

System: MAC, II, PLUS, SE, XL
Minimum Memory: 512K
Requires: Modem.
Medium: 3 1/2-inch disk
ISPN: 26725-175   **Price: $299.00**

DOW JONES & CO., INC.

DOW JONES MARKET MANAGER PLUS (VER. 2.0)

Manages one or more portfolios and accesses up-to-date prices. Tracks stocks, bonds, options, mutual funds and treasury issues.

System: MAC, II, PLUS, SE, XL
Minimum Memory: 512K
Requires: Modem.
Medium: 3 1/2-inch disk
ISPN: 26725-200   **Price: $299.00**

DOW JONES & CO., INC.

DOW JONES SPREADSHEET LINK

Connects with Dow Jones News/Retrieval and downloads information directly into a spreadsheet template set up for desired analysis.

System: MAC, II, PLUS, SE, XL
Minimum Memory: 128K
Requires: Straight Talk (ISPN 26725-425), Multiplan (ISPN 35087-400).
Medium: 3 1/2-inch disk
ISPN: 26725-400 **Price: $99.00**

DOW JONES & CO., INC.

DOW JONES STRAIGHT TALK (VER. 2.0)

Designed to help the user obtain, store and organize information from Dow Jones News/Retrieval.

System: MAC, II, PLUS, SE, XL
Minimum Memory: 512K
Medium: 3 1/2-inch disk
ISPN: 26725-425 **Price: $95.00**

HEIZER SOFTWARE

DOW MONTH-BY-MONTH SET

A database format of four Dow averages for industrials, utilities, transportation and composites for over thirty-five years.

System: MAC, II, PLUS, SE, XL
Minimum Memory: 512K
Requires: Microsoft Excel (ISPN 53150-270), Microsoft Works (ISPN 53150-740) or HyperCard (ISPN 03900-300).
Medium: 3 1/2-inch disk
ISPN: 35175-383 **Price: $25.00**

HEIZER SOFTWARE

EASY QUOTES

Automatically converts downloaded stock market quotes from text format to numeric format.

System: MAC, II, PLUS, SE, XL
Minimum Memory: 512K
Requires: Microsoft Excel (ISPN 53150-270).
Medium: 3 1/2-inch disk
ISPN: 35175-513 **Price: $9.00**

HEIZER SOFTWARE

EDUCATION FINANCING ANALYSIS

Projects the approximate cost of a child's college education based on age, current cost, inflation and investment rate assumptions.

System: MAC, II, PLUS, SE, XL
Minimum Memory: 512K
Requires: Microsoft Works (ISPN 53150-740) or Microsoft Excel (ISPN 53150-740).
Medium: 3 1/2-inch disk
ISPN: 35175-834 **Price: $14.00**

LARRY ROSEN CO.

FINANCIAL AND INTEREST CALCULATOR

Includes studies on loan amortization schedules, internal rate of return, and studies with multiple cash flows per year.

System: MAC, II, PLUS, SE, XL
Minimum Memory: 512K
Medium: 3 1/2-inch disk
ISPN: 66987-375 **Price: $89.00**

HEIZER SOFTWARE

GOLD COIN CALCULATOR

Calculates premiums for twenty-three widely traded gold coins from the current market prices of coins and gold.

System: MAC, II, PLUS, SE, XL
Minimum Memory: 512K
Requires: Microsoft Excel (ISPN 53150-270), Microsoft Works (ISPN 53150-740) or HyperCard (ISPN 03900-300).
Medium: 3 1/2-inch disk
ISPN: 35175-395 **Price: $7.00**

LARRY ROSEN CO.

INVESTMENT ANALYSIS-AFTER TAX (VER. 1.7B)

Evaluates existing and proposed real estate, stock and bond investments by internal rate of return analysis after taxes.

System: MAC, II, PLUS, SE, XL
Minimum Memory: 128K
Requires: Spreadsheet.
Medium: 3 1/2-inch disk
ISPN: 66987-425 **Price: $89.00**

P3, INC.

INVESTOR

A full-featured portfolio management system which gives the user control over financial holdings.

System: MAC, II, PLUS, SE, XL
Minimum Memory: 512K
Medium: 3 1/2-inch disk
ISPN: 59250-350 **Price: $150.00**

SMITH MICRO SOFTWARE

MARKET LINK

Accesses Dow Jones News/Retrieval and The Source. Defines up to 120 security symbols for stocks, bonds, mutual funds, treasury issues.

System: MAC, II, PLUS, SE, XL
Minimum Memory: 512K
Requires: Apple or Hayes compatible modem.
Medium: 3 1/2-inch disk
ISPN: 71606-400 **Price: $85.00**

HEIZER SOFTWARE

METALS DATABASE

A database indicating the weekly prices for copper, silver, gold, and platinum.

System: MAC, II, PLUS, SE, XL
Minimum Memory: 512K
Requires: Microsoft Excel (ISPN 53150-270) or Microsoft Works (ISPN 53150-740).
Medium: 3 1/2-inch disk
ISPN: 35175-962 **Price: $20.00**

DYNACOMP, INC.

MICROCOMPUTER BOND PROGRAM

Estimates price and yield of fixed income securities under a broad range of assumptions and provides estimates about the future.

System: MAC, II, PLUS, SE, XL
Minimum Memory: 512K
Medium: 3 1/2-inch disk
ISPN: 27050-485 **Price: $64.95**

DYNACOMP, INC.

MICROCOMPUTER STOCK PROGRAM

Provides timing signals for stock purchases and sales.

System: MAC, II, PLUS, SE, XL
Minimum Memory: 512K
Medium: 3 1/2-inch disk
ISPN: 27050-486 **Price: $64.95**

HEIZER SOFTWARE

MUTUAL FUND REINVESTMENT

Tracks the number of shares, capital gains, total investment, average share price and the growth rate of mutual funds.

System: MAC, II, PLUS, SE, XL
Minimum Memory: 512K
Requires: Microsoft Excel (ISPN 53150-270) or Microsoft Works (ISPN 53150-740).
Medium: 3 1/2-inch disk
ISPN: 35175-377 **Price: $15.00**

HEIZER SOFTWARE

NAIC STOCK SELECTION GUIDE

Performs the calculations required to arrive at a buy-sell or hold-sell recommendation.

System: MAC, II, PLUS, SE, XL
Minimum Memory: 512K
Requires: Microsoft Excel (ISPN 53150-270) or Microsoft Works (ISPN 53150-740).
Medium: 3 1/2-inch disk
ISPN: 35175-378 **Price: $20.00**

HEIZER SOFTWARE

OPTION EXPIRATION DATES

Calculates the third-Friday option expiration dates for nine months.

System: MAC, II, PLUS, SE, XL
Minimum Memory: 512K
Requires: Microsoft Excel (ISPN 53150-270).
Medium: 3 1/2-inch disk
ISPN: 35175-389 **Price: $8.00**

HEIZER SOFTWARE

OPTION SPREADS

Calculates profit or loss and return on investment using bull and bear Call Option spreads and Put Option spreads.

System: MAC, II, PLUS, SE, XL
Minimum Memory: 512K
Requires: Microsoft Excel (ISPN 53150-270).
Medium: 3 1/2-inch disk
ISPN: 35175-379 **Price: $25.00**

HEIZER SOFTWARE

OPTION SYMBOL CONVERTER

An option symbol converter for stock options or index options.

System: MAC, II, PLUS, SE, XL
Minimum Memory: 512K
Requires: Microsoft Excel (ISPN 53150-270).
Medium: 3 1/2-inch disk
ISPN: 35175-388   **Price: $7.00**

HEIZER SOFTWARE

OPTION-WARRANT ANALYZER-BLACK SCHOLES

Calculates the theoretical values of up to six stock options and warrants.

System: MAC, II, PLUS, SE, XL
Minimum Memory: 512K
Requires: Microsoft Excel (ISPN 53150-270).
Medium: 3 1/2-inch disk
ISPN: 35175-397   **Price: $30.00**

HEIZER SOFTWARE

OPTION-WARRANT ANALYZER-THORP AND KASSOUF

Calculates theoretical values of up to six stock options and warrants based on the Thorp and Kassouf analysis.

System: MAC, II, PLUS, SE, XL
Minimum Memory: 512K
Requires: Microsoft Excel (ISPN 53150-270).
Medium: 3 1/2-inch disk
ISPN: 35175-398   **Price: $25.00**

HEIZER SOFTWARE

OPTION-WARRANTS COMBO

Combines two methods which calculate the theoretical values for stock options and warrants.

System: MAC, II, PLUS, SE, XL
Minimum Memory: 512K
Requires: Microsoft Excel (ISPN 53150-270).
Medium: 3 1/2-inch disk
ISPN: 35175-399   **Price: $49.00**

DYNACOMP, INC.

OPTIONS ANALYSIS

Provides analyses for Put and Call prices as a function of both stock prices and time to expiration based on investment strategies.

System: MAC, II, PLUS, SE, XL
Minimum Memory: 512K
Medium: 3 1/2-inch disk
ISPN: 27050-523   **Price: $104.95**

HEIZER SOFTWARE

OPTIONS COVERED

Calculates profit or loss and return on investment using margin or cash covered call writing positions.

System: MAC, II, PLUS, SE, XL
Minimum Memory: 512K
Requires: Microsoft Excel (ISPN 53150-270).
Medium: 3 1/2-inch disk
ISPN: 35175-380   **Price: $25.00**

DISK-COUNT SOFTWARE, INC.

PORTFOLIO MANAGER

Updates and manages securities portfolios, including stocks, bonds, options, mutual funds, and treasury notes.

System: MAC, II, PLUS, SE, XL
Minimum Memory: 512K
Requires: ImageWriter, ImageWriter II, or LaserWriter printer, modem.
Medium: 3 1/2-inch disk
ISPN: 26189-666   **Price: $34.95**

HEIZER SOFTWARE

S & P 1957-87 MONTHLY

The Standard and Poors monthly averages back to 1957 with year by year charts.

System: MAC, II, PLUS, SE, XL
Minimum Memory: 1024K
Requires: Microsoft Excel (ISPN 53150-270), Microsoft Works (ISPN 53150-740) or HyperCard (ISPN 03900-300).
Medium: 3 1/2-inch disk
ISPN: 35175-408   **Price: $12.00**

HEIZER SOFTWARE

SECURITIES PORTFOLIO

Organizes stocks, bonds and option portfolios. Values portfolio and individual securities at any point of time.

System: MAC, II, PLUS, SE, XL
Minimum Memory: 1024K
Requires: HyperCard (ISPN 03900-300).
Medium: 3 1/2-inch disk
ISPN: 35175-108   **Price: $25.00**

MENU® also publishes directories for the **IBM® PC & compatibles** and **Apple® II** and **COMMODORE®** computers. There's a directory for **Local Area Networks**, too.

HEIZER SOFTWARE

SECURITY TRANSACTION CALCULATOR-SCHWAB

Calculates stocks, warrants and listed options transaction costs using Charles Schwab's March, 1988, commission schedule.

System: MAC, II, PLUS, SE, XL
Minimum Memory: 512K
Requires: Microsoft Excel (ISPN 53150-270).
Medium: 3 1/2-inch disk
ISPN: 35175-394   **Price: $12.00**

HEIZER SOFTWARE

STANDARD AND POOR 1957 TO 1987 MONTHLY

A database format including the Standard and Poors average from the year 1957.

System: MAC, II, PLUS, SE, XL
Minimum Memory: 512K
Requires: Microsoft Excel (ISPN 53150-270) or Microsoft Works (ISPN 53150-740).
Medium: 3 1/2-inch disk
ISPN: 35175-385   **Price: $12.00**

HEIZER SOFTWARE

STANDARD AND POOR DAILY-1953 TO 1987

Standard and Poors composite daily closing prices for every trading day from January 1, 1953 to December 31, 1987.

System: MAC, II, PLUS, SE, XL
Minimum Memory: 512K
Requires: Microsoft Excel (ISPN 53150-270) or Microsoft Works (ISPN 53150-740).
Medium: 3 1/2-inch disk
ISPN: 35175-387   **Price: $99.00**

HEIZER SOFTWARE

STANDARD AND POOR DAILY-1980'S

Standard and Poors composite daily closing prices for every trading day from January 1, 1980 to December 31, 1987.

System: MAC, II, PLUS, SE, XL
Minimum Memory: 512K
Requires: Microsoft Excel (ISPN 53150-270) or Microsoft Works (ISPN 53150-740).
Medium: 3 1/2-inch disk
ISPN: 35175-386   **Price: $39.00**

HEIZER SOFTWARE

STOCK DIVIDEND REINVESTMENT

Keeps track of the value of the holdings of a stock with a dividend reinvestment plan.

System: MAC, II, PLUS, SE, XL
Minimum Memory: 512K
Requires: Microsoft Excel (ISPN 53150-270).
Medium: 3 1/2-inch disk
ISPN: 35175-371   **Price: $15.00**

HEIZER SOFTWARE

STOCK INDEX MAKER

Designs and tracks price, value or equal-weighted stock indices based on stocks chosen by an individual.

System: MAC, II, PLUS, SE, XL
Minimum Memory: 512K
Requires: Microsoft Excel (ISPN 53150-270).
Medium: 3 1/2-inch disk
ISPN: 35175-393   **Price: $10.00**

HEIZER SOFTWARE

STOCK OPTION RECORD

Keeps records for each stock option granted and subsequently exercised.

System: MAC, II, PLUS, SE, XL
Minimum Memory: 512K
Requires: Microsoft Excel (ISPN 53150-270).
Medium: 3 1/2-inch disk
ISPN: 35175-990   **Price: $12.00**

HEIZER SOFTWARE
STOCK OPTIONS DATABASE

A database of 440 stocks having options. Includes stock's name and symbol, option's exchange, volatility, beta and expiration cycle.

System: MAC, II, PLUS, SE, XL
Minimum Memory: 512K
Requires: Microsoft Excel (ISPN 53150-270) or HyperCard (ISPN 03900-300).
Medium: 3 1/2-inch disk
ISPN: 35175-373
Price: $15.00

HEIZER SOFTWARE
STOCK PORTFOLIO

Records buy/sell dates and prices, commissions, dividends and overall portfolio performance statistics.

System: MAC, II, PLUS, SE, XL
Minimum Memory: 512K
Requires: Microsoft Excel (ISPN 53150-270) or Microsoft Works (ISPN 53150-740).
Medium: 3 1/2-inch disk
ISPN: 35175-485
Price: $15.00

SMITH MICRO SOFTWARE
STOCK PORTFOLIO SYSTEM

An investment accounting, recordkeeping, and control system which includes certificate of deposit and money market investments.

System: MAC, II, PLUS, SE, XL
Minimum Memory: 512K
Medium: 3 1/2-inch disk
ISPN: 71606-700
Price: $225.00

HEIZER SOFTWARE
STOCK VALUATION

Computes the theoretical price of a stock to determine whether the stock is over or under valued.

System: MAC, II, PLUS, SE, XL
Minimum Memory: 512K
Requires: Microsoft Excel (ISPN 53150-270) or Microsoft Works (ISPN 53150-740).
Medium: 3 1/2-inch disk
ISPN: 35175-381
Price: $25.00

HEIZER SOFTWARE
STOCK VALUATION H-MODEL

Determines the expected rate of return on a dividend-paying stock.

System: MAC, II, PLUS, SE, XL
Minimum Memory: 512K
Requires: Microsoft Excel (ISPN 53150-270) or Microsoft Works (ISPN 53150-740).
Medium: 3 1/2-inch disk
ISPN: 35175-382
Price: $10.00

ENCYCLOWARE
STOCK WATCH

Allows users to keep track of a stock portfolio.

System: MAC, II, PLUS, SE, XL
Minimum Memory: 512K
Medium: 3 1/2-inch disk
ISPN: 29087-300
Price: $39.00

HEIZER SOFTWARE
STOCKS WITH INCREASING DIVIDENDS

A database of 370 stocks from the New York Stock Exchange and Over the Counter stocks with a ten-year history of increasing dividends.

System: MAC, II, PLUS, SE, XL
Minimum Memory: 1024K
Requires: Microsoft Excel (ISPN 53150-270) or HyperCard (ISPN 03900-300).
Medium: 3 1/2-inch disk
ISPN: 35175-396
Price: $30.00

HEIZER SOFTWARE
TECHNICAL MARKET ANALYSIS

Automatically performs twelve key, technical calculations including on-balance volume, relative strength and ease of movement.

System: MAC, II, PLUS, SE, XL
Minimum Memory: 512K
Requires: Microsoft Excel (ISPN 53150-270).
Medium: 3 1/2-inch disk
ISPN: 35175-392
Price: $20.00

VALUE LINE SOFTWARE
VALUE/SCREEN PLUS (QUARTERLY SUBSCRIPTION)

A multi-screen, stock selection and portfolio management system.

System: MAC, II, PLUS, SE, XL
Minimum Memory: 512K
Medium: 3 1/2-inch disk
ISPN: 84762-520
Price: $211.00

VALUE LINE SOFTWARE
VALUE/SCREEN PLUS (VER. 1.12)

Contains a stock selection and portfolio management system.

System: MAC, II, PLUS, SE, XL
Minimum Memory: 512K
Medium: 3 1/2-inch disk
ISPN: 84762-600
Price: $95.00

PRO PLUS SOFTWARE
WALL STREET INVESTOR (VER. 3.0)

A fully integrated portfolio management and Security Analysis system.

System: MAC, II, SE, XL
Minimum Memory: 1024K
Requires: Two disk drives or a hard disk, modem.
Medium: 3 1/2-inch disk
ISPN: 12181-525
Price: $695.00

SMITH MICRO SOFTWARE
WALL STREET TECHNIQUES (VER. 1.04)

Includes an easy to use format to provide complete stock charting and market momentum analysis.

System: MAC, II, PLUS, SE, XL
Minimum Memory: 512K
Medium: 3 1/2-inch disk
ISPN: 71606-925
Price: $295.00

MICRO TRADING SOFTWARE LTD.
WALL STREET WATCHER (VER. 2.68)

Provides technical analysis with charting windows, multiple indicators, and manual or automatic updating of information.

System: MAC, II, PLUS, SE, XL
Minimum Memory: 1024K
Requires: Hayes compatible modem.
Medium: 3 1/2-inch disk
ISPN: 51553-800
Price: $495.00

143 PRODUCTIVITY/ INVOICING/ORDER ENTRY

CET, INC.
A/E BILLINGS

Provides multiple invoicing formats and monitors project costs.

System: MAC, II, PLUS, SE, XL
Minimum Memory: 512K
Requires: Omnis 3 Plus/Express (ISPN 58775-515).
Medium: 3 1/2-inch disk
ISPN: 90915-100
Price: $495.00

LAKE AVE. SOFTWARE
ASSISTANT CONTROLLER SERIES-ORDER ENTRY/ INVOICING

Enters orders for pick ticket/packing slip, invoicing, or shipping labels.

System: MAC, II, PLUS, SE, XL
Minimum Memory: 512K
Medium: 3 1/2-inch disk
ISPN: 43418-156
Price: $495.00

FLEXWARE, INC.
FLEXWARE ORDER ENTRY

Speeds processing and filling, reduces bad debt and inventory problems.

System: MAC
Minimum Memory: 256K
Medium: 3 1/2-inch disk
ISPN: 52468-300
Price: $795.00

GREAT PLAINS SOFTWARE
GREAT PLAINS ACCT SERIES-ORDER ENTRY W/POS 4.2

Handles cash and account sales, returns, quotes, prepayments and deposits.

System: MAC, II, PLUS, SE, XL
Minimum Memory: 512K
Requires: 20 MB hard disk, 800K disk drive, 132-column printer, or 80-column printer with condensed print.
Medium: 3 1/2-inch disk
ISPN: 33475-825
Price: $795.00

SYNEX

MACINVOICE (VER. 1.0)

Designed for small businesses and individuals to fill in, print, and save invoices.

System: MAC, II, PLUS, SE, XL
Minimum Memory: 512K
Requires: 800K disk drive, printer.
Medium: 3 1/2-inch disk
ISPN: 77712-450 **Price: $69.95**

PRECISION COMPUTER SYSTEMS

PRECISION INVENTORY CONTROL & ORDER ENTRY

Includes receiving of new stock items, shipping, reordering, tracking year-to-date sales and backordering of stock items.

System: MAC, II, PLUS, SE, XL
Minimum Memory: 1024K
Requires: 800K disk drive or hard disk, ImageWriter printer, Omnis 3 Plus/Express (ISPN 58775-515).
Medium: 3 1/2-inch disk
ISPN: 61720-350 **Price: $1295.00**

SBT CORP.

SBT DINVOICE-COMPILED (VER. 6.20)

Provides a billing and inventory control system that includes customer and inventory labels and reports for inventory reordering.

System: MAC, II, PLUS, SE, XL
Minimum Memory: 512K
Medium: 3 1/2-inch disk
ISPN: 68057-101 **Price: $295.00**

SBT CORP.

SBT DINVOICE-STANDARD (VER. 6.20)

Provides a billing and inventory control system that includes customer and inventory labels and reports for inventory reordering.

System: MAC, II, PLUS, SE, XL
Minimum Memory: 512K
Medium: 3 1/2-inch disk
ISPN: 68057-100 **Price: $395.00**

SBT CORP.

SBT DINVOICE/DSTATEMENTS-COMPILED (VER. 6.20)

Provides a billing and inventory system and an accounts receivable system.

System: MAC, II, PLUS, SE, XL
Minimum Memory: 512K
Medium: 3 1/2-inch disk
ISPN: 68057-850 **Price: $295.00**

SBT CORP.

SBT DINVOICE/DSTATEMENTS-STANDARD (VER. 6.20)

Provides a billing and inventory system and an accounts receivable system.

System: MAC, II, PLUS, SE, XL
Minimum Memory: 512K
Medium: 3 1/2-inch disk
ISPN: 68057-800 **Price: $395.00**

SBT CORP.

SBT DORDERS-COMPILED (VER. 6.20)

Generates schedules and maintains sales orders and order backlog information. Creates invoices when items are shipped.

System: MAC, II, PLUS, SE, XL
Minimum Memory: 512K
Medium: 3 1/2-inch disk
ISPN: 68057-121 **Price: $295.00**

SBT CORP.

SBT DORDERS-STANDARD (VER. 6.20)

Generates schedules and maintains sales orders and order backlog information. Creates invoices when items are shipped.

System: MAC, II, PLUS, SE, XL
Minimum Memory: 512K
Medium: 3 1/2-inch disk
ISPN: 68057-120 **Price: $395.00**

NATIONAL TELE-PRESS

SUPER MOM (VER. 2.0)

Features includes order entry, accounts receivable, inventory, report generator and free utilities disk.

System: MAC, II, PLUS, SE, XL
Minimum Memory: 512K
Requires: 800K disk drive.
Medium: 3 1/2-inch disk
ISPN: 94203-700 **Price: $795.00**

NATIONAL TELE-PRESS

SUPER MOM (VER. 2.0)

Features includes order entry, accounts receivable, inventory, report generator and free utilities disk.

System: MAC, II, PLUS, SE, XL
Minimum Memory: 512K
Requires: 1-5 users.
Medium: 3 1/2-inch disk
ISPN: 94203-700 **Price: $1795.00**

148 PRODUCTIVITY/ MAILING LISTS

SATORI SOFTWARE

BULK MAILER + (VER. 3.23)

Version of Bulk Mailer program that allows your mailing list to grow to 90,000 names.

System: MAC, II, PLUS, SE, XL
Minimum Memory: 512K
Requires: 800K disk drive. Hard disk or two disk drives.
Medium: 3 1/2-inch disk
ISPN: 68024-105 **Price: $350.00**

HEIZER SOFTWARE

CHAMBERS OF COMMERCE

Contains the names and addresses of 1900 United States Chambers of Commerce.

System: MAC, II, PLUS, SE, XL
Minimum Memory: 512K
Requires: Microsoft Excel (ISPN 53150-270) or Microsoft Works (ISPN 53150-740).
Medium: 3 1/2-inch disk
ISPN: 35175-164 **Price: $20.00**

HEIZER SOFTWARE

ENVELOPE ADDRESSER

Addresses individual envelopes on an ImageWriter or LaserWriter without leaving the Microsoft Excel program.

System: MAC, II, PLUS, SE, XL
Minimum Memory: 512K
Requires: Microsoft Excel (ISPN 53150-270).
Medium: 3 1/2-inch disk
ISPN: 35175-931 **Price: $15.00**

HEIZER SOFTWARE

MAC ADVERTISERS INDEX

A database of names, addresses, phone numbers and products of over 500 companies with advertisements in recent issues of Macworld.

System: MAC, II, PLUS, SE, XL
Minimum Memory: 512K
Requires: Microsoft Excel (ISPN 53150-270), Microsoft Works (ISPN 53150-740) or HyperCard (ISPN 03900-300).
Medium: 3 1/2-inch disk
ISPN: 35175-789 **Price: $12.00**

HEIZER SOFTWARE

MAC PUBLICATIONS DATABASE

A database of over one-hundred Macintosh publications which can be used for mail merge or printing address labels.

System: MAC, II, PLUS, SE, XL
Minimum Memory: 512K
Requires: Microsoft Excel (ISPN 53150-270), Microsoft Works (ISPN 53150-740) or HyperCard (ISPN 03900-300).
Medium: 3 1/2-inch disk
ISPN: 35175-533 **Price: $20.00**

HEIZER SOFTWARE

MAC USERS GROUPS DATABASE

A database with over 450 Macintosh user groups which can be used for mail merge or printing address labels.

System: MAC, II, PLUS, SE, XL
Minimum Memory: 512K
Requires: Microsoft Excel (ISPN 53150-270), Microsoft Works (ISPN 53150-740) or HyperCard (ISPN 03900-300).
Medium: 3 1/2-inch disk
ISPN: 35175-534 **Price: $25.00**

PECAN SOFTWARE SYSTEMS
MACADVANTAGE-MAIL MANAGER

Handles one label across at time, lists, letters and more. records. File size is limited only by available disk space.

System: MAC, II, PLUS, SE, XL
Minimum Memory: 512K
Requires: MacWrite (ISPN 12784-530) or Microsoft Word (ISPN 53150-732) to run reports.
Medium: 3 1/2-inch disk
ISPN: 60356-560 **Price: $99.95**

SYNEX
MACENVELOPE (VER. 4.1)

Prints envelopes and labels with postal bar coding, provides batch printing and allows for variable envelope layout and font choices.

System: MAC, II, PLUS, SE, XL
Minimum Memory: 512K
Requires: 800K disk drive. ImageWriter I or II, LaserWriter, LaserWriter Plus or II, or any dot-matrix printer.
Medium: 3 1/2-inch disk
ISPN: 77712-410 **Price: $89.95**

ARTWORX SOFTWARE CO., INC.
MAIL LIST

Manages mail lists from several hundred to several thousand names and can also be used as a mini database manager.

System: MAC, II, PLUS, SE, XL
Minimum Memory: 512K
Medium: 3 1/2-inch disk
ISPN: 05437-300 **Price: $24.95**

VIKING TECHNOLOGIES
MAIL MAGIC

Prints labels and reports. Sorts by name or zip code. Records can be edited or deleted. Provides MacWrite file importing/exporting.

System: MAC, II, PLUS, SE, XL
Minimum Memory: 512K
Medium: 3 1/2-inch disk
ISPN: 85231-510 **Price: $19.95**

EXCEIVER CORP.
MAILBASE (VER. 2.0)

Handles mailing list management with label printing and mail-merge with word processing documents.

System: MAC, II, PLUS, SE, XL
Minimum Memory: 512K
Requires: Omnis 3 Plus/Express (ISPN 58775-515) or Omnis Runtime.
Medium: 3 1/2-inch disk
ISPN: 91574-500 **Price: $149.00**

HEIZER SOFTWARE
MAILING LABEL MACRO

Automatically prepares mailing labels from a database, including one-up and multi-column labels of any size.

System: MAC, II, PLUS, SE, XL
Minimum Memory: 512K
Requires: Microsoft Excel (ISPN 53150-270).
Medium: 3 1/2-inch disk
ISPN: 35175-501 **Price: $15.00**

HEIZER SOFTWARE
MAILING LABEL TEMPLATE

Prints individualized form letters or mailing labels using the Microsoft Works 'Print Merge' command.

System: MAC, II, PLUS, SE, XL
Minimum Memory: 512K
Requires: Microsoft Works (ISPN 53150-740), ImageWriter printer for mailing labels.
Medium: 3 1/2-inch disk
ISPN: 35175-902 **Price: $6.00**

HEIZER SOFTWARE
MAILING LABELS

A HyperCard stack which prints mailing labels. Includes buttons that sort, specify which names to print, and merge information.

System: MAC, II, PLUS, SE, XL
Minimum Memory: 512K
Requires: HyperCard (ISPN 03900-300) Ver-1.2.
Medium: 3 1/2-inch disk
ISPN: 35175-958 **Price: $15.00**

PAUL MACE SOFTWARE
NVELOPE (VER. 1.0)

Provides a memory resident envelope and label addressing application for single or bulk mailings.

System: MAC, II, PLUS, SE, XL
Minimum Memory: 512K
Requires: Printer.
Medium: 3 1/2-inch disk
ISPN: 59790-355 **Price: $69.00**

JANAC ENTERPRISES
OMNIMAILER (VER. 1.02)

Offers a variety of search, select and sorting modes.

System: MAC, II, PLUS, SE, XL
Minimum Memory: 512K
Requires: Omnis 3 Plus/Express (ISPN 58775-515) or Runtime.
Medium: 3 1/2-inch disk
ISPN: 41438-099 **Price: $54.95**

JANAC ENTERPRISES
OMNIMAILER (VER. 1.02) (CANADA VERSION)

Mailing list manager offering a wide variety of search, select and sorting modes. The user defines fields and default entries.

System: MAC, II, PLUS, SE, XL
Minimum Memory: 512K
Requires: Omnis 3 Plus/Express (ISPN 58775-515), or Omnis 3 Plus Runtime.
Medium: 3 1/2-inch disk
ISPN: 41438-100 **Price: $54.95**

CE SOFTWARE
QUICKMAIL

Provides real-time conferencing, custom forms, prioritizing, personalized directories, printers and more.

System: MAC, II, PLUS, SE, XL
Minimum Memory: 512K
Requires: 800K disk drive.
Medium: 3 1/2-inch disk
ISPN: 11725-600 **Price: $300.00**

EQUAL PLUS
ROLOBASE PLUS

Contains an information organizer to be used for filing cards, label, envelope, and continuous-feed postcard addressing.

System: MAC, II, PLUS, SE, XL
Minimum Memory: 512K
Requires: Two disk drives or a hard disk.
Medium: 3 1/2-inch disk
ISPN: 29584-200 **Price: $39.99**

SILICON BEACH SOFTWARE
SILICON PRESS (VER. 1.1)

Label, envelope and card maker. Good mix of text and graphics. In color on an Imagewriter II.

System: MAC, II, PLUS, SE, XL
Minimum Memory: 512K
Medium: 3 1/2-inch disk
ISPN: 70237-450 **Price: $79.95**

AJL SYSTEMS, INC.
SUPERMAILER

A bulk mailing list manager which can search and sort on any of eighteen entry fields. Holds up to 200,000 entries.

System: MAC, II, PLUS, SE, XL
Minimum Memory: 512K
Requires: Printer.
Medium: 3 1/2-inch disk
ISPN: 02121 300 **Price: $309.00**

AJL SYSTEMS, INC.
SUPERMAILER

A bulk mailing list manager which can search and sort on any of eighteen entry fields. Holds up to 200,000 entries.

System: MAC, II, PLUS, SE, XL
Minimum Memory: 512K
Requires: 1-10 users. Printer.
Medium: 3 1/2-inch disk
ISPN: 02121-300 **Price: $839.00**

AJL SYSTEMS, INC.
SUPERMAILER

A bulk mailing list manager which can search and sort on any of eighteen entry fields. Holds up to 200,000 entries.

System: MAC, II, PLUS, SE, XL
Minimum Memory: 512K
Requires: 1-32 users. Printer.
Medium: 3 1/2-inch disk
ISPN: 02121-300 **Price: $1369.00**

AJL SYSTEMS, INC.
SUPERMAILER II

Sorts on any field. Provides a 2nd Class Zone Table and 2nd Class Mail Report based on user's local post office Official Zone Chart.

System: MAC, II, PLUS, SE, XL
Minimum Memory: 512K
Requires: Printer.
Medium: 3 1/2-inch disk
ISPN: 02121-305 **Price: $409.00**

AJL SYSTEMS, INC.

SUPERMAILER II

Sorts on any field. Provides a 2nd Class Zone Table and 2nd Class Mail Report based on user's local post office Official Zone Chart.

System: MAC, II, PLUS, SE, XL
Minimum Memory: 512K
Requires: 1-10 users. Printer.
Medium: 3 1/2-inch disk
ISPN: 02121-305   **Price: $939.00**

AJL SYSTEMS, INC.

SUPERMAILER II

Sorts on any field. Provides a 2nd Class Zone Table and 2nd Class Mail Report based on user's local post office Official Zone Chart.

System: MAC, II, PLUS, SE, XL
Minimum Memory: 512K
Requires: 1-32 users. Printer.
Medium: 3 1/2-inch disk
ISPN: 02121-305   **Price: $1469.00**

JAMES RIVER GROUP, INC.

T-MAN

Files any type of information for quick access. Name or subject oriented with 15 lines of notes per name.

System: MAC, II, PLUS, SE, XL
Minimum Memory: 512K
Medium: 3 1/2-inch disk
ISPN: 41412-900   **Price: $60.00**

151 PRODUCTIVITY/ MARKETING/SALES

CHANG LABORATORIES, INC.

C*A*T (VER. 2.04)

Integrates management of contacts, activities and time.

System: MAC, II, PLUS, SE, XL
Minimum Memory: 512K
Medium: 3 1/2-inch disk
ISPN: 12200-200   **Price: $399.95**

HEIZER SOFTWARE

CHART USA

A chart for presenting relative sales by state, the relation of population between state and the relative number of retail outlets.

System: MAC, II, PLUS, SE, XL
Minimum Memory: 512K
Requires: Microsoft Excel (ISPN 53150-270).
Medium: 3 1/2-inch disk
ISPN: 35175-001   **Price: $15.00**

HEIZER SOFTWARE

CIRCULATION/RENEWAL RESPONSE

Tracks the costs and results of subscription renewal mailings to existing subscribers.

System: MAC, II, PLUS, SE, XL
Minimum Memory: 512K
Requires: Microsoft Excel (ISPN 53150-270) or Microsoft Works (ISPN 53150-740).
Medium: 3 1/2-inch disk
ISPN: 35175-671   **Price: $12.00**

MICROSERVE, INC.

ESTIMATOR PLUS (VER. 1.0)

Provides complete estimating and job costing functions including mark-up on variable costs and the budgeted hourly method.

System: MAC, II, PLUS, SE, XL
Minimum Memory: 512K
Requires: Omnis 3 Plus/Express (ISPN 58775-515).
Medium: 3 1/2-inch disk
ISPN: 53112-250   **Price: $695.00**

PSRC SOFTWARE

FIELDER

Contains the interview portion of the MacATI program and allows users to perform telemarketing and telephone surveys.

System: MAC, II, PLUS, SE, XL
Minimum Memory: 5120K
Requires: MacATI (ISPN 63684-500).
Medium: 3 1/2-inch disk
ISPN: 63684-300   **Price: $200.00**

MULTI SOLUTIONS, INC.

HYPER-ACTION (VER. 1.0)

Provides monthly sales projections, conversions of leads to prospects, client time billing, and letter management.

System: MAC, II, PLUS, SE, XL
Minimum Memory: 1024K
Requires: HyperCard (ISPN 03900-300).
Medium: 3 1/2-inch disk
ISPN: 55676-300   **Price: $94.50**

PSRC SOFTWARE

MACATI

Provides a telephone interviewing package for survey researchers which can handle surveys of up to 500 questions.

System: MAC, II, PLUS, SE, XL
Minimum Memory: 512K
Requires: Supervisor needs two disk drives or disk drive and hard disk.
Medium: 3 1/2-inch disk
ISPN: 63684-500   **Price: $795.00**

ERICH BREITSCHWERDT + PARTNER

MACINTERVIEW FOR MARKETING

Enables users to analyze various polls, surveys, questionnaires, tests, and evaluations.

System: MAC, II, PLUS, SE, XL
Minimum Memory: 512K
Medium: 3 1/2-inch disk
ISPN: 29593-525   **Price: $950.00**

BREAKTHROUGH PRODUCTIONS

MARKET MASTER FOR THE MACINTOSH (VER. II+)

Performs automatic inquiry and lead follow up where a regular marketing strategy is maintained and leads arrive continuously.

System: MAC, II, PLUS, SE, XL
Minimum Memory: 1024K
Requires: Hard disk.
Medium: 3 1/2-inch disk
ISPN: 90659-299   **Price: $295.00**

BREAKTHROUGH PRODUCTIONS

MARKET MASTER MANAGER (VER. II+)

Performs automatic inquiry lead follow-up for an entire sales force and produces management reports.

System: MAC, II, PLUS, SE, XL
Minimum Memory: 1024K
Requires: 1-3 users. Hard disk.
Medium: 3 1/2-inch disk
ISPN: 90659-350   **Price: $595.00**

BREAKTHROUGH PRODUCTIONS

MARKET MASTER MANAGER (VER. II+)

Performs automatic inquiry lead follow-up for an entire sales force and produces management reports.

System: MAC, II, PLUS, SE, XL
Minimum Memory: 1024K
Requires: 1-10 users. Hard disk.
Medium: 3 1/2-inch disk
ISPN: 90659-350   **Price: $895.00**

BREAKTHROUGH PRODUCTIONS

MARKET MASTER MANAGER (VER. II+)

Performs automatic inquiry lead follow-up for an entire sales force and produces management reports.

System: MAC, II, PLUS, SE, XL
Minimum Memory: 1024K
Requires: 1-20 users. Hard disk.
Medium: 3 1/2-inch disk
ISPN: 90659-350   **Price: $1295.00**

BREAKTHROUGH PRODUCTIONS

MARKET MASTER MANAGER (VER. II+)

Performs automatic inquiry lead follow-up for an entire sales force and produces management reports.

System: MAC, II, PLUS, SE, XL
Minimum Memory: 1024K
Requires: Unlimited users. Hard disk.
Medium: 3 1/2-inch disk
ISPN: 90659-350   **Price: $1995.00**

BREAKTHROUGH PRODUCTIONS

MARKET MASTER R/A (VER. II+)

Performs automatic inquiry lead follow up where a regular marketing strategy is maintained, and leads arrive continuously.

System: MAC, II, PLUS, SE, XL
Minimum Memory: 1024K
Requires: Hard disk.
Medium: 3 1/2-inch disk
ISPN: 90659-399   **Price: $395.00**

LIONHEART PRESS
SALES AND MARKET FORECASTING

Applies forecasting techniques to business problems.
System: MAC, II, PLUS, SE, XL
Minimum Memory: 512K
Medium: 3 1/2-inch disk
ISPN: 44900-050   **Price: $145.00**

PALO ALTO SOFTWARE
SALES AND MARKET FORECASTING TOOLKIT (VER. 1.0)

Covers forecasting techniques which include customer poll, market share model, product life cycle and linear regression.
System: MAC, II, PLUS, SE, XL
Minimum Memory: 512K
Requires: Microsoft Excel (ISPN 53150-270), Multiplan (ISPN 53150-550), or Appleworks (ISPN 12784-100).
Medium: 3 1/2-inch disk
ISPN: 37443-238   **Price: $69.95**

HEIZER SOFTWARE
SALES AND RECEIVABLES

A model database for tracking sales and accounts receivables.
System: MAC, II, PLUS, SE, XL
Minimum Memory: 512K
Requires: Microsoft Works (ISPN 53150-740).
Medium: 3 1/2-inch disk
ISPN: 35175-043   **Price: $10.00**

HEIZER SOFTWARE
SALES COMMISSION RECORD

Contains a template which can be modified to reflect specific commission schedules.
System: MAC, II, PLUS, SE, XL
Minimum Memory: 512K
Requires: Microsoft Excel (ISPN 53150-270) or Microsoft Works (ISPN 53150-740).
Medium: 3 1/2-inch disk
ISPN: 35175-161   **Price: $6.00**

HEIZER SOFTWARE
SALES PROSPECTING

Tracks sales prospects from the original contact through the final sale, or to the end of a no-sale situation.
System: MAC, II, PLUS, SE, XL
Minimum Memory: 512K
Requires: Microsoft Works (ISPN 53150-740).
Medium: 3 1/2-inch disk
ISPN: 35175-940   **Price: $10.00**

HEIZER SOFTWARE
SALES TRACKING

Sets up an annual forecast by product and area, and provides a method for tracking sales commissions.
System: MAC, II, PLUS, SE, XL
Minimum Memory: 512K
Requires: Microsoft Excel (ISPN 53150-270).
Medium: 3 1/2-inch disk
ISPN: 35175-009   **Price: $30.00**

HEIZER SOFTWARE
SALESMAN ANALYSIS

Computes total sales, amounts, expenses, commissions and average sales.
System: MAC, II, PLUS, SE, XL
Minimum Memory: 512K
Requires: Microsoft Excel (ISPN 53150-270) or Microsoft Works (ISPN 53150-740).
Medium: 3 1/2-inch disk
ISPN: 35175-160   **Price: $8.00**

REMOTE CONTROL, INC.
TELEMAGIC-DUTCH

Organizes and facilitates all aspects of sales and management in the Dutch language. Includes word processor, filer and mailmerge.
System: MAC, II, PLUS, SE, XL
Minimum Memory: 512K
Requires: Modem for autodialer.
Medium: 3 1/2-inch disk
ISPN: 95416-090   **Price: $495.00**

REMOTE CONTROL, INC.
TELEMAGIC-ENGLISH (VER. 10.0)

Organizes and facilitates all aspects of sales and management. Includes a word processor, filer, autodialer, and mailmerge.
System: MAC, II, PLUS, SE, XL
Minimum Memory: 512K
Requires: Modem for autodialer.
Medium: 3 1/2-inch disk
ISPN: 95416-100   **Price: $495.00**

REMOTE CONTROL, INC.
TELEMAGIC-FRENCH

Organizes and facilitates all aspects of sales and management in the French language. Includes word processor, filer and mailmerge.
System: MAC, II, PLUS, SE, XL
Minimum Memory: 512K
Requires: Modem for autodialer.
Medium: 3 1/2-inch disk
ISPN: 95416-150   **Price: $495.00**

REMOTE CONTROL, INC.
TELEMAGIC-PORTUGUESE

Organizes and facilitates all aspects of sales and management in the Portuguese language. Includes a word processor and mailmerge.
System: MAC, II, PLUS, SE, XL
Minimum Memory: 512K
Requires: Modem for autodialer.
Medium: 3 1/2-inch disk
ISPN: 95416-175   **Price: $495.00**

REMOTE CONTROL, INC.
TELEMAGIC-SWEDISH

Organizes and facilitates all aspects of sales and management in the Swedish language. Includes a word processor, filer & mailmerge.
System: MAC, II, PLUS, SE, XL
Minimum Memory: 512K
Requires: Modem for autodialer.
Medium: 3 1/2-inch disk
ISPN: 95416-200   **Price: $495.00**

HEIZER SOFTWARE
UNITED STATES MAP

Prepares a regional sales report, marketing plan or travel itinerary using Microsoft Works.
System: MAC, II, PLUS, SE, XL
Minimum Memory: 512K
Requires: Microsoft Works (ISPN 53150-740).
Medium: 3 1/2-inch disk
ISPN: 35175-457   **Price: $5.00**

HEIZER SOFTWARE
WORKS FOR SMALL BUSINESSES

Model templates for setting up sales and expenses, quotation and estimating forms and a breakeven analysis.
System: MAC, II, PLUS, SE, XL
Minimum Memory: 512K
Requires: Microsoft Works (ISPN 53150-740).
Medium: 3 1/2-inch disk
ISPN: 35175-908   **Price: $50.00**

153 PRODUCTIVITY/ MISCELLANEOUS PRODUCTIVITY

ALDUS CORP.
ALDUS PERSUASION

A complete desktop presentation system which streamlines the entire process from outline to finished overheads, 35mm slides and notes.
System: MAC, II, PLUS, SE, XL
Minimum Memory: 512K
Requires: One 800K disk drive and hard disk.
Medium: 3 1/2-inch disk
ISPN: 02226-800   **Price: $495.00**

HEIZER SOFTWARE
AREA CODE DATABASE

Decodes phone bills by supplying the United States and Canadian area codes.
System: MAC, II, PLUS, SE, XL
Minimum Memory: 512K
Requires: Microsoft Excel (ISPN 53150-270) or Microsoft Works (ISPN 53150-740).
Medium: 3 1/2-inch disk
ISPN: 35175-192   **Price: $8.00**

HEIZER SOFTWARE
AUTO EXPENSE REPORT

Calculates mileage and costs on a monthly basis.
System: MAC, II, PLUS, SE, XL
Minimum Memory: 512K
Requires: Microsoft Excel (ISPN 53150-270) or Microsoft Works (ISPN 53150-740).
Medium: 3 1/2-inch disk
ISPN: 35175-171   **Price: $6.00**

MACPDS

BEST OF MAC PDS (VOL. 1)

Contains a five disk set of Public Domain Software (Over 100 titles) with comprehensive 64-page manual.

System: MAC, II, PLUS, SE, XL
Minimum Memory: 512K
Medium: 3 1/2-inch disk
ISPN: 93905-050   **Price: $39.95**

MACPDS

BEST OF MAC PDS (VOL. 2)

Contains a five disk set of over 150 Public Domain Software titles and a 64-page manual.

System: MAC, II, PLUS, SE, XL
Minimum Memory: 512K
Medium: 3 1/2-inch disk
ISPN: 93905-150   **Price: $39.95**

HEIZER SOFTWARE

BUSINESS TRAVEL PLANNER

Plans and organizes business travel including flights, reservations and meetings.

System: MAC, II, PLUS, SE, XL
Minimum Memory: 512K
Requires: Microsoft Excel (ISPN 53150-270) or Microsoft Works (ISPN 53150-740).
Medium: 3 1/2-inch disk
ISPN: 35175-168   **Price: $6.00**

DUBL-CLICK SOFTWARE, INC.

CALCULATOR CONSTRUCTION SET (VER. 1.04)

Design custom calculators that install as desk accessories on your disks.

System: MAC, II, PLUS, SE, XL
Minimum Memory: 128K
Requires: 800K disk drive.
Medium: 3 1/2-inch disk
ISPN: 26806-100   **Price: $59.95**

MAINSTAY

CLICKPASTE (VER. 1.0)

Stores and retrieves frequently used text, graphics and other items.

System: MAC, II, PLUS, SE, XL
Minimum Memory: 512K
Medium: 3 1/2-inch disk
ISPN: 46041-105   **Price: $99.95**

SOFTWORKS, INC. (CT)

CLIENT (VER. 1.1)

A HyperCard stack that maintains clients, business interests, financial and contact history. Includes HyperCard 1.2.

System: MAC, II, PLUS, SE, XL
Minimum Memory: 1024K
Medium: 3 1/2-inch disk
ISPN: 74165-100   **Price: $195.00**

GENERATION FOUR

COMMCENTER (VER. 1.1)

Provides a customizable telephone directory with E-Mail, a message center, contact log, and mail merge.

System: MAC, II, PLUS, SE, XL
Minimum Memory: 1024K
Requires: Hard disk.
Medium: 3 1/2-inch disk
ISPN: 92117-100   **Price: $249.00**

HEIZER SOFTWARE

COUNT-BY-STATE MACROS

Counts and tabulates the database by occurrences of state abbreviations or state names.

System: MAC, II, PLUS, SE, XL
Minimum Memory: 512K
Requires: Microsoft Excel (ISPN 53150-270).
Medium: 3 1/2-inch disk
ISPN: 35175-191   **Price: $6.00**

KANODE ASSOCIATES

ELECTRONIC CALL SCREENING

A HyperCard stack with digitized phrases that can be used to screen calls which sounds like an executive secretary.

System: MAC, II, PLUS, SE, XL
Minimum Memory: 1024K
Requires: HyperCard (ISPN 03900-300), Hyperdialer.
Medium: 3 1/2-inch disk
ISPN: 42331-200   **Price: $49.95**

KINKOS ACADEMIC COURSEWARE EXCHANGE

GLOSSARY MAKER (VER. 1.0)

A HyperCard stack that allows the user to create a glossary to be used with any other stack.

System: MAC, II, PLUS, SE, XL
Minimum Memory: 1024K
Requires: HyperCard (ISPN 03900-300).
Medium: 3 1/2-inch disk
ISPN: 43025-215   **Price: $14.00**

CERES SOFTWARE, INC.

INSPIRATION (VER. 2.0)

Helps you capture, organize and communicate ideas and information in diagrams, outlines, complete documents, reports or articles.

System: MAC, II, PLUS, SE, XL
Minimum Memory: 512K
Requires: 800K disk drive.
Medium: 3 1/2-inch disk
ISPN: 12053-300   **Price: $195.00**

LIONHEART PRESS

INVENTORIES AND QUEUES

Contains standard procedures for the study of inventories with deterministic and probabilistic demand.

System: MAC, II, PLUS, SE, XL
Minimum Memory: 512K
Medium: 3 1/2-inch disk
ISPN: 44900-243   **Price: $95.00**

JAPANESE LANGUAGE SERVICES

JAPANESE ATTACHMENT TO MACINTOSH (JAM) (VER. 3.5)

Allows input of Japanese text into almost any application program.

System: MAC, II, PLUS, SE, XL
Minimum Memory: 1024K
Requires: ImageWriter or LaserWriter.
Medium: 3 1/2-inch disk
ISPN: 20012-325   **Price: $249.00**

CAUZIN SYSTEMS, INC.

LASER ARCHIVIST

Enables LaserJet and LaserWriter customers to print electronically readable data strips on standard bond paper.

System: MAC, II, PLUS, SE, XL
Minimum Memory: 512K
Requires: Apple LaserWriter with System 3.2 and Finder 5.3 or later.
Medium: 3 1/2-inch disk
ISPN: 11571-400   **Price: $79.95**

SPINNAKER SOFTWARE

M.U.D. (MACROMIND UTILITY DISK)

A utility disk designed to enhance and speed your creativity with almost any Macintosh application.

System: MAC, II, PLUS, SE, XL
Minimum Memory: 512K
Medium: 3 1/2-inch disk
ISPN: 75300-174   **Price: $49.95**

SOFTWARE FOR RECOGNITION TECHNOLOGIES

MAC SIGMA QN/EQUATION PROCESSOR (VER. 2.1.3)

A desk accessory equation processor that allows inclusion of complicated mathematical equations into technical documents.

System: MAC, II, PLUS, SE, XL
Minimum Memory: 512K
Medium: 3 1/2-inch disk
ISPN: 72943-100   **Price: $44.95**

IDEAFORM, INC.

MACLABELER (VER. 2.2)

Reads document, application and folder names and automatically prints them on wrap-around labels.

System: MAC, PLUS, SE, XL
Minimum Memory: 128K
Requires: ImageWriter printer.
Medium: 3 1/2-inch disk
ISPN: 37059-500   **Price: $49.95**

PARAGON CONCEPTS, INC.

MACQWERTY FOR MACINTOSH

Enables normal keyboard to become Dvorak keyboard. Also user can change location of any character on keyboard.

System: MAC, II, PLUS, SE, XL
Minimum Memory: 512K
Medium: 3 1/2-inch disk
ISPN: 59740-450   **Price: $45.00**

COMGRAFIX

MAPGRAFIX

An intelligent mapping and decision-making system for land use, demographic analysis, impact analysis, zoning enforcement and more.

System: MAC, II, PLUS, SE, XL
Minimum Memory: 1024K
Requires: Digitizer, plotter/printer, hard disk and relational database program.
Medium: 3 1/2-inch disk
ISPN: 13843-500   **Price: $8500.00**

HEIZER SOFTWARE

MONTHLY TRAVEL EXPENSE

Keeps track of monthly travel expenses.

System: MAC, II, PLUS, SE, XL
Minimum Memory: 512K
Requires: Microsoft Excel (ISPN 53150-270) or Microsoft Works (ISPN 53150-740).
Medium: 3 1/2-inch disk
ISPN: 35175-170   **Price: $6.00**

SYMANTEC

MORE II

Provides outline processing and a presentation system to organize and develop ideas, lists, projects and desktop presentations.

System: MAC, II, PLUS, SE, XL
Minimum Memory: 1024K
Medium: 3 1/2-inch disk
ISPN: 77413-400   **Price: $395.00**

WILLIAMS AND MACIAS

MYDISKLABELER (VER. 2.5) (BLACK/WHITE AND COLOR)

Produces black and white or color labels for 3.5-inch disks.

System: MAC, II, PLUS, SE, XL
Minimum Memory: 128K
Requires: ImageWriter I or ImageWriter II with color ribbon.
Medium: 3 1/2-inch disk
ISPN: 86506-476   **Price: $54.95**

WILLIAMS AND MACIAS

MYDISKLABLER (VER. 2.5) (LASER OPTION)

Prints 3.5-inch disk labels on LaserWriter or LaserWriter Plus and prints in black and white or color on ImageWriters.

System: MAC, II, PLUS, SE, XL
Minimum Memory: 128K
Requires: LaserWriter or LaserWriter Plus printer.
Medium: 3 1/2-inch disk
ISPN: 86506-477   **Price: $64.95**

HEIZER SOFTWARE

PHONE NAME NUMBERS

Converts seven-character combinations of letters and digits to the equivalent seven-digit phone number.

System: MAC, PLUS, SE, XL
Minimum Memory: 512K
Requires: Microsoft Excel (ISPN 53150-270).
Medium: 3 1/2-inch disk
ISPN: 35175-193   **Price: $3.00**

HEIZER SOFTWARE

PHONE NUMBER NAMES

Calculates the 'words' which can be made with the letter combinations of any seven-digit phone number.

System: MAC, II, PLUS, SE, XL
Minimum Memory: 1024K
Requires: Microsoft Excel (ISPN 53150-270).
Medium: 3 1/2-inch disk
ISPN: 35175-194   **Price: $9.00**

S & J ENTERPRISES

PREVENTIVE MAINTENANCE (VER. 2.1)

Tracks preventive maintenance work due and finished as well as parts inventory.

System: MAC, II, PLUS, SE, XL
Minimum Memory: 1024K
Medium: 3 1/2-inch disk
ISPN: 67356-600   **Price: $1250.00**

STATSOFT, INC.

Q-FAST

Computerizes questionnaires, surveys and interviews.

System: MAC, PLUS, SE, XL
Minimum Memory: 512K
Medium: 3 1/2-inch disk
ISPN: 75992-600   **Price: $299.00**

HIGH PERFORMANCE SYSTEMS

STELLA FOR BUSINESS (VER. 2.0)

Software for modeling and simulating business issues ranging from operations analysis, to human resources, to strategic planning.

System: MAC, II, PLUS, SE, XL
Minimum Memory: 512K
Requires: 800K disk drive.
Medium: 3 1/2-inch disk
ISPN: 35638-800   **Price: $350.00**

HIGH PERFORMANCE SYSTEMS

STELLA FOR BUSINESS (VER. 2.0)

Software for modeling and simulating business issues ranging from operations analysis, to human resources, to strategic planning.

System: II
Minimum Memory: 512K
Requires: 800K disk drive.
Medium: 3 1/2-inch disk
ISPN: 35638-800   **Price: $425.00**

MAINSTAY

THINK 'N TIME

Visual organization tool for developing and organizing ideas, projects, tasks, meetings, schedules, estimates and reports.

System: MAC, II, PLUS, SE, XL
Minimum Memory: 1024K
Medium: 3 1/2-inch disk
ISPN: 46041-720   **Price: $99.95**

SYMANTEC

THINKTANK (VER. 2.0)

Provides outline processing, integrated word processing and graphics capabilities for planning, strategizing and writing.

System: MAC, II, PLUS, SE, XL
Minimum Memory: 512K
Medium: 3 1/2-inch disk
ISPN: 77413-100   **Price: $195.00**

KINKOS ACADEMIC COURSEWARE EXCHANGE

TIPS DESK ACCESSORY (VER. 1.0)

A desk accessory used for storing and displaying tips or other information while running an application.

System: MAC, II, PLUS, SE, XL
Minimum Memory: 512K
Medium: 3 1/2-inch disk
ISPN: 43025-890   **Price: $21.50**

APPLIED SYSTEMS & TECHNOLOGIES, INC.

TRAID-NAMES (VER. 1.0)

Assists you in the development of new product, new business or new service names.

System: MAC, II, PLUS, SE, XL
Minimum Memory: 512K
Medium: 3 1/2-inch disk
ISPN: 04768-500   **Price: $159.00**

GALLIE COMPUTERS

UNITS! UNITS! UNITS!

Involves printable tables relating over 500 units of measure to each other en masse, for engineering and business.

System: MAC, II, PLUS, SE, XL
Minimum Memory: 128K
Medium: 3 1/2-inch disk
ISPN: 32200-100   **Price: $35.00**

S & J ENTERPRISES

WATER-SEWER-TRASH MANAGEMENT (VER. 3.2)

Computes and prints water, sewer, and garbage bills maintaining a list of customers and monitors accounts receivable and water usage.

System: MAC, II, PLUS, SE, XL
Minimum Memory: 512K
Medium: 3 1/2-inch disk
ISPN: 67356-800   **Price: $500.00**

HEIZER SOFTWARE

WEEKLY TRAVEL EXPENSE

Creates weekly expense reports.

System: MAC, II, PLUS, SE, XL
Minimum Memory: 512K
Requires: Microsoft Excel (ISPN 53150-270) or Microsoft Works (ISPN 53150-740).
Medium: 3 1/2-inch disk
ISPN: 35175-169   **Price: $6.00**

FIRST ROW SOFTWARE PUBLISHING

ZAP..THE CODEFINDER

A memory resident zip code directory.

System: MAC, II, PLUS, SE, XL
Minimum Memory: 512K
Medium: 3 1/2-inch disk
ISPN: 91839-900   **Price: $24.95**

HEIZER SOFTWARE

ZIP CODE

Assigns state names and abbreviations based on ZIP code.

System: MAC, II, PLUS, SE, XL
Minimum Memory: 512K
Requires: Microsoft Excel (ISPN 53150-270) or HyperCard (ISPN 03900-300).
Medium: 3 1/2-inch disk
ISPN: 35175-190   **Price: $8.00**

157 PRODUCTIVITY/ PAYROLL

AATRIX SOFTWARE

AATRIX PAYROLL PLUS (VER. 3.02)

Keeps access of employee data, write checks, and provides a check ledger, special contractors files and expanded functions.

System: MAC, II, PLUS, SE, XL
Minimum Memory: 512K
Medium: 3 1/2-inch disk
ISPN: 00281-610   **Price: $295.00**

LAKE AVE. SOFTWARE

ASSISTANT CONTROLLER SERIES-PAYROLL

Handles payroll calculations, prints payroll checks and/or stubs and generates the necessary information for federal and state tax.

System: MAC, II, PLUS, SE, XL
Minimum Memory: 512K
Medium: 3 1/2-inch disk
ISPN: 43418-124   **Price: $495.00**

BAKER GRAPHICS

BAKERFORMS FOR PAYROLL

Allows user to keep accurate records and process pin-feed payroll checks.

System: MAC, II, PLUS, SE, XL
Minimum Memory: 512K
Requires: Microsoft Works (ISPN 53150-740) and Imagewriter printer.
Medium: 3 1/2-inch disk
ISPN: 06712-205   **Price: $49.95**

CHECKMARK SOFTWARE, INC.

CHECKMARK PAYROLL (VER. 3.1)

Performs payroll tax calculations, generates and prints paychecks, earnings, check registers, and W-2's.

System: MAC, II, PLUS, SE, XL
Minimum Memory: 512K
Medium: 3 1/2-inch disk
ISPN: 04612-525   **Price: $295.00**

FLEXWARE, INC.

FLEXWARE PAYROLL

Automatic payroll processing functions, with manual over-rides to handle very unusual situations.

System: MAC, II, PLUS, SE, XL
Minimum Memory: 512K
Requires: 20MB hard disk.
Medium: 3 1/2-inch disk
ISPN: 52468-350   **Price: $795.00**

GREAT PLAINS SOFTWARE

GREAT PLAINS ACCOUNTING SERIES-PAYROLL 4.1

Allows a breakdown of payroll expenses by department, with customer defined departments and job descriptions.

System: MAC, II, PLUS, SE, XL
Minimum Memory: 512K
Requires: 20 MB hard disk, 800K disk drive, 132-column printer or 80-column printer with condensed print.
Medium: 3 1/2-inch disk
ISPN: 33475-830   **Price: $795.00**

LAKE AVE. SOFTWARE

MULTI COMPANY-PAYROLL

Handles payroll calculations, print payroll checks and/or stubs and generate the necessary information for Federal and State Tax.

System: MAC, II, PLUS, SE, XL
Minimum Memory: 512K
Medium: 3 1/2-inch disk
ISPN: 43418-806   **Price: $695.00**

JANAC ENTERPRISES

OMNIPAY TEMPLATE FOR OMNIS 3+

A flexible payroll system which handles hourly salary and piecework wages.

System: MAC, II, PLUS, SE, XL
Minimum Memory: 512K
Requires: Omnis 3 Plus/Express (ISPN 58775-515) or Runtime, 800K disk drive.
Medium: 3 1/2-inch disk
ISPN: 41438-033   **Price: $79.95**

CHAMPION BUSINESS SYSTEMS

PAYROLL

Produces payroll for all fifty states.

System: MAC, II, PLUS, SE, XL
Minimum Memory: 1024K
Requires: 800K hard disk.
Medium: 3 1/2-inch disk
ISPN: 12175-650   **Price: $395.00**

AATRIX SOFTWARE

PAYROLL (VER. 3.01)

Retains employee data and allows users to write checks at any time. Includes all of the state and federal tax tables.

System: MAC, II, PLUS, SE, XL
Minimum Memory: 512K
Medium: 3 1/2-inch disk
ISPN: 00281-600   **Price: $179.00**

SOFTWARE BRIDGE, INC.

PAYROLL BRIDGE II (VER. 5.0)

Multi-user payroll/personnel management system. Calculates gross pay, federal, state and local tax withholding.

System: MAC, II, PLUS, SE, XL
Minimum Memory: 1024K
Requires: Hard disk.
Medium: 3 1/2-inch disk
ISPN: 72468-601   **Price: $595.00**

SOFTWARE BRIDGE, INC.

PAYROLL BRIDGE II (VER. 5.0)

Multi-user payroll/personnel management system. Calculates gross pay, federal, state and local tax withholding.

System: MAC, II, PLUS, SE, XL
Minimum Memory: 1024K
Requires: Multiuser. Hard disk.
Medium: 3 1/2-inch disk
ISPN: 72468-601   **Price: $795.00**

HEIZER SOFTWARE

PAYROLL PARTNER

Calculates all federal and FICA taxes, provides full summary and detail data for each period and employee and prints paychecks.

System: MAC, II, PLUS, SE, XL
Minimum Memory: 1024K
Requires: Microsoft Excel (ISPN 53150-270).
Medium: 3 1/2-inch disk
ISPN: 35175-610   **Price: $99.00**

HEIZER SOFTWARE

PAYROLL TEMPLATES BI-WEEKLY

Handles bi-weekly state and federal payroll for up to twenty employees.

System: MAC, II, PLUS, SE, XL
Minimum Memory: 512K
Requires: Microsoft Works (ISPN 53150-740).
Medium: 3 1/2-inch disk
ISPN: 35175-806   **Price: $75.00**

HEIZER SOFTWARE

PAYROLL TEMPLATES SEMI-MONTHLY

Handles semi-monthly state and federal payroll for up to twenty-five employees.

System: MAC, II, PLUS, SE, XL
Minimum Memory: 512K
Requires: Microsoft Works (ISPN 53150-740).
Medium: 3 1/2-inch disk
ISPN: 35175-807   **Price: $75.00**

HEIZER SOFTWARE
PAYROLL TEMPLATES-MONTHLY

Handles monthly state and federal payroll for up to thirty-five employees.

System: MAC, II, PLUS, SE, XL
Minimum Memory: 512K
Requires: Microsoft Works (ISPN 53150-740).
Medium: 3 1/2-inch disk
ISPN: 35175-808　　　　　**Price: $75.00**

HEIZER SOFTWARE
PAYROLL TEMPLATES-WEEKLY

Handles weekly state and federal payroll for sixteen employees.

System: MAC, II, PLUS, SE, XL
Minimum Memory: 512K
Requires: Microsoft Works (ISPN 53150-740).
Medium: 3 1/2-inch disk
ISPN: 35175-805　　　　　**Price: $75.00**

SOFTWARE BRIDGE, INC.
PAYROLL-BRIDGE PLUS (VER. 4.0)

Comprehensive payroll and personnel system for businesses having any number of employees.

System: MAC, II, PLUS, SE, XL
Minimum Memory: 512K
Requires: Two 800K disk drives or a hard disk.
Medium: 3 1/2-inch disk
ISPN: 72468-600　　　　　**Price: $295.00**

SEXTANT CORP.
RMS PLUS PAYROLL (VER. 1.3)

Permits unlimited earnings and deductions, recurring time cards for salaried employees, tip allocation, minimum wage adjustments.

System: MAC, II, PLUS, SE, XL
Minimum Memory: 1024K
Medium: 3 1/2-inch disk
ISPN: 42575-601　　　　　**Price: $395.00**

SBT CORP.
SBT DPAYROLL-COMPILED (VER. 6.15)

A compiled version which performs the entry, calculation, and maintenance functions of payroll and labor distribution.

System: MAC, II, PLUS, SE, XL
Minimum Memory: 512K
Medium: 3 1/2-inch disk
ISPN: 68057-326　　　　　**Price: $295.00**

SBT CORP.
SBT DPAYROLL-STANDARD (VER. 6.15)

Performs the entry, calculation, and maintenance of payroll and labor distribution including tax calculations and deductions.

System: MAC, II, PLUS, SE, XL
Minimum Memory: 512K
Medium: 3 1/2-inch disk
ISPN: 68057-325　　　　　**Price: $395.00**

WESTERN SOFTWARE ASSOCIATES
TIME-SAVER PAYROLL SYSTEM (VER. 5.0)

A Microsoft Excel template that provides a full featured payroll system that prints checks, W-2 forms and quarterly reports.

System: MAC, II, PLUS, SE, XL
Minimum Memory: 512K
Requires: Microsoft Excel (ISPN 53150-270).
Medium: 3 1/2-inch disk
ISPN: 86131-100　　　　　**Price: $99.50**

HEIZER SOFTWARE
TIMEKEEPER

A time card template which handles regular time entries, lunch time and calculates regular, overtime and double time hours.

System: MAC, II, PLUS, SE, XL
Minimum Memory: 512K
Requires: Microsoft Excel (ISPN 53150-270).
Medium: 3 1/2-inch disk
ISPN: 35175-602　　　　　**Price: $50.00**

---

160 PRODUCTIVITY/ PROJECT MANAGEMENT

AEC MANAGEMENT SYSTEMS, INC.
AEC INFORMATION MANAGER (VER. 1.21)

Designed for the management and tracking of projects, activities, documents, scheduled processes and people.

System: MAC, II, PLUS, SE, XL
Minimum Memory: 512K
Medium: 3 1/2-inch disk
ISPN: 01716-100　　　　　**Price: $695.00**

LAKE AVE. SOFTWARE
ASSISTANT CONTROLLER SERIES-JOB COSTING

Enables users to monitor labor, material and sub-contractor costs against budget by project/job number.

System: MAC, II, PLUS, SE, XL
Minimum Memory: 512K
Medium: 3 1/2-inch disk
ISPN: 43418-372　　　　　**Price: $495.00**

HEIZER SOFTWARE
BID ANALYZER

Provides a model for analyzing bids and quotations.

System: MAC, II, PLUS, SE, XL
Minimum Memory: 512K
Requires: Microsoft Works (ISPN 53150-740).
Medium: 3 1/2-inch disk
ISPN: 35175-455　　　　　**Price: $8.00**

SOFTOUCH SOFTWARE, INC.
COST MANAGEMENT SYSTEM II

Offers cost estimating, job costing, cost variance reporting, export with management reporting and change order management.

System: MAC, II, PLUS, SE, XL
Minimum Memory: 1024K
Medium: 3 1/2-inch disk
ISPN: 72162-160　　　　　**Price: $495.00**

HEIZER SOFTWARE
COST-ESTIMATING FORM

Estimates job costs, based on unit costs and hours.

System: MAC, II, PLUS, SE, XL
Minimum Memory: 512K
Requires: Microsoft Works (ISPN 53150-740) or Microsoft Excel (ISPN 53150-270).
Medium: 3 1/2-inch disk
ISPN: 35175-458　　　　　**Price: $10.00**

HEIZER SOFTWARE
COSTED BILL OF MATERIALS

Calculates the total costs of bill of materials from labor and cost data in a master table.

System: MAC, II, PLUS, SE, XL
Minimum Memory: 512K
Requires: Microsoft Excel (ISPN 53150-270) or Microsoft Works (ISPN 53150-740).
Medium: 3 1/2-inch disk
ISPN: 35175-555　　　　　**Price: $30.00**

SOFTOUCH SOFTWARE, INC.
CUSTOMER PROFILE SYSTEM (CPS)

Provides executive management the capability to review key aspects of their customer database and to monitor critical aspects.

System: MAC, II, PLUS, SE, XL
Minimum Memory: 1024K
Requires: Oracle host based database, Oracle for the Macintosh, (ISPN 58667-555) HyperCard (ISPN 03900-300).
Medium: 3 1/2-inch disk
ISPN: 72162-200
Price: Please contact the software publisher.

HEIZER SOFTWARE
DECISION ASSISTANT

Assists decision-making by ranking the relative importance of up to 14 criteria including tasks, objectives, or alternatives.

System: MAC, II, PLUS, SE, XL
Minimum Memory: 1024K
Requires: HyperCard (ISPN 03900-300).
Medium: 3 1/2-inch disk
ISPN: 35175-428　　　　　**Price: $25.00**

SOFTSTYLE, INC.
DECISIONMAP

A modeling tool to help you make the best decision and back it up.

System: MAC, II, PLUS, SE, XL
Minimum Memory: 512K
Medium: 3 1/2-inch disk
ISPN: 72235-020　　　　　**Price: $145.00**

BRODERBUND SOFTWARE, INC.

DTP ADVISOR

A HyperCard-based tutorial on design and graphic arts issues and a project management tool with a database calendar and forms.

System: MAC, II, PLUS, SE, XL
Minimum Memory: 1024K
Medium: 3 1/2-inch disk
ISPN: 08850-200 **Price: $79.95**

GREAT PLAINS SOFTWARE

EXECUTIVE ADVISOR

Generates business ratios and analyses in graph, chart and table formats drawing from information in Great Plains Accounting Series.

System: MAC, II, PLUS, SE, XL
Minimum Memory: 1024K
Requires: Great Plains Accounting Series module 4.2 or later, 20 MB hard disk, 132-column printer or 80-column with condensed print.
Medium: 3 1/2-inch disk
ISPN: 33475-300 **Price: $595.00**

SOFTOUCH SOFTWARE, INC.

EXECUTIVE INFORMATION SYSTEMS EXPLORER

Allows executives to review, evaluate and use EISE business applications systems and key computing technologies.

System: MAC, II, PLUS, SE, XL
Minimum Memory: 1024K
Requires: HyperCard (ISPN 03900-300).
Medium: 3 1/2-inch disk
ISPN: 72162-250 **Price: $195.00**

DECISION SCIENCE SOFTWARE

EXPERT

Enables the analyst to solve problems using PERT expression and solution. Defines a network of up to 250 activities.

System: MAC, II, PLUS, SE, XL
Minimum Memory: 512K
Requires: Printer.
Medium: 3 1/2-inch disk
ISPN: 24325-150 **Price: $125.00**

AEC MANAGEMENT SYSTEMS, INC.

FASTTRACK SCHEDULE

Draws Gantt schedules for presentations.

System: MAC, II, PLUS, SE, XL
Minimum Memory: 1024K
Medium: 3 1/2-inch disk
ISPN: 01716-200 **Price: $195.00**

FLEXWARE, INC.

FLEXWARE JOB COSTING

Automatically records costs and revenues through general ledger to provide instant access to variance analysis.

System: MAC
Minimum Memory: 256K
Medium: 3 1/2-inch disk
ISPN: 52468-250 **Price: $795.00**

LINDO SYSTEMS

LINDO/PC

Interactive program for solving linear, integer and quadratic programming problems.

System: MAC, II, PLUS, SE, XL
Minimum Memory: 1024K
Medium: 3 1/2-inch disk
ISPN: 44737-200 **Price: $90.00**

OITC, INC.

MACOMO (VER. 2.0)

Provides a management tool to predict software costs and scheduling.

System: MAC, II, PLUS, SE, XL
Minimum Memory: 512K
Requires: 800K disk drive.
Medium: 3 1/2-inch disk
ISPN: 94527-220 **Price: $185.00**

CLARIS CORP.

MACPROJECT II

Provides project management tools to help plan, control, and present projects of any size.

System: MAC, II, PLUS, SE, XL
Minimum Memory: 512K
Medium: 3 1/2-inch disk
ISPN: 12784-520 **Price: $495.00**

MICROSERVE, INC.

MACPROSPECT (VER. 2.0)

Provides a professional sales and prospecting management system with a client and prospect database.

System: MAC, II, PLUS, SE, XL
Minimum Memory: 512K
Requires: Omnis 3 Plus/Express (ISPN 58775-515), two disk drives or a hard disk and a printer.
Medium: 3 1/2-inch disk
ISPN: 53112-500 **Price: $395.00**

MAINSTAY

MACSCHEDULE

Creates and revises bar schedule charts. (Gantt)

System: MAC, II, PLUS, SE, XL
Minimum Memory: 1024K
Medium: 3 1/2-inch disk
ISPN: 46041-560 **Price: $195.00**

LEGALWARE, INC.

MATTER ORGANIZER (VER. 1.7)

Designed to assist business professionals in organizing projects such as business incorporation and hiring personnel.

System: MAC, II, PLUS, SE, XL
Minimum Memory: 512K
Medium: 3 1/2-inch disk
ISPN: 44063-600 **Price: $599.00**

MICRO PLANNING INT'L.

MICRO PLANNER PLUS (VER. 6.0)

Contains critical path (PERT) and powerful resource management capability to help managers finish projects on time and on budget.

System: MAC, II, PLUS, SE, XL
Minimum Memory: 512K
Requires: Two disk drives or hard disk, printer.
Medium: 3 1/2-inch disk
ISPN: 50912-550 **Price: $595.00**

HEIZER SOFTWARE

MINI EXPERT SYSTEM

An evaluation program based on information entered by the user to predict the most probable alternative.

System: MAC, II, PLUS, SE, XL
Minimum Memory: 512K
Requires: Microsoft Excel (ISPN 53150-270).
Medium: 3 1/2-inch disk
ISPN: 35175-163 **Price: $35.00**

LAKE AVE. SOFTWARE

MULTI COMPANY-JOB COSTING

Enables you to monitor labor material and sub-contractor costs against budget by project/job number.

System: MAC, II, PLUS, SE, XL
Minimum Memory: 512K
Medium: 3 1/2-inch disk
ISPN: 43418-744 **Price: $695.00**

LIONHEART PRESS

OPTIMIZATION

Addresses the wide variety of problems in business and technology, usually non-linear, which require optimization.

System: MAC, II, PLUS, SE, XL
Minimum Memory: 512K
Medium: 3 1/2-inch disk
ISPN: 44900-600 **Price: $145.00**

HEIZER SOFTWARE

ORGANIZATION CHART MAKER

Creates a vertical, outline format organization chart.

System: MAC, II, PLUS, SE, XL
Minimum Memory: 512K
Requires: Microsoft Excel (ISPN 53150-270).
Medium: 3 1/2-inch disk
ISPN: 35175-172 **Price: $8.00**

HEIZER SOFTWARE

PROJECT COST TRACKING

Tracks and summarizes the labor and materials costs for a project.

System: MAC, II, PLUS, SE, XL
Minimum Memory: 512K
Requires: Microsoft Excel (ISPN 53150-270) or Microsoft Works (ISPN 53150-740).
Medium: 3 1/2-inch disk
ISPN: 35175-558 **Price: $30.00**

LIONHEART PRESS
PROJECT PLANNER (PERT & CPM)

Handles the specific problems of job shop scheduling and optimum assignments.

System: MAC, II, PLUS, SE, XL
Minimum Memory: 512K
Medium: 3 1/2-inch disk
ISPN: 44900-700   **Price: $145.00**

HEIZER SOFTWARE
PURCHASES AND PAYABLES

Tracks orders, cash disbursements, payables and individual cost areas utilizing Microsoft Works' database.

System: MAC, II, PLUS, SE, XL
Minimum Memory: 512K
Requires: Microsoft Works (ISPN 53150-740)
Medium: 3 1/2-inch disk
ISPN: 35175-044   **Price: $10.00**

SBT CORP.
SBT DMATERIALS-COMPILED (VER. 6.10)

Bill of materials manufacturing planning maintenance and explosion to gross requirements based on orders entered for assemblies.

System: MAC, II, PLUS, SE, XL
Minimum Memory: 512K
Medium: 3 1/2-inch disk
ISPN: 68057-251   **Price: $295.00**

SBT CORP.
SBT DMATERIALS-STANDARD (VER. 6.10)

Bill of materials manufacturing planning maintenance and explosion to gross requirements based on orders entered for assemblies.

System: MAC, II, PLUS, SE, XL
Minimum Memory: 512K
Medium: 3 1/2-inch disk
ISPN: 68057-250   **Price: $395.00**

SBT CORP.
SBT DPROJECT-COMPILED (VER. 6.20)

Provides a fast and flexible budgeting and cost accounting tool for project and job cost management.

System: MAC, II, PLUS, SE, XL
Minimum Memory: 512K
Requires: 20MB hard disk.
Medium: 3 1/2-inch disk
ISPN: 68057-351   **Price: $295.00**

SBT CORP.
SBT DPROJECT-STANDARD (VER. 6.20)

Provides a fast and flexible budgeting and cost accounting tool for project and job cost management.

System: MAC, II, PLUS, SE, XL
Minimum Memory: 512K
Medium: 3 1/2-inch disk
ISPN: 68057-350   **Price: $395.00**

DECISION SCIENCE SOFTWARE
SHORTEST PATH

Solves problems using the shortest path solution to a network of directed arcs with known lengths.

System: MAC, II, PLUS, SE, XL
Minimum Memory: 512K
Medium: 3 1/2-inch disk
ISPN: 24325-900   **Price: $50.00**

SOFTOUCH SOFTWARE, INC.
SYSTEMS PLANNING NAVIGATOR

Helps management and staff understand, develop and produce a strategic systems plan, a plan for selecting the best systems.

System: MAC, II, PLUS, SE, XL
Minimum Memory: 1024K
Requires: HyperCard (ISPN 03900-300).
Medium: 3 1/2-inch disk
ISPN: 72162-700   **Price: $195.00**

HEIZER SOFTWARE
TRACKER

A project tracking system which indicates the completion status of each component within a project.

System: MAC, II, PLUS, SE, XL
Minimum Memory: 1024K
Requires: HyperCard (ISPN 03900-300).
Medium: 3 1/2-inch disk
ISPN: 35175-431   **Price: $25.00**

DECISION SCIENCE SOFTWARE
TRANSPORTATION

Enables the analyst to solve problems of expression and solution using the transportation approach.

System: MAC, II, PLUS, SE, XL
Minimum Memory:
Medium: 3 1/2-inch disk
ISPN: 24325-950   **Price: $65.00**

SOFTSTREAM INT'L., INC.
ULTRASPEC

Manages the publication process and determines size and space needed, time tables, budgets, and staffing required for projects.

System: MAC, II, PLUS, SE, XL
Minimum Memory: 1024K
Requires: HyperCard (ISPN 03900-300).
Medium: 3 1/2-inch disk
ISPN: 72232-600   **Price: $149.95**

162 PRODUCTIVITY/ PURCHASING/ INVENTORY

LAKE AVE. SOFTWARE
ASSISTANT CONTROLLER SERIES-INVENTORY MODULE

Features automatic or override calculation of economic order quantities, reorder points and standard costs and more.

System: MAC, II, PLUS, SE, XL
Minimum Memory: 512K
Medium: 3 1/2-inch disk
ISPN: 43418-315   **Price: $495.00**

LAKE AVE. SOFTWARE
ASSISTANT CONTROLLER SERIES-PURCHASE ORDER

Prints and tracks purchase orders from requisition to receipt of merchandise.

System: MAC, II, PLUS, SE, XL
Minimum Memory: 512K
Medium: 3 1/2-inch disk
ISPN: 43418-376   **Price: $495.00**

BAKER GRAPHICS
BAKERFORMS FOR PURCHASING

Allows the user to keep accurate records and process pin-feed purchase orders.

System: MAC, II, PLUS, SE, XL
Minimum Memory: 512K
Requires: Microsoft Works (ISPN 53150-740) and ImageWriter printer.
Medium: 3 1/2-inch disk
ISPN: 06712 210   **Price: $49.95**

FLEXWARE, INC.
FLEXWARE INVENTORY CONTROL

Optimizes inventory with automatic restocking, cross reference of parts and reorder/backorder processing.

System: MAC
Minimum Memory: 256K
Medium: 3 1/2-inch disk
ISPN: 52468-200   **Price: $795.00**

FLEXWARE, INC.
FLEXWARE PURCHASING

Automatic reorder point and quantity calculations, with automatic features and manual controls.

System: MAC
Minimum Memory: 256K
Medium: 3 1/2-inch disk
ISPN: 52468-400   **Price: $795.00**

GREAT PLAINS SOFTWARE
GREAT PLAINS ACCOUNTING SERIES-INVENTORY 4.2

Accommodates 6000 inventory items efficiently, allowing for part numbers up to 15 characters.

System: MAC, II, PLUS, SE, XL
Minimum Memory: 1024K
Requires: 20 MB hard disk, 800K disk drive, 132-column printer or 80-column printer with condensed print.
Medium: 3 1/2-inch disk
ISPN: 33475-820   **Price: $795.00**

GREAT PLAINS SOFTWARE
GREAT PLAINS ACCOUNTING SERIES-PURCHASE ORDER 4.2

Handles four types of purchase orders which include regular, recurring or 'standing' orders, drop-ship, and blanket.

System: MAC, II, PLUS, SE, XL
Minimum Memory: 1024K
Requires: 20 MB hard disk, 800K disk drive, 132-column printer or 80-column printer with condensed print.
Medium: 3 1/2-inch disk
ISPN: 33475-875   **Price: $795.00**

LAYERED, INC.
INSIGHT EXPERT INVENTORY (VER. 1.0)

Manages inventory control with movement tracking, flexible valuation methods, reorder capabilities and physical count control.

System: MAC, II, PLUS, SE, XL
Minimum Memory: 1024K
Requires: Two 800K disk drives or a disk drive and a hard disk.
Medium: 3 1/2-inch disk
ISPN: 43760-655   **Price: $695.00**

JAMES RIVER GROUP, INC.
INVENTORY

Allows up to 4,000 parts (10,000 optional). Features indexed files and search routines allowing very fast searches.

System: MAC, II, PLUS, SE, XL
Minimum Memory: 512K
Medium: 3 1/2-inch disk
ISPN: 41412-500   **Price: $125.00**

CHAMPION BUSINESS SYSTEMS
INVENTORY

Maintains inventory master list, inventory history, planning report, adjustments journal and reorder report.

System: MAC, II, PLUS, SE, XL
Minimum Memory: 1024K
Requires: 800K hard disk.
Medium: 3 1/2-inch disk
ISPN: 12175-500   **Price: $395.00**

BLACK BANANA, INC.
INVENTORY CONTROL

An inventory database with audit trails, worksheets, reports and array windows.

System: MAC, II, PLUS, SE, XL
Minimum Memory: 512K
Requires: Two 800K disk drives or hard disk drive.
Medium: 3 1/2-inch disk
ISPN: 07838-300   **Price: $250.00**

HEIZER SOFTWARE
INVENTORY TRACKER

Provides fields for initial quantity, quantities added, used and currently on-hand, latest price paid and source of supply.

System: MAC, II, PLUS, SE, XL
Minimum Memory: 512K
Requires: Microsoft Excel (ISPN 53150-270).
Medium: 3 1/2-inch disk
ISPN: 35175-166   **Price: $20.00**

HEIZER SOFTWARE
LABOR COST REPORT

Tracks burdened and unburdened labor costs as various parts go through the fabrication cycle.

System: MAC, II, PLUS, SE, XL
Minimum Memory: 512K
Requires: Microsoft Excel (ISPN 53150-270) or Microsoft Works (ISPN 53150-740).
Medium: 3 1/2-inch disk
ISPN: 35175-557   **Price: $40.00**

HEIZER SOFTWARE
MASTER SCHEDULE

Calculates the finished goods inventory level over a period of time, based on committed and planned component purchases.

System: MAC, II, PLUS, SE, XL
Minimum Memory: 512K
Requires: Microsoft Excel (ISPN 53150-270) or Microsoft Works (ISPN 53150-740).
Medium: 3 1/2-inch disk
ISPN: 35175-556   **Price: $20.00**

HEIZER SOFTWARE
QUOTATION FROM INVENTORY

Prints quotations using a priced or costed inventory database.

System: MAC, II, PLUS, SE, XL
Minimum Memory: 512K
Requires: Microsoft Excel (ISPN 53150-270) or Microsoft Works (ISPN 53150-740).
Medium: 3 1/2-inch disk
ISPN: 35175-167   **Price: $15.00**

CHANG LABORATORIES, INC.
RAGS TO RICHES-INVENTORY (VER. 3.0)

Tracks purchase orders, receiving of goods, returns, consignment, COD purchases, transfers, adjustments. Includes POS capability.

System: MAC, II, PLUS, SE, XL
Minimum Memory: 512K
Medium: 3 1/2-inch disk
ISPN: 12200-746   **Price: $399.95**

SBT CORP.
SBT DPURCHASE-COMPILED (VER. 6.20)

Provides a complete purchasing and inventory control system, includes publisher and inventory labels and inventory reports.

System: MAC, II, PLUS, SE, XL
Minimum Memory: 512K
Medium: 3 1/2-inch disk
ISPN: 68057-077   **Price: $295.00**

SBT CORP.
SBT DPURCHASE-STANDARD (VER. 6.20)

Provides a purchase and inventory control system that includes publisher and inventory labels and inventory reports.

System: MAC, II, PLUS, SE, XL
Minimum Memory: 512K
Medium: 3 1/2-inch disk
ISPN: 68057-079   **Price: $395.00**

---

166 PRODUCTIVITY/ SPREADSHEET SUPPORT

INDIVIDUAL SOFTWARE, INC.
101 MACROS FOR EXCEL

Provides 101 prewritten, ready-to-run, all purpose macros to enhance the operation of Microsoft Excel.

System: MAC, II, PLUS, SE, XL
Minimum Memory: 512K
Requires: Microsoft Excel (ISPN 53150-270).
Medium: 3 1/2-inch disk
ISPN: 37275-015   **Price: $69.95**

HEIZER SOFTWARE
ACCOUNTING SPREADSHEET

Performs all formatting functions when creating a new basic, cross-footed spreadsheet.

System: MAC, II, PLUS, SE, XL
Minimum Memory: 512K
Requires: Microsoft Works (ISPN 53150-740).
Medium: 3 1/2-inch disk
ISPN: 35175-904   **Price: $9.00**

HEIZER SOFTWARE
ADVANCED CHART TUTORIAL III

Illustrates a scatter chart plotting technique for producing smooth curves rather than normal straight-line scatter plots.

System: MAC, II, PLUS, SE, XL
Minimum Memory: 512K
Requires: Microsoft Excel (ISPN 53150-270).
Medium: 3 1/2-inch disk
ISPN: 35175-337   **Price: $15.00**

HEIZER SOFTWARE
ANIMATED INTRODUCTIONS

Illustrates eight methods for adding graphic introductions to Excel programs.

System: MAC, II, PLUS, SE, XL
Minimum Memory: 512K
Requires: Microsoft Excel (ISPN 53150-270).
Medium: 3 1/2-inch disk
ISPN: 35175-346   **Price: $6.00**

HEIZER SOFTWARE
AUTOSAVE MACRO
An adjustable macro which helps prevent data loss.
System: MAC, II, PLUS, SE, XL
Minimum Memory: 512K
Requires: Microsoft Excel (ISPN 53150-270).
Medium: 3 1/2-inch disk
ISPN: 35175-525　　　　**Price: $3.00**

HEIZER SOFTWARE
BASIC ACCOUNTING WORKSHEET MACRO
Sets up a worksheet with numbered rows and columns, title and total areas, borders and number formats.
System: MAC, II, PLUS, SE, XL
Minimum Memory: 512K
Requires: Microsoft Excel (ISPN 53150-270).
Medium: 3 1/2-inch disk
ISPN: 35175-350　　　　**Price: $9.00**

HEIZER SOFTWARE
BASIC EDITING MACROS
Contains forty-eight command macros to expedite worksheet editing.
System: MAC, II, PLUS, SE, XL
Minimum Memory: 512K
Requires: Microsoft Excel (ISPN 53150-270).
Medium: 3 1/2-inch disk
ISPN: 35175-509　　　　**Price: $9.00**

HEIZER SOFTWARE
BEST ANSWER
Utilizes linear programming to determine which combination of variables on a spreadsheet will produce the best possible result.
System: MAC, II, PLUS, SE, XL
Minimum Memory: 1024K
Requires: Microsoft Excel (ISPN 53150-270) or Microsoft Works (ISPN 53150-740).
Medium: 3 1/2-inch disk
ISPN: 35175-100　　　　**Price: $99.00**

HEIZER SOFTWARE
BREAKEVEN ANALYSIS TEMPLATE
Allows an individual to enter data for a breakeven analysis.
System: MAC, II, PLUS, SE, XL
Minimum Memory: 512K
Requires: Microsoft Excel (ISPN 53150-270) or Microsoft Works (ISPN 53150-740).
Medium: 3 1/2-inch disk
ISPN: 35175-530　　　　**Price: $8.00**

PALO ALTO SOFTWARE
BUSINESS PLAN TOOLKIT (VER. 3.0)
Aids in the development of business plans. Includes tables, graphs and pre-programmed macros.
System: MAC, II, PLUS, SE, XL
Minimum Memory: 512K
Requires: Microsoft Excel (ISPN 53150-270), Multiplan (ISPN 53150-550), or Appleworks (ISPN 12784-100).
Medium: 3 1/2-inch disk
ISPN: 37443-010　　　　**Price: $99.95**

HEIZER SOFTWARE
CARPET CHART TUTORIAL
Creates 'carpet' charts to plot data of the form 'z = function of x & y', to produce a 3-D illusion and still exhibit accurate values.
System: MAC, II, PLUS, SE, XL
Minimum Memory: 512K
Requires: Microsoft Excel (ISPN 53150-270).
Medium: 3 1/2-inch disk
ISPN: 35175-338　　　　**Price: $18.00**

HEIZER SOFTWARE
CHART DATA COMPRESS
Provides two methods to compress over one hundred points of data to one hundred points, either equal or optimized.
System: MAC, II, PLUS, SE, XL
Minimum Memory: 512K
Requires: Microsoft Excel (ISPN 53150-270).
Medium: 3 1/2-inch disk
ISPN: 35175-518　　　　**Price: $10.00**

HEIZER SOFTWARE
CHART DATA GRABBER
A macro which selects data from various rows or columns for charting.
System: MAC, II, PLUS, SE, XL
Minimum Memory: 512K
Requires: Microsoft Excel (ISPN 53150-270).
Medium: 3 1/2-inch disk
ISPN: 35175-516　　　　**Price: $10.00**

HEIZER SOFTWARE
DATES IN THE FUTURE
Calculates a starting date in relation to an earlier date when the number of years, months and days between the two dates are known.
System: MAC, II, PLUS, SE, XL
Minimum Memory: 512K
Requires: Microsoft Excel (ISPN 53150-270).
Medium: 3 1/2-inch disk
ISPN: 35175-185　　　　**Price: $10.00**

HEIZER SOFTWARE
DATES IN THE PAST
Calculates a starting date in relation to a later date when the number of years, months and days between the two dates are known.
System: MAC, II, PLUS, SE, XL
Minimum Memory: 512K
Requires: Microsoft Excel (ISPN 53150-270).
Medium: 3 1/2-inch disk
ISPN: 35175-184　　　　**Price: $10.00**

HEIZER SOFTWARE
DATES PAST AND FUTURE
Calculates a starting date in relation to a later or earlier date when the number of years, months and days between are known.
System: MAC, II, PLUS, SE, XL
Minimum Memory: 512K
Requires: Microsoft Excel (ISPN 53150-270).
Medium: 3 1/2-inch disk
ISPN: 35175-183　　　　**Price: $15.00**

HEIZER SOFTWARE
DOCUMENT!
Demonstrates several ways to hide built-in documentation to an Excel application.
System: MAC, II, PLUS, SE, XL
Minimum Memory: 512K
Requires: Microsoft Excel (ISPN 53150-270).
Medium: 3 1/2-inch disk
ISPN: 35175-341　　　　**Price: $5.00**

HEIZER SOFTWARE
DOUBLE-TRIPLE SPACE
Automatically adds and deletes, double or triple spaces, to/from a worksheet Print Area.
System: MAC, II, PLUS, SE, XL
Minimum Memory: 512K
Requires: Microsoft Excel (ISPN 53150-270).
Medium: 3 1/2-inch disk
ISPN: 35175-512　　　　**Price: $10.00**

HEIZER SOFTWARE
EXCELLENT EXCHANGE PERSONAL RESOURCE
Provides macros and templates to provide for a checkbook, personal budgeting, expense logs, mortgage calculation, net worth, and more.
System: MAC, II, PLUS, SE, XL
Minimum Memory: 1024K
Requires: Microsoft Excel (ISPN 53150-270).
Medium: 3 1/2-inch disk
ISPN: 35175-200　　　　**Price: $49.00**

HEIZER SOFTWARE
EXCELLENT EXCHANGE SAMPLE DISK
Consists of one program and fifteen Demos of the user's choice, from Excel's inventory.
System: MAC, II, PLUS, SE, XL
Minimum Memory: 512K
Requires: Microsoft Excel (ISPN 53150-270).
Medium: 3 1/2-inch disk
ISPN: 35175-347　　　　**Price: $4.00**

HEIZER SOFTWARE
EXCELLENT EXCHANGE UTILITIES
Contains ten macros and templates that include generating mailing labels, time-saving macros, custom databases and more.
System: MAC, II, PLUS, SE, XL
Minimum Memory: 512K
Requires: Microsoft Excel (ISPN 53150-270).
Medium: 3 1/2-inch disk
ISPN: 35175-210　　　　**Price: $49.00**

HEIZER SOFTWARE
EXCELLENT GRAPHICS
A worksheet program which shows the potential of adding graphic titles to Excel programs.
System: MAC, II, PLUS, SE, XL
Minimum Memory: 512K
Requires: Microsoft Excel (ISPN 53150-270).
Medium: 3 1/2-inch disk
ISPN: 35175-345　　　　**Price: $2.00**

HEIZER SOFTWARE

FILL UP/FILL LEFT

Command macros which duplicate Fill Down and Fill Right.

System: MAC, II, PLUS, SE, XL
Minimum Memory: 512K
Requires: Microsoft Excel (ISPN 53150-270).
Medium: 3 1/2-inch disk
ISPN: 35175-524 **Price: $6.00**

REALDATA, INC.

FINANCIAL ANALYSIS (VER. 4.0)

Contains 18 useful and sophisticated models (templates) and a user's guide.

System: MAC, II, PLUS, SE, XL
Minimum Memory: 512K
Requires: Microsoft Excel (53150-270), Jazz (ISPN 45525-025) or Microsoft Works (ISPN 53150-740).
Medium: 3 1/2-inch disk
ISPN: 65462-300 **Price: $195.00**

HEIZER SOFTWARE

FIND FACTORS

Determines if an integer within Excel's range of accuracy is prime, and if not, finds its factors.

System: MAC, II, PLUS, SE, XL
Minimum Memory: 512K
Requires: Microsoft Excel (ISPN 53150-270).
Medium: 3 1/2-inch disk
ISPN: 35175-568 **Price: $8.00**

HEIZER SOFTWARE

FIND PRIME

Determines if an integer within Excel's range of accuracy is a prime number.

System: MAC, II, PLUS, SE, XL
Minimum Memory: 512K
Requires: Microsoft Excel (ISPN 53150-270).
Medium: 3 1/2-inch disk
ISPN: 35175-567 **Price: $4.00**

HEIZER SOFTWARE

FRACTIONS MACROS

Converts decimals to fractions using functional macros.

System: MAC, II, PLUS, SE, XL
Minimum Memory: 512K
Requires: Microsoft Excel (ISPN 53150-270).
Medium: 3 1/2-inch disk
ISPN: 35175-317 **Price: $4.00**

HEIZER SOFTWARE

HOT SPOT MACROS

Designates a cell on a worksheet as a 'hot spot' which can be accessed from any other point in the worksheet.

System: MAC, II, PLUS, SE, XL
Minimum Memory: 512K
Requires: Microsoft Excel (ISPN 53150-270).
Medium: 3 1/2-inch disk
ISPN: 35175-514 **Price: $5.00**

HEIZER SOFTWARE

ITERATION ON A MACRO

Tutors on iteration methods which allow the user to control the order of cell recalculation.

System: MAC, II, PLUS, SE, XL
Minimum Memory: 512K
Requires: Microsoft Excel (ISPN 53150-270).
Medium: 3 1/2-inch disk
ISPN: 35175-342 **Price: $7.00**

HEIZER SOFTWARE

MACROS ON THE FLY

Command macros which analyze a worksheet without entering formulas.

System: MAC, II, PLUS, SE, XL
Minimum Memory: 512K
Requires: Microsoft Excel (ISPN 53150-270).
Medium: 3 1/2-inch disk
ISPN: 35175-507 **Price: $9.00**

SYMANTEC

MACSQZ

Compacts the size of Microsoft Excel spreadsheets up to 95 percent, and adds backup and file-level password protection.

System: MAC, II, PLUS, SE, XL
Minimum Memory: 512K
Requires: Microsoft Excel (ISPN 53150-270).
Medium: 3 1/2-inch disk
ISPN: 77413-510 **Price: $79.95**

MICROTEMP

MICROTEMP FINANCIAL CALCULATORS

Provides a series of 45 custom built financial calculators for use with Microsoft Excel or Microsoft Works.

System: MAC, II, PLUS, SE, XL
Minimum Memory: 512K
Requires: Microsoft Excel (ISPN 53150-270) or Microsoft Works (ISPN 53150-270).
Medium: 3 1/2-inch disk
ISPN: 53668-500 **Price: $79.95**

HEIZER SOFTWARE

MIND READER

Deceives players into concluding that the Macintosh is psychic.

System: MAC, II, PLUS, SE, XL
Minimum Memory: 512K
Requires: Microsoft Excel (ISPN 53150-270) or HyperCard (ISPN 03900-300).
Medium: 3 1/2-inch disk
ISPN: 35175-244 **Price: $10.00**

HEIZER SOFTWARE

MOVING AVERAGE MACRO

Calculates the moving average of any list of numbers for any moving period.

System: MAC, II, PLUS, SE, XL
Minimum Memory: 512K
Requires: Microsoft Excel (ISPN 53150-270).
Medium: 3 1/2-inch disk
ISPN: 35175-511 **Price: $10.00**

HEIZER SOFTWARE

NAME REVERSER

Allows user to keep full names in one database field and still meet the needs of sorting and printing.

System: MAC, II, PLUS, SE, XL
Minimum Memory: 512K
Requires: Microsoft Excel (ISPN 53150-270).
Medium: 3 1/2-inch disk
ISPN: 35175-528 **Price: $8.00**

HEIZER SOFTWARE

NEW WORKSHEET MACRO

Utilizes a macro to create a new worksheet within Microsoft Excel.

System: MAC, II, PLUS, SE, XL
Minimum Memory: 512K
Requires: Microsoft Excel (ISPN 53150-270).
Medium: 3 1/2-inch disk
ISPN: 35175-967 **Price: $6.00**

LAYERED, INC.

NOTES FOR JAZZ

Includes Notes, installed as a desk accessory on the system disk, and Business Companion installs as a desk accessory on Jazz system.

System: MAC, II, PLUS, SE, XL
Minimum Memory: 512K
Requires: Jazz (ISPN 45525-025).
Medium: 3 1/2-inch disk
ISPN: 43760-675 **Price: $79.00**

LAYERED, INC.

NOTES FOR MICROSOFT EXCEL

Makes learning and using Excel easier for both beginners and experts. Installs as a desk accessory on the system disk.

System: MAC, II, PLUS, SE, XL
Minimum Memory: 512K
Requires: Microsoft Excel Ver-1.03 (ISPN 53150-270).
Medium: 3 1/2-inch disk
ISPN: 43760-700 **Price: $79.00**

LAYERED, INC.

NOTES FOR MICROSOFT WORKS

Provides help, advice, tips and templates to make learning and using Works easier for both beginners and experts.

System: MAC, II, PLUS, SE, XL
Minimum Memory: 512K
Requires: Microsoft Works (ISPN 53150-740).
Medium: 3 1/2-inch disk
ISPN: 43760-730 **Price: $79.00**

HEIZER SOFTWARE

NUMBER UPDATE MACROS

Changes or updates a cell on a worksheet. Contains an Undo feature which allows the user to do rapid 'what if' analysis.

System: MAC, II, PLUS, SE, XL
Minimum Memory: 512K
Requires: Microsoft Excel (ISPN 53150-270).
Medium: 3 1/2-inch disk
ISPN: 35175-521 **Price: $8.00**

HEIZER SOFTWARE
NUMBERED TICKETS

Issues sequentially numbered tickets for events, meals, raffles or coupons.

System: MAC, II, PLUS, SE, XL
Minimum Memory: 512K
Requires: Microsoft Excel (ISPN 53150-270).
Medium: 3 1/2-inch disk
ISPN: 35175-246   **Price: $8.00**

REALDATA, INC.
ON SCHEDULE (VER. 2.0)

Economic critical path model templates create a month-by-month plan of how and when a development loan is drawn and used.

System: MAC, II, PLUS, SE, XL
Minimum Memory: 512K
Requires: Excel (ISPN 53150-270), Jazz (ISPN 45525-025) or Microsoft (ISPN 53150-740)
Medium: 3 1/2-inch disk
ISPN: 65462-600   **Price: $195.00**

HEIZER SOFTWARE
PLOT OVER 100 POINTS

Plots over one hundred points on an Excel chart.

System: MAC, II, PLUS, SE, XL
Minimum Memory: 512K
Requires: Microsoft Excel (ISPN 53150-270).
Medium: 3 1/2-inch disk
ISPN: 35175-517   **Price: $15.00**

REBUS DEVELOPMENT
PMTALK (VER. 1.0)

Communications interface that provides input of data directly into the spreadsheet from other computer systems and data loggers.

System: MAC, II, PLUS, SE, XL
Minimum Memory: 512K
Requires: Parameter Manager Plus (ISPN 76600-055).
Medium: 3 1/2-inch disk
ISPN: 76600-060   **Price: $295.00**

HEIZER SOFTWARE
PRINT-ALL MACRO

Automatically prints all open Excel documents.

System: MAC, II, PLUS, SE, XL
Minimum Memory: 512K
Requires: Microsoft Excel (ISPN 53150-270).
Medium: 3 1/2-inch disk
ISPN: 35175-527   **Price: $5.00**

HEIZER SOFTWARE
REMINDER MAKER

Uses a macro to build another macro which gives messages for weekdays and dates specified by the user.

System: MAC, II, PLUS, SE, XL
Minimum Memory: 512K
Requires: Microsoft Excel (ISPN 53150-270).
Medium: 3 1/2-inch disk
ISPN: 35175-529   **Price: $15.00**

HEIZER SOFTWARE
REMOVE PAGE BREAK MACRO

Automatically removes defined page breaks using a macro.

System: MAC, II, PLUS, SE, XL
Minimum Memory: 512K
Requires: Microsoft Excel (ISPN 53150-270).
Medium: 3 1/2-inch disk
ISPN: 35175-505   **Price: $8.00**

HEIZER SOFTWARE
ROOTS MACROS

Solves equations from a worksheet for all of the real and imaginary roots of non-linear quadratic, cubic and quartic equations.

System: MAC, II, PLUS, SE, XL
Minimum Memory: 512K
Requires: Microsoft Excel (ISPN 53150-270).
Medium: 3 1/2-inch disk
ISPN: 35175-573   **Price: $20.00**

HEIZER SOFTWARE
ROTARY FILE CARD MACROS

Prints the database on standard, pin-feed card forms which can be used with Rolodex rotary card files.

System: MAC, II, PLUS, SE, XL
Minimum Memory: 512K
Requires: Microsoft Excel (ISPN 53150-270), ImageWriter.
Medium: 3 1/2-inch disk
ISPN: 35175-520   **Price: $15.00**

HEIZER SOFTWARE
RUN TIME MACROS

Command macros which report the recalculation time of the Excel desktop, while adding speed.

System: MAC, II, PLUS, SE, XL
Minimum Memory: 512K
Requires: Microsoft Excel (ISPN 53150-270).
Medium: 3 1/2-inch disk
ISPN: 35175-519   **Price: $4.00**

HEIZER SOFTWARE
SAVE-ALL MACROS

Macros which automatically save, or save and close, all open documents.

System: MAC, II, PLUS, SE, XL
Minimum Memory: 512K
Requires: Microsoft Excel (ISPN 53150-270).
Medium: 3 1/2-inch disk
ISPN: 35175-526   **Price: $5.00**

SDG DECISION SYSTEMS
SENSITIVITY (VER. 5.3)

Performs sensitivity analysis on all variables in spreadsheet models, and calculates baseline, and high and low variable changes.

System: MAC, II, PLUS, SE, XL
Minimum Memory: 1024K
Medium: 3 1/2-inch disk
ISPN: 76475-605   **Price: $175.00**

HEIZER SOFTWARE
SIGNIFICANT DIGITS

Rounds values to a user-specified number of significant digits for data presentation.

System: MAC, II, PLUS, SE, XL
Minimum Memory: 512K
Requires: Microsoft Excel (ISPN 53150-270).
Medium: 3 1/2-inch disk
ISPN: 35175-569   **Price: $7.00**

HEIZER SOFTWARE
SIMULTANEOUS EQUATION MACROS

Solves two to nine simultaneous equations and can handle up to twenty-five equations when necessary.

System: MAC, II, PLUS, SE, XL
Minimum Memory: 512K
Requires: Microsoft Excel (ISPN 53150-270).
Medium: 3 1/2-inch disk
ISPN: 35175-577   **Price: $36.00**

HEIZER SOFTWARE
SMALL BUSINESS ACCOUNTING SYSTEM

Allows entry of accounting information into a single worksheet to produce a balance sheet or an income statement with Excel.

System: MAC, II, PLUS, SE, XL
Minimum Memory: 512K
Requires: Microsoft Excel (ISPN 53150-270).
Medium: 3 1/2-inch disk
ISPN: 35175-730   **Price: $79.00**

ALLEGRO SOFTWARE (MA)
SOFT START BUSINESS ANALYSIS

Multiplan templates for break even analysis, cash flow budget, financial statement analysis, and more.

System: MAC, II, PLUS, SE, XL
Minimum Memory: 512K
Requires: Multiplan (ISPN 64928-500) or Microsoft Excel (ISPN 53150-270).
Medium: 3 1/2-inch disk
ISPN: 59003-200   **Price: $49.95**

ALLEGRO SOFTWARE (MA)
SOFT START PERSONAL FINANCE

Set of 12 templates for personal finance including Investments, Budgeting, Property and Cash Management.

System: MAC, II, PLUS, SE, XL
Minimum Memory: 512K
Requires: Microsoft Multiplan (ISPN 53150-550) or Microsoft Excel (ISPN 53150-270).
Medium: 3 1/2-inch disk
ISPN: 59003-600   **Price: $49.95**

HEIZER SOFTWARE

SUBTOTAL MACROS

Sorts data in one column and automatically subtotals numerical data in a second column for each subgroup of the first column.

System: MAC, II, PLUS, SE, XL
Minimum Memory: 512K
Requires: Microsoft Excel (ISPN 53150-270).
Medium: 3 1/2-inch disk
ISPN: 35175-502   **Price: $15.00**

HEIZER SOFTWARE

TEXTUAL BAR GRAPH TUTORIAL

Tutors on how to create bar graphs of textual strings for a visual feedback of some relationship between entry lists of numbers.

System: MAC, II, PLUS, SE, XL
Minimum Memory: 512K
Requires: Microsoft Excel (ISPN 53150-270).
Medium: 3 1/2-inch disk
ISPN: 35175-339   **Price: $15.00**

HEIZER SOFTWARE

TIP SHEET

A collection of tips, tricks and ideas about Excel programs which were gathered form Excel's authors and customers.

System: MAC, II, PLUS, SE, XL
Minimum Memory: 512K
Requires: Microsoft Excel (ISPN 53150-270).
Medium: 3 1/2-inch disk
ISPN: 35175-348   **Price: $9.00**

HEIZER SOFTWARE

TOGGLE MACROS

Command macros which use on and off keystrokes to adjust style, border and alignment for selected cells.

System: MAC, II, PLUS, SE, XL
Minimum Memory: 512K
Requires: Microsoft Excel (ISPN 53150-270).
Medium: 3 1/2-inch disk
ISPN: 35175-508   **Price: $5.00**

HEIZER SOFTWARE

TRANSPOSE MACRO

Transposes the cell contents of any rectangular group of cells, interchanging rows and columns.

System: MAC, II, PLUS, SE, XL
Minimum Memory: 512K
Requires: Microsoft Excel (ISPN 53150-270).
Medium: 3 1/2-inch disk
ISPN: 35175-994   **Price: $15.00**

HEIZER SOFTWARE

UTILITY WORKS

Provides templates for databases, business forms and outlining, mailing labels and font tools using Microsoft Works.

System: MAC, II, PLUS, SE, XL
Minimum Memory: 512K
Requires: Microsoft Works (ISPN 53150-740).
Medium: 3 1/2-inch disk
ISPN: 35175-700   **Price: $50.00**

LINDO SYSTEMS

VINO-VISUAL INTERACTIVE OPTIMIZER

Provides optimization capabilities for spreadsheet programs Lotus 1-2-3, Multiplan, and Visicalc.

System: MAC, II, PLUS, SE, XL
Minimum Memory: 1024K
Medium: 3 1/2-inch disk
ISPN: 44737-300   **Price: $375.00**

HEIZER SOFTWARE

WORD WRAP MACRO

Rearranges text on an Excel worksheet so each row has only a specified number of characters.

System: MAC, II, PLUS, SE, XL
Minimum Memory: 512K
Requires: Microsoft Excel (ISPN 53150-270).
Medium: 3 1/2-inch disk
ISPN: 35175-504   **Price: $20.00**

LUNDEEN AND ASSOCIATES

WORKSPLUS COMMAND (VER. 1.1A)

Provides macro-recording and programming capabilities for Microsoft Works.

System: MAC, II, PLUS, SE, XL
Minimum Memory: 512K
Requires: Microsoft Works (ISPN 53150-740).
Medium: 3 1/2-inch disk
ISPN: 45593-700   **Price: $99.95**

169 PRODUCTIVITY/ SPREADSHEETS

MICRO SYSTEMS SOFTWARE (FLA)

ANALYZE! (VER. 2.11)

Transfers data from a personal budget or check register to a company's general ledger and bank reconciliation statement.

System: MAC, II, PLUS, SE, XL
Minimum Memory: 512K
Medium: 3 1/2-inch disk
ISPN: 51534-122   **Price: $149.95**

BRAVO TECHNOLOGIES, INC.

MACCALC

Allows each cell to have its own font, format, size, and style for presentation-quality reports and tables.

System: MAC, II, PLUS, SE, XL
Minimum Memory: 512K
Requires: 800K disk drive.
Medium: 3 1/2-inch disk
ISPN: 90657-500   **Price: $139.00**

MICROSOFT CORP.

MICROSOFT EXCEL (VER. 1.5)

A financial analysis tool which is linked with business graphics and a database for interpretation of vast quantities of numbers.

System: MAC, II, PLUS, SE, XL
Minimum Memory: 512K
Medium: 3 1/2-inch disk
ISPN: 53150-270   **Price: $495.00**

MICROSOFT CORP.

MICROSOFT MULTIPLAN (VER. 4.1)

Spreadsheet for numeric modeling and planning. Allows linked worksheets to share information.

System: MAC, II, PLUS, SE, XL
Minimum Memory: 512K
Medium: 3 1/2-inch disk
ISPN: 53150-550   **Price: $195.00**

REBUS DEVELOPMENT

PARAMETER MANAGER PLUS (VER. 3.0)

A specialized spreadsheet that stores data chronologically by time or sequence, with graphic analysis commands selected from a menu.

System: MAC, II, PLUS, SE, XL
Minimum Memory: 512K
Requires: 800K disk drive and a hard disk, ImageWriter or LaserWriter.
Medium: 3 1/2-inch disk
ISPN: 76600-055   **Price: $595.00**

HEIZER SOFTWARE

STACKCALC

A mini-spreadsheet complete with cell references and a function library. Used as a starting point for organizing calculations.

System: MAC, II, PLUS, SE, XL
Minimum Memory: 1024K
Requires: HyperCard (ISPN 03900-300).
Medium: 3 1/2-inch disk
ISPN: 35175-091   **Price: $15.00**

INFORMIX SOFTWARE, INC. (KS)

WINGZ

A true graphic environment spreadsheet with advanced charts and graphs, full color support, 3-D capabilities and more.

System: MAC, II, PLUS, SE, XL
Minimum Memory: 1024K
Medium: 3 1/2-inch disk
ISPN: 38500-800   **Price: $395.00**

172 PRODUCTIVITY/ STATISTICS

LIONHEART PRESS

ANOVA (VER. 5.0)

Provides a set of analysis of variance algorithms for replicated factorials, unbalanced and nested factorials, and repeat measures.

System: MAC, II, PLUS, SE, XL
Minimum Memory: 512K
Medium: 3 1/2-inch disk
ISPN: 44900-563   **Price: $95.00**

LIONHEART PRESS

ARIMA TECHNIQUES (VER. 5.0)

Contains a set of programs which allows the transformation of time-series and calculates the coefficients of correlation.

System: MAC, II, PLUS, SE, XL
Minimum Memory: 512K
Medium: 3 1/2-inch disk
ISPN: 44900-065   **Price: $95.00**

DYNACOMP, INC.

BASIC SCIENTIFIC SUBROUTINES (VOL. 3) CHAPTER TWO

Features text which deals with statistical subroutines, including data handling.

System: MAC, II, PLUS, SE, XL
Minimum Memory: 512K
Medium: 3 1/2-inch disk
ISPN: 27050-025   **Price: $34.95**

HEIZER SOFTWARE

BINOMIAL DISTRIBUTION

Evaluates and charts the binomial distribution of n things in groups of k with probability p.

System: MAC, II, PLUS, SE, XL
Minimum Memory: 512K
Requires: Microsoft Excel (ISPN 53150-270).
Medium: 3 1/2-inch disk
ISPN: 35175-736   **Price: $7.00**

HEIZER SOFTWARE

BINOMIAL DISTRIBUTION MACROS

Function macros and a command macro give cumulative probability and calculates confidence limits for binomial parameters.

System: MAC, II, PLUS, SE, XL
Minimum Memory: 512K
Requires: Microsoft Excel (ISPN 53150-270).
Medium: 3 1/2-inch disk
ISPN: 35175-725   **Price: $12.00**

SOF-WARE TOOLS

BIOMEDICAL RESEARCH CHART TOOL KIT (VER. 4.01)

Records numeric research data, and then translates this data into meaningful graphic forms and statistics.

System: MAC, II, PLUS, SE, XL
Minimum Memory: 512K
Requires: ImageWriter or LaserWriter, 800K disk drive.
Medium: 3 1/2-inch disk
ISPN: 71803-150   **Price: $199.00**

LIONHEART PRESS

BIOMETRICS (VER. 5.0)

Contains a statistical analysis program for the life sciences, which includes stem and leaf displays, boxplots, and coded tables.

System: MAC, II, PLUS, SE, XL
Minimum Memory: 512K
Medium: 3 1/2-inch disk
ISPN: 44900-852   **Price: $145.00**

LIONHEART PRESS

BUSINESS STATISTICS

Contains a collection of statistical problems that occur in business situations.

System: MAC, II, PLUS, SE, XL
Minimum Memory: 512K
Medium: 3 1/2-inch disk
ISPN: 44900-150   **Price: $145.00**

LIONHEART PRESS

BUSINESS STATISTICS AND EXPERIMENTAL STATISTICS

Helps improve management skills with a collection of statistical problems that occur in business situations.

System: MAC, II, PLUS, SE, XL
Minimum Memory: 512K
Medium: 3 1/2-inch disk
ISPN: 44900-100   **Price: $190.00**

TRUE BASIC, INC.

CHIPENDALE

A menu-driven program for the statistical analysis of contingency tables. Use stored data sets or create new data sets.

System: MAC, II, PLUS, SE, XL
Minimum Memory: 512K
Medium: 3 1/2-inch disk
ISPN: 82789-200   **Price: $49.95**

CLEAR LAKE RESEARCH, INC.

CLR ANOVA

Compute up to a 10-way design including means, plots of interactions, simple effects, range tests, and contrasts.

System: MAC, II, PLUS, SE, XL
Minimum Memory: 512K
Medium: 3 1/2-inch disk
ISPN: 12891-100   **Price: $75.00**

LIONHEART PRESS

CLUSTER ANALYSIS

Provides a collection of all the major cluster analysis algorithms.

System: MAC, II, PLUS, SE, XL
Minimum Memory: 512K
Medium: 3 1/2-inch disk
ISPN: 44900-175   **Price: $145.00**

HEIZER SOFTWARE

COMBINATIONS

Evaluates the number of combinations of n things in groups of k.

System: MAC, II, PLUS, SE, XL
Minimum Memory: 512K
Requires: Microsoft Excel (ISPN 53150-270).
Medium: 3 1/2-inch disk
ISPN: 35175-734   **Price: $3.00**

HEIZER SOFTWARE

CPI-U MONTHLY 35 YEAR

A monthly Consumer Price Index database which covers the past thirty-five years.

System: MAC, II, PLUS, SE, XL
Minimum Memory: 512K
Requires: Microsoft Works (ISPN 53150-740), Microsoft Excel (ISPN 53150-270) or HyperCard (ISPN 03900-300).
Medium: 3 1/2-inch disk
ISPN: 35175-464   **Price: $12.00**

ODESTA CORP.

DATA DESK PROFESSIONAL II (VER. 2.0)

Allows users to explore and analyze data by asking questions visually with graphics backed up by analytic functions.

System: MAC, II, PLUS, SE, XL
Minimum Memory: 512K
Requires: Two 800K disk drives or one disk drive and a hard disk.
Medium: 3 1/2-inch disk
ISPN: 57709-100   **Price: $495.00**

LIONHEART PRESS

DECISION TREES AND TABLES (VER. 5.0)

Assists in decision making under uncertain conditions by applying local and statistical principles.

System: MAC, II, PLUS, SE, XL
Minimum Memory: 512K
Medium: 3 1/2-inch disk
ISPN: 44900-163   **Price: $95.00**

SYSTAT, INC.

DESIGN

Provides sample size estimation design, table of expected mean squares for balanced experiments and randomization plans design.

System: MAC, II, PLUS, SE, XL
Minimum Memory: 1024K
Medium: 3 1/2-inch disk
ISPN: 77843-200   **Price: $90.00**

LIONHEART PRESS

ECONOMETRICS (VER. 5.0)

Covers statistical distributions and inference, multilinear regression such as weighted regression and ridge regression models.

System: MAC, II, PLUS, SE, XL
Minimum Memory: 512K
Medium: 3 1/2-inch disk
ISPN: 44900-123   **Price: $145.00**

HEIZER SOFTWARE

ERROR BARS

Calculates and draws error bars for scatter charts.

System: MAC, II, PLUS, SE, XL
Minimum Memory: 512K
Requires: Microsoft Excel (ISPN 53150-270).
Medium: 3 1/2-inch disk
ISPN: 35175-731   **Price: $15.00**

LIONHEART PRESS

EXPERIMENTAL STATISTICS

Allows users to develop a useful understanding of statistics to improve management skills.

System: MAC, II, PLUS, SE, XL
Minimum Memory: 512K
Medium: 3 1/2-inch disk
ISPN: 44900-300   **Price: $145.00**

LIONHEART PRESS

EXPLORATORY DATA ANALYSIS

Allows user to examine letter-value displays and boxplots of data instead of pie charts and histograms.

System: MAC, II, PLUS, SE, XL
Minimum Memory: 512K
Medium: 3 1/2-inch disk
ISPN: 44900-350   **Price: $85.00**

SELECT MICRO SYSTEMS, INC.

EXSTATIX

Statistical analysis with full regression analysis, correlations, descriptive statistics, ANOVA, and presentation graphics.

System: MAC, II, PLUS, SE, XL
Minimum Memory: 512K
Requires: 800K disk drive.
Medium: 3 1/2-inch disk
ISPN: 69106-200   **Price: $349.00**

HEIZER SOFTWARE

FACTORIAL

Computes the factorial for integers up to 170.

System: MAC, II, PLUS, SE, XL
Minimum Memory: 512K
Requires: Microsoft Excel (ISPN 53150-270).
Medium: 3 1/2-inch disk
ISPN: 35175-735   **Price: $3.00**

SYSTAT, INC.

FASTAT (VER. 1.0)

Statistics and graphics program that will handle up to 50 variables and unlimited cases.

System: MAC, II, PLUS, SE, XL
Minimum Memory: 1024K
Requires: Hard disk.
Medium: 3 1/2-inch disk
ISPN: 77843-300   **Price: $195.00**

SYSTAT, INC.

FASTAT (VER. 1.0)

Statistics and graphics program that will handle up to 50 variables and unlimited cases.

System: II
Minimum Memory: 2048K
Requires: Hard disk. 68881 math co-processor.
Medium: 3 1/2-inch disk
ISPN: 77843-300   **Price: $195.00**

LIONHEART PRESS

FORECASTING AND TIME-SERIES

Covers the statistical analysis of time-series.

System: MAC, II, PLUS, SE, XL
Minimum Memory: 512K
Medium: 3 1/2-inch disk
ISPN: 44900-400   **Price: $145.00**

LIONHEART PRESS

FORECASTING AND TIME-SERIES/SALES AND MARKET

Covers the statistical analysis of time-series and applies forecasting techniques to business problems.

System: MAC, II, PLUS, SE, XL
Minimum Memory: 512K
Medium: 3 1/2-inch disk
ISPN: 44900-450   **Price: $200.00**

DECISION SCIENCE SOFTWARE

FUTURE

Contains an interactive computer model that forecasts using time series data.

System: MAC, II, PLUS, SE, XL
Minimum Memory:
Medium: 3 1/2-inch disk
ISPN: 24325-200   **Price: $75.00**

HEIZER SOFTWARE

HISTOGRAM/PARETO DIAGRAM

Utilizes numerical or text data to prepares a histogram and or a Pareto diagram.

System: MAC, II, PLUS, SE, XL
Minimum Memory: 512K
Requires: Microsoft Excel (ISPN 53150-270).
Medium: 3 1/2-inch disk
ISPN: 35175-726   **Price: $16.00**

HEIZER SOFTWARE

HYPERGEOMETRIC DISTRIBUTION

A function macro for standard evaluation of hypergeometric probabilities.

System: MAC, II, PLUS, SE, XL
Minimum Memory: 512K
Requires: Microsoft Excel (ISPN 53150-270).
Medium: 3 1/2-inch disk
ISPN: 35175-737   **Price: $10.00**

LIONHEART PRESS

INFERENCE (VER. 5.0)

Calculates direct, inverse and non-central statistical distributions and provides calculation of Type II errors.

System: MAC, II, PLUS, SE, XL
Minimum Memory: 512K
Medium: 3 1/2-inch disk
ISPN: 44900-632   **Price: $95.00**

MATHEMATICAL SOFTWARE CO.

INTERACTIVE MULTIPLE PREDICTION

Accepts as input a data-set made up of one criterion variable and up to 79 predictor variables.

System: MAC, II, PLUS, SE, XL
Minimum Memory: 512K
Medium: 3 1/2-inch disk
ISPN: 47775-375   **Price: $49.95**

SOF-WARE TOOLS

LAB PARTNER (VER. 1.1)

A systematic approach to experimental design and analysis. Attacks the problem of poor quality due to excessive variation.

System: MAC, II, PLUS, SE, XL
Minimum Memory: 1024K
Medium: 3 1/2-inch disk
ISPN: 71803-444   **Price: $500.00**

HEIZER SOFTWARE

LEAST SQUARES

Calculates and draws linear least squares regression. Allows regression through zero.

System: MAC, II, PLUS, SE, XL
Minimum Memory: 512K
Requires: Microsoft Excel (ISPN 53150-270).
Medium: 3 1/2-inch disk
ISPN: 35175-732   **Price: $15.00**

DREWS PROGRAMS

LEAST SQUARES ANALYSIS

Fits up to 10th order polynomials to data points, and fits bell curves, mean and standard deviation, Handles up to 1800 points.

System: MAC, II, PLUS, SE, XL
Minimum Memory: 512K
Medium: 3 1/2-inch disk
ISPN: 26771-475   **Price: $75.00**

HEIZER SOFTWARE

LINEAR REGRESSION

Works the same as the Microsoft Excel 'Linest' function, with the addition of regression statistics.

System: MAC, II, PLUS, SE, XL
Minimum Memory: 512K
Requires: Microsoft Excel (ISPN 53150-270) or Microsoft Works (ISPN 53150-740).
Medium: 3 1/2-inch disk
ISPN: 35175-724   **Price: $7.00**

SYSTAT, INC.

LOGIT

Offers logistic regression for binary and multinomial dependent variables estimated by maximum likelihood.

System: MAC, II, PLUS, SE, XL
Minimum Memory: 1024K
Medium: 3 1/2-inch disk
ISPN: 77843-400   **Price: $90.00**

DATA MANAGEMENT ASSOCIATES

MAC-QCV (VER. 1.0)

A quality control/statistical analysis package for doctors, physicians and/or clinical laboratories.

System: MAC, II, PLUS, SE, XL
Minimum Memory: 512K
Medium: 3 1/2-inch disk
ISPN: 17245-500 **Price: $995.00**

TESSERACT EDUCATIONAL SYSTEMS

MACFITS

A data analysis package to transfer/ manipulate data with other programs.

System: MAC, II, PLUS, SE, XL
Minimum Memory: 512K
Medium: 3 1/2-inch disk
ISPN: 81206-500 **Price: $39.95**

VAR ECONOMETRICS, INC.

MACRATS

Provides time series analysis and econometrics.

System: MAC, II, PLUS, SE, XL
Minimum Memory: 512K
Requires: System 4.2 or later.
Medium: 3 1/2-inch disk
ISPN: 84879-600 **Price: $300.00**

D2 SOFTWARE

MACSPIN (VER. 1.5)

A data planetarium disguised as a three dimensional statistical analysis program.

System: MAC, II, PLUS, SE, XL
Minimum Memory: 512K
Medium: 3 1/2-inch disk
ISPN: 21975-480 **Price: $250.00**

STATSOFT, INC.

MACSS

A comprehensive and powerful statistical and forecasting package.

System: MAC, PLUS, SE, XL
Minimum Memory: 512K
Medium: 3 1/2-inch disk
ISPN: 75992-300 **Price: $245.00**

LIONHEART PRESS

MARKETING STATISTICS (VER. 5.0)

Provides statistical techniques for market research which include data collection and sampling, and tabulation of questionnaire data.

System: MAC, II, PLUS, SE, XL
Minimum Memory: 512K
Medium: 3 1/2-inch disk
ISPN: 44900-900 **Price: $145.00**

HEIZER SOFTWARE

MEGA CALENDAR

A HyperCard stack which produces a calendar for any month of any year from September, 1752, through December, 2099.

System: MAC, II, PLUS, SE, XL
Minimum Memory: 512K
Requires: HyperCard (ISPN 03900-300).
Medium: 3 1/2-inch disk
ISPN: 35175-960 **Price: $10.00**

ACTUARIAL MICRO SOFTWARE

MONTE CARLO SIMULATIONS-ADVANCED (VER. 2.0)

Enables users to analyze raw data, fit a curve and create mathematical models with random variables.

System: MAC, II, PLUS, SE, XL
Minimum Memory: 512K
Medium: 3 1/2-inch disk
ISPN: 00844-500 **Price: $595.00**

DYNACOMP, INC.

MULTILINEAR REGRESSION

Treats multi-variate situations with no limit on the number of dimensions.

System: MAC, II, PLUS, SE, XL
Minimum Memory: 512K
Medium: 3 1/2-inch disk
ISPN: 27050-490 **Price: $33.95**

MATHEMATICAL SOFTWARE CO.

MULTIPLE FACTOR ANALYSIS (VER. 4.0)

Analyzes masses of research data for principle sources of variance or influence.

System: MAC, II, PLUS, SE, XL
Minimum Memory: 512K
Requires: Hard disk.
Medium: 3 1/2-inch disk
ISPN: 47775-100 **Price: $149.95**

BIOSOFT

MULTISTAT (VER. 1.0)

A statistics with graphics program which generates random numbers from 4 distributions – uniform, normal, poisson and exponential.

System: MAC, II, PLUS, SE, XL
Minimum Memory:
Medium: 3 1/2-inch disk
ISPN: 28881-925 **Price: $250.00**

LIONHEART PRESS

MULTIVARIATE ANALYSIS

Provides statistical techniques for the analysis of data which includes subjects and responses.

System: MAC, II, PLUS, SE, XL
Minimum Memory: 512K
Medium: 3 1/2-inch disk
ISPN: 44900-575 **Price: $125.00**

HEIZER SOFTWARE

NOBEL LAUREATES

Contains a list of over 500 Nobel Prize winners, including the awardee's birth data, the year won, and the country represented.

System: MAC, II, PLUS, SE, XL
Minimum Memory: 512K
Requires: Microsoft Excel (ISPN 53150-270) or Microsoft Works (ISPN 53150-740).
Medium: 3 1/2-inch disk
ISPN: 35175-968 **Price: $15.00**

HEIZER SOFTWARE

PERMUTATIONS

Evaluates the number of permutations of n things in groups of k.

System: MAC, II, PLUS, SE, XL
Minimum Memory: 512K
Requires: Microsoft Excel (ISPN 53150-270).
Medium: 3 1/2-inch disk
ISPN: 35175-733 **Price: $3.00**

HEIZER SOFTWARE

POLYNOMIAL REGRESSION

Uses a function macro, worksheet and chart to find curve-fitting coefficients.

System: MAC, II, PLUS, SE, XL
Minimum Memory: 512K
Requires: Microsoft Excel (ISPN 53150-270).
Medium: 3 1/2-inch disk
ISPN: 35175-723 **Price: $10.00**

SYSTAT, INC.

PROBIT

Estimates multiple regression model or analysis of covariance when dependent variables are categorical and take one of two values.

System: MAC, II, PLUS, SE, XL
Minimum Memory: 1024K
Medium: 3 1/2-inch disk
ISPN: 77843-600 **Price: $90.00**

SOF-WARE TOOLS

PROCESS CONTROL CHART TOOL KIT (VER. 3.0)

Provides graphics based on Deming's philosophy of statistical quality control systems.

System: MAC, II, PLUS, SE, XL
Minimum Memory: 512K
Requires: ImageWriter or LaserWriter printer, 800K disk drive.
Medium: 3 1/2-inch disk
ISPN: 71803-700 **Price: $199.00**

HEIZER SOFTWARE

RANDOM SELECTION WITHOUT DUPLICATION

Chooses unique numbers from a range of specified numbers.

System: MAC, II, PLUS, SE, XL
Minimum Memory: 512K
Requires: Microsoft Excel (ISPN 53150-270) or Microsoft Works (ISPN 53150-740).
Medium: 3 1/2-inch disk
ISPN: 35175-565 **Price: $8.00**

LIONHEART PRESS

REGRESSION

Provides procedures based on the least squares technique.

System: MAC, PLUS, SE, XL
Minimum Memory: 512K
Medium: 3 1/2-inch disk
ISPN: 44900-620   **Price: $95.00**

UNIVERSITY OF BRITISH COLUMBIA

SHAZAM (VER. 6.1)

Provides an econometric estimation program with extensive data manipulation commands.

System: MAC, II, PLUS, SE, XL
Minimum Memory: 512K
Requires: 68881 or 68882 co-processor.
Medium: 3 1/2-inch disk
ISPN: 83987-100   **Price: $275.00**

HEIZER SOFTWARE

STATISTICAL FUNCTION PACKAGE

A set of function macros which include Normal Distribution, Chi-Square Distribution and t-Distribution.

System: MAC, II, PLUS, SE, XL
Minimum Memory: 512K
Requires: Microsoft Excel (ISPN 53150-270).
Medium: 3 1/2-inch disk
ISPN: 35175-721   **Price: $30.00**

HEIZER SOFTWARE

STATISTICAL MACRO PACKAGE (VER. 1.0)

Provides statistical analysis templates which run on Microsoft Excel.

System: MAC, II, PLUS, SE, XL
Minimum Memory: 512K
Requires: Microsoft Excel (ISPN 53150-270).
Medium: 3 1/2-inch disk
ISPN: 35175-740   **Price: $79.00**

HEIZER SOFTWARE

STATISTICAL TEST PACKAGE

A set of statistical tests which include Correlations, Equal Proportion test, Medians, and Repeated measures.

System: MAC, II, PLUS, SE, XL
Minimum Memory: 512K
Requires: Microsoft Excel (ISPN 53150-270).
Medium: 3 1/2-inch disk
ISPN: 35175-722   **Price: $30.00**

SOF-WARE TOOLS

STATS TOOL KIT-STK (VER. 3.0)

Records research data and generates statistical analysis reports for physicians, researchers, and scientists.

System: MAC, II, PLUS, SE, XL
Minimum Memory: 512K
Requires: ImageWriter printer or Laserwriter, 800K disk drive.
Medium: 3 1/2-inch disk
ISPN: 71803-800   **Price: $99.00**

DYNACOMP, INC.

STATTEST

Performs statistical tests of hypotheses. Includes t-tests, chi-square tests and F-tests as well as simple regression.

System: MAC, II, PLUS, SE, XL
Minimum Memory: 512K
Medium: 3 1/2-inch disk
ISPN: 27050-602   **Price: $38.95**

BRAINPOWER, INC.

STATVIEW

Interactive visual data analysis package designed to take advantage of the Macintosh windows, pull-down menus, and the mouse.

System: MAC, II, PLUS, SE, XL
Minimum Memory: 512K
Medium: 3 1/2-inch disk
ISPN: 08413-475   **Price: $49.95**

BRAINPOWER, INC.

STATVIEW 512+ (VER. 1.1)

Adds step-wise regression to Statview Multivariate analysis with orthogonal and oblique transformations.

System: MAC, II, PLUS, SE, XL
Minimum Memory: 512K
Requires: Two disk drives.
Medium: 3 1/2-inch disk
ISPN: 08413-480   **Price: $349.95**

ABACUS CONCEPTS, INC.

STATVIEW II (VER. 1.03)

Statistical analysis with color presentation graphics for the Macintosh.

System: MAC, II, PLUS, SE, XL
Minimum Memory: 1024K
Requires: Two 800K disk drives, or hard disk and disk drive, 68881 and 68020 processors.
Medium: 3 1/2-inch disk
ISPN: 00319-100   **Price: $495.00**

ABACUS CONCEPTS, INC.

STATVIEW SE+ GRAPHICS (VER. 1.03)

Statistical analysis with color presentation graphics for the Macintosh.

System: MAC, PLUS, SE, XL
Minimum Memory: 1024K
Requires: 800K disk drive.
Medium: 3 1/2-inch disk
ISPN: 00319-110   **Price: $399.00**

ABACUS CONCEPTS, INC.

SUPERANOVA

A full featured general linear modelling program which is revolutionary in its power and ease of use.

System: MAC, II, PLUS, SE, XL
Minimum Memory: 1024K
Medium: 3 1/2-inch disk
ISPN: 00319-120   **Price: $495.00**

SYSTAT, INC.

SYSTAT (VER. 3.2)

Provides a comprehensive statistics, high-resolution graphics and data management package.

System: MAC, II, PLUS, SE, XL
Minimum Memory: 1024K
Requires: Two 800K disk drives or a hard disk, 2 MB RAM on a Macintosh II.
Medium: 3 1/2-inch disk
ISPN: 77843-100   **Price: $595.00**

SYSTAT, INC.

TESTAT

Provides test summary statistics, reliability coefficients, standard errors of measurement for selected score intervals.

System: MAC, PLUS, SE, XL
Minimum Memory: 1024K
Medium: 3 1/2-inch disk
ISPN: 77843-800   **Price: $90.00**

HEIZER SOFTWARE

TIME SERIES

Performs a correlation analysis on sequences of equally spaced data known as time series.

System: MAC, II, PLUS, SE, XL
Minimum Memory: 512K
Requires: Microsoft Excel (ISPN 53150-270).
Medium: 3 1/2-inch disk
ISPN: 35175-729   **Price: $20.00**

TRUE BASIC, INC.

TRUESTAT (VER. 1.2)

Provides an interactive statistical analysis system, stressing simulation of various distributions and graphic output.

System: MAC, II, PLUS, SE, XL
Minimum Memory: 512K
Medium: 3 1/2-inch disk
ISPN: 82789-725   **Price: $49.95**

SMALL BUSINESS COMPUTERS OF NEW ENGLAND

WORMSTAT (VER. 1.1)

Provides a statistical package using a MacPaint-like format to perform 16 statistical analyses.

System: MAC, II, PLUS, SE, XL
Minimum Memory: 512K
Medium: 3 1/2-inch disk
ISPN: 71101-750   **Price: $19.95**

175 PRODUCTIVITY/ TAXES

HEIZER SOFTWARE
1988 BUSINESS FEDERAL TAX TEMPLATES

Includes several forms and schedules for the categories of Corporate, S Corporations, Partnership, and Fudiciary.
System: MAC, II, PLUS, SE, XL
Minimum Memory: 512K
Requires: Microsoft Excel (ISPN 53150-270), ImageWriter, LQ or LaserWriter printer.
Medium: 3 1/2-inch disk
ISPN: 35175-149   **Price: $45.00**

HEIZER SOFTWARE
1988 PERSONAL FEDERAL TAX TEMPLATES

Contains Steve Willet's tax templates. Forms are approved for IRS submission in both LaserWriter and ImageWriter formats.
System: MAC, II, PLUS, SE, XL
Minimum Memory: 512K
Requires: Microsoft Excel (ISPN 53150-270) or Microsoft Works (ISPN 53150-740), ImageWriter, LaserWriter or LQ printer.
Medium: 3 1/2-inch disk
ISPN: 35175-741   **Price: $35.00**

HEIZER SOFTWARE
1988 STATE TAX SUPPLEMENT-CALIFORNIA

Contains California state tax forms 540, 540H, 540ES, and Schedules CA, D and FTB 3885.
System: MAC, II, PLUS, SE, XL
Minimum Memory: 512K
Requires: Microsoft Excel (ISPN 53150-270) or Microsoft Works (ISPN 53150-740), 1988 Personal Federal Tax Templates (ISPN 35175-741).
Medium: 3 1/2-inch disk
ISPN: 35175-742   **Price: $15.00**

HEIZER SOFTWARE
1988 STATE TAX SUPPLEMENT-MINNESOTA

Contains Minnesota state tax forms M-1 and M-1A, and Schedules M-1CD, M-1CR, M-1MT and M-1NR.
System: MAC, II, PLUS, SE, XL
Minimum Memory: 512K
Requires: Microsoft Excel (ISPN 53150-270), 1988 Personal Federal Tax Templates (ISPN 35175-741).
Medium: 3 1/2-inch disk
ISPN: 35175-744   **Price: $15.00**

HEIZER SOFTWARE
1988 STATE TAX SUPPLEMENT-NEW YORK

Contains New York state tax forms and schedules IT-201, IT-201-ATT, IT-250, and IT-270.
System: MAC, II, PLUS, SE, XL
Minimum Memory: 512K
Requires: Microsoft Excel (ISPN 53150-270) or Microsoft Works (ISPN 53150-740), 1988 Personal Federal Tax Templates (ISPN 35175-741).
Medium: 3 1/2-inch disk
ISPN: 35175-743   *   **Price: $15.00**

HEIZER SOFTWARE
1988 W-4 CALCULATOR

Performs the mathematic calculations necessary to complete W-4 forms.
System: MAC, II, PLUS, SE, XL
Minimum Memory: 512K
Requires: Microsoft Excel (ISPN 53150-270).
Medium: 3 1/2-inch disk
ISPN: 35175-749   **Price: $12.00**

COMPUCRAFT (CO)
BOTTOMLINE TAX TEMPLATES

Assists in calculating personal and business tax returns. Includes over 50 tax forms, associated schedules and worksheets.
System: MAC, II, PLUS, SE, XL
Minimum Memory: 512K
Requires: Microsoft Excel (ISPN 53150-270).
Medium: 3 1/2-inch disk
ISPN: 15178-175   **Price: $79.95**

HEIZER SOFTWARE
DEPENDENT SUPPORT TEST

A guide through five tests applied by the Internal Revenue Service to determine whether a person can be claimed as a dependent.
System: MAC, II, PLUS, SE, XL
Minimum Memory: 512K
Requires: Microsoft Works (ISPN 53150-740).
Medium: 3 1/2-inch disk
ISPN: 35175-887   **Price: $10.00**

TAXCALC SOFTWARE, INC.
ESTATE TAX PLANNER

Contains an estate planning program which follows the IRS Form 706 for both input of assumptions and calculation of results.
System: MAC, II, PLUS, SE, XL
Minimum Memory: 512K
Requires: 800K disk drive, Microsoft Excel (ISPN 53150-270).
Medium: 3 1/2-inch disk
ISPN: 79843-210   **Price: $100.00**

EZWARE CORP.
EZTAX-PLAN BUSINESS EDITION

Performs personal and corporate tax planning, and includes depreciation.
System: MAC, II, PLUS, SE, XL
Minimum Memory: 512K
Requires: Microsoft Excel (ISPN 53150-270).
Medium: 3 1/2-inch disk
ISPN: 30578-205   **Price: $295.00**

EZWARE CORP.
EZTAX-PREP 1040

Features 26 IRS forms simulated on screen. Generates IRS approved printouts, uses an IRS 1040 overlay or optional laser printing.
System: MAC, II, PLUS, SE, XL
Minimum Memory: 512K
Requires: Microsoft Multiplan (ISPN 53150-550) or Microsoft Excel (ISPN 53150-550).
Medium: 3 1/2-inch disk
ISPN: 30578-700   **Price: $99.95**

EZWARE CORP.
EZTAX-PREP 1065

Prepares partnership income tax returns. Generates and prints forms, letters, invoices and mailing labels.
System: MAC, PLUS, SE, XL
Minimum Memory: 512K
Requires: Microsoft Excel (ISPN 53150-270).
Medium: 3 1/2-inch disk
ISPN: 30578-705   **Price: $250.00**

EZWARE CORP.
EZTAX-PREP STATE SUPPLEMENT

Prepares state tax returns using Lotus 1-2-3, or Excel. Available in CA, NY or PA. Used with EZTax-PREP 1040.
System: MAC, II, PLUS, SE, XL
Minimum Memory: 512K
Requires: Microsoft Excel (ISPN 53150-270).
Medium: 3 1/2-inch disk
ISPN: 30578-750   **Price: $69.00**

HEIZER SOFTWARE
FORM 1099 PRINTER (1988)

Covers Tax Form 1099-DIV and Tax Form 1099-INT.
System: MAC, II, PLUS, SE, XL
Minimum Memory: 512K
Requires: Microsoft Excel (ISPN 53150-270).
Medium: 3 1/2-inch disk
ISPN: 35175-925   **Price: $15.00**

HEIZER SOFTWARE
LUMP SUM 5/10-YEAR AVERAGING

A two-page analysis to determine the best tax treatment of lump sum distributions from qualified pension and profit-sharing plans.
System: MAC, II, PLUS, SE, XL
Minimum Memory: 512K
Requires: Microsoft Excel (ISPN 53150-270).
Medium: 3 1/2-inch disk
ISPN: 35175-957   **Price: $10.00**

SOFTVIEW, INC.
MACINTAX FEDERAL 1988

1988 Federal income tax preparation program that utilizes the exact authorized and approved IRS forms, schedules and worksheets.
System: MAC, II, PLUS, SE, XL
Minimum Memory: 512K
Requires: 800K disk drive.
Medium: 3 1/2-inch disk
ISPN: 74106-500   **Price: $119.00**

SOFTVIEW, INC.
MACINTAX PLANNER

1987-1991 income tax planning supplement that utilizes all new tables and IRS rules under the Tax Reform Act.
System: MAC, II, PLUS, SE, XL
Minimum Memory: 512K
Requires: Two disk drives.
Medium: 3 1/2-inch disk
ISPN: 74106-510   **Price: $79.00**

SOFTVIEW, INC.

MACINTAX/TAXVIEW CALIFORNIA STATE SUPPLEMENT

1987 California state income tax preparation that works with the MacInTax Federal or TaxView.

System: MAC, II, PLUS, SE, XL
Minimum Memory: 512K
Requires: MacInTax Federal (ISPN 74106-500) or TaxView Federal (ISPN 74106-600).
Medium: 3 1/2-inch disk
ISPN: 74106-700   **Price: $65.00**

SOFTVIEW, INC.

MACINTAX/TAXVIEW NEW YORK STATE SUPPLEMENT

Contains New York State tax forms and all IRS forms and schedules formally approved by the IRS for signature and submission.

System: MAC, II, PLUS, SE, XL
Minimum Memory: 512K
Requires: MacInTax Federal (ISPN 74106-500).
Medium: 3 1/2-inch disk
ISPN: 74106-705   **Price: $65.00**

HEIZER SOFTWARE

SCHEDULE C ACCOUNTING SYSTEM

Enables sole proprietors to keep business records which meet the requirements of the Internal Revenue Service's Schedule C.

System: MAC, II, PLUS, SE, XL
Minimum Memory: 512K
Requires: Microsoft Excel (ISPN 53150-270) or Microsoft Works (ISPN 53150-740).
Medium: 3 1/2-inch disk
ISPN: 35175-936   **Price: $25.00**

HEIZER SOFTWARE

TAX PLANNER

Calculates taxes, personal exemptions and standard deduction vs. itemized deductions automatically.

System: MAC, II, PLUS, SE, XL
Minimum Memory: 512K
Requires: Microsoft Excel (ISPN 53150-270) or Microsoft Works (ISPN 53150-740).
Medium: 3 1/2-inch disk
ISPN: 35175-748   **Price: $20.00**

STACKWORKS, INC.

TAX STACKS

A Federal Income tax preparation program with a tax questionaire, forms, schedules, tax tables and worksheets. Includes HyperCard.

System: MAC, II, PLUS, SE, XL
Minimum Memory: 1024K
Requires: Two disk drives or a hard disk, ImageWriter or LaserWriter printer.
Medium: 3 1/2-inch disk
ISPN: 75627-700   **Price: $69.95**

TAXCALC SOFTWARE, INC.

TAXCALC PROFESSIONAL TAX PLANNER-MULTI YEAR

Automatically computes tax limitations. Plays 'what if,' makes changes or additions, recalculates and selects lowest tax option.

System: MAC, II, PLUS, SE, XL
Minimum Memory: 512K
Requires: Microsoft Excel (ISPN 53150-270).
Medium: 3 1/2-inch disk
ISPN: 79843-100   **Price: $395.00**

ISLAND COMPUTER SERVICES

TAXMASTER 1988

Provides spreadsheet templates containing updated IRS forms and schedules for easy tax preparation and increased understanding.

System: MAC, II, PLUS, SE, XL
Minimum Memory: 512K
Requires: Microsoft Excel (ISPN 53150-270) or Microsoft Works (ISPN 53150-740).
Medium: 3 1/2-inch disk
ISPN: 40815-600   **Price: $50.00**

ISLAND COMPUTER SERVICES

TAXMASTER PRO

Consists of the main Taxmaster template and a number of stripped down templates and simplified 1040 forms for faster processing.

System: MAC, II, PLUS, SE, XL
Minimum Memory: 512K
Requires: Microsoft Excel (ISPN 53150-270) or Microsoft Works (ISPN 53150-740).
Medium: 3 1/2-inch disk
ISPN: 40815-650   **Price: $75.00**

FUTURE VEST

TAXPLAN '89

Tax preparation package to be used with Microsoft Excel.

System: MAC, II, PLUS, SE, XL
Minimum Memory: 512K
Requires: Microsoft Excel (ISPN 53150-270).
Medium: 3 1/2-inch disk
ISPN: 91863-750   **Price: $59.00**

SOFTVIEW, INC.

TAXVIEW PLANNER (1988-1992)

Forecasts income taxes from 1987 to 1991 using the new tables and Internal Revenue Service rules under the Tax Reform Act.

System: MAC, PLUS, SE, XL
Minimum Memory: 512K
Medium: 3 1/2-inch disk
ISPN: 74106-610   **Price: $119.00**

HEIZER SOFTWARE

W-2 FORM PRINTER (1988)

Utilizes a macro to print W-2 forms, using standard data which has been entered by the user.

System: MAC, II, PLUS, SE, XL
Minimum Memory: 512K
Requires: Microsoft Excel (ISPN 53150-270).
Medium: 3 1/2-inch disk
ISPN: 35175-998   **Price: $15.00**

HEIZER SOFTWARE

ZERO COUPON TAXABLE INTEREST CALCULATOR

An Internal Revenue Service interest calculator for taxable and non-taxable zero coupon bond tax reports.

System: MAC, II, PLUS, SE, XL
Minimum Memory: 512K
Requires: Microsoft Excel (ISPN 53150-270).
Medium: 3 1/2-inch disk
ISPN: 35175-372   **Price: $15.00**

178 PRODUCTIVITY/ TIME MANAGEMENT

HEIZER SOFTWARE

ANNUAL CALENDAR

Calculates and prints a specified year's full twelve months for any year from 1905 through 2039.

System: MAC, II, PLUS, SE, XL
Minimum Memory: 512K
Requires: Microsoft Excel (ISPN 53150-270) or Microsoft Works (ISPN 35175-740).
Medium: 3 1/2-inch disk
ISPN: 35175-176   **Price: $6.00**

KINKOS ACADEMIC COURSEWARE EXCHANGE

ARABIC DATES (VER. 1.0)

A desk accessory to covert dates between Arabic and English formats.

System: MAC, II, PLUS, SE, XL
Minimum Memory: 128K
Requires: Finder (Ver. 5.3).
Medium: 3 1/2-inch disk
ISPN: 43025-060   **Price: $10.00**

HEIZER SOFTWARE

BUSINESS MONTH CALENDAR

Calculates and prints a seven-day week appointment calendar for any month from February 1904 to December 2039.

System: MAC, PLUS, SE, XL
Minimum Memory: 512K
Requires: Microsoft Excel (ISPN 53150-270).
Medium: 3 1/2-inch disk
ISPN: 35175-179   **Price: $10.00**

HEIZER SOFTWARE

BUSINESS WEEK CALENDAR

Calculates and prints a Monday through Friday appointment calendar for any month from February, 1904 through December 2039.

System: MAC, II, PLUS, SE, XL
Minimum Memory: 512K
Requires: Microsoft Excel (ISPN 53150-270).
Medium: 3 1/2-inch disk
ISPN: 35175-180   **Price: $8.00**

LEGALWARE, INC.
CALCULATOR

Assists the user in determining how many days there are between two dates.

System: MAC, II, PLUS, SE, XL
Minimum Memory: 128K
Medium: 3 1/2-inch disk
ISPN: 44063-200   **Price: $99.00**

POWER UP SOFTWARE CORP.
CALENDAR CREATOR

Lets your computer take over your calendar, ensuring that any calendar, from corporate to personal, is always neat and accurate.

System: MAC, II, PLUS, SE, XL
Minimum Memory: 512K
Requires: Graphics printer, 80-column monitor, double-sided disk drive.
Medium: 3 1/2-inch disk
ISPN: 61687-100   **Price: $59.95**

CE SOFTWARE
CALENDARMAKER (VER. 3.0)

Creates presentation-quality calendars, and includes a utility program for moving, editing, or designing icons.

System: MAC, II, PLUS, SE, XL
Minimum Memory: 512K
Requires: ImageWriter, ImageWriter II, or LaserWriter printer.
Medium: 3 1/2-inch disk
ISPN: 11725-150   **Price: $49.95**

HEIZER SOFTWARE
CEO-CORPORATE EXECUTIVE ORGANIZER

A HyperCard stack which helps maintain daily and week-at-a-glance calendars, and notifies executives of up-coming appointments.

System: MAC, II, PLUS, SE, XL
Minimum Memory: 512K
Requires: HyperCard (03900-300).
Medium: 3 1/2-inch disk
ISPN: 35175-921   **Price: $79.00**

LAYERED, INC.
FRONT DESK (VER. 6.10)

Integrates schedules for up to 30 people, then reports or projects productivity and revenue by person in any business environment.

System: MAC, II, PLUS, SE, XL
Minimum Memory: 512K
Medium: 3 1/2-inch disk
ISPN: 43760-500   **Price: $99.00**

HEIZER SOFTWARE
HYPER ALARMS

A HyperCard based reminder system which sounds an audible alarm and displays a reminder card for scheduled events.

System: MAC, II, PLUS, SE, XL
Minimum Memory: 1024K
Requires: HyperCard (ISPN 03900-300).
Medium: 3 1/2-inch disk
ISPN: 35175-429   **Price: $10.00**

HEIZER SOFTWARE
LINEAR CALENDAR

A horizontally arranged calendar for long-term planning on a five or seven-day week basis.

System: MAC, II, PLUS, SE, XL
Minimum Memory: 512K
Requires: Microsoft Excel (ISPN 53150-270) or Microsoft Works (ISPN 53150-740).
Medium: 3 1/2-inch disk
ISPN: 35175-174   **Price: $8.00**

ERICH BREITSCHWERDT + PARTNER
MACCONTROL FOR CONTROLLING

A controlling program for people dealing with a lot of data, mainly time series.

System: MAC, PLUS, SE, XL
Minimum Memory: 512K
Medium: 3 1/2-inch disk
ISPN: 29593-500   **Price: $1950.00**

GARAJO LOUIS M
MACDATE (VER. 1.3)

Calendar/appointment program, providing for daily, weekly, monthly and yearly planning.

System: MAC, II, PLUS, SE, XL
Minimum Memory: 512K
Medium: 3 1/2-inch disk
ISPN: 32308-515   **Price: $39.00**

GARAJO LOUIS M
MACDATE (VER. 1.3) (FRENCH)

Calendar and appointment program that provides for daily, weekly, monthly and yearly planning.

System: MAC, II, PLUS, SE, XL
Minimum Memory: 512K
Medium: 3 1/2-inch disk
ISPN: 32308-516   **Price: $39.00**

GARAJO LOUIS M
MACDATE (VER. 1.3) (GERMAN)

Contains a calendar and appointment program that provides for daily, weekly, monthly and yearly planning.

System: MAC, PLUS, SE, XL
Minimum Memory: 512K
Medium: 3 1/2-inch disk
ISPN: 32308-517   **Price: $39.00**

GARAJO LOUIS M
MACDATE (VER. 1.3) (ITALIAN)

Contains a calendar and appointment program that provides for daily, weekly, monthly and yearly planning.

System: MAC, II, PLUS, SE, XL
Minimum Memory: 512K
Medium: 3 1/2-inch disk
ISPN: 32308-519   **Price: $39.00**

GARAJO LOUIS M
MACDATE (VER. 1.3) (SPANISH)

Contains a calendar and appointment program that provides for daily, weekly, monthly and yearly planning.

System: MAC, II, PLUS, SE, XL
Minimum Memory: 512K
Medium: 3 1/2-inch disk
ISPN: 32308-518   **Price: $39.00**

SOFTVIEW, INC.
MACINTAX BUNDLE

Combination of MacInTax Federal tax program and The MaxInTax Planner.

System: MAC, II, PLUS, SE, XL
Minimum Memory: 512K
Medium: 3 1/2-inch disk
ISPN: 74106-520   **Price: $178.00**

ADVANCED LOGIC SYSTEMS
MIGHTY MAC

Organizes events, reminders, appointments, directory information and notes. Retrieves in alphabetical or date/time sequence.

System: MAC, II, PLUS, SE, XL
Minimum Memory:
Medium: 3 1/2-inch disk
ISPN: 01312-500   **Price: $59.95**

HEIZER SOFTWARE
MONTH/YEAR CALENDAR

A combination calendar which prints the specified month in large type and the appropriate year in small type.

System: MAC, II, PLUS, SE, XL
Minimum Memory: 512K
Requires: Microsoft Excel (ISPN 53150-270) or Microsoft Works (ISPN 53150-740).
Medium: 3 1/2-inch disk
ISPN: 35175-178   **Price: $10.00**

HEIZER SOFTWARE
MONTHLY CALENDAR

Prints an appointment calendar for any month from February 1904 to December 2039.

System: MAC, II, PLUS, SE, XL
Minimum Memory: 512K
Requires: Microsoft Excel (ISPN 53150-270) or Microsoft Works (ISPN 53150-740).
Medium: 3 1/2-inch disk
ISPN: 35175-175   **Price: $6.00**

MACSHACK ENTERPRISES
MY TIME DA

Provides access to My Time Manager data through a desk accessory.

System: MAC, PLUS, SE, XL
Minimum Memory: 128K
Medium: 3 1/2-inch disk
ISPN: 45910-140   **Price: $25.00**

MACSHACK ENTERPRISES

MY TIME MANAGER

Gives a glimpse at seven-day periods with the ability to scroll through 24 hours per day vertically or horizontally.

System: MAC
Minimum Memory: 128K
Medium: 3 1/2-inch disk
ISPN: 45910-150   **Price: $25.00**

REBUS DEVELOPMENT

PARAMETER MANAGER

Desktop analysis for collecting, storing, trending and analyzing your time, date or sample based technical data.

System: MAC, PLUS, SE, XL
Minimum Memory: 512K
Medium: 3 1/2-inch disk
ISPN: 76600-050   **Price: $495.00**

HEIZER SOFTWARE

PROJECT SCHEDULER

A horizontally arranged scheduler for long term planning on a five or seven-day week basis.

System: MAC, II, PLUS, SE, XL
Minimum Memory: 512K
Requires: Microsoft Excel (ISPN 53150-270).
Medium: 3 1/2-inch disk
ISPN: 35175-165   **Price: $15.00**

ESSEX SYSTEMS

PROJECT/TIME MANAGEMENT

Customizable project time and cost tracker designed for grant-based research projects.

System: MAC, II, PLUS, SE, XL
Minimum Memory: 512K
Medium: 3 1/2-inch disk
ISPN: 29837-500   **Price: $1850.00**

PMC TELESYSTEMS

RENDEZVOUS (VER. 2.0)

A unified electronic appointment diary system with automatic reminder and automatic task forwarding.

System: MAC, II, PLUS, SE, XL
Minimum Memory: 128K
Medium: 3 1/2-inch disk
ISPN: 61403-600   **Price: $200.00**

JAM SOFTWARE

SMART ALARMS AND APPOINTMENT DIARY

A complete desk accessory system that schedules time and sets personalized screen reminders for up to 25 users.

System: MAC, II, PLUS, SE, XL
Minimum Memory: 512K
Medium: 3 1/2-inch disk
ISPN: 41381-700   **Price: $99.00**

JAM SOFTWARE

SMART ALARMS AND APPOINTMENT DIARY

A complete desk accessory system that schedules time and sets personalized screen reminders for up to 25 users.

System: MAC, II, PLUS, SE, XL
Minimum Memory: 512K
Requires: 1-4 users.
Medium: 3 1/2-inch disk
ISPN: 41381-700   **Price: $199.00**

JAM SOFTWARE

SMART ALARMS AND APPOINTMENT DIARY

A complete desk accessory system that schedules time and sets personalized screen reminders for up to 25 users.

System: MAC, II, PLUS, SE, XL
Minimum Memory: 512K
Requires: 5-8 users.
Medium: 3 1/2-inch disk
ISPN: 41381-700   **Price: $299.00**

JAM SOFTWARE

SMART ALARMS AND APPOINTMENT DIARY

A complete desk accessory system that schedules time and sets personalized screen reminders for up to 25 users.

System: MAC, II, PLUS, SE, XL
Minimum Memory: 512K
Requires: 9-15 users.
Medium: 3 1/2-inch disk
ISPN: 41381-700   **Price: $399.00**

JAM SOFTWARE

SMART ALARMS AND APPOINTMENT DIARY

A complete desk accessory system that schedules time and sets personalized screen reminders for up to 25 users.

System: MAC, II, PLUS, SE, XL
Minimum Memory: 512K
Requires: 16-25 users.
Medium: 3 1/2-inch disk
ISPN: 41381-700   **Price: $599.00**

SOURCEVIEW SOFTWARE INT'L.

TASKMASTER

Allows user to organize time and projects. Two files are created, one called Things-To-Do-Today and one called Future Tasks.

System: MAC, II, PLUS, SE, XL
Minimum Memory: 512K
Medium: 3 1/2-inch disk
ISPN: 70675-651   **Price: $99.99**

HEIZER SOFTWARE

THREE-YEAR CALENDAR

Prints a full calendar for any three consecutive years from 1904 through 2040.

System: MAC, II, PLUS, SE, XL
Minimum Memory: 512K
Requires: Microsoft Excel (ISPN 53150-270).
Medium: 3 1/2-inch disk
ISPN: 35175-177   **Price: $12.00**

HEIZER SOFTWARE

TIME MANAGEMENT AND PRODUCTIVITY ANALYSIS

Tracks and analyzes time for up to ten work areas on a daily basis, with a month-by-month summary.

System: MAC, II, PLUS, SE, XL
Minimum Memory: 512K
Requires: Microsoft Excel (ISPN 53150-270) or Microsoft Works (ISPN 53150-740).
Medium: 3 1/2-inch disk
ISPN: 35175-008   **Price: $20.00**

HEIZER SOFTWARE

US GOVERNMENT FISCAL YEAR CALENDAR

Prints an October through September appointment calendar for any year from 1904-1905 through 2038-2039.

System: MAC, II, PLUS, SE, XL
Minimum Memory: 512K
Requires: Microsoft Excel (ISPN 53150-270) or Microsoft Works (ISPN 53150-740).
Medium: 3 1/2-inch disk
ISPN: 35175-181   **Price: $6.00**

180 PRODUCTIVITY/ TIME/CLIENT BILLING

AATRIX SOFTWARE

AATRIX TIMEMINDER (VER. 1.7)

Provides automatic time tracking of projects, tasks, meetings or other activities for billing or productivity analysis.

System: MAC, II, PLUS, SE, XL
Minimum Memory: 512K
Requires: Two 800K disk drives or one 800K disk drive and a hard disk.
Medium: 3 1/2-inch disk
ISPN: 00281-100   **Price: $199.00**

LAKE AVE. SOFTWARE

ASSISTANT CONTROLLER SERIES-PROF.TIME & INVOICING

Allows the user to monitor staff time and expense charges by project and client number.

System: MAC, II, PLUS, SE, XL
Minimum Memory: 512K
Medium: 3 1/2-inch disk
ISPN: 43418-375   **Price: $495.00**

LAYERED, INC.

INSIGHT EXPERT TIME BILLING (VER. 2.00)

Tracks billable time and produces detailed invoices.

System: MAC, II, PLUS, SE, XL
Minimum Memory: 1024K
Requires: Hard disk, 800K disk drive and ImageWriter II, ImageWriter LQ, LaserWriter Plus or LaserWriter II.
Medium: 3 1/2-inch disk
ISPN: 43760-615   **Price: $695.00**

LAKE AVE. SOFTWARE

MULTI COMPANY-PROFESSIONAL TIME & INVOICING

Allows monitoring of staff time and expense charges by project/client number.

System: MAC, II, PLUS, SE, XL
Minimum Memory: 512K
Medium: 3 1/2-inch disk
ISPN: 43418-868   **Price: $695.00**

SATORI SOFTWARE

PROJECT BILLING (VER. 1.56)

Designed for ad agencies, designers, architects, engineers and other professionals that bill for time and expense.

System: MAC, II, PLUS, SE, XL
Minimum Memory: 512K
Requires: 800K disk drive.
Medium: 3 1/2-inch disk
ISPN: 68024-825   **Price: $595.00**

CHANG LABORATORIES, INC.

RAGS TO RICHES-PROFESSIONAL BILLING (VER. 3.0)

Time and Cost billing for lawyers, CPA's, architects, engineers, designers, advertising agencies, photographers, and other services.

System: MAC, II, PLUS, SE, XL
Minimum Memory: 512K
Medium: 3 1/2-inch disk
ISPN: 12200-775   **Price: $399.95**

SBT CORP.

SBT DPROFESSIONAL-COMPILED (VER. 6.10)

Provides time and billing accounting with a balance forward accounts receivable. Features interactive data entry and query.

System: MAC, II, PLUS, SE, XL
Minimum Memory: 512K
Medium: 3 1/2-inch disk
ISPN: 68057-065   **Price: $295.00**

SBT CORP.

SBT DPROFESSIONAL-STANDARD (VER. 6.10)

Performs time and billing functions with a balance forward accounts receivable and features interactive data entry and query.

System: MAC, II, PLUS, SE, XL
Minimum Memory: 512K
Medium: 3 1/2-inch disk
ISPN: 68057-060   **Price: $395.00**

EXCEIVER CORP.

TIME BILLING (VER. 1.5)

A comprehensive and versatile time-billing and cost/billing, tracking and analysis system for professionals.

System: MAC, II, PLUS, SE, XL
Minimum Memory: 512K
Requires: Two disk drives or one disk drive and a hard disk.
Medium: 3 1/2-inch disk
ISPN: 91574-600   **Price: $950.00**

EXCEIVER CORP.

TIME BILLING AND ACCOUNTING

A comprehensive and versatile time-billing and cost/billing, tracking and analysis system with accounting. For professionals.

System: MAC, II, PLUS, SE, XL
Minimum Memory: 512K
Requires: Two disk drives or a hard disk.
Medium: 3 1/2-inch disk
ISPN: 91574-601   **Price: $2130.00**

HEIZER SOFTWARE

TIME BILLING LOG AND INVOICE

Keeps track of total hours for professionals who bill clients based on time.

System: MAC, II, PLUS, SE, XL
Minimum Memory: 512K
Requires: Microsoft Excel (ISPN 53150-270).
Medium: 3 1/2-inch disk
ISPN: 35175-162   **Price: $12.00**

HEIZER SOFTWARE

TIMECARDS

Tracks use of the computer by user, client, task and software. Calculates charges based on user rates and produces reports.

System: MAC, II, PLUS, SE, XL
Minimum Memory: 1024K
Requires: HyperCard (ISPN 03900-300).
Medium: 3 1/2-inch disk
ISPN: 35175-432   **Price: $75.00**

---

184 PRODUCTIVITY/ TYPING TUTORIALS

SPINNAKER SOFTWARE

BETTER WORKING-TYPING MADE EASY

Teaches touch typing by beginning with simple skills and progressing to more difficult exercises.

System: MAC, II, PLUS, SE, XL
Minimum Memory: 512K
Medium: 3 1/2-inch disk
ISPN: 75300-700   **Price: $49.95**

PALANTIR, INC.

MACTYPE

Interactive graphic, mouse driven, touch typing tutorial designed for Kindergarten children to adults.

System: MAC, II, PLUS, SE, XL
Minimum Memory: 128K
Medium: 3 1/2-inch disk
ISPN: 59624-075   **Price: $59.95**

MINDSCAPE, INC.

MASTERTYPE

Teaches typing and improves keyboard skills. Uses arcade game action and includes 18 levels from letters to words to symbols.

System: MAC, II, PLUS, SE, XL
Minimum Memory: 512K
Requires: Lab pack.
Medium: 3 1/2-inch disk
ISPN: 54375-029   **Price: $79.90**

MINDSCAPE, INC.

MASTERTYPE

Teaches typing and improves keyboard skills. Uses arcade game action and includes 18 levels from letters to words to symbols.

System: MAC, II, PLUS, SE, XL
Minimum Memory: 128K
Medium: 3 1/2-inch disk
ISPN: 54375-029   **Price: $39.95**

ELECTRONIC ARTS

MAVIS BEACON TEACHES TYPING

Teaches typing skills with lessons from a database of interesting passages.

System: MAC, II, PLUS, SE, XL
Minimum Memory: 512K
Medium: 3 1/2-inch disk
ISPN: 28512-013   **Price: $49.95**

BRODERBUND SOFTWARE, INC.

TYPE!

Grades 5-12: Teaches typing skills through the use of real words and sentences. Saves and prints out progress reports.

System: MAC, II, PLUS, SE, XL
Minimum Memory: 512K
Requires: Consumer edition.
Medium: 3 1/2-inch disk
ISPN: 08850-180   **Price: $29.95**

BRODERBUND SOFTWARE, INC.

TYPE!

Grades 5-12: Teaches typing skills through the use of real words and sentences. Saves and prints out progress reports.

System: MAC, II, PLUS, SE, XL
Minimum Memory: 512K
Requires: School edition.
Medium: 3 1/2-inch disk
ISPN: 08850-180   **Price: $39.95**

BRODERBUND SOFTWARE, INC.

TYPE!

Grades 5-12: Teaches typing skills through the use of real words and sentences. Saves and prints out progress reports.

System: MAC, II, PLUS, SE, XL
Minimum Memory: 512K
Requires: Lab Pack.
Medium: 3 1/2-inch disk
ISPN: 08850-180   **Price: $49.95**

INDIVIDUAL SOFTWARE, INC.
TYPING INSTRUCTOR ENCORE

Uses the computer's graphics capabilities to teach typing skills in a self-paced manner.

System: MAC, II, PLUS, SE, XL
Minimum Memory: 512K
Medium: 3 1/2-inch disk
ISPN: 37275-400   **Price: $49.95**

MACTRONICS
TYPING TEACHER (VER. 1.1)

Designed for anyone wanting to develop or improve typing skills. Counts words, speed and errors.

System: MAC, II, PLUS, SE, XL
Minimum Memory: 512K
Requires: 400K disk drive.
Medium: 3 1/2-inch disk
ISPN: 93904-701   **Price: $29.95**

SIMON AND SCHUSTER
ELECTRONIC PUBLISHING GROUP
TYPING TUTOR IV

Adapts lessons to an individual's specific typing skills and learning needs. Picks up where Typing Tutor III leaves off.

System: MAC, PLUS, SE, XL
Minimum Memory: 128K
Medium: 3 1/2-inch disk
ISPN: 70387-750   **Price: $59.95**

187 PRODUCTIVITY/ WORD PROCESSING

GLPS PRODUCTS
ABTOP III

Allows dual-language word processing in modern Russian and English with Cyrillic and Latin fonts.

System: MAC, II, PLUS, SE, XL
Minimum Memory: 512K
Medium: 3 1/2-inch disk
ISPN: 32956-100   **Price: $40.00**

EASTERN LANGUAGE SYSTEMS
ALKAATIB

Provides an Arabic and Persian right to left word processor.

System: MAC, II, PLUS, SE, XL
Minimum Memory: 512K
Medium: 3 1/2-inch disk
ISPN: 04837-050   **Price: $199.00**

HABA/ARRAYS SYSTEMS, INC.
BUSINESS LETTERS

Contains fifty professionally written, pre-defined letter and memo formats.

System: MAC, II, PLUS, SE, XL
Minimum Memory: 512K
Medium: 3 1/2-inch disk
ISPN: 33987-015   **Price: $29.95**

JAPANESE LANGUAGE SERVICES
EGWORD (VER. 3.0)

A Japanese word processing program allowing full text entry access of all written components of the language.

System: MAC, II, PLUS, SE, XL
Minimum Memory: 2048K
Requires: Hard disk.
Medium: 3 1/2-inch disk
ISPN: 20012-300   **Price: $499.00**

VIKING TECHNOLOGIES
EZ TYPER

Turns the Mac into a high powered memory typewriter to produce notes, letters, address envelopes, fill out forms and memos.

System: MAC, II, PLUS, SE, XL
Minimum Memory:
Medium: 3 1/2-inch disk
ISPN: 85231-250   **Price: $19.95**

WU CORP.
FEIMA-P (VER. 4.0)

A Chinese word processing system designed for those who know Chinese. Offers all standard word processing features.

System: MAC, PLUS, SE, XL
Minimum Memory: 1024K
Requires: Two 800K disk drives or hard disk.
Medium: 3 1/2-inch disk
ISPN: 87029-080   **Price: $585.00**

WU CORP.
FEIMA-S (VER. 2.8)

A Chinese word processing system designed specifically for students who are learning Chinese.

System: PLUS, SE
Minimum Memory: 1024K
Requires: Two 800K disk drives or a hard disk.
Medium: 3 1/2-inch disk
ISPN: 87029-100   **Price: $295.00**

WU CORP.
FEIMA-S EDUCATIONAL PROGRAM (VER. 2.8)

A Chinese word processing system designed to offer productivity and economy to schools that teach Chinese.

System: MAC, PLUS, SE, XL
Minimum Memory: 1024K
Requires: Two 800K disk drives or hard disk.
Medium: 3 1/2-inch disk
ISPN: 87029-105   **Price: $2000.00**

KNOWLEDGE ENGINEERING
JUSTTEXT (VER. 1.2)

A professional level word processor and page makeup program that generates PostScript output.

System: MAC, II, PLUS, SE, XL
Minimum Memory: 512K
Requires: PostScript printer.
Medium: 3 1/2-inch disk
ISPN: 93342-300   **Price: $395.00**

CLARIS CORP.
MACWRITE II (VER. 1.0)

Combines all of the essential tools needed for professional quality word processing with original MacWrite accessibility.

System: MAC, II, PLUS, SE, XL
Minimum Memory: 1024K
Medium: 3 1/2-inch disk
ISPN: 12784-530   **Price: $259.00**

MICROSOFT CORP.
MICROSOFT WORD (VER. 4.0)

A powerful word processor featuring outlining, indexing, generation of a table of contents, column manipulation and more.

System: MAC, PLUS, SE, XL
Minimum Memory: 512K
Requires: 800K disk drive.
Medium: 3 1/2-inch disk
ISPN: 53150-732   **Price: $395.00**

MICROSOFT CORP.
MICROSOFT WRITE

Creates straightforward, lightly formatted documents with word processing capabilities. Includes an 80000 word spell checker.

System: MAC, II, PLUS, SE, XL
Minimum Memory: 512K
Medium: 3 1/2-inch disk
ISPN: 53150-800   **Price: $175.00**

ACCESS TECHNOLOGY, INC.
ACCESS/MINDWORK DIVISION
MINDWRITE (VER. 2.0)

Outliner and integrated word processor that allows a document to develop naturally from ideas to polished documents.

System: MAC, II, PLUS, SE, XL
Minimum Memory: 512K
Requires: Two 800K disk drives or a hard disk.
Medium: 3 1/2-inch disk
ISPN: 00506-500   **Price: $195.00**

ACCESS TECHNOLOGY, INC.
ACCESS/MINDWORK DIVISION
MINDWRITEEXPRESS

Provides integrated outlining with application-to-application connectivity solutions between PC's, mini computers and mainframes.

System: MAC, II, PLUS, SE, XL
Minimum Memory: 512K
Requires: Two 800K disk drives or a hard disk, network.
Medium: 3 1/2-inch disk
ISPN: 00506-510   **Price: $250.00**

PARAGON CONCEPTS, INC.
NISUS (VER. 1.01)

A full-featured text editing package that includes integrated graphics tools.

System: MAC, II, PLUS, SE, XL
Minimum Memory: 512K
Medium: 3 1/2-inch disk
ISPN: 59740-100   **Price: $395.00**

WORKING SOFTWARE, INC.
QUICKLETTER (VER.1.01)

A desk accessory based word processing program designed for writing letters and printing envelopes.

System: MAC, II, PLUS, SE, XL
Minimum Memory: 512K
Requires: 800K disk drive.
Medium: 3 1/2-inch disk
ISPN: 92154-600   **Price: $124.95**

DAVKA CORP.
RAV-K'TAV (VER. 1.2)

Provides bilingual, bidirectional Hebrew/English word processing with both English and Hebrew fonts.

System: MAC, II, PLUS, SE, XL
Minimum Memory: 512K
Medium: 3 1/2-inch disk
ISPN: 91205-670   **Price: $350.00**

PREFERRED PUBLISHERS, INC.
VANTAGE

A full-featured word processor that includes macros, an 80,000 word spell checker and allows up to 16 windows to be open at once.

System: MAC, II, PLUS, SE, XL
Minimum Memory: 128K
Medium: 3 1/2-inch disk
ISPN: 61825-100   **Price: $99.95**

ADVANCED LOGIC SYSTEMS
WORD HANDLER FOR THE MACINTOSH

Incorporates the easy-to-use features of MacWrite with the power of Microsoft Word.

System: MAC, II, PLUS, SE, XL
Minimum Memory: 512K
Medium: 3 1/2-inch disk
ISPN: 01312-760   **Price: $79.95**

NEW HORIZONS SOFTWARE
WORDMAKER (VER. 1.0)

Features text flow around graphics, print merge, color text and graphics output, and a 100,000 word spelling checker.

System: MAC, PLUS, SE, XL
Minimum Memory: 512K
Medium: 3 1/2-inch disk
ISPN: 56703-650   **Price: $124.95**

WORDPERFECT CORP.
WORDPERFECT FOR THE MACINTOSH (VER. 1.0.2)

Provides word processing with a speller, thesaurus, macros, merge capability, and automatic footnoting and outlining.

System: MAC, II, PLUS, SE, XL
Minimum Memory: 512K
Requires: 800K disk drive.
Medium: 3 1/2-inch disk
ISPN: 68012-615   **Price: $395.00**

T/MAKER CO.
WRITENOW MACINTOSH (VER. 2.0)

Provides WYSIWYG editing, embedded graphics, spelling checker, four-column capability, and font sizes up to 127 points.

System: MAC, PLUS, SE, XL
Minimum Memory: 512K
Requires: 800K disk drive.
Medium: 3 1/2-inch disk
ISPN: 79465-900   **Price: $195.00**

---

188 PRODUCTIVITY/ WORD PROCESSING SUPPORT

1ST DESK SYSTEMS, INC.
1STMERGE (VER. 3.5)

Mail Merge and file handling system. Works as a stand alone or with 1ST file. Outputs data to any word processor supporting Macwrite.

System: MAC, II, PLUS, SE, XL
Minimum Memory: 128K
Medium: 3 1/2-inch disk
ISPN: 81083-595   **Price: $95.00**

1ST DESK SYSTEMS, INC.
1STMERGE (VER. 4.0)

Provides a full-featured list manager and mail merge program.

System: MAC, II, PLUS, SE, XL
Minimum Memory: 512K
Medium: 3 1/2-inch disk
ISPN: 81083-596   **Price: $195.00**

DENEBA SOFTWARE
BIGTHESAURUS (VER. 2.0)

Provides an electronic version of Merriam-Webster's Thesaurus with 1400000 synonyms, antonyms, related and contrasting words.

System: MAC, II, PLUS, SE, XL
Minimum Memory: 512K
Requires: 800K disk drive.
Medium: 3 1/2-inch disk
ISPN: 24765-150   **Price: $99.95**

INNOVISION
CALLIOPE PLUS (VER. 2.0)

A tool for the capture and refinement of ideas of all kinds. Uses clustering and hypertext.

System: MAC, II, PLUS, SE, XL
Minimum Memory: 512K
Medium: 3 1/2-inch disk
ISPN: 38531-200   **Price: $99.00**

MEDINA SOFTWARE, INC.
CORRECTAMENT (VER. 2.0)

A Spanish spelling dictionary that works with Microsoft Word and its main dictionary. Contains 100000 words.

System: MAC, PLUS, SE, XL
Minimum Memory: 512K
Requires: Microsoft Word (ISPN 53150-732), 800K disk drive.
Medium: 3 1/2-inch disk
ISPN: 48842-205   **Price: $32.95**

ADVANCED SOFTWARE, INC.
DOCUCOMP (VER. 1.12)

Compares any two versions of a word processor or ASCII document and shows all the changes made going from one version to the other.

System: MAC, II, PLUS, SE, XL
Minimum Memory: 512K
Medium: 3 1/2-inch disk
ISPN: 01446-200   **Price: $159.95**

LEGALWARE, INC.
DOCUMENT COMPARE

Allows the user to compare any two MacWrite, Microsoft Word, or ASCII documents and allows output that shows modifications.

System: MAC, II, PLUS, SE, XL
Minimum Memory: 512K
Medium: 3 1/2-inch disk
ISPN: 44063-210   **Price: $99.00**

AEGIS DEVELOPMENT, INC.
DOUG CLAPP'S WORD TOOLS (VER. 1.02)

Takes MacWrite, Word, or text files and runs them through an inter- active analysis for style, punctuation, word counts and other data.

System: MAC, II, PLUS, SE, XL
Minimum Memory:
Medium: 3 1/2-inch disk
ISPN: 01718-150   **Price: $79.95**

TECHNOLOGY TRAINING ASSOCIATES
ELECTRONIC ENGLISH HANDBOOK (THE)

Enables users to look up English rules in a window while in a word processing program. Covers punctuation, mechanics, usage and more.

System: MAC, II, PLUS, SE, XL
Minimum Memory: 128K
Medium: 3 1/2-inch disk
ISPN: 80612-200   **Price: $29.95**

HABA/ARRAYS SYSTEMS, INC.
HABA/PERSONAL PUBLISHER

Contains an integrated desktop publishing system with enhanced word processing including full graphics, paint and draw.

System: MAC, II, PLUS, XL
Minimum Memory: 512K
Medium: 3 1/2-inch disk
ISPN: 33987-075   **Price: $275.00**

SPINNAKER SOFTWARE

HAYDEN SPELLER

Contains 97% of the most-used words in the English language and an add your own 'personal dictionary' feature.

System: MAC, PLUS, SE, XL
Minimum Memory: 512K
Requires: MacWrite (ISPN 12784-530).
Medium: 3 1/2-inch disk
ISPN: 75300-173   **Price: $39.95**

HYPERPRESS PUBLISHING CORP

HYPERSPELL

Provides a spelling verifier and corrector for HyperCard.

System: MAC, II, PLUS, SE, XL
Minimum Memory: 1024K
Requires: HyperCard (ISPN 03900-300).
Medium: 3 1/2-inch disk
ISPN: 36737-250   **Price: $79.95**

DATAPAK SOFTWARE, INC.

LIBERTY SPELL-II

A spell-checker that checks for spelling errors as you type plus can check completed documents and works with most word processors.

System: MAC, PLUS, SE, XL
Minimum Memory: 512K
Medium: 3 1/2-inch disk
ISPN: 23762-200   **Price: $49.00**

WORKING SOFTWARE, INC.

LOOKUP (VER. 1.0C)

Provides a spell checker that can be accessed at any time from any MacIntosh program.

System: MAC, II, PLUS, SE, XL
Minimum Memory: 512K
Requires: 800K disk drive.
Medium: 3 1/2-inch disk
ISPN: 92154-757   **Price: $59.95**

LONDON PRIDE, INC.

LPTEXT

Creates effects and allows user to modify postscript programs to display customized graphics.

System: MAC, II, PLUS, SE, XL
Minimum Memory: 512K
Requires: Pagemaker (ISPN 02226-700), Ready Set Go! (ISPN 46612-495), Microsoft Word (ISPN 53150-732) or any other page makeup program.
Medium: 3 1/2-inch disk
ISPN: 45503-200   **Price: $99.00**

ENTERSET

MACGAS (VER. 1.06)

Spelling checker, thesaurus, glossary and word-lookup. 80,000 word dictionary, 5,000 synonyms and antonyms.

System: MAC, II, PLUS, SE, XL
Minimum Memory: 512K
Requires: 800K disk drive.
Medium: 3 1/2-inch disk
ISPN: 29481-400   **Price: $99.00**

LINGUIST'S SOFTWARE, INC.

MACGREEK NEW TESTAMENT DICTIONARY (VER. 2.0)

Exhaustive spell checking dictionary that checks all forms of all words occurring in the Greek New Testament.

System: MAC, II, PLUS, SE, XL
Minimum Memory: 512K
Requires: Microsoft Word (ISPN 53150-732).
Medium: 3 1/2-inch disk
ISPN: 44825-805   **Price: $49.95**

LINGUIST'S SOFTWARE, INC.

MACKANJI (VER. 2.0)

A Romaji based Japanese input system and Japanese font for English systems, with Kanji Talk 2.0, MiniWriter and a system switcher.

System: MAC, II, PLUS, SE, XL
Minimum Memory: 1024K
Requires: PostScript printer.
Medium: 3 1/2-inch disk
ISPN: 44825-165   **Price: $99.95**

AVENUE SOFTWARE, INC.

MACKEYMELEON (VER. 1.6)

Allows users to re-assign any letter to another key and to make superimposed two key combinations.

System: MAC, PLUS, SE, XL
Minimum Memory: 512K
Medium: 3 1/2-inch disk
ISPN: 06418-500   **Price: $69.95**

LEXPERTISE, USA, INC.

MACPROOF (VER. 3.2)

A desk accessory that detects errors in spelling, style and usage. Works with most major word processors.

System: MAC, II, PLUS, SE, XL
Minimum Memory: 1024K
Medium: 3 1/2-inch disk
ISPN: 44474-100   **Price: $195.00**

MAINSTAY

MARKUP (VER. 1.0)

Enables several users to simultaneously comment on a document electronically. Includes tools to rewrite, annotate and highlight.

System: MAC, II, PLUS, SE, XL
Minimum Memory: 1024K
Medium: 3 1/2-inch disk
ISPN: 46041-566   **Price: $245.00**

MAINSTAY

MARKUP (VER. 1.0)

Enables several users to simultaneously comment on a document electronically. Includes tools to rewrite, annotate and highlight.

System: MAC, II, PLUS, SE, XL
Minimum Memory: 1024K
Requires: Two users.
Medium: 3 1/2-inch disk
ISPN: 46041-566   **Price: $495.00**

MAINSTAY

MARKUP (VER. 1.0)

Enables several users to simultaneously comment on a document electronically. Includes tools to rewrite, annotate and highlight.

System: MAC, II, PLUS, SE, XL
Minimum Memory: 1024K
Requires: Three to five users.
Medium: 3 1/2-inch disk
ISPN: 46041-566   **Price: $995.00**

LAYERED, INC.

NOTES FOR PAGEMAKER

Provides help, advice, tips and templates to make learning and using PageMaker easier for both beginners and experts.

System: MAC, II, PLUS, SE, XL
Minimum Memory: 512K
Requires: PageMaker (ISPN 2226-700).
Medium: 3 1/2-inch disk
ISPN: 43760-725   **Price: $79.00**

HEIZER SOFTWARE

OUTLINING TEMPLATE

An outline format system with a special combination of tabs for use in word processor documents.

System: MAC, II, PLUS, SE, XL
Minimum Memory: 512K
Requires: Microsoft Works (ISPN 53150-740).
Medium: 3 1/2-inch disk
ISPN: 35175-905   **Price: $3.00**

ENTERSET

QUICKWORD

Time-saving shorthand expander that allows users to type abbreviations for common and/or lengthy phrases. A desk accessory.

System: MAC, II, PLUS, SE, XL
Minimum Memory: 128K
Medium: 3 1/2-inch disk
ISPN: 29481-750   **Price: $59.00**

OLDUVAI CORP.

READ-IT! OCR (VER. 2.0)

Provides a trainable optical character recognition program that converts scanned images into text files.

System: MAC, II, PLUS, SE, XL
Minimum Memory: 1024K
Requires: Scanner.
Medium: 3 1/2-inch disk
ISPN: 57812-200   **Price: $395.00**

OLDUVAI CORP.

READ-IT! TS

Converts Thunderscan files into text files.

System: MAC, II, PLUS, SE, XL
Minimum Memory: 1024K
Medium: 3 1/2-inch disk
ISPN: 57812-100   **Price: $149.00**

FOR MORE DETAILED INFORMATION, CALL (412) 746-MENU

HEIZER SOFTWARE
SEARCH AND REPLACE

Performs global search and replace for whole or partial words in a HyperCard stack.

System: MAC, II, PLUS, SE, XL
Minimum Memory: 1024K
Requires: HyperCard (ISPN 03900-300).
Medium: 3 1/2-inch disk
ISPN: 35175-096 **Price: $12.00**

SENSIBLE SOFTWARE, INC.
SENSIBLE GRAMMAR

Provides a proofreading program designed to check word processing files for common writing errors.

System: MAC, II, PLUS, SE, XL
Minimum Memory: 512K
Medium: 3 1/2-inch disk
ISPN: 69200-450 **Price: $99.95**

HEIZER SOFTWARE
SPECIAL CHARTING

Uses the Draw option of Microsoft Works word processor to plot data when both X and Y vary over wide ranges.

System: MAC, II, PLUS, SE, XL
Minimum Memory: 512K
Requires: Microsoft Works (ISPN 53150-740).
Medium: 3 1/2-inch disk
ISPN: 35175-903 **Price: $6.00**

CHAMPION SWIFTWARE
SPELLING CHAMPION

Provides a spelling checker for MacWrite and Microsoft Word.

System: MAC, II, PLUS, SE, XL
Minimum Memory: 512K
Requires: MacWrite (ISPN 12784-530) or Microsoft Word (ISPN 53150-732).
Medium: 3 1/2-inch disk
ISPN: 12178-600 **Price: $39.95**

DENEBA SOFTWARE
SPELLING COACH (VER. 3.0)

Provides an interactive spelling and batch file spelling desk accessory.

System: MAC, II, PLUS, SE, XL
Minimum Memory: 512K
Medium: 3 1/2-inch disk
ISPN: 24765-610 **Price: $99.95**

DENEBA SOFTWARE
SPELLING COACH PROFESSIONAL (VER. 3.0)

Provides spelling verification, on-line reference, hyphenation, and a thesaurus and dictionary with definitions.

System: MAC, II, PLUS, SE, XL
Minimum Memory: 512K
Requires: 800K disk drive.
Medium: 3 1/2-inch disk
ISPN: 24765-600 **Price: $99.95**

WORKING SOFTWARE, INC.
SPELLSWELL (VER. 2.0G)

A spelling checker for the Macintosh that reads MacWrite, ACTA, Microsoft Word, Thinktank, More, Jazz, Quickletter and Text Files.

System: MAC, II, PLUS, SE, XL
Minimum Memory: 512K
Requires: 800K disk drive.
Medium: 3 1/2-inch disk
ISPN: 92154-750 **Price: $74.95**

WORKING SOFTWARE, INC.
SPELLSWELL MEDICAL DICTIONARY

Medical dictionary for Spellswell Spelling checker, contains over 40,000 unique entries.

System: MAC, II, PLUS, SE, XL
Minimum Memory: 512K
Requires: 800K disk drive. Spellswell (ISPN 92154-750).
Medium: 3 1/2-inch disk
ISPN: 92154-755 **Price: $99.95**

HEIZER SOFTWARE
STICKY BUTTONS TUTORIAL

Teaches users how to attach buttons to words in scrolling text fields.

System: MAC, II, PLUS, SE, XL
Minimum Memory: 1024K
Requires: HyperCard (ISPN 03900-300).
Medium: 3 1/2-inch disk
ISPN: 35175-080 **Price: $8.00**

HEIZER SOFTWARE
STRIPPER BUTTON

Strips trailing and leading quotes, double quotes, trailing and leading spaces from data.

System: MAC, II, PLUS, SE, XL
Minimum Memory: 1024K
Requires: HyperCard (ISPN 03900-300).
Medium: 3 1/2-inch disk
ISPN: 35175-088 **Price: $12.00**

TOOL MASTERS, LTD./DIV OF INT'L. TELESYSTEMS CORP.
TEXSYS

Track and record all your text file revisions.

System: MAC, II, PLUS, SE, XL
Minimum Memory: 512K
Medium: 3 1/2-inch disk
ISPN: 82278-750 **Price: $69.00**

ELECTRONIC ARTS
THUNDER (VER. 1.1)

Contains a real-time 50000 word spelling checker that corrects spelling as it is typed, or an entire document when finished.

System: MAC, II, PLUS, SE, XL
Minimum Memory: 512K
Medium: 3 1/2-inch disk
ISPN: 28512-037 **Price: $49.95**

LINGUIST'S SOFTWARE, INC.
TLG MACGREEK CONVERTER AND TEXT EDITOR (VER. 1.1)

Converts any Greek text in the Thesauras Linguae Graecai into Super Greek. Includes the text editor, 'Edit'.

System: MAC, II, PLUS, SE, XL
Minimum Memory: 512K
Requires: MacGreek (ISPN 44825-580), LaserGreek (ISPN 44825-50), or MacGreek, Hebrew and Phonetics (ISPN 44825-590).
Medium: 3 1/2-inch disk
ISPN: 44825-710 **Price: $79.95**

MAINSTAY
TYPENOW

Turns the Macintosh and ImageWriter into a memory typewriter, doing jobs that are difficult to do with a word processor.

System: MAC, II, PLUS, SE, XL
Minimum Memory: 128K
Medium: 3 1/2-inch disk
ISPN: 46041-750 **Price: $39.95**

MICROLYTICS, INC.
WORD FINDER (VER. 4.0)

A 220,000-synonym, highly compatible electronic thesaurus.

System: MAC, II, PLUS, SE, XL
Minimum Memory: 512K
Medium: 3 1/2-inch disk
ISPN: 52573-850 **Price: $59.95**

LUNDEEN AND ASSOCIATES
WORKSPLUS SPELL (VER. 2.0)

Piggybacks on top of Microsoft Works providing additional commands for spell checking, glossary substitution and hyphenation.

System: MAC, II, PLUS, SE, XL
Minimum Memory: 512K
Requires: Microsoft Works (ISPN 53150-740).
Medium: 3 1/2-inch disk
ISPN: 45593-800 **Price: $79.95**

---

202 EDUCATION/ ADDITION/ SUBTRACTION

QUEUE
HOW MANY

Introduces young children to counting, number recognition, addition and subtraction.

System: MAC, II, PLUS, SE, XL
Minimum Memory: 128K
Medium: 3 1/2-inch disk
ISPN: 64387-355 **Price: $34.95**

QUEUE

MACFLASH

Provides a simulation of traditional flashcard techniques to help children learn basic arithmetic facts. Grades 1-2.

System: MAC, II, PLUS, SE, XL
Minimum Memory: 128K
Medium: 3 1/2-inch disk
ISPN: 64387-490   **Price: $59.95**

MINDPLAY

MATH MAGIC

Grades K-4: Provides games and guided practice that build skill with numbers and increase eye/hand coordination.

System: MAC, II, PLUS, SE, XL
Minimum Memory: 512K
Requires: Home and school version.
Medium: 3 1/2-inch disk
ISPN: 54362-500   **Price: $49.99**

MINDPLAY

MATH MAGIC

Grades K-4: Provides games and guided practice that build skill with numbers and increase eye/hand coordination.

System: MAC, II, PLUS, SE, XL
Minimum Memory: 512K
Requires: Lab pack (includes 6 disks).
Medium: 3 1/2-inch disk
ISPN: 54362-500   **Price: $120.00**

204 EDUCATION/ ADMINISTRATION

HEIZER SOFTWARE

ATTENDANCE RECORD

Tracks student attendance and overall class attendance.

System: MAC, II, PLUS, SE, XL
Minimum Memory: 512K
Requires: Microsoft Excel (ISPN 53150-270) or Microsoft Works (ISPN 53150-740).
Medium: 3 1/2-inch disk
ISPN: 35175-229   **Price: $10.00**

KINKOS ACADEMIC COURSEWARE EXCHANGE

BRAINCHILD GRADE

An electronic gradebook designed for educators at all grade levels. Replaces conventional paper-based gradebook.

System: MAC, II, PLUS, SE, XL
Minimum Memory: 512K
Requires: 800K disk drive, Finder (Ver. 5.2 or later).
Medium: 3 1/2-inch disk
ISPN: 43025-100   **Price: $25.00**

RIGHT TRACK SOFTWARE, INC.

CORPORATE REGISTRAR

Complete student record keeping for business training.

System: MAC, II, PLUS, SE, XL
Minimum Memory: 512K
Medium: 3 1/2-inch disk
ISPN: 66475-200   **Price: $2995.00**

CHANCERY SOFTWARE

CSL ATTENDANCE

Provides both the reports that administrators require and efficiently highlights attendance trends.

System: MAC, II, PLUS, SE, XL
Minimum Memory: 1024K
Requires: Single-user.
Medium: 3 1/2-inch disk
ISPN: 12182-102   **Price: $750.00**

CHANCERY SOFTWARE

CSL ATTENDANCE

Provides both the reports that administrators require and efficiently highlights attendance trends.

System: MAC, II, PLUS, SE, XL
Minimum Memory: 1024K
Requires: Multi-user.
Medium: 3 1/2-inch disk
ISPN: 12182-102   **Price: $900.00**

CHANCERY SOFTWARE

CSL MARKS

Gradebook program for individual teachers that produces comprehensive grade reports

System: MAC, II, PLUS, SE, XL
Minimum Memory: 1024K
Requires: Single-user. Multi-user.
Medium: 3 1/2-inch disk
ISPN: 12182-104   **Price: $375.00**

CHANCERY SOFTWARE

CSL REPORTS CARDS AND TRANSCRIPTS

Transcripts, honor roles, failing lists, class rankings, mailing labels and GPA's can be produced at any time.

System: MAC, II, PLUS, SE, XL
Minimum Memory: 1024K
Requires: Single-user. CSL Attendance (ISPN 12182-102) and CSL Marks (ISPN 12182-104).
Medium: 3 1/2-inch disk
ISPN: 12182-103   **Price: $500.00**

CHANCERY SOFTWARE

CSL REPORTS CARDS AND TRANSCRIPTS

Transcripts, honor roles, failing lists, class rankings, mailing labels and GPA's can be produced at any time.

System: MAC, II, PLUS, SE, XL
Minimum Memory: 1024K
Requires: Multi-user. CSL Attendance (ISPN 12182-102) and CSL Marks (ISPN 12182-104.
Medium: 3 1/2-inch disk
ISPN: 12182-103   **Price: $600.00**

CHANCERY SOFTWARE

CSL SCHEDULING

Schedules students in up to eight terms at one time.

System: MAC, II, PLUS, SE, XL
Minimum Memory: 1024K
Requires: Single-user.
Medium: 3 1/2-inch disk
ISPN: 12182-101   **Price: $750.00**

CHANCERY SOFTWARE

CSL SCHEDULING

Schedules students in up to eight terms at one time.

System: MAC, II, PLUS, SE, XL
Minimum Memory: 1024K
Requires: Multi-user.
Medium: 3 1/2-inch disk
ISPN: 12182-101   **Price: $900.00**

DA POMA, INC.

DA POMA GB-ELEMENTARY VERSION

Allows a teacher to record and calculate grades. Scores can be weighted individually or by type, grade and standard break points.

System: MAC, II, PLUS, SE, XL
Minimum Memory: 128K
Requires: Two 400K drives or one 800k drive.
Medium: 3 1/2-inch disk
ISPN: 22125-225   **Price: $75.00**

DA POMA, INC.

DA POMA GB-UNIVERSITY VERSION

Gradebook management program designed for teachers and professors at the university level who have classes up to 350 students.

System: MAC, II, PLUS, SE, XL
Minimum Memory: 512K
Requires: Two 400K drives or one 800k drive.
Medium: 3 1/2-inch disk
ISPN: 22125-275   **Price: $150.00**

PRECISION COMPUTER SYSTEMS

EDUCATIONAL BUDGET MGMT. SYSTEM (VER. 1.3.4)

Creates and configures school budgets with a budget development model.

System: MAC, II, PLUS, SE, XL
Minimum Memory: 512K
Requires: Two disk drives or a hard disk, ImageWriter or LaserWriter printer.
Medium: 3 1/2-inch disk
ISPN: 61720-200   **Price: $1495.00**

ASSOCIATED COMPUTER SERVICES

GRADE MANAGER (VER. 2.0)

Assists in the accurate recording and reporting of student grades.

System: MAC, II, PLUS, SE, XL
Minimum Memory: 512K
Medium: 3 1/2-inch disk
ISPN: 05543-300   **Price: $89.95**

HEIZER SOFTWARE
GRADE POINT AVERAGE

Records a student's class history and grades, and calculates the Grade Point Average over a four-year period.

System: MAC, II, PLUS, SE, XL
Minimum Memory: 512K
Requires: Microsoft Excel (ISPN 53150-270) or Microsoft Works (ISPN 53150-740).
Medium: 3 1/2-inch disk
ISPN: 35175-941   **Price: $6.00**

BOBBING SOFTWARE
GRADEBOOK (VER. 1.1)

Allows educators to record, edit, average, plot and report grades. Screen display looks like a paper gradebook.

System: MAC, II, PLUS, SE, XL
Minimum Memory: 512K
Medium: 3 1/2-inch disk
ISPN: 08075-600   **Price: $99.00**

EMA SOFTWARE
GRADEBOOK PLUS-MACINTOSH EDITION

Provides and individual teacher with a gradebook that keeps records and generates statistical information for a class or student.

System: MAC, II, PLUS, SE, XL
Minimum Memory: 512K
Medium: 3 1/2-inch disk
ISPN: 28900-299   **Price: $59.95**

HEIZER SOFTWARE
GRADING AND ATTENDANCE SET

Records individual homework, lab and test scores, and attendance for an unlimited number of students.

System: MAC, II, PLUS, SE, XL
Minimum Memory: 512K
Requires: Microsoft Excel (ISPN 53150-270) or Microsoft Works (ISPN 53150-740).
Medium: 3 1/2-inch disk
ISPN: 35175-230   **Price: $30.00**

CHANCERY SOFTWARE
MAC SCHOOL-COMPLETE SYSTEM

Integrated school administration system that handles all student records in public and private schools.

System: MAC, II, PLUS, SE, XL
Minimum Memory: 1024K
Requires: Single-user.
Medium: 3 1/2-inch disk
ISPN: 12182-500   **Price: $2450.00**

CHANCERY SOFTWARE
MAC SCHOOL-COMPLETE SYSTEM

Integrated school administration system that handles all student records in public and private schools.

System: MAC, II, PLUS, SE, XL
Minimum Memory: 1024K
Requires: Multi-user.
Medium: 3 1/2-inch disk
ISPN: 12182-500   **Price: $2950.00**

COOKE PUBLICATIONS
MACREGISTRAR

Contains a database for maintaining course records, numeric and letter, as well as free-form text for up to 2,600 students.

System: MAC, II, PLUS, SE, XL
Minimum Memory: 512K
Requires: Note: University site license available.
Medium: 3 1/2-inch disk
ISPN: 19659-550   **Price: $49.95**

PARAGON CONCEPTS, INC.
MACTAG (VER. 2.03)

A teacher's assistant on the Macintosh. Keeps track of class records, calculates the composite scores and more.

System: MAC, II, PLUS, SE, XL
Minimum Memory: 512K
Medium: 3 1/2-inch disk
ISPN: 59740-460   **Price: $65.00**

RIGHT TRACK SOFTWARE, INC.
MAIN OFFICE

Complete student record keeping for grades K-12.

System: MAC, II, PLUS, SE, XL
Minimum Memory: 512K
Medium: 3 1/2-inch disk
ISPN: 66475-450   **Price: $2995.00**

CHARIOT SOFTWARE GROUP
MICROGRADE (VER. 1.03)

Applicable for any grade level or subject: A teacher gradebook with complete flexibility and advanced features.

System: MAC, II, PLUS, SE, XL
Minimum Memory: 512K
Medium: 3 1/2-inch disk
ISPN: 12237-400   **Price: $95.00**

CHARIOT SOFTWARE GROUP
MICROTEST III

Creates, updates, generates and stores a variety of tests. MacWrite and MacPaint compatible files for word processing and graphics.

System: MAC, II, PLUS, SE, XL
Minimum Memory: 512K
Requires: Two disk drives, PostScript printer.
Medium: 3 1/2-inch disk
ISPN: 12237-500   **Price: $139.00**

COMPUTER RESOURCES, INC. (NH)
MMS-ATTENDANCE REPORTING SYSTEM (VER. 2.0)

Allows administrators to record, process and report both period-by-period and daily attendance.

System: MAC, II, PLUS, SE, XL
Minimum Memory: 512K
Requires: MMS-Student Master File System (ISPN 17293-300).
Medium: 3 1/2-inch disk
ISPN: 17293-105   **Price: $749.00**

COMPUTER RESOURCES, INC. (NH)
MMS-DISCIPLINE REPORTING SYSTEM

Allows administrators to record and report disciplinary infractions and actions taken.

System: MAC, II, PLUS, SE, XL
Minimum Memory: 512K
Requires: Multi-user version. MMS-Student Master File System (ISPN 17293-300), 132-column printer.
Medium: 3 1/2-inch disk
ISPN: 17293-225   **Price: $599.00**

COMPUTER RESOURCES, INC. (NH)
MMS-DISCIPLINE REPORTING SYSTEM

Allows administrators to record and report disciplinary infractions and actions taken.

System: MAC, II, PLUS, SE, XL
Minimum Memory: 512K
Requires: MMS-Student Master File system (ISPN 17293-300), 132-column printer.
Medium: 3 1/2-inch disk
ISPN: 17293-225   **Price: $449.00**

COMPUTER RESOURCES, INC. (NH)
MMS-GRADE REPORTING SYSTEM (VER. 2.0)

Allows administrators to record, process, and report grades that students receive in their classes.

System: MAC, II, PLUS, SE, XL
Minimum Memory: 512K
Requires: MMS-Student Master File System (ISPN 17293-300), 132-column printer.
Medium: 3 1/2-inch disk
ISPN: 17293-400   **Price: $1199.00**

COMPUTER RESOURCES, INC. (NH)
MMS-GRADE REPORTING SYSTEM (VER. 2.0)

Allows administrators to record, process, and report grades that students receive in their classes.

System: MAC, II, PLUS, SE, XL
Minimum Memory: 512K
Requires: Multi-user version. MMS-Student Master File System (ISPN 17293-300), 132-column printer.
Medium: 3 1/2-inch disk
ISPN: 17293-400   **Price: $1649.00**

COMPUTER RESOURCES, INC. (NH)
MMS-STUDENT MASTER FILE SYSTEM (VER. 2.0)

Allows administrators to edit, sort and display student biographical information.

System: MAC, II, PLUS, SE, XL
Minimum Memory: 512K
Requires: 132-column printer.
Medium: 3 1/2-inch disk
ISPN: 17293-300   **Price: $499.00**

COMPUTER RESOURCES, INC. (NH)

MMS-STUDENT MASTER FILE SYSTEM (VER. 2.0)

Allows administrators to edit, sort and display student biographical information.

System: MAC, II, PLUS, SE, XL
Minimum Memory: 512K
Requires: Multi-user version. 132-column printer.
Medium: 3 1/2-inch disk
ISPN: 17293-300   **Price: $699.00**

COMPUTER RESOURCES, INC. (NH)

MMS-STUDENT SCHEDULING SYSTEM (VER. 2.0)

Allows administrators to create a working Course Master Schedule and schedule their students accordingly.

System: MAC, II, PLUS, SE, XL
Minimum Memory: 512K
Requires: MMS-Student Master File System (ISPN 17293-300), 132-column printer.
Medium: 3 1/2-inch disk
ISPN: 17293-500   **Price: $1399.00**

COMPUTER RESOURCES, INC. (NH)

MMS-STUDENT SCHEDULING SYSTEM (VER. 2.0)

Allows administrators to create a working Course Master Schedule and schedule their students accordingly.

System: MAC, II, PLUS, SE, XL
Minimum Memory: 512K
Requires: Multi-user version. MMS-Student Master File System (ISPN 17293-300), 132-column printer.
Medium: 3 1/2-inch disk
ISPN: 17293-500   **Price: $1949.00**

COMPUTER RESOURCES, INC. (NH)

MMS-TUITION/FEE ACCOUNTING SYSTEM (VER. 1.0)

Allows administrators to track debits and credits to individual student accounts for items such as tuition, book and lab fees.

System: MAC, II, PLUS, SE, XL
Minimum Memory: 512K
Requires: MMS-Student Master File System (ISPN 17293-300), 132-column printer.
Medium: 3 1/2-inch disk
ISPN: 17293-510   **Price: $549.00**

HEIZER SOFTWARE

MULTIPLE CHOICE TEST

An on-line testing and grading program for students with up to fifty-four multiple choice questions.

System: MAC, II, PLUS, SE, XL
Minimum Memory: 512K
Requires: Microsoft Excel (ISPN 53150-270).
Medium: 3 1/2-inch disk
ISPN: 35175-231   **Price: $20.00**

LEARNING SKILLS, INC.

NOTEPRO

An educational package for college and high school that teaches users to organize and make best use of their notes.

System: MAC, II, PLUS, SE, XL
Minimum Memory:
Medium: 3 1/2-inch disk
ISPN: 43875-800   **Price: $59.95**

PRECISION COMPUTER SYSTEMS

PRECISION SCHOOL MANAGEMENT SYSTEM (VER. 1.4)

Maintains current records relating to the management of school operations.

System: MAC, II, PLUS, SE, XL
Minimum Memory: 512K
Requires: Omnis 3 Plus/Express (ISPN 58775-515), two disk drives or a hard disk, ImageWriter or LaserWriter printer.
Medium: 3 1/2-inch disk
ISPN: 61720-360   **Price: $995.00**

RIGHT TRACK SOFTWARE, INC.

REGISTRAR'S OFFICE

Student registration and academic administration for higher education.

System: MAC, II, PLUS, SE, XL
Minimum Memory: 512K
Medium: 3 1/2-inch disk
ISPN: 66475-600   **Price: $9995.00**

COMPUTER SOLUTIONS (WA)

STUDENT INFORMATION MGMT SYSTEM (SIMS) (VER. 2.0)

Schedules students, tracks attendance data, and prepares transcripts and report cards.

System: MAC, II, PLUS, SE, XL
Minimum Memory: 512K
Requires: Single user version. Two 800K disk drives or a hard disk, LaserWriter or ImageWriter printer.
Medium: 3 1/2-inch disk
ISPN: 17606-650   **Price: $3500.00**

COMPUTER SOLUTIONS (WA)

STUDENT INFORMATION MGMT SYSTEM (SIMS) (VER. 2.0)

Schedules students, tracks attendance data, and prepares transcripts and report cards.

System: MAC, II, PLUS, SE, XL
Minimum Memory: 512K
Requires: Multi-user version. Two 800K disk drives or a hard disk, LaserWriter or ImageWriter printer.
Medium: 3 1/2-inch disk
ISPN: 17606-650   **Price: $4500.00**

208 EDUCATION/ APTITUDE TESTING/ COUNSELING

SPINNAKER SOFTWARE

ACHIEVEMENT TEST

Contains Achievement Test, English Composition and Math Level One.

System: MAC, II, PLUS, SE, XL
Minimum Memory: 128K
Medium: 3 1/2-inch disk
ISPN: 75300-529   **Price: $99.95**

QUEUE

ANALOGIES I

Teaches students to analyze and solve analogies to help students taking aptitude tests.

System: MAC, II, PLUS, SE, XL
Minimum Memory: 128K
Medium: 3 1/2-inch disk
ISPN: 64387-130   **Price: $65.00**

QUEUE

ANALOGIES II

Helps prepare students for the analogies section of college aptitude tests.

System: MAC, II, PLUS, SE, XL
Minimum Memory: 128K
Medium: 3 1/2-inch disk
ISPN: 64387-118   **Price: $65.00**

QUEUE

ANTONYMS

Provides students with examples and practice exercises on antonyms covered on standardized college aptitude exams.

System: MAC, II, PLUS, SE, XL
Minimum Memory: 128K
Medium: 3 1/2-inch disk
ISPN: 64387-120   **Price: $34.95**

BARRON'S EDUCATIONAL SERIES, INC.

BARRON'S COMPUTER STUDY PROGRAM FOR THE SAT

Provides a diagnostic SAT containing a verbal and math review with 2500 practice exercises and a 3000 word vocabulary builder.

System: MAC, PLUS, XL
Minimum Memory: 512K
Medium: 3 1/2-inch disk
ISPN: 06931-100   **Price: $49.95**

QUEUE

COLLEGE APTITUDE READING COMPREHENSION EXERCISES

Grades 9 and up: Helps students prepare for college aptitude tests reading comprehension using SAT style exercises.

System: MAC, PLUS, XL
Minimum Memory: 128K
Medium: 3 1/2-inch disk
ISPN: 64387-211   **Price: $65.00**

MINDSCAPE, INC.

PERFECT COLLEGE

Produces a list of the schools to match the user's needs by letting him or her specify the college criteria that is important.

System: MAC, II, PLUS, SE, XL
Minimum Memory:
Medium: 3 1/2-inch disk
ISPN: 54375-495   **Price: $19.95**

MINDSCAPE, INC.

PERFECT SCORE SAT W/ PERFECT COLLEGE

Provides an actual timed SAT exam and an extensive database for the college student.

System: MAC, II, PLUS, SE, XL
Minimum Memory: 128K
Medium: 3 1/2-inch disk
ISPN: 54375-499   **Price: $69.95**

MINDSCAPE, INC.

PERFECT SCORE-COMPUTER PREPARATION FOR THE SAT

Grades 10-12: Covers subjects and categories to prepare students for the PSAT and SAT exams using a timed exam.

System: MAC, PLUS, XL
Minimum Memory:
Medium: 3 1/2-inch disk
ISPN: 54375-500   **Price: $79.95**

HEIZER SOFTWARE

PSYCH-FILES

Converts, compares, graphs and reports results of any battery of individual psycho-educational tests.

System: MAC, II, PLUS, SE, XL
Minimum Memory: 512K
Requires: Microsoft Excel (ISPN 53150-270) or Microsoft Works (ISPN 53150-740).
Medium: 3 1/2-inch disk
ISPN: 35175-222   **Price: $60.00**

HEI, INC.

TOPSCORE (VER. 1.4)

Scans and corrects tests, organizes results and prepares reports. Transfers hard data from a sheet of paper to a diskette file.

System: MAC, II, PLUS, SE, XL
Minimum Memory: 384K
Requires: Optical mark page reader, HEI 360, NCS or Scantron.
Medium: 3 1/2-inch disk
ISPN: 35150-450   **Price: $395.00**

DAVIDSON AND ASSOCIATES, INC.

WORD ATTACK! SAT DATA DISK

Grades 9-12: Provides an additional data disk for use with the Word Attack! program.

System: MAC, PLUS, SE, XL
Minimum Memory: 512K
Requires: Word Attack! (ISPN 24075-300).
Medium: 3 1/2-inch disk
ISPN: 24075-325   **Price: $19.95**

---

212 EDUCATION/ COGNITIVE DEVELOPMENT

ARBORWORKS, INC.

LEARNING TOOL (VER. 1.0)

Designed specifically to help students study any subject.

System: MAC, II, PLUS, SE, XL
Minimum Memory: 512K
Requires: Available exclusively through Kinko's Academic Courseware Exchange at (800)235-6919 or (800)292-6640 in CA.
Medium: 3 1/2-inch disk
ISPN: 04925-400   **Price: $30.00**

NORDIC SOFTWARE, INC.

MACKIDS-COINWORKS

Seven lessons cover counting coins, making change, knowing if there is enough money for a purchase and more. Ages 4-12.

System: MAC, II, PLUS, SE, XL
Minimum Memory: 512K
Medium: 3 1/2-inch disk
ISPN: 57028-035   **Price: $39.95**

NORDIC SOFTWARE, INC.

MACKIDS-FLASHWORKS

Utilizes both visual and verbal stimuli to tutor the child in math drills, geography, foreign language and more. Ages 6-adult.

System: MAC, II, PLUS, SE, XL
Minimum Memory: 512K
Medium: 3 1/2-inch disk
ISPN: 57028-075   **Price: $39.95**

COMPU-TEACH, INC.

ONCE UPON A TIME II

Ages 6-12: Children can design and publish their very own storybooks with characters from three new scenes.

System: MAC, II, PLUS, SE, XL
Minimum Memory: 512K
Medium: 3 1/2-inch disk
ISPN: 15081-125   **Price: $39.95**

HEIZER SOFTWARE

PIAGET-A LOGIC GAME

A game which tests and improves logic skills in both children and adults.

System: MAC, II, PLUS, SE, XL
Minimum Memory: 512K
Requires: HyperCard (ISPN 03900-300).
Medium: 3 1/2-inch disk
ISPN: 35175-976   **Price: $8.00**

BAUDVILLE

RAINY DAY GAMES

Introduces Ted Bear, a companion with which a child can play Concentration, Old Maid and Go Fish. Develops strategy skills.

System: MAC, II, PLUS, SE, XL
Minimum Memory: 512K
Medium: 3 1/2-inch disk
ISPN: 07087-510   **Price: $19.95**

COMPU-TEACH, INC.

STEPPING STONES BONUS PACK (LEVELS I & II)

Ages 2-4: Helps children master essential concepts of math, reading and language.

System: MAC, II, PLUS, SE, XL
Minimum Memory: 512K
Medium: 3 1/2-inch disk
ISPN: 15081-760   **Price: $49.95**

BRAINPOWER, INC.

THINKFAST

Measures and helps improve short and long term memory in both hemispheres of the brain.

System: MAC, II, PLUS, SE, XL
Minimum Memory: 512K
Medium: 3 1/2-inch disk
ISPN: 08413-100   **Price: $39.95**

---

215 EDUCATION/ COMPOSITION/ GRAMMAR

QUEUE

ADJECTIVES-ADDING TO NOUNS AND PRONOUNS

Covers use of adjectives, kinds of adjectives and comparison of adjectives.

System: MAC, PLUS, SE, XL
Minimum Memory: 128K
Medium: 3 1/2-inch disk
ISPN: 64387-010   **Price: $39.95**

QUEUE

ADVERBIAL CLAUSES

Lets you review subordinate conjunctions, kinds of adverbial clauses and words used as subordinate conjunctions.

System: MAC, PLUS, SE, XL
Minimum Memory: 128K
Medium: 3 1/2-inch disk
ISPN: 64387-064   **Price: $34.95**

QUEUE

ADVERBS-MODIFIERS OF VERBS/ADJECTIVES/ADVERBS

Grades 4-8: Students will cover adverb forms, comparison of adverbs and correct use of adjectives and adverbs.

System: MAC, II, PLUS, SE, XL
Minimum Memory: 128K
Medium: 3 1/2-inch disk
ISPN: 64387-020   **Price: $39.95**

QUEUE

AGREEMENT OF SUBJECT AND VERB

Covers agreement in person and number, agreement of verb with compound subject and agreement of verb with collective nouns.

System: MAC, II, PLUS, SE, XL
Minimum Memory: 128K
Medium: 3 1/2-inch disk
ISPN: 64387-056　　　　　　**Price: $34.95**

QUEUE

CASE AND GENDER OF NOUNS AND PRONOUNS

Covers subjects, predicate nouns and pronouns, object of verbs, prepositions, verbals and subjects of infinitives.

System: MAC, II, PLUS, SE, XL
Minimum Memory: 128K
Medium: 3 1/2-inch disk
ISPN: 64387-038　　　　　　**Price: $44.95**

QUEUE

CLAUSES AND WHOLE SENTENCES

Helps students identify clauses and learn to use them correctly in sentences.

System: MAC, II, PLUS, SE, XL
Minimum Memory: 128K
Medium: 3 1/2-inch disk
ISPN: 64387-037　　　　　　**Price: $44.95**

QUEUE

COMPARING GERUND, PARTICIPLE AND INFINITIVE PHRASE

Discusses nouns, verbs and participles – also noun, verb, participle, adverbial, prepositional and gerund phrases.

System: MAC, II, PLUS, SE, XL
Minimum Memory: 128K
Medium: 3 1/2-inch disk
ISPN: 64387-036　　　　　　**Price: $44.95**

QUEUE

COMPLETE PRACTICAL COMPOSITION SERIES

Includes Practical Composition I, II, III, IV and V.

System: MAC, II, PLUS, SE, XL
Minimum Memory: 128K
Medium: 3 1/2-inch disk
ISPN: 64387-556　　　　　　**Price: $229.95**

QUEUE

COMPLETE PRACTICAL GRAMMAR PART I

Includes thirteen disks and a text with programs such as parts of speech, modifiers, adjectives and principal parts of verbs.

System: MAC, II, PLUS, SE, XL
Minimum Memory: 128K
Medium: 3 1/2-inch disk
ISPN: 64387-007　　　　　　**Price: $375.00**

QUEUE

COMPLETE PRACTICAL GRAMMAR PART II

Covers tenses of verbs, voice and mood and agreement of subject and verb. Includes fourteen disks and a manual.

System: MAC, II, PLUS, SE, XL
Minimum Memory: 128K
Medium: 3 1/2-inch disk
ISPN: 64387-050　　　　　　**Price: $395.00**

QUEUE

COMPLETE PRACTICAL GRAMMAR PART III

Includes programs such as patterns of sentences, eight parts of speech, comparing gerunds, clauses and whole sentences.

System: MAC, II, PLUS, SE, XL
Minimum Memory: 128K
Medium: 3 1/2-inch disk
ISPN: 64387-031　　　　　　**Price: $224.95**

QUEUE

COMPLEX SENTENCE-ADJECTIVE CLAUSES

Covers the complex sentence, kinds of subordinate clauses and adjective clauses.

System: MAC, II, PLUS, SE, XL
Minimum Memory: 128K
Medium: 3 1/2-inch disk
ISPN: 64387-062　　　　　　**Price: $34.95**

QUEUE

COMPOUND SENTENCE

Covers kind of clauses, simple sentences, compound sentence and coordinate conjunctions.

System: MAC, II, PLUS, SE, XL
Minimum Memory: 128K
Medium: 3 1/2-inch disk
ISPN: 64387-060　　　　　　**Price: $34.95**

QUEUE

COMPREHENSIVE GRAMMAR REVIEW I

Grades 7-12: Provides exercises to identify parts of speech, locate the subject and predicate, and correct sentence fragments.

System: MAC, PLUS, SE, XL
Minimum Memory: 128K
Medium: 3 1/2-inch disk
ISPN: 64387-217　　　　　　**Price: $54.95**

QUEUE

COMPREHENSIVE GRAMMAR REVIEW II

Grades 7-12: Exercises on subject and predicate, complements of verbs, kinds of sentences, verb forms and identifying phrases.

System: MAC, II, PLUS, SE, XL
Minimum Memory: 128K
Medium: 3 1/2-inch disk
ISPN: 64387-218　　　　　　**Price: $54.95**

QUEUE

DEVELOPING WRITING SKILLS

Grades 6-9: Provides an introductory tutorial and drill on writing effective sentences and paragraphs. Includes a teacher's manual.

System: MAC, II, PLUS, SE, XL
Minimum Memory: 128K
Medium: 3 1/2-inch disk
ISPN: 64387-276　　　　　　**Price: $135.00**

QUEUE

EIGHT PARTS OF SPEECH

Teachers and students: Provides a comprehensive overview of all eight parts of speech.

System: MAC, II, PLUS, SE, XL
Minimum Memory: 128K
Medium: 3 1/2-inch disk
ISPN: 64387-034　　　　　　**Price: $44.95**

QUEUE

GERUNDS

Covers the gerund phrase, complements of gerunds and adverbial gerunds.

System: MAC, II, PLUS, SE, XL
Minimum Memory: 128K
Medium: 3 1/2-inch disk
ISPN: 64387-070　　　　　　**Price: $34.95**

QUEUE

INFINITIVES

Explains uses of infinitives as adverbs and adjectives and also the infinitive phrase.

System: MAC, II, PLUS, SE, XL
Minimum Memory: 128K
Medium: 3 1/2-inch disk
ISPN: 64387-072　　　　　　**Price: $34.95**

QUEUE

MANAGING THE SENTENCE

Teachers and students: Covers kinds of sentences, faults in the sentence structure, dangling modifiers and subject verb agreement.

System: MAC, II, PLUS, SE, XL
Minimum Memory: 128K
Medium: 3 1/2-inch disk
ISPN: 64387-039　　　　　　**Price: $44.95**

CLINES RAYMOND AND BARKER ELLEN

MINDSTORM-A COMPUTER WORKBOOK (VER. 1.0)

Contains a series of imaginative exercises to remediate major grammatical errors and punctuation mistakes made by basic writers.

System: MAC
Minimum Memory: 128K
Medium: 3 1/2-inch disk
ISPN: 65262-550　　　　　　**Price: $75.00**

QUEUE
NOT LIKE THE OTHERS
Preschool program which teaches children to recognize similarities and differences. An excellent program for non-readers.
System: MAC, II, PLUS, SE, XL
Minimum Memory: 128K
Medium: 3 1/2-inch disk
ISPN: 64387-535 **Price: $49.95**

QUEUE
NOUN CLAUSES
Learn the function of a noun clause, omission of connecting words and even clauses used as appositives.
System: MAC, II, PLUS, SE, XL
Minimum Memory: 128K
Medium: 3 1/2-inch disk
ISPN: 64387-066 **Price: $34.95**

QUEUE
NOUNS-WORDS USED AS NAMES
Grades 4-8: Helps students recognize nouns, kinds of nouns, capitalization of proper nouns and plurals of nouns.
System: MAC, II, PLUS, SE, XL
Minimum Memory: 128K
Medium: 3 1/2-inch disk
ISPN: 64387-540 **Price: $39.95**

QUEUE
PARTICIPLES
Covers the nature of verbs, modifiers and forms of the participles plus the participle phrase.
System: MAC, II, PLUS, SE, XL
Minimum Memory: 128K
Medium: 3 1/2-inch disk
ISPN: 64387-068 **Price: $34.95**

QUEUE
PATTERN OF SENTENCES
Provides a comprehensive overview of the way words are ordered.
System: MAC, II, PLUS, SE, XL
Minimum Memory: 128K
Medium: 3 1/2-inch disk
ISPN: 64387-033 **Price: $44.95**

QUEUE
PATTERNS OF SENTENCES
Learn to construct proper sentences.
System: MAC, PLUS, SE, XL
Minimum Memory: 128K
Medium: 3 1/2-inch disk
ISPN: 64387-041 **Price: $44.95**

QUEUE
PRACTICAL COMPOSITION PART I-MAKING WORDS WORK
Aids writers in choosing the 'right' word – discusses denotations, connotations, emotional and unemotional words.
System: MAC, II, PLUS, SE, XL
Minimum Memory: 128K
Medium: 3 1/2-inch disk
ISPN: 64387-545 **Price: $44.95**

QUEUE
PRACTICAL COMPOSITION PART II-LOGICAL SENTENCES
Offers tutorial on sentence sense, coordination and subordination, sentence length, incorrect omissions and comparisons.
System: MAC, II, PLUS, SE, XL
Minimum Memory: 128K
Medium: 3 1/2-inch disk
ISPN: 64387-547 **Price: $74.95**

QUEUE
PRACTICAL COMPOSITION PART III-SELECTING APPROACH
Tutors you in four types of composition – also includes personal and impersonal styles.
System: MAC, II, PLUS, SE, XL
Minimum Memory: 128K
Medium: 3 1/2-inch disk
ISPN: 64387-548 **Price: $44.95**

QUEUE
PRACTICAL COMPOSITION PART IV-MAKING SENTENCES
Grades 7-12: Provides tutorials and drills on 'managing' the sentence.
System: MAC, PLUS, SE, XL
Minimum Memory: 128K
Medium: 3 1/2-inch disk
ISPN: 64387-552 **Price: $44.95**

QUEUE
PRACTICAL COMPOSITION PART V-USING WORDS CORRECTLY
Grades 7-12: Aids writers with words and phrases often misused in writing and conversation.
System: MAC, II, PLUS, SE, XL
Minimum Memory: 128K
Medium: 3 1/2-inch disk
ISPN: 64387-553 **Price: $44.95**

QUEUE
PRACTICAL COMPOSITION-SERIES
A five-program series combining rules of good writing with practice material that develops the student's ability to write.
System: MAC, II, PLUS, SE, XL
Minimum Memory: 128K
Medium: 3 1/2-inch disk
ISPN: 64387-543 **Price: $229.95**

QUEUE
PRACTICAL GRAMMAR II
Grades 7-12: Instructs students in tenses of verbs, voice and mood, compound and complex sentences and punctuation.
System: MAC, II, PLUS, SE, XL
Minimum Memory: 128K
Medium: 3 1/2-inch disk
ISPN: 64387-499 **Price: $395.00**

QUEUE
PRACTICAL GRAMMAR III
Grades 7-12: Covers parts of speech, gerund, participle and infinitive phrases, clauses, whole sentences and gender of nouns.
System: MAC, II, PLUS, SE, XL
Minimum Memory: 128K
Medium: 3 1/2-inch disk
ISPN: 64387-501 **Price: $224.95**

QUEUE
PREPOSITIONAL PHRASES
Includes adjective and adverb phrases, commonly used prepositions and compound or phrasal prepositions.
System: MAC, II, PLUS, SE, XL
Minimum Memory: 128K
Medium: 3 1/2-inch disk
ISPN: 64387-058 **Price: $34.95**

QUEUE
PROBLEMS IN THE USE OF INFINITIVES
Covers infinitive clauses, the verb 'to be', the split infinitive and special uses.
System: MAC, II, PLUS, SE, XL
Minimum Memory: 128K
Medium: 3 1/2-inch disk
ISPN: 64387-074 **Price: $34.95**

QUEUE
PRONOUNS-SUBSTITUTES FOR NOUNS
Grades 4-8: Helps students recognize pronouns, kinds of pronouns, personal, interrogative, demonstrative, indefinite and relative.
System: MAC, II, PLUS, SE, XL
Minimum Memory: 128K
Medium: 3 1/2-inch disk
ISPN: 64387-570 **Price: $39.95**

QUEUE
PUNCTUATION REVIEW
Grades 7-12: Covers periods, commas, semicolons, parenthesis, dashes, brackets, question marks and exclamation marks.
System: MAC, II, PLUS, SE, XL
Minimum Memory: 128K
Medium: 3 1/2-inch disk
ISPN: 64387-675 **Price: $34.95**

SMART COMMUNICATIONS, INC.
SMART EXPERT EDITOR (VER. 2.0)
Critiques written texts for grammar, syntax, vocabulary and comprehension using artificial intelligence techniques.
System: MAC, II, PLUS, SE, XL
Minimum Memory: 1024K
Medium: 3 1/2-inch disk
ISPN: 71412-075 **Price: $12500.00**

QUEUE
TENSES OF VERBS
Covers the six tenses, the simple tenses, the perfect tenses, the verb 'to be' and progressive forms of verbs.
System: MAC, II, PLUS, SE, XL
Minimum Memory: 128K
Medium: 3 1/2-inch disk
ISPN: 64387-052   **Price: $34.95**

QUEUE
VERB VOICE-TENSE AND MOOD
Grades 7-12: Study verb tense and mood.
System: MAC, II, PLUS, SE, XL
Minimum Memory: 128K
Medium: 3 1/2-inch disk
ISPN: 64387-681   **Price: $34.95**

QUEUE
VERBS-ACTION AND LINKING WORDS
Helps build skill with transitive and intransitive verbs, active and passive verbs and tense of verbs.
System: MAC, II, PLUS, SE, XL
Minimum Memory: 128K
Medium: 3 1/2-inch disk
ISPN: 64387-920   **Price: $39.95**

QUEUE
VERBS-VOICE AND MOOD
Covers active and passive voice and six tenses of 'call'.
System: MAC, II, PLUS, SE, XL
Minimum Memory: 128K
Medium: 3 1/2-inch disk
ISPN: 64387-054   **Price: $34.95**

QUEUE
VERBS: VOICE AND MOOD
Covers active and passive voice, how passive voice is formed, six tenses of the verb 'call', mood of verbs and more.
System: MAC, II, PLUS, SE, XL
Minimum Memory: 128K
Medium: 3 1/2-inch disk
ISPN: 64387-055   **Price: $34.95**

DAVIDSON AND ASSOCIATES, INC.
WORD ATTACK DATA DISK-ROOTS AND PREFIXES
Grades 4-12: A vocabulary expander.
System: MAC, PLUS, SE, XL
Minimum Memory: 512K
Requires: Word Attack! (ISPN 24075-300).
Medium: 3 1/2-inch disk
ISPN: 24075-323   **Price: $19.95**

CONDUIT
WRITER'S HELPER-STAGE II
Contains a collection of tools for writing and revising any type of writing assignment.
System: MAC, II, PLUS, SE, XL
Minimum Memory: 512K
Requires: 800K disk.
Medium: 3 1/2-inch disk
ISPN: 19050-800   **Price: $120.00**

CONDUIT
WRITER'S HELPER-STAGE II
Contains a collection of tools for writing and revising any type of writing assignment.
System: MAC, II, PLUS, SE, XL
Minimum Memory: 512K
Requires: EdPack 6 (six disks). 800K disk.
Medium: 3 1/2-inch disk
ISPN: 19050-800   **Price: $170.00**

CONDUIT
WRITER'S HELPER-STAGE II
Contains a collection of tools for writing and revising any type of writing assignment.
System: MAC, II, PLUS, SE, XL
Minimum Memory: 512K
Requires: EdPack 15 (fifteen disks). 800K disk.
Medium: 3 1/2-inch disk
ISPN: 19050-800   **Price: $285.00**

CONDUIT
WRITER'S HELPER-STAGE II
Contains a collection of tools for writing and revising any type of writing assignment.
System: MAC, II, PLUS, SE, XL
Minimum Memory: 512K
Requires: EdPack 25 (twenty-five disks). 800K disk.
Medium: 3 1/2-inch disk
ISPN: 19050-800   **Price: $425.00**

219 EDUCATION/ COMPUTER LITERACY

1ST DESK SYSTEMS, INC.
1STSTEP (VER. 3.4)
Contains 1stFile, and 1stPort(all versions 4.0) and limited to 25 records with 1stBook of data for education
System: MAC, II, PLUS, SE, XL
Minimum Memory: 128K
Medium: 3 1/2-inch disk
ISPN: 81083-650
Price: Please contact the software publisher.

BROWNBAG SOFTWARE
31 ALL-TIME FAVORITE PROGRAMS FOR THE MACINTOSH
Includes 31 games, business and finance programs, utilities, education and science programs.
System: MAC, II, PLUS, SE, XL
Minimum Memory: 512K
Requires: QuickBasic (ISPN 53150-205).
Medium: 3 1/2-inch disk
ISPN: 08993-100   **Price: $29.95**

KINKOS ACADEMIC COURSEWARE EXCHANGE
BINARY TREES (VER. 2.3)
Allows users to experiment with binary trees in a graphical, interactive fashion.
System: MAC, II, PLUS, SE, XL
Minimum Memory: 128K
Medium: 3 1/2-inch disk
ISPN: 43025-090   **Price: $7.00**

VENTURA EDUCATIONAL SYSTEMS
COMPUTER CONCEPTS (VER. 2.0)
Grades 7 and up: Introduces the basic and essential concepts necessary for understanding the computer.
System: MAC, II, PLUS, SE, XL
Minimum Memory: 512K
Requires: Lab pack (5 copies of the program).
Medium: 3 1/2-inch disk
ISPN: 84911-180   **Price: $89.95**

VENTURA EDUCATIONAL SYSTEMS
COMPUTER CONCEPTS (VER. 2.0)
Grades 7 and up: Introduces the basic and essential concepts necessary for understanding the computer.
System: MAC, PLUS, SE, XL
Minimum Memory: 512K
Medium: 3 1/2-inch disk
ISPN: 84911-180   **Price: $49.95**

FLIPTRACK LEARNING SYSTEMS
HOW TO OPERATE THE MAC II
An interactive course that teaches how to operate the Macintosh II computer on four audio cassettes. Includes document disk.
System: II
Minimum Memory: 1024K
Requires: 800K disk drive, audio cassette player.
Medium: 3 1/2-inch disk
ISPN: 30881-091   **Price: $109.00**

FLIPTRACK LEARNING SYSTEMS
HOW TO OPERATE THE MACINTOSH
An interactive course on three audio cassettes that teaches first time users how to operate the Macintosh Plus or SE computer.
System: MAC, PLUS, SE, XL
Minimum Memory: 1024K
Requires: Two 800K disk drives or one 800K disk drive and a hard disk, audio cassette player.
Medium: 3 1/2-inch disk
ISPN: 30881-090   **Price: $89.00**

FLIPTRACK LEARNING SYSTEMS
HOW TO USE MICROSOFT EXCEL
An audio cassette course that teaches the development of an Excel spreadsheet, and commands and functions to manipulate it.
System: MAC, II, PLUS, SE, XL
Minimum Memory: 512K
Requires: Microsoft Excel (ISPN 53150-270), 800K disk drive, audio cassette player.
Medium: 3 1/2-inch disk
ISPN: 30881-312   **Price: $119.00**

FLIPTRACK LEARNING SYSTEMS

HOW TO USE MICROSOFT WORD

Contains an interactive course with four audio cassettes that teaches first time users how to operate Microsoft Word.

System: MAC, II, PLUS, SE, XL
Minimum Memory: 512K
Requires: Microsoft Word(ISPN 53150-732), printer, two 400K disk drives or one 400K disk drive and hard disk, audio cassette player.
Medium: 3 1/2-inch disk
ISPN: 30881-310   **Price: $99.00**

FLIPTRACK LEARNING SYSTEMS

HOW TO USE PAGEMAKER (VER. 3.0)

An audio cassette course that teaches page layout and desktop publishing using Aldus Pagemaker (Ver. 3.0).

System: MAC, II, PLUS, SE, XL
Minimum Memory: 512K
Requires: Pagemaker (ISPN 02226-740), 800K disk drive, audio cassette player.
Medium: 3 1/2-inch disk
ISPN: 30881-600   **Price: $195.00**

PROFESSOR CORP.

MAC'S CORE PART I

Learn Microsoft Basic programming on the Macintosh.

System: MAC, II, PLUS, SE, XL
Minimum Memory: 128K
Requires: Microsoft QuickBasic (ISPN 53150-205).
Medium: 3 1/2-inch disk
ISPN: 62925-801   **Price: $69.95**

PROFESSOR CORP.

MAC'S CORE PART II

The second program in the Mac's Core series. Learn more Microsoft Basic programming on the Macintosh.

System: MAC, PLUS, SE, XL
Minimum Memory: 128K
Requires: Microsoft QuickBasic (ISPN 53150-205).
Medium: 3 1/2-inch disk
ISPN: 62925-795   **Price: $84.95**

STAX, INC.

MACINTOSH BIBLE-S*T*A*X EDITION

A stackware edition of The Macintosh Bible on three diskettes that contains hints, tips, shortcuts and Macintosh information.

System: MAC, II, PLUS, SE, XL
Minimum Memory: 1024K
Requires: HyperCard (ISPN 03900-300), two disk drives or one disk drive and a hard disk
Medium: 3 1/2-inch disk
ISPN: 75998-300   **Price: $79.95**

FREEMAN W H AND CO.

MACINTOSH PASCAL SOLUTION DISKETTE

Solution diskette to be used by instructors who use the text Macintosh Pascal. Part of a complete intro to Pascal programming.

System: MAC, II, PLUS, SE, XL
Minimum Memory:
Requires: Macintosh Pascal text.
Medium: 3 1/2-inch disk
ISPN: 17298-758   **Price: $20.00**

FREEMAN W H AND CO.

MACINTOSH PASCAL STUDENTS DISKETTE

Convenience diskette with sample programs to be used with the text, Macintosh Pascal, providing a complete intro to Pascal programming.

System: MAC, II, PLUS, SE, XL
Minimum Memory:
Requires: Macintosh Pascal text.
Medium: 3 1/2-inch disk
ISPN: 17298-755   **Price: $20.00**

ORION COMPUTER TRAINING SYSTEMS

MASTER

Teaches beginning programming with Microsoft BASIC.

System: MAC, II, PLUS, SE, XL
Minimum Memory: 512K
Requires: Microsoft Basic (Ver. 1.0 or 2.0).
Medium: 3 1/2-inch disk
ISPN: 58862-666   **Price: $99.95**

AMERICAN TRAINING INT'L. (ATI)

TEACH YOURSELF MACCOACH

Interactive tutorial program that introduces the beginner to the various functions and operations of the computer.

System: MAC, II, PLUS, SE, XL
Minimum Memory: 512K
Medium: 3 1/2-inch disk
ISPN: 03156-083   **Price: $75.00**

BAUDVILLE

TED BEAR GAMES

Ages 4-5: Children play Concentration, Old Maid and Go Fish while being introduced to the computer.

System: MAC, II, PLUS, SE, XL
Minimum Memory: 512K
Medium: 3 1/2-inch disk
ISPN: 07087-800   **Price: $19.95**

BORLAND INT'L.

TURBO PASCAL TUTOR (VER. 1.0) (MACINTOSH)

Guides user through a wide variety of Turbo Pascal programs. Includes 300 page manual and disk.

System: MAC, II, PLUS, SE, XL
Minimum Memory: 512K
Medium: 3 1/2-inch disk
ISPN: 08225-201   **Price: $69.95**

---

224 EDUCATION/ CURRICULUM DEVELOPMENT/ AUTHORING

KINKOS ACADEMIC COURSEWARE EXCHANGE

ATLAS AND OVERLAY (VER. 1.0)

An authoring tool for creating and manipulating atlases of images.

System: MAC, II, PLUS, SE, XL
Minimum Memory: 512K
Medium: 3 1/2-inch disk
ISPN: 43025-075   **Price: $12.50**

KINKOS ACADEMIC COURSEWARE EXCHANGE

CASEMAKER (VER. 1.0)

Poses questions to students after they have read the case, then interactively permits them to choose from a number of responses.

System: MAC, II, PLUS, SE, XL
Minimum Memory: 128K
Requires: Finder (Ver. 4.1 or 5.3), word processing program that saves documents as 'text only'.
Medium: 3 1/2-inch disk
ISPN: 43025-105   **Price: $12.00**

FIRST REFERENCE, INC.

CBT DEVELOPMENT STACKS

Provides templates and tools for generating computer based training programs using HyperCard.

System: MAC, II, PLUS, SE, XL
Minimum Memory: 1024K
Requires: HyperCard (ISPN 03900-300), two disk drives or a disk drive and a hard disk.
Medium: 3 1/2-inch disk
ISPN: 91834-100   **Price: $135.00**

MINDPLAY

COTTON WORKS

Grades K-2: Provides 50 prepared worksheets where the child can fill in ready-made grids with Cotton graphics to make worksheets.

System: MAC, II, PLUS, SE, XL
Minimum Memory: 512K
Medium: 3 1/2-inch disk
ISPN: 54362-364   **Price: $29.99**

TELEROBOTICS INT'L., INC.
COURSE BUILDER (VER. 3.0)

A visual authoring language that enables user to create interactive courseware as stand alone applications.
System: MAC, II, PLUS, SE, XL
Minimum Memory: 1024K
Requires: Two 800K disk drives or hard disk.
Medium: 3 1/2-inch disk
ISPN: 80981-100 **Price: $395.00**

TELEROBOTICS INT'L., INC.
COURSE BUILDER COLOR (VER. 3.0)

A visual authoring language that enables users to create stand alone interactive courseware in color to run on the Macintosh II.
System: MAC, II, PLUS, SE, XL
Minimum Memory: 1024K
Requires: Two 800K disk drives or hard disk. 2048K RAM is required for authoring mode.
Medium: 3 1/2-inch disk
ISPN: 80981-110 **Price: $695.00**

TELEROBOTICS INT'L., INC.
COURSE BUILDER FRENCH (VER. 3.0)

A visual language that enables users to create interactive courseware as stand alone applications in French.
System: MAC, II, PLUS, SE, XL
Minimum Memory: 1024K
Requires: Two 800K disk drives or hard disk.
Medium: 3 1/2-inch disk
ISPN: 80981-120 **Price: $395.00**

KINKOS ACADEMIC COURSEWARE EXCHANGE
DRILL (VER. 2.2)

A general question-and-answer drill program with text and pictures, modeless help and multiple windows.
System: MAC, II, PLUS, SE, XL
Minimum Memory: 128K
Requires: MacWrite (ISPN 12784-530), MacPaint (ISPN 12784-510).
Medium: 3 1/2-inch disk
ISPN: 43025-108 **Price: $7.00**

INDIVIDUAL SOFTWARE, INC.
FLASH & MATCH

Contains customizable electronic flash cards.
System: MAC, II, PLUS, SE, XL
Minimum Memory: 512K
Medium: 3 1/2-inch disk
ISPN: 37275-210 **Price: $39.95**

MENLO BUSINESS SYSTEMS, INC.
FOUNDATION COMPUTER BASED TRAINING (CBT)

Integrates the authoring power of the Macintosh with the OLTP power of the Tandem computer to meet the training needs of organizations.
System: MAC, II, PLUS, SE, XL
Minimum Memory:
Medium: 3 1/2-inch disk
ISPN: 48969-175
Price: Please contact the software publisher.

KINKOS ACADEMIC COURSEWARE EXCHANGE
LESSON WRITER (VER. 2.2)

Helps teachers create tutorials, tests and quizzes containing questions of varying detail and sophistication.
System: MAC, II, PLUS, SE, XL
Minimum Memory: 128K
Requires: Finder (Ver. 4.1 or later).
Medium: 3 1/2-inch disk
ISPN: 43025-350 **Price: $30.00**

KINKOS ACADEMIC COURSEWARE EXCHANGE
LESSON WRITER FOR CHEMISTRY LESSONS (VER. 2.2)

Helps teachers create tutorials, tests and quizzes for chemistry. Includes lessons on inorganic nomenclature.
System: MAC, II, PLUS, SE, XL
Minimum Memory: 128K
Requires: Finder (Ver. 4.1 or later).
Medium: 3 1/2-inch disk
ISPN: 43025-351 **Price: $34.00**

LOGIC EXTENSION RESOURCES
LXR TEST (VER. 3.1) (SCORING EDITION)

A specialized desktop publishing program for generating and scoring exams.
System: MAC, II, PLUS, SE, XL
Minimum Memory: 512K
Medium: 3 1/2-inch disk
ISPN: 45225-300 **Price: $799.00**

LOGIC EXTENSION RESOURCES
LXR TEST (VER. 4.0) (FULL EDITION)

A specialized desktop publishing program for generating exams that is limited to 500 questions.
System: MAC, II, PLUS, SE, XL
Minimum Memory: 512K
Medium: 3 1/2-inch disk
ISPN: 45225-350 **Price: $499.00**

LOGIC EXTENSION RESOURCES
LXR TEST (VER. 4.0) SITE EDITION (COMMERCIAL)

Combines text and graphics to generate tests with scoring capabilities. For commercial site use.
System: MAC, II, PLUS, SE, XL
Minimum Memory: 512K
Medium: 3 1/2-inch disk
ISPN: 45225-370 **Price: $2500.00**

LOGIC EXTENSION RESOURCES
LXR TEST (VER. 4.0) SITE EDITION (EDUCATIONAL)

Combines text and graphics to generate tests with scoring capability. For educational site use.
System: MAC, II, PLUS, SE, XL
Minimum Memory: 512K
Medium: 3 1/2-inch disk
ISPN: 45225-360 **Price: $1500.00**

EDUDISC
MACAUTHOR (VER. 3.4)

Helps teacher in designing interactive computer-aided lessons.
System: MAC, II, PLUS, SE, XL
Minimum Memory: 512K
Requires: 800K disk drive.
Medium: 3 1/2-inch disk
ISPN: 28068-200 **Price: $195.00**

KINKOS ACADEMIC COURSEWARE EXCHANGE
MACLANG (VER. 3.2)

Helps teachers prepare computer exercises in French, Spanish, Italian, Portuguese, German, Rumanian, Russian and Greek.
System: MAC, II, PLUS, SE, XL
Minimum Memory: 512K
Medium: 3 1/2-inch disk
ISPN: 43025-390 **Price: $30.00**

KINKOS ACADEMIC COURSEWARE EXCHANGE
MACLANG (VER. 3.2)

Helps teachers prepare computer exercises in French, Spanish, Italian, Portuguese, German, Rumanian, Russian and Greek.
System: MAC, II, PLUS, SE, XL
Minimum Memory: 512K
Requires: Site license.
Medium: 3 1/2-inch disk
ISPN: 43025-390 **Price: $300.00**

DYNACOMP, INC.
MASTER DRILL

Allows the user to set up multiple choice drills on any subject desired by responding to prompts.
System: MAC, II, PLUS, SE, XL
Minimum Memory: 512K
Medium: 3 1/2-inch disk
ISPN: 27050-491 **Price: $34.95**

KINKOS ACADEMIC COURSEWARE EXCHANGE
MATCHMAKER AND MATCHMAKER UTILITY (VER. 1.1)

Helps teachers create matching-type quizzes, and then interactively presents, checks and scores the quizzes.
System: MAC, II, PLUS, SE, XL
Minimum Memory: 128K
Requires: 800K disk, Finder (Ver. 4.1 or 5.3).
Medium: 3 1/2-inch disk
ISPN: 43025-425 **Price: $12.00**

EDUDISC
MENTOR/MACVIDEO (VER. 3.4)

Authoring software for educators and trainers to design interactive videodisc courseware. Includes interface to video players.
System: MAC, II, PLUS, SE, XL
Minimum Memory: 512K
Requires: Panasonic OMDR TQ-2023F, TQ-2024F, TQ2026F, TQ2027F, or Pioneer LD-V4200, 6000(A), 6010(A), or Sony LDP-1000(A), 2000 and monitor.
Medium: 3 1/2-inch disk
ISPN: 28068-300 **Price: $595.00**

POSEIDON, INC.
OYSTER (VER. 2.02)

Provides an instructional authoring system to create educational experiences including tutorials, guided analysis and role playing.
System: MAC, II, PLUS, SE, XL
Minimum Memory: 512K
Medium: 3 1/2-inch disk
ISPN: 61619-575   **Price: $79.95**

TELEROBOTICS INT'L., INC.
VIDEO BUILDER (VER. 3.0)

Visual language that enables creation of interactive courseware as stand alone applications and provides video disk support.
System: MAC, II, PLUS, SE, XL
Minimum Memory: 1024K
Requires: Two 800K disk drives or hard disk.
Medium: 3 1/2-inch disk
ISPN: 80981-700   **Price: $695.00**

TELEROBOTICS INT'L., INC.
VIDEO BUILDER COLOR (VER. 3.0)

Enables you to create interactive color courseware. Allows access and control of video disc players and video tape players.
System: MAC, II, PLUS, SE, XL
Minimum Memory: 1024K
Requires: Two 800K disk drives or hard disk.
   2048K RAM is required for authoring mode.
Medium: 3 1/2-inch disk
ISPN: 80981-710   **Price: $995.00**

226 EDUCATION/ DECIMALS/FRACTIONS/ PERCENTS/RATIOS

UNICORN SOFTWARE CO.
DECIMAL DUNGEON

Grades 5-9: Multi-level arcade game and guide to decimals, fractions and percents.
System: MAC, II, PLUS, SE, XL
Minimum Memory: 512K
Medium: 3 1/2-inch disk
ISPN: 83562-075   **Price: $49.95**

UNICORN SOFTWARE CO.
FRACTION ACTION

Teaches addition, multiplication, subtraction and division of fractions.
System: MAC, II, PLUS, SE, XL
Minimum Memory: 512K
Medium: 3 1/2-inch disk
ISPN: 83562-100   **Price: $49.95**

QUEUE
FRACTION WORD PROBLEMS

Grades 7-9: Gives complete instructions on addition, subtraction, multiplication and fractional division.
System: MAC, II, PLUS, SE, XL
Minimum Memory: 128K
Medium: 3 1/2-inch disk
ISPN: 64387-359   **Price: $34.95**

FIRST BYTE, INC.
MATHTALK FRACTIONS

Tutor and game program introduces children to fractions, decimals and percents.
System: MAC, II, PLUS, SE, XL
Minimum Memory: 512K
Medium: 3 1/2-inch disk
ISPN: 30836-350   **Price: $49.95**

QUEUE
RATIOS AND PROPORTIONS

Grades 7-9: A step-by-step guide for calculating ratios and proportions.
System: MAC, II, PLUS, SE, XL
Minimum Memory: 128K
Medium: 3 1/2-inch disk
ISPN: 64387-530   **Price: $29.95**

QUEUE
SPORTS PROBLEMS III

Grades 7-9: Use sports problems to reinforce math skills.
System: MAC, II, PLUS, SE, XL
Minimum Memory: 128K
Medium: 3 1/2-inch disk
ISPN: 64387-881   **Price: $39.95**

228 EDUCATION/EARLY CHILDHOOD DEVELOPMENT

BRIGHT STAR TECHNOLOGY
ALPHABET BLOCKS (VER. 1.0)

A talking elf on the screen teaches phonic sounds and lcttcr names to even the youngest user.
System: MAC, II, PLUS, SE, XL
Minimum Memory: 1024K
Medium: 3 1/2-inch disk
ISPN: 08459-100   **Price: $59.95**

SPRINGBOARD SOFTWARE, INC.
EARLY GAMES FOR YOUNG CHILDREN

Ages 2-6: Teaches children a variety of basic skills with a collection of nine individual learning games.
System: MAC, II, PLUS, SE, XL
Minimum Memory: 512K
Medium: 3 1/2-inch disk
ISPN: 75309-083   **Price: $49.95**

SPRINGBOARD SOFTWARE, INC.
EASY AS ABC

Ages 3-6: Approaches learning the alphabet in a variety of ways with a series of five games.
System: MAC, II, PLUS, SE, XL
Minimum Memory: 512K
Medium: 3 1/2-inch disk
ISPN: 75309-166   **Price: $49.95**

FIRST BYTE, INC.
FIRST SHAPES

Ages 3-8: Introduces children to the concepts of form and shape with games and a Bear.
System: MAC, II, PLUS, SE, XL
Minimum Memory: 512K
Medium: 3 1/2-inch disk
ISPN: 30836-150   **Price: $49.95**

HEIZER SOFTWARE
FLASHCARDS FOR KIDS-READING

A HyperCard stack which includes ten sets of customizable flash cards and speech capabilities.
System: MAC, II, PLUS, SE, XL
Minimum Memory: 512K
Requires: HyperCard (ISPN 03900-300) Ver-1.2.
Medium: 3 1/2-inch disk
ISPN: 35175-912   **Price: $12.00**

GREAT WAVE SOFTWARE
KIDSTIME (VER. 1.2)

Ages 3-8: Includes five exciting games which encourage creativity and early learning.
System: MAC, II, PLUS, SE, XL
Minimum Memory: 512K
Medium: 3 1/2-inch disk
ISPN: 33476-155   **Price: $49.95**

FIRST BYTE, INC.
KIDTALK

A talking notebook with letter by letter, word by word, sentence by sentence spoken texts that aid children in learning to communicate.
System: MAC, II, PLUS, SE, XL
Minimum Memory: 512K
Medium: 3 1/2-inch disk
ISPN: 30836-200   **Price: $49.95**

OHM SOFTWARE
KIERAN (VER. 1.8)

Teaches children aged 2-6 the alphabet, counting, letters and time telling with speech and graphics.
System: MAC, II, PLUS, SE
Minimum Memory: 128K
Medium: 3 1/2-inch disk
ISPN: 57781-450   **Price: $39.95**

HEIZER SOFTWARE
LEARNING COUNTING

A HyperCard stack which teaches preschool children the basics of counting.
System: MAC, II, PLUS, SE, XL
Minimum Memory: 512K
Requires: HyperCard (ISPN 03900-300).
Medium: 3 1/2-inch disk
ISPN: 35175-952   **Price: $8.00**

HEIZER SOFTWARE

LEARNING SHAPES

A HyperCard stack which teaches children to recognize shapes such as circles, squares, and hearts.

System: MAC, II, PLUS, SE, XL
Minimum Memory: 512K
Requires: HyperCard (ISPN 03900-300).
Medium: 3 1/2-inch disk
ISPN: 35175-953   **Price: $8.00**

VIKING TECHNOLOGIES

LEARNING TIME

Includes Mac 'n' States (US geography quiz), Shape Art (building blocks program), ABSpeaks (talking alphabet tutor) and Time Teller.

System: MAC, II, PLUS, SE
Minimum Memory:
Medium: 3 1/2-inch disk
ISPN: 85231-400   **Price: $19.95**

UNICORN SOFTWARE CO.

MAC ROBOTS

Animated robots teach pre-reading, addition and subtraction, counting numbers and upper/lower case letter recognition.

System: MAC, II, PLUS, SE, XL
Minimum Memory: 512K
Medium: 3 1/2-inch disk
ISPN: 83562-245   **Price: $49.95**

NORDIC SOFTWARE, INC.

MACKIDS-ALPHABETIZER

Ages 7 and up: Teaches children to sort different types of lists alphabetically, numerically and chronologically.

System: MAC, II, PLUS, SE, XL
Minimum Memory: 128K
Medium: 3 1/2-inch disk
ISPN: 57028-001   **Price: $39.95**

NORDIC SOFTWARE, INC.

MACKIDS-CLOCKWORKS

Ages 4-10: Includes vocabulary lessons and lessons on telling time on analog and digital clock faces.

System: MAC, II, PLUS, SE, XL
Minimum Memory: 128K
Medium: 3 1/2-inch disk
ISPN: 57028-025   **Price: $39.95**

NORDIC SOFTWARE, INC.

MACKIDS-PRESCHOOL DISK I

Ages 3-7: Teaches letter recognition, how to complete a picture and counting skills by matching numbers with groups of objects.

System: MAC, II, PLUS, SE, XL
Minimum Memory: 128K
Medium: 3 1/2-inch disk
ISPN: 57028-350   **Price: $39.95**

NORDIC SOFTWARE, INC.

MACKIDS-PRESCHOOL DISK II

Ages 3-7: Three programs teach shapes and sizes, numbers and short term memory skills. Contains a bonus game called Tic-Tac-Toe.

System: MAC, II, PLUS, SE, XL
Minimum Memory: 128K
Medium: 3 1/2-inch disk
ISPN: 57028-352   **Price: $39.95**

TEACH YOURSELF BY COMPUTER SOFTWARE, INC.

MATCH-ON-A-MAC

Eleven games help children match letters, numbers, pictures, shapes, and quantities.

System: MAC, II, PLUS, SE, XL
Minimum Memory: 512K
Medium: 3 1/2-inch disk
ISPN: 82981-440   **Price: $39.95**

BRIGHT STAR TECHNOLOGY

TALKING TILES (VER. 1.0)

Uses an animated 'talking tutor' to teach word sounds, letters and how words are phonetically put together.

System: MAC, II, PLUS, SE, XL
Minimum Memory: 1024K
Requires: Two 800K disk drives or a hard disk.
Medium: 3 1/2-inch disk
ISPN: 08459-700   **Price: $129.95**

GREAT WAVE SOFTWARE

TIMEMASTERS

Entertaining way of learning time concepts for children ages 4-10. Also helpful for children having trouble mastering clock time.

System: MAC, II, PLUS, SE, XL
Minimum Memory:
Medium: 3 1/2-inch disk
ISPN: 33476-177   **Price: $39.95**

QUEUE

WHAT COMES NEXT?

Designed to introduce children from age 3 – 6 to story sequences and mathematical progressions.

System: MAC, II, PLUS, SE, XL
Minimum Memory: 128K
Medium: 3 1/2-inch disk
ISPN: 64387-960   **Price: $44.95**

---

229 EDUCATION/ ENGLISH AS A SECOND LANGUAGE

PEMD EDUCATION GROUP

EXERCISOR

Instructs student in learning the vocabulary and grammatical forms required for mastery of English.

System: MAC, II, PLUS, SE, XL
Minimum Memory: 512K
Requires: 800K disk drive.
Medium: 3 1/2-inch disk
ISPN: 60424-200   **Price: $150.00**

---

232 EDUCATION/ FOREIGN LANGUAGE (MISCELLANEOUS)

DAVKA CORP.

HYPERHEBREW (VER. 1.0)

A HyperCard stack that introduces Hebrew language basics with digitized Hebrew speech.

System: MAC, II, PLUS, SE, XL
Minimum Memory: 1024K
Requires: HyperCard (ISPN 03900-300).
Medium: 3 1/2-inch disk
ISPN: 91205-310   **Price: $39.95**

HYPERGLOT SOFTWARE CO.

INTRODUCTION TO RUSSIAN

A HyperCard stack that teaches Russian with digitized sound of native Russian speakers.

System: MAC, II, PLUS, SE, XL
Minimum Memory: 1024K
Requires: HyperCard (VER. 1.2.1) (ISPN 03900-300).
Medium: 3 1/2-inch disk
ISPN: 36734-600   **Price: $39.95**

QUEUE 2

ITALIAN GRAMMAR REVIEW I

Grades 9 and up: A review and practice of Italian grammar structure including subject pronouns, adjective agreement and idioms.

System: MAC, II, PLUS, SE, XL
Minimum Memory: 128K
Medium: 3 1/2-inch disk
ISPN: 64393-052   **Price: $49.95**

QUEUE 2

LATIN GRAMMAR REVIEW I

Grades 9 and up: Provides students with review and practice involving grammar points covered in first-year Latin.

System: MAC, II, PLUS, SE, XL
Minimum Memory: 128K
Medium: 3 1/2-inch disk
ISPN: 64393-084   **Price: $49.95**

DAVKA CORP.

LEARNING TO READ HEBREW (VER. 4.2)

Teaches reading of Hebrew to those who have no prior knowledge of Hebrew alphabet. Contains 14 units, including letters and vowels.

System: MAC, II, PLUS, SE, XL
Minimum Memory: 512K
Medium: 3 1/2-inch disk
ISPN: 91205-400   **Price: $39.95**

EASTERN LANGUAGE SYSTEMS

MU'ALLIM ALMUFRADAAT

Provides an Arabic Vocabulary tutor.

System: MAC, II, PLUS, SE, XL
Minimum Memory: 1024K
Requires: HyperCard (ISPN 03900-300).
Medium: 3 1/2-inch disk
ISPN: 04837-500   **Price: $30.00**

HYPERGLOT SOFTWARE CO.

RUSSIAN NOUN TUTOR

A complete tutorial and series of drills on gender, number and irregularities on over 300 noun forms with translations.

System: MAC, II, PLUS, SE, XL
Minimum Memory: 1024K
Requires: HyperCard (VER. 1.2.1) (ISPN 03900-300).
Medium: 3 1/2-inch disk
ISPN: 36734-610   **Price: $29.95**

HYPERGLOT SOFTWARE CO.

RUSSIAN VERBAL ASPECT

Provides 200 sentences to drill you on 40 verbs (20 aspectual pair) using HyperCard. For first or second year Russian students.

System: MAC, II, PLUS, SE, XL
Minimum Memory: 1024K
Requires: HyperCard (VER. 1.2.1) (ISPN 03900-300).
Medium: 3 1/2-inch disk
ISPN: 36734-620   **Price: $29.95**

HYPERGLOT SOFTWARE CO.

RUSSIAN WORD TORTURE

An automated vocabulary drill with over 1400 accented verbs, nouns, adjectives, comparatives and function words.

System: MAC, II, PLUS, SE, XL
Minimum Memory: 1024K
Requires: HyperCard (VER. 1.2.1) (ISPN 03900-300).
Medium: 3 1/2-inch disk
ISPN: 36734-630   **Price: $19.95**

DAVKA CORP.

ULPAN DAVKA (VER. 1.0)

A Hebrew vocabulary program with digitized speech.

System: MAC, II, PLUS, SE, XL
Minimum Memory: 1024K
Requires: HyperCard (ISPN 03900-300).
Medium: 3 1/2-inch disk
ISPN: 91205-750   **Price: $39.95**

---

233 EDUCATION/ FRENCH

INDIVIDUAL SOFTWARE, INC.

FLASH & MATCH FRENCH

Provides customizable electronic flash cards with an 1800 word French/English database to help build foreign language vocabulary.

System: MAC, II, PLUS, SE, XL
Minimum Memory: 512K
Requires: 800K disk drive.
Medium: 3 1/2-inch disk
ISPN: 37275-215   **Price: $59.95**

QUEUE

FRENCH GRAMMAR I

Instructs French students on use of the noun, the definite article, the indefinite article and prepositions.

System: MAC, II, PLUS, SE, XL
Minimum Memory: 128K
Medium: 3 1/2-inch disk
ISPN: 64387-361   **Price: $34.95**

QUEUE 2

FRENCH GRAMMAR I-IX

A nine-program, progressive series which instructs students in the major points of French grammar and usage.

System: MAC, II, PLUS, SE, XL
Minimum Memory: 128K
Medium: 3 1/2-inch disk
ISPN: 64393-010   **Price: $285.00**

QUEUE

FRENCH GRAMMAR II

Instructs French students in the use of qualifying adjectives, interrogative and negative forms and negative interrogative forms.

System: MAC, II, PLUS, SE, XL
Minimum Memory: 128K
Medium: 3 1/2-inch disk
ISPN: 64387-362   **Price: $34.95**

QUEUE

FRENCH GRAMMAR III

Instructs French students in the use of first, second and third conjugation, regular verbs and imperative forms.

System: MAC
Minimum Memory: 128K
Medium: 3 1/2-inch disk
ISPN: 64387-363   **Price: $34.95**

QUEUE 2

FRENCH GRAMMAR IV

Instructs students in French grammar and usage, including demonstrative, possessive, and interrogative adjectives.

System: MAC, II, PLUS, SE, XL
Minimum Memory: 128K
Medium: 3 1/2-inch disk
ISPN: 64393-007   **Price: $34.95**

QUEUE 2

FRENCH GRAMMAR IX

Instructs students in French grammar and usage, including short and long forms of interrogative pronouns, and demonstrative pronouns.

System: MAC, II, PLUS, SE, XL
Minimum Memory: 128K
Medium: 3 1/2-inch disk
ISPN: 64393-006   **Price: $34.95**

QUEUE 2

FRENCH GRAMMAR REVIEW I

Grades 9 and up: A review and practice in basic French grammar, which includes present tense of regular and irregular verbs.

System: MAC, II, PLUS, SE, XL
Minimum Memory: 128K
Medium: 3 1/2-inch disk
ISPN: 64393-046   **Price: $49.95**

QUEUE 2

FRENCH GRAMMAR REVIEW II

Grades 9 and up: A review and practice in French grammar, including passe compose, imperfect, future, conditional and subjunctive.

System: MAC, II, PLUS, SE, XL
Minimum Memory: 128K
Medium: 3 1/2-inch disk
ISPN: 64393-050   **Price: $49.95**

QUEUE 2

FRENCH GRAMMAR V

Instructs students in French grammar and usage, including the form and position of direct and indirect object pronouns.

System: MAC, II, PLUS, SE, XL
Minimum Memory: 128K
Medium: 3 1/2-inch disk
ISPN: 64393-004   **Price: $34.95**

QUEUE 2

FRENCH GRAMMAR VI

Instructs students in French grammar and usage, including form and use of the future and future perfect tenses.

System: MAC, II, PLUS, SE, XL
Minimum Memory: 128K
Medium: 3 1/2-inch disk
ISPN: 64393-008   **Price: $34.95**

QUEUE 2
FRENCH GRAMMAR VII

Instructs students in French grammar and usage, including adverbs which indicate time, place, manner, and quantity.

System: MAC, II, PLUS, SE
Minimum Memory: 128K
Medium: 3 1/2-inch disk
ISPN: 64393-005 **Price: $34.95**

QUEUE 2
FRENCH GRAMMAR VIII

Instructs students in French grammar and usage, including relative pronouns and adverbs, and possessive pronouns.

System: MAC, II, PLUS, SE, XL
Minimum Memory: 128K
Medium: 3 1/2-inch disk
ISPN: 64393-009 **Price: $34.95**

HYPERGLOT SOFTWARE CO.
FRENCH VERB TUTOR

Provides 200 sentences to drill you on 20 verbs using HyperText capabilities.

System: MAC, II, PLUS, SE, XL
Minimum Memory: 1024K
Requires: HyperCard (VER. 1.2.1) (ISPN 03900-300).
Medium: 3 1/2-inch disk
ISPN: 36734-200 **Price: $29.95**

HYPERGLOT SOFTWARE CO.
FRENCH WORD TORTURE

An automated vocabulary drill with over 1600 french verbs, nouns, adjectives, adverbs, comparatives and function words.

System: MAC, II, PLUS, SE, XL
Minimum Memory: 1024K
Requires: HyperCard (VER. 1.2.1) (ISPN 03900-300).
Medium: 3 1/2-inch disk
ISPN: 36734-210 **Price: $19.95**

LES EDITIONS/AD LIB, INC.
LE CONJUGUEUR

A desk accessory which supplies the correct conjuation of all French verbs.

System: MAC, PLUS, XL
Minimum Memory: 512K
Medium: 3 1/2-inch disk
ISPN: 44287-425 **Price: $49.95**

LE COQ BRANCHE
LE COQ BRANCHE NUMBER 7

Designed as a quarterly magazine on disk to provide information in French from French sources to help users practice reading skills.

System: MAC, PLUS, XL
Minimum Memory: 128K
Requires: 800K disk drive.
Medium: 3 1/2-inch disk
ISPN: 43783-400 **Price: $29.00**

ARTWORX SOFTWARE CO., INC.
LINKWORD-FRENCH

Teaches up to 400 words of French grammar and pronunciation.

System: MAC, II, PLUS, SE, XL
Minimum Memory: 512K
Medium: 3 1/2-inch disk
ISPN: 05437-265 **Price: $29.95**

AVENUE SOFTWARE, INC.
MENTOR (VER. 1.23)

Checks words to see if they pertain to the active WordBank. If they do, an appropriate explanation and examples are displayed.

System: MAC, II, PLUS, SE, XL
Minimum Memory: 128K
Requires: Single user.
Medium: 3 1/2-inch disk
ISPN: 06418-550 **Price: $195.00**

AVENUE SOFTWARE, INC.
MENTOR (VER. 1.23)

Checks words to see if they pertain to the active WordBank. If they do, an appropriate explanation and examples are displayed.

System: MAC, II, PLUS, SE, XL
Minimum Memory: 128K
Requires: 2-3 users.
Medium: 3 1/2-inch disk
ISPN: 06418-550 **Price: $295.00**

AVENUE SOFTWARE, INC.
MENTOR (VER. 1.23)

Checks words to see if they pertain to the active WordBank. If they do, an appropriate explanation and examples are displayed.

System: MAC, II, PLUS, SE, XL
Minimum Memory: 128K
Requires: 4-8 users.
Medium: 3 1/2-inch disk
ISPN: 06418-550 **Price: $395.00**

AVENUE SOFTWARE, INC.
MENTOR (VER. 1.23)

Checks words to see if they pertain to the active WordBank. If they do, an appropriate explanation and examples are displayed.

System: MAC, II, PLUS, SE, XL
Minimum Memory: 128K
Requires: 9-50 users.
Medium: 3 1/2-inch disk
ISPN: 06418-550 **Price: $495.00**

GESSLER EDUCATIONAL SOFTWARE
WHODUNIT (CANAL MEURTRE-FRENCH)

An educational program in a game format that teaches vocabulary and reading comprehension for intermediate to advanced students.

System: MAC, II, PLUS, SE, XL
Minimum Memory: 512K
Medium: 3 1/2-inch disk
ISPN: 32819-670 **Price: $49.95**

238 EDUCATION/ GEOGRAPHY

IMAGE MAPPING SYSTEMS
AFRICA BY COUNTRY

A digital map file for use with MacChoro that includes all the outlines of all countries in Africa.

System: MAC, II, PLUS, SE, XL
Minimum Memory: 512K
Requires: MacChoro (ISPN 37156-100)
Medium: 3 1/2-inch disk
ISPN: 37156-130 **Price: $50.00**

GREAT WAVE SOFTWARE
AMERICAN DISCOVERY (VER. 2.1)

Provides interactive instructions for learning geography, trivia and history of the United States. Recommended for ages 10 and up.

System: MAC, II, PLUS, SE, XL
Minimum Memory: 512K
Medium: 3 1/2-inch disk
ISPN: 33476-040 **Price: $49.95**

IMAGE MAPPING SYSTEMS
ANY OF 48 STATES BY COUNTY (ALABAMA-WYOMING)

A digital map file for use with MacChord that includes all of the county outlines for any one of 48 states, from Alabama to Wyoming.

System: MAC, II, PLUS, SE, XL
Minimum Memory: 512K
Requires: MacChoro (ISPN 37156-100).
Medium: 3 1/2-inch disk
ISPN: 37156-105 **Price: $50.00**

IMAGE MAPPING SYSTEMS
ASIA BY COUNTRY

A digital map file for use with MacChoro that includes all the outlines of countries in Asia.

System: MAC, II, PLUS, SE, XL
Minimum Memory: 512K
Requires: MacChoro (ISPN 37156-100).
Medium: 3 1/2-inch disk
ISPN: 37156-135 **Price: $50.00**

IMAGE MAPPING SYSTEMS
CANADA BY PROVINCE

A digital map file for use with MacChoro that includes all the outlines for the provinces in Canada.

System: MAC, II, PLUS, SE, XL
Minimum Memory: 512K
Requires: MacChoro (ISPN 37156-100).
Medium: 3 1/2-inch disk
ISPN: 37156-110   **Price: $50.00**

HEIZER SOFTWARE
CANADIAN DATABASE

Contains over forty fields of data for each province in Canada, including population and area.

System: MAC, II, PLUS, SE, XL
Minimum Memory: 512K
Requires: Microsoft Excel (ISPN 53150-270) or Microsoft Works (ISPN 53150-740).
Medium: 3 1/2-inch disk
ISPN: 35175-917   **Price: $10.00**

IMAGE MAPPING SYSTEMS
EUROPE BY COUNTRY

A digital map file for use with MacChoro that includes all of the outlines for countries in Europe.

System: MAC, II, PLUS, SE, XL
Minimum Memory: 512K
Requires: MacChoro (ISPN 37156-100).
Medium: 3 1/2-inch disk
ISPN: 37156-125   **Price: $50.00**

QUEUE
EUROPE-PART II

Grades 4 and up: Students learn to identify the capital, largest cities, rivers, and noteworthy geographical features.

System: MAC, II, PLUS, SE, XL
Minimum Memory: 128K
Medium: 3 1/2-inch disk
ISPN: 64387-981   **Price: $59.95**

QUEUE
GEOGRAPHY OF THE AMERICAS

Improves knowledge of the geography of North, Central and South America with comprehensive multiple-choice review questions.

System: MAC, II, PLUS, SE, XL
Minimum Memory: 128K
Medium: 3 1/2-inch disk
ISPN: 64387-300   **Price: $34.95**

MICROMAPS SOFTWARE, INC.
HYPERATLAS

Allows users to access geographically based data in HyperCard stacks and includes a set of maps that cover the whole world.

System: MAC, II, PLUS, SE, XL
Minimum Memory: 1024K
Requires: HyperCard (ISPN 03900-300).
Medium: 3 1/2-inch disk
ISPN: 50675-300   **Price: $99.00**

HEIZER SOFTWARE
HYPERATLAS USA

A series of HyperCard stacks containing maps of the United States and all individual fifty states.

System: MAC, II, PLUS, SE, XL
Minimum Memory: 512K
Requires: HyperCard (ISPN 03900-300).
Medium: 3 1/2-inch disk
ISPN: 35175-948   **Price: $30.00**

HEIZER SOFTWARE
HYPERATLAS WORLD

A series of HyperCard stacks containing maps of the world, which are linked to information cards for every country.

System: MAC, II, PLUS, SE, XL
Minimum Memory: 512K
Requires: HyperCard (ISPN 03900-300).
Medium: 3 1/2-inch disk
ISPN: 35175-949   **Price: $30.00**

SOFT HORIZON
KNOW YOUR WORLD

Teaches countries, capitals and major cities using continent and USA maps and five learning activities.

System: MAC, II, PLUS, SE, XL
Minimum Memory: 512K
Medium: 3 1/2-inch disk
ISPN: 71808-400   **Price: $39.95**

IMAGE MAPPING SYSTEMS
MACCHORO

A menu-driven data classification and statistical mapping program for the creation of maps.

System: MAC, II, PLUS, SE, XL
Minimum Memory: 512K
Requires: 800K disk drive.
Medium: 3 1/2-inch disk
ISPN: 37156-100   **Price: $295.00**

NORDIC SOFTWARE, INC.
MACKIDS-EARTHWORKS

Teaches geography and related topics and the names of Capitals, States and major cities. Ages 10-adult.

System: MAC, II, PLUS, SE, XL
Minimum Memory: 512K
Medium: 3 1/2-inch disk
ISPN: 57028-065   **Price: $39.95**

QUEUE
NORTH & SOUTH AMERICA-PART I

Grades 4 and up: Students learn to identify the capital, largest cities, rivers, and noteworthy geographical features.

System: MAC, II, PLUS, SE, XL
Minimum Memory: 128K
Medium: 3 1/2-inch disk
ISPN: 64387-979   **Price: $59.95**

IMAGE MAPPING SYSTEMS
NORTH AMERICA BY COUNTRY

A digital map file for use with MacChoro that includes all the outlines of the countries in North America.

System: MAC, II, PLUS, SE, XL
Minimum Memory: 512K
Requires: MacChoro (ISPN 37156-100).
Medium: 3 1/2-inch disk
ISPN: 37156-115   **Price: $50.00**

IMAGE MAPPING SYSTEMS
POLYEXTRACT

To be used with MacChoro to extract individual state with counties. Extracts up to 400 counties.

System: MAC, II, PLUS, SE, XL
Minimum Memory: 512K
Requires: MacChoro (ISPN 37156-100).
Medium: 3 1/2-inch disk
ISPN: 37156-300   **Price: $60.00**

IMAGE MAPPING SYSTEMS
SOUTH AMERICA BY COUNTRY

A digital map file for use with MacChoro that includes all the outlines of the countries in South America.

System: MAC, II, PLUS, SE, XL
Minimum Memory: 512K
Requires: MacChoro (ISPN 37156-100).
Medium: 3 1/2-inch disk
ISPN: 37156-120   **Price: $50.00**

HEIZER SOFTWARE
STATE QUIZZES

Includes two HyperCard stacks which teach students the names and locations of all the states in the United States.

System: MAC, II, PLUS, SE, XL
Minimum Memory: 512K
Requires: HyperCard (ISPN 03900-300).
Medium: 3 1/2-inch disk
ISPN: 35175-989   **Price: $6.00**

HYPERFORMANCE
STATE-SMART

A hypercard stack of maps and information and topography of each state in the U.S.

System: MAC, II, PLUS, SE, XL
Minimum Memory: 1024K
Requires: 800K disk drive. HyperCard (ISPN 03900-300) Ver. 1.2 or higher.
Medium: 3 1/2-inch disk
ISPN: 36732-700   **Price: $59.95**

VENTURA EDUCATIONAL SYSTEMS
STATES (VER. 2.0)

Grades 4 and up: A geography study unit to learn and identify all of the fifty states and their respective capitals and facts.

System: MAC, II, PLUS, SE, XL
Minimum Memory: 512K
Medium: 3 1/2-inch disk
ISPN: 84911-722   **Price: $49.95**

P PRODUCTIONS

STATESFACTS (VER. 2.0)

A HyperCard stack that contains drawings and information on the 50 states.

System: MAC, II, PLUS, SE, XL
Minimum Memory: 1024K
Requires: HyperCard (ISPN 03900-300).
Medium: 3 1/2-inch disk
ISPN: 59187-720   **Price: $39.00**

P PRODUCTIONS

STATESFACTS (VER. 2.0)

A HyperCard stack that contains drawings and information on the 50 states.

System: MAC, II, PLUS, SE, XL
Minimum Memory: 1024K
Requires: Small School district license (under 5,000 students). HyperCard (ISPN 03900-300).
Medium: 3 1/2-inch disk
ISPN: 59187-720   **Price: $99.00**

P PRODUCTIONS

STATESFACTS (VER. 2.0)

A HyperCard stack that contains drawings and information on the 50 states.

System: MAC, II, PLUS, SE, XL
Minimum Memory: 1024K
Requires: Large school district license. HyperCard (ISPN 03900-300).
Medium: 3 1/2-inch disk
ISPN: 59187-720   **Price: $249.00**

KINKOS ACADEMIC COURSEWARE EXCHANGE

STUDENT ATLAS-COUNTIES (VER. 1.0)

A three-disk set of 8- by 10-inch state maps, showing all county borders, in MacPaint format.

System: MAC, II, PLUS, SE, XL
Minimum Memory: 128K
Requires: MacPaint (ISPN 12784-510) or compatible program.
Medium: 3 1/2-inch disk
ISPN: 43025-840   **Price: $20.50**

KINKOS ACADEMIC COURSEWARE EXCHANGE

STUDENT ATLAS-COUNTIES (VER. 1.0)

A three-disk set of 8- by 10-inch state maps, showing all county borders, in MacPaint format.

System: MAC, II, PLUS, SE, XL
Minimum Memory: 128K
Requires: Site license.
Medium: 3 1/2-inch disk
ISPN: 43025-840   **Price: $750.00**

KINKOS ACADEMIC COURSEWARE EXCHANGE

STUDENT ATLAS-U.S.A. (VER. 1.0)

Includes twenty maps of the U.S.A. showing state borders, major cities and state abbreviations, in MacPaint format.

System: MAC, II, PLUS, SE, XL
Minimum Memory: 128K
Requires: MacPaint (ISPN 12784-510) or compatible program.
Medium: 3 1/2-inch disk
ISPN: 43025-841   **Price: $16.00**

KINKOS ACADEMIC COURSEWARE EXCHANGE

STUDENT ATLAS-U.S.A. (VER. 1.0)

Includes twenty maps of the U.S.A. showing state borders, major cities and state abbreviations, in MacPaint format.

System: MAC, II, PLUS, SE, XL
Minimum Memory: 128K
Requires: Site license. MacPaint (ISPN 12784-510) or compatible program.
Medium: 3 1/2-inch disk
ISPN: 43025-841   **Price: $600.00**

KINKOS ACADEMIC COURSEWARE EXCHANGE

STUDENT ATLAS-WORLD (VER. 1.0)

Contains sixteen maps of the world in MacPaint format.

System: MAC, II, PLUS, SE, XL
Minimum Memory: 128K
Requires: MacPaint (ISPN 12784-510) or compatible program.
Medium: 3 1/2-inch disk
ISPN: 43025-842   **Price: $16.00**

KINKOS ACADEMIC COURSEWARE EXCHANGE

STUDENT ATLAS-WORLD (VER. 1.0)

Contains sixteen maps of the world in MacPaint format.

System: MAC, II, PLUS, SE, XL
Minimum Memory: 128K
Requires: Site license. MacPaint (ISPN 12784-510) or compatible program.
Medium: 3 1/2-inch disk
ISPN: 43025-842   **Price: $600.00**

QUEUE

U.S. GEOGRAPHY ADVENTURE

Travel to all 50 states plus Washington, D.C., Puerto Rico, Guam and the Virgin Islands as students learn to identify each state.

System: MAC, II, PLUS, SE, XL
Minimum Memory: 128K
Medium: 3 1/2-inch disk
ISPN: 64387-900   **Price: $59.95**

IMAGE MAPPING SYSTEMS

WORLD BY COUNTRY

A digital map file for use with MacChoro that includes all the outlines for countries in the world.

System: MAC, II, PLUS, SE, XL
Minimum Memory: 512K
Medium: 3 1/2-inch disk
ISPN: 37156-140   **Price: $50.00**

P PRODUCTIONS

WORLD FACTS

A group of six interactive HyperCard stacks that contains information on 140 United Nations recognized countries.

System: MAC, II, PLUS, SE, XL
Minimum Memory: 1024K
Requires: HyperCard (ISPN 03900-300).
Medium: 3 1/2-inch disk
ISPN: 59187-800   **Price: $39.00**

P PRODUCTIONS

WORLD FACTS

A group of six interactive HyperCard stacks that contains information on 140 United Nations recognized countries.

System: MAC, II, PLUS, SE, XL
Minimum Memory: 1024K
Requires: Small school district license (under 5,000 students). HyperCard (ISPN 03900-300).
Medium: 3 1/2-inch disk
ISPN: 59187-800   **Price: $99.00**

P PRODUCTIONS

WORLD FACTS

A group of six interactive HyperCard stacks that contains information on 140 United Nations recognized countries.

System: MAC, II, PLUS, SE, XL
Minimum Memory: 1024K
Requires: Large school district license. HyperCard (ISPN 03900-300).
Medium: 3 1/2-inch disk
ISPN: 59187-800   **Price: $249.00**

QUEUE

WORLD GEOGRAPHY ADVENTURE I

Students travel to each country and must learn capitals, largest cities, rivers and other noteworthy geographical features.

System: MAC, II, PLUS, SE, XL
Minimum Memory: 128K
Medium: 3 1/2-inch disk
ISPN: 64387-970   **Price: $59.95**

QUEUE

WORLD GEOGRAPHY ADVENTURE II

Students see every country in Europe while learning the geography, cities, capitals, rivers and learn their relationships.

System: MAC, II, PLUS, SE, XL
Minimum Memory: 128K
Medium: 3 1/2-inch disk
ISPN: 64387-980   **Price: $59.95**

---

239 EDUCATION/ GERMAN

INDIVIDUAL SOFTWARE, INC.

FLASH & MATCH GERMAN

Provides customizable electronic flashcards with an 1800 word German/English database to help build foreign language vocabulary.

System: MAC, II, PLUS, SE, XL
Minimum Memory: 512K
Requires: 800K disk drive.
Medium: 3 1/2-inch disk
ISPN: 37275-225   **Price: $59.95**

QUEUE 2

GERMAN CONTESTS-LEVELS I AND II

Grades 9 and up: Provides 200 multiple-choice questions on German grammar and culture, with explanatory comments in English.

System: MAC, II, PLUS, SE, XL
Minimum Memory: 128K
Medium: 3 1/2-inch disk
ISPN: 64393-072   **Price: $39.95**

QUEUE 2

GERMAN GRAMMAR REVIEW I

Grades 9 and up: Provides review lessons in German, followed by extensive drill and practice on 14 different topics.

System: MAC, II, PLUS, SE, XL
Minimum Memory: 128K
Medium: 3 1/2-inch disk
ISPN: 64393-070   **Price: $49.95**

QUEUE 2

GERMAN GRAMMAR REVIEW II

Grades 9 and up: Provides review lessons in German, followed by extensive drill and practice on 14 topics.

System: MAC, II, PLUS, SE, XL
Minimum Memory: 128K
Medium: 3 1/2-inch disk
ISPN: 64393-071   **Price: $49.95**

HYPERGLOT SOFTWARE CO.

GERMAN VERB TUTOR

Provides 200 sentences to drill you on 20 verbs using HyperText capabilities.

System: MAC, II, PLUS, SE, XL
Minimum Memory: 1024K
Requires: HyperCard (VER. 1.2.1) (ISPN 03900-300).
Medium: 3 1/2-inch disk
ISPN: 36734-300   **Price: $29.95**

HYPERGLOT SOFTWARE CO.

GERMAN WORD TORTURE

An automated vocabulary drill with over 1600 verbs, adverbs, nouns, adjectives, comparatives and function words.

System: MAC, II, PLUS, SE, XL
Minimum Memory: 1024K
Requires: HyperCard (VER. 1.2.1) (ISPN 03900-300).
Medium: 3 1/2-inch disk
ISPN: 36734-310   **Price: $19.95**

ARTWORX SOFTWARE CO., INC.

LINKWORD-GERMAN

Teaches up to 400 words of German grammar, and pronunciation.

System: MAC, II, PLUS, SE, XL
Minimum Memory: 128K
Medium: 3 1/2-inch disk
ISPN: 05437-270   **Price: $29.95**

GESSLER EDUCATIONAL SOFTWARE

WHODUNIT (FERNSEHKRIMI-GERMAN)

An educational program in a game format that teaches vocabulary and reading comprehension for intermediate and advanced students.

System: MAC, II, PLUS, SE, XL
Minimum Memory: 512K
Medium: 3 1/2-inch disk
ISPN: 32819-680   **Price: $49.95**

241 EDUCATION/ GOVERNMENT/ ECONOMICS

HEIZER SOFTWARE

ACADEMIC CALENDAR

Prints a July to June appointment calendar for any school year from 1904-1905 through 2038-2039.

System: MAC, II, PLUS, SE, XL
Minimum Memory: 512K
Requires: Microsoft Excel (ISPN 53150-270) or Microsoft Works (ISPN 53150-740).
Medium: 3 1/2-inch disk
ISPN: 35175-227   **Price: $6.00**

QUEUE

AMERICAN GOVERNMENT I

Includes Democracy in America, the American political system and the constitution.

System: MAC, II, PLUS, SE, XL
Minimum Memory: 128K
Medium: 3 1/2-inch disk
ISPN: 64387-082   **Price: $34.95**

QUEUE

AMERICAN GOVERNMENT II

Includes Federalism, The First Amendment Freedoms, and other Civil Liberties.

System: MAC, II, PLUS, SE, XL
Minimum Memory: 128K
Medium: 3 1/2-inch disk
ISPN: 64387-084   **Price: $34.95**

QUEUE

AMERICAN GOVERNMENT III

Includes public opinion, elections, selecting our leaders, and how to win an election.

System: MAC, II, PLUS, SE, XL
Minimum Memory: 128K
Medium: 3 1/2-inch disk
ISPN: 64387-086   **Price: $34.95**

QUEUE

AMERICAN GOVERNMENT IV

Includes political parties, the presidential leadership, power, work, structure of congress, bills becoming law.

System: MAC, II, PLUS, SE, XL
Minimum Memory: 128K
Medium: 3 1/2-inch disk
ISPN: 64387-088   **Price: $34.95**

QUEUE

AMERICAN GOVERNMENT PACKAGE

Grades 7-12: Provides students with an understanding of the development and processes of the American governmental system.

System: MAC, II, PLUS, SE, XL
Minimum Memory: 128K
Medium: 3 1/2-inch disk
ISPN: 64387-961   **Price: $150.00**

QUEUE

AMERICAN GOVERNMENT V

Includes The Judiciary, The Supreme Court and The Bureaucracy.

System: MAC, II, PLUS, SE, XL
Minimum Memory: 128K
Medium: 3 1/2-inch disk
ISPN: 64387-092   **Price: $34.95**

P PRODUCTIONS

AMERICAN PRESIDENTS (VER. 1.0)

A HyperCard based database that contains information on all of the United States Presidents.

System: MAC, II, PLUS, SE, XL
Minimum Memory: 1024K
Requires: HyperCard (ISPN 03900-300).
Medium: 3 1/2-inch disk
ISPN: 59187-100   **Price: $39.00**

P PRODUCTIONS

AMERICAN PRESIDENTS (VER. 1.0)

A HyperCard based database that contains information on all of the United States Presidents.

System: MAC, II, PLUS, SE, XL
Minimum Memory: 1024K
Requires: Large school district license. HyperCard (ISPN 03900-300).
Medium: 3 1/2-inch disk
ISPN: 59187-100   **Price: $249.00**

P PRODUCTIONS

AMERICAN PRESIDENTS (VER. 1.0)

A HyperCard based database that contains information on all of the United States Presidents.

System: MAC, II, PLUS, SE, XL
Minimum Memory: 1024K
Requires: Small school district license (under 5,000 students). HyperCard (ISPN 03900-300).
Medium: 3 1/2-inch disk
ISPN: 59187-100   **Price: $99.00**

HEIZER SOFTWARE

ECONOMIC INDICATORS

Covers twenty-five years of annual US economic data for more than thirty-five areas. Includes unemployment, wages, prices and money.

System: MAC, II, PLUS, SE, XL
Minimum Memory: 512K
Requires: Microsoft Excel (ISPN 53150-270), Microsoft Works (ISPN 53150-740) or HyperCard (ISPN 03900-300).
Medium: 3 1/2-inch disk
ISPN: 35175-201   **Price: $25.00**

JP CONSULTING, INC.

FORSAL 29-HINDSIGHT

Simulates the conditions that appear to have caused the great depression of 1929.

System: MAC, PLUS, SE, XL
Minimum Memory: 128K
Medium: 3 1/2-inch disk
ISPN: 42125-260   **Price: $59.00**

QUEUE

HOW A BILL BECOMES LAW

Teaches students about the legislative system using the simulation of a Congressman trying to pass a bill in the U.S. Congress.

System: MAC, II, PLUS, SE, XL
Minimum Memory: 128K
Medium: 3 1/2-inch disk
ISPN: 64387-391   **Price: $49.95**

NORDIC SOFTWARE, INC.

MACKIDS-LEMONADE STAND

An economic simulation that assists young entrepreneurs learn to make solid business decisions at an early age. Ages 6-16.

System: MAC, II, PLUS, SE, XL
Minimum Memory: 128K
Medium: 3 1/2-inch disk
ISPN: 57028-105   **Price: $39.95**

QUEUE

MACROECONOMICS

Interactive tutorial on the basic principles of macroeconomics.

System: MAC, II, PLUS, SE, XL
Minimum Memory: 128K
Medium: 3 1/2-inch disk
ISPN: 64387-492   **Price: $39.95**

QUEUE

MACROECONOMICS-QUEUE

Covers the nature of economics, national income accounting and income determination.

System: MAC, PLUS, SE, XL
Minimum Memory: 128K
Medium: 3 1/2-inch disk
ISPN: 64387-449   **Price: $39.95**

QUEUE

MICROECONOMICS

Covers supply, demand schedule and curve, substitution of income effects, the law of diminishing return and more.

System: MAC, II, PLUS, SE, XL
Minimum Memory: 128K
Medium: 3 1/2-inch disk
ISPN: 64387-522   **Price: $39.95**

HEIZER SOFTWARE

PRESIDENTIAL CANDIDATES

A database of over 400 presidential candidates involved in every United States presidential election from 1789 through 1984.

System: MAC, II, PLUS, SE, XL
Minimum Memory: 512K
Requires: Microsoft Excel (ISPN 53150-270) or Microsoft Works (ISPN 53150-270).
Medium: 3 1/2-inch disk
ISPN: 35175-977   **Price: $15.00**

HEIZER SOFTWARE

PRESIDENTIAL DATABASE

Contains over forty different fields of data on all United States presidents.

System: MAC, II, PLUS, SE, XL
Minimum Memory: 512K
Requires: Microsoft Excel (ISPN 53150-270), Microsoft Works (ISPN 53150-740) or HyperCard (ISPN 03900-300).
Medium: 3 1/2-inch disk
ISPN: 35175-226   **Price: $8.00**

HEIZER SOFTWARE

PRESIDENTIAL ELECTIONS

A database containing the complete presidential vote results for every United States election from 1789 through 1984.

System: MAC, II, PLUS, SE, XL
Minimum Memory: 512K
Requires: Microsoft Excel (ISPN 53150-270) or Microsoft Works (ISPN 53150-270).
Medium: 3 1/2-inch disk
ISPN: 35175-979   **Price: $25.00**

HEIZER SOFTWARE

REAL MONEY CALCULATOR

Annual Consumer Price Index data for the past thirty-five years. Shows any 'base' year price in terms of all other years' amounts.

System: MAC, II, PLUS, SE, XL
Minimum Memory: 512K
Requires: Microsoft Excel (ISPN 53150-270), Microsoft Works (ISPN 53150-740) or HyperCard (ISPN 03900-300).
Medium: 3 1/2-inch disk
ISPN: 35175-216   **Price: $12.00**

HEIZER SOFTWARE

SENATORS AND REPRESENTATIVES DATABASE

Includes the names, states, districts, committees and seniority of all 435 senators and representatives.

System: MAC, II, PLUS, SE, XL
Minimum Memory: 512K
Requires: Microsoft Excel (ISPN 53150-270), Microsoft Works (ISPN 53150-740) or HyperCard (ISPN 03900-300).
Medium: 3 1/2-inch disk
ISPN: 35175-225   **Price: $15.00**

HEIZER SOFTWARE

STATES OF THE UNION DATABASE

Covers more than thirty fields including geography, government and economy for all fifty states.

System: MAC, II, PLUS, SE, XL
Minimum Memory: 512K
Requires: Microsoft Excel (ISPN 53150-270) or Microsoft Works (ISPN 53150-740).
Medium: 3 1/2-inch disk
ISPN: 35175-224   **Price: $15.00**

HEIZER SOFTWARE

UNITED STATES DATABASE

Covers over 30 fields for each of the 50 states including geography, government, economy, state flower and state motto.

System: MAC, II, PLUS, SE, XL
Minimum Memory: 1024K
Requires: HyperCard (ISPN 03900-300).
Medium: 3 1/2-inch disk
ISPN: 35175-061   **Price: $20.00**

HEIZER SOFTWARE

WORLD COUNTRY DATABASE

Covers the people, geography, government and economies of more than 160 countries, updated every sixty days.

System: MAC, PLUS, SE, XL
Minimum Memory: 512K
Requires: Microsoft Excel (ISPN 53150-270), Microsoft Works (ISPN 53150-740) or HyperCard (ISPN 03900-300).
Medium: 3 1/2-inch disk
ISPN: 35175-223   **Price: $20.00**

245 EDUCATION/ HISTORY

QUEUE

AMERICAN HISTORY ADVENTURE

Enables students to research history books in order to succeed at the game.

System: MAC, II, PLUS, SE, XL
Minimum Memory: 128K
Medium: 3 1/2-inch disk
ISPN: 64387-128   **Price: $59.95**

HEIZER SOFTWARE
DINOSAURS

Contains a picture and information about a dinosaur or pre-historic animal in 26 cards.

System: MAC, II, PLUS, SE, XL
Minimum Memory: 1024K
Requires: HyperCard (ISPN 03900-300).
Medium: 3 1/2-inch disk
ISPN: 35175-064   **Price: $12.00**

VISATEX CORP.
FACTS AND FACES OF U.S. PRESIDENTS (VER. 1.0)

A HyperCard stack which provides information about U.S. presidents. in a game format where the user answers multiple choice questions.

System: MAC, II, PLUS, SE, XL
Minimum Memory: 1024K
Requires: HyperCard (ISPN 03900-300).
Medium: 3 1/2-inch disk
ISPN: 85340-200   **Price: $49.50**

HEIZER SOFTWARE
RISE AND FALL

An animated map of Europe from 1933 to 1945 showing Germany's expansion before and during World War II and her eventual defeat.

System: MAC, II, PLUS, SE, XL
Minimum Memory: 1024K
Requires: HyperCard (ISPN 03900-300).
Medium: 3 1/2-inch disk
ISPN: 35175-059   **Price: $12.00**

KINKOS ACADEMIC COURSEWARE EXCHANGE
TREATY OF VERSAILLES (VER. 1.0)

A series of exercises to help students understand the main problems confronting the diplomats who drafted the treaties ending WWI.

System: MAC, II, PLUS, SE, XL
Minimum Memory: 128K
Requires: Finder (Ver. 4.1 or later).
Medium: 3 1/2-inch disk
ISPN: 43025-925   **Price: $15.50**

KINKOS ACADEMIC COURSEWARE EXCHANGE
WOULD-BE GENTLEMAN (THE) (VER. 4.1)

A simulation of social mobility in the France of King Louis XIV.

System: MAC, II, PLUS, SE, XL
Minimum Memory: 128K
Requires: Finder (Ver. 4.1 or later).
Medium: 3 1/2-inch disk
ISPN: 43025-960   **Price: $7.00**

249 EDUCATION/ HUMANITIES

KINKOS ACADEMIC COURSEWARE EXCHANGE
ARISTOTLE'S GREEK TRAGEDY CONSTRUCTION KIT

An electronic book – a non-linear, non-sequential study of Aristotle's Poetics that serves as a tutorial and reference guide.

System: MAC, II, PLUS, SE, XL
Minimum Memory: 1024K
Requires: HyperCard (ISPN 03900-300).
Medium: 3 1/2-inch disk
ISPN: 43025-064   **Price: $17.00**

TISCHREDE SOFTWARE
LEXEGETE-LUKE (VER. 2.0)

A 3-disk set of theological documents designed for exegetical analysis of Luke in sermon preparation.

System: MAC, II, PLUS, SE, XL
Minimum Memory: 512K
Requires: MacWrite (ISPN 12784-530) or Microsoft Word (ISPN 53150-732).
Medium: 3 1/2-inch disk
ISPN: 82132-400   **Price: $59.95**

VOYAGER CO.
LOUVRE DISCGUIDE (VOL. 1) PAINTINGS AND DRAWINGS

A comprehensive index to The Louvre (Vol. 1) Paintings and Drawings laser disc.

System: MAC, II, PLUS, SE, XL
Minimum Memory: 1024K
Requires: Hard disk, HyperCard (ISPN 03900-300).
Medium: 3 1/2-inch disk
ISPN: 96647-400   **Price: $99.95**

VOYAGER CO.
LOUVRE DISCGUIDE (VOL. 3) ANTIQUITIES

A comprehensive index to The Louvre (Vol. 3) Antiquities laser disc.

System: MAC, II, PLUS, SE, XL
Minimum Memory: 1024K
Requires: Hard disk, HyperCard (ISPN 03900-300).
Medium: 3 1/2-inch disk
ISPN: 96647-420   **Price: $99.95**

VOYAGER CO.
LOUVRE DISCGUIDE (VOL.2) SCULPTURE AND OBJETSD'ART

A comprehensive index to The Louvre (Vol 2.) Sculpture and ObjetsD'Art laser disc.

System: MAC, II, PLUS, SE, XL
Minimum Memory: 1024K
Requires: Hard disk, HyperCard (ISPN 03900-300).
Medium: 3 1/2-inch disk
ISPN: 96647-410   **Price: $99.95**

LINGUIST'S SOFTWARE, INC.
MACGREEK NEW TESTAMENT (VER. 2.4)

Consists of the entire text of the UBS 3rd edition of Greek New Testament in Super Greek on three disks.

System: MAC, II, PLUS, SE, XL
Minimum Memory: 512K
Requires: MacWrite (ISPN 12784-530), Microsoft Word (ISPN 53150-732), WriteNow (ISPN 79465-900), or MacGreek (ISPN 44825-580).
Medium: 3 1/2-inch disk
ISPN: 44825-800   **Price: $99.95**

LINGUIST'S SOFTWARE, INC.
MACGREEK OLD TESTAMENT (VER. 1.6)

A complete Greek text of Rahlfs edition of the Septuagint, the Greek Old Testament, in SuperGreek on seven 800K diskettes.

System: MAC, II, PLUS, SE, XL
Minimum Memory: 512K
Requires: MacGreek (ISPN 44825-580), LaserGreek (ISPN 44825-050) or MacGreek, Hebrew and Phonetics (ISPN 44825-590).
Medium: 3 1/2-inch disk
ISPN: 44825-810   **Price: $99.95**

LINGUIST'S SOFTWARE, INC.
MACHEBREW SCRIPTURES (B.H.S.) (VER. 2.4)

The entire text of the Biblia Hebraica Stuttgartensia formatted for MacHebrew, including Ketiv and Qere readings.

System: MAC, PLUS, SE, XL
Minimum Memory: 512K
Requires: MacWrite (ISPN 12784-530) or Microsoft Word (ISPN 53150-732) MacHebrew (ISPN 44825-350) or LaserHebrew (ISPN 44825-035).
Medium: 3 1/2-inch disk
ISPN: 44825-820   **Price: $99.95**

LINGUIST'S SOFTWARE, INC.
MACHEBREW SCRIPTURES CONVERTER (VER. 2.3)

Creates ten optional text formats for non-accented or consonantal Hebrew or transliterated, plus or minus morphological divisions.

System: MAC, II, PLUS, SE, XL
Minimum Memory: 512K
Requires: MacHebrew Scriptures (ISPN 44825-820), MacHebrew (ISPN 44825-350), LaserHebrew (ISPN 44825-035) or MacGreek, Hebrew and Phonetics.
Medium: 3 1/2-inch disk
ISPN: 44825-825   **Price: $79.95**

VOYAGER CO.
NATIONAL GALLERY OF ART LASERGUIDE (VER. 1.2)

A HyperCard based laserguide for the National Gallery of Art Laserdisc.

System: MAC, II, PLUS, SE, XL
Minimum Memory: 1024K
Requires: HyperCard (ISPN 03900-300).
Medium: 3 1/2-inch disk
ISPN: 96647-500   **Price: $59.95**

VOYAGER CO.
VINCENT VAN GOGH LASERGUIDE

A HyperCard guide and index to the Van Gogh Revisited laserdisc.

System: MAC, II, PLUS, SE, XL
Minimum Memory: 1024K
Requires: HyperCard (ISPN 03900-300).
Medium: 3 1/2-inch disk
ISPN: 96647-800   **Price: $59.95**

---

253 EDUCATION/ LIBRARY MANAGEMENT/ REFERENCE

SENSIBLE SOFTWARE, INC.
BOOKENDS MACINTOSH (VER. 1)

A specialized database for books and journals. Import data can be downloaded from Dialog, Medline and BRS.

System: MAC, II, PLUS, SE, XL
Minimum Memory: 1024K
Requires: Hypercard (ISPN 03900-300).
Medium: 3 1/2-inch disk
ISPN: 69200-111   **Price: $99.95**

DYNACOMP, INC.
CATALOG CARD AND LABEL WRITER

Contains a specialized word processor that automatically formats and prints catalog cards, book pockets and spine labels.

System: MAC, II, PLUS, SE, XL
Minimum Memory: 48K
Medium: 3 1/2-inch disk
ISPN: 27050-078   **Price: $159.95**

RIGHT ON PROGRAMS
CATALOG CARDER

Creates catalog card set which conform to AACR II rules. Provides simple directions and immediate start up time.

System: MAC, II, PLUS, SE, XL
Minimum Memory: 512K
Medium: 3 1/2-inch disk
ISPN: 66450-122   **Price: $99.00**

CHANCERY SOFTWARE
CSL LIBRARY

Allows a school to track up to 30,000 books and up to 4,000 borrowers.

System: MAC, II, PLUS, SE, XL
Minimum Memory: 1024K
Requires: Single-user. 20MB hard drive.
Medium: 3 1/2-inch disk
ISPN: 12182-100   **Price: $1500.00**

CHANCERY SOFTWARE
CSL LIBRARY

Allows a school to track up to 30,000 books and up to 4,000 borrowers.

System: MAC, II, PLUS, SE, XL
Minimum Memory: 1024K
Requires: Multi-user. 20MB hard drive.
Medium: 3 1/2-inch disk
ISPN: 12182-100   **Price: $1900.00**

FRIEDMAN COMPUTING & PUBLISHING
HYPERLIBRARY (VER. 2.0)

A HyperCard stack library reference tool for grade K-12 which conducts a biographical search.

System: II
Minimum Memory: 1024K
Requires: HyperCard (ISPN 3900-300).
Medium: 3 1/2-inch disk
ISPN: 31465-300   **Price: $15.00**

CASPR
MAC LIBRARY SYSTEM (MLS)

Complete library management system which integrates cataloging, circulation and aquisitions.

System: MAC, II, PLUS, SE, XL
Minimum Memory: 1024K
Requires: Multiuser. Hard disk, ImageWriter or LaserWRiter printer. AppleShare and AppleTalk cabling system.
Medium: 3 1/2-inch disk
ISPN: 11566-510   **Price: $4995.00**

CASPR
MAC LIBRARY SYSTEM (MLS)

Complete library management system which integrates cataloging, circulation and aquisitions.

System: MAC, II, PLUS, SE, XL
Minimum Memory: 1024K
Requires: ImageWriter or LaserWriter printer, hard disk.
Medium: 3 1/2-inch disk
ISPN: 11566-510   **Price: $1695.00**

COMPANION CONSULTING
MACBOOK

Contains the basic elements of library management including patron control, collection control, fines and overdue notices.

System: MAC, II, PLUS, SE, XL
Minimum Memory: 1024K
Requires: 20MB hard disk, ImageWriter or LaserWriter printer, barcode reader.
Medium: 3 1/2-inch disk
ISPN: 14331-500   **Price: $995.00**

COMPANION CONSULTING
MACBOOK

Contains the basic elements of library management including patron control, collection control, fines and overdue notices.

System: MAC, II, PLUS, SE, XL
Minimum Memory: 1024K
Requires: 1-5 users. 20MB hard disk, ImageWriter or LaserWriter printer, barcode reader.
Medium: 3 1/2-inch disk
ISPN: 14331-500   **Price: $1995.00**

COMPANION CONSULTING
MACBOOK II

Tracks patron information, collection information, fines, holds, reserves requests, and collection usage statistics.

System: MAC, II, PLUS, SE, XL
Minimum Memory: 1024K
Requires: 1-10 users. 20MB hard disk, ImageWriter or LaserWriter printer.
Medium: 3 1/2-inch disk
ISPN: 14331-510   **Price: $4995.00**

COMPANION CONSULTING
MACBOOK II

Tracks patron information, collection information, fines, holds, reserves requests, and collection usage statistics.

System: MAC, II, PLUS, SE, XL
Minimum Memory: 1024K
Requires: 20MB hard disk, ImageWriter or LaserWriter printer.
Medium: 3 1/2-inch disk
ISPN: 14331-510   **Price: $1995.00**

COMPANION CONSULTING
MACBOOK II

Tracks patron information, collection information, fines, holds, reserves requests, and collection usage statistics.

System: MAC, II, PLUS, SE, XL
Minimum Memory: 1024K
Requires: 1-5 users. 20MB hard disk, ImageWriter or LaserWriter printer.
Medium: 3 1/2-inch disk
ISPN: 14331-510   **Price: $3995.00**

COMPANION CONSULTING
MACBOOK II PLUS

Contains a patron access on-line catalogue, extensive reporting capabilities, import/export capabilities and more.

System: MAC, II, PLUS, SE, XL
Minimum Memory: 1024K
Requires: 1-10 users. 20MB hard disk, ImageWriter or LaserWriter printer.
Medium: 3 1/2-inch disk
ISPN: 14331-501   **Price: $7495.00**

COMPANION CONSULTING
MACBOOK II PLUS

Contains a patron access on-line catalogue, extensive reporting capabilities, import/export capabilities and more.

System: MAC, II, PLUS, SE, XL
Minimum Memory: 1024K
Requires: 1-25 users. 20MB hard disk, ImageWriter or LaserWriter printer.
Medium: 3 1/2-inch disk
ISPN: 14331-501   **Price: $8995.00**

COMPANION CONSULTING
MACBOOK II PLUS

Contains a patron access on-line catalogue, extensive reporting capabilities, import/export capabilities and more.

System: MAC, II, PLUS, SE, XL
Minimum Memory: 1024K
Requires: 20MB hard disk, ImageWriter or LaserWriter printer.
Medium: 3 1/2-inch disk
ISPN: 14331-501   **Price: $2995.00**

COMPANION CONSULTING
MACBOOK II PLUS

Contains a patron access on-line catalogue, extensive reporting capabilities, import/export capabilities and more.

System: MAC, II, PLUS, SE, XL
Minimum Memory: 1024K
Requires: 1-5 users. 20MB hard disk, ImageWriter or LaserWriter printer.
Medium: 3 1/2-inch disk
ISPN: 14331-501   **Price: $5995.00**

CASPR
MACCARDS

A catalog card and label production system with full editing capabilities and database commands.

System: MAC, II, PLUS, SE, XL
Minimum Memory: 512K
Medium: 3 1/2-inch disk
ISPN: 11566-500   **Price: $269.00**

MOUSETRAP SOFTWARE
MACDEWEY

A card catalog circulation system for home, school, office and community libraries.

System: MAC, II, PLUS, SE, XL
Minimum Memory: 512K
Requires: Two disk drives or one disk drive and a hard disk.
Medium: 3 1/2-inch disk
ISPN: 55484-100   **Price: $79.95**

MECKLERSOFT
MEDIA CIRCULATION SYSTEM

Provides the user with a system for managing a media center and/or a film library.

System: MAC, II, PLUS, SE, XL
Minimum Memory: 64K
Medium: 3 1/2-inch disk
ISPN: 93919-300   **Price: $64.95**

RIGHT ON PROGRAMS
ON-LINE CATALOG

Provides the ability to catalog information designed for special libraries, private collections, small public libraries or museums.

System: MAC, II, PLUS, SE, XL
Minimum Memory: 512K
Medium: 3 1/2-inch disk
ISPN: 66450-525   **Price: $199.00**

JAM TECHNOLOGIES
TECHNOFILE (VER. 1.0)

A HyperCard based bibliographic referencing system which could also be used to organize recipes and record collections.

System: MAC, II, PLUS, SE, XL
Minimum Memory: 1024K
Requires: HyperCard (ISPN 3900-300).
Medium: 3 1/2-inch disk
ISPN: 41388-710   **Price: $39.00**

---

259 EDUCATION/MATH (ADVANCED)

TRUE BASIC, INC.
ALGEBRA (VER. 3.0)

Covers topics in beginning algebra, review of arithmetic concepts and introduction of intermediate topics.

System: MAC, II, PLUS, SE, XL
Minimum Memory: 512K
Medium: 3 1/2-inch disk
ISPN: 82789-095   **Price: $49.95**

VENTURA EDUCATIONAL SYSTEMS
ALGEBRA CONCEPTS

Introduces the terminology associated with fundamental algebra concepts in a game-like format.

System: MAC, II, PLUS, SE, XL
Minimum Memory: 512K
Medium: 3 1/2-inch disk
ISPN: 84911-090   **Price: $49.95**

VENTURA EDUCATIONAL SYSTEMS
ALGEBRA CONCEPTS

Introduces the terminology associated with fundamental algebra concepts in a game-like format.

System: MAC, II, PLUS, SE, XL
Minimum Memory: 512K
Requires: Lab pack (includes 5 copies).
Medium: 3 1/2-inch disk
ISPN: 84911-090   **Price: $89.95**

QUEUE
ALGEBRA WORD PROBLEMS

Contains word problems which require algebraic solutions. Each wrong answer draws a step-by-step explanation.

System: MAC, II, PLUS, SE, XL
Minimum Memory: 128K
Medium: 3 1/2-inch disk
ISPN: 64387-080   **Price: $49.95**

TRUE BASIC, INC.
ALGEBRAIC PROPOSER (VER. 1.0)

Builds models that students can use to dissect word problems into mathematical components.

System: MAC, II, PLUS, SE, XL
Minimum Memory: 512K
Medium: 3 1/2-inch disk
ISPN: 82789-120   **Price: $99.95**

BRODERBUND SOFTWARE, INC.
CALCULUS

Presents a full year of introductory calculus. Lets students create and graph functions and their derivatives.

System: MAC, II, PLUS, SE, XL
Minimum Memory: 512K
Requires: School Edition (includes back-up disk and teacher's guide).
Medium: 3 1/2-inch disk
ISPN: 08850-020   **Price: $109.95**

BRODERBUND SOFTWARE, INC.
CALCULUS

Presents a full year of introductory calculus. Lets students create and graph functions and their derivatives.

System: MAC, II, PLUS, SE, XL
Minimum Memory: 512K
Requires: Lab Pack (includes five disks and teacher's guide).
Medium: 3 1/2-inch disk
ISPN: 08850-020   **Price: $219.95**

TRUE BASIC, INC.
CALCULUS (VER. 3.0)

Performs symbolic differentiation routine for calculus functions. Operations are equivalent to first year calculus program.

System: MAC, II, PLUS, SE, XL
Minimum Memory: 512K
Medium: 3 1/2-inch disk
ISPN: 82789-212   **Price: $49.95**

HEIZER SOFTWARE
CIRCLE SECTOR SOLUTIONS

A HyperCard stack which determines solutions of the sector and segment of a circle.

System: MAC, II, PLUS, SE, XL
Minimum Memory: 512K
Requires: HyperCard (ISPN 03900-300).
Medium: 3 1/2-inch disk
ISPN: 35175-922   **Price: $14.00**

KINKOS ACADEMIC COURSEWARE EXCHANGE
DIFFERENTIAL EQUATIONS (VER. 1.0)

An exploratory tool for viewing solutions to first-order scaler differential equations.

System: MAC, II, PLUS, SE, XL
Minimum Memory: 512K
Requires: Finder (Ver. 5.5).
Medium: 3 1/2-inch disk
ISPN: 43025-103   **Price: $30.00**

TRUE BASIC, INC.

DISCRETE MATHEMATICS (VER. 1.0)

Constructs truth tables, Venn diagrams, recursive functions and elementary combinatorics. Includes graph theory.

System: MAC, II, PLUS, SE, XL
Minimum Memory: 512K
Medium: 3 1/2-inch disk
ISPN: 82789-250   **Price: $49.95**

QUEUE

ECONOMICS AND BUSINESS PACKAGE

A four-program series covering accounting, starting a new business, Macroeconomics, and Microeconomics.

System: MAC, II, PLUS, SE, XL
Minimum Memory: 128K
Medium: 3 1/2-inch disk
ISPN: 64387-742   **Price: $155.00**

KINKOS ACADEMIC COURSEWARE EXCHANGE

FUNPLOT (VER. 3.0)

Plots functions and illustrates calculus problems. Images can be printed or saved and used with MacPaint or MacWrite.

System: MAC, II, PLUS, SE, XL
Minimum Memory: 512K
Medium: 3 1/2-inch disk
ISPN: 43025-170   **Price: $15.00**

KINKOS ACADEMIC COURSEWARE EXCHANGE

FUNPLOT (VER. 3.0)

Plots functions and illustrates calculus problems. Images can be printed or saved and used with MacPaint or MacWrite.

System: MAC, II, PLUS, SE, XL
Minimum Memory: 512K
Requires: Site license.
Medium: 3 1/2-inch disk
ISPN: 43025-170   **Price: $1000.00**

KINKOS ACADEMIC COURSEWARE EXCHANGE

FUNPLOT-3D (VER. 2.0)

Functions of two variables can be drawn in Cartesian or polar coordinates and in four different modes.

System: MAC, II, PLUS, SE, XL
Minimum Memory: 512K
Medium: 3 1/2-inch disk
ISPN: 43025-171   **Price: $25.00**

KINKOS ACADEMIC COURSEWARE EXCHANGE

FUNPLOT-3D (VER. 2.0)

Functions of two variables can be drawn in Cartesian or polar coordinates and in four different modes.

System: MAC, II, PLUS, SE, XL
Minimum Memory: 512K
Requires: Site license.
Medium: 3 1/2-inch disk
ISPN: 43025-171   **Price: $1500.00**

BRODERBUND SOFTWARE, INC.

GEOMETRY

Grades 9-12: Abstract mathematical theories come to life on the screen in this interactive program.

System: MAC, II, PLUS, SE, XL
Minimum Memory: 512K
Medium: 3 1/2-inch disk
ISPN: 08850-070   **Price: $99.95**

BRODERBUND SOFTWARE, INC.

GEOMETRY

Grades 9-12: Abstract mathematical theories come to life on the screen in this interactive program.

System: MAC, II, PLUS, SE, XL
Minimum Memory: 512K
Requires: School edition.
Medium: 3 1/2-inch disk
ISPN: 08850-070   **Price: $109.95**

BRODERBUND SOFTWARE, INC.

GEOMETRY

Grades 9-12: Abstract mathematical theories come to life on the screen in this interactive program.

System: MAC, II, PLUS, SE, XL
Minimum Memory: 512K
Requires: Lab pack.
Medium: 3 1/2-inch disk
ISPN: 08850-070   **Price: $219.95**

VENTURA EDUCATIONAL SYSTEMS

GEOMETRY CONCEPTS (VER. 2.0)

Grades 7 and up: Provides an introduction to geometry terms and concepts.

System: MAC, II, PLUS, SE, XL
Minimum Memory: 512K
Requires: Lab pack (five disks).
Medium: 3 1/2-inch disk
ISPN: 84911-320   **Price: $89.95**

VENTURA EDUCATIONAL SYSTEMS

GEOMETRY CONCEPTS (VER. 2.0)

Grades 7 and up: Provides an introduction to geometry terms and concepts.

System: MAC, PLUS, SE, XL
Minimum Memory: 512K
Medium: 3 1/2-inch disk
ISPN: 84911-320   **Price: $49.95**

HEIZER SOFTWARE

GRADING PROGRAM

Records individual homework, lab and test scores for an unlimited number of students.

System: MAC, II, PLUS, SE, XL
Minimum Memory: 512K
Requires: Microsoft Excel (ISPN 53150-270) or Microsoft Works (ISPN 53150-740).
Medium: 3 1/2-inch disk
ISPN: 35175-228   **Price: $30.00**

MISSING LINK SOFTWARE, INC.

HOMEWORK TUTOR SERIES-ALGEBRA I/SIMPLIFY

Handles first semester Algebra I problems and allows students to complete and print homework with the help of a built-in tutor.

System: MAC, II, PLUS, SE, XL
Minimum Memory: 512K
Medium: 3 1/2-inch disk
ISPN: 54785-100   **Price: $79.95**

KINKOS ACADEMIC COURSEWARE EXCHANGE

LINEAR PROGRAMMING BY FRACTIONS FOR THE MACINTOSH

Aids students in learning the simplex method and solving linear programming problems in the familiar format of fractions.

System: MAC, II, PLUS, SE, XL
Minimum Memory: 512K
Requires: Finder (Ver. 5.3).
Medium: 3 1/2-inch disk
ISPN: 43025-358   **Price: $20.00**

HEIZER SOFTWARE

LOGARITHMAC

Contains 76 MacPaint based semi-log and log-log templates, with up to five by seven cycles in three scales.

System: MAC, II, PLUS, SE, XL
Minimum Memory: 512K
Requires: MacPaint (ISPN 12784-510).
Medium: 3 1/2-inch disk
ISPN: 35175-400   **Price: $39.95**

FREEMAN W H AND CO.

MACALGEBRA DISKETTE WITH BOOK

Contains all programs used in the text MacAlgebra: Basic Algebra on the Macintosh and solutions to all programming exercises.

System: MAC, II, PLUS, SE, XL
Minimum Memory: 128K
Medium: 3 1/2-inch disk
ISPN: 17298-750   **Price: $49.95**

COOKE PUBLICATIONS

MACELASTIC (VER. 1.0) (STUDENT)

Solves two-dimensional and axisymmetric problems in classical elasticity, limited to 300 degrees of freedom.

System: MAC, II, PLUS, SE, XL
Minimum Memory: 512K
Medium: 3 1/2-inch disk
ISPN: 19659-300   **Price: $99.95**

TRUE BASIC, INC.

MACFUNCTION (VER. 1.0)

Performs Macintosh interface. Allows input of 2 or 3-D graph, show or remove lines, plot derivatives, adjust eye level, resolve grid.

System: MAC, II, PLUS, SE, XL
Minimum Memory: 512K
Medium: 3 1/2-inch disk
ISPN: 82789-305   **Price: $49.95**

KINKOS ACADEMIC COURSEWARE EXCHANGE

MACSIMPLEX (VER. 1.62)

Teaches students how linear programming problems are solved. Also useful for other topics in linear algebra.

System: MAC, II, PLUS, SE, XL
Minimum Memory: 128K
Requires: Word processor that saves documents as 'text only,' printer.
Medium: 3 1/2-inch disk
ISPN: 43025-406 **Price: $12.00**

BROOKS/COLE PUBLISHING

MAPLE (VER. 4.2)

A symbolic computation system – an interactive tool developed by experts at the University of Waterloo.

System: MAC, II, PLUS, SE, XL
Minimum Memory: 1024K
Medium: 3 1/2-inch disk
ISPN: 08962-450 **Price: $395.00**

WOLFRAM RESEARCH, INC.

MATHEMATICA (VER. 1.1)

Performs numeric, symbolic, and graphic computation using a symbolic programming language.

System: MAC, II, PLUS, SE, XL
Minimum Memory: 2560K
Medium: 3 1/2-inch disk
ISPN: 86956-500 **Price: $495.00**

WOLFRAM RESEARCH, INC.

MATHEMATICA (VER. 1.1)

Performs numeric, symbolic, and graphic computation using a symbolic programming language.

System: II
Minimum Memory: 2560K
Requires: 68881 math-coprocessor.
Medium: 3 1/2-inch disk
ISPN: 86956-500 **Price: $795.00**

TRUE BASIC, INC.

MATHEMATICIAN'S TOOLKIT (VER. 1.0)

Gives complete double precision floating point accuracy to calculations that can be raised to 100,000 digits.

System: MAC, II, PLUS, SE, XL
Minimum Memory: 512K
Requires: True Basic Language System (ISPN 82789-671).
Medium: 3 1/2-inch disk
ISPN: 82789-310 **Price: $69.95**

E & M SOFTWARE

MATHLAB

Symbolic algebra for multivariate polynomials and transcendental functions.

System: MAC, II, PLUS, SE, XL
Minimum Memory: 512K
Medium: 3 1/2-inch disk
ISPN: 27331-500 **Price: $49.95**

DESIGN SCIENCE, INC.

MATHTYPE (VER. 2.0)

Provides a desk accessory for use with any word processor or page layout program for the creation of mathematical equations.

System: MAC, II, PLUS, SE, XL
Minimum Memory: 512K
Medium: 3 1/2-inch disk
ISPN: 24875-500 **Price: $149.00**

COOKE PUBLICATIONS

MATHWRITER (VER. 1.4)

Compose complex mathematical equations. An interactive editor for use with a word processor.

System: MAC, II, PLUS, SE, XL
Minimum Memory: 512K
Medium: 3 1/2-inch disk
ISPN: 19659-400 **Price: $79.95**

LIONHEART PRESS

MATRIX OPERATIONS (VER. 5.0)

Includes matrix entry, routines, addition, multiplication, inverse, transposition, and the Cholesky decomposition of matrices.

System: MAC, II, PLUS, SE, XL
Minimum Memory: 512K
Medium: 3 1/2-inch disk
ISPN: 44900-862 **Price: $95.00**

CENTRAL PRODUCTS CORP.

POWERMATH II

Solves mathematic problems from basic math to calculus.

System: MAC, II, PLUS, SE, XL
Minimum Memory: 512K
Medium: 3 1/2-inch disk
ISPN: 11963-600 **Price: $149.95**

TRUE BASIC, INC.

PRE-CALCULUS WITH TRIGONOMETRY (VER. 3.0)

Illustrates concepts in Pre-Calculus and Trigonometry. Provides a function plotting routine and light topic routines.

System: MAC, II, PLUS, SE, XL
Minimum Memory: 512K
Medium: 3 1/2-inch disk
ISPN: 82789-475 **Price: $49.95**

TRUE BASIC, INC.

PROBABILITY THEORY (VER. 1.0)

Introduction to probability theory and decision making processes. Includes simulations and Baye's theorem.

System: MAC, II, PLUS, SE, XL
Minimum Memory: 512K
Medium: 3 1/2-inch disk
ISPN: 82789-500 **Price: $49.95**

KINKOS ACADEMIC COURSEWARE EXCHANGE

PROBLEM SOLVING INTERPRETER

College level: A simple interpretive language designed for problem solving, calculations and graphical modeling.

System: MAC, II, PLUS, SE, XL
Minimum Memory: 128K
Requires: Finder (Ver. 4.1 or later).
Medium: 3 1/2-inch disk
ISPN: 43025-615 **Price: $20.50**

KINKOS ACADEMIC COURSEWARE EXCHANGE

PROBLEM SOLVING INTERPRETER

College level: A simple interpretive language designed for problem solving, calculations and graphical modeling.

System: MAC, II, PLUS, SE, XL
Minimum Memory: 128K
Requires: Site license. Finder (Ver. 4.1 or later).
Medium: 3 1/2-inch disk
ISPN: 43025-615 **Price: $3000.00**

HEIZER SOFTWARE

SOLVE TRIANGLES

A HyperCard stack which solves plane triangles, given one side and two angles, or any of five other variations.

System: MAC, II, PLUS, SE, XL
Minimum Memory: 512K
Requires: HyperCard (ISPN 03900-300).
Medium: 3 1/2-inch disk
ISPN: 35175-985 **Price: $14.00**

QUEUE

SPECIAL TOPICS IN MATHEMATICS SERIES-COMPLETE

Grades 7-9: A six-program tutorial that explains mathematic processes, such as powers and roots, and ratios and proportion.

System: MAC, II, PLUS, SE, XL
Minimum Memory: 128K
Medium: 3 1/2-inch disk
ISPN: 64387-758 **Price: $155.00**

PROBABILTY DISTRIBUTION

SPECTRAL ANALYSIS

Provides four basic functions: forward and inverse transform, power spectrum, and autocorrelation.

System: MAC
Minimum Memory: 256K
Medium: 3 1/2-inch disk
ISPN: 65993-775 **Price: $75.00**

SDG DECISION SYSTEMS

SUPERTREE STUDENT (VER. 5.3)

Performs probabilistic analysis of complex decision trees. Developed for schools and includes a textbook.

System: MAC, II, PLUS, SE, XL
Minimum Memory: 512K
Medium: 3 1/2-inch disk
ISPN: 76475-700 **Price: $65.00**

TRUE BASIC, INC.

TRIGONOMETRY (VER. 1.0)

Includes graphs, tables, finding roots of trigonometric functions, solving triangles and trig identities.

System: MAC, II, PLUS, SE, XL
Minimum Memory: 512K
Medium: 3 1/2-inch disk
ISPN: 82789-650　　　　**Price: $49.95**

264 EDUCATION/MATH (BASIC, GENERAL)

TRUE BASIC, INC.

ARITHMETIC (VER. 1.0)

Supplements basic arithmetic topics such as fractions, percents, and square roots, allowing student easy access to any one topic.

System: MAC, II, PLUS, SE, XL
Minimum Memory: 512K
Medium: 3 1/2-inch disk
ISPN: 82789-196　　　　**Price: $49.95**

HEIZER SOFTWARE

ARITHO-THE MATH ADVENTURE GAME

A HyperCard stack which includes a math game with mathematic questions and speech capabilities.

System: MAC, II, PLUS, SE, XL
Minimum Memory: 512K
Requires: HyperCard (ISPN 03900-300).
Medium: 3 1/2-inch disk
ISPN: 35175-911　　　　**Price: $15.00**

QUEUE

AVERAGES

Grades 7-9: Offers step-by-step tutor program that explains how to calculate an average.

System: MAC, II, PLUS, SE, XL
Minimum Memory: 128K
Medium: 3 1/2-inch disk
ISPN: 64387-145　　　　**Price: $29.95**

DAVIDSON AND ASSOCIATES, INC.

MATH BLASTER

Grades 1-6: Learn math arcade-style.

System: MAC, PLUS, SE, XL
Minimum Memory: 512K
Medium: 3 1/2-inch disk
ISPN: 24075-075　　　　**Price: $49.95**

HEIZER SOFTWARE

MATH ELIMINATOR

An arithmetic game which requires each player to design an equation that equals a number from one to fifty.

System: MAC, II, PLUS, SE, XL
Minimum Memory: 512K
Requires: HyperCard (ISPN 03900-300).
Medium: 3 1/2-inch disk
ISPN: 35175-959　　　　**Price: $8.00**

UNICORN SOFTWARE CO.

MATH WIZARD

Teaches basic functions of math, including math word problems.

System: MAC, II, PLUS, SE, XL
Minimum Memory: 512K
Medium: 3 1/2-inch disk
ISPN: 83562-120　　　　**Price: $49.95**

QUEUE

MATH WORD PROBLEMS-COMPLETE

Grades 2-8: An eight-program series which guides students through problems one step at a time, producing hints to solving problems.

System: MAC, II, PLUS, SE, XL
Minimum Memory: 128K
Medium: 3 1/2-inch disk
ISPN: 64387-749　　　　**Price: $195.00**

QUEUE

MATHEMATICS WORD PROBLEMS GRADE 4

A step-by-step guide that covers addition, subtraction, multiplication and division of numbers up to 7 places.

System: MAC, II, PLUS, SE, XL
Minimum Memory: 128K
Medium: 3 1/2-inch disk
ISPN: 64387-512　　　　**Price: $34.95**

QUEUE

MATHEMATICS WORD PROBLEMS-GRADE 2

A step-by-step guide with color graphics.

System: MAC, II, PLUS, SE, XL
Minimum Memory: 128K
Medium: 3 1/2-inch disk
ISPN: 64387-459　　　　**Price: $34.95**

QUEUE

MATHEMATICS WORD PROBLEMS-GRADE 3

A step-by-step guide with color graphics.

System: MAC, PLUS, SE, XL
Minimum Memory: 128K
Medium: 3 1/2-inch disk
ISPN: 64387-510　　　　**Price: $34.95**

QUEUE

MATHEMATICS WORD PROBLEMS-GRADE 5

A step-by-step guide with color graphics that covers addition, subtraction, multiplication and division.

System: MAC, II, PLUS, SE, XL
Minimum Memory: 128K
Medium: 3 1/2-inch disk
ISPN: 64387-514　　　　**Price: $34.95**

QUEUE

MATHEMATICS WORD PROBLEMS-GRADE 6

A step-by-step guide that covers addition, subtraction, division and multiplication questions.

System: MAC, II, PLUS, SE, XL
Minimum Memory: 128K
Medium: 3 1/2-inch disk
ISPN: 64387-516　　　　**Price: $34.95**

QUEUE

MATHEMATICS WORD PROBLEMS-GRADE 7

A step-by-step guide with color graphics and more than 100 questions.

System: MAC, II, PLUS, SE, XL
Minimum Memory: 128K
Medium: 3 1/2-inch disk
ISPN: 64387-518　　　　**Price: $34.95**

QUEUE

MATHEMATICS WORD PROBLEMS-GRADE 8

Includes lessons on area, perimeter, adding, subtraction and multiplication of fractions.

System: MAC, II, PLUS, SE, XL
Minimum Memory: 128K
Medium: 3 1/2-inch disk
ISPN: 64387-520　　　　**Price: $34.95**

FIRST BYTE, INC.

MATHTALK

Increases a student's ability to solve basic addition, subtraction, multiplication and division problems.

System: MAC, PLUS, SE, XL
Minimum Memory: 512K
Medium: 3 1/2-inch disk
ISPN: 30836-300　　　　**Price: $49.95**

GREAT WAVE SOFTWARE

NUMBERMAZE (VER. 1)

Ages 5-12: Includes counting, addition, subtraction, multiplication and word problems. Exciting graphics, solving mazes and sound.

System: MAC, II, PLUS, SE, XL
Minimum Memory: 512K
Medium: 3 1/2-inch disk
ISPN: 33476-500　　　　**Price: $49.95**

QUEUE

POWERS AND ROOTS

Grades 7-9: An interactive step-by-step tutorial.

System: MAC, II, PLUS, SE, XL
Minimum Memory: 128K
Medium: 3 1/2-inch disk
ISPN: 64387-496　　　　**Price: $29.95**

QUEUE
ROUNDING AND ESTIMATION

Grades 7-9: Step-by-step tutorial and drill exercises to reinforce rounding and estimating skills.

System: MAC, II, PLUS, SE, XL
Minimum Memory: 128K
Medium: 3 1/2-inch disk
ISPN: 64387-594   **Price: $29.95**

QUEUE
SPORTS PROBLEMS I

Grades 3-4: Use sports problems to develop math skills.

System: MAC, II, PLUS, SE, XL
Minimum Memory: 128K
Medium: 3 1/2-inch disk
ISPN: 64387-870   **Price: $39.95**

QUEUE
SPORTS PROBLEMS II

Grades 5-7: Use sports problems to develop math skills.

System: MAC, II, PLUS, SE, XL
Minimum Memory: 128K
Medium: 3 1/2-inch disk
ISPN: 64387-872   **Price: $39.95**

QUEUE
SPORTS PROBLEMS PACKAGE

Grades 4-9: A three-program series of sports-based word problems in addition, subtraction, decimals, fractions, and percentages.

System: MAC, II, PLUS, SE, XL
Minimum Memory: 128K
Medium: 3 1/2-inch disk
ISPN: 64387-752   **Price: $95.00**

DYNACOMP, INC.
TEACHER'S AIDE

Grades 1-6: A drill program to develop math skills.

System: MAC, II, PLUS, SE, XL
Minimum Memory: 512K
Requires: Microsoft QuickBasic (ISPN 53150-205).
Medium: 3 1/2-inch disk
ISPN: 27050-620   **Price: $22.95**

NORDIC SOFTWARE, INC.
TURBO MATH FACTS

Ages 6-9: Teaches basic math functions, short memory skills and outcome visualization.

System: MAC, II, PLUS, SE, XL
Minimum Memory: 512K
Medium: 3 1/2-inch disk
ISPN: 57028-930   **Price: $39.95**

269 EDUCATION/ MISCELLANEOUS EDUCATION

AUTHORWARE, INC.
BEST COURSE OF ACTION (THE)

A visual software construction kit used by non-programmers to create multi-media interactive learning experiences.

System: MAC, II, PLUS, SE, XL
Minimum Memory: 512K
Requires: Commercial version.
Medium: 3 1/2-inch disk
ISPN: 06031-100   **Price: $2499.00**

AUTHORWARE, INC.
BEST COURSE OF ACTION (THE)

A visual software construction kit used by non-programmers to create multi-media interactive learning experiences.

System: MAC, PLUS, SE, XL
Minimum Memory: 512K
Requires: Educational version.
Medium: 3 1/2-inch disk
ISPN: 06031-100   **Price: $499.00**

MINDPLAY
COTTON TALES

Pre-school to grade 3: A picture menu introduction to word processing and desktop publishing.

System: MAC, II, PLUS, SE, XL
Minimum Memory: 512K
Requires: Home and school edition.
Medium: 3 1/2-inch disk
ISPN: 54362-360   **Price: $49.99**

MINDPLAY
COTTON TALES

Pre-school to grade 3: A picture menu introduction to word processing and desktop publishing.

System: MAC, PLUS, SE, XL
Minimum Memory: 512K
Requires: Lab pack (6 copies of the program).
Medium: 3 1/2-inch disk
ISPN: 54362-360   **Price: $120.00**

MINDSCAPE, INC.
CROSSWORD MAGIC-EDUCATIONAL VERSION

Grades 2-12: Creates customized crossword puzzles, which can be used repeatedly by students. Includes a teacher's manual.

System: MAC, II, PLUS, SE, XL
Minimum Memory: 48K
Medium: 3 1/2-inch disk
ISPN: 54375-157   **Price: $49.95**

HEIZER SOFTWARE
DEFENSE ACRONYMS

Contains over 6500 Department of Defense, Military and Electronic acronyms and their meanings.

System: MAC, II, PLUS, SE, XL
Minimum Memory: 512K
Requires: Microsoft Excel (ISPN 53150-270) or Microsoft Works (ISPN 53150-740).
Medium: 3 1/2-inch disk
ISPN: 35175-599   **Price: $20.00**

KINKOS ACADEMIC COURSEWARE EXCHANGE
DREXEL PLOT (VER. 1.3)

Plots line and/or scatter plots. User can enter up to four paired sets of data, and place as many as four lines on the same graph.

System: MAC, II, PLUS, SE, XL
Minimum Memory: 128K
Requires: Finder (Ver. 4.1 or 5.3).
Medium: 3 1/2-inch disk
ISPN: 43025-107   **Price: $11.00**

SPINNAKER SOFTWARE
HAYDEN SCORE IMPROVEMENT SYSTEM FOR THE SAT

Includes a complete math module, verbal module and practice exams module.

System: MAC, II, PLUS, SE, XL
Minimum Memory: 512K
Medium: 3 1/2-inch disk
ISPN: 75300-146   **Price: $99.95**

THINK EDUCATIONAL SOFTWARE
MACEDGE

Contains eight reading and math programs for basic skills. Five and three reading programs on one disk, for children 4-14.

System: MAC, II, PLUS, SE, XL
Minimum Memory: 128K
Medium: 3 1/2-inch disk
ISPN: 81375-475   **Price: $49.95**

THINK EDUCATIONAL SOFTWARE
MACEDGE II

Enhances development of math & reading skills from primary to junior high. Includes eight programs.

System: MAC, II, PLUS, SE, XL
Minimum Memory: 128K
Medium: 3 1/2-inch disk
ISPN: 81375-500   **Price: $49.95**

T & M SYSTEMS, INC.
MACLUNCHROOM

Provides a hot lunch tracking system with reporting capabilities. Utilizes a barcode reader to replace punching student lunch cards.

System: MAC, II, PLUS, SE, XL
Minimum Memory: 1024K
Requires: ImageWriter or LaserWriter printer, 20 MB hard disk.
Medium: 3 1/2-inch disk
ISPN: 79401-500   **Price: $1490.00**

HEIZER SOFTWARE
MORSE CODE TUTORIAL

Teaches the basics of International Morse code with Codes, Memory Test, and a Translator.

System: MAC, II, PLUS, SE, XL
Minimum Memory: 1024K
Requires: HyperCard (ISPN 03900-300).
Medium: 3 1/2-inch disk
ISPN: 35175-054   **Price: $12.00**

HEIZER SOFTWARE

OH! CANADA

Has over 25 data fields for each province in Canada including population, land area, unemployment, number of schools and motto.

System: MAC, II, PLUS, SE, XL
Minimum Memory: 1024K
Requires: HyperCard (ISPN 03900-300).
Medium: 3 1/2-inch disk
ISPN: 35175-065   **Price: $10.00**

KINKOS ACADEMIC COURSEWARE EXCHANGE

REED APPLICATIONS I

College level: Includes several utility, academic and picturesque applications created with the Rascal Development System.

System: MAC, II, PLUS, SE, XL
Minimum Memory: 128K
Requires: Finder (Ver. 4.1 or later).
Medium: 3 1/2-inch disk
ISPN: 43025-700   **Price: $14.00**

KINKOS ACADEMIC COURSEWARE EXCHANGE

REED APPLICATIONS II

College level: Contains several utility, academic and picturesque applications created with the Rascal Development System.

System: MAC, II, PLUS, SE, XL
Minimum Memory: 128K
Requires: Finder (Ver. 4.1 or later).
Medium: 3 1/2-inch disk
ISPN: 43025-701   **Price: $14.00**

KINKOS ACADEMIC COURSEWARE EXCHANGE

TORTS EXERCISES (VER. 1.0)

Presents questions with alternative answers to aid in the development of legal reasoning.

System: MAC, II, PLUS, SE, XL
Minimum Memory: 512K
Requires: 800K disk drive.
Medium: 3 1/2-inch disk
ISPN: 43025-910   **Price: $12.00**

KINKOS ACADEMIC COURSEWARE EXCHANGE

TORTS EXERCISES (VER. 1.0)

Presents questions with alternative answers to aid in the development of legal reasoning.

System: MAC, II, PLUS, SE, XL
Minimum Memory: 512K
Requires: Site license. 800K disk drive.
Medium: 3 1/2-inch disk
ISPN: 43025-910   **Price: $2400.00**

---

271 EDUCATION/ MULTIPLICATION/ DIVISION

MINDPLAY

ROBOMATH

An arcade game that builds multiplication and division skills.

System: MAC, II, PLUS, SE, XL
Minimum Memory: 512K
Requires: Lab pack (includes 6 disks).
Medium: 3 1/2-inch disk
ISPN: 54362-650   **Price: $120.00**

MINDPLAY

ROBOMATH

An arcade game that builds multiplication and division skills.

System: MAC, II, PLUS, SE, XL
Minimum Memory: 512K
Requires: Home and school edition.
Medium: 3 1/2-inch disk
ISPN: 54362-650   **Price: $49.99**

---

273 EDUCATION/ READING/VOCABULARY

QUEUE

BEGINNER READER

Grades K-2: Helps students recognize when words rhyme and when words don't rhyme.

System: MAC, II, PLUS, SE, XL
Minimum Memory: 128K
Medium: 3 1/2-inch disk
ISPN: 64387-158   **Price: $24.95**

QUEUE

COMPLETE LESSONS IN READING AND REASONING

Introduces many types of fallacies and shows the user how to recognize them in his/her own thinking and others arguments.

System: MAC, II, PLUS, SE, XL
Minimum Memory: 512K
Medium: 3 1/2-inch disk
ISPN: 64387-475   **Price: $149.95**

QUEUE

COMPREHENSIVE GRAMMAR REVIEW PART II

Contains over 200 exercises on the parts of speech, subject and predicate, complements of verbs, and kinds of sentences.

System: MAC, II, PLUS, SE, XL
Minimum Memory: 128K
Medium: 3 1/2-inch disk
ISPN: 64387-946   **Price: $54.95**

MINDPLAY

COTTON PLUS

Graphics to expand your 'Cotton Tales Picture Library.'

System: MAC, II, PLUS, SE, XL
Minimum Memory: 512K
Requires: Cotton Tales Picture Library (ISPN 54362-360).
Medium: 3 1/2-inch disk
ISPN: 54362-362   **Price: $29.99**

MINDPLAY

COTTON PLUS

Graphics to expand your 'Cotton Tales Picture Library.'

System: MAC, II, PLUS, SE, XL
Minimum Memory: 512K
Requires: Lab Pack (Includes 6 data disks). Cotton Tales Picture Library (ISPN 54362-360).
Medium: 3 1/2-inch disk
ISPN: 54362-362   **Price: $72.00**

QUEUE

EARLY READER

Reading education program through matching easy-to-read sentences with attractive pictures.

System: MAC, II, PLUS, SE, XL
Minimum Memory: 128K
Medium: 3 1/2-inch disk
ISPN: 64387-280   **Price: $34.95**

QUEUE

EIGHTH GRADE READING COMPREHENSION I

Features reading comprehension exercises at the eighth grade level.

System: MAC, II, PLUS, SE, XL
Minimum Memory: 128K
Medium: 3 1/2-inch disk
ISPN: 64387-285   **Price: $65.00**

QUEUE

FABLES, MYTHS AND POEMS

Grades 2-3: Instructs students with reading and comprehension skills – through Aesop's Fables and humorous poems.

System: MAC
Minimum Memory: 128K
Medium: 3 1/2-inch disk
ISPN: 64387-342   **Price: $49.95**

QUEUE

FIFTH GRADE READING COMPREHENSION

Includes fifth grade level reading comprehension exercises.

System: MAC, II, PLUS, SE, XL
Minimum Memory: 128K
Medium: 3 1/2-inch disk
ISPN: 64387-347   **Price: $65.00**

FIRST BYTE, INC.
FIRST LETTERS AND WORDS

Helps young children learn to recognize upper and lower case letters and words.

System: MAC, II, PLUS, SE, XL
Minimum Memory: 512K
Medium: 3 1/2-inch disk
ISPN: 30836-125   **Price: $49.95**

QUEUE
FOURTH GRADE READING COMPREHENSION

Contains fourth grade level reading comprehension exercises.

System: MAC, II, PLUS, SE, XL
Minimum Memory: 128K
Medium: 3 1/2-inch disk
ISPN: 64387-357   **Price: $65.00**

QUEUE
HOW TO SPELL

Grades 4-7: A tutorial on the principles of correct spelling (illustrative graphics).

System: MAC
Minimum Memory: 128K
Medium: 3 1/2-inch disk
ISPN: 64387-393   **Price: $39.95**

COMPU-TEACH, INC.
JOSHUA'S READING MACHINE

Ages 4-7: Joshua the giraffe introduces his reading machine with 37 Mother Goose rhymes, children's songs and Aesop's fables.

System: MAC, II, PLUS, SE, XL
Minimum Memory: 512K
Medium: 3 1/2-inch disk
ISPN: 15081-075   **Price: $39.95**

QUEUE
LESSONS IN READING AND REASONING I

Develops critical reading skills and helps students detect fallacies and errors in what they read.

System: MAC, II, PLUS, SE, XL
Minimum Memory: 128K
Medium: 3 1/2-inch disk
ISPN: 64387-893   **Price: $39.95**

QUEUE
LESSONS IN READING AND REASONING II

Learn to detect fallacies in what you read.

System: MAC, II, PLUS, SE, XL
Minimum Memory: 128K
Medium: 3 1/2-inch disk
ISPN: 64387-430   **Price: $39.95**

QUEUE
LESSONS IN READING AND REASONING III

How to detect fallacies and errors in what you read.

System: MAC, II, PLUS, SE, XL
Minimum Memory: 128K
Medium: 3 1/2-inch disk
ISPN: 64387-431   **Price: $39.95**

QUEUE
LESSONS IN READING AND REASONING IV

Covers advanced lessons on the sexism fallacy, the rationalization fallacy and correct and fallacious reasoning.

System: MAC, II, PLUS, SE, XL
Minimum Memory: 128K
Medium: 3 1/2-inch disk
ISPN: 64387-432   **Price: $59.95**

QUEUE
LESSONS IN READING AND REASONING PACKAGE

Instructions cover the shifty word fallacy, the either-or fallacy, and circular reasoning fallacy. High school and college level.

System: MAC, II, PLUS, SE, XL
Minimum Memory: 128K
Medium: 3 1/2-inch disk
ISPN: 64387-433   **Price: $149.95**

QUEUE
MYTHS

Grades 4-6: Builds comprehension skills through the use of mythic figures and stories.

System: MAC, II, PLUS, SE, XL
Minimum Memory: 128K
Medium: 3 1/2-inch disk
ISPN: 64387-527   **Price: $39.95**

COMPU-TEACH, INC.
ONCE UPON A TIME

Ages 6-12: Allows children to design and publish their own illustrated books. Contains hundreds of graphic images.

System: MAC, II, PLUS, SE, XL
Minimum Memory: 512K
Medium: 3 1/2-inch disk
ISPN: 15081-120   **Price: $39.95**

QUEUE
PRACTICAL VOCABULARY

Grades 9-12: Vocabulary drill on recognition and use of synonyms, definitions, antonyms, vocabulary, word roots and prefixes.

System: MAC, II, PLUS, SE, XL
Minimum Memory: 128K
Medium: 3 1/2-inch disk
ISPN: 64387-554   **Price: $54.95**

UNICORN SOFTWARE CO.
READ-A-RAMA

Ages 5-8: An early learning and reading readiness program. Spelling lists can be entered into the program.

System: MAC, II, PLUS, SE, XL
Minimum Memory: 512K
Medium: 3 1/2-inch disk
ISPN: 83562-110   **Price: $59.95**

LEARNING CO. (THE)
READER RABBIT

Ages 4-7: Animated games that improve letter, word and memory skill.

System: MAC, PLUS, SE, XL
Minimum Memory: 512K
Requires: 800K disk drive.
Medium: 3 1/2-inch disk
ISPN: 43870-487   **Price: $39.95**

QUEUE
READING ADVENTURE I-3 PONIES, 4 FRIENDS

Grades 2-3: Lets students create-a-story as you read.

System: MAC, II, PLUS, SE, XL
Minimum Memory: 128K
Medium: 3 1/2-inch disk
ISPN: 64387-534   **Price: $39.95**

QUEUE
READING ADVENTURE II-CASE OF THE LOST MUSIC BOX

Grades 4-6: Presents a reading adventure in which players become a detective investigating the disappearance of a music box.

System: MAC, II, PLUS, SE, XL
Minimum Memory: 128K
Medium: 3 1/2-inch disk
ISPN: 64387-536   **Price: $59.95**

QUEUE
READING ADVENTURE III-SWITCHING SIBLINGS

Grades 6-8: Provides a tale of two siblings with normal rivalries, constantly reversing roles from younger to older sibling.

System: MAC, II, PLUS, SE, XL
Minimum Memory: 128K
Medium: 3 1/2-inch disk
ISPN: 64387-537   **Price: $59.95**

QUEUE
READING ADVENTURE-COMPLETE SERIES

Grades 2-8: A three-program adventure series which provides practice in comprehension skills.

System: MAC, II, PLUS, SE, XL
Minimum Memory: 128K
Medium: 3 1/2-inch disk
ISPN: 64387-838   **Price: $130.00**

QUEUE

READING AND THINKING I

Grades 2-3: Reading exercises which require students to think inferentially to figure out what is not explicitly stated.

System: MAC, II, PLUS, SE, XL
Minimum Memory: 128K
Medium: 3 1/2-inch disk
ISPN: 64387-770   **Price: $54.95**

QUEUE

READING AND THINKING II

Grades 4-5: Reading exercises which require students to think inferentially to figure out what is not explicitly stated.

System: MAC, II, PLUS, SE, XL
Minimum Memory: 128K
Medium: 3 1/2-inch disk
ISPN: 64387-773   **Price: $54.95**

QUEUE

READING AND THINKING III

Grades 6-8: Inferential reading practice.

System: MAC, II, PLUS, SE, XL
Minimum Memory: 128K
Medium: 3 1/2-inch disk
ISPN: 64387-775   **Price: $54.95**

QUEUE

READING COMPREHENSION SERIES-GRADES 2-8

Grades 2-8: Improves both factual recall and inferential thinking through a series of programs by grade level.

System: MAC, PLUS, SE, XL
Minimum Memory: 128K
Medium: 3 1/2-inch disk
ISPN: 64387-833   **Price: $425.00**

QUEUE

SECOND GRADE READING COMPREHENSION

Grades 2-3: Contains 20 lessons of reading passages using fables, mystery stories and passages on foreign countries and animals.

System: MAC
Minimum Memory: 128K
Medium: 3 1/2-inch disk
ISPN: 64387-600   **Price: $65.00**

QUEUE

SEVENTH GRADE READING COMPREHENSION

Includes seventh grade level reading comprehension exercises.

System: MAC, II, PLUS, SE, XL
Minimum Memory: 128K
Medium: 3 1/2-inch disk
ISPN: 64387-604   **Price: $85.00**

QUEUE

SIXTH GRADE READING COMPREHENSION

Includes sixth grade level reading comprehension exercises.

System: MAC, II, PLUS, SE, XL
Minimum Memory: 128K
Medium: 3 1/2-inch disk
ISPN: 64387-607   **Price: $65.00**

ADDISON WESLEY PUBLISHING CO.

SMART WORDS-COLLEGE PREP VOCABULARY

Increases your knowledge and understanding of words.

System: MAC, PLUS, XL
Minimum Memory: 512K
Medium: 3 1/2-inch disk
ISPN: 00900-700   **Price: $49.95**

ADDISON WESLEY PUBLISHING CO.

SMART WORDS-ESSENTIAL BUSINESS VOCABULARY

Word exercises for business professionals – the most commonly used and misused words.

System: MAC, PLUS, XL
Minimum Memory: 512K
Medium: 3 1/2-inch disk
ISPN: 00900-725   **Price: $49.95**

QUEUE

THIRD GRADE READING COMPREHENSION

Tests and reinforces comprehension by offering students a variety of passages to read.

System: MAC, II, PLUS, SE, XL
Minimum Memory: 128K
Medium: 3 1/2-inch disk
ISPN: 64387-661   **Price: $65.00**

QUEUE

VOCABULARY ADVENTURE I – CASTLE OF TREASURE

Vocabulary tutorial in adventure game scenario.

System: MAC, II, PLUS, SE, XL
Minimum Memory: 128K
Medium: 3 1/2-inch disk
ISPN: 64387-930   **Price: $59.95**

QUEUE

VOCABULARY ADVENTURE II-THE LABYRINTH

Grades 7-9: Adventure designed to encourage students to learning the meaning of new words. Over 1000 new words are introduced.

System: MAC, II, PLUS, SE, XL
Minimum Memory: 128K
Medium: 3 1/2-inch disk
ISPN: 64387-940   **Price: $59.95**

QUEUE

VOCABULARY ADVENTURE III-MARAUDERS OF ARK

Grades 10-12: Score points by searching for treasures on the ark, moving to a new location after solving a vocabulary mystery.

System: MAC, II, PLUS, SE, XL
Minimum Memory: 128K
Medium: 3 1/2-inch disk
ISPN: 64387-942   **Price: $59.95**

KINKOS ACADEMIC COURSEWARE EXCHANGE

VOCABULARY DRILL (VER. 1.0)

A vocabulary exercise to accompany the study of chapters 16 through 25 of McKay's 'A History of Western Society'.

System: MAC, II, PLUS, SE, XL
Minimum Memory: 128K
Requires: Finder (Ver. 4.1 or 5.3).
Medium: 3 1/2-inch disk
ISPN: 43025-947   **Price: $20.00**

ADVANCED IDEAS, INC.

WIZARD OF WORDS

Ages 5 and up: Build word skills interacting with medieval enchantment.

System: MAC, II, PLUS, SE, XL
Minimum Memory: 512K
Medium: 3 1/2-inch disk
ISPN: 15700-900   **Price: $49.95**

DAVIDSON AND ASSOCIATES, INC.

WORD ATTACK!

Grades 4-12: Multi-level word games help students acquire a way with words.

System: MAC, PLUS, SE, XL
Minimum Memory: 512K
Medium: 3 1/2-inch disk
ISPN: 24075-300   **Price: $49.95**

DAVIDSON AND ASSOCIATES, INC.

WORD ATTACK! VOCABULARY DATA DISK-GRADES 6-7

Introduces 500 new words for use with Word Attack!

System: MAC, PLUS, XL
Minimum Memory: 512K
Requires: Word Attack! (ISPN 24075-300).
Medium: 3 1/2-inch disk
ISPN: 24075-327   **Price: $19.95**

DAVIDSON AND ASSOCIATES, INC.

WORD ATTACK!-VOCABULARY DATA DISK-GRADES 2-3

Introduces 500 new words for use with Word Attack!.

System: MAC, II, PLUS, SE, XL
Minimum Memory: 512K
Requires: Word Attack! (ISPN 24075-300)
Medium: 3 1/2-inch disk
ISPN: 24075-324   **Price: $19.95**

FOR MORE DETAILED INFORMATION, CALL (412) 746-MENU

DAVIDSON AND ASSOCIATES, INC.

WORD ATTACK!-VOCABULARY DATA DISK-GRADES 4-5

Provides 500 new words for use with Word Attack!

System: MAC, PLUS, SE, XL
Minimum Memory: 512K
Requires: Word Attack! (ISPN 24075-300).
Medium: 3 1/2-inch disk
ISPN: 24075-326 **Price: $19.95**

DAVIDSON AND ASSOCIATES, INC.

WORD ATTACK!-VOCABULARY DATA DISK-GRADES 8-9

Introduces 500 new words for use with Word Attack!

System: MAC, PLUS, SE, XL
Minimum Memory: 512K
Requires: Word Attack! (ISPN 24075-300).
Medium: 3 1/2-inch disk
ISPN: 24075-328 **Price: $19.95**

278 EDUCATION/ SCIENCE

OAKLEAF SYSTEMS

ANIMAL BEHAVIOR DATA SIMULATION

Provides 25 simulations, including the influence of flock size on vigilance in starlings and single gene mutant and fruitfly memory.

System: MAC, II, PLUS, SE, XL
Minimum Memory: 128K
Medium: 3 1/2-inch disk
ISPN: 57587-175 **Price: $59.95**

OAKLEAF SYSTEMS

AQUATIC ECOLOGY DATA SIMULATION

Provides 25 simulations suitable for the college level, including production at different depths in Lake Tahoe.

System: MAC, II, PLUS, SE, XL
Minimum Memory: 128K
Medium: 3 1/2-inch disk
ISPN: 57587-150 **Price: $59.95**

VOYAGER CO.

BIO SCI LASERGUIDE

A HyperCard based laserguide for the Bio Sci laserdisc.

System: MAC, II, PLUS, SE, XL
Minimum Memory: 1024K
Requires: HyperCard (ISPN 03900-300).
Medium: 3 1/2-inch disk
ISPN: 96647-100 **Price: $99.95**

QUEUE

BIOLOGY I

Interactive tutorial with quizzes. Topics are development and organismal biology, embryology and respiratory system.

System: MAC, II, PLUS, SE, XL
Minimum Memory: 128K
Medium: 3 1/2-inch disk
ISPN: 64387-151 **Price: $79.95**

QUEUE

BIOLOGY II

Grades 9 and up: Provides instructions for students in molecular biology, enzymes, bioenergetics, nucleic acids and biosynthesis.

System: MAC, PLUS, SE, XL
Minimum Memory: 128K
Medium: 3 1/2-inch disk
ISPN: 64387-163 **Price: $79.95**

OAKLEAF SYSTEMS

BREEDING BIRD SURVEY DATA SIMULATION

Provides information on population trends for 50 bird species, including the Mourning Dove, Downy Woodpecker and Barn Swallow.

System: MAC, II, PLUS, SE, XL
Minimum Memory: 128K
Medium: 3 1/2-inch disk
ISPN: 57587-250 **Price: $69.95**

AAH COMPUTER GRAPHIC PRODUCTIONS

DINOSAUR BYTES

A carefully crafted image collection, suitable for educational use.

System: MAC, II, PLUS, SE, XL
Minimum Memory: 128K
Requires: MacPaint (ISPN 12784-510) or Paint-compatible program.
Medium: 3 1/2-inch disk
ISPN: 00181-150 **Price: $29.95**

OAKLEAF SYSTEMS

ECOLOGICAL DATA SIMULATION

Includes 25 simulations suitable for undergraduate biology students, including rainfall and primary production.

System: MAC, II, PLUS, SE, XL
Minimum Memory: 128K
Medium: 3 1/2-inch disk
ISPN: 57587-205 **Price: $59.95**

QUEUE

ELECTRICITY

Grades 7-9: Explains the sources of electricity, magnetism, charges, circuits, kinds of current and transistors.

System: MAC, II, PLUS, SE, XL
Minimum Memory: 128K
Medium: 3 1/2-inch disk
ISPN: 64387-288 **Price: $34.95**

QUEUE

ELEMENTARY BIOLOGY I

Grades 7-9: An interactive tutorial which introduces students to biology, zoology, ecology, botany and plant reproduction.

System: MAC, II, PLUS, SE, XL
Minimum Memory: 128K
Medium: 3 1/2-inch disk
ISPN: 64387-293 **Price: $34.95**

QUEUE

ELEMENTARY BIOLOGY II

Grades 7-9: Explains the circulatory system, the lymph system, the nervous system, and the endocrine system.

System: MAC, II, PLUS, SE, XL
Minimum Memory: 128K
Medium: 3 1/2-inch disk
ISPN: 64387-296 **Price: $34.95**

QUEUE

ELEMENTARY CHEMISTRY

Grades 7-9: Designed as an introduction to chemistry, covering elements, compounds and mixtures, chemical bonds and gases.

System: MAC, II, PLUS, SE, XL
Minimum Memory: 128K
Medium: 3 1/2-inch disk
ISPN: 64387-301 **Price: $34.95**

QUEUE

ELEMENTARY PHYSICS

Grades 4-5: Designed as an introduction to physics for students.

System: MAC, PLUS, SE, XL
Minimum Memory: 128K
Medium: 3 1/2-inch disk
ISPN: 64387-311 **Price: $34.95**

KINKOS ACADEMIC COURSEWARE EXCHANGE

ENERGETICS AND METABOLISM (VER. 1.0)

Illustrates the interactions among the several metabolic compartments of a cell by using diagrams of biochemical pathways.

System: MAC, II, PLUS, SE, XL
Minimum Memory: 512K
Requires: 800K disk, Atlas (ISPN 43025-075).
Medium: 3 1/2-inch disk
ISPN: 43025-109 **Price: $11.50**

KINKOS ACADEMIC COURSEWARE EXCHANGE

EVOLUTION (VER. 1.03)

Illustrates the relations among organisms of many kinds, emphasizing the history and mechanics of their evolutionary change.

System: MAC, II, PLUS, SE, XL
Minimum Memory: 512K
Requires: 800K disk, Atlas (ISPN 43025-075).
Medium: 3 1/2-inch disk
ISPN: 43025-120 **Price: $11.50**

OAKLEAF SYSTEMS

EVOLUTION: A SIMULATION

Allows users to see the effects of mutation, gene flow, natural selection and genetic drift on population.

System: MAC, II, PLUS, SE, XL
Minimum Memory: 128K
Medium: 3 1/2-inch disk
ISPN: 57587-300   **Price: $49.95**

QUEUE

EXPLORING SCIENCE II-COMPLETE SERIES

Grades 7-9: Contains six programs including electricity, physics, chemistry, biology I and II, and behavioral sciences.

System: MAC, II, PLUS, SE, XL
Minimum Memory: 128K
Medium: 3 1/2-inch disk
ISPN: 64387-004   **Price: $195.00**

OAKLEAF SYSTEMS

FISHERIES BIOLOGY DATA SIMULATION

Provides 25 simulations, including production by algae and herbivores and herring survival in the Gulf of Maine.

System: MAC, II, PLUS, SE, XL
Minimum Memory: 128K
Medium: 3 1/2-inch disk
ISPN: 57587-600   **Price: $59.95**

OAKLEAF SYSTEMS

GENERAL BIOLOGY DATA SIMULATION

Provides 25 simulations, including years since infection and proportion with AIDS, and relative growth rates of root tissue.

System: MAC, II, PLUS, SE, XL
Minimum Memory: 128K
Medium: 3 1/2-inch disk
ISPN: 57587-350   **Price: $59.95**

QUEUE

GENERAL CHEMISTRY I

A comprehensive interactive tutorial with quizzes. Each wrong answer branches to further explanation.

System: MAC, II, PLUS, SE, XL
Minimum Memory: 128K
Medium: 3 1/2-inch disk
ISPN: 64387-165   **Price: $79.95**

QUEUE

GENERAL CHEMISTRY II

A comprehensive interactive tutorial with quizzes. Each wrong answer branches to further explanation.

System: MAC, II, PLUS, SE, XL
Minimum Memory: 128K
Medium: 3 1/2-inch disk
ISPN: 64387-166   **Price: $79.95**

KINKOS ACADEMIC COURSEWARE EXCHANGE

GENERAL CHEMISTRY, MULTIPLAN TEMPLATES (VER. 1.0)

Contains four templates: percentage composition, equilibrium concentrations, acid-base titration curves and linear regression.

System: MAC, II, PLUS, SE, XL
Minimum Memory: 128K
Requires: Microsoft Multiplan (ISPN 53150-550).
Medium: 3 1/2-inch disk
ISPN: 43025-200   **Price: $14.50**

COMPRESS, DIV. OF QUEUE

IR SIMULATOR

Displays the control panel and plotting area of an IR Spectrometer. Contains a library of spectra designed for use with the Simulator.

System: MAC, II, PLUS, SE, XL
Minimum Memory: 512K
Medium: 3 1/2-inch disk
ISPN: 14850-006   **Price: $75.00**

COMPRESS, DIV. OF QUEUE

IR SIMULATOR

Displays the control panel and plotting area of an IR Spectrometer. Contains a library of spectra designed for use with the Simulator.

System: MAC, II, PLUS, SE, XL
Minimum Memory: 512K
Requires: Lab pack (includes 5 copies).
Medium: 3 1/2-inch disk
ISPN: 14850-006   **Price: $135.00**

ADVANCED GEOGRAPHIC SYSTEMS

MAC CHEMISTRY

Custom font, MacPaint artwork, Indexed text and graphics scrapbook plus titration simulator. Senior High School and College.

System: MAC, II, PLUS, SE, XL
Minimum Memory: 128K
Medium: 3 1/2-inch disk
ISPN: 31215-200   **Price: $145.00**

NORDIC SOFTWARE, INC.

MACKIDS-BODYWORKS

Ages 10 and up: Teaches children to identify different parts of the human anatomy.

System: MAC, II, PLUS, SE, XL
Minimum Memory: 512K
Medium: 3 1/2-inch disk
ISPN: 57028-015   **Price: $39.95**

KINKOS ACADEMIC COURSEWARE EXCHANGE

MACMENDELEEV (VER. 1.0)

Places information about the periodic table at your fingertips. Includes the tools necessary to begin to comprehend the table.

System: MAC, II, PLUS, SE, XL
Minimum Memory: 512K
Requires: Finder (Ver. 4.1 or 5.3).
Medium: 3 1/2-inch disk
ISPN: 43025-395   **Price: $17.00**

KINKOS ACADEMIC COURSEWARE EXCHANGE

MACPRIMATE.VERVET (VER. 1.0)

Models eighteen behavioral activities of vervet monkeys from birth to adulthood.

System: MAC, II, PLUS, SE, XL
Minimum Memory: 512K
Medium: 3 1/2-inch disk
ISPN: 43025-400   **Price: $17.50**

KINKOS ACADEMIC COURSEWARE EXCHANGE

MACSTEREO (R/S) (VER. 3.31)

Illustrates the Cahn-Ingold-Prelog stereochemical designation system.

System: MAC, II, PLUS, SE, XL
Minimum Memory: 128K
Requires: Finder (Ver. 4.1 or 5.3).
Medium: 3 1/2-inch disk
ISPN: 43025-408   **Price: $17.00**

HEIZER SOFTWARE

MOLECULAR WEIGHT CALCULATOR

Calculates the molecular weight of any molecule when entered as an Excel formula.

System: MAC, II, PLUS, SE, XL
Minimum Memory: 512K
Requires: Microsoft Excel (ISPN 53150-270).
Medium: 3 1/2-inch disk
ISPN: 35175-702   **Price: $12.00**

COMPRESS, DIV. OF QUEUE

NMR SIMULATOR

Designed as a tool to teach students how to operate an NMR spectrometer and how to use the instrument in the laboratory.

System: MAC, II, PLUS, SE, XL
Minimum Memory: 512K
Medium: 3 1/2-inch disk
ISPN: 14850-866 **Price: $95.00**

COMPRESS, DIV. OF QUEUE

NMR SIMULATOR

Designed as a tool to teach students how to operate an NMR spectrometer and how to use the instrument in the laboratory.

System: MAC, II, PLUS, SE, XL
Minimum Memory: 512K
Requires: Lab pack (includes 5 copies).
Medium: 3 1/2-inch disk
ISPN: 14850-866 **Price: $155.00**

COMPRESS, DIV. OF QUEUE

ORGANIC STEREOCHEMISTRY

Covers the concepts of stereochemistry as they are applied to organic molecules.

System: MAC, II, PLUS, SE, XL
Minimum Memory: 512K
Medium: 3 1/2-inch disk
ISPN: 14850-667 **Price: $75.00**

COMPRESS, DIV. OF QUEUE

ORGANIC STEREOCHEMISTRY

Covers the concepts of stereochemistry as they are applied to organic molecules.

System: MAC, II, PLUS, SE, XL
Minimum Memory: 512K
Requires: Lab pack (includes 5 copies).
Medium: 3 1/2-inch disk
ISPN: 14850-667 **Price: $135.00**

KINKOS ACADEMIC COURSEWARE EXCHANGE

PERICHART (VER. 1.3)

A database of atoms and elements that can be searched through interaction with an electronic display of the periodic chart.

System: MAC, II, PLUS, SE, XL
Minimum Memory: 128K
Requires: 800K disk, Finder (Ver. 4.1 or 5.3).
Medium: 3 1/2-inch disk
ISPN: 43025-570 **Price: $22.00**

BRODERBUND SOFTWARE, INC.

PHYSICS

Grades 9-12: Provides a private tutor that complements an introductory course in classical mechanics.

System: MAC, II, PLUS, SE, XL
Minimum Memory: 512K
Medium: 3 1/2-inch disk
ISPN: 08850-114 **Price: $99.95**

BRODERBUND SOFTWARE, INC.

PHYSICS

Grades 9-12: Provides a private tutor that complements an introductory course in classical mechanics.

System: MAC, II, PLUS, SE, XL
Minimum Memory: 512K
Requires: School edition.
Medium: 3 1/2-inch disk
ISPN: 08850-114 **Price: $109.95**

BRODERBUND SOFTWARE, INC.

PHYSICS

Grades 9-12: Provides a private tutor that complements an introductory course in classical mechanics.

System: MAC, II, PLUS, SE, XL
Minimum Memory: 512K
Requires: Lab pack.
Medium: 3 1/2-inch disk
ISPN: 08850-114 **Price: $219.95**

OAKLEAF SYSTEMS

PHYSIOLOGICAL DATA SIMULATION

Provides 25 simulations, including enzyme activity and amount of substrate, and ejected volume and blood pressure in a frog.

System: MAC, II, PLUS, SE, XL
Minimum Memory: 128K
Medium: 3 1/2-inch disk
ISPN: 57587-500 **Price: $59.95**

OAKLEAF SYSTEMS

PLANT BIOLOGY DATA SIMULATION

Provides 25 simulations, including light attenuation by plant canopies and near ground temperature profiles.

System: MAC, II, PLUS, SE, XL
Minimum Memory: 128K
Medium: 3 1/2-inch disk
ISPN: 57587-225 **Price: $59.95**

KINKOS ACADEMIC COURSEWARE EXCHANGE

PLANT PAINT (VER. 1.0)

A set of 36 graphic images which illustrate concepts in plant biology.

System: MAC, II, PLUS, SE, XL
Minimum Memory: 128K
Requires: MacPaint (ISPN 12784-510) or compatible program.
Medium: 3 1/2-inch disk
ISPN: 43025-600 **Price: $17.50**

KINKOS ACADEMIC COURSEWARE EXCHANGE

PLANT PAINT (VER. 1.0)

A set of 36 graphic images which illustrate concepts in plant biology.

System: MAC, II, PLUS, SE, XL
Minimum Memory: 128K
Requires: Site license. MacPaint (ISPN 12784-510) or compatible program.
Medium: 3 1/2-inch disk
ISPN: 43025-600 **Price: $300.00**

VENTURA EDUCATIONAL SYSTEMS

PROTOZOA (VER. 2.0)

An introduction to microorganisms within the protozoa phylum.

System: MAC, II, PLUS, SE, XL
Minimum Memory: 512K
Medium: 3 1/2-inch disk
ISPN: 84911-627 **Price: $49.95**

VENTURA EDUCATIONAL SYSTEMS

PROTOZOA (VER. 2.0)

An introduction to microorganisms within the protozoa phylum.

System: MAC, PLUS, SE, XL
Minimum Memory: 512K
Requires: Lab pack (five disks).
Medium: 3 1/2-inch disk
ISPN: 84911-627 **Price: $89.95**

QUEUE

SCIENTIFIC NOTATION

Contains an interactive, step-by-step tutorial with drill and practice on scientific notation.

System: MAC, II, PLUS, SE, XL
Minimum Memory: 128K
Medium: 3 1/2-inch disk
ISPN: 64387-599 **Price: $29.95**

AAH COMPUTER GRAPHIC PRODUCTIONS

SEA LIFE

Accurately drawn images of a wide variety of sea creatures, educational as well as enjoyable.

System: MAC, II, PLUS, SE, XL
Minimum Memory: 128K
Requires: MacPaint (ISPN 12784-510) or program that can read MacPaint format.
Medium: 3 1/2-inch disk
ISPN: 00181-175 **Price: $29.95**

VENTURA EDUCATIONAL SYSTEMS

SENSES (VER. 2.0)

Grades 7 and up: A 'Physiology Study Unit' to become familiar with the various aspects of the human sense organs.

System: MAC, II, PLUS, SE, XL
Minimum Memory: 512K
Medium: 3 1/2-inch disk
ISPN: 84911-721 **Price: $49.95**

VENTURA EDUCATIONAL SYSTEMS

SENSES (VER. 2.0)

Grades 7 and up: A 'Physiology Study Unit' to become familiar with the various aspects of the human sense organs.

System: MAC, PLUS, SE, XL
Minimum Memory: 512K
Requires: Lab pack (includes 5 disks).
Medium: 3 1/2-inch disk
ISPN: 84911-721 **Price: $89.95**

AAH COMPUTER GRAPHIC PRODUCTIONS

SKY BYTES

A carefully crafted collection of aerospace graphics.

System: MAC, II, PLUS, SE, XL
Minimum Memory: 128K
Requires: MacPaint (ISPN 12784-510) or Paint-compatible program.
Medium: 3 1/2-inch disk
ISPN: 00181-200   **Price: $29.95**

DELTRON

SKY TRAVEL

Graphic astronomy program, a window on the universe, stars, deep sky objects, sun, moon, all planets.

System: MAC, II, PLUS, SE, XL
Minimum Memory: 250K
Medium: 3 1/2-inch disk
ISPN: 24681-700   **Price: $62.95**

COOKE PUBLICATIONS

STOMATETUTOR (VER. 2.0)

An interactive video animation of the mechanism used by plants to regulate their gaseous environment.

System: MAC, II, PLUS, SE, XL
Minimum Memory: 512K
Requires: Hypercard (ISPN 03900-300).
Medium: 3 1/2-inch disk
ISPN: 19659-600   **Price: $19.95**

VENTURA EDUCATIONAL SYSTEMS

VISIFROG (VER. 2.0)

Grades 7 and up: A vertebrate anatomy learning program using computer graphics that display the anatomy of the frog.

System: MAC, II, PLUS, SE, XL
Minimum Memory: 512K
Medium: 3 1/2-inch disk
ISPN: 84911-800   **Price: $49.95**

VENTURA EDUCATIONAL SYSTEMS

VISIFROG (VER. 2.0)

Grades 7 and up: A vertebrate anatomy learning program using computer graphics that display the anatomy of the frog.

System: MAC, PLUS, SE, XL
Minimum Memory: 512K
Requires: Lab pack (includes 5 disks).
Medium: 3 1/2-inch disk
ISPN: 84911-800   **Price: $89.95**

UNICORN SOFTWARE CO.

WONDERS OF THE ANIMAL KINGDOM

Ages 6-12: An early science program that helps enhance language arts, reading development and memory skills. One to four players.

System: MAC, II, PLUS, SE, XL
Minimum Memory: 512K
Medium: 3 1/2-inch disk
ISPN: 83562-050   **Price: $49.95**

VENTURA EDUCATIONAL SYSTEMS

WORM (VER. 2.0)

The phylum 'Annelida' is brought to life on the screen to help the user learn more about the anatomy of the worm.

System: MAC, II, PLUS, SE, XL
Minimum Memory: 512K
Medium: 3 1/2-inch disk
ISPN: 84911-850   **Price: $49.95**

VENTURA EDUCATIONAL SYSTEMS

WORM (VER. 2.0)

The phylum 'Annelida' is brought to life on the screen to help the user learn more about the anatomy of the worm.

System: MAC, PLUS, SE, XL
Minimum Memory: 512K
Requires: Lab pack (five disks).
Medium: 3 1/2-inch disk
ISPN: 84911-850   **Price: $89.95**

283 EDUCATION/SOCIAL SCIENCE

QUEUE

BEHAVIORAL SCIENCES

Grades 7-9: Provides an introduction to and review of psychology, sociology, and anthropology.

System: MAC, II, PLUS, SE, XL
Minimum Memory: 128K
Medium: 3 1/2-inch disk
ISPN: 64387-160   **Price: $34.95**

QUEUE

INTRODUCTION TO BEHAVIORAL SCIENCES

Grades 7-9: Provides an introduction to and review of psychology, sociology and anthropology.

System: MAC, II, PLUS, SE, XL
Minimum Memory: 128K
Medium: 3 1/2-inch disk
ISPN: 64387-407   **Price: $34.95**

TRUE BASIC, INC.

PATHFINDER (VER. 1.0)

Estimates causal statistical relationships using correlation coefficients as inputs.

System: MAC, II, PLUS, SE, XL
Minimum Memory: 512K
Medium: 3 1/2-inch disk
ISPN: 82789-315   **Price: $49.95**

285 EDUCATION/ SPANISH

QUEUE

COMPLETE SPANISH GRAMMAR SERIES

Grades 7 and up: An eleven-program series which provides instruction in all major points of Spanish grammar and usage.

System: MAC, II, PLUS, SE, XL
Minimum Memory: 128K
Medium: 3 1/2-inch disk
ISPN: 64387-825   **Price: $335.00**

INDIVIDUAL SOFTWARE, INC.

FLASH & MATCH SPANISH

Provides customizable electronic flashcards with an 1800 word Spanish/English database to help build foreign vocabulary skills.

System: MAC, II, PLUS, SE, XL
Minimum Memory: 512K
Requires: 800K disk drive.
Medium: 3 1/2-inch disk
ISPN: 37275-220   **Price: $59.95**

ARTWORX SOFTWARE CO., INC.

LINKWORD-SPANISH

Teaches up to 400 words of Spanish grammar, and pronunciation.

System: MAC, II, PLUS, SE, XL
Minimum Memory: 512K
Medium: 3 1/2-inch disk
ISPN: 05437-280   **Price: $29.95**

QUEUE

SPANISH GRAMMAR I

Grades 7 and up: Includes gender of nouns, definite and indefinite articles, plural of nouns, contradictions, regular verbs and more.

System: MAC, II, PLUS, SE, XL
Minimum Memory: 128K
Medium: 3 1/2-inch disk
ISPN: 64387-850   **Price: $34.95**

QUEUE

SPANISH GRAMMAR II

Grades 7 and up: Includes agreement of adjectives, gender of adjectives, plural of adjectives, and adjectives used as nouns.

System: MAC, II, PLUS, SE, XL
Minimum Memory: 128K
Medium: 3 1/2-inch disk
ISPN: 64387-860   **Price: $34.95**

QUEUE

SPANISH GRAMMAR III

Grades 7 and up: Provides instruction in Spanish grammar, including the preterit tense of regular, irregular, and stem-changing verbs.

System: MAC, II, PLUS, SE, XL
Minimum Memory: 128K
Medium: 3 1/2-inch disk
ISPN: 64387-799   **Price: $34.95**

QUEUE
SPANISH GRAMMAR IV

Grades 7 and up: Instructs students in Spanish grammar, including imperfect versus preterit tenses, and present progressive tense.

System: MAC, II, PLUS, SE, XL
Minimum Memory: 128K
Medium: 3 1/2-inch disk
ISPN: 64387-815   **Price: $34.95**

QUEUE
SPANISH GRAMMAR IX

Grades 9 and up: Instructs students in Spanish grammar, including interrogatives used as pronouns, adjectives and exclamations.

System: MAC, II, PLUS, SE, XL
Minimum Memory: 128K
Medium: 3 1/2-inch disk
ISPN: 64387-802   **Price: $34.95**

QUEUE 2
SPANISH GRAMMAR REVIEW I

Grades 9 and up: Provides review and practice in Spanish grammar structure, including subject pronouns and adjective agreement.

System: MAC, II, PLUS, SE, XL
Minimum Memory: 128K
Medium: 3 1/2-inch disk
ISPN: 64393-061   **Price: $49.95**

QUEUE 2
SPANISH GRAMMAR REVIEW II

Grades 9 and up: Provides review and practice in Spanish grammar structure, including negatives, interrogatives and preterite tense.

System: MAC, II, PLUS, SE, XL
Minimum Memory: 128K
Medium: 3 1/2-inch disk
ISPN: 64393-065   **Price: $49.95**

QUEUE
SPANISH GRAMMAR V

Grades 7 and up: Provides instruction in Spanish grammar, including the subjunctive to express feeling or emotion, & past participles.

System: MAC, II, PLUS, SE, XL
Minimum Memory: 128K
Medium: 3 1/2-inch disk
ISPN: 64387-800   **Price: $34.95**

QUEUE
SPANISH GRAMMAR VI

Grades 7 and up: Instructs students in Spanish grammar, including the subjunctive to express uncertainty and unreality.

System: MAC, II, PLUS, SE, XL
Minimum Memory: 128K
Medium: 3 1/2-inch disk
ISPN: 64387-818   **Price: $34.95**

QUEUE
SPANISH GRAMMAR VII

Grades 7 and up: Provides instruction in Spanish, including impersonal expressions that call for subjunctive or indicative mood

System: MAC, II, PLUS, SE, XL
Minimum Memory: 128K
Medium: 3 1/2-inch disk
ISPN: 64387-801   **Price: $34.95**

QUEUE
SPANISH GRAMMAR VIII

Grades 7 and up: Provides instruction in Spanish grammar, including the active voice versus the passive voice.

System: MAC, II, PLUS, SE, XL
Minimum Memory: 128K
Medium: 3 1/2-inch disk
ISPN: 64387-820   **Price: $34.95**

QUEUE
SPANISH GRAMMAR X

Grades 9 and up: Provides instruction in Spanish grammar and usage, including diminutives and augmentatives.

System: MAC, II, PLUS, SE, XL
Minimum Memory: 128K
Medium: 3 1/2-inch disk
ISPN: 64387-821   **Price: $34.95**

QUEUE
SPANISH GRAMMAR XI

Grades 9 and up: A review of the most frequently used Spanish idioms.

System: MAC, II, PLUS, SE, XL
Minimum Memory: 128K
Medium: 3 1/2-inch disk
ISPN: 64387-810   **Price: $34.95**

HYPERGLOT SOFTWARE CO.
SPANISH VERB TUTOR

Provides 200 sentences to drill you on 20 verbs using HyperText capabilities.

System: MAC, II, PLUS, SE, XL
Minimum Memory: 1024K
Requires: HyperCard (VER. 1.2.1) (ISPN 03900-300).
Medium: 3 1/2-inch disk
ISPN: 36734-700   **Price: $29.95**

HYPERGLOT SOFTWARE CO.
SPANISH WORD TORTURE

An automated vocabulary drill with over 1600 verbs, adverbs, nouns, adjectives, comparatives and function words.

System: MAC, II, PLUS, SE, XL
Minimum Memory: 1024K
Requires: HyperCard (VER. 1.2.1) (ISPN 03900-300).
Medium: 3 1/2-inch disk
ISPN: 36734-710   **Price: $19.95**

HEIZER SOFTWARE
SPEED SPANISH

A HyperCard stack which includes six strategies for developing speed and vocabulary skills in basic Spanish.

System: MAC, II, PLUS, SE, XL
Minimum Memory: 512K
Requires: HyperCard (ISPN 03900-300).
Medium: 3 1/2-inch disk
ISPN: 35175-986   **Price: $20.00**

287 EDUCATION/ SPECIAL EDUCATION

BERKELEY SYSTEMS
INLARGE (VER. 1.1)

Magnifies anything on the Macintosh screen by 2 to 16 times. The magnified display can cover the whole screen.

System: MAC, PLUS, SE, XL
Minimum Memory: 512K
Medium: 3 1/2-inch disk
ISPN: 07441-400   **Price: $95.00**

BERKELEY SYSTEMS
INTOUCH

Allows TSI's Opticon II (a tactile imaging device) to display any information on the Macintosh screen.

System: MAC, II, PLUS, SE, XL
Minimum Memory: 1024K
Medium: 3 1/2-inch disk
ISPN: 07441-450   **Price: $395.00**

BERKELEY SYSTEMS
OUTSPOKEN: THE TALKING MACINTOSH INTERFACE

Allows blind users to work with text-based programs such as word processors and spreadsheets using navigational key commands.

System: MAC, II, PLUS, SE, XL
Minimum Memory: 1024K
Medium: 3 1/2-inch disk
ISPN: 07441-500   **Price: $395.00**

QUEUE 2
PACKAGE A

Grade 3 reading level: Contains three stories which help improve student's factual recall and inferential thinking ability.

System: MAC, II, PLUS, SE, XL
Minimum Memory: 128K
Medium: 3 1/2-inch disk
ISPN: 64393-018   **Price: $65.00**

QUEUE 2
PACKAGE B

Grade 4 reading level: Contains stories which help improve a student's factual recall and inferential thinking ability.

System: MAC, II, PLUS, SE, XL
Minimum Memory: 128K
Medium: 3 1/2-inch disk
ISPN: 64393-022   **Price: $65.00**

QUEUE 2
PACKAGE BB

Grade 2 reading level: Presents factual and inferential questions on topics such as countries, animals and well-known fables.

System: MAC, PLUS, SE, XL
Minimum Memory: 128K
Medium: 3 1/2-inch disk
ISPN: 64393-021   **Price: $65.00**

QUEUE 2
PACKAGE C

Grade 5 reading level: A reading comprehension program to help improve a student's factual recall & inferential thinking ability.

System: MAC, II, PLUS, SE, XL
Minimum Memory: 128K
Medium: 3 1/2-inch disk
ISPN: 64393-019   **Price: $65.00**

QUEUE 2
PACKAGE D

Grade 6 reading level: Contains 30 lessons to help improve a student's factual recall and inferential thinking ability.

System: MAC, II, PLUS, SE, XL
Minimum Memory: 128K
Medium: 3 1/2-inch disk
ISPN: 64393-023   **Price: $65.00**

QUEUE 2
PACKAGE E

Grade 7 reading level: Contains 40 lessons to help improve a student's factual recall and inferential thinking ability.

System: MAC, II, PLUS, SE, XL
Minimum Memory: 128K
Medium: 3 1/2-inch disk
ISPN: 64393-020   **Price: $65.00**

QUEUE 2
PACKAGE F

Grade 8 reading level: Concentrates on helping students to improve factual recall and inferential thinking abilities.

System: MAC, II, PLUS, SE, XL
Minimum Memory: 128K
Medium: 3 1/2-inch disk
ISPN: 64393-024   **Price: $65.00**

QUEUE 2
REMEDIAL READING COMPREHENSION SERIES

An interactive seven-program series in reading comprehension to improve factual recall and inferential thinking ability.

System: MAC, II, PLUS, SE, XL
Minimum Memory: 128K
Medium: 3 1/2-inch disk
ISPN: 64393-016   **Price: $425.00**

289 EDUCATION/SPEED READING

TIMEWORKS, INC.
EVELYN WOOD DYNAMIC READER

Ages 14 and up: Improves reading comprehension, retention and speed.

System: MAC, II, PLUS, SE, XL
Minimum Memory: 128K
Medium: 3 1/2-inch disk
ISPN: 82000-215   **Price: $49.95**

ADDISON WESLEY PUBLISHING CO.
SMART EYES

Age 13 and up: Focuses on increasing reading comprehension as well as speed.

System: MAC, PLUS, XL
Minimum Memory: 128K
Medium: 3 1/2-inch disk
ISPN: 00900-695   **Price: $49.95**

DAVIDSON AND ASSOCIATES, INC.
SPEED READER II

Improves reading skills by increasing speed and maintaining or improving comprehension.

System: MAC, PLUS, SE, XL
Minimum Memory: 512K
Medium: 3 1/2-inch disk
ISPN: 24075-125   **Price: $69.95**

DAVIDSON AND ASSOCIATES, INC.
SPEED READER II DATA DISK GRADES 5-6

Grades 5-6: Designed to help increase reading speed and improve comprehension.

System: MAC, PLUS, SE, XL
Minimum Memory: 512K
Requires: Speed Reader II (ISPN 24075-125).
Medium: 3 1/2-inch disk
ISPN: 24075-126   **Price: $19.95**

DAVIDSON AND ASSOCIATES, INC.
SPEED READER II DATA DISK GRADES 7-8

Grades 7-8: Designed to help increase reading speed and improve comprehension.

System: MAC, PLUS, SE, XL
Minimum Memory: 512K
Requires: Speed Reader II (ISPN 24075-125).
Medium: 3 1/2-inch disk
ISPN: 24075-127   **Price: $19.95**

DAVIDSON AND ASSOCIATES, INC.
SPEED READER II DATA DISK- COLLEGE AND ADULT LEVEL

Adult level: Designed to help increase reading speed and improve comprehension.

System: MAC, PLUS, SE, XL
Minimum Memory: 512K
Requires: Speed Reader II (ISPN 24075-125).
Medium: 3 1/2-inch disk
ISPN: 24075-129   **Price: $19.95**

DAVIDSON AND ASSOCIATES, INC.
SPEED READER II DATA DISK- GRADES 9-12

Grades 9-12: Designed to help increase reading speed and improve comprehension.

System: MAC, PLUS, SE, XL
Minimum Memory: 512K
Requires: Speed Reader II (ISPN 24075-125).
Medium: 3 1/2-inch disk
ISPN: 24075-128   **Price: $19.95**

SIMON AND SCHUSTER
ELECTRONIC PUBLISHING GROUP
SPEED READING TUTOR IV

A personal reading acceleration program for students, business people and pleasure readers.

System: MAC, PLUS, SE, XL
Minimum Memory: 128K
Medium: 3 1/2-inch disk
ISPN: 70387-705   **Price: $49.95**

290 EDUCATION/ SPELLING

FIRST BYTE, INC.
SPELLER BEE

A talking notebook to teach spelling and pronunciation.

System: MAC, II, PLUS, SE, XL
Minimum Memory: 512K
Medium: 3 1/2-inch disk
ISPN: 30836-600   **Price: $49.95**

292 EDUCATION/ VOCATIONAL/BUSINESS SKILLS

ILAR SYSTEMS, INC.
BOTTOMLINE CAPITALIST (VER. 2.1)

A four team business simulation balancing market share, ROI and company growth, while maintaining cash flow.

System: MAC, II, PLUS, SE, XL
Minimum Memory: 512K
Requires: Printer.
Medium: 3 1/2-inch disk
ISPN: 37131-100   **Price: $125.00**

HARVARD ASSOCIATES, INC.
MACMANAGER (VER. 2.1)

Management simulation. Make business decisions based on financial data and try to maximize a hypothetical companies profits.

System: MAC, II, PLUS, SE, XL
Minimum Memory: 128K
Medium: 3 1/2-inch disk
ISPN: 34579-075   **Price: $19.95**

DYNACOMP, INC.
MANAGEMENT SIMULATOR

Each player or team controls a company which manufactures three products and competes against companies with similar products.
System: MAC, II, PLUS, SE, XL
Minimum Memory: 512K
Medium: 3 1/2-inch disk
ISPN: 27050-481 **Price: $44.95**

QUEUE
REVIEW QUESTIONS IN ACCOUNTING

Multiple choice questions on accumulation of financial data, periodic adjustments and the accounting cycle.
System: MAC, II, PLUS, SE, XL
Minimum Memory: 128K
Medium: 3 1/2-inch disk
ISPN: 64387-805 **Price: $39.95**

QUEUE
STARTING A NEW BUSINESS

Learn the ins and outs of starting a new business venture. Make decisions about trade name, partnership agreement and more.
System: MAC, II, PLUS, SE, XL
Minimum Memory: 128K
Medium: 3 1/2-inch disk
ISPN: 64387-890 **Price: $59.95**

ADDISON WESLEY PUBLISHING CO.
TEACH YOURSELF ESSENTIALS OF ACCOUNTING

Gives users solid understanding of essential accounting terminology and principles with an interactive course.
System: MAC, PLUS, XL
Minimum Memory: 512K
Requires: 800K disk drive.
Medium: 3 1/2-inch disk
ISPN: 00900-830 **Price: $49.95**

301 INDUSTRIES/ AEROSPACE

MICRONEERING
SAMBAS

A finite element program for Structural Analysis of Multibody Axial Symetric objects.
System: MAC
Minimum Memory: 512K
Medium: 3 1/2-inch disk
ISPN: 52818-700 **Price: $4500.00**

305 INDUSTRIES/ AGRICULTURE

AG PLUS SOFTWARE
AG COUNT EXTRA

A farm accounting package featuring cash flows, budgets, net worth & profit-and-loss statements, tax estimates and management reports.
System: MAC, II, PLUS, SE, XL
Minimum Memory: 512K
Medium: 3 1/2-inch disk
ISPN: 01759-105 **Price: $495.00**

AG-WARE
AG-BUSINESS MANAGER (VER. 3.0)

A farm or ranch financial management program. It can be set up to match the production cost and income categories of your farm/ranch.
System: MAC, II, PLUS, SE, XL
Minimum Memory: 512K
Requires: 132-column printer, HFS operating system.
Medium: 3 1/2-inch disk
ISPN: 01760-100 **Price: $895.00**

DOANE INFORMATION SERVICES, DIV. OF CONTROL DATA
AGDISK CROP-LIVESTOCK PROFIT PROJECTOR

Calculates crop and livestock profit based on expected projection costs and current market conditions.
System: MAC, II, PLUS, SE, XL
Minimum Memory: 128K
Medium: 3 1/2-inch disk
ISPN: 34425-105 **Price: $95.00**

HEIZER SOFTWARE
ALFALFA STANDS

Determines the time to replace an existing stand of alfalfa with a new seeding.
System: MAC, PLUS, XL
Minimum Memory: 512K
Requires: Microsoft Excel (ISPN 53150-270) or Microsoft Works (ISPN 53150-740).
Medium: 3 1/2-inch disk
ISPN: 35175-111 **Price: $8.00**

HEIZER SOFTWARE
BEEF CATTLE FEEDLOT ANALYSIS

Calculates the expected gain of sending cattle to a feedlot.
System: MAC, II, PLUS, SE, XL
Minimum Memory: 512K
Requires: Microsoft Excel (ISPN 53150-270) or Microsoft Works (ISPN 53150-740).
Medium: 3 1/2-inch disk
ISPN: 35175-123 **Price: $8.00**

HEIZER SOFTWARE
BEEF COW VALUE

Provides estimates of economic payback for any cow in a commercial herd-producing weanlings or yearlings.
System: MAC, II, PLUS, SE, XL
Minimum Memory: 512K
Requires: Microsoft Excel (ISPN 53150-270) or Microsoft Works (ISPN 53150-740).
Medium: 3 1/2-inch disk
ISPN: 35175-112 **Price: $12.00**

HEIZER SOFTWARE
BEEF SIRE VALUE

Estimates economic return for beef sires used in commercial herds which are producing yearlings or weanlings.
System: MAC, II, PLUS, SE, XL
Minimum Memory: 512K
Requires: Microsoft Excel (ISPN 53150-270) or Microsoft Works (ISPN 53150-740).
Medium: 3 1/2-inch disk
ISPN: 35175-113 **Price: $12.00**

AGRICULTURAL SOFTWARE CONSULTANTS, INC.
COMPFEED (VER. 1.0)

Balances protein and energy for user-defined milk increments while calculating the necessary grains for those increments.
System: MAC, PLUS, XL
Minimum Memory: 512K
Requires: MIXIT programs produced by Vendor (01950) with MSDOS option.
Medium: 3 1/2-inch disk
ISPN: 01950-175
Price: Please contact the software publisher.

AG PLUS SOFTWARE
CROP PRODUCTION ANALYSIS

Analyzes up to six individual crops to determine cash flow and profitability.
System: MAC, II, PLUS, SE, XL
Minimum Memory: 512K
Medium: 3 1/2-inch disk
ISPN: 01759-200 **Price: $99.00**

HEIZER SOFTWARE
CROP RETURNS

Calculates total and per acre income, expenses and profit.
System: MAC, II, PLUS, SE, XL
Minimum Memory: 512K
Requires: Microsoft Excel (ISPN 53150-270) or Microsoft Works (ISPN 53150-740).
Medium: 3 1/2-inch disk
ISPN: 35175-114 **Price: $12.00**

HEIZER SOFTWARE
FARM TRUCK COSTS

Provides total annual costs and per mile costs of operations.
System: MAC, II, PLUS, SE, XL
Minimum Memory: 512K
Requires: Microsoft Excel (ISPN 53150-270) or Microsoft Works (ISPN 53150-740).
Medium: 3 1/2-inch disk
ISPN: 35175-115 **Price: $8.00**

HEIZER SOFTWARE
FEED MIX CALCULATOR

Replaces the Pearson Square 'box' method of calculating feed mix.
System: MAC, II, PLUS, SE, XL
Minimum Memory: 512K
Requires: Microsoft Excel (ISPN 53150-270) or Microsoft Works (ISPN 53150-740).
Medium: 3 1/2-inch disk
ISPN: 35175-122 **Price: $9.00**

HEIZER SOFTWARE
FEEDER CATTLE BREAK-EVEN

Calculates the break-even price per pound, profit or loss per head, and total profit or loss.

System: MAC, II, PLUS, SE, XL
Minimum Memory: 512K
Requires: Microsoft Excel (ISPN 53150-270) or Microsoft Works (ISPN 53150-740).
Medium: 3 1/2-inch disk
ISPN: 35175-116   **Price: $12.00**

AG PLUS SOFTWARE
LAND PURCHASE

Determines cash flow and the profitability of purchasing land.

System: MAC, II, PLUS, SE, XL
Minimum Memory: 512K
Medium: 3 1/2-inch disk
ISPN: 01759-400   **Price: $50.00**

AGRICULTURAL SOFTWARE CONSULTANTS, INC.
LAYER (VER. 1.0)

Formulates feed rations for laying chickens when used with any MIXIT program.

System: MAC, II, PLUS, SE, XL
Minimum Memory: 256K
Requires: MS-DOS option.
Medium: 3 1/2-inch disk
ISPN: 01950-475   **Price: $195.00**

HEIZER SOFTWARE
LIVESTOCK SHRINKAGE

Calculates the shrinkage of livestock when the actual pounds are known or when estimating.

System: MAC, II, PLUS, SE, XL
Minimum Memory: 512K
Requires: Microsoft Excel (ISPN 53150-270) or Microsoft Works (ISPN 53150-740).
Medium: 3 1/2-inch disk
ISPN: 35175-121   **Price: $5.00**

AG PLUS SOFTWARE
LOAN REPAYMENT

Program determines payment required for a loan using amortization method.

System: MAC, II, PLUS, SE, XL
Minimum Memory: 512K
Medium: 3 1/2-inch disk
ISPN: 01759-500   **Price: $35.00**

DAPPLE-TECH COMPUTERS
MAC HORSE (VER. 4.5)

Complete horse farm management system for veterinarians, breeders, trainers, and show horse operators.

System: MAC, II, PLUS, SE, XL
Minimum Memory: 512K
Requires: Hard disk, ImageWriter printer.
Medium: 3 1/2-inch disk
ISPN: 22281-500   **Price: $1495.00**

HEIZER SOFTWARE
MARKET GRAIN

Discusses the benefits of trucking grain to a distant terminal.

System: MAC, II, PLUS, SE, XL
Minimum Memory: 512K
Requires: Microsoft Excel (ISPN 53150-270) or Microsoft Works (ISPN 53150-740).
Medium: 3 1/2-inch disk
ISPN: 35175-118   **Price: $8.00**

HEIZER SOFTWARE
PUREBRED COW PRICE

Provides a break-even purchase price for purebred beef heifers or cows.
System: MAC, II, PLUS, SE, XL
Minimum Memory: 512K
Requires: Microsoft Excel (ISPN 53150-270) or Microsoft Works (ISPN 53150-740).
Medium: 3 1/2-inch disk
ISPN: 35175-119   **Price: $6.00**

HEIZER SOFTWARE
RELATIVE FORAGE VALUE

Rates hay according to the University of Wisconsin system.
System: MAC, II, PLUS, SE, XL
Minimum Memory: 512K
Requires: Microsoft Excel (ISPN 53150-270) or Microsoft Works (ISPN 53150-740).
Medium: 3 1/2-inch disk
ISPN: 35175-117   **Price: $8.00**

HEIZER SOFTWARE
RETAINED OWNERSHIP OF CALVES

Calculates the profitability of selling calves at weaning time as opposed to alternative methods.
System: MAC, PLUS, XL
Minimum Memory: 512K
Requires: Microsoft Excel (ISPN 53150-270) or Microsoft Works (ISPN 53150-740).
Medium: 3 1/2-inch disk
ISPN: 35175-120   **Price: $8.00**

AG PLUS SOFTWARE
SERIES 110

Contains three programs for agriculture including grain storage costs, and cattle and hog break-evens.
System: MAC, II, PLUS, SE, XL
Minimum Memory: 512K
Medium: 3 1/2-inch disk
ISPN: 01759-600   **Price: $90.00**

HEIZER SOFTWARE
SWINE ENTERPRISE ANALYSIS

Tracks cost input for pork production, including feed by ingredient.
System: MAC, II, PLUS, SE, XL
Minimum Memory: 512K
Requires: Microsoft Excel (ISPN 53150-270).
Medium: 3 1/2-inch disk
ISPN: 35175-778   **Price: $40.00**

310 INDUSTRIES/ AUTOMOTIVE

SOFTWARE DEVELOPMENT GROUP
FLEET MANAGER (VER. 2.0)

Monitors scheduled maintenance, theft detection, performance analyses and provides information to help mechanics.

System: MAC, PLUS, XL
Minimum Memory: 1024K
Medium: 3 1/2-inch disk
ISPN: 72681-200   **Price: $1495.00**

315 INDUSTRIES/ AVIATION

HEIZER SOFTWARE
ANNUAL PLANE EXPENSES

A cumulative breakdown record of all yearly costs associated with owning an airplane.

System: MAC, II, PLUS, SE, XL
Minimum Memory: 512K
Requires: Microsoft Excel (ISPN 53150-270) or Microsoft Works (ISPN 53150-740).
Medium: 3 1/2-inch disk
ISPN: 35175-205   **Price: $9.00**

HEIZER SOFTWARE
AVIATION LOGBOOK

Keeps year-to-date and total flight-hour recordings for day, night, Instrument Flight Rules hood time, dual, solo and pilot in command.

System: MAC, II, PLUS, SE, XL
Minimum Memory: 512K
Requires: Microsoft Excel (ISPN 53150-270) or Microsoft Works (ISPN 53150-740).
Medium: 3 1/2-inch disk
ISPN: 35175-207   **Price: $7.00**

HEIZER SOFTWARE
AVIATION MAINTENANCE LOG

Records general aviation dates, tachometer readings, ID, the task accomplished, date when next due and cost.

System: MAC, II, PLUS, SE, XL
Minimum Memory: 512K
Requires: Microsoft Excel (ISPN 53150-270) or Microsoft Works (ISPN 53150-740).
Medium: 3 1/2-inch disk
ISPN: 35175-208   **Price: $7.00**

HEIZER SOFTWARE
CITY TO CITY TABLE

Creates a table showing the distance between each pair of cities in statute miles, nautical miles or kilometers.

System: MAC, II, PLUS, SE, XL
Minimum Memory: 512K
Requires: Microsoft Excel (ISPN 53150-270).
Medium: 3 1/2-inch disk
ISPN: 35175-215   **Price: $15.00**

HEIZER SOFTWARE
COURSE NAVIGATOR

Calculates great circle straight line course between any two points on Earth.

System: MAC, II, PLUS, SE, XL
Minimum Memory: 512K
Requires: Microsoft Excel (ISPN 53150-270).
Medium: 3 1/2-inch disk
ISPN: 35175-214   **Price: $10.00**

HEIZER SOFTWARE
FIND MECCA

Calculates the great circle direction and distance to Mecca.

System: MAC, PLUS, XL
Minimum Memory: 512K
Requires: Microsoft Excel (ISPN 53150-270).
Medium: 3 1/2-inch disk
ISPN: 35175-211   **Price: $8.00**

HEIZER SOFTWARE
FLIGHT LOG

Keeps track of air travel and puts the data to use. Useful for participants of an airlines 'frequent flyer' program.

System: MAC, II, PLUS, SE, XL
Minimum Memory: 512K
Requires: Microsoft Works (ISPN 53150-740).
Medium: 3 1/2-inch disk
ISPN: 35175-034   **Price: $8.00**

HEIZER SOFTWARE
GREAT CIRCLE

Calculates the distance between any two points on Earth.

System: MAC, II, PLUS, SE, XL
Minimum Memory: 512K
Requires: Microsoft Excel (ISPN 53150-270), Microsoft Works (ISPN 53150-740) or HyperCard (ISPN 03900-300).
Medium: 3 1/2 inch disk
ISPN: 35175-212   **Price: $6.00**

HEIZER SOFTWARE
IFR FLIGHT PLANNING

Figures mileage remaining after each leg of the flight, plugs in ground speed and calculates point-to-point and cumulative times.

System: MAC, II, PLUS, SE, XL
Minimum Memory: 512K
Requires: Microsoft Excel (ISPN 53150-270) or Microsoft Works (ISPN 53150-740).
Medium: 3 1/2-inch disk
ISPN: 35175-209   **Price: $9.00**

HEIZER SOFTWARE
NAVIGATOR

Calculates the great circle headings and distances for trips with as many as ten legs.

System: MAC, II, PLUS, SE, XL
Minimum Memory: 512K
Requires: Microsoft Excel (ISPN 53150-270).
Medium: 3 1/2-inch disk
ISPN: 35175-213   **Price: $10.00**

HEIZER SOFTWARE
PLANE OWNERSHIP COSTS

Calculates cost per hour and per mile of flying, including percentage of ownership, depreciation and cost of money.

System: MAC, II, PLUS, SE, XL
Minimum Memory: 512K
Requires: Microsoft Excel (ISPN 53150-270) or Microsoft Works (ISPN 53150-740).
Medium: 3 1/2-inch disk
ISPN: 35175-204   **Price: $9.00**

HEIZER SOFTWARE
WEIGHT AND BALANCE

A template which can be customized to provide loaded weight and center of gravity figures.

System: MAC, II, PLUS, SE, XL
Minimum Memory: 512K
Requires: Microsoft Excel (ISPN 53150-270).
Medium: 3 1/2-inch disk
ISPN: 35175-206   **Price: $10.00**

319 INDUSTRIES/ CHEMICAL

CAMBRIDGE SCIENTIFIC COMPUTING
CHEM 3D (VER. 2.0)

A molecular modeling package that aids professional scientists and scientific authors in analyzing chemical models.

System: MAC, II, PLUS, SE, XL
Minimum Memory: 1024K
Requires: Consumer version. 800K disk drive.
Medium: 3 1/2-inch disk
ISPN: 10862-150   **Price: $595.00**

CAMBRIDGE SCIENTIFIC COMPUTING
CHEM 3D (VER. 2.0)

A molecular modeling package that aids professional scientists and scientific authors in analyzing chemical models.

System: MAC, II, PLUS, SE, XL
Minimum Memory: 1024K
Requires: Academic version. 800K disk drive.
Medium: 3 1/2-inch disk
ISPN: 10862-150   **Price: $396.00**

CAMBRIDGE SCIENTIFIC COMPUTING
CHEM 3D+ (VER. 2.0)

A superset of the Chem 3D program which includes color and MM2 minimization for use in analyzing chemical models.

System: MAC, II, PLUS, SE, XL
Minimum Memory: 1024K
Requires: Consumer version. 800K disk drive.
Medium: 3 1/2-inch disk
ISPN: 10862-155   **Price: $895.00**

CAMBRIDGE SCIENTIFIC COMPUTING
CHEM 3D+ (VER. 2.0)

A superset of the Chem 3D program which includes color and MM2 minimization for use in analyzing chemical models.

System: MAC, II, PLUS, SE, XL
Minimum Memory: 1024K
Requires: Academic version. 800K disk drive.
Medium: 3 1/2-inch disk
ISPN: 10862-155   **Price: $595.00**

CAMBRIDGE SCIENTIFIC COMPUTING
CHEMDRAW (VER. 2.1.1)

Aids scientists and scientific authors in drawing difficult chemical structure formulas.

System: MAC, II, PLUS, SE, XL
Minimum Memory: 512K
Requires: Consumer version. 800K disk drive.
Medium: 3 1/2-inch disk
ISPN: 10862-100   **Price: $595.00**

CAMBRIDGE SCIENTIFIC COMPUTING
CHEMDRAW (VER. 2.1.1)

Aids scientists and scientific authors in drawing difficult chemical structure formulas.

System: MAC, II, PLUS, SE, XL
Minimum Memory: 512K
Requires: Academic version. 800K disk drive.
Medium: 3 1/2-inch disk
ISPN: 10862-100   **Price: $396.00**

325 INDUSTRIES/ COMPUTER-AIDED DESIGN (CAD)

COMPU-ARCH
ADS-MGMSTATION- ARCHITECTURE (VER. 1.2)

An extensive collection of architectural symbols that conform to ANSI standards, arranged in more than 20 distinct libraries.

System: MAC, II, PLUS, SE, XL
Minimum Memory: 1024K
Requires: MGMStation (ISPN 49818-220).
Medium: 3 1/2-inch disk
ISPN: 15066-105   **Price: $195.00**

COMPU-ARCH
ADS-MGMSTATION-ELECTRONIC (VER. 1.2)

An extensive collection of electrical and electronic symbols arranged in more than 15 distinct libraries.

System: MAC, II, PLUS, SE, XL
Minimum Memory: 1024K
Requires: MGMStation (ISPN 49818-220).
Medium: 3 1/2-inch disk
ISPN: 15066-110   **Price: $195.00**

COMPU-ARCH

ADS-MGMSTATION-INTERIORS (VER. 1.2)

An extensive collection of interior design symbols that conform to ANSI standards, arranged in more than 20 distinct libraries.

System: MAC, II, PLUS, SE, XL
Minimum Memory: 1024K
Requires: MGMStation (ISPN 49818-220).
Medium: 3 1/2-inch disk
ISPN: 15066-115   **Price: $195.00**

COMPU-ARCH

ADS-MGMSTATION-MECHANICAL (VER. 1.2)

An extensive collection of mechanical design symbols that conform to MIL standards arranged in more than 20 distinct libraries.

System: MAC, II, PLUS, SE, XL
Minimum Memory: 1024K
Requires: MGMStation (ISPN 49818-220).
Medium: 3 1/2-inch disk
ISPN: 15066-100   **Price: $195.00**

ABVENT

ARCHICAD (VER. 3.5)

Provides automatic surface and solids modeling of architectural floor plans, and generates a Bill of Materials.

System: II
Minimum Memory: 2048K
Requires: Hard disk, and printer or plotter.
Medium: 3 1/2-inch disk
ISPN: 00437-100   **Price: $3950.00**

KANDU SOFTWARE

CADMOVER (VER. 3.0)

Provides the ability to read, translate and write a variety of graphic files formats.

System: MAC, II, PLUS, SE, XL
Minimum Memory: 512K
Medium: 3 1/2-inch disk
ISPN: 42307-100   **Price: $495.00**

CLARIS CORP.

CLARIS CAD

Two dimensional design and drafting with geometric construction and support of ANSI Y14.5, ISO, DIN, JIS, and BS308 standards.

System: MAC, II, PLUS, SE, XL
Minimum Memory: 1024K
Requires: System Software 6.02 or higher (ISPN 03900-700).
Medium: 3 1/2-inch disk
ISPN: 12784-150   **Price: $799.00**

KLEX SOFTWARE, INC.

COMPUGRAPH (VER. 1.0)

Provides multi-dimensional spacial design features, 3-D modeling and real-time dynamic rotation.

System: II, PLUS, XL
Minimum Memory: 512K
Medium: 3 1/2-inch disk
ISPN: 43107-100   **Price: $395.00**

SOLARSOFT

DAYLITE (VER. 2.1)

Quantifies the natural illumination levels in buildings and calculates glare and contrast values.

System: MAC, II, PLUS, SE, XL
Minimum Memory: 512K
Medium: 3 1/2-inch disk
ISPN: 74262-400   **Price: $289.00**

VISUAL INFORMATION, INC.

DESIGNS-DIMENSIONS (BLACK AND WHITE)

Three dimensional CAD system and surface design program in black and white.

System: MAC, II, PLUS, SE, XL
Minimum Memory: 1024K
Medium: 3 1/2-inch disk
ISPN: 85412-100   **Price: $750.00**

VISUAL INFORMATION, INC.

DESIGNS-DIMENSIONS (COLOR)

Three dimensional CAD system and surface design program in color.

System: MAC, II, PLUS, SE, XL
Minimum Memory: 1024K
Requires: 800K external disk drive.
Medium: 3 1/2-inch disk
ISPN: 85412-110   **Price: $1395.00**

DOUGLAS ELECTRONICS

DOUGLAS PROFESSIONAL CAD/CAM SYSTEM

Contains a schematic, layout and autorouter package to allow user to design from the schematic to the final circuit board.

System: MAC, II, PLUS, SE, XL
Minimum Memory: 1024K
Medium: 3 1/2-inch disk
ISPN: 26668-250   **Price: $2900.00**

DOUGLAS ELECTRONICS

DOUGLAS PROFESSIONAL SYSTEM-AUTOROUTER (VER. 1.2)

Allows for full integration of The Professional system by automatically completing board connection.

System: MAC, II, PLUS, SE, XL
Minimum Memory: 1024K
Requires: Schematic (ISPN 26668-600) and Professional Layout (ISPN 26668-400).
Medium: 3 1/2-inch disk
ISPN: 26668-150   **Price: $700.00**

INNOVATIVE DATA DESIGN, INC.

DREAMS

Consists of a family of design tools, and features advanced text handling, a high-performance zoom, and PostScript compatability.

System: II
Minimum Memory: 2048K
Requires: Hard disk drive.
Medium: 3 1/2-inch disk
ISPN: 37053-207   **Price: $500.00**

INNOVATIVE DATA DESIGN, INC.

DREAMS

Consists of a family of design tools, and features advanced text handling, a high-performance zoom, and PostScript compatability.

System: MAC, II, PLUS, SE, XL
Minimum Memory: 1024K
Requires: Hard disk drive.
Medium: 3 1/2-inch disk
ISPN: 37053-207   **Price: $500.00**

ENABLING TECHNOLOGIES, INC.

EASY3D

Allows even novices to create realistic three dimensional objects.

System: MAC, PLUS, SE, XL
Minimum Memory: 512K
Medium: 3 1/2-inch disk
ISPN: 29051-100   **Price: $149.00**

BRIDGEPORT MACHINES

EZ-DRAFT

A full-featured professional drafting system which has the ability to separate a drawing into top, front, left, and right views.

System: MAC, II, PLUS, SE, XL
Minimum Memory: 512K
Medium: 3 1/2-inch disk
ISPN: 90656-500   **Price: $2500.00**

GENERIC SOFTWARE, INC.

GENERIC CADD LEVEL I

A 'first step' for learning CADD. Enables the user to create flow charts, organization charts, graphs, and presentations.

System: MAC, II, PLUS, SE, XL
Minimum Memory: 1024K
Requires: Two 800K disk drives or a hard disk.
Medium: 3 1/2-inch disk
ISPN: 32537-330   **Price: $149.95**

INFINITE GRAPHICS, INC.

IN-CAD

Provides 3-D design, 2-D drafting and solids modeling with Dynamic Sizing, 2 programming languages and 2 translators.

System: II
Minimum Memory: 2048K
Requires: Math co-processor.
Medium: 3 1/2-inch disk
ISPN: 37387-375   **Price: $2495.00**

LIONSHEAD SOFTWARE, INC.

LSI PENTAGON CAD (VER. 1.2)

Creates two dimensional object based drawings with layering, editing, symbols and plotter support.

System: MAC, II, PLUS, SE, XL
Minimum Memory: 512K
Requires: MacWorks Plus (ISPN 77034-500).
Medium: 3 1/2-inch disk
ISPN: 44912-400   **Price: $99.00**

VAMP, INC.

M.G.M.S. MECHANICAL DRAFTING PACKAGE (VER. 2.51)

Professional drafting tool offering design analysis, a scientific calculator and automatic dimensioning.

System: MAC, II, PLUS, SE, XL
Minimum Memory: 512K
Requires: ImageWriter I or II, LaserWriter, or Pen Plotters.
Medium: 3 1/2-inch disk
ISPN: 84771-465   **Price: $995.00**

VAMP, INC.

M.G.M.S. MECHANICAL DRAFTING PACKAGE (VER. 2.52)

Professional color drafting tool offering design analysis, a scientific calculator and automatic dimensioning.

System: II
Minimum Memory: 1024K
Requires: ImageWriter I or II, LaserWriter, or pen plotters.
Medium: 3 1/2-inch disk
ISPN: 84771-466   **Price: $1395.00**

GIMEOR, INC.

MAC ARCHITRION (VER. 3.5E)

Consists of Real Volumetric 3D, 2D and Quantifier Bill of Materials modules.

System: MAC, II, PLUS, SE, XL
Minimum Memory: 1024K
Medium: 3 1/2-inch disk
ISPN: 32907-500   **Price: $1499.00**

CHALLENGER SOFTWARE

MAC3D (VER. 2.1)

A two-and three-dimensional graphics package for technical and free-form drawing, designing, modeling and desktop publishing.

System: MAC, II, PLUS, SE, XL
Minimum Memory: 512K
Requires: Two 400K disk drives or one 800K disk drive.
Medium: 3 1/2-inch disk
ISPN: 12093-500   **Price: $249.00**

COMPSERVCO

MACCAD-FLOW CHARTS AND LOGIC

Minicad Templates which include analog, digital logic, IC components, information system, and mechanical flow.

System: MAC, II, PLUS, SE, XL
Minimum Memory: 512K
Requires: Please specify version when ordering: PICT Version, MiniCad Version, MacDraw Version or MacDraft Version.
Medium: 3 1/2-inch disk
ISPN: 15025-228   **Price: $149.00**

COMPSERVCO

MACCAD-RULED ISOMETRIC WITH OVALS

Minicad Templates for drawing isometric views on a 30 degree grid using 3/32 inch thru 10 inch ovals and cylinders.

System: MAC, II, PLUS, SE, XL
Minimum Memory: 512K
Requires: Please specify version when ordering: PICT Version, MacDraw Version or MacDraft Version.
Medium: 3 1/2-inch disk
ISPN: 15025-684   **Price: $149.00**

INNOVATIVE DATA DESIGN, INC.

MACDRAFT (VER. 1.2B)

Creates scaled drawings, schematic diagrams, organizational charts, and business illustrations, as well as personal greeting cards.

System: MAC, II, PLUS, SE, XL
Minimum Memory: 1024K
Medium: 3 1/2-inch disk
ISPN: 37053-400   **Price: $269.00**

GRAPHIC MAGIC

MACSURF

Computer aided design and surface modelling techniques using B-spline for use by naval architect or drawing office.

System: MAC, II, PLUS, SE, XL
Minimum Memory: 512K
Medium: 3 1/2-inch disk
ISPN: 33421-400   **Price: $2450.00**

MICRO CAD/CAM SYSTEMS, INC.

MGMSTATION CAD (VER. 2.5 I)

Provides basic and expanded drawing functions, and allows creation of unlimited symbol libraries.

System: MAC, II, PLUS, SE, XL
Minimum Memory: 1024K
Medium: 3 1/2-inch disk
ISPN: 49818-220   **Price: $999.00**

MICRO CAD/CAM SYSTEMS, INC.

MGMSTATION CAD (VER. 2.5 II) COLOR

Utilizes color, provides basic and expanded drawing functions, and allows creation of unlimited symbol libraries.

System: II
Minimum Memory: 1024K
Medium: 3 1/2-inch disk
ISPN: 49818-221   **Price: $1399.00**

MICRO CAD/CAM SYSTEMS, INC.

MGMSTATION IGES/DXF

Enables drawing files to be exported to, or imported from, CAD programs that run on different computers.

System: MAC, II, PLUS, SE, XL
Minimum Memory: 512K
Requires: Hard disk.
Medium: 3 1/2-inch disk
ISPN: 49818-225   **Price: $500.00**

DYNACOMP, INC.

MICRO CAP II

Allows the user to design and predict the performance of a circuit without having to actually build it.

System: MAC, II, PLUS, SE, XL
Minimum Memory: 512K
Requires: Two disk drives.
Medium: 3 1/2-inch disk
ISPN: 27050-105   **Price: $749.95**

GRAPHSOFT, INC.

MINICAD +

Fully integrated 2D/3D CAD program with hot-lined spreadsheet designed for architects, engineers and graphic artists.

System: MAC, II, PLUS, SE, XL
Minimum Memory: 1024K
Medium: 3 1/2-inch disk
ISPN: 25184-500   **Price: $495.00**

GRAPHSOFT, INC.

MINICAD +

Fully integrated 2D/3D CAD program with hot-lined spreadsheet designed for architects, engineers and graphic artists.

System: MAC, II, PLUS, SE, XL
Minimum Memory: 1024K
Requires: 1-5 users.
Medium: 3 1/2-inch disk
ISPN: 25184-500   **Price: $1237.50**

MODACAD, INC.

MODACAD SKETCH (VER. 1.2)

An automated fashion design and manufacturing system for the apparel industry.

System: II
Minimum Memory: 2048K
Requires: Price stated is base price. Price varies according to options.
Medium: 3 1/2-inch disk
ISPN: 54848-500   **Price: $3000.00**

DELTASOFT, INC.

ORIGINS

A 2-D and 3-D with real-time rotation and multiple surface construction, solid modeling, 256 layers and solid modeling.

System: MAC, II, PLUS, SE, XL
Minimum Memory: 512K
Requires: 800K disk drive.
Medium: 3 1/2-inch disk
ISPN: 24667-500   **Price: $495.00**

DELTASOFT, INC.

ORIGINS

A 2-D and 3-D with real-time rotation and multiple surface construction, solid modeling, 256 layers and solid modeling.

System: II
Minimum Memory: 512K
Requires: 800K disk drive. Color version.
Medium: 3 1/2-inch disk
ISPN: 24667-500   **Price: $595.00**

IGC TECHNOLOGY CORP.
PEGASYS I (VER. 3.2.4)

A two-dimensional CADD package intended for use in mechanical, architectural, civil, piping and electrical industries.

System: MAC, II, PLUS, SE, XL
Minimum Memory: 1024K
Requires: Hard disk.
Medium: 3 1/2-inch disk
ISPN: 37106-200   **Price: $695.00**

IGC TECHNOLOGY CORP.
PEGASYS II (VER. 3.2.3)

Provides mainframe speed in design and drafting operations. Takes advantage of 68020 & MC68881 math coprocessor & full color support.

System: II, MAC, PLUS, XL
Minimum Memory: 1024K
Requires: Hard disk.
Medium: 3 1/2-inch disk
ISPN: 37106-220   **Price: $1795.00**

ENGINEERED SOFTWARE
POWERDRAW (VER. 2.0)

Provides a Computer Aided Design (CAD) tool for the professional.

System: MAC, II, PLUS, SE, XL
Minimum Memory: 1024K
Requires: Two disk drives or one disk drive and hard disk, printer or plotter.
Medium: 3 1/2-inch disk
ISPN: 17509-700   **Price: $795.00**

ENGINEERED SOFTWARE
POWERDRAW DXF TRANSLATOR

Allows 2-way exchange of drawings between PowerDraw and other CAD platforms.

System: MAC, II, PLUS, SE, XL
Minimum Memory: 1024K
Requires: 800K disk drive.
Medium: 3 1/2-inch disk
ISPN: 17509-710   **Price: $195.00**

ENABLING TECHNOLOGIES, INC.
PRO3D/MAC

A high end sophisticated three-dimensional shaded modelling system for the design, examination and presentation of 3-D images.

System: MAC, PLUS, SE, XL
Minimum Memory: 512K
Requires: LaserWriter or ImageWriter I or II printer.
Medium: 3 1/2-inch disk
ISPN: 29051-400   **Price: $349.00**

BISHOP GRAPHICS, INC.
QUIK CIRCUIT (VER. 4.2)

A CAD/CAM system for designing printed circuit boards. Produces precision artwork.

System: MAC, II, PLUS, SE, XL
Minimum Memory: 512K
Medium: 3 1/2-inch disk
ISPN: 07787-750   **Price: $525.00**

MFE ASSOCIATES
SIZER/ADJACENCY

Increases the accessible accuracy of MacDraw.

System: MAC, II, PLUS, SE, XL
Minimum Memory: 128K
Requires: MacDraw 1.9 or earlier (ISPN 12784-500), 800K disk drive.
Medium: 3 1/2-inch disk
ISPN: 49331-800   **Price: $69.00**

WILLIAMS AG PRODUCTS
SKETCH-TO-SCALE PLUS (VER. 1.0)

For anyone interested in making 'to scale' drawings. Almost all architectural and engineering scales are possible.

System: MAC, II, PLUS, SE, XL
Minimum Memory: 128K
Medium: 3 1/2-inch disk
ISPN: 86503-500   **Price: $74.95**

FORTHOUGHT, INC.
SNAP! (VER. 3.0)

A 2-D CAD system with auto-dimensioning, built-in plotter and LaserWriter drivers. Includes symbol libraries with nested symbols.

System: MAC, PLUS, SE, XL
Minimum Memory: 1024K
Medium: 3 1/2-inch disk
ISPN: 22380-700   **Price: $695.00**

FORTHOUGHT, INC.
SNAP! / INTERGRAPH TRANSLATOR

Provides conversion of drawings between the Snap! format and the 2-D Intergraph IGDS format.

System: MAC, II, PLUS, SE, XL
Minimum Memory: 1024K
Medium: 3 1/2-inch disk
ISPN: 22380-705   **Price: $195.00**

VISUAL INFORMATION, INC.
SOLID DIMENSIONS (BLACK AND WHITE)

Solid surface design for creating wireframe designs and solid objects in black and white.

System: MAC, II, PLUS, SE, XL
Minimum Memory: 1024K
Requires: Two 800K disk drives.
Medium: 3 1/2-inch disk
ISPN: 85412-700   **Price: $395.00**

VISUAL INFORMATION, INC.
SOLID DIMENSIONS (COLOR)

Solid surface design with color rendering.

System: MAC, PLUS, SE, XL
Minimum Memory: 1024K
Requires: Two 800K disk drives.
Medium: 3 1/2-inch disk
ISPN: 85412-710   **Price: $1295.00**

ABVENT
SPACE EDIT

A fully integrated 2 and 3D package that allows engineers and architects to design any object and then visualize it.

System: MAC, II, PLUS, SE, XL
Minimum Memory: 512K
Medium: 3 1/2-inch disk
ISPN: 00437-510   **Price: $395.00**

ABVENT
SPACE EDIT (VER. 2.5)

A fully integrated 2 and 3D color package that allows engineers and architects to design any object and then visualize it.

System: MAC, II, XL
Minimum Memory: 1024K
Medium: 3 1/2-inch disk
ISPN: 00437-515   **Price: $495.00**

GENERIC SOFTWARE, INC.
SYMBOLS LIBRARY-BASIC HOME DESIGN

Contains over 120 pre-drawn symbols, for use in drawing plans and elevation views of home designs.

System: MAC, II, PLUS, SE, XL
Minimum Memory: 1024K
Requires: Generic Cadd (ISPN 32537-330, or 340), two 800K disk drives or a hard disk.
Medium: 3 1/2-inch disk
ISPN: 32537-700   **Price: $49.95**

GENERIC SOFTWARE, INC.
SYMBOLS LIBRARY-BATHROOM DESIGN

Provides over 450 symbols for bathroom cabinets and fixtures, in both plan and elevation views.

System: MAC, II, PLUS, SE, XL
Minimum Memory: 1024K
Requires: Generic Cadd (ISPN 32537-330 or 340), two 800K disk drives or a hard disk.
Medium: 3 1/2-inch disk
ISPN: 32537-711   **Price: $74.95**

GENERIC SOFTWARE, INC.
SYMBOLS LIBRARY-COMMERCIAL RESIDENTIAL ELECTRICAL

Contains over 120 pre-drawn symbols, with most conforming to NECA wiring symbols standards.

System: MAC, II, PLUS, SE, XL
Minimum Memory: 1024K
Requires: Generic Cadd (ISPN 32537-330 or 340), two 800K disk drives or a hard disk.
Medium: 3 1/2-inch disk
ISPN: 32537-705   **Price: $49.95**

GENERIC SOFTWARE, INC.
SYMBOLS LIBRARY-COMMERCIAL RESIDENTIAL PLUMBING

Contains over 100 pre-drawn symbols for use in designing and drawing plumbing systems.

System: MAC, II, PLUS, SE, XL
Minimum Memory: 1024K
Requires: Generic Cadd (ISPN 32537-330, or 340), two 800K disk drives or a hard disk.
Medium: 3 1/2-inch disk
ISPN: 32537-715   **Price: $49.95**

DYNACOMP, INC.
TOLCULATOR

Provides a computer aided tolerancing system.

System: PLUS
Minimum Memory: 512K
Requires: Two disk drives, Microsoft Excel (ISPN 53150-270).
Medium: 3 1/2-inch disk
ISPN: 27050-157   **Price: $175.00**

DYNACOMP, INC.
TOLCULATOR

Provides a computer aided tolerancing system.

System: MAC
Minimum Memory: 512K
Requires: Two disk drives, Microsoft Excel (ISPN 53150-270).
Medium: 3 1/2-inch disk
ISPN: 27050-157   **Price: $149.95**

VERSACAD CORP.
VERSACAD/MACINTOSH EDITION (VER. 2.1)

Contains a fully integrated CAD system for mechanical, architectural and educational design requirements.

System: MAC, II, PLUS, SE, XL
Minimum Memory: 2048K
Requires: Hard disk, math co-processor.
Medium: 3 1/2-inch disk
ISPN: 79543-380   **Price: $1995.00**

330 INDUSTRIES/COMPUTER-AIDED MANUFACTURING (CAM)

META SOFTWARE CORP.
DESIGN/IDEF

Allows automation of Computer Integrated Manufacturing(CIM) planning and modelling.

System: MAC, II, PLUS, SE, XL
Minimum Memory: 1024K
Medium: 3 1/2-inch disk
ISPN: 49215-270   **Price: $2000.00**

MICRO CAD/CAM SYSTEMS, INC.
MGMSTATION CAD/CAM

Integrates full-function design and NC/CNC milling and turning simulation, control and processing.

System: MAC, II, PLUS, SE, XL
Minimum Memory: 512K
Requires: Hard disk.
Medium: 3 1/2-inch disk
ISPN: 49818-223   **Price: $7000.00**

LIONHEART PRESS
QUALITY CONTROL AND INDUSTRIAL EXPERIMENTS

Provides programs for the traditional production quality control analysis, covers Taguchi methods and topic of experiments.

System: MAC, II, PLUS, SE, XL
Minimum Memory: 512K
Medium: 3 1/2-inch disk
ISPN: 44900-775   **Price: $150.00**

335 INDUSTRIES/CONSTRUCTION/CONTRACTING

SOFTWARE CONSTRUCTORS, INC.
ACCOUNTING AND CONSTRUCTION (VER. 1.0)

Provides a complete accounting package centered on job cost.

System: II, SE
Minimum Memory: 1024K
Requires: ImageWriter or ImageWriter II.
Medium: 3 1/2-inch disk
ISPN: 72556-190   **Price: $2000.00**

HEIZER SOFTWARE
BEAM ANALYSIS

Performs an analysis of a specific load, and determines wood and steel beam sizes due to varying loading configurations.

System: MAC, II, PLUS, SE, XL
Minimum Memory: 512K
Requires: Microsoft Excel (ISPN 53150-270).
Medium: 3 1/2-inch disk
ISPN: 35175-938   **Price: $99.00**

HEIZER SOFTWARE
COMPLETE CONSTRUCTION COST ESTIMATOR

Estimates the cost of house and apartment construction using a square foot calculation.

System: MAC, II, PLUS, SE, XL
Minimum Memory: 512K
Requires: Microsoft Excel (ISPN 53150-270) or Microsoft Works (ISPN 53150-740).
Medium: 3 1/2-inch disk
ISPN: 35175-133   **Price: $79.00**

HEIZER SOFTWARE
CONCRETE ESTIMATOR

Calculates cubic yardage based on the desired dimensions of the concrete pour.

System: MAC, II, PLUS, SE, XL
Minimum Memory: 512K
Requires: Microsoft Excel (ISPN 53150-270) or Microsoft Works (ISPN 53150-740).
Medium: 3 1/2-inch disk
ISPN: 35175-135   **Price: $20.00**

SOFTOUCH SOFTWARE, INC.
CONSTRUCTIMATOR II

Develops complete cost estimates or actual jobs costs of commercial industrial or residential building construction projects.

System: MAC, II, PLUS, SE, XL
Minimum Memory: 1024K
Requires: Microsoft Excel (ISPN 53150-270).
Medium: 3 1/2-inch disk
ISPN: 72162-110   **Price: $195.00**

EXCEIVER CORP.
CONSTRUCTION CONTRACTOR MGMT W/ACCTG (VER. 2.0)

Includes estimating job costing and tracking, with full integrated accounting.

System: MAC, II, PLUS, SE, XL
Minimum Memory: 512K
Requires: 800K disk drive.
Medium: 3 1/2-inch disk
ISPN: 91574-250   **Price: $2230.00**

EXCEIVER CORP.
CONSTRUCTION CONTRACTOR MGMT WITHOUT ACCT

For general contractors including estimating job costing and tracking.

System: MAC, II, PLUS, SE, XL
Minimum Memory: 512K
Requires: 800K disk drive.
Medium: 3 1/2-inch disk
ISPN: 91574-260   **Price: $1050.00**

HEIZER SOFTWARE
CONSTRUCTION COST ESTIMATOR-RESIDENTIAL

Automatically calculates extensions and summaries based on the quantities and prices for the residence.

System: MAC, II, PLUS, SE, XL
Minimum Memory: 512K
Requires: Microsoft Excel (ISPN 53150-270) or Microsoft Works (ISPN 53150-740).
Medium: 3 1/2-inch disk
ISPN: 35175-134   **Price: $40.00**

MESA RESEARCH
CONSTRUCTION ESTIMATOR

Estimates costs, compares material and lumber costs, performs calculations, provides worksheets and recalculates all entries.

System: MAC, II, PLUS, SE, XL
Minimum Memory: 128K
Requires: Spreadsheet program.
Medium: 3 1/2-inch disk
ISPN: 49177-100   **Price: $69.95**

SOFTWARE CONSTRUCTORS, INC.

CONSTRUCTION MARKETING (VER. 1.0)

Includes marketing efforts for Construction or Architectural companies to produce reports keep track of clients and more.

System: MAC
Minimum Memory: 512K
Requires: Corvus Omninet local area network and hard disk system.
Medium: 3 1/2-inch disk
ISPN: 72556-200   **Price: $298.00**

SOFTOUCH SOFTWARE, INC.

CONSTRUCTION PROJECT MANAGEMENT SYSTEM II

Designed for a construction firm to produce accurate biddings, estimates, and will help with cost control and more.

System: MAC, II, PLUS, SE, XL
Minimum Memory: 512K
Requires: Excel (ISPN 53150-270).
Medium: 3 1/2-inch disk
ISPN: 72162-100   **Price: $95.00**

UNICOM SOFTWARE DEVELOPMENT GROUP

DBPERMIT (VER. 1.0)

Keeps track of all building, electrical, plumbing or mechanical permits, and computerizes the filing system.

System: MAC, PLUS, SE
Minimum Memory: 640K
Medium: 3 1/2-inch disk
ISPN: 83550-110   **Price: $995.00**

TURTLE CREEK SOFTWARE

HYPER-ESTIMATOR (VER. 1.1)

Calculates project dimensions and sets specifications for new residential constructions, additions, and remodeling.

System: MAC, II, PLUS, SE, XL
Minimum Memory: 1024K
Requires: HyperCard (ISPN 03900-300).
Medium: 3 1/2-inch disk
ISPN: 82925-300   **Price: $95.00**

TURTLE CREEK SOFTWARE

HYPER-REMODELER (VER. 1.1)

Used for remodeling projects, repairs. Projects best handled on a 'room by room' basis.

System: MAC, II, PLUS, SE, XL
Minimum Memory: 1024K
Requires: HyperCard (ISPN 03900-300).
Medium: 3 1/2-inch disk
ISPN: 82925-301   **Price: $95.00**

SOFTWARE CONSTRUCTORS, INC.

JOB COST 4 CONSTRUCTION

Created by a construction company for contractors to track job costs.

System: MAC, II, PLUS, SE, XL
Minimum Memory: 512K
Requires: 800k disk drive
Medium: 3 1/2-inch disk
ISPN: 72556-400   **Price: $595.00**

TURTLE CREEK SOFTWARE

MACNAIL (VER. 2.2)

Helps construction managers to prepare bids, schedule jobs, order materials, monitor costs, and organize punch lists.

System: MAC, II, PLUS, SE, XL
Minimum Memory: 1024K
Requires: Microsoft Excel (ISPN 53150-270).
Medium: 3 1/2-inch disk
ISPN: 82925-500   **Price: $295.00**

HEIZER SOFTWARE

STAIR CALCULATOR

Calculates stair tread and riser proportions of straight run and scissor stairs for variable floor-to-floor heights.

System: MAC, II, PLUS, SE, XL
Minimum Memory: 512K
Requires: Microsoft Excel (ISPN 53150-270) or Microsoft Works (ISPN 53150-740).
Medium: 3 1/2-inch disk
ISPN: 35175-136   **Price: $10.00**

SOFTWARE CONSTRUCTORS, INC.

TOOLBOX (VER. 1.0)

Assists construction managers in better controlling projects through bids, reports and more.

System: MAC
Minimum Memory: 512K
Medium: 3 1/2-inch disk
ISPN: 72556-575   **Price: $398.00**

---

339 INDUSTRIES/ ENERGY (OIL, GAS, ALTERNATIVE, ETC)

ROCKWARE, INC.

FIN-AL (VER 3.0)

Provides an oil and gas cashflow. Calculates on a monthly basis, and then summarizes the monthly information into annual figures.

System: MAC, II, PLUS, SE, XL
Minimum Memory: 512K
Requires: Multiplan or Excel, Imagewriter dot matrix printer or Laserwriter.
Medium: 3 1/2-inch disk
ISPN: 66643-203   **Price: $339.00**

LOGIC GROUP

FLUID CALC

Computes fluid properties for gas, oil, and water such as Z-factors and formation volume factors.

System: MAC, II, PLUS, SE, XL
Minimum Memory: 65K
Medium: 3 1/2-inch disk
ISPN: 45237-220   **Price: $125.00**

HEIZER SOFTWARE

FUEL ENERGY AND COST CONVERTER

Allows rapid dollars per million BTU comparisons of eight common fuels.

System: MAC, II, PLUS, SE, XL
Minimum Memory: 512K
Requires: Microsoft Excel (ISPN 53150-270) or Microsoft Works (ISPN 53150-740).
Medium: 3 1/2-inch disk
ISPN: 35175-320   **Price: $10.00**

LOGIC GROUP

MACDIGI

Provides an interface between a Macintosh and a digitizing tablet to facilitate well log data entry.

System: MAC, II, PLUS, SE, XL
Minimum Memory: 420K
Requires: Summa Graphics digitizing tablet or Kurta digitizing tablet.
Medium: 3 1/2-inch disk
ISPN: 45237-150   **Price: $700.00**

JIM YARMCHUK

OIL IN ONE

Provides a series of 21 templates, oil and gas tax, accounting, tracking and engineering that can be customized.

System: MAC, II, PLUS, SE, XL
Minimum Memory: 512K
Requires: Microsoft Multiplan (ISPN 53150-550) or Microsoft Excel (ISPN 53150-270).
Medium: 3 1/2-inch disk
ISPN: 87237-652   **Price: $135.00**

HOUSTON DIRECTIONAL SOFTWARE

OIL WELL BLOWOUT

Helps oil-well drilling firms plan their drilling activities.

System: MAC, II, PLUS, SE, XL
Minimum Memory: 128K
Medium: 3 1/2-inch disk
ISPN: 36318-100   **Price: $2000.00**

HOUSTON DIRECTIONAL SOFTWARE

PETROLEUM INDUSTRY DIRECTIONAL WELL PACKAGE

A Well drilling package.

System: MAC, II, PLUS, SE, XL
Minimum Memory: 128K
Medium: 3 1/2-inch disk
ISPN: 36318-250   **Price: $18000.00**

SOLARSOFT

SUNPAS/SUNOP (VER. 4.03)

Contains a menu driven program that calculates both heating and cooling loads in residential and light commercial buildings.

System: MAC, II, PLUS, SE, XL
Minimum Memory: 512K
Medium: 3 1/2-inch disk
ISPN: 74262-810   **Price: $189.00**

HOUSTON DIRECTIONAL SOFTWARE
SURVEY CALCULATION PROGRAM

Offers a plan that allows a user to survey for petroleum for well drilling.

System: MAC, II, PLUS, SE, XL
Minimum Memory: 128K
Medium: 3 1/2-inch disk
ISPN: 36318-200   **Price: $2500.00**

LOGIC GROUP
UNIT CONVERT

Performs unit conversions, displays conversion factors, and allows multiple conversions through equation mode.

System: MAC, II, PLUS, SE, XL
Minimum Memory: 64K
Medium: 3 1/2-inch disk
ISPN: 45237-860   **Price: $65.00**

345 INDUSTRIES/ ENGINEERING (CIVIL/ STRUCTURAL)

DYNACOMP, INC.
ANALYSIS OF PLANE TRUSSES- APT

Analyzes determinate and indeterminate plane truss structures.

System: MAC, II, PLUS, SE, XL
Minimum Memory: 512K
Requires: Microsoft QuickBasic (ISPN 53150-205).
Medium: 3 1/2-inch disk
ISPN: 27050-038   **Price: $54.95**

COMPUNEERING, INC.
BEAM MAC

Analyze any simple beam with any combination of loads. Shows load, shear, moment, deflection diagrams, text, etc.

System: MAC, II, PLUS, SE, XL
Minimum Memory: 512K
Medium: 3 1/2-inch disk
ISPN: 03746-150   **Price: $145.00**

COMPUNEERING, INC.
BEAM MAC II

Analyze any beam with any combination of loads by showing load, tension, shear, moment, deflection diagrams, text, etc.

System: MAC, II, PLUS, SE, XL
Minimum Memory: 512K
Medium: 3 1/2-inch disk
ISPN: 03746-250   **Price: $345.00**

DYNACOMP, INC.
BEAM-COLUMN ANALYSIS

Contains a user-interactive program for solving multiple-span beams and columns in the elastic range.

System: MAC, II, PLUS, SE, XL
Minimum Memory: 512K
Medium: 3 1/2-inch disk
ISPN: 27050-042   **Price: $74.95**

J.J. JORDAN ARCHITECT-ENGINEER
BEAMJOIS

Provides selections of wood beams or joists for simple or canilever members with various loadings.

System: MAC, II, PLUS, SE, XL
Minimum Memory: 512K
Requires: 80 column printer.
Medium: 3 1/2-inch disk
ISPN: 42025-100   **Price: $96.96**

J.J. JORDAN ARCHITECT-ENGINEER
BIGBEAMS

Computes simple and cantilever spans using GLU-LAM and/or steel beams with various loadings.

System: MAC, II, PLUS, SE, XL
Minimum Memory: 512K
Medium: 3 1/2-inch disk
ISPN: 42025-150   **Price: $96.96**

ECOM ASSOCIATES, INC.
CD-1 CONCRETE BEAM DESIGN

Designs reinforced concrete beams by either the ultimate strength or working stress method of ACI 318.

System: MAC, II, PLUS, SE, XL
Minimum Memory: 512K
Medium: 3 1/2-inch disk
ISPN: 27600-020   **Price: $525.00**

ECOM ASSOCIATES, INC.
CD-2 REINFCD CONCRETE COLUMN

Designs or checks the capacity of a reinforced concrete column in accordance with ACI 318 with bending in either direction.

System: MAC, II, PLUS, SE, XL
Minimum Memory: 512K
Medium: 3 1/2-inch disk
ISPN: 27600-040   **Price: $525.00**

ECOM ASSOCIATES, INC.
CD-3 FLAT SLAB ANALYSIS

Analyzes and designs flat slab or waffle slab floors in accordance with ACI 318.

System: MAC, II, PLUS, SE, XL
Minimum Memory: 512K
Medium: 3 1/2-inch disk
ISPN: 27600-060   **Price: $500.00**

SHEEHAN ASSOCIATES
DESIGNER SOFTWARE SERIES

A collection of design templates for wood frame building projects structural analysis and design.

System: MAC, II, PLUS, SE, XL
Minimum Memory: 512K
Requires: Microsoft Multiplan (ISPN 53150-550) or Microsoft Excel (ISPN 53150-270).
Medium: 3 1/2-inch disk
ISPN: 95724-075   **Price: $195.00**

J.J. JORDAN ARCHITECT-ENGINEER
DIAFRAMS (VER. 1.1)

Calculates wind loads, determines plywood class, thickness, grade and fastening for roof and floor diaphragms.

System: MAC, II, PLUS, SE, XL
Minimum Memory: 512K
Requires: 80-column printer.
Medium: 3 1/2-inch disk
ISPN: 42025-200   **Price: $96.96**

ECOM ASSOCIATES, INC.
FA-3 PLANE FRAME & TRUSS ANALYSIS

Determines critical moments, shears, axial loads, & the displacements at all joints for a plane frame of any configuration.

System: MAC
Minimum Memory: 256K
Medium: 3 1/2-inch disk
ISPN: 27600-080   **Price: $600.00**

KELIX SOFTWARE SYSTEMS
FLOW NETWORK ANALYSIS

Determines unknown nodal pressures and internodal flow rates for arbitrary N node pipe networks.

System: MAC, II, PLUS, SE, XL
Minimum Memory: 512K
Medium: 3 1/2-inch disk
ISPN: 42550-300   **Price: $395.00**

COMPUNEERING, INC.
FRAME MAC

Analyzes 2-D frame, truss and beam analysis. Any combination and number of nodes, restraints, hinges, loads. Diagrams, text.

System: MAC, II, PLUS, SE, XL
Minimum Memory: 512K
Medium: 3 1/2-inch disk
ISPN: 03746-325   **Price: $595.00**

DYNACOMP, INC.
LINEAR PROGRAMMER MINIMAX

Treats over- and under- constrained problems, has maximized objective function and solves simultaneous equations.

System: MAC, II, PLUS, SE, XL
Minimum Memory: 512K
Medium: 3 1/2-inch disk
ISPN: 27050-513   **Price: $54.95**

LIONSHEAD SOFTWARE, INC.
LSI PENTAGON CAD WITH COGO ADDITION (VER. 1.2)

Two dimensional CAD with COGO (professional coordinate geometry tools) capabilities.

System: MAC, II, PLUS, SE, XL
Minimum Memory: 512K
Requires: MacWorks Plus (ISPN 77034-500).
Medium: 3 1/2-inch disk
ISPN: 44912-410   **Price: $499.00**

COMPSERVCO

MACCAD-MECHANICAL DESIGN

Minicad Template Library includes HVAC fluid power, valve symbols, welding symbols, fastener and spring tool kits and more.

System: MAC, II, PLUS, SE, XL
Minimum Memory: 512K
Requires: Please specify version when ordering: PICT Version, MiniCad Version, MacDraft Version or MacDraw Version.
Medium: 3 1/2-inch disk
ISPN: 15025-532   **Price: $169.00**

DESIGN SOURCE SOFTWARE

MACFRAME2D (ENGLISH)

Plane frame analysis application based on stiffness matrix methods.

System: MAC, II, PLUS, SE, XL
Minimum Memory: 512K
Medium: 3 1/2-inch disk
ISPN: 24901-500   **Price: $150.00**

DESIGN SOURCE SOFTWARE

MACFRAME2D (METRIC)

Plane frame analysis application based on stiffness matrix methods.

System: MAC, II, PLUS, SE, XL
Minimum Memory: 512K
Medium: 3 1/2-inch disk
ISPN: 24901-550   **Price: $150.00**

COMPUNEERING, INC.

MACSHAPES (VER. 1.01)

List and sum structural and geometric properties of shapes. Draw and manipulate shapes in MacDraw-like fashion, and/or with keys.

System: MAC, II, PLUS, SE, XL
Minimum Memory: 512K
Requires: 800K disk drive.
Medium: 3 1/2-inch disk
ISPN: 03746-500   **Price: $145.00**

GRAPHIC MAGIC

MULTIFRAME (VER. 1.0)

A structural design and analysis system with an integrated database and calculation sheet.

System: MAC, II, PLUS, SE, XL
Minimum Memory: 512K
Requires: 800K disk drive.
Medium: 3 1/2-inch disk
ISPN: 33421-504   **Price: $895.00**

HEIZER SOFTWARE

POLYGON AREA CALCULATOR

Calculates the area of a polygon, regular or irregular, from the x and y coordinates of each corner.

System: MAC, II, PLUS, SE, XL
Minimum Memory: 512K
Requires: Microsoft Excel (ISPN 53150-270).
Medium: 3 1/2-inch disk
ISPN: 35175-316   **Price: $10.00**

J.J. JORDAN ARCHITECT-ENGINEER

RETWALLS (VER. 1.2)

Determines the construction requirements of a poured concrete or or concrete block retaining wall.

System: MAC, II, PLUS, SE, XL
Minimum Memory: 512K
Medium: 3 1/2-inch disk
ISPN: 42025-400   **Price: $96.96**

ECOM ASSOCIATES, INC.

SD-1 STEEL BEAM DESIGN

Designs or checks steel sections subjected to loads and end moments per the AISC code (LRFD or ASD).

System: MAC, II, PLUS, SE, XL
Minimum Memory: 640K
Medium: 3 1/2-inch disk
ISPN: 27600-120   **Price: $325.00**

ECOM ASSOCIATES, INC.

SD-2 STEEL COLUMN DESIGN

Designs or checks sections subjected to axial loads with or without bending moments applied about axes of the column.

System: MAC
Minimum Memory: 256K
Medium: 3 1/2-inch disk
ISPN: 27600-140   **Price: $375.00**

ECOM ASSOCIATES, INC.

SD-3 COMPOSITE STEEL BEAM DESIGN

Designs or checks simple span beams of composite steel and concrete construction.

System: MAC, II, PLUS, SE, XL
Minimum Memory: 512K
Medium: 3 1/2-inch disk
ISPN: 27600-260   **Price: $500.00**

J.J. JORDAN ARCHITECT-ENGINEER

SHERWALL (VER. 1.1)

Calculates building seismic loads and determines shear wall material, fastening and panel hold-downs.

System: MAC, II, PLUS, SE, XL
Minimum Memory: 512K
Medium: 3 1/2-inch disk
ISPN: 42025-500   **Price: $96.96**

MICROSOFT STRUCTURAL SYSTEMS

SKELETON

Plane frame/truss analysis. it pinned, rigid, or a mixture of joints.

System: MAC, II, PLUS, SE, XL
Minimum Memory: 512K
Medium: 3 1/2-inch disk
ISPN: 53250-400   **Price: $350.00**

MICROSOFT STRUCTURAL SYSTEMS

SKELETON (VER. 5.0)

Provides an analysis of of a two dimensional plan frame under any type of loading.

System: MAC, II, PLUS, SE, XL
Minimum Memory: 512K
Requires: Graphics printer.
Medium: 3 1/2-inch disk
ISPN: 53250-425   **Price: $1150.00**

MICROSOFT STRUCTURAL SYSTEMS

SKELETON II

Plane Frame Linear Analysis of any skeletal structure, any loading, comprehensive output.

System: MAC, II, PLUS, SE, XL
Minimum Memory: 512K
Medium: 3 1/2-inch disk
ISPN: 53250-450   **Price: $450.00**

HEIZER SOFTWARE

SLANTED TANK VOLUME

Calculates the volume of liquid in a slanted cylindrical tank for any depth of fill and angle of inclination.

System: MAC, II, PLUS, SE, XL
Minimum Memory: 512K
Requires: Microsoft Works (ISPN 53150-740).
Medium: 3 1/2-inch disk
ISPN: 35175-475   **Price: $40.00**

HEIZER SOFTWARE

STEAM FUNCTION MACRO SET

A set of five function macros which allow complex thermodynamic models to be set up, modeled and solved.

System: MAC, II, PLUS, SE, XL
Minimum Memory: 512K
Requires: Microsoft Excel (ISPN 53150-270).
Medium: 3 1/2-inch disk
ISPN: 35175-706   **Price: $35.00**

HEIZER SOFTWARE

STRUCTURAL STEEL

Includes 241 structural steel beams with over twenty design parameters for each.

System: MAC, II, PLUS, SE, XL
Minimum Memory: 512K
Requires: Microsoft Excel (ISPN 53150-270) or Microsoft Works (ISPN 53150-740).
Medium: 3 1/2-inch disk
ISPN: 35175-314   **Price: $9.00**

---

350 INDUSTRIES/ ENGINEERING (ELECTRICAL/ ELECTRONIC)

DYNACOMP, INC.

AC CIRCUIT ANALYSIS (ACNAP3)

A menu-driven package that calculates magnitude, phase, and delay at any node and supports up to 50 nodes with 200 components.

System: MAC, II, PLUS, SE, XL
Minimum Memory: 512K
Medium: 3 1/2-inch disk
ISPN: 27050-201　　　　　**Price: $119.95**

DYNACOMP, INC.

AC CIRCUIT ANALYSIS (ACNAP3)

A menu-driven package that calculates magnitude, phase, and delay at any node and supports up to 50 nodes with 200 components.

System: MAC, II, PLUS, SE, XL
Minimum Memory: 512K
Requires: PC Plot (ISPN 27050-164) or PDP (ISPN 27050-176).
Medium: 3 1/2-inch disk
ISPN: 27050-201　　　　　**Price: $189.95**

BV ENGINEERING

ACNAP AC NETWORK ANALYSIS PROGRAM (VER. 3.0)

Provides general purpose electronic circuit analysis program, worst case, Monte-Carlo, sensitivities, linear or logarithmic sweeps.

System: MAC, II, PLUS, SE, XL
Minimum Memory: 512K
Medium: 3 1/2-inch disk
ISPN: 09875-100　　　　　**Price: $349.95**

BV ENGINEERING

ACTFIL2-ACTIVE FILTER DESIGN/REALIZATION PROGRAM

Provides solutions for active lowpass, highpass, bandpass, and band-reject filters.

System: MAC, II, PLUS, SE, XL
Minimum Memory: 512K
Medium: 3 1/2-inch disk
ISPN: 09875-110　　　　　**Price: $124.95**

KASK LABS

BODEMLT

Performs a frequency domain analysis of the system transfer function to be analyzed.

System: MAC, II, PLUS, SE, XL
Minimum Memory: 128K
Medium: 3 1/2-inch disk
ISPN: 42400-100　　　　　**Price: $45.00**

MICROCODE ENGINEERING

CIRCUITMAKER (VER. 2.0)

Provides digital logic design, simulation, and schematic generation.

System: MAC, II, PLUS, SE, XL
Minimum Memory: 512K
Medium: 3 1/2-inch disk
ISPN: 51737-100　　　　　**Price: $100.00**

DYNACOMP, INC.

DC CIRCUIT ANALYSIS

Calculates responses for all node voltages, branch currents, element power dissipation, and node impedances.

System: MAC, II, PLUS, SE, XL
Minimum Memory: 512K
Medium: 3 1/2-inch disk
ISPN: 27050-202　　　　　**Price: $89.95**

DYNACOMP, INC.

DC CIRCUIT ANALYSIS

Calculates responses for all node voltages, branch currents, element power dissipation, and node impedances.

System: MAC, II, PLUS, SE, XL
Minimum Memory: 512K
Requires: PC Plot (ISPN 27050-164) or PDP (ISPN 27050-176).
Medium: 3 1/2-inch disk
ISPN: 27050-202　　　　　**Price: $149.95**

BV ENGINEERING

DC NETWORK ANALYSIS PROGRAM DCNAP2

Contains DC circuit analysis program which analyzes passive and active circuits consisting of resistors, voltage sources and more.

System: MAC, II, PLUS, SE, XL
Minimum Memory: 512K
Medium: 3 1/2-inch disk
ISPN: 09875-500　　　　　**Price: $199.95**

BRAINPOWER, INC.

DESIGNSCOPE

Provides an electronic system-design simulation to design and simulate component circuitry.

System: MAC, II, PLUS, SE, XL
Minimum Memory: 512K
Medium: 3 1/2-inch disk
ISPN: 08413-225　　　　　**Price: $249.95**

CAPILANO COMPUTING SYSTEMS LTD.

DESIGNWORKS (VER. 1.1)

Allows users to create, document and test electronic circuit design.

System: MAC, II, PLUS, SE, XL
Minimum Memory: 1024K
Requires: 800K disk.
Medium: 3 1/2-inch disk
ISPN: 11162-200　　　　　**Price: $685.00**

DOUGLAS ELECTRONICS

DOUGLAS CAD/CAM-BASIC (VER. 4.3)

Two dimensional CAD/CAM printed circuit board drawing program.

System: MAC, II, PLUS, SE, XL
Minimum Memory: 512K
Medium: 3 1/2-inch disk
ISPN: 26668-200　　　　　**Price: $95.00**

DOUGLAS ELECTRONICS

DOUGLAS CAD/CAM-PLOT VER-4.3

Two-dimensional CAD/CAM printed circuit board drawing program for use with plotters.

System: MAC, II, PLUS, SE, XL
Minimum Memory: 512K
Requires: Plotter.
Medium: 3 1/2-inch disk
ISPN: 26668-220　　　　　**Price: $525.00**

DOUGLAS ELECTRONICS

DOUGLAS CAD/CAM-PRINT (VER. 4.4)

Two dimensional CAD/CAM printed circuit board drawing program with printing capabilities.

System: MAC, II, PLUS, SE, XL
Minimum Memory: 512K
Requires: Apple ImageWriter or LaserWriter printer.
Medium: 3 1/2-inch disk
ISPN: 26668-210　　　　　**Price: $395.00**

DOUGLAS ELECTRONICS

DOUGLAS PROFESSIONAL SYSTEM LAYOUT (VER. 5.2)

Provides a parts placement facility for component positioning.

System: MAC, II, PLUS, SE, XL
Minimum Memory: 512K
Medium: 3 1/2-inch disk
ISPN: 26668-400　　　　　**Price: $1500.00**

DOUGLAS ELECTRONICS

DOUGLAS PROFESSIONAL SYSTEM-SCHEMATIC (VER. 1.2)

An interactive, digital logic drawing and simulation package.

System: MAC, II, PLUS, SE, XL
Minimum Memory: 1024K
Medium: 3 1/2-inch disk
ISPN: 26668-600　　　　　**Price: $700.00**

DOUGLAS ELECTRONICS

DRILL TAPE CREATOR (VER. 1.0)

Generates drill tapes from layout files created on the Douglas CAD/ CAM System.

System: MAC, II, PLUS, SE, XL
Minimum Memory: 512K
Requires: Douglas CAD/CAM Print (ISPN 26668-210), Plot (ISPN 26668-220), Layout (ISPN 26668-400), or Professional System (ISPN 26668-250).
Medium: 3 1/2-inch disk
ISPN: 26668-500　　　　　**Price: $150.00**

HEIZER SOFTWARE

ELECTRICAL PANEL SCHEDULE

Develops electrical panel schedules used in architectural and engineering drawings.

System: MAC, II, PLUS, SE, XL
Minimum Memory: 512K
Requires: Microsoft Excel (ISPN 53150-270).
Medium: 3 1/2-inch disk
ISPN: 35175-132　　　　　**Price: $25.00**

MEDINA SOFTWARE, INC.

ELECTRO BITS-ENGLISH

A graphics tool containing a library of several hundred electronic elements and computer symbols that employs the MacPaint function.

System: MAC, II, PLUS, SE, XL
Minimum Memory: 128K
Requires: MacPaint (ISPN 03900-413), MacBillboard (ISPN 11725-205), FullPaint (ISPN 90343-375) or Picturebase (ISPN 77437-550).
Medium: 3 1/2-inch disk
ISPN: 48842-300   **Price: $24.95**

PARAGON CONCEPTS, INC.

ELECTROFONTS

Special character font which allows you to type diagrams of analog circuits. A microspace allows you to position circuits.

System: MAC, II, PLUS, SE, XL
Minimum Memory: 512K
Medium: 3 1/2-inch disk
ISPN: 59740-300   **Price: $99.00**

DYNACOMP, INC.

FOURIER ANALYZER

Examines the frequency spectrum characteristics of defined duration signals, such as groups of pulses, etc.

System: MAC, II, PLUS, SE, XL
Minimum Memory: 512K
Medium: 3 1/2-inch disk
ISPN: 27050-330   **Price: $28.95**

DOUGLAS ELECTRONICS

GERBER FILE CREATOR (VER. 4.4)

Reads a Douglas CAD/CAM layout file and an aperture file to drive a Gerber(or Gerber compatible) photoplotter.

System: MAC, II, PLUS, SE, XL
Minimum Memory: 512K
Requires: Douglas CAD/CAM Print (ISPN 26668-210), Plot (ISPN 26668-220), Layout (ISPN 26668-400), or Professional System (ISPN 26668-250).
Medium: 3 1/2-inch disk
ISPN: 26668-550   **Price: $250.00**

HEIZER SOFTWARE

HORSEPOWER CALCULATOR

Converts horsepower to other units of power and calculates output horsepower from electric and hydraulic motors.

System: MAC, II, PLUS, SE, XL
Minimum Memory: 512K
Requires: Microsoft Excel (ISPN 53150-270) or Microsoft Works (ISPN 53150-740).
Medium: 3 1/2-inch disk
ISPN: 35175-311   **Price: $12.00**

NATIONAL INSTRUMENTS CORP.

LABVIEW (VER. 2.0)

A scientific software system for data acquisition and instrument control with an interactive graphical programming environment.

System: MAC, II, PLUS, SE, XL
Minimum Memory: 1024K
Requires: Hard disk.
Medium: 3 1/2-inch disk
ISPN: 56100-410   **Price: $1995.00**

BV ENGINEERING

LCFIL-PASSIVE FILTER DESIGN/ ANALYSIS PROGRAM

Expedites the design, synthesis and/or analysis of L-C filters.

System: MAC, II, PLUS, SE, XL
Minimum Memory: 512K
Medium: 3 1/2-inch disk
ISPN: 09875-340   **Price: $149.95**

CAPILANO COMPUTING SYSTEMS LTD.

LOGICWORKS

An integrated schematic diagram and digital logic simulation package used to create, document and test circuit designs.

System: MAC, II, PLUS, SE, XL
Minimum Memory: 512K
Requires: 800K disk.
Medium: 3 1/2-inch disk
ISPN: 11162-175   **Price: $200.00**

PARAGON CONCEPTS, INC.

LOGIFONT

Contains all standard symbols, logic gates, etc, to type logic circuits and includes capital alphabet for use in labelling.

System: MAC, II, PLUS, SE, XL
Minimum Memory: 512K
Medium: 3 1/2-inch disk
ISPN: 59740-445   **Price: $40.00**

KINKOS ACADEMIC COURSEWARE EXCHANGE

LOGIMAC (VER. 1.3)

Helps you create, test and document logic circuits.

System: MAC, II, PLUS, SE, XL
Minimum Memory: 128K
Medium: 3 1/2-inch disk
ISPN: 43025-365   **Price: $28.00**

KINKOS ACADEMIC COURSEWARE EXCHANGE

LOGIMAC (VER. 1.3)

Helps you create, test and document logic circuits.

System: MAC, II, PLUS, SE, XL
Minimum Memory: 128K
Requires: Site license.
Medium: 3 1/2-inch disk
ISPN: 43025-365   **Price: $5000.00**

CAPILANO COMPUTING SYSTEMS LTD.

LPLC (PROGRAMMABLE LOGIC DEVICE COMPILER)

Allows the user to generate and test code for Programmable Logic Devices such as PLA's or PROM's.

System: MAC, II, PLUS, SE, XL
Minimum Memory: 1024K
Requires: 800K disk.
Medium: 3 1/2-inch disk
ISPN: 11162-125   **Price: $535.00**

BV ENGINEERING

LSP-LOGIC SIMULATOR PROGRAM

Provides digital logic simulation.

System: MAC, II, PLUS, SE, XL
Minimum Memory: 512K
Medium: 3 1/2-inch disk
ISPN: 09875-320   **Price: $124.95**

KINKOS ACADEMIC COURSEWARE EXCHANGE

MACBODE (VER. S1.0) AND MACLOCUS (VER. S2.0)

An interactive environment to analyze linear control systems using Bode plot and Root Locus techniques.

System: MAC, II, PLUS, SE, XL
Minimum Memory: 128K
Medium: 3 1/2-inch disk
ISPN: 43025-383   **Price: $29.50**

COMPSERVCO

MACCAD-ELECTRICAL AND ELECTRONIC

Minicad Templates with virtually all ANSII electrical and electronic symbols in three sizes and includes logic symbols.

System: MAC, II, PLUS, SE, XL
Minimum Memory: 512K
Requires: Please specify version when ordering: PICT Version, MiniCad Version, MacDraw Version or MacDraft Version.
Medium: 3 1/2-inch disk
ISPN: 15025-152   **Price: $169.00**

SOURCEVIEW SOFTWARE INT'L.

MACROCIRCUITS

Electronic circuit design and emulation system with laser output.

System: MAC, II, PLUS, SE, XL
Minimum Memory: 512K
Medium: 3 1/2-inch disk
ISPN: 70675-330   **Price: $99.99**

CAPILANO COMPUTING SYSTEMS LTD.

MACSPICE

A full implementation of SPICE3 that simulates circuits consisting of resistors, capacitors, inductors, and mutual inductors.

System: MAC, II, PLUS, SE, XL
Minimum Memory: 1024K
Requires: 800K disk.
Medium: 3 1/2-inch disk
ISPN: 11162-250   **Price: $1500.00**

VAMP, INC.

MCCAD EDS I (VER. 1.1)

Integrated electronic design program with schematic capture, printed circuit board design, Routing and Gerber Translator.

System: II
Minimum Memory: 1024K
Requires: Color monitor, hard disk.
Medium: 3 1/2-inch disk
ISPN: 84771-495 **Price: $1495.00**

VAMP, INC.

MCCAD EDS II (VER. 1.1)

Includes schematic capture, digital simulation, printed circuit board layout, autorouting and gerber translator.

System: MAC, II, PLUS, SE, XL
Minimum Memory: 1024K
Requires: Two 800K disk drives or one 800K disk drive and a hard disk.
Medium: 3 1/2-inch disk
ISPN: 84771-496 **Price: $1895.00**

VAMP, INC.

MCCAD PCB I (VER. 3.2)

Tool for designing, creating, editing and revising printed circuit board drawings.

System: MAC, II, PLUS, SE, XL
Minimum Memory: 512K
Requires: 800K disk drive. ImageWriter, Apple LaserWriter, or Pen plotter.
Medium: 3 1/2-inch disk
ISPN: 84771-500 **Price: $395.00**

VAMP, INC.

MCCAD PCB ST (VER. 1.1)

Tool for designing, creating, editing and revising printed circuit board drawings with linkage to McCad Schematics.

System: MAC, II, PLUS, SE, XL
Minimum Memory: 1024K
Requires: 800K disk drive. ImageWriter, Apple LaserWriter, Pen Plotter, or Gerber type Photoplotter.
Medium: 3 1/2-inch disk
ISPN: 84771-510 **Price: $995.00**

VAMP, INC.

MCCAD SCHEMATICS (VER. 3.1)

Allows electronic designers to easily create and revise electronic digital or analog circuit designs directly on the Macintosh.

System: MAC, II, PLUS, SE, XL
Minimum Memory: 1024K
Requires: Two 800K disk drives, Imagewriter I or II, Apple LaserWriter, or Pen Plotter.
Medium: 3 1/2-inch disk
ISPN: 84771-475 **Price: $495.00**

VAMP, INC.

MCCAD SCHEMATICS-D.S. (VER. 1.1)

Allows electronic designers to simulate digital circuits, and create and revise electronic digital or analog circuits.

System: MAC, II, PLUS, SE, XL
Minimum Memory: 1024K
Requires: Two 800K disk drives or one 800K disk drive and a hard disk.
Medium: 3 1/2-inch disk
ISPN: 84771-480 **Price: $895.00**

SPECTRUM SOFTWARE

MICRO-CAP II (VER. 4.0)

Provides analog schematic drawing and simulation with electronic circuit analysis.

System: MAC
Minimum Memory: 512K
Requires: Two disk drives, printer.
Medium: 3 1/2-inch disk
ISPN: 75200-610 **Price: $895.00**

DYNACOMP, INC.

MICROCOMPUTER CIRCUIT ANALYSIS PROGRAM (VER. 2.0)

Contains a professional design tool created to enhance the productivity of electronics design.

System: MAC, II, PLUS, SE, XL
Minimum Memory: 512K
Requires: Two disk drives.
Medium: 3 1/2-inch disk
ISPN: 27050-514 **Price: $895.00**

KASK LABS

NETAZ

A linear network analysis program that handles passive and active network elements, and accomodates transmission-line analysis.

System: MAC, II, PLUS, SE, XL
Minimum Memory: 128K
Medium: 3 1/2-inch disk
ISPN: 42400-480 **Price: $25.00**

KASK LABS

NETMATCHS I

Optimizes L-C and Micro-Stripline (Wheeler) ladder matching type networks over a user specified range of frequencies.

System: MAC, II, PLUS, SE, XL
Minimum Memory: 128K
Medium: 3 1/2-inch disk
ISPN: 42400-500 **Price: $40.00**

DYNACOMP, INC.

PASSIVE FILTER DESIGN AND ANALYSIS-LCFIL

Allows user to design and analyze complex multi-stage low, high, and band-pass filters with up to 21 poles.

System: MAC, II, PLUS, SE, XL
Minimum Memory: 512K
Medium: 3 1/2-inch disk
ISPN: 27050-222 **Price: $89.95**

DYNACOMP, INC.

PASSIVE FILTER DESIGN AND ANALYSIS-LCFIL

Allows user to design and analyze complex multi-stage low, high, and band-pass filters with up to 21 poles.

System: MAC, II, PLUS, SE, XL
Minimum Memory: 512K
Requires: PC Plot (ISPN 27050-164) or PDP (ISPN 27050-176), and SSP (ISPN 27050-630).
Medium: 3 1/2-inch disk
ISPN: 27050-222 **Price: $249.95**

KINKOS ACADEMIC COURSEWARE EXCHANGE

SIGNAL OPERATIONS (VER. 1.21)

An interactive exploratory tool to visualize and experiment with theoretical and applied concepts in discrete signals and systems.

System: MAC, II, PLUS, SE, XL
Minimum Memory: 128K
Requires: Finder (Ver. 4.1 or later).
Medium: 3 1/2-inch disk
ISPN: 43025-780 **Price: $25.00**

KASK LABS

SPDES

Provides an interactive program used for the design of small signal RF transistor amplifier circuits.

System: MAC, II, PLUS, SE, XL
Minimum Memory: 128K
Medium: 3 1/2-inch disk
ISPN: 42400-300 **Price: $35.00**

BV ENGINEERING

SPP2

Contains a general purpose signal processing program which analyzes linear/non-linear systems, La Place and FFT.

System: MAC, II, PLUS, SE, XL
Minimum Memory: 512K
Medium: 3 1/2-inch disk
ISPN: 09875-400 **Price: $149.95**

KINKOS ACADEMIC COURSEWARE EXCHANGE

TLS: TRANSMISSION LINE SIMULATOR (VER. 2.3)

Simulates both transient and steady-state behavior of transmission lines, and provides dynamic displays of voltage and current waves.

System: MAC, II, PLUS, SE, XL
Minimum Memory: 128K
Medium: 3 1/2-inch disk
ISPN: 43025-900 **Price: $20.00**

KINKOS ACADEMIC COURSEWARE EXCHANGE

TLS: TRANSMISSION LINE SIMULATOR (VER. 2.3)

Simulates both transient and steady-state behavior of transmission lines, and provides dynamic displays of voltage and current waves.

System: MAC, II, PLUS, SE, XL
Minimum Memory: 128K
Requires: Site license.
Medium: 3 1/2-inch disk
ISPN: 43025-900 **Price: $490.00**

KINKOS ACADEMIC COURSEWARE EXCHANGE

TRANSFORMS, WINDOWS, MODULATION... (VER. 1.01)

An interactive exploratory tool to visualize and experiment with theoretical and applied concepts in discrete signals and systems.

System: MAC, II, PLUS, SE, XL
Minimum Memory: 512K
Requires: Finder (Ver. 4.1 or later).
Medium: 3 1/2-inch disk
ISPN: 43025-920   **Price: $40.00**

KINKOS ACADEMIC COURSEWARE EXCHANGE

VLSI MAGICIAN (VER. 1.1A)

Allows you to do trial circuit layouts on the Macintosh. Completed designs can be downloaded to a VAX 11/780 host computer.

System: MAC, II, PLUS, SE, XL
Minimum Memory: 128K
Requires: Finder (Ver. 4.1 or 5.3).
Medium: 3 1/2-inch disk
ISPN: 43025-950   **Price: $18.50**

355 INDUSTRIES/ ENGINEERING (MECHANICAL)

HEIZER SOFTWARE
BOLT CIRCLES

Calculates the rectangular coordinates and the angular positions of equally spaced holes on a bolt circle.

System: MAC, II, PLUS, SE, XL
Minimum Memory: 512K
Requires: Microsoft Excel (ISPN 53150-270) or Microsoft Works (ISPN 53150-740).
Medium: 3 1/2-inch disk
ISPN: 35175-321   **Price: $14.00**

J.J. JORDAN ARCHITECT-ENGINEER
HEATCOOL (VER. 1.2)

Provides an involved, yet flexible program to determine the BTUH and CFM requirements for heating and cooling of any building.

System: MAC, II, PLUS, SE, XL
Minimum Memory: 512K
Requires: 80-column printer.
Medium: 3 1/2-inch disk
ISPN: 42025-300   **Price: $96.96**

TECHWARE, INC. (KS)
HVAC LOAD FORECASTING

Provides an accurate method of calculating air conditioning loads with limited input enabling the user to print out or save to disk.

System: MAC, II, PLUS, SE, XL
Minimum Memory: 512K
Medium: 3 1/2-inch disk
ISPN: 04778-500   **Price: $495.00**

COMPSERVCO

MACCAD-DOUBLE LINE ORTHOGRAPHIC PIPING

Minicad Template libraries of pipe fittings, and valve symbols in 1/4 inch to 24 inch and in 3 orthogonal views.

System: MAC, II, PLUS, SE, XL
Minimum Memory: 512K
Requires: Please specify version when ordering: PICT Version, MiniCad Version, MacDraw Version or MacDraft Version.
Medium: 3 1/2-inch disk
ISPN: 15025-912   **Price: $249.00**

COMPSERVCO

MACCAD-SINGLE LINE ISOMETRIC PIPING

Isometric sheets with ovals and valves, pipe and fittings (flanged, screwed, etc.) drawn in isometric and more.

System: MAC, II, PLUS, SE, XL
Minimum Memory: 512K
Requires: Please specify version when ordering: PICT Version, MacDraw Version or MacDraft Version.
Medium: 3 1/2-inch disk
ISPN: 15025-760   **Price: $249.00**

COMPSERVCO

MACCAD-SINGLE LINE ORTHOGRAPHIC PIPING

Minicad Template libraries of pipe fittings and valve symbols from 1/4 inch to 24 inch with 3 orthogonal views.

System: MAC, II, PLUS, SE, XL
Minimum Memory: 512K
Requires: Please specify version when ordering: PICT Version, MiniCad Version, MacDraft Version or MacDraw Version.
Medium: 3 1/2-inch disk
ISPN: 15025-836   **Price: $249.00**

KINKOS ACADEMIC COURSEWARE EXCHANGE

PIPE FLOW (VER. 2.6)

Helps solve a practical problem in fluid mechanics: incompressible flow through pipes and ducts.

System: MAC, II, PLUS, SE, XL
Minimum Memory: 512K
Medium: 3 1/2-inch disk
ISPN: 43025-580   **Price: $17.00**

HEIZER SOFTWARE

PSYCHOMETRY

Utilizes altitude, wet and dry bulb, dew point and relative humidity to calculate enthalpy, humidity ratios and volume.

System: MAC, II, PLUS, SE, XL
Minimum Memory: 512K
Requires: Microsoft Excel (ISPN 53150-270).
Medium: 3 1/2-inch disk
ISPN: 35175-328   **Price: $15.00**

ARGOSY SERVICES

SCM (VER. 2.0)

Energy budget calculation program for nonresidential buildings. Certified by California Energy Commission for Compliance Calc.

System: MAC, II, PLUS, SE, XL
Minimum Memory: 512K
Requires: Two 400K drives or single 800K drive and ImageWriter printer or compatible.
Medium: 3 1/2-inch disk
ISPN: 05181-400   **Price: $105.00**

INTERNATIONAL GEOMETRIC TOLERANCING INSTITUTE

SOFTGAGE

Use in lieu of selected Positional Functional Gages with an X, Y Coordinate Measuring Machine.

System: MAC, II, PLUS, SE, XL
Minimum Memory: 512K
Requires: Microsoft Excel (ISPN 53150-270).
Medium: 3 1/2-inch disk
ISPN: 67746-600   **Price: $99.95**

DYNACOMP, INC.

STATIC THERMAL ANALYSIS (STAP)

A general-purpose, two-dimensional steady-state heat-transfer program that analyzes heat sinks in the electronic packaging field.

System: MAC, II, PLUS, SE, XL
Minimum Memory: 512K
Medium: 3 1/2-inch disk
ISPN: 27050-227   **Price: $89.95**

ARGOSY SERVICES

SUN/SHADE I (VER. 1.02)

Solar utility to compute sun position shading and transmitted radiation through glazing.

System: MAC, II, PLUS, SE, XL
Minimum Memory: 512K
Requires: ImageWriter compatible printer.
Medium: 3 1/2-inch disk
ISPN: 05181-650   **Price: $85.00**

INTERNATIONAL GEOMETRIC TOLERANCING INSTITUTE

TOLCULATOR (VER. 3.0)

Provides automated geometric tolerance and mechanical design analysis per ANSI and ISO standards for design and inspection.

System: MAC, II, PLUS, SE, XL
Minimum Memory: 512K
Requires: Microsoft Excel (ISPN 55150-270).
Medium: 3 1/2-inch disk
ISPN: 67746-630   **Price: $175.00**

INTERNATIONAL GEOMETRIC
TOLERANCING INSTITUTE
TOLCULATOR-W/ APPLIED GEOMETRIC TOLERANCING MANUAL

Geometric tolerancing per ANSI standards and automatic sampling, positional tolerance, gage formulas and tolerance circuits.

System: MAC, II, PLUS, SE, XL
Minimum Memory: 512K
Requires: Microsoft Excel (ISPN 55150-270).
Medium: 3 1/2-inch disk
ISPN: 67746-631   **Price: $225.00**

360 INDUSTRIES/ ENGINEERING (MISCELLANEOUS)

HEIZER SOFTWARE
3-D PIPE CLEARANCE

Computes the clearance or interface between two non-parallel straight pipes or lines.

System: MAC, II, PLUS, SE, XL
Minimum Memory: 512K
Requires: Microsoft Excel (ISPN 53150-270) or Microsoft Works (ISPN 53150-740).
Medium: 3 1/2-inch disk
ISPN: 35175-312   **Price: $14.00**

DYNACOMP, INC.
ACTFIL ACTIVE FILTER DESIGN/ REALIZATION

Provides detailed design parameters and transfer function coefficients given the desired characteristics.

System: MAC, II, PLUS, SE, XL
Minimum Memory: 512K
Medium: 3 1/2-inch disk
ISPN: 27050-058   **Price: $69.95**

INTERCEPT SOFTWARE
COMPACT HEAT EXCHANGER DESIGN (VER. 2.1)

Allows engineers to design heat based on the book 'Compact Heat Exchangers' by Kays and London.

System: MAC, II, PLUS, SE, XL
Minimum Memory: 512K
Medium: 3 1/2-inch disk
ISPN: 39562-100   **Price: $395.00**

DYNACOMP, INC.
DIGITAL FILTER

Provides a comprehensive data processing program which permits the user to design his own filter function or choose from a menu.

System: MAC, II, PLUS, SE, XL
Minimum Memory: 512K
Medium: 3 1/2-inch disk
ISPN: 27050-241   **Price: $58.95**

DM SYSTEMS
DRAFT MATH 512

Produces two-dimensional drawings by allowing an engineer or designer to draw with freehand or digital entry.

System: MAC, II, PLUS, SE, XL
Minimum Memory: 512K
Requires: Microsoft QuickBasic (ISPN 53150-205).
Medium: 3 1/2-inch disk
ISPN: 26512-250   **Price: $60.00**

EPCON
ENGINEER'S AIDE (VER. 1.2)

Provides an engineering package of nine programs designed to meet the principle needs of chemical/process engineers.

System: MAC, II, PLUS, SE
Minimum Memory: 512K
Medium: 3 1/2-inch disk
ISPN: 29256-100   **Price: $695.00**

SOF-WARE TOOLS
ENGINEERING TOOL KIT-ETK (VER. 4.01)

Provides database, statistics and graphs, scientific calculator. Includes curve fitting capabilities.

System: MAC, II, PLUS, SE, XL
Minimum Memory: 512K
Requires: Two disk drives, ImageWriter or LaserWriter.
Medium: 3 1/2-inch disk
ISPN: 71803-300   **Price: $199.00**

SOF-WARE TOOLS
ENGINEERING TOOLKIT SUPPLEMENT (VER. 4.01)

Allows for eight scatter plots on the same graph and six polynomial plots on the same graph.

System: MAC
Minimum Memory: 512K
Requires: Engineering Tool Kit (ISPN 71803-300), 800K disk drive.
Medium: 3 1/2-inch disk
ISPN: 71803-325   **Price: $79.00**

IMAGINE THAT, INC.
EXTEND (VER. 1.1)

Modeling and simulation program which supports continuous and discrete behavioral simulations.

System: MAC, II, PLUS, SE, XL
Minimum Memory: 1024K
Requires: Two 800K disk drives or a hard disk.
Medium: 3 1/2-inch disk
ISPN: 37194-200   **Price: $495.00**

KINKOS ACADEMIC COURSEWARE
EXCHANGE
FEMG: A FINITE ELEMENT MESH GENERATOR (VER. 1.15)

An interactive finite element mesh generator and editor for generating two-dimensional finite element meshes.

System: MAC, II, PLUS, SE, XL
Minimum Memory: 512K
Medium: 3 1/2-inch disk
ISPN: 43025-163   **Price: $20.00**

KINKOS ACADEMIC COURSEWARE
EXCHANGE
FEMG: A FINITE ELEMENT MESH GENERATOR (VER. 1.15)

An interactive finite element mesh generator and editor for generating two-dimensional finite element meshes.

System: MAC, II, PLUS, SE, XL
Minimum Memory: 512K
Medium: 3 1/2-inch disk
ISPN: 43025-163   **Price: $300.00**

LINDO SYSTEMS
GINO (GENERAL INTERACTIVE OPTIMIZER)

Solves general nonlinear equation and inequality systems.

System: MAC, II, PLUS, SE, XL
Minimum Memory: 1024K
Medium: 3 1/2-inch disk
ISPN: 44737-050   **Price: $195.00**

HEIZER SOFTWARE
HARMONIC ANALYSIS

Determines an empiricle equation for periodic experimental data.

System: MAC, II, PLUS, SE, XL
Minimum Memory: 512K
Requires: Microsoft Excel (ISPN 53150-270).
Medium: 3 1/2-inch disk
ISPN: 35175-322   **Price: $18.00**

HEIZER SOFTWARE
HORIZONTAL CYLINDRICAL TANK LIQUID VOLUME

Calculates liquid volume versus depth for horizontal or cylindrical tanks with flat ends.

System: MAC, II, PLUS, SE, XL
Minimum Memory: 512K
Requires: Microsoft Excel (ISPN 53150-270) or Microsoft Works (ISPN 53150-740).
Medium: 3 1/2-inch disk
ISPN: 35175-326   **Price: $12.00**

SOF-WARE TOOLS
LAB PARTNER (VER. 1.0)

Offers a systematic approach to experimental design and analysis based on the techniques and philosophy of Dr. Genichi Taguchi.

System: MAC, II, PLUS, SE, XL
Minimum Memory: 1024K
Requires: 800K disk drive.
Medium: 3 1/2-inch disk
ISPN: 71803-400   **Price: $500.00**

LINDO SYSTEMS
LINGO (VER. 1.04)

An interactive modeling system for linear and integer programming problems.

System: MAC, II, PLUS, SE, XL
Minimum Memory: 1024K
Medium: 3 1/2-inch disk
ISPN: 44737-150   **Price: $495.00**

MFE ASSOCIATES

MACEARTHWORKS

Calculates cut fill volume using the average-and-area method. Features mouse spaced editing. Used by Engineers and Architects.

System: MAC, II, PLUS, SE, XL
Minimum Memory: 512K
Medium: 3 1/2-inch disk
ISPN: 49331-500   **Price: $295.00**

HEIZER SOFTWARE

MOMENT OF INERTIA

Determines the moments of inertia of any cross-section having an outline definable by a series of ordered coordinate points.

System: MAC, II, PLUS, SE, XL
Minimum Memory: 512K
Requires: Microsoft Excel (ISPN 53150-270).
Medium: 3 1/2-inch disk
ISPN: 35175-324   **Price: $30.00**

HEIZER SOFTWARE

PERFORMANCE CURVE FIT TUTORIAL

Provides step-by-step procedures for creating tabular performance results.

System: MAC, II, PLUS, SE, XL
Minimum Memory: 512K
Requires: Microsoft Excel (ISPN 53150-270).
Medium: 3 1/2-inch disk
ISPN: 35175-250   **Price: $20.00**

KINKOS ACADEMIC COURSEWARE EXCHANGE

PIPELINE DESIGN KIT (VER. 1.0)

Uses a paradigm of graphic objects that can be manipulated with the Macintosh mouse.

System: MAC, II, PLUS, SE, XL
Minimum Memory: 512K
Requires: Finder (Ver. 5.5).
Medium: 3 1/2-inch disk
ISPN: 43025-585   **Price: $21.50**

HEIZER SOFTWARE

PROCESS MODELS

Includes three increasingly complex models of industrial processes.

System: MAC, II, PLUS, SE, XL
Minimum Memory: 512K
Requires: Microsoft Excel (ISPN 53150-270).
Medium: 3 1/2-inch disk
ISPN: 35175-313   **Price: $15.00**

HEIZER SOFTWARE

RELIABILITY ANALYSIS

Predicts failure frequency trends based on fitting limited reliability data to the Weibull distribution.

System: MAC, II, PLUS, SE, XL
Minimum Memory: 512K
Requires: Microsoft Excel (ISPN 53150-270).
Medium: 3 1/2-inch disk
ISPN: 35175-251   **Price: $25.00**

ABVENT

SIMUL

Graphically simulates any object or concept that moves, and provides animation up to 3000 frames per second.

System: MAC, II, PLUS, SE, XL
Minimum Memory: 512K
Requires: 800K disk drive.
Medium: 3 1/2-inch disk
ISPN: 00437-505   **Price: $495.00**

HEIZER SOFTWARE

SLANTED TANK LIQUID VOLUME

Calculates the volume of liquid in a slanted cylindrical tank for any depth of fill and angle of inclination.

System: MAC, II, PLUS, SE, XL
Minimum Memory: 512K
Requires: Microsoft Excel (ISPN 53150-270) or Microsoft Works (ISPN 53150-740).
Medium: 3 1/2-inch disk
ISPN: 35175-325   **Price: $40.00**

HEIZER SOFTWARE

SOLAR POSITION

Tabulates and charts the hourly sun positions for any day at any North American time zone location in worksheet and chart format.

System: MAC, II, PLUS, SE, XL
Minimum Memory: 512K
Requires: Microsoft Excel (ISPN 53150-270).
Medium: 3 1/2-inch disk
ISPN: 35175-137   **Price: $24.00**

HEIZER SOFTWARE

SPHERICAL TANK LIQUID VOLUME

Calculates liquid volume versus depth and liquid and tank surface areas for spherical tanks.

System: MAC, II, PLUS, SE, XL
Minimum Memory: 512K
Requires: Microsoft Excel (ISPN 53150-270) or Microsoft Works (ISPN 53150-740).
Medium: 3 1/2-inch disk
ISPN: 35175-327   **Price: $15.00**

HEIZER SOFTWARE

THICKNESS REDUCTION

Determines the economical material thickness reduction on a product re-design.

System: MAC, II, PLUS, SE, XL
Minimum Memory: 512K
Requires: Microsoft Excel (ISPN 53150-270).
Medium: 3 1/2-inch disk
ISPN: 35175-323   **Price: $14.00**

PUMA SOFTWARE, INC.

TIMDOM/MAC

A computer-aided design program that performs control engineering mathematical functions.

System: MAC, II, PLUS, SE, XL
Minimum Memory: 512K
Medium: 3 1/2-inch disk
ISPN: 63768-300   **Price: $295.00**

---

365 INDUSTRIES/ INVENTORY INDUSTRIES

HEIZER SOFTWARE

INVENTORY MODELING

Models manufacturing inventory, using ABC ordering rules for maximum inventory turns and minimal risks of shortages and delays.

System: MAC, II, PLUS, SE, XL
Minimum Memory: 512K
Requires: Microsoft Excel (ISPN 53150-270).
Medium: 3 1/2-inch disk
ISPN: 35175-550   **Price: $45.00**

HEIZER SOFTWARE

INVENTORY/SUPPLIES MANAGER

A method for small businesses and offices to acquire supplies or inventory under conditions set by the user.

System: MAC, II, PLUS, SE, XL
Minimum Memory: 512K
Requires: Microsoft Excel (ISPN 53150-270).
Medium: 3 1/2-inch disk
ISPN: 35175-551   **Price: $20.00**

---

367 INDUSTRIES/ LUMBER

BENNETT & PETERS, INC.

TIMBER INVENTORY (VER. 3.0)

Complete system for entering, editing, calculating and printing results of the timber inventories in South East United States.

System: MAC, II, PLUS, SE, XL
Minimum Memory: 1024K
Requires: 132-character printer.
Medium: 3 1/2-inch disk
ISPN: 07420-700   **Price: $495.00**

---

369 INDUSTRIES/ MANUFACTURING

DECISION SCIENCE SOFTWARE
LOT

An interactive model that determines the optimal lot size using several different rules to meet the schedule of demand.

System: MAC, II, PLUS, SE, XL
Minimum Memory: 512K
Medium: 3 1/2-inch disk
ISPN: 24325-400 **Price: $85.00**

HEIZER SOFTWARE
MANUFACTURING FINANCIAL MODEL

Includes financial and resource scheduling, and inventory balancing in mass production manufacturing operations.

System: MAC, II, PLUS, SE, XL
Minimum Memory: 512K
Requires: Microsoft Excel (ISPN 53150-270).
Medium: 3 1/2-inch disk
ISPN: 35175-554 **Price: $45.00**

DECISION SCIENCE SOFTWARE
MRP

An interactive program to demonstrate all features of industrial production control by the inventory file management system.

System: MAC, II, PLUS, SE, XL
Minimum Memory: 512K
Medium: 3 1/2-inch disk
ISPN: 24325-600 **Price: $125.00**

380 INDUSTRIES/ MISCELLANEOUS INDUSTRIES

GRAPHIC MAGIC
MACRATE

An IOR rating calculation program that allows the user to generate a rating certificate that made be viewed and then edited on screen.

System: MAC, II, PLUS, SE, XL
Minimum Memory: 512K
Medium: 3 1/2-inch disk
ISPN: 33421-300 **Price: $450.00**

385 INDUSTRIES/ SURVEYING

HEIZER SOFTWARE
DEGREE CONVERT

Converts decimal degrees to properly formatted degrees, minutes and seconds or vice versa in a single cell.

System: MAC, II, PLUS, SE, XL
Minimum Memory: 512K
Requires: Microsoft Excel (ISPN 53150-270).
Medium: 3 1/2-inch disk
ISPN: 35175-315 **Price: $5.00**

COMPUNEERING, INC.
LANDESIGN (VER. 1.1)

Provides professional coordinate geometry tools for land, road, and subdivision layout, and land surveying.

System: MAC, II, PLUS, SE, XL
Minimum Memory: 512K
Requires: 800K disk drive.
Medium: 3 1/2-inch disk
ISPN: 03746-300 **Price: $595.00**

LIONSHEAD SOFTWARE, INC.
LSI SURVEYOR

Allows the user to operate on points and figures, and calculate various quantities of interest in surveying and engineering.

System: MAC, II, PLUS, SE, XL
Minimum Memory: 512K
Requires: MacWorks Plus (ISPN 77034-500).
Medium: 3 1/2-inch disk
ISPN: 44912-409 **Price: $1999.00**

389 INDUSTRIES/ TRANSPORTATION

H & D LEASING, INC.
FUEL TAX SPECIALIST VER-1.0

An over-the-road trucking program which tracks fuel and mileage on each truck for each trip made.

System: MAC, II, PLUS, SE, XL
Minimum Memory: 1024K
Requires: 20 MB hard disk.
Medium: 3 1/2-inch disk
ISPN: 33851-300 **Price: $2900.00**

H & D LEASING, INC.
KEEP ON TRUCKING (VER. 3.0)

Provides a dispatch program with billing entry, driver trip information, settlement and payroll, and truck owner options.

System: MAC, II, PLUS, SE, XL
Minimum Memory: 1024K
Requires: 20 MB hard disk.
Medium: 3 1/2-inch disk
ISPN: 33851-400 **Price: $2990.00**

AD ASTRA
MACFLEET

A private vehicle control system which tracks and distributes operations and maintenance cost information. Multi-user compatible.

System: MAC, II, PLUS, SE, XL
Minimum Memory: 512K
Medium: 3 1/2-inch disk
ISPN: 00848-400 **Price: $2950.00**

EXCEIVER CORP.
TRANSPORTATION BROKERAGE MANAGEMENT (VER. 1.0)

A management system for trucking brokers. A package including full accounting is also available.

System: MAC, II, PLUS, SE, XL
Minimum Memory: 512K
Requires: Two disk drives or a hard disk.
Medium: 3 1/2-inch disk
ISPN: 91574-650 **Price: $480.00**

EXCEIVER CORP.
TRANSPORTATION BROKERAGE MANAGEMENT AND ACCOUNTING

A management system for trucking brokers with full accounting package.

System: MAC, II, PLUS, SE, XL
Minimum Memory: 512K
Requires: Two disk drives or a hard disk.
Medium: 3 1/2-inch disk
ISPN: 91574-651 **Price: $1660.00**

407 PERSONAL/ ASTROLOGY AND DIVINATION

TIME CYCLES RESEARCH
ADVANCED GRAPHIC ASTROLOGY (VER. 8.3)

Utilizing Macintosh interface and resolution: calculates displays and prints natal and derivative charts.

System: MAC, PLUS, SE, XL
Minimum Memory: 512K
Medium: 3 1/2-inch disk
ISPN: 81875-100 **Price: $129.50**

ASTROLABE, INC.
ASTRO-SCOPE

Understand horoscopes and interpret planet positions.

System: MAC, II, PLUS, SE, XL
Minimum Memory: 512K
Requires: Two disk drives.
Medium: 3 1/2-inch disk
ISPN: 02000-100 **Price: $39.95**

ASTROLABE, INC.
ASTRO-SCOPE REPORT

Prints a horoscope wheel and aspect list, then prints ten pages or more of natal interpretation by Steve Blake.

System: MAC, II, PLUS, SE, XL
Minimum Memory: 512K
Requires: 80-column printer, two disk drives.
Medium: 3 1/2-inch disk
ISPN: 02000-300 **Price: $195.00**

HEIZER SOFTWARE
BIORHYTHM CALCULATOR
Calculates and charts biorhythms.
System: MAC, II, PLUS, SE, XL
Minimum Memory: 512K
Requires: Microsoft Excel (ISPN 53150-270) or Microsoft Works (ISPN 53150-740).
Medium: 3 1/2-inch disk
ISPN: 35175-263   **Price: $5.00**

ASTROLABE, INC.
CCRS HOROSCOPE PROGRAM 88
A multi-function horoscope calculation program emphasizing research and experimental techniques and high-precision ephemeris.
System: MAC, II, PLUS, SE, XL
Minimum Memory: 1024K
Requires: Two disk drives, printer.
Medium: 3 1/2-inch disk
ISPN: 02000-230   **Price: $225.00**

TIME CYCLES RESEARCH
CHART INTERPRETER (VER. 1.2)
Calculates and displays chart and a 15 to 17 page natal interpretation.
System: MAC, II, PLUS, SE, XL
Minimum Memory: 1024K
Requires: Two disk drives or a hard disk.
Medium: 3 1/2-inch disk
ISPN: 81875-150   **Price: $199.00**

ASTROLABE, INC.
COMPOSITE ASTRO REPORT
Generates astrological compatibility reports. Mainly treats romance but also includes friendships and other relationships.
System: MAC, II, PLUS, SE, XL
Minimum Memory: 512K
Requires: Two disk drives, printer.
Medium: 3 1/2-inch disk
ISPN: 02000-220   **Price: $295.00**

ASTROLABE, INC.
CONTACT ASTRO REPORT
Computes the horoscopes of two people, then prints a detailed 25-page analysis of their relationship potential.
System: MAC, II, PLUS, SE, XL
Minimum Memory: 512K
Requires: 80-column printer, two disk drives.
Medium: 3 1/2-inch disk
ISPN: 02000-250   **Price: $295.00**

ASTROLABE, INC.
DAILY ASTRO REPORT-ELECTIONAL TEXT
Suggests appropriate activities for the current aspects, helping people find the best times for important actions.
System: MAC, PLUS, SE, XL
Minimum Memory: 512K
Requires: Two disk drives, 80-column printer.
Medium: 3 1/2-inch disk
ISPN: 02000-282   **Price: $295.00**

ASTROLABE, INC.
DAILY ASTRO REPORT-KEYWORD TEXT
Shows how symbolism of transiting aspects can work out at many levels.
System: MAC, II, PLUS, SE, XL
Minimum Memory: 512K
Requires: Two disk drives, 80-column printer.
Medium: 3 1/2-inch disk
ISPN: 02000-281   **Price: $295.00**

ASTROLABE, INC.
DAILY ASTRO REPORT-RELATIONSHIP TEXT
Forecasts how one will react to people at different times, can serve as a guide to improving relationships.
System: MAC, II, PLUS, SE, XL
Minimum Memory: 512K
Requires: Two disk drives, 80-column printer.
Medium: 3 1/2-inch disk
ISPN: 02000-283   **Price: $295.00**

ASTROLABE, INC.
DAILY ASTRO REPORT-STANDARD TEXT
Prints out forecast reports on the relation of present planetary positions to positions in the birth chart.
System: MAC, II, PLUS, SE, XL
Minimum Memory: 512K
Requires: Two disk drives, 80-column printer.
Medium: 3 1/2-inch disk
ISPN: 02000-280   **Price: $295.00**

TIME CYCLES RESEARCH
GAMMA BASIC (VER. 1.0)
Produces Natal chart, data page and an interpretation page utility.
System: MAC, II, PLUS, SE, XL
Minimum Memory: 512K
Requires: 800K disk drive.
Medium: 3 1/2-inch disk
ISPN: 81875-070   **Price: $59.50**

TIME CYCLES RESEARCH
GAMMA EDITION (VER. 2.21)
Includes transit search for any year, report files, nine house systems, tropical, and Heliocentric and Sidereal Zodiacs.
System: MAC, II, PLUS, SE, XL
Minimum Memory: 512K
Requires: 800K disk drive.
Medium: 3 1/2-inch disk
ISPN: 81875-060   **Price: $199.50**

TIME CYCLES RESEARCH
GRAPHIC ASTROLOGY (VER. 2.3)
Calculates, displays and prints a natal chart as well as data and interpretation pages utilizing Macintosh Interface and resolution.
System: MAC, PLUS, SE, XL
Minimum Memory: 512K
Medium: 3 1/2-inch disk
ISPN: 81875-050   **Price: $39.50**

MAGNUM SOFTWARE
GYPSY
The Computer Oracle provides several on-screen 'Answer Boards' where the mystic Pointer reveals its messages.
System: MAC, II, PLUS, XL
Minimum Memory: 512K
Medium: 3 1/2-inch disk
ISPN: 46032-040   **Price: $59.95**

ASTROLABE, INC.
MONTHLY ASTRO-REPORT
Produces monthly, bi-monthly or weekly astrological forecasts based on natal horoscope and lunar return.
System: MAC, II, PLUS, SE, XL
Minimum Memory: 512K
Requires: 80-column printer, two disk drives.
Medium: 3 1/2-inch disk
ISPN: 02000-350   **Price: $295.00**

TIME CYCLES RESEARCH
NATAL INTERPRETER (VER. 1.0)
Produces chart and a 12-18 page Natal Interpretation. Interpreting covers sign positions, house positions and planetary aspects.
System: MAC, II, PLUS, SE, XL
Minimum Memory: 1024K
Medium: 3 1/2-inch disk
ISPN: 81875-500   **Price: $199.00**

ASTROLABE, INC.
PERSONAL NUMEROLOGY
An on-screen outline of long-term trends using numbers.
System: MAC, II, PLUS, SE, XL
Minimum Memory: 512K
Requires: Two disk drives.
Medium: 3 1/2-inch disk
ISPN: 02000-670   **Price: $39.95**

ASTROLABE, INC.
PERSONAL NUMEROLOGY REPORT
Provides calculations and interpretations and prints a seven page numerology report based on name and birthdate.
System: MAC, II, PLUS, SE, XL
Minimum Memory: 512K
Requires: 80-column printer, two disk drives.
Medium: 3 1/2-inch disk
ISPN: 02000-400   **Price: $195.00**

ASTROLABE, INC.
SEX-O-SCOPE
Interpret lovemaking styles and tastes.
System: MAC, II, PLUS, SE, XL
Minimum Memory: 512K
Requires: Two disk drives.
Medium: 3 1/2-inch disk
ISPN: 02000-550   **Price: $39.95**

ASTROLABE, INC.

SEX-O-SCOPE REPORT

Prints a natal horoscope wheel, then a witty interpretation by John Townley of lovemaking styles and preferences.

System: MAC, II, PLUS, SE, XL
Minimum Memory: 512K
Requires: 80-column printing, two disk drives.
Medium: 3 1/2-inch disk
ISPN: 02000-310　　　**Price: $195.00**

HEIZER SOFTWARE

TAROT PACK

A HyperCard stack which contains the complete Tarot deck.

System: MAC, II, PLUS, SE, XL
Minimum Memory: 512K
Requires: HyperCard (ISPN 03900-300).
Medium: 3 1/2-inch disk
ISPN: 35175-993　　　**Price: $25.00**

414 PERSONAL/CAREER DEVELOPMENT

REALITY TECHNOLOGIES

BUSINESS WEEK'S BUSINESS ADVANTAGE

Develops users' business skills through interactive case studies based on cover stories from Business Week magazine.

System: MAC, II, PLUS, SE, XL
Minimum Memory: 512K
Requires: 800K disk drive.
Medium: 3 1/2-inch disk
ISPN: 65487-200　　　**Price: $69.95**

MICROMASH

CPA REVIEW

Contains over 2000 multiple-choice questions and over 50 essay problems from recent CPA exams. Hard copy reference manual included

System: MAC, II, PLUS, SE, XL
Minimum Memory: 800K
Requires: Two disk drives.
Medium: 3 1/2-inch disk
ISPN: 52590-025　　　**Price: $650.00**

MICROMASH

CPE SERIES (VER. 687)

Twenty-two Continuing Professional Education courses, each eight hours in length and covering distinct topics.

System: MAC, II, PLUS, SE, XL
Minimum Memory: 800K
Medium: 3 1/2-inch disk
ISPN: 52590-275　　　**Price: $99.95**

KINKOS ACADEMIC COURSEWARE EXCHANGE

PERSONAL RESUME WRITER

Helps you create a near 'type set quality resume' which can be customized to your personal specifications.

System: MAC, II, PLUS, SE, XL
Minimum Memory: 512K
Requires: Finder (Ver. 3.2 or later).
Medium: 3 1/2-inch disk
ISPN: 43025-573　　　**Price: $30.00**

HEIZER SOFTWARE

PROFESSIONAL RECRUITER

A HyperCard stack for tracking job applicants. Lists the the applicant's references, experience and personnel information.

System: MAC, II, PLUS, SE, XL
Minimum Memory: 1024K
Requires: HyperCard (ISPN 03900-300).
Medium: 3 1/2-inch disk
ISPN: 35175-051　　　**Price: $20.00**

BOOTWARE SOFTWARE CO., INC.

PROFESSIONAL RESUMEWRITER (VER. 1.0)

A professional software application for the creation of customized personal resumes with a minimum of time, effort and cost.

System: MAC, II, PLUS, SE, XL
Minimum Memory: 512K
Medium: 3 1/2-inch disk
ISPN: 08220-675　　　**Price: $100.00**

BOOTWARE SOFTWARE CO., INC.

STUDENT RESUMEWRITER (VER. 1.0)

Professional software application for creating four different types of resume formats, with several types of fonts to choose from.

System: MAC, II, PLUS, SE, XL
Minimum Memory: 512K
Medium: 3 1/2-inch disk
ISPN: 08220-700　　　**Price: $30.00**

419 PERSONAL/ COOKING AND DIET

DISK-COUNT SOFTWARE, INC.

8-WEEK CHOLESTEROL CURE

A database of foods for tracking the consumption of fats, calories, and cholesterol. Includes the book, 'The 8-Week Cholesterol Cure.'

System: MAC, II, PLUS, SE, XL
Minimum Memory: 512K
Requires: Two 400K disk drives, or one 400K disk drive and a hard drive.
Medium: 3 1/2-inch disk
ISPN: 26189-222　　　**Price: $39.95**

CONCEPT DEVELOPMENT ASSOCIATES, INC.

AMERICA COOKS AMERICAN

Cook like America's premier chefs of American cuisine.

System: MAC, II, PLUS, SE, XL
Minimum Memory: 512K
Medium: 3 1/2-inch disk
ISPN: 18875-010　　　**Price: $14.95**

CONCEPT DEVELOPMENT ASSOCIATES, INC.

AMERICA COOKS CHINESE

Cook like America's premier chefs of Chinese cuisine.

System: MAC, II, PLUS, SE, XL
Minimum Memory: 512K
Medium: 3 1/2-inch disk
ISPN: 18875-015　　　**Price: $14.95**

CONCEPT DEVELOPMENT ASSOCIATES, INC.

AMERICA COOKS FRENCH

Cook like America's premier chefs of French cuisine.

System: MAC, II, PLUS, SE, XL
Minimum Memory: 512K
Medium: 3 1/2-inch disk
ISPN: 18875-020　　　**Price: $14.95**

CONCEPT DEVELOPMENT ASSOCIATES, INC.

AMERICA COOKS ITALIAN

Cook like America's premier chefs of Italian cuisine.

System: MAC, II, PLUS, SE, XL
Minimum Memory: 512K
Medium: 3 1/2-inch disk
ISPN: 18875-025　　　**Price: $14.95**

CONCEPT DEVELOPMENT ASSOCIATES, INC.

AMERICA COOKS MEXICAN

Cook like America's premier chefs of Mexican cuisine.

System: MAC, II, PLUS, SE, XL
Minimum Memory: 512K
Medium: 3 1/2-inch disk
ISPN: 18875-030　　　**Price: $14.95**

CONCEPT DEVELOPMENT ASSOCIATES, INC.

AWARD WINNING WINES

A wine book on disk for use with 'Wine Companion.'

System: MAC, II, PLUS, SE, XL
Minimum Memory: 512K
Medium: 3 1/2-inch disk
ISPN: 18875-040　　　**Price: $14.95**

CONCEPT DEVELOPMENT ASSOCIATES, INC.
BORDEAUX
Part of the World of Wines LADV Collectors Series.
System: MAC, II, PLUS, SE, XL
Minimum Memory: 512K
Medium: 3 1/2-inch disk
ISPN: 18875-080 **Price: $14.95**

CONCEPT DEVELOPMENT ASSOCIATES, INC.
CALVERT'S CEDAR STREET
Sauce and exotic recipes from Rita Calvert.
System: MAC, II, PLUS, XL
Minimum Memory: 512K
Medium: 3 1/2-inch disk
ISPN: 18875-200 **Price: $14.95**

CONCEPT DEVELOPMENT ASSOCIATES, INC.
CHACHIE DUPUY'S NEW ORLEANS HOME COOKING
Home style recipes for Creole dishes.
System: MAC, II, PLUS, SE, XL
Minimum Memory: 512K
Medium: 3 1/2-inch disk
ISPN: 18875-240 **Price: $14.95**

CONCEPT DEVELOPMENT ASSOCIATES, INC.
CHAMPAGNE
Part of the World of Wines LADV Collectors Series.
System: MAC, II, PLUS, SE, XL
Minimum Memory: 512K
Medium: 3 1/2-inch disk
ISPN: 18875-280 **Price: $14.95**

CONCEPT DEVELOPMENT ASSOCIATES, INC.
CHARDONNAY
Part of the World of Wines LADV Collectors Series.
System: MAC, II, PLUS, SE, XL
Minimum Memory: 512K
Medium: 3 1/2-inch disk
ISPN: 18875-160 **Price: $14.95**

CONCEPT DEVELOPMENT ASSOCIATES, INC.
CLASSIC COMPANIONS
Choose the proper wine for your meals.
System: MAC, II, PLUS, SE, XL
Minimum Memory: 512K
Medium: 3 1/2-inch disk
ISPN: 18875-320 **Price: $14.95**

CONCEPT DEVELOPMENT ASSOCIATES, INC.
CONTEMPORARY CUISINE
A collection of recipes from Katherine Lacy.
System: MAC, II, PLUS, SE, XL
Minimum Memory: 512K
Medium: 3 1/2-inch disk
ISPN: 18875-400 **Price: $14.95**

CONCEPT DEVELOPMENT ASSOCIATES, INC.
COOKING WITH KIDS
Introduce your child to cooking.
System: MAC, II, PLUS, SE, XL
Minimum Memory: 512K
Medium: 3 1/2-inch disk
ISPN: 18875-440 **Price: $14.95**

ALSOFT, INC.
DIETICIAN
Allows user to design meal plans, examining more than 700 foods and evaluating with criteria from vitamins to carbohydrates.
System: MAC, II, PLUS, XL
Minimum Memory:
Medium: 3 1/2-inch disk
ISPN: 02506-200 **Price: $94.95**

CONCEPT DEVELOPMENT ASSOCIATES, INC.
DINING IN-MANHATTAN
Recipes from New York restaurants.
System: MAC, II, PLUS, SE, XL
Minimum Memory: 512K
Medium: 3 1/2-inch disk
ISPN: 18875-480 **Price: $14.95**

CONCEPT DEVELOPMENT ASSOCIATES, INC.
DINING IN-SAN FRANCISCO
Recipes from San Francisco restaurants.
System: MAC, II, PLUS, SE, XL
Minimum Memory: 512K
Medium: 3 1/2-inch disk
ISPN: 18875-520 **Price: $14.95**

RUBICON PUBLISHING
DINNER AT EIGHT
A comprehensive helper for fine dining.
System: MAC, II, PLUS, SE, XL
Minimum Memory: 128K
Medium: 3 1/2-inch disk
ISPN: 95463-300 **Price: $49.95**

RUBICON PUBLISHING
ENCORE EDITION (VER. 1.03)
Recipes of gourmet cuisine.
System: MAC, II, PLUS, SE, XL
Minimum Memory: 128K
Requires: Dinner at Eight (ISPN 95463-300).
Medium: 3 1/2-inch disk
ISPN: 95463-350 **Price: $15.95**

ESHA RESEARCH
FOOD PROCESSOR II
Nutrition analysis of daily intakes, diet plans, menus and recipes. Includes 2400 foods, 30 nutrients and text graphics.
System: MAC, II, PLUS, SE, XL
Minimum Memory: 512K
Medium: 3 1/2-inch disk
ISPN: 29781-250 **Price: $295.00**

CONCEPT DEVELOPMENT ASSOCIATES, INC.
GREAT CHEFS OF PBS (VOL. 1.1) (VER. 2.11)
Recipes from PBS's 'Great Tastes of the Southwest.'
System: MAC, II, PLUS, XL
Minimum Memory: 512K
Medium: 3 1/2-inch disk
ISPN: 18875-582 **Price: $24.95**

CONCEPT DEVELOPMENT ASSOCIATES, INC.
GREAT CHEFS OF PBS (VOL. 1.2) (VER. 2.11)
Enjoy 'Great Tastes of the Southwest' recipes, plus numerous cooking tips, chef biographies and more.
System: MAC, II, PLUS, SE, XL
Minimum Memory: 512K
Medium: 3 1/2-inch disk
ISPN: 18875-584 **Price: $24.95**

CONCEPT DEVELOPMENT ASSOCIATES, INC.
GREAT CHEFS OF PBS (VOL. 1.3) (VER. 2.11)
Enjoy 'Great Tastes of the Southwest' recipes, plus numerous cooking tips, chef biographies and more.
System: MAC, II, PLUS, SE, XL
Minimum Memory: 512K
Medium: 3 1/2-inch disk
ISPN: 18875-586 **Price: $24.95**

CONCEPT DEVELOPMENT ASSOCIATES, INC.
GREAT CHEFS OF PBS MASTER-PAK (VOL. 1-3)(VER. 2.1)
Enjoy three volumes of 'Great Tastes of the Southwest' recipes, numerous cooking tips and more.
System: MAC, II, PLUS, SE, XL
Minimum Memory: 512K
Medium: 3 1/2-inch disk
ISPN: 18875-590 **Price: $24.95**

CONCEPT DEVELOPMENT ASSOCIATES, INC.
GREAT VINTAGE YEARS
Take suggestions from leading experts on 100 wines from great vintage years.
System: MAC, II, PLUS, SE, XL
Minimum Memory: 512K
Medium: 3 1/2-inch disk
ISPN: 18875-600 **Price: $14.95**

HEIZER SOFTWARE
HEALTHY HOME COOKSTACK
Contains 70 tried-and-true recipes for those who want a low-fat, low-cholesterol diet.
System: MAC, II, PLUS, SE, XL
Minimum Memory: 1024K
Requires: HyperCard (ISPN 03900-300).
Medium: 3 1/2-inch disk
ISPN: 35175-076 **Price: $30.00**

BRIGHT IDEAS, INC.

HYPER CHEF (VER. 1.07)

Provides a cookbook in a HyperCard stack with 250 New England recipes.

System: MAC, II, PLUS, SE, XL
Minimum Memory: 1024K
Requires: HyperCard (ISPN 03900-300).
Medium: 3 1/2-inch disk
ISPN: 08456-400 **Price: $49.95**

HEIZER SOFTWARE

HYPERDIET

Allows up to four users to record and maintain their food intake and activity output. Keeps track of calorie and nutrient intakes.

System: MAC, II, PLUS, SE, XL
Minimum Memory: 1024K
Requires: HyperCard (ISPN 03900-300).
Medium: 3 1/2-inch disk
ISPN: 35175-078 **Price: $25.00**

MICROMEDX

MACNUTRIPLAN

Analyzes meals and daily intake for nutritional values in 21 nutrients including calories, protein, fats, carbohydrates, etc.

System: MAC, II, PLUS, SE, XL
Minimum Memory: 512K
Medium: 3 1/2-inch disk
ISPN: 52737-200 **Price: $75.00**

CONCEPT DEVELOPMENT ASSOCIATES, INC.

MICRO KITCHEN COMPANION

Select recipes by preparation time, ingredients on hand and even the pan or utensils required.

System: MAC, II, PLUS, SE, XL
Minimum Memory: 512K
Medium: 3 1/2-inch disk
ISPN: 18875-640 **Price: $39.95**

CONCEPT DEVELOPMENT ASSOCIATES, INC.

MICRO WINE COMPANION

Choose the right wine from thousands of brands and labels – every occasion and price range.

System: MAC, II, PLUS, SE, XL
Minimum Memory: 512K
Medium: 3 1/2-inch disk
ISPN: 18875-920 **Price: $49.95**

CONCEPT DEVELOPMENT ASSOCIATES, INC.

MR. BOSTON ABRIDGED

Prepare drinks like a 'seasoned' bartender with this collection of more than 200 American favorites.

System: MAC, II, PLUS, SE, XL
Minimum Memory: 512K
Medium: 3 1/2-inch disk
ISPN: 18875-660 **Price: $14.95**

CAMDE CORP.

NUTRI-CALC MACINTOSH (VER. 2.4)

Analyzes meals and diets for nutritional content. Includes 900+ foods, RDA analysis, extensive graphics. Full Mac user interface.

System: MAC, II, PLUS, SE, XL
Minimum Memory: 128K
Medium: 3 1/2-inch disk
ISPN: 10875-600 **Price: $65.00**

N-SQUARED COMPUTING

NUTRITIONIST II (VER. 4.5)

Provides an interactive program with which one can analyze single foods, food combinations, meals or specialty diets.

System: MAC, II, PLUS, SE, XL
Minimum Memory: 512K
Medium: 3 1/2-inch disk
ISPN: 55907-110 **Price: $295.00**

N-SQUARED COMPUTING

NUTRITIONIST III (VER. 3.0) (COMPILED VERSION)

A comprehensive and flexible nutrition and exercise analysis program and includes all the features of Nutritionist I and II.

System: MAC, II, PLUS, XL
Minimum Memory: 1024K
Requires: 800K disk drive.
Medium: 3 1/2-inch disk
ISPN: 55907-120 **Price: $495.00**

CONCEPT DEVELOPMENT ASSOCIATES, INC.

OFFICIAL MR. BOSTON MICRO BARTENDER'S GUIDE DELUXE

Access a database of more than 1,000 mixed drink recipes, plus a listing of wine and beer selections.

System: MAC, II, PLUS, SE, XL
Minimum Memory: 512K
Medium: 3 1/2-inch disk
ISPN: 18875-680 **Price: $19.95**

CONCEPT DEVELOPMENT ASSOCIATES, INC.

SOUTHERN COOKING

Enjoy authentic Southern recipes from Maryland to Texas.

System: MAC, II, PLUS, SE, XL
Minimum Memory: 512K
Medium: 3 1/2-inch disk
ISPN: 18875-800 **Price: $14.95**

CONCEPT DEVELOPMENT ASSOCIATES, INC.

SPICE HUNTER

Learn to identify and use a wide range of spices.

System: MAC, II, PLUS, XL
Minimum Memory: 512K
Medium: 3 1/2-inch disk
ISPN: 18875-840 **Price: $14.95**

HEIZER SOFTWARE

VITAMIN AND MINERAL DATABASE

A list of vitamins and minerals which covers common, letter names, B family, Lipotropic factor, RDA and natural sources.

System: MAC, II, PLUS, SE, XL
Minimum Memory: 512K
Requires: Microsoft Excel (ISPN 53150-270), Microsoft Works (ISPN 53150-740) or HyperCard (ISPN 03900-300).
Medium: 3 1/2-inch disk
ISPN: 35175-620 **Price: $5.00**

RUBICON PUBLISHING

WEEKNIGHT GOURMET (VER. 1.03)

A collection of recipes for quick gourmet meals.

System: MAC, II, PLUS, SE, XL
Minimum Memory: 128K
Requires: Dinner at Eight (ISPN 95463-300).
Medium: 3 1/2-inch disk
ISPN: 95463-800 **Price: $15.95**

CONCEPT DEVELOPMENT ASSOCIATES, INC.

WINES OF AUSTRALIA

Read expert Les Amis du Vin reviews and taste notes on more than 100 Australian wines.

System: MAC, II, PLUS, SE, XL
Minimum Memory: 512K
Medium: 3 1/2-inch disk
ISPN: 18875-960 **Price: $14.95**

CONCEPT DEVELOPMENT ASSOCIATES, INC.

WINES OF GERMANY

Part of the World of Wines LADV Collectors series.

System: MAC, II, PLUS, SE, XL
Minimum Memory: 512K
Medium: 3 1/2-inch disk
ISPN: 18875-560 **Price: $14.95**

---

424 PERSONAL/ ELECTRONIC PUBLICATIONS

HIGHLIGHTED DATA, INC.

CONGRESS STACK

An electronic directory of the 100th Congress that includes data on congressmen, districts, committees and pictures.

System: MAC, II, PLUS, XL
Minimum Memory: 1024K
Requires: HyperCard (ISPN 03900-300), 20MB hard disk.
Medium: 3 1/2-inch disk
ISPN: 35775-100 **Price: $159.95**

OWL INTERNATIONAL, INC.

GUIDE (VER. 2.0)

A hypertext system for personal computers. Creates electronic documents with hidden levels of detail and hooks them together.

System: MAC, II, PLUS, SE, XL
Minimum Memory: 512K
Medium: 3 1/2-inch disk
ISPN: 58987-300   **Price: $199.95**

OWL INTERNATIONAL, INC.

GUIDE ENVELOPE

Creates personalized hypertext applications.

System: MAC, II, PLUS, SE, XL
Minimum Memory: 512K
Medium: 3 1/2-inch disk
ISPN: 58987-301   **Price: $199.95**

APDA

INSIDE MACINTOSH X-REF ON DISK (VER. 1.0)

Contains the entire text of the book 'Inside Macintosh X-Ref', which is stored as Macintosh Programmer's Workshop text files.

System: MAC, II, PLUS, SE, XL
Minimum Memory: 512K
Requires: Any Macintosh text editor.
Medium: 3 1/2-inch disk
ISPN: 03749-311   **Price: $10.00**

HEIZER SOFTWARE

MAC MAGAZINE PRODUCT INDEX 84/85/86

A database of software and hardware articles in MacWorld and MacUser for 1984, 1985 and 1986.

System: MAC, II, PLUS, SE, XL
Minimum Memory: 1024K
Requires: Microsoft Excel (ISPN 53150-270), Microsoft Works (ISPN 53150-740) or HyperCard (ISPN 03900-300).
Medium: 3 1/2-inch disk
ISPN: 35175-416   **Price: $7.00**

MACPOINT PUBLICATIONS

MACINDEX (VER. 2.0)

Definitive index to all published Macintosh information, with extensive, precision-updated lists of publishers, products and more.

System: MAC, II, PLUS, SE, XL
Minimum Memory: 128K
Medium: 3 1/2-inch disk
ISPN: 45902-250   **Price: $75.00**

MEDINA SOFTWARE, INC.

MACMUNDO (INSIDE U.S./ ANNUAL SUBSCRIPTION)

A quarterly disk-based magazine designed for the Spanish speaking Macintosh users in the world. Program is for annual subscription.

System: MAC, II, PLUS, SE, XL
Minimum Memory: 128K
Requires: MacWrite (ISPN 12784-530). Microsoft Word (ISPN 53150-732) or compatible. MacPaint (ISPN 12784-510) or compatible.
Medium: 3 1/2-inch disk
ISPN: 48842-526   **Price: $36.00**

MEDINA SOFTWARE, INC.

MACMUNDO (INSIDE U.S./PER DISK)

A quarterly disk-based magazine designed for the Spanish speaking Macintosh users in the world. Program sold by disk quarterly.

System: MAC, II, PLUS, SE, XL
Minimum Memory: 128K
Requires: MacWrite (ISPN 12784-530) Microsoft Word (ISPN 53150-732), or compatible. MacPaint (ISPN 12784-510) or compatible.
Medium: 3 1/2-inch disk
ISPN: 48842-525   **Price: $10.00**

MEDINA SOFTWARE, INC.

MACMUNDO (OUTSIDE U.S./ ANNUAL SUBSCRIPTION)

A quarterly disk-based magazine designed for the Spanish speaking Macintosh users in the world. Program for annual subscription.

System: MAC, II, PLUS, XL
Minimum Memory: 128K
Requires: MacWrite (ISPN 12784-530), Microsoft Word (ISPN 53150-732) or compatible. MacPaint (ISPN 12784-510) or compatible.
Medium: 3 1/2-inch disk
ISPN: 48842-528   **Price: $44.00**

MEDINA SOFTWARE, INC.

MACMUNDO (OUTSIDE U.S./PER DISK)

A quarterly disk-based magazine designed for the Spanish speaking Macintosh users in the world. Program sold by disk quarterly.

System: MAC, II, PLUS, SE, XL
Minimum Memory: 128K
Requires: MacWrite (ISPN 12784-530), Microsoft Word (ISPN 53150-732) or compatible. MacPaint (ISPN 12784-510) or compatible.
Medium: 3 1/2-inch disk
ISPN: 48842-527   **Price: $13.00**

MAC AMERICA (CA)

SOFT SPOT MAGAZINE

Publication on disk listing editorial comments, stand alone software in several areas, such as visual effects, and more.

System: MAC
Minimum Memory: 128K
Medium: 3 1/2-inch disk
ISPN: 71848-600   **Price: $24.95**

HEIZER SOFTWARE

STACK EXCHANGE SAMPLE DISK

Heizer's disk-based version of the Stack Exchange Catalog which contains sample cards from many stacks.

System: MAC, II, PLUS, XL
Minimum Memory: 1024K
Requires: HyperCard (ISPN 03900-300).
Medium: 3 1/2-inch disk
ISPN: 35175-081   **Price: $3.00**

HEIZER SOFTWARE

TYPEFACES OF DESKTOP PUBLISHING

Includes information on all PostScript typefaces available as of November 1987.

System: MAC, II, PLUS, SE, XL
Minimum Memory: 1024K
Requires: HyperCard (ISPN 03900-300).
Medium: 3 1/2-inch disk
ISPN: 35175-435   **Price: $25.00**

VIKING TECHNOLOGIES

UPTIME MAC ISSUES

Magazine disk that features new programs each month for a year.

System: MAC, II, PLUS, SE, XL
Minimum Memory: 128K
Medium: 3 1/2-inch disk
ISPN: 85231-850   **Price: $19.95**

428 PERSONAL/ FINANCIAL/LEGAL

HEIZER SOFTWARE

ASSET MANAGEMENT AND FINANCIAL INDEPENDENCE

Coordinates assets into a personal balance sheet, calculates weighted average rate of return and analyzes a portfolio.

System: MAC, II, PLUS, SE, XL
Minimum Memory: 512K
Requires: Microsoft Excel (ISPN 53150-270) or Microsoft Works (ISPN 53150-740).
Medium: 3 1/2-inch disk
ISPN: 35175-631   **Price: $34.00**

HEIZER SOFTWARE

AUTO FINANCE ANALYZER

Analyzes the true purchase cost and actual interest charged as compared to the cash price.

System: MAC, II, PLUS, SE, XL
Minimum Memory: 512K
Requires: Microsoft Excel (ISPN 53150-270) or Microsoft Works (ISPN 53150-740).
Medium: 3 1/2-inch disk
ISPN: 35175-624   **Price: $9.00**

HEIZER SOFTWARE

BALANCE IT!

A personal budgeting and checkbook balancing tool that tracks spending and produces reports by budget categories.

System: MAC, II, PLUS, SE, XL
Minimum Memory: 1024K
Requires: HyperCard (ISPN 03900-300).
Medium: 3 1/2-inch disk
ISPN: 35175-422   **Price: $15.00**

HEIZER SOFTWARE

CHECK BOOK

Applies full database and command macro features to a checking account to allow a wide range of transaction analyses.

System: MAC, II, PLUS, SE, XL
Minimum Memory: 512K
Requires: Microsoft Excel (ISPN 53150-270) or Microsoft Works (ISPN 53150-740).
Medium: 3 1/2-inch disk
ISPN: 35175-605   **Price: $15.00**

ORION COMPUTER TRAINING SYSTEMS

CHECKWRITER (VER. 4.0)

Includes multiple checking accounts, auto pay, prints checks, auto deposit, bank statement reconciliation, auto balance and more.

System: MAC, II, PLUS, SE, XL
Minimum Memory: 512K
Requires: Two disk drives.
Medium: 3 1/2-inch disk
ISPN: 58862-333   **Price: $69.95**

HEIZER SOFTWARE

CREDIT CARD ANALYZER

Analyzes the current status of credit cards, the weighted interest rate and payments.

System: MAC, II, PLUS, XL
Minimum Memory: 512K
Requires: Microsoft Excel (ISPN 53150-270), Microsoft Works (ISPN 53150-740) or HyperCard (ISPN 03900-300).
Medium: 3 1/2-inch disk
ISPN: 35175-613   **Price: $7.00**

HEIZER SOFTWARE

DAILY INCOME AND EXPENSE LOG

Performs daily income and expense transactions.

System: MAC, II, PLUS, SE, XL
Minimum Memory: 512K
Requires: Microsoft Excel (ISPN 53150-270) or Microsoft Works (ISPN 53150-740).
Medium: 3 1/2-inch disk
ISPN: 35175-607   **Price: $8.00**

HEIZER SOFTWARE

DISABILITY INSURANCE NEEDS

Estimates the replacement income coverage an individual would need in case of disability, based on actual expense requirements.

System: MAC, II, PLUS, SE, XL
Minimum Memory: 512K
Requires: Microsoft Excel (ISPN 53150-270).
Medium: 3 1/2-inch disk
ISPN: 35175-930   **Price: $12.00**

MONOGRAM SOFTWARE, INC.

DOLLARS AND SENSE (VER. 4.1C) (MAC)

Provides financial management for personal and small business use.

System: MAC, II, PLUS, SE, XL
Minimum Memory: 512K
Requires: 800K disk drive.
Medium: 3 1/2-inch disk
ISPN: 55240-205   **Price: $149.95**

HEIZER SOFTWARE

ESTATE ANALYSIS

Provides current and proposed estimates of estate settlement costs and cash liquidity needs.

System: MAC, II, PLUS, SE, XL
Minimum Memory: 512K
Requires: Microsoft Excel (ISPN 53150-270) or Microsoft Works (ISPN 53150-740).
Medium: 3 1/2-inch disk
ISPN: 35175-635   **Price: $16.00**

EZWARE CORP.

EZTAX-PLAN PERSONAL EDITION

Computes comprehensive tax plans for individuals and projects up to 45 years.

System: MAC, II, PLUS, XL
Minimum Memory: 512K
Requires: Microsoft Excel (ISPN 53150-270).
Medium: 3 1/2-inch disk
ISPN: 30578-200   **Price: $95.00**

ELECTRONIC ARTS

FINANCIAL COOKBOOK

Contains financial 'recipes' ranging from monthly mortgage schedules to investment analysis for personal financial planning.

System: MAC, II, PLUS, SE, XL
Minimum Memory: 128K
Medium: 3 1/2-inch disk
ISPN: 28512-050   **Price: $19.95**

NOLO PRESS

FOR THE RECORD (VER. 1.0)

Records personal, financial and legal information.

System: MAC, II, PLUS, SE, XL
Minimum Memory: 48K
Medium: 3 1/2-inch disk
ISPN: 44075-950   **Price: $49.95**

HABA/ARRAYS SYSTEMS, INC.

HOME ACCOUNTANT

Home accounting program designed to keep track of checking, bills and expenses.

System: MAC, II, PLUS, SE, XL
Minimum Memory: 512K
Medium: 3 1/2-inch disk
ISPN: 33987-020   **Price: $59.95**

HABA/ARRAYS SYSTEMS, INC.

HOME ACCOUNTANT & FINANCIAL PLANNER FOR MACINTOSH

Home financial planner that tracks daily expenses, maintains current financial situation and creates reports and graphs.

System: MAC
Minimum Memory: 512K
Medium: 3 1/2-inch disk
ISPN: 33987-425   **Price: $59.95**

HEIZER SOFTWARE

HOME INVENTORY

A database which keeps track of physical assets including insurance or warranty problems.

System: MAC, II, PLUS, SE, XL
Minimum Memory: 512K
Requires: Microsoft Excel (ISPN 53150-270) or Microsoft Works (ISPN 53150-740).
Medium: 3 1/2-inch disk
ISPN: 35175-617   **Price: $6.00**

HEIZER SOFTWARE

INSURANCE ANALYSIS

Provides a summary of insurance contracts and analyzes the family's cash flow needs in case of disability or death.

System: MAC, II, PLUS, XL
Minimum Memory: 512K
Requires: Microsoft Excel (ISPN 53150-270) or Microsoft Works (ISPN 53150-740).
Medium: 3 1/2-inch disk
ISPN: 35175-633   **Price: $16.00**

HEIZER SOFTWARE

IRA ANALYSIS

Calculates the future value of Individual Retirement Account contributions.

System: MAC, II, PLUS, SE, XL
Minimum Memory: 512K
Requires: Microsoft Excel (ISPN 53150-270), Microsoft Works (ISPN 53150-740) or HyperCard (ISPN 03900-300).
Medium: 3 1/2-inch disk
ISPN: 35175-640   **Price: $6.00**

HEIZER SOFTWARE

IRA DEDUCTION CALCULATOR

Calculates the amount which can be contributed to and/or deducted from an Individual Retirement Account, under current tax laws.

System: MAC, II, PLUS, SE, XL
Minimum Memory: 512K
Requires: Microsoft Excel (ISPN 53150-270) or Microsoft Works (ISPN 53150-740).
Medium: 3 1/2-inch disk
ISPN: 35175-641   **Price: $12.00**

HEIZER SOFTWARE
IRA ORGANIZER

Discusses the new tax law and the changes to Individual Retirement Account qualification and record-keeping requirements.
System: MAC, II, PLUS, SE, XL
Minimum Memory: 512K
Requires: Microsoft Excel (ISPN 53150-270) or Microsoft Works (ISPN 53150-740).
Medium: 3 1/2-inch disk
ISPN: 35175-642   **Price: $15.00**

HEIZER SOFTWARE
LIFE INSURANCE POLICY PROJECTION

Projects the rates of return on a life insurance policy for future years, based on inflation and assumed policy performance.
System: MAC, II, PLUS, SE, XL
Minimum Memory: 512K
Requires: Microsoft Excel (ISPN 53150-270).
Medium: 3 1/2-inch disk
ISPN: 35175-954   **Price: $25.00**

HEIZER SOFTWARE
LOAN PAYOFF ANALYSIS

Analyzes loans using both cash flow and net worth perspectives.
System: MAC, II, PLUS, SE, XL
Minimum Memory: 512K
Requires: Microsoft Excel (ISPN 53150-270) or Microsoft Works (ISPN 53150-740).
Medium: 3 1/2-inch disk
ISPN: 35175-611   **Price: $6.00**

QUADMATION, INC.
MAC PERSONAL CLASS (VER. 1.80)

A HyperCard stack used for recording vital personal information including family data, assets, documents, and investment data.
System: MAC, II, PLUS, XL
Minimum Memory: 1024K
Requires: HyperCard (ISPN 3900-300).
Medium: 3 1/2-inch disk
ISPN: 63981-500   **Price: $59.00**

SURVIVOR SOFTWARE LTD.
MACMONEY (VER. 3.02)

A checkbook and financial planner with up to 250 bank account, credit card, cash, expense, income, asset and liability categories.
System: MAC, II, PLUS, SE, XL
Minimum Memory: 512K
Requires: 800K disk drive.
Medium: 3 1/2-inch disk
ISPN: 77227-600   **Price: $119.95**

MECA VENTURES, INC.
MANAGING YOUR MONEY

An integrated money management package designed by Andrew Tobias.
System: MAC, II, PLUS, SE, XL
Minimum Memory: 512K
Requires: Two disk drives.
Medium: 3 1/2-inch disk
ISPN: 50231-100   **Price: $219.98**

HEIZER SOFTWARE
MEDICAL EXPENSE RECORDER

Tracks routine expenses, status of claims and provides data for preparing tax returns.
System: MAC, II, PLUS, SE, XL
Minimum Memory: 512K
Requires: Microsoft Excel (ISPN 53150-270).
Medium: 3 1/2-inch disk
ISPN: 35175-609   **Price: $10.00**

HEIZER SOFTWARE
MONEY MORTALITY

Calculates the remaining life from insurance and IRS tables and computes equal annual savings withdrawals during that time.
System: MAC, II, PLUS, SE, XL
Minimum Memory: 512K
Requires: Microsoft Excel (ISPN 53150-270) or Microsoft Works (ISPN 53150-740).
Medium: 3 1/2-inch disk
ISPN: 35175-612   **Price: $8.00**

DISK-COUNT SOFTWARE, INC.
MULTIPLE CHECKBOOK SYSTEM

Organizes personal and business checking accounts by categories, and prints reports on all checking transactions.
System: MAC, II, PLUS, SE, XL
Minimum Memory: 512K
Requires: Two 400K disk drives, or one 400K disk drive and a hard drive.
Medium: 3 1/2-inch disk
ISPN: 26189-555   **Price: $29.95**

HEIZER SOFTWARE
NET WORTH CALCULATOR

Calculates current net worth, previous net worth and changes for the period.
System: MAC, II, PLUS, SE, XL
Minimum Memory: 512K
Requires: Microsoft Excel (ISPN 53150-270) or Microsoft Works (ISPN 53150-740).
Medium: 3 1/2-inch disk
ISPN: 35175-608   **Price: $10.00**

OPTIONS-80
OPTIONS-80A-ADVANCED STOCK OPTION ANALYZER

Provides an option analyzer for individual investors to maximize returns on portfolio.
System: MAC, II, PLUS, SE, XL
Minimum Memory: 512K
Medium: 3 1/2-inch disk
ISPN: 58660-200   **Price: $170.00**

PROVUE DEVELOPMENT CORP.
OVERVUE MAIL MANAGER TEMPLATE

A template that works with Overvue to print labels, form letters, and other mailing list tasks.
System: MAC, II, PLUS, SE, XL
Minimum Memory: 128K
Requires: Overvue (ISPN 63531-700).
Medium: 3 1/2-inch disk
ISPN: 63531-500   **Price: $39.95**

PROVUE DEVELOPMENT CORP.
OVERVUE PERSONAL FINANCE TEMPLATE (VER. 1.0)

Will store, analyze, and print personal finance transactions in one convenient file.
System: MAC, II, PLUS, SE, XL
Minimum Memory: 128K
Requires: Overvue (ISPN 63531-700).
Medium: 3 1/2-inch disk
ISPN: 63531-550   **Price: $39.95**

SOFTSYNC, INC.
PERSONAL ACCOUNTANT (VER. 3.0)

Manages all basic home accounting tasks using double-entry bookkeeping and generates reports, financial statements and graphs.
System: MAC, II, PLUS, SE, XL
Minimum Memory: 512K
Requires: 800K disk drive.
Medium: 3 1/2-inch disk
ISPN: 72240-460   **Price: $49.95**

DYNACOMP, INC.
PERSONAL BALANCE SHEET

Creates a statement of the user's financial position such as the assets and liabilities.
System: MAC, II, PLUS, SE, XL
Minimum Memory: 512K
Requires: 80-column printer.
Medium: 3 1/2-inch disk
ISPN: 27050-802   **Price: $34.95**

HEIZER SOFTWARE
PERSONAL BUDGET

Tracks income, expenses, net worth and cash flow changes monthly, quarterly, annually and cumulatively.
System: MAC, II, PLUS, SE, XL
Minimum Memory: 512K
Requires: Microsoft Excel (ISPN 53150-270) or Microsoft Works (ISPN 53150-740).
Medium: 3 1/2-inch disk
ISPN: 35175-606   **Price: $15.00**

HEIZER SOFTWARE
PERSONAL CHECK PRINTER

Prints on pin-feed check forms that can be used with ImageWriter. Includes payee, date, and the check amount in numbers and text.
System: MAC, II, PLUS, XL
Minimum Memory: 512K
Requires: Microsoft Excel (ISPN 53150-270).
Medium: 3 1/2-inch disk
ISPN: 35175-604   **Price: $15.00**

HEIZER SOFTWARE
PERSONAL FINANCIAL PLANNING SET

A series of five programs which include asset management, insurance analysis, education financing, tax/cash flow and estate analysis.
System: MAC, II, PLUS, SE, XL
Minimum Memory: 512K
Requires: Microsoft Excel (ISPN 53150-270) or Microsoft Works (ISPN 53150-740).
Medium: 3 1/2-inch disk
ISPN: 35175-630   **Price: $96.00**

HEIZER SOFTWARE
PERSONAL NET WORTH

Indicates current and previous net worth and changes in personal net worth for a specified period of time.

System: MAC, II, PLUS, SE, XL
Minimum Memory: 512K
Requires: Microsoft Works (ISPN 53150-740).
Medium: 3 1/2-inch disk
ISPN: 35175-813   **Price: $10.00**

DECISION SCIENCE SOFTWARE
PROJECT INVESTMENT ANALYSIS

Provides an interactive model which evaluates investment projects.

System: MAC, II, PLUS, SE, XL
Minimum Memory: 512K
Medium: 3 1/2-inch disk
ISPN: 24325-160   **Price: $110.00**

DECISION SCIENCE SOFTWARE
PROJECT SELECTION (PROSEL)

Provides an interactive system designed to perform selection of investment projects.

System: MAC, II, PLUS, SE, XL
Minimum Memory: 512K
Medium: 3 1/2-inch disk
ISPN: 24325-170   **Price: $90.00**

INTUIT
QUICKEN

A checking and financial package including the Quicken-AppleWorks link letting users transfer data to spreadsheets in Appleworks.

System: MAC, II, PLUS, XL
Minimum Memory: 512K
Requires: Printer.
Medium: 3 1/2-inch disk
ISPN: 40562-700   **Price: $49.95**

HEIZER SOFTWARE
RETIREMENT ANALYZER

Predicts estimated income needed at retirement, spending needs, sources of retirement income and capital accumulation.

System: MAC, II, PLUS, SE, XL
Minimum Memory: 512K
Requires: Microsoft Excel (ISPN 53150-270) or Microsoft Works (ISPN 53150-740).
Medium: 3 1/2-inch disk
ISPN: 35175-644   **Price: $25.00**

HEIZER SOFTWARE
RETIREMENT PLAN FEASIBILITY

A template which analyzes tax status and age to determine whether it is beneficial to set up a retirement plan.

System: MAC, II, PLUS, SE, XL
Minimum Memory: 512K
Requires: Microsoft Excel (ISPN 53150-270) or Microsoft Works (ISPN 53150-740).
Medium: 3 1/2-inch disk
ISPN: 35175-643   **Price: $10.00**

HEIZER SOFTWARE
SIMPLIFIED RETIREMENT ANALYSIS

Determines retirement needs and goals using the standards and formats of the College of Financial Planning.

System: MAC, II, PLUS, SE, XL
Minimum Memory: 512K
Requires: Microsoft Excel (ISPN 53150-270) or Microsoft Works (ISPN 53150-740).
Medium: 3 1/2-inch disk
ISPN: 35175-645   **Price: $15.00**

HEIZER SOFTWARE
SOCIAL SECURITY BENEFIT CALCULATOR

Estimates Social Security benefits, including eligibility, three retirement, three survivor and two disability benefit categories.

System: MAC, II, PLUS, XL
Minimum Memory: 512K
Requires: Microsoft Excel (ISPN 53150-270) or Microsoft Works (ISPN 53150-740).
Medium: 3 1/2-inch disk
ISPN: 35175-646   **Price: $12.00**

SUNRISE SOFTWARE
TAX MINI-MISER

Computes up to sixteen different tax strategies and projects their effect for sixteen years.

System: MAC, II, PLUS, SE, XL
Minimum Memory: 512K
Medium: 3 1/2-inch disk
ISPN: 77043-100   **Price: $295.00**

HEIZER SOFTWARE
TAX/CASH FLOW

Analyzes federal and state taxes and cash flow and determines ways of minimizing taxes and maximizing cash flows.

System: MAC, II, PLUS, SE, XL
Minimum Memory: 512K
Requires: Microsoft Excel (ISPN 53150-270) or Microsoft Works (ISPN 53150-740).
Medium: 3 1/2-inch disk
ISPN: 35175-634   **Price: $36.00**

HEIZER SOFTWARE
TRUTH IN LENDING

Calculates the true annual interest rate when points and front-end fees cloud the issue.

System: MAC, II, PLUS, SE, XL
Minimum Memory: 512K
Requires: Microsoft Excel (ISPN 53150-270) or Microsoft Works (ISPN 53150-740).
Medium: 3 1/2-inch disk
ISPN: 35175-615   **Price: $9.00**

NOLO PRESS
WILLMAKER (VER. 3.0)

Uses a rule-based system to create wills valid in all states except Louisiana. Complete book on wills and estate planning included.

System: MAC, II, PLUS, SE, XL
Minimum Memory: 512K
Requires: 800K disk drive.
Medium: 3 1/2-inch disk
ISPN: 44075-900   **Price: $59.95**

HABA/ARRAYS SYSTEMS, INC.
WILLS

Provides 14 different legally prepared wills for every need and a guidebook to help users along.

System: MAC, II, PLUS, SE, XL
Minimum Memory: 512K
Medium: 3 1/2-inch disk
ISPN: 33987-800   **Price: $29.95**

432 PERSONAL/ GAMBLING

SOFTWARE EXCHANGE
ADVANCED GREYHOUND RACING ANALYSIS SYSTEM

Handicap greyhounds using up to nine years of data.

System: MAC, II, PLUS, SE, XL
Minimum Memory: 512K
Medium: 3 1/2-inch disk
ISPN: 72868-075   **Price: $74.95**

SOFTWARE EXCHANGE
ADVANCED HARNESS RACING ANALYSIS SYSTEM

Handicap harness racing using up to nine years of data.

System: MAC, II, PLUS, SE, XL
Minimum Memory: 64K
Medium: 3 1/2-inch disk
ISPN: 72868-080   **Price: $64.95**

SOFTWARE EXCHANGE
ADVANCED QUARTER HORSE RACING SYSTEM

Handicap sprint races using up to nine years of data.

System: MAC, II, PLUS, SE, XL
Minimum Memory: 64K
Medium: 3 1/2-inch disk
ISPN: 72868-090   **Price: $64.95**

SOFTWARE EXCHANGE
ADVANCED RACING SYSTEM 2

Handicaps and predicts thoroughbred, harness, and greyhound racing based on past performance data.

System: MAC, II, PLUS, XL
Minimum Memory: 64K
Medium: 3 1/2-inch disk
ISPN: 72868-100   **Price: $184.95**

SOFTWARE EXCHANGE
ADVANCED RACING SYSTEM 3

Handicaps Thoroughbred, Harness and Quarter Horse races for up to 26 horses.

System: MAC, II, PLUS, SE, XL
Minimum Memory: 64K
Medium: 3 1/2-inch disk
ISPN: 72868-110   **Price: $174.95**

SOFTWARE EXCHANGE

ADVANCED RACING SYSTEM 4

Provides handicapping for Harness, Thoroughbred, Quarter Horse, and Greyhound racing.

System: MAC, II, PLUS, SE, XL
Minimum Memory: 64K
Medium: 3 1/2-inch disk
ISPN: 72868-120 **Price: $239.95**

SOFTWARE EXCHANGE

ADVANCED THOROUGHBRED RACING ANALYSIS SYSTEM

Handicap thoroughbred racing using up to nine years of data.

System: MAC, II, PLUS, SE, XL
Minimum Memory: 64K
Medium: 3 1/2-inch disk
ISPN: 72868-085 **Price: $64.95**

PDS SPORTS

BASEBALL DATA DISK-PAST YEARS

Compilation of past statistics for handicapping.

System: MAC, II, PLUS, SE, XL
Minimum Memory: 512K
Requires: Pro Baseball Handicapping and Statistics System (ISPN 60137-020).
Medium: 3 1/2-inch disk
ISPN: 60137-080 **Price: $19.95**

PDS SPORTS

BASEBALL DATA DISK-YEAR-TO-DATE

Specific yearly statistics for handicapping purposes.

System: MAC, II, PLUS, SE, XL
Minimum Memory: 512K
Requires: Pro Baseball Handicapping and Statistics System (ISPN 60137-020).
Medium: 3 1/2-inch disk
ISPN: 60137-082 **Price: $19.95**

HEIZER SOFTWARE

DICE ROLLER

Demonstrates probability on track results and rolling dice.

System: MAC, II, PLUS, SE, XL
Minimum Memory: 512K
Requires: Microsoft Excel (ISPN 53150-270).
Medium: 3 1/2-inch disk
ISPN: 35175-260 **Price: $4.00**

PROFESSIONAL HANDICAPPING SYSTEMS

FOOTBALL PREDICTOR

Football analysis program.

System: MAC, II, PLUS, SE, XL
Minimum Memory: 128K
Requires: Microsoft QuickBasic (ISPN 53150-205).
Medium: 3 1/2-inch disk
ISPN: 62912-200 **Price: $99.95**

PDS SPORTS

GREYHOUND HANDICAPPING SYSTEM

Provides a complete statistical handicapping system for greyhound racing.

System: MAC, II, PLUS, SE, XL
Minimum Memory: 512K
Medium: 3 1/2-inch disk
ISPN: 60137-090 **Price: $129.00**

DYNACOMP, INC.

HANDICAPPER

A handicapping scheme for thoroughbred races.

System: MAC, II, PLUS, SE, XL
Minimum Memory: 512K
Requires: Microsoft QuickBasic (ISPN 53150-205).
Medium: 3 1/2-inch disk
ISPN: 27050-440 **Price: $38.95**

DYNACOMP, INC.

HANDICAPPER II

A complete handicapping system for horse racing.

System: MAC, II, PLUS, SE, XL
Minimum Memory: 512K
Requires: Microsoft QuickBasic (ISPN 53150-205).
Medium: 3 1/2-inch disk
ISPN: 27050-442 **Price: $58.95**

PDS SPORTS

HARNESS DRIVER STATISTICS SYSTEM (RELEASE 2.5)

Rate the driver's ability.

System: MAC, II, PLUS, SE, XL
Minimum Memory: 512K
Medium: 3 1/2-inch disk
ISPN: 60137-065 **Price: $39.95**

PDS SPORTS

HARNESS HORSE HANDICAPPING SYSTEM (RELEASE 2.5)

Handicaps harness races using past performance and current horse and track information.

System: MAC, II, PLUS, SE, XL
Minimum Memory: 512K
Medium: 3 1/2-inch disk
ISPN: 60137-035 **Price: $129.00**

PDS SPORTS

HARNESS HORSE RACING PACKAGE (RELEASE 2.5)

Contains harness horse handicapping system plus Driver and Trainer statistics programs.

System: MAC, II, PLUS, SE, XL
Minimum Memory: 512K
Medium: 3 1/2-inch disk
ISPN: 60137-040 **Price: $189.00**

PDS SPORTS

JOCKEY STATISTICS SYSTEM (RELEASE 2.5)

Rate the jockey's ability.

System: MAC, II, PLUS, SE, XL
Minimum Memory: 512K
Medium: 3 1/2-inch disk
ISPN: 60137-055 **Price: $39.95**

SOFT-BYTE COMPUTER PROGRAMS

LOTTO PROGRAM (VER. 2.1)

Pick the most likely winning lotto number.

System: MAC, II, PLUS, SE, XL
Minimum Memory: 128K
Medium: 3 1/2-inch disk
ISPN: 95753-600 **Price: $29.95**

HOT DATA, INC.

LOTTOMATION (VER. 1.05)

Pick your winning lotto numbers.

System: MAC, II, PLUS, SE, XL
Minimum Memory: 128K
Medium: 3 1/2-inch disk
ISPN: 36246-400 **Price: $29.95**

HEIZER SOFTWARE

LOTTOMAX

Creates a twenty-five year plan for lottery winners, including how much the winnings would be worth in today's dollars.

System: MAC, II, PLUS, SE, XL
Minimum Memory: 512K
Requires: Microsoft Excel (ISPN 53150-270).
Medium: 3 1/2-inch disk
ISPN: 35175-249 **Price: $9.00**

HEIZER SOFTWARE

LOTTOPIC'R

Selects six unique lottery numbers at random.

System: MAC, II, PLUS, SE, XL
Minimum Memory: 512K
Requires: Microsoft Excel (ISPN 53150-270) or HyperCard (ISPN 03900-300).
Medium: 3 1/2-inch disk
ISPN: 35175-248 **Price: $5.00**

PDS SPORTS

NBA DATA DISK-PAST YEARS

Past performance statistics for handicapping.

System: MAC, II, PLUS, SE, XL
Minimum Memory: 512K
Requires: Pro Basketball Handicapping and Statistics System (ISPN 60137-015).
Medium: 3 1/2-inch disk
ISPN: 60137-086 **Price: $19.95**

PDS SPORTS

NBA DATA DISK-YEAR TO DATE

Provides past statistics for comparison in handicapping.

System: MAC, II, PLUS, SE, XL
Minimum Memory: 512K
Requires: Pro Basketball Handicapping and Statistics System (ISPN 60137-015).
Medium: 3 1/2-inch disk
ISPN: 60137-085 **Price: $19.95**

PDS SPORTS

NFL DATA DISKS-PAST YEARS

Compilation of past performance records.

System: MAC, II, PLUS, XL
Minimum Memory: 512K
Requires: Pro Football Handicapping and
   Statistics System (ISPN 60137-010).
Medium: 3 1/2-inch disk
ISPN: 60137-075   **Price: $19.95**

PDS SPORTS

NFL DATA DISKS-YEAR-TO-DATE

Compilation of records and statistics for
handicapping.

System: MAC, II, PLUS, SE, XL
Minimum Memory: 512K
Requires: Pro Football Handicapping and
   Statistics System (ISPN 60137-010).
Medium: 3 1/2-inch disk
ISPN: 60137-076   **Price: $19.95**

DYNACOMP, INC.

NFL HANDICAPPER

Statistically handicap the national football
league.

System: MAC, II, PLUS, SE, XL
Minimum Memory: 512K
Medium: 3 1/2-inch disk
ISPN: 27050-537   **Price: $64.95**

PDS SPORTS

PRO BASEBALL HANDICAPPING AND STATISTICAL SYSTEM

Compare team performances against a
variety of factors.

System: MAC, II, PLUS, SE, XL
Minimum Memory: 512K
Medium: 3 1/2-inch disk
ISPN: 60137-020   **Price: $69.95**

PDS SPORTS

PRO BASKETBALL HANDICAP. & STAT. SYS.(RELEASE 2.5)

Assistance in predicting NBA game
outcome.

System: MAC, II, PLUS, SE, XL
Minimum Memory: 512K
Medium: 3 1/2-inch disk
ISPN: 60137-015   **Price: $69.95**

PDS SPORTS

PRO FOOTBALL HANDICAP. & STAT. SYS. (RELEASE 3.0)

Evaluate offense and defense and forecast
outcome.

System: MAC, II, PLUS, SE, XL
Minimum Memory: 512K
Medium: 3 1/2-inch disk
ISPN: 60137-010   **Price: $69.95**

PDS SPORTS

QUARTER HORSE HANDICAPPING SYSTEM

Handicaps quarter horse races using past
performances and current track
information.

System: MAC, II, PLUS, SE, XL
Minimum Memory: 512K
Medium: 3 1/2-inch disk
ISPN: 60137-045   **Price: $129.00**

PDS SPORTS

QUARTER HORSE RACING PACKAGE

Contains Quarter Horse handicapping
system plus Jockey and Trainer statistics
programs.

System: MAC, II, PLUS, SE, XL
Minimum Memory: 512K
Medium: 3 1/2-inch disk
ISPN: 60137-050   **Price: $189.00**

PDS SPORTS

THOROUGHBRED HANDICAPPING SYSTEM

Provides a thoroughbred handicapping
system based on past performance and
current jockey, trainer and track
information.

System: MAC, II, PLUS, XL
Minimum Memory: 512K
Medium: 3 1/2-inch disk
ISPN: 60137-025   **Price: $129.00**

PDS SPORTS

THOROUGHBRED RACING PACKAGE

Consists of a thoroughbred handicapping
system plus jockey and trainer statistics
programs.

System: MAC, II, PLUS, SE, XL
Minimum Memory: 512K
Medium: 3 1/2-inch disk
ISPN: 60137-030   **Price: $189.00**

PDS SPORTS

TRAINER STATISTICS SYSTEM (RELEASE 2.5)

Rate the horse trainer's ability.

System: MAC, II, PLUS, SE, XL
Minimum Memory: 512K
Medium: 3 1/2-inch disk
ISPN: 60137-060   **Price: $39.95**

HEIZER SOFTWARE

UNIVERSAL LOTTERY CHECKER

A HyperCard stack which supports sixty-
three different lottery games and keeps
track of an individual's lottery bets.

System: MAC, II, PLUS, SE, XL
Minimum Memory: 512K
Requires: HyperCard (ISPN 03900-300).
Medium: 3 1/2-inch disk
ISPN: 35175-996   **Price: $10.00**

---

436 PERSONAL/ GENEALOGY/FAMILY HISTORY

STARCOM MICROSYSTEMS

FAMILY HERITAGE FILE

A comprehensive personal genealogy
management system, powerful enough for
the serious genealogist, easy for the
beginner.

System: MAC, II, PLUS, SE, XL
Minimum Memory: 512K
Medium: 3 1/2-inch disk
ISPN: 75815-300   **Price: $149.00**

QUINSEPT, INC.

FAMILY ROOTS (VER. 1.3) (MACINTOSH)

A comprehensive genealogical research
program which prints lists, group sheets,
person sheets and charts.

System: MAC, II, PLUS, SE, XL
Minimum Memory: 512K
Requires: 800K disk drive.
Medium: 3 1/2-inch disk
ISPN: 64475-110   **Price: $135.00**

COMPSERVCO

HYPERGENE (VER. 1.0)

A genealogy program to store your
complete family history. Includes charts,
information sheets, and receives scanned-
in photographs.

System: MAC, II, PLUS, SE, XL
Minimum Memory: 512K
Requires: Hypercard (ISPN 03900-300).
Medium: 3 1/2-inch disk
ISPN: 15025-050   **Price: $89.00**

STARCOM MICROSYSTEMS

LIFE HISTORY DISK

Contains a comprehensive life history
format and extensive instructions on how
to produce significant life histories.

System: MAC, II, PLUS, SE, XL
Minimum Memory: 128K
Requires: MacWrite (ISPN 12784-530) or
   Microsoft Word (ISPN 53150-732) or other
   word processor.
Medium: 3 1/2-inch disk
ISPN: 75815-500   **Price: $19.95**

APPLIED IDEAS, INC.

MACGENE (VER. 3.0)

A genealogy program which features descendant, pedigree, family tree, mail-list, history log, LDS and user-defined fields.

System: MAC, II, PLUS, SE, XL
Minimum Memory: 512K
Medium: 3 1/2-inch disk
ISPN: 04512-200   **Price: $145.00**

HEIZER SOFTWARE

MACGENIE

Helps gather, store, arrange and access information about the user's family.

System: MAC, II, PLUS, SE, XL
Minimum Memory: 1024K
Requires: HyperCard (ISPN 03900-300).
Medium: 3 1/2-inch disk
ISPN: 35175-419   **Price: $20.00**

ACCURATE COMPUTER SEARCH

TIME SCROLLS

Print histories of what happened on any date such as news, sports, cost of living and famous birthdays.

System: MAC, II, PLUS, SE, XL
Minimum Memory: 512K
Medium: 3 1/2-inch disk
ISPN: 00582-150   **Price: $39.95**

442 PERSONAL/HEALTH/ SELF-IMPROVEMENT

COMPUTER SPIRIT GRAPHICS, INC.

AIDS-A PROGRAM ABOUT HEALTH

Grades 6-11: Combines graphics, synthesized speech, and instructional techniques to inform about AIDS.

System: MAC, II, PLUS, XL
Minimum Memory: 512K
Medium: 3 1/2-inch disk
ISPN: 17675-304   **Price: $89.00**

HEIZER SOFTWARE

BIKING CALORIE COUNTER

Calculates tables for 'gear inches', miles-per-hour, and calories-per-hour for bicycling.

System: MAC, II, PLUS, SE, XL
Minimum Memory: 512K
Requires: Microsoft Excel (ISPN 53150-270) or HyperCard (ISPN 03900-300).
Medium: 3 1/2-inch disk
ISPN: 35175-714   **Price: $4.00**

INTRACORP, INC.

BIRDS N BEES FOR 7-12 YEAR OLDS

Ages 7-12: The facts of life in a clear, simple manner.

System: MAC, II, PLUS, SE, XL
Minimum Memory: 512K
Medium: 3 1/2-inch disk
ISPN: 40531-250   **Price: $14.95**

QUEUE

CONTRACEPTION

Grades 7 and up: Various types of contraception.

System: MAC, II, PLUS, SE, XL
Minimum Memory: 128K
Medium: 3 1/2-inch disk
ISPN: 64387-275   **Price: $34.95**

QUEUE

DRUG ABUSE

Describes various aspects of drug abuse.

System: MAC, II, PLUS, XL
Minimum Memory: 128K
Medium: 3 1/2-inch disk
ISPN: 64387-278   **Price: $39.95**

LUNDIN LABORATORIES, INC.

FAMILYCARE SOFTWARE (VER. 1.05)

Models the diagnostic process used by doctors to help parents with their childrens medical problems.

System: MAC, II, PLUS, SE, XL
Minimum Memory: 512K
Medium: 3 1/2-inch disk
ISPN: 45596-100   **Price: $99.00**

HEIZER SOFTWARE

FAST FOOD CALCULATOR

A HyperCard stack which provides nutrition and ingredient information for major fast food chains and has speech capabilities.

System: MAC, II, PLUS, SE, XL
Minimum Memory: 512K
Requires: HyperCard (ISPN 03900-300).
Medium: 3 1/2-inch disk
ISPN: 35175-932   **Price: $15.00**

MINDSCAPE, INC.

LUSCHER PROFILE

Examine your responses to preferences.

System: MAC, II, PLUS, SE, XL
Minimum Memory:
Medium: 3 1/2-inch disk
ISPN: 54375-130   **Price: $39.95**

REASON HOUSE

MAC PSYCH ADMINISTRATOR (VER. 1.01)

Administers House-Tree-Person, Human Figure and Kinetic Family Drawing tests and Bender Visual-Motor Gestalt Test.

System: MAC, II, PLUS, SE, XL
Minimum Memory: 128K
Medium: 3 1/2-inch disk
ISPN: 65635-500   **Price: $79.00**

TECH 2000 SOFTWARE, INC.

MACMUSCLE

Generates exercise schedules based on subject's muscle group selection and provides animated instruction for chosen exercises.

System: MAC
Minimum Memory: 128K
Medium: 3 1/2-inch disk
ISPN: 80212-500   **Price: $64.95**

QUEUE

NEW BABY CARE

Grades 7-12: New baby care discussions designed for expectant families.

System: MAC, II, PLUS, SE, XL
Minimum Memory: 128K
Medium: 3 1/2-inch disk
ISPN: 64387-532   **Price: $34.95**

HEIZER SOFTWARE

OVERWEIGHT

A HyperCard stack which calculates an individual's Body Mass Index, and determines the risk of obesity.

System: MAC, II, PLUS, SE, XL
Minimum Memory: 512K
Requires: HyperCard (ISPN 03900-300) (Ver. 1.2).
Medium: 3 1/2-inch disk
ISPN: 35175-972   **Price: $6.00**

QUEUE

PREGNANCY SERIES

Grades 7-12: Prenatal care discussions for older children.

System: MAC, II, PLUS, SE, XL
Minimum Memory: 128K
Medium: 3 1/2-inch disk
ISPN: 64387-786   **Price: $59.95**

QUEUE

SEX EDUCATION PACKAGE

Grades 7 and up: Sex education discussions.

System: MAC, II, PLUS, SE, XL
Minimum Memory: 128K
Medium: 3 1/2-inch disk
ISPN: 64387-783   **Price: $65.00**

DYNACOMP, INC.

UNDERSTAND YOURSELF

Determine the real 'you'.

System: MAC, II, PLUS, SE, XL
Minimum Memory: 512K
Medium: 3 1/2-inch disk
ISPN: 27050-719   **Price: $29.95**

QUEUE

VENEREAL DISEASE

Learn about various types of venereal disease.

System: MAC, II, PLUS, SE, XL
Minimum Memory: 128K
Medium: 3 1/2-inch disk
ISPN: 64387-915   **Price: $34.95**

448 PERSONAL/HOBBIES

COMPU-QUOTE
CARD/FAX-DONRUSS

Inventory and evaluate your Donruss card collection.

System: MAC, II, PLUS, SE, XL
Minimum Memory: 512K
Requires: One 800K disk drive or hard disk.
Medium: 3 1/2-inch disk
ISPN: 15387-220 **Price: $95.00**

COMPU-QUOTE
CARD/FAX-FLEER

Inventory and evaluate your fleer card collection.

System: MAC, II, PLUS, SE, XL
Minimum Memory: 512K
Requires: One 800K disk drive or hard disk.
Medium: 3 1/2-inch disk
ISPN: 15387-240 **Price: $95.00**

COMPU-QUOTE
CARD/FAX-TOPPS

Inventory and evaluate your topps card collection.

System: MAC, II, PLUS, SE, XL
Minimum Memory: 512K
Requires: One 800K disk drive or hard disk.
Medium: 3 1/2-inch disk
ISPN: 15387-200 **Price: $95.00**

JS GRAPHICS
COIN COLLECTION (VER. 1.0)

HyperCard based organizer for listing a coin collection and making notes about each coin or set.

System: MAC, II, PLUS, SE, XL
Minimum Memory: 1024K
Requires: HyperCard (ISPN 03900-300).
Medium: 3 1/2-inch disk
ISPN: 93058-100 **Price: $14.95**

COMPU-QUOTE
COINS (VER. 1.01)

Inventory and evaluate your coin collection.

System: MAC, II, PLUS, SE, XL
Minimum Memory: 512K
Requires: Two disk drives, printer.
Medium: 3 1/2-inch disk
ISPN: 15387-100 **Price: $95.00**

COMPU-QUOTE
COINS/PLUS

Inventory and evaluate your U.S. coin collection.

System: MAC, II, PLUS, SE, XL
Minimum Memory: 512K
Requires: One 800K disk drive or hard disk.
Medium: 3 1/2-inch disk
ISPN: 15387-110 **Price: $95.00**

ORTHO INFORMATION SERVICES
COMPUTERIZED GARDENING

A personalized gardening program that adjusts itself to any zip code in the country to tell when to plant and type of care needed.

System: MAC, II, PLUS, SE, XL
Minimum Memory: 512K
Medium: 3 1/2-inch disk
ISPN: 58887-200 **Price: $49.95**

CIASA
HANDWRITING ANALYST

Analyze the secrets manifested in your handwriting.

System: MAC, II, PLUS, SE, XL
Minimum Memory: 512K
Medium: 3 1/2-inch disk
ISPN: 12543-050 **Price: $69.95**

HEIZER SOFTWARE
HOMEBREW AND BREW RECORDS

A set of two HyperCard stacks which contains step-by-step instructions for brewing beer.

System: MAC, II, PLUS, SE, XL
Minimum Memory: 512K
Requires: HyperCard (ISPN 03900-300).
Medium: 3 1/2-inch disk
ISPN: 35175-945 **Price: $15.00**

ABRACADATA LTD.
MACINOOGA CHOO CHOO

Simulates a complete toy train set. Includes signals, switches, scenery, carriages, and three locomotives.

System: MAC, PLUS, SE, XL
Minimum Memory: 512K
Medium: 3 1/2-inch disk
ISPN: 00366-275 **Price: $49.95**

FINE S SOFTWARE
MACKET (VER. 1.2)

A terminal program for amateur radio operators who operate packet radio with a terminal node controller.

System: MAC, II, PLUS, SE, XL
Minimum Memory: 512K
Requires: Terminal Node Controller with an RS-232 port.
Medium: 3 1/2-inch disk
ISPN: 91835-500 **Price: $39.95**

TRIPLE-D SOFTWARE
MOM'S KNITTING COMPUTER PROGRAM (VER. 2.0)

Designed to assist the knitter when charting curves, collars, sleeves, necklines, and other patterns.

System: MAC, II, PLUS, SE, XL
Minimum Memory: 512K
Medium: 3 1/2-inch disk
ISPN: 82737-450 **Price: $49.95**

HEIZER SOFTWARE
MOVING GAME LEADS

Provides a table to figure the lead to allow at a distance of ten to 400 yards with game moving ten to 50 miles per hour.

System: MAC, II, PLUS, SE, XL
Minimum Memory: 512K
Requires: Microsoft Excel (ISPN 53150-270) or Microsoft Works (ISPN 53150-740).
Medium: 3 1/2-inch disk
ISPN: 35175-712 **Price: $5.00**

HEIZER SOFTWARE
RELATIVE STOPPING POWER

Figures the stopping power of any hand-loaded or commercial cartridge for either handguns or rifles.

System: MAC, II, PLUS, SE, XL
Minimum Memory: 512K
Requires: Microsoft Excel (ISPN 53150-270) or Microsoft Works (ISPN 53150-740).
Medium: 3 1/2-inch disk
ISPN: 35175-713 **Price: $5.00**

COMPU-QUOTE
REPORTER-COINS/PLUS VERSION

Customize reports for your Coins Plus program.

System: MAC, II, PLUS, SE, XL
Minimum Memory: 512K
Requires: One 800K disk drive or hard disk, Coins/Plus (ISPN 15387-110).
Medium: 3 1/2-inch disk
ISPN: 15387-554 **Price: $45.00**

COMPU-QUOTE
REPORTER-DONRUSS CARD/FAX VERSION

Customize reports for your Donruss Card/Fax program.

System: MAC, II, PLUS, SE, XL
Minimum Memory: 512K
Requires: One 800K disk drive or hard disk, Donruss Card/Fax (ISPN 15387-220).
Medium: 3 1/2-inch disk
ISPN: 15387-550 **Price: $45.00**

COMPU-QUOTE
REPORTER-FLEER CARD/FAX VERSION

Customize reports for your fleer Card/Fax program.

System: MAC, II, PLUS, SE, XL
Minimum Memory: 512K
Requires: One 800K disk drive or hard disk, Fleer Card/Fax (ISPN 15387-240).
Medium: 3 1/2-inch disk
ISPN: 15387-551 **Price: $45.00**

COMPU-QUOTE
REPORTER-STAMPS VERSION

Customize reports for your Stamps program.

System: MAC, II, PLUS, SE, XL
Minimum Memory: 512K
Requires: One 800K disk drive or hard disk, Stamps (ISPN 15387-600).
Medium: 3 1/2-inch disk
ISPN: 15387-553 **Price: $45.00**

COMPU-QUOTE

REPORTER-TOPPS CARD/FAX VERSION

Customize reports for your Topps Card/Fax program.

System: MAC, II, PLUS, SE, XL
Minimum Memory: 512K
Requires: One 800K disk drive or hard disk, Topps Card/Fax (ISPN 15387-200).
Medium: 3 1/2-inch disk
ISPN: 15387-552   **Price: $45.00**

COMPU-QUOTE

STAMPS (VER. 1.15)

Inventory and evaluate your U.S. stamp collection.

System: MAC, II, PLUS, SE, XL
Minimum Memory: 512K
Requires: One 800K disk drive or hard disk, printer.
Medium: 3 1/2-inch disk
ISPN: 15387-600   **Price: $95.00**

COMPU-QUOTE

STAMPS WORLD

Inventory and evaluate your world-wide and topical stamp collection.

System: MAC, II, PLUS, SE, XL
Minimum Memory: 512K
Requires: One 800K disk drive or hard disk.
Medium: 3 1/2-inch disk
ISPN: 15387-605   **Price: $65.00**

ZIHUA

ZIHUA MORSE (VER. 2.0)

Provides Morse code instructions. Users can send from keyboard, file, or randomly. User can adjust speed and characters.

System: MAC, II, PLUS, SE, XL
Minimum Memory: 512K
Medium: 3 1/2-inch disk
ISPN: 87412-900   **Price: $39.95**

450 PERSONAL/ HOUSEHOLD MANAGEMENT

HEIZER SOFTWARE

COMPARATIVE SHOPPER

A worksheet which records comparative costs on various items needed for a project.

System: MAC, PLUS, SE, XL
Minimum Memory: 512K
Requires: Microsoft Excel (ISPN 53150-270) or Microsoft Works (ISPN 53150-740).
Medium: 3 1/2-inch disk
ISPN: 35175-618   **Price: $8.00**

X-10 (USA), INC.

HOME CONTROL SOFTWARE

Uses a CP290 interface to program lights and appliances to turn on and off at preset times. Works with X-10 modules.

System: MAC, II, PLUS, SE, XL
Minimum Memory: 128K
Requires: Includes CP290 interface.
Medium: 3 1/2-inch disk
ISPN: 87034-800   **Price: $49.99**

HEIZER SOFTWARE

HOME UTILITY RECORDER

Records and analyzes gas and electric bills and seasonal consumption.

System: MAC, II, PLUS, SE, XL
Minimum Memory: 512K
Requires: Microsoft Excel (ISPN 53150-270) or Microsoft Works (ISPN 53150-740).
Medium: 3 1/2-inch disk
ISPN: 35175-616   **Price: $5.00**

HEIZER SOFTWARE

WALLPAPER CALCULATOR

Calculates the number of single and double wallpaper rolls required for a room.

System: MAC, II, PLUS, SE, XL
Minimum Memory: 512K
Requires: Microsoft Excel (ISPN 53150-270).
Medium: 3 1/2-inch disk
ISPN: 35175-619   **Price: $10.00**

453 PERSONAL/ MISCELLANEOUS PERSONAL

METACOMET SOFTWARE

ACCU-WEATHER FORECASTER

Uses telecommunications to access live weather information and forecasts.

System: MAC, II, PLUS, SE, XL
Minimum Memory: 1024K
Requires: Hayes compatible modem.
Medium: 3 1/2-inch disk
ISPN: 49223-100   **Price: $89.95**

QUEUE

ADDRESS BOOK/CARD FILE

Maintains a file of friends, clients and contacts.

System: MAC, II, PLUS, SE, XL
Minimum Memory: 128K
Medium: 3 1/2-inch disk
ISPN: 64387-005   **Price: $39.95**

HEIZER SOFTWARE

AUTO GAS RECORDER

Records and analyzes gas consumption, miles per gallon, and daily mileage.

System: MAC, II, PLUS, SE, XL
Minimum Memory: 512K
Requires: Microsoft Excel (ISPN 53150-270) or Microsoft Works (ISPN 53150-740).
Medium: 3 1/2-inch disk
ISPN: 35175-623   **Price: $5.00**

HEIZER SOFTWARE

AUTO LEASE VERSUS BUY

A comparative financial analysis for deciding whether to buy or lease a car.

System: MAC, II, PLUS, SE, XL
Minimum Memory: 512K
Requires: Microsoft Excel (ISPN 53150-270) or Microsoft Works (ISPN 53150-740).
Medium: 3 1/2-inch disk
ISPN: 35175-622   **Price: $10.00**

HEIZER SOFTWARE

BABY NAME SCRAMBLER

Prints possible combinations of first and middle names.

System: MAC, II, PLUS, SE, XL
Minimum Memory: 512K
Requires: Microsoft Excel (ISPN 53150-270).
Medium: 3 1/2-inch disk
ISPN: 35175-628   **Price: $9.00**

QUEUE

BABYSITTER'S MANUAL

Learn all about baby care.

System: MAC, II, PLUS, SE, XL
Minimum Memory: 128K
Medium: 3 1/2-inch disk
ISPN: 64387-134   **Price: $34.95**

LINGUIST'S SOFTWARE, INC.

BIBLE-KJV (VER. 1.0)

Contains the complete text of the King James Version of the Holy Bible, Old and New Testaments, and the Apocrypha.

System: MAC, II, PLUS, SE, XL
Minimum Memory: 512K
Requires: 800K disk drive.
Medium: 3 1/2-inch disk
ISPN: 44825-020   **Price: $9.95**

LINGUIST'S SOFTWARE, INC.

BIBLE-NIV (VER. 1.2)

Contains the complete text of the New International Version of the Bible, including the Old and New Testaments.

System: MAC, II, PLUS, SE, XL
Minimum Memory: 512K
Requires: 800K disk drive.
Medium: 3 1/2-inch disk
ISPN: 44825-022   **Price: $99.95**

LINGUIST'S SOFTWARE, INC.

BIBLE-RSV (VER. 1.0)

The complete text of the Revised Standard Version of the Bible on 7 800K diskettes.

System: MAC, II, PLUS, SE, XL
Minimum Memory: 512K
Requires: Microsoft Word (ISPN 53150-732).
Medium: 3 1/2-inch disk
ISPN: 44825-517   **Price: $99.95**

ALPHA & OMEGA

BIBLE-STACK KING JAMES VERSION

A HyperCard version of the King James Version of the Bible with chapter and verse search capabilities.

System: MAC, II, PLUS, SE, XL
Minimum Memory: 1024K
Requires: HyperCard (ISPN 03900-300), hard disk.
Medium: 3 1/2-inch disk
ISPN: 02330-100   **Price: $120.00**

ALPHA & OMEGA

BIBLE-STACK NIV VERSION

A HyperCard version of the New International Version of the Bible with chapter and verse search capabilities.

System: MAC, II, PLUS, SE, XL
Minimum Memory: 1024K
Requires: HyperCard (ISPN 03900-300), hard disk.
Medium: 3 1/2-inch disk
ISPN: 02330-110   **Price: $120.00**

LINGUIST'S SOFTWARE, INC.

BIBLE-VULGATE (VER. 1.0)

The entire text of the Latin Vulgate translation of the Bible with Old and New Testaments, Apocrypha and textual notations of variants

System: MAC, II, PLUS, SE, XL
Minimum Memory: 512K
Requires: Microsoft Word (ISPN 53150-732).
Medium: 3 1/2-inch disk
ISPN: 44825-190   **Price: $99.95**

HEIZER SOFTWARE

BIRTH COUNTDOWN

Calculates and prints a dated, week-by-week calendar which covers stages in the development of the fetus.

System: MAC, II, PLUS, SE, XL
Minimum Memory: 512K
Requires: Microsoft Excel (ISPN 53150-270) or Microsoft Works (ISPN 53150-740).
Medium: 3 1/2-inch disk
ISPN: 35175-626   **Price: $8.00**

HEIZER SOFTWARE

BIRTH COUNTDOWN AND BIRTH PLAN CHECKLIST

Calculates and prints out a dated, week-by-week calendar which covers fetus development. Includes a checklist of birth options.

System: MAC, PLUS, SE, XL
Minimum Memory: 512K
Requires: Microsoft Excel (ISPN 53150-270) or Microsoft Works (ISPN 53150-740).
Medium: 3 1/2-inch disk
ISPN: 35175-627   **Price: $12.00**

HEIZER SOFTWARE

CAR OPERATING COSTS

Calculates the total annual costs and per mile vehicle operation costs.

System: MAC, II, PLUS, SE, XL
Minimum Memory: 512K
Requires: Microsoft Excel (ISPN 53150-270) or Microsoft Works (ISPN 53150-740).
Medium: 3 1/2-inch disk
ISPN: 35175-621   **Price: $8.00**

BIBLE RESEARCH SYSTEMS

CHAIN REFERENCE

Provides over 55,000 chains that associate a specific word in a verse with a list of other verses from which references are added.

System: MAC, II, PLUS, SE, XL
Minimum Memory: 512K
Requires: The Word Processor (ISPN 07546-any version).
Medium: 3 1/2-inch disk
ISPN: 07546-240   **Price: $49.95**

BIBLE RESEARCH SYSTEMS

CHRONOLOGICAL BIBLE

Gives a chronological view of the Bible.

System: MAC, II, PLUS, SE, XL
Minimum Memory: 512K
Requires: The Word Processor (ISPN 07546-any version).
Medium: 3 1/2-inch disk
ISPN: 07546-250   **Price: $49.95**

HEIZER SOFTWARE

DATE OF EASTER

Computes the day and month of Easter for any year after 1582.

System: MAC, II, PLUS, SE, XL
Minimum Memory: 512K
Requires: Microsoft Excel (ISPN 53150-270) or Microsoft Works (ISPN 53150-740).
Medium: 3 1/2-inch disk
ISPN: 35175-182   **Price: $3.00**

MEDINA SOFTWARE, INC.

ELECTRO BITS (SPANISH VERSION)

A graphic tool containing a library of several hundred electronic elements and computer symbols that employ the MacPaint function.

System: MAC, II, PLUS, SE, XL
Minimum Memory: 128K
Requires: MacPaint (ISPN 12784-510) or any program that can read MacPaint format files.
Medium: 3 1/2-inch disk
ISPN: 48842-301   **Price: $24.95**

CHATEAU SOFTWARE

FIND A MATE

This program enables user to determine from several options which mate is best suited.

System: PLUS
Minimum Memory: 512K
Requires: Speech Synthesizer and speech editor.
Medium: 3 1/2-inch disk
ISPN: 12400-100   **Price: $110.00**

HEIZER SOFTWARE

FREQUENT FLYER FLIGHT LOG-US

Keeps track of flights, mileage, bonus miles, purpose of trip and class of service for United States and major Canadian airports.

System: MAC, II, PLUS, SE, XL
Minimum Memory: 1024K
Requires: Microsoft Excel (ISPN 53150-270).
Medium: 3 1/2-inch disk
ISPN: 35175-202   **Price: $25.00**

HEIZER SOFTWARE

FREQUENT FLYER FLIGHT LOG-US AND FOREIGN

Keeps track of flights, mileage, bonus miles, purpose of trip and class of service for all major airports around the world.

System: MAC, II, PLUS, SE, XL
Minimum Memory: 1024K
Requires: Microsoft Excel (ISPN 53150-270).
Medium: 3 1/2-inch disk
ISPN: 35175-203   **Price: $35.00**

STAR SOFTWARE, INC.

GREEK NEW TESTAMENT MODULE

Contains the Greek New Testament UBS Third Edition (corrected) for use with ThePerfectWORD.

System: MAC, II, PLUS, SE, XL
Minimum Memory: 1024K
Requires: ThePerfectWORD (ISPN 96954-700). Two 800K disk drives or a hard disk.
Medium: 3 1/2-inch disk
ISPN: 75856-300   **Price: $150.00**

BIBLE RESEARCH SYSTEMS

GREEK TRANSLITERATOR

The King James Version of the Bible with Strongs reference numbers assigned to the English words.

System: MAC, II, PLUS, SE, XL
Minimum Memory: 512K
Medium: 3 1/2-inch disk
ISPN: 07546-320   **Price: $199.95**

STAR SOFTWARE, INC.

HEBREW BIBLE MODULE

Contains the Biblia Hebraica Stuttgartensia version of the Hebrew Bible for use with ThePerfectWORD.

System: MAC, II, PLUS, SE, XL
Minimum Memory: 1024K
Requires: ThePerfectWORD (ISPN 96954-700). Hard disk.
Medium: 3 1/2-inch disk
ISPN: 75856-350   **Price: $180.00**

BIBLE RESEARCH SYSTEMS

HEBREW TRANSLITERATOR

Helps the individual without a great knowledge of Hebrew to study the Old Testament.

System: MAC, II, PLUS, SE, XL
Minimum Memory: 512K
Medium: 3 1/2-inch disk
ISPN: 07546-330   **Price: $249.95**

BERT MONROY
HUMANFORMS

Approximately 1000 drawings of individual parts of the human body. Assemble the parts in MacPaint to create various illustrations.
System: MAC, II, PLUS, SE, XL
Minimum Memory: 128K
Requires: MacPaint (ISPN 12784-510) or program that can read MacPaint files.
Medium: 3 1/2-inch disk
ISPN: 65712-100   **Price: $59.95**

BRIGHT IDEAS, INC.
HYPER CHRISTMAS CARD (VER. 1.0)

Contains an interactive Christmas card with carols, stories and an Advent Calendar, with graphics, designed as a HyperCard stack.
System: MAC, II, PLUS, SE, XL
Minimum Memory: 1024K
Requires: HyperCard (ISPN 03900-300).
Medium: 3 1/2-inch disk
ISPN: 08456-410   **Price: $39.95**

BEACON TECHNOLOGY, INC.
HYPERBIBLE (KJV) (VER. 1.0)

A HyperCard adaptation of the King James Version of the Thompson Chain Reference Bible. Includes a copy of HyperCard Version 1.21.
System: MAC, II, PLUS, SE, XL
Minimum Memory: 1024K
Requires: Hard disk.
Medium: 3 1/2-inch disk
ISPN: 07156-300   **Price: $229.95**

BEACON TECHNOLOGY, INC.
HYPERBIBLE (NIV) (VER. 1.0)

A HyperCard adaptation of the New International Version of the Thompson Chain Reference Bible. Includes HyperCard (Ver. 1.21).
System: MAC, II, PLUS, SE, XL
Minimum Memory: 1024K
Requires: Hard disk.
Medium: 3 1/2-inch disk
ISPN: 07156-305   **Price: $279.95**

DAVKA CORP.
HYPERSEDER (VER. 1.0)

A Judaic HyperCard stack that describes and teaches about Passover.
System: MAC, II, PLUS, SE, XL
Minimum Memory: 1024K
Requires: HyperCard (ISPN 03900-300).
Medium: 3 1/2-inch disk
ISPN: 91205-295   **Price: $34.95**

CAMTRONICS, INC.
HYPERSHOPPER (VER. 1.0)

Lists over 1000 mail order companies and factory outlets. Helps find suppliers of unique or specific products.
System: MAC, II, PLUS, SE, XL
Minimum Memory: 1024K
Requires: Two disk drives, HyperCard (ISPN 03900-300).
Medium: 3 1/2-inch disk
ISPN: 10923-300   **Price: $19.95**

MEDIAGENIC/TENPOINT0
HYPERWARE BIRTHDAY BUNDLE

Contains the Focal Point and Business Class Hypercard stacks which tracks information and provides information on 65 countries.
System: MAC, II, PLUS, SE, XL
Minimum Memory: 1024K
Requires: Hypercard (ISPN 03900-300).
Medium: 3 1/2-inch disk
ISPN: 48702-300   **Price: $99.95**

BIBLE RESEARCH SYSTEMS
INSTANT ACCESS

Find any word or phrase in the Bible.
System: MAC, II, PLUS, SE, XL
Minimum Memory: 512K
Requires: The Word Processor (ISPN 07546-any version).
Medium: 3 1/2-inch disk
ISPN: 07546-350   **Price: $49.95**

STAR SOFTWARE, INC.
KING JAMES VERSION MODULE

The entire King James Version of the Bible for use with ThePerfectWORD.
System: MAC, II, PLUS, SE, XL
Minimum Memory: 1024K
Requires: ThePerfectWORD (ISPN 96954-700). Two 800K disk drives or a hard disk.
Medium: 3 1/2-inch disk
ISPN: 75856-400   **Price: $75.00**

TISCHREDE SOFTWARE
LEXEGETE-MATTHEW (VER. 1.1)

A 3-disk set of bible research documents based on the Gospel of Matthew by 35 scholars, useful in sermon preparation.
System: MAC, PLUS, SE, XL
Minimum Memory: 512K
Requires: MacWrite (ISPN 12784-530) or Microsoft Word (ISPN 53150-732).
Medium: 3 1/2-inch disk
ISPN: 82132-600   **Price: $59.95**

HEIZER SOFTWARE
LIFE PLANNER

A spreadsheet set up to plot major events which occur in a lifetime.
System: MAC, II, PLUS, SE, XL
Minimum Memory: 512K
Requires: Microsoft Works (ISPN 53150-740) or Microsoft Excel (ISPN 53150-270).
Medium: 3 1/2-inch disk
ISPN: 35175-830   **Price: $2.00**

ENCYCLOWARE
MACBIBLE-KING JAMES VERSION

A 25-disk file set of the King James version of the Bible. Complete Old and New Testaments.
System: MAC, II, PLUS, SE, XL
Minimum Memory: 128K
Medium: 3 1/2-inch disk
ISPN: 29087-450   **Price: $119.00**

ENCYCLOWARE
MACBIBLE-NEW INTERNATIONAL VERSION

Provides a 25 disk file set of the New International Version of the Bible.
System: MAC, II, PLUS, SE, XL
Minimum Memory: 128K
Medium: 3 1/2-inch disk
ISPN: 29087-260   **Price: $119.00**

MEDINA SOFTWARE, INC.
MACCONCORD I

Concordance of the New Testament. Features more than 10,000 references from the King James Bible.
System: MAC, II, PLUS, SE, XL
Minimum Memory: 128K
Requires: MacWrite (ISPN 12784-530), Microsoft Word (ISPN 53150-732) or compatible word processor.
Medium: 3 1/2-inch disk
ISPN: 48842-500   **Price: $24.95**

MEDINA SOFTWARE, INC.
MACGOSPEL (KING JAMES VERSION)

Contains the gospels according to Matthew, Mark, Luke and John.
System: MAC, II, PLUS, SE, XL
Minimum Memory: 128K
Requires: MacWrite (ISPN 12784-530), Microsoft Word (ISPN 53150-732) or HyperCard ISPN 03900-300).
Medium: 3 1/2-inch disk
ISPN: 48842-515   **Price: $24.95**

MEDINA SOFTWARE, INC.
MACSCRIPTURE I-NEW TESTAMENT (KJV)

Contains the King James version of the New Testament.
System: MAC, PLUS, SE, XL
Minimum Memory: 512K
Requires: MacWrite (ISPN 03900-417), Microsoft Word (ISPN 53150-732) or compatible word processor, 800K disk drive.
Medium: 3 1/2-inch disk
ISPN: 48842-550   **Price: $39.95**

MEDINA SOFTWARE, INC.
MACSCRIPTURE II-OLD TESTAMENT (KJV)

Contains the Old Testament. (King James Version).
System: MAC, II, PLUS, SE, XL
Minimum Memory: 512K
Requires: MacWrite (ISPN 12784-530), Microsoft Word (ISPN 53150-732) or compatible word processor.
Medium: 3 1/2-inch disk
ISPN: 48842-555   **Price: $79.95**

MEDINA SOFTWARE, INC.

MACSCRIPTURE-OLD AND NEW TESTAMENTS (KING JAMES)

Contains both the Old and New Testaments.

System: MAC, II, PLUS, SE, XL
Minimum Memory: 512K
Requires: MacWrite (ISPN 12784-530), Microsoft Word (ISPN 53150-732) or compatible word processor. Specify 400K or 800K disks in order.
Medium: 3 1/2-inch disk
ISPN: 48842-545 **Price: $99.95**

HEIZER SOFTWARE

MOVIE MINDER

Manages home-video cassette libraries with title year, comments, tape numbers and locations on tapes.

System: MAC, II, PLUS, SE, XL
Minimum Memory: 1024K
Requires: HyperCard (ISPN 03900-300).
Medium: 3 1/2-inch disk
ISPN: 35175-418 **Price: $20.00**

STAR SOFTWARE, INC.

NEW INTERNATIONAL VERSION MODULE

Contains the entire New International Version of the Bible for use with ThePerfectWORD.

System: MAC, PLUS, SE, XL
Minimum Memory: 1024K
Requires: ThePerfectWORD (ISPN 96954-700). Two 800K disk drives or a hard disk.
Medium: 3 1/2-inch disk
ISPN: 75856-500 **Price: $75.00**

BIBLE RESEARCH SYSTEMS

PEOPLE

Find a frequently referenced biblical person.

System: MAC, II, PLUS, SE, XL
Minimum Memory: 512K
Requires: The Word Processor (ISPN 07546-any version).
Medium: 3 1/2-inch disk
ISPN: 07546-500 **Price: $49.95**

BIBLE RESEARCH SYSTEMS

PERSONAL COMMENTARY

Provides a full-featured text editor for entering, editing, saving, retrieving and printing commentary for any verse in the Bible.

System: MAC, II, PLUS, SE, XL
Minimum Memory: 512K
Requires: The Word Processor (ISPN 07546-any version), Greek Transliterator (ISPN 07546-320) or Hebrew Transliterator (ISPN 07546-330).
Medium: 3 1/2-inch disk
ISPN: 07546-600 **Price: $49.95**

HEIZER SOFTWARE

PERSONAL PRODUCTIVITY WORKS

Contains twelve programs including personal budget, checkbook, mortgage/loan calculations, about expense log, & vacation planner.

System: MAC, II, PLUS, SE, XL
Minimum Memory: 512K
Requires: Microsoft Works (ISPN 53150-740).
Medium: 3 1/2-inch disk
ISPN: 35175-600 **Price: $50.00**

VIKING TECHNOLOGIES

PHOTO TIME

Unique digitized pictures of jets, helicopters, music, children and symbols.

System: MAC, II, PLUS, SE, XL
Minimum Memory: 128K
Medium: 3 1/2-inch disk
ISPN: 85231-600 **Price: $19.95**

CASADY & GREENE, INC.

QUICKDEX (VER. 1.4A)

A free-form database desk accessory with auto-dialer that allows users to find data instantly from within any program.

System: MAC, II, PLUS, SE, XL
Minimum Memory: 512K
Medium: 3 1/2-inch disk
ISPN: 11556-700 **Price: $60.00**

MEDINA SOFTWARE, INC.

RELIGIOUS ART PORTFOLIO (VOL. 1) (ENGLISH)

A selected collection of historic Christian symbols and digitized images of the life of Jesus Christ.

System: MAC, II, PLUS, SE, XL
Minimum Memory: 128K
Requires: MacPaint (ISPN 12784-510), MacBillboard (ISPN 11725-205), Picturebase (ISPN 77437-550) or HyperCard (ISPN 03900-300).
Medium: 3 1/2-inch disk
ISPN: 48842-590 **Price: $24.95**

MEDINA SOFTWARE, INC.

RELIGIOUS ART PORTFOLIO (VOL. 1) (SPANISH)

A selected collection of historic Christian symbols and digitized images of the life of Jesus Christ.

System: MAC, II, PLUS, SE, XL
Minimum Memory: 128K
Requires: MacPaint (ISPN 12784-510), MacBillboard (ISPN 11725-205), PictureBase (ISPN 77437-550) or HyperCard (ISPN 03900-300).
Medium: 3 1/2-inch disk
ISPN: 48842-591 **Price: $24.95**

STAR SOFTWARE, INC.

REVISED STANDARD VERSION MODULE

The Revised Standard Version of the Bible for use with ThePerfectWORD.

System: MAC, II, PLUS, SE, XL
Minimum Memory: 1024K
Requires: ThePerfectWORD (ISPN 96954-700). Two 800K disk drives or a hard disk.
Medium: 3 1/2-inch disk
ISPN: 75856-600 **Price: $75.00**

MEDINA SOFTWARE, INC.

SCRIPTURE BITS (ENGLISH)

A series of MacWrite documents containing scripture references that include 360 quotes under 200 topics from Old and New Testaments.

System: MAC, II, PLUS, SE, XL
Minimum Memory: 128K
Requires: MacWrite (ISPN 12784-530), Microsoft Word (ISPN 53150-732) or compatible word processor.
Medium: 3 1/2-inch disk
ISPN: 48842-600 **Price: $22.00**

MEDINA SOFTWARE, INC.

SCRIPTURE BITS (SPANISH VERSION)

A series of MacWrite documents containing scripture references including 360 quotes under 200 topics from Old and New Testament.

System: MAC, II, PLUS, SE, XL
Minimum Memory: 128K
Requires: MacWrite (ISPN 12784-530), Microsoft Word (ISPN 53150-732) or compatible word processing program.
Medium: 3 1/2-inch disk
ISPN: 48842-601 **Price: $22.00**

ANDROS SOFTWEAR

SEWSOFT BASIC BODICE (VER. 1.6)

Provides consistent sewing patterns based on user input of specific dimensions.

System: MAC, PLUS, SE, XL
Minimum Memory: 512K
Requires: 800K disk drive, printer.
Medium: 3 1/2-inch disk
ISPN: 03648-700 **Price: $79.95**

MEDINA SOFTWARE, INC.

SPELLING DICTIONARY (VER. 1.0)

A 20,000 plus word medical, religious and technical dictionary used with Microsoft Word.

System: MAC, II, PLUS, SE, XL
Minimum Memory: 512K
Requires: Microsoft Word (ISPN 53150-732).
Medium: 3 1/2-inch disk
ISPN: 48842-565 **Price: $24.95**

STAR SOFTWARE, INC.
THEPERFECTWORD (VER. 2.0)

Designed for Bible study and research, which gives rapid word and phrase search capability, verse text display and word counts.

System: MAC, II, PLUS, SE, XL
Minimum Memory: 1024K
Requires: Two 800K disk drives or a hard disk. Requires one or more of five available modules.
Medium: 3 1/2-inch disk
ISPN: 75856-700   **Price: $224.00**

BIBLE RESEARCH SYSTEMS
TOPICS

A topical cross-reference of the Bible.

System: MAC, II, PLUS, SE, XL
Minimum Memory: 512K
Requires: The Word Processor (ISPN 07564-any version).
Medium: 3 1/2-inch disk
ISPN: 07546-700   **Price: $49.95**

DAVKA CORP.
VEZOT HATORAH (VER. 1.0)

Reveals reasons behind sacred traditions of the Torah Reading Service.

System: MAC, II, PLUS, SE, XL
Minimum Memory: 1024K
Medium: 3 1/2-inch disk
ISPN: 91205-800   **Price: $39.95**

HEIZER SOFTWARE
VIDEO COUNT TO TIME

Converts Video Cassette Recording to time remaining on tape.

System: MAC, II, PLUS, SE, XL
Minimum Memory: 512K
Requires: Microsoft Excel (ISPN 53150-270).
Medium: 3 1/2-inch disk
ISPN: 35175-266   **Price: $14.00**

INTRACORP, INC.
VIDEO WIZARD (VER. 1.2)

Your VCR and your computer – a new partnership.

System: MAC, II, PLUS, SE, XL
Minimum Memory: 512K
Medium: 3 1/2-inch disk
ISPN: 40531-800   **Price: $29.95**

HEIZER SOFTWARE
WEDDING PLANNER

A checklist which covers dress fitting, buying the ring, renting tuxedos and arranging for a church.

System: MAC, II, PLUS, SE, XL
Minimum Memory: 512K
Requires: Microsoft Excel (ISPN 53150-270), Microsoft Works (ISPN 53150-740) or HyperCard (ISPN 03900-300).
Medium: 3 1/2-inch disk
ISPN: 35175-625   **Price: $10.00**

BIBLE RESEARCH SYSTEMS
WORD PROCESSOR-KING JAMES VERSION

Entire text of the Bible with ability to search for words or phrases, great permanent cross references useful to personal study.

System: MAC, II, PLUS, SE, XL
Minimum Memory: 512K
Medium: 3 1/2-inch disk
ISPN: 07546-100   **Price: $199.95**

BIBLE RESEARCH SYSTEMS
WORD PROCESSOR-NEW INTERNATIONAL VERSION

Contains the text of the Bible. Provides the ability to search for words or phrases, or create permanent cross references.

System: MAC, II, PLUS, SE, XL
Minimum Memory: 512K
Medium: 3 1/2-inch disk
ISPN: 07546-150   **Price: $199.95**

BIBLE RESEARCH SYSTEMS
WORD PROCESSOR-NEW KING JAMES VERSION

Provides an extensive analytical tool for the New King James version of the Bible.

System: MAC, PLUS, SE, XL
Minimum Memory: 512K
Medium: 3 1/2-inch disk
ISPN: 07546-110   **Price: $199.95**

BIBLE RESEARCH SYSTEMS
WORD PROCESSOR-RSV WITH APOCRYPHA

Provides an extensive analytical tool for the text of the Revised Standard Version (RSV) including Apocrypha.

System: MAC, PLUS, SE, XL
Minimum Memory: 512K
Medium: 3 1/2-inch disk
ISPN: 07546-170   **Price: $199.95**

---

456 PERSONAL/MUSIC

SONUS
7TH HEAVEN

Incorporates artificial intelligence into a music generator and educational music product.

System: MAC, II, PLUS, SE, XL
Minimum Memory: 512K
Requires: Sonus Macface MIDI interface.
Medium: 3 1/2-inch disk
ISPN: 74679-700   **Price: $79.95**

GREAT WAVE SOFTWARE
ART OF FUGUE IN D MINOR (VOL. 2)

The complete Art of Fugue by Johann Sebastian Bach.

System: MAC, II, PLUS, SE, XL
Minimum Memory: 512K
Medium: 3 1/2-inch disk
ISPN: 33476-050   **Price: $15.00**

BAUDVILLE
AUDIO CASSETTE LABELER

Shows an information window where you may enter the artist, title, company, recording year and up to twelve songs for each cassette.

System: MAC, II, PLUS, SE, XL
Minimum Memory: 512K
Medium: 3 1/2-inch disk
ISPN: 07087-050   **Price: $49.95**

MACMIDI
BROADWAY SHOWTUNES-VIRTUOSO PIANIST LIBRARY

A collection of digitized children's tunes, Broadway show tunes, movie themes, and holiday music in a MIDI format.

System: MAC, II, PLUS, SE, XL
Minimum Memory: 512K
Requires: Virtuoso Pianist (ISPN 55865-700), MIDI synthesizer, MacMIDI compatible interface.
Medium: 3 1/2-inch disk
ISPN: 55865-102   **Price: $199.00**

GREAT WAVE SOFTWARE
CHRISTMAS FAVORITES (VOL. 3)

Contains a collection of Christmas songs, including a large section from Handel's Messiah.

System: MAC, II, PLUS, SE, XL
Minimum Memory: 512K
Medium: 3 1/2-inch disk
ISPN: 33476-075   **Price: $15.00**

MACMIDI
CLASSICAL PIANO-VIRTUOSO PIANIST LIBRARY

A collection of digitized classical piano performances in the MIDI format.

System: MAC, II, PLUS, SE, XL
Minimum Memory: 512K
Requires: Virtuoso Pianist (ISPN 55865-700), MIDI synthesizer, MacMIDI compatible interface.
Medium: 3 1/2-inch disk
ISPN: 55865-100   **Price: $199.00**

GREAT WAVE SOFTWARE
CLASSICAL SELECTIONS (VOL. 5)

Provides a collection of favorite classical music, including the complete Four Seasons by Vivaldi.

System: MAC, II, PLUS, SE, XL
Minimum Memory: 512K
Medium: 3 1/2-inch disk
ISPN: 33476-080   **Price: $15.00**

PASSPORT DESIGNS, INC.
CLICKTRACKS

Provides a tool for scoring music to 'hits' on video or film. Can be used alone or in conjunction with a MIDI sequencer.

System: II, PLUS, SE, XL
Minimum Memory: 512K
Medium: 3 1/2-inch disk
ISPN: 59781-025   **Price: $495.00**

GREAT WAVE SOFTWARE
CONCERTWARE MUSIC (VOL. 6) POPULAR MUSIC 1900-1930

Provides a collection of popular songs from 1900 to 1930.

System: MAC, II, PLUS, SE, XL
Minimum Memory: 512K
Requires: Concertware + (ISPN 33476-151).
Medium: 3 1/2-inch disk
ISPN: 33476-140   **Price: $15.00**

GREAT WAVE SOFTWARE
CONCERTWARE+ (VER. 4) (REGULAR)

Create, edit, print and play music files as well as create new instrument sounds. Some music and instruments included.

System: MAC, II, PLUS, SE, XL
Minimum Memory: 512K
Medium: 3 1/2-inch disk
ISPN: 33476-151   **Price: $69.95**

GREAT WAVE SOFTWARE
CONCERTWARE+MIDI (VER. 4.0)

Using a MIDI adapter , compose, edit, and play music through a compatible synthesizer.

System: MAC, II, PLUS, SE, XL
Minimum Memory: 512K
Requires: One or more MIDI-equipped instruments, any Macintosh MIDI interface.
Medium: 3 1/2-inch disk
ISPN: 33476-160   **Price: $149.95**

MACMIDI
CONTEMPORARY-VIRTUOSO PIANIST LIBRARY

A collection of digitized contemporary performances in the MIDI format.

System: II, PLUS, SE, XL
Minimum Memory: 512K
Requires: Virtuoso Pianist (ISPN 55865-700), MIDI synthesizer, MacMIDI compatible interface.
Medium: 3 1/2-inch disk
ISPN: 55865-106   **Price: $199.00**

SONUS
D-50 DESIGN

Contains a mouse-based editor/librarian for the Roland D-50.

System: MAC, II, PLUS, SE, XL
Minimum Memory: 512K
Requires: Any major Macintosh MIDI interface (Includes Sonus MacFace Interface), Roland D-50 or D-550 synthesizer
Medium: 3 1/2-inch disk
ISPN: 74679-220   **Price: $149.95**

ELECTRONIC ARTS
DELUXE MUSIC CONSTRUCTION SET (VER. 2.0)

Teaches music without having to learn a musical instrument, redesigned to take full advantage of the Macintosh.

System: MAC, PLUS, SE, XL
Minimum Memory: 128K
Medium: 3 1/2-inch disk
ISPN: 28512-080   **Price: $99.95**

ELECTRONIC ARTS
DELUXE MUSIC CONSTRUCTION SET-MIDI

Gives the user better control over composition with a range of musical options and mouse control.

System: MAC, II, PLUS, SE, XL
Minimum Memory: 128K
Medium: 3 1/2-inch disk
ISPN: 28512-106   **Price: $129.95**

PRIMERA SOFTWARE
DIFFERENT DRUMMER (VER. 1.0)

Turns your Mac into a drum machine. Plays over Mac, MIDI, writes MIDI files and includes a visual interface.

System: MAC, II, PLUS, SE, XL
Minimum Memory: 512K
Requires: Two 800K drives.
Medium: 3 1/2-inch disk
ISPN: 62018-100   **Price: $99.95**

DIGITAL MUSIC SERVICES
DMP11 PRO

Works with the Yamaha DMP11 (Digital Music Processor) to make it easier to use, and adds features not on the DMP11 itself.

System: MAC, II, PLUS, SE, XL
Minimum Memory: 1024K
Requires: Yamaha DMP11 and a MIDI interface.
Medium: 3 1/2-inch disk
ISPN: 25450-211   **Price: $295.00**

DIGITAL MUSIC SERVICES
DMP7 PRO

Works with the Yamaha DMP7 (Digital Music Processor) to make its features easier to use and adds important features not on the DMP7.

System: MAC, II, PLUS, SE, XL
Minimum Memory: 1024K
Requires: Yamaha DMP7 and a MIDI interface.
Medium: 3 1/2-inch disk
ISPN: 25450-207   **Price: $395.00**

OPCODE SYSTEMS
DX/TX EDITOR/LIBRARIAN

Eases the programming digital FM synthesis algorithms by displaying every parameter of a sound on a high-resolution Macintosh.

System: MAC, II, PLUS, SE, XL
Minimum Memory: 512K
Medium: 3 1/2-inch disk
ISPN: 58384-525   **Price: $200.00**

DIGITAL MUSIC SERVICES
DX7 II PRO

An integrated editor/librarian for the Yamaha DX7 II synthesizer with voices, performances, microtunings and systems setups.

System: MAC, II, PLUS, SE, XL
Minimum Memory: 512K
Requires: Yamaha DX7 II and a MIDI interface.
Medium: 3 1/2-inch disk
ISPN: 25450-235   **Price: $199.00**

GREAT WAVE SOFTWARE
EARLY MUSIC (VOL. 4)

A collection of music from the Renaissance period.

System: MAC, II, PLUS, SE, XL
Minimum Memory: 512K
Medium: 3 1/2-inch disk
ISPN: 33476-161   **Price: $15.00**

RAECREATIONS SOFTWARE
EARLY MUSIC FOR MUSICWORKS

Contains more than 60 music files of early music of many different styles, sounds and moods.

System: MAC, II, PLUS, SE, XL
Minimum Memory: 512K
Requires: 800K disk drive.
Medium: 3 1/2-inch disk
ISPN: 64887-250   **Price: $15.00**

PASSPORT DESIGNS, INC.
ENCORE (VER. 1.0)

A music transcription program for composing and transcribing sequencer files into notation.

System: MAC, II, PLUS, SE, XL
Minimum Memory: 512K
Requires: ImageWriter, LaserWriter or PostScript compatible printer.
Medium: 3 1/2-inch disk
ISPN: 59781-030   **Price: $495.00**

DIGITAL MUSIC SERVICES
FB PRO

A voicing and librarian for the Yamaha FB-01 with hundreds of supplied voices.

System: MAC, PLUS, SE, XL
Minimum Memory: 512K
Requires: Yamaha FB-01 and a MIDI interface.
Medium: 3 1/2-inch disk
ISPN: 25450-220   **Price: $129.00**

CODA MUSIC SOFTWARE, DIV. OF WENGER CORP.
FINALE

Allows musicians and composers to transcribe musical notations from ideas to paper using MIDI equipment, pointing devices or keyboards.

System: MAC, II, PLUS, SE, XL
Minimum Memory: 1024K
Requires: SCSI hard drive.
Medium: 3 1/2-inch disk
ISPN: 55862-267   **Price: $1000.00**

DIGIDESIGN, INC.
FX DESIGNER (VER. 1.0)

Edits effects, provide MIDI patching capabilities, and saves user created patches for the Lexicon PCM 70 Digital Effects Processor.

System: MAC, II, PLUS, SE, XL
Minimum Memory: 512K
Requires: MIDI interface.
Medium: 3 1/2-inch disk
ISPN: 25212-220   **Price: $295.00**

MACMIDI

GREAT POPULAR COMPOSERS-VIRTUOSO PIANIST LIBRARY

A collection of digitized Gershwin, Porter and Lennon-McCartney performances in the MIDI format.

System: MAC, II, PLUS, SE, XL
Minimum Memory: 512K
Requires: Virtuoso Pianist (ISPN 55865-700), MIDI synthesizer, MacMIDI compatible interface.
Medium: 3 1/2-inch disk
ISPN: 55865-103   **Price: $199.00**

NAPPO SOFTWARE

GUITAR TUTOR

Program for the Macintosh to teach beginning guitarists the correct finger positions of basic chords.

System: MAC, II, PLUS, SE, XL
Minimum Memory: 512K
Medium: 3 1/2-inch disk
ISPN: 55956-300   **Price: $49.95**

BAUDVILLE

GUITAR WIZARD

Learn and analyze the fingerings and fretboard patterns for all types of chords and scales, from the simple to the exotic.

System: MAC, II, PLUS, SE, XL
Minimum Memory: 128K
Medium: 3 1/2-inch disk
ISPN: 07087-200   **Price: $34.95**

FROG PEAK MUSIC

HMSL

A programming language for experiments in music composition with object oriented extensions to Forth for MIDI synthesizers.

System: MAC, II, PLUS, SE, XL
Minimum Memory: 1024K
Requires: MIDI synthesizer, MIDI interface, and Mach2 FORTH (ISPN 52546-400).
Medium: 3 1/2-inch disk
ISPN: 91854-350   **Price: $150.00**

MACMIDI

IMPROVASATIONAL ARTS-VIRTUOSO PIANIST LIBRARY

A collection of digitized jazz, ragtime, stride, swing and boogie performances in the MIDI format.

System: MAC, II, PLUS, SE, XL
Minimum Memory: 512K
Requires: Virtuoso Pianist (ISPN 55865-700), MIDI synthesizer, MacMIDI compatible interface.
Medium: 3 1/2-inch disk
ISPN: 55865-101   **Price: $199.00**

GREAT WAVE SOFTWARE

INSTRUMENTAL FAVORITES (VOL. 1)

A collection of favorite classical and ragtime music.

System: MAC, PLUS, SE, XL
Minimum Memory: 512K
Medium: 3 1/2-inch disk
ISPN: 33476-163   **Price: $15.00**

INTELLIGENT MUSIC

JAM FACTORY (VER. 1.32)

Consists of four 'players' which 'learn' from material played on a MIDI keyboard. Users can improvise, perform and compose music.

System: MAC, II, PLUS, SE, XL
Minimum Memory: 512K
Requires: MIDI interface, MIDI synthesizer.
Medium: 3 1/2-inch disk
ISPN: 39007-400   **Price: $200.00**

BRODERBUND SOFTWARE, INC.

JAM SESSION

Enables anyone to play professional-sounding music without having a musical background.

System: MAC, II, PLUS, SE, XL
Minimum Memory: 512K
Medium: 3 1/2-inch disk
ISPN: 08850-112   **Price: $49.95**

SOUTHWORTH MUSIC SYSTEMS

JAMBOX/4

A four input for output MIDI merger, muting device and SMPTE reader generator, and synchronizer.

System: MAC, II, PLUS, SE, XL
Minimum Memory:
Medium: 3 1/2-inch disk
ISPN: 75101-300   **Price: $389.00**

DR. T'S MUSIC SOFTWARE

KEYBOARD CONTROLLED SEQUENCER (KCS) LEVEL II W-PVG

Allows chaining of music sequences together to form songs using the Track, Open and Song modes and a Programmable Variations Generator.

System: MAC, II, PLUS, SE, XL
Minimum Memory: 512K
Medium: 3 1/2-inch disk
ISPN: 26762-400   **Price: $349.00**

RESONATE

LISTEN (VER. 2.0 REV. 2.1)

Interactive music program providing melodic and harmonic ear training. Piano and guitar on screen or MIDI.

System: MAC, II, PLUS, SE, XL
Minimum Memory: 128K
Medium: 3 1/2-inch disk
ISPN: 37193-400   **Price: $99.00**

INTELLIGENT MUSIC

M (VER. 2.0)

Allows user to shape or change any aspect of a composition while hearing it.

System: MAC, II, PLUS, SE, XL
Minimum Memory: 512K
Requires: MIDI interface and MIDI synthesizer.
Medium: 3 1/2-inch disk
ISPN: 39007-500   **Price: $250.00**

PARK ROW SOFTWARE

MACCAROLS (VER. 2.0)

Contains a Christmas disk with the ability to sing or play twenty popular Christmas carols in eight languages.

System: MAC, II, PLUS, SE, XL
Minimum Memory: 128K
Medium: 3 1/2-inch disk
ISPN: 59755-130   **Price: $19.95**

CODA MUSIC SOFTWARE, DIV. OF WENGER CORP.

MACDRUMS

A self-contained, full programmable, 4-voice polyphonic drum synthesizer and sequencer.

System: MAC, PLUS, SE, XL
Minimum Memory: 512K
Medium: 3 1/2-inch disk
ISPN: 55862-517   **Price: $59.95**

UTOPIAN SOFTWARE

MACMUSIC

Allows users to compose and edit songs and then play them through either the Mac's speaker or its sound port in the back.

System: MAC
Minimum Memory: 128K
Medium: 3 1/2-inch disk
ISPN: 84675-500   **Price: $89.95**

IMPULSE, INC.

MACNIFTY AUDIO DIGITIZER WITH SOUNDCAP

Plays sounds backward, reverberates and flanges sounds, ramps up and down, and generally creates special effects.

System: MAC, II, PLUS, SE, XL
Minimum Memory: 512K
Medium: 3 1/2-inch disk
ISPN: 93906-100   **Price: $199.97**

FARALLON COMPUTING

MACRECORDER (VER. 1.1)

Provides hardware and software that allows users to record, edit and play live or pre-recorded sound on the Macintosh.

System: MAC, II, PLUS, SE, XL
Minimum Memory: 1024K
Medium: 3 1/2-inch disk
ISPN: 91809-500   **Price: $199.00**

PASSPORT DESIGNS, INC.

MASTER TRACK JR.

Provides tools for composing, recording and editing music with a graphical user interface.

System: II, PLUS, SE, XL
Minimum Memory: 512K
Requires: Passport MIDI Interface (ISPN 59781-800) or compatible. One or more MIDI equipped instruments.
Medium: 3 1/2-inch disk
ISPN: 59781-050   **Price: $149.95**

PASSPORT DESIGNS, INC.

MASTER TRACKS PRO (VER. 3.0)

A professional sequencing program that provides 64 tracks of real-time and step-time input and graphic song editing.

System: MAC, II, PLUS, SE, XL
Minimum Memory: 512K
Requires: Passport MIDI interface or compatible, MIDI cables.
Medium: 3 1/2-inch disk
ISPN: 59781-430 **Price: $395.00**

MACMIDI

MIDI MINUS ONE (CLASSICAL)-VIRTUOSO PIANIST

A collection of digitized classical performances in the MIDI format.

System: MAC, II, PLUS, SE, XL
Minimum Memory: 512K
Requires: Virtuoso Pianist (ISPN 55865-700), MIDI synthesizer, MacMIDI compatible interface.
Medium: 3 1/2-inch disk
ISPN: 55865-108 **Price: $199.00**

MACMIDI

MIDI MINUS ONE (IMPROVISATION)-VIRTUOSO PIANIST

A collection of improvisational performances in the MIDI format.

System: MAC, II, PLUS, SE, XL
Minimum Memory: 512K
Requires: Virtuoso Pianist (ISPN 55865-700), MIDI synthesizer, MacMIDI compatible interface.
Medium: 3 1/2-inch disk
ISPN: 55865-109 **Price: $199.00**

PASSPORT DESIGNS, INC.

MIDI TRANSPORT

Provides user with a dual MIDI Interface that incorporates SMPTE to MIDI Time Code conversion.

System: MAC, II, PLUS, SE, XL
Minimum Memory: 512K
Requires: MIDI cables, compatible MIDI software, MIDI synthesizer or equipment capable of sending and/or receiving MIDI data.
Medium: 3 1/2-inch disk
ISPN: 59781-080 **Price: $495.00**

OPCODE SYSTEMS

MIDIMAC SEQUENCER (VER. 2.0)

Allows the user to create, edit, store, and play music made with a MIDI instrument(s).

System: MAC, II, PLUS, SE, XL
Minimum Memory: 512K
Requires: One or more MIDI-equipped instruments, any Macintosh MIDI interface.
Medium: 3 1/2-inch disk
ISPN: 58384-380 **Price: $250.00**

SOUTHWORTH MUSIC SYSTEMS

MIDIPAINT (VER. 1.0)

A full-featured professional MIDI sequencer that includes graphic note editing, 16000 tracks, complete quantization and SMPTE lock.

System: MAC, II, PLUS, SE, XL
Minimum Memory: 1024K
Requires: 1 MHz MIDI interface.
Medium: 3 1/2-inch disk
ISPN: 75101-500 **Price: $149.00**

HEIZER SOFTWARE

MUSIC BUSINESS MANAGEMENT

Tracks expenses, invoices, track sheets, audio and sound libraries, mileage, technical notes, and inventory.

System: MAC, II, PLUS, SE, XL
Minimum Memory: 1024K
Requires: HyperCard (ISPN 3900-300).
Medium: 3 1/2-inch disk
ISPN: 35175-052 **Price: $59.00**

HEIZER SOFTWARE

MUSIC KEYBOARD

A HyperCard stack which provides a keyboard that can be played using a mouse.

System: MAC, II, PLUS, SE, XL
Minimum Memory: 512K
Requires: HyperCard (ISPN 03900-300).
Medium: 3 1/2-inch disk
ISPN: 35175-966 **Price: $12.00**

OPCODE SYSTEMS

MUSIC MOUSE

Enables the user to make music by playing complex four-voice sounds.

System: MAC, II, PLUS, SE, XL
Minimum Memory:
Medium: 3 1/2-inch disk
ISPN: 58384-390 **Price: $60.00**

SHAHERAZAM

MUSIC TYPE (VER. 2.0)

Turns the Macintosh into a music typewriter, 300 notes and symbols can be typed directly from the keyboard.

System: MAC, II, PLUS, SE, XL
Minimum Memory: 512K
Requires: MacPaint (ISPN 12784-510).
Medium: 3 1/2-inch disk
ISPN: 69425-500 **Price: $59.95**

SPINNAKER SOFTWARE

MUSIC WORKS

Create, edit and listen to musical compositions. Features 8 instruments playable in up to 4 voices.

System: MAC, II, PLUS, SE, XL
Minimum Memory: 512K
Medium: 3 1/2-inch disk
ISPN: 75300-170 **Price: $49.95**

PASSPORT DESIGNS, INC.

NOTEWRITER (VER. 1.0)

A music publishing program offering a variety of powerful input methods.

System: MAC, II, PLUS, SE, XL
Minimum Memory: 512K
Requires: ImageWriter, LaserWriter or PostScript compatible printer.
Medium: 3 1/2-inch disk
ISPN: 59781-600 **Price: $295.00**

MACMIDI

OLD FASHIONED SING ALONG-VIRTUOSO PIANIST LIBRARY

A collection of old fashioned sing-along performances in the MIDI format.

System: MAC, II, PLUS, SE, XL
Minimum Memory: 512K
Requires: Virtuoso Pianist (ISPN 55865-700), MIDI synthesizer, MacMIDI compatible interface.
Medium: 3 1/2-inch disk
ISPN: 55865-105 **Price: $199.00**

INTELLIGENT MUSIC

OVALTUNE (VER. 1.0)

Works with graphics taken from any Macintosh graphics program and transforms them in synchronization with music.

System: MAC, II, PLUS, SE, XL
Minimum Memory: 800K
Requires: MIDI applications require MIDI interface and MIDI synthesizer.
Medium: 3 1/2-inch disk
ISPN: 39007-550 **Price: $145.00**

OPCODE SYSTEMS

PATCH LIBRARIAN (VER. 4.0)

Stores synthesizer 'voice' patches in files on disk. Each file has a window on the screen, displaying the names of the patches.

System: MAC, II, PLUS, SE
Minimum Memory: 512K
Medium: 3 1/2-inch disk
ISPN: 58384-555 **Price: $100.00**

OPCODE SYSTEMS

PATCH LIBRARIAN-CASIO CZ

Made for the Casio CZ synthesizer with several banks of patches to store thousands of sounds with MIDI capabilities.

System: MAC, II, PLUS, SE
Minimum Memory: 512K
Medium: 3 1/2-inch disk
ISPN: 58384-540 **Price: $75.00**

OPCODE SYSTEMS

PATCH LIBRARIAN-CZ EDITOR

Turns a Macintosh into a complete voicing and librarian system for any CZ instrument.

System: MAC, II, PLUS, SE, XL
Minimum Memory: 512K
Medium: 3 1/2-inch disk
ISPN: 58384-530 **Price: $125.00**

OPCODE SYSTEMS
PATCH LIBRARIAN-FENDER CHROMA

Allows use of Macintosh disks to store thousands of sound 'patches' for the Fender Chroma synthesizer.

System: MAC, II, PLUS, SE, XL
Minimum Memory: 512K
Medium: 3 1/2-inch disk
ISPN: 58384-480   **Price: $75.00**

OPCODE SYSTEMS
PATCH LIBRARIAN-FENDER POLARIS

Made for the Fender Polaris synthesizer with several sound banks of patches to store thousands of sounds.

System: MAC, II, PLUS, SE, XL
Minimum Memory: 512K
Medium: 3 1/2-inch disk
ISPN: 58384-541   **Price: $75.00**

OPCODE SYSTEMS
PATCH LIBRARIAN-JUNO-1 AND 2

Allows use of Macintosh disks to store thousands of sound 'patches' for the Juno synthesizer.

System: MAC, II, PLUS, SE, XL
Minimum Memory: 512K
Medium: 3 1/2-inch disk
ISPN: 58384-425   **Price: $75.00**

OPCODE SYSTEMS
PATCH LIBRARIAN-KORG DW-8000

Allows use of Macintosh disks to store thousands of sound 'patches' for the Korg synthesizer.

System: MAC, II, PLUS, SE, XL
Minimum Memory: 512K
Medium: 3 1/2-inch disk
ISPN: 58384-475   **Price: $75.00**

OPCODE SYSTEMS
PATCH LIBRARIAN-LINN DRUM

Allows use of Macintosh disks to store thousands of sound 'patches' for the Linn Drum synthesizer.

System: MAC, II, PLUS, SE, XL
Minimum Memory: 512K
Medium: 3 1/2-inch disk
ISPN: 58384-490   **Price: $50.00**

OPCODE SYSTEMS
PATCH LIBRARIAN-OBERHEIM MATRIX-6

Allows use of Macintosh disks to store thousands of sound patches for the Oberheim Matrix synthesizer.

System: MAC, II, PLUS, SE, XL
Minimum Memory: 512K
Medium: 3 1/2-inch disk
ISPN: 58384-500   **Price: $75.00**

OPCODE SYSTEMS
PATCH LIBRARIAN-OBERHEIM OB-8

Allows use of Macintosh disks to store thousands of sound patches for the Oberheim OB synthesizer.

System: MAC, II, PLUS, SE, XL
Minimum Memory: 512K
Medium: 3 1/2-inch disk
ISPN: 58384-550   **Price: $75.00**

OPCODE SYSTEMS
PATCH LIBRARIAN-OBERHEIM XPANDER/MATRIX-12

Made for the Oberheim Xpander with several banks of patches that can store thousands of sounds with MIDI capabilities.

System: MAC, II, PLUS, SE, XL
Minimum Memory: 512K
Medium: 3 1/2-inch disk
ISPN: 58384-543   **Price: $75.00**

OPCODE SYSTEMS
PATCH LIBRARIAN-ROLAND JUNO-106

Made for the Roland Juno synthesizer with several banks of patches to store thousands of sounds with MIDI capabilities.

System: MAC, II, PLUS, SE, XL
Minimum Memory: 512K
Medium: 3 1/2-inch disk
ISPN: 58384-544   **Price: $75.00**

OPCODE SYSTEMS
PATCH LIBRARIAN-ROLAND JX-8P

Made for the Roland JX synthesizer with several patches to store thousands of sounds with MIDI capabilities.

System: MAC, II, PLUS, SE, XL
Minimum Memory: 512K
Medium: 3 1/2-inch disk
ISPN: 58384-545   **Price: $75.00**

OPCODE SYSTEMS
PATCH LIBRARIAN-ROLAND SUPER JUPITER

Allows use of Macintosh disks to store thousands of sound 'patches' for the Roland Super Jupiter synthesizer.

System: MAC, II, PLUS, SE, XL
Minimum Memory: 512K
Medium: 3 1/2-inch disk
ISPN: 58384-450   **Price: $75.00**

OPCODE SYSTEMS
PATCH LIBRARIAN-YAMAHA DX/TX/TX816 BULK

Made for the Yamaha synthesizer with several banks of patches to store thousands of sounds with MIDI capabilities.

System: MAC, II, PLUS, SE, XL
Minimum Memory: 512K
Medium: 3 1/2-inch disk
ISPN: 58384-546   **Price: $100.00**

OPCODE SYSTEMS
PATCH LIBRARIAN-YAMAHA DX21/27/100

Allows use of Macintosh disks to store thousands of sound 'patches' for the Yamaha DX synthesizer.

System: MAC, II, PLUS, SE
Minimum Memory: 512K
Medium: 3 1/2-inch disk
ISPN: 58384-400   **Price: $75.00**

RESONATE
PATCHWORKS (VER. 1.0)

Converts patches into other patch bay's, thus making configuration upgrades seamless.

System: MAC, II, PLUS, SE, XL
Minimum Memory: 512K
Requires: System 4.1 or higher (supplied).
Medium: 3 1/2-inch disk
ISPN: 37193-600   **Price: $125.00**

CODA MUSIC SOFTWARE, DIV. OF WENGER CORP.
PERCEIVE

A personal musical ear-training course that combines listening, reading and writing and includes a textbook and workbook.

System: MAC, PLUS, SE, XL
Minimum Memory: 512K
Medium: 3 1/2-inch disk
ISPN: 55862-611   **Price: $99.99**

MARK OF THE UNICORN
PERFORMER (VER. 2.0)

A powerful MIDI sequencer, editor, and performance tool for the Apple Macintosh.

System: MAC, II, PLUS, SE, XL
Minimum Memory: 512K
Requires: One or more MIDI-equipped instruments, any Macintosh MIDI interface.
Medium: 3 1/2-inch disk
ISPN: 47250-360   **Price: $395.00**

MACMIDI
PERFORMING MUSICIAN

Comes with Megatrack XL, MidiWork-which will translate other programs to Megatrack XL, sample tapes, and hardware.

System: MAC, II, PLUS, SE, XL
Minimum Memory: 512K
Medium: 3 1/2-inch disk
ISPN: 55865-475   **Price: $299.00**

MACMIDI
PIANO TECHNIQUE-VIRTUOSO PIANIST LIBRARY

A collection of Czerny and Hanon performances in the MIDI format.

System: MAC, PLUS, SE, XL
Minimum Memory: 512K
Requires: Virtuoso Pianist (ISPN 55865-700), MIDI synthesizer, MacMIDI compatible interface.
Medium: 3 1/2-inch disk
ISPN: 55865-107   **Price: $199.00**

ARS NOVA SOFTWARE
PRACTICA MUSICA (VER. 2.0)

Trains users in interval and chord spelling, provides ear training for intervals, melody and rhythm.

System: MAC, II, PLUS, SE
Minimum Memory: 512K
Requires: 800K disk drive.
Medium: 3 1/2-inch disk
ISPN: 60542-100 **Price: $125.00**

MARK OF THE UNICORN
PROFESSIONAL COMPOSER (VER. 2.3)

A music notation program which lets you create everything from lead sheets to scores with up to 40 staves.

System: MAC, II, PLUS, SE
Minimum Memory: 512K
Medium: 3 1/2-inch disk
ISPN: 47250-375 **Price: $495.00**

MACMIDI
PROFESSIONAL MUSICIAN MACMIDI SYSTEM

Comes with Megatrack XL, MidiWord-which will translate from other programs to Megatrack XL, librarians, sample tapes, and hardware.

System: MAC, II, PLUS, SE, XL
Minimum Memory: 512K
Medium: 3 1/2-inch disk
ISPN: 55865-500 **Price: $549.00**

DIGIDESIGN, INC.
Q-SHEET A/V

Automates any MIDI device while synchronized to precise SMPTE time code.

System: MAC, II, PLUS, SE, XL
Minimum Memory: 512K
Requires: SMPTE/MIDI time code converter, MIDI interface.
Medium: 3 1/2-inch disk
ISPN: 25212-550 **Price: $995.00**

MACMIDI
RELIGIOUS AND GOSPEL-VIRTUOSO PIANIST LIBRARY

A collection of digitized religious and gospel performances in the MIDI format.

System: MAC, II, PLUS, SE, XL
Minimum Memory: 512K
Requires: Virtuoso Pianist (ISPN 55865-700), MIDI synthesizer, MacMIDI compatible interface.
Medium: 3 1/2-inch disk
ISPN: 55865-104 **Price: $199.00**

DR. T'S MUSIC SOFTWARE
ROLAND D-50 EDITOR-LIBRARIAN

Contains a music Editor and Librarian for use with the Roland D-50 synthesizer.

System: MAC, II, PLUS, SE, XL
Minimum Memory: 512K
Medium: 3 1/2-inch disk
ISPN: 26762-150 **Price: $149.00**

OPCODE SYSTEMS
SEQUENCER (VER. 2.0) (WITH STEP ENTRY)

A real-time musical performance and composition system.

System: MAC, II, PLUS, SE, XL
Minimum Memory: 512K
Medium: 3 1/2-inch disk
ISPN: 58384-551 **Price: $200.00**

OPCODE SYSTEMS
SEQUENCER (VER. 2.5)

Allows files to be transcribed using Deluxe Music Constr. Set (Elec. Arts) or Profess. Comp. (Mark of Unicorn) Plus 2.0 features.

System: MAC, II, PLUS, SE, XL
Minimum Memory: 512K
Medium: 3 1/2-inch disk
ISPN: 58384-553 **Price: $250.00**

DIGIDESIGN, INC.
SOFTSYNTH

Uses the Macintosh to synthesize sounds designed by the user.

System: MAC, II, PLUS, SE, XL
Minimum Memory: 512K
Requires: Any Macintosh MIDI interface (RS-422 cable must be used for Emulator II).
Medium: 3 1/2-inch disk
ISPN: 25212-450 **Price: $295.00**

DIGIDESIGN, INC.
SOUND DESIGNER II

An audio-editing program for Digidesign's Sound Tools hard disk digital recording.

System: SE, II
Minimum Memory: 1024K
Requires: Sound Tools.
Medium: 3 1/2-inch disk
ISPN: 25212-502 **Price: $995.00**

DIGIDESIGN, INC.
SOUND DESIGNER II SK

A graphic editor for editing stereo waveforms.

System: MAC, II, PLUS, SE, XL
Minimum Memory: 1024K
Medium: 3 1/2-inch disk
ISPN: 25212-501 **Price: $595.00**

DIGIDESIGN, INC.
SOUND DESIGNER UNIVERSAL

Offers digital sample editing and processing features, and displays up to three sound waveforms in high-resolution on the screen.

System: MAC, II, PLUS, SE, XL
Minimum Memory: 1024K
Requires: 800K disk drive, MIDI Interface.
Medium: 3 1/2-inch disk
ISPN: 25212-500 **Price: $395.00**

DR. T'S MUSIC SOFTWARE
SOUND FILE (MAC)

Provides a complete sound and sequence librarian for the Ensoniq ESQ-1 Digital Wave Synthesizer.

System: MAC, II, PLUS, SE, XL
Minimum Memory: 512K
Requires: MIDI interface and cable, Ensoniq-1 (ROM (Ver. 2.0) or higher).
Medium: 3 1/2-inch disk
ISPN: 26762-190 **Price: $99.95**

DR. T'S MUSIC SOFTWARE
SOUND LAB

Provides editing for visual waveforms and voice parameters, audio processing, and a wavesample librarian for the ENSONIQ Mirage.

System: MAC, II, PLUS, SE, XL
Minimum Memory: 512K
Requires: Mirage Digital Sampling Keyboard or Digital Multi-Sampler, Macintosh MIDI interface, Mirage Advanced Sampler's Guide.
Medium: 3 1/2-inch disk
ISPN: 26762-180 **Price: $299.95**

BOGAS PUBLICATIONS
STUDIO SESSION (VER. 1.0)

Will give a user true music output by using its library of digitized instruments to output six voices through the Macintosh.

System: MAC, PLUS, SE, XL
Minimum Memory: 512K
Medium: 3 1/2-inch disk
ISPN: 08160-100 **Price: $89.95**

GREAT WAVE SOFTWARE
TERPSICHORE

Contains 181 Renaissance/Baroque musical selections for exclusive use with Concertware+ and Concertware+MIDI on the Macintosh.

System: MAC, II, PLUS, SE, XL
Minimum Memory: 512K
Requires: Concertware+ (ISPN 33476-151) or Concertware+MIDI (ISPN 33476-160).
Medium: 3 1/2-inch disk
ISPN: 33476-175 **Price: $49.95**

DIGIDESIGN, INC.
TURBOSYNTH

A graphically-oriented modular synthesis and sample processing program that allows users to create interesting sounds.

System: MAC, II, PLUS, SE, XL
Minimum Memory: 1024K
Requires: MIDI interface.
Medium: 3 1/2-inch disk
ISPN: 25212-700 **Price: $349.00**

DIGITAL MUSIC SERVICES
TX802 PRO

An integrated editor and librarian for the Yamaha TX802 synthesizer with voices, performances, microtunings and system setups.

System: MAC, II, PLUS, SE, XL
Minimum Memory: 512K
Requires: Yamaha TX802 and a MIDI interface.
Medium: 3 1/2-inch disk
ISPN: 25450-240 **Price: $249.00**

DIGITAL MUSIC SERVICES
TX81Z PRO

An integrated voice editor and librarian for the Yamaha TX81Z to alphabetize and arrange hundreds of voices and performances.

System: MAC, II, PLUS, SE, XL
Minimum Memory: 512K
Requires: Yamaha TX81Z and a MIDI interface.
Medium: 3 1/2-inch disk
ISPN: 25450-225   **Price: $139.00**

INTELLIGENT MUSIC
UPBEAT (VER. 1.2)

Provides a rhythm programmer for all MIDI drum machines and synthesizers to record and edit up to 32 tracks of music.

System: MAC, II, PLUS, SE, XL
Minimum Memory: 512K
Requires: MIDI interface and MIDI drum machine or synthesizer.
Medium: 3 1/2-inch disk
ISPN: 39007-700   **Price: $150.00**

MACMIDI
VIRTUOSO PIANIST

Allows you to adapt music of any style or difficulty to your own level. Master performances by having your improvement challenged.

System: MAC, II, PLUS, SE, XL
Minimum Memory: 512K
Requires: MIDI keyboard synthesizer, MIDI interface.
Medium: 3 1/2-inch disk
ISPN: 55865-700   **Price: $549.00**

---

468 PERSONAL/SPORTS

HEIZER SOFTWARE
BASEBALL STATISTICS 1986-1987

Eight databases of 1986 and 1987 baseball statistics with pitchers and hitters for the American and National League.

System: MAC, II, PLUS, SE, XL
Minimum Memory: 512K
Requires: Microsoft Excel (ISPN 53150-270), Microsoft Works (ISPN 53150-740) or HyperCard (ISPN 03900-300).
Medium: 3 1/2-inch disk
ISPN: 35175-708   **Price: $30.00**

HEIZER SOFTWARE
BASEBALL STATISTICS 1987

A database of 1987 baseball statistics on pitchers and hitters, for both the American League and National League.

System: MAC, PLUS, SE, XL
Minimum Memory: 512K
Requires: Microsoft Works (ISPN 53150-740) or HyperCard (ISPN 03900-300).
Medium: 3 1/2-inch disk
ISPN: 35175-881   **Price: $20.00**

HEIZER SOFTWARE
BASKETBALL STATWHIZ

Features automatic tabulation of team and individual totals, point totals, percentages and averages for basketball teams.

System: MAC, PLUS, SE, XL
Minimum Memory: 512K
Requires: Microsoft Excel (ISPN 53150-270).
Medium: 3 1/2-inch disk
ISPN: 35175-711   **Price: $25.00**

HEIZER SOFTWARE
BOWLING LEAGUE MANAGER

Handles up to four teams of five players each, three games per week. Provides averages and summary statistics.

System: MAC, II, PLUS, SE, XL
Minimum Memory: 512K
Requires: Microsoft Excel (ISPN 53150-270) or Microsoft Works (ISPN 53150-740).
Medium: 3 1/2-inch disk
ISPN: 35175-715   **Price: $35.00**

JGR SPORTS SOFTWARE
BRACKETS AND SCHEDULES (VER. 1.0) (MAC VERSION)

Allows you to quickly develop and outline many combinations of team or player schedules and tournament brackets.

System: II, PLUS, SE
Minimum Memory: 512K
Requires: Microsoft Excel (ISPN 53150-270).
Medium: 3 1/2-inch disk
ISPN: 41634-200   **Price: $99.50**

ARTWORX SOFTWARE CO., INC.
DAILY DOUBLE HORSE RACING

Includes past race histories of 180 horses and 12 jockeys competing in nearly 400 races.

System: MAC, II, PLUS, SE, XL
Minimum Memory: 512K
Medium: 3 1/2-inch disk
ISPN: 05437-070   **Price: $29.95**

LAKE AVE. SOFTWARE
GOLF HANDICAPPING

Calculate golf handicaps based on USGA rules.

System: MAC, II, PLUS, SE, XL
Minimum Memory: 512K
Medium: 3 1/2-inch disk
ISPN: 43418-400   **Price: $89.00**

LAKE AVE. SOFTWARE
GOLF TOURNAMENT SCORING

Calculate your golf score 16 different ways.

System: MAC, II, PLUS, SE, XL
Minimum Memory: 512K
Medium: 3 1/2-inch disk
ISPN: 43418-425   **Price: $89.00**

HEIZER SOFTWARE
HORSE RACE ANALYZER

Determines the horse most likely to win a race.

System: MAC, II, PLUS, SE, XL
Minimum Memory: 512K
Requires: Microsoft Excel (ISPN 53150-270), Microsoft Works (ISPN 53150-740) or HyperCard (ISPN 03900-300).
Medium: 3 1/2-inch disk
ISPN: 35175-717   **Price: $15.00**

HEIZER SOFTWARE
MACRUN RUNNER'S LOG

Computes a runner's mileage, and average pace and shoe mileage.

System: MAC, II, PLUS, SE, XL
Minimum Memory: 512K
Requires: Microsoft Excel (ISPN 53150-270).
Medium: 3 1/2-inch disk
ISPN: 35175-716   **Price: $60.00**

UNLIMITED SOFTWARE
MATCH TRAC (VER. 5.0)

Analyze your tennis strengths and weaknesses.

System: MAC
Minimum Memory: 512K
Medium: 3 1/2-inch disk
ISPN: 96343-100   **Price: $195.95**

HEIZER SOFTWARE
MEN'S GYMNASTIC SCORING

Handles all individual entries and events, and individual and team scoring.

System: II, PLUS, SE
Minimum Memory: 512K
Requires: Microsoft Excel (ISPN 53150-270).
Medium: 3 1/2-inch disk
ISPN: 35175-601   **Price: $40.00**

BAUDVILLE
SPORTS AWARD LIBRARY (VER. 31801)

A supplemental library for use with Award Maker Plus, which includes ten new borders and four new text styles.

System: MAC, II, PLUS, SE, XL
Minimum Memory: 512K
Medium: 3 1/2-inch disk
ISPN: 07087-300   **Price: $29.95**

---

472 PERSONAL/TRAVEL

MEDIAGENIC/TENPOINT0
BUSINESS CLASS

A Hypercard stack travel planner that provides information about 65 countries, from hotels and transportation to customs and currency.

System: MAC, II, PLUS, SE, XL
Minimum Memory: 1024K
Requires: HyperCard (ISPN 03900-300).
Medium: 3 1/2-inch disk
ISPN: 48702-080   **Price: $49.95**

FOR MORE DETAILED INFORMATION, CALL (412) 746-MENU

MEDIAGENIC/TENPOINT0
CITY TO CITY

A Hypercard stack that is a customizable business and personal travel planner for the United States.

System: MAC, II, PLUS, SE, XL
Minimum Memory: 1024K
Requires: HyperCard (ISPN 03900-300).
Medium: 3 1/2-inch disk
ISPN: 48702-125   **Price: $49.95**

HEIZER SOFTWARE
FLASH CARD SPANISH

A stack of 1500 vocabulary words which can be used as Spanish to English, English to Spanish, or as a dictionary for meanings.

System: MAC, II, PLUS, SE, XL
Minimum Memory: 1024K
Requires: HyperCard (ISPN 03900-300).
Medium: 3 1/2-inch disk
ISPN: 35175-410   **Price: $15.00**

HEIZER SOFTWARE
JAPANESE ENGINEER

Over 1000 Japanese words that are taught in first-year Japanese classes. Words are displayed in English, Japanese or Kanji.

System: MAC, II, PLUS, SE, XL
Minimum Memory: 1024K
Requires: HyperCard (ISPN 03900-300).
Medium: 3 1/2-inch disk
ISPN: 35175-411   **Price: $30.00**

MEDINA SOFTWARE, INC.
ORLANDO A LA CARTE (ENGLISH)

An up-to-date alphabetical listing of hundreds of Central Florida's restaurants arranged according to cuisine.

System: MAC, II, PLUS, SE, XL
Minimum Memory: 128K
Requires: MacWrite (ISPN 12784-530), Microsoft Word (ISPN 53150-732) or compatible word processor.
Medium: 3 1/2-inch disk
ISPN: 48842-575   **Price: $19.95**

HEIZER SOFTWARE
VACATION PLANNER

Plans and organizes flights, reservations and ground transfers.

System: MAC, II, PLUS, SE, XL
Minimum Memory: 512K
Requires: Microsoft Excel (ISPN 53150-270) or Microsoft Works (ISPN 53150-740).
Medium: 3 1/2-inch disk
ISPN: 35175-268   **Price: $5.00**

510 ENTERTAINMENT/ ADULT

DESKTOP VIDEO PRODUCTIONS
CLIP ANIMATION-EROTICA (VER. 1.0) (SELF-RUNNING)

Contains animated clip sequences of erotic and romantic pictures.

System: MAC, II, PLUS, SE, XL
Minimum Memory: 512K
Requires: 800K disk drive.
Medium: 3 1/2-inch disk
ISPN: 46012-535   **Price: $59.95**

RAINBIRD, DIV. OF MEDIAGENIC
CORRUPTION

An illustrated, interactive adventure game about power, profit, double-dealing and deceit.

System: MAC, II, PLUS, SE, XL
Minimum Memory: 512K
Medium: 3 1/2-inch disk
ISPN: 91828-064   **Price: $44.95**

SIERRA ON-LINE, INC.
LEISURE SUIT LARRY II- LOOKING FOR LOVE

Join Larry as he wins the lottery, dream cruise on the 'Lover's Boat,' and a date on 'The Dating Connection.'

System: MAC, II, PLUS, SE, XL
Minimum Memory: 512K
Medium: 3 1/2-inch disk
ISPN: 69925-305   **Price: $49.95**

SIERRA ON-LINE, INC.
LEISURE SUIT LARRY IN THE LAND OF LOUNGE LIZARDS

Slip into a leisure suit and guide Larry through singles bars, discos and restaurants while he looks for love.

System: MAC
Minimum Memory: 512K
Medium: 3 1/2-inch disk
ISPN: 69925-304   **Price: $39.95**

ARTWORX SOFTWARE CO., INC.
STRIP POKER

Pits your poker skills against Suzi and Melissa, two gorgeous opponents each with their own style of play.

System: MAC, II, PLUS, SE, XL
Minimum Memory: 512K
Medium: 3 1/2-inch disk
ISPN: 05437-430   **Price: $29.95**

520 ENTERTAINMENT/ ADVENTURE

INFOCOM, INC.
A MIND FOREVER VOYAGING

Enter the year 2031 and the years to come as a humanized mega-computer.

System: MAC, II, PLUS, SE, XL
Minimum Memory: 512K
Medium: 3 1/2-inch disk
ISPN: 37413-005   **Price: $14.95**

JAMES ASSOCIATES
ADVENTURE

Enables the player to become the master adventurer.

System: MAC, II, PLUS, SE, XL
Minimum Memory: 512K
Medium: 3 1/2-inch disk
ISPN: 41400-075   **Price: $29.95**

DATASOFT/INTELLICREATIONS, INC.
ALTERNATE REALITY-THE CITY

Survive the City in this role-playing fantasy adventure.

System: II, PLUS, SE
Minimum Memory: 512K
Medium: 3 1/2-inch disk
ISPN: 23850-100   **Price: $39.95**

BRODERBUND SOFTWARE, INC.
ANCIENT ART OF WAR AT SEA

Enjoy real-time excitement and intellectual challenge as you command a navy.

System: MAC, II, PLUS, SE, XL
Minimum Memory: 512K
Medium: 3 1/2-inch disk
ISPN: 08850-016   **Price: $44.95**

AEGIS DEVELOPMENT, INC.
ARAZOK'S TOMB (VER. 1.0)

In this program with sound and graphs you unravel this mystery from beyond the mists of time where evil is rediscovered.

System: MAC, PLUS, SE, XL
Minimum Memory: 512K
Medium: 3 1/2-inch disk
ISPN: 01718-125   **Price: $39.95**

INFOCOM, INC.
BALLYHOO

Someone's kidnapped the circus owner's daughter and you must rescue her.

System: MAC, II, PLUS, SE, XL
Minimum Memory: 512K
Medium: 3 1/2-inch disk
ISPN: 37413-007   **Price: $14.95**

INFOCOM, INC.
BEYOND ZORK

Go beyond Zork in a variety of ways with this text adventure.

System: MAC, II, PLUS, SE, XL
Minimum Memory: 512K
Medium: 3 1/2-inch disk
ISPN: 37413-115   **Price: $49.95**

INFOCOM, INC.
BORDER ZONE

Become an American spy, a businessman and a KGB agent all entangled in an diplomat's assassination.

System: MAC, II, PLUS, SE, XL
Minimum Memory: 512K
Medium: 3 1/2-inch disk
ISPN: 37413-120   **Price: $39.95**

MINDSCAPE, INC.

COLONY

Players must discover what has happened to this once thriving space colony and rescue survivors from aliens that overran the planet.

System: MAC, II, PLUS, SE, XL
Minimum Memory: 512K
Medium: 3 1/2-inch disk
ISPN: 54375-039   **Price: $49.95**

POLARWARE PENGUIN SOFTWARE

CRIMSON CROWN

Return to Wallachia with a desperate princess and crown prince in search of the Crimson Crown.

System: MAC, II, PLUS, SE, XL
Minimum Memory: 512K
Medium: 3 1/2-inch disk
ISPN: 60425-070   **Price: $19.95**

INFOCOM, INC.

CUTTHROATS

Dive for sunken riches while dodging cutthroats in this seaborne adventure.

System: MAC, II, PLUS, SE, XL
Minimum Memory: 512K
Medium: 3 1/2-inch disk
ISPN: 37413-015   **Price: $14.95**

INFOCOM, INC.

DEADLINE

Experience the thrills of a real-life adventure.

System: MAC, II, PLUS, SE, XL
Minimum Memory:
Medium: 3 1/2-inch disk
ISPN: 37413-020   **Price: $9.95**

CINEMAWARE CORP.

DEFENDERS OF THE CROWN

Win the crown of England and the love of many damsels.

System: MAC, II, PLUS, SE, XL
Minimum Memory: 512K
Medium: 3 1/2-inch disk
ISPN: 12656-010   **Price: $49.95**

ICOM SIMULATIONS, INC.

DEJA VU II-LOST IN LAS VEGAS

An interactive graphic adventure mystery where you remember nothing but you fear the worst.

System: MAC, II, PLUS, SE, XL
Minimum Memory: 512K
Medium: 3 1/2-inch disk
ISPN: 82194-200   **Price: $49.95**

MINDSCAPE, INC.

DEJA VU-A NIGHTMARE COMES TRUE

Ages teens to adults: Explore this Chandleresque murder mystery - everything seems vaguely familiar, yet you remember nothing.

System: MAC, PLUS, SE, XL
Minimum Memory: 512K
Medium: 3 1/2-inch disk
ISPN: 54375-048   **Price: $49.95**

SOFTWARE INVESTMENT PLUS, INC.

DESTINY (VER. 1.0)

You are trying to find the crystal key to open your destiny. It is a difficult adventure graphics game.

System: MAC, II, PLUS, SE, XL
Minimum Memory: 128K
Medium: 3 1/2-inch disk
ISPN: 73106-150   **Price: $29.95**

FIRST ROW SOFTWARE PUBLISHING

DR. DUMONT'S WILD P.A.R.T.I.

Dr. Dumont has found a way to hook the human mind directly to a machine. You must teach the machine to perceive reality.

System: MAC, PLUS, SE, XL
Minimum Memory: 512K
Medium: 3 1/2-inch disk
ISPN: 91839-200   **Price: $39.95**

SILICON BEACH SOFTWARE

ENCHANTED SCEPTERS

You undertake a quest for the enchanted sceptres to save the tiny kingdom of Callion. Includes 200+ detailed scenes and RealSound.

System: MAC, II, PLUS, SE, XL
Minimum Memory: 128K
Medium: 3 1/2-inch disk
ISPN: 70237-250   **Price: $39.95**

INFOCOM, INC.

ENCHANTER

You, the novice magician, must match spells with the Evil Warlock.

System: MAC, II, PLUS, SE, XL
Minimum Memory: 128K
Requires: 400K formatted disks to save games in progress.
Medium: 3 1/2-inch disk
ISPN: 37413-025   **Price: $14.95**

INFOCOM, INC.

ENCHANTER TRILOGY

Defeat your magical enemies in three text adventures: Enchanter, Sorceror and Spell Breaker.

System: MAC, II, PLUS, SE, XL
Minimum Memory: 512K
Medium: 3 1/2-inch disk
ISPN: 37413-029   **Price: $29.85**

ADDISON WESLEY PUBLISHING CO.

FELLOWSHIP OF THE RING

Traverse the mysterious paths of middle earth in these two Tolkienian adventures.

System: MAC, II, PLUS, SE, XL
Minimum Memory: 512K
Requires: 800K disk drive.
Medium: 3 1/2-inch disk
ISPN: 00900-215   **Price: $39.95**

MILES COMPUTING, INC.

FOOL'S ERRAND

A fantasy puzzle about the Fool, whom in his search for wisdom, must rebuild the Sun's Map to regain that which has been lost.

System: MAC, II, PLUS, SE, XL
Minimum Memory: 512K
Requires: Two 400K disk drives or a hard disk.
Medium: 3 1/2-inch disk
ISPN: 54075-100   **Price: $49.95**

UNICORN SOFTWARE CO.

FUTURIA

A graphic adventure/strategy game that takes you into the future and lets you survive in a city where you are looking for your ship.

System: MAC, II, PLUS, SE, XL
Minimum Memory: 128K
Medium: 3 1/2-inch disk
ISPN: 83562-175   **Price: $44.95**

SIERRA ON-LINE, INC.

GOLD RUSH!

Relive one of America's most exciting eras as you seek to reach the West Coast and pan for gold.

System: MAC, II, PLUS, SE, XL
Minimum Memory: 512K
Medium: 3 1/2-inch disk
ISPN: 69925-230   **Price: $39.95**

ARTWORX SOFTWARE CO., INC.

GRAILQUEST

An interactive graphics adventure that puts the player inside the legendary world of King Arthur and the Knights of the Round Table.

System: MAC, II, PLUS, SE, XL
Minimum Memory: 512K
Requires: 800K disk drive.
Medium: 3 1/2-inch disk
ISPN: 05437-093   **Price: $29.95**

MEDIAGENIC/SOLID GOLD SOFTWARE

HACKER II-THE DOOMSDAY PAPERS

A diabolical plot exists to destroy the United States and the game player must save the day.

System: MAC, PLUS, SE, XL
Minimum Memory: 512K
Medium: 3 1/2-inch disk
ISPN: 48693-210   **Price: $19.95**

INFOCOM, INC.

HITCHHIKER'S GUIDE TO THE GALAXY

Be Arthur Dent, a hapless earthling who tries to hitchhike across the galaxy in this fantasy game.

System: MAC, II, PLUS, SE, XL
Minimum Memory:
Medium: 3 1/2-inch disk
ISPN: 37413-027   **Price: $14.95**

ADDISON WESLEY PUBLISHING CO.

HOBBIT

Become the hobbit Bilbo Baggins and enter the world of Middle Earth, trolls and Wilderland.

System: MAC, II, PLUS, SE, XL
Minimum Memory: 512K
Requires: 800K disk drive.
Medium: 3 1/2-inch disk
ISPN: 00900-230   **Price: $39.95**

INFOCOM, INC.

HOLLYWOOD HIJINX

Explore Hollywood at its zaniest while searching for ten treasures from Uncle Buddy's wacky 'B' movies.

System: MAC, II, PLUS, SE, XL
Minimum Memory:
Medium: 3 1/2-inch disk
ISPN: 37413-024   **Price: $14.95**

INFOCOM, INC.

INFIDEL

Search for a great lost pyramid in the heart of the Egyptian desert.

System: MAC, II, PLUS, SE, XL
Minimum Memory: 512K
Medium: 3 1/2-inch disk
ISPN: 37413-030   **Price: $9.95**

CINEMAWARE CORP.

KING OF CHICAGO

Sweep forces of the 1930's Al Capone gang out of Chicago.

System: MAC, II, PLUS, SE, XL
Minimum Memory:
Medium: 3 1/2-inch disk
ISPN: 12656-020   **Price: $49.95**

SIERRA ON-LINE, INC.

KING'S QUEST I

Become Sir Graham as you search for the lost treasures of Daventry.

System: MAC
Minimum Memory: 512K
Medium: 3 1/2-inch disk
ISPN: 69925-290   **Price: $49.95**

SIERRA ON-LINE, INC.

KING'S QUEST II-ROMANCING THE THRONE (VER. 1.1H)

Travel with King Graham to rescue the beautiful maiden.

System: MAC, II, PLUS, SE, XL
Minimum Memory: 512K
Medium: 3 1/2-inch disk
ISPN: 69925-295   **Price: $49.95**

RAECREATIONS SOFTWARE

LAWMAN (VER. 1.06)

You're the Sheriff of an 1880's frontier town. Deal with robberies and showdowns, gunfights and surprises. Includes digitized sounds.

System: MAC, II, PLUS, SE, XL
Minimum Memory: 512K
Requires: 800K disk drive.
Medium: 3 1/2-inch disk
ISPN: 64887-400   **Price: $49.95**

CHALLENGER SOFTWARE

LEGACY

Interactive fiction, unique graphics on 2/3 of screen, accepts full sentence commands.

System: MAC, II, PLUS, SE, XL
Minimum Memory: 128K
Medium: 3 1/2-inch disk
ISPN: 12093-300   **Price: $45.00**

BRODERBUND SOFTWARE, INC.

LODE RUNNER

Run, jump and drill new passages – escape your enemies and gain gold chests.

System: MAC, II, PLUS, SE, XL
Minimum Memory: 512K
Requires: Consumer edition.
Medium: 3 1/2-inch disk
ISPN: 08850-089   **Price: $9.95**

BRODERBUND SOFTWARE, INC.

LODE RUNNER

Run, jump and drill new passages – escape your enemies and gain gold chests.

System: MAC, II, PLUS, SE, XL
Minimum Memory: 512K
Requires: School edition.
Medium: 3 1/2-inch disk
ISPN: 08850 089   **Price: $14.95**

BRODERBUND SOFTWARE, INC.

LODE RUNNER

Run, jump and drill new passages – escape your enemies and gain gold chests.

System: MAC, II, PLUS, SE, XL
Minimum Memory: 512K
Requires: Lab Pack.
Medium: 3 1/2-inch disk
ISPN: 08850-089   **Price: $39.95**

NORDIC SOFTWARE, INC.

MACKIDS-NAVAL BATTLE

Ages 6 to adult: Teaches the fundamentals of coordinate geometry and strategy while trying to sink the user's fleet.

System: MAC, II, PLUS, SE, XL
Minimum Memory: 128K
Medium: 3 1/2-inch disk
ISPN: 57028-200   **Price: $39.95**

SIERRA ON-LINE, INC.

MANHUNTER-NEW YORK

Step into the role of manhunter, spy and assassin as you work for aliens that have taken over the Earth.

System: MAC, II, PLUS, SE, XL
Minimum Memory: 512K
Medium: 3 1/2-inch disk
ISPN: 69925-306   **Price: $49.95**

NEW WORLD COMPUTING, INC.

MIGHT AND MAGIC-THE SECRET OF THE INNER SANCTUM

Create up to six characters and adventure through towns, castles, mountains, caverns and dungeons.

System: MAC, II, PLUS, SE, XL
Minimum Memory: 512K
Requires: 800K disk drive.
Medium: 3 1/2-inch disk
ISPN: 56744-500   **Price: $59.95**

DAR SYSTEMS INT'L.

MINES OF MORIA

You stand at the gates of Moria – head into the mine and then search for the way out in this tricky text venture.

System: MAC, II, PLUS, SE, XL
Minimum Memory: 512K
Medium: 3 1/2-inch disk
ISPN: 22287-500   **Price: $19.95**

DAR SYSTEMS INT'L.

MINES OF MORIA, PART TWO

A sequel to the Mines of Moria text adventure game.

System: MAC, II, PLUS, SE, XL
Minimum Memory: 512K
Requires: 128K ROM.
Medium: 3 1/2-inch disk
ISPN: 22287-510   **Price: $19.95**

ORIGIN SYSTEMS, INC.

MOEBIUS I-THE ORB OF CELESTIAL HARMONY

You must recover the stolen Orb of Celestial Harmony or chaos will erupt.

System: MAC, II, PLUS, SE
Minimum Memory: 512K
Medium: 3 1/2-inch disk
ISPN: 58793-750   **Price: $39.95**

INFOCOM, INC.

MOONMIST

Solve a classic gothic mystery set in a haunted castle on the mist shrouded seacoast of Cornwall.

System: MAC, II, PLUS, SE, XL
Minimum Memory: 512K
Medium: 3 1/2-inch disk
ISPN: 37413-045   **Price: $14.95**

INTRACORP, INC.

MURDER ON THE ATLANTIC (VER. 1.0)

Return to 1938 to solve a murder mystery that takes place on the SS Bourgogne.

System: MAC, II, PLUS, SE, XL
Minimum Memory: 512K
Medium: 3 1/2-inch disk
ISPN: 40531-444   **Price: $39.95**

OMNITREND SOFTWARE, INC.

PALADIN (VER. 1.0)

Return to the time of the Paladins, where only the bravest swordsman survived.

System: MAC, II, PLUS, SE, XL
Minimum Memory: 512K
Medium: 3 1/2-inch disk
ISPN: 58198-600   **Price: $39.95**

DAR SYSTEMS INT'L.

PITS OF DOOM!

Gather treasures from caverns which are guarded by monstrous creatures like medusas, balrogs and minotaurs.

System: MAC, II, PLUS, SE, XL
Minimum Memory: 512K
Medium: 3 1/2-inch disk
ISPN: 22287-600   **Price: $19.95**

INFOCOM, INC.

PLANETFALL

You, a lowly ensign, are exploded off your ship into a mysterious, deserted and sometimes humorous world.

System: MAC, II, PLUS, SE, XL
Minimum Memory: 128K
Requires: 400K formatted disks to save games in progress.
Medium: 3 1/2-inch disk
ISPN: 37413-050   **Price: $14.95**

INFOCOM, INC.

PLUNDERED HEARTS

Roam the high seas and bunk with pirates in this 17th century adventure.

System: MAC, II, PLUS, SE, XL
Minimum Memory:
Medium: 3 1/2-inch disk
ISPN: 37413-055   **Price: $39.95**

SIERRA ON-LINE, INC.

POLICE QUEST II-THE VENGEANCE

Follow the bloody trail of Jessie Bains (the Death Angel) as you play police detective Sonny Bonds.

System: MAC, II, PLUS, SE, XL
Minimum Memory: 512K
Medium: 3 1/2-inch disk
ISPN: 69925-535   **Price: $49.95**

OMNITREND SOFTWARE, INC.

SCROLLS OF TALMOUTH (THE)

A quest disk for Paladin, with 16 different games, all linked to form one grand quest to test you on your path to knighthood.

System: MAC, II, PLUS, SE, XL
Minimum Memory: 512K
Requires: Paladin (ISPN 58198-600).
Medium: 3 1/2-inch disk
ISPN: 58198-764   **Price: $24.95**

CINEMAWARE CORP.

SDI-STRATEGIC DEFENSE INITIATIVE

Get caught up in space combat as well as romance and intrigue of the near future.

System: MAC, II, PLUS, SE, XL
Minimum Memory: 128K
Medium: 3 1/2-inch disk
ISPN: 12656-030   **Price: $49.95**

MINDSCAPE, INC.

SHADOWGATE

Seek out and destroy the warlock before he carries out his evil deed.

System: MAC, II, PLUS, SE, XL
Minimum Memory: 512K
Medium: 3 1/2-inch disk
ISPN: 54375-639   **Price: $49.95**

ADDISON WESLEY PUBLISHING CO.

SHADOWS OF MORDOR

Keep the ring away from the greedy wizard, Sauron, in this adventure based on the Lord of the Rings.

System: MAC, II, PLUS, SE, XL
Minimum Memory: 512K
Requires: 800K disk drive.
Medium: 3 1/2-inch disk
ISPN: 00900-660   **Price: $39.95**

INFOCOM, INC.

SHERLOCK-THE RIDDLE OF THE CROWN JEWELS

You, Dr. Watson, must close the deadly trap that the evil Moriarty has set for your friend Sherlock Holmes.

System: MAC, II, PLUS, SE
Minimum Memory: 512K
Medium: 3 1/2-inch disk
ISPN: 37413-060   **Price: $39.95**

INFOCOM, INC.

SORCERER

A mystical clue starts you on a magical tour through the dark side of Zorkian enchantment.

System: MAC, II, PLUS, SE, XL
Minimum Memory: 128K
Requires: 400K formatted disks to save games in progress.
Medium: 3 1/2-inch disk
ISPN: 37413-070   **Price: $14.95**

SIERRA ON-LINE, INC.

SPACE QUEST III-THE PIRATES OF PESTULON

Become Roger Wilco and save two software developers from a fate worse than death.

System: MAC, II, PLUS, SE, XL
Minimum Memory: 512K
Medium: 3 1/2-inch disk
ISPN: 69925-642   **Price: $49.95**

INFOCOM, INC.

SPELLBREAKER

Enjoy the riveting conclusion to the Enchanter trilogy as you try to learn why magic is on the wane.

System: MAC, II, PLUS, SE, XL
Minimum Memory: 128K
Requires: 400K formatted disk to save games in progress.
Medium: 3 1/2-inch disk
ISPN: 37413-074   **Price: $14.95**

SIMON AND SCHUSTER ELECTRONIC PUBLISHING GROUP

STAR TREK-THE KOBAYASHI ALTERNATIVE

You must discover the location of a threatening 'Bermuda Triangle' in space. Work fast, it has already claimed a hospital ship.

System: MAC, II, PLUS, SE
Minimum Memory: 128K
Medium: 3 1/2-inch disk
ISPN: 70387-745   **Price: $39.95**

INFOCOM, INC.

STARCROSS

A science fiction interactive story/game where the moves that the player makes affect the outcome of the story.

System: MAC, II, PLUS, SE, XL
Minimum Memory:
Medium: 3 1/2-inch disk
ISPN: 37413-075   **Price: $9.95**

INFOCOM, INC.

STATION FALL

Join Floyd, the unforgettable robot, in a text adventure where the fate of the galaxy rests in your hands.

System: MAC, II, PLUS, SE, XL
Minimum Memory: 128K
Requires: 400K formatted disks to save games in progress.
Medium: 3 1/2-inch disk
ISPN: 37413-076   **Price: $39.95**

INFOCOM, INC.

SUSPECT

Go from being an unsuspecting news reporter to a murder suspect.

System: MAC, II, PLUS, SE, XL
Minimum Memory:
Medium: 3 1/2-inch disk
ISPN: 37413-713   **Price: $14.95**

INFOCOM, INC.

SUSPENDED

You awaken from a cryogenic state to find your planet 'gone mad' in this text adventure.

System: MAC, II, PLUS, SE, XL
Minimum Memory:
Medium: 3 1/2-inch disk
ISPN: 37413-080   **Price: $9.95**

EPYX COMPUTER SOFTWARE
TEMPLE OF APSHAI TRILOGY

Three quests bring you classic graphic adventure.

System: MAC
Minimum Memory: 512K
Medium: 3 1/2-inch disk
ISPN: 29575-810 **Price: $9.95**

POLARWARE PENGUIN SOFTWARE
TRANSYLVANIA

Put the clues together in time and Princess Sabrina is saved. Fail, and she dies at dawn.

System: MAC, II, PLUS, SE, XL
Minimum Memory: 64K
Medium: 3 1/2-inch disk
ISPN: 60425-300 **Price: $19.95**

INFOCOM, INC.
TRINITY

See what it's like to tour London when WWIII breaks out.

System: MAC, XL
Minimum Memory: 512K
Medium: 3 1/2-inch disk
ISPN: 37413-082 **Price: $14.95**

PARAGON SOFTWARE CORP.
TWILIGHT'S RANSOM

Become Ron Mulligan, who must save his girlfriend from the weird characters populating a decaying metropolis.

System: MAC, II, PLUS, SE, XL
Minimum Memory: 512K
Medium: 3 1/2-inch disk
ISPN: 53429-100 **Price: $34.95**

ORIGIN SYSTEMS, INC.
ULTIMA III-EXODUS

Step into a new fantasy world and use your skill and wit to find and destroy the insidious Exodus.

System: MAC, PLUS, SE, XL
Minimum Memory: 512K
Medium: 3 1/2-inch disk
ISPN: 58793-400 **Price: $59.95**

MINDSCAPE, INC.
UNINVITED

Take a trip through a demon-filled mansion where only the fearless can survive.

System: MAC, II, PLUS, SE, XL
Minimum Memory: 512K
Medium: 3 1/2-inch disk
ISPN: 54375-850 **Price: $49.95**

OMNITREND SOFTWARE, INC.
UNIVERSE II

As a deep-cover agent for the Federated Worlds, you will be called upon to carry out missions within enemy territory.

System: MAC, II, PLUS, SE, XL
Minimum Memory: 512K
Medium: 3 1/2-inch disk
ISPN: 58198-905 **Price: $49.95**

UNICORN SOFTWARE CO.
UTOPIA

A graphic adventure/strategy game that crashes you on a distant planet on the hostile side. You must get to the peaceful island.

System: MAC, II, PLUS, SE, XL
Minimum Memory: 512K
Medium: 3 1/2-inch disk
ISPN: 83562-750 **Price: $44.95**

REALITY TECHNOLOGIES
VENTURE MAGAZINES BUSINESS SIMULATOR

Provides the user with the various business experience, of running a company for 25 simulated years, from start to maturity.

System: MAC, II, PLUS, SE, XL
Minimum Memory: 512K
Requires: Two 800K disk drives or a hard disk.
Medium: 3 1/2-inch disk
ISPN: 65487-800 **Price: $69.95**

BRODERBUND SOFTWARE, INC.
WHERE IN THE WORLD IS CARMEN SANDIEGO?

Ages 10 and up: Solve the mystery, learn about geography and other cultures in an international chase.

System: MAC, II, PLUS, SE, XL
Minimum Memory: 512K
Medium: 3 1/2-inch disk
ISPN: 08850-701 **Price: $49.95**

BRODERBUND SOFTWARE, INC.
WHERE IN THE WORLD IS CARMEN SANDIEGO?

Ages 10 and up: Solve the mystery, learn about geography and other cultures in an international chase.

System: MAC, II, PLUS, SE, XL
Minimum Memory: 512K
Requires: School edition.
Medium: 3 1/2-inch disk
ISPN: 08850-701 **Price: $59.95**

BRODERBUND SOFTWARE, INC.
WHERE IN THE WORLD IS CARMEN SANDIEGO?

Ages 10 and up: Solve the mystery, learn about geography and other cultures in an international chase.

System: MAC, II, PLUS, SE, XL
Minimum Memory: 512K
Requires: Lab pack.
Medium: 3 1/2-inch disk
ISPN: 08850-701 **Price: $119.95**

INFOCOM, INC.
WISHBRINGER

You are an ordinary mail clerk – until one day when you deliver a note an elderly woman.

System: MAC, II, PLUS, SE, XL
Minimum Memory:
Medium: 3 1/2-inch disk
ISPN: 37413-095 **Price: $14.95**

INFOCOM, INC.
WITNESS

Your job as Chief Detective, is to solve a murder in this normally quiet L.A. Suburb.

System: MAC, II, PLUS, SE, XL
Minimum Memory: 512K
Medium: 3 1/2-inch disk
ISPN: 37413-801 **Price: $9.95**

SIR-TECH SOFTWARE, INC.
WIZARDRY I-PROVING GROUNDS OF THE MAD OVERLORD

Your job is to create and assemble a diverse crew of adventurers to retrieve the amulet.

System: MAC, PLUS, SE, XL
Minimum Memory: 128K
Medium: 3 1/2-inch disk
ISPN: 70750-400 **Price: $59.95**

INFOCOM, INC.
ZORK I-SOLID GOLD

Perils and predicaments ranging from the mystical to the macabre will dog your steps in this text adventure.

System: MAC, II, PLUS, SE, XL
Minimum Memory: 128K
Requires: 400K formatted disks to save games in progress.
Medium: 3 1/2-inch disk
ISPN: 37413-098 **Price: $14.95**

INFOCOM, INC.
ZORK II

Volcanoes, princesses, unicorns and a myriad of other objects test your inventivity in this text adventure.

System: MAC, II, PLUS, SE, XL
Minimum Memory: 128K
Requires: 400K formatted disk to save games in progress.
Medium: 3 1/2-inch disk
ISPN: 37413-100 **Price: $14.95**

INFOCOM, INC.
ZORK III

Your odyssey culminates in an encounter with the dungeon master himself.

System: MAC, II, PLUS, SE, XL
Minimum Memory: 128K
Requires: 400K formatted disk to save games in progress.
Medium: 3 1/2-inch disk
ISPN: 37413-105 **Price: $14.95**

INFOCOM, INC.
ZORK TRILOGY

Enjoy one of the most popular sequences of text adventures: Zork I, II and III.

System: MAC, PLUS, SE, XL
Minimum Memory:
Medium: 3 1/2-inch disk
ISPN: 37413-110   **Price: $49.95**

530 ENTERTAINMENT/ ARCADE/SIMULATION

HJC SOFTWARE, INC.
AIR TRAFFIC CONTROL SIMULATION

Real-time simulation places the user in the role of an Air Traffic Control specialist.

System: MAC, II, PLUS, SE, XL
Minimum Memory: 512K
Medium: 3 1/2-inch disk
ISPN: 92430-100   **Price: $49.95**

SILICON BEACH SOFTWARE
AIRBORNE!

Use an antiaircraft gun and a mortar to ward off waves of enemy paratroopers, tanks and jets.

System: MAC, PLUS, SE, XL
Minimum Memory: 128K
Medium: 3 1/2-inch disk
ISPN: 70237-100   **Price: $34.95**

SILICON BEACH SOFTWARE
APACHE STRIKE

You fly an attack helicopter through a maze of skyscrapers to evade enemy choppers and tanks and destroy deadly strategic computers.

System: MAC, II, PLUS, SE, XL
Minimum Memory: 1024K
Medium: 3 1/2-inch disk
ISPN: 70237-110   **Price: $49.95**

DISCOVERY SOFTWARE INT'L.
ARKANOID

Challenges the user to take charge of the Arkanoid, a galactic cruise ship, which has been attached by an alien drone ship.

System: MAC, II, PLUS, SE, XL
Minimum Memory: 512K
Medium: 3 1/2-inch disk
ISPN: 26178-100   **Price: $49.95**

SILICON BEACH SOFTWARE
BEYOND DARK CASTLE

A fast paced arcade style sequel to Dark Castle in which you control the hero as he battles his way through the castle again.

System: MAC, II, PLUS, SE, XL
Minimum Memory: 512K
Requires: 800K disk drive.
Medium: 3 1/2-inch disk
ISPN: 70237-015   **Price: $49.95**

RAINBIRD, DIV. OF MEDIAGENIC
CARRIER COMMAND

Capture over 60 islands while at the helm of a futuristic aircraft carrier equipped with multiple weapons.

System: MAC, II, PLUS, SE, XL
Minimum Memory: 512K
Medium: 3 1/2-inch disk
ISPN: 91828-070   **Price: $49.95**

ELECTRONIC ARTS
CHUCK YEAGER'S ADVANCED FLIGHT TRAINER

Test your flying skills with real and experimental aircraft at mach speeds.

System: MAC, II, PLUS, SE, XL
Minimum Memory: 512K
Medium: 3 1/2-inch disk
ISPN: 28512-026   **Price: $49.95**

CASADY & GREENE, INC.
CRITTEREDITOR

Gives you the power to create your own style of arcade game or change the world of Crystal Quest.

System: MAC, II, PLUS, SE, XL
Minimum Memory: 512K
Requires: Crystal Quest (ISPN 11556-200) (Ver. 2.2).
Medium: 3 1/2-inch disk
ISPN: 11556-195   **Price: $40.00**

CASADY & GREENE, INC.
CRYSTAL QUEST (VER. 2.2)

Players must collect all the crystals, while avoiding mines, bullets, and 12 varieties of 'super-nasties.'

System: MAC, II, PLUS, SE, XL
Minimum Memory: 512K
Requires: When ordering, specify 400K or 800K disk.
Medium: 3 1/2-inch disk
ISPN: 11556-200   **Price: $49.95**

CASADY & GREENE, INC.
CRYSTAL QUEST WITH CRITTEREDITOR

Collect all the crystals and avoid all the mines, bullets and 12 varieties of super-nasties. Create your own style arcade game.

System: MAC, II, PLUS, SE, XL
Minimum Memory: 1024K
Medium: 3 1/2-inch disk
ISPN: 11556-201   **Price: $79.95**

SILICON BEACH SOFTWARE
DARK CASTLE

A fast paced arcade-style action game in which you control the hero as he battles his way through the castle.

System: MAC, II, PLUS, SE, XL
Minimum Memory: 1024K
Requires: 800K disk drive.
Medium: 3 1/2-inch disk
ISPN: 70237-010   **Price: $49.95**

BULLSEYE SOFTWARE
FERRARI GRAND PRIX

Formula one race car simulator. Climb in, put your helmet on, strap yourself down. Ferrari Grand Prix is about to begin.

System: MAC, II, PLUS, SE, XL
Minimum Memory: 512K
Medium: 3 1/2-inch disk
ISPN: 09168-400   **Price: $59.95**

MICROILLUSIONS
FIRE POWER

Rescue your men, capture the enemy flag and avoid the enemy's shells in this arcade tank battle.

System: MAC, II, PLUS, SE, XL
Minimum Memory: 512K
Medium: 3 1/2-inch disk
ISPN: 50425-250   **Price: $29.95**

DYNACOMP, INC.
FLIGHT SIMULATOR (NON-GRAPHIC)

Enjoy the takeoff, flight, navigation and landing of an airplane in this mathematical simulation.

System: MAC, II, PLUS, SE, XL
Minimum Memory: 512K
Medium: 3 1/2-inch disk
ISPN: 27050-272   **Price: $28.95**

SPECTRUM HOLOBYTE, DIV. OF SPHERE, INC.
GATO

Captain a WWII attack sub in 3-D and real-time.

System: MAC, II, PLUS, SE, XL
Minimum Memory: 512K
Medium: 3 1/2-inch disk
ISPN: 75175-400   **Price: $49.95**

STRATEGIC SIMULATIONS, INC.
GEMSTONE WARRIOR

A strategic adventure game where the player's goal is to find the five missing pieces of the stolen Gemstone.

System: MAC
Minimum Memory: 128K
Medium: 3 1/2-inch disk
ISPN: 76500-625   **Price: $14.95**

MEDIAGENIC/SOLID GOLD SOFTWARE
HACKER

Challenging simulation of what a computer user might experience if he were to accidentally stumble into an unfamiliar computer system.

System: MAC, II, PLUS, SE, XL
Minimum Memory: 512K
Medium: 3 1/2-inch disk
ISPN: 48693-200   **Price: $19.95**

MILES COMPUTING, INC.

HARRIER STRIKE MISSION II

Simulates the flight of the Harrier JumpJet with flight combat, six scenarios and realistic 3-D action.

System: MAC, II, PLUS, SE, XL
Minimum Memory: 512K
Medium: 3 1/2-inch disk
ISPN: 54075-300 **Price: $49.95**

SUBLOGIC CORP.

JET (68000-BASED)

Puts you at the controls of an f-16 fighting Falcon or a carrier based F-18 Hornet.

System: MAC, II, PLUS, SE, XL
Minimum Memory: 512K
Medium: 3 1/2-inch disk
ISPN: 76950-121 **Price: $49.95**

PRACTICAL COMPUTER APPLICATIONS, INC.

LUNAR RESCUE (VER. 1.0)

The player searches for stolen control crystals that maintain the automated lunar defense network which has gone haywire.

System: MAC, PLUS, SE, XL
Minimum Memory: 512K
Requires: 800K disk drive.
Medium: 3 1/2-inch disk
ISPN: 59081-400 **Price: $59.95**

SOFTSTREAM INT'L., INC.

MAC MAN

Mac Man gobbles all the apples in each of 16 mazes, while the nasty PC's are hot on his trail.

System: MAC, PLUS, SE, XL
Minimum Memory: 512K
Medium: 3 1/2-inch disk
ISPN: 72232-500 **Price: $35.95**

OLDUVAI CORP.

MAZE SURVIVAL

Your mission is to keep a growing colony of bugs alive inside a changing maze. Features the capability for digitized sound effect.

System: MAC, II, PLUS, SE, XL
Minimum Memory: 128K
Medium: 3 1/2-inch disk
ISPN: 57812-500 **Price: $39.95**

MACRO MIND PUBLISHING

MAZE WARS +

Multiple player game via a modem or AppleTalk networks. Fight your way with a robot friend (or enemy) through waves of attacking foes.

System: MAC, PLUS, SE, XL
Minimum Memory: 512K
Medium: 3 1/2-inch disk
ISPN: 45904-200 **Price: $50.00**

MICROSOFT CORP.

MICROSOFT FLIGHT SIMULATOR (VER. 3.0)

The granddaddy of them all puts the stick of a Cassna 182 in your hands.

System: MAC, II, PLUS, SE, XL
Minimum Memory: 512K
Medium: 3 1/2-inch disk
ISPN: 53150-356 **Price: $49.95**

ISM, INC.

MIGHTY NERD

The player provides the super powers to the hero and defeats the super villains.

System: MAC, II, PLUS, SE, XL
Minimum Memory: 1024K
Medium: 3 1/2-inch disk
ISPN: 40882-500 **Price: $49.95**

ISM, INC.

MIGHTY NERD

The player provides the super powers to the hero and defeats the super villains.

System: II
Minimum Memory: 1024K
Medium: 3 1/2-inch disk
ISPN: 40882-500 **Price: $59.95**

DYNACOMP, INC.

MOONPROBE

Navigate your lunar lander to a precise and hopefully safe landing on the surface of the moon.

System: MAC, II, PLUS, SE, XL
Minimum Memory: 512K
Medium: 3 1/2-inch disk
ISPN: 27050-489 **Price: $21.95**

MARK OF THE UNICORN

MOUSE STAMPEDE

A pack of rabid mice is on the attack, and headed your way. If they run into a moldy piece of cheese they go wild and head for you.

System: MAC, II, PLUS, SE, XL
Minimum Memory: 512K
Medium: 3 1/2-inch disk
ISPN: 47250-325 **Price: $39.95**

CREATIVE SOLUTIONS, INC.

ORBITAL MECH

Simulates real-time spaceflight with rotational and translational thrusters activated by mouse or keyboard.

System: MAC, II, PLUS, SE, XL
Minimum Memory: 512K
Medium: 3 1/2-inch disk
ISPN: 20700-750 **Price: $49.95**

SPECTRUM HOLOBYTE, DIV. OF SPHERE, INC.

ORBITER

Move smoothly through launch, orbit, de-orbit and landing in this shuttle simulation.

System: MAC, II, PLUS, SE, XL
Minimum Memory: 512K
Medium: 3 1/2-inch disk
ISPN: 75175-500 **Price: $49.95**

BULLSEYE SOFTWARE

P51 MUSTANG FLIGHT SIMULATOR

Set during World War II, you pilot the most successful fighter of that era, the P51 Mustang.

System: MAC, II, PLUS, SE, XL
Minimum Memory: 1024K
Medium: 3 1/2-inch disk
ISPN: 09168-600 **Price: $59.95**

ELECTRONIC ARTS

PINBALL CONSTRUCTION SET

Be a pinball wizard on a machine you design, or play on one of five provided.

System: MAC, II, PLUS, SE, XL
Minimum Memory: 128K
Medium: 3 1/2-inch disk
ISPN: 28512-085 **Price: $19.95**

ADVANCED SIMULATION SYSTEMS

PROFESSIONAL AIR TRAFFIC CONTROLLER SIMULATOR

Simulation of the operation of an Federal Aviation Administration air traffic controller's radar screen.

System: MAC, II, PLUS, SE, XL
Minimum Memory: 512K
Requires: 40 or more users.
Medium: 3 1/2-inch disk
ISPN: 01438-600 **Price: $35.00**

ADVANCED SIMULATION SYSTEMS

PROFESSIONAL AIR TRAFFIC CONTROLLER SIMULATOR

Simulation of the operation of an Federal Aviation Administration air traffic controller's radar screen.

System: MAC, PLUS, XL
Minimum Memory: 512K
Requires: 1-40 users.
Medium: 3 1/2-inch disk
ISPN: 01438-600 **Price: $15.00**

CREATIVE SOLUTIONS, INC.

RACE CAR SIMULATOR

A 3-D game and toolkit.

System: MAC, II, PLUS, SE, XL
Minimum Memory: 512K
Medium: 3 1/2-inch disk
ISPN: 20700-600 **Price: $39.95**

PRACTICAL COMPUTER APPLICATIONS, INC.

ROAD RACER (VER. 1.0)

A high performance 1965 Corvette graphic simulation, driving through five environments from deserts to mountain roads.

System: MAC, II, PLUS, SE, XL
Minimum Memory: 1024K
Medium: 3 1/2-inch disk
ISPN: 59081-600 **Price: $69.95**

SUBLOGIC CORP.

SCENERY DISK 10 BILLINGS-TWIN-CITIES-GREEN BAY

Take a trip over the Billings/Twin Cities/Green Bay area with your flight simulator.

System: MAC, II, PLUS, SE, XL
Minimum Memory: 512K
Requires: Microsoft Flight Simulator (ISPN 53150-356), Jet (ISPN 76950-315).
Medium: 3 1/2-inch disk
ISPN: 76950-520 **Price: $29.95**

SUBLOGIC CORP.

SCENERY DISK 11 LAKE HURON-DETROIT

Take a trip over the Lake Huron/Detroit area with your flight simulator.

System: MAC, II, PLUS, SE, XL
Minimum Memory: 512K
Requires: Microsoft Flight Simulator (ISPN 53150-356) or Jet (ISPN 76950-315)
Medium: 3 1/2-inch disk
ISPN: 76950-522 **Price: $29.95**

SUBLOGIC CORP.

SCENERY DISK 12 HALIFAX-MONTREAL-NEW YORK

Take a trip over the Halifax/Montreal/New York area with your flight simulator.

System: MAC, II, PLUS, SE, XL
Minimum Memory: 512K
Requires: Microsoft Flight Simulator (ISPN 53150-356) or Jet (ISPN 76950-315).
Medium: 3 1/2-inch disk
ISPN: 76950-524 **Price: $29.95**

SUBLOGIC CORP.

SCENERY DISK 7 WASHINGTON-CHARLOTTE-MIAMI

Take a trip over the Washington/Charlotte/Miami area with your flight simulator.

System: MAC, II, PLUS, SE, XL
Minimum Memory: 512K
Requires: Microsoft Flight Simulator (ISPN 53150-356) or Jet (ISPN 76950-315).
Medium: 3 1/2-inch disk
ISPN: 76950-514 **Price: $29.95**

SUBLOGIC CORP.

SCENERY DISK 7-12 EASTERN U.S.

Expands the potential flying environment of the flight simulator programs. Includes radio-navigation aids and major airports.

System: MAC, II, PLUS, SE, XL
Minimum Memory: 512K
Requires: Microsoft Flight Simulator (ISPN 53150-356) or Jet (ISPN 76950-315).
Medium: 3 1/2-inch disk
ISPN: 76950-526 **Price: $149.95**

SUBLOGIC CORP.

SCENERY DISK 9 ST LOUIS-CHICAGO-CINCINNATI

Take a trip over the St Louis/Chicago/Cincinnati area with your flight simulator.

System: MAC, II, PLUS, SE, XL
Minimum Memory: 512K
Requires: Microsoft Flight Simulator (ISPN 53150-356) or Jet (ISPN 76950-315).
Medium: 3 1/2-inch disk
ISPN: 76950-518 **Price: $29.95**

SUBLOGIC CORP.

SCENERY DISK-JAPAN

Take an aerial excursion from Tokyo to Osaka.

System: MAC, II, PLUS, SE, XL
Minimum Memory: 512K
Requires: Flight Simulator II (ISPN 76950-215) or Jet (ISPN 76950-315).
Medium: 3 1/2-inch disk
ISPN: 76950-122 **Price: $29.95**

SUBLOGIC CORP.

SCENERY DISK-SAN FRANCISCO

Take an aerial trip over San Francisco, San Jose and Oakland.

System: MAC, II, PLUS, SE, XL
Minimum Memory: 512K
Requires: Flight Simulator II (ISPN 76950-215) or Jet (ISPN 76950-315).
Medium: 3 1/2-inch disk
ISPN: 76950-101 **Price: $29.95**

SUBLOGIC CORP.

SCENERY DISK-WESTERN EUROPEAN TOUR

Take an aerial excursion of England, France, West Germany and more.

System: MAC, II, PLUS, SE, XL
Minimum Memory: 512K
Requires: Flight Simulator II (ISPN 76950-215) or Jet (ISPN 76950-315).
Medium: 3 1/2-inch disk
ISPN: 76950-102 **Price: $29.95**

BRODERBUND SOFTWARE, INC.

SHUFFLEPUCK CAFE

Simulation of air hockey that pits the player against nine opponents, each with their own personality and skills.

System: MAC, II, PLUS, SE, XL
Minimum Memory: 512K
Requires: 800K disk drive.
Medium: 3 1/2-inch disk
ISPN: 08850-750 **Price: $39.95**

SIERRA ON-LINE, INC.

SILPHEED

Begin with a quote from Shakespeare and become the super dogfighter of the planet.

System: MAC, II, PLUS, SE, XL
Minimum Memory: 512K
Medium: 3 1/2-inch disk
ISPN: 69925-537 **Price: $34.95**

ELECTRONIC ARTS

SKYFOX

Contains a flight simulation in which you alone can save your colony from the invaders. For one player.

System: MAC, II, PLUS, SE, XL
Minimum Memory: 512K
Medium: 3 1/2-inch disk
ISPN: 28512-125 **Price: $19.95**

HEIZER SOFTWARE

SLOT MACHINE

A game which 'pays' on winning combinations and keeps a record of plays, the amount bet and won.

System: MAC, II, PLUS, SE, XL
Minimum Memory: 512K
Requires: Microsoft Excel (ISPN 53150-270).
Medium: 3 1/2-inch disk
ISPN: 35175-243 **Price: $5.00**

PRIMERA SOFTWARE

SMASH HIT RACQUETBALL (VER. 1.3)

A realistic, challenging game with animation, digitized sound, four ability levels, instant replay and more.

System: MAC, II, PLUS, SE, XL
Minimum Memory: 512K
Medium: 3 1/2-inch disk
ISPN: 62018-800 **Price: $19.95**

DYNACOMP, INC.

STARBASE 3.2

Battle 'new and improved' Croylin starships in this enhanced offshoot of the classic space simulation.

System: MAC, II, PLUS, SE, XL
Minimum Memory: 512K
Medium: 3 1/2-inch disk
ISPN: 27050-583 **Price: $22.95**

EPYX COMPUTER SOFTWARE

SUB BATTLE SIMULATOR

Direct six U.S. or German subs in the Atlantic or Pacific oceans during World War II.

System: MAC, PLUS, SE, XL
Minimum Memory: 512K
Medium: 3 1/2-inch disk
ISPN: 29575-668 **Price: $39.95**

SIGNAL COMPUTER CONSULTANTS

TRAIN DISPATCHER

In an accelerated eight-hour shift – move up to 12 trains in both directions through 150 miles of track.

System: MAC, PLUS, SE, XL
Minimum Memory: 512K
Medium: 3 1/2-inch disk
ISPN: 70125-875 **Price: $30.00**

RAINBIRD, DIV. OF MEDIAGENIC

UNIVERSAL MILITARY SIMULATOR

Features a 3-D grid landscape which gives a topographical battlefield of five historical battles.

System: MAC, PLUS, SE, XL
Minimum Memory: 512K
Medium: 3 1/2-inch disk
ISPN: 91828-860 **Price: $49.95**

THREE-SIXTY PACIFIC, INC.

WARLOCK

You alone have been chosen to rescue the stolen Karna from the depths of darkness. Journey through 20 levels to locate the jewel.

System: MAC, II, PLUS, SE, XL
Minimum Memory: 512K
Medium: 3 1/2-inch disk
ISPN: 81693-800 **Price: $44.95**

BETHESDA SOFTWORKS

WAYNE GRETZKY HOCKEY

Play, coach or watch a most realistic hockey simulation on a microcomputer.

System: MAC, II, PLUS, SE, XL
Minimum Memory: 512K
Medium: 3 1/2-inch disk
ISPN: 07542-100 **Price: $49.95**

535 ENTERTAINMENT/ ANIMATION/DRAWING/ MOVIE MAKING

ANIMCALC

ANIMCALC

Produce the same smooth moves on your hand animation stand as the new computer driven stands.

System: MAC, II, PLUS, SE, XL
Minimum Memory: 1024K
Medium: 3 1/2-inch disk
ISPN: 03656-100 **Price: $59.95**

MACRO MIND PUBLISHING

BLACK AND WHITE MOVIES

Contains 17 animated black and white movies designed for use with Videoworks II.

System: MAC, II, PLUS, SE, XL
Minimum Memory: 512K
Requires: VideoWorks II (ISPN 45904-440), two disk drives or one disk drive and hard disk.
Medium: 3 1/2-inch disk
ISPN: 45904-080 **Price: $49.95**

MACRO MIND PUBLISHING

CLIP ANIMATIONS

Contains 70 short animations for Overview presentations and Video Works II applications.

System: MAC, II, PLUS, SE, XL
Minimum Memory: 512K
Requires: VideoWorks II (ISPN 45904-440), two disk drives or one disk drive and hard disk.
Medium: 3 1/2-inch disk
ISPN: 45904-100 **Price: $59.95**

MACRO MIND PUBLISHING

CLIP SOUNDS

Contains 16 sounds and a Sound-to-Video program that allows users to import sounds to either VideoWorks II or HyperCard.

System: MAC, II, PLUS, SE, XL
Minimum Memory: 512K
Requires: VideoWorks II (ISPN 45904-440), or HyperCard (ISPN 3900-300), two disk drives or one disk drive and a hard disk.
Medium: 3 1/2-inch disk
ISPN: 45904-110 **Price: $59.95**

FREEMYERS DESIGN

CLIP VIDEO ART-ANIMATION EFFECTS

Provides animated clip art special effect graphics for use with VideoWorks II.

System: MAC, II, PLUS, SE, XL
Minimum Memory: 512K
Requires: Two 800K disk drives or hard disk, VideoWorks II (ISPN 45904-440).
Medium: 3 1/2-inch disk
ISPN: 31415-250 **Price: $59.95**

FREEMYERS DESIGN

CLIP VIDEO ART-PRESENTATION ANIMATION (VER. 1.0)

Has animated clip art graphic symbols including pie charts, bar charts and special effect graphics for enhancing presentations.

System: MAC, II, PLUS, SE, XL
Minimum Memory: 512K
Requires: Two 800K disk drives or a hard disk, VideoWorks II (ISPN 45904-440).
Medium: 3 1/2-inch disk
ISPN: 31415-255 **Price: $59.95**

MINDSCAPE, INC.

COMICWORKS

A paint program, a drawing tool, a text editor, and a page layout program in which the user can create comics, storyboards and more.

System: MAC, II, PLUS, SE, XL
Minimum Memory: 512K
Medium: 3 1/2-inch disk
ISPN: 54375-020 **Price: $79.95**

VOYAGER CO.

DREAM MACHINE DISCGUIDE (VER. 1.0)

Indexes motion-picture sequences on Dream Machine Videodisc.

System: MAC, II, PLUS, SE, XL
Minimum Memory: 1024K
Requires: HyperCard (ISPN 03900-300).
Medium: 3 1/2-inch disk
ISPN: 96647-200 **Price: $59.95**

BRIGHT STAR TECHNOLOGY

HYPERANIMATOR (VER. 1.0)

Creates and controls lip-synchronized talking actors or other sound-synchronized images using a random access animation tool.

System: MAC, II, PLUS, SE, XL
Minimum Memory: 1024K
Requires: HyperCard (ISPN 3900-300).
Medium: 3 1/2-inch disk
ISPN: 08459-300 **Price: $199.95**

BECK TECH

MACMOVIES

An image processor that provides full screen animation at speeds up to 30 screens per second.

System: MAC, II, PLUS, SE, XL
Minimum Memory: 512K
Medium: 3 1/2-inch disk
ISPN: 07225-500 **Price: $99.95**

MEDIAGENIC/ACTIVISION ENTERTAINMENT

MANHOLE

Ages 3-10: A Hypercard stack for children which features an animated story with animal sounds and digitized speech.

System: MAC, II, PLUS, SE, XL
Minimum Memory: 1024K
Requires: Hard disk, HyperCard (ISPN 03900-300).
Medium: 3 1/2-inch disk
ISPN: 48679-335 **Price: $49.95**

TELEROBOTICS INT'L., INC.

MUSIC AND SOUND SUPPLEMENT ONE

Contains 80 sounds for use in Course Builder or Video Builder in SoundCap/ SoundEdit format.

System: MAC, II, PLUS, SE, XL
Minimum Memory: 1024K
Requires: Course Builder (Ver. 3.0) (ISPN 80981-100) or Video Builder (Ver. 3.0) (ISPN 80981-700).
Medium: 3 1/2-inch disk
ISPN: 80981-600 **Price: $10.00**

IMAGE WORLD, INC.

SILHOUETTES AND SHADOWS

Silhouettes from old paper cutouts, shadow grams, drawings and prints were created for family entertainment and more.

System: MAC, II, PLUS, SE, XL
Minimum Memory: 128K
Medium: 3 1/2-inch disk
ISPN: 37181-450 **Price: $30.00**

UNICOM SOFTWARE DEVELOPMENT GROUP

STIX

Visual pattern entertainment program.

System: MAC
Minimum Memory: 128K
Medium: 3 1/2-inch disk
ISPN: 83550-004 **Price: $14.95**

SILICON BEACH SOFTWARE

SUPER 3D (VER. 2.0)

A three dimensional graphics editor that allows modeling and animation. Supports color and black and white graphics.

System: MAC, II, PLUS, SE, XL
Minimum Memory: 512K
Medium: 3 1/2-inch disk
ISPN: 70237-500 **Price: $495.00**

SOURCEVIEW SOFTWARE INT'L.

TALKSHOW

Branching slide show and graphic presentation with electronic voice accompaniment.

System: MAC, II, PLUS, SE, XL
Minimum Memory: 512K
Medium: 3 1/2-inch disk
ISPN: 70675-650 **Price: $49.99**

KINKOS ACADEMIC COURSEWARE EXCHANGE

THEATERGAME (THE) (VER. 1.0)

A theater-blocking simulation using characters from Hamlet.

System: MAC, II, PLUS, SE, XL
Minimum Memory: 512K
Requires: Finder (Ver. 4.1 or later).
Medium: 3 1/2-inch disk
ISPN: 43025-886 **Price: $25.00**

HEIZER SOFTWARE

US FLAG MACRO

Features a 'patriotic' command macro to construct a United States flag.

System: MAC, II, PLUS, SE, XL
Minimum Memory: 512K
Requires: Microsoft Excel (ISPN 53150-270).
Medium: 3 1/2-inch disk
ISPN: 35175-267 **Price: $3.00**

HEIZER SOFTWARE

VALENTINE MACRO

Uses a macro to build a Valentine's Day card.

System: MAC, II, PLUS, SE, XL
Minimum Memory: 512K
Requires: Microsoft Excel (ISPN 53150-270).
Medium: 3 1/2-inch disk
ISPN: 35175-264 **Price: $2.00**

SPINNAKER SOFTWARE

VIDEO WORKS

A full-featured animation program for presentations, training, storyboards, movies or cartoons.

System: MAC, II, PLUS, SE, XL
Minimum Memory: 512K
Medium: 3 1/2-inch disk
ISPN: 75300-171 **Price: $99.95**

MACRO MIND PUBLISHING

VIDEOWORKS II

An animation package that features advanced animation techniques, a text editor, improved graphics and color capabilities.

System: MAC, PLUS, SE, XL
Minimum Memory: 512K
Medium: 3 1/2-inch disk
ISPN: 45904-440 **Price: $295.00**

MACRO MIND PUBLISHING

VIDEOWORKS II ACCELERATOR

Takes any VideoWorks II movie and allows it to run at 40 frames per second.

System: MAC, II, PLUS, SE, XL
Minimum Memory: 1024K
Requires: VideoWorks II (ISPN 45904-440), two disk drives or one disk drive and a hard disk.
Medium: 3 1/2-inch disk
ISPN: 45904-510 **Price: $195.00**

MACRO MIND PUBLISHING

VIDEOWORKS II HYPERCARD DRIVER

Allows the playing of VideoWorks II movies from within a HyperCard stack.

System: MAC, II, PLUS, SE, XL
Minimum Memory: 1024K
Requires: HyperCard (ISPN 03900-300).
Medium: 3 1/2-inch disk
ISPN: 45904-500 **Price: $99.95**

MACRO MIND PUBLISHING

VIDEOWORKS PROFESSIONAL

An animation package that supports color cycling, 24-bit color, multiple palettes, and MIDI interfaces.

System: MAC, II, PLUS, SE, XL
Minimum Memory: 1024K
Requires: Two 800K disk drives or a hard disk.
Medium: 3 1/2-inch disk
ISPN: 45904-460 **Price: $695.00**

SILICON BEACH SOFTWARE

WORLD BUILDER

Allows the user to create text, graphic and digitized sound games and programs.

System: MAC, II, PLUS, SE, XL
Minimum Memory: 512K
Medium: 3 1/2-inch disk
ISPN: 70237-030 **Price: $79.95**

536 ENTERTAINMENT/ MISCELLANEOUS ENTERTAINMENT

VOYAGER CO.

AMANDA STORIES (VOL. 2) (VER. 1.0)

The adventures of Your Faithful Camel, a trustworthy pal on the road to good fortune, trips to deserts and the North Pole.

System: MAC, II, PLUS, SE, XL
Minimum Memory: 1024K
Requires: 800K disk drive, HyperCard (ISPN 03900-300).
Medium: 3 1/2-inch disk
ISPN: 96647-060 **Price: $19.95**

VOYAGER CO.

AMANDA STORIES VOL 1 (VER. 1.0)

HyperCard based adventures that features Inigo, the spunky and endearing cat in a series of four adventures.

System: MAC, II, PLUS, SE, XL
Minimum Memory: 1024K
Requires: 800K disk drive, HyperCard (ISPN 03900-300).
Medium: 3 1/2-inch disk
ISPN: 96647-050 **Price: $19.95**

XOR CORP.

BERMUDA SQUARE (VER. 1.0)

Find the best fit of squares in this puzzle game.

System: MAC, PLUS, SE, XL
Minimum Memory: 512K
Medium: 3 1/2-inch disk
ISPN: 87125-110 **Price: $29.95**

INTRACORP, INC.

BUMPER STICKER MAKER

Design and create your own bumper stickers.

System: MAC, II, PLUS, SE, XL
Minimum Memory: 512K
Medium: 3 1/2-inch disk
ISPN: 40531-700 **Price: $59.95**

HEIZER SOFTWARE

BUNNY RACE

Players set the number of bunnies, race speed and the length of time the pari-mutual window is open.

System: MAC, II, PLUS, SE, XL
Minimum Memory: 512K
Requires: Microsoft Excel (ISPN 53150-270).
Medium: 3 1/2-inch disk
ISPN: 35175-242 **Price: $5.00**

FIRST BYTE, INC.

COMPUTER MAD LIBS

Fill in the missing blanks from one of eight stories to create a hilarious twist to an old plot.

System: MAC, II, PLUS, SE, XL
Minimum Memory: 512K
Medium: 3 1/2-inch disk
ISPN: 30836-250 **Price: $19.95**

CENTRON SOFTWARE
CRAPSMASTER (VER. 3.2)

Place your bets and cash in your chips, just as they do in a Las Vegas casino.

System: MAC, II, PLUS, SE, XL
Minimum Memory: 512K
Medium: 3 1/2-inch disk
ISPN: 35869-300 **Price: $39.00**

ARTIFICIAL INTELLIGENCE RESEARCH GROUP
ELIZA (VER. 3.0)

Indulge in non-directive therapy or show off the artificial intelligence potential of your Personal Computer.

System: MAC, II, PLUS, SE, XL
Minimum Memory: 128K
Requires: QuickBasic (ISPN 53150-205).
Medium: 3 1/2-inch disk
ISPN: 05412-100 **Price: $45.00**

VISATEX CORP.
FACTS & FACES OF HOLLYWOOD GREATS (VER. 1.0)

A HyperCard stack with information and trivial about the great stars of Hollywood.

System: MAC, II, PLUS, SE, XL
Minimum Memory: 1024K
Requires: 800K disk drive, HyperCard (ISPN 03900-300).
Medium: 3 1/2-inch disk
ISPN: 85340-180 **Price: $49.50**

BROWNBAG SOFTWARE
MAC-FAIR

Seven programs along with 42 picture files that are utilized within these programs. Includes: Shooting Gallery, Dart Throw and more.

System: MAC, PLUS, SE, XL
Minimum Memory: 512K
Medium: 3 1/2-inch disk
ISPN: 08993-500 **Price: $39.95**

VIDEX, INC.
MACINTOSH FUNPAK

Games included are Sevens, Solitaire, King Albert, Klondike, and Four-in-a-row.

System: MAC, II, PLUS, SE, XL
Minimum Memory: 128K
Medium: 3 1/2-inch disk
ISPN: 85150-071 **Price: $39.00**

NORDIC SOFTWARE, INC.
MACKIDS-WORD SEARCH

Ages 6 to adult: Generates word puzzles and allows the user to create personalized word puzzles.

System: MAC, PLUS, SE, XL
Minimum Memory: 512K
Medium: 3 1/2-inch disk
ISPN: 57028-900 **Price: $39.95**

THINK EDUCATIONAL SOFTWARE
MIND OVER MAC

Contains five complete entertainment programs: Master Code, Destroyer, On-The-Contrary, Trivial Intrigue and Third Dimension.

System: MAC, II, PLUS, SE, XL
Minimum Memory: 128K
Medium: 3 1/2-inch disk
ISPN: 81375-550 **Price: $49.95**

HEIZER SOFTWARE
OSCAR NOMINEES DATABASE

A database of over 1700 Oscar nominees from 1928 to 1987.

System: MAC, PLUS, SE, XL
Minimum Memory: 1024K
Requires: Microsoft Excel (ISPN 53150-270), Microsoft Works (ISPN 53150-740) or HyperCard (ISPN 03900-300).
Medium: 3 1/2-inch disk
ISPN: 35175-067 **Price: $15.00**

FIRST ROW SOFTWARE PUBLISHING
PRIME TIME

Gives players the chance to run a TV network.

System: MAC, II, PLUS, SE, XL
Minimum Memory: 512K
Medium: 3 1/2-inch disk
ISPN: 91839-600 **Price: $39.95**

ADDISON WESLEY PUBLISHING CO.
PUPPY LOVE

Allows the user to build, train and invent their own tricks for training a puppy and create routines for puppies to perform.

System: MAC, PLUS, XL
Minimum Memory: 512K
Medium: 3 1/2-inch disk
ISPN: 00900-650 **Price: $29.95**

MILES COMPUTING, INC.
QUINTETTE

Master this 4000 year old Chinese game by aligning five stones in a row or by capturing five pairs of your opponent' stones.

System: MAC, PLUS, SE, XL
Minimum Memory: 512K
Medium: 3 1/2-inch disk
ISPN: 54075-600 **Price: $39.95**

MINDSCAPE, INC.
RACTER

Venture into the little known realm of artificial insanity with a computer conversationalist.

System: MAC, II, PLUS, SE, XL
Minimum Memory: 128K
Medium: 3 1/2-inch disk
ISPN: 54375-575 **Price: $44.95**

HEIZER SOFTWARE
RANDOM

Illustrates the graphics potential of an Excel worksheet.

System: MAC, II, PLUS, SE, XL
Minimum Memory: 512K
Requires: Microsoft Excel (ISPN 53150-270).
Medium: 3 1/2-inch disk
ISPN: 35175-344 **Price: $2.00**

ELECTRONIC ARTS
SOFTWARE GOLDEN OLDIES (VOL. 1) (VER. 2.4)

Play these four 'historic' computer game programs: Adventure, Eliza, Life and Pong.

System: MAC, PLUS, SE, XL
Minimum Memory: 512K
Medium: 3 1/2-inch disk
ISPN: 28512-120 **Price: $19.95**

MINDSCAPE, INC.
TRUST AND BETRAYAL-THE LEGACY OF SIBOOT

An icon based program where the user has to try to get information about other characters to win in mental combat and triumph.

System: MAC, II, PLUS, SE, XL
Minimum Memory: 512K
Medium: 3 1/2-inch disk
ISPN: 54375-785 **Price: $49.95**

545 ENTERTAINMENT/ SPORTS GAMES

LANCE HAFFNER GAMES
3 IN 1 COLLEGE AND PRO FOOTBALL

Enjoy endless hours of gridiron glory as you line up college and pro teams.

System: MAC, II, PLUS, SE, XL
Minimum Memory: 512K
Medium: 3 1/2-inch disk
ISPN: 43487-003 **Price: $39.99**

ACCOLADE
4TH & INCHES

Gives you all of the hard-hitting action of real football: the bombs, the blitzing, and the goal line stands.

System: MAC, PLUS, SE, XL
Minimum Memory: 512K
Medium: 3 1/2-inch disk
ISPN: 00543-620 **Price: $44.95**

ACCOLADE
4TH & INCHES-TEAM CONSTRUCTION DISK

Create any team and any type of player for your 4th & Inches pro football game.

System: MAC, PLUS, SE, XL
Minimum Memory: 512K
Requires: 4th & Inches (ISPN 00543-620).
Medium: 3 1/2-inch disk
ISPN: 00543-625 **Price: $14.95**

SIERRA ON-LINE, INC.
CHAMPIONSHIP BOXING

Recreate history's greatest bouts or stage a custom fight from a list of over 50 famous boxers.

System: MAC, II, PLUS, SE, XL
Minimum Memory: 512K
Medium: 3 1/2-inch disk
ISPN: 69925-029   **Price: $39.95**

SOFTSTREAM INT'L., INC.
COLOR BILLIARDS

Includes Billiards, Straight Pool, Snooker, 8-Ball, 9-Ball, Slop and lag. Includes sound, English, scoring caroms and full color.

System: MAC, II, PLUS, SE, XL
Minimum Memory: 512K
Medium: 3 1/2-inch disk
ISPN: 72232-100   **Price: $59.95**

MILES COMPUTING, INC.
DOWNHILL RACER

You are put on the cutting edge of hi-tech racing with all of the thrill and excitement of world-class competition.

System: MAC, PLUS, SE, XL
Minimum Memory: 512K
Medium: 3 1/2-inch disk
ISPN: 54075-002   **Price: $39.95**

ACCESS SOFTWARE, INC.
FAMOUS COURSES DISK (VOL. 1)

Link World Class Leader Board to Harbour Town and Dorado Beach.

System: MAC, II, PLUS, SE, XL
Minimum Memory: 512K
Requires: World Class Leader Board (ISPN 00525-600), joystick.
Medium: 3 1/2-inch disk
ISPN: 00525-028   **Price: $19.95**

ACCESS SOFTWARE, INC.
FAMOUS COURSES DISK (VOL. 2)

Lets you play on three of the world's most prestigious courses: Pebble Beach, Muirfield and Colonial Country Club.

System: MAC, II, PLUS, SE, XL
Minimum Memory: 512K
Requires: World Class Leader Board (ISPN 00525-600), joystick.
Medium: 3 1/2-inch disk
ISPN: 00525-015   **Price: $19.95**

ACCESS SOFTWARE, INC.
FAMOUS COURSES DISK (VOL. 3)

Link World Class Leader Board to Firestone, Sawgrass, Banff Springs or the Royal St. George's courses.

System: MAC, II, PLUS, SE, XL
Minimum Memory: 512K
Requires: World Class Leader Board (ISPN 00525-600), joystick.
Medium: 3 1/2-inch disk
ISPN: 00525-016   **Price: $19.95**

INFINITY SOFTWARE
GRAND SLAM TENNIS

A true tennis simulation game that feels and looks like a real live tennis match. Created by Tom Maremaa, a former professional player.

System: MAC, II, PLUS, SE, XL
Minimum Memory: 512K
Medium: 3 1/2-inch disk
ISPN: 92744-300   **Price: $49.95**

ACCOLADE
HARDBALL

Play on the field as you coach from the dugout on a 3-D baseball field.

System: MAC, II, PLUS, SE, XL
Minimum Memory: 512K
Medium: 3 1/2-inch disk
ISPN: 00543-405   **Price: $44.95**

ELECTRONIC ARTS
JULIUS ERVING AND LARRY BIRD GO ONE-ON-ONE

Play one-on-one as an NBA star with realistic dunks, turn around jump shots, fakes and dribbles.

System: MAC, II, PLUS, SE, XL
Minimum Memory: 512K
Medium: 3 1/2-inch disk
ISPN: 28512-040   **Price: $19.95**

PRACTICAL COMPUTER APPLICATIONS, INC.
MACCOURSES (VER. 1.0)

An application program with four courses (72 individual holes). Each course is par 72 and challenges the professional MacGolfer.

System: MAC, II, PLUS, SE, XL
Minimum Memory: 1024K
Requires: MacGolf (ISPN 59081-300).
Medium: 3 1/2-inch disk
ISPN: 59081-175   **Price: $34.95**

PRACTICAL COMPUTER APPLICATIONS, INC.
MACGOLF (VER. 2.0)

The ultimate graphic golf simulation game. Digitized golfing figure, real-life digitized sounds. Two 18-hole courses.

System: MAC, II, PLUS, SE, XL
Minimum Memory: 512K
Medium: 3 1/2-inch disk
ISPN: 59081-300   **Price: $59.95**

PRACTICAL COMPUTER APPLICATIONS, INC.
MACGOLF CLASSIC (VER. 3.0)

Provides digitized golfing with sound, color support for the Mac II , and includes the program MacCourses with extra ranges.

System: MAC, II, PLUS, SE, XL
Minimum Memory: 1024K
Requires: 800K disk drive.
Medium: 3 1/2-inch disk
ISPN: 59081-325   **Price: $94.90**

PRACTICAL COMPUTER APPLICATIONS, INC.
MACRACQUETBALL (VER. 2.0)

A challenging and accurate simulation of racquetball with a 3-D court, players and a ball. A mouse gives the user full control.

System: MAC, II, PLUS, SE, XL
Minimum Memory: 1024K
Medium: 3 1/2-inch disk
ISPN: 59081-350   **Price: $59.95**

ACCOLADE
MEAN 18-ULTIMATE GOLF

Learn the mechanics of a scratch game and try your skills on Pebble Beach, St. Andrews and Augusta.

System: MAC, II, PLUS, SE, XL
Minimum Memory: 512K
Medium: 3 1/2-inch disk
ISPN: 00543-650   **Price: $44.95**

XOR CORP.
NFL CHALLENGE

Football action with offensive plays and defensive sets based on NFL playbooks, plus complete updatable rosters for all 28 teams.

System: MAC, II, PLUS, SE, XL
Minimum Memory: 1024K
Requires: 800K disk drive.
Medium: 3 1/2-inch disk
ISPN: 87125-300   **Price: $99.95**

XOR CORP.
NFL CHALLENGE 1984 SEASON TEAM DISK

Replay the 1984 season with all the original players and teams.

System: MAC, PLUS, SE, XL
Minimum Memory: 1024K
Requires: NFL Challenge (ISPN 87125-300).
Medium: 3 1/2-inch disk
ISPN: 87125-350   **Price: $14.95**

XOR CORP.
NFL CHALLENGE 1985 SEASON TEAM DISK

Use the player ratings and rosters from each team in the 1985 season.

System: MAC, II, PLUS, SE, XL
Minimum Memory: 1024K
Requires: NFL Challenge (ISPN 87125-300).
Medium: 3 1/2-inch disk
ISPN: 87125-360   **Price: $14.95**

XOR CORP.
NFL CHALLENGE 1986 SEASON TEAM DISK

Relive the players, rosters and stats of the 1986 season with this disk and NFL Challenge.

System: MAC, II, PLUS, SE, XL
Minimum Memory: 1024K
Requires: NFL Challenge (ISPN 87125-300).
Medium: 3 1/2-inch disk
ISPN: 87125-320   **Price: $19.95**

FOR MORE DETAILED INFORMATION, CALL (412) 746-MENU

XOR CORP.
NFL CHALLENGE 1987 SEASON TEAM DISK
Relive the players, rosters and stats of the 1987 season with this disk and NFL challenge.
System: MAC, II, PLUS, SE, XL
Minimum Memory: 1024K
Requires: NFL Challenge (ISPN 87125-300).
Medium: 3 1/2-inch disk
ISPN: 87125-322 **Price: $19.95**

XOR CORP.
NFL CHALLENGE 1988 PRE-SEASON TEAM DISK
Relive the players, rosters and stats of the 1988 pre-season with this disk and NFL Challenge.
System: MAC, II, PLUS, SE, XL
Minimum Memory: 1024K
Requires: NFL Challenge (ISPN 87125-300).
Medium: 3 1/2-inch disk
ISPN: 87125-324 **Price: $19.95**

XOR CORP.
NFL CHALLENGE ALL-STAR DISK
Coach the greatest players from each team regardless of the years they played with this disk and NFL Challenge.
System: MAC, II, PLUS, SE, XL
Minimum Memory: 1024K
Requires: NFL Challenge (ISPN 87125-300).
Medium: 3 1/2-inch disk
ISPN: 87125-315 **Price: $24.95**

XOR CORP.
NFL CHALLENGE GAME SITUATION DEVELOPMENT SYSTEM
Create 'what if' game scenarios, replay a 'bad call' using your own game plan and re-do football history.
System: MAC, II, PLUS, SE, XL
Minimum Memory: 1024K
Requires: NFL Challenge (ISPN 87125-300).
Medium: 3 1/2-inch disk
ISPN: 87125-340 **Price: $19.95**

XOR CORP.
NFL CHALLENGE GREATEST TEAMS DISK
Play the best teams of each NFL franchise from the past 21 seasons.
System: MAC, II, PLUS, SE, XL
Minimum Memory: 1024K
Requires: NFL Challenge (ISPN 87125-300).
Medium: 3 1/2-inch disk
ISPN: 87125-310 **Price: $24.95**

XOR CORP.
NFL CHALLENGE ROSTER EDITOR DISK
Keep your team rosters current with the latest trades, retirements, cuts, injuries and lineup changes.
System: MAC, II, PLUS, SE, XL
Minimum Memory: 1024K
Requires: NFL Challenge (ISPN 87125-300).
Medium: 3 1/2-inch disk
ISPN: 87125-330 **Price: $19.95**

XOR CORP.
PRO CHALLENGE
Enjoy a coach's perspective on NFL football.
System: MAC, PLUS, SE, XL
Minimum Memory: 1024K
Medium: 3 1/2-inch disk
ISPN: 87125-400 **Price: $49.95**

PRIMERA SOFTWARE
SMASH HIT RACQUETBALL II
A realistic game with animation, digitized sound, and four ability levels for play by two users on separate Macintoshes.
System: MAC, II, PLUS, SE, XL
Minimum Memory: 512K
Medium: 3 1/2-inch disk
ISPN: 62018-810 **Price: $39.95**

EPYX COMPUTER SOFTWARE
WINTER GAMES
Bobsled, ski jump, figure skate, free style skate, aerial and finish the biathlon on your way to a medal.
System: MAC
Minimum Memory: 512K
Medium: 3 1/2-inch disk
ISPN: 29575-870 **Price: $19.95**

ACCESS SOFTWARE, INC.
WORLD CLASS LEADER BOARD
Take on the traps, trees and hazards of four courses: St. Andrews, Doral Country Club, Cypress Creek and Gauntlet Country Club.
System: MAC, II, PLUS, SE, XL
Minimum Memory: 512K
Requires: Joystick.
Medium: 3 1/2-inch disk
ISPN: 00525-600 **Price: $49.95**

550 ENTERTAINMENT/ STRATEGY

BRODERBUND SOFTWARE, INC.
ANCIENT ART OF WAR
Carry out entire military campaigns (not just battles) as you choose an army and challenge a military genius.
System: MAC, II, PLUS, SE, XL
Minimum Memory: 128K
Medium: 3 1/2-inch disk
ISPN: 08850-015 **Price: $44.95**

ELECTRONIC ARTS
ARCHON
Think strategically and tactically in this game of medieval fantasy.
System: MAC, PLUS, SE, XL
Minimum Memory: 512K
Medium: 3 1/2-inch disk
ISPN: 28512-010 **Price: $19.95**

JOKER SOFTWARE INT'L.
AUSSIE JOKER POKER
Play against the computer, or compete with up to 90 other players.
System: MAC, II, PLUS, SE, XL
Minimum Memory: 512K
Medium: 3 1/2-inch disk
ISPN: 41975-400 **Price: $49.95**

MINDSCAPE, INC.
BALANCE OF POWER
Players can be the American President or Soviet General Secretary, and must maintain the balance of power and prevent World War III.
System: MAC, II, PLUS, SE, XL
Minimum Memory: 512K
Requires: Lab pack (includes 5 disks).
Medium: 3 1/2-inch disk
ISPN: 54375-036 **Price: $109.90**

MINDSCAPE, INC.
BALANCE OF POWER
Players can be the American President or Soviet General Secretary, and must maintain the balance of power and prevent World War III.
System: MAC, II, PLUS, SE, XL
Minimum Memory: 64K
Medium: 3 1/2-inch disk
ISPN: 54375-036 **Price: $39.95**

MINDSCAPE, INC.
BALANCE OF POWER-THE 1990 EDITION
Players can be the American President or Soviet General Secretary and must maintain the balance of power and prevent World War III.
System: MAC, II, PLUS, SE, XL
Minimum Memory: 512K
Medium: 3 1/2-inch disk
ISPN: 54375-200 **Price: $49.95**

BRITANNICA SOFTWARE-BLUE CHIP SOFTWARE DIVISION
BARON
Teaches about investing in commercial, residential, and undeveloped property through the use of a real estate market simulation.
System: MAC, II, PLUS, SE, XL
Minimum Memory: 512K
Medium: 3 1/2-inch disk
ISPN: 07970-050 **Price: $49.95**

TIMELINE LTD.
BATTLE STATIONS
For one or two players. You command a fleet trying to hunt down and sink the enemy's fleet before he sinks you.
System: MAC, XL
Minimum Memory:
Medium: 3 1/2-inch disk
ISPN: 81981-100 **Price: $30.00**

DYNACOMP, INC.

BATTLEFIELD

Choose from eight battle terrains in this tactical clash of armor and infantry.

System: MAC, II, PLUS, SE, XL
Minimum Memory: 512K
Medium: 3 1/2-inch disk
ISPN: 27050-020   **Price: $24.95**

GARDE

BLUE POWDER GREY SMOKE

Take command of an army in three battles of the American Civil War including Antietam, Gettysburg and Chicamauga.

System: MAC, II, PLUS, SE, XL
Minimum Memory: 512K
Medium: 3 1/2-inch disk
ISPN: 92110-128   **Price: $49.95**

OMNITREND SOFTWARE, INC.

BREACH (VER. 1.0)

Guide a squad leader and squad of space marines through a variety of missions – or create your own.

System: MAC
Minimum Memory: 512K
Medium: 3 1/2-inch disk
ISPN: 58198-175   **Price: $39.95**

ARTWORX SOFTWARE CO., INC.

BRIDGE (VER. 5.0)

You and your computer partner play against two computer opponents to try and control the bid.

System: MAC, II, PLUS, SE, XL
Minimum Memory: 512K
Medium: 3 1/2-inch disk
ISPN: 05437-055   **Price: $34.95**

GREAT GAME PRODUCTS

BRIDGE BARON II

Play a complete game of bridge from over 1,000,000,000 random but repeatable deals.

System: MAC, II, PLUS, SE, XL
Minimum Memory: 512K
Medium: 3 1/2-inch disk
ISPN: 33443-755   **Price: $49.95**

HEIZER SOFTWARE

BRIDGE CONVENTIONS

Includes overviews and information on usage for 30 common bridge conventions. Details of the point count system is included.

System: MAC, II, PLUS, SE, XL
Minimum Memory: 1024K
Requires: HyperCard (ISPN 3900-300).
Medium: 3 1/2-inch disk
ISPN: 35175-066   **Price: $15.00**

HEIZER SOFTWARE

BRIDGE DEALER

Shuffles, deals and arranges by suit, four hands of bridge.

System: MAC, II, PLUS, SE, XL
Minimum Memory: 512K
Requires: Microsoft Excel (ISPN 53150-270).
Medium: 3 1/2-inch disk
ISPN: 35175-261   **Price: $3.00**

DYNACOMP, INC.

BRIDGE MASTER

Explore several bidding strategies – play a savvy team of PC opponents with a PC player on your side.

System: MAC, II, PLUS, SE, XL
Minimum Memory: 512K
Medium: 3 1/2-inch disk
ISPN: 27050-059   **Price: $34.95**

INFOCOM, INC.

BUREAUCRACY

Control frustrations and keep your blood pressure down by handling bureaucratic red tape.

System: MAC, II, PLUS, SE, XL
Minimum Memory: 512K
Medium: 3 1/2-inch disk
ISPN: 37413-008   **Price: $14.95**

DATAPAK SOFTWARE, INC.

CASINO CLASSICS

Contains four games, Blackjack (21), Poker (five card draw), Slots and Keno in one package and provides graphics and animation.

System: MAC, II, PLUS, SE, XL
Minimum Memory: 512K
Medium: 3 1/2-inch disk
ISPN: 23762-025   **Price: $39.95**

ELECTRONIC ARTS

CHESSMASTER 2000

Switch from among 12 play levels as you challenge a chess algorithm that stocks 71,000 moves.

System: MAC, PLUS, SE, XL
Minimum Memory: 512K
Medium: 3 1/2-inch disk
ISPN: 28512-025   **Price: $44.95**

ARTWORX SOFTWARE CO., INC.

COMPUBRIDGE

Based on a popular bridge text and consists of ten tutorials and eight computer generated quizzes to aid you in the game of bridge.

System: MAC, II, PLUS, SE, XL
Minimum Memory: 512K
Medium: 3 1/2-inch disk
ISPN: 05437-056   **Price: $19.95**

STRATEGIC SIMULATIONS, INC.

COMPUTER AMBUSH (VER. 1.0)

Features a game of man-to-man combat as the player commands a squad of soldiers in World War II.

System: MAC, II, PLUS, SE, XL
Minimum Memory: 512K
Medium: 3 1/2-inch disk
ISPN: 76500-200   **Price: $59.95**

MINDSCAPE, INC.

CROSSWORD MAGIC-CONSUMER VERSION

Create customized crossword puzzles that you can use over again.

System: MAC, II, PLUS, SE, XL
Minimum Memory: 48K
Medium: 3 1/2-inch disk
ISPN: 54375-045   **Price: $49.95**

HEIZER SOFTWARE

FIVE CARD STUD DEALER

Uses a macro to shuffle and deal eight hands of stud poker in three seconds.

System: MAC, II, PLUS, SE, XL
Minimum Memory: 512K
Requires: Microsoft Excel (ISPN 53150-270).
Medium: 3 1/2-inch disk
ISPN: 35175-265   **Price: $3.00**

HEIZER SOFTWARE

GAME WORDS

A database of all two, three and four-letter words in the Merriam Webster Dictionary and Official Scrabble Player's Dictionaries.

System: MAC, PLUS, SE, XL
Minimum Memory: 512K
Requires: Microsoft Excel (ISPN 53150-270) or Microsoft Works (ISPN 53150-740).
Medium: 3 1/2-inch disk
ISPN: 35175-241   **Price: $15.00**

INFINITY SOFTWARE

GO

Captures the excitement and challenge of the legendary game of strategy from the Orient.

System: MAC, II, PLUS, SE, XL
Minimum Memory: 512K
Requires: 800K disk drive.
Medium: 3 1/2-inch disk
ISPN: 92744-260   **Price: $49.95**

ARTSCI, INC.

HEARTS

Hearts card game with the Macintosh as your opponent. The Macintosh shuffles, deals and keeps score. Select the cards you want to pass.

System: MAC, II, PLUS, SE, XL
Minimum Memory: 512K
Medium: 3 1/2-inch disk
ISPN: 05425-025   **Price: $19.95**

FOR MORE DETAILED INFORMATION, CALL (412) 746-MENU

DATASOFT/INTELLICREATIONS, INC.

HUNT FOR RED OCTOBER

Command a Russian sub in a bid to defect to the United States.

System: MAC, II, PLUS, SE, XL
Minimum Memory: 512K
Medium: 3 1/2-inch disk
ISPN: 23850-410 **Price: $49.95**

HEIZER SOFTWARE

HYPERCHESS ARCHIVES

A software chess book and chess 'movie' projector which contains 100 famous short games of chess.

System: MAC, II, PLUS, SE, XL
Minimum Memory: 1024K
Requires: HyperCard (ISPN 3900-300).
Medium: 3 1/2-inch disk
ISPN: 35175-070 **Price: $20.00**

HEIZER SOFTWARE

IDEA MAKER

Produces random word pairs to generate ideas and product names.

System: MAC, II, PLUS, SE, XL
Minimum Memory: 512K
Requires: Microsoft Excel (ISPN 53150-270) or Microsoft Works (ISPN 53150-740).
Medium: 3 1/2-inch disk
ISPN: 35175-247 **Price: $9.00**

GREAT WAVE SOFTWARE

LOC

Fun educational games for young children and challenging strategy games for adults.

System: MAC, II, PLUS, SE, XL
Minimum Memory: 512K
Medium: 3 1/2-inch disk
ISPN: 33476-170 **Price: $29.95**

VIDEX, INC.

MAC CHECKERS AND REVERSI

Includes two games, checkers and reversi where players plot to trap and capture opponents pieces.

System: MAC, II, PLUS, SE, XL
Minimum Memory: 128K
Medium: 3 1/2-inch disk
ISPN: 85150-065 **Price: $49.00**

VIDEX, INC.

MAC GAMMON AND CRIBBAGE

A game of blended luck and skill, choose from a variety of strategies and playing levels to build your skills.

System: MAC, PLUS, SE, XL
Minimum Memory: 128K
Medium: 3 1/2-inch disk
ISPN: 85150-067 **Price: $49.00**

VIDEX, INC.

MAC VEGAS (VER. 1.3)

Challenge your skill and cunning at the gaming table. Includes: Roulette, Poker, Blackjack, Baccarat, Slots, Craps and Keno.

System: MAC, PLUS, SE, XL
Minimum Memory: 128K
Medium: 3 1/2-inch disk
ISPN: 85150-069 **Price: $59.00**

DATAPAK SOFTWARE, INC.

MAC-JACK II

Black Jack card game which has 1, 2, 4, and 6 deck selection, sound effects, speed deal option and Las Vegas rules.

System: MAC, PLUS, SE, XL
Minimum Memory: 128K
Medium: 3 1/2-inch disk
ISPN: 23762-250 **Price: $25.00**

DATAPAK SOFTWARE, INC.

MAC-POKER

Five-card draw poker game that features animated graphics, wild betting action and is mouse controlled.

System: MAC, II, PLUS, SE, XL
Minimum Memory: 128K
Medium: 3 1/2-inch disk
ISPN: 23762-525 **Price: $25.00**

EXPERT SOFTWARE SYSTEMS, INC.

MACGAMMON

Realistic game at expert level, an understanding of backgammon essentials: key points, blocking, timing, running and doubling.

System: MAC, II, PLUS, SE, XL
Minimum Memory:
Medium: 3 1/2-inch disk
ISPN: 30471-500 **Price: $19.95**

BRITANNICA SOFTWARE-BLUE CHIP SOFTWARE DIVISION

MILLIONAIRE I

Teaches about financial investment in this stock market simulation.

System: MAC, II, PLUS, SE, XL
Minimum Memory: 512K
Medium: 3 1/2-inch disk
ISPN: 07970-100 **Price: $49.95**

DYNACOMP, INC.

MONARCH

Budget your country's resources or your monarchy could topple.

System: MAC, II, PLUS, SE, XL
Minimum Memory: 512K
Medium: 3 1/2-inch disk
ISPN: 27050-488 **Price: $23.95**

NEWSOFT

NEWGAMMON

Computer Backgammon. Play against the Mac or another opponent. Tournament scoring, adjustable skill levels and doubling cube.

System: MAC, PLUS, SE, XL
Minimum Memory: 128K
Medium: 3 1/2-inch disk
ISPN: 56762-500 **Price: $39.95**

INFOCOM, INC.

NORD AND BERT COULDN'T MAKE HEAD OR TAIL OF IT

When you live in the town of Punster, expect word play and verbal tricks.

System: MAC, II, PLUS, SE, XL
Minimum Memory: 64K
Medium: 3 1/2-inch disk
ISPN: 37413-046 **Price: $39.95**

ORIGIN SYSTEMS, INC.

OGRE (VER. 1.14)

Defend a command post against a cybernetic supertank bristling with weapons.

System: MAC, XL
Minimum Memory: 128K
Medium: 3 1/2-inch disk
ISPN: 58793-300 **Price: $29.95**

XOR CORP.

OLIGOPOLY (VER. 1.0)

Dominate the globe as you establish worldwide monopolies.

System: MAC, II, PLUS, SE, XL
Minimum Memory: 512K
Requires: Two 400k disk drives or a hard disk.
Medium: 3 1/2-inch disk
ISPN: 87125-390 **Price: $49.95**

ELECTRONIC ARTS

PATTON VS. ROMMEL

The Allies have a fingernail-hold on the beach. It's D-Day and you as Patton or Rommel must push your troops to victory.

System: MAC, II, PLUS, SE, XL
Minimum Memory: 512K
Medium: 3 1/2-inch disk
ISPN: 28512-099 **Price: $19.95**

GREAT GAME PRODUCTS

PLAY BRIDGE WITH DOROTHY TRUSCOTT

Learn the secrets of winning play from Dorothy Truscott, renowned bridge player.

System: MAC, II, PLUS, SE, XL
Minimum Memory: 256K
Medium: 3 1/2-inch disk
ISPN: 33443-770 **Price: $29.95**

GREAT GAME PRODUCTS

PLAY BRIDGE WITH SHEINWOLD

Learn the secrets of winning play from Alfred Sheinwold, reknowned bridge player.

System: MAC, II, PLUS, SE, XL
Minimum Memory: 256K
Medium: 3 1/2-inch disk
ISPN: 33443-751 **Price: $29.95**

CENTRON SOFTWARE

POKER MASTER

Take your initial stake of $10,000 and win or go broke in this video poker recreation.

System: MAC, II, PLUS, SE, XL
Minimum Memory: 512K
Medium: 3 1/2-inch disk
ISPN: 35869-115 **Price: $39.00**

PSION, INC.

PSION CHESS

1984 World Micro Champion. Makes superb use of graphics and the Macintosh Interface. Switch between six languages for variety.

System: MAC, XL
Minimum Memory: 128K
Medium: 3 1/2-inch disk
ISPN: 63681-600 **Price: $59.95**

SPECTRUM HOLOBYTE, DIV. OF SPHERE, INC.

PT-109 (VER. 1.1)

Take the PT boat, WWII's most daring vessel, on Pacific and Mediterranean hunts.

System: MAC, II, PLUS, SE, XL
Minimum Memory: 1024K
Medium: 3 1/2-inch disk
ISPN: 75175-550 **Price: $49.95**

HEIZER SOFTWARE

PUZZLE

Presents the original Macintosh Puzzle desk accessory.

System: MAC, XL
Minimum Memory: 512K
Requires: Microsoft Excel (ISPN 53150-270).
Medium: 3 1/2-inch disk
ISPN: 35175-262 **Price: $5.00**

INFOCOM, INC.

QUARTERSTAFF

You have been recruited for a brave mission to discover 'what fate has befallen the gentle souls' of the Tree Druid colony.

System: MAC, II, PLUS, SE, XL
Minimum Memory: 512K
Medium: 3 1/2-inch disk
ISPN: 37413-150 **Price: $49.95**

STRATEGIC STUDIES GROUP

REACH FOR THE STARS (VER. 3.0)

A game of colonization, expansion and conflict in a hypothetical galaxy.

System: MAC, II, PLUS, SE, XL
Minimum Memory: 512K
Medium: 3 1/2-inch disk
ISPN: 76525-650 **Price: $44.95**

SPINNAKER SOFTWARE

SARGON III

Chess for players of all ages, interests and skill, includes nine levels of play, 68,000 moves, novice instruction and brain teasers.

System: MAC, II, PLUS, SE, XL
Minimum Memory: 128K
Medium: 3 1/2-inch disk
ISPN: 75300-041 **Price: $49.95**

ELECTRONIC ARTS

SCRABBLE

Experience board game fun at your PC.

System: MAC, II, PLUS, SE, XL
Minimum Memory: 512K
Medium: 3 1/2-inch disk
ISPN: 28512-101 **Price: $39.95**

OMNITREND SOFTWARE, INC.

SERAYACHI CAMPAIGN (THE)

Test your mettle against a challenging set of opponents and conditions with this combat disk. Contains 16 different scenarios.

System: MAC, II, PLUS, SE, XL
Minimum Memory: 512K
Requires: Breach (ISPN 58198-175).
Medium: 3 1/2-inch disk
ISPN: 58198-783 **Price: $24.95**

ELECTRONIC ARTS

SEVEN CITIES OF GOLD

The Conquistador's dilemma-trade or fight-needs your solution.

System: MAC, PLUS, SE, XL
Minimum Memory: 512K
Medium: 3 1/2-inch disk
ISPN: 28512-100 **Price: $19.95**

MEDIAGENIC/SOLID GOLD SOFTWARE

SHANGHAI

Captivating strategy challenge devised from the ancient Chinese game of Mah Jongg.

System: MAC, II, PLUS, SE, XL
Minimum Memory: 512K
Requires: 800K disk drive.
Medium: 3 1/2-inch disk
ISPN: 48693-500 **Price: $19.95**

MAXIS SOFTWARE, INC.

SIMCITY

A simulation strategy game where the user is mayor and city planner of a simulated city.

System: MAC, II, PLUS, SE, XL
Minimum Memory: 512K
Medium: 3 1/2-inch disk
ISPN: 47900-710 **Price: $49.95**

HEIZER SOFTWARE

SOLITAIRE

Play the game of Solitaire using a Microsoft Excel macro.

System: MAC, II, PLUS, SE, XL
Minimum Memory: 512K
Requires: Microsoft Excel (ISPN 53150-270).
Medium: 3 1/2-inch disk
ISPN: 35175-984 **Price: $7.00**

SOFTSTREAM INT'L., INC.

SOLITAIRE DA

A desk accessory game including Klondike, the Boston variation, or Pyramid. Includes on-line help, replay, new game, undo and look.

System: MAC, II, PLUS, SE, XL
Minimum Memory: 512K
Medium: 3 1/2-inch disk
ISPN: 72232-700 **Price: $35.95**

SPECTRUM HOLOBYTE, DIV. OF SPHERE, INC.

SOLITAIRE ROYALE

Play solitaires: Pyramid, Golf, Klondike, Canfield, Corners, Calculation, three Shuffles and a Draw and Reno.

System: II
Minimum Memory: 1024K
Requires: 800K double-sided disk drive.
Medium: 3 1/2-inch disk
ISPN: 75175-610 **Price: $34.95**

SPECTRUM HOLOBYTE, DIV. OF SPHERE, INC.

SOLITAIRE ROYALE

Play solitaires: Pyramid, Golf, Klondike, Canfield, Corners, Calculation, three Shuffles and a Draw and Reno.

System: MAC, II, XL
Minimum Memory: 512K
Requires: 400K single-sided disk drive.
Medium: 3 1/2-inch disk
ISPN: 75175-610 **Price: $34.95**

DYNACOMP, INC.

SPACE EVACUATION

Evacuate as many people as possible before the sun explodes.

System: MAC, II, PLUS, SE, XL
Minimum Memory: 512K
Medium: 3 1/2-inch disk
ISPN: 27050-565 **Price: $24.95**

BRITANNICA SOFTWARE-BLUE CHIP SOFTWARE DIVISION

SQUIRE

A financial planning simulation which is both entertaining and educational.

System: MAC, II, PLUS, SE, XL
Minimum Memory: 512K
Medium: 3 1/2-inch disk
ISPN: 07970-200   **Price: $49.95**

DYNACOMP, INC.

STAR CON

Conquer the planets before they conquer you.

System: MAC, II, PLUS, SE, XL
Minimum Memory: 512K
Medium: 3 1/2-inch disk
ISPN: 27050-574   **Price: $24.95**

INTERSTEL CORP.

STAR FLEET I-THE WAR BEGINS

The United Galactic Alliance is counting on you to destroy the dangerous Krellans and savage Zaldrons.

System: MAC, II, PLUS, SE, XL
Minimum Memory: 512K
Medium: 3 1/2-inch disk
ISPN: 21751-800   **Price: $54.95**

PBI SOFTWARE

STRATEGIC CONQUEST PLUS

A strategic tactical game which the user commands and army, navy, and air force to conquer the enemy and challenge the computer.

System: MAC, II, PLUS, SE, XL
Minimum Memory: 1024K
Medium: 3 1/2-inch disk
ISPN: 59937-600   **Price: $59.95**

SPECTRUM HOLOBYTE, DIV. OF SPHERE, INC.

TETRIS

Manipulate odd shaped pieces into position as they descend from the top of the screen to the bottom.

System: MAC, II, PLUS, SE, XL
Minimum Memory: 512K
Medium: 3 1/2-inch disk
ISPN: 75175-650   **Price: $34.95**

SPECTRUM HOLOBYTE, DIV. OF SPHERE, INC.

TETRIS

Manipulate odd shaped pieces into position as they descend from the top of the screen to the bottom.

System: II
Minimum Memory: 1024K
Requires: RGB color monitor.
Medium: 3 1/2-inch disk
ISPN: 75175-650   **Price: $39.95**

CALIFORNIA DREAMS

TRIANGO

Capture the excitement, as well as your opponent's stones, in this Oriental classic game with a new twist.

System: MAC, II, PLUS, SE, XL
Minimum Memory: 512K
Medium: 3 1/2-inch disk
ISPN: 10575-727   **Price: $39.95**

BRITANNICA SOFTWARE-BLUE CHIP SOFTWARE DIVISION

TYCOON

Teaches the user about the commodities market through a challenging simulation.

System: MAC, II, PLUS, SE, XL
Minimum Memory: 512K
Medium: 3 1/2-inch disk
ISPN: 07970-300   **Price: $49.95**

PALANTIR, INC.

WORDPLAY

Powerful tool for solving word puzzles of all sorts, featuring crossword and puzzles without diagrams.

System: MAC, II, PLUS, SE, XL
Minimum Memory: 512K
Medium: 3 1/2-inch disk
ISPN: 59624-800   **Price: $49.95**

INFOCOM, INC.

ZORK ZERO

Covers a century of time and explores the collapse of the great underground empire. Has as many puzzles as the entire Zork Trilogy.

System: MAC, II, PLUS, SE, XL
Minimum Memory: 512K
Medium: 3 1/2-inch disk
ISPN: 37413-125   **Price: $59.95**

615 SCIENCES/ ASTRONOMY

E & M SOFTWARE

ASTRONOMY (VER. 2.8)

Plots the solar system and an image of the heavens for a given date time, longitude, and latitude.

System: MAC, XL
Minimum Memory: 512K
Medium: 3 1/2-inch disk
ISPN: 27331-076   **Price: $19.95**

HEIZER SOFTWARE

DEEP SKY OBJECTS

Twelve fields of information on over 1000 objects, which include galaxies, bright nebula, dark nebula, and geostellar poles.

System: MAC, II, PLUS, SE, XL
Minimum Memory: 512K
Requires: Microsoft Works (ISPN 53150-740) or Microsoft Excel (ISPN 53150-270).
Medium: 3 1/2-inch disk
ISPN: 35175-873   **Price: $25.00**

HEIZER SOFTWARE

HYPERSKY

Allows user to scan the heavens from the display screen, and includes over 70 percent of the sky.

System: MAC, XL
Minimum Memory: 1024K
Requires: HyperCard (ISPN 03900-300).
Medium: 3 1/2-inch disk
ISPN: 35175-446   **Price: $25.00**

ETLON SOFTWARE

MACSTRONOMY (VER. 1.2B)

Provides views of the sky for any date, time, or field of view location on earth.

System: MAC, II, PLUS, SE, XL
Minimum Memory: 128K
Medium: 3 1/2-inch disk
ISPN: 29937-500   **Price: $75.00**

HEIZER SOFTWARE

MOON PHASE CALCULATOR

Calculates the moon phase for any date.

System: MAC, II, PLUS, SE, XL
Minimum Memory: 512K
Requires: Microsoft Excel (ISPN 53150-270).
Medium: 3 1/2-inch disk
ISPN: 35175-148   **Price: $9.00**

MACTRAK SOFTWARE

SATELLITE HELPER (VER. 1.3)

Calculates and displays positions of orbiting earth satellites. Offers both graphic and tabular data displays.

System: MAC, II, PLUS, SE, XL
Minimum Memory: 512K
Requires: 800K disk drive.
Medium: 3 1/2-inch disk
ISPN: 65131-500   **Price: $59.95**

MACTRAK SOFTWARE

SATELLITE PRO (VER. 1.0)

Calculates and displays positions of orbiting earth satellites.

System: MAC, II, PLUS, SE, XL
Minimum Memory: 1024K
Requires: 800K disk drive.
Medium: 3 1/2-inch disk
ISPN: 65131-700   **Price: $99.95**

HEIZER SOFTWARE

SATELLITES OF JUPITER

Calculates the position of the sun, Jupiter and Jupiter's four brightest satellites.

System: MAC, II, PLUS, SE, XL
Minimum Memory: 512K
Requires: Microsoft Excel (ISPN 53150-270).
Medium: 3 1/2-inch disk
ISPN: 35175-146   **Price: $12.00**

MICROILLUSIONS

SKY TRAVEL

Provides accurate mathematical models of the solar system and a database of thousands of celestial objects.

System: SE
Minimum Memory: 512K
Medium: 3 1/2-inch disk
ISPN: 50425-725   **Price: $69.95**

HEIZER SOFTWARE

SOLAR SYSTEM CALCULATOR

Calculates the location of the sun, moon and principal planets.

System: MAC, II, PLUS, SE, XL
Minimum Memory: 512K
Requires: Microsoft Excel (ISPN 53150-270).
Medium: 3 1/2-inch disk
ISPN: 35175-145   **Price: $25.00**

MOUSETRAP SOFTWARE

STARGAZER

A display and quiz astronomy program for 1200 stars and the shapes of major constellations.

System: MAC, II, PLUS, SE, XL
Minimum Memory:
Medium: 3 1/2-inch disk
ISPN: 55484-150   **Price: $24.95**

ARKTOS ENTERPRISES

STARVIEW I

Includes stars through magnitude 3.5. Displays a 180 degree view of the sky for any desired time, location, date, and direction.

System: MAC, II, PLUS, SE, XL
Minimum Memory: 128K
Requires: QuickBasic (ISPN 53150-205)
Medium: 3 1/2-inch disk
ISPN: 05256-575   **Price: $24.50**

ARKTOS ENTERPRISES

STARVIEW II

Computer planetarium shows positions of stars and planets for any location or time to a magnitude of 4.99.

System: MAC, II, PLUS, SE, XL
Minimum Memory: 128K
Medium: 3 1/2-inch disk
ISPN: 05256-600   **Price: $37.50**

HEIZER SOFTWARE

SUN AND MOON/RISE AND SET

Calculates the positions of the sun and moon for any location on Earth for any date and time.

System: MAC, II, PLUS, SE, XL
Minimum Memory: 512K
Requires: Microsoft Excel (ISPN 53150-270).
Medium: 3 1/2-inch disk
ISPN: 35175-147   **Price: $12.00**

SPECTRUM HOLOBYTE, DIV. OF SPHERE, INC.

TELLSTAR LEVEL II (VER. 1.03)

Contains three detailed star tables covering the Northern and Southern hemispheres and all of the Messier objects.

System: MAC, II, PLUS, SE, XL
Minimum Memory: 512K
Medium: 3 1/2-inch disk
ISPN: 75175-625   **Price: $19.95**

---

620 SCIENCES/BIOLOGY

BIOSOFT

ASSAYZAP (VER. 1.1)

Provides a universal assay calculator for handling large assays and maintaining a record of assays for comparisons.

System: MAC, II, PLUS, SE, XL
Minimum Memory: 512K
Medium: 3 1/2-inch disk
ISPN: 28881-140   **Price: $249.00**

NORTON W.W.

BLIND WATCHMAKER (VER. 1.0)

Compresses the evolutionary time line to demonstrate the process of natural selection. Includes the book, 'The Blind Watchmaker'.

System: MAC, II, PLUS, SE, XL
Minimum Memory: 512K
Medium: 3 1/2-inch disk
ISPN: 57290-100   **Price: $17.90**

TEXTCO

DNA INSPECTOR IIE (VER. 3.01)

A DNA analysis program for molecular geneticists which contains standard analysis routines and is HFS compatible.

System: MAC, PLUS, SE, XL
Minimum Memory: 1024K
Medium: 3 1/2-inch disk
ISPN: 81277-251   **Price: $345.00**

TEXTCO

GENE COMMUNICATOR (VER. 1.10)

Accessory program for DNA Inspector II, II+ and IIE.

System: MAC, II, PLUS, SE, XL
Minimum Memory: 1024K
Requires: DNA Inspector IIE (ISPN 81277-251).
Medium: 3 1/2-inch disk
ISPN: 81277-300   **Price: $199.00**

UNIVERSITY OF MINNESOTA

MACCHROMOSOME (VER. 3.0)

Reduces chromosome measuring time by converting the process from ruler-on-photo to a computer.

System: MAC, II, PLUS, SE, XL
Minimum Memory: 512K
Requires: Scanner that will create a paint document.
Medium: 3 1/2-inch disk
ISPN: 84215-500   **Price: $145.00**

SOFTWARE DEVELOPMENT GROUP

PISCES (VER. 3.0)

Automatically calculates oxygen saturation, estimated biomass, and recommended feeding percentages for aquaculture research.

System: MAC, II, PLUS, SE, XL
Minimum Memory: 1024K
Medium: 3 1/2-inch disk
ISPN: 72681-600   **Price: $185.00**

---

625 SCIENCES/ CHEMISTRY

MODERN GRAPHICS

CHEMSTACK (VER. 1.0)

A HyperCard stack for constructing and indexing chemical structures, also includes a large indexed structure library.

System: MAC, II, PLUS, SE, XL
Minimum Memory: 1024K
Requires: HyperCard (ISPN 03900-300).
Medium: 3 1/2-inch disk
ISPN: 54925-200   **Price: $79.95**

INTERACTIVE MICROWARE, INC.

CHROMAC (VER. 5.01)

An easy-to-use, mouse-driven chromatography data acquisition, display and analysis package.

System: MAC, II, PLUS, SE, XL
Minimum Memory: 512K
Medium: 3 1/2-inch disk
ISPN: 39300-111   **Price: $3500.00**

ROCKWARE, INC.

ELEMENTARY DATA PERIODIC TABLE (VER. 2.0)

Yields chemical and geological data on all the known elements in the Periodic Table.

System: MAC, II, PLUS, SE, XL
Minimum Memory: 128K
Medium: 3 1/2-inch disk
ISPN: 66643-202   **Price: $75.00**

E & M SOFTWARE

EQUILIBRIUM (VER. 1.0)

Calculates equilibrium concentrations for up to 18 species involved in up to 18 reaction equations.

System: MAC, II, PLUS, SE, XL
Minimum Memory: 512K
Requires: Microsoft QuickBasic (ISPN 53150-205).
Medium: 3 1/2-inch disk
ISPN: 27331-300   **Price: $28.00**

KINKOS ACADEMIC COURSEWARE EXCHANGE
HUCKEL MOLECULAR ORBITALS (VER. 2.2)

Calculates energy eigenvalues, eigenvectors, pi-electron charge densities, and pi-electron orders using HMO theory.

System: MAC, PLUS, SE, XL
Minimum Memory: 512K
Medium: 3 1/2-inch disk
ISPN: 43025-230 **Price: $20.00**

KINKOS ACADEMIC COURSEWARE EXCHANGE
KSIMS

A simulation for determining the rate law and the reaction rate of a chemical reaction.

System: MAC, PLUS, SE, XL
Minimum Memory: 128K
Requires: Finder (Ver. 4.1 or 5.3).
Medium: 3 1/2-inch disk
ISPN: 43025-300 **Price: $21.50**

ROCKWARE, INC.
MINERAL DATA BASE-HAND SPECIMEN (VER. 2.0)

Includes physical properties such as color, luster, streak, hardness and habit for the common minerals.

System: MAC, II, PLUS, SE, XL
Minimum Memory: 512K
Requires: Microsoft File, Filemaker Plus (ISPN 55970-375).
Medium: 3 1/2-inch disk
ISPN: 66643-502 **Price: $50.00**

ROCKWARE, INC.
MINERAL DATA BASE-THIN SECTION (VER. 2.0)

Includes optical orientation diagrams for over 2/3 of the minerals. Allows you to sort on relief, birefringence, elongation and more.

System: MAC, II, PLUS, SE, XL
Minimum Memory: 512K
Requires: Microsoft File, Filemaker Plus (ISPN 55970-375).
Medium: 3 1/2-inch disk
ISPN: 66643-501 **Price: $75.00**

KINKOS ACADEMIC COURSEWARE EXCHANGE
MOLECULAR EDITOR (VER. 1.1)

A construction kit for building molecules and crystals that can be represented by interconnected points or spheres in 3-D.

System: MAC, II, PLUS, SE, XL
Minimum Memory: 512K
Requires: 800K disk, Finder (Ver. 4.1 or later).
Medium: 3 1/2-inch disk
ISPN: 43025-490 **Price: $30.50**

MODERN GRAPHICS
ORGANIC FONTS (VER. 1.2)

Allows users to create professional quality chemical structures, within any graphics or word processing program.

System: MAC, II, PLUS, SE, XL
Minimum Memory: 512K
Medium: 3 1/2-inch disk
ISPN: 54925-600 **Price: $79.95**

E & M SOFTWARE
REACTIONS (VER. 1.0)

Chemical Reaction Rate program. Calculates time-varying species concentrations for up to 18 species and 18 reaction equations.

System: MAC, II, PLUS, SE, XL
Minimum Memory: 512K
Requires: Microsoft QuickBasic (ISPN 53150-205).
Medium: 3 1/2-inch disk
ISPN: 27331-700 **Price: $28.00**

HEIZER SOFTWARE
SEAWATER PROPERTIES

Measures density, boiling point elevation and specific heat of seawater concentrates as functions of salinity and temperature.

System: MAC, II, PLUS, SE, XL
Minimum Memory: 512K
Requires: Microsoft Excel (ISPN 53150-270).
Medium: 3 1/2-inch disk
ISPN: 35175-705 **Price: $20.00**

635 SCIENCES/EARTH

KINKOS ACADEMIC COURSEWARE EXCHANGE
GEOSTRUCTURES (VER. 1.2)

Helps students of geology understand and interpret the full 3-D expression of geologic structures.

System: MAC, II, PLUS, SE, XL
Minimum Memory: 512K
Medium: 3 1/2-inch disk
ISPN: 43025-205 **Price: $8.00**

ROCKWARE, INC.
MACGRIDZO (VER. 1.1)

Provides gridding and contouring from user-selected data.

System: MAC, II, PLUS, SE, XL
Minimum Memory: 512K
Requires: 800K disk drive.
Medium: 3 1/2-inch disk
ISPN: 66643-490 **Price: $325.00**

ROCKWARE, INC.
MACMOHR

A circle calculation program providing graphic displays of Mohr's circles, and analytical information concerning stress parameters.

System: MAC, II, PLUS, SE, XL
Minimum Memory: 128K
Medium: 3 1/2-inch disk
ISPN: 66643-500 **Price: $75.00**

ROCKWARE, INC.
MACSECTION (VER. 1.0)

Plots strip-logs, cross-sections, and fence diagrams. Includes 50 customizable lithology patterns.

System: MAC, PLUS, SE, XL
Minimum Memory: 512K
Medium: 3 1/2-inch disk
ISPN: 66643-505 **Price: $300.00**

HEIZER SOFTWARE
PAINT USA MAP

A HyperCard stack which produces a scaled map of the United States within a defined area, by clicking the mouse twice.

System: MAC, II, PLUS, SE, XL
Minimum Memory: 512K
Requires: HyperCard (ISPN 03900-300).
Medium: 3 1/2-inch disk
ISPN: 35175-974 **Price: $15.00**

ROCKWARE, INC.
PIPER-STIFF (VER. 1.0)

Plots Piper and Stiff diagrams for hydrology. Includes adjustable scales, titles, well name and label options.

System: MAC, II, PLUS, SE, XL
Minimum Memory: 512K
Medium: 3 1/2-inch disk
ISPN: 66643-655 **Price: $225.00**

ROCKWARE, INC.
ROSY

Two dimensional orientation analysis program.

System: MAC, II, PLUS, SE, XL
Minimum Memory: 512K
Medium: 3 1/2-inch disk
ISPN: 66643-690 **Price: $150.00**

ROCKWARE, INC.
STEREO

A stereographic projection program.

System: MAC, II, PLUS, SE, XL
Minimum Memory: 512K
Requires: Word processor, ImageWriter.
Medium: 3 1/2-inch disk
ISPN: 66643-700 **Price: $199.00**

ROCKWARE, INC.
STRAIN-GRAPH

Strain-Graph, Deform-A-Pic, and Shear Zone which perform various types of strain on 2-D images on the screen.

System: MAC, II, PLUS, SE, XL
Minimum Memory: 512K
Requires: ImageWriter printer, Microsoft QuickBasic (ISPN 53150-205), MacPaint (ISPN 12784-510).
Medium: 3 1/2-inch disk
ISPN: 66643-750 **Price: $100.00**

PAZ GRAPHICS

TERNARY PLOT (VER. 3.0)

Contains a graphic plotting package that normalizes and plots three values on a triangular diagram.

System: MAC, II, PLUS, SE, XL
Minimum Memory: 512K
Medium: 3 1/2-inch disk
ISPN: 59912-500   **Price: $100.00**

PAZ GRAPHICS

VECTOR ROSE (VER. 1.0)

Calculates vector statistics and plots a circular histogram for any set of directional data.

System: MAC, II, PLUS, SE, XL
Minimum Memory: 512K
Medium: 3 1/2-inch disk
ISPN: 59912-800   **Price: $100.00**

660 SCIENCES/ MATHEMATICS

DYNACOMP, INC.

ADAM OSBORNE SOFTWARE COLLECTION-DOUBLE DENSITY

Contains four disks on topics including average growth rate, prime factors, integration and tax depreciation.

System: MAC, II, PLUS, SE, XL
Minimum Memory: 512K
Requires: Microsoft QuickBasic (ISPN 53150-205).
Medium: 3 1/2-inch disk
ISPN: 27050-085   **Price: $47.95**

KINKOS ACADEMIC COURSEWARE EXCHANGE

ALPAL (VER. 1.0)

Presents linear programming by three methods: graphical, algebraic and simplex. Features sensitivity analysis and duality.

System: MAC, II, PLUS, SE, XL
Minimum Memory: 128K
Requires: Finder (Ver. 4.1 or later).
Medium: 3 1/2-inch disk
ISPN: 43025-050   **Price: $21.50**

DYNACOMP, INC.

BASIC SCIENTIFIC SUBROUTINES (VOL. 1) CHAPTER 4

Consists of Table Interpolation, Differentiation and Integration that is keyed to Chapter 5 in the BASIC Scientific Subroutine text.

System: MAC, II, PLUS, SE, XL
Minimum Memory: 512K
Medium: 3 1/2-inch disk
ISPN: 27050-048   **Price: $23.95**

DYNACOMP, INC.

BASIC SCIENTIFIC SUBROUTINES (VOL. 2) CHAPTER 1

Contains least squares approximation keyed to Chapter I in the BASIC Scientific Subroutines McGraw-Hill text.

System: MAC, II, PLUS, SE, XL
Minimum Memory: 512K
Medium: 3 1/2-inch disk
ISPN: 27050-044   **Price: $23.95**

DYNACOMP, INC.

BASIC SCIENTIFIC SUBROUTINES (VOL. 2) CHAPTER 2

Provides scientific subroutines written in Basic.

System: MAC, II, PLUS, SE, XL
Minimum Memory: 512K
Medium: 3 1/2-inch disk
ISPN: 27050-045   **Price: $23.95**

DYNACOMP, INC.

BASIC SCIENTIFIC SUBROUTINES (VOL. 2) CHAPTER 3

Functional approximations by iteration and recursion relates to the BASIC Scientific Subroutines (Vol. II) text by McGraw-Hill.

System: MAC, II, PLUS, SE, XL
Minimum Memory: 512K
Medium: 3 1/2-inch disk
ISPN: 27050-046   **Price: $23.95**

DYNACOMP, INC.

BASIC SCIENTIFIC SUBROUTINES (VOL. 2) CHAPTER 4

Approximation techniques and alternatives corresponding to Chapter four in the BASIC Scientific Subroutines (Vol. II) text.

System: MAC, II, PLUS, SE, XL
Minimum Memory: 512K
Medium: 3 1/2-inch disk
ISPN: 27050-047   **Price: $23.95**

DYNACOMP, INC.

BASIC SCIENTIFIC SUBROUTINES (VOL. 2) CHAPTER 6

Finding the Real Roots of Functions corresponds to Chapter six in the BASIC Scientific Subroutines (Vol. II) text by McGraw-Hill.

System: MAC, PLUS, SE, XL
Minimum Memory: 512K
Medium: 3 1/2-inch disk
ISPN: 27050-049   **Price: $23.95**

DYNACOMP, INC.

BASIC SCIENTIFIC SUBROUTINES (VOL. 2) CHAPTER 7

Finding the Complex Roots of Functions corresponds to the BASIC Scientific Subroutines (Vol. II) text by McGraw-Hill.

System: MAC, II, PLUS, SE, XL
Minimum Memory: 512K
Medium: 3 1/2-inch disk
ISPN: 27050-050   **Price: $23.95**

DYNACOMP, INC.

BASIC SCIENTIFIC SUBROUTINES (VOL. 2) CHAPTER 8

Optimization by Steepest Descent corresponding to the BASIC Scientific Subroutine (Vol. II) text by McGraw-Hill.

System: MAC, II, PLUS, SE, XL
Minimum Memory: 512K
Medium: 3 1/2-inch disk
ISPN: 27050-051   **Price: $23.95**

DYNACOMP, INC.

BASIC SCIENTIFIC SUBROUTINES (VOL. 3) CHAPTER 1

Provides subroutines to calculate the probability of density, cumulative and inverse cumulative distributions.

System: MAC, II, PLUS, SE, XL
Minimum Memory: 512K
Medium: 3 1/2-inch disk
ISPN: 27050-806   **Price: $34.95**

DYNACOMP, INC.

BASIC SCIENTIFIC SUBROUTINES (VOL.1) COLLECTION II

A package that is keyed to Chapter four of Basic Scientific Subroutines (Vol. I).

System: MAC, II, PLUS, SE, XL
Minimum Memory: 512K
Medium: 3 1/2-inch disk
ISPN: 27050-804   **Price: $25.95**

DYNACOMP, INC.

BASIC SCIENTIFIC SUBROUTINES (VOL.1)COLLECTION III

A package that is keyed to Chapters five and six of Basic Scientific Subroutines (Vol. I).

System: MAC, II, PLUS, SE, XL
Minimum Memory: 512K
Medium: 3 1/2-inch disk
ISPN: 27050-805   **Price: $25.95**

KINKOS ACADEMIC COURSEWARE EXCHANGE

BIG ALPAL (VER. 1.0)

A tool to be used in solving linear programming problems with up to 800 variables and constraints with sensitivity analysis.

System: MAC, PLUS, SE, XL
Minimum Memory: 128K
Requires: Finder (Ver. 4.1 or 5.3).
Medium: 3 1/2-inch disk
ISPN: 43025-088　　　　　**Price: $21.50**

HEIZER SOFTWARE

BINARY CONVERTER

Contains two macros which convert Arabic to binary numbers and binary numbers to Arabic.

System: MAC, II, PLUS, SE, XL
Minimum Memory: 512K
Requires: Microsoft Excel (ISPN 53150-270).
Medium: 3 1/2-inch disk
ISPN: 35175-510　　　　　**Price: $10.00**

SPECTRUM COMPUTING, INC.

CHAMELEON (VER. 2.2)

Encyclopedic weights and measures conversion program for education, engineering and science. Over 100 million conversions are possible.

System: MAC
Minimum Memory: 128K
Medium: 3 1/2-inch disk
ISPN: 75162-100　　　　　**Price: $69.95**

HEIZER SOFTWARE

CIRCLE BY THREE POINTS

Determines the radius and center of a circle or arc, given any three points.

System: MAC, II, PLUS, SE, XL
Minimum Memory: 512K
Requires: Microsoft Excel (ISPN 53150-270).
Medium: 3 1/2-inch disk
ISPN: 35175-564　　　　　**Price: $14.00**

HEIZER SOFTWARE

CIRCLE INTERSECTION

Features array function macros which determine the point of intersection between two circles, or a circle and a straight line.

System: MAC, II, PLUS, SE, XL
Minimum Memory: 512K
Requires: Microsoft Excel (ISPN 53150-270).
Medium: 3 1/2-inch disk
ISPN: 35175-560　　　　　**Price: $15.00**

HEIZER SOFTWARE

CIRCLE SECTOR

Provides chord and arc length, segment rise, center to chord, radius and angle when given any two dimensions.

System: MAC, II, PLUS, SE, XL
Minimum Memory: 512K
Requires: Microsoft Excel (ISPN 53150-270) or Microsoft Works (ISPN 53150-740).
Medium: 3 1/2-inch disk
ISPN: 35175-562　　　　　**Price: $14.00**

JAM TECHNOLOGIES

CONVERT

A desk accessory that converts values to and from the metric system.

System: MAC, II, PLUS, SE, XL
Minimum Memory: 1024K
Medium: 3 1/2-inch disk
ISPN: 41388-150　　　　　**Price: $15.00**

HEIZER SOFTWARE

CUBIC DATA INTERPOLATION MACRO

Function macros which interpolate and differentiate, or determine the slope of tabular data.

System: MAC, II, PLUS, SE, XL
Minimum Memory: 512K
Requires: Microsoft Excel (ISPN 53150-270).
Medium: 3 1/2-inch disk
ISPN: 35175-571　　　　　**Price: $18.00**

HEIZER SOFTWARE

CUBIC VLOOKUP (VALUE AND SLOPE)

Interpolates values between table entries and differentiates or determines the slope between table entries.

System: MAC, II, PLUS, SE, XL
Minimum Memory: 512K
Requires: Microsoft Excel (ISPN 53150-270).
Medium: 3 1/2-inch disk
ISPN: 35175-578　　　　　**Price: $24.00**

KINKOS ACADEMIC COURSEWARE EXCHANGE

DEGRAPH (VER. 1.04)

Graphs differential equations with a MacPaint-style interface.

System: MAC, II, PLUS, SE, XL
Minimum Memory: 512K
Medium: 3 1/2-inch disk
ISPN: 43025-106　　　　　**Price: $22.00**

DECISION SCIENCE SOFTWARE

DYNAM

Computer model designed to solve the 'knapsack' version of Dynamic Programming.

System: MAC, II, PLUS, SE, XL
Minimum Memory:
Medium: 3 1/2-inch disk
ISPN: 24325-125　　　　　**Price: $50.00**

MICROMOTION

FLOATING POINT

Includes trigonometric, logarithmic and hyperbolic functions.

System: MAC, II, PLUS, SE, XL
Minimum Memory: 512K
Requires: MasterForth (ISPN 52750-520).
Medium: 3 1/2-inch disk
ISPN: 52750-080　　　　　**Price: $60.00**

HEIZER SOFTWARE

GEOMETRIC PROGRESSION

Determines the most favorable size series when specifying prominent design characteristics.

System: MAC, II, PLUS, SE, XL
Minimum Memory: 512K
Requires: Microsoft Excel (ISPN 53150-270).
Medium: 3 1/2-inch disk
ISPN: 35175-318　　　　　**Price: $14.00**

HEIZER SOFTWARE

GEOMETRIC SOLIDS

Determines the relationships between dimensional proportions, volumes and surface areas for 12 geometric solids.

System: MAC, II, PLUS, SE, XL
Minimum Memory: 1024K
Requires: HyperCard (ISPN 03900-300).
Medium: 3 1/2-inch disk
ISPN: 35175-441　　　　　**Price: $15.00**

HEIZER SOFTWARE

INTEGRATION-SIMPSON'S RULE

Calculates the area under the curve for continuous functions according to Simpson's Rule, using parabolic curve fitting.

System: MAC, II, PLUS, SE, XL
Minimum Memory: 512K
Requires: Microsoft Works (ISPN 53150-740) or Microsoft Excel (ISPN 53150-270).
Medium: 3 1/2-inch disk
ISPN: 35175-796　　　　　**Price: $20.00**

KINKOS ACADEMIC COURSEWARE EXCHANGE

IVP (VER. 1.0)

A collection of Microsoft BASIC templates that enables the user to make graphical studies of initial-value problems.

System: MAC, II, PLUS, SE, XL
Minimum Memory: 512K
Requires: Microsoft BASIC.
Medium: 3 1/2-inch disk
ISPN: 43025-240　　　　　**Price: $16.50**

LIONHEART PRESS

LINEAR & NON-LINEAR PROGRAMMING

Enables the user to solve mathematical problems with linear, non-linear and quadratic programming techniques.

System: MAC, PLUS, SE, XL
Minimum Memory: 512K
Medium: 3 1/2-inch disk
ISPN: 44900-500　　　　　**Price: $95.00**

DYNACOMP, INC.

LINEAR PROGRAMMER

Solves the standard linear programming inequality problem.

System: MAC, II, PLUS, SE, XL
Minimum Memory: 512K
Medium: 3 1/2-inch disk
ISPN: 27050-470　　　　　**Price: $38.95**

DECISION SCIENCE SOFTWARE
LINEAR REGRESSION

Provides linear regression operations which enables the analyst to solve problems.

System: MAC, II, PLUS, SE, XL
Minimum Memory:
Medium: 3 1/2-inch disk
ISPN: 24325-850   **Price: $65.00**

DECISION SCIENCE SOFTWARE
LINPRO

Generalizes implementation of the Simplex technique of solving mathematical problems which may be formulated as linear programs.

System: MAC, II, PLUS, SE, XL
Minimum Memory:
Medium: 3 1/2-inch disk
ISPN: 24325-300   **Price: $80.00**

BV ENGINEERING
LOCIPRO-ROOT LOCUS ANALYSIS PROGRAM

Determines closed loop system stability from a description of the open loop LaPlace transfer functions.

System: MAC, II, PLUS, SE, XL
Minimum Memory: 512K
Medium: 3 1/2-inch disk
ISPN: 09875-300   **Price: $145.95**

COOKE PUBLICATIONS
MACELASTIC (VER. 1.0) (PROFESSIONAL)

Solves 2-D and axisymmetric problems in classical elasticity and is limited only by RAM available.

System: MAC, PLUS, SE, XL
Minimum Memory: 512K
Medium: 3 1/2-inch disk
ISPN: 19659-305   **Price: $495.00**

COHERENT COGNITION (CA)
MACMATHPASCAL

A HyperCard stack containing a collection of source listings for Pascal programs. Performs complex mathematical equations.

System: MAC, II, PLUS, SE, XL
Minimum Memory: 128K
Requires: HyperCard (ISPN 03900-300), Pascal compiler.
Medium: 3 1/2-inch disk
ISPN: 13419-500   **Price: $100.00**

COOKE PUBLICATIONS
MACPOISSON (VER. 1.0)

Provides a visual interface for the formulation, solution, and presentation result of Poisson Partial Differential Equations.

System: MAC, II, PLUS, SE, XL
Minimum Memory: 512K
Requires: Professional version.
Medium: 3 1/2-inch disk
ISPN: 19659-505   **Price: $495.00**

COOKE PUBLICATIONS
MACPOISSON (VER. 1.0)

Provides a visual interface for the formulation, solution, and presentation result of Poisson Partial Differential Equations.

System: MAC, II, PLUS, SE, XL
Minimum Memory: 512K
Requires: Student version.
Medium: 3 1/2-inch disk
ISPN: 19659-505   **Price: $99.95**

DECISION SCIENCE SOFTWARE
MARKOV

An interactive computer model that analyzes Basic Markov processes.

System: MAC, II, PLUS, SE, XL
Minimum Memory:
Medium: 3 1/2-inch disk
ISPN: 24325-500   **Price: $50.00**

HEIZER SOFTWARE
MATH FUNCTION MACRO SET

Twenty-eight mathematical function macros including Bessel Functions, Elliptical Integrals and Exponential Integrals.

System: MAC, II, PLUS, SE, XL
Minimum Memory: 512K
Requires: Microsoft Excel (ISPN 53150-270).
Medium: 3 1/2-inch disk
ISPN: 35175-570   **Price: $60.00**

BRAINPOWER, INC.
MATHVIEW PROFESSIONAL

Handles wide range of math problems such as function evaluation, linear and non-linear equations, Fast Fourier transformations.

System: MAC, II, PLUS, SE, XL
Minimum Memory: 1024K
Medium: 3 1/2-inch disk
ISPN: 08413-200   **Price: $249.95**

DECISION SCIENCE SOFTWARE
MATRIX

Collection of matrix manipulation operations enabling the analyst to solve problems using matrix algebra.

System: MAC, II, PLUS, SE, XL
Minimum Memory:
Medium: 3 1/2-inch disk
ISPN: 24325-650   **Price: $65.00**

HEIZER SOFTWARE
MATRIX MACROS

Performs matrix operations, including copying a matrix to a new location and generating a transposition of the matrix.

System: MAC, II, PLUS, SE, XL
Minimum Memory: 512K
Requires: Microsoft Excel (ISPN 53150-270).
Medium: 3 1/2-inch disk
ISPN: 35175-561   **Price: $25.00**

PUMA SOFTWARE, INC.
MATRIX WORKSHOP (VER. 1.0)

Manipulates and preforms calculations on matrices and vectors using a command driven analysis program.

System: MAC, II, PLUS, SE, XL
Minimum Memory: 512K
Medium: 3 1/2-inch disk
ISPN: 63768-500   **Price: $295.00**

MACNEAL-SCHWENDLER CORP.
MSC/PAL (VER. 1.986)

Performs finite element analysis for the stress and vibration analysis of structures and mechanical components.

System: MAC, II, PLUS, SE, XL
Minimum Memory: 1024K
Medium: 3 1/2-inch disk
ISPN: 45900-320   **Price: $1495.00**

HEIZER SOFTWARE
MULTIPLE LINEAR REGRESSION

Performs multiple linear regression for up to 25 independent variables.

System: MAC, II, PLUS, SE, XL
Minimum Memory: 512K
Requires: Microsoft Excel (ISPN 53150-270).
Medium: 3 1/2-inch disk
ISPN: 35175-965   **Price: $25.00**

DECISION SCIENCE SOFTWARE
MULTIPLE LINEAR REGRESSION

Computer model designed to solve the multi-regression problem with up to 30 independent variables.

System: MAC, II, PLUS, SE, XL
Minimum Memory: 512K
Medium: 3 1/2-inch disk
ISPN: 24325-675   **Price: $95.00**

HEIZER SOFTWARE
NUMERIC INTEGRATION/ DIFFERENTIATION

Calculates the derivative (slope) of Y with respect to X, and the integral of Y over the range of X (area under the curve).

System: MAC, II, PLUS, SE, XL
Minimum Memory: 512K
Requires: Microsoft Excel (ISPN 53150-270).
Medium: 3 1/2-inch disk
ISPN: 35175-971   **Price: $25.00**

CAMBRIDGE UNIVERSITY PRESS
NUMERICAL RECIPES (FORTRAN) (VER. 1.1)

Provides 200 Fortran subroutines in all areas of scientific computing, for use in user programs.

System: MAC, II, PLUS, SE, XL
Minimum Memory: 512K
Requires: Fortran compiler.
Medium: 3 1/2-inch disk
ISPN: 57462-575   **Price: $39.00**

CAMBRIDGE UNIVERSITY PRESS
NUMERICAL RECIPES (PASCAL) (VER. 1.1)

Provides 200 Pascal procedures in all areas of scientific computing, for use in user programs.

System: MAC, II, PLUS, SE, XL
Minimum Memory: 512K
Requires: Pascal compiler.
Medium: 3 1/2-inch disk
ISPN: 57462-600 **Price: $39.00**

CAMBRIDGE UNIVERSITY PRESS
NUMERICAL RECIPES EXAMPLE DISKETTE (FORTRAN)

Demonstration and example programs which use the Fortran Numerical Recipes.

System: MAC, II, PLUS, SE, XL
Minimum Memory: 128K
Requires: Fortran compiler.
Medium: 3 1/2-inch disk
ISPN: 57462-615 **Price: $29.00**

CAMBRIDGE UNIVERSITY PRESS
NUMERICAL RECIPES EXAMPLES PASCAL (VER. 1.0)

Demonstration and example programs which use the Pascal Numerical Recipes.

System: MAC, II, PLUS, SE, XL
Minimum Memory: 128K
Requires: Pascal compiler.
Medium: 3 1/2-inch disk
ISPN: 57462-610 **Price: $29.00**

E & M SOFTWARE
POLYMATH

Symbolic algebra for univariate polynomials.

System: MAC, II, PLUS, SE, XL
Minimum Memory: 512K
Medium: 3 1/2-inch disk
ISPN: 27331-600 **Price: $19.95**

DYNACOMP, INC.
REGRESSION II (PARAFIT)

A parametric least squares regression program that determines the non-linear coefficients in complicated math expressions.

System: MAC, II, PLUS, SE, XL
Minimum Memory: 512K
Medium: 3 1/2-inch disk
ISPN: 27050-540 **Price: $28.95**

HEIZER SOFTWARE
ROOTS OF EQUATIONS

Solves all of the roots of non-linear quadratic, cubic and quartic equations.

System: MAC, II, PLUS, SE, XL
Minimum Memory: 512K
Requires: Microsoft Excel (ISPN 53150-270) or Microsoft Works (ISPN 53150-740).
Medium: 3 1/2-inch disk
ISPN: 35175-572 **Price: $14.00**

HEIZER SOFTWARE
ROSETTE STRAIN GAGES

Determines the principal and maximum shear stress conditions by reducing data from three types of rosette strain gages.

System: MAC, II, PLUS, SE, XL
Minimum Memory: 512K
Requires: Microsoft Excel (ISPN 53150-270).
Medium: 3 1/2-inch disk
ISPN: 35175-319 **Price: $18.00**

HEIZER SOFTWARE
ROUND TO ANY NUMBER

A function macro which allows user to round numbers to the nearest multiple of any number.

System: MAC, II, PLUS, SE, XL
Minimum Memory: 512K
Requires: Microsoft Excel (ISPN 53150-270).
Medium: 3 1/2-inch disk
ISPN: 35175-566 **Price: $5.00**

KINKOS ACADEMIC COURSEWARE EXCHANGE
SCIENTIST'S SPREADSHEET (VER. 2.17)

An interactive data-analysis application which performs complex mathematical and statistical operations on a table of numbers.

System: MAC, II, PLUS, SE, XL
Minimum Memory: 512K
Medium: 3 1/2-inch disk
ISPN: 43025-770 **Price: $10.00**

KINKOS ACADEMIC COURSEWARE EXCHANGE
SCIENTIST'S SPREADSHEET (VER. 2.17)

An interactive data-analysis application which performs complex mathematical and statistical operations on a table of numbers.

System: MAC, II, PLUS, SE, XL
Minimum Memory: 512K
Requires: Site license.
Medium: 3 1/2-inch disk
ISPN: 43025-770 **Price: $300.00**

HEIZER SOFTWARE
SIMULTANEOUS EQUATIONS SPREADSHEET

Solves a system of N linear equations in N unknowns for N up to nine.

System: MAC, II, PLUS, SE, XL
Minimum Memory: 512K
Requires: Microsoft Excel (ISPN 53150-270).
Medium: 3 1/2-inch disk
ISPN: 35175-574 **Price: $18.00**

HEIZER SOFTWARE
TRIANGLES

Solves plane triangles, given one side and two angles.

System: MAC, II, PLUS, SE, XL
Minimum Memory: 512K
Requires: Microsoft Excel (ISPN 53150-270) or Microsoft Works (ISPN 53150-740).
Medium: 3 1/2-inch disk
ISPN: 35175-563 **Price: $14.00**

668 SCIENCES/ MISCELLANEOUS SCIENCES

DECISION SCIENCE SOFTWARE
ASSIGN

An interactive computer model which solves the assignment algorithm.

System: MAC, II, PLUS, SE, XL
Minimum Memory:
Medium: 3 1/2-inch disk
ISPN: 24325-025 **Price: $50.00**

DYNACOMP, INC.
BASIC SCIENTIFIC SUBROUTINES (VOL. 1) COLLECTION 1

Provides a key to Chapters two and three of the Basic Scientific Subroutine (Vol. I) text.

System: MAC, II, PLUS, SE, XL
Minimum Memory: 512K
Medium: 3 1/2-inch disk
ISPN: 27050-803 **Price: $25.95**

DYNACOMP, INC.
BASIC SCIENTIFIC SUBROUTINES (VOL. 1) COMPLETE

Consists of a package keyed to Basic Scientific Subroutines (Vol. I) that is organized by chapter.

System: MAC, II, PLUS, SE, XL
Minimum Memory: 512K
Medium: 3 1/2-inch disk
ISPN: 27050-017 **Price: $58.95**

DYNACOMP, INC.
BASIC SCIENTIFIC SUBROUTINES (VOL. 2) COMPLETE

Contains a program keyed to the text Basic Scientific Subroutines (Vol. 2) exploring input and output parameters and algorithms.

System: MAC, II, PLUS, SE, XL
Minimum Memory: 512K
Medium: 3 1/2-inch disk
ISPN: 27050-018 **Price: $134.95**

GW INSTRUMENTS, INC.

MACASIOS MANAGER II (VER. 1.52)

Used to create, view, edit experiments, cut, copy and paste waveform segments.

System: II, PLUS, SE, XL
Minimum Memory: 512K
Requires: MacADIOS data acquisition hardware.
Medium: 3 1/2-inch disk
ISPN: 33837-501   **Price: $890.00**

GW INSTRUMENTS, INC.

MACINSTRUMENTS (VER. 1.0)

Converts the Macintosh into an oscilloscope, chart reader, scan-line recorder and scrolling strip chart recorder.

System: MAC, II, PLUS, SE, XL
Minimum Memory: 1024K
Medium: 3 1/2-inch disk
ISPN: 33837-510   **Price: $790.00**

GW INSTRUMENTS, INC.

MACSPEECH LAB I (VER. 2.0)

Provides acquisition and analysis of speech waveforms. Allows full editing, playback, printout and save to disk.

System: MAC, PLUS, SE, XL
Minimum Memory: 512K
Requires: MacAdios model 411 hardware.
Medium: 3 1/2-inch disk
ISPN: 33837-525   **Price: $300.00**

BIO-RAD LABORATORIES, INC.

MICROPLATE MANAGER (VER. 1.0)

Data acquisition and analysis program for Bio-Rad's Model 2550 EIA Reader.

System: MAC, II, PLUS, SE, XL
Minimum Memory: 1024K
Requires: Bio-Rad's Model 2550 EIA Reader.
Medium: 3 1/2-inch disk
ISPN: 07762-100   **Price: $750.00**

KINKOS ACADEMIC COURSEWARE EXCHANGE

MODEL NEURON (VER. 1.21)

Simulates the behavior of an isolated excitable cell under user-specified conditions.

System: MAC, II, PLUS, SE, XL
Minimum Memory: 512K
Requires: Finder (Ver. 4.1 or later).
Medium: 3 1/2-inch disk
ISPN: 43025-475   **Price: $14.00**

KINKOS ACADEMIC COURSEWARE EXCHANGE

MODEL NEURON (VER. 1.21)

Simulates the behavior of an isolated excitable cell under user-specified conditions.

System: MAC, II, PLUS, SE, XL
Minimum Memory: 512K
Requires: Site license.
Medium: 3 1/2-inch disk
ISPN: 43025-475   **Price: $400.00**

HEIZER SOFTWARE

PERIODIC TABLE DATABASE

Professional and educational use: Database of the Periodic Table with over 15 related information fields.

System: MAC, II, PLUS, SE, XL
Minimum Memory: 512K
Requires: Microsoft Excel (ISPN 53150-270), Microsoft Works (ISPN 53150-740) or HyperCard (ISPN 03900-300).
Medium: 3 1/2-inch disk
ISPN: 35175-701   **Price: $25.00**

HEIZER SOFTWARE

SCIENTIFIC NOTATION FUNCTIONS

A HyperCard stack of a set of six functions that facilitate working with numbers expressed in scientific notations.

System: MAC, II, PLUS, SE, XL
Minimum Memory: 512K
Requires: HyperCard (ISPN 03900-300).
Medium: 3 1/2-inch disk
ISPN: 35175-982   **Price: $8.00**

PERCEPTICS

TCL-IMAGE (VER. 1.0)

Scientific, quantitative image processing and analysis software with a toolbox of image processing functions.

System: II
Minimum Memory: 4096K
Requires: Hard disk.
Medium: 3 1/2-inch disk
ISPN: 60512-700   **Price: $3500.00**

HEIZER SOFTWARE

TIDE CALCULATOR

Calculates and charts the heights and times of high and low tides for any body of water which opens to the ocean.

System: MAC, II, PLUS, SE, XL
Minimum Memory: 512K
Requires: Microsoft Excel (ISPN 53150-270).
Medium: 3 1/2-inch disk
ISPN: 35175-939   **Price: $20.00**

ZIHUA

TIDE GUIDE 89

Ocean tide predictor for 1989 with 300 plus locations on the East, West and Gulf coasts. Shows moon phases, sunrise and sunset times.

System: MAC, II, PLUS, SE, XL
Minimum Memory: 512K
Medium: 3 1/2-inch disk
ISPN: 87412-700   **Price: $19.95**

GTFS, INC.

ULTIMAGE

Performs image processing and analysis. Processes images acquired from scanners, cameras, microscopes, and echographs.

System: II
Minimum Memory: 2048K
Requires: Hard disk, Apple or compatible 8-bit graphic board and color monitor with 256 color display.
Medium: 3 1/2-inch disk
ISPN: 33690-500   **Price: $2990.00**

HEIZER SOFTWARE

UNIVERSAL CONVERSION CALCULATOR

A HyperCard stack which converts any unit of measure to any other unit of measure.

System: MAC, II, PLUS, SE, XL
Minimum Memory: 512K
Requires: HyperCard (ISPN 03900-300).
Medium: 3 1/2-inch disk
ISPN: 35175-995   **Price: $10.00**

---

685 SCIENCES/PHYSICS

GW INSTRUMENTS, INC.

MACADIOS SYSTEM I (VER. 1.0)

Coordinates many tasks performed in the laboratory environment. Includes data acquisition and waveform synthesis.

System: MAC, PLUS, SE, XL
Minimum Memory: 128K
Requires: MacADIOS (Macintosh Analog/ Digital Input/Output System) hardware.
Medium: 3 1/2-inch disk
ISPN: 33837-500   **Price: $2500.00**

---

705 PROFESSIONS/ SERVICES/ ARCHITECTURE/ INTERIOR DESIGN

GARDNER PARTNERSHIP ARCHITECTS

ARCHACCOUNT (VER. 2.07)

Provides a billing and job costing program for small architectural firms.

System: MAC, II, PLUS, SE, XL
Minimum Memory: 512K
Medium: 3 1/2-inch disk
ISPN: 32318-020   **Price: $295.00**

HEIZER SOFTWARE

ARCHITECT'S FEE ESTIMATOR

Prepares estimates for providing design services. Covers design development, schematics, working drawings and bidding.

System: MAC, PLUS, SE, XL
Minimum Memory: 512K
Requires: Microsoft Excel (ISPN 53150-270).
Medium: 3 1/2-inch disk
ISPN: 35175-131   **Price: $50.00**

FOR MORE DETAILED INFORMATION, CALL (412) 746-MENU

HEIZER SOFTWARE

ARCHITECT'S OFFICE MGMT. AND FEE CALCULATION

A series of templates which calculates benefits factor, direct personnel expenses, direct salary expenses and overhead rates.

System: MAC, II, PLUS, SE, XL
Minimum Memory: 512K
Requires: Microsoft Excel (ISPN 53150-270).
Medium: 3 1/2-inch disk
ISPN: 35175-130   **Price: $225.00**

ABVENT

BUILD (VER. 1.3)

Enables you to design a house from floor plan to four views elevation. Organizes information about each client and site.

System: MAC, II, PLUS, SE, XL
Minimum Memory: 1024K
Medium: 3 1/2-inch disk
ISPN: 00437-175   **Price: $295.00**

SPINNAKER SOFTWARE

BUILDING BLOCKS-DA VINCI SERIES

A system of detailed interchangeable units which draw from a variety of architectural design and landscaping examples.

System: MAC, II, PLUS, SE, XL
Minimum Memory: 512K
Medium: 3 1/2-inch disk
ISPN: 75300-177   **Price: $79.95**

SPINNAKER SOFTWARE

COMMERCIAL INTERIORS-DA VINCI SERIES

A tool for space planning in a business environment. Contains scaled images of objects needed in restaurants, offices & theaters.

System: MAC, II, PLUS, SE, XL
Minimum Memory: 512K
Medium: 3 1/2-inch disk
ISPN: 75300-175   **Price: $199.95**

ABRACADATA LTD.

DESIGN YOUR OWN HOME-ARCHITECTURE

Enables the user to draw floor plans, side view building plans and structural details. Calculates measurement automatically.

System: MAC, II, PLUS, SE, XL
Minimum Memory: 640K
Medium: 3 1/2-inch disk
ISPN: 00366-100   **Price: $99.95**

ABRACADATA LTD.

DESIGN YOUR OWN HOME-INTERIORS

Create space plans and color schemes for home or office. Draw a floor plan, add furniture, appliances and plants. Top or side view

System: MAC, II, PLUS, SE, XL
Minimum Memory: 640K
Medium: 3 1/2-inch disk
ISPN: 00366-150   **Price: $99.95**

ABRACADATA LTD.

DESIGN YOUR OWN HOME-LANDSCAPE

Plan the grounds around your home or office. Includes dozens of pre-drawn plants that you can 'grow' and view from four sides.

System: MAC, II, PLUS, SE, XL
Minimum Memory: 640K
Medium: 3 1/2-inch disk
ISPN: 00366-175   **Price: $99.95**

SPINNAKER SOFTWARE

HOME DESIGN-DA VINCI SERIES

Offers carefully drawn and scaled 3-D images for 'hands on' exploration of your design idea in an easy-to-visualize format.

System: MAC, II, PLUS, SE, XL
Minimum Memory: 512K
Medium: 3 1/2-inch disk
ISPN: 75300-176   **Price: $79.95**

MENU® also publishes directories for the **IBM® PC & compatibles** and **Apple® II** and **COMMODORE®** computers. There's a directory for **Local Area Networks**, too.

ALTERNATIVE ENTERPRISES

HOUSEBUILDER (VER. 1.1)

Architectural graphics package-allows the user to produce and modify plans, elevations, interiors and landscapes.

System: MAC, II, PLUS, SE, XL
Minimum Memory: 128K
Requires: MacPaint (ISPN 12784-510).
Medium: 3 1/2-inch disk
ISPN: 02577-275   **Price: $55.00**

COMPSERVCO

MAC INTERIORS

A 3-D interior design tool for designing room layouts that allow elevations, plans and perspectives to be printed.

System: MAC, II, PLUS, SE, XL
Minimum Memory: 512K
Medium: 3 1/2-inch disk
ISPN: 15025-900   **Price: $295.00**

COMPSERVCO

MACCAD-COMMERCIAL ARCHITECTURAL DESIGN

Provides templates of building components, details, fixtures, and equipment. All templates are in plan and elevated views.

System: MAC, PLUS, SE, XL
Minimum Memory: 512K
Requires: Please specify version when ordering: PICT Version, MiniCad Version, MacDraw Version or MacDraft Version.
Medium: 3 1/2-inch disk
ISPN: 15025-100   **Price: $169.00**

COMPSERVCO

MACCAD-DRAFTING TOOLKIT

MacDraw, MacDraft & Minicad templates with 30 drafting sheets (A-E sizes) for plotters, LaserWriter & ImageWriter & drafting symbols.

System: MAC, II, PLUS, SE, XL
Minimum Memory: 512K
Requires: Please specify version when ordering: PICT Version, MiniCad Version, MacDraw Version or MacDraft Version.
Medium: 3 1/2-inch disk
ISPN: 15025-456   **Price: $69.00**

COMPSERVCO

MACCAD-LAYOUT PLANNER

MacDraw, MacDraft and Minicad template libraries for layouts of offices, stores and restaurants drawn in plan and elevation views.

System: MAC, II, PLUS, SE, XL
Minimum Memory: 512K
Requires: Please specify version when ordering: PICT Version, MiniCad Version, MacDraw Version or MacDraft Version.
Medium: 3 1/2-inch disk
ISPN: 15025-380   **Price: $149.00**

COMPSERVCO

MACCAD-RESIDENTIAL ARCHITECTURAL DESIGN

MacDraw, MacDraft and Minicad template Library includes symbols in plan and elevation views for designing homes.

System: MAC, II, PLUS, SE, XL
Minimum Memory: 512K
Requires: Please specify version when ordering: PICT Version, MiniCad Version, MacDraw Version or MacDraft Version.
Medium: 3 1/2-inch disk
ISPN: 15025-680   **Price: $169.00**

KNICK DRAFTING, INC.

MACPERSPECTIVE (VER. 4.0)

Allows architects, draftsmen and artists to construct perspective drawings of houses or other objects from dimensioned drawings.

System: MAC, II, PLUS, SE, XL
Minimum Memory: 512K
Medium: 3 1/2-inch disk
ISPN: 43110-500   **Price: $295.00**

WILLIAMS AG PRODUCTS
PROFESSIONAL SERIES DRAFTING SYMBOLS (VER. 1.0)

A collection of the most commonly used architectural drafting symbols. Contains Modules One, Two and Three.

System: MAC, II, PLUS, SE, XL
Minimum Memory: 512K
Requires: 800K disk drive, Minicad (ISPN 25184-500) or any program that reads PICT format.
Medium: 3 1/2-inch disk
ISPN: 86503-300   **Price: $195.00**

WILLIAMS AG PRODUCTS
PROFESSIONAL SERIES-MODULE 1-ARCHITECTURAL SYMBOLS

Contains a collection of common architectural symbols created with Minicad or PICT format.

System: MAC, II, PLUS, SE, XL
Minimum Memory: 512K
Requires: 800K disk drive, Minicad (ISPN 25184-500) or any program that reads PICT format.
Medium: 3 1/2-inch disk
ISPN: 86503-200   **Price: $95.00**

WILLIAMS AG PRODUCTS
PROFESSIONAL SERIES-MODULE 2-CABINETWORK

Contains a collection of common architectural drafting symbols showing cabinetwork created with Minicad in a PICT format.

System: MAC, II, PLUS, SE, XL
Minimum Memory: 512K
Requires: 800K disk drive, Minicad (ISPN 25184-500) or any program that reads PICT format.
Medium: 3 1/2-inch disk
ISPN: 86503-210   **Price: $75.00**

WILLIAMS AG PRODUCTS
PROFESSIONAL SERIES-MODULE 3-DOORS/WINDOWS

Contains a collection of common architectural drafting symbols created with Minicad in a PICT format detailing doors and windows.

System: MAC, II, PLUS, SE, XL
Minimum Memory: 512K
Requires: 800K disk drive, Minicad (ISPN 25184-500) or any program that reads PICT format.
Medium: 3 1/2-inch disk
ISPN: 86503-220   **Price: $75.00**

ARCH SOFTWARE
SIMPLESPAN (VER. 2.5)

Desk accessory to size simple wood and steel beams without tables. Can accommodate multiple loading conditions.

System: MAC, II, PLUS, SE, XL
Minimum Memory: 512K
Medium: 3 1/2-inch disk
ISPN: 04959-100   **Price: $99.00**

ARCH SOFTWARE
SIMPLESPAN UTILITIES I

Sizes simply-supported or cantilevered wood beams under multiple loading conditions. Simple span sizes WF beams.

System: MAC, II, PLUS, SE, XL
Minimum Memory: 512K
Medium: 3 1/2-inch disk
ISPN: 04959-050   **Price: $149.00**

---

709 PROFESSIONS/ SERVICES/BANKING

SULCUS COMPUTER CORP.
FINANCIAL MARKETPLACE (LOAN MANAGEMENT) SYSTEM

Handles loan processing and servicing businesses. Includes loan applications, commitment to closing and portfolio and sold loans.

System: MAC, II, PLUS, SE, XL
Minimum Memory:
Medium: 3 1/2-inch disk
ISPN: 77006-200
Price: Please contact the software publisher.

---

713 PROFESSIONS/ SERVICES/ COMMUNICATIONS/ MEDIA

HEIZER SOFTWARE
2001 QUOTES

Includes 2001 quotations for use by writers and speakers.

System: MAC, II, PLUS, SE, XL
Minimum Memory: 512K
Requires: Microsoft Excel (ISPN 53150-270), Microsoft Works (ISPN 53150-740) or HyperCard (ISPN 03900-300).
Medium: 3 1/2-inch disk
ISPN: 35175-667   **Price: $25.00**

MAX 3, INC.
CINEWRITE (VER. 2.0)

The word processor and storyboarder designed for advertising, film, and television professionals.

System: MAC, II, PLUS, SE, XL
Minimum Memory: 512K
Medium: 3 1/2-inch disk
ISPN: 59754-175   **Price: $495.00**

HEIZER SOFTWARE
CITATION LOG

A database which configures to technical journals' footnote formats.

System: MAC, II, PLUS, SE, XL
Minimum Memory: 512K
Requires: Microsoft Excel (ISPN 53150-270) or HyperCard (ISPN 03900-300).
Medium: 3 1/2-inch disk
ISPN: 35175-675   **Price: $5.00**

HEIZER SOFTWARE
COPYFIT

A template which estimates space requirements for articles. Takes into account the number of characters, columns and pages.

System: MAC, II, PLUS, SE, XL
Minimum Memory: 512K
Requires: Microsoft Excel (ISPN 53150-270) or Microsoft Works (ISPN 53150-270).
Medium: 3 1/2-inch disk
ISPN: 35175-676   **Price: $12.00**

HEIZER SOFTWARE
EDIT-AD RATIOS

Supplies low, medium and high editorial-to-ad ratio results for the number of total pages and editorial pages needed to print.

System: MAC, II, PLUS, SE, XL
Minimum Memory: 512K
Requires: Microsoft Excel (ISPN 53150-270) or Microsoft Works (ISPN 53150-740).
Medium: 3 1/2-inch disk
ISPN: 35175-672   **Price: $8.00**

HEIZER SOFTWARE
FIGURE CPM CHANGES

Calculates cost per thousand and shows the effect of ad rate or circulation change.

System: MAC, II, PLUS, SE, XL
Minimum Memory: 512K
Requires: Microsoft Excel (ISPN 53150-270) or Microsoft Works (ISPN 53150-740).
Medium: 3 1/2-inch disk
ISPN: 35175-673   **Price: $5.00**

SELECT MICRO SYSTEMS, INC.
FLOWMASTER (VER. 1.1)

Allows development, printing and storing of media flowcharts.

System: MAC, II, PLUS, SE, XL
Minimum Memory: 512K
Medium: 3 1/2-inch disk
ISPN: 69106-400   **Price: $495.00**

EDUDISC
PORTFOLIO

Picture archiving software to record, catalog and retrieve still images on videodisc.

System: MAC, II, PLUS, SE, XL
Minimum Memory: 512K
Requires: 800K disk drive, Panasonic, Pioneer and/or Sony videodisc players.
Medium: 3 1/2-inch disk
ISPN: 28068-700   **Price: $750.00**

AMERICAN INTELLIWARE CORP.
SCRIPTWRITER (VER. 1.1)

A versatile, stand-alone scriptwriting tool designed to address the particular needs of film, advertising and television writers.

System: MAC, PLUS, SE, XL
Minimum Memory: 512K
Medium: 3 1/2-inch disk
ISPN: 02896-415　　　　　**Price: $495.00**

HEIZER SOFTWARE
SIGNATURE COLLATOR

Generates a page layout for signatures when the user enters the number of pages in the publication.

System: MAC, II, PLUS, SE, XL
Minimum Memory: 512K
Requires: Microsoft Excel (ISPN 53150-270).
Medium: 3 1/2-inch disk
ISPN: 35175-670　　　　　**Price: $9.00**

AMERICAN INTELLIWARE CORP.
STORYBOARDER

Designed for the film, advertising and television professional to simplify and speed up production, reduce costs and be creative.

System: MAC, II, PLUS, SE, XL
Minimum Memory: 512K
Medium: 3 1/2-inch disk
ISPN: 02896-500　　　　　**Price: $495.00**

SAGE PRODUCTIONS, INC.
SUBSCRIPTION MANAGER

Provides professional level subscription and mailing list management that can track up to 200,000 subscribers.

System: MAC, II, PLUS, SE, XL
Minimum Memory: 1024K
Requires: Hard disk.
Medium: 3 1/2-inch disk
ISPN: 63857-600　　　　　**Price: $1995.00**

MAGNUM SOFTWARE
TELEFLEX (VER. 1.0)

A hardware/software combination that provides voice mail, answering machine, trace and page function and electronic reminders.

System: MAC, II, PLUS, SE, XL
Minimum Memory: 1024K
Requires: 20MB hard disk.
Medium: 3 1/2-inch disk
ISPN: 46032-300　　　　　**Price: $3495.00**

HEIZER SOFTWARE
WRITING RECORDS

Maintains records of articles, submissions, dates, payment dates and amounts.

System: MAC, II, PLUS, SE, XL
Minimum Memory: 512K
Requires: Microsoft Excel (ISPN 53150-270) or Microsoft Works (ISPN 53150-740).
Medium: 3 1/2-inch disk
ISPN: 35175-674　　　　　**Price: $5.00**

721 PROFESSIONS/ SERVICES/FOOD/ RESTAURANT

RESTAURANTCOMP
FOOD AND BEVERAGE INVENTORY

Organizes, calculates and writes inventory reports regarding food, beverage, beer, wine, and liquor supplies.

System: MAC, II, PLUS, SE, XL
Minimum Memory: 1024K
Medium: 3 1/2-inch disk
ISPN: 66181-300　　　　　**Price: $1195.00**

RESTAURANTCOMP
RECIPE PROFIT ANALYZER

Monitors profitability of regular menu items, and can be used for planning new menu items, specials, banquets and catering menus.

System: MAC, II, PLUS, SE, XL
Minimum Memory: 1024K
Requires: Food and Beverage Inventory (ISPN 66181-300).
Medium: 3 1/2-inch disk
ISPN: 66181-640　　　　　**Price: $495.00**

SEXTANT CORP.
RMS PLUS (VER. 1.3)

Provides Inventory Control, Menu Management, Accounts Payable, Restaurant Payroll and General Ledger modules for restaurants.

System: MAC, II, PLUS, SE, XL
Minimum Memory: 1024K
Requires: 20MB hard disk.
Medium: 3 1/2-inch disk
ISPN: 42575-675　　　　　**Price: $1995.00**

RESTAURANTCOMP
SALES AND FOOD COST ANALYZER

Provides a detailed analysis of sales, gross profits, food costs, and perpetual inventory.

System: MAC, II, PLUS, SE, XL
Minimum Memory: 1024K
Requires: Food and Beverage Inventory (ISPN 66181-300) and Recipe Profit Analyzer (ISPN 66181-640).
Medium: 3 1/2-inch disk
ISPN: 66181-700　　　　　**Price: $195.00**

725 PROFESSIONS/ SERVICES/ GOVERNMENT/ MUNICIPALITIES

SYSTEMS SERVICES ENGINEERING
BENCH SHEET SYSTEM
Laboratory data management for water and wastewater treatment operations.
System: MAC, PLUS, SE, XL
Minimum Memory: 512K
Medium: 3 1/2-inch disk
ISPN: 78968-300　　　　　**Price: $795.00**

VISATEX CORP.
COMPUSKETCH
Does composite sketches of criminal suspects from witness interview.
System: MAC, II, PLUS, SE, XL
Minimum Memory: 1024K
Requires: Hard disk.
Medium: 3 1/2-inch disk
ISPN: 85340-800　　　　　**Price: $4500.00**

SHAHERAZAM
MAC-A-MUG
Allows a user to create human faces by scrolling through and choosing from hundreds of individual facial features.
System: MAC, II, PLUS, SE, XL
Minimum Memory: 512K
Requires: Two 800K disk drives or a hard disk.
Medium: 3 1/2-inch disk
ISPN: 69425-400　　　　　**Price: $59.95**

HEIZER SOFTWARE
SPEED FROM SKIDS
Determines the speed of vehicles involved in traffic accidents from skidmarks and other physical evidence.
System: MAC, II, PLUS, SE, XL
Minimum Memory: 1024K
Requires: HyperCard (ISPN 03900-300).
Medium: 3 1/2-inch disk
ISPN: 35175-421　　　　　**Price: $15.00**

729 PROFESSIONS/ SERVICES/HOSPITAL MANAGEMENT

H & D LEASING, INC.
MACNURSE (VER. 2.0)
Provides an admissions and plan of care system for nursing homes.
System: MAC, II, PLUS, SE, XL
Minimum Memory: 1024K
Requires: 20MB hard disk.
Medium: 3 1/2-inch disk
ISPN: 33851-500   **Price: $3500.00**

733 PROFESSIONS/ SERVICES/HOTEL/ MOTEL

ELIOT SOFTWARE CO.
MACINN
Lodging management including reservations, check in and out, folio control, automatic posting, night audit, A/R and A/P.
System: MAC, II, PLUS, SE, XL
Minimum Memory: 1024K
Requires: ImageWriter I, ImageWriter II or LaserWriter, hard disk.
Medium: 3 1/2-inch disk
ISPN: 34937-100   **Price: $1495.00**

737 PROFESSIONS/ SERVICES/INSURANCE

MERRY MAID, INC./BUSINESS SYSTEMS GROUP
AGENTBASE (VER. 1.5)
A fully integrated office management package designed to automate marketing and customer service functions.
System: MAC, II, PLUS, SE, XL
Minimum Memory: 1024K
Medium: 3 1/2-inch disk
ISPN: 49169-050   **Price: $1500.00**

ORION COMPUTER TRAINING SYSTEMS
ORION INSURANCE ADMINISTRATOR (VER. 1.0)
Provides contract tracking and invoicing by employer within insurance groups.
System: MAC, II, PLUS, SE, XL
Minimum Memory: 1024K
Medium: 3 1/2-inch disk
ISPN: 58862-540   **Price: $2995.00**

741 PROFESSIONS/ SERVICES/LEASING/ RENTAL

WRITE HAND, INC.
MANAGE-U-STORE
Allows a manager of a self-serve storage complex to keep accurate track of rentals and clients.
System: MAC, PLUS, SE, XL
Minimum Memory: 1024K
Requires: ImageWriter printer, hard disk.
Medium: 3 1/2-inch disk
ISPN: 87006-500   **Price: $1500.00**

745 PROFESSIONS/ SERVICES/LEGAL

ELAN ASSOCIATES
CADENCE WITH PPM
An on-disk office policy and procedure manual. Also has staff selection guides.
System: MAC, II, PLUS, SE, XL
Minimum Memory: 512K
Requires: Word Processer compatible with MacWrite files.
Medium: 3 1/2-inch disk
ISPN: 28288-201   **Price: $49.50**

CALIFORNIA CONTINUING EDUCATION OF THE BAR
CALIFORNIA JUDICIAL COUNCIL FAMILY LAW FORMS
Contains over 49 official forms approved by the Judicial Council which includes Order to Show Cause and Temporary Restraining Order.
System: MAC
Minimum Memory: 256K
Requires: Microsoft Word (ISPN 53150-732).
Medium: 3 1/2-inch disk
ISPN: 10612-030   **Price: $100.00**

CALIFORNIA CONTINUING EDUCATION OF THE BAR
CALIFORNIA TRUST DRAFTING TRUSTMASTER SYSTEM
Contains a set of ten master intervivos trust forms in word processing format for lawyers to modify for specific client needs.
System: MAC
Minimum Memory: 256K
Requires: Microsoft Word (ISPN 53150-732).
Medium: 3 1/2-inch disk
ISPN: 10612-185   **Price: $395.00**

CALIFORNIA CONTINUING EDUCATION OF THE BAR
CALIFORNIA WILL DRAFTING WILLMASTER
Contains a set of 16 master will forms in word processing format for lawyers to modify for specific client needs.
System: MAC, II, PLUS, SE, XL
Minimum Memory: 512K
Requires: Microsoft Word (ISPN 53150-732).
Medium: 3 1/2-inch disk
ISPN: 10612-190   **Price: $395.00**

ELAN ASSOCIATES
CLIENT PORTRAIT (VER. 1.0)
Attorney's and professional's client information, marketing and conflicts-of-interest system.
System: MAC, II, PLUS, SE, XL
Minimum Memory: 512K
Requires: Double Helix (ISPN 57709-150).
Medium: 3 1/2-inch disk
ISPN: 28288-200   **Price: $69.50**

CALIFORNIA CONTINUING EDUCATION OF THE BAR
CORPSYSTEM W/MANUAL
Includes more than 100 corporate forms in word processing format for lawyers to modify for client need.
System: MAC, II, PLUS, SE, XL
Minimum Memory: 512K
Requires: Microsoft Word (ISPN 53150-732).
Medium: 3 1/2-inch disk
ISPN: 10612-350   **Price: $395.00**

PRODUCTS DIVERSIFIED, INC.
DISCOVERY MASTER (VER. 1.0)
A litigation support tool that provides large-scale document management and full text retrieval.
System: MAC, II, PLUS, SE, XL
Minimum Memory: 1024K
Requires: Freeform, ShareBase server.
Medium: 3 1/2-inch disk
ISPN: 62334-150   **Price: $5000.00**

KINKOS ACADEMIC COURSEWARE EXCHANGE
HARRIS VS. KLONDIKE KLIMBER, INC.
A series of nine tutorials that lead the student through the preparation of a products liability lawsuit.
System: MAC, II, PLUS, SE, XL
Minimum Memory: 512K
Requires: 800K disk drive.
Medium: 3 1/2-inch disk
ISPN: 43025-225   **Price: $14.00**

KINKOS ACADEMIC COURSEWARE EXCHANGE
HARRIS VS. KLONDIKE KLIMBER, INC.
A series of nine tutorials that lead the student through the preparation of a products liability lawsuit.
System: MAC, II, PLUS, SE, XL
Minimum Memory: 512K
Requires: Site license. 800K disk drive.
Medium: 3 1/2-inch disk
ISPN: 43025-225   **Price: $2400.00**

SULCUS COMPUTER CORP.
LAW OFFICE MANAGEMENT SYSTEM
Includes a complete ABA approved program designed to automate law practices.
System: MAC, II, PLUS, SE, XL
Minimum Memory:
Medium: 3 1/2-inch disk
ISPN: 77006-470
Price: Please contact the software publisher.

INTERNET

LEGAL AIDE (VER. 1.0)

A comprehensive legal office time, billing and data management system.

System: MAC, II, PLUS, SE, XL
Minimum Memory: 512K
Medium: 3 1/2-inch disk
ISPN: 40257-150
Price: $795.00

SATORI SOFTWARE

LEGAL BILLING II (VER. 2.56)

Advanced legal billing package. Specifically designed for professional time billing. ABA approved.

System: MAC, II, PLUS, SE, XL
Minimum Memory: 512K
Requires: 800K disk drive.
Medium: 3 1/2-inch disk
ISPN: 68024-310
Price: $595.00

SATORI SOFTWARE

LEGAL BILLING II + (VER. 2.56)

Advanced multi-user legal billing package specifically designed for professional time billing. ABA approved.

System: MAC, II, PLUS, SE, XL
Minimum Memory: 512K
Requires: 800K disk drive.
Medium: 3 1/2-inch disk
ISPN: 68024-320
Price: $995.00

SYSCOM, INC.

LEGAL EAGLE

Provides the law office with time and disbursement management in a single or multiuser environment.

System: MAC, II, PLUS, SE, XL
Minimum Memory: 512K
Requires: Single user.
Medium: 3 1/2-inch disk
ISPN: 77822-400
Price: $995.00

SYSCOM, INC.

LEGAL EAGLE

Provides the law office with time and disbursement management in a single or multiuser environment.

System: MAC, II, PLUS, SE, XL
Minimum Memory: 1024K
Requires: Multi-user.
Medium: 3 1/2-inch disk
ISPN: 77822-400
Price: $1495.00

PRODUCTS DIVERSIFIED, INC.

LEGAL TEXT ANALYSIS TOOL (VER. 1.0)

Assists in the preparation and trial phase of a law suit. Allows you to search and analyze large volumes of text data.

System: MAC, II, PLUS, SE, XL
Minimum Memory: 1024K
Requires: HyperCard (ISPN 03900-300).
Medium: 3 1/2-inch disk
ISPN: 62334-450
Price: $595.00

SHAHERAZAM

MAC-A-MUG-PRO

Complete professional system for generating composite human faces.

System: MAC, II, PLUS, SE, XL
Minimum Memory: 512K
Medium: 3 1/2-inch disk
ISPN: 69425-450
Price: $495.00

PROGRESSIVE PERIPHERALS AND SOFTWARE

MICROLAWYER

Contains approximately 100 legal forms including leases, mortgages, marital agreements, contracts and power of attorneys.

System: MAC
Minimum Memory:
Medium: 3 1/2-inch disk
ISPN: 63225-215
Price: $59.95

ADVOCATE SOFTWARE

PI-ECONOMIST (VER. 2.0)

Calculates the present value of past and future losses for personal injury, medical malpractice and product liability cases.

System: MAC, II, PLUS, SE, XL
Minimum Memory: 312K
Medium: 3 1/2-inch disk
ISPN: 01715-600
Price: $250.00

749 PROFESSIONS/ SERVICES/MEDICAL (DIAGNOSIS/ANALYSIS)

REASON HOUSE

CHILD DIAGNOSTIC SCREENING BATTERY (VER. 1.03)

Used to generate a psychological five axle diagnosis for children ages 2-17.

System: MAC, II, PLUS, SE, XL
Minimum Memory: 128K
Medium: 3 1/2-inch disk
ISPN: 65635-140
Price: $195.00

MFE ASSOCIATES

EXCHANGE CALCULATOR

Calculates diabetic exchanges from analysis information.

System: MAC, II, PLUS, SE, XL
Minimum Memory: 512K
Requires: Single user.
Medium: 3 1/2-inch disk
ISPN: 49331-480
Price: $35.00

MFE ASSOCIATES

EXCHANGE CALCULATOR

Calculates diabetic exchanges from analysis information.

System: MAC, II, PLUS, SE, XL
Minimum Memory: 512K
Requires: Multiuser or Institution.
Medium: 3 1/2-inch disk
ISPN: 49331-480
Price: $150.00

N-SQUARED COMPUTING

INTERNIST (VER. 4.0)

Performs differential diagnoses on any combination of over 538 symptoms for 337 diseases or disorders.

System: MAC, II, PLUS, SE, XL
Minimum Memory: 512K
Medium: 3 1/2-inch disk
ISPN: 55907-500
Price: $145.00

N-SQUARED COMPUTING

INTERNIST +

A computer assisted medical diagnostic/ differential diagnostic package.

System: MAC, II, PLUS, SE, XL
Minimum Memory: 512K
Medium: 3 1/2-inch disk
ISPN: 55907-510
Price: $295.00

BIOSOFT

KINETIC EBDA LIGAND LOWRY

Maintains a collection of radioligand binding analysis programs.

System: MAC
Minimum Memory: 1024K
Medium: 3 1/2-inch disk
ISPN: 28881-215
Price: $249.00

CHARIOT SOFTWARE GROUP

LUNG CANCER STAGING

A visual introduction to the International TNM Staging Lung Cancer and the American Thoracic Society's Lymph Node classifications.

System: MAC, II, PLUS, SE, XL
Minimum Memory: 512K
Medium: 3 1/2-inch disk
ISPN: 12237-350
Price: $75.00

IATROCOM

MAC-ON-CALL

An interactive, knowledge-based expert medical diagnostic system that intuitively relates information for rapid analysis.

System: MAC, II, PLUS, SE, XL
Minimum Memory: 1024K
Requires: Apple System (Ver. 6.02 or later), external disk drive.
Medium: 3 1/2-inch disk
ISPN: 36755-500
Price: $595.00

DATA MANAGEMENT ASSOCIATES

MAC-TALLY (VER. 1.0)

Used in Hematology laboratories to maintain Leukocyte differential counts.

System: MAC, II, PLUS, SE, XL
Minimum Memory: 1024K
Medium: 3 1/2-inch disk
ISPN: 17245-550
Price: $129.95

MACMEDIC PUBLICATIONS, INC.
MACANATOMY (VOL. 1)

An electronic atlas of human anatomy presented on disk covering the head and neck, abdomen and pelvis and the gastrointestinal tract.

System: MAC, II, PLUS, SE, XL
Minimum Memory: 512K
Medium: 3 1/2-inch disk
ISPN: 45845-500   **Price: $95.00**

MACMEDIC PUBLICATIONS, INC.
MACANATOMY (VOL. 2)

An electronic atlas of human anatomy presented on disk covering the heart and lungs, thorax and the nervous system.

System: MAC, II, PLUS, SE, XL
Minimum Memory: 512K
Medium: 3 1/2-inch disk
ISPN: 45845-505   **Price: $95.00**

MACMEDIC PUBLICATIONS, INC.
MACANATOMY (VOL. 3)

An electronic atlas of human anatomy presented on disk covering the upper limbs and lower limbs. Comes on two disks.

System: MAC, II, PLUS, SE, XL
Minimum Memory: 512K
Medium: 3 1/2-inch disk
ISPN: 45845-510   **Price: $95.00**

MACMEDIC PUBLICATIONS, INC.
MACANATOMY (VOL. 4)

An electronic atlas of human anatomy presented on disk covering the bones and joints and cross sections.

System: MAC, II, PLUS, SE, XL
Minimum Memory: 512K
Medium: 3 1/2-inch disk
ISPN: 45845-515   **Price: $95.00**

MACMEDIC PUBLICATIONS, INC.
MACANATOMY-COMPLETE SET (VOLS. 1-4)

Complete electronic atlas of human anatomy on disk in MacPaint document form.

System: MAC, II, PLUS, SE, XL
Minimum Memory: 512K
Medium: 3 1/2-inch disk
ISPN: 45845-520   **Price: $350.00**

MACPDS
MEDICAL APPLICATION CLIPART (VOL. 1.0)

Collection of over 100 medically related bit-mapped images stored in MacPaint format.

System: MAC, II, PLUS, SE, XL
Minimum Memory: 512K
Requires: 800K disk drive.
Medium: 3 1/2-inch disk
ISPN: 93905-500   **Price: $89.95**

CAMDE CORP.
NUTRI-CALC PLUS

Nutritional analysis program for dietitians and professionals and includes 1700+ foods, 32 nutrients, RDA analysis, user histories.

System: MAC, II, PLUS, SE, XL
Minimum Memory: 512K
Requires: Internal 800K double-sided disk drive or two 400K single-sided disk drives.
Medium: 3 1/2-inch disk
ISPN: 10875-625   **Price: $225.00**

IATROCOM
SENIOR CONSULTANT

An add-on to Mac-On-Call that allows the user to customize the diagnoses and manifestations.

System: MAC, II, PLUS, SE, XL
Minimum Memory: 1024K
Requires: Apple System (Ver. 6.02 or later), external disk drive, Mac-On-Call (ISPN 36755-500).
Medium: 3 1/2-inch disk
ISPN: 36755-700   **Price: $395.00**

754 PROFESSIONS/ SERVICES/MEDICAL/ DENTAL (OFFICE MANAGEMENT)

CMA MICRO COMPUTER DIVISION
CMA DENTAL FOR MACINTOSH

Includes private patient accounts receivable and claim form preparation.

System: MAC, II, PLUS, SE, XL
Minimum Memory: 512K
Requires: Hard disk, printer.
Medium: 3 1/2-inch disk
ISPN: 13112-198   **Price: $1995.00**

CMA MICRO COMPUTER DIVISION
CMA MEDICAL FOR THE MACINTOSH

Includes a private patient accounts receivable, claim form appointments with patient recall, chart and financial histories.

System: MAC, II, PLUS, SE, XL
Minimum Memory: 512K
Requires: Hard disk, compatible printer.
Medium: 3 1/2-inch disk
ISPN: 13112-349   **Price: $1995.95**

UNICOM SOFTWARE DEVELOPMENT GROUP
DBMED-MEDICAL OFFICE MANAGER (VER. 2.21)

Provides office automation for medical offices that allows inexperienced computer operators to maximize efficiency.

System: PLUS, SE, II
Minimum Memory: 1024K
Requires: 800K disk drive, hard disk. 800K disk drive.
Medium: 3 1/2-inch disk
ISPN: 83550-210   **Price: $1995.00**

CMA MICRO COMPUTER DIVISION
DENTAL OFFICE MANAGEMENT FOR MACINTOSH

Offers a wide range of office management and billing features.

System: XL
Minimum Memory: 512K
Requires: 5MB Hard disk, 132-column printer.
Medium: 3 1/2-inch disk
ISPN: 13112-199   **Price: $7995.95**

CMA MICRO COMPUTER DIVISION
DENTAL OFFICE MANAGEMENT IIP

Integrates private patient accounts receivables, claim form preparation and appointment scheduling.

System: MAC, II, PLUS, SE, XL
Minimum Memory: 512K
Requires: Hard disk, printer.
Medium: 3 1/2-inch disk
ISPN: 13112-192   **Price: $1995.95**

INTERNET
DONOR ROOM

Comprehensive blood donor management program for hospitals and blood banks.

System: MAC, II, PLUS, SE, XL
Minimum Memory: 512K
Medium: 3 1/2-inch disk
ISPN: 40257-175   **Price: $9995.00**

EASY PRACTICE
EASY PRACTICE (VER. 1.0)

Provides a solution for integrated management of a dental office by running every operation on a single command or macro.

System: MAC, II, PLUS, SE, XL
Minimum Memory: 128K
Requires: OverVue (ISPN 87500-100), FrontDesk (ISPN 43760-500).
Medium: 3 1/2-inch disk
ISPN: 91503-250   **Price: $89.95**

SYSTEC COMPUTER SERVICES
FRONT OFFICE (VER. 2.0)

Provides billing, claims processing, patient history, reports, appointments and receipts.

System: MAC, II, PLUS, SE, XL
Minimum Memory: 1024K
Requires: Omnis 3 Plus/Express (ISPN 58775-515), hard disk.
Medium: 3 1/2-inch disk
ISPN: 95775-200   **Price: $2895.00**

NUMERISATION SERVICES S.A.
HYPERMED

A HyperCard-based medicine management system for general practitioners in France.

System: MAC, II, PLUS, SE, XL
Minimum Memory: 2048K
Requires: Hypercard (ISPN 03900-300).
Medium: 3 1/2-inch disk
ISPN: 90916-360   **Price: $1000.00**

INTERNET
MAC BACK

A comprehensive scheduling and billing system for the chiropractic office.

System: MAC, II, PLUS, SE, XL
Minimum Memory: 512K
Medium: 3 1/2-inch disk
ISPN: 40257-225
Price: Please contact the software publisher.

NEWHOUSE MEDICAL SYSTEMS LTD.
MACMED (VER. 4.02)

A medical office record keeping, billing, appointments and practice evaluation program for practices with one to twelve physicians.

System: MAC, II, PLUS, SE, XL
Minimum Memory: 1024K
Requires: Multi-user version. 10MB hard disk.
Medium: 3 1/2-inch disk
ISPN: 56753-500　　　　**Price: $3450.00**

NEWHOUSE MEDICAL SYSTEMS LTD.
MACMED (VER. 4.02)

A medical office record keeping, billing, appointments and practice evaluation program for practices with one to twelve physicians.

System: MAC, II, PLUS, SE, XL
Minimum Memory: 1024K
Requires: Single user version. 10MB hard disk.
Medium: 3 1/2-inch disk
ISPN: 56753-500　　　　**Price: $2250.00**

DAPPLE-TECH COMPUTERS
MED QUEST

Provides a complete medical office management system.

System: MAC, II, PLUS, SE, XL
Minimum Memory:
Medium: 3 1/2-inch disk
ISPN: 22281-600　　　　**Price: $2495.00**

JAM TECHNOLOGIES
MEDICAL ELECTRONIC DESKTOP (MACMED) (VER. 1.1)

Manages direct patient care and maintains patient medical records.

System: MAC, II, PLUS, SE, XL
Minimum Memory: 1024K
Requires: Hard disk.
Medium: 3 1/2-inch disk
ISPN: 41388-500　　　　**Price: $2500.00**

SYNAPSE SOFTWARE
OMNI-MED

Provides a medical office management system, utilizing the database Omnis 3 Plus/Express.

System: MAC, II, PLUS, SE, XL
Minimum Memory: 512K
Requires: 1-5 users. Omnis 3 Plus/Express (ISPN 58775-515).
Medium: 3 1/2-inch disk
ISPN: 77487-100　　　　**Price: $2495.00**

SYNAPSE SOFTWARE
OMNI-MED

Provides a medical office management system, utilizing the database Omnis 3 Plus/Express.

System: MAC, II, PLUS, SE, XL
Minimum Memory: 512K
Requires: One user. Omnis 3 Plus/Express (ISPN 58775-515).
Medium: 3 1/2-inch disk
ISPN: 77487-100　　　　**Price: $1495.00**

EYECARE DATA SERVICES
OPTISYSTEMS-APAY

Allows the optometry office to perform accounts payable functions.

System: MAC, II, PLUS, SE, XL
Minimum Memory: 128K
Medium: 3 1/2-inch disk
ISPN: 30560-100　　　　**Price: $195.00**

EYECARE DATA SERVICES
OPTISYSTEMS-PIBS

Provides patient information and billing system.

System: MAC, II, PLUS, SE, XL
Minimum Memory: 128K
Medium: 3 1/2-inch disk
ISPN: 30560-200　　　　**Price: $395.00**

OR-D SYSTEMS
OR-D CHIROPRACTIC SYSTEM-COMPLETE MGMT. SYSTEM

Starter system for the complete practice management system for the chiropractic practice.

System: MAC, II, PLUS, SE, XL
Minimum Memory: 512K
Requires: Hard disk.
Medium: 3 1/2-inch disk
ISPN: 58663-052　　　　**Price: $3500.00**

OR-D SYSTEMS
OR-D DENTAL MANAGEMENT SYSTEM COMPLETE MGMT SYSTEM

Starter system for the complete office management system for a dental practice.

System: MAC, II, PLUS, SE, XL
Minimum Memory: 512K
Medium: 3 1/2-inch disk
ISPN: 58663-102　　　　**Price: $990.00**

OR-D SYSTEMS
OR-D MEDICAL MANAGEMENT SYSTEM (VER. 1.1.A)

Complete office management system for a medical practice which performs per visit billing, diagnosis, treatment and prescription.

System: MAC, II, PLUS, SE, XL
Minimum Memory: 512K
Medium: 3 1/2-inch disk
ISPN: 58663-300　　　　**Price: $990.00**

OR-D SYSTEMS
OR-D OB-GYN SYSTEM

A complete practice management system for obstetrics and gynecology.

System: MAC, II, PLUS, SE, XL
Minimum Memory: 512K
Medium: 3 1/2-inch disk
ISPN: 58663-350　　　　**Price: $3500.00**

OR-D SYSTEMS
OR-D OPTOMETRIC SYSTEM

Complete office management system for an optometric office which performs per visit billing, diagnosis, practice building and more.

System: MAC
Minimum Memory: 512K
Medium: 3 1/2-inch disk
ISPN: 58663-400　　　　**Price: $3500.00**

OR-D SYSTEMS
OR-D ORTHODONTIC SYSTEM (VER. 1.1B)

Office management for orthodontic office which performs visit billing, diagnosis, practice building, contract billing, and more.

System: MAC
Minimum Memory: 512K
Medium: 3 1/2-inch disk
ISPN: 58663-450　　　　**Price: $990.00**

ORION COMPUTER TRAINING SYSTEMS
ORION DENTAL (VER. 2.5)

Handles dental office management, scheduling, patient information, receivables, payables, and patient recall.

System: MAC, II, PLUS, SE, XL
Minimum Memory: 1024K
Requires: ImageWriter II, 20MB hard disk.
Medium: 3 1/2-inch disk
ISPN: 58862-500　　　　**Price: $3995.00**

ORION COMPUTER TRAINING SYSTEMS
ORION DENTAL (VER. 2.5)

Handles dental office management, scheduling, patient information, receivables, payables, and patient recall.

System: MAC, II, PLUS, SE, XL
Minimum Memory: 1024K
Requires: 2-5 users. ImageWriter II, 20MB hard disk.
Medium: 3 1/2-inch disk
ISPN: 58862-500　　　　**Price: $6995.00**

ORION COMPUTER TRAINING SYSTEMS
ORION FAMILY PRACTICE (VER. 2.5)

Handles medical office management, scheduling, patient information, receivables, payables and electronic claims.

System: MAC, II, PLUS, SE, XL
Minimum Memory: 1024K
Requires: ImageWriter II, 20MB hard disk.
Medium: 3 1/2-inch disk
ISPN: 58862-510　　　　**Price: $3995.00**

ORION COMPUTER TRAINING SYSTEMS

ORION FAMILY PRACTICE (VER. 2.5)

Handles medical office management, scheduling, patient information, receivables, payables and electronic claims.

System: MAC, II, PLUS, SE, XL
Minimum Memory: 1024K
Requires: 2-5 users. ImageWriter II, 20MB hard disk.
Medium: 3 1/2-inch disk
ISPN: 58862-510 **Price: $6995.00**

ORION COMPUTER TRAINING SYSTEMS

ORION OPTICIAN'S LAB

Provides automation of management with order entry, billing, accounts payable, accounts receivable and reports.

System: MAC, II, PLUS, SE, XL
Minimum Memory: 1024K
Medium: 3 1/2-inch disk
ISPN: 58862-550 **Price: $2595.00**

ORION COMPUTER TRAINING SYSTEMS

ORION OPTOMETRIC (VER. 3.0)

Provides office management with scheduling, patient information, accounts payable, accounts receivable and electronic claims.

System: MAC, II, PLUS, SE, XL
Minimum Memory: 1024K
Requires: ImageWriter II printer, 20MB hard disk, Microcom AX modem with MNP protocol for electronic claim submission.
Medium: 3 1/2-inch disk
ISPN: 58862-560 **Price: $3995.00**

ORION COMPUTER TRAINING SYSTEMS

ORION OPTOMETRIC (VER. 3.0)

Provides office management with scheduling, patient information, accounts payable, accounts receivable and electronic claims.

System: MAC, II, PLUS, SE, XL
Minimum Memory: 1024K
Requires: 2-5 users. ImageWriter II printer, 20MB hard disk, Microcom AX modem with MNP protocol for electronic claim submission.
Medium: 3 1/2-inch disk
ISPN: 58862-560 **Price: $6995.00**

ORION COMPUTER TRAINING SYSTEMS

ORION SURGICAL (VER. 3.2)

Provides scheduling, maintaining patient information, accounts payable, accounts receivable, and electronic claims.

System: MAC, II, PLUS, SE, XL
Minimum Memory: 1024K
Requires: ImageWriter II, 20MB hard disk, Microcom AX modem with MNP protocol for electronic claim submission.
Medium: 3 1/2-inch disk
ISPN: 58862-570 **Price: $3995.00**

ORION COMPUTER TRAINING SYSTEMS

ORION SURGICAL (VER. 3.2)

Provides scheduling, maintaining patient information, accounts payable, accounts receivable, and electronic claims.

System: MAC, II, PLUS, SE, XL
Minimum Memory: 1024K
Requires: 2-5 users. ImageWriter II, 20MB hard disk, Microcom AX modem with MNP protocol for electronic claim submission.
Medium: 3 1/2-inch disk
ISPN: 58862-570 **Price: $6995.00**

REASON HOUSE

PRACTICE MANAGER (VER. 1.07)

Built around services provided and fees associated with services in a clinical practice.

System: MAC, II, PLUS, SE, XL
Minimum Memory: 512K
Requires: 800K disk drive, hard disk, Double Helix II (ISPN 57709-160).
Medium: 3 1/2-inch disk
ISPN: 65635-550 **Price: $795.00**

ORION COMPUTER TRAINING SYSTEMS

PULSE POINT

Complete for medical office management, scheduling, patient information, receivables, payables, electronic claims and more.

System: MAC, II, PLUS, SE, XL
Minimum Memory: 512K
Requires: 20MB hard disk, Modem with MNP Protocol and 2400 baud rate, ImageWriter II printer.
Medium: 3 1/2-inch disk
ISPN: 58862-999 **Price: $7200.00**

SIMPLICITY DENTAL SOFTWARE SYSTEMS, INC.

SIMPLICITY DENTAL SOFTWARE (VER. 7.404)

Handles over 10,000 patients and 40,000 transaction records and is capable of finding a patient record in a fraction of a second.

System: MAC, II, PLUS, SE, XL
Minimum Memory: 1024K
Requires: 20MB hard disk, ImageWriter or LaserWriter printer, Omnis 3 Plus (ISPN 58775-515)
Medium: 3 1/2-inch disk
ISPN: 70438-700 **Price: $2450.00**

T & M SYSTEMS, INC.

T & M OPTOMETRIC PLUS (VER. 3.3)

Provides a complete optometric office management system including accounts receivable, records, ICD codes, insurance and reports.

System: MAC, II, PLUS, SE, XL
Minimum Memory: 1024K
Requires: 20MB hard disk, ImageWriter or Okidata printer.
Medium: 3 1/2-inch disk
ISPN: 79401-700 **Price: $3000.00**

WABASH MEDICAL RESOURCES

TESSSYSTEM ONE (VER. 2.0.3)

Designed for the medical office to provide accounts receivable, insurance reporting and appointment scheduling.

System: MAC, II, PLUS, SE, XL
Minimum Memory: 1024K
Requires: 800K disk drive, 20MB hard disk, ImageWriter or other printer.
Medium: 3 1/2-inch disk
ISPN: 81175-700 **Price: $650.00**

WABASH MEDICAL RESOURCES

TESSSYSTEM ONE PLUS

Unlimited number of CPT codes, suitable for surgeons, radiologists, pathologists who use CPT codes. Expandable to Multi-Doctor System.

System: MAC, II, PLUS, SE, XL
Minimum Memory: 512K
Requires: 10MB hard disk, ImageWriter printer.
Medium: 3 1/2-inch disk
ISPN: 81175-710 **Price: $3599.00**

WABASH MEDICAL RESOURCES

TESSSYSTEM TWO (VER. 1.4)

Provides accounts receivable, billing and insurance filing for a single physician, or up to ten physicians.

System: MAC, II, PLUS, SE, XL
Minimum Memory: 1024K
Requires: Includes electronic claims. 800K disk drive, 20MB hard disk, ImageWriter or other printer.
Medium: 3 1/2-inch disk
ISPN: 81175-715 **Price: $4390.00**

WABASH MEDICAL RESOURCES

TESSSYSTEM TWO (VER. 1.4)

Provides accounts receivable, billing and insurance filing for a single physician, or up to ten physicians.

System: MAC, II, PLUS, SE, XL
Minimum Memory: 1024K
Requires: 800K disk drive, 20MB hard disk, ImageWriter or other printer.
Medium: 3 1/2-inch disk
ISPN: 81175-715 **Price: $2995.00**

WABASH MEDICAL RESOURCES

TESSSYSTEM TWO (VER. 1.4)

Provides accounts receivable, billing and insurance filing for a single physician, or up to ten physicians.

System: MAC, II, PLUS, SE, XL
Minimum Memory: 1024K
Requires: 2-4 doctors. 800K disk drive, 20MB hard disk, ImageWriter or other printer.
Medium: 3 1/2-inch disk
ISPN: 81175-715 **Price: $3995.00**

CLASS ONE, INC.

TOOTHPICS (VER. 2.1)

A patient management system for dental offices, with 'on screen' dental charting, self contained networking capabilities.

System: MAC, II, PLUS, SE, XL
Minimum Memory: 1024K
Medium: 3 1/2-inch disk
ISPN: 12881-700   **Price: $2750.00**

758 PROFESSIONS/ SERVICES/ MISCELLANEOUS PROFESSIONS/ SERVICES

MACHUNTER

MACHUNTER RMS (VER. 1.8)

Manages information for personnel recruitment with activity tracking, time management and a relational database.

System: MAC, II, PLUS, SE, XL
Minimum Memory: 1024K
Requires: Hard disk. 2-4 users $1095 per user. 5-7 users $895 per user, 8-10 users $795 per user, 11-20 users $695 per user, 20 + users $595.
Medium: 3 1/2-inch disk
ISPN: 45825-500   **Price: $1295.00**

MACMEDIC PUBLICATIONS, INC.

MACSURGERY (VER. 1.0)

An interactive, self-educational program in general surgery, for continuing medical education and board preparation.

System: MAC, II, PLUS, SE, XL
Minimum Memory: 1024K
Requires: HyperCard (ISPN 3900-300).
Medium: 3 1/2-inch disk
ISPN: 45845-530   **Price: $125.00**

ESSEX SYSTEMS

OMNITRAX

Comprehensive management product for retail video business.

System: MAC, II, PLUS, SE, XL
Minimum Memory: 512K
Medium: 3 1/2-inch disk
ISPN: 29837-100   **Price: $2795.00**

763 PROFESSIONS/ SERVICES/NON-PROFIT/ ASSOCIATIONS

SPECIALTY SOFTWARE

CHURCH MANAGEMENT SYSTEM (VER. 4.4)

Includes Contribution Records, Church Finance, Membership Record, Visitation Files, and Sunday School Records.

System: MAC, II, PLUS, SE, XL
Minimum Memory: 1024K
Requires: 800K disk drive.
Medium: 3 1/2-inch disk
ISPN: 95752-050   **Price: $395.00**

SOFTWARE DEVELOPMENT GROUP

CHURCH MASTER (VER. 1.0)

Tracks and maintains information on church members and includes fund and group management.

System: MAC, II, PLUS, SE, XL
Minimum Memory: 1024K
Medium: 3 1/2-inch disk
ISPN: 72681-100   **Price: $245.00**

SPECIALTY SOFTWARE

CHURCH ORGANIZATIONAL MANAGEMENT SYSTEM (VER. 2.1)

Includes an advanced organizational management program for churches of any size.

System: MAC, II, PLUS, SE, XL
Minimum Memory: 1024K
Requires: 800K disk drive.
Medium: 3 1/2-inch disk
ISPN: 95752-605   **Price: $395.00**

H & D LEASING, INC.

CHURCH STEWARDSHIP (VER. 2.5)

Tracks church members, visitors, and prospective members' addresses, phone numbers, group affiliations and contributions.

System: MAC, II, PLUS, SE, XL
Minimum Memory: 512K
Requires: 20MB hard disk.
Medium: 3 1/2-inch disk
ISPN: 33851-100   **Price: $495.00**

CAMPAGNE ASSOCIATES LTD.

COMMTACT/COMMUNITY CONTACT SYSTEM (VER. 2.0)

An approach and solution for non-profits to increase public relations, marketing and fund-raising activities in the community.

System: MAC, II, PLUS, SE, XL
Minimum Memory: 1024K
Requires: Omnis 3 Plus (ISPN 58775-320).
Medium: 3 1/2-inch disk
ISPN: 10905-100   **Price: $2990.00**

LITURGICAL PUBLICATIONS, INC.

CONCENSUS (VER. 1.51)

A contribution and census management system for churches, featuring detailed family and member records and reporting capabilities.

System: MAC, II, PLUS, SE, XL
Minimum Memory: 512K
Requires: Hard disk.
Medium: 3 1/2-inch disk
ISPN: 93628-150   **Price: $995.00**

LITURGICAL PUBLICATIONS, INC.

CONCENSUS (VER. 1.51)

A contribution and census management system for churches, featuring detailed family and member records and reporting capabilities.

System: MAC, II, PLUS, SE, XL
Minimum Memory: 512K
Requires: 1-10 users. Hard disk.
Medium: 3 1/2-inch disk
ISPN: 93628-150   **Price: $1695.00**

GIFTS CONSULTANTS, INC.

CONSULTANT (VER. 6.0)

Provides menu-driven campaign and special event managing, report generating, membership and pledge/contribution tracking.

System: MAC, II, PLUS, SE, XL
Minimum Memory: 1024K
Medium: 3 1/2-inch disk
ISPN: 32837-700   **Price: $2995.00**

DAVKA CORP.

MACSHAMMES

Complete synagogue and administrative management system. Maintains membership, Yahrtzeit records and synagogue mailing lists.

System: MAC, II, PLUS, SE, XL
Minimum Memory: 512K
Medium: 3 1/2-inch disk
ISPN: 91205-500   **Price: $995.00**

772 PROFESSIONS/ SERVICES/PUBLISHING/ PRINTING

CRICKET SOFTWARE

CRICKET GRAPH (VER. 1.2)

Professional color graphics presentation/ desktop publishing software for science and business.

System: MAC, II, PLUS, SE, XL
Minimum Memory: 512K
Medium: 3 1/2-inch disk
ISPN: 35512-025   **Price: $195.00**

IDEAFORM, INC.

HYPERBOOK MAKER

A utility program that brings desktop publishing capability to HyperCard and allows printing in a variety of formats.

System: MAC, II, PLUS, SE, XL
Minimum Memory: 1024K
Requires: HyperCard (ISPN 03900-300).
Medium: 3 1/2-inch disk
ISPN: 37059-400   **Price: $59.95**

BOSTON PUBLISHING SYSTEMS

MACPUBLISHER II

Personal publishing system that offers professional features including variable letter spacing and kerning.

System: MAC, II, PLUS, SE, XL
Minimum Memory: 512K
Requires: LaserWriter, ImageWriter, Allied l-100, Allied L-300 or Data Products LZR-2665 printers.
Medium: 3 1/2-inch disk
ISPN: 08268-475   **Price: $195.00**

BOSTON PUBLISHING SYSTEMS

MACPUBLISHER III

Allows text editing and sophisticated graphics drawing directly on the layout page, including multi-line rules, multi-pattern borders.

System: MAC, II, PLUS, SE, XL
Minimum Memory: 512K
Requires: Two disk drives or a disk drive and a hard disk.
Medium: 3 1/2-inch disk
ISPN: 08268-480   **Price: $99.95**

NEW IMAGE TECHNOLOGY, INC.

MACSCAN (VER. 1.49)

Digitizes any printed image including logos, halftones photos, maps, and forms in less than 15 seconds at 300 dots per inch.

System: MAC, II, PLUS, SE, XL
Minimum Memory: 1024K
Medium: 3 1/2-inch disk
ISPN: 56706-450   **Price: $1547.00**

BRAUCH SOFTWARE, INC.

MACSUB

Provides a subscription fulfillment and circulation management system for periodical publications.

System: MAC, II, PLUS, SE, XL
Minimum Memory: 1024K
Requires: 132-column dot matrix printer, minimum of 3MB per 1000 subscribers hard disk space. Microsoft Excel (ISPN 53150-270).
Medium: 3 1/2-inch disk
ISPN: 90660-500   **Price: $3100.00**

FTL SYSTEMS, INC.

MACTEX

Professional typesetting software package that uses a full implementation of the TEX typesetting language.

System: MAC, II, PLUS, SE, XL
Minimum Memory: 1024K
Medium: 3 1/2-inch disk
ISPN: 91860-400   **Price: $750.00**

TELETYPESETTING CO.

MICROSETTER II (VER. 2.0)

Converts document output to allow for direct phototypesetting with 'What you see is what you get' viewing.

System: MAC, II, PLUS, SE, XL
Minimum Memory: 1024K
Requires: Serial connection to typesetter.
Medium: 3 1/2-inch disk
ISPN: 81055-500   **Price: $1490.00**

MCCUTCHEON GRAPHICS, INC.

PAGE ONE

Eliminates book production problems like book design, typesetting and proofreading of typeset galleys automatically.

System: MAC, II, PLUS, SE, XL
Minimum Memory: 1024K
Requires: 20MB hard disk.
Medium: 3 1/2-inch disk
ISPN: 48212-600   **Price: $1200.00**

ALDUS CORP.

PAGEMAKER (VER. 3.0)

Design and produce publication pages in an office environment. Pages can be assembled from stored word processing and graphics.

System: MAC, II, PLUS, SE, XL
Minimum Memory: 512K
Requires: MacWrite (ISPN 12784-530), MacDraw (ISPN 12784-500), or Microsoft Word (ISPN 53150-732) and a LaserWriter printer.
Medium: 3 1/2-inch disk
ISPN: 02226-700   **Price: $595.00**

ALDUS CORP.

PAGEMAKER CLASSROOM

Complete set of introductory training materials on desktop publishing using PageMaker.

System: MAC, II, PLUS, SE, XL
Minimum Memory: 512K
Medium: 3 1/2-inch disk
ISPN: 02226-725   **Price: $795.00**

ALDUS CORP.

PAGEMAKER PORTFOLIO-DESIGNS FOR NEWSLETTERS

Twenty one different newsletter formats designed to help PageMaker users produce better-looking publications.

System: MAC, II, PLUS, SE, XL
Minimum Memory: 512K
Requires: PageMaker (ISPN 02226-700).
Medium: 3 1/2-inch disk
ISPN: 02226-740   **Price: $99.00**

STRIDER SOFTWARE

POSTERMAKER PLUS (VER. 2.5)

A graphics scaling program with fancy text styling capabilities for use in making posters, banners, signs and headlines.

System: MAC, II, PLUS, SE, XL
Minimum Memory: 512K
Requires: Printer.
Medium: 3 1/2-inch disk
ISPN: 76569-551   **Price: $99.95**

RCO COMPUTER SERVICES, INC.

QU*EST

Performs quoting, estimating, invoicing, and reports for the professional printers management problems.

System: MAC, II, PLUS, SE, XL
Minimum Memory: 512K
Medium: 3 1/2-inch disk
ISPN: 64606-300   **Price: $1250.00**

DESKTOP COMPOSITION SYSTEM, INC.

STYLO-TYPE I

A quality typesetting program which drives CRTronic/Linotronic typesetters in their native Dewsy command language.

System: MAC, II, PLUS, SE, XL
Minimum Memory: 512K
Medium: 3 1/2-inch disk
ISPN: 83187-100   **Price: $295.00**

BLUE SKY RESEARCH

TEXTURES

Allows users to accurately typeset scientific and mathematical material for presentation quality output.

System: MAC, II, PLUS, SE, XL
Minimum Memory: 1024K
Requires: Two disk drives.
Medium: 3 1/2-inch disk
ISPN: 42587-700   **Price: $495.00**

FUTURESOFT SYSTEM DESIGNS, INC.

WRITERS WORKSHOP (VER. 1.0)

Track ideas, manuscripts, set layouts, submissions, evaluate publisher's rates, enter one query letter send to all publishers.

System: MAC, II, PLUS, SE, XL
Minimum Memory: 512K
Medium: 3 1/2-inch disk
ISPN: 31694-200   **Price: $99.00**

776 PROFESSIONS/ SERVICES/REAL ESTATE/PROPERTY MANAGEMENT

YARDI SYSTEMS, INC.

BASIC PROPERTY MANAGEMENT (VER. 3.1)

Designed to manage single family dwellings and apartment buildings.

System: MAC, II, PLUS, SE, XL
Minimum Memory: 512K
Medium: 3 1/2-inch disk
ISPN: 87225-160   **Price: $395.00**

HEIZER SOFTWARE

BUSINESS VALUATION

Determines the value of a closely-held business for sale, estate, insurance or borrowing purposes.

System: MAC, II, PLUS, SE, XL
Minimum Memory: 512K
Requires: Microsoft Excel (ISPN 53150-270), Microsoft Works (ISPN 53150-740) or HyperCard (ISPN 03900-300).
Medium: 3 1/2-inch disk
ISPN: 35175-531   **Price: $15.00**

HEIZER SOFTWARE
BUYER'S CLOSING COSTS
Calculates the estimated closing costs for a prospective buyer.
System: MAC, II, PLUS, SE, XL
Minimum Memory: 512K
Requires: Microsoft Works (ISPN 53150-740).
Medium: 3 1/2-inch disk
ISPN: 35175-869   **Price: $15.00**

HEIZER SOFTWARE
CAPITALIZATION OF AN INVESTMENT PROPERTY
Prepares a pro-forma analysis of a residential rental property for a potential buyer.
System: MAC, II, PLUS, SE, XL
Minimum Memory: 512K
Requires: Microsoft Works (ISPN 53150-740).
Medium: 3 1/2-inch disk
ISPN: 35175-871   **Price: $12.00**

HEIZER SOFTWARE
CEILING PRICE CALCULATOR
Computes the maximum equitable purchase price for a residence or any commercial real estate.
System: MAC, II, PLUS, SE, XL
Minimum Memory: 512K
Requires: Microsoft Excel (ISPN 53150-270) or Microsoft Works (ISPN 53150-740).
Medium: 3 1/2-inch disk
ISPN: 35175-919   **Price: $10.00**

REALDATA, INC.
COMMERCIAL/INDUSTRIAL/ REAL ESTATE APPLICATIONS
Provides spreadsheet templates which produce reports, cost analysis and budget pro-forma to present to lenders.
System: MAC, II, PLUS, SE, XL
Minimum Memory: 512K
Requires: Multiplan (ISPN 35087-400), Microsoft Works (ISPN 53150-740) or Microsoft Excel (ISPN 53150-270).
Medium: 3 1/2-inch disk
ISPN: 65462-200   **Price: $100.00**

HEIZER SOFTWARE
COMPARISON OF REAL ESTATE PROPERTIES
A comparison of several properties with a focus on cash flow and internal financial return.
System: MAC, II, PLUS, SE, XL
Minimum Memory: 512K
Requires: Microsoft Excel (ISPN 53150-270) or Microsoft Works (ISPN 53150-740).
Medium: 3 1/2-inch disk
ISPN: 35175-680   **Price: $20.00**

YARDI SYSTEMS, INC.
DELUXE PROPERTY MANAGEMENT (VER. 3.821)
Manages residential and commercial rental and condominium association properties.
System: MAC, II, PLUS, SE, XL
Minimum Memory: 1024K
Requires: System 6.0 or higher.
Medium: 3 1/2-inch disk
ISPN: 87225-200   **Price: $1195.00**

HMS COMPUTER CO.
HMSCALC
Series of programs designed to qualify buyers by loan type. Displays loan type, annual income, loan amount, term, rate, & more.
System: MAC, II, PLUS, SE, XL
Minimum Memory: 512K
Medium: 3 1/2-inch disk
ISPN: 35873-200   **Price: $89.95**

HEIZER SOFTWARE
INVESTMENT REAL ESTATE ANALYZER/RECORDER
A template which projects and/or records income and expenses for a residential investment property on a monthly basis.
System: MAC, II, PLUS, SE, XL
Minimum Memory: 512K
Requires: Microsoft Excel (ISPN 53150-270) or Microsoft Works (ISPN 53150-740).
Medium: 3 1/2-inch disk
ISPN: 35175-678   **Price: $15.00**

HEIZER SOFTWARE
LIMITED PARTNERSHIP ANALYZER
Determines the net cash flow and taxable income to limited partners along with the internal rate of return on investment.
System: MAC, II, PLUS, SE, XL
Minimum Memory: 512K
Requires: Microsoft Excel (ISPN 53150-270) or Microsoft Works (ISPN 53150-740).
Medium: 3 1/2-inch disk
ISPN: 35175-682   **Price: $20.00**

REALDATA, INC.
LISTING/PROSPECT DATA MANAGEMENT
Provides a series of ready-made database templates for use with Microsoft File.
System: MAC, II, PLUS, SE, XL
Minimum Memory: 512K
Requires: Microsoft File (53150-275).
Medium: 3 1/2-inch disk
ISPN: 65462-440   **Price: $195.00**

FINANCIAL MICROWARE
LOAN QUALIFIER (VER. 1.5)
Assists in the sales, quotation and qualifying process used in providing prospective clients with mortgage loan details.
System: MAC, II, PLUS, SE, XL
Minimum Memory: 128K
Requires: Spreadsheet program such as Excel (ISPN 53150-270), Multiplan (ISPN 53150-55) or Crunch.
Medium: 3 1/2-inch disk
ISPN: 91833-475   **Price: $99.00**

SOFTFLAIR, INC.
LOANLEASE LIBRARY (VER. 1.01)
Tracks loan or rental payments and receipts and generates professional customized reports.
System: MAC, II, PLUS, SE, XL
Minimum Memory: 512K
Medium: 3 1/2-inch disk
ISPN: 95747-400   **Price: $69.95**

SOFTFLAIR, INC.
LOANLEASE LIBRARY (VER. 1.01)
Tracks loan or rental payments and receipts and generates professional customized reports.
System: MAC, II, PLUS, SE, XL
Minimum Memory: 512K
Requires: Loan only version. Lease only version.
Medium: 3 1/2-inch disk
ISPN: 95747-400   **Price: $49.95**

MACLORD SYSTEMS, INC.
MACLORD PROFESSIONAL PROPERTY MANAGEMENT
Integrates property management Accounting, Leasing, and Repairs into one package.
System: MAC, II, PLUS, SE, XL
Minimum Memory: 512K
Requires: Two disk drives or a hard disk, printer.
Medium: 3 1/2-inch disk
ISPN: 93907-500   **Price: $1295.00**

TRONSOFT, INC.
MAXILOAN (VER. 2.1)
Performs depreciation evaluation, income/ sales analysis, and fixed rate and variable loans for up to 30 years.
System: MAC, II, PLUS, SE, XL
Minimum Memory: 128K
Medium: 3 1/2 inch disk
ISPN: 82788-500   **Price: $395.00**

REALDATA, INC.
MORTGAGE QUALIFIER
Easy-to-use system intended for real estate agents, mortgage lenders and home builders.
System: MAC, II, PLUS, SE, XL
Minimum Memory: 512K
Requires: Microsoft Excel (ISPN 53150-270).
Medium: 3 1/2-inch disk
ISPN: 65462-500   **Price: $195.00**

HEIZER SOFTWARE
MULTI-UNIT PROPERTY MANAGEMENT
Keeps records on income-producing properties, including apartment buildings, mini-warehouses, office buildings and shopping centers.
System: MAC, II, PLUS, SE, XL
Minimum Memory: 512K
Requires: Microsoft Excel (ISPN 53150-270) or Microsoft Works (ISPN 53150-740).
Medium: 3 1/2-inch disk
ISPN: 35175-677   **Price: $40.00**

METROPOLIS SOFTWARE, INC.
PROANALYSIS (VER. 1.10)
Provides real estate investment analysis.
System: MAC, II, PLUS, SE, XL
Minimum Memory: 512K
Medium: 3 1/2-inch disk
ISPN: 80218-675   **Price: $295.00**

HMS COMPUTER CO.

PROCLASS (PROSPECT CLOSING ASSISTANT) (VER. 2.1)

Interactive sales tool designed to prepare home purchase price, and a proposal and purchase agreement for home buyers.

System: MAC, II, PLUS, SE, XL
Minimum Memory: 1024K
Medium: 3 1/2-inch disk
ISPN: 35873-300   **Price: $495.00**

REALDATA, INC.

PROPERTY MANAGEMENT LEVEL I

Designed for real estate management for owners and managers. Helps keep track of important information about rental property.

System: MAC, II, PLUS, SE, XL
Minimum Memory: 512K
Requires: Microsoft Excel (ISPN 53150-270).
Medium: 3 1/2-inch disk
ISPN: 65462-580   **Price: $250.00**

REALDATA, INC.

PROPERTY MANAGEMENT LEVEL II

Expands Property Management Level I providing increased capacity for tracking information about rental property.

System: MAC, II, PLUS, SE, XL
Minimum Memory: 1024K
Requires: Microsoft Excel (ISPN 53150-270).
Medium: 3 1/2-inch disk
ISPN: 65462-585   **Price: $295.00**

MPM COMPUTING

PROPERTY MANAGER

A complete property management system that is supported and can be customized by a national network of Omnis developers.

System: MAC, II, PLUS, SE, XL
Minimum Memory: 512K
Requires: Omnis 3 Plus/Express (ISPN 58875-515).
Medium: 3 1/2-inch disk
ISPN: 93916-600   **Price: $995.00**

MPM COMPUTING

PROPERTY MANAGER

A complete property management system that is supported and can be customized by a national network of Omnis developers.

System: MAC, II, PLUS, SE, XL
Minimum Memory: 512K
Requires: 2-5 users. Omnis 3 Plus/Express (ISPN 58775-515).
Medium: 3 1/2-inch disk
ISPN: 93916-600   **Price: $1795.00**

METROPOLIS SOFTWARE, INC.

PROPERTY MANAGER (VER. 1.01)

An accounting system for multiple rental property management.

System: MAC, II, PLUS, SE, XL
Minimum Memory: 1024K
Requires: 4th Dimension (ISPN 90311-200) or 4D Runtime Unit, hard disk.
Medium: 3 1/2-inch disk
ISPN: 80218-800   **Price: $195.00**

TRONSOFT, INC.

PROPERTY MASTER (VER. 1.2)

Manages new and existing rental properties from duplexes to apartment houses with thousands of units.

System: MAC, II, PLUS, SE, XL
Minimum Memory: 1024K
Requires: FileMaker (ISPN 12784-200).
Medium: 3 1/2-inch disk
ISPN: 82788-590   **Price: $1295.00**

HMS COMPUTER CO.

PROSPECT TRACKING SYSTEM

Includes prospect profile, tracking, mailings, market research analysis used to track prospects and report to management.

System: MAC, II, PLUS, SE, XL
Minimum Memory: 512K
Medium: 3 1/2-inch disk
ISPN: 35873-310   **Price: $395.00**

HEIZER SOFTWARE

REAL ESTATE ANALYSIS

Follows the National Association of Realtors' standard format for evaluation of income-producing properties.

System: MAC, II, PLUS, SE, XL
Minimum Memory: 512K
Requires: Microsoft Excel (ISPN 53150-270) or Microsoft Works (ISPN 53150-740).
Medium: 3 1/2-inch disk
ISPN: 35175-679   **Price: $30.00**

METROPOLIS SOFTWARE, INC.

REAL ESTATE EDGE FORMING SYSTEM (VER. 1.0)

Farming system designed specifically for residential salespeople interested in generating more listings.

System: MAC, II, PLUS, SE, XL
Minimum Memory: 1024K
Requires: 800K disk drive, hard drive, Fourth Dimension (ISPN 90311-200) or Fourth Dimension Runtime.
Medium: 3 1/2-inch disk
ISPN: 80218-600   **Price: $295.00**

REALDATA, INC.

REAL ESTATE INVESTMENT ANALYSIS (VER. 6.0)

Enables user to handle new passive loss rules, carry-forward of suspended losses, and changes in capital gain rules.

System: MAC, II, PLUS, SE, XL
Minimum Memory: 512K
Requires: Microsoft Excel (ISPN 53150-270), Microsoft Works (ISPN 53150-740) or Jazz (ISPN 45525-090).
Medium: 3 1/2-inch disk
ISPN: 65462-650   **Price: $195.00**

REALDATA, INC.

REAL ESTATE INVESTMENT ANALYSIS 1988 TAX (VER 6.0)

Handle cash flow/sensitivity analysis, annual operating statement, loan amortization schedule and internal rate of return calculator.

System: MAC, II, PLUS, SE, XL
Minimum Memory: 512K
Requires: Microsoft Excel (ISPN 53150-270) or Microsoft Works (ISPN 53150-740).
Medium: 3 1/2-inch disk
ISPN: 65462-700   **Price: $250.00**

SULCUS COMPUTER CORP.

REAL ESTATE MANAGEMENT SYSTEM

Provides the total needs of the real estate business including loan closings, document preparation, deeds, mortgages and notes.

System: MAC, II, PLUS, SE, XL
Minimum Memory:
Medium: 3 1/2-inch disk
ISPN: 77006-600
Price: **Please contact the software publisher.**

TRONSOFT, INC.

REAL ESTATE MASTER (VER. 3.46)

Provides complete analysis of any real estate venture, preparing a report ready for the bank or partners.

System: MAC, II, PLUS, SE, XL
Minimum Memory: 1024K
Requires: Microsoft Excel (ISPN 53150-270).
Medium: 3 1/2-inch disk
ISPN: 82788-605   **Price: $1295.00**

HEIZER SOFTWARE

REAL ESTATE OFFICE FINANCIAL TEMPLATES

Eight templates for realtors on mortgages, houses, FHA and VA qualifications, buying and closing, and mortgage amortization.

System: MAC, II, PLUS, SE, XL
Minimum Memory: 512K
Requires: Microsoft Excel (ISPN 53150-270) or Microsoft Works (ISPN 53150-740).
Medium: 3 1/2-inch disk
ISPN: 35175-691   **Price: $99.00**

TAXCALC SOFTWARE, INC.

REAL ESTATE PLANNER

Evaluates the economics of a real estate investment over a period of one to ten years.

System: MAC, II, PLUS, SE, XL
Minimum Memory: 512K
Requires: Microsoft Excel (ISPN 53150-270).
Medium: 3 1/2-inch disk
ISPN: 79843-060   **Price: $150.00**

HEIZER SOFTWARE

REAL ESTATE ROI PROJECTIONS

Projects return on investment for a single property with a focus on cash flow and internal financial return.

System: MAC, II, PLUS, SE, XL
Minimum Memory: 512K
Requires: Microsoft Excel (ISPN 53150-270) or Microsoft Works (ISPN 53150-740).
Medium: 3 1/2-inch disk
ISPN: 35175-854   **Price: $20.00**

AD ASTRA

REAL ESTATE TRACKER

Tracks real estate owner, buyer, seller and property information and finds properties which match buyer's needs.

System: MAC, II, PLUS, SE, XL
Minimum Memory: 1024K
Requires: Hard disk, Fourth Dimension (ISPN 90311-200) or Fourth Dimension Runtime.
Medium: 3 1/2-inch disk
ISPN: 00848-500   **Price: $350.00**

AD ASTRA

REAL ESTATE TRACKER (WITH FOURTH DIMENSION)

Tracks real estate owner, buyer, seller and property information and finds properties which match buyer's needs.

System: MAC, II, PLUS, SE, XL
Minimum Memory: 1024K
Requires: Hard disk.
Medium: 3 1/2-inch disk
ISPN: 00848-505   **Price: $425.00**

HEIZER SOFTWARE

RENT VERSUS BUY

Analyzes a residential rental versus purchase option for an individual, based on interest, tax bracket, and inflation.

System: MAC, II, PLUS, SE, XL
Minimum Memory: 512K
Requires: Microsoft Excel (ISPN 53150-270), Microsoft Works (ISPN 53150-740) or HyperCard (ISPN 03900-300).
Medium: 3 1/2-inch disk
ISPN: 35175-684   **Price: $9.00**

UNICOM SOFTWARE DEVELOPMENT GROUP

RENTAL/UTILITY MANAGER SYSTEM

Provides a complete custom invoice system to manage the rent and utilities of building owners.

System: PLUS, SE
Minimum Memory: 640K
Medium: 3 1/2-inch disk
ISPN: 83550-600   **Price: $895.00**

METROPOLIS SOFTWARE, INC.

SALES ASSOCIATE (VER. 1.10)

Provides a records management system that enables real estate salespeople to keep track of contacts and properties.

System: MAC, II, PLUS, SE, XL
Minimum Memory: 1024K
Requires: 4th Dimension (ISPN 90311-200), or 4D Runtime Unit, hard disk.
Medium: 3 1/2-inch disk
ISPN: 80218-700   **Price: $395.00**

SBT CORP.

SBT DPROPERTY-COMPILED (VER. 6.10)

Performs the accounts receivable functions for property management including maintenance of tenant, unit, and property records.

System: MAC, II, PLUS, SE, XL
Minimum Memory: 512K
Medium: 3 1/2-inch disk
ISPN: 68057-361   **Price: $295.00**

SBT CORP.

SBT DPROPERTY-STANDARD (VER. 6.10)

Performs the accounts receivable functions for property management including maintenance of tenant, unit and property records.

System: MAC, II, PLUS, SE, XL
Minimum Memory: 512K
Medium: 3 1/2-inch disk
ISPN: 68057-360   **Price: $395.00**

HEIZER SOFTWARE

SECOND RESIDENCE TAX TREATMENT

Helps to determine the most advantageous tax treatment for a second residence.

System: MAC, II, PLUS, SE, XL
Minimum Memory: 512K
Requires: Microsoft Excel (ISPN 53150-270).
Medium: 3 1/2-inch disk
ISPN: 35175-983   **Price: $10.00**

HEIZER SOFTWARE

SELLER'S CLOSING COSTS

Calculates estimated closing costs for potential sellers.

System: MAC, II, PLUS, SE, XL
Minimum Memory: 512K
Requires: Microsoft Works (ISPN 53150-740).
Medium: 3 1/2-inch disk
ISPN: 35175-870   **Price: $15.00**

---

786 PROFESSIONS/ SERVICES/RETAIL/ WHOLESALE

DB SOLUTIONS, INC.

AUTOMATIC ITEM KEY UTILITY

Subdivides the inventory number into user-defined logical supplements for use with db:$ Retailer's Advantage.

System: MAC, II, PLUS, SE, XL
Minimum Memory: 1024K
Medium: 3 1/2-inch disk
ISPN: 24094-210   **Price: $295.00**

VIDEX, INC.

BARCODE LABELER (VER. 1.1)

Prints bar code labels (code 3 of 9), mailing labels, inventory tags or virtually any type of label your business requires.

System: MAC, II, PLUS, SE, XL
Minimum Memory: 512K
Requires: ImageWriter or LaserWriter printer.
Medium: 3 1/2-inch disk
ISPN: 85150-051   **Price: $89.00**

TPS ELECTRONICS

BARCODE PRINTING (VER. 1.5)

An inexpensive means for on-site generation of Code 3 of 9 bar code labels. A LaserWriter of ImageWriter may be used.

System: MAC, II, PLUS, SE, XL
Minimum Memory: 512K
Requires: 800K disk drive. A 400K disk can be requested.
Medium: 3 1/2-inch disk
ISPN: 82421-100   **Price: $200.00**

DB SOLUTIONS, INC.

CREDIT CUSTOMER

Maintains customer balances, applies payments to invoices and generates statements. For use with db:$ Retailer's Advantage.

System: MAC, II, PLUS, SE, XL
Minimum Memory: 1024K
Medium: 3 1/2-inch disk
ISPN: 24094-225   **Price: $395.00**

DB SOLUTIONS, INC.

DB:$ RETAILERS ADVANTAGE

A retail full function point of sale management system.

System: MAC, II, PLUS, SE, XL
Minimum Memory: 1024K
Medium: 3 1/2-inch disk
ISPN: 24094-200   **Price: $1795.00**

DB SOLUTIONS, INC.

FLEXSHARE

Reduces network usage 50 to 80 times for reading and writing records to a database.

System: MAC, II, PLUS, SE, XL
Minimum Memory: 1024K
Medium: 3 1/2-inch disk
ISPN: 24094-250   **Price: $295.00**

S & J ENTERPRISES

MAC FLORIST (VER. 2.01)

Provides order management for retail florist operations with data entry of local, wire out, and wire in orders.

System: MAC, II, PLUS, SE, XL
Minimum Memory: 512K
Medium: 3 1/2-inch disk
ISPN: 67356-500   **Price: $400.00**

CHANG LABORATORIES, INC.

MACINTOSH PROFESSIONAL 3-PAK (VER. 3.0)

Includes general ledger, accounts payable, and professional billing modules.

System: MAC, II, PLUS, SE, XL
Minimum Memory: 512K
Medium: 3 1/2-inch disk
ISPN: 12200-082   **Price: $649.95**

CHANG LABORATORIES, INC.

MACINTOSH RETAIL 3-PAK (VER. 3.0)

Includes General Ledger, Accounts Payable, and Inventory Modules.

System: MAC, II, PLUS, SE, XL
Minimum Memory: 512K
Medium: 3 1/2-inch disk
ISPN: 12200-085   **Price: $649.95**

SMALL BUSINESS COMPUTER CONSULTING

MACJEWEL (VER. 1.70)

Provides point-of-sale inventory management for jewelry stores.

System: MAC, II, PLUS, SE, XL
Minimum Memory: 1024K
Requires: 800K disk drive, 20MB hard disk.
Medium: 3 1/2-inch disk
ISPN: 71037-500   **Price: $4995.00**

DB SOLUTIONS, INC.

MULTIPLE PRICE & QUANTITY DISCOUNT LEVELS

Implements complex pricing policies for up to five levels. For use with db:$ Retailer's Advantage.

System: MAC, II, PLUS, SE, XL
Minimum Memory: 1024K
Medium: 3 1/2-inch disk
ISPN: 24094-220   **Price: $495.00**

GRAFTECH

PREMIERE VIDEO RENTAL

Video rental point of sale system manages inventory of customers and movies.

System: MAC, II, PLUS, SE, XL
Minimum Memory: 1024K
Requires: Hard disk, ImageWriter I or II.
Medium: 3 1/2-inch disk
ISPN: 33375-100   **Price: $995.00**

INOVATIC

READSTAR II PLUS

Reads typed and typeset characters at constant or proportional pitch, including kerned characters and non-conventional characters.

System: MAC, II, PLUS, SE, XL
Minimum Memory: 2048K
Requires: Hard disk, scanner, System 5.5 or later.
Medium: 3 1/2-inch disk
ISPN: 92746-600   **Price: $4500.00**

HOULBERG DEVELOPMENT

RETAIL ENGINE (VER. 2.5)

Enables point of sale, cash management, barcode scanning, inventory management, purchasing, and receiving for small apparel retailers.

System: MAC, II, PLUS, SE, XL
Minimum Memory: 1024K
Requires: Hard disk.
Medium: 3 1/2-inch disk
ISPN: 36268-600   **Price: $1295.00**

HOULBERG DEVELOPMENT

RETAIL ENGINE (VER. 2.5)

Enables point of sale, cash management, barcode scanning, inventory management, purchasing, and receiving for small apparel retailers.

System: MAC, II, PLUS, SE, XL
Minimum Memory: 1024K
Requires: 2-10 users. Hard disk, printer.
Medium: 3 1/2-inch disk
ISPN: 36268-600   **Price: $2395.00**

DB SOLUTIONS, INC.

SERIALIZATION

Inventory items can be stored and sold in the system by its own serial number. For use with db:$ Retailer's Advantage.

System: MAC, II, PLUS, SE, XL
Minimum Memory: 1024K
Medium: 3 1/2-inch disk
ISPN: 24094-215   **Price: $395.00**

SOFTWARE DEVELOPMENT GROUP

SERVICES RENDERED (VER. 2.0)

A billing and customer tracking system that includes payment dispersal, account aging and bill configuring functions.

System: MAC, II, PLUS, SE, XL
Minimum Memory: 1024K
Medium: 3 1/2-inch disk
ISPN: 72681-700   **Price: $1200.00**

SHOPKEEPER SOFTWARE

SHOPKEEPER III

Integrated accounts receivable, billing, inventory, invoicing, point of sale for the Macintosh.

System: MAC, II, PLUS, SE, XL
Minimum Memory: 512K
Requires: Two 800K disk drives or a disk drive and a hard disk, 80-column printer.
Medium: 3 1/2-inch disk
ISPN: 69805-630   **Price: $195.00**

---

790 PROFESSIONS/SERVICES/VETERINARY PRACTICE

HEIZER SOFTWARE

MACPETIGREE

A HyperCard pedigree program for animals which shows name, registration number, parents, offspring, color, breeder and prizes.

System: MAC, II, PLUS, SE, XL
Minimum Memory: 1024K
Requires: HyperCard (ISPN 03900-300).
Medium: 3 1/2-inch disk
ISPN: 35175-420   **Price: $20.00**

---

805 SYSTEMS/ARTIFICIAL INTELLIGENCE/EXPERT SYSTEMS

APPLIED LOGIC SYSTEMS, INC.

ALS PROLOG COMPILER-MACINTOSH VERSION

Provides a Prolog compiler environment for fast, multi-windowed development of AI and Expert systems applications.

System: MAC, II, PLUS, SE, XL
Minimum Memory: 1024K
Requires: 800K disk drive.
Medium: 3 1/2-inch disk
ISPN: 04560-100   **Price: $349.00**

COSMIC (GA)

C LANGUAGE INTEGRATED PRODUCTION SYSTEM-CLIPS

A shell for developing expert systems. Allows for AI research, development and delivery on conventional computers.

System: MAC, II, PLUS, SE, XL
Minimum Memory: 512K
Medium: 3 1/2-inch disk
ISPN: 19888-165   **Price: $250.00**

PERIDOM, INC.

COGNATE (VER. 1.5)

Provides an environment and language for constructing knowledge based systems such as expert systems.

System: MAC, II, PLUS, SE, XL
Minimum Memory: 512K
Requires: 800K disk drive.
Medium: 3 1/2-inch disk
ISPN: 60537-100 **Price: $150.00**

PERIDOM, INC.

COGNATE DEVELOPER'S KIT

Supplies the inference engine object code so users can extend Cognate to fit their needs.

System: MAC, II, PLUS, SE, XL
Minimum Memory: 2048K
Requires: Macintosh Programmer's Workshop (ISPN 03749-500), MPW Pascal (ISPN 03749-510), MPW C (ISPN 03749-505), MacApp (ISPN 03749-511).
Medium: 3 1/2-inch disk
ISPN: 60537-110 **Price: $250.00**

EXPERTELLIGENCE, INC.

EXPERFACTS

Flexible Expert Systems building tool featuring forward and backward chaining with easy to use syntax.

System: MAC, II, PLUS, SE, XL
Minimum Memory: 512K
Requires: ExperLisp (Ver. 1.5) (ISPN 30473-300), external disk drive or hard disk.
Medium: 3 1/2-inch disk
ISPN: 30473-750 **Price: $495.00**

EXPERTELLIGENCE, INC.

EXPERPROLOG II (VER. 2.4)

A language using graphics, pull-down menus, multiple windows, and ad facilities to 'extend' the languages of Prolog II and Pascal.

System: MAC, II, PLUS, SE, XL
Minimum Memory: 512K
Requires: External disk drive or hard disk.
Medium: 3 1/2-inch disk
ISPN: 30473-850 **Price: $495.00**

LOGIC PROGRAMMING ASSOCIATES LTD.

FLEX EXPERT SYSTEM TOOLKIT (VER. 1.2)

Object-orientated frame-based expert system toolkit written in Prolog.

System: MAC, II, PLUS, SE, XL
Minimum Memory: 1024K
Requires: LPA MacProlog (ISPN 45287-520).
Medium: 3 1/2-inch disk
ISPN: 45287-250 **Price: $495.00**

COGNITION TECHNOLOGY

HYPERSMARTS

Allows non-programmers to convert HyperCard stacks into expert systems.

System: MAC, II, PLUS, SE, XL
Minimum Memory: 512K
Requires: HyperCard (ISPN 03900-300).
Medium: 3 1/2-inch disk
ISPN: 13396-150 **Price: $99.95**

HUMAN INTELLECT SYSTEMS (HIS)

INSTANT-EXPERT (VER. 2.0)

Expert system development tool provides advice, decisions, solves problems and offers selections after entry of experts' knowledge.

System: MAC, II, PLUS, SE, XL
Minimum Memory: 512K
Medium: 3 1/2-inch disk
ISPN: 36563-300 **Price: $69.95**

HUMAN INTELLECT SYSTEMS (HIS)

INSTANT-EXPERT PLUS (VER. 1.6)

Allows user to build an expert system by using natural language rules which can link with graphics and text.

System: MAC, II, PLUS, SE, XL
Minimum Memory: 512K
Medium: 3 1/2-inch disk
ISPN: 36563-310 **Price: $498.00**

LOGIC PROGRAMMING ASSOCIATES LTD.

LPA MACPROLOG (VER. 1.0)

Prolog compiler set in a multi-window environment with windows and dialogue primitives.

System: MAC, II, PLUS, SE, XL
Minimum Memory: 512K
Medium: 3 1/2-inch disk
ISPN: 45287-530 **Price: $195.00**

LOGIC PROGRAMMING ASSOCIATES LTD.

LPA MACPROLOG (VER. 2.5)

A compact, fast Prolog compiler that is fully integrated with the Macintosh interface.

System: MAC, II, PLUS, SE, XL
Minimum Memory: 1024K
Medium: 3 1/2-inch disk
ISPN: 45287-520 **Price: $495.00**

COGNITION TECHNOLOGY

MACSMARTS (VER. 3.02)

Powerful logical tool based on Prolog, the fifth generation language for expert systems with two-way links to HyperCard.

System: MAC, II, PLUS, SE, XL
Minimum Memory: 512K
Medium: 3 1/2-inch disk
ISPN: 13396-500 **Price: $195.00**

COGNITION TECHNOLOGY

MACSMARTS PROFESSIONAL

Features a spreadsheet-like interface that uses fill-in-the-blank forms. Performs computations and can interface with databases.

System: MAC, II, PLUS, SE, XL
Minimum Memory: 512K
Medium: 3 1/2-inch disk
ISPN: 13396-510 **Price: $495.00**

SOURCEVIEW SOFTWARE INT'L.

MICRO MIND KNOWLEDGE ENGINEERING TOOL (VER. 2.0)

Enables designers to create knowledge based expert systems.

System: MAC
Minimum Memory: 512K
Medium: 3 1/2-inch disk
ISPN: 70675-390 **Price: $99.00**

NEURON DATA, INC.

NEXPERT OBJECT

An expert system development tool which is rule and object based with access to external programs.

System: MAC, II, PLUS, SE, XL
Minimum Memory: 1024K
Medium: 3 1/2-inch disk
ISPN: 56569-550 **Price: $5000.00**

HUMAN INTELLECT SYSTEMS (HIS)

NEXUS (VER. 1.7)

Combines, in a single development environment, conventional programming and knowledge engineering.

System: MAC, II, PLUS, SE, XL
Minimum Memory: 512K
Medium: 3 1/2-inch disk
ISPN: 36563-533 **Price: $4800.00**

AVENUE SOFTWARE, INC.

OURSE (VER. 1.0)

A shell for the production of expert systems using a knowledge representation model and a reasoning model (SL-resolution).

System: MAC, II, PLUS, SE, XL
Minimum Memory: 1024K
Medium: 3 1/2-inch disk
ISPN: 06418-525 **Price: $4000.00**

AVENUE SOFTWARE, INC.

PROLOG II (VER. 2.4)

An artificial intelligence language for building expert systems in either English or French. Features natural language processing.

System: MAC, II, PLUS, SE, XL
Minimum Memory: 128K
Medium: 3 1/2-inch disk
ISPN: 06418-600 **Price: $495.00**

AVENUE SOFTWARE, INC.

PROLOG II+ COMPILER

Responds to professional developer needs for large applications higher performance, open architecture and standardization.

System: MAC, II, PLUS, SE, XL
Minimum Memory: 128K
Medium: 3 1/2-inch disk
ISPN: 06418-650 **Price: $1295.00**

SOFTSYNC, INC.
SUPER EXPERT

Features an example-based expert system
shell using a spreadsheet like interface.
System: MAC, II, PLUS, SE, XL
Minimum Memory: 512K
Requires: 800K disk drive.
Medium: 3 1/2-inch disk
ISPN: 72240-601   **Price: $199.95**

810 SYSTEMS/
ASSEMBLERS

CONSULAIR CORP.
68000 DEVELOPMENT SYSTEM

Provides software tools for developing
assembly language programs and includes
a multiple-window editor with an undo
feature.
System: MAC, II, PLUS, SE, XL
Minimum Memory: 512K
Medium: 3 1/2-inch disk
ISPN: 19231-223   **Price: $79.95**

METARESEARCH, INC.
**ASSEMBLER/EDITOR/LOADER
MACINTOSH (AELM-51)**

Enables efficient programming of Intel
8051/8031/8751 micro-controllers.
System: MAC, II, PLUS, SE, XL
Minimum Memory: 512K
Medium: 3 1/2-inch disk
ISPN: 49225-015   **Price: $99.00**

PECAN SOFTWARE SYSTEMS
**MACADVANTAGE-68000
ASSEMBLER**

32-bit macro assembler.
System: MAC, II, PLUS, SE, XL
Minimum Memory: 512K
Medium: 3 1/2-inch disk
ISPN: 60356-570   **Price: $99.95**

MAINSTAY
MACASM

Gives the programmer the power to
produce his own application, and develop
turn-key applications using integrated
resource compiler.
System: MAC, II, PLUS, SE, XL
Minimum Memory: 128K
Medium: 3 1/2-inch disk
ISPN: 46041-500   **Price: $125.00**

PALO ALTO SHIPPING CO.
MACH 2 FORTH (VER. 2.14)

Integrated, interactive, multi-tasking
environment for the development of stand-
alone Macintosh applications.
System: MAC, II, PLUS, SE, XL
Minimum Memory: 512K
Medium: 3 1/2-inch disk
ISPN: 59681-300   **Price: $99.95**

APDA
**MACINTOSH PROGRAMMER'S
WORKSHOP ASSEMBLER (VER.
3)**

A full-featured assembler that generates
code for current members of the MC68000
family, when used with MPW
Development Environment.
System: MAC, II, PLUS, SE, XL
Minimum Memory: 1024K
Requires: Hard disk, 800K disk drive, MPW
    Development Environment (Ver. 3.0).
Medium: 3 1/2-inch disk
ISPN: 03749-515   **Price: $100.00**

APDA
MPW IIGS ASSEMBLER

Provides the software tools needed to
develop assembly language Apple IIGS
applications, desk accessories and APW
utilities.
System: MAC, II, PLUS, SE, XL
Minimum Memory: 1024K
Requires: Macintosh Programmers Workshop-
    MPW (ISPN 03749-500) and MPW IIGS Tools
    (ISPN 03749-301), hard disk and an 800K disk
    drive.
Medium: 3 1/2-inch disk
ISPN: 03749-295   **Price: $150.00**

MICRO DIALECTS, INC.
UASM-1802

Provides an eight bit macro cross
assembler that assembles code for the
1802, 1804, 1805, 1805A and 1806
microprocessors.
System: MAC, II, PLUS, SE, XL
Minimum Memory: 512K
Medium: 3 1/2-inch disk
ISPN: 50226-735   **Price: $129.95**

MICRO DIALECTS, INC.
UASM-400

Provides an eight bit macro cross
assembler that assembles code for the
COP400 family microprocessors.
System: MAC, II, PLUS, SE, XL
Minimum Memory: 512K
Medium: 3 1/2-inch disk
ISPN: 50226-740   **Price: $129.95**

MICRO DIALECTS, INC.
UASM-6502

Provides an eight bit macro cross
assembler that assembles code for the
6502, 65C02, and the 65C00
microprocessors.
System: MAC, II, PLUS, SE, XL
Minimum Memory: 512K
Medium: 3 1/2-inch disk
ISPN: 50226-745   **Price: $129.95**

MICRO DIALECTS, INC.
UASM-6801

Provides an eight bit macro cross
assembler that assembles code for the
6801, 6301, 6803, 6800, 6802, and 6808
microprocessors.
System: MAC, II, PLUS, SE, XL
Minimum Memory: 512K
Medium: 3 1/2-inch disk
ISPN: 50226-700   **Price: $129.95**

MICRO DIALECTS, INC.
UASM-6804

Provides an eight bit macro cross
assembler that assembles code for the
6804 and 68HC04 microprocessors.
System: MAC, II, PLUS, SE, XL
Minimum Memory: 512K
Medium: 3 1/2-inch disk
ISPN: 50226-710   **Price: $129.95**

MICRO DIALECTS, INC.
UASM-6805

Provides an eight bit macro cross
assembler that assembles code for the
6805, 6305, 146805, and 68HC05
microprocessors.
System: MAC, II, PLUS, SE, XL
Minimum Memory: 512K
Medium: 3 1/2-inch disk
ISPN: 50226-715   **Price: $129.95**

MICRO DIALECTS, INC.
UASM-6809

Provides an eight bit macro cross
assembler that assembles code for the
6809 and 6309 microprocessors.
System: MAC, II, PLUS, SE, XL
Minimum Memory: 512K
Medium: 3 1/2-inch disk
ISPN: 50226-720   **Price: $129.95**

MICRO DIALECTS, INC.
UASM-8048

Provides an eight bit macro cross
assembler that assembles code for the
8048, 80C48, 8049, 8050, 8044, 8021, and
8022 microprocessors.
System: MAC, II, PLUS, SE, XL
Minimum Memory: 512K
Medium: 3 1/2-inch disk
ISPN: 50226-725   **Price: $129.95**

MICRO DIALECTS, INC.
UASM-8051

Provides an eight bit macro cross
assembler that assembles code for the
8051, 80C51 and 8052 microprocessors.
System: MAC, II, PLUS, SE, XL
Minimum Memory: 512K
Medium: 3 1/2-inch disk
ISPN: 50226-730   **Price: $129.95**

MICRO DIALECTS, INC.
UASM-8085
Provides an eight bit macro cross assembler that assembles code for the 8085 and 8080 microprocessors.
System: MAC, II, PLUS, SE, XL
Minimum Memory: 512K
Medium: 3 1/2-inch disk
ISPN: 50226-702   **Price: $129.95**

MICRO DIALECTS, INC.
UASM-8096
Provides an eight bit macro cross assembler that assembles code for the 809 and 80C196 microprocessors.
System: MAC, II, PLUS, SE, XL
Minimum Memory: 512K
Medium: 3 1/2-inch disk
ISPN: 50226-701   **Price: $129.95**

MICRO DIALECTS, INC.
UASM-HC11
Provides an eight bit macro cross assembler that assembles code for the 68HC11, 6801, 6803, 6800, 6802, and 6808 microprocessors.
System: MAC, II, PLUS, SE, XL
Minimum Memory: 512K
Medium: 3 1/2-inch disk
ISPN: 50226-705   **Price: $129.95**

MICRO DIALECTS, INC.
UASM-Z8
Provides an eight bit macro cross assembler that assembles code for the Z8 family of microprocessors.
System: MAC, II, PLUS, SE, XL
Minimum Memory: 512K
Medium: 3 1/2-inch disk
ISPN: 50226-750   **Price: $129.95**

MICRO DIALECTS, INC.
UASM-Z80
Provides an eight bit macro cross assembler that assembles code for the Z80, and the Z180/HD64180 microprocessors.
System: MAC, II, PLUS, SE, XL
Minimum Memory: 512K
Medium: 3 1/2-inch disk
ISPN: 50226-755   **Price: $129.95**

815 SYSTEMS/ COMMUNICATIONS/ SYSTEM EMULATION

1ST DESK SYSTEMS, INC.
1STPORT (VER. 4.0)
Provides communication, file conversion, reformatting and matching and text editor through a multi-purpose transport system.
System: MAC, II, PLUS, SE, XL
Minimum Memory: 512K
Requires: Appropriate cable for computer.
Medium: 3 1/2-inch disk
ISPN: 81083-600   **Price: $295.00**

LAMIR SOFTWARE CORP.
ACKNOWLEDGE (VER. 1.0)
A communications toolkit for creating stand-alone Macintosh applications.
System: MAC, II, PLUS, SE, XL
Minimum Memory: 512K
Requires: 800K disk drive.
Medium: 3 1/2-inch disk
ISPN: 43453-100   **Price: $495.00**

SUPERMAC SOFTWARE
ACKNOWLEDGE (VER. 1.0)
A communications toolkit that allows creation of customized communication programs for users.
System: MAC, II, PLUS, SE, XL
Minimum Memory: 512K
Requires: 800K disk drive.
Medium: 3 1/2-inch disk
ISPN: 77125-100
Price: Please contact the software publisher.

LAMIR SOFTWARE CORP.
ACKNOWLEDGE GATEWAY
A communications tool palette with icon buttons, scripting, phone book and built-in 'gateway' to major on-line services.
System: MAC, II, PLUS, SE, XL
Minimum Memory: 1024K
Medium: 3 1/2-inch disk
ISPN: 43453-200   **Price: $195.00**

ALISA SYSTEMS, INC.
ALISATALK
Provides file sharing, transferring, printing and terminal emulation services for networked systems on an AppleTalk network.
System: MAC, II, PLUS, SE, XL
Minimum Memory: 512K
Requires: Kinetics Fast Path.
Medium: 3 1/2-inch disk
ISPN: 02265-100
Price: Please contact the software publisher.

RACAL VADIC
APPLE MACINTOSH COMMUNIKIT
Includes MacGeorge, a communications program with standard terminal functions, electronic mailbox, and database management capability.
System: MAC, II, PLUS, SE, XL
Minimum Memory:
Medium: 3 1/2-inch disk
ISPN: 64725-100   **Price: $79.00**

APPLE COMPUTER, INC.
APPLESHARE FILESERVER (VER. 2.01)
Turns a dedicated Macintosh Plus, SE, or II with one or more hard disks into a dedicated file server for the AppleTalk network.
System: MAC, II, PLUS, SE, XL
Minimum Memory: 512K
Requires: 1-32 users. Hard disk, 1MB of RAM required on the server.
Medium: 3 1/2-inch disk
ISPN: 03900-100   **Price: $799.00**

SOLUTIONS INT'L.
BACKFAX (VER. 1.02)
Provides background communications for the Apple Fax modem.
System: MAC, II, PLUS, SE, XL
Minimum Memory: 1024K
Requires: 800K disk drive. Apple Fax modem.
Medium: 3 1/2-inch disk
ISPN: 74437-040   **Price: $245.00**

HEIZER SOFTWARE
BBS TRACKER
A HyperCard-based database of over 3,500 Electronic Bulletin Board Systems.
System: MAC, II, PLUS, SE, XL
Minimum Memory: 1024K
Requires: HyperCard (ISPN 3900-300).
Medium: 3 1/2-inch disk
ISPN: 35175-053   **Price: $30.00**

PERSONAL BIBLIOGRAPHIC SOFTWARE, INC.
BIBLIO-LINK
Contains companion programs to the Pro-Cite programs which transfer records downloaded from online database systems.
System: MAC, II, PLUS, SE, XL
Minimum Memory: 1024K
Requires: Pro-Cite for the Macintosh (ISPN 60587-240).
Medium: 3 1/2-inch disk
ISPN: 60587-050   **Price: $195.00**

COMMUNICATIONS RESEARCH GROUP, INC.
BLAST II
Can automatically connect different types of computers with different operating systems.
System: MAC, II, PLUS, SE, XL
Minimum Memory: 128K
Medium: 3 1/2-inch disk
ISPN: 23100-125   **Price: $150.00**

TYMLABS CORP.
BUSINESS SESSION (VER. 3.0)
Hewlett Packard 2392 Block Mode terminal emulator. Includes intelligent, high-speed file transfer.
System: MAC, II, PLUS, SE, XL
Minimum Memory: 512K
Medium: 3 1/2-inch disk
ISPN: 83125-200   **Price: $199.00**

TRUE BASIC, INC.
COMMUNICATIONS LIBRARY (VER. 1.1)
Allows True BASIC programs to send and receive data via RS232/ modem ports.
System: MAC, II, PLUS, SE, XL
Minimum Memory: 512K
Medium: 3 1/2-inch disk
ISPN: 82789-210   **Price: $69.95**

TECHNOLOGY CONCEPTS
COMMUNITY-MAC (VER. 1.3)
Enables the Macintosh to communicate with DEC computers and other CommUnity systems on a DECnet Phase IV through ethernet networks.
System: MAC, II, PLUS, SE, XL
Minimum Memory: 1024K
Requires: 800K disk drive. Includes documentation, media, license.
Medium: 3 1/2-inch disk
ISPN: 80569-100   **Price: $495.00**

TECHNOLOGY CONCEPTS
COMMUNITY-MAC (VER. 1.3)
Enables the Macintosh to communicate with DEC computers and other CommUnity systems on a DECnet Phase IV through ethernet networks.
System: MAC, II, PLUS, SE, XL
Minimum Memory: 1024K
Requires: 800K disk drive. Includes license.
Medium: 3 1/2-inch disk
ISPN: 80569-100   **Price: $350.00**

COMPUSERVE
COMPUSERVE NAVIGATOR
Automates access to CompuServe by giving users a set of selection tiles that represent the topics, forums or menus available.
System: MAC, II, PLUS, SE, XL
Minimum Memory: 512K
Requires: One double-sided 800K disk drive and a hard disk or two 800K double sided disk drives, System 4.1 or higher.
Medium: 3 1/2-inch disk
ISPN: 15388-500   **Price: $79.95**

ALIVE SYSTEMS, INC.
COMPUTER CO-PILOT
Assists the user at communication tasks while learning about the user and user's relation to the world.
System: SE
Minimum Memory: 4096K
Requires: 80MB hard disk and telephone voice interface.
Medium: 3 1/2-inch disk
ISPN: 02273-175   **Price: $900.00**

AVENUE SOFTWARE, INC.
CONTACT (VER. 1.20)
Provides DEC VT52, VT100, VT220, IBM 3270 (with protocol converter), Burroughs TD730, TD830, MT and ET families, and TTY emulation.
System: MAC, II, PLUS, SE, XL
Minimum Memory: 512K
Medium: 3 1/2-inch disk
ISPN: 06418-120   **Price: $395.00**

AVENUE SOFTWARE, INC.
CONTACT FILE XPRESS
Add-on module to Contact that makes format conversions between host and micro applications, including file transfers.
System: MAC, II, PLUS, SE, XL
Minimum Memory: 512K
Requires: Contact (ISPN 06418-120).
Medium: 3 1/2-inch disk
ISPN: 06418-135   **Price: $250.00**

MCTEL, INC.
ELECTRONIC ENVELOPE (VER. 1.8)
Prepares binary files for data transmission over public and private E-Mail systems.
System: MAC, II, PLUS, SE, XL
Minimum Memory: 64K
Medium: 3 1/2-inch disk
ISPN: 60925-050   **Price: $49.95**

NILES AND ASSOCIATES
ENDLINK (VER. 1.0)
Allows you to import references downloaded from online databases into EndNote (Ver. 1.1).
System: MAC, II, PLUS, SE, XL
Minimum Memory: 512K
Requires: Modem, communication program, EndNote (Ver. 1.1) (ISPN 56952-200).
Medium: 3 1/2-inch disk
ISPN: 56952-202   **Price: $99.00**

COMPUTER LEARNING SYSTEMS, INC.
EXCHANGE (VER. 4)
Displays Xenix/Unix PicoSpan conferences an icons, allows checking, dragging and editing of conferences.
System: MAC, II, PLUS, SE, XL
Minimum Memory: 512K
Requires: Picospan on a Unix/Xenix system.
Medium: 3 1/2-inch disk
ISPN: 16917-200   **Price: $39.95**

EXPERTELLIGENCE, INC.
EXPERLINK
Offers text file transfer between a Symbolics Lisp machine and an Apple Macintosh computer configured with ExperLisp.
System: MAC, II, PLUS, SE, XL
Minimum Memory: 512K
Requires: Experlisp (ISPN 30473-300).
Medium: 3 1/2-inch disk
ISPN: 30473-250   **Price: $600.00**

OLDUVAI CORP.
FONTSHARE VER-1.1
Allows all Macintoshes on a network to share downloadable PostScript fonts that reside on a server.
System: MAC, II, PLUS, SE, XL
Minimum Memory: 512K
Requires: Network file server.
Medium: 3 1/2-inch disk
ISPN: 57812-250   **Price: $295.00**

MENLO BUSINESS SYSTEMS, INC.
FOUNDATION GRAPHICS TOOLBOX (VER. 1.0)
Directly integrates data and/or text applications into Tandem Pathway applications using Macintosh workstations.
System: MAC, II, PLUS, SE, XL
Minimum Memory:
Medium: 3 1/2-inch disk
ISPN: 48969-250
Price: Please contact the software publisher.

KAZ BUSINESS SYSTEMS
FRONTEND VER-1.1
Communications program which makes the Macintosh interface able to host computer applications.
System: MAC, II, PLUS, SE, XL
Minimum Memory:
Medium: 3 1/2-inch disk
ISPN: 42446-195   **Price: $120.00**

TYMLABS CORP.
GRAPHIC SESSION (VER. 3.0)
Adds HP 2393 monochrome graphics capability to Tymlabs' Business Session (formerly MAC 2624) product.
System: MAC, II, PLUS, SE, XL
Minimum Memory: 512K
Medium: 3 1/2-inch disk
ISPN: 83125-400   **Price: $299.00**

INFRASTRUCTURE SOFTWARE
GRAPHTERM
A 'glass tty' terminal emulator which acquires and displays Tektronix 4010/4014 format graphics vectors.
System: MAC
Minimum Memory: 128K
Medium: 3 1/2-inch disk
ISPN: 38257-375   **Price: $100.00**

METARESEARCH, INC.
GRIFFINTERMINAL
Turns a Macintosh into a text and graphics terminal.
System: MAC, II, PLUS, SE, XL
Minimum Memory: 512K
Medium: 3 1/2-inch disk
ISPN: 49225-070   **Price: $89.00**

METARESEARCH, INC.
GRIFFINTERMINAL 100 EXMODEM
Emulates either a Tektronix 4012 Graphics Terminal or a VT100 terminal when linked to a mainframe or host computer.
System: MAC, II, PLUS, SE, XL
Minimum Memory: 512K
Medium: 3 1/2-inch disk
ISPN: 49225-150   **Price: $99.00**

COMPUTER APPLICATIONS, INC. (NC)
II IN A MAC (VER. 2.53)
Run Apple II software on the Macintosh without modification. User has the capability to run Apple DOS 3.3 on the Macintosh.
System: MAC, II, PLUS, SE, XL
Minimum Memory: 512K
Medium: 3 1/2-inch disk
ISPN: 16012-700   **Price: $149.95**

MARVELIN CORP.
IMPORT/EXPORT UTILITY FOR BUSINESS FILEVISION

Allows Business Filevision users to exchange data with existing Macintosh and MS-DOS programs.

System: MAC, II, PLUS, SE, XL
Minimum Memory: 512K
Requires: Business Filevision (ISPN 47483-045).
Medium: 3 1/2-inch disk
ISPN: 47483-055				**Price: $50.00**

TOPS
INBOX (VER. 2.0)

Allows users on AppleTalk networks, while in an application, to transfer files, create, send and receive phone and E-mail messages.

System: MAC, II, PLUS, SE, XL
Minimum Memory: 512K
Requires: One user. AppleTalk network. Starter Kit is required.
Medium: 3 1/2-inch disk
ISPN: 11962-300				**Price: $69.00**

TOPS
INBOX (VER. 2.0)

Allows users on AppleTalk networks, while in an application, to transfer files, create, send and receive phone and E-mail messages.

System: MAC, II, PLUS, SE, XL
Minimum Memory: 512K
Requires: Starter kit. 1-3 users. AppleTalk Network.
Medium: 3 1/2-inch disk
ISPN: 11962-300				**Price: $249.00**

SYMANTEC
INBOX (VER. 2.2)

Allows users on AppleTalk networks, while in an application, to transfer files, create, send and receive phone messages.

System: MAC, II, PLUS, SE, XL
Minimum Memory: 512K
Requires: One user. AppleTalk network.
Medium: 3 1/2-inch disk
ISPN: 77413-310				**Price: $125.00**

SYMANTEC
INBOX (VER. 2.2)

Allows users on AppleTalk networks, while in an application, to transfer files, create, send and receive phone messages.

System: MAC, II, PLUS, SE, XL
Minimum Memory: 512K
Requires: 1-3 users. AppleTalk Network.
Medium: 3 1/2-inch disk
ISPN: 77413-310				**Price: $350.00**

WESTERN UNION CORP.
INSTANT MAIL MANAGER FOR THE MACINTOSH

Contains an integrated word processing, address list, and communications package for Western Union Easylink users.

System: MAC, II, PLUS, SE, XL
Minimum Memory: 512K
Requires: 800K disk drive.
Medium: 3 1/2-inch disk
ISPN: 86146-300				**Price: $195.00**

TRAVELING SOFTWARE, INC.
LAPLINK MAC (VER. 2.0)

Transfers files between a Macintosh and an IBM PC or compatible.

System: MAC, II, PLUS, SE, XL
Minimum Memory: 512K
Medium: 3 1/2-inch disk
ISPN: 82540-460				**Price: $139.95**

KINKOS ACADEMIC COURSEWARE EXCHANGE
LASERTERMINAL

College level: Facilitates the use of the LaserWriter with a host or mainframe computer via the Macintosh.

System: MAC, II, PLUS, SE, XL
Minimum Memory: 128K
Requires: Finder (Ver. 4.1 or later), LaserWriter printer.
Medium: 3 1/2-inch disk
ISPN: 43025-340				**Price: $20.00**

INFOSPHERE, INC.
LIAISON (VER. 1.0.1)

Enables remote users to dial into remote AppleTalk or Ethernet networks over existing telecommunications equipment.

System: MAC, II, PLUS, SE
Minimum Memory: 512K
Requires: 800K disk drive, Hayes compatible modem.
Medium: 3 1/2-inch disk
ISPN: 38212-040				**Price: $295.00**

UNGERMANN-BASS
LINKWARE INFORMATION SERVER

Offers a solution to the problem of information transfer among dissimilar computers.

System: MAC, II, PLUS, SE, XL
Minimum Memory: 512K
Medium: 3 1/2-inch disk
ISPN: 83481-100				**Price: $500.00**

CAMBRIDGE COMPUTER CORP.
MAC 73/78 (VER. 1.08)

Emulates the Honeywell VIP 7200, VIP 7300 and VIP 7800 series of asynchronous terminals.

System: MAC, II, PLUS, SE, XL
Minimum Memory: 1024K
Requires: Asynchronous communications adapter.
Medium: 3 1/2-inch disk
ISPN: 10775-500				**Price: $295.00**

MENLO BUSINESS SYSTEMS, INC.
MAC MENLO LEAR SIEGLER ADM2

Supports block mode applications for host computer environments that use the Lear Siegler ADM2 terminal or its equivalent.

System: MAC, II, PLUS, SE, XL
Minimum Memory:
Medium: 3 1/2-inch disk
ISPN: 48969-500				**Price: $395.00**

MENLO BUSINESS SYSTEMS, INC.
MAC MENLO T65XX

Supports block mode applications for the Tandem host computer environment by emulating the T65xx line of terminals.

System: MAC, II, PLUS, SE, XL
Minimum Memory: 512K
Medium: 3 1/2-inch disk
ISPN: 48969-530				**Price: $395.00**

TRI DATA
MAC MOVER (VER. 5.0)

Host file transfer system which allows the Macintosh to send or receive text, Macdocument or Binary (IBM/PC) files.

System: MAC, II, PLUS, SE, XL
Minimum Memory: 512K
Requires: Netway Presentation Services (Ver. 5.0).
Medium: 3 1/2-inch disk
ISPN: 82556-500				**Price: $995.00**

TRI DATA
MAC WINDOWS 3270

Turns a single Macintosh personal computer into a multiscreen IBM 3270 terminal with concurrent access to multiple host computers.

System: MAC, PLUS
Minimum Memory: 512K
Requires: Netway 1000A communications server.
Medium: 3 1/2-inch disk
ISPN: 82556-400				**Price: $125.00**

ICC INT'L. COMPUTER CONSULTANTS
MAC-3000 (VER. 3.2)

Provides full HP-3000 block mode terminal emulation. Offers all the features of the HP-2392A terminal, DEC VT-100, TTY, IBM 3278.

System: MAC, II, PLUS, SE, XL
Minimum Memory: 512K
Medium: 3 1/2-inch disk
ISPN: 36841-510				**Price: $150.00**

WHITE PINE SOFTWARE, INC.
MAC220

Fully emulates DEC's VT220 graphics terminals as well as the VT220 text terminals.

System: MAC, II, PLUS, SE, XL
Minimum Memory:
Medium: 3 1/2-inch disk
ISPN: 86315-200				**Price: $129.00**

WHITE PINE SOFTWARE, INC.
MAC240 (VER. 2.0)

A DEC VT240 emulator that provides DEC compatible text and graphics emulation.

System: MAC, II, PLUS, SE, XL
Minimum Memory: 128K
Medium: 3 1/2-inch disk
ISPN: 86315-100				**Price: $199.00**

WHITE PINE SOFTWARE, INC.
MAC241

Emulates the Dec VT241 providing a range of color capabilities.

System: MAC, II, PLUS, SE, XL
Minimum Memory:
Medium: 3 1/2-inch disk
ISPN: 86315-300 **Price: $299.00**

COMMUNICATIONS RESEARCH GROUP, INC.
MACBLAST

Provides VT100/220, DG D200, TTY emulation, background file transfer, auto-dialing and login, and connectivity with 30 systems.

System: MAC, II, PLUS, SE, XL
Minimum Memory: 1024K
Medium: 3 1/2-inch disk
ISPN: 23100-500 **Price: $195.00**

VANO ASSOCIATES, INC.
MACCHUCK (VER. 1.5)

Allows a PC to be operated from a window on a Macintosh via a standard serial cable connecting them.

System: MAC, II, PLUS, SE, XL
Minimum Memory: 512K
Requires: 800K disk drive, IBM PC AT/XT with mono or CGA. Serial port on PC, MS-DOS 3.0 + . PC, MS-DOS 3.0 + .
Medium: 3 1/2-inch disk
ISPN: 84878-100 **Price: $99.95**

TOUCHSTONE SOFTWARE CORP.
MACLINE (VER. 2.01)

Connects a Macintosh workstation to Unix/Xenix systems as a VT100/52, ANSI or TTY terminal.

System: MAC, II, PLUS, SE, XL
Minimum Memory: 128K
Requires: RS232-C interface cable or modem.
Medium: 3 1/2-inch disk
ISPN: 82400-050 **Price: $145.00**

DATAVIZ, INC.
MACLINK PLUS (VER. 3.0)

Provides file transfer and conversion with IBM PC's. Includes software for both machines and a direct connect cable.

System: MAC, II, PLUS, SE, XL
Minimum Memory: 512K
Medium: 3 1/2-inch disk
ISPN: 23962-600 **Price: $195.00**

DATAVIZ, INC.
MACLINK PLUS/NBI (VER. 3.0)

Provides two-way exchange and conversion of formatted word processing documents between the Macintosh and NBI word processors.

System: MAC, II, PLUS, SE, XL
Minimum Memory: 1024K
Medium: 3 1/2-inch disk
ISPN: 23962-650 **Price: $495.00**

DATAVIZ, INC.
MACLINK PLUS/TRANSLATORS (VER. 2.12)

A library of over 46 different translation combinations that extend the translation capabilities of the Apple File Exchange utility.

System: MAC, II, PLUS, SE, XL
Minimum Memory: 512K
Requires: Apple File Exchange.
Medium: 3 1/2-inch disk
ISPN: 23962-610 **Price: $159.00**

DATAVIZ, INC.
MACLINK PLUS/WANG VS (VER. 3.0)

Provides Wang VS workstation emulation, file transfer, and document conversion capabilities.

System: MAC, II, PLUS, SE, XL
Minimum Memory: 1024K
Requires: Wang ADC or EADC port via RS-232 cable, modem or access paths established via AppleTalk network for the Macintosh.
Medium: 3 1/2-inch disk
ISPN: 23962-630 **Price: $395.00**

AVATAR TECHNOLOGIES, INC. (MA)
MACMAINFRAME DX

Provides 3278 emulation for Apple Macintosh with file transfer.

System: MAC, II, PLUS, SE, XL
Minimum Memory: 512K
Medium: 3 1/2-inch disk
ISPN: 06409-600 **Price: $1195.00**

AVATAR TECHNOLOGIES, INC. (MA)
MACMAINFRAME II

Internal card and software package that connects the Apple Macintosh II to IBM mainframes running 3270 protocol.

System: II
Minimum Memory: 1024K
Requires: IND$FILE or Avatar's Host file Transfer on host.
Medium: 3 1/2-inch disk
ISPN: 06409-800 **Price: $995.00**

AVATAR TECHNOLOGIES, INC. (MA)
MACMAINFRAME SE

Hardware and software communications program that provides IBM 3278 /7 emulation with file transfer.

System: SE
Minimum Memory: 1024K
Requires: Host file transfer software residing on the IBM mainframe, unit via MACMAINFRAME hardware unit.
Medium: 3 1/2-inch disk
ISPN: 06409-700 **Price: $795.00**

ELECTROHOME LTD.
MACNAPLPS (VER. 1.4)

Allows users to connect to a remote database that supports the NAPLPS coding syntax.

System: MAC, II, PLUS, SE, XL
Minimum Memory: 512K
Requires: Hayes 1200 baud modem or compatible.
Medium: 3 1/2-inch disk
ISPN: 28425-100 **Price: $99.00**

CONNECT, INC.
MACNET (VER. 1.0)

Provides organizations with electronic mail and information forums via an on-line information service that is accessed via MACNET.

System: MAC, II, PLUS, SE, XL
Minimum Memory: 512K
Requires: 800K disk drive, 1200, 2400, or 9600 bps modem, external disk drive or hard disk.
Medium: 3 1/2-inch disk
ISPN: 90947-500 **Price: $49.95**

CONNECT, INC.
MACNET (VER. 1.0)

Provides organizations with electronic mail and information forums via an on-line information service that is accessed via MACNET.

System: MAC, II, PLUS, SE, XL
Minimum Memory: 512K
Requires: 20 users. 800K disk drive, 1200, 2400, or 9600 bps modem, external disk drive or hard disk.
Medium: 3 1/2-inch disk
ISPN: 90947-500 **Price: $999.00**

INFOSPHERE, INC.
MACSERVE (VER. 2.4)

Hard disk support software for single users or for sharing files over an Apple Talk network.

System: MAC, II, PLUS, SE, XL
Minimum Memory: 512K
Medium: 3 1/2-inch disk
ISPN: 38212-050 **Price: $250.00**

BASELINE
MACTELL (VER. 3.4)

Communications software with ASCII and Minitel modes. Multiple file transfer protocols, script learning mode, optional bulletin board.

System: MAC, II, PLUS, SE, XL
Minimum Memory: 512K
Requires: 800K disk drive, modem.
Medium: 3 1/2-inch disk
ISPN: 06943-500 **Price: $97.00**

APPLE COMPUTER, INC.
MACTERMINAL (VER. 2.3)

Transfer data between Macintosh and other computers or tap into online services. Available only through authorized Apple dealers.

System: MAC, II, PLUS, SE, XL
Minimum Memory: 128K
Medium: 3 1/2-inch disk
ISPN: 03900-415 **Price: $125.00**

SUN REMARKETING
MACWORKS PLUS

Emulates the Macintosh Plus and supports MultiFinder and other Apple system software.

System: XL
Minimum Memory:
Medium: 3 1/2-inch disk
ISPN: 77034-500 **Price: $200.00**

VIDEX, INC.
MAIL CENTER (VER. 1.8)
Allows users connected via the AppleTalk Personal Network to communicate by means of computerized mail.

System: MAC, II, PLUS, SE, XL
Minimum Memory: 512K
Requires: 2 users. AppleTalk network.
Medium: 3 1/2-inch disk
ISPN: 85150-090   **Price: $299.00**

VIDEX, INC.
MAIL CENTER (VER. 1.8)
Allows users connected via the AppleTalk Personal Network to communicate by means of computerized mail.

System: MAC, II, PLUS, SE, XL
Minimum Memory: 512K
Requires: 6 users. AppleTalk network.
Medium: 3 1/2-inch disk
ISPN: 85150-090   **Price: $499.00**

MENLO BUSINESS SYSTEMS, INC.
MAX
Tandem host-based file exchange process that facilitates file transfer between a Macintosh workstation and a Tandem mainframe.

System: MAC, II, PLUS, SE, XL
Minimum Memory: 128K
Requires: Tandem compatible terminal device.
Medium: 3 1/2-inch disk
ISPN: 48969-550
Price: Please contact the software publisher.

MICRO PLANNING INT'L.
MICRO PLANNER PROJECT EXCHANGE
Allows user to transfer data to and from Micro Planner Plus and applications such as wordprocessors and spreadsheets.

System: MAC, II, PLUS, SE, XL
Minimum Memory: 512K
Requires: Two disk drives, or a disk drive and a hard disk.
Medium: 3 1/2-inch disk
ISPN: 50912-575   **Price: $100.00**

SOFTWARE VENTURES CORP.
MICROPHONE II (VER. 3.0)
Powerful telecommunications software for the Macintosh, which automates the entire telecommunication process using macros.

System: MAC, II, PLUS, SE, XL
Minimum Memory: 128K
Medium: 3 1/2-inch disk
ISPN: 73963-550   **Price: $295.00**

MICROSOFT CORP.
MICROSOFT MAIL (VER. 1.35)
Allows users to send and receive files and messages electronically on an AppleTalk network.

System: MAC, II, PLUS, SE, XL
Minimum Memory: 512K
Requires: 1-4 users. AppleTalk compatible network and hard disk.
Medium: 3 1/2-inch disk
ISPN: 53150-810   **Price: $299.95**

MICROSOFT CORP.
MICROSOFT MAIL (VER. 1.35)
Allows users to send and receive files and messages electronically on an AppleTalk network.

System: MAC, II, PLUS, SE, XL
Minimum Memory: 512K
Requires: 5-10 users. AppleTalk compatible network and hard disk.
Medium: 3 1/2-inch disk
ISPN: 53150-810   **Price: $499.00**

TRI DATA
NETWAY 1000 EMULATOR (VER. 5.0)
Emulates the IBM 3278 terminal.

System: II, PLUS, SE
Minimum Memory: 512K
Requires: Netway 1000 hardware.
Medium: 3 1/2-inch disk
ISPN: 82556-600   **Price: $3195.00**

MEDIAGENIC/TENPOINT0
OPEN IT!
A desk accessory that allows users to share files between incompatible programs.

System: MAC, II, PLUS, SE, XL
Minimum Memory: 512K
Medium: 3 1/2-inch disk
ISPN: 48702-400   **Price: $89.95**

PACER SOFTWARE, INC.
PACERLINK
Integrates Macintosh and IBM PC's with VAX and UNIX systems over Ethernet, Apple LocalTalk or Asynchronous with VT220/240.

System: MAC, II, PLUS, SE, XL
Minimum Memory: 512K
Medium: 3 1/2-inch disk
ISPN: 59306-100   **Price: $2000.00**

DYNAMIC MICROPROCESSOR ASSOCIATES
PC MACTERM
Enables the user to run a PC from a Macintosh, either through a modem, direct cable connection, or on an AppleTalk network.

System: MAC, II, PLUS, SE, XL
Minimum Memory: 128K
Requires: IBM compatible running pcAnywhere (ISPN 27200-150).
Medium: 3 1/2-inch disk
ISPN: 27200-175   **Price: $99.00**

TANGENT TECHNOLOGIES
PC MACTXT (VER. 1.0)
Converts IBM PC files to a format useable by Apple Macintosh available as a desk accessory on Macintosh and as PC programs.

System: MAC, II, PLUS, SE, XL
Minimum Memory: 128K
Medium: 3 1/2-inch disk
ISPN: 79646-600   **Price: $50.00**

DILITHIUM PRESS SOFTWARE
PC TO MAC AND BACK WITH CABLE
Transfers Basic programs, ASCII text and binary files immediately and directly between the IBM PC and Macintosh.

System: MAC, II, PLUS, SE, XL
Minimum Memory: 512K
Requires: RS-232 serial port on IBM PC, modem recommended for transfer of data over phone lines.
Medium: 3 1/2-inch disk
ISPN: 25900-480   **Price: $149.95**

FARALLON COMPUTING
PHONENET STAR CONTROLLER WITH STARCOMMAND
Allows network manager to turn any or all of the 12 ports of the starcontroller on or off and to communicate from remote locations.

System: MAC, II, PLUS, SE, XL
Minimum Memory: 512K
Requires: PhoneNet Star Controller with StarController wiring kit.
Medium: 3 1/2-inch disk
ISPN: 91809-600   **Price: $1695.00**

VIDEX, INC.
PHRASEMAKER
A Macintosh desk accessory that allows bar codes data to be integrated directly into a third party databases, and spreadsheets.

System: MAC, II, PLUS, SE, XL
Minimum Memory: 512K
Requires: Videx TimeWand Bar Code reader, TimeWand Recharger and cable.
Medium: 3 1/2-inch disk
ISPN: 85150-092   **Price: $299.00**

PROMETHEUS PRODUCTS, INC.
PROCOM-M (VER. 1.85)
Telecommunications with Xmodem, MacBinary, text editor, log-on macros and phone directory with log.

System: MAC, II, PLUS, SE, XL
Minimum Memory: 128K
Medium: 3 1/2-inch disk
ISPN: 63273-405   **Price: $49.00**

SMITH MICRO SOFTWARE
QUICK LINK
Generalizer terminal emulator provides Xmodem and text file transfers.

System: II, PLUS, SE
Minimum Memory: 512K
Requires: Hayes or Apple compatible modem (800, 1200 or 2400 baud).
Medium: 3 1/2-inch disk
ISPN: 71606-490   **Price: $45.00**

COMPUTER VECTORS, INC.
RCOM-2/PC (VER. 2.32)
Transfers files from micro to mainframe and from PC to PC.

System: II, PLUS, SE
Minimum Memory: 512K
Requires: Modem.
Medium: 3 1/2-inch disk
ISPN: 18106-100   **Price: $159.95**

FREESOFT CO.
RED RYDER (VER. 10.3)
Complete communications package supporting speeds up to 57,600 bps.
System: II, PLUS, SE
Minimum Memory: 512K
Requires: Modem.
Medium: 3 1/2-inch disk
ISPN: 31420-200   **Price: $80.00**

FREESOFT CO.
RED RYDER HOST (VER. 2.0)
Contains a complete Bulletin board system construction program that gives you a small version of your own CompuServe.
System: MAC, II, PLUS, SE, XL
Minimum Memory: 512K
Requires: Hard disk and modem.
Medium: 3 1/2-inch disk
ISPN: 31420-220   **Price: $135.00**

WALKER, RICHER & QUINN, INC.
REFLECTION 1 FOR THE MACINTOSH (VER. 3.2)
Contains a terminal emulation/data communications software package that emulates a HP 2392 A terminal.
System: MAC, II, PLUS, SE, XL
Minimum Memory: 512K
Requires: Imagewriter, LaserWriter or Macintosh supported printer.
Medium: 3 1/2-inch disk
ISPN: 96905-604   **Price: $249.00**

WALKER, RICHER & QUINN, INC.
REFLECTION 3 FOR THE MACINTOSH (VER. 3.2)
Contains a terminal emulation/data communications package that allows the Macintosh to act like an HP 2393A graphics terminal.
System: MAC, II, PLUS, SE, XL
Minimum Memory: 512K
Requires: ImageWriter, LaserWriter or Macintosh supported printer.
Medium: 3 1/2-inch disk
ISPN: 96905-700   **Price: $349.00**

HAYES MICROCOMPUTER PRODUCTS
SMARTCOM II FOR MACINTOSH (VER. 3.0)
Telecommunications that supports 2400 bps communications terminal emulation (VT 52/VT 102), Hayes verification and X modem protocols.
System: MAC, II, PLUS, SE, XL
Minimum Memory: 512K
Medium: 3 1/2-inch disk
ISPN: 34950-500   **Price: $145.00**

INSIGNIA SOLUTIONS, INC.
SOFTPC (VER. 1.3)
Enables IBM PC software to run without modification on the Macintosh SE/30, II, IIx, IIcx and 68020-accelerated SE.
System: SE, II
Minimum Memory: 1700K
Requires: 68020 processor and hard disk.
Medium: 3 1/2-inch disk
ISPN: 38546-700   **Price: $399.00**

MAINSTAY
TELESCAPE
Features an integrated communications directory, intelligent macros, universal terminal emulation and more.
System: MAC, II, PLUS, SE, XL
Minimum Memory: 128K
Medium: 3 1/2-inch disk
ISPN: 46041-700   **Price: $125.00**

MAINSTAY
TELESCAPE PRO VT100
Features include a communication directory, 40 programmable soft keys on screen and both text and XMODEM file-transfer capabilities.
System: MAC, II, PLUS, SE, XL
Minimum Memory:
Requires: Hayes-compatible modem.
Medium: 3 1/2-inch disk
ISPN: 46041-710   **Price: $125.00**

MESA GRAPHICS, INC.
TEXT TERM AND GRAPHICS (VER. 1.02)
A graphic terminal featuring VT100 commands, VT640 commands, Tektronix 4104 and 4105, file transfer and editor.
System: MAC, II, PLUS, SE, XL
Minimum Memory: 512K
Requires: Modem or direct RS232 connection to a host computer.
Medium: 3 1/2-inch disk
ISPN: 49173-700   **Price: $195.00**

GRAFPOINT
TGRAF-07
Provides a terminal emulation package that accesses both alpha numeric and graphic applications and a micro to mainframe link.
System: MAC, II, PLUS, SE, XL
Minimum Memory: 512K
Medium: 3 1/2-inch disk
ISPN: 33362-350   **Price: $995.00**

FARALLON COMPUTING
TIMBUKTU (VER. 2.0.1)
Allows users to view and operate other Macintosh computers over AppleTalk. Several users can connect to the same computer.
System: MAC, II, PLUS, SE, XL
Minimum Memory: 512K
Requires: AppleTalk, or compatible networking systems.
Medium: 3 1/2-inch disk
ISPN: 91809-700   **Price: $99.95**

FARALLON COMPUTING
TIMBUKTU (VER. 2.0.1)
Allows users to view and operate other Macintosh computers over AppleTalk. Several users can connect to the same computer.
System: MAC, II, PLUS, SE, XL
Minimum Memory: 512K
Requires: 1-6 users. AppleTalk, or compatible networking systems.
Medium: 3 1/2-inch disk
ISPN: 91809-700   **Price: $495.00**

GRAFPOINT
TNET: MICRO-TO-MAINFRAME THROUGH NETWORKS
Includes a high-performance Textonix 4105/07/09/15 emulation software package that connect PC's and mainframes on a LAN.
System: MAC, II, PLUS, SE, XL
Minimum Memory: 4096K
Medium: 3 1/2-inch disk
ISPN: 33362-700
Price: Please contact the software publisher.

HUMAN COMPUTER INTERFACE LTD.
TOPMAIL (VER. 3.2)
Send messages or files across AppleTalk without leaving an application. Mail server runs in background.
System: MAC, II, PLUS, SE, XL
Minimum Memory:
Requires: AppleTalk Personal Network.
Medium: 3 1/2-inch disk
ISPN: 82310-300   **Price: $375.00**

TOPS
TOPS FOR THE MACINTOSH (VER. 2.1)
Local area network offering distributed file server architecture and interoperating system connectivity.
System: MAC, II, PLUS, SE, XL
Minimum Memory: 512K
Medium: 3 1/2-inch disk
ISPN: 11962-700   **Price: $249.00**

FARALLON COMPUTING
TRAFFICWATCH
Comprehensive network analysis utility designed to aid network managers in optimizing network loads.
System: MAC, II, PLUS, SE, XL
Minimum Memory: 512K
Medium: 3 1/2-inch disk
ISPN: 91809-625   **Price: $195.00**

ALISA SYSTEMS, INC.
TSSNET (VER. 1.3.2)
Enables Macintosh computers to communicate with DECnet networks as a Phase IV end node.
System: MAC, II, PLUS, SE, XL
Minimum Memory: 1024K
Medium: 3 1/2-inch disk
ISPN: 02265-500   **Price: $495.00**

TOUCHSTONE SOFTWARE CORP.
UNIHOST
Allows a Unix/Xenix system to act as a command server, respond to file transfer, electronic mail or other requests from workstations.
System: MAC, II, PLUS, SE, XL
Minimum Memory: 128K
Medium: 3 1/2-inch disk
ISPN: 82400-850   **Price: $395.00**

PERIPHERALS COMPUTERS
SUPPLIES, INC.

VERSATERM (VER. 3.2)

A text and graphics communication
program offering VT100, DG200, and
Tektronix 4014 emulations.

System: MAC, II, PLUS, SE, XL
Minimum Memory: 512K
Requires: Any auto answer autodial modem or
  direct connection to a host computer.
Medium: 3 1/2-inch disk
ISPN: 60539-900 **Price: $99.00**

PERIPHERALS COMPUTERS
SUPPLIES, INC.

VERSATERM-PRO (VER. 2.2)

Text and color graphics terminal emulator
which emulates Tektronix 4105, 4014,
DEC VT100, and Data General D200
terminals.

System: MAC, II, PLUS, SE, XL
Minimum Memory: 512K
Requires: 800K disk drive, ImageWriter I/II or
  LaserWriter printer.
Medium: 3 1/2-inch disk
ISPN: 60539-895 **Price: $295.00**

M/H GROUP

VSCOM

Provides Wang VS 2110 and VT100
terminal emulation for PCs and
Macintoshes and document/file conversion
to and from Wang VS.

System: MAC, II, PLUS, SE, XL
Minimum Memory: 1024K
Requires: Finder 5.5 or higher.
Medium: 3 1/2-inch disk
ISPN: 45637-800 **Price: $395.00**

M/H GROUP

VSCOM-TERMINAL EMULATION

Provides Wang VS 2110 and VT100
terminal emulation.

System: MAC, II, PLUS, SE, XL
Minimum Memory: 1024K
Requires: Finder 5.5 or higher.
Medium: 3 1/2-inch disk
ISPN: 45637-810 **Price: $195.00**

WATCOM PRODUCTS, INC.

WATERLOO MACJANET (VER. 2.0)

A local area network (LAN) with
LaserWriter/ImageWriter print spooler
features designed specifically for academic
institutions.

System: MAC, II, PLUS, SE, XL
Minimum Memory: 512K
Medium: 3 1/2-inch disk
ISPN: 85718-900 **Price: $1450.00**

820 SYSTEMS/ COMPILERS/ INTERPRETERS/ LANGUAGES

ADVANCED A.I. SYSTEMS, INC.

AAIS PROLOG (VER. M-2.0)

Programming language that provides
compatiblility with DEC 10/20 and C-
Prolog, including function, arg, bagof, setof
and sort.

System: MAC, II, PLUS, SE, XL
Minimum Memory: 1024K
Requires: 800K disk drive.
Medium: 3 1/2-inch disk
ISPN: 01065-600 **Price: $298.00**

MERIDIAN SOFTWARE SYSTEMS,
INC.

ADASTARTER

An entry level Ada compiler limited to
ten library units, each with up to 200
executable statements. Limits program size
to 4000 lines.

System: MAC, II, PLUS, SE, XL
Minimum Memory: 2048K
Requires: 20MB hard disk, System File 4.1,
  Finder 5.5.
Medium: 3 1/2-inch disk
ISPN: 49106-250 **Price: $99.00**

MERIDIAN SOFTWARE SYSTEMS,
INC.

ADAVANTAGE COMPILER (VER. 2.1)

A production quality, U.S. DoD-validated,
Ada compiler with low and high-level
object linker, run-time library and
configuration tools.

System: MAC, II, PLUS, SE, XL
Minimum Memory: 2048K
Requires: 20MB hard disk, System File 4.1,
  Finder 5.5.
Medium: 3 1/2-inch disk
ISPN: 49106-100 **Price: $795.00**

MERIDIAN SOFTWARE SYSTEMS,
INC.

ADAVANTAGE COMPILER (VER. 2.1) WITH OPTIMIZER

A production quality, U.S. DoD-validated
Ada compiler with low and high-level
linker, run-time library and optimizer.

System: MAC, II, PLUS, SE, XL
Minimum Memory: 2048K
Requires: 20MB hard disk, System File 4.1,
  Finder 5.5.
Medium: 3 1/2-inch disk
ISPN: 49106-125 **Price: $1195.00**

CORAL SOFTWARE CORP.

ALLEGRO COMMON LISP (VER. 1.2)

A complete implementation of Common
Lisp, including an efficient compiler,
object-oriented extensions and many
programming tools.

System: MAC, II, PLUS, SE, XL
Minimum Memory: 1024K
Medium: 3 1/2-inch disk
ISPN: 19756-090 **Price: $600.00**

CORAL SOFTWARE CORP.

ALLEGRO FLAVORS (VER. 1.0)

Provides compatibility with Symbolics (Ver.
6.1), and extends Allegro Common Lisp
(Ver. 1.1 and 1.2).

System: MAC, II, PLUS, SE, XL
Minimum Memory: 2048K
Medium: 3 1/2-inch disk
ISPN: 19756-080 **Price: $350.00**

CORAL SOFTWARE CORP.

ALLEGRO FOREIGN FUNCTION INTERFACE (VER. 1.0)

Gives users access to MPW C, Pascal, and
assembly language from within Allegro
Common Lisp programs.

System: MAC, II, PLUS, SE, XL
Minimum Memory: 2048K
Medium: 3 1/2-inch disk
ISPN: 19756-085 **Price: $200.00**

CORAL SOFTWARE CORP.

ALLEGRO STAND-ALONE APPLICATION GENERATOR(VER.1.0)

Produces applications which can be
distributed and run outside of the Allegro
Common Lisp environment.

System: MAC, II, PLUS, SE, XL
Minimum Memory: 2048K
Medium: 3 1/2-inch disk
ISPN: 19756-100 **Price: $600.00**

STRAWBERRY TREE, INC.

ANALOG CONNECTION WORKBENCH (VER. 3.0)

Icon-based object-oriented programming
language for configuring data acquisition
equipment and equipment control
software.

System: II, SE
Minimum Memory: 1024K
Requires: Data aquisition plug-in card.
Medium: 3 1/2-inch disk
ISPN: 76550-105 **Price: $995.00**

STSC, INC.

APL*PLUS MAC SYSTEM

Language interpreter combining the power
of the APL language with advanced
problem-solving features.

System: MAC
Minimum Memory:
Medium: 3 1/2-inch disk
ISPN: 76925-050 **Price: $395.00**

SPENCER ORGANIZATION, INC.

APL.68000 (VER. 7.0)

An interpreted modular programming
language with full Apple Macintosh
integration and native file access.

System: MAC, II, PLUS, SE, XL
Minimum Memory: 1024K
Requires: 800K disk drive.
Medium: 3 1/2-inch disk
ISPN: 75215-120 **Price: $149.00**

SPENCER ORGANIZATION, INC.

APL.68000 (VER. 7.0)

An interpreted modular programming language with full Apple Macintosh integration and native file access.

System: II
Minimum Memory: 1024K
Requires: 68881 or 68882 co-processor.
Medium: 3 1/2-inch disk
ISPN: 75215-120   **Price: $399.00**

ALSYS, INC.

APPLE MACINTOSH II A/UX ADA COMPILER (VER. 4.3)

Converts each compilation unit into object code allowing ADA development on the Macintosh.

System: II
Minimum Memory: 4096K
Requires: Apple A/UX operating system.
Medium: 3 1/2-inch disk
ISPN: 02509-150   **Price: $3095.00**

MANX SOFTWARE SYSTEMS

AZTEC C

Includes an Aztec shell, compiler, 68000 macro assembler, overlay linker, and a full Macintosh toolbox interface.

System: MAC, II, PLUS, SE, XL
Minimum Memory: 512K
Medium: 3 1/2-inch disk
ISPN: 46856-602   **Price: $125.00**

MANX SOFTWARE SYSTEMS

AZTEC C + MPW

Includes MPW shell, Aztec shell, compiler, 680x0 macro assembler, overlay linker, librarian, run-time libraries, and a profiler.

System: MAC, II, PLUS, SE, XL
Minimum Memory: 512K
Medium: 3 1/2-inch disk
ISPN: 46856-300   **Price: $189.00**

MANX SOFTWARE SYSTEMS

AZTEC C + SDB

Includes a source level debugger, an Aztec shell, compiler, overlay linker, and 68000 macro assembler.

System: MAC, II, PLUS, SE, XL
Minimum Memory: 512K
Medium: 3 1/2-inch disk
ISPN: 46856-603   **Price: $189.00**

MANX SOFTWARE SYSTEMS

AZTEC C LIBRARY SOURCE

Provides the source code to all routines found in the Aztec runtime libraries.

System: MAC, II, PLUS, SE, XL
Minimum Memory: 512K
Medium: 3 1/2-inch disk
ISPN: 46856-720   **Price: $250.00**

MANX SOFTWARE SYSTEMS

AZTEC C UNITOOLS

Includes the utilities Z (vi editor), make, diff, and grep.

System: MAC, II, PLUS, SE, XL
Minimum Memory: 512K
Medium: 3 1/2-inch disk
ISPN: 46856-710   **Price: $125.00**

SOFTWORKS LTD.

BUSINESS BASIC

Basic language system oriented to business programming needs.

System: MAC, II, PLUS, SE, XL
Minimum Memory: 512K
Medium: 3 1/2-inch disk
ISPN: 74175-200   **Price: $295.00**

CONSULAIR CORP.

CONSULAIR DIRECT 68020/68881 ACCESS COMPILER

Makes applications up to 100 times faster by using floating point hardware on the Macintosh II.

System: MAC, II, PLUS, SE, XL
Minimum Memory: 1024K
Medium: 3 1/2-inch disk
ISPN: 19231-225   **Price: $600.00**

CONSULAIR CORP.

CONSULAIR MACC/MACC TOOLKIT

Complete C development system which includes the compiler, assembler, a support library and examples.

System: MAC, II, PLUS, SE, XL
Minimum Memory: 512K
Medium: 3 1/2-inch disk
ISPN: 19231-500   **Price: $425.00**

EXPERTELLIGENCE, INC.

EXPERCOMMON LISP FOREIGN FUNCTION INTERFACE

Enables the creation of new versions of Expercommon Lisp language containing functions written in C, Pascal, or assembler.

System: MAC, II, PLUS, SE, XL
Minimum Memory: 1024K
Requires: Expercommon Lisp (ISPN 30473-225) or Expercommon Lisp II (ISPN 30473-230).
Medium: 3 1/2-inch disk
ISPN: 30473-240   **Price: $295.00**

EXPERTELLIGENCE, INC.

EXPERCOMMON LISP II

Allows for future Macintosh II specific enhancements.

System: II
Minimum Memory: 2048K
Medium: 3 1/2-inch disk
ISPN: 30473-230   **Price: $1195.00**

EXPERTELLIGENCE, INC.

EXPERCOMMONOPS5

Provides implementation of OPS5. Integrates with Expercommon Lisp.

System: MAC, II, PLUS, SE, XL
Minimum Memory:
Requires: Expercommon Lisp (ISPN 30473-225) or Expercommon Lisp II (ISPN 30473-230).
Medium: 3 1/2-inch disk
ISPN: 30473-245   **Price: $625.00**

EXPERTELLIGENCE, INC.

EXPERLISP (VER. 1.5)

Modern high performance, compiled version of LISP containing the features that serious LISP programmers require.

System: MAC, II, PLUS, SE, XL
Minimum Memory: 512K
Requires: Two disk drives or a disk drive and a hard disk.
Medium: 3 1/2-inch disk
ISPN: 30473-300   **Price: $495.00**

EXPERTELLIGENCE, INC.

EXPERLOGO PLUS (VER. 2.0)

Powerful adaptation of the Logo computer language.

System: MAC, II, PLUS, SE, XL
Minimum Memory: 512K
Medium: 3 1/2-inch disk
ISPN: 30473-500   **Price: $150.00**

LANGUAGE SYSTEMS CORP.

FORTRAN COMPILER (VER. 1.2)

Supports Apple's SANE floating point routines, INTEGER*1, COMPLEX*16, Pascal type strings and DEC Vax compatible extensions.

System: MAC, II, PLUS, SE, XL
Minimum Memory: 1024K
Requires: Hard disk, Macintosh Programmer's Workshop (ISPN 03749-500).
Medium: 3 1/2-inch disk
ISPN: 43576-405   **Price: $249.00**

LANGUAGE SYSTEMS CORP.

FORTRAN COMPILER WITH MPW (VER. 1.2)

Supports Apple's SANE floating point routines, INTEGER*1, COMPLEX*16, Pascal type strings and Dec Vax compatible extensions.

System: MAC, II, PLUS, SE, XL
Minimum Memory: 1024K
Requires: Hard disk.
Medium: 3 1/2-inch disk
ISPN: 43576-400   **Price: $345.00**

PECAN SOFTWARE SYSTEMS

FORTRAN-77 COMPILER WITH POWER SYSTEM

Ansi Fortran 77 Compiler including integrated power system development environment and compiler.

System: MAC, II, PLUS, SE, XL
Minimum Memory: 512K
Medium: 3 1/2-inch disk
ISPN: 60356-250   **Price: $99.95**

PECAN SOFTWARE SYSTEMS
FORTRAN-77 COMPILER WITHOUT POWER SYSTEM

Ansi Fortran 77 Compiler.

System: MAC, II, PLUS, SE, XL
Minimum Memory: 512K
Medium: 3 1/2-inch disk
ISPN: 60356-260   **Price: $79.95**

MENLO BUSINESS SYSTEMS, INC.
FOUNDATION VISTA TRANSLATOR (VER. 3.1)

Automatically interfaces compiled Vista designs with the Tandem environment by generating Pathway screen definitions.

System: MAC, II, PLUS, SE, XL
Minimum Memory: 1024K
Medium: 3 1/2-inch disk
ISPN: 48969-200
Price: Please contact the software publisher.

TDI SOFTWARE
KERMIT

Contains a source to the utility of Modula-2. Runs from a window, has single character IO and a receive mode for text and code files.

System: MAC
Minimum Memory: 512K
Medium: 3 1/2-inch disk
ISPN: 79965-400   **Price: $29.95**

SYMANTEC
LIGHTSPEED C (VER. 3.0)

A high performance C compiler which includes a Macintosh-style source level debugger.

System: MAC, II, PLUS, SE, XL
Minimum Memory: 512K
Medium: 3 1/2-inch disk
ISPN: 77413-240   **Price: $175.00**

SYMANTEC
LIGHTSPEED PASCAL (VER. 1.1A)

Provides debugging features and is seamlessly integrated with a high performance compiler, linker and project management.

System: MAC, II, PLUS, SE, XL
Minimum Memory: 512K
Medium: 3 1/2-inch disk
ISPN: 77413-250   **Price: $125.00**

PROGRAMMING LOGIC SYSTEMS, INC.
MAC PROLOG

Contains edit windows, and can paste, find and replace and is capable of initiating a command or query plus much more.

System: MAC, II, PLUS, SE, XL
Minimum Memory: 512K
Medium: 3 1/2-inch disk
ISPN: 63173-100   **Price: $295.00**

MEGAMAX, INC.
MAC-TO-GS C

A C compiler which creates Apple IIGS applications, enabling Apple developers to utilize the power of Macintosh hardware and software.

System: MAC, II, PLUS, SE, XL
Minimum Memory: 512K
Requires: Macintosh Programmer's Workshop (ISPN 03749-500).
Medium: 3 1/2-inch disk
ISPN: 48887-200   **Price: $500.00**

PECAN SOFTWARE SYSTEMS
MACADVANTAGE-UCSD PASCAL

Designed specifically to take advantage of the Macintosh features. Includes compiler, editor, debugger, ROM interface units and more.

System: MAC, II, PLUS, SE, XL
Minimum Memory: 512K
Medium: 3 1/2-inch disk
ISPN: 60356-600   **Price: $99.95**

HUMAN COMPUTER INTERFACE LTD.
MACBCPL (VER. 2.0)

A complete development system for the BCPL language for Macintosh applications.

System: MAC, II, PLUS, SE, XL
Minimum Memory:
Medium: 3 1/2-inch disk
ISPN: 82310-200   **Price: $225.00**

CONSULAIR CORP.
MACC JR.

An introductory C language development system for the Macintosh user who wants to learn to develop real applications.

System: MAC, II, PLUS, SE, XL
Minimum Memory: 1024K
Medium: 3 1/2-inch disk
ISPN: 19231-520   **Price: $79.95**

CREATIVE SOLUTIONS, INC.
MACFORTH PLUS (VER. 3.53)

Interactive, multi-tasking programming environment for the Apple Macintosh.

System: MAC, II, PLUS, SE, XL
Minimum Memory: 512K
Medium: 3 1/2-inch disk
ISPN: 20700-590   **Price: $199.00**

ABSOFT CORP.
MACFORTRAN (VER. 2.4)

Mainframe quality full ANSI Fortran 77 compiler with debugger for Macintosh.

System: MAC, II, PLUS, SE, XL
Minimum Memory: 512K
Medium: 3 1/2-inch disk
ISPN: 00368-500   **Price: $295.00**

ABSOFT CORP.
MACFORTRAN/020 (VER. 2.4)

ANSI Fortran 77 compiler with debugger for Macintosh II and 68020/30 upgrades.

System: MAC, II, PLUS, SE, XL
Minimum Memory: 512K
Medium: 3 1/2-inch disk
ISPN: 00368-525   **Price: $495.00**

ABSOFT CORP.
MACFORTRAN/MPW (VER. 1.0)

A full ANSI Fortran 77 compiler with VAX and Fortran 8X extensions for Macintosh Programmer's Workshop.

System: MAC, II, PLUS, SE, XL
Minimum Memory: 1024K
Requires: Macintosh Programmer's Workshop (Ver. 3.0), 68020 microprocessor, 68881 co-processor.
Medium: 3 1/2-inch disk
ISPN: 00368-570   **Price: $495.00**

APDA
MACINTOSH PROGRAMMER'S WORKSHOP (VER. 3.0)

A MC68020 development system including assembler, shell/editor, resource compiler, and utilities.

System: MAC, II, PLUS, SE, XL
Minimum Memory: 1024K
Medium: 3 1/2-inch disk
ISPN: 03749-500   **Price: $400.00**

APDA
MACINTOSH PROGRAMMER'S WORKSHOP C (VER. 3.0)

A 'C' programming language for use with the Macintosh Programmer's Workshop that can generate MC68020 and MC68881 object code.

System: MAC, II, PLUS, SE, XL
Minimum Memory: 1024K
Requires: Macintosh Programmer's Workshop (ISPN 03749-500).
Medium: 3 1/2-inch disk
ISPN: 03749-505   **Price: $150.00**

APDA
MACINTOSH PROGRAMMER'S WORKSHOP PASCAL (VER. 2.02)

Contains the Pascal programming language for the Macintosh Programmer's Workshop.

System: MAC, II, PLUS, SE, XL
Minimum Memory: 1024K
Requires: Macintosh Programmer's Workshop (ISPN 3749-500).
Medium: 3 1/2-inch disk
ISPN: 03749-510   **Price: $150.00**

MODULA CORP.
MACMETH (VER. 2.0)

Modula-2 language system that features fast compilation and execution, relocatable object code, integrated editors and more.

System: MAC, II, PLUS, SE, XL
Minimum Memory: 512K
Medium: 3 1/2-inch disk
ISPN: 55068-400   **Price: $100.00**

MODULA CORP.

MACMODULA-2 (WITH BOOK)

Provides access to all built-in quickdraw graphics procedures, resource files, menus and windows with over 400 toolbox routines.

System: MAC, II, PLUS, SE, XL
Minimum Memory: 512K
Medium: 3 1/2-inch disk
ISPN: 55068-505   **Price: $166.95**

MODULA CORP.

MACMODULA-2 (WITHOUT BOOK)

Provides access to all built-in QuickDraw graphics procedures, resource files, menus and windows. Over 400 ToolBox routines.

System: MAC, II, PLUS, SE, XL
Minimum Memory: 512K
Medium: 3 1/2-inch disk
ISPN: 55068-500   **Price: $150.00**

MGLOBAL

MACMUMPS

Used to create and manage large filing systems.

System: MAC, II, PLUS, SE, XL
Minimum Memory: 512K
Medium: 3 1/2-inch disk
ISPN: 49375-100   **Price: $199.95**

LIGHTSHIP SOFTWARE

MACSCHEME (VER. 1.5)

Implementation of Lisp for the 512K Macintosh. Features a fast reliable byte code interpreter, editor, debugger and tracer.

System: MAC, II, PLUS, SE, XL
Minimum Memory: 512K
Medium: 3 1/2-inch disk
ISPN: 69162-500   **Price: $125.00**

DCM DATA PRODUCTS

MACTRAN PLUS (VER. 3.0)

An integrated ANSI 77 Fortran environment with editor, compiler, linker, and symbolic debugger. Generates inline 68020/688881 code.

System: MAC, II, PLUS, SE, XL
Minimum Memory: 512K
Medium: 3 1/2-inch disk
ISPN: 24196-610   **Price: $399.00**

DCM DATA PRODUCTS

MACTRAN77 (VER. 2.0)

An integrated Editor, Compiler and Symbolic Debugger with High Level Interface to Macintosh ToolBox and library to support 68881.

System: MAC, II, PLUS, SE, XL
Minimum Memory: 512K
Medium: 3 1/2-inch disk
ISPN: 24196-600   **Price: $199.00**

MICROMOTION

MASTERFORTH (VER. 1.1)

Implements the Forth programming language. Includes a full-file interface, macro assembler, screen editor, and debugger.

System: MAC, II, PLUS, SE, XL
Minimum Memory: 512K
Medium: 3 1/2-inch disk
ISPN: 52750-520   **Price: $125.00**

MICROMOTION

MASTERFORTH TARGET APPLICATION GENERATION SYSTEM

Produces optimized application programs for virtually any programming environment.

System: MAC, II, PLUS, SE, XL
Minimum Memory: 512K
Medium: 3 1/2-inch disk
ISPN: 52750-525   **Price: $495.00**

MEGAMAX, INC.

MEGAMAX C COMPILER (VER. 3.0)

Featuring in-line assembly, one pass compilation, full access of Macintosh toolbox routines, support of dynamic overlays and more.

System: MAC, II, PLUS, SE, XL
Minimum Memory: 512K
Medium: 3 1/2-inch disk
ISPN: 48887-100   **Price: $299.95**

METROPOLIS COMPUTER NETWORKS, INC.

METCOM MODULA-2

An integrated Modula-2 development system comprised of a text editor, native code compiler, dynamic liner and source debugger.

System: MAC, II, PLUS, SE, XL
Minimum Memory: 1024K
Requires: 800K disk drive.
Medium: 3 1/2-inch disk
ISPN: 49287-500   **Price: $245.00**

MICROSOFT CORP.

MICROSOFT QUICKBASIC (VER. 1.0)(MACINTOSH)

Provides a complete BASIC programming language development environment for the Macintosh computer.

System: MAC, II, PLUS, SE, XL
Minimum Memory: 512K
Requires: 800K disk drive.
Medium: 3 1/2-inch disk
ISPN: 53150-205   **Price: $99.00**

TDI SOFTWARE

MODULA II

Provides a language that encourages users to write in modules which makes programs easy to design, write and maintain.

System: MAC
Minimum Memory: 512K
Medium: 3 1/2-inch disk
ISPN: 79965-500   **Price: $495.00**

TDI SOFTWARE

MODULA II-COMMERCIAL VERSION

Demonstrates how to write complex modules using Modula II.

System: MAC
Minimum Memory: 512K
Medium: 3 1/2-inch disk
ISPN: 79965-520   **Price: $495.00**

TDI SOFTWARE

MODULA II-DEVELOPER VERSION

Provides a language that encourages users to write in modules.

System: MAC
Minimum Memory: 512K
Medium: 3 1/2-inch disk
ISPN: 79965-510   **Price: $495.00**

APDA

MPW IIGS C

A cross-development system C compiler for the Apple IIGS which runs in the MPW environment on the Macintosh.

System: MAC, II, PLUS, SE, XL
Minimum Memory: 1024K
Requires: Macintosh Programmer's Workshop (ISPN 03749-500) and MPW IIGS Tools (ISPN 03749-301), hard disk and an 800K disk drive.
Medium: 3 1/2-inch disk
ISPN: 03749-300   **Price: $150.00**

COOKE PUBLICATIONS

MW2TEX (VER. 1.0)

Translates the mathematical expressions of MathWriter into the mathematical language TeX (used in mathematical sciences).

System: MAC, II, PLUS, SE, XL
Minimum Memory: 512K
Requires: MathWriter (ISPN 19659-400).
Medium: 3 1/2-inch disk
ISPN: 19659-410   **Price: $49.95**

CORAL SOFTWARE CORP.

OBJECT LOGO (VER. 2.0)

An extended version of Logo that maintains compatability with standard dialects. Includes compiler and object-oriented features.

System: MAC, II, PLUS, SE, XL
Minimum Memory: 1024K
Requires: 800K disk drive.
Medium: 3 1/2-inch disk
ISPN: 19756-500   **Price: $125.00**

PTERODACTYL SOFTWARE

PC MAC BASIC (VER. 2.01)

This BASIC compiler for the Macintosh is compatible with BASICA on the IBM PC. Best used for research files and large programs.

System: MAC, II, PLUS, SE, XL
Minimum Memory: 512K
Medium: 3 1/2-inch disk
ISPN: 63737-090   **Price: $39.95**

PECAN SOFTWARE SYSTEMS

PDQ PASCAL

Provides an introductory teaching tool for learning Pascal and specifically USCD Pascal. Compiler, editor and filer are included.

System: MAC, II, PLUS, SE, XL
Minimum Memory: 512K
Medium: 3 1/2-inch disk
ISPN: 60356-625 **Price: $69.95**

CORAL SOFTWARE CORP.

PEARL LISP (VER. 1.0)

A Lisp compiler, including object-oriented programming system, Macintosh interface tools, Emacs-like editor, and file-compiler.

System: MAC, II, PLUS, SE, XL
Minimum Memory: 1024K
Medium: 3 1/2-inch disk
ISPN: 19756-095 **Price: $175.00**

PECAN SOFTWARE SYSTEMS

POWER SYSTEM-UCSD PASCAL COMPILER

An implementation of the UCSD p-system which includes a Pascal compiler, access ProDOS files, and uses SANE numbers.

System: MAC, II, PLUS, SE, XL
Minimum Memory: 512K
Requires: Designer Series Development System.
Medium: 3 1/2-inch disk
ISPN: 60356-860 **Price: $79.95**

PROLOGIA LUMINY

PROLOG II (VER. 2.0)

Provides an interpreter for the Prolog programming language.

System: MAC, II, PLUS, SE, XL
Minimum Memory: 512K
Medium: 3 1/2-inch disk
ISPN: 63268-100 **Price: $495.00**

METARESEARCH, INC.

RASCAL (VER. 3.0)

Real-time, compiled, I/O-oriented language based on Pascal and C.

System: MAC, II, PLUS, SE, XL
Minimum Memory: 512K
Requires: 400K disk version. 800K disk version.
Medium: 3 1/2-inch disk
ISPN: 49225-200 **Price: $149.00**

CACI PRODUCTS CO.

SIMSCRIPT II.5

Includes a free-form, English-like simulation language designed to simplify writing programs for simulation modeling.

System: II
Minimum Memory: 3072K
Requires: Hard disk with at least 3MB.
Medium: 3 1/2-inch disk
ISPN: 10300-100 **Price: $15000.00**

KINKOS ACADEMIC COURSEWARE EXCHANGE

SMALLGOL COMPILER (VER. 1.0)

An animated compiler that displays animated, dynamic pictures that reveal how a compiler works.

System: MAC, II, PLUS, SE, XL
Minimum Memory: 128K
Requires: Finder (Ver. 4.1 or later).
Medium: 3 1/2-inch disk
ISPN: 43025-820 **Price: $16.50**

DIGITALK, INC.

SMALLTALK/V MAC (VER. 1.0)

Provides a Smalltalk object-oriented programming environment for the Macintosh.

System: MAC, II, PLUS, SE, XL
Minimum Memory: 1536K
Medium: 3 1/2-inch disk
ISPN: 25687-250 **Price: $199.95**

FIRST BYTE, INC.

SMOOTHTALKER (VER. 2.O)

Provides a speech synthesizer that converts English text into high quality, natural sounding speech. No extra hardware needed.

System: MAC, II, PLUS, SE, XL
Minimum Memory: 512K
Medium: 3 1/2-inch disk
ISPN: 30836-500 **Price: $49.95**

TERRAPIN, INC.

TERRAPIN LOGO FOR THE MACINTOSH

Features include 25,000 nodes of workspace, improved ability to simulate graphics animation, plus multiple turtles and arrays.

System: MAC, II, PLUS, SE, XL
Minimum Memory: 512K
Medium: 3 1/2-inch disk
ISPN: 81150-350 **Price: $99.95**

TERRAPIN, INC.

TERRAPIN LOGO FOR THE MACINTOSH

Features include 25,000 nodes of workspace, improved ability to simulate graphics animation, plus multiple turtles and arrays.

System: MAC, II, PLUS, SE, XL
Minimum Memory: 512K
Requires: Ten-pack.
Medium: 3 1/2-inch disk
ISPN: 81150-350 **Price: $299.95**

TML SYSTEMS, INC.

TML MODULA II

Modula-2 compiler creates stand-alone Macintosh applications, simple terminal input/output programs and accessories.

System: MAC, II, PLUS, SE, XL
Minimum Memory: 1024K
Medium: 3 1/2-inch disk
ISPN: 82182-400 **Price: $99.95**

TML SYSTEMS, INC.

TML PASCAL FOR THE MACINTOSH

A native code Pascal compiler designed to be used for creating stand-alone, double-clickable applications.

System: MAC, II, PLUS, SE
Minimum Memory: 512K
Medium: 3 1/2-inch disk
ISPN: 82182-500 **Price: $99.95**

TRUE BASIC, INC.

TRUE BASIC LANGUAGE SYSTEM (VER. 2.0)

Fully structured, easy-to-use, programming language. Produces a compact and fast intermediate code.

System: MAC, II, PLUS, SE, XL
Minimum Memory: 512K
Medium: 3 1/2-inch disk
ISPN: 82789-673 **Price: $99.95**

BORLAND INT'L.

TURBO PASCAL FOR THE MAC

Includes a complete development environment with a built-in editor and the ability to run programs while you run the compiler.

System: MAC, II, PLUS, SE, XL
Minimum Memory: 512K
Medium: 3 1/2-inch disk
ISPN: 08225-125 **Price: $99.95**

MAINSTAY

V.I.P. (VISUAL INTERACTIVE PROGRAMMING) (VER. 2.5)

See the programming right on the screen. Features include an icon based, visual language, visual, source level debugger and more.

System: MAC, II, PLUS, SE, XL
Minimum Memory: 1024K
Medium: 3 1/2-inch disk
ISPN: 46041-950 **Price: $149.95**

ZEDCOR, INC.

ZBASIC (VER. 4.01)

Compiles Basic coding into machine language with complete event trapping.

System: MAC, II, PLUS, SE
Minimum Memory: 512K
Medium: 3 1/2-inch disk
ISPN: 70625-200 **Price: $199.95**

---

827 SYSTEMS/ CONVERSIONS/CROSS COMPILERS

INTERPROGRAM

BLUE LOAD (VER. 4.6.01)

Creates an ASCII coded file from any Blues module data dictionary.

System: II, PLUS, SE, XL
Minimum Memory: 512K
Requires: Any of the Blues modules (ISPN 40293-100 thru 40293-150).
Medium: 3 1/2-inch disk
ISPN: 40293-160　　　　　**Price: $375.00**

CORVUS SYSTEMS, INC.

CONSTELLATION III-MACINTOSH (RELEASE 2.0)

An enhanced, high-performance network management system which combines speed and reliability in a menu-driven Omninet network.

System: MAC, II, PLUS, SE, XL
Minimum Memory: 200K
Medium: 3 1/2-inch disk
ISPN: 19884-500　　　　　**Price: $495.00**

ZEDCOR, INC.

CONVERSION PROGRAM

Allows people to convert programs written in Microsoft Basic, Basic Basica, etc. where commands do not respond to ZBasic Syntax.

System: MAC, II, PLUS, SE, XL
Minimum Memory:
Medium: 3 1/2-inch disk
ISPN: 70625-210　　　　　**Price: $29.95**

CONSULAIR CORP.

MAC TO GS ASSEMBLER/ LINKER

A cross-development system that allows the user to develop Apple IIGS assembly-language programs on the Macintosh.

System: MAC, II, PLUS, SE, XL
Minimum Memory: 512K
Medium: 3 1/2-inch disk
ISPN: 19231-540　　　　　**Price: $195.00**

JASIK DESIGNS

MACNOSY PLUS DEBUGGER UNIVERSAL VERSION

Two programs enable the user to recover source code of an Macintosh application file, ROM or code type resources and debug.

System: MAC, II, PLUS, SE, XL
Minimum Memory: 128K
Medium: 3 1/2-inch disk
ISPN: 41462-505　　　　　**Price: $350.00**

MENLO BUSINESS SYSTEMS, INC.

MENLOCOM (VER. 1.0)

Transfers presentation services from Tandem to the Macintosh.

System: MAC, II, PLUS, SE, XL
Minimum Memory: 512K
Medium: 3 1/2-inch disk
ISPN: 48969-600　　　　　**Price: $125.00**

ALSOFT, INC.

PROLINK

Transfer AppleWorks data and other Apple II text files to your Macintosh or Macintosh text files to your Apple II.

System: MAC, II, PLUS, SE, XL
Minimum Memory: 512K
Medium: 3 1/2-inch disk
ISPN: 02506-600　　　　　**Price: $49.95**

WHITE PINE SOFTWARE, INC.

REGGIE (VER. 1.1)

Converts MacDraw, MacPaint and Clipboard images for output on DEC graphics terminals and laser printers.

System: MAC, II, PLUS, SE, XL
Minimum Memory: 512K
Medium: 3 1/2-inch disk
ISPN: 86315-600　　　　　**Price: $149.00**

MAINSTAY

V.I.P. TO LIGHTSPEED C

Translates and interprets code from LightSpeed C.

System: II, PLUS, SE, XL
Minimum Memory: 1024K
Requires: Lightspeed C (Ver. 2.15), 800K drive or two 400K drives.
Medium: 3 1/2-inch disk
ISPN: 46041-952　　　　　**Price: $89.95**

MAINSTAY

V.I.P. TO LIGHTSPEED PASCAL

Translates programs written with V.I.P. to Lightspeed Pascal source code.

System: MAC, II, PLUS, SE, XL
Minimum Memory: 1024K
Requires: Lightspeed Pascal (ISPN 81387-300).
Medium: 3 1/2-inch disk
ISPN: 46041-956　　　　　**Price: $89.95**

MAINSTAY

V.I.P. TO MPW C

Translates programs written with V.I.P. to MPW C source code.

System: MAC, II, PLUS, SE, XL
Minimum Memory: 1024K
Requires: MPW C.
Medium: 3 1/2-inch disk
ISPN: 46041-960　　　　　**Price: $89.95**

MAINSTAY

V.I.P. TO MPW PASCAL

Translates programs written with V.I.P. to MPW Pascal source code.

System: MAC, II, PLUS, SE, XL
Minimum Memory: 1024K
Requires: MPW Pascal (ISPN 03749-510).
Medium: 3 1/2-inch disk
ISPN: 46041-958　　　　　**Price: $89.95**

MAINSTAY

V.I.P. TO TURBO PASCAL

Translates programs written with V.I.P. to Turbo Pascal source code.

System: MAC, II, PLUS, SE, XL
Minimum Memory: 1024K
Requires: 800K disk drive, Turbo Pascal (ISPN 08225-125).
Medium: 3 1/2-inch disk
ISPN: 46041-954　　　　　**Price: $89.95**

---

830 SYSTEMS/DATA ENTRY

NEW IMAGE TECHNOLOGY, INC.

TEXTSCAN (VER. 2.15)

Uses Optical Character Recognition that allows users to create word processing files from a scanned image.

System: MAC, II, PLUS, SE, XL
Minimum Memory: 1024K
Requires: Scanner.
Medium: 3 1/2-inch disk
ISPN: 56706-700　　　　　**Price: $295.00**

---

835 SYSTEMS/DATABASE MANAGEMENT SYSTEMS (ADVANCED)

1ST DESK SYSTEMS, INC.

1STGATE (VER. 4.0)

Provides a remote access, programmable relational database and bulletin board.

System: MAC, II, PLUS, SE, XL
Minimum Memory: 512K
Requires: Modem.
Medium: 3 1/2-inch disk
ISPN: 81083-620　　　　　**Price: $495.00**

1ST DESK SYSTEMS, INC.

1STTEAM (VER. 4.0)

Contains a multi-user automated, macro-programmable power database.

System: II, PLUS, SE, XL
Minimum Memory: 512K
Medium: 3 1/2-inch disk
ISPN: 81083-610　　　　　**Price: $795.00**

BROCK SOFTWARE PRODUCTS, INC.

BROCK KEYSTROKE RELATIONAL DATABASE

Relational database program with multi-file capabilities. Includes free-design, re-design, and field formatting functions.

System: MAC, II, PLUS, SE, XL
Minimum Memory: 512K
Medium: 3 1/2-inch disk
ISPN: 08825-600　　　　　**Price: $99.00**

BROCK SOFTWARE PRODUCTS, INC.

BROCK KEYSTROKE RELATIONAL DATABASE/ADV. ENCRYPTED

Has password protection. Features free-design input form up to nine screens in size.

System: MAC, II, PLUS, SE, XL
Minimum Memory: 512K
Medium: 3 1/2-inch disk
ISPN: 08825-650   **Price: $149.00**

MARVELIN CORP.

BUSINESS FILEVISION

Integrated graphics database includes linking, drawing, filing and reporting for business professionals.

System: MAC, II, PLUS, SE, XL
Minimum Memory: 512K
Medium: 3 1/2-inch disk
ISPN: 47483-045   **Price: $395.00**

PREFERRED PUBLISHERS, INC.

DATABASE

A full-function database desk accessory for pictures, text and forms.

System: MAC, II, PLUS, SE, XL
Minimum Memory: 512K
Requires: 800K disk drive.
Medium: 3 1/2-inch disk
ISPN: 61825-200   **Price: $129.95**

RAIMA CORP.

DB-VISTA

Provides a database management system for use by C language applications programmers.

System: MAC, II, PLUS, SE, XL
Minimum Memory: 256K
Requires: C compiler.
Medium: 3 1/2-inch disk
ISPN: 77831-100   **Price: $695.00**

DESKTOP AI

DBX TRANSLATOR

Allows the user to run dBASE applications in any environment where the C language is available.

System: MAC, II, PLUS, SE, XL
Minimum Memory: 512K
Medium: 3 1/2-inch disk
ISPN: 24940-200   **Price: $750.00**

ODESTA CORP.

DOUBLE HELIX II

Provides a relational database/applications generator for users with little or no programming knowledge.

System: MAC, II, PLUS, SE, XL
Minimum Memory: 1024K
Requires: Hard disk.
Medium: 3 1/2-inch disk
ISPN: 57709-160   **Price: $595.00**

CLARIS CORP.

FILEMAKER II

Provides data management, layout and drawing, and extended report generation.

System: II, PLUS, SE, XL
Minimum Memory: 512K
Requires: Two 800K drives or a hard disk.
Medium: 3 1/2-inch disk
ISPN: 12784-200   **Price: $299.00**

ACIUS

FOURTH DIMENSION

A relational database with layout graphics and programming language plus runtime, multi-user and customization.

System: MAC, II, PLUS, SE, XL
Minimum Memory: 1024K
Requires: Hard disk.
Medium: 3 1/2-inch disk
ISPN: 90311-200   **Price: $695.00**

FOX SOFTWARE, INC.

FOXBASE +/MAC (VER. 1.10)

A dBASE III compatible applications development system with an integrated compiler and a true Macintosh interface.

System: MAC, II, PLUS, SE, XL
Minimum Memory: 1024K
Requires: Hard disk.
Medium: 3 1/2-inch disk
ISPN: 31262-285   **Price: $395.00**

FOX SOFTWARE, INC.

FOXBASE +/MAC-RUNTIME (VER. 1.10)

Enables programs developed on Foxbase +/Mac to run as stand-alone applications.

System: MAC, II, PLUS, SE, XL
Minimum Memory: 1024K
Requires: Hard disk.
Medium: 3 1/2-inch disk
ISPN: 31262-290   **Price: $300.00**

ODESTA CORP.

GEOQUERY

Uses existing or imported information to create maps that show the geographic relationships in data.

System: MAC, II, PLUS, SE, XL
Minimum Memory: 1024K
Requires: Two 800K disk drives or one 800K disk drive and hard disk.
Medium: 3 1/2-inch disk
ISPN: 57709-180   **Price: $349.00**

INFORMIX SOFTWARE, INC.

INFORMIX-4GL (VER. 1.1)

Fourth-generation database application development language based on industry-standard SQL query language.

System: MAC, II, PLUS, SE, XL
Minimum Memory:
Medium: 3 1/2-inch disk
ISPN: 65750-045
Price: Please contact the software publisher.

INFORMIX SOFTWARE, INC.

INFORMIX-ESQL/C (VER. 2.1)

Allows 'C' programmers to create and manipulate databases from within application programs written in 'C'.

System: MAC, II, PLUS, SE, XL
Minimum Memory:
Medium: 3 1/2-inch disk
ISPN: 65750-055
Price: Please contact the software publisher.

INFORMIX SOFTWARE, INC.

INFORMIX-SQL (VER. 2.1)

A relational database management system that provides the tools required for sophisticated application building.

System: MAC, II, PLUS, SE, XL
Minimum Memory:
Medium: 3 1/2-inch disk
ISPN: 65750-050
Price: Please contact the software publisher.

SHANA CORP.

INSIDE OUT

A development tool which performs the database functions of an application.

System: MAC, II, PLUS, SE, XL
Minimum Memory: 512K
Requires: Multi-user.
Medium: 3 1/2-inch disk
ISPN: 69475-002   **Price: $595.00**

SHANA CORP.

INSIDE OUT

A development tool which performs the database functions of an application.

System: MAC, II, PLUS, SE
Minimum Memory: 512K
Requires: Single user.
Medium: 3 1/2-inch disk
ISPN: 69475-002   **Price: $395.00**

TML SYSTEMS, INC.

MACLANGUAGE SERIES DATABASE TOOLKIT

Library of Pascal procedures that locates, inserts or deletes records in a database using an Indexed Sequential Access Method.

System: MAC, II, PLUS, SE, XL
Minimum Memory: 512K
Medium: 3 1/2-inch disk
ISPN: 82182-300   **Price: $89.95**

NANTUCKET CORP.

MCMAX (VER. 2.0)

Provides a database management system for the Macintosh that supports dBASE III and dBASE III+ files and applications.

System: MAC, II, PLUS, SE, XL
Minimum Memory: 512K
Requires: Hard disk or two disk drives.
Medium: 3 1/2-inch disk
ISPN: 55949-500   **Price: $295.00**

MICROSOFT CORP.

MICROSOFT FILE (VER. 2.0)

Gives user control to record, organize, manage and sort information or to change and reshape that information as needs change.

System: MAC, II, PLUS, SE, XL
Minimum Memory:
Medium: 3 1/2-inch disk
ISPN: 53150-275   **Price: $195.00**

BLYTH SOFTWARE, INC.

OMNIS 3 PLUS/EXPRESS (VER. 3.25)

Provides a relational, programmable database that comes with an applications generator that automates building of an Omnis library.

System: MAC, II, PLUS, SE, XL
Minimum Memory: 512K
Requires: Hard disk.
Medium: 3 1/2-inch disk
ISPN: 58775-515   **Price: $249.00**

BLYTH SOFTWARE, INC.

OMNIS 3 PLUS/EXPRESS (VER. 3.3)

A relational, programmable database with an applications generator and supports Apple's CL/1 language and major Local Area Networks.

System: MAC, II, PLUS, SE, XL
Minimum Memory: 1024K
Requires: 1-3 users. Hard disk.
Medium: 3 1/2-inch disk
ISPN: 58775-320   **Price: $795.00**

ORACLE CORP.

ORACLE FOR MACINTOSH

Provides access to a relational database residing on the Macintosh using the SQL language within the HyperCard environment.

System: MAC, II, PLUS, SE, XL
Minimum Memory: 2048K
Requires: Hard disk drive, HyperCard (ISPN 03900-300) (Ver. 1.2 or higher).
Medium: 3 1/2-inch disk
ISPN: 58667-555   **Price: $999.00**

PERSONAL BIBLIOGRAPHIC SOFTWARE, INC.

PRO-CITE FOR THE MACINTOSH

Contains a specialized database and text management system which enables the user to generate formatted bibliographies.

System: MAC, II, PLUS, SE, XL
Minimum Memory: 512K
Medium: 3 1/2-inch disk
ISPN: 60587-240   **Price: $395.00**

BORLAND INT'L.

REFLEX FOR THE MAC (VER. 1.0)

Relational database with various flexible layouts and calculation capabilities.

System: MAC, II, PLUS, SE, XL
Minimum Memory: 512K
Medium: 3 1/2-inch disk
ISPN: 08225-083   **Price: $99.95**

BORLAND INT'L.

REFLEX PLUS-THE DATABASE MANAGER

Relational database that gives user ability to create databases, access data, and produce reports.

System: MAC, II, PLUS, SE, XL
Minimum Memory: 512K
Medium: 3 1/2-inch disk
ISPN: 08225-086   **Price: $279.00**

SILENTPARTNER

SILENTPARTNER (VER. 2.0)

Maintains information on client and company information, and accounting functions for photographers.

System: MAC, II, PLUS, SE, XL
Minimum Memory: 512K
Requires: 800K disk drive.
Medium: 3 1/2-inch disk
ISPN: 07841-700   **Price: $1200.00**

VIDEX, INC.

TIMEWAND MANAGER (VER. 4.01)

Contains relational database with the ability to utilize bar code entries with the Videx TimeWand.

System: MAC, II, PLUS, SE, XL
Minimum Memory: 512K
Requires: Timewand Bar Code Reader, Timewand recharger and cable.
Medium: 3 1/2-inch disk
ISPN: 85150-097   **Price: $489.00**

---

838 SYSTEMS/DATABASE MANAGEMENT SYSTEMS (BASIC)

1ST DESK SYSTEMS, INC.

1STFILE (VER. 3.5)

Relational database and report generator, mailing labels, and powerful mail list manager. Programmable in English.

System: MAC, II, PLUS, SE, XL
Minimum Memory: 128K
Medium: 3 1/2-inch disk
ISPN: 81083-590   **Price: $95.00**

1ST DESK SYSTEMS, INC.

1STFILE (VER. 4.0)

Create files, enter and edit data, sort multiple fields, and produce reports from single or relational files.

System: MAC, II, PLUS, SE, XL
Minimum Memory: 512K
Medium: 3 1/2-inch disk
ISPN: 81083-550   **Price: $295.00**

HEIZER SOFTWARE

501 QUOTES

A collection of 501 quotations for use by writers and speakers.

System: MAC, II, PLUS, SE, XL
Minimum Memory: 512K
Requires: Microsoft Excel (ISPN 53150-270), Microsoft Works (ISPN 53150-740) or HyperCard (ISPN 03900-300).
Medium: 3 1/2-inch disk
ISPN: 35175-668   **Price: $12.00**

LASER DIGITAL CORP.

ARCHE TYPER (VER. 1.04)

A pre-programmed user interface and development shell for use with Fourth Dimension.

System: MAC, II, PLUS, SE, XL
Minimum Memory: 1024K
Requires: Hard disk, Fourth Dimension (ISPN 90311-200).
Medium: 3 1/2-inch disk
ISPN: 43660-100   **Price: $195.00**

BRAINPOWER, INC.

ARCHITEXT

A text retrieval, analysis, management and presentation package for organizing text.

System: MAC, II, PLUS, SE, XL
Minimum Memory: 1024K
Requires: Finder 6.0 or later.
Medium: 3 1/2-inch disk
ISPN: 08413-050   **Price: $349.95**

BROCK SOFTWARE PRODUCTS, INC.

BROCK KEYSTROKE FILER

Features Free-design input form up to nine screens in size.

System: MAC, II, PLUS, SE, XL
Minimum Memory: 512K
Medium: 3 1/2-inch disk
ISPN: 08825-400   **Price: $49.00**

HEIZER SOFTWARE

CONVERT STATE MACROS

Converts state abbreviations in the database to full state names and vice versa.

System: MAC, II, PLUS, SE, XL
Minimum Memory: 512K
Requires: Microsoft Excel (ISPN 53150-270).
Medium: 3 1/2-inch disk
ISPN: 35175-522   **Price: $8.00**

HEIZER SOFTWARE

CREDIT CARD DATABASE

A database containing information on sixty banks which offer low interest and/or no-fee Visa and MasterCards.

System: MAC, II, PLUS, SE, XL
Minimum Memory: 512K
Requires: Microsoft Excel (ISPN 53150-270), Microsoft Works (ISPN 53150-740) or HyperCard (ISPN 03900-300).
Medium: 3 1/2-inch disk
ISPN: 35175-614   **Price: $9.00**

HEIZER SOFTWARE
CUSTOMER DATABASE

Keeps records of customer number, name, billing address, contact, phone number and shipping address.

System: MAC, II, PLUS, SE, XL
Minimum Memory: 512K
Requires: Microsoft Excel (ISPN 53150-270).
Medium: 3 1/2-inch disk
ISPN: 35175-006   **Price: $8.00**

HEIZER SOFTWARE
DATA VIEW FORM

Shows how to set up a form on a worksheet, by using a model which displays all data in a database record at the same time.

System: MAC, II, PLUS, SE, XL
Minimum Memory: 512K
Requires: Microsoft Excel (ISPN 53150-270).
Medium: 3 1/2-inch disk
ISPN: 35175-343   **Price: $7.00**

GARY HOLMES
DATABASE MANAGER

Stores tax receipt and other tax data in files created and formatted by the user, following computer-generated promptings.

System: MAC, II, PLUS, SE, XL
Minimum Memory: 512K
Medium: 3 1/2-inch disk
ISPN: 92104-250   **Price: $8.00**

STONE EDGE TECHNOLOGIES, INC.
DB MASTER MACINTOSH

Easy-to-learn, easy-to-use database management system that supports large records and files.

System: MAC, II, PLUS, SE, XL
Minimum Memory: 512K
Medium: 3 1/2-inch disk
ISPN: 76400-150   **Price: $59.95**

ASHTON-TATE
DBASE MAC

A highly advanced database to help make heads and tails out of even the most complicated data management tasks.

System: MAC, II, PLUS, SE, XL
Minimum Memory: 512K
Requires: Two 800K disk drives, or one 400K disk drive and one 800 disk drive or disk drive and hard disk.
Medium: 3 1/2-inch disk
ISPN: 05500-168   **Price: $495.00**

HEIZER SOFTWARE
EVENTS DAY-BY-DAY

A database with access to the dates of birth and death of over 3,000 famous people.

System: MAC, II, PLUS, SE, XL
Minimum Memory: 512K
Requires: Microsoft Excel (ISPN 53150-270), Microsoft Works (ISPN 53150-740) or HyperCard (ISPN 03900-300).
Medium: 3 1/2-inch disk
ISPN: 35175-666   **Price: $35.00**

HEIZER SOFTWARE
EXTREMELY HAZARDOUS SUBSTANCES-EHS

Covers all 406 chemicals named in the Community Right to Know Act of 1986.

System: MAC, II, PLUS, SE, XL
Minimum Memory: 512K
Requires: Microsoft Excel (ISPN 53150-270), Microsoft Works (ISPN 53150-740) or HyperCard (ISPN 03900-300).
Medium: 3 1/2-inch disk
ISPN: 35175-704   **Price: $25.00**

HEIZER SOFTWARE
FONT CATALOGS

Catalogs 256 Macintosh characters of fonts.

System: MAC, II, PLUS, SE, XL
Minimum Memory: 512K
Requires: Microsoft Excel (ISPN 53150-270).
Medium: 3 1/2-inch disk
ISPN: 35175-538   **Price: $7.00**

APPLE COMPUTER, INC.
HYPERCARD (VER. 1.22)

Enables users to customize storage and retrieval of both text and graphics, and organize large amounts of data.

System: MAC, II, PLUS, SE, XL
Minimum Memory: 1024K
Requires: Two 800K disk drives or one 800K disk drive and hard disk.
Medium: 3 1/2-inch disk
ISPN: 03900-300   **Price: $49.00**

SPINNAKER SOFTWARE
I KNOW IT'S HERE SOMEWHERE!

Create your own customized form layout. Includes sort, search and print options.

System: MAC, II, PLUS, SE, XL
Minimum Memory: 512K
Medium: 3 1/2-inch disk
ISPN: 75300-172   **Price: $29.95**

HEIZER SOFTWARE
MAC MAGAZINE PRODUCT INDEX 87/88

A database of over 850 software and hardware articles from every 1987 and 1988 Macworld and MacUser issue.

System: MAC, II, PLUS, SE, XL
Minimum Memory: 512K
Requires: Microsoft Excel (ISPN 53150-270), Microsoft Works (ISPN 53150-740) or HyperCard (ISPN 03900-300).
Medium: 3 1/2-inch disk
ISPN: 35175-536   **Price: $10.00**

JAM SOFTWARE
MACLIST (VER. 1.02)

A disk accessory database for sorting and searching files, allowing unlimited rows and columns, with import and export capability.

System: MAC, II, PLUS, SE, XL
Minimum Memory: 512K
Requires: 800K disk drive.
Medium: 3 1/2-inch disk
ISPN: 41381-510   **Price: $20.00**

HEIZER SOFTWARE
NATIONAL GEOGRAPHIC INDEX

A collection of over 2,000 names of articles taken from the spine of each magazine. Includes search and extract features.

System: MAC, II, PLUS, SE, XL
Minimum Memory: 512K
Requires: Microsoft Excel (ISPN 53150-270), Microsoft Works (ISPN 53150-740) or HyperCard (ISPN 03900-300).
Medium: 3 1/2-inch disk
ISPN: 35175-703   **Price: $10.00**

DAVKA CORP.
OTZAR

Contains a treasury of Judaic wit and wisdom on almost any subject, taken from the Talmud, the Midrash and Hasidic tales.

System: MAC
Minimum Memory: 48K
Requires: Microsoft Works (ISPN 53150-740).
Medium: 3 1/2-inch disk
ISPN: 91205-550   **Price: $29.95**

PARK ROW SOFTWARE
PUBLISH OR PERISH (VER. 4.0)

Bibliographic database program that allows you to find and format references. Can import and export text files.

System: MAC, II, PLUS, SE, XL
Minimum Memory: 512K
Medium: 3 1/2-inch disk
ISPN: 59755-100   **Price: $74.95**

SOFTWARE DISCOVERIES INC
RECORD HOLDER (VER. 2.2B)

Full-function data management system designed for both business and home applications.

System: MAC, II, PLUS, SE, XL
Minimum Memory: 512K
Medium: 3 1/2-inch disk
ISPN: 72775-675   **Price: $69.95**

SOFTWARE DISCOVERIES INC
RECORD HOLDER PLUS (VER. 3.0)

Single file data manager that allows variable length text data, color and graphics. Useful for forms and mailing labels.

System: MAC, II, PLUS, SE, XL
Minimum Memory: 512K
Medium: 3 1/2-inch disk
ISPN: 72775-501   **Price: $69.95**

EXODUS SOFTWARE
RETRIEVER (VER. 1.01)

A desk accessory non-relational database that allows the user to access lists of information from any application.

System: MAC, II, PLUS, SE, XL
Minimum Memory: 512K
Medium: 3 1/2-inch disk
ISPN: 91576-600   **Price: $89.95**

SPECIALTY SOFTWARE
SPECIALTY DATA DORGANIZER (VER. 1.1)

Allows the user to design reports and labels, mail-merge files, sort data, and create databases.

System: MAC, II, PLUS, SE, XL
Minimum Memory: 1023K
Requires: 800K disk drive, hard disk, Church Organizational Management System (ISPN 95752-605) or Minister Management System (ISPN 95752-060).
Medium: 3 1/2-inch disk
ISPN: 95752-675   **Price: $150.00**

HEIZER SOFTWARE
SUPPLIER DATABASE

Keeps records of supplier number, name, billing address, contact, phone number and shipping address.

System: MAC, II, PLUS, SE, XL
Minimum Memory: 512K
Requires: Microsoft Excel (ISPN 53150-270).
Medium: 3 1/2-inch disk
ISPN: 35175-154   **Price: $8.00**

WOS DATA SYSTEMS, INC.
WOSBASE

Includes facilities for file design, data entry, reporting, mass updates, and exchanging information with other programs.

System: MAC, II, PLUS, SE, XL
Minimum Memory: 512K
Requires: 1-45 users. Hard disk.
Medium: 3 1/2-inch disk
ISPN: 96946-610   **Price: $495.00**

WOS DATA SYSTEMS, INC.
WOSBASE

Includes facilities for file design, data entry, reporting, mass updates, and exchanging information with other programs.

System: MAC, II, PLUS, SE
Minimum Memory: 512K
Requires: Single user. Hard disk.
Medium: 3 1/2-inch disk
ISPN: 96946-610   **Price: $195.00**

845 SYSTEMS/DEVICE/ UTILITY CONTROLLERS

SOFTSTYLE, INC.
BLUESTART (VER. 2.5)

Modifies the Macintosh printer drivers of application software to support printing from a Macintosh on the IBM printers.

System: MAC, II, PLUS, SE, XL
Minimum Memory: 512K
Medium: 3 1/2-inch disk
ISPN: 72235-010   **Price: $45.00**

MAINSTAY
CAPTURE

Saves screen images as a picture in the clipboard or as a PICT file.

System: MAC, II, PLUS, SE, XL
Minimum Memory: 1024K
Medium: 3 1/2-inch disk
ISPN: 46041-100   **Price: $59.95**

T/MAKER CO.
CLICKART-EFFECTS

Consists of four tools, rotation, slant, perspective, and distort, that work with images in files from MacPaint (Ver. 1.5 or earlier).

System: MAC, II, PLUS, SE, XL
Minimum Memory: 128K
Requires: MacPaint (Ver. 1.5 or earlier).
Medium: 3 1/2-inch disk
ISPN: 79465-040   **Price: $49.95**

I O DESIGN INC.
COLORCHART

Stand alone business graphics program that will print and plot color charts and graphs.

System: MAC, II, PLUS, SE, XL
Minimum Memory: 512K
Medium: 3 1/2-inch disk
ISPN: 36753-090   **Price: $39.95**

SOFTSTYLE, INC.
COLORMATE (VER. 2.151)

Coloring and color printing software for the Macintosh, the ImageWriter II and the NEC Color Pinwriter.

System: MAC, II, PLUS, SE, XL
Minimum Memory: 512K
Medium: 3 1/2-inch disk
ISPN: 72235-014   **Price: $75.00**

I O DESIGN INC.
COLORPRINT

Allows you to print MacPaint and MacDraw documents in color using any ImageWriter printer.

System: MAC, II, PLUS, SE, XL
Minimum Memory: 512K
Medium: 3 1/2-inch disk
ISPN: 36753-095   **Price: $29.95**

DIGITAL VISION, INC.
COMPUTEREYES

Provides a slow-scan video digitizer that connects to any standard video source.

System: MAC, II, PLUS, SE, XL
Minimum Memory: 1024K
Medium: 3 1/2-inch disk
ISPN: 25665-100   **Price: $249.95**

BRAINPOWER, INC.
DATASCAN

Reads bit mapped pictures of graphs and determines the coordinate value of the points.

System: MAC, II, PLUS, SE, XL
Minimum Memory: 512K
Requires: Scanner.
Medium: 3 1/2-inch disk
ISPN: 08413-210   **Price: $199.95**

SOFTSTYLE, INC.
EPSTART (VER. 2.5)

Allows Epson FX-80, FX-100 or JX-80: LQ 800, LQ 1000, LQ 1500, LQ 2500 printers to be used with the Macintosh.

System: MAC, II, PLUS, SE, XL
Minimum Memory: 512K
Medium: 3 1/2-inch disk
ISPN: 72235-025   **Price: $45.00**

ORANGE MICRO, INC.
GRAPPLER LQ (VER. 1.7)

Allows you to connect Macintosh Plus, SE or II computers with 24-pin dot matrix printers and parallel laser printers.

System: MAC, II, PLUS, SE, XL
Minimum Memory: 1024K
Medium: 3 1/2-inch disk
ISPN: 58668-140   **Price: $149.00**

ORANGE MICRO, INC.
GRAPPLER LS (VER. 1.7)

A printer interface for Hewlett Packard DeskJet, LaserJet or Serial Laser printers to connect with Macintosh Plus, SE or II computers.

System: MAC, II, PLUS, SE, XL
Minimum Memory: 1024K
Medium: 3 1/2-inch disk
ISPN: 58668-150   **Price: $149.00**

GDT SOFTWORKS, INC.
JETLINK EXPRESS (VER. 1.0)

A Macintosh printer driver for the Hewlett Packard DeskJet, LaserJet Series and compatible laser printers.

System: MAC, II, PLUS, SE, XL
Minimum Memory: 1024K
Requires: Hard disk, 1MB on laser printer.
Medium: 3 1/2-inch disk
ISPN: 92112-400   **Price: $149.00**

SOFTSTYLE, INC.
JETSTART (VER. 2.5)

Modifies the Macintosh printer drivers to support ThinkJet. Will also reverse the process.

System: MAC, II, PLUS, SE, XL
Minimum Memory: 512K
Requires: Standard Macintosh printer cable and a ThinkJet serial printer.
Medium: 3 1/2-inch disk
ISPN: 72235-035   **Price: $45.00**

SYMANTEC
LASERSPEED (VER. 1.5)

A no-wait print spooler software for the Apple LaserWriter.

System: MAC, II, PLUS, SE, XL
Minimum Memory: 512K
Requires: 1-5 users. LaserWriter.
Medium: 3 1/2-inch disk
ISPN: 77413-200   **Price: $499.00**

SYMANTEC
LASERSPEED (VER. 1.5)

A no-wait print spooler software for the Apple LaserWriter.

System: MAC, II, PLUS, SE, XL
Minimum Memory: 512K
Requires: LaserWriter.
Medium: 3 1/2-inch disk
ISPN: 77413-200   **Price: $99.00**

SOFTSTYLE, INC.
LASERSTART (VER. 2.5) (WITH CABLE)

Software to modify the Macintosh printer drivers to fully support the LaserJet. Supports all Macintosh text and graphics.

System: MAC, II, PLUS, SE, XL
Minimum Memory: 512K
Medium: 3 1/2-inch disk
ISPN: 72235-045   **Price: $95.00**

THUNDERWARE, INC.
LIGHTNINGSCAN (VER. 5.0)

A hand help scanner with software that features real-time display, image editing tools, and contrast and brightness controls.

System: II, PLUS, SE, XL
Minimum Memory: 512K
Requires: 800K disk drive. System 6.02 or greater.
Medium: 3 1/2-inch disk
ISPN: 81750-400   **Price: $549.00**

GRAMMAR ENGINE, INC.
LOADROM

A microprocessor cross development tool that accepts binary and popular hex record formats for loading ROM code.

System: MAC, II, PLUS, SE, XL
Minimum Memory: 512K
Medium: 3 1/2-inch disk
ISPN: 33407-475
Price: Please contact the software publisher.

GDT SOFTWORKS, INC.
MAC DAISY LINK (VER. 1.1.3)

A single universal printer driver which can be used with nearly any daisywheel printer or properly interfaced typewriter.

System: II, PLUS, SE, XL
Minimum Memory: 128K
Requires: Serial to parallel converter for parallel printer.
Medium: 3 1/2-inch disk
ISPN: 92112-600   **Price: $82.00**

GDT SOFTWORKS, INC.
MAC DAISY LINK (VER. 1.1.3) (WITH CABLE)

A single universal printer driver and cable which can be used with any daisywheel printer or properly interfaced typewriter.

System: MAC, II, PLUS, SE, XL
Minimum Memory: 512K
Requires: 400K disk, serial to parallel converter for parallel printer. Must specify Macintosh model, printer model and number when ordering.
Medium: 3 1/2-inch disk
ISPN: 92112-605   **Price: $104.95**

SOFTSTYLE, INC.
MACENHANCER

Allows connection of printers, plotters, computers and AppleTalk Artwork to your Macintosh. Combined hardware and software.

System: MAC, II, PLUS, SE, XL
Minimum Memory:
Medium: 3 1/2-inch disk
ISPN: 72235-050   **Price: $245.00**

CREATIVE SOLUTIONS, INC.
MACFORTH TOOLS DISK I

Window/control/menu builder, smart controls, fast floating point, and many other utilities. Runs with MacForth Plus.

System: MAC, II, PLUS, SE, XL
Minimum Memory: 512K
Medium: 3 1/2-inch disk
ISPN: 20700-595   **Price: $30.00**

COMPSERVCO
MACPALETTE (VER. 1.2)

A color printer driver prints graphics and text from almost all Macintosh programs using the ImageWriter II and four color ribbons.

System: MAC, II, PLUS, SE, XL
Minimum Memory: 512K
Medium: 3 1/2-inch disk
ISPN: 15025-705   **Price: $69.00**

COMPSERVCO
MACPALLETTE LQ (VER. 1.0)

Color printer driver prints object oriented graphics and text using the ImageWriter LQ four-color ribbon.

System: II, PLUS, SE, XL
Minimum Memory: 512K
Requires: ImageWriter LQ.
Medium: 3 1/2-inch disk
ISPN: 15025-700   **Price: $149.00**

COMPUTER PHONE SOLUTIONS
MACPBX (VER. 1.0)

Integrates an Apple Macintosh computer with any PBX system to simplify the control of PBX features.

System: MAC, II, PLUS, SE, XL
Minimum Memory: 512K
Medium: 3 1/2-inch disk
ISPN: 17216-500   **Price: $249.00**

COMPSERVCO
MACPLOT PROFESSIONAL (VER. 3.4.5)

Interfaces Macintosh object oriented programs with 57 A to E size plotters. Easily plots color even with single pen plotters.

System: MAC, II, PLUS, SE, XL
Minimum Memory: 512K
Medium: 3 1/2-inch disk
ISPN: 15025-800   **Price: $399.00**

COMPSERVCO
MACPLOT STANDARD

Interfaces Macintosh object oriented graphics programs with 25 A and B size plotters. Plots color even with single pen plotters.

System: MAC, II, PLUS, SE, XL
Minimum Memory: 512K
Medium: 3 1/2-inch disk
ISPN: 15025-805   **Price: $199.00**

STAR MICRONICS AMERICA, INC.
MACSTAR II

Hardware/software package that enables Macintosh users to use the company's line of printers.

System: MAC
Minimum Memory: 128K
Medium: 3 1/2-inch disk
ISPN: 75831-500   **Price: $99.95**

VAMP, INC.
MCCAD GERBER VIEW/ TRANSLATOR (VER. 1.0)

Translates Gerber Photoplot files into McCad format for viewing prior to plot or editing on McCad PCB software.

System: MAC, II, PLUS, SE, XL
Minimum Memory: 512K
Medium: 3 1/2-inch disk
ISPN: 84771-460   **Price: $895.00**

VAMP, INC.
MCCAD TO GERBER TRANSLATOR

Covert McCad print circuit design database to Gerber Database for photoplotting. Selection of single or multiple aperture mode.

System: MAC, II, PLUS, SE, XL
Minimum Memory: 512K
Medium: 3 1/2-inch disk
ISPN: 84771-520   **Price: $175.00**

MESA GRAPHICS, INC.
MESA GRAPHICS PLOTTER UTILITY

A plotting application that produces accurate engineering and architectural drawing, and high-quality scientific plots in color.

System: MAC, II, PLUS, SE, XL
Minimum Memory: 512K
Requires: MacPaint or application that can save as a Pict document, copy to clipboard, or save as a MacPaint document, plotter w/RS232C opt.
Medium: 3 1/2-inch disk
ISPN: 49173-550   **Price: $125.00**

CAERE CORP.
OMNIPAGE

Gives desktop scanners the capability of recognizing any page, plus a mix of images, fonts and variable font sizes.

System: MAC, II, PLUS, SE, XL
Minimum Memory: 1024K
Requires: Scanner.
Medium: 3 1/2-inch disk
ISPN: 10394-500   **Price: $795.00**

BV ENGINEERING
PDP2-SCIENTIFIC/FINANCIAL GRAPH PLOTTING PROGRAM

Makes multi-color scientific and financial graphs on pen plotters.

System: II, PLUS, SE, XL
Minimum Memory: 512K
Medium: 3 1/2-inch disk
ISPN: 09875-600   **Price: $95.00**

SOFTSTYLE, INC.
PLOTSTART (VER. 2.55)

A color plotter driver for the Macintosh which supports the HP ColorPro, 7440A, and 7550A plotters.

System: II, PLUS, SE, XL
Minimum Memory:
Medium: 3 1/2-inch disk
ISPN: 72235-225   **Price: $125.00**

STEVENS CREEK SOFTWARE
PLOTVIEW (VER. 1.2)

HP plotter emulation which takes Hewlett Packard Graphics Language commands and converts them into PICT images.

System: MAC, II, PLUS, SE, XL
Minimum Memory: 512K
Medium: 3 1/2-inch disk
ISPN: 76253-500   **Price: $79.95**

STEVENS CREEK SOFTWARE
PLOTVIEW (VER. 1.2)

HP plotter emulation which takes Hewlett Packard Graphics Language commands and converts them into PICT images.

System: MAC, II, PLUS, SE, XL
Minimum Memory: 512K
Requires: Mini-Site license includes 5 disks and manuals.
Medium: 3 1/2-inch disk
ISPN: 76253-500   **Price: $279.95**

GDT SOFTWORKS, INC.
PRINT LINK

Allows a choice of dot matrix or ink jet printers to function with the Macintosh computer. Each printer requires a different driver.

System: MAC, II, PLUS, SE, XL
Minimum Memory: 512K
Requires: Serial to parallel converter for parallel printers. Must specify printer type and Macintosh model when ordering.
Medium: 3 1/2-inch disk
ISPN: 92112-650   **Price: $62.00**

GDT SOFTWORKS, INC.
PRINT LINK (WITH CABLE)

Allows a choice of popular Dot Matrix or Ink Jet printers with the Macintosh Personal Computer. Price includes cable.

System: MAC, II, PLUS, SE, XL
Minimum Memory: 512K
Requires: 400K disk, serial to parallel converter for parallel printers. Must specify Macintosh model, printer model and number when ordering.
Medium: 3 1/2-inch disk
ISPN: 92112-651   **Price: $84.95**

DATAPAK SOFTWARE, INC.
PRINTER INTERFACE II (VER. 1.0)

A printer driver construction set that allows the Macintosh to print text from non-Apple, serial interface printers.

System: MAC, II, PLUS, SE, XL
Minimum Memory: 128K
Medium: 3 1/2-inch disk
ISPN: 23762-600   **Price: $89.00**

DATAPAK SOFTWARE, INC.
PRINTER INTERFACE III (VER. 1.0)

A printer driver construction kit that allows the Macintosh or Amiga to print from Hewlett Packard's Deskjet printer.

System: MAC, II, PLUS, SE, XL
Minimum Memory: 128K
Requires: Special cable from DataPak for $29.95.
Medium: 3 1/2-inch disk
ISPN: 23762-610   **Price: $125.00**

DATAPAK SOFTWARE, INC.
PRINTER INTERFACE IV (VER. 1.0)

Allows the Macintosh to print using any HP LaserJet, combines the LaserJet's built-in and cartridge fonts with any Mac fonts.

System: MAC, II, PLUS, SE, XL
Minimum Memory: 512K
Medium: 3 1/2-inch disk
ISPN: 23762-620   **Price: $125.00**

SOFTSTYLE, INC.
PRINTWORKS FOR MAC-DAISYWHEEL VERSION (VER. 3.0)

Printer driver package that allows gives daisywheel printing compatibility with all Macintosh applications which print text.

System: MAC
Minimum Memory: 512K
Medium: 3 1/2-inch disk
ISPN: 72235-005   **Price: $95.00**

SOFTSTYLE, INC.
PRINTWORKS FOR MAC-DOT MATRIX VERSION (VER. 3.5)

Printer driver package for Macintosh users allowing full support of over 20 dot matrix and inkjet printers including the HP PaintJet.

System: MAC, II, PLUS, SE, XL
Minimum Memory: 512K
Requires: Macintosh XL-under MacWorks (ISPN 77034-500) environment. Standard Mac supports only ImageWriter or compatible dot-matrix printers.
Medium: 3 1/2-inch disk
ISPN: 72235-085   **Price: $75.00**

SOFTSTYLE, INC.
PRINTWORKS FOR MAC-LASER VERSION (VER. 3.0)

Printer driver package allowing full support of laser printers such as the HP LaserJet, Canon, Epson, NCR, Xerox and compatibles.

System: MAC, II, PLUS, SE, XL
Minimum Memory: 512K
Medium: 3 1/2-inch disk
ISPN: 72235-090   **Price: $145.00**

MAGNUM SOFTWARE
SLIDE SHOW MAGICIAN (VER. 1.3) SE

Make and run professional looking presentations on the Macintosh including sound, and music.

System: MAC, II, PLUS, SE, XL
Minimum Memory: 512K
Medium: 3 1/2-inch disk
ISPN: 46032-150   **Price: $59.95**

NEC INFORMATION SYSTEMS, INC.
SPINMAC

Allows letter quality printing with a NEC Spinwriter. Price includes cable.

System: MAC, II, PLUS, SE, XL
Minimum Memory: 128K
Medium: 3 1/2-inch disk
ISPN: 56400-900   **Price: $99.00**

MENLO BUSINESS SYSTEMS, INC.
SPOOL-AT

Integrates Tandem document spooling and printing with the Macintosh standard printing capabilities.

System: MAC, II, PLUS, SE, XL
Minimum Memory:
Medium: 3 1/2-inch disk
ISPN: 48969-650   **Price: $1290.00**

SUPERMAC SOFTWARE
SUPERSPOOL (VER. 5.0)

Print spooler designed for use with the direct-connect ImageWriter that works with all Macintosh applications.

System: MAC, PLUS, SE, XL
Minimum Memory: 512K
Requires: 800K disk drive.
Medium: 3 1/2-inch disk
ISPN: 77125-800   **Price: $99.95**

PERIPHERALS COMPUTERS SUPPLIES, INC.
TEKPRINT (VER. 2.0)
Zooms, rotates and prints high-resolution Tektronix 4014 graphics on ImageWriter or LaserWriter printers.

System: MAC, II, PLUS, SE, XL
Minimum Memory: 128K
Requires: Versaterm (ISPN 60539-900) or Versaterm-Pro (ISPN 60539-650).
Medium: 3 1/2-inch disk
ISPN: 60539-650   **Price: $79.00**

CTA, INC.
TEXTPERT (VER. 3.0)
Captures and stores text and symbols from a wide range of media including typed documents, newspapers and books from scanned input.

System: MAC, II, PLUS, SE, XL
Minimum Memory: 1024K
Requires: Scanner.
Medium: 3 1/2-inch disk
ISPN: 20969-700   **Price: $995.00**

THUNDERWARE, INC.
THUNDERSCAN FOR THE MACINTOSH (VER. 5.0)
High-resolution digitizer for Macintosh. Turns any ImageWriter printer into a graphics tool by replacing ribbon cartridge.

System: II, PLUS, SE
Minimum Memory: 1024K
Requires: ImageWriter or ImageWriter II. State which Macintosh is being used when ordering.
Medium: 3 1/2-inch disk
ISPN: 81750-750   **Price: $249.00**

SOFTSTYLE, INC.
TI-START (VER. 2.5) (WITH CABLE)
Completely compatible printer driver for the Macintosh to support Texas Instrument printers. Supports Macintosh text and graphics.

System: MAC, II, PLUS, SE, XL
Minimum Memory: 512K
Requires: TI 850/860, TI 850XL/860XL or TI 855/865 printer.
Medium: 3 1/2-inch disk
ISPN: 72235-150   **Price: $75.00**

SOFTSTYLE, INC.
TOSHSTART (VER. 2.5)
Completely compatible printer driver for the Macintosh to support Toshiba printers. Supports all Macintosh text and graphics.

System: MAC, II, PLUS, SE, XL
Minimum Memory: 512K
Medium: 3 1/2-inch disk
ISPN: 72235-200   **Price: $45.00**

VOYAGER CO.
VOYAGER VIDEO DA (VER. 1.0)
A laserdisc player remote control desk accessory.

System: MAC, II, PLUS, SE, XL
Minimum Memory: 1024K
Requires: Laserdisc player with RS 232 interface.
Medium: 3 1/2-inch disk
ISPN: 96647-850   **Price: $49.95**

VOYAGER CO.
VOYAGER VIDEOSTACK (VER. 2.0)
A toolkit for controlling videodiscs from Hypercard with sets of video drivers for Sony, Pioneer and most RS-232 videodisc players.

System: II, PLUS, SE
Minimum Memory: 1024K
Requires: HyperCard (ISPN 03900-300).
Medium: 3 1/2-inch disk
ISPN: 96647-900   **Price: $99.95**

851 SYSTEMS/ DIAGNOSTICS/ ANALYSIS

SOURCEVIEW SOFTWARE INT'L.
INTERACTIVE EVALUATION
Evaluates the quality of software along 16 criterion dimensions.

System: MAC, II, PLUS, SE, XL
Minimum Memory: 512K
Medium: 3 1/2-inch disk
ISPN: 70675-305   **Price: $999.00**

855 SYSTEMS/ INFORMATION RETRIEVAL

BIOSOFT
AUTOBIBLIO (VER. 1.1)
Provides a bibliographic storage and retrieval system for the creation of literature databases.

System: II, PLUS, SE
Minimum Memory: 800K
Medium: 3 1/2-inch disk
ISPN: 28881-130   **Price: $199.00**

SOFTFOCUS
BTREE/ISAM
Contains C function libraries that are intended to be incorporated within application programs. Indexed filesystems can be created.

System: MAC, II, PLUS, SE, XL
Minimum Memory: 512K
Medium: 3 1/2-inch disk
ISPN: 95759-200   **Price: $115.00**

FAIRCOM CORP.
C-TREE AND R-TREE
File handler to store, update and retrieve data written in C language. Also general purpose report generator.

System: MAC, II, PLUS, SE, XL
Minimum Memory: 512K
Medium: 3 1/2-inch disk
ISPN: 91808-300   **Price: $650.00**

NILES AND ASSOCIATES
ENDNOTE (VER. 1.1)
Contains a reference database and bibliography maker that holds up to 32000 references, and builds bibliographies automatically.

System: II, PLUS, SE
Minimum Memory: 512K
Requires: 800K disk drive.
Medium: 3 1/2-inch disk
ISPN: 56952-200   **Price: $129.00**

HEIZER SOFTWARE
FILE RECOVERY MACRO
Automatically recovers all the values from a damaged file and enters them in a new macro or worksheet.

System: II, PLUS, SE
Minimum Memory: 512K
Requires: Microsoft Excel (ISPN 53150-270).
Medium: 3 1/2-inch disk
ISPN: 35175-506   **Price: $18.00**

NASHOBA SYSTEMS
FILEMAKER PLUS (VER. 2.1)
Finds, records, indexes and formats fields, text or graphics.

System: MAC, II, PLUS, SE, XL
Minimum Memory: 512K
Requires: Two 400K drives or one 800K drive.
Medium: 3 1/2-inch disk
ISPN: 55970-375   **Price: $295.00**

MICROLYTICS, INC.
GOFER (VER. 1.0)
Finds and retrieves files and text within floppy or hard disks. Reduces files, searches and copies text.

System: MAC, II, PLUS, SE, XL
Minimum Memory: 512K
Medium: 3 1/2-inch disk
ISPN: 52573-500   **Price: $79.95**

TDI SOFTWARE
GRID
Used to store and access variable length records in a file by variable length key strings.

System: MAC
Minimum Memory: 512K
Medium: 3 1/2-inch disk
ISPN: 79965-300   **Price: $49.95**

INT'L. DATA ACQUISITION & CONTROL, INC.
MACONTROL-IDAC/1000
Makes data acquisition and control as simple as using a spreadsheet.

System: MAC, II, PLUS, SE, XL
Minimum Memory: 512K
Medium: 3 1/2-inch disk
ISPN: 39793-100   **Price: $695.00**

SYMMETRY CORP.

PICTUREBASE (VER. 1.2)

Organizes Macintosh clip art (paint, pict or pict/embedded postscript) and documents into a library of pictures.

System: MAC, II, PLUS, SE, XL
Minimum Memory: 512K
Medium: 3 1/2-inch disk
ISPN: 77437-550   **Price: $99.00**

VIRGINIA SYSTEMS SOFTWARE

ROUNDUP! (VER. 3.0)

Searches the contents of a disk for a given search string, eliminating the need to remember file names.

System: MAC, II, PLUS, SE, XL
Minimum Memory: 1024K
Requires: 800K disk drive.
Medium: 3 1/2-inch disk
ISPN: 85284-050   **Price: $49.95**

VIRGINIA SYSTEMS SOFTWARE

SONAR (VER. 4.8)

Scans thousands of documents at one time, searches at over 15,000 pages per minute on a Mac II, and indexes and analyzes documents.

System: MAC, II, PLUS, SE, XL
Minimum Memory: 1024K
Requires: 800K disk drive.
Medium: 3 1/2-inch disk
ISPN: 85284-100   **Price: $295.00**

VIRGINIA SYSTEMS SOFTWARE

SONAR PROFESSIONAL (VER. 2.0)

A high-speed text retrieval system capable of searching an entire disk for all references to a particular topic, word or phrase.

System: MAC, II, PLUS, SE, XL
Minimum Memory: 1024K
Requires: 800K disk drive.
Medium: 3 1/2-inch disk
ISPN: 85284-110   **Price: $795.00**

861 SYSTEMS/ OPERATING SYSTEMS

APDA

ARABIC MACINTOSH SYSTEM SOFTWARE (VER. 1.1)

A transparent Arabic system enabling the input, display and editing of Arabic characters when using existing Macintosh applications.

System: MAC, II, PLUS, SE, XL
Minimum Memory: 1024K
Medium: 3 1/2-inch disk
ISPN: 03749-115   **Price: $12.25**

APDA

AUSTRALIAN MACINTOSH SYSTEM SOFTWARE X-5.0

Contains an Australian version of Macintosh System Software (Ver. 5.0). Includes extensive release notes.

System: MAC, II, PLUS, SE, XL
Minimum Memory: 512K
Medium: 3 1/2-inch disk
ISPN: 03749-157   **Price: $17.50**

APDA

BRITISH MACINTOSH SYSTEM SOFTWARE B-5.0

Contains a British version of the Macintosh System Software (Ver. 5.0). Includes extensive release notes.

System: II, PLUS, SE
Minimum Memory: 512K
Medium: 3 1/2-inch disk
ISPN: 03749-158   **Price: $17.50**

APDA

CANADIAN FRENCH MACINTOSH SYSTEM SOFTWARE C-5.0

Contains a French-Canadian version of the Macintosh System Software (Ver. 5.0). Includes extensive release notes.

System: MAC, II, PLUS, SE, XL
Minimum Memory: 512K
Medium: 3 1/2-inch disk
ISPN: 03749-160   **Price: $17.50**

APDA

DANISH MACINTOSH SYSTEM SOFTWARE DK-5.0

Contains a Danish version of the Macintosh System Software (Ver. 5.0). Includes extensive release notes.

System: MAC, II, PLUS, SE, XL
Minimum Memory: 512K
Medium: 3 1/2-inch disk
ISPN: 03749-257   **Price: $17.50**

PBI SOFTWARE

DESKSCENE

Utility that customizes the Macintosh desktop screen.

System: MAC, II, PLUS, SE, XL
Minimum Memory:
Medium: 3 1/2-inch disk
ISPN: 59937-175   **Price: $29.95**

APDA

DUTCH MACINTOSH SYSTEM SOFTWARE N-5.0

Contains a Dutch version of the Macintosh System Software (Ver. 5.0). Includes extensive release notes.

System: MAC, II, PLUS, SE, XL
Minimum Memory: 512K
Medium: 3 1/2-inch disk
ISPN: 03749-258   **Price: $17.50**

APDA

FINNISH MACINTOSH SYSTEM SOFTWARE K-5.0

Contains a Finnish version of the Macintosh System Software (Ver. 5.0). Includes extensive release notes.

System: MAC, II, PLUS, SE, XL
Minimum Memory: 512K
Medium: 3 1/2-inch disk
ISPN: 03749-259   **Price: $17.50**

APDA

FLEMISH MACINTOSH SYSTEM SOFTWARE FN-5.0

Contains a Flemish version of the Macintosh System Software (Ver. 5.0). Includes extensive release notes.

System: MAC, II, PLUS, SE, XL
Minimum Memory: 512K
Medium: 3 1/2-inch disk
ISPN: 03749-260   **Price: $17.50**

APDA

FRENCH MACINTOSH SYSTEM SOFTWARE F-5.1.

Contains a French version of the Macintosh System Software (Ver. 5.0). Includes extensive release notes.

System: MAC, II, PLUS, SE, XL
Minimum Memory: 512K
Medium: 3 1/2-inch disk
ISPN: 03749-261   **Price: $17.50**

APDA

GERMAN MACINTOSH SYSTEM SOFTWARE D-5.0

Contains a German version of the Macintosh System Software (Ver. 5.0). Includes extensive release notes.

System: MAC, II, PLUS, SE, XL
Minimum Memory: 512K
Medium: 3 1/2-inch disk
ISPN: 03749-357   **Price: $17.50**

PBI SOFTWARE

HFS LOCATOR PLUS

Desk accessory which expands the versatility of the Macintosh HFS by locating, deleting, copying, launching and renaming files.

System: II, PLUS, SE
Minimum Memory: 512K
Medium: 3 1/2-inch disk
ISPN: 59937-360   **Price: $39.95**

APDA

ICELANDIC MACINTOSH SYSTEM SOFTWARE SK 5.0

Contains an Icelandic version of the Macintosh System Software (Ver. 5.0). Includes extensive release notes.

System: MAC, II, PLUS, SE, XL
Minimum Memory: 512K
Medium: 3 1/2-inch disk
ISPN: 03749-358   **Price: $17.50**

APDA

ITALIAN MACINTOSH SYSTEM SOFTWARE T-5.1

Contains an Italian version of the Macintosh System Software (Ver. 5.0). Includes extensive release notes.

System: MAC, II, PLUS, SE, XL
Minimum Memory: 512K
Medium: 3 1/2-inch disk
ISPN: 03749-359   **Price: $17.50**

APDA

KANJI MACINTOSH SYSTEM SOFTWARE (VER. 1.1)

A transparent Japanese system, enabling the input, display, and editing of Japanese characters in existing Macintosh applications.

System: MAC, II, PLUS, SE, XL
Minimum Memory: 1024K
Medium: 3 1/2-inch disk
ISPN: 03749-401   **Price: $12.25**

APPLE COMPUTER, INC.

MACINTOSH SYSTEM SOFTWARE (VER. 6.02)

Contains the current Macintosh operating system and utility programs such as Font/DA mover, Disk First Aid and MacroMaker.

System: MAC, II, PLUS, SE, XL
Minimum Memory: 1024K
Medium: 3 1/2-inch disk
ISPN: 03900-700   **Price: $49.00**

MICROSTAR SOFTWARE LTD.

MVDI-T DEVELOPMENT TOOLKIT

A NAPLPS Virtual Device Interface toolkit for application developers. Supports over 80% of video adapters on the market.

System: MAC, II, PLUS, SE, XL
Minimum Memory: 512K
Medium: 3 1/2-inch disk
ISPN: 53437-200   **Price: $949.00**

APDA

NORWEGIAN MACINTOSH SYSTEM SOFTWARE H-5.0

Contains a Norwegian version of the Macintosh System Software (Ver. 5.0). Includes extensive release notes.

System: II, PLUS, SE
Minimum Memory: 512K
Medium: 3 1/2-inch disk
ISPN: 03749-557   **Price: $17.50**

APDA

SPANISH MACINTOSH SYSTEM SOFTWARE E-5.0

Contains a Spanish version of the Macintosh System Software (Ver. 5.0). Includes extensive release notes.

System: MAC, II, PLUS, SE, XL
Minimum Memory: 512K
Medium: 3 1/2-inch disk
ISPN: 03749-756   **Price: $17.50**

APDA

SWEDISH MACINTOSH SYSTEM SOFTWARE S-5.0

Contains a Swedish version of the Macintosh System Software (Ver. 5.0). Includes extensive release notes.

System: MAC, II, PLUS, SE, XL
Minimum Memory: 512K
Medium: 3 1/2-inch disk
ISPN: 03749-759   **Price: $17.50**

APDA

SWISS FRENCH MACINTOSH SYSTEM SOFTWARE SF-5.0

Contains a Swiss-French version of the Macintosh System Software (Ver. 5.0). Includes extensive release notes.

System: MAC, II, PLUS, SE, XL
Minimum Memory: 512K
Medium: 3 1/2-inch disk
ISPN: 03749-757   **Price: $17.50**

APDA

SWISS GERMAN MACINTOSH SYSTEM SOFTWARE SD-5.0

Contains a Swiss-German version of the Macintosh System Software (Ver. 5.0). Includes extensive release notes.

System: MAC, II, PLUS, SE, XL
Minimum Memory: 512K
Medium: 3 1/2-inch disk
ISPN: 03749-758   **Price: $17.50**

865 SYSTEMS/ PROGRAM/REPORT GENERATORS

MENLO BUSINESS SYSTEMS, INC.

CDUX

Allows users to list (in a variety of ways) the COBOL/Screen COBOL programs affected by a given module or data element change.

System: MAC, II, PLUS, SE, XL
Minimum Memory:
Medium: 3 1/2-inch disk
ISPN: 48969-100   **Price: $4500.00**

HYPERPRESS PUBLISHING CORP

DAN SHAFER'S SCRIPT EXPERT

A HyperCard stack that allows users to write HyperCard scripts by pushing buttons and answering questions.

System: MAC, II, PLUS, SE, XL
Minimum Memory: 1024K
Requires: HyperCard (ISPN 03900-300).
Medium: 3 1/2-inch disk
ISPN: 36737-700   **Price: $79.95**

NORDIC SOFTWARE, INC.

HYPERCONTROL VER-1.0

Increases the printing options for HyperCard and allows more versatility and variety when printing labels and reports.

System: MAC, II, PLUS, SE, XL
Minimum Memory: 1024K
Requires: HyperCard (ISPN 03900-300).
Medium: 3 1/2-inch disk
ISPN: 57028-010   **Price: $59.95**

PRODUCTS DIVERSIFIED, INC.

MAC/FREEFORM (VER. 5.3)

A fourth generation high level programming development interface for ShareBase Relational Database Server Systems from Britton-Lee.

System: MAC, II, PLUS, SE, XL
Minimum Memory: 1024K
Requires: 1-8 users. ShareBase server, modem or other interface to the Britton Lee shared database.
Medium: 3 1/2-inch disk
ISPN: 62334-500   **Price: $11500.00**

ABRAXAS SOFTWARE, INC.

MACYACC (VER. 2.0)

Generates ANSI C source code for building assemblers, compilers, browsers, page description/query languages, language translators.

System: MAC, II, PLUS, SE, XL
Minimum Memory: 512K
Requires: Personal version.
Medium: 3 1/2-inch disk
ISPN: 00367-200   **Price: $139.00**

ABRAXAS SOFTWARE, INC.

MACYACC (VER. 2.0)

Generates ANSI C source code for building assemblers, compilers, browsers, page description/query languages, language translators.

System: MAC, II, PLUS, SE, XL
Minimum Memory: 512K
Requires: Professional version.
Medium: 3 1/2-inch disk
ISPN: 00367-200   **Price: $395.00**

FAIRCOM CORP.

R-TREE REPORT GENERATOR

Works with C-tree File Handler to permit complex, multi-line reports to be produced from single or multiple C-tree data files.

System: MAC, II, PLUS, SE, XL
Minimum Memory: 512K
Medium: 3 1/2-inch disk
ISPN: 91808-500   **Price: $295.00**

MEDIAGENIC/TENPOINT0

REPORTS (VER. 1.2)

Provides a report generator for Hypercard, adding fourteen printing functions.

System: MAC, II, PLUS, SE, XL
Minimum Memory: 1024K
Requires: HyperCard (ISPN 03900-300).
Medium: 3 1/2-inch disk
ISPN: 48702-540 **Price: $99.95**

870 SYSTEMS/ PROGRAMMING DEVELOPMENT AIDS/ TUTORIALS

INDIVIDUAL SOFTWARE, INC.

101 SCRIPTS & BUTTONS FOR HYPERCARD

A collection of HyperCard tools including external commands, games, painting, buttons, scripts, animation and text processing.

System: MAC, II, PLUS, SE, XL
Minimum Memory: 1024K
Requires: HyperCard (ISPN 3900-300).
Medium: 3 1/2-inch disk
ISPN: 37275-010 **Price: $69.95**

TRUE BASIC, INC.

3-DIMENSIONAL GRAPHICS (VER. 1.0)

Contains a graphics library with parallel and perspective projections and calling sequences for simple 3-D work.

System: MAC, II, PLUS, SE, XL
Minimum Memory: 512K
Requires: True Basic Language System (ISPN 82789-671).
Medium: 3 1/2-inch disk
ISPN: 82789-066 **Price: $69.95**

ICONIX SOFTWARE ENGINEERING, INC.

ADA FLOW

An object oriented design tool with Buhr diagrams and a language sensitive editor.

System: MAC, II, PLUS, SE, XL
Minimum Memory: 1024K
Medium: 3 1/2-inch disk
ISPN: 37012-125 **Price: $1995.00**

MERIDIAN SOFTWARE SYSTEMS, INC.

ADAVANTAGE DEBUGGER

Contains a interactive, source-level debugger that sets breakpoints subprogram traces, single-stepping, and subprogram call backtraces.

System: MAC, II, PLUS, SE, XL
Minimum Memory: 2048K
Requires: AdaVantage Compiler (ISPN 49106-100) or AdaVantage Optimizing Compiler (ISPN 49106-125).
Medium: 3 1/2-inch disk
ISPN: 49106-150 **Price: $495.00**

TRUE BASIC, INC.

ADVANCED STRING LIBRARY (VER. 1.0)

Contains tools for pattern matching expression scanning, parsing, text manipulation and associative memories.

System: MAC, II, PLUS, SE, XL
Minimum Memory: 512K
Medium: 3 1/2-inch disk
ISPN: 82789-690 **Price: $69.95**

ADVANCED LOGICAL SOFTWARE

ANATOOL (VER. 3.1)

A case tool implementing structured system analysis which creates dataflow diagrams, data dictionary and pseudo-code specifications.

System: MAC, II, PLUS, SE, XL
Minimum Memory: 512K
Medium: 3 1/2-inch disk
ISPN: 01318-100 **Price: $925.00**

APDA

APPLE FILE EXCHANGE TECH. REF. PACKAGE (VER. 1.0)

Contains the source code and support files to help the user write a translator that can be used with the Apple File Exchange utility.

System: MAC, II, PLUS, SE, XL
Minimum Memory: 512K
Requires: Macintosh System Software (Ver. 5.0).
Medium: 3 1/2-inch disk
ISPN: 03749-045 **Price: $19.95**

APDA

APPLETALK MANAGER UPDATE (VER. 1.0)

Describes changes and bug fixes to the AppleTalk Pascal Interface and contains notes on the AppleTalk Drivers (Ver. 48) and the XPP.

System: MAC, II, PLUS, SE, XL
Minimum Memory: 512K
Requires: Appletalk.
Medium: 3 1/2-inch disk
ISPN: 03749-111 **Price: $13.50**

BOWERS DEVELOPMENT CORP.

APPMAKER-THE APPLICATION GENERATOR (VER. 1.0)

Cuts development time for Macintosh applications by automatically programming user interface (menus, windows, dialogs and alerts).

System: MAC, II, PLUS, SE, XL
Minimum Memory: 512K
Requires: Macintosh Programmer's Workshop C (ISPN 03749-505) or Macintosh Programmer's Workshop Pascal (ISPN 03749-510).
Medium: 3 1/2-inch disk
ISPN: 08326-100 **Price: $295.00**

HEIZER SOFTWARE

AUTOCOMPACTOR

Installs in Home Stack and automatically compacts stacks that are being closed.

System: MAC, II, PLUS, SE, XL
Minimum Memory: 1024K
Requires: HyperCard (ISPN 03900-300).
Medium: 3 1/2-inch disk
ISPN: 35175-105 **Price: $8.00**

JAM TECHNOLOGIES

AUTODIALOG

A set of routines and data types that provide a way to run dialogs specified by the resource editor instead of by programmer code.

System: MAC, II, PLUS, SE, XL
Minimum Memory: 1024K
Medium: 3 1/2-inch disk
ISPN: 41388-100 **Price: $79.00**

MANX SOFTWARE SYSTEMS

AZTEC SDB

An interactive source level debugger which examines variables from any active function and displays values of passed parameters.

System: MAC, II, PLUS, SE, XL
Minimum Memory: 512K
Medium: 3 1/2-inch disk
ISPN: 46856-601 **Price: $125.00**

INTERPROGRAM

BLUE/10-PRECEDENCE ANALYSIS (VER. 4.0)

Deals with precedence analysis and is used at the information and functional design phase for MIS professionals.

System: II, PLUS, SE, XL
Minimum Memory: 512K
Medium: 3 1/2-inch disk
ISPN: 40293-100 **Price: $1875.00**

INTERPROGRAM

BLUE/20-SYSTEM FLOW (VER. 4.0)

Presents an overview of the automated administration with system flowcharts in the technical design phase.

System: II, PLUS, SE, XL
Minimum Memory: 512K
Medium: 3 1/2-inch disk
ISPN: 40293-110 **Price: $1875.00**

INTERPROGRAM

BLUE/30-CHAPIN CHARTS (VER. 2.17)

Creates and maintains Nassi Shneiderman/ Chapin diagrams for computer software development.

System: II, PLUS, SE, XL
Minimum Memory: 512K
Medium: 3 1/2-inch disk
ISPN: 40293-120 **Price: $1875.00**

INTERPROGRAM

BLUE/50-DATAFLOW DIAGRAM (VER. 4.0)

Diagrams data flow according to the Yourdon method for MIS professionals.

System: II, PLUS, SE, XL
Minimum Memory: 512K
Medium: 3 1/2-inch disk
ISPN: 40293-130   **Price: $1875.00**

INTERPROGRAM

BLUE/60-DATA MODEL (VER. 4.01)

Creates and maintains data models for computer software development.

System: II, PLUS, SE, XL
Minimum Memory: 512K
Medium: 3 1/2-inch disk
ISPN: 40293-140   **Price: $1875.00**

INTERPROGRAM

BLUE/80-PROCEDURE FLOW (VER. 4.0)

Creates and maintains procedure flow diagrams for preliminary investigations and feasibility studies.

System: II, PLUS, SE, XL
Minimum Memory: 512K
Medium: 3 1/2-inch disk
ISPN: 40293-150   **Price: $1875.00**

APDA

BOSTON MACWORLD KIOSK HYPERCARD STACKS (VER. 1.3)

A set of HyperCard stacks used at the Boston MacWorld show which can be used as an example for creating new HyperCard stacks.

System: MAC, II, PLUS, SE, XL
Minimum Memory: 1024K
Requires: Two 800K disk drives or a hard disk, HyperCard (ISPN 03900-300).
Medium: 3 1/2-inch disk
ISPN: 03749-143   **Price: $10.00**

TRUE BASIC, INC.

BUSINESS GRAPHICS TOOLKIT (VER. 2.0)

Contains a collection of True BASIC subroutines for generating business graphics.

System: MAC, II, PLUS, SE, XL
Minimum Memory: 512K
Requires: True BASIC Language System (ISPN 82789-671).
Medium: 3 1/2-inch disk
ISPN: 82789-900   **Price: $69.95**

WORKING COMPUTER

BUSINESS TOOLS FOR OMNIS 3 PLUS

A customizable business application which provides customer tracking, inventory control and invoicing.

System: MAC, II, PLUS, SE, XL
Minimum Memory: 1024K
Requires: 800K disk drive, Omnis 3 Plus/Express (ISPN 58775-515).
Medium: 3 1/2-inch disk
ISPN: 96949-100   **Price: $299.95**

TRIO SYSTEMS

C-INDEX/PLUS

A complete data management library for development of data, text and graphic oriented applications in the C language.

System: MAC
Minimum Memory: 25K
Medium: 3 1/2-inch disk
ISPN: 82712-100   **Price: $395.00**

FAIRCOM CORP.

C-TREE FILE HANDLER

Offers portable B+Tree functions in Language C source code, which provide multi-key ISAM file management for C programs.

System: MAC, II, PLUS, SE, XL
Minimum Memory: 512K
Medium: 3 1/2-inch disk
ISPN: 91808-200   **Price: $395.00**

HEIZER SOFTWARE

CALCULATED FIELDS STACK

Creates stacks with calculated fields using a short-hand method for writing and storing formulas in HyperCard.

System: II, PLUS, SE, XL
Minimum Memory: 1024K
Requires: HyperCard (ISPN 03900-300).
Medium: 3 1/2-inch disk
ISPN: 35175-102   **Price: $12.00**

SYMANTEC

CAPPS' PROFESSIONAL EDITOR CONSTRUCTION KIT

Provides programmers with a set of tools for adding line-oriented text editing capabilities to their programs.

System: MAC, II, PLUS, SE, XL
Minimum Memory: 512K
Requires: LightSpeed C (ISPN 77413-240).
Medium: 3 1/2-inch disk
ISPN: 77413-070   **Price: $75.00**

HEIZER SOFTWARE

CLIP IT BUTTONS

Selects and copies artwork into the clipboard.

System: MAC, II, PLUS, SE, XL
Minimum Memory: 1024K
Requires: HyperCard (ISPN 03900-300).
Medium: 3 1/2-inch disk
ISPN: 35175-097   **Price: $5.00**

CLEAR LAKE RESEARCH, INC.

CLR GRAPH 3D LIB

Extension to Basic allowing two and three dimensional rotation, translation and scaling of objects in one or more axes at once.

System: MAC, II, PLUS, SE, XL
Minimum Memory: 512K
Requires: QuickBasic (ISPN 53150-205).
Medium: 3 1/2-inch disk
ISPN: 12891-200   **Price: $35.00**

CLEAR LAKE RESEARCH, INC.

CLR MATHSTATLIB

Extends QuickBasic with more than 20 sorting utilities, matrix operations, statistical functions.

System: MAC, II, PLUS, SE, XL
Minimum Memory: 512K
Requires: QuickBasic (ISPN 53150-205).
Medium: 3 1/2-inch disk
ISPN: 12891-300   **Price: $35.00**

CLEAR LAKE RESEARCH, INC.

CLR SPEECH LIB

Extends QuickBasic to create synthesized speech. Phonetic and English text can be spoken with speech rate, pitch and volume.

System: MAC, II, PLUS, SE, XL
Minimum Memory: 512K
Requires: QuickBasic (ISPN 53150-205).
Medium: 3 1/2-inch disk
ISPN: 12891-400   **Price: $35.00**

CLEAR LAKE RESEARCH, INC.

CLR VW LIB

Plays sophisticated sound-enhanced animation sequences created by VideoWorks from QuickBasic.

System: MAC, II, PLUS, SE, XL
Minimum Memory: 512K
Requires: VideoWorks (ISPN 34925-475) and QuickBasic (ISPN 53150-205).
Medium: 3 1/2-inch disk
ISPN: 12891-500   **Price: $50.00**

CONSULAIR CORP.

CONSULAIR EXAMPLES II

Set of utility programs for Apple Macintosh developers.

System: MAC, II, PLUS, SE, XL
Minimum Memory: 512K
Medium: 3 1/2-inch disk
ISPN: 19231-280   **Price: $50.00**

CONSULAIR CORP.

CONSULAIR UTILITIES

Enhanced utilities package for Consulair C and Apple's Macintosh Development System (MDS).

System: MAC, II, PLUS, SE, XL
Minimum Memory: 512K
Medium: 3 1/2-inch disk
ISPN: 19231-275   **Price: $50.00**

HEIZER SOFTWARE

COUNT BUTTON

Counts the number of occurrences of an item in any field on a specified card, or on all cards with the same background.

System: MAC, II, PLUS, SE, XL
Minimum Memory: 1024K
Requires: HyperCard (ISPN 03900-300).
Medium: 3 1/2-inch disk
ISPN: 35175-099   **Price: $12.00**

HEIZER SOFTWARE

DATA SELECTION METHODS

Contains three methods of selecting and marking information within HyperCard.

System: II, PLUS, SE, XL
Minimum Memory: 512K
Requires: HyperCard (ISPN 03900-300).
Medium: 3 1/2-inch disk
ISPN: 35175-927　　　　**Price: $8.00**

HEIZER SOFTWARE

DATA STATEMENTS TUTORIAL

Presents a method for storing variables in scripts rather than in global variables.

System: MAC, II, PLUS, SE, XL
Minimum Memory: 1024K
Requires: HyperCard (ISPN 3900-300).
Medium: 3 1/2-inch disk
ISPN: 35175-086　　　　**Price: $6.00**

HEIZER SOFTWARE

DATABASE SHELL

Generic database shell ready for uses to import data from an outside source or to enter data.

System: MAC, II, PLUS, SE, XL
Minimum Memory: 1024K
Requires: HyperCard (ISPN 3900-300).
Medium: 3 1/2-inch disk
ISPN: 35175-089　　　　**Price: $6.00**

RAIMA CORP.

DB-QUERY

Provides an SQL-based ad hoc query and report writing system for use with db-VISTA databases.

System: MAC, II, PLUS, SE, XL
Minimum Memory: 256K
Requires: C compiler.
Medium: 3 1/2-inch disk
ISPN: 77831-150　　　　**Price: $695.00**

RAIMA CORP.

DB-REVISE

Allows users to redesign their database, and provides restructuring capabilities for developers.

System: MAC, II, PLUS, SE, XL
Minimum Memory: 256K
Requires: C compiler.
Medium: 3 1/2-inch disk
ISPN: 77831-175　　　　**Price: $695.00**

META SOFTWARE CORP.

DESIGN + DA DEVELOPMENT SYSTEM

Permits writing of desk accessories which interact with a special version of Design to modify text and graphic operations.

System: MAC, II, PLUS, SE, XL
Minimum Memory: 1024K
Requires: C compiler program.
Medium: 3 1/2-inch disk
ISPN: 49215-260　　　　**Price: $2000.00**

TDI SOFTWARE

EDITOR

Contains the source of full screen editor. User may modify source to include any additional features.

System: MAC
Minimum Memory: 512K
Medium: 3 1/2-inch disk
ISPN: 79965-200　　　　**Price: $49.95**

KINKOS ACADEMIC COURSEWARE EXCHANGE

EVENT TUTOR (VER. 1.1)

Helps you learn about 'events,' a concept important in Macintosh programming.

System: II, PLUS, SE, XL
Minimum Memory: 128K
Medium: 3 1/2-inch disk
ISPN: 43025-117　　　　**Price: $7.00**

TDI SOFTWARE

EXAMPLES

Modula-2 example programs showing advanced programming techniques and C programs from ROM Kernel/Intuition translated into Modula-2.

System: MAC
Minimum Memory: 512K
Medium: 3 1/2-inch disk
ISPN: 79965-210　　　　**Price: $24.95**

EXPERTELLIGENCE, INC.

EXPERCOMMON LISP

Programming environment well suited for training and development.

System: MAC, II, PLUS, SE, XL
Minimum Memory: 1024K
Requires: Two disk drives.
Medium: 3 1/2-inch disk
ISPN: 30473-225　　　　**Price: $995.00**

EVOLUTIONARY COMMERCIAL SYSTEMS

EXPRESSFORM

Handles data conversion to and from text, check the input data for validity, size or range, and automatically turns controls on/off.

System: MAC, II, PLUS, SE, XL
Minimum Memory: 128K
Medium: 3 1/2-inch disk
ISPN: 30266-200　　　　**Price: $94.95**

HEIZER SOFTWARE

EXTRACT BUTTON

Copies cards matching specified criteria from one stack into a new stack.

System: MAC, II, PLUS, SE, XL
Minimum Memory: 1024K
Requires: HyperCard (ISPN 03900-300).
Medium: 3 1/2-inch disk
ISPN: 35175-098　　　　**Price: $10.00**

HEIZER SOFTWARE

FAST-FIND SCRIPT

A script that allows users to double-click on any word in a locked field to find the next occurence of that word.

System: MAC, II, PLUS, SE, XL
Minimum Memory: 1024K
Requires: HyperCard (ISPN 03900-300).
Medium: 3 1/2-inch disk
ISPN: 35175-106　　　　**Price: $6.00**

ICONIX SOFTWARE ENGINEERING, INC.

FASTTASK (VER. 1.0)

Provides graphic modeling of finite state machine for real-time system analysis.

System: MAC, II, PLUS, SE, XL
Minimum Memory: 1024K
Medium: 3 1/2-inch disk
ISPN: 37012-080　　　　**Price: $995.00**

FLEXWARE, INC.

FLEXWARE DEVELOPMENT SYSTEM

Allows users to quickly develop customized systems for fast penetration of new markets.

System: MAC
Minimum Memory: 256K
Medium: 3 1/2-inch disk
ISPN: 52468-125　　　　**Price: $795.00**

HEIZER SOFTWARE

FORMAT NUMBER SCRIPT

Converts numerical values to dollar amounts for use in stacks which create reports.

System: MAC, II, PLUS, SE, XL
Minimum Memory: 1024K
Requires: HyperCard (ISPN 03900-300).
Medium: 3 1/2-inch disk
ISPN: 35175-107　　　　**Price: $6.00**

OHM SOFTWARE

FORMS PROGRAMMER (VER. 1.01)

Generates source code of drawn images for printing or display.

System: MAC, II, PLUS, SE, XL
Minimum Memory: 512K
Requires: 400K disk drive.
Medium: 3 1/2-inch disk
ISPN: 57781-200　　　　**Price: $99.00**

KINKOS ACADEMIC COURSEWARE EXCHANGE

FORTHTALK KERNEL

Provides a complete interactive object-based programming environment on the Macintosh computer.

System: II, PLUS, SE, XL
Minimum Memory: 512K
Requires: MacForth (Ver. 3.5 or later).
Medium: 3 1/2-inch disk
ISPN: 43025-165　　　　**Price: $30.00**

KINKOS ACADEMIC COURSEWARE EXCHANGE

FORTHTALK LIBRARY (VER. 1.81F)

A collection of flavors that supports the ForthTalk Kernel program.

System: II, PLUS, SE, XL
Minimum Memory: 512K
Requires: MacForth (Ver. 3.5 or later), ForthTalk Kernel (ISPN 43025-165).
Medium: 3 1/2-inch disk
ISPN: 43025-166 **Price: $25.00**

MENLO BUSINESS SYSTEMS, INC.

FOUNDATION BASYS (VER. 3.6)

A comprehensive on-line transaction processing (OLTP) application development tool box and environment.

System: II, PLUS, SE, XL
Minimum Memory:
Medium: 3 1/2-inch disk
ISPN: 48969-150
Price: Please contact the software publisher.

MENLO BUSINESS SYSTEMS, INC.

FOUNDATION SQL (VER. 1.0)

Helps database administrators control the environment, and gives developers the power to develop effective NonStop SQL applications.

System: II, PLUS, SE, XL
Minimum Memory:
Medium: 3 1/2-inch disk
ISPN: 48969-275
Price: Please contact the software publisher.

BUZZWORDS INT'L., INC.

FOXTOOLBOX (VER. 1.1B)

Converts single-user Foxbase + to a multi-user application with the development tools included.

System: MAC, II, PLUS, SE, XL
Minimum Memory: 1024K
Requires: Foxbase +/Mac (ISPN 31262-285).
Medium: 3 1/2-inch disk
ISPN: 09868-300 **Price: $295.00**

TECHALLIANCE

FREDITOR FORTRAN SOURCE CODE EDITOR (VER. 1.0)

A Macintosh text editor for creating and modifying Fortran source code.

System: II, PLUS, SE, XL
Minimum Memory: 512K
Requires: 800K disk drive.
Medium: 3 1/2-inch disk
ISPN: 80216-200 **Price: $79.95**

ICONIX SOFTWARE ENGINEERING, INC.

FREEFLOW (VER. 3.0)

Computer aided software development tool that supports DeMarco conventions for structured analysis.

System: MAC, II, PLUS, SE, XL
Minimum Memory: 1024K
Medium: 3 1/2-inch disk
ISPN: 37012-100 **Price: $995.00**

HEIZER SOFTWARE

FULL-PAGE SCROLLER

Creates stacks with full-page graphics editing. Allows users to link two cards together and treat them as one card.

System: MAC, II, PLUS, SE, XL
Minimum Memory: 1024K
Requires: HyperCard (ISPN 3900-300).
Medium: 3 1/2-inch disk
ISPN: 35175-090 **Price: $15.00**

MAINSTAY

GRID MANAGER

External procedure that adds grid procedures to V.I.P.

System: MAC, II, PLUS, SE, XL
Minimum Memory: 1024K
Requires: V.I.P. (ISPN 46041-950).
Medium: 3 1/2-inch disk
ISPN: 46041-225 **Price: $59.95**

OWL INTERNATIONAL, INC.

GUIDANCE

Provides context-sensitive access to hypertext documents for developers' Window's (Ver. 2.0) or Macintosh programs.

System: II, PLUS, SE, XL
Minimum Memory: 512K
Requires: Two disk drives.
Medium: 3 1/2-inch disk
ISPN: 58987-357 **Price: $500.00**

HEIZER SOFTWARE

HYPER EXTERNALS I

A HyperCard stack which includes twelve external commands and external functions.

System: MAC, II, PLUS, SE, XL
Minimum Memory: 512K
Requires: HyperCard (ISPN 03900-300).
Medium: 3 1/2-inch disk
ISPN: 35175-947 **Price: $25.00**

ZONE1, INC.

HYPER-XCALL (VER. 1.03)

Enables Fortran subroutines to be called from within HyperCard.

System: MAC, II, PLUS, SE, XL
Minimum Memory: 1024K
Requires: Hard disk or access to file server, HyperCard (ISPN 03900-300) and MacFortran (00368-500).
Medium: 3 1/2-inch disk
ISPN: 87459-300 **Price: $99.00**

ZONE1, INC.

HYPER-XREMOTE (VER. 1.0)

Provides a means to click buttons and perform other functions by remote control with the Kodak DataShow Presentation Remote.

System: MAC, II, PLUS, SE, XL
Minimum Memory: 1024K
Requires: Kodak DataShow Presentation Remote, HyperCard (ISPN 03900-300).
Medium: 3 1/2-inch disk
ISPN: 87459-305 **Price: $65.00**

APDA

HYPERCARD DEVELOPER'S TOOLKIT (VER. 1.0)

Provides information and examples for creating HyperCard stacks and for writing external commands and external functions.

System: MAC, II, PLUS, SE, XL
Minimum Memory: 512K
Requires: MacWrite (ISPN 12784-530), HyperCard (ISPN 03900-300).
Medium: 3 1/2-inch disk
ISPN: 03749-305 **Price: $10.00**

SOFTSTREAM INT'L., INC.

HYPERHIT

Creates structured files that can be randomly searched in fractions of seconds. Makes use of keyed or indexed sequential access files.

System: II, PLUS, SE, XL
Minimum Memory: 1024K
Requires: HyperCard (ISPN 03900-300).
Medium: 3 1/2-inch disk
ISPN: 72232-350 **Price: $195.95**

HEIZER SOFTWARE

HYPERTALK TRICKS

Provides ten useful scripting tricks and techniques including intelligent buttons that know when they were copied.

System: MAC, II, PLUS, SE, XL
Minimum Memory: 1024K
Requires: HyperCard (ISPN 3900-300).
Medium: 3 1/2-inch disk
ISPN: 35175-085 **Price: $10.00**

SOFTWORKS, INC. (CT)

HYPERTOOLS I

Provides 16 tools to aid developers and users in the design of HyperCard stacks. Includes HyperCard 1.2.

System: MAC, II, PLUS, SE, XL
Minimum Memory: 1024K
Medium: 3 1/2-inch disk
ISPN: 74165-300 **Price: $99.95**

SOFTWORKS, INC. (CT)

HYPERTOOLS II

Aids developers and users in the design of HyperCard stacks with 16 additional tools. Includes HyperCard 1.2.

System: II, PLUS, SE, XL
Minimum Memory: 1024K
Medium: 3 1/2-inch disk
ISPN: 74165-310 **Price: $99.95**

POWER UP SOFTWARE CORP.

HYPERTUTOR (VER. 2.0)

A tutorial of HyperCard's programming language, HyperTalk, with 41 lessons that cover all the points of scripting.

System: MAC, II, PLUS, SE, XL
Minimum Memory: 1024K
Requires: HyperCard (ISPN 03900-300).
Medium: 3 1/2-inch disk
ISPN: 61687-300 **Price: $49.95**

OLDUVAI CORP.

ICON-IT! (VER. 1.1)

Assigns familiar icons to represent frequently used menu items, desk accessories, and F Keys.

System: MAC, II, PLUS, SE, XL
Minimum Memory: 512K
Requires: 800K disk drive.
Medium: 3 1/2-inch disk
ISPN: 57812-300   **Price: $79.95**

KINKOS ACADEMIC COURSEWARE EXCHANGE

KAREL GENIE (VER. 1.0)

An integrated, language-oriented environment for Karel the Robot.

System: II, PLUS, SE, XL
Minimum Memory: 512K
Requires: Finder (Ver. 5.5), two disk drives.
Medium: 3 1/2-inch disk
ISPN: 43025-275   **Price: $28.00**

EMERALD CITY SOFTWARE

LASERTALK

Gives user interactive debugging of the PostScript interpreter in the LaserWriter.

System: MAC, II, PLUS, SE, XL
Minimum Memory: 1024K
Requires: PostScript printer connected over AppleTalk.
Medium: 3 1/2-inch disk
ISPN: 28902-400   **Price: $249.00**

INFORMATION BUILDERS, INC.

LEVEL5

Provides an expert-system shell for developing custom applications built around a set of rules and facts.

System: MAC, II, PLUS, SE, XL
Minimum Memory: 512K
Medium: 3 1/2-inch disk
ISPN: 37675-610   **Price: $685.00**

LOGIC PROGRAMMING ASSOCIATES LTD.

LPA SAAG (VER. 1.0)

Combines with LPA MacPROLOG to form a complete general-purpose Macintosh development environment.

System: MAC, II, PLUS, SE, XL
Minimum Memory: 1024K
Requires: LPA MacPROLOG (Ver. 2.5) (ISPN 45287-520).
Medium: 3 1/2-inch disk
ISPN: 45287-400   **Price: $895.00**

CREATIVE SOLUTIONS, INC.

MAC II TOOLS (VER. 3.5X)

Provides MacForth Plus extensions that adds color graphics, 68020 assembler, and 68881 co-processor support.

System: II
Minimum Memory: 1024K
Requires: MacForth Plus (ISPN 20700-590).
Medium: 3 1/2-inch disk
ISPN: 20700-200   **Price: $79.00**

PROFESSOR CORP.

MAC'S CORE SERIES

Teaches how to use and program the Macintosh using Microsoft Basic.

System: II, PLUS, SE, XL
Minimum Memory: 128K
Requires: Microsoft QuickBasic (ISPN 53150-205).
Medium: 3 1/2-inch disk
ISPN: 62925-800   **Price: $139.95**

EXCEL SOFTWARE

MACANALYST (VER. 1.0)

A CASE tool for producing data and control flow diagrams, process specifications, data dictionary and verification reports.

System: II, PLUS, SE, XL
Minimum Memory: 1024K
Medium: 3 1/2-inch disk
ISPN: 91573-450   **Price: $795.00**

APDA

MACAPP-THE EXPANDABLE MAC APPLICATION (VER. 1.1.1)

An object-oriented programming library which implements the standard features common to most Macintosh application programs.

System: MAC, II, PLUS, SE, XL
Minimum Memory: 1024K
Requires: Hard disk, 800K disk drive, Macintosh Programmer's Workshop (ISPN 03749-500) (Ver. 2.0.2), MPW Pascal (ISPN 03749-510) (Ver. 2.0.2).
Medium: 3 1/2-inch disk
ISPN: 03749-511   **Price: $100.00**

EXCEL SOFTWARE

MACDESIGNER (VER. 2.0)

Provides tools for producing data dictionary, structure charts, tree diagrams, cross-reference lists and module descriptions.

System: MAC, II, PLUS, SE, XL
Minimum Memory: 512K
Requires: ImageWriter or LaserWriter printer, 800K disk drive.
Medium: 3 1/2-inch disk
ISPN: 91573-500   **Price: $795.00**

ALSOFT, INC.

MACEXPRESS-LIGHTSPEED C AND PASCAL VERSION

Implements the main event loop, menu-handling, panels, views, splitting, scaling (1-2000 percent), and resizing.

System: MAC, II, PLUS, SE, XL
Minimum Memory:
Medium: 3 1/2-inch disk
ISPN: 02506-410   **Price: $195.00**

ALSOFT, INC.

MACEXPRESS-MPW C AND PASCAL VERSION

Implements the main event loop, menu-handling, panels, views, splitting, scaling (1-2000 percent), and resizing.

System: MAC, II, PLUS, SE, XL
Minimum Memory:
Medium: 3 1/2-inch disk
ISPN: 02506-400   **Price: $195.00**

CREATIVE SOLUTIONS, INC.

MACFORTH PLUS STUDENT

A high speed interactive programming language and operating system that is optimized to take advantage of hardware specifics.

System: MAC, II, PLUS, SE, XL
Minimum Memory: 512K
Medium: 3 1/2-inch disk
ISPN: 20700-592   **Price: $89.00**

APDA

MACINTOSH DEVELOPMENT UTILITIES (VER. 1.0)

Contains 17 tools and utilities for developing, examining, and modifying an application.

System: MAC, II, PLUS, SE, XL
Minimum Memory: 128K
Medium: 3 1/2-inch disk
ISPN: 03749-400   **Price: $25.00**

APDA

MACINTOSH SMALLTALK-80 (VER. 0.4)

Consists of the Smalltalk-80 object-oriented programming language, an integrated programming environment, and a library of utilities.

System: MAC, II, PLUS, SE, XL
Minimum Memory: 1024K
Requires: 800K disk drive.
Medium: 3 1/2-inch disk
ISPN: 03749-509   **Price: $75.00**

JASIK DESIGNS

MACNOSY & DEBUGGER, MAC+/ SE VERSION

Symbolic debugger presents information in formats that are natural and allows user to recognize any underlying patterns.

System: MAC, II, PLUS, SE, XL
Minimum Memory: 512K
Medium: 3 1/2-inch disk
ISPN: 41462-150   **Price: $170.00**

APDA

MACSBUG (VER. 6.0) (BETA)

An assembly-language debugger customized for the Macintosh family of computers.

System: MAC, II, PLUS, SE, XL
Minimum Memory: 512K
Medium: 3 1/2-inch disk
ISPN: 03749-519   **Price: $12.00**

LIGHTSHIP SOFTWARE
MACSCHEME + TOOSMITH (VER. 1.0)

Complete software development featuring the Scheme programming language, a dialect of LISP to develop stand-alone programs.

System: MAC, II, PLUS, SE, XL
Minimum Memory: 1024K
Medium: 3 1/2-inch disk
ISPN: 69162-550   **Price: $395.00**

MANOR OF MICRO, INC.
MANORTOOLS

Adds tools including icon editing, cursor editing, and sound importing and exporting features to HyperCard.

System: MAC, II, PLUS, SE, XL
Minimum Memory: 1024K
Requires: HyperCard (ISPN 03900-300).
Medium: 3 1/2-inch disk
ISPN: 46631-500   **Price: $59.95**

TRUE BASIC, INC.
MATHEMATICIAN'S TOOLKIT (VER. 2.0)

Contains a collection of True BASIC subroutines for mathematical applications.

System: MAC, II, PLUS, SE, XL
Minimum Memory: 512K
Requires: True BASIC Language System (ISPN 82789-671).
Medium: 3 1/2-inch disk
ISPN: 82789-850   **Price: $69.95**

MAINSTAY
MATRIX MANAGER (VER. 1.0)

Adds matrix manipulation and computation capability to V.I.P.

System: MAC, II, PLUS, SE, XL
Minimum Memory: 1024K
Requires: V.I.P. (ISPN 46041-950).
Medium: 3 1/2-inch disk
ISPN: 46041-530   **Price: $95.00**

MMC AD SYSTEMS
MCCLINT (REV. 1.10)

Provides a complete C programming language editing and semantic checking system for program debugging.

System: MAC, II, PLUS, SE, XL
Minimum Memory: 1024K
Medium: 3 1/2-inch disk
ISPN: 54835-130   **Price: $99.95**

MMC AD SYSTEMS
MCCPRINT (REV. 1.02)

Reformats C programming language source code into a user selected format and includes editor and source code highlighting system.

System: II, PLUS, SE, XL
Minimum Memory: 1024K
Medium: 3 1/2-inch disk
ISPN: 54835-140   **Price: $59.95**

APDA
MDS 2.1 UPDATE (VER. 2.1)

Consists of Apple's final update to the Macintosh 68000 Development System, including improvements to selected files.

System: MAC, II, PLUS, SE, XL
Minimum Memory: 512K
Medium: 3 1/2-inch disk
ISPN: 03749-507   **Price: $10.00**

APDA
MEGACORP DEMO STACK (VER. 1.0) (BETA)

Shows developers how to use various features of HyperCard to create stacks or to use as a platform for business-market applications.

System: MAC, II, PLUS, SE, XL
Minimum Memory: 1024K
Requires: 800K disk drive, HyperCard (ISPN 03900-300) (Ver. 1.1 or higher).
Medium: 3 1/2-inch disk
ISPN: 03749-521   **Price: $10.00**

SOFTPLUS
MEMORY MAP (VER. 2.5)

A desk accessory which displays Macintosh global variables, data structures, heaps, resource maps, and general memory information.

System: II, PLUS, SE, XL
Minimum Memory: 512K
Medium: 3 1/2-inch disk
ISPN: 72171-500   **Price: $59.95**

META SOFTWARE CORP.
METADESIGN (VER. 2.3)

Powerful graphics and text processing program for the analysis and design of complex systems.

System: MAC, II, PLUS, SE, XL
Minimum Memory: 512K
Requires: 800K disk drive.
Medium: 3 1/2-inch disk
ISPN: 49215-250   **Price: $250.00**

EXPERT SOFTWARE SYSTEMS N.V.
MIRA

A computer aided software engineering tool for the development of interactive or batch software products in Ada, PL1, Pascal or C.

System: MAC, II, PLUS, SE, XL
Minimum Memory: 128K
Medium: 3 1/2-inch disk
ISPN: 30465-525   **Price: $12500.00**

PALOMAR SOFTWARE, INC.
MPW EXAMPLES

Provides source code examples from 'Programming with Macintosh Programmer's Workshop by Joel West (Bantam).

System: MAC, II, PLUS, SE, XL
Minimum Memory: 512K
Medium: 3 1/2-inch disk
ISPN: 59684-300   **Price: $19.95**

PALOMAR SOFTWARE, INC.
MPW EXAMPLES – WITH BOOK

Provides the book 'Programming with Macintosh Programmer's Workshop' by Joel West (Bantam) and source code disk.

System: MAC, II, PLUS, SE, XL
Minimum Memory: 512K
Medium: 3 1/2-inch disk
ISPN: 59684-305   **Price: $39.95**

APDA
MULTIFINDER DEVELOPMENT PACKAGE (VER. 1.0)

Contains Assembly, C, and Pascal interface files for MultiFinder, and describes how to write MultiFinder compatible applications.

System: MAC, II, PLUS, SE, XL
Minimum Memory: 512K
Medium: 3 1/2-inch disk
ISPN: 03749-570   **Price: $12.50**

HEIZER SOFTWARE
MY PLACE BUTTON

A HyperCard button used to mark a spot within any stack.

System: MAC, II, PLUS, SE, XL
Minimum Memory: 1024K
Requires: HyperCard (ISPN 03900-300).
Medium: 3 1/2-inch disk
ISPN: 35175-092   **Price: $8.00**

MINDCRAFT PUBLISHING CORP.
NIBBLE MAC UTILITY PAK

Basic programming utilities that assist the user with aid of sound waves, windows, patterns, cursors, and more.

System: II, PLUS, SE, XL
Minimum Memory: 512K
Requires: Microsoft QuickBasic (ISPN 53150-205).
Medium: 3 1/2-inch disk
ISPN: 53425-780   **Price: $29.95**

HEIZER SOFTWARE
NOTES BUTTON

Operates in the background, allowing users to add pop-up notes anywhere on a card for future reference.

System: MAC, II, PLUS, SE, XL
Minimum Memory: 1024K
Requires: HyperCard (ISPN 03900-300).
Medium: 3 1/2-inch disk
ISPN: 35175-093   **Price: $8.00**

HEIZER SOFTWARE
NUMBER STUFF

A HyperCard stack which can convert numbers to words and set up multiple columns in a single field.

System: MAC, II, PLUS, SE, XL
Minimum Memory: 512K
Requires: HyperCard (ISPN 03900-300).
Medium: 3 1/2-inch disk
ISPN: 35175-970   **Price: $11.00**

KINKOS ACADEMIC COURSEWARE EXCHANGE
PASCAL POINTERS (VER. 1.5)

Interprets and displays pictorially the results of Pascal commands that use pointers and dynamic variables.

System: MAC, II, PLUS, SE, XL
Minimum Memory: 128K
Requires: 800K disk, Finder (Ver. 4.1 or later).
Medium: 3 1/2-inch disk
ISPN: 43025-530   **Price: $17.00**

PALOMAR SOFTWARE, INC.
PICT DETECTIVE (VER. 2.0)

Gives a complete description of any valid QuickDraw picture which can then be modified and recompiled.

System: MAC, II, PLUS, SE, XL
Minimum Memory: 1024K
Requires: Macintosh Programmer's Workshop (ISPN 03749-500).
Medium: 3 1/2-inch disk
ISPN: 59684-400   **Price: $69.95**

HEIZER SOFTWARE
PORT AUTHORITY

A file import/export utility that works like the Font/DA mover to transfer data separated by tabs into and out of HyperCard.

System: MAC, II, PLUS, SE, XL
Minimum Memory: 1024K
Requires: HyperCard (ISPN 3900-300).
Medium: 3 1/2-inch disk
ISPN: 35175-087   **Price: $25.00**

ICONIX SOFTWARE ENGINEERING, INC.
POWER PDL (VER. 1.4)

Contributes to analysis design and maintenance phases of software development, uses pseudo code as design language.

System: MAC, II, PLUS, SE, XL
Minimum Memory: 1024K
Medium: 3 1/2-inch disk
ISPN: 37012-300   **Price: $995.00**

ICONIX SOFTWARE ENGINEERING, INC.
POWERTOOLS (VER. 2.0)

CASE tool set of five programs which span the entire software life cycle and includes real-time support.

System: MAC, II, PLUS, SE, XL
Minimum Memory: 1024K
Medium: 3 1/2-inch disk
ISPN: 37012-350   **Price: $4495.00**

EXPERTELLIGENCE, INC.
PROCYON COMMON LISP (VER. 2.0)

Features full implementation of the Common Lisp standard.

System: MAC, II, PLUS, SE, XL
Minimum Memory: 2048K
Medium: 3 1/2-inch disk
ISPN: 30473-860   **Price: $620.00**

PECAN SOFTWARE SYSTEMS
PROFESSIONAL DEVELOPMENT PACK

Includes a symbolic debugger, print spooler, applications service interface, and compiler. For use with development systems.

System: MAC, II, PLUS, SE, XL
Minimum Memory: 512K
Medium: 3 1/2-inch disk
ISPN: 60356-040   **Price: $199.95**

INVENTION SOFTWARE CORP. (MI)
PROFESSIONAL EXTENDER (VOL. 2) (LIGHTSPEED C)

Provides additional high level Lightspeed C routines to support application development including graphics and lists.

System: MAC, II, PLUS, SE, XL
Minimum Memory: 512K
Requires: Programmers Extender (Vol. 1) (ISPN 38337-205), 800K disk drive.
Medium: 3 1/2-inch disk
ISPN: 38337-305   **Price: $119.95**

MENU® also publishes directories for the **IBM® PC & compatibles** and **Apple® II** and **COMMODORE®** computers. There's a directory for **Local Area Networks**, too.

INVENTION SOFTWARE CORP. (MI)
PROFESSIONAL PROGRAMMER'S EXTENDER (L. PASCAL)

Provides 100% source code version of Volume One and Two of the Programmer's Extender for Lightspeed Pascal.

System: MAC, II, PLUS, SE, XL
Minimum Memory: 512K
Requires: 800K disk drive.
Medium: 3 1/2-inch disk
ISPN: 38337-115   **Price: $395.00**

INVENTION SOFTWARE CORP. (MI)
PROFESSIONAL PROGRAMMER'S EXTENDER (LIGHTSPEED C)

Provides 100% source code version of Volume One and Two of the Programmer's Extender for LightSpeed C.

System: MAC, II, PLUS, SE, XL
Minimum Memory: 512K
Requires: 800K disk drive.
Medium: 3 1/2-inch disk
ISPN: 38337-105   **Price: $395.00**

INVENTION SOFTWARE CORP. (MI)
PROFESSIONAL PROGRAMMER'S EXTENDER (MPW C)

Provides 100% source code version of Volume One and Two of the Programmer's Extender for Turbo Pascal.

System: MAC, II, PLUS, SE, XL
Minimum Memory: 512K
Requires: 800K disk drive.
Medium: 3 1/2-inch disk
ISPN: 38337-130   **Price: $395.00**

INVENTION SOFTWARE CORP. (MI)
PROFESSIONAL PROGRAMMER'S EXTENDER (MPW PASCAL)

Provides 100% source code version of Volume One and Two of the Programmer's Extender for MPW Pascal.

System: MAC, II, PLUS, SE, XL
Minimum Memory: 512K
Requires: 800K disk drive.
Medium: 3 1/2-inch disk
ISPN: 38337-120   **Price: $395.00**

INVENTION SOFTWARE CORP. (MI)
PROFESSIONAL PROGRAMMER'S EXTENDER (TML PASCAL)

Provides 100% source code version of Volume One and Two of the Programmer's Extender for TML Pascal.

System: MAC, II, PLUS, SE, XL
Minimum Memory: 512K
Requires: 800K disk drive.
Medium: 3 1/2-inch disk
ISPN: 38337-125   **Price: $395.00**

INVENTION SOFTWARE CORP. (MI)
PROGRAMMER'S EXTENDER (VOL. 1) (L. PASCAL)

Contains a compiled library of routines in Lightspeed Pascal designed to simplify and enhance Macintosh interface programming.

System: MAC, II, PLUS, SE, XL
Minimum Memory: 512K
Requires: 800K disk drive.
Medium: 3 1/2-inch disk
ISPN: 38337-215   **Price: $119.95**

INVENTION SOFTWARE CORP. (MI)
PROGRAMMER'S EXTENDER (VOL. 1) (MPW PASCAL)

Provides a compiled library of routines in MPW Pascal designed to simplify and enhance Macintosh interface programming.

System: MAC, II, PLUS, SE, XL
Minimum Memory: 512K
Requires: 800K disk drive.
Medium: 3 1/2-inch disk
ISPN: 38337-220   **Price: $119.95**

INVENTION SOFTWARE CORP. (MI)
PROGRAMMER'S EXTENDER (VOL. 1) (TML PASCAL)

Contains a compiled library of routines in TML Pascal designed to simplify and enhance Macintosh interface programming.

System: MAC, II, PLUS, SE, XL
Minimum Memory: 512K
Requires: 800K disk drive.
Medium: 3 1/2-inch disk
ISPN: 38337-225   **Price: $119.95**

INVENTION SOFTWARE CORP. (MI)

PROGRAMMER'S EXTENDER (VOL. 1) (VER. 3.07) (MPW C

Compiled library of routines in MPW C designed to simplify and enhance Macintosh interface programming.

System: MAC, II, PLUS, SE, XL
Minimum Memory: 512K
Requires: 800K disk drive.
Medium: 3 1/2-inch disk
ISPN: 38337-200 **Price: $119.95**

INVENTION SOFTWARE CORP. (MI)

PROGRAMMER'S EXTENDER (VOL. 1) LIGHTSPEED C

Contains compiled library of routines in Lightspeed C designed to simplify and enhance Macintosh interface programming.

System: MAC, II, PLUS, SE, XL
Minimum Memory: 512K
Requires: 800K disk drive.
Medium: 3 1/2-inch disk
ISPN: 38337-205 **Price: $119.95**

INVENTION SOFTWARE CORP. (MI)

PROGRAMMER'S EXTENDER (VOL. 2) (MPW C)

Provides additional high level MPW C routines to support application development including graphics and lists.

System: MAC, II, PLUS, SE, XL
Minimum Memory: 512K
Requires: Programmers Extender (Vol. 1) (ISPN 38337-210), 800K disk drive.
Medium: 3 1/2-inch disk
ISPN: 38337-310 **Price: $119.95**

INVENTION SOFTWARE CORP. (MI)

PROGRAMMER'S EXTENDER (VOL. 2) (MPW PASCAL)

Provides additional high level MPW Pascal routines to support application development including graphics and lists.

System: MAC, II, PLUS, SE, XL
Minimum Memory: 512K
Requires: Programmers Extender (Vol. 1) (ISPN 38337-220), 800K disk drive.
Medium: 3 1/2-inch disk
ISPN: 38337-320 **Price: $119.95**

INVENTION SOFTWARE CORP. (MI)

PROGRAMMER'S EXTENDER (VOL. 2) (TML PASCAL)

Provides additional high level TML Pascal routines to support application development including graphics and lists.

System: MAC, II, PLUS, SE, XL
Minimum Memory: 512K
Requires: Programmers Extender (Vol. 1) (ISPN 38337-225), 800K disk drive.
Medium: 3 1/2-inch disk
ISPN: 38337-325 **Price: $119.95**

INVENTION SOFTWARE CORP. (MI)

PROGRAMMER'S EXTENDER (VOL. 2) LIGHTSPEED PASCAL

Provides additional high level Lightspeed Pascal routines to support application development including graphics and lists.

System: MAC, II, PLUS, SE, XL
Minimum Memory: 512K
Requires: Programmers Extender (Vol. 1) (ISPN 38337-215), 800K disk drive.
Medium: 3 1/2-inch disk
ISPN: 38337-315 **Price: $119.95**

ADDISON WESLEY PUBLISHING CO.

PROGRAMMER'S ONLINE COMPANION (VER. 2.0)

RAM resident database utility for Macintosh developers based upon volumes I-V of Inside Macintosh.

System: MAC, II, PLUS, SE, XL
Minimum Memory: 512K
Requires: 800K disk drive or hard disk
Medium: 3 1/2-inch disk
ISPN: 00900-640 **Price: $49.95**

GUNAKARA SUN SYSTEMS LTD.

PROGRAPH EDITOR/ INTERPRETER (VER. 1.11)

A fully pictorial, very high-level, object-oriented language and programming environment.

System: MAC, II, PLUS, SE, XL
Minimum Memory: 1024K
Medium: 3 1/2-inch disk
ISPN: 33812-600 **Price: $195.00**

SMETHERSBARNES

PROTOTYPER (VER. 2.0)

Allows users to create a Macintosh program in C or Pascal by designing the program with a MacDraw style environment.

System: MAC, II, PLUS, SE, XL
Minimum Memory: 512K
Requires: 800K disk drive, C or Pascal compiler.
Medium: 3 1/2-inch disk
ISPN: 71463-600 **Price: $249.00**

PARAGON CONCEPTS, INC.

QUED (VER. 1.5)

Screen-based programming editor with features specific to programming convenience.

System: MAC, II, PLUS, SE, XL
Minimum Memory: 512K
Medium: 3 1/2-inch disk
ISPN: 59740-700 **Price: $65.00**

CE SOFTWARE

QUICKEYS (VER. 1.1)

A keyboard enhancer which allows the user to define an action on any key on a Macintosh keyboard.

System: MAC, II, PLUS, SE, XL
Minimum Memory: 512K
Requires: 800K double-sided disk drives, ImageWriter, ImageWriter II, or LaserWriter printer.
Medium: 3 1/2-inch disk
ISPN: 11725-400 **Price: $99.95**

MICROMOTION

RELOCATOR

Includes utilities and transient definitions, which makes it possible to run substantial software packages on the Macintosh.

System: MAC, II, PLUS, SE, XL
Minimum Memory: 512K
Requires: MasterForth (ISPN 52750-520).
Medium: 3 1/2-inch disk
ISPN: 52750-650 **Price: $60.00**

TRUE BASIC, INC.

SCIENTIFIC GRAPHICS TOOLKIT (VER. 2.0)

Contains a collection of True BASIC subroutines for generating scientific graphics.

System: MAC, II, PLUS, SE, XL
Minimum Memory: 512K
Requires: True Basic Language System (ISPN 82789-671).
Medium: 3 1/2-inch disk
ISPN: 82789-800 **Price: $69.95**

APDA

SCRIPT MANAGER DEVELOPER'S PACKAGE (VER. 1.0)

Provides hints on writing applications using Script Manager and hints on testing applications for Script Manager compatibility.

System: MAC, II, PLUS, SE, XL
Minimum Memory: 512K
Medium: 3 1/2-inch disk
ISPN: 03749-724 **Price: $25.00**

APDA

SCSI DEVELOPMENT PACKAGE (VER. 1.0)

Contains a sample Small Computer System Interface driver and describes patches to the SCSI Manager in the Macintosh Plus.

System: MAC, II, PLUS, SE, XL
Minimum Memory: 512K
Medium: 3 1/2-inch disk
ISPN: 03749-740 **Price: $10.00**

ARBORWORKS, INC.

SCSI TOOL (VER. 1.1)

Assists in the development of SCSI hardware and software and provides a programming language for executing SCSI Tool procedures.

System: MAC, II, PLUS, SE, XL
Minimum Memory: 512K
Medium: 3 1/2-inch disk
ISPN: 04925-500 **Price: $175.00**

MACTRONICS

SERIAL SHORTCUTS (VER. 1.1)

Contains an application with complete source code in Pascal for programers who want to make use of Mac's serial ports.

System: MAC, II, PLUS, SE, XL
Minimum Memory: 512K
Requires: 400K disk drive.
Medium: 3 1/2-inch disk
ISPN: 93904-700 **Price: $29.95**

PEAT MARWICK ADVANCED TECHNOLOGY
SILVERRUN-DFD (VER. 1.1)

A tool that integrates the creation of data flow diagrams and their documentation.

System: MAC, II, PLUS, SE, XL
Minimum Memory: 1024K
Medium: 3 1/2-inch disk
ISPN: 60287-200 **Price: $1775.00**

PEAT MARWICK ADVANCED TECHNOLOGY
SILVERRUN-ERM

Creates documented and normalized entity-relationship data models.

System: MAC, II, PLUS, SE, XL
Minimum Memory: 512K
Medium: 3 1/2-inch disk
ISPN: 60287-100 **Price: $1775.00**

PEAT MARWICK ADVANCED TECHNOLOGY
SILVERRUN-LDM (VER. 1.0)

Helps database administrators produce data models. Performs integrity checking to identify logical design problems.

System: MAC, II, PLUS, SE, XL
Minimum Memory: 1024K
Medium: 3 1/2-inch disk
ISPN: 60287-300 **Price: $1775.00**

KINKOS ACADEMIC COURSEWARE EXCHANGE
SKEL (VER. 2.4)

A skeleton Macintosh program (written in Lisa Pascal) providing a source code that can be studied and modified.

System: MAC, II, PLUS, SE, XL
Minimum Memory: 128K
Medium: 3 1/2-inch disk
ISPN: 43025-800 **Price: $7.00**

ICONIX SOFTWARE ENGINEERING, INC.
SMARTCHART (VER. 1.0)

Automatically generates structure charts. Contains language sensitive editor.

System: MAC, II, PLUS, SE, XL
Minimum Memory: 1024K
Medium: 3 1/2-inch disk
ISPN: 37012-400 **Price: $995.00**

HEIZER SOFTWARE
SORTLINES BUTTON

Sorts the lines of highlighted text. Can also be installed as a function for scripts to sort the lines of a specified field.

System: MAC, II, PLUS, SE, XL
Minimum Memory: 1024K
Requires: HyperCard (ISPN 03900-300).
Medium: 3 1/2-inch disk
ISPN: 35175-101 **Price: $8.00**

MAINSTAY
SPEECH MANAGER (VER. 1.0)

External procedure set that adds MacInTalk compatible speech procedures to V.I.P.

System: MAC, II, PLUS, SE, XL
Minimum Memory: 1024K
Requires: V.I.P. (ISPN 46041-655).
Medium: 3 1/2-inch disk
ISPN: 46041-655 **Price: $49.95**

HEIZER SOFTWARE
STACK DETECTIVE

Analyzes a stack and provides information on scripts and field values and outputs to a text file.

System: MAC, II, PLUS, SE, XL
Minimum Memory: 1024K
Requires: HyperCard (ISPN 03900-300).
Medium: 3 1/2-inch disk
ISPN: 35175-104 **Price: $10.00**

HEIZER SOFTWARE
STACK EDITOR

Allows the developer to browse, copy, and edit scripts from several HyperCard stacks at once without using the HyperCard script editor.

System: MAC, II, PLUS, SE, XL
Minimum Memory: 512K
Requires: HyperCard (ISPN 03900-300).
Medium: 3 1/2-inch disk
ISPN: 35175-987 **Price: $15.00**

HEIZER SOFTWARE
STACK STATS BUTTON

Documents the properties of all buttons, fields, cards, and backgrounds for any stack.

System: MAC, II, PLUS, SE, XL
Minimum Memory: 1024K
Requires: HyperCard (ISPN 03900-300).
Medium: 3 1/2-inch disk
ISPN: 35175-094 **Price: $12.00**

STAX, INC.
STAX HELPER

Provides a three disk set of hints, tips, buttons, scripts and stacks to assist in the building of a HyperCard stack.

System: MAC, II, PLUS, SE, XL
Minimum Memory: 1024K
Requires: HyperCard (ISPN 03900-300).
Medium: 3 1/2-inch disk
ISPN: 75998-310 **Price: $59.95**

STAX, INC.
STAX SOUND EFFECTS STUDIO

Contains a Soundcap to SND converter, a pitch and speed modifier, a sound library, database, and sound inserter for stackware design.

System: MAC, II, PLUS, SE, XL
Minimum Memory: 1024K
Requires: HyperCard (ISPN 03900-300).
Medium: 3 1/2-inch disk
ISPN: 75998-320 **Price: $59.95**

HEIZER SOFTWARE
SUPER FIND/DELETE

A HyperCard stack which contains two scripts for finding information and deleting cards.

System: MAC, II, PLUS, SE, XL
Minimum Memory: 512K
Requires: HyperCard (ISPN 03900-300).
Medium: 3 1/2-inch disk
ISPN: 35175-991 **Price: $11.00**

ICOM SIMULATIONS, INC.
TMON (VER. 2.8.2)

Tool for examining in detail the inner workings of a Macintosh program, providing a multi-window debugger.

System: MAC, II, PLUS, SE, XL
Minimum Memory: 512K
Medium: 3 1/2-inch disk
ISPN: 82194-650 **Price: $149.95**

CREATIVE SOLUTIONS, INC.
TOOL DISK II

Provides a set of MacForth Plus extensions that include block file browser, MacForth Queues, and Windows lists.

System: MAC, II, PLUS, SE, XL
Minimum Memory: 512K
Requires: MacForth Plus (ISPN 20700-590).
Medium: 3 1/2-inch disk
ISPN: 20700-730 **Price: $30.00**

APDA
TOOLBOX INTERFACE REFERENCE PACKAGE (VER. 2.0.2)

Contains the Assembly Equate files, C Header files, and Pascal Interface files from the Macintosh Programmer's Workshop.

System: MAC, II, PLUS, SE, XL
Minimum Memory: 512K
Medium: 3 1/2-inch disk
ISPN: 03749-704 **Price: $12.00**

KAETRON SOFTWARE CORP.
TOPDOWN (VER. 1.1)

A design tool that helps you create data flow diagrams, structure charts, flow charts, graphic outlines, documentation & procedures.

System: MAC, II, PLUS, SE, XL
Minimum Memory: 1024K
Medium: 3 1/2-inch disk
ISPN: 42296-100 **Price: $295.00**

DISK SOFTWARE, INC.
TURBOGEOMETRY LIBRARY (VER. 2.0)

A library of 2- and 3-D Pascal and C geometric routines for CAD, CAM, CAE and graphics programmers.

System: MAC, II, PLUS, SE, XL
Minimum Memory: 512K
Requires: Turbo Pascal (ISPN 8225-125).
Medium: 3 1/2-inch disk
ISPN: 26225-700 **Price: $149.95**

SHANA CORP.

USER GUIDE

Allows non-programmers to implement on-line help and instructions used through a desk accessory. Supports text/graphics.

System: MAC, II, PLUS, SE, XL
Minimum Memory: 512K
Medium: 3 1/2-inch disk
ISPN: 69475-790 **Price: $79.00**

MERIDIAN SOFTWARE SYSTEMS, INC.

UTILITY LIBRARY

Enables programmer to access command line arguments, perform bit manipulation, transcendental functions and string manipulation.

System: MAC, II, PLUS, SE, XL
Minimum Memory: 1024K
Requires: AdaVantage Compiler (ISPN 49106-100) or AdaVantage Optimizing Compiler (ISPN 46106-125).
Medium: 3 1/2-inch disk
ISPN: 49106-225 **Price: $50.00**

MACRO MIND PUBLISHING

VIDEOWORK OBJECT CODE

Source code of VideoWorks II that programmers can use with their own programming language to access animations.

System: MAC, II, PLUS, SE, XL
Minimum Memory: 512K
Medium: 3 1/2-inch disk
ISPN: 45904-450 **Price: $500.00**

MACRO MIND PUBLISHING

VIDEOWORKS INTERACTIVE

A high-end animation program for creating interactive animations for training, simulations, prototypes, and presentations.

System: MAC, II, PLUS, SE, XL
Minimum Memory: 1024K
Medium: 3 1/2-inch disk
ISPN: 45904-400 **Price: $500.00**

HEIZER SOFTWARE

VISUAL EFFECTS BUILDER

A HyperCard stack which allows users to experiment with different combinations of visual effects.

System: MAC, II, PLUS, SE, XL
Minimum Memory: 512K
Requires: HyperCard (ISPN 03900-300).
Medium: 3 1/2-inch disk
ISPN: 35175-997 **Price: $6.00**

HEIZER SOFTWARE

WORDWISE

Creates custom indexes for HyperCard stacks to be kept on file for reference and instant access.

System: MAC, II, PLUS, SE, XL
Minimum Memory: 512K
Requires: HyperCard (ISPN 03900-300) (Ver. 1.2).
Medium: 3 1/2-inch disk
ISPN: 35175-999 **Price: $30.00**

---

880 SYSTEMS/ SECURITY/ ENCRYPTION, COPY/ RESTORE

MAINSTAY

ANTITOXIN (VER. 1.1)

Provides both decontamination and protection from known viral strains.

System: MAC, II, PLUS, SE, XL
Minimum Memory: 1024K
Medium: 3 1/2-inch disk
ISPN: 46041-050 **Price: $99.95**

MAGIC SOFTWARE, INC.

AUTOSAVE II

Automatically saves the file that you are working on while you work, transparently at a time interval you set.

System: MAC, II, PLUS, SE, XL
Minimum Memory: 1024K
Requires: 800K disk drive.
Medium: 3 1/2-inch disk
ISPN: 45962-102 **Price: $49.95**

CENTRAL POINT SOFTWARE, INC.

COPY II MAC (VER. 7.2)

For archival backups of most protected software without parameter changes. Includes set of utilities, and disk recovery features.

System: MAC, II, PLUS, SE, XL
Minimum Memory: 512K
Medium: 3 1/2-inch disk
ISPN: 11950-500 **Price: $39.95**

OITC, INC.

DECLASS (VER. 2.2)

A data processing support tool for classified data processing to declassify ADP equipment used for national security information.

System: MAC, II, PLUS, SE, XL
Minimum Memory: 512K
Medium: 3 1/2-inch disk
ISPN: 94527-200 **Price: $225.00**

ALSOFT, INC.

DISK EXPRESS (VER. 1.5)

Optimizes the information saved on disks, and gathers all the pieces of files and puts them into contiguous blocks.

System: MAC, II, PLUS, SE, XL
Minimum Memory: 512K
Medium: 3 1/2-inch disk
ISPN: 02506-100 **Price: $49.95**

SUPERMAC SOFTWARE

DISKFIT (VER. 1.5)

A hard disk back-up utility which fits data onto a 'smart set' of floppy disks.

System: MAC, II, PLUS, SE, XL
Minimum Memory: 512K
Requires: Single user. 800K disk drive, hard drive.
Medium: 3 1/2-inch disk
ISPN: 77125-200 **Price: $99.95**

MAGNA

EMPOWER

Protects data by providing both full-featured access control and transparent encryption.

System: MAC, II, PLUS, SE, XL
Minimum Memory: 1024K
Medium: 3 1/2-inch disk
ISPN: 45987-200 **Price: $395.00**

NUVO LABS

FASTTAPE (VER. 3.21)

Backup and restore with the speed, security and convenience that you never thought possible.

System: MAC, II, PLUS, SE, XL
Minimum Memory: 1024K
Requires: Tape drive.
Medium: 3 1/2-inch disk
ISPN: 57484-200 **Price: $129.00**

MAC MASTER

FEDIT PLUS

Will recapture files that have been accidentally deleted.

System: MAC, II, PLUS, SE, XL
Minimum Memory: 512K
Medium: 3 1/2-inch disk
ISPN: 45784-050 **Price: $40.00**

NASHOBA SYSTEMS

FILEFINDER (VER. 2.0)

Desk accessory that lets users copy, delete, rename and get information about files within an application.

System: MAC, II, PLUS, SE, XL
Minimum Memory: 128K
Medium: 3 1/2-inch disk
ISPN: 55970-300 **Price: $24.95**

NEMESIS SYSTEMS

GUARD DOG (VER. 2.0)

A control panel device to protect the desktop. Files may not be moved, duplicated or trashed without using a user-defined sequence.

System: MAC, II, PLUS, SE, XL
Minimum Memory: 512K
Medium: 3 1/2-inch disk
ISPN: 56512-300   **Price: $20.00**

MACTRONICS

GUARDIAN (VER. 1.1)

Protects your files from intruders, by rewriting them according to a code word.

System: MAC, II, PLUS, SE, XL
Minimum Memory: 512K
Requires: 400K disk drive.
Medium: 3 1/2-inch disk
ISPN: 93904-300   **Price: $29.95**

FWB, INC.

HARD DISK DEADBOLT (VER. 1.0)

Protects a hard disk from tampering through encryption. Includes BlackOut, a feature that locks up the computer when not used.

System: MAC, II, PLUS, SE, XL
Minimum Memory: 512K
Requires: Hard disk.
Medium: 3 1/2-inch disk
ISPN: 31697-350   **Price: $89.95**

FWB, INC.

HARD DISK PARTITION (VER. 2.0)

Allows a user to structure any HFS volume into smaller MFS of HFS volumes, separating data files from program files.

System: MAC, II, PLUS, SE, XL
Minimum Memory: 512K
Requires: 800K disk drive.
Medium: 3 1/2-inch disk
ISPN: 31697-395   **Price: $69.95**

FWB, INC.

HARD DISK UTIL

Upload protected software to a hard disk. Compatible with any hard disk.

System: MAC, II, PLUS, SE, XL
Minimum Memory: 128K
Requires: Hard disk.
Medium: 3 1/2-inch disk
ISPN: 31697-400   **Price: $89.95**

PBI SOFTWARE

HD BACK-UP

Back-up utility which copies all data from hard disk drives and other peripherals to floppy disks for all Macintosh computers.

System: MAC, II, PLUS, SE, XL
Minimum Memory: 512K
Medium: 3 1/2-inch disk
ISPN: 59937-350   **Price: $49.95**

PERSONAL COMPUTER PERIPHERALS CORP.

HFS BACKUP (VER. 2.02)

Allows user to backup data from hard disks, save or restore entire disk, selected files, or changes since the last backup.

System: MAC, II, PLUS, SE, XL
Minimum Memory: 512K
Medium: 3 1/2-inch disk
ISPN: 60612-400   **Price: $49.95**

TESSERACT DISTRIBUTING, INC.

MACCOPY (VER. 2.0)

Back-up nearly all of the Macintosh software on the market and deprotects software for hard disk use.

System: MAC, II, PLUS, SE, XL
Minimum Memory: 512K
Medium: 3 1/2-inch disk
ISPN: 81204-500   **Price: $49.95**

KENT MARSH LTD., INC.

MACSAFE (VER. 1.3)

Allows users to protect files by placing them in a 'safe' area of a disk with a password known only to the user.

System: MAC, II, PLUS, SE, XL
Minimum Memory: 512K
Medium: 3 1/2-inch disk
ISPN: 47462-500   **Price: $149.95**

CE SOFTWARE

MASSCOPIER

Turns the Macintosh into an affordable, effective bulk disk duplicator for 400K or 800K diskettes.

System: MAC, II, PLUS, SE, XL
Minimum Memory: 512K
Requires: Systems that use 800K diskettes require 1MB of RAM.
Medium: 3 1/2-inch disk
ISPN: 11725-210   **Price: $20.00**

SUPERMAC SOFTWARE

NETWORK DISKFIT (VER. 1.5)

Utility that backs up and restores AppleShare servers and Tops volumes with access privileges and folder hierarchies intact.

System: MAC, II, PLUS, SE, XL
Minimum Memory: 512K
Requires: 800K hard drive. Network running AppleShare (ISPN 03900-100) or Tops(ISPN 119620-700).
Medium: 3 1/2-inch disk
ISPN: 77125-500   **Price: $395.00**

KENT MARSH LTD., INC.

NIGHTWATCH (VER. 1.03)

A password system that uses six files and two programs to guard the Macintosh even when turned off.

System: MAC, II, PLUS, SE, XL
Minimum Memory: 512K
Requires: 800K disk drive.
Medium: 3 1/2-inch disk
ISPN: 47462-550   **Price: $149.95**

MCTEL, INC.

P/C PRIVACY

Encrypts files to provide privacy 'security' for local storage or transmission over electronic mail systems.

System: MAC, II, PLUS, SE, XL
Minimum Memory: 128K
Medium: 3 1/2-inch disk
ISPN: 60925-600   **Price: $95.00**

BOBBING SOFTWARE

PACKER (VER. 1.0)

Simple utility that compresses files. It can be used to save disk space and also encrypt files.

System: MAC, II, PLUS, SE, XL
Minimum Memory: 128K
Medium: 3 1/2-inch disk
ISPN: 08075-700   **Price: $29.00**

CENTRAL POINT SOFTWARE, INC.

PC TOOLS DELUXE FOR THE MACINTOSH

Contains data recovery, hard disk backup, and disk management tools.

System: MAC, II, PLUS, SE, XL
Minimum Memory: 512K
Medium: 3 1/2-inch disk
ISPN: 11950-605   **Price: $79.00**

FIRST BYTE, INC.

PRO*TEK COPY PROTECTION

A patent-protected copy protection technique which has been tested on several retail products where security has not been broken.

System: MAC, II, PLUS, SE, XL
Minimum Memory: 512K
Medium: 3 1/2-inch disk
ISPN: 30836-400   **Price: $350.00**

SBT CORP.

SBT DMENU/BACKUP-COMPILED (VER. 6.10)

Provides a central user-defined menu for all dBASE applications and a comprehensive backup utility for dBASE data files.

System: MAC, II, PLUS, SE, XL
Minimum Memory: 512K
Medium: 3 1/2-inch disk
ISPN: 68057-076   **Price: $45.00**

SBT CORP.

SBT DMENU/BACKUP-STANDARD (VER. 6.10)

Provides a central user-defined menu for all dBASE applications and a comprehensive backup utility for dBASE data files.

System: MAC, II, PLUS, SE, XL
Minimum Memory: 512K
Medium: 3 1/2-inch disk
ISPN: 68057-075   **Price: $65.00**

SUPERMAC SOFTWARE
SENTINEL (VER. 2.0)

Protects documents, leaving them to remain in original format so they can be backed up and copied without being unlocked.

System: MAC, II, PLUS, SE, XL
Minimum Memory: 512K
Requires: 800K disk drive.
Medium: 3 1/2-inch disk
ISPN: 77125-700　　　　**Price: $295.95**

CREATIVITY PLUS SOFTWARE
SERVER MASC (VER. 1.02)

Multi-launch version of MASC fully AppleShare compatible.

System: MAC, II, PLUS, SE, XL
Minimum Memory: 1024K
Requires: AppleShare FileServer (ISPN 03900-100).
Medium: 3 1/2-inch disk
ISPN: 20762-700　　　　**Price: $195.00**

SYMANTEC
SYMANTEC ANTIVIRUS FOR MACINTOSH (SAM)

A comprehensive virus protection, detection, and elimination program with four protection levels.

System: MAC, II, PLUS, SE, XL
Minimum Memory: 512K
Requires: 800K disk drive. Finder 6.0 or later.
Medium: 3 1/2-inch disk
ISPN: 77413-530　　　　**Price: $99.95**

SYMANTEC
SYMANTEC UTILITIES FOR MACINTOSH (SUM)

Provides utility tools for diagnostics, recovery of deleted files, repair of disks, copying of disks, optimization and partitioning.

System: MAC, II, PLUS, SE, XL
Minimum Memory: 512K
Requires: 800K disk drive.
Medium: 3 1/2-inch disk
ISPN: 77413-525　　　　**Price: $99.95**

SOFTGUARD SYSTEMS, INC.
TRIALDISC (VER. 1.0)

Creates full-function evaluation copies of software which does not require source code changes, and disables after a preset time.

System: MAC, II, PLUS, SE, XL
Minimum Memory: 512K
Requires: Requires format meter disk available from Softguard.
Medium: 3 1/2-inch disk
ISPN: 95751-700　　　　**Price: $400.00**

HJC SOFTWARE, INC.
VIREX (VER. 1.4)

Detects the presence of computer viruses and repairs infected programs. Combats all known Mac viruses.

System: MAC, II, PLUS, SE, XL
Minimum Memory: 512K
Medium: 3 1/2-inch disk
ISPN: 92430-800
Price: Please contact the software publisher.

885 SYSTEMS/SORTING/MERGING

HEIZER SOFTWARE
MAIL MERGE MACRO

A macro for printing customized form letters using data drawn from database records.

System: MAC, II, PLUS, SE, XL
Minimum Memory: 512K
Requires: Microsoft Excel (ISPN 53150-270).
Medium: 3 1/2-inch disk
ISPN: 35175-503　　　　**Price: $15.00**

TRUE BASIC, INC.
SORTING AND SEARCHING LIBRARY (VER. 1.0)

Includes fourteen subroutines for sorting arrays, quicksorts, heapsorts and multi-key sorts.

System: MAC, II, PLUS, SE, XL
Minimum Memory: 512K
Requires: True Basic Language System (ISPN 82789-671).
Medium: 3 1/2-inch disk
ISPN: 82789-575　　　　**Price: $69.95**

HEIZER SOFTWARE
STACK SORTER BUTTON

Performs multi-level sorts on any combination of background fields in a HyperCard stack.

System: MAC, II, PLUS, SE, XL
Minimum Memory: 1024K
Requires: HyperCard (ISPN 03900-300).
Medium: 3 1/2-inch disk
ISPN: 35175-095　　　　**Price: $12.00**

HEIZER SOFTWARE
TILER MACROS

Arranges all open Excel files into tiles, or a cascading set of overlapped files, on the screen, with two macros.

System: MAC, II, PLUS, SE, XL
Minimum Memory: 512K
Requires: Microsoft Excel (ISPN 53150-270).
Medium: 3 1/2-inch disk
ISPN: 35175-515　　　　**Price: $10.00**

890 SYSTEMS/SYSTEM ADMINISTRATION

DOGSTAR SOFTWARE
ARCMAC

Packs, unpacks and maintains groups of files in an archive format.

System: MAC, II, PLUS, SE, XL
Minimum Memory: 512K
Requires: 800K disk drive.
Medium: 3 1/2-inch disk
ISPN: 91246-100　　　　**Price: $40.00**

BROCK SOFTWARE PRODUCTS, INC.
BROCK DISKETTE LIBRARIAN

Disk utility program for cataloging and labeling Macintosh diskettes.

System: MAC, II, PLUS, SE, XL
Minimum Memory: 128K
Medium: 3 1/2-inch disk
ISPN: 08825-300　　　　**Price: $29.95**

PARAGON CONCEPTS, INC.
DISKORDER

Organizes Macintosh files on diskettes and on the hard disk.

System: MAC, II, PLUS, SE, XL
Minimum Memory: 512K
Medium: 3 1/2-inch disk
ISPN: 59740-200　　　　**Price: $55.00**

IDEAFORM, INC.
DISKQUICK (VER. 2.10)

The Macintosh disk librarian exports catalog to data base or word processor. Catalogs hard disk and floppies.

System: MAC, II, PLUS, SE, XL
Minimum Memory: 512K
Medium: 3 1/2-inch disk
ISPN: 37059-200　　　　**Price: $49.95**

B T COMPUTING CORP.
HEAPSHOW (VER. 3.0)

Memory management provides a graphic representation of what goes on inside both the system and application heaps and more.

System: MAC, II, PLUS, SE, XL
Minimum Memory: 512K
Medium: 3 1/2-inch disk
ISPN: 06562-300　　　　**Price: $79.00**

ODESTA CORP.
HELIX MULTIUSER KIT

An add-on networking package that upgrades single user Double Helix II to support multiuser applications.

System: MAC, II, PLUS, SE, XL
Minimum Memory: 1024K
Requires: One MB of RAM and hard disk for host, 512K RAM and one disk drive for guests.
Medium: 3 1/2-inch disk
ISPN: 57709-350　　　　**Price: $495.00**

HEIZER SOFTWARE
LIBRARY STACK

Keeps tracks of borrowed and owned books, and records the due date of library books. Prints a summary report of maintained database.

System: MAC, II, PLUS, SE, XL
Minimum Memory: 1024K
Requires: HyperCard (ISPN 03900-300).
Medium: 3 1/2-inch disk
ISPN: 35175-434　　　　**Price: $20.00**

SOFTVIEW, INC.

MACINUSE (VER. 2.0)

Tracks useage of Macintosh records name application, start time, duration, category and other user-defined data.

System: MAC, II, PLUS, SE, XL
Minimum Memory: 512K
Medium: 3 1/2-inch disk
ISPN: 74106-750   **Price: $79.00**

NEW CANAAN MICROCODE

MDC FINDER

A desk accessory companion to MDC II disk cataloging utility, the DA lets the user search MDC II catalogs from the Apple menu.

System: MAC, II, PLUS, SE, XL
Minimum Memory: 512K
Medium: 3 1/2-inch disk
ISPN: 56573-400   **Price: $29.95**

NEW CANAAN MICROCODE

MDC II (MAC DISK CATALOG II)

A disk cataloging utility for organizing large collections of disks and files for rapid search and retrieval.

System: MAC, II, PLUS, SE, XL
Minimum Memory: 512K
Medium: 3 1/2-inch disk
ISPN: 56573-525   **Price: $49.95**

EXECUCOM SYSTEMS CORP.

MINDSIGHT (VER. 1.2) (APPLE)

A planning and analysis system provides direct access to computer modeling and problem-solving.

System: MAC, II, PLUS, SE, XL
Minimum Memory: 512K
Medium: 3 1/2-inch disk
ISPN: 30400-525   **Price: $249.00**

HEIZER SOFTWARE

SYSTEM INSTALLATION TRACKER

Keeps track of computer networks with a visual schematic, and maintains information on each device on the network.

System: MAC, II, PLUS, SE, XL
Minimum Memory: 1024K
Requires: HyperCard (ISPN 03900-300).
Medium: 3 1/2-inch disk
ISPN: 35175-427   **Price: $25.00**

892 SYSTEMS/SYSTEM UTILITIES

1ST AID SOFTWARE, INC.

1ST AID KIT-HFS (VER. 2.5)

Provides file and disk recovery for diskettes and hard disks including detailed troubleshooting for operating problems.

System: MAC, II, PLUS, SE, XL
Minimum Memory: 512K
Requires: 800K disk drive.
Medium: 3 1/2-inch disk
ISPN: 91829-500   **Price: $99.95**

ICONIX SOFTWARE ENGINEERING, INC.

ASCII BRIDGE

Allows import, export and merge of Freeflow and Fastask files.

System: MAC, II, PLUS, SE, XL
Minimum Memory: 1024K
Medium: 3 1/2-inch disk
ISPN: 37012-150   **Price: $995.00**

BIBLE RESEARCH SYSTEMS

ASCII UTILITY

Transfers The Word text to a ASCII file for use in a word processing program.

System: MAC, II, PLUS, SE, XL
Minimum Memory: 512K
Requires: The Word Processor (ISPN 07546-any version), Greek Transliterator (ISPN 07546-320) or Hebrew Transliterator (ISPN 07546-330).
Medium: 3 1/2-inch disk
ISPN: 07546-200   **Price: $49.95**

APDA

ASYNCHRONOUS LASERWRITER DRIVER (VER. 4.0)

An asynchronous connection which allows the Macintosh computer to print using the LaserWriter and LaserWriter Plus printers.

System: MAC, II, PLUS, SE, XL
Minimum Memory: 512K
Requires: LaserWriter or LaserWriter Plus printer.
Medium: 3 1/2-inch disk
ISPN: 03749-171   **Price: $10.00**

MAGIC SOFTWARE, INC.

AUTOSAVE DA

Will periodically invoke the save command within any program at user defined time intervals. Works with all software programs.

System: MAC, II, PLUS, SE, XL
Minimum Memory: 128K
Medium: 3 1/2-inch disk
ISPN: 45962-050   **Price: $49.95**

INTELLISOFT INT'L.

BOOKMARK (VER. 1.2)

Prevents the accidental loss of work in progress by saving data to a hard disk in the event of loss of power, or a system crash.

System: PLUS, SE
Minimum Memory: 1024K
Requires: 10MB hard disk.
Medium: 3 1/2-inch disk
ISPN: 39038-100   **Price: $99.95**

INTELLISOFT INT'L.

BOOKMARK (VER. 1.2) (FRENCH VERSION)

Prevents the accidental loss of work in progress by saving data to a hard disk in the event of loss of power or system crash.

System: PLUS, SE
Minimum Memory: 1024K
Requires: 10MB hard disk.
Medium: 3 1/2-inch disk
ISPN: 39038-106   **Price: $99.95**

CTEX

BRICKPLATE II

Hard-disk compatible copy protection. Prices varies.

System: MAC, II, PLUS, SE, XL
Minimum Memory:
Medium: 3 1/2-inch disk
ISPN: 20971-100
Price: Please contact the software publisher.

PHOENIX SPECIALITIES, INC.

CAT MAC (VER. 1.2.6)

Catalog file utility that contains three text features, universally compatible with hard disk drives.

System: MAC, II, PLUS, SE, XL
Minimum Memory: 128K
Medium: 3 1/2-inch disk
ISPN: 61012-100   **Price: $24.95**

OLDUVAI CORP.

CLIPSHARE (VER. 1.0)

Allows any user on a network to send their clipboard to any other user on the same network.

System: MAC, II, PLUS, SE, XL
Minimum Memory: 512K
Requires: 800K disk drive.
Medium: 3 1/2-inch disk
ISPN: 57812-150   **Price: $195.00**

HEIZER SOFTWARE

DATABASE MACROS

Creates a database with space for the number of fields and records indicated by the user, including criteria and extract areas.

System: MAC, II, PLUS, SE, XL
Minimum Memory: 512K
Requires: Microsoft Excel (ISPN 53150-270).
Medium: 3 1/2-inch disk
ISPN: 35175-349   **Price: $9.00**

ONTRACK COMPUTER SYSTEMS, INC.

DISK MANAGER MAC

Installs most SCSI hard drives into the Mac SE, Mac II, or Mac Plus.

System: MAC, II, PLUS, SE, XL
Minimum Memory: 1024K
Medium: 3 1/2-inch disk
ISPN: 58380-225   **Price: $99.95**

DESIGN SOFTWARE, INC./DIV. OF DS TECHNOLOGIES

DS BACKUP (VER. 4.0)

A hard disk backup utility that backs up files to either diskettes or to another hard disk.

System: MAC, II, PLUS, SE, XL
Minimum Memory: 512K
Requires: Hard disk.
Medium: 3 1/2-inch disk
ISPN: 91215-210 **Price: $69.95**

PERSONAL COMPUTER PERIPHERALS CORP.

EUREKA! (VER. 1.0)

Provides a file finder desk accessory which displays the location of the file in an easy to read heirarchical graphic display.

System: MAC, II, PLUS, SE, XL
Minimum Memory: 512K
Medium: 3 1/2-inch disk
ISPN: 60612-250 **Price: $24.95**

EXPERTELLIGENCE, INC.

EXPEROPS5 +

Complete implementation of the OPS5 Expert System building tool. Includes graphics and dialog boxes.

System: MAC, II, PLUS, SE, XL
Minimum Memory: 512K
Requires: ExperLisp (Ver. 1.5) (ISPN 30473-300), external disk drive or hard disk.
Medium: 3 1/2-inch disk
ISPN: 30473-800 **Price: $495.00**

FIFTH GENERATION SYSTEMS, INC.

FASTBACK FOR THE MACINTOSH (VER. 1.3)

Provides high speed back-up of files from a hard disk to diskettes or tape.

System: MAC, II, PLUS, SE, XL
Minimum Memory: 512K
Requires: System 4.2 or later.
Medium: 3 1/2-inch disk
ISPN: 30787-200 **Price: $99.95**

SOFTPLUS

FILE EDIT (VER. 1.1)

A file editing and file management desk accessory for the Macintosh.

System: MAC, II, PLUS, SE, XL
Minimum Memory: 512K
Requires: 800K disk drive.
Medium: 3 1/2-inch disk
ISPN: 72171-275 **Price: $39.95**

WORKING SOFTWARE, INC.

FINDSWELL (VER.2.0)

Remembers and locates frequently used folders and documents on the disk and opens them.

System: MAC, II, PLUS, SE, XL
Minimum Memory: 512K
Requires: 800K disk drive.
Medium: 3 1/2-inch disk
ISPN: 92154-760 **Price: $59.95**

ALSOFT, INC.

FONT/DA JUGGLER PLUS (VER. 1.10)

Provides access to fonts, desk accessories, files, and sounds which remain in their Font/DA or FKey/Sound mover files.

System: MAC, II, PLUS, SE, XL
Minimum Memory: 512K
Medium: 3 1/2-inch disk
ISPN: 02506-240 **Price: $59.95**

GRAPHIC MAGIC

FULLPLOT

A utility with multisheet and roll feed capability which directs precise output of MacSurf designs to printers and plotters.

System: MAC, II, PLUS, SE, XL
Minimum Memory:
Requires: MacSurf (ISPN 33421-400).
Medium: 3 1/2-inch disk
ISPN: 33421-100 **Price: $500.00**

FWB, INC.

HARD DISK JOCKEY

Purges and organizes files and folders on a hard disk.

System: MAC, II, PLUS, SE, XL
Minimum Memory: 1024K
Requires: Hard disk.
Medium: 3 1/2-inch disk
ISPN: 31697-380 **Price: $69.95**

SYMANTEC

HFS NAVIGATOR

Finds buried folders and document, creates new folders and renames and deletes files instantly.

System: MAC, II, PLUS, SE, XL
Minimum Memory: 512K
Medium: 3 1/2-inch disk
ISPN: 77413-350 **Price: $59.95**

INTELLIGENT ENGINEERED SYSTEMS

I.E.S. DISKSURGEON (VER. 2.0)

Enables a user to access disk files and directories directly for editing, file recovery and disk repair.

System: MAC, II, PLUS, SE, XL
Minimum Memory: 512K
Medium: 3 1/2-inch disk
ISPN: 39006-400 **Price: $19.95**

MAC AMERICA (CA)

LASER SPOOL (VER. 4.0)

Utility program inserted as desk-top accessory that print spools documents on LaserWriter or LaserWriter Plus.

System: MAC, II, PLUS, SE, XL
Minimum Memory: 512K
Medium: 3 1/2-inch disk
ISPN: 71848-400 **Price: $50.00**

INFOSPHERE, INC.

LASERSERVE (VER. 2.0)

Allows users to continue to use the Macintosh while printing to the LaserWriter printer.

System: MAC, II, PLUS, SE, XL
Minimum Memory: 512K
Medium: 3 1/2-inch disk
ISPN: 38212-030 **Price: $95.00**

INFOSPHERE, INC.

LASERSERVE (VER. 2.0)

Allows users to continue to use the Macintosh while printing to the LaserWriter printer.

System: MAC, II, PLUS, SE
Minimum Memory: 512K
Requires: Five pack (includes 5 copies).
Medium: 3 1/2-inch disk
ISPN: 38212-030 **Price: $295.00**

NEMESIS SYSTEMS

MACBACKUP (VER. 8.0)

Duplicates protected and unprotected software and allows protected software and software that needs a 'key' to run on a hard disk.

System: MAC, II, PLUS, SE, XL
Minimum Memory: 512K
Requires: 800K disk drive.
Medium: 3 1/2-inch disk
ISPN: 56512-200 **Price: $49.95**

GRAPHIC MAGIC

MACHYDRO

A Hydrostatics and Stability program specifically designed to work with MacSurf.

System: MAC, II, PLUS, SE, XL
Minimum Memory:
Requires: MacSurf (ISPN 33421-400).
Medium: 3 1/2-inch disk
ISPN: 33421-200 **Price: $750.00**

DATAVIZ, INC.

MACLINK PLUS/WANG OIS (VER. 2.12)

Provides file transfer and conversion of formatted word processing processing documents between the Macintosh and Wang OIS.

System: MAC, II, PLUS, SE, XL
Minimum Memory: 512K
Requires: Includes software for PC's or compatibles and Wang OIS.
Medium: 3 1/2-inch disk
ISPN: 23962-640 **Price: $495.00**

VIKING TECHNOLOGIES

MACTALKER

Program allows the Macintosh to read text only files aloud or have the Macintosh talk as users type.

System: MAC, II, PLUS, SE, XL
Minimum Memory: 512K
Medium: 3 1/2-inch disk
ISPN: 85231-500 **Price: $19.95**

GO TECHNOLOGY, INC.
MACTREE PLUS

Displays files in folders in a graphic 'tree' showing exactly where programs are stored on a hard disk.

System: MAC, II, PLUS, SE, XL
Minimum Memory: 512K
Requires: Hard disk.
Medium: 3 1/2-inch disk
ISPN: 33131-500   **Price: $69.95**

APDA
MPW IIGS TOOLS

Cross-development tools that run in the Macintosh Programmer's Workshop (MPW) environment.

System: MAC, II, PLUS, SE, XL
Minimum Memory: 512K
Requires: Macintosh Programmer's Workshop-MPW (ISPN 03749-500), and a compatible language translator.
Medium: 3 1/2-inch disk
ISPN: 03749-301   **Price: $50.00**

ICOM SIMULATIONS, INC.
ON CUE (VER. 1.3)

A file launching utility that lets the user move from one program to another without having to return to the desktop.

System: MAC, II, PLUS, SE, XL
Minimum Memory: 512K
Medium: 3 1/2-inch disk
ISPN: 82194-500   **Price: $59.95**

MICRO DYNAMICS. LTD.
POST HASTE

An interactive PostScript language programming utility for both extended graphical effects and for stand-alone programming.

System: MAC, II, PLUS, SE, XL
Minimum Memory: 512K
Medium: 3 1/2-inch disk
ISPN: 50227-600   **Price: $59.95**

AMERICAN POWER CONVERSION CORP.
POWERCHUTE

An Uninterruptible Power Supply (UPS) monitoring program for AppleShare networks which is installed in the control panel.

System: MAC, II, PLUS, SE, XL
Minimum Memory: 1024K
Requires: AppleShare (Ver. 2.0) (ISPN 03900-100) and APC UPS model 110SE, 520ES, 800RT or 1200VX with computer interface.
Medium: 3 1/2-inch disk
ISPN: 03009-100   **Price: $99.00**

MAGIC SOFTWARE, INC.
POWERMENUS (VER. 1.01)

Makes the pulldown menus from the top of the screen available where ever the mouse is positioned.

System: MAC, II, PLUS, SE, XL
Minimum Memory: 1024K
Medium: 3 1/2-inch disk
ISPN: 45962-600   **Price: $79.95**

MICROSEEDS PUBLISHING, INC.
SCREEN GEMS

A collection of utilities for the Macintosh II that provides for color desktop changes, screen dimmers, and a screen mode switcher.

System: II
Minimum Memory: 1024K
Requires: Color monitor.
Medium: 3 1/2-inch disk
ISPN: 53093-700   **Price: $79.00**

DIVERSIFIED I/O
SOFTBACKUP-MULTI USER VERSION

Permits automatic backup of data on a data bank when convenient for the user and allows up to 32 people on the network.

System: MAC, II, PLUS, SE, XL
Minimum Memory: 512K
Medium: 3 1/2-inch disk
ISPN: 26465-705   **Price: $139.95**

DIVERSIFIED I/O
SOFTBACKUP-SINGLE USER VERSION

Permits automatic backup of information and input data on a data bank when convenient for the user.

System: MAC, II, PLUS, SE, XL
Minimum Memory: 512K
Medium: 3 1/2-inch disk
ISPN: 26465-700   **Price: $69.95**

MINDCRAFT PUBLISHING CORP.
SPEED DISK

Creates fast simulated disk drives in the Macintosh memory greatly speeding up many applications.

System: MAC, II, PLUS, SE, XL
Minimum Memory: 512K
Requires: 800K disk drive.
Medium: 3 1/2-inch disk
ISPN: 53425-850   **Price: $29.95**

BERKELEY SYSTEMS
STEPPING OUT (VER. 1.3)

Extends Macintosh display features to give the feel and features of full page display plus reduction and enlargement options.

System: MAC, PLUS, SE, XL
Minimum Memory: 512K
Requires: 800K disk drive.
Medium: 3 1/2-inch disk
ISPN: 07441-700   **Price: $95.00**

BERKELEY SYSTEMS
STEPPING OUT II (VER. 2.01)

Extends the capabilities of the standard Macintosh display to give it the features of a full-page display.

System: MAC, II, PLUS, SE, XL
Minimum Memory: 1024K
Medium: 3 1/2-inch disk
ISPN: 07441-725   **Price: $95.00**

CAUZIN SYSTEMS, INC.
STRIPPER-DOT MATRIX PRINTER VERSION

Provides a data strip program that allows the user to strip disk files onto paper.

System: MAC, II, PLUS, SE, XL
Minimum Memory: 128K
Requires: ImageWriter printer.
Medium: 3 1/2-inch disk
ISPN: 11571-800   **Price: $29.95**

SUPERMAC SOFTWARE
SUPERLASERSPOOL (VER. 2.0)

Allows users to go on to other applications while printing without waiting for the printing operation to be completed.

System: MAC, II, PLUS, SE, XL
Minimum Memory: 512K
Requires: Single user. 800K disk drive.
Medium: 3 1/2-inch disk
ISPN: 77125-810   **Price: $149.95**

SUPERMAC SOFTWARE
SUPERLASERSPOOL (VER. 2.0)

Allows users to go on to other applications while printing without waiting for the printing operation to be completed.

System: MAC, II, PLUS, SE
Minimum Memory: 512K
Requires: 1-5 users. 800K disk drive.
Medium: 3 1/2-inch disk
ISPN: 77125-810   **Price: $395.00**

AFFINITY MICROSYSTEMS LIMITED
TEMPO (VER. 1.2)

Automates word processing, graphics, desktop communications, databases, spreadsheets and nearly every Macintosh program.

System: MAC, II, PLUS, SE, XL
Minimum Memory: 512K
Medium: 3 1/2-inch disk
ISPN: 90318-700   **Price: $99.00**

AFFINITY MICROSYSTEMS LIMITED
TEMPO II

Creates macros to automate word processing, graphics, databases, spreadsheets and nearly every Macintosh program.

System: MAC, II, PLUS, SE, XL
Minimum Memory: 1024K
Medium: 3 1/2-inch disk
ISPN: 90318-710   **Price: $149.95**

ADVANCED INTERFACE PROGRAMMING
TOM-INIT

A combination INIT/CDEV that provides tear-off menu capability for the entire Macintosh family.

System: MAC, II, PLUS, SE, XL
Minimum Memory: 1024K
Requires: 800K disk drive.
Medium: 3 1/2-inch disk
ISPN: 01293-700   **Price: $79.95**

CORTLAND COMPUTER
TOP DESK (VER. 3.0)

Seven desk accessories including background printer, encryption program, macroprogram, screen saver and more.

System: MAC, II, PLUS, SE, XL
Minimum Memory: 512K
Medium: 3 1/2-inch disk
ISPN: 19878-675   **Price: $59.95**

VIKING TECHNOLOGIES
UTILITY TIME

Includes Macros, Filecopy, Utility Time, DeleteFile DA, Launch DA, and PrintFile.

System: MAC, II, PLUS, SE, XL
Minimum Memory:
Medium: 3 1/2-inch disk
ISPN: 85231-800   **Price: $19.95**

MESSENGER SOFTWARE, INC.
XFER (VER. 1.1)

A PC to and from Macintosh file/folder/ directory transfer and utility. Supports direct and modem connections.

System: MAC, II, PLUS, SE, XL
Minimum Memory: 512K
Requires: 800K disk drive.
Medium: 3 1/2-inch disk
ISPN: 49196-800   **Price: $99.95**

MESSENGER SOFTWARE, INC.
XFER (VER. 1.1)

A PC to and from Macintosh file/folder/ directory transfer and utility. Supports direct and modem connections.

System: MAC, II, PLUS, SE, XL
Minimum Memory: 512K
Requires: Includes cables to connect to PC or PC compatible. 800K disk drive.
Medium: 3 1/2-inch disk
ISPN: 49196-800   **Price: $129.95**

INDEX BY PRODUCT

D

E

G

H

I

M

N

Q

T

U

V

W

X

Y

Z

INDEX BY PUBLISHER

R

S

T

PUBLISHER DIRECTORY

A

1ST AID SOFTWARE, INC. (617) 782-4676
MENU PUBLISHER NUMBER 91829
42 RADNOR RD.
BOSTON, MA 02135 USA

1ST DESK SYSTEMS, INC. (508) 533-2203
MENU PUBLISHER NUMBER 81083 *FAX:* (508) 533-5691
7 INDUSTRIAL PARK RD.
MEDWAY, MA 02053 USA

3G GRAPHICS (800) 456-0234
MENU PUBLISHER NUMBER 00062
11410 N.E. 124TH ST.
SUITE 6155
KIRKLAND, WA 98034 USA

AAH COMPUTER GRAPHIC PRODUCTIONS (408) 980-7363
MENU PUBLISHER NUMBER 00181
P.O. BOX 610667
SAN JOSE, CA 95161 USA

AATRIX SOFTWARE (701) 746-7202
MENU PUBLISHER NUMBER 00281
405 BRUCE AVE.
GRAND FORKS, ND 58201 USA

ABACOUNT, INC. (612) 374-9131
MENU PUBLISHER NUMBER 00293
1599 SELBY AVE.
SUITE 22
ST. PAUL, MN 55104 USA

ABACUS CONCEPTS, INC. (415) 540-1949
MENU PUBLISHER NUMBER 00319
1984 BONITA AVE.
BERKLEY, CA 94704 USA

ABRA MACDABRA SOFTWARE (408) 737-9454
MENU PUBLISHER NUMBER 90306
485 PALA AVE.
SUNNYVALE, CA 94806 USA

ABRACADATA LTD. (503) 342-3030
MENU PUBLISHER NUMBER 00366
P.O. BOX 2440
EUGENE, OR 97402 USA

ABRAXAS SOFTWARE, INC. (503) 244-5253
MENU PUBLISHER NUMBER 00367 *FAX:* (503) 244-8375
7033 S.W. MACADAM AVE.
PORTLAND, OR 97219 USA

ABSOFT CORP. (313) 853-0050
MENU PUBLISHER NUMBER 00368 *TELEX:* 235608
2781 BOND ST. *FAX:* (313) 853-0108
ROCHESTER HILLS, MI 48309 USA

ABVENT (714) 380-0333
MENU PUBLISHER NUMBER 00437 *TELEX:* 4949496
23331 EL TORO RD. *FAX:* (714) 380-0858
SUITE 209
EL TORO, CA 92630 USA

ACCESS SOFTWARE, INC. (800) 824-2549
MENU PUBLISHER NUMBER 00525 *FAX:* (801) 298-9160
545 WEST 500 SOUTH
SUITE 130
BOUNTIFUL, UT 84010 USA

ACCESS TECHNOLOGY, INC. ACCESS/ MINDWORK DIVISION (800) 367-4334
MENU PUBLISHER NUMBER 00506 *FAX:* (408) 375-7396
200 G HERITAGE HARBOR
MONTEREY, CA 939402483 USA

ACCOLADE (408) 985-1700
MENU PUBLISHER NUMBER 00543 *FAX:* (408) 246-0885
550 S. WINCHESTER BLVD.
SUITE 200
SAN JOSE, CA 95128 USA

ACCURATE COMPUTER SEARCH (619) 726-7136
MENU PUBLISHER NUMBER 00582
993C S. SANTA FE AVE.
VISTA, CA 92084 USA

ACIUS (408) 252-4444
MENU PUBLISHER NUMBER 90311
20300 STEVENS CREEK BLVD.
SUITE 495
CUPERTINO, CA 95014 USA

ACTUARIAL MICRO SOFTWARE (919) 773-1313
MENU PUBLISHER NUMBER 00844
8025 N. POINT BLVD.
SUITE 215E
WINSTON-SALEM, NC 27106 USA

AD ASTRA (619) 660-0356
MENU PUBLISHER NUMBER 00848
10148 DIAMOND HEAD CT.
SPRING VALLEY, CA 92077 USA

ADDISON WESLEY PUBLISHING CO. (617) 944-3700
MENU PUBLISHER NUMBER 00900 *TELEX:* 989572
ROUTE 128 *FAX:* (617) 944-9338
READING, MA 01867 USA

ADH SOFTWARE
MENU PUBLISHER NUMBER 00915
P.O. BOX 67129
LOS ANGELES, CA 900670129 USA

ADOBE SYSTEMS, INC. (415) 961-4400
MENU PUBLISHER NUMBER 01012 *FAX:* (415) 961-3769
1585 CHARLESTON RD.
P.O. BOX 7900
MOUNTAIN VIEW, CA 940397900
USA

ADVANCED A.I. SYSTEMS, INC.
MENU PUBLISHER NUMBER 01065
P.O. BOX 39-0360
MOUNTAIN VIEW, CA 940390360
USA
(415) 948-8658

ADVANCED GEOGRAPHIC SYSTEMS
MENU PUBLISHER NUMBER 31215
16742 GOTHARD ST.
SUITE 213
HUNTINGTON BEACH, CA 92647
USA
(714) 841-1562
FAX: (714) 842-7336

ADVANCED IDEAS, INC.
MENU PUBLISHER NUMBER 15700
2902 SAN PABLO AVE.
BERKELEY, CA 94702 USA
(415) 526-9100
TELEX: 278-559 MUHA UR
FAX: (415) 548-4731

ADVANCED INTERFACE PROGRAMMING
MENU PUBLISHER NUMBER 01293
1224 2ND AVE.
NEBRASKA CITY, NE 68410 USA
(800) MAC-TOSH
FAX: (402) 873-7755

ADVANCED LOGIC SYSTEMS
MENU PUBLISHER NUMBER 01312
1211 ALDERWOOD AVE.
SUNNYVALE, CA 94089 USA
(408) 747-1988

ADVANCED LOGICAL SOFTWARE
MENU PUBLISHER NUMBER 01318
9903 SANTA MONICA BLVD.
SUITE 108
BEVERLY HILLS, CA 90212 USA
(213) 653-5786
APPLELINK: D0870

ADVANCED SIMULATION SYSTEMS
MENU PUBLISHER NUMBER 01458
4231 N. SHORE DR.
PRINCE FREDERICK, MD 20678 USA
(301) 535-3474

ADVANCED SOFTWARE, INC.
MENU PUBLISHER NUMBER 01446
1905 E. DUANE AVE.
SUITE 212
SUNNYVALE, CA 94086 USA
(408) 733-0745

ADVOCATE SOFTWARE
MENU PUBLISHER NUMBER 01715
350 HANOVER AVE.
SUITE 102
OAKLAND, CA 94606 USA
(415) 268-1525

AEC MANAGEMENT SYSTEMS, INC.
MENU PUBLISHER NUMBER 01716
20524 AMETHYST LANE
GERMANTOWN, MD 20874 USA
(301) 428-3694

AEGIS DEVELOPMENT, INC.
MENU PUBLISHER NUMBER 01718
2210 WILSHIRE BLVD.
SUITE 277
SANTA MONICA, CA 90403 USA
(213) 392-9972
TELEX: 6502861171

AFFINITY MICROSYSTEMS LIMITED
MENU PUBLISHER NUMBER 90318
1050 WALNUT ST.
SUITE 425
BOULDER, CO 80302 USA
(303) 442-4840
FAX: 303-443-0500

AG PLUS SOFTWARE
MENU PUBLISHER NUMBER 01759
410-1/2 2ND ST.
IDA GROVE, IA 51445 USA
(712) 364-2885

AG-WARE
MENU PUBLISHER NUMBER 01760
P.O. BOX 1503
KEARNEY, NE 68848 USA
(308) 234-9538

AGRICULTURAL SOFTWARE CONSULTANTS, INC.
MENU PUBLISHER NUMBER 01950
P.O. BOX 32
KINGSVILLE, TX 78363 USA
(512) 595-1937
TELEX: 6713995 ASC. KING
FAX: (512) 595-0446

AJL SYSTEMS, INC.
MENU PUBLISHER NUMBER 02121
100 COLONY SQ.
SUITE 200
ATLANTA, GA 30361 USA
(404) 872-4330

ALDUS CORP.
MENU PUBLISHER NUMBER 02226
411 FIRST AVE. S.
SUITE 200
SEATTLE, WA 981042258 USA
(206) 622-5500
TELEX: (650) 210-6205
FAX: (206) 343-4316

ALISA SYSTEMS, INC.
MENU PUBLISHER NUMBER 02265
221 E. WALNUT ST.
SUITE 175
PASADENA, CA 91101 USA
(818) 792-9474
TELEX: 881268 ALISA
SYSTEMS

ALIVE SYSTEMS, INC.
MENU PUBLISHER NUMBER 02273
33307-B DECKER SCHOOL RD.
MALIBU, CA 90265 USA
(213) 457-6634
TELEX: 6502154406 MCI

ALLAN BONADIO ASSOCIATES
MENU PUBLISHER NUMBER 08168
814 CASTRO ST.
SAN FRANCISCO, CA 94114 USA
(415) 282-5864

ALLEGRO SOFTWARE (MA)
MENU PUBLISHER NUMBER 59003
79 MILK ST.
SUITE 1108
BOSTON, MA 02109 USA
(617) 879-7048

ALLIED COMPUTER SERVICE
MENU PUBLISHER NUMBER 90337
255 W. 98TH ST.
NEW YORK, NY 10025 USA
(212) 222-5665

ALLOTYPE TYPOGRAPHICS
MENU PUBLISHER NUMBER 90338
1600 PACKARD RD.
SUITE 5
ANN ARBOR, MI 48104 USA
(313) 663-1989

ALPHA & OMEGA
MENU PUBLISHER NUMBER 02330
P.O. BOX 81056
SOUTH BURNABY, BC V5H 4K2
CANADA
(604) 732-7171

ALPHABETS, INC.
MENU PUBLISHER NUMBER 02406
804 DEMPSTER ST.
EVANSTON, IL 60202 USA
(312) 328-2733

ALSOFT, INC.
MENU PUBLISHER NUMBER 02506
P.O. BOX 927
SPRING, TX 773830927 USA
(713) 353-4090

ALSYS, INC.
MENU PUBLISHER NUMBER 02509
ONE BURLINGTON BUSINESS CENTER
67 SOUTH BEDFORD ST.
BURLINGTON, MA 018035152 USA
(617) 270-0030
FAX: (617) 270-6882

ALTERNATIVE ENTERPRISES
MENU PUBLISHER NUMBER 02577
3300 JARRETTSVILLE PIKE
MONKTON, MD 21111 USA
(301) 557-9670

ALTSYS CORP.   (214) 424-4888
MENU PUBLISHER NUMBER 02675   *TELEX:* 271 8914 MCI
720 AVE. F
SUITE 108
PLANO, TX 75074 USA

AMERICAN INTELLIWARE CORP.   (213) 533-4040
MENU PUBLISHER NUMBER 02896
P.O. BOX 6980
TORRANCE, CA 90504 USA

AMERICAN POWER CONVERSION CORP.   (401) 789-5735
MENU PUBLISHER NUMBER 03009   *APPLELINK:* D3016
350 COLUMBIA ST.   *FAX:* (401) 789-3710
PEACE DALE, RI 02883 USA

AMERICAN TRAINING INT'L. (ATI)   (213) 823-1129
MENU PUBLISHER NUMBER 03156   *TELEX:* (650) 291-4736
12638 BEATRICE ST.
LOS ANGELES, CA 90066 USA

ANAMATRIX, INC.   (801) 546-1616
MENU PUBLISHER NUMBER 03468
1219 W. GENTILE ST.
LAYTON, UT 84041 USA

ANDROS SOFTWEAR   (415) 728-3553
MENU PUBLISHER NUMBER 03648
P.O. BOX 782
MOSS BEACH, CA 94038 USA

ANIMCALC   (503) 254-7622
MENU PUBLISHER NUMBER 03656
895 N.E. 90TH AVE.
PORTLAND, OR 97220 USA

ANTIC PUBLISHING, INC.   (800) 234-7001
MENU PUBLISHER NUMBER 03735   *FAX:* (415) 882-9502
544 SECOND ST.
SAN FRANCISCO, CA 94107 USA

APDA   (206) 251-5222
MENU PUBLISHER NUMBER 03749
290 S.W. 43RD ST.
RENTON, WA 98055 USA

APPLE COMPUTER, INC.   (408) 252-2775
MENU PUBLISHER NUMBER 03900   *TELEX:* 171-576
20525 MARIANI AVE.
CUPERTINO, CA 95014 USA

APPLIED IDEAS, INC.   (213) 545-2996
MENU PUBLISHER NUMBER 04512
P.O. BOX 3225
MANHATTAN BEACH, CA 90266 USA

APPLIED LOGIC SYSTEMS, INC.   (315) 471-3900
MENU PUBLISHER NUMBER 04560   *FAX:* (315) 471-2606
P.O. BOX 90
UNIVERSITY STATION
SYRACUSE, NY 13210 USA

APPLIED SYSTEMS & TECHNOLOGIES, INC.   (315) 675-8584
MENU PUBLISHER NUMBER 04768
227 M HALLENBECK RD.
CLEVELAND, NY 13042 USA

ARBORWORKS, INC.   (800) 346-6980
MENU PUBLISHER NUMBER 04925   *FAX:* (313) 747-8775
431 VIRGINIA AVE.
ANN ARBOR, MI 48103 USA

ARCH SOFTWARE   (513) 681-1642
MENU PUBLISHER NUMBER 04959
1642 PULLAN AVE.
CINCINNATI, OH 45223 USA

ARGOSY SERVICES   (602) 282-3222
MENU PUBLISHER NUMBER 05181
150 COLOR COVE RD.
SEDONA, AZ 86336 USA

ARKTOS ENTERPRISES   (415) 654-8204
MENU PUBLISHER NUMBER 05256
130 WILDING LANE
OAKLAND, CA 94618 USA

ARS NOVA SOFTWARE   (800) 445-4866
MENU PUBLISHER NUMBER 60542   *TELEX:* (800) 445-8749
BOX 40629
SANTA BARBARA, CA 93140 USA

ARTBASE COMPUTER GRAPHIC SERVICES   (604) 255-8077
MENU PUBLISHER NUMBER 05324
815 PRINCESS AVE.
VANCOUVER, BC V6A 3E5 CANADA

ARTFACTORY   (714) 793-7346
MENU PUBLISHER NUMBER 90358
414 TENNESSEE PLAZA
SUITE A
REDLANDS, CA 92373 USA

ARTIFICIAL INTELLIGENCE RESEARCH GROUP   (213) 656-7368
MENU PUBLISHER NUMBER 05412
921 N. LA JOLLA AVE.
LOS ANGELES, CA 90046 USA

ARTSCI, INC.   (818) 843-4080
MENU PUBLISHER NUMBER 05425   *FAX:* (818) 846-2298
P.O. BOX 1848
BURBANK, CA 91505 USA

ARTWARE SYSTEMS, INC.   (919) 872-6511
MENU PUBLISHER NUMBER 05432
3741 BENSON DR.
RALEIGH, NC 27609 USA

ARTWORX SOFTWARE CO., INC.   (800) 828-6573
MENU PUBLISHER NUMBER 05437   *FAX:* (716) 385-1603
1844 PENFIELD RD.
PENFIELD, NY 14526 USA

ASHTON-TATE   (213) 329-8000
MENU PUBLISHER NUMBER 05500   *TELEX:* 664228 ASHTATE
20101 HAMILTON AVE.   TOR
TORRANCE, CA 905021319 USA   *FAX:* (213) 538-7998

ASSOCIATED COMPUTER SERVICES   (417) 887-9923
MENU PUBLISHER NUMBER 05543
1306 E. SUNSHINE
SPRINGFIELD, MO 65804 USA

ASTROLABE, INC.   (800) 255-0510
MENU PUBLISHER NUMBER 02000   *FAX:* (508) 255-0932
P.O. BOX 28
45 S. ORLEANS RD.
ORLEANS, MA 02653 USA

AUTHORWARE, INC.   (612) 921-8555
MENU PUBLISHER NUMBER 06031   *FAX:* (612) 921-8556
8500 NORMANDALE LAKE BLVD.
SUITE 900
MINNEAPOLIS, MN 55437 USA

AVALON DEVELOPMENT GROUP   (617) 661-1405
MENU PUBLISHER NUMBER 06337
1000 MASSACHUSETTS AVE.
CAMBRIDGE, MA 02138 USA

AVATAR TECHNOLOGIES, INC. (MA)
MENU PUBLISHER NUMBER 06409
99 SOUTH ST.
HOPKINTON, MA 01748 USA
(617) 435-6872
TELEX: 710 390 0375
FAX: (617) 435-2470

AVENUE SOFTWARE, INC.
MENU PUBLISHER NUMBER 06418
1173 W. CHAREST BLVD.
SUITE 390
QUEBEC CITY, QUEBEC G1N 2C9
CANADA
(418) 682-3088
FAX: (418) 681-1055

B

B T COMPUTING CORP.
MENU PUBLISHER NUMBER 06562
P.O. BOX 1465
EULESS, TX 76039 USA
(817) 267-1415

BAKER GRAPHICS
MENU PUBLISHER NUMBER 06712
P.O. BOX G-826
NEW BEDFORD, MA 02742 USA
(800) 338-1753
FAX: (617) 997-9523

BANTAM ELECTRONIC PUBLISHING
MENU PUBLISHER NUMBER 06781
C/O BANTAM BOOKS, INC.
666 FIFTH AVE.
NEW YORK, NY 10103 USA
(800) 223-6834
TELEX: 1-2402

BARRON'S EDUCATIONAL SERIES, INC.
MENU PUBLISHER NUMBER 06931
250 WIRELESS BLVD.
MAUPPAUGE, NY 11788 USA
(800) 645-3476
TELEX: 143160

BASELINE
MENU PUBLISHER NUMBER 06943
838 BROADWAY
NEW YORK, NY 10003 USA
(212) 254-8235

BAUDVILLE
MENU PUBLISHER NUMBER 07087
5380 52ND ST. S.E.
GRAND RAPIDS, MI 49508 USA
(616) 698-0888
FAX: (616) 698-0325

BEACON TECHNOLOGY, INC.
MENU PUBLISHER NUMBER 07156
3550 STEVENS CREEK BLVD.
SUITE 305
SAN JOSE, CA 95117 USA
(408) 296-4884

BEAR ROCK SOFTWARE CO., INC.
MENU PUBLISHER NUMBER 07196
6069 ENTERPRISE DR.
PLACERVILLE, CA 95667 USA
(916) 622-4640
FAX: (916) 622-4775

BECK TECH
MENU PUBLISHER NUMBER 07225
41 TUNNEL RD.
P.O. BOX 5027
BERKELEY, CA 947050027 USA
(415) 548-4054
FAX: (415) 548-4059

BEDE TECH
MENU PUBLISHER NUMBER 07237
8327 CLINTON RD.
CLEVELAND, OH 44144 USA
(216) 631-1441
FAX: (216) 631-1452

BEDFORD SOFTWARE
MENU PUBLISHER NUMBER 07243
15311 N.E. 90TH
REDMOND, WA 980523522 USA
(206) 883-0074

BENNETT & PETERS, INC.
MENU PUBLISHER NUMBER 07420
8313 O'HARA CT.
BATON ROUGE, LA 70806 USA
(504) 927-3500

BERKELEY SYSTEMS
MENU PUBLISHER NUMBER 07441
1700 SHATTUCK AVE.
BERKELEY, CA 94709 USA
(415) 540-5537

BERT MONROY
MENU PUBLISHER NUMBER 65712
50 THIRD ST.
BROOKLYN, NY 11231 USA
(212) 713-5195

BETHESDA SOFTWORKS
MENU PUBLISHER NUMBER 07542
15235 SHADY GROVE RD.
SUITE 100
ROCKVILLE, MD 20850 USA
(301) 926-8300
FAX: (301) 926-8010

BEYOND, INC.
MENU PUBLISHER NUMBER 90615
6069 E. GRANT RD.
TUCSON, AZ 85712 USA
(602) 290-9790

BIBLE RESEARCH SYSTEMS
MENU PUBLISHER NUMBER 07546
2013 WELLS BRANCH PKWY.
SUITE 304
AUSTIN, TX 78728 USA
(512) 251-7541

BIO-RAD LABORATORIES, INC.
MENU PUBLISHER NUMBER 07762
CHEMICAL DIVISION
1414 HARBOUR WAY S.
RICHMOND, CA 94804 USA
(415) 232-7000

BIOSOFT
MENU PUBLISHER NUMBER 28881
22 HILLS RD.
CAMBRIDGE CB2 1JP
UNITED KINGDOM
44-0223-68622
TELEX: 9312130806 BS G
FAX: 265451 MONREF

BISHOP GRAPHICS, INC.
MENU PUBLISHER NUMBER 07787
5388 STERLING CTR. DR.
WESTLAKE VILLAGE, CA 91359 USA
(818) 991-2600
TELEX: 66-2400(BISHOP WKVG)
FAX: (818) 889-3744

BITMAP, INC.
MENU PUBLISHER NUMBER 07834
P.O. BOX 237
WESTWEGO, LA 70094 USA
(504) 347-6317

BITSTREAM, INC.
MENU PUBLISHER NUMBER 07836
ATHENAEUM HOUSE
215 FIRST ST.
CAMBRIDGE, MA 02142 USA
(800) 522-3668
TELEX: 467-237
FAX: (617) 868-4732

BLACK BANANA, INC.
MENU PUBLISHER NUMBER 07838
201 N. 3RD ST.
PHILADELPHIA, PA 19106 USA
(215) 928-9044

BLUE SKY RESEARCH
MENU PUBLISHER NUMBER 42587
534 S.W. THIRD AVE.
PORTLAND, OR 97204 USA
(800) 622-8398
TELEX: 9102900911 BLUE SKY
FAX: (503) 243-3923

BLYTH SOFTWARE, INC.
MENU PUBLISHER NUMBER 58775
2929 CAMPUS DR.
SUITE 425
SAN MATEO, CA 94403 USA
(415) 571-0222
TELEX: 650 2738152 MCI
FAX: (415) 571-1132

BOBBING SOFTWARE
MENU PUBLISHER NUMBER 08075
67 COUNTRY OAKS DR.
BUDA, TX 78610 USA
(512) 295-5045

BOGAS PUBLICATIONS (415) 332-6427
MENU PUBLISHER NUMBER 08160
1520 PACIFIC AVE.
SAN FRANCISCO, CA 94109 USA

BOOTWARE SOFTWARE CO., INC. (818) 706-3887
MENU PUBLISHER NUMBER 08220
28024 DOROTHY DR.
AGOURA HILLS, CA 91301 USA

BORLAND INT'L. (408) 438-8400
MENU PUBLISHER NUMBER 08225 TELEX: 172373
4585 SCOTTS VALLEY DR.
SCOTTS VALLEY, CA 95066 USA

BOSTON PUBLISHING SYSTEMS (617) 267-4747
MENU PUBLISHER NUMBER 08268
115 PORTER ST.
EAST BOSTON, MA 021282118 USA

BOWERS DEVELOPMENT CORP. (617) 259-8428
MENU PUBLISHER NUMBER 08326 FAX: (508) 881-1532
P.O. BOX 9
LINCOLN CENTER, MA 01773 USA

BRAINPOWER, INC. (818) 884-6911
MENU PUBLISHER NUMBER 08413
24009 VENTURA BLVD.
SUITE 250
CALABASAS, CA 91302 USA

BRAUCH SOFTWARE, INC. (416) 471-1766
MENU PUBLISHER NUMBER 90660 FAX: (416) 479-8433
550 ALDEN RD.
SUITE 105
MARKHAM, ONTARIO L3R 6A8
CANADA

BRAVO TECHNOLOGIES, INC. (415) 841-8552
MENU PUBLISHER NUMBER 90657
P.O. BOX 10078
BERKELEY, CA 947090078 USA

BREAKTHROUGH PRODUCTIONS (619) 281-6174
MENU PUBLISHER NUMBER 90659
10659 CAMINITO CASCARA
SAN DIEGO, CA 92108 USA

BRIDGEPORT MACHINES (203) 367-3651
MENU PUBLISHER NUMBER 90656
500 LINDLEY ST.
P.O. BOX 32
BRIDGEPORT, CT 06606 USA

BRIGHT IDEAS, INC. (800) 272-1330
MENU PUBLISHER NUMBER 08456 FAX: (207) 767-6033
87A OCEAN ST.
SOUTH PORTLAND, ME 04106 USA

BRIGHT STAR TECHNOLOGY (206) 885-5446
MENU PUBLISHER NUMBER 08459
14450 N. E. 29TH PL.
SUITE 220
BELLEVUE, WA 98007 USA

BRITANNICA SOFTWARE-BLUE CHIP (415) 546-1866
SOFTWARE DIVISION FAX: (415) 546-1887
MENU PUBLISHER NUMBER 07970
345 FOURTH ST.
SAN FRANCISCO, CA 94107 USA

BROCK SOFTWARE PRODUCTS, INC. (815) 459-4210
MENU PUBLISHER NUMBER 08825 TELEX: 722-469 BROCK CRYS
8603 PYOTT RD. FAX: (815) 455-0025
P.O. BOX 799
CRYSTAL LAKE, IL 60014 USA

BRODERBUND SOFTWARE, INC. (415) 492-3200
MENU PUBLISHER NUMBER 08850 TELEX: 172029 SPX SRFL
17 PAUL DR. FAX: (415) 499-8661
SAN RAFAEL, CA 949032101 USA

BROOKS/COLE PUBLISHING (408) 373-0728
MENU PUBLISHER NUMBER 08962 FAX: (408) 375-6414
511 FOREST LODGE RD.
PACIFIC GROVE, CA 93950 USA

BROWNBAG SOFTWARE (309) 692-7786
MENU PUBLISHER NUMBER 08993
DIV. OF MICROCOMPUTER SERVICE
8208 N. UNIVERSITY ST.
PEORIA, IL 61615 USA

BULLSEYE SOFTWARE (702) 265-2298
MENU PUBLISHER NUMBER 09168
P.O. DRAWER 7900
INCLINE VILLAGE, NV 89450 USA

BUZZWORDS INT'L., INC. (314) 334-2518
MENU PUBLISHER NUMBER 09868
BELLA VISTA LOT 29
BOX 112G
JACKSON, MO 63755 USA

BV ENGINEERING (714) 781-0252
MENU PUBLISHER NUMBER 09875 TELEX: 6503089864
2023 CHICAGO AVE.
SUITE B-13
RIVERSIDE, CA 92507 USA

C

CACI PRODUCTS CO. (619) 457-9681
MENU PUBLISHER NUMBER 10300 FAX: (619) 457-1184
3344 N. TORREY PINES CT.
LA JOLLA, CA 92037 USA

CAERE CORP. (408) 395-7000
MENU PUBLISHER NUMBER 10394
100 COOPER CT.
LOS GATOS, CA 95030 USA

CALIFORNIA CONTINUING EDUCATION (415) 642-6025
OF THE BAR
MENU PUBLISHER NUMBER 10612
2300 SHATTUCK AVE.
BERKELEY, CA 94704 USA

CALIFORNIA DREAMS (408) 435-1445
MENU PUBLISHER NUMBER 10575 FAX: (408) 435-7355
780 MONTAGUE EXPWY.
SUITE 403
SAN JOSE, CA 95131 USA

CAMBRIDGE COMPUTER CORP. (203) 288-6004
MENU PUBLISHER NUMBER 10775 TELEX: (650) 223-6599
80 MT. SANFORD RD.
MT. CARMEL, CT 06518 USA

CAMBRIDGE SCIENTIFIC COMPUTING (617) 491-6862
MENU PUBLISHER NUMBER 10862 FAX: (617) 354-7027
875 MASSACHUSETTS AVE.
SUITE 41
CAMBRIDGE, MA 02139 USA

CAMBRIDGE UNIVERSITY PRESS (212) 688-8888
MENU PUBLISHER NUMBER 57462
32 E. 57TH ST.
NEW YORK, NY 10022 USA

CAMDE CORP.   (602) 821-2310
MENU PUBLISHER NUMBER 10875
4435 S. RURAL RD.
SUITE 331
TEMPE, AZ 85282 USA

CAMPAGNE ASSOCIATES LTD.   (603) 595-8774
MENU PUBLISHER NUMBER 10905   *APPLELINK:* DSV0001
491 AMHERST ST.   *FAX:* (603) 595-8776
NASHUA, NH 03063 USA

CAMTRONICS, INC.   (503) 445-2824
MENU PUBLISHER NUMBER 10923
P.O. BOX 1
CAMAS VALLEY, OR 97416 USA

CAPILANO COMPUTING SYSTEMS LTD.   (604) 669-6343
MENU PUBLISHER NUMBER 11162
1168 HAMILTON ST.
SUITE 501
VANCOUVER, BC V6B2S2 CANADA

CASADY & GREENE, INC.   (408) 624-8716
MENU PUBLISHER NUMBER 11556   *TELEX:* 6975771
P.O. BOX 223779   *FAX:* (408) 624-7865
CARMEL, CA 93922 USA

CASEYS PAGE MILL   (303) 220-1463
MENU PUBLISHER NUMBER 11563
6528 S. ONEIDA CT.
ENGLEWOOD, CO 80111 USA

CASHMASTER BUSINESS SYSTEMS, INC.   (800) 999-4593
MENU PUBLISHER NUMBER 90903
12345 LAKE CITY WAY N.E.
SUITE 220
SEATTLE, WA 98125 USA

CASPR   (408) 446-3075
MENU PUBLISHER NUMBER 11566
10311 S. DE ANZA BLVD.
SUITE 4
CUPERTINO, CA 95014 USA

CAUZIN SYSTEMS, INC.   (800) 533-7323
MENU PUBLISHER NUMBER 11571   *FAX:* (203) 597-9762
835 S. MAIN ST.
WATERBURY, CT 06706 USA

CE SOFTWARE   (515) 224-1995
MENU PUBLISHER NUMBER 11725   *APPLELINK:* D0048
1854 FULLER RD.   *FAX:* (515) 224-4534
P.O. BOX 65580
WEST DES MOINES, IA 50265 USA

CENTRAL POINT SOFTWARE, INC.   (503) 690-8090
MENU PUBLISHER NUMBER 11950   *TELEX:* 757710
15220 N.W. GREENBRIER PKWY.   *FAX:* (503) 690-8083
SUITE 200
BEAVERTON, OR 97006 USA

CENTRAL PRODUCTS CORP.   (713) 529-1080
MENU PUBLISHER NUMBER 11963
221 NORFOLK
SUITE 518
HOUSTON, TX 77098 USA

CENTRON SOFTWARE   (407) 392-3678
MENU PUBLISHER NUMBER 35869
P.O. BOX 2121
7718 LA MIRADA DR.
BOCA RATON, FL 33433 USA

CERES SOFTWARE, INC.   (503) 245-9011
MENU PUBLISHER NUMBER 12053
9498 S.W. BARBUR BLVD.
SUITE 103
PORTLAND, OR 97219 USA

CET, INC.   (717) 232-2266
MENU PUBLISHER NUMBER 90915
3113 N. FRONT ST.
HARRISBURG, PA 17110 USA

CHALLENGER SOFTWARE   (312) 957-3475
MENU PUBLISHER NUMBER 12093   *TELEX:* 6502262952
18350 KEDZIE AVE.   *FAX:* (312) 957-1282
HOMEWOOD, IL 60430 USA

CHAMPION BUSINESS SYSTEMS   (303) 278-8666
MENU PUBLISHER NUMBER 12175
17301 W. COLFAX AVE.
SUITE 250
GOLDEN, CO 80401 USA

CHAMPION SWIFTWARE   (608) 833-1777
MENU PUBLISHER NUMBER 12178
6617 GETTYSBURG DR.
MADISON, WI 53705 USA

CHANCERY SOFTWARE   (604) 685-2041
MENU PUBLISHER NUMBER 12182
1168 HAMILTON ST.
SUITE 500
VANCOUVER, BC V6B 2S2 CANADA

CHANG LABORATORIES, INC.   (408) 246-8020
MENU PUBLISHER NUMBER 12200   *TELEX:* 296653 (RCA)
5300 STEVENS CREEK BLVD.   *FAX:* 408-247-8751
SAN JOSE, CA 951291088 USA

CHARIOT SOFTWARE GROUP   (800) 242-7468
MENU PUBLISHER NUMBER 12237   *FAX:* (619) 491-0021
3659 INDIA ST.
SUITE 100A
SAN DIEGO, CA 92103 USA

CHATEAU SOFTWARE
MENU PUBLISHER NUMBER 12400
7817 HOLLOW OAK
SAN ANTONIO, TX 78233 USA

CHECKMARK SOFTWARE, INC.   (303) 484-3541
MENU PUBLISHER NUMBER 04612
1520 E. MULBERRY
SUITE 200
FT. COLLINS, CO 80524 USA

CHRIS TIGGES   (303) 490-1380
MENU PUBLISHER NUMBER 81781
C/O DAVE GUENTHER
673 ORANGE ST., SUITE 7
NEW HAVEN, CT 06511 USA

CIASA   (415) 644-2771
MENU PUBLISHER NUMBER 12543
2017 CEDAR ST.
BERKELEY, CA 94709 USA

CINEMAWARE CORP.   (805) 495-6515
MENU PUBLISHER NUMBER 12656   *FAX:* (312) 940-8517
2275 HALF DAY RD.
SUITE 350
BANNOCKBURN, IL 60015 USA

CIRCO BUSINESS SOLUTIONS   (408) 998-1132
MENU PUBLISHER NUMBER 12676
1725-A LITTLE ORCHARD ST.
SAN JOSE, CA 95125 USA

CLARIS CORP.   (415) 960-1500
MENU PUBLISHER NUMBER 12784   *FAX:* (415) 960-2764
440 CLYDE AVE.
MOUNTAIN VIEW, CA 94043 USA

CLASS ONE, INC. (602) 820-3696
MENU PUBLISHER NUMBER 12881
431 E. ELLIS DR.
TEMPE, AZ 85282 USA

CLEAR LAKE RESEARCH, INC. (713) 523-7842
MENU PUBLISHER NUMBER 12891
5615 MORNINGSIDE
SUITE 127
HOUSTON, TX 77005 USA

CLINES RAYMOND AND BARKER ELLEN (317) 288-7818
MENU PUBLISHER NUMBER 65262
2104 W. EUCLID AVE.
MUNCIE, IN 47304 USA

CMA MICRO COMPUTER DIVISION (619) 365-9718
MENU PUBLISHER NUMBER 13112
55888 YUCCA TRAIL
P.O. BOX 2080
YUCCA VALLEY, CA 922862080 USA

CODA MUSIC SOFTWARE, DIV. OF WEN- (612) 854-1288
GER CORP. *FAX:* (612) 854-4631
MENU PUBLISHER NUMBER 55862
1401 E. 79TH ST.
BLOOMINGTON, MN 55425 USA

CODY COMPUTERS (801) 225-3731
MENU PUBLISHER NUMBER 13340
23 S. 1160 W.
OREM, UT 84058 USA

COGNITION TECHNOLOGY (617) 492-0246
MENU PUBLISHER NUMBER 13396
55 WHEELER ST.
CAMBRIDGE, MA 02138 USA

COHERENT COGNITION (CA) (619) 278-4141
MENU PUBLISHER NUMBER 13419
P.O. BOX 24114
SAN DIEGO, CA 92124 USA

COLLIER SOFTWARE (512) 476-1110
MENU PUBLISHER NUMBER 13456
1616 RIO GRANDE
AUSTIN, TX 78701 USA

COMGRAFIX (813) 443-6807
MENU PUBLISHER NUMBER 13843
302 SOUTH GARDEN AVE.
CLEARWATER, FL 34616 USA

COMMUNICATIONS RESEARCH GROUP, (504) 923-0888
INC. *TELEX:* 759985
MENU PUBLISHER NUMBER 23100 *FAX:* (504) 926-2155
5615 CORPORATE BLVD.
BATON ROUGE, LA 70808 USA

COMPANION CONSULTING (408) 446-9779
MENU PUBLISHER NUMBER 14331
10101 BUBB RD.
CUPERTINO, CA 95014 USA

COMPLAN SOFTWARE SYSTEM, INC. (615) 370-4380
MENU PUBLISHER NUMBER 14587
9310 CROCKETT RD.
BRENTWOOD, TN 37027 USA

COMPRESS, DIV. OF QUEUE (800) 232-2224
MENU PUBLISHER NUMBER 14850
562 BOSTON AVE.
BRIDGEPORT, CT 06610 USA

COMPSERVCO (504) 649-0484
MENU PUBLISHER NUMBER 15025
1921 CORPORATE SQ.
SUITE 1
SLIDELL, LA 70458 USA

COMPU-ARCH (213) 281-5933
MENU PUBLISHER NUMBER 15066 *FAX:* (213) 444-9577
9348 CIVIC CENTER DR.
BEVERLY HILLS, CA 90210 USA

COMPU-QUOTE (818) 348-3662
MENU PUBLISHER NUMBER 15387
6914 BERQUIST AVE.
CANOGA PARK, CA 91307 USA

COMPU-TEACH, INC. (800) 448-3224
MENU PUBLISHER NUMBER 15081 *FAX:* (203) 624-0900
78 OLIVE ST.
NEW HAVEN, CT 06510 USA

COMPUCRAFT (CO) (303) 791-2077
MENU PUBLISHER NUMBER 15178
P.O. BOX 3155
ENGLEWOOD, CO 80155 USA

COMPUGRAPHICS CORP. (508) 658-5600
MENU PUBLISHER NUMBER 15303
TYPE DIVISION
90 INDUSTRIAL WAY
WILMINGTON, MA 01887 USA

COMPUNEERING, INC. (416) 738-4601
MENU PUBLISHER NUMBER 03746
113 MCCABE CRESCENT
THORNHILL, ONTARIO L4J 2S6
CANADA

COMPUSERVE (800) 848-8199
MENU PUBLISHER NUMBER 15388
5000 ARLINGTON CENTRE BLVD.
P.O. BOX 20212
COLUMBUS, OH 43220 USA

COMPUTER APPLICATIONS, INC. (NC) (919) 846-1411
MENU PUBLISHER NUMBER 16012
12813 LINDLEY DR.
RALEIGH, NC 27614 USA

COMPUTER ASSOCIATES/MICRO (408) 432-1727
PRODUCTS DIVISION *FAX:* (408) 432-0614
MENU PUBLISHER NUMBER 74700
1240 MCKAY DR.
SAN JOSE, CA 95131 USA

COMPUTER FRIENDS (503) 626-2291
MENU PUBLISHER NUMBER 16839 *TELEX:* 4949559CF
14250 N. W. SCIENCE PARK DR. *FAX:* (503) 643-5379
PORTLAND, OR 97229 USA

COMPUTER LEARNING SYSTEMS, INC. (603) 783-4708
MENU PUBLISHER NUMBER 16917
R.F.D. 8
BOX 375
CONCORD, NH 03301 USA

COMPUTER PHONE SOLUTIONS (305) 653-4500
MENU PUBLISHER NUMBER 17216
17630 N. E. 8TH PL.
N. MIAMI BEACH, FL 33162 USA

COMPUTER RESOURCES, INC. (NH) (603) 664-5811
MENU PUBLISHER NUMBER 17293
BARRINGTON OFFICE MALL
P.O. BOX D
BARRINGTON, NH 03825 USA

COMPUTER SOLUTIONS (WA) (206) 456-1888
MENU PUBLISHER NUMBER 17606
7044 MILL CT. S. E.
OLYMPIA, WA 98503 USA

COMPUTER SPIRIT GRAPHICS, INC. (716) 881-6706
MENU PUBLISHER NUMBER 17675
1001 JEFFERSON AVE.
BUFFALO, NY 14204 USA

COMPUTER VECTORS, INC. (800) 262-7266
MENU PUBLISHER NUMBER 18106 FAX: (800) 329-6523
74-5617 PAWAI PLACE
SUITE 102
KAILUA-KONA, HI 96740 USA

COMPUTRAC (800) 535-7990
MENU PUBLISHER NUMBER 18537
1017 PLEASANT ST.
NEW ORLEANS, LA 70115 USA

CONCEPT DEVELOPMENT ASSOCIATES, (904) 825-0220
INC. *TELEX:* 650 256 5000 MCI
MENU PUBLISHER NUMBER 18875 *FAX:* (904) 825-0223
63 ORANGE ST.
ST. AUGUSTINE, FL 32084 USA

CONDUIT (319) 335-4100
MENU PUBLISHER NUMBER 19050 *TELEX:* 2813491 MCI
UNIVERSITY OF IOWA
OAKDALE CAMPUS
IOWA CITY, IA 52242 USA

CONNECT, INC. 408-973-0110
MENU PUBLISHER NUMBER 90947
10101 BUBB RD.
CUPERTINO, CA 95014 USA

CONSULAIR CORP. (208) 726-5846
MENU PUBLISHER NUMBER 19231 *APPLELINK:* X0051
P.O. BOX 2192
KETCHUM, ID 83340 USA

COOKE PUBLICATIONS (800) 482-4438
MENU PUBLISHER NUMBER 19659
P.O. BOX 4448
ITHACA, NY 14852 USA

CORAL SOFTWARE CORP. (617) 547-2662
MENU PUBLISHER NUMBER 19756
P.O. BOX 307
CAMBRIDGE, MA 02142 USA

CORTLAND COMPUTER (415) 845-1142
MENU PUBLISHER NUMBER 19878
P.O. BOX 9916
BERKLEY, CA 94709 USA

CORVUS SYSTEMS, INC. (408) 281-4100
MENU PUBLISHER NUMBER 19884 *FAX:* (408) 578-4102
160 GREAT OAKS BLVD.
SAN JOSE, CA 951191347 USA

COSMIC (GA) (404) 542-3265
MENU PUBLISHER NUMBER 19888 *TELEX:* 490-999-1619
382 E. BROAD ST. *FAX:* (404) 542-4807
UNIVERSITY OF GEORGIA
ATHENS, GA 30602 USA

CRAIG MANAGEMENT, INC. (504) 291-6348
MENU PUBLISHER NUMBER 20309
16717 MONITOR AVE.
BATON ROUGE, LA 70817 USA

CREATIVE SOLUTIONS, INC. (301) 984-0262
MENU PUBLISHER NUMBER 20700 *FAX:* (301) 770-1675
4701 RANDOLPH RD.
SUITE 12
ROCKVILLE, MD 20852 USA

CREATIVITY PLUS SOFTWARE (415) 631-0883
MENU PUBLISHER NUMBER 20762
P.O. BOX 1333
LAFAYETTE, CA 94549 USA

CRICKET SOFTWARE (215) 251-9890
MENU PUBLISHER NUMBER 35512 *FAX:* (215) 251-0678
40 VALLEY STREAM PKWY.
MALVERN, PA 19355 USA

CTA, INC. (800) 252-1442
MENU PUBLISHER NUMBER 20969 *TELEX:* 429292 TNTDC
747 3RD AVE. *FAX:* (212) 935-2272
3RD FLOOR
NEW YORK, NY 10017 USA

CTEX (415) 788-5505
MENU PUBLISHER NUMBER 20971
582 MARKET ST.
SUITE 216
SAN FRANCISCO, CA 94104 USA

D

D2 SOFTWARE (512) 454-7746
MENU PUBLISHER NUMBER 21975
5609 B ADAMS AVE.
AUSTIN, TX 78756 USA

DA POMA, INC. (512) 426-5932
MENU PUBLISHER NUMBER 22125
P.O. DRAWER H
1101 21ST ST.
HONDO, TX 78861 USA

DAPPLE-TECH COMPUTERS (301) 792-2735
MENU PUBLISHER NUMBER 22281
P.O. BOX 220
LAUREL, MD 20707 USA

DAR SYSTEMS INT'L. (305) 529-3572
MENU PUBLISHER NUMBER 22287 *TELEX:* 6502802624
P.O. BOX 164933
MIAMI, FL 331164933 USA

DATA MANAGEMENT ASSOCIATES (914) 565-6262
MENU PUBLISHER NUMBER 17245
275 N. PLANK RD.
NEWBURGH, NY 12550 USA

DATAPAK SOFTWARE, INC. (818) 905-6419
MENU PUBLISHER NUMBER 23762 *TELEX:* 6503038268
14011 VENTURA BLVD. *FAX:* (800) 935-0518
SUITE 507
SHERMAN OAKS, CA 914233587 USA

DATASOFT/INTELLICREATIONS, INC. (818) 885-9000
MENU PUBLISHER NUMBER 23850 *FAX:* (818) 772-6809
19808 NORDHOFF PL.
CHATSWORTH, CA 91311 USA

DATAVIZ, INC. (203) 268-0030
MENU PUBLISHER NUMBER 23962 *TELEX:* (510) 100-4900
35 CORPORATE DR.
TRUMBULL, CT 06611 USA

DAVIDSON AND ASSOCIATES, INC. (213) 534-4070
MENU PUBLISHER NUMBER 24075 *FAX:* (213) 534-3169
3135 KASHIWA ST.
TORRANCE, CA 90505 USA

DAVKA CORP.
MENU PUBLISHER NUMBER 91205
845 N. MICHIGAN AVE.
SUITE 843
CHICAGO, IL 60611 USA
(800) 621-8227
FAX: (312) 787-7865

DAZZL
MENU PUBLISHER NUMBER 91213
2 CHANDLER CT.
COLUMBIA, MO 65201 USA
(314) 874-8657

DB SOLUTIONS, INC.
MENU PUBLISHER NUMBER 24094
230 LINK RD.
SUITE C-300
FAIRFIELD, CA 94585 USA
(707) 864-4246
APPLELINK: D2240

DCM DATA PRODUCTS
MENU PUBLISHER NUMBER 24196
610, ONE TANDY CTR.
FORT WORTH, TX 76102 USA
(817) 870-2202
TELEX: 756916

DECISION SCIENCE SOFTWARE
MENU PUBLISHER NUMBER 24325
P.O. BOX 1483
SUGAR LAND, TX 77487 USA
(713) 491-0073

DELTASOFT, INC.
MENU PUBLISHER NUMBER 24667
P.O. BOX 55089
TULSA, OK 74155 USA
(918) 250-5594

DELTRON
MENU PUBLISHER NUMBER 24681
155 DEER HILL RD.
LEBANON, NJ 08833 USA
(201) 236-2928

DENEBA SOFTWARE
MENU PUBLISHER NUMBER 24765
3305 N. W. 74TH AVE.
MIAMI, FL 33122 USA
(305) 594-6965
FAX: (305) 594-1959

DESIGN SCIENCE, INC.
MENU PUBLISHER NUMBER 24875
6475-B E. PACIFIC COAST HWY.
SUITE 392
LONG BEACH, CA 90803 USA
(213) 433-0685

DESIGN SOFTWARE, INC./DIV. OF DS TECHNOLOGIES
MENU PUBLISHER NUMBER 91215
1275 W. ROOSEVELT RD.
WEST CHICAGO, IL 60185 USA
(800) 231-3088
FAX: (312) 293-727

DESIGN SOURCE SOFTWARE
MENU PUBLISHER NUMBER 24901
P.O. BOX 91219
HOUSTON, TX 772917026 USA
(713) 820-7026

DESKTOP AI
MENU PUBLISHER NUMBER 24940
303 LINWOOD AVE.
FAIRFIELD, CT 06430 USA
(203) 255-3400
TELEX: (650) 297-2226 (MCI)
FAX: (203) 259-8853

DESKTOP COMPOSITION SYSTEM, INC.
MENU PUBLISHER NUMBER 83187
P.O. BOX 5279
RENO, NV 89513 USA
(702) 355-7503

DESKTOP ENGINEERING
MENU PUBLISHER NUMBER 24943
P.O. BOX 2401
STANFORD, CA 94309 USA
(415) 326-4222

DESKTOP GRAPHICS
MENU PUBLISHER NUMBER 23555
268 E. 16TH ST.
SUITE 6
COSTA MESA, CA 92627 USA
(714) 642-3269

DESKTOP VIDEO PRODUCTIONS
MENU PUBLISHER NUMBER 46012
1000 BROADWAY
SUITE 292
OAKLAND, CA 94607 USA
(415) 763-6243
FAX: (415) 839-7916

DEVONIAN INT'L. SOFTWARE CO.
MENU PUBLISHER NUMBER 24987
P.O. BOX 2351
MONTCLAIR, CA 91763 USA
(714) 621-0973

DIGIDESIGN, INC.
MENU PUBLISHER NUMBER 25212
1360 WILLOW RD.
SUITE 101
MENLO PARK, CA 94025 USA
(415) 327-8811
FAX: (415) 327-0777

DIGITAL MUSIC SERVICES
MENU PUBLISHER NUMBER 25450
23010 LAKE FOREST DR.
SUITE D334
LAGUNA HILLS, CA 92653 USA
714-951-1159

DIGITAL VISION, INC.
MENU PUBLISHER NUMBER 25665
66 EASTERN AVE.
DEDHAM, MA 02026 USA
(617) 329-5400

DIGITALK, INC.
MENU PUBLISHER NUMBER 25687
9841 AIRPORT BLVD.
LOS ANGELES, CA 90045 USA
(213) 645-1082

DILITHIUM PRESS SOFTWARE
MENU PUBLISHER NUMBER 25900
P.O. BOX 606
BEAVERTON, OR 97075 USA
(503) 243-3313

DISCOVERY SOFTWARE INT'L.
MENU PUBLISHER NUMBER 26178
163 CONDUIT ST.
ANNAPOLIS, MD 214012512 USA
(800) 34-AMIGA
FAX: (301) 268-2367

DISK SOFTWARE, INC.
MENU PUBLISHER NUMBER 26225
2116 E. ARAPAHO
SUITE 487
RICHARDSON, TX 75081 USA
(214) 423-7288
FAX: (214) 423-4465

DISK-COUNT SOFTWARE, INC.
MENU PUBLISHER NUMBER 26189
1751 WEST COUNTY RD. B
SUITE 107
SAINT PAUL, MN 55113 USA
(612) 633-0730

DIVERSIFIED I/O
MENU PUBLISHER NUMBER 26465
766 SAN ALESO AVE.
SUNNYVALE, CA 94086 USA
(408) 745-0344
FAX: (408) 745-7017

DM SYSTEMS
MENU PUBLISHER NUMBER 26512
752 HILLTOP CT.
CORAM, NY 11727 USA
(516) 732-9884

DOANE INFORMATION SERVICES, DIV. OF CONTROL DATA
MENU PUBLISHER NUMBER 34425
8800 QUEEN AVE. S.
BLOOMINGTON, MN 554311996 USA
(612) 921-6345
FAX: (612) 921-6869

DOGSTAR SOFTWARE (812) 333-5616
MENU PUBLISHER NUMBER 91246
P.O. BOX 302
BLOOMINGTON, IN 47402 USA

DOUGLAS ELECTRONICS (415) 483-8770
MENU PUBLISHER NUMBER 26668
718 MARINA BLVD.
SAN LEANDRO, CA 94577 USA

DOW JONES & CO., INC. (609) 520-4000
MENU PUBLISHER NUMBER 26725 FAX: (609) 520-4660
P.O. BOX 300
PRINCETON, NJ 08540 USA

DR. T'S MUSIC SOFTWARE (617) 244-6954
MENU PUBLISHER NUMBER 26762 FAX: (617) 244-5243
220 BOYLSTON ST.
SUITE 306
CHESTNUT HILL, MA 02167 USA

DREAM MAKER SOFTWARE (800) 876-5665
MENU PUBLISHER NUMBER 91255 FAX: (213) 223-8580
4020 PAIGE ST.
LOS ANGELES, CA 90031 USA

DREWS PROGRAMS (303) 442-6957
MENU PUBLISHER NUMBER 26771
3120 CORONA TRAIL, NO. 206
BOULDER, CO 80301 USA

DUBL-CLICK SOFTWARE, INC. (818) 700-9525
MENU PUBLISHER NUMBER 26806 APPLELINK: DO255
9316 DEERING AVE. FAX: (818) 700-9727
CHATSWORTH, CA 91311 USA

DV FRANKS (919) 872-5379
MENU PUBLISHER NUMBER 26925 FAX: (919) 878-6123
3721 SUE ELLEN DR.
RALEIGH, NC 276044245 USA

DYNACOMP, INC. (716) 265-4040
MENU PUBLISHER NUMBER 27050
178 PHILLIPS RD.
WEBSTER, NY 14580 USA

DYNAMIC GRAPHICS, INC. (IL) (800) 255-8800
MENU PUBLISHER NUMBER 27181 TELEX: 269331 DGUS UR
6000 N. FOREST PARK DR. FAX: (309) 688-3075
P.O. BOX 1901
PEORIA, IL 616561901 USA

DYNAMIC MICROPROCESSOR (212) 687-7115
ASSOCIATES
MENU PUBLISHER NUMBER 27200
545 FIFTH AVE.
SUITE 1103
NEW YORK, NY 10017 USA

E

E & M SOFTWARE (508) 251-7451
MENU PUBLISHER NUMBER 27331
95 RICHARDSON RD.
NORTH CHELMSFORD, MA 01863
USA

EASTERN LANGUAGE SYSTEMS (801) 377-4558
MENU PUBLISHER NUMBER 04837 TELEX: 6502594091 MCIUW
39 W. 300 N. FAX: (801) 377-2200
PROVO, UT 84601 USA

EASY PRACTICE (514) 288-3093
MENU PUBLISHER NUMBER 91503
1414 DRUMMOND ST.
SUITE 1019
MONTREAL, QUEBEC H3G 1W1
CANADA

ECOM ASSOCIATES, INC. (414) 354-0243
MENU PUBLISHER NUMBER 27600 FAX: (414) 351-4617
8634 W. BROWN DEER RD.
MILWAUKEE, WI 53224 USA

EDUDISC (615) 373-2506
MENU PUBLISHER NUMBER 28068
1400 TYNE BLVD.
NASHVILLE, TN 37215 USA

ELAN ASSOCIATES (312) 782-6496
MENU PUBLISHER NUMBER 28288 TELEX: MCIMAIL=KEGAN
GREENLIGHT DIVISION FAX: (312) 782-6494
79 W. MONROE, SUITE 1320
CHICAGO, IL 606034969 USA

ELECTROHOME LTD. (519) 744-7111
MENU PUBLISHER NUMBER 28425
809 WELLINGTON ST. N.
KITCHENER, ONTARIO N2G 4J6
CANADA

ELECTRONIC ARTS (415) 571-7171
MENU PUBLISHER NUMBER 28512 TELEX: 709204
1820 GATEWAY DR.
SAN MATEO, CA 94404 USA

ELECTRONIC PUBLISHER, INC. (816) 637-7233
MENU PUBLISHER NUMBER 28553
215 S. ST.
EXCELSIOR SPRINGS, MO 64024
USA

ELIOT SOFTWARE CO. (207) 439-9361
MENU PUBLISHER NUMBER 34937 FAX: (207) 439-5704
159 STATE RD.
P.O. BOX 337
ELIOT, ME 03903 USA

EMA SOFTWARE (415) 969-4679
MENU PUBLISHER NUMBER 28900
P.O. BOX 339
LOS ALTOS, CA 94023 USA

EMDASH (312) 441-6699
MENU PUBLISHER NUMBER 28901
P.O. BOX 8256
NORTHFIELD, IL 60093 USA

EMERALD CITY SOFTWARE (415) 368-8303
MENU PUBLISHER NUMBER 28902
P.O. BOX 2103
MENLO PARK, CA 94026 USA

ENABLING TECHNOLOGIES, INC. (312) 427-0386
MENU PUBLISHER NUMBER 29051
600 S. DEARBORN
SUITE 1304
CHICAGO, IL 60605 USA

ENCYCLOWARE (919) 746-4961
MENU PUBLISHER NUMBER 29087
715 WASHINGTON ST.
AYDEN, NC 28513 USA

ENGINEERED SOFTWARE (919) 299-4843
MENU PUBLISHER NUMBER 17509 FAX: (919) 852-2067
P.O. BOX 18344
GREENSBORO, NC 27419 USA

ENTERSET   (415) 549-0539
MENU PUBLISHER NUMBER 29481
2380 ELLSWORTH
BERKELEY, CA 94704 USA

EPCON   (800) 367-3585
MENU PUBLISHER NUMBER 29256
P.O. BOX 270
WOODSFIELD, OH 43793 USA

EPYX COMPUTER SOFTWARE   (415) 368-3200
MENU PUBLISHER NUMBER 29575
600 GALVESTON DR.
P.O. BOX 8020
REDWOOD CITY, CA 94063 USA

EQUAL PLUS   (512) 327-5484
MENU PUBLISHER NUMBER 29584
1406 CAMP CRAFT RD.
SUITE 106
AUSTIN, TX 78746 USA

ERICH BREITSCHWERDT + PARTNER   0211/718 2232
MENU PUBLISHER NUMBER 29593
PAULSMUHLENSTRABE 41-4000
DUSSELDORF, 13 WEST GERMANY

ESHA RESEARCH   (503) 585-6242
MENU PUBLISHER NUMBER 29781   *FAX:* (503) 585-5543
P.O. BOX 13028
SALEM, OR 97309 USA

ESSEX SYSTEMS   (201) 743-1818
MENU PUBLISHER NUMBER 29837
P.O. BOX 1818
BLOOMFIELD, NJ 070031818 USA

ETLON SOFTWARE   (303) 665-3444
MENU PUBLISHER NUMBER 29937
1936 QUAIL CIR.
LOUISVILLE, CO 80027 USA

EVOLUTIONARY COMMERCIAL SYSTEMS   (713) 996-0061
MENU PUBLISHER NUMBER 30266
1201 BAYOU OAK DR.
FRIENDSWOOD, TX 77546 USA

EXCEIVER CORP.   (612) 938-3361
MENU PUBLISHER NUMBER 91574   *FAX:* (612) 935-5358
P.O. BOX 671
HOPKINS, MN 55343 USA

EXCEL SOFTWARE   (515) 752-5359
MENU PUBLISHER NUMBER 91573
P.O. BOX 1414
MARSHALLTOWN, IA 50158 USA

EXECUCOM SYSTEMS CORP.   (512) 346-4980
MENU PUBLISHER NUMBER 30400   *TELEX:* 166982 EXECOM AUS
9442 CAPTIAL OF TEXAS HWY.   *FAX:* (512) 345-7915
ARBORETUM PLAZA ONE
AUSTIN, TX 78759 USA

EXODUS SOFTWARE   (513) 522-0011
MENU PUBLISHER NUMBER 91576
8620 WINTON RD.
SUITE 304
CINCINATTI, OH 45231 USA

EXPERT SOFTWARE SYSTEMS N.V.   +32(91)210383
MENU PUBLISHER NUMBER 30465   *TELEX:* 12570 EXSOFT B
BLDG. 'DE SCHELDE'   *FAX:* +32(91)203191
MOUTSTRAAT 100
B-9000 GENT BELGIUM

EXPERT SOFTWARE SYSTEMS, INC.   (407) 725-5614
MENU PUBLISHER NUMBER 30471
P.O. BOX 2352
1301 DONNA MARIE DR.
MELBOURNE, FL 32902 USA

EXPERTELLIGENCE, INC.   (800) 828-0113
MENU PUBLISHER NUMBER 30473   *FAX:* (805) 964-8448
5638 HOLLISTER AVE.
SUITE 302
GOLETA, CA 93117 USA

EYECARE DATA SERVICES   (218) 233-6111
MENU PUBLISHER NUMBER 30560
1110 S. 16TH ST.
MOORHEAD, MN 56560 USA

EZWARE CORP.   (215) 667-4064
MENU PUBLISHER NUMBER 30578
P.O. BOX 620
29 BALA AVE., SUITE 206
BALA CYNWYD, PA 19004 USA

F

FAIRCOM CORP.   (800) 234-8180
MENU PUBLISHER NUMBER 91808   *FAX:* (314) 445-9698
4006 W. BROADWAY
COLUMBIA, MO 65203 USA

FARALLON COMPUTING   (415) 849-2331
MENU PUBLISHER NUMBER 91809   *FAX:* (415) 841-5770
2201 DWIGHT WAY
BERKELEY, CA 94704 USA

FGM, INC.   (703) 478-9881
MENU PUBLISHER NUMBER 30774
131 ELDEN RD.
SUITE 108
HERNDON, VA 22070 USA

FIFTH GENERATION SYSTEMS, INC.   (800) 225-2775
MENU PUBLISHER NUMBER 30787   *FAX:* (504) 295-3268
11200 INDUSTRIPLEX BLVD.
BATON ROUGE, LA 70809 USA

FINANCIAL MICROWARE   (408) 446-5639
MENU PUBLISHER NUMBER 91833
P.O. BOX 40
CUPERTINO, CA 95015 USA

FINDER AIDS
MENU PUBLISHER NUMBER 91837
19333 SUMMERLIN RD.
LOT 772
FT. MYERS, FL 339085207 USA

FINE S SOFTWARE   (814) 234-3766
MENU PUBLISHER NUMBER 91835
P.O. BOX 6037
STATE COLLEGE, PA 16801 USA

FINGERTIP SOFTWARE   (213) 438-0772
MENU PUBLISHER NUMBER 30831
3111 MARIQUITA
LONG BEACH, CA 90803 USA

FIRST BYTE, INC.   (213) 595-7006
MENU PUBLISHER NUMBER 30836   *FAX:* (213) 426-2556
DIV. OF ELECTRONIC ARTS
3333 E. SPRING ST., SUITE 302
LONG BEACH, CA 90806 USA

FIRST REFERENCE, INC.   (212) 730-8211
MENU PUBLISHER NUMBER 91834
516 FIFTH AVE.
SUITE 706
NEW YORK, NY 10036 USA

FIRST ROW SOFTWARE PUBLISHING   (215) 662-1400
MENU PUBLISHER NUMBER 91839   *FAX:* (215) 662-9912
3624 MARKET ST.
PHILADELPHIA, PA 19104 USA

FLEXWARE, INC.   (818) 961-0237
MENU PUBLISHER NUMBER 52468   *TELEX:* (650) 210-8672 MCI
15404 E. VALLEY BLVD.
CITY OF INDUSTRY, CA 91746 USA

FLIPTRACK LEARNING SYSTEMS   (312) 790-1117
MENU PUBLISHER NUMBER 30881   *FAX:* (312) 469-8313
999 MAIN
SUITE 200
GLEN ELLYN, IL 60137 USA

FOLKSTONE DESIGN, INC.   (604) 886-4502
MENU PUBLISHER NUMBER 31108
P.O. BOX 44
GRANTHAM'SLANDING, BC V0N1X0
CANADA

FORTHOUGHT, INC.   (803) 878-7484
MENU PUBLISHER NUMBER 22380
P.O. BOX 32
SUNSET, SC 29685 USA

FOUNDATION PUBLISHING   (612) 925-6027
MENU PUBLISHER NUMBER 42743
5100 EDEN AVE.
SUITE 307
EDINA, MN 55436 USA

FOX SOFTWARE, INC.   (419) 874-0162
MENU PUBLISHER NUMBER 31262   *FAX:* (419) 874-8678
118 W. S. BOUNDARY
PERRYSBURG, OH 43551 USA

FREEMAN W H AND CO.   (801) 973-4660
MENU PUBLISHER NUMBER 17298   *FAX:* (301) 762-7627
4419 W. 1980 S.
SALT LAKE CITY, UT 84104 USA

FREEMYERS DESIGN   (916) 533-9365
MENU PUBLISHER NUMBER 31415
575 NELSON AVE.
OROVILLE, CA 95965 USA

FREESOFT CO.   (412) 846-2700
MENU PUBLISHER NUMBER 31420   *FAX:* (412) 847-4436
150 HICKORY DR.
BEAVER FALLS, PA 15010 USA

FRIEDMAN COMPUTING & PUBLISHING   (813) 924-3238
MENU PUBLISHER NUMBER 31465
2347 PINE TERRACE
SARASOTA, FL 34231 USA

FROG PEAK MUSIC   (415) 485-6867
MENU PUBLISHER NUMBER 91854
P.O. BOX 1051
SAN RAFAEL, CA 94915 USA

FTL SYSTEMS, INC.   (416) 487-2142
MENU PUBLISHER NUMBER 91860   *TELEX:* 6502995979
234 EGLINTON AVE. E.
SUITE 205
TORONTO, ONTARIO M4P 1K5
CANADA

FUTURE DESIGN SOFTWARE   (714) 891-9796
MENU PUBLISHER NUMBER 91864
17280 NEWHOPE ST.
FOUNTAIN VALLEY, CA 92708 USA

FUTURE VEST   (212) 228-6680
MENU PUBLISHER NUMBER 91863
P.O. BOX 20223
NEW YORK, NY 10025 USA

FUTURESOFT SYSTEM DESIGNS, INC.   (212) 674-5195
MENU PUBLISHER NUMBER 31694
P.O. BOX 132
NEW YORK, NY 100120132 USA

FWB, INC.   (415) 474-8055
MENU PUBLISHER NUMBER 31697   *FAX:* (415) 775-2125
2040 POLK ST.
SUITE 215
SAN FRANCISCO, CA 94109 USA

G

GALLIE COMPUTERS   (312) 863-8591
MENU PUBLISHER NUMBER 32200
4726 W. 13TH ST.
SUITE 2
CHICAGO, IL 60650 USA

GARAJO LOUIS M   031534594
MENU PUBLISHER NUMBER 32308
35 SCHAUFELWEG
3098 BERNE SWITZERLAND

GARDE   (203) 245-9089
MENU PUBLISHER NUMBER 92110
8 BISHOP LANE
MADISON, CT 06443 USA

GARDNER PARTNERSHIP ARCHITECTS   (801) 586-9494
MENU PUBLISHER NUMBER 32318
P.O. BOX 549
CEDAR CITY, UT 84720 USA

GARY HOLMES   (804) 293-4688
MENU PUBLISHER NUMBER 92104
384-327A GOOCH HOUSE
BOX 11-314, STATION 2
CHARLOTESVILLE, VA 22904 USA

GDT SOFTWORKS, INC.   (800) 663-6222
MENU PUBLISHER NUMBER 92112   *FAX:* (604) 291-9689
4664 LOUGHEED HWY.
SUITE 188
BURNABY, BC V5C 6B7 CANADA

GENERATION FOUR   (505) 294-3210
MENU PUBLISHER NUMBER 92117
3232 SAN MATEO N. E.
SUITE 199
ALBEQUERQUE, NM 87110 USA

GENERIC SOFTWARE, INC.   (800) 228-3601
MENU PUBLISHER NUMBER 32537   *FAX:* (206) 483-6969
11911 NORTH CREEK PKWY S.
BOTHELL, WA 98011 USA

GENNY SOFTWARE   (409) 860-5817
MENU PUBLISHER NUMBER 32612
P.O. BOX 5909
BEAUMONT, TX 77706 USA

GESSLER EDUCATIONAL SOFTWARE   (212) 627-0099
MENU PUBLISHER NUMBER 32819   *TELEX:* 503770
55 W. 13 ST.   *FAX:* (212) 627-5548
NEW YORK, NY 10011 USA

GIFTS CONSULTANTS, INC. — (817) 284-3566
MENU PUBLISHER NUMBER 32837
3248 MATTHEWS
FORT WORTH, TX 76118 USA

GIMEOR, INC. — (202) 223-4373 / *FAX:* (202) 659-9852
MENU PUBLISHER NUMBER 32907
1815 H ST. N.W.
WASHINGTON, DC 20006 USA

GLPS PRODUCTS — (919) 933-6530
MENU PUBLISHER NUMBER 32956
P.O. BOX 3454
CHAPEL HILL, NC 27515 USA

GO TECHNOLOGY, INC. — (702) 831-3100 / *FAX:* (701) 831-3118
MENU PUBLISHER NUMBER 33131
850 TANAGER, SUITE 4
P.O. BOX 4535
INCLINE VILLAGE, NV 89450 USA

GOLDMIND PUBLISHING — (714) 785-8685
MENU PUBLISHER NUMBER 33256
12155 MAGNOLIA AVE.
SUITE 3-B
RIVERSIDE, CA 92503 USA

GOOD SOFTWARE CORP. — (214) 239-6085 / *FAX:* (214) 239-4643
MENU PUBLISHER NUMBER 33278
13601 PRESTON RD.
SUITE 500 W.
DALLAS, TX 75240 USA

GRAFPOINT — (408) 446-1919 / *TELEX:* 650-2748289 MCI / *FAX:* (408) 446-0666
MENU PUBLISHER NUMBER 33362
1485 SARATOGA AVE.
SAN JOSE, CA 95129 USA

GRAFTECH — (408) 373-5273 / *APPLELINK:* D1187 / *MACNET:* GRAFTE
MENU PUBLISHER NUMBER 33375
993 SHORT ST.
PACIFIC GROVE, CA 93950 USA

GRAHAM SOFTWARE (CO) — (303) 422-0757
MENU PUBLISHER NUMBER 33406
8609 INGALLS CIR.
ARVADA, CO 80003 USA

GRAMMAR ENGINE, INC. — (614) 471-1113
MENU PUBLISHER NUMBER 33407
3314 MORSE RD.
COLUMBUS, OH 43231 USA

GRAPHIC ENHANCEMENTS, INC.
MENU PUBLISHER NUMBER 33419
P.O. BOX 543
WRIGHT BROTHERS STATION
DAYTON, OH 454090543 USA

GRAPHIC MAGIC — 61 9383 2114 / *TELEX:* 10718626 GMBT / *FAX:* 01161 9 38400
MENU PUBLISHER NUMBER 33421
P.O. BOX 185
COTTESLOE, PERTH AUSTRALIA

GRAPHSOFT, INC. — (301) 461-9488 / *FAX:* (301) 461-9345
MENU PUBLISHER NUMBER 25184
8370 COURT AVE.
SUITE 202
ELLICOTT CITY, MD 21043 USA

GREAT GAME PRODUCTS — (800) 426-3748
MENU PUBLISHER NUMBER 33443
8804 CHALON DR.
BETHESDA, MD 20817 USA

GREAT PLAINS SOFTWARE — (701) 281-0550 / *FAX:* (701) 282-4826
MENU PUBLISHER NUMBER 33475
1701 S.W. 38TH ST.
FARGO, ND 58103 USA

GREAT WAVE SOFTWARE — (408) 438-1990
MENU PUBLISHER NUMBER 33476
5353 SCOTTS VALLEY DR.
SCOTTS VALLEY, CA 95066 USA

GTFS, INC. — (707) 579-1733 / *FAX:* (707) 578-3195
MENU PUBLISHER NUMBER 33690
2455 BENNETT VALLEY RD.
SUITE 100C
SANTA ROSA, CA 95404 USA

GUNAKARA SUN SYSTEMS LTD. — (902) 429-5642 / *FAX:* (902) 429-9983
MENU PUBLISHER NUMBER 33812
1127 BARRINGTON ST.
SUITE 19
HALIFAX, NOVA SCOTIA B3H 2P8
CANADA

GW INSTRUMENTS, INC. — (617) 625-4096 / *TELEX:* 940-103 / *FAX:* (617) 625-1322
MENU PUBLISHER NUMBER 33837
35 MEDFORD ST.
CAMBRIDGE, MA 02143 USA

H

H & D LEASING, INC. — (505) 762-3324 / *TELEX:* (505) 762-3325
MENU PUBLISHER NUMBER 33851
5500 MABRY DR.
CLOVIS, NM 88101 USA

HABA/ARRAYS SYSTEMS, INC. — (818) 994-1899
MENU PUBLISHER NUMBER 33987
6711 VALJEAN AVE.
VAN NUYS, CA 91406 USA

HARVARD ASSOCIATES, INC. — (617) 492-0660 / *TELEX:* 880792 HARV AS / *FAX:* (617) 492-4610
MENU PUBLISHER NUMBER 34579
10 HOLWORTHY ST.
CAMBRIDGE, MA 02138 USA

HAYES MICROCOMPUTER PRODUCTS — (404) 449-8791 / *TELEX:* 703500 HAYES USA
MENU PUBLISHER NUMBER 34950
705 WESTECH
NORCROSS, GA 30092 USA

HEI, INC. — (612) 443-2500 / *FAX:* (612) 443-2668
MENU PUBLISHER NUMBER 35150
1495 STEIGER LAKE LANE
VICTORIA, MN 55386 USA

HEIZER SOFTWARE — (415) 943-7667 / *FAX:* (415) 943-6882
MENU PUBLISHER NUMBER 35175
1941 OAK PARK BLVD.
SUITE 30
PLEASANT HILL, CA 94523 USA

HELP SOFTWARE, INC. — (408) 257-3815 / *TELEX:* 650 3155428
MENU PUBLISHER NUMBER 35212
10659A MAPLEWOOD RD.
CUPERTINO, CA 95014 USA

HIGH PERFORMANCE SYSTEMS — (603) 795-4857
MENU PUBLISHER NUMBER 35638
13 DARTMOUTH COLLEGE HWY.
LYME, NH 03768 USA

HIGHLIGHTED DATA, INC. — (703) 241-1180
MENU PUBLISHER NUMBER 35775
6628 MIDHILL PL.
FALLS CHURCH, VA 22043 USA

HJC SOFTWARE, INC. (919) 490-1277
MENU PUBLISHER NUMBER 92430
P.O. BOX 51816
DURHAM, NC 27717 USA

HMS COMPUTER CO. (612) 452-5928
MENU PUBLISHER NUMBER 35873
2401 PILOT KNOB RD.
SUITE 108
MENDOTA HEIGHTS, MN 55120 USA

HOT DATA, INC. (213) 393-6405
MENU PUBLISHER NUMBER 36246
1021 LINCOLN BLVD.
SANTA MONICA, CA 90403 USA

HOULBERG DEVELOPMENT (619) 287-7444
MENU PUBLISHER NUMBER 36268
P.O. BOX 151501
SAN DIEGO, CA 92115 USA

HOUSTON DIRECTIONAL SOFTWARE (800) 835-0213
MENU PUBLISHER NUMBER 36318
7127 MOBUD DR.
HOUSTON, TX 77074 USA

HUMAN COMPUTER INTERFACE LTD. 817911 TOPEXP G
MENU PUBLISHER NUMBER 82310
11 BRUNSWICK WALK
CAMBRIDGE, ENGLAND CB5 8AD
UNITED KINGDOM

HUMAN INTELLECT SYSTEMS (HIS) (415) 571-5939
MENU PUBLISHER NUMBER 36563 *TELEX:* 349-420
1670 S. AMPHLETT BLVD. *FAX:* (415) 571-0696
SUITE 326
SAN MATEO, CA 94402 USA

HYPERFORMANCE (503) 758-3429
MENU PUBLISHER NUMBER 36732
P.O. BOX 1591
CORVALLIS, OR 97339 USA

HYPERGLOT SOFTWARE CO. (615) 558-8270
MENU PUBLISHER NUMBER 36734
505 FOREST HILLS BLVD.
KNOXVILLE, TN 37919 USA

HYPERPRESS PUBLISHING CORP (415) 345-4620
MENU PUBLISHER NUMBER 36737
P.O. BOX 8243
FOSTER CITY, CA 94404 USA

I

I O DESIGN INC. 215-524-7277
MENU PUBLISHER NUMBER 36753
924 SPRINGDALE DR.
P.O. BOX 156
EXTON, PA 19341 USA

IATROCOM (619) 698-6927
MENU PUBLISHER NUMBER 36755
7159 NAVAJO RD.
SUITE E
SAN DIEGO, CA 92119 USA

ICC INT'L. COMPUTER CONSULTANTS (707) 765-9200
MENU PUBLISHER NUMBER 36841 *FAX:* (707) 765-1231
1311 CLEGG ST.
PETALUMA, CA 94952 USA

ICOM SIMULATIONS, INC. (312) 520-4440
MENU PUBLISHER NUMBER 82194
648 S. WHEELING RD.
WHEELING, IL 60090 USA

ICONIX SOFTWARE ENGINEERING, INC. (213) 458-0092
MENU PUBLISHER NUMBER 37012 *FAX:* (213) 396-3454
2800 TWENTY-EIGHTH ST.
SUITE 320
SANTA MONICA, CA 90405 USA

IDEAFORM, INC. (515) 472-7256
MENU PUBLISHER NUMBER 37059
P.O. BOX 1540
FAIRFIELD, IA 52556 USA

IGC TECHNOLOGY CORP. (415) 945-7300
MENU PUBLISHER NUMBER 37106 *FAX:* (415) 943-6477
305 LENNON LANE
WALNUT CREEK, CA 94598 USA

ILAR SYSTEMS, INC. (714) 759-8987
MENU PUBLISHER NUMBER 37131 *TELEX:* 295-603
334 BAYWOOD DR. *FAX:* (714) 756-8648
NEWPORT BEACH, CA 92660 USA

IMAGE CLUB GRAPHICS (403) 250-1969
MENU PUBLISHER NUMBER 37146 *FAX:* (403) 291-4053
2915 19TH ST. N. E.
SUITE 206
CALGARY, ALBERTA T2E 7A2
CANADA

IMAGE MAPPING SYSTEMS (402) 553-2246
MENU PUBLISHER NUMBER 37156
P.O. BOX 31593
OMAHA, NE 68131 USA

IMAGE WORLD, INC. (800) 457-6633
MENU PUBLISHER NUMBER 37181
310 WOODCUTTER WAY
P.O. BOX 10415
EUGENE, OR 97405 USA

IMAGINE SOFTWARE (415) 453-3944
MENU PUBLISHER NUMBER 41387
19 BOLINAS RD.
FAIRFAX, CA 94930 USA

IMAGINE THAT, INC. (408) 365-0305
MENU PUBLISHER NUMBER 37194 *FAX:* (408) 226-6013
7109 VIA CARMELA
SAN JOSE, CA 95139 USA

IMPULSE, INC. (800) 328-0184
MENU PUBLISHER NUMBER 93906
6870 SHINGLE CREEK PKWY.
MINNEAPOLIS, MN 55430 USA

INDIVIDUAL SOFTWARE, INC. (800) 331-3313
MENU PUBLISHER NUMBER 37275 *TELEX:* 595-1497
125 SHOREWAY DR. *FAX:* (415) 595-5619
SUITE 3000
SAN CARLOS, CA 94070 USA

INFINITE GRAPHICS, INC. (612) 721-6283
MENU PUBLISHER NUMBER 37387
4611 E. LAKE ST.
MINNEAPOLIS, MN 55406 USA

INFINITY SOFTWARE (415) 420-1551
MENU PUBLISHER NUMBER 92744 *FAX:* (415) 420-1729
1144 65TH ST.
SUITE C
EMERYVILLE, CA 94608 USA

INFOCOM, INC. (617) 492-6000
MENU PUBLISHER NUMBER 37413
125 CAMBRIDGE PARK DR.
CAMBRIDGE, MA 02140 USA

INFORMATION BUILDERS, INC.
MENU PUBLISHER NUMBER 37675
1250 BROADWAY
NEW YORK, NY 10001 USA
(212) 736-4433
TELEX: UW661558
INFOBLD

INFORMIX SOFTWARE, INC.
MENU PUBLISHER NUMBER 65750
4100 BOHANNON DR.
MENLO PARK, CA 94025 USA
(415) 322-4100
TELEX: 361834
FAX: (415) 322-4571

INFORMIX SOFTWARE, INC. (KS)
MENU PUBLISHER NUMBER 38500
9875 WIDMER RD.
LENEXA, KS 662159990 USA
(800) 438-7627
TELEX: 209542
FAX: (913) 492-2965

INFOSPHERE, INC.
MENU PUBLISHER NUMBER 38212
4730 S.W. MACADAM AVE.
PORTLAND, OR 97201 USA
(800) 445-7085
TELEX: 282829
FAX: (503) 226-6543

INFRASTRUCTURE SOFTWARE
MENU PUBLISHER NUMBER 38257
9 LEYTON CIR.
MADISON, WI 53713 USA
(608) 273-8805

INNOVATIVE DATA DESIGN, INC.
MENU PUBLISHER NUMBER 37053
2280 BATES AVE.
SUITE A
CONCORD, CA 94520 USA
(415) 680-6818
FAX: (415) 680-1165

INNOVISION
MENU PUBLISHER NUMBER 38531
DEPT. A
P.O. BOX 1317 .
LOS ALTOS, CA 940231317 USA
(415) 964-2885

INOVATIC
MENU PUBLISHER NUMBER 92746
1911 N. FORT MYER DR.
SUITE 708
ARLINGTON, VA 22209 USA
(703) 522-3053
FAX: (703) 522-6724

INSIGNIA SOLUTIONS, INC.
MENU PUBLISHER NUMBER 38546
787 LUCERNE DR.
SUNNYVALE, CA 94086 USA
(408) 446-2228
FAX: (408) 773-9541

INT'L. DATA ACQUISITION & CONTROL, INC.
MENU PUBLISHER NUMBER 39793
4 LIMBO LANE
AMHERST, NH 03031 USA
(603) 673-0765

INTELLIGENT ENGINEERED SYSTEMS
MENU PUBLISHER NUMBER 39006
4954 E. 56TH ST.
SUITE 8
INDIANAPOLIS, IN 462205769 USA
(317) 545-6618

INTELLIGENT MUSIC
MENU PUBLISHER NUMBER 39007
116 N. LAKE AVE.
ALBANY, NY 12206 USA
(518) 434-4110
FAX: (518) 434-0308

INTELLISOFT INT'L.
MENU PUBLISHER NUMBER 39038
70 DIGITAL DR.
P.O. BOX 5055
NOVATO, CA 94948 USA
(415) 883-1188
FAX: (415) 883-2646

INTERACTIVE MICROWARE, INC.
MENU PUBLISHER NUMBER 39300
P.O. BOX 139
STATE COLLEGE, PA 16804 USA
(800) 832-3021
TELEX: 705250
FAX: (814) 238-1120

INTERCEPT SOFTWARE
MENU PUBLISHER NUMBER 39562
DIV. OF S. LEVY, INC.
3425 S. BASCOM AVE.
CAMPBELL, CA 95008 USA
(408) 377-4998
TELEX: 752172
FAX: (408) 371-6804

INTERLEAF, INC.
MENU PUBLISHER NUMBER 39678
TEN CANAL PARK
CAMBRIDGE, MA 02141 USA
(617) 577-9800

INTERNATIONAL GEOMETRIC TOLERANCING INSTITUTE
MENU PUBLISHER NUMBER 67746
2943 CORTINA DR.
SAN JOSE, CA 95132 USA
(408) 251-7058

INTERNET
MENU PUBLISHER NUMBER 40257
11 LONG MEADOW RD.
LINCOLN, MA 01773 USA
(617) 259-1320

INTERPROGRAM
MENU PUBLISHER NUMBER 40293
WILDENBORCH 3
1112 XB
DIEMEN NETHERLANDS
31-20-996121

INTERSTEL CORP.
MENU PUBLISHER NUMBER 21751
P.O. BOX 57825
WEBSTER, TX 77598 USA
(713) 486-4163
FAX: (713) 488-1149

INTRACORP, INC.
MENU PUBLISHER NUMBER 40531
14160 S.W. 139TH CT.
MIAMI, FL 33186 USA
(800) 468-7226
FAX: (305) 255-1205

INTUIT
MENU PUBLISHER NUMBER 40562
540 UNIVERSITY AVE.
PALO ALTO, CA 94301 USA
(415) 322-0573
FAX: (415) 322-1597

INVENTION SOFTWARE CORP. (MI)
MENU PUBLISHER NUMBER 38337
P.O. BOX 3168
ANN ARBOR, MI 48106 USA
(313) 996-8108

ISLAND COMPUTER SERVICES
MENU PUBLISHER NUMBER 40815
3501 E. YACHT DR.
LONG BEACH, NC 28461 USA
(919) 278-9483

ISM, INC.
MENU PUBLISHER NUMBER 40882
P.O. BOX 247
PHOENIX, MD 21131 USA
(301) 527-1988
APPLELINK: D0071

J

J.J. JORDAN ARCHITECT-ENGINEER
MENU PUBLISHER NUMBER 42025
5236 OVERBROOK WAY
SACRAMENTO, CA 95841 USA
(916) 332-6610

JAM SOFTWARE
MENU PUBLISHER NUMBER 41381
P.O. BOX 1345
POINT REYES STATION, CA 94956
USA
(415) 663-1041

JAM TECHNOLOGIES
MENU PUBLISHER NUMBER 41388
685 MARKET ST.
SUITE 860
SAN FRANCISCO, CA 94105 USA
(415) 442-0795

JAMES ASSOCIATES (303) 484-5296
MENU PUBLISHER NUMBER 41400
1525 E. COUNTY RD.
SUITE 58
FT COLLINS, CO 80524 USA

JAMES RIVER GROUP, INC. (612) 339-2521
MENU PUBLISHER NUMBER 41412
125 N. FIRST ST.
MINNEAPOLIS, MN 55401 USA

JANAC ENTERPRISES (815) 648-2492
MENU PUBLISHER NUMBER 41438 *FAX:* (815) 648-2657
11214 N. RT. 47
P.O. BOX 394
HEBRON, IL 60034 USA

JAPANESE LANGUAGE SERVICES (617) 338-2211
MENU PUBLISHER NUMBER 20012 *TELEX:* ITT 494-8540
186 LINCOLN ST. *FAX:* (617) 386-4611
BOSTON, MA 02111 USA

JASIK DESIGNS (415) 322-1386
MENU PUBLISHER NUMBER 41462
343 TRENTON WAY
MENLO PARK, CA 94025 USA

JGR SPORTS SOFTWARE (801) 896-9292
MENU PUBLISHER NUMBER 41634
SOUTHERN UTAH COMPUTER SYSTEMS
25 S. MAIN
RICHFIELD, UT 84701 USA

JIM YARMCHUK (817) 332-8774
MENU PUBLISHER NUMBER 87237
810 HOUSTON ST.
SUITE 610
FORT WORTH, TX 76102 USA

JOKER SOFTWARE INT'L. (800) 24-JOKER
MENU PUBLISHER NUMBER 41975 *TELEX:* AUST.011-619-
C/O D.P.A.S. 3876507
50 VAN NESS AVE. *FAX:* (415) 863-2686
SAN FRANCISCO, CA 94102 USA

JP CONSULTING, INC. (218) 722-2602
MENU PUBLISHER NUMBER 42125
NORTHSTAR PHYSICIANS PLAN
1017 E. FIRST ST.
DULUTH, MN 55805 USA

JS GRAPHICS
MENU PUBLISHER NUMBER 93058
2472 N. BARTLETT AVE.
MILWAUKEE, WI 53211 USA

K

KAETRON SOFTWARE CORP. (713) 320-0278
MENU PUBLISHER NUMBER 42296
11318 ERICSTON DR.
HOUSTON, TX 77070 USA

KANDU SOFTWARE (703) 532-0213
MENU PUBLISHER NUMBER 42307 *FAX:* (703) 533-0291
2305 N. KENTUCKY ST.
ARLINGTON, VA 22205 USA

KANODE ASSOCIATES (602) 482-3155
MENU PUBLISHER NUMBER 42331
4709 E. SANDRA TERRACE
PHOENIX, AZ 85032 USA

KASK LABS (602) 831-1420
MENU PUBLISHER NUMBER 42400
1207 E. SECRETARIAT DR.
TEMPE, AZ 85284 USA

KAZ BUSINESS SYSTEMS (212) 757-9566
MENU PUBLISHER NUMBER 42446 *FAX:* (212) 265-9248
10 COLUMBUS CIR.
SUITE 1620
NY, NY 10019 USA

KELIX SOFTWARE SYSTEMS (504) 769-6785
MENU PUBLISHER NUMBER 42550
11814 COURSEY BLVD.
#220
BATON ROUGE, LA 70816 USA

KENT MARSH LTD., INC. (800) 325-3587
MENU PUBLISHER NUMBER 47462 *TELEX:* WUT792333 VIA
1200 POST OAK BLVD. TLXHOU
SUITE 210
HOUSTON, TX 77056 USA

KEVIN J. DOYLE, COMPUTER SYSTEMS (508) 745-2679
CONSULTANT *APPLELINK:* V0289
MENU PUBLISHER NUMBER 26752
27 CONGRESS ST.
SALEM, MA 01970 USA

KINGSLEY/ATF SOFTWARE DIVISION (800) 289-8973
MENU PUBLISHER NUMBER 43012
2559-2 E. BROADWAY
TUCSON, AZ 85716 USA

KINKOS ACADEMIC COURSEWARE (800) 235-6919
EXCHANGE
MENU PUBLISHER NUMBER 43025
255 W. STANLEY AVE., SUITE A
P.O. BOX 8000
VENTURA, CA 930028000 USA

KLEX SOFTWARE, INC. (313) 477-6800
MENU PUBLISHER NUMBER 43107
25633 BRANCHASTER
FARMINGTON HILLS, MI 48018 USA

KNICK DRAFTING, INC. (407) 777-0275
MENU PUBLISHER NUMBER 43110
1275 S. PATRICK DR.
SUITE P
SATELLITE BEACH, FL 32937 USA

KNOWLEDGE ENGINEERING (203) 622-8770
MENU PUBLISHER NUMBER 93342 *FAX:* (203) 622-0688
G.P.O. BOX 2139
NEW YORK, NY 10116 USA

L

L & L PRODUCTS, INC. (603) 643-4503
MENU PUBLISHER NUMBER 43306
WHEELER PROFESSIONAL PARK
P.O. BOX A-57
HANOVER, NH 03755 USA

LAKE AVE. SOFTWARE (818) 351-5483
MENU PUBLISHER NUMBER 43418 *FAX:* (818) 351-5497
650 SIERRA MADRE VILLA
SUITE 204
PASADENA, CA 911072013 USA

LAMIR SOFTWARE CORP. (707) 448-5901
MENU PUBLISHER NUMBER 43453
336 CERNON ST.
VACAVILLE, CA 95688 USA

LANCE HAFFNER GAMES   (615) 242-2617
MENU PUBLISHER NUMBER 43487
P.O. BOX 100594
NASHVILLE, TN 37210 USA

LANGUAGE SYSTEMS CORP.   (703) 478-0181
MENU PUBLISHER NUMBER 43576   *FAX:* (703) 689-9593
441 CARLISLE DR.
HERNDON, VA 22070 USA

LARRY ROSEN CO.   (502) 228-4343
MENU PUBLISHER NUMBER 66987
7008 SPRINGDALE RD.
LOUISVILLE, KY 40241 USA

LASER DIGITAL CORP.   (800) 338-4259
MENU PUBLISHER NUMBER 43660
P.O. BOX 11169
EUGENE, OR 97440 USA

LASERWARE, INC.   (800) 367-6898
MENU PUBLISHER NUMBER 27734
P.O. BOX 668
SAN RAFAEL, CA 94915 USA

LAYERED, INC.   (617) 242-7700
MENU PUBLISHER NUMBER 43760
SCHRAFF CENTER
529 MAIN ST.
BOSTON, MA 02129 USA

LE COQ BRANCHE   (619) 568-6773
MENU PUBLISHER NUMBER 43783
73450 COUNTRY CLUB DR.
#291
PALM DESERT, CA 92260 USA

LEARNING CO. (THE)   (415) 792-2101
MENU PUBLISHER NUMBER 43870   *FAX:* (415) 792-9628
6493 KAISER DR.
FREMONT, CA 94555 USA

LEARNING SKILLS, INC.   (702) 747-2277
MENU PUBLISHER NUMBER 43875
P.O. BOX 8038
RENO, NV 89507 USA

LEGALWARE, INC.   (416) 863-6906
MENU PUBLISHER NUMBER 44063
135 KING ST. E.
TORONTO, ONTARIO M5C 1G6
CANADA

LES EDITIONS/AD LIB, INC.   (800) 463-2686
MENU PUBLISHER NUMBER 44287   *FAX:* (418) 529-1159
220, GRANDE-ALLEE EST
BUREAU 960
QUEBEC, QUEBEC G1R 2J1
CANADA

LETRASET   (201) 845-6100
MENU PUBLISHER NUMBER 44293
40 EISENHOWER DR.
PARAMUS, NJ 07653 USA

LEXPERTISE, USA, INC.   (800) 354-5656
MENU PUBLISHER NUMBER 44474   *FAX:* (801) 350-9051
175 E. 400 SOUTH
SUITE 1000
SALT LAKE CITY, UT 84111 USA

LIGHTSHIP SOFTWARE   (503) 643-4539
MENU PUBLISHER NUMBER 69162
4470 S.W. HALL ST.
SUITE 340
BEAVERTON, OR 97005 USA

LINDO SYSTEMS   (312) 871-2524
MENU PUBLISHER NUMBER 44737
P.O. BOX 148231
CHICAGO, IL 60614 USA

LINGUIST'S SOFTWARE, INC.   (206) 775-1130
MENU PUBLISHER NUMBER 44825
P.O. BOX 580
EDMONDS, WA 980200580 USA

LIONHEART PRESS   (514) 933-4918
MENU PUBLISHER NUMBER 44900
P.O. BOX 379
ALBURG, VT 05440 USA

LIONSHEAD SOFTWARE, INC.   (407) 790-1157
MENU PUBLISHER NUMBER 44912
1911 HOLLYHOCK RD.
WEST PALM BEACH, FL 33414 USA

LIPA SOFTWARE   (415) 366-0547
MENU PUBLISHER NUMBER 44925
165 HARCROSS RD.
WOODSIDE, CA 94062 USA

LITURGICAL PUBLICATIONS, INC.   (414) 785-1188
MENU PUBLISHER NUMBER 93628
1025 S. MOORLAND RD.
SUITE 300
BROOKFIELD, WI 53005 USA

LOGIC EXTENSION RESOURCES   (714) 980-0046
MENU PUBLISHER NUMBER 45225   *FAX:* (714) 987-8706
9651 BUSINESS CENTER DR.
SUITE C
RANCHO CUCAMONGA, CA 91730
USA

LOGIC GROUP   (512) 474-4641
MENU PUBLISHER NUMBER 45237
P.O. BOX 50499
AUSTIN, TX 78763 USA

LOGIC PROGRAMMING ASSOCIATES   44-187-12016
LTD.   *TELEX:* 9312110461 (LPG)
MENU PUBLISHER NUMBER 45287   *FAX:* 44-187-40449
ROYAL VICTORIA PATRIOTIC BLVD.
STUDIO 4, TRINITY RD.
LONDON SW18 3SX ENGLAND

LONDON PRIDE, INC.   (203) 866-4806
MENU PUBLISHER NUMBER 45503
#1 BIRCH ST.
NORWALK, CT 068519990 USA

LOTUS DEVELOPMENT CORP.   (617) 577-8500
MENU PUBLISHER NUMBER 45525
55 CAMBRIDGE PKWY.
CAMBRIDGE, MA 02142 USA

LUNDEEN AND ASSOCIATES   (800) 233-6851
MENU PUBLISHER NUMBER 45593   *FAX:* (415) 769-2078
1000 ATLANTIC AVE.
SUITE 107
ALAMEDA, CA 94501 USA

LUNDIN LABORATORIES, INC.   (800) 426-8426
MENU PUBLISHER NUMBER 45596   *FAX:* (313) 443-5191
29451 GREENFIELD RD.
SOUTHFIELD, MI 48076 USA

M

M/H GROUP
(312) 443-1222
MENU PUBLISHER NUMBER 45637
TELEX: 650 3306745
222 W. ADAMS ST.
FAX: (312) 443-1377
#1410
CHICAGO, IL 60606 USA

MAC AMERICA (CA)
(714) 779-2922
MENU PUBLISHER NUMBER 71848
18032-C LEMAY DR.
YORBA LINDA, CA 92686 USA

MAC MASTER
(408) 773-9834
MENU PUBLISHER NUMBER 45784
108 E. FREEMONT AVE.
SUITE 37
SUNNYVILLE, CA 94087 USA

MACHUNTER
(213) 393-7006
MENU PUBLISHER NUMBER 45825
228 SANTA MONICA BLVD.
SUITE 7
SANTA MONICA, CA 90401 USA

MACLORD SYSTEMS, INC.
(714) 687-1919
MENU PUBLISHER NUMBER 93907
9487 MAGNOLIA AVE.
RIVERSIDE, CA 92503 USA

MACMEDIC PUBLICATIONS, INC.
(713) 977-2655
MENU PUBLISHER NUMBER 45845
FAX: (713) 784-1271
7530 HARWIN DR.
HOUSTON, TX 77036 USA

MACMIDI
(617) 266-2886
MENU PUBLISHER NUMBER 55865
18 HAVILAND ST.
BOSTON, MA 02115 USA

MACNEAL-SCHWENDLER CORP.
(213) 258-9111
MENU PUBLISHER NUMBER 45900
FAX: (213) 259-3838
815 COLORADO BLVD.
LOS ANGELES, CA 90041 USA

MACPDS
(206) 367-1129
MENU PUBLISHER NUMBER 93905
TELEX: 6503075508
P.O. BOX 85097
VIA WUI
SEATTLE, WA 98105 USA
FAX: (206) 367-1129

MACPOINT PUBLICATIONS
(312) 955-1954
MENU PUBLISHER NUMBER 45902
1374 E. 57TH ST., #3
CHICAGO, IL 60637 USA

MACRO MIND PUBLISHING
(312) 871-0987
MENU PUBLISHER NUMBER 45904
FAX: (312) 871-6448
1028 W. WOLFRAM
CHICAGO, IL 60657 USA

MACSHACK ENTERPRISES
(617) 876-0165
MENU PUBLISHER NUMBER 45910
19 HARRINGTON RD.
CAMBRIDGE, MA 02140 USA

MACTOGRAPHY
(301) 424-1357
MENU PUBLISHER NUMBER 00031
702 TWINBROOK PKWY.
ROCKVILLE, MD 20851 USA

MACTRAK SOFTWARE
(206) 871-1111
MENU PUBLISHER NUMBER 65131
P.O. BOX 1590
PORT ORCHARD, WA 98366 USA

MACTRONICS
(214) 520-1570
MENU PUBLISHER NUMBER 93904
4416 TRAVIS
#105
DALLAS, TX 75205 USA

MAGIC SOFTWARE, INC.
(402) 291-0670
MENU PUBLISHER NUMBER 45962
FAX: (402) 291-1121
1602 CASCIO DR.
BELLEVUE, NE 68005 USA

MAGNA
(408) 433-5467
MENU PUBLISHER NUMBER 45987
2540 N. FIRST ST.
SUITE 302
SAN JOSE, CA 95131 USA

MAGNUM SOFTWARE
(818) 700-0510
MENU PUBLISHER NUMBER 46032
21115 DEVONSHIRE ST.
SUITE 337
CHATSWORTH, CA 91311 USA

MAINSTAY
(818) 991-6540
MENU PUBLISHER NUMBER 46041
TELEX: 696191
5311-B DERRY AVE.
AGOURA HILLS, CA 91301 USA

MANOR OF MICRO, INC.
(612) 426-5606
MENU PUBLISHER NUMBER 46631
6827 BLACK DUCK CIR.
LINO LAKES, MN 55014 USA

MANX SOFTWARE SYSTEMS
(201) 542-2121
MENU PUBLISHER NUMBER 46856
FAX: (201) 542-8386
P.O. BOX 55
SHREWSBURY, NJ 07701 USA

MARK OF THE UNICORN
(617) 576-2760
MENU PUBLISHER NUMBER 47250
TELEX: 499 6346 UNICORN
222 3RD ST.
CAMBRIDGE, MA 02142 USA

MARKET ENGINEERING CORP.
(800) 289-2550
MENU PUBLISHER NUMBER 47365
1675 LARIMER ST.
SUITE 640
DENVER, CO 80202 USA

MARVELIN CORP.
(213) 450-6813
MENU PUBLISHER NUMBER 47483
3420 OCEAN PARK BLVD.
#3020
SANTA MONICA, CA 90405 USA

MATHEMATICAL SOFTWARE CO.
(619) 940-0343
MENU PUBLISHER NUMBER 47775
P.O. BOX 12349
EL CAJON, CA 92022 USA

MAX 3, INC.
(213) 398-3771
MENU PUBLISHER NUMBER 59754
FAX: (213) 276-7740
3021 AIRPORT AVE.
SUITE 112
SANTA MONICA, CA 90405 USA

MAXIS SOFTWARE, INC.
(415) 376-6434
MENU PUBLISHER NUMBER 47900
953 MT. VIEW DR.
SUITE 113
LAFAYETTE, CA 94549 USA

MCCUTCHEON GRAPHICS, INC.
(416) 636-6070
MENU PUBLISHER NUMBER 48212
88 ST. REGIS CRESCENT
NORTH YORK, ONTARIO M3J 1Y8
CANADA

MCTEL, INC.
(215) 668-0983
MENU PUBLISHER NUMBER 60925
TELEX: TLX-467515
5070 PARKSIDE AVE.
SUITE 1300
PHILADELPHIA, PA 19131 USA

MECA VENTURES, INC.
MENU PUBLISHER NUMBER 50231
355 RIVERSIDE AVE.
WESTPORT, CT 06880 USA
(203) 226-2426
FAX: (203) 222-6540

MECKLERSOFT
MENU PUBLISHER NUMBER 93919
11 FERRY LANE W.
WESTPORT, CT 068805808 USA
(203) 226-6967
FAX: (203) 454-5840

MEDIAGENIC/ACTIVISION ENTERTAINMENT
MENU PUBLISHER NUMBER 48679
3885 BOHANNON DR.
MENLO PARK, CA 94025 USA
(415) 329-0500
TELEX: 172758
FAX: (415) 322-0260

MEDIAGENIC/SOLID GOLD SOFTWARE
MENU PUBLISHER NUMBER 48693
3885 BOHANNON DR.
MENLO PARK, CA 94025 USA
(415) 329-0500
TELEX: 172758
FAX: (415) 329-0260

MEDIAGENIC/TENPOINT0
MENU PUBLISHER NUMBER 48702
3885 BOHANNON DR.
MENLO PARK, CA 94025 USA
(415) 329-0500
TELEX: 172758
FAX: (415) 322-0260

MEDINA SOFTWARE, INC.
MENU PUBLISHER NUMBER 48842
P.O. BOX 521917
LONGWOOD, FL 327521917 USA
(407) 260-1676

MEGAMAX, INC.
MENU PUBLISHER NUMBER 48887
BOX 851521
RICHARDSON, TX 750851521 USA
(214) 987-4931

MEGATHERIUM ENTERPRISES
MENU PUBLISHER NUMBER 48961
P.O. BOX 7000-417
REDONDO BEACH, CA 90277 USA
(213) 545-5913

MENLO BUSINESS SYSTEMS, INC.
MENU PUBLISHER NUMBER 48969
201 MAIN ST.
LOS ALTOS, CA 94022 USA
(415) 948-7920
FAX: (415) 948-5824

MERIDIAN SOFTWARE SYSTEMS, INC.
MENU PUBLISHER NUMBER 49106
23141 VERDUGO DR.
SUITE 105
LAGUNA HILLS, CA 92653 USA
(714) 380-9800
FAX: (714) 380-1683

MERRY MAID, INC./BUSINESS SYSTEMS GROUP
MENU PUBLISHER NUMBER 49169
P.O. BOX 228
25 MESSENGER ST.
BANGOR, PA 18013 USA
(215) 588-0927

MESA GRAPHICS, INC.
MENU PUBLISHER NUMBER 49173
P.O. BOX 600
LOS ALAMOS, NM 87544 USA
(505) 672-1998
APPLELINK: D0194

MESA RESEARCH
MENU PUBLISHER NUMBER 49177
R-12, BOX 480
WACO, TX 76712 USA
(817) 848-5272

MESSENGER SOFTWARE, INC.
MENU PUBLISHER NUMBER 49196
180 W. STREETSBORO RD.
SUITE 302
HUDSON, OH 44236 USA
(216) 656-3679

META SOFTWARE CORP.
MENU PUBLISHER NUMBER 49215
150 CAMBRIDGE PARK DR.
CAMBRIDGE, MA 02140 USA
(617) 576-6920
FAX: (617) 576-0519

METACOMET SOFTWARE
MENU PUBLISHER NUMBER 49223
P.O. BOX 31337
HARTFORD, CT 06103 USA
(800) 345-9111

METARESEARCH, INC.
MENU PUBLISHER NUMBER 49225
516 S.E. MORRISON
SUITE M-1
PORTLAND, OR 97214 USA
(503) 238-5728

METROPOLIS COMPUTER NETWORKS, INC.
MENU PUBLISHER NUMBER 49287
THE TRIMEX BLDG.
ROUTE 11
MOOERS, NY 12958 USA
(514) 866-4776
FAX: (514) 871-1269

METROPOLIS SOFTWARE, INC.
MENU PUBLISHER NUMBER 80218
499 HAMILTON AVE.
SUITE 202
PALO ALTO, CA 94301 USA
(415) 322-2001

MFE ASSOCIATES
MENU PUBLISHER NUMBER 49331
BOX 851
AMHERST, MA 01004 USA
(413) 549-7626
TELEX: 37-94190 MFEDK
FAX: (413) 549-7542

MGI
MENU PUBLISHER NUMBER 49362
4401 DOMINION BLVD.
SUITE 210
GLEN ALLEN, VA 230603379 USA
(804) 747-6991
FAX: (804) 747-0879

MGLOBAL
MENU PUBLISHER NUMBER 49375
3618 MT. VERNON
SUITE D
HOUSTON, TX 77006 USA
(713) 529-4858

MICRO CAD/CAM SYSTEMS, INC.
MENU PUBLISHER NUMBER 49818
5900 SEPULVEDA BLVD.
VAN NUYS, CA 91411 USA
(818) 376-0008
TELEX: 650-3107078
MCI UW
FAX: (818) 901-0617

MICRO DIALECTS, INC.
MENU PUBLISHER NUMBER 50226
P.O. BOX 30014
CINCINNATI, OH 45230 USA
(513) 271-9100

MICRO DYNAMICS. LTD.
MENU PUBLISHER NUMBER 50227
8555 16TH ST.
SUITE 802
SILVER SPRING, MD 20910 USA
(301) 589-6300

MICRO PLANNING INT'L.
MENU PUBLISHER NUMBER 50912
235 MONTGOMERY ST.
SUITE 840
SAN FRANCISCO, CA 94104 USA
(415) 788-3324
FAX: (415) 788-3405

MICRO SYSTEMS SOFTWARE (FLA)
MENU PUBLISHER NUMBER 51534
12798 W. FOREST HILL BLVD.
SUITE 202
W. PALM BEACH, FL 33414 USA
(800) 327-8724

MICRO TRADING SOFTWARE LTD.
MENU PUBLISHER NUMBER 51553
123 HULDA HILL RD.
WILTON, CT 06897 USA
(203) 762-7820

MICROCODE ENGINEERING (801) 226-4470
MENU PUBLISHER NUMBER 51737
1943 N. 205 W.
SUITE 1
OREM, UT 84057 USA

MICROILLUSIONS (800) 522-2041
MENU PUBLISHER NUMBER 50425 FAX: (818) 360-1464
17408 CHATSWORTH ST.
GRANADA HILLS, CA 91344 USA

MICROLYTICS, INC. (716) 248-9620
MENU PUBLISHER NUMBER 52573 FAX: (716) 248-3868
ONE TOBEY VILLAGE OFFICE PARK
PITTSFORD, NY 14534 USA

MICROMAPS SOFTWARE, INC. (609) 397-1611
MENU PUBLISHER NUMBER 50675
P.O. BOX 757
LAMBERTVILLE, NJ 08530 USA

MICROMASH (800) 241-9700
MENU PUBLISHER NUMBER 52590 FAX: (303) 799-1425
14 INVERNESS DR. E.
SUITE F-104
ENGLEWOOD, CO 80112 USA

MICROMEDX (800) 535-3438
MENU PUBLISHER NUMBER 52737
187 GARDINERS AVE.
LEVITTOWN, NY 11756 USA

MICROMOTION (213) 821-4340
MENU PUBLISHER NUMBER 52750
8726 S. SEPULVEDA BLVD.
SUITE A171
LOS ANGELES, CA 90045 USA

MICRONEERING (800) 423-0814
MENU PUBLISHER NUMBER 52818
211 E. CULVER BLVD.
SUITE Q
PLAYA DEL REY, CA 90293 USA

MICROSEEDS PUBLISHING, INC. (813) 882-8635
MENU PUBLISHER NUMBER 53093
7030-B W. HILLSBOROUGH AVE.
TAMPA, FL 33615 USA

MICROSERVE, INC. (512) 343-0180
MENU PUBLISHER NUMBER 53112
4412 SPICEWOOD SPRINGS
SUITE F-1000
AUSTIN, TX 78759 USA

MICROSOFT CORP. (206) 882-8080
MENU PUBLISHER NUMBER 53150 FAX: (206) 883-8101
16011 N.E. 36TH WAY
BOX 97017
REDMOND, WA 980739717 USA

MICROSOFT STRUCTURAL SYSTEMS 61-928-9047
MENU PUBLISHER NUMBER 53250
29 THE DOWNS
ALTRINGHAM, MANCHESTER WA14
2QD
ENGLAND

MICROSTAR SOFTWARE LTD. (613) 727-5696
MENU PUBLISHER NUMBER 53437 FAX: (613) 727-9491
34 COLONNADE RD. N.
SUITE 100
NEPEAN, ONTARIO K2E 7J6
CANADA

MICROTEK LAB, INC. (213) 321-2121
MENU PUBLISHER NUMBER 53662 TELEX: 797880 MICRO
16901 SOUTH WESTERN AVE.
GARDENA, CA 90247 USA

MICROTEMP (707) 575-1459
MENU PUBLISHER NUMBER 53668
318 MENDOCINO AVE.
SANTA ROSA, CA 95404 USA

MIGENT SOFTWARE CORP. (702) 832-3700
MENU PUBLISHER NUMBER 87037 FAX: (702) 832-3725
865 TAHOE BLVD.
CALL BOX 6
INCLINE VILLAGE, NV 894506062
USA

MILES COMPUTING, INC. (818) 340-6300
MENU PUBLISHER NUMBER 54075
5115 DOUGLAS FIR RD.
SUITE I
CALABASAS, CA 91302 USA

MINDCRAFT PUBLISHING CORP. (508) 371-1660
MENU PUBLISHER NUMBER 53425
52 DOMINO DR.
CONCORD, MA 01742 USA

MINDPLAY (800) 221-7911
MENU PUBLISHER NUMBER 54362
100 CONIFER HILL DR.
BLDG. 3, SUITE 301
DANVERS, MA 01923 USA

MINDSCAPE, INC. (800) 221-9884
MENU PUBLISHER NUMBER 54375 TELEX: 206699
3444 DUNDEE RD. FAX: (312) 480-0496
NORTHBROOK, IL 60062 USA

MISSING LINK SOFTWARE, INC. (201) 721-2569
MENU PUBLISHER NUMBER 54785
BOX 3280
SOUTH AMBOY, NJ 08879 USA

MLT SOFTWARE (503) 245-7093
MENU PUBLISHER NUMBER 54834
P.O. BOX 98041
6325 S.W. CAPITAL HWY.
PORTLAND, OR 97201 USA

MMC AD SYSTEMS (408) 263-0781
MENU PUBLISHER NUMBER 54835
BOX 360845
MILPITAS, CA 95035 USA

MODACAD, INC. (213) 312-6632
MENU PUBLISHER NUMBER 54848 FAX: (313) 444-9577
1954 COTNER AVE.
LOS ANGELES, CA 90025 USA

MODERN GRAPHICS (317) 253-4316
MENU PUBLISHER NUMBER 54925
P.O. BOX 21366
INDIANAPOLIS, IN 462210366 USA

MODULA CORP. (801) 224-8999
MENU PUBLISHER NUMBER 55068
1121 S. OREM BLVD.
OREM, UT 84058 USA

MONOGRAM SOFTWARE, INC. (213) 533-5120
MENU PUBLISHER NUMBER 55240
531 VAN NESS AVE.
TORRANCE, CA 905011420 USA

MOUSETRAP SOFTWARE (412) 372-9004
MENU PUBLISHER NUMBER 55484
336 COLEMAN DR.
MONROEVILLE, PA 15146 USA

MPM COMPUTING   (213) 254-2806
MENU PUBLISHER NUMBER 93916
6135 YORK BLVD.
LOS ANGELES, CA 90042 USA

MULTI SOLUTIONS, INC.   (609) 896-4100
MENU PUBLISHER NUMBER 55676   *TELEX:* 821073
123 FRANKLIN CORNER RD.
LAWRENCEVILLE, NJ 08648 USA

N

N-SQUARED COMPUTING   (503) 873-5906
MENU PUBLISHER NUMBER 55907
5318 FOREST RIDGE RD.
SILVERTON, OR 97381 USA

NANTUCKET CORP.   (213) 390-7923
MENU PUBLISHER NUMBER 55949   *FAX:* (213) 397-5469
12555 W. JEFFERSON BLVD.
LOS ANGELES, CA 90066 USA

NAPPO SOFTWARE   203-878-8770
MENU PUBLISHER NUMBER 55956
284 NAUGATUCK AVE.
P.O. BOX 4116
MILFORD, CT 06406 USA

NASHOBA SYSTEMS   (800) 274-0610
MENU PUBLISHER NUMBER 55970   *FAX:* (415) 578-8901
1157 TRITON DR.
SUITE A
FOSTER CITY, CA 94404 USA

NATIONAL INSTRUMENTS CORP.   (512) 250-9119
MENU PUBLISHER NUMBER 56100   *TELEX:* 756737
12109 TECHNOLOGY BLVD.   *FAX:* (512) 250-0382
AUSTIN, TX 787276204 USA

NATIONAL TELE-PRESS   (707) 937-2848
MENU PUBLISHER NUMBER 94203
44651 WOODSTOCK RD.
MENDOCINO, CA 95460 USA

NEC INFORMATION SYSTEMS, INC.   (617) 635-4000
MENU PUBLISHER NUMBER 56400   *TELEX:* (617) 635-4400
155 SWANSON
FOXBOROUGH, MA 01719 USA

NEMESIS SYSTEMS   (612) 535-7485
MENU PUBLISHER NUMBER 56512
P.O. BOX 33268
MINNEAPOLIS, MN 55433 USA

NEOSCRIBE INT'L.   (203) 467-9880
MENU PUBLISHER NUMBER 56537
P.O. BOX 633
EAST HAVEN, CT 06512 USA

NEURON DATA, INC.   (415) 321-4488
MENU PUBLISHER NUMBER 56569   *FAX:* (415) 321-9648
444 HIGH ST.
PALO ALTO, CA 94301 USA

NEW CANAAN MICROCODE   (203) 966-6969
MENU PUBLISHER NUMBER 56573   *TELEX:* (023) 6502910484
136 BEECH RD.
NEW CANAAN, CT 06840 USA

NEW HORIZONS SOFTWARE   (512) 328-6650
MENU PUBLISHER NUMBER 56703   *TELEX:* (650) 287-6117
P.O. BOX 43167
AUSTIN, TX 78745 USA

NEW IMAGE TECHNOLOGY, INC.   (301) 731-2000
MENU PUBLISHER NUMBER 56706   *FAX:* (301) 731-4760
9701 PHILADELPHIA CT.
LANHAM, MD 20706 USA

NEW WEST SOFTWARE   (714) 898-1039
MENU PUBLISHER NUMBER 94216
5462 OCEANUS
SUITE B
HUNTINGTON BEACH, CA 92649
USA

NEW WORLD COMPUTING, INC.   (818) 785-0519
MENU PUBLISHER NUMBER 56744   *FAX:* (818) 785-5034
14922 CALVERT ST.
VAN NUYS, CA 91411 USA

NEWHOUSE MEDICAL SYSTEMS LTD.   (800) 323-3002
MENU PUBLISHER NUMBER 56753
50 S. 18TH ST.
EASTON, PA 18042 USA

NEWSOFT   (714) 646-9949
MENU PUBLISHER NUMBER 56762
P.O. BOX 3046
NEWPORT BEACH, CA 92663 USA

NIKROM TECHNICAL PRODUCTS, INC.   (508) 537-9970
MENU PUBLISHER NUMBER 56950
176 FORT POND RD.
SHIRLEY, MA 01464 USA

NILES AND ASSOCIATES   (415) 655-6666
MENU PUBLISHER NUMBER 56952
2200 POWELL ST.
SUITE 765
EMERYVILLE, CA 94608 USA

NOLO PRESS   (415) 549-1976
MENU PUBLISHER NUMBER 44075   *FAX:* (415) 548-5902
950 PARKER ST.
BERKELEY, CA 94710 USA

NORDIC SOFTWARE, INC.   (402) 466-6502
MENU PUBLISHER NUMBER 57028
3939 N. 48TH ST.
LINCOLN, NE 68504 USA

NORTON W.W.   (212) 354-5500
MENU PUBLISHER NUMBER 57290
500 5TH AVE.
NEW YORK, NY 10110 USA

NUEQUATION, INC.   (214) 699-7747
MENU PUBLISHER NUMBER 57416
1701 N. GREENVILLE AVE.
SUITE 703
RICHARDSON, TX 75081 USA

NUMERISATION SERVICES S.A.   (331) 43368686
MENU PUBLISHER NUMBER 90916   *FAX:* (331) 45358833
73-77 RUE PASCAL
PARIS 75013 FRANCE

NUVO LABS   (805) 544-5766
MENU PUBLISHER NUMBER 57484
245A TANK FARM RD.
SAN LUIS OBISPO, CA 93401 USA

O

OAKLEAF SYSTEMS   (319) 382-4320
MENU PUBLISHER NUMBER 57587
P.O. BOX 472
DECORAH, IA 52101 USA

ODESTA CORP.   (312) 498-5615
MENU PUBLISHER NUMBER 57709
4084 COMMERCIAL AVE.
NORTHBROOK, IL 60062 USA

OHM SOFTWARE   (401) 253-9354
MENU PUBLISHER NUMBER 57781
163 RICHARD DR.
TIVERTON, RI 02878 USA

OITC, INC.   (407) 984-3714
MENU PUBLISHER NUMBER 94527   *FAX:* (407) 723-8484
P.O. BOX 73
MELBOURNE BEACH, FL 32951 USA

OLDUVAI CORP.   (305) 665-4665
MENU PUBLISHER NUMBER 57812
7520 RED RD.
SUITE A
SOUTH MIAMI, FL 33143 USA

OMNITREND SOFTWARE, INC.   (203) 658-6917
MENU PUBLISHER NUMBER 58198
P.O. BOX 733
WEST SIMSBURY, CT 06092 USA

ONTRACK COMPUTER SYSTEMS, INC.   (800) 752-1333
MENU PUBLISHER NUMBER 58380   *TELEX:* 910 240 0196
6231 BURY DR.   *FAX:* (612) 937-5815
SUITES 16-19
EDEN PRAIRIE, MN 55346 USA

OPCODE SYSTEMS   (415) 321-8977
MENU PUBLISHER NUMBER 58384   *TELEX:* 9102400541OPCODE
1024 HAMILTON CT.   PLA
MENLO PARK, CA 94025 USA

OPTIONS-80   (808) 874-3534
MENU PUBLISHER NUMBER 58660
P.O. BOX 674
KIHEI, HI 96753 USA

OR-D SYSTEMS   (609) 795-8300
MENU PUBLISHER NUMBER 58663
1414 BRACE RD.
CHERRY HILL, NJ 08034 USA

ORACLE CORP.   (415) 598-8000
MENU PUBLISHER NUMBER 58667   *TELEX:* 171437
MARKETING DIV.   *FAX:* (415) 595-0630
20 DAVIS DR.
BELMONT, CA 94002 USA

ORANGE MICRO, INC.   (714) 779-2772
MENU PUBLISHER NUMBER 58668
1400 N. LAKEVIEW AVE.
ANAHEIM, CA 92807 USA

ORIGIN SYSTEMS, INC.   (603) 644-3360
MENU PUBLISHER NUMBER 58793
136 HARVEY RD.
BLDG. B
LONDONDERRY, NH 03053 USA

ORION COMPUTER TRAINING SYSTEMS   (800) 451-5059
MENU PUBLISHER NUMBER 58862
2591 S. QUEEN ST.
YORK, PA 17402 USA

ORTHO INFORMATION SERVICES   (415) 842-5537
MENU PUBLISHER NUMBER 58887   *FAX:* (415) 842-5518
6001 BOLLINGER CANYON RD.
BUILDING T
SAN RAMON, CA 94583 USA

OWL INTERNATIONAL, INC.   (800) 34-HYPER
MENU PUBLISHER NUMBER 58987   *FAX:* (206) 641-9367
2800-156TH S.E.
BELLEVUE, WA 98007 USA

P

P PRODUCTIONS
MENU PUBLISHER NUMBER 59187
2514 ILLINOIS ST.
RACINE, WI 53405 USA

P3, INC.   (312) 729-2555
MENU PUBLISHER NUMBER 59250
246 NOTTINGHAM AVE.
GLENVIEW, IL 60025 USA

PACER SOFTWARE, INC.   (508) 898-3300
MENU PUBLISHER NUMBER 59306   *FAX:* (508) 366-1356
1900 W. PARK DR.
SUITE 280
WESTBOROUGH, MA 01581 USA

PAGE STUDIO GRAPHICS   (602) 839-2763
MENU PUBLISHER NUMBER 59575
3175 N. PRICE RD.
SUITE 1050
CHANDLER, AZ 85224 USA

PALANTIR, INC.   (800) 368-3797
MENU PUBLISHER NUMBER 59624   *TELEX:* 790510
17314 TOMBALL PKWY.   *FAX:* (713) 955-8924
SUITE 101
HOUSTON, TX 770641108 USA

PALO ALTO SHIPPING CO.   (800) 443-6784
MENU PUBLISHER NUMBER 59681   *FAX:* (415) 363-8511
P.O. BOX 7430
MENLO PARK, CA 94026 USA

PALO ALTO SOFTWARE   (415) 325-3190
MENU PUBLISHER NUMBER 37443   *TELEX:* (650) 203-3525 (MCI)
260 SHERIDAN AVE.
SUITE 219
PALO ALTO, CA 94306 USA

PALOMAR SOFTWARE, INC.   (619) 721-7000
MENU PUBLISHER NUMBER 59684
P.O. BOX 2635
VISTA, CA 92083 USA

PAPERBACK SOFTWARE INT'L.   (415) 644-2116
MENU PUBLISHER NUMBER 59721   *TELEX:* 5106014700
2830 NINTH ST.   *FAX:* (415) 644-8241
BERKELEY, CA 94710 USA

PARAGON CONCEPTS, INC.   (619) 481-1477
MENU PUBLISHER NUMBER 59740   *APPLELINK:* D0405
4954 SUN VALLEY RD.
DEL MAR, CA 92014 USA

PARAGON SOFTWARE CORP.   (412) 838-1166
MENU PUBLISHER NUMBER 53429   *TELEX:* 709204
600 RUGH ST.   *FAX:* (412) 838-1169
GREENSBURG, PA 15601 USA

PARK ROW SOFTWARE   (619) 581-6778
MENU PUBLISHER NUMBER 59755
4640 JEWELL ST.
#232
SAN DIEGO, CA 92109 USA

PASSPORT DESIGNS, INC.   (415) 726-0280
MENU PUBLISHER NUMBER 59781
625 MIRAMONTES ST.
SUITE 103
HALF MOON BAY, CA 94019 USA

PAUL MACE SOFTWARE   (503) 488-0224
MENU PUBLISHER NUMBER 59790   *FAX:* (503) 488-1549
400 WILLIAMSON WAY
ASHLAND, OR 97520 USA

PAUL RAPOPORT   (416) 648-2181
MENU PUBLISHER NUMBER 95403
7 CRADOCK CT.
ANCASTER, ONTARIO L9G 3Z5
CANADA

PAZ GRAPHICS   (416) 766-4077
MENU PUBLISHER NUMBER 59912
60 MOUNTVIEW AVE.
#410
TORONTO, ONTARIO M6P 2L4
CANADA

PBI SOFTWARE   (415) 349-8765
MENU PUBLISHER NUMBER 59937   *FAX:* (415) 573-9586
1163 TRITON DR.
FOSTER CITY, CA 94404 USA

PDS SPORTS   (213) 212-7788
MENU PUBLISHER NUMBER 60137
P.O. BOX E
TORRANCE, CA 90507 USA

PEACHTREE SOFTWARE, INC.   (800) 247-3224
MENU PUBLISHER NUMBER 60150   *FAX:* (404) 564-5888
4355 SHACKLEFORD RD.
NORCROSS, GA 30093 USA

**PEAT MARWICK ADVANCED
TECHNOLOGY**   (514) 646-0600
MENU PUBLISHER NUMBER 60287   *FAX:* (514) 646-8167
1111 ST. CHARLES W.
SUITE 600
LONGUEVIL, QUEBEC J4K 5G4
CANADA

PECAN SOFTWARE SYSTEMS   (718) 851-3100
MENU PUBLISHER NUMBER 60356   *TELEX:* 494-8910
1410 39TH ST.
BROOKLYN, NY 11218 USA

PEMD EDUCATION GROUP   01 915 0861
MENU PUBLISHER NUMBER 60424
AROSA STR. 6
8008
ZURICH, SWITZERLAND

PERCEPTICS   (615) 966-9200
MENU PUBLISHER NUMBER 60512   *FAX:* (615) 966-9330
725 PELLISSIPPI PARKWAY
P.O. BOX 22991
KNOXVILLE, TN 379330991 USA

PERIDOM, INC.   (301) 390-9570
MENU PUBLISHER NUMBER 60537
P.O. BOX 1812
BOWIE, MD 20716 USA

**PERIPHERALS COMPUTERS SUPPLIES,
INC.**   (215) 779-0522
                                                            FAX: (215) 370-0548
MENU PUBLISHER NUMBER 60539
2457 PERKIOMEN AVE.
READING, PA 19606 USA

**PERSONAL BIBLIOGRAPHIC SOFTWARE,
INC.**   (313) 996-1580
                                                            TELEX: 9102502461
                                                            FAX: (313) 996-4672
MENU PUBLISHER NUMBER 60587
P.O. BOX 4250
ANN ARBOR, MI 48106 USA

**PERSONAL COMPUTER PERIPHERALS
CORP.**   (813) 884-3092
                                                            FAX: (813) 886-052
MENU PUBLISHER NUMBER 60612
4710 EISENHOWER BLVD.
BLDG. A
TAMPA, FL 33634 USA

PERSONAL SOFTWARE, INC.   (804) 766-2625
MENU PUBLISHER NUMBER 05440
22 NATALIE DR.
HAMPTON, VA 23666 USA

PERSONAL TRAINING SYSTEMS   (408) 559-8635
MENU PUBLISHER NUMBER 94817   *FAX:* (408) 977-1166
P.O. BOX 54240
SAN JOSE, CA 95124 USA

PHOENIX SPECIALITIES, INC.   (408) 733-9625
MENU PUBLISHER NUMBER 61012
2981 CORVIN DR.
SANTA CLARA, CA 95051 USA

PLEASANT GRAPHIC WARE   (503) 345-5796
MENU PUBLISHER NUMBER 61360
P.O. BOX 506
PLEASANT HILL, OR 97455 USA

PMC TELESYSTEMS   (604) 925-3787
MENU PUBLISHER NUMBER 61403
P.O. BOX 5127
VANCOUVER, BC V6B 4A9 CANADA

POLARWARE PENGUIN SOFTWARE   (800) 323-0884
MENU PUBLISHER NUMBER 60425   *TELEX:* 5106009287
1055 PARAMOUNT PKWY.   *FAX:* (312) 232-0711
SUITE A
BATAVIA, IL 60510 USA

POSEIDON, INC.   (312) 382-7272
MENU PUBLISHER NUMBER 61619
200 W. STATION ST.
BARRINGTON, IL 60010 USA

POSTCRAFT INT'L., INC.   (805) 257-1797
MENU PUBLISHER NUMBER 81203   *FAX:* (805) 257-1759
27811 AVE.
HOPKINS #6
VALENCIA, CA 91355 USA

POWER UP SOFTWARE CORP.   (415) 345-5900
MENU PUBLISHER NUMBER 61687   *FAX:* (415) 349-1356
2929 CAMPUS DR., SUITE 400
P.O. BOX 7600
SAN MATEO, CA 94403 USA

**PRACTICAL COMPUTER APPLICATIONS,
INC.**   (612) 427-4789
MENU PUBLISHER NUMBER 59081
1305 JEFFERSON HWY.
CHAMPLIN, MN 55316 USA

PRECISION COMPUTER SYSTEMS   (602) 779-5341
MENU PUBLISHER NUMBER 61720
575 W. RIORDAN RD.
FLAGSTAFF, AZ 86001 USA

PREFERRED PUBLISHERS, INC.   (800) 446-6393
MENU PUBLISHER NUMBER 61825   *FAX:* (901) 683-4983
5100 POPLAR AVE.
SUITE 617
MEMPHIS, TN 38137 USA

PRIMERA SOFTWARE (415) 525-3000
MENU PUBLISHER NUMBER 62018
650 CRAGMONT AVE.
BERKELEYON, CA 94708 USA

PRO PLUS SOFTWARE (602) 461-3296
MENU PUBLISHER NUMBER 12181 *FAX:* (602) 834-0461
2150 E. BROWN RD.
MESA, AZ 85203 USA

PROBABILTY DISTRIBUTION (512) 837-4689
MENU PUBLISHER NUMBER 65993
P.O. BOX 27276
AUSTIN, TX 787551276 USA

PRODUCTS DIVERSIFIED, INC. (713) 771-8357
MENU PUBLISHER NUMBER 62334 *FAX:* (713) 981-6283
9720 BEECHNUT
SUITE 406
HOUSTON, TX 77036 USA

PROFESSIONAL AUTOMATION RESOURCES (206) 694-1539
MENU PUBLISHER NUMBER 59723
P.O. BOX 1309
VANCOUVER, WA 98666 USA

PROFESSIONAL HANDICAPPING SYSTEMS (208) 342-6939
MENU PUBLISHER NUMBER 62912
1940 W. STATE ST.
BOISE, ID 83702 USA

PROFESSOR CORP. (305) 427-5090
MENU PUBLISHER NUMBER 62925
3411 N.W. 21ST ST.
COCONUT CREEK, FL 33066 USA

PROGRAMMING LOGIC SYSTEMS, INC. (203) 877-7988
MENU PUBLISHER NUMBER 63173
31 CRESCENT DR.
MILFORD, CT 06460 USA

PROGRESSIVE PERIPHERALS AND SOFTWARE (303) 825-4144
MENU PUBLISHER NUMBER 63225 *TELEX:* 888837
464 KALAMATH ST. *FAX:* (303) 893-6938
DENVER, CO 80204 USA

PROLOGIA LUMINY 91-26-8636
MENU PUBLISHER NUMBER 63268 *TELEX:* PROLOG 402094F
CASE 919
13288 MARSEILLE CEDEX 09
MARSEILLE 13005 FRANCE

PROMETHEUS PRODUCTS, INC. (503) 624-0571
MENU PUBLISHER NUMBER 63273 *FAX:* (503) 624-0843
7225 S.W. BONITA RD.
TIGARD, OR 97223 USA

PROVUE DEVELOPMENT CORP. (714) 892-8199
MENU PUBLISHER NUMBER 63531
15180 TRANSISTOR LANE
HUNTINGTON BEACH, CA 92649
USA

PSION, INC. (203) 274-7521
MENU PUBLISHER NUMBER 63681
32O SYLVAN LAKE RD.
WATERTOWN, CT 06779 USA

PSRC SOFTWARE (419) 372-2497
MENU PUBLISHER NUMBER 63684
BOWLING GREEN STATE UNIVERSITY
BOWLING GREEN, OH 43403 USA

PTERODACTYL SOFTWARE (415) 388-4827
MENU PUBLISHER NUMBER 63737
905 W. CALIFORNIA ST.
MILL VALLEY, CA 94941 USA

PUBLISHING INT'L. (408) 738-4311
MENU PUBLISHER NUMBER 63743 *FAX:* (408) 773-1791
333 W. EL CAMINO REAL
SUITE 222
SUNNYVALE, CA 94087 USA

PUMA SOFTWARE, INC. (505) 265-5270
MENU PUBLISHER NUMBER 63768
P.O. BOX 35373
ALBUQUERQUE, NM 87176 USA

Q

QUADMATION, INC. (408) 985-8984
MENU PUBLISHER NUMBER 63981
1016 EL CAMINO REAL
SUITE 160
SUNNYVALE, CA 94087 USA

QUARK, INC. (415) 967-6796
MENU PUBLISHER NUMBER 64285 *FAX:* (415) 967-0424
1983 LANDINGS DR.
MOUNTAIN VIEW, CA 94043 USA

QUEUE (203) 335-0908
MENU PUBLISHER NUMBER 64387
562 BOSTON AVE.
BRIDGEPORT, CT 066101705 USA

QUEUE 2 (203) 335-0908
MENU PUBLISHER NUMBER 64393
562 BOSTON AVE.
BRIDGEPORT, CT 066101705 USA

QUINSEPT, INC. (617) 641-2930
MENU PUBLISHER NUMBER 64475
P.O. BOX 216
LEXINGTON, MA 02173 USA

R

RACAL VADIC (408) 432-8008
MENU PUBLISHER NUMBER 64725
1525 MCCARTHY BLVD.
MILPITAS, CA 95035 USA

RAECREATIONS SOFTWARE (317) 823-1164
MENU PUBLISHER NUMBER 64887
7371 PEBBLEBROOKE W. DR.
INDIANAPOLIS, IN 462368938 USA

RAIMA CORP. (206) 828-4636
MENU PUBLISHER NUMBER 77831 *TELEX:* 6503018237 MCI UW
3055 112TH AVE., N.E. *FAX:* (206) 747-1991
BELLEVUE, WA 98004 USA

RAINBIRD, DIV. OF MEDIAGENIC (415) 322-0412
MENU PUBLISHER NUMBER 91828 *FAX:* (415) 322-0260
3885 BOHANNON DR.
MENLO PARK, CA 94025 USA

RCO COMPUTER SERVICES, INC. (616) 956-9474
MENU PUBLISHER NUMBER 64606
2750 BIRCHCREST S.E.
GRAND RAPIDS, MI 49506 USA

REALDATA, INC.   (203) 255-2732
MENU PUBLISHER NUMBER 65462   *FAX:* (203) 852-9083
78 N. MAIN ST.
S. NORWALK, CT 06854 USA

REALITY TECHNOLOGIES   (215) 387-6055
MENU PUBLISHER NUMBER 65487
3624 MARKET ST.
PHILADELPHIA, PA 19104 USA

REAS NABLE SOFTWARE   (208) 529-0378
MENU PUBLISHER NUMBER 65634
779 ELEVENTH ST.
IDAHO FALLS, ID 83404 USA

REASON HOUSE   (301) 321-7270
MENU PUBLISHER NUMBER 65635
204 E. JOPPA RD.
PENTHOUSE SUITE 10
TOWSON, MD 21204 USA

REBUS DEVELOPMENT   (408) 727-0110
MENU PUBLISHER NUMBER 76600   *TELEX:* 4990967
2330 B WALSH AVE.   *FAX:* (408) 263-3925
SANTA CLARA, CA 95051 USA

REMOTE CONTROL, INC.   (619) 481-8577
MENU PUBLISHER NUMBER 95416   *FAX:* (619) 481-0311
514 VIA DE LA VALLE
SUITE 306
SOLANA BEACH, CA 92075 USA

RESONATE   (415) 323-5022
MENU PUBLISHER NUMBER 37193   *FAX:* (415) 323-1827
P.O. BOX 996
MENLO PARK, CA 94026 USA

RESTAURANTCOMP   (415) 924-6300
MENU PUBLISHER NUMBER 66181
5 ECHO PL.
LARKSPUR, CA 94939 USA

RH COMMUNICATIONS, INC.   (619) 480-5641
MENU PUBLISHER NUMBER 66287
P.O. BOX 271177
ESCONDIDO, CA 92027 USA

RIGHT ON PROGRAMS   (516) 424-7777
MENU PUBLISHER NUMBER 66450   *FAX:* (516) 424-7207
755 NEW YORK AVE.
SUITE 210
HUNTINGTON, NY 11743 USA

RIGHT TRACK SOFTWARE, INC.   (415) 652-3320
MENU PUBLISHER NUMBER 66475
5550 LAWTON AVE.
OAKLAND, CA 94618 USA

ROCKWARE, INC.   (303) 423-6171
MENU PUBLISHER NUMBER 66643
4251 KIPLING ST.
SUITE 595
WHEAT RIDGE, CO 80033 USA

RUBICON PUBLISHING   (512) 448-4133
MENU PUBLISHER NUMBER 95463
2111 DICKSON DR.
SUITE 30
AUSTIN, TX 78704 USA

S

S & J ENTERPRISES   (319) 332-4166
MENU PUBLISHER NUMBER 67356
P.O. BOX 1134
BETTENDORF, IA 527221134 USA

SAGE PRODUCTIONS, INC.   (619) 455-7513
MENU PUBLISHER NUMBER 63857
5677 OBERLIN DR.
SUITE 100
SAN DIEGO, CA 92121 USA

SATORI SOFTWARE   (206) 443-0765
MENU PUBLISHER NUMBER 68024   *FAX:* (206) 728-4411
2815 SECOND AVE.
SUITE 560
SEATTLE, WA 98121 USA

SBT CORP.   (415) 331-9900
MENU PUBLISHER NUMBER 68057   *TELEX:* 9102404708
ONE HARBOR DR. #300   *FAX:* (415) 331-1951
SAUSALITO, CA 94965 USA

SDG DECISION SYSTEMS   (800) 852-1236
MENU PUBLISHER NUMBER 76475   *FAX:* (415) 854-6718
2440 SAND HILL RD.
MENLO PARK, CA 940256900 USA

SELECT MICRO SYSTEMS, INC.   (914) 245-4670
MENU PUBLISHER NUMBER 69106
PROFESSIONAL BLDG.
SUITE 211, 40 TRIANGLE CTR.
YORKTOWN HEIGHTS, NY 10598
USA

SENSIBLE SOFTWARE, INC.   (313) 528-1950
MENU PUBLISHER NUMBER 69200
335 E. BIG BEAVER
SUITE 207
TROY, MI 48083 USA

SEXTANT CORP.   (800) 262-6665
MENU PUBLISHER NUMBER 42575
3516 27 PKWY.
SARASOTA, FL 34235 USA

SHAHERAZAM   (414) 442-7503
MENU PUBLISHER NUMBER 69425
P O BOX 26731
MILWAUKEE, WI 53210 USA

SHANA CORP.   (403) 463-3330
MENU PUBLISHER NUMBER 69475   *FAX:* (403) 428-5376
#105, 9650-20 AVE.
EDMONTON, ALBERTA T6N 1G1
CANADA

SHEEHAN ASSOCIATES   (805) 985-5318
MENU PUBLISHER NUMBER 95724
3509 OCEAN DR.
OXNARD, CA 93035 USA

SHOPKEEPER SOFTWARE   (904) 222-8808
MENU PUBLISHER NUMBER 69805
630 E. CALL ST.
P.O. BOX 38160
TALLAHASSEE, FL 323158160 USA

SIERRA ON-LINE, INC.   (209) 683-6858
MENU PUBLISHER NUMBER 69925   *TELEX:* 754727
P.O. BOX 485
COARSEGOLD, CA 93614 USA

SIGNAL COMPUTER CONSULTANTS   (412) 655-7727
MENU PUBLISHER NUMBER 70125   *FAX:* (412) 655-1893
P.O. BOX 18222
PITTSBURGH, PA 15236 USA

SILENTPARTNER   (215) 829-0911
MENU PUBLISHER NUMBER 07841
32 N. THIRD ST.
PHILADELPHIA, PA 19106 USA

SILICON BEACH SOFTWARE (619) 695-6956
MENU PUBLISHER NUMBER 70237
9770 CARROLL CENTER RD. #J
P.O. BOX 261430
SAN DIEGO, CA 92126 USA

SIMON AND SCHUSTER ELECTRONIC (212) 373-8880
PUBLISHING GROUP
MENU PUBLISHER NUMBER 70387
ONE GULF AND WESTERN PLAZA
NEW YORK, NY 10023 USA

SIMPLICITY DENTAL SOFTWARE SYS- (215) 646-3382
TEMS, INC.
MENU PUBLISHER NUMBER 70438
9 S. RIDGE AVE.
AMBLER, PA 19002 USA

SIR-TECH SOFTWARE, INC. (315) 393-6633
MENU PUBLISHER NUMBER 70750 FAX: (315) 393-1525
CHARLESTON/OGDENSBURG MALL
P.O. BOX 245
OGDENSBURG, NY 13669 USA

SMALL BUSINESS COMPUTER (307) 362-9325
CONSULTING
MENU PUBLISHER NUMBER 71037
613 WALNUT
ROCK SPRINGS, WY 82901 USA

SMALL BUSINESS COMPUTERS OF NEW (603) 673-0228
ENGLAND
MENU PUBLISHER NUMBER 71101
P.O. BOX 397
4 LIMBO LANE
AMHERST, NH 03031 USA

SMART COMMUNICATIONS, INC. (212) 486-1894
MENU PUBLISHER NUMBER 71412 TELEX: 220883 TAUR
825 THIRD AVE., 30TH FLOOR FAX: (212) 752-6441
P.O. BOX 963
NEW YORK, NY 10022 USA

SMETHERSBARNES (800) 237-3611
MENU PUBLISHER NUMBER 71463
P.O. BOX 639
PORTLAND, OR 97207 USA

SMITH MICRO SOFTWARE (714) 964-0412
MENU PUBLISHER NUMBER 71606
P.O. BOX 7137
HUNTINGTON BEACH, CA 92615
USA

SMK (312) 947-9157
MENU PUBLISHER NUMBER 95739
5760 S. BLACKSTONE
CHICAGO, IL 60637 USA

SOF-WARE TOOLS (208) 343-1437
MENU PUBLISHER NUMBER 71803 FAX: (208) 336-2536
P.O. BOX 8751
BOISE, ID 83707 USA

SOFT HORIZON (817) 699-0493
MENU PUBLISHER NUMBER 71808
P.O. BOX 2115
HARKER HEIGHTS, TX 76543 USA

SOFT-BYTE COMPUTER PROGRAMS (513) 278-1110
MENU PUBLISHER NUMBER 95753
P.O. BOX 556
FOREST PARK
DAYTON, OH 45405 USA

SOFTFLAIR, INC. (414) 797-4490
MENU PUBLISHER NUMBER 95747
8753 PARK VIEW
MILWAUKEE, WI 53226 USA

SOFTFOCUS (416) 825-0903
MENU PUBLISHER NUMBER 95759 FAX: (416) 825-1025
1343 STANBURY DR.
OAKVILLE, ONTARIO L6L 2J5
CANADA

SOFTGUARD SYSTEMS, INC. (408) 773-9680
MENU PUBLISHER NUMBER 95751 TELEX: 5101006989
710 LAKEWAY FAX: (408) 773-1405
SUITE 200
SUNNYVILLE, CA 94086 USA

SOFTOUCH SOFTWARE, INC. (503) 241-1841
MENU PUBLISHER NUMBER 72162
2066 N.W. IRVING
SUITE 2
PORTLAND, OR 97209 USA

SOFTPLUS (301) 540-6552
MENU PUBLISHER NUMBER 72171
14500 CHRISMAN HILL DR.
BOIDS, MD 20841 USA

SOFTSTREAM INT'L., INC. (609) 866-1187
MENU PUBLISHER NUMBER 72232 FAX: (609) 866-7517
19 WHITE CHAPEL DR.
MT. LAUREL, NJ 08054 USA

SOFTSTYLE, INC. (800) 367-5600
MENU PUBLISHER NUMBER 72235 TELEX: 353338(SOFSTYLEUD)
6600 KALANIANAOLE HWY. FAX: (808) 395-8972
SUITE 200
HONOLULU, HI 96825 USA

SOFTSYNC, INC. (212) 685-2080
MENU PUBLISHER NUMBER 72240 FAX: (212) 685-6322
162 MADISON AVE.
NEW YORK, NY 10016 USA

SOFTVIEW, INC. (805) 388-2626
MENU PUBLISHER NUMBER 74106
4820 ADHOR LANE
SUITE F
CAMARILLO, CA 93010 USA

SOFTWARE APPLE CATIONS (208) 345-0547
MENU PUBLISHER NUMBER 72325
1934 RIDGE POINT WAY
BOISE, ID 83712 USA

SOFTWARE BRIDGE, INC. (801) 562-2625
MENU PUBLISHER NUMBER 72468
6925 UNION PARK CTR.
SUITE 145
MIDVALE, UT 84047 USA

SOFTWARE CONSTRUCTORS, INC. (615) 385-1612
MENU PUBLISHER NUMBER 72556
2416 HILLSBORO RD.
NASHVILLE, TN 37212 USA

SOFTWARE DEVELOPMENT GROUP (504) 343-8437
MENU PUBLISHER NUMBER 72681
1890 KERR GULCH
EVERGREEN, CO 80439 USA

SOFTWARE DISCOVERIES, INC. (203) 872-1024
MENU PUBLISHER NUMBER 72775 FAX: (203) 247-1681
137 KRAWSKI DR.
SOUTH WINDSOR, CT 06074 USA

SOFTWARE EXCHANGE (313) 626-7208
MENU PUBLISHER NUMBER 72868
P.O. BOX 5382
W. BLOOMFIELD, MI 48033 USA

SOFTWARE FOR RECOGNITION
TECHNOLOGIES
MENU PUBLISHER NUMBER 72943
55 ACADEMY DR.
ROCHESTER, NY 14623 USA
(716) 334-4207

SOFTWARE INVESTMENT PLUS, INC.
MENU PUBLISHER NUMBER 73106
502 OPERA HOUSE LANE
ODESSA, MO 64076 USA
(816) 633-8529

SOFTWARE VENTURES CORP.
MENU PUBLISHER NUMBER 73963
2907 CLAREMONT AVE.
SUITE 220
BERKELEY, CA 94705 USA
(415) 644-3232
FAX: (415) 848-0885

SOFTWORKS LTD.
MENU PUBLISHER NUMBER 74175
607 W. WELLINGTON
CHICAGO, IL 60657 USA
(312) 975-4030
FAX: (312) 975-9849

SOFTWORKS, INC. (CT)
MENU PUBLISHER NUMBER 74165
P.O. BOX 2285
HUNTINGTON, CT 06484 USA
(203) 926-1116

SOLAR SYSTEMS SOFTWARE
MENU PUBLISHER NUMBER 74212
8105 SHELTER CREEK
SAN BRUNO, CA 94066 USA
(415) 952-2375

SOLARSOFT
MENU PUBLISHER NUMBER 74262
1406 BURLINGAME
SUITE 31
BURLINGAME, CA 94010 USA
(415) 342-3338

SOLUTIONS INT'L.
MENU PUBLISHER NUMBER 74437
30 COMMERCE ST.
WILLISTON, VT 05495 USA
(802) 658-5506
FAX: (802) 865-9961

SONUS
MENU PUBLISHER NUMBER 74679
21430 STRATHERN
SUITE H
CANOGA PARK, CA 91304 USA
(818) 702-0992
FAX: (818) 704-0638

SOURCEVIEW SOFTWARE INT'L.
MENU PUBLISHER NUMBER 70675
P.O. BOX 578
CONCORD, CA 945220578 USA
(415) 686-VIEW
FAX: (415) 686-8436

SOUTHWORTH MUSIC SYSTEMS
MENU PUBLISHER NUMBER 75101
91 ANN LEE RD.
HARVARD, MA 01451 USA
(508) 772-9471
FAX: (508) 772-4603

SPECIALTY SOFTWARE
MENU PUBLISHER NUMBER 95752
P.O. BOX 5494
EVANSVILLE, IN 47715 USA
(217) 234-3531

SPECTRUM COMPUTING, INC.
MENU PUBLISHER NUMBER 75162
P.O. BOX 141097
CORAL GABLES, FL 33114 USA
(305) 665-0404

SPECTRUM HOLOBYTE, DIV. OF
SPHERE, INC.
MENU PUBLISHER NUMBER 75175
2061 CHALLENGER DR.
ALAMEDA, CA 94501 USA
(415) 522-3584
TELEX: 517628
FAX: (415) 522-3587

SPECTRUM SOFTWARE
MENU PUBLISHER NUMBER 75200
1021 S. WOLFE RD.
SUITE 130
SUNNYVALE, CA 94086 USA
(408) 738-4387
TELEX: 3716987
FAXTEL SNJ
FAX: (408) 738-470

SPENCER ORGANIZATION, INC.
MENU PUBLISHER NUMBER 75215
366 KINDERKAMAK RD.
P.O. BOX 248
WESTWOOD, NJ 07675 USA
(201) 666-6011
FAX: (201) 266-5626

SPINNAKER SOFTWARE
MENU PUBLISHER NUMBER 75300
ONE KENDALL SQ.
CAMBRIDGE, MA 02139 USA
(617) 494-1200

SPRINGBOARD SOFTWARE, INC.
MENU PUBLISHER NUMBER 75309
7808 CREEKRIDGE CIR.
MINNEAPOLIS, MN 55435 USA
(612) 944-3915
FAX: (612) 944-1832

STACKWORKS, INC.
MENU PUBLISHER NUMBER 75627
P.O. BOX 426
URBANA, IL 61801 USA
(217) 328-5257

STAR MICRONICS AMERICA, INC.
MENU PUBLISHER NUMBER 75831
200 PARK AVE.
SUITE 3510
NEW YORK, NY 10133 USA
(212) 986-6770

STAR SOFTWARE, INC.
MENU PUBLISHER NUMBER 75856
229 LIVE OAKS BLVD.
CASSELBERRY, FL 32707 USA
(407) 831-8050

STARCOM MICROSYSTEMS
MENU PUBLISHER NUMBER 75815
WINDSOR PARK E.
25 W. 1480 N.
OREM, UT 84057 USA
(801) 225-1480

STATSOFT, INC.
MENU PUBLISHER NUMBER 75992
2325 E. 13TH ST.
TULSA, OK 74104 USA
(918) 583-4149
FAX: (918) 583-4376

STAX, INC.
MENU PUBLISHER NUMBER 75998
8008 SHOAL CREEK BLVD.
AUSTIN, TX 78758 USA
(512) 467-4550
APPLELINK: X0381

STEVENS CREEK SOFTWARE
MENU PUBLISHER NUMBER 76253
21346 RUMFORD DR.
CUPERTINO, CA 95014 USA
(408) 725-0424

STONE EDGE TECHNOLOGIES, INC.
MENU PUBLISHER NUMBER 76400
P.O. BOX 200
MAPLE GLEN, PA 19002 USA
(215) 641-1825

STORM KING TECHNOLOGY
MENU PUBLISHER NUMBER 76406
37 DRAGON DR.
LEAVENWORTH, KS 66027 USA
(800) 331-4460

STRATEGIC LOCATIONS PLANNING
MENU PUBLISHER NUMBER 76481
4030 MOORPARK AVE.
SUITE 123
SAN JOSE, CA 95117 USA
(408) 985-7400

STRATEGIC PLANNING SYSTEMS (818) 784-6863
MENU PUBLISHER NUMBER 76493
15233 VENTURA BLVD.
SUITE 708
SHERMAN OAKS, CA 91403 USA

STRATEGIC SIMULATIONS, INC. (415) 964-1353
MENU PUBLISHER NUMBER 76500 *TELEX:* 989631
1046 N. RENGSTORFF AVE. *FAX:* (415) 961-6716
MOUNTAIN VIEW, CA 940431716
USA

STRATEGIC STUDIES GROUP (415) 932-3019
MENU PUBLISHER NUMBER 76525
1747 ORLEANS CT.
WALNUT CREEK, CA 94598 USA

STRAWBERRY TREE, INC. (408) 736-8800
MENU PUBLISHER NUMBER 76550 *TELEX:* 650 317-2834 MCI
160 S. WOLFE RD. *FAX:* (408) 736-1041
SUNNYVALE, CA 94086 USA

STRIDER SOFTWARE (715) 324-5487
MENU PUBLISHER NUMBER 76569
BEECHER LAKE RD.
PEMBINE, WI 54156 USA

STSC, INC. (301) 984-5488
MENU PUBLISHER NUMBER 76925 *TELEX:* (301) 984-5000
2115 E. JEFFERSON ST.
ROCKVILLE, MD 20852 USA

SUBLOGIC CORP. (800) 637-4983
MENU PUBLISHER NUMBER 76950 *TELEX:* 206995
501 KENYON RD. *FAX:* (217) 352-1472
CHAMPAIGN, IL 61820 USA

SULCUS COMPUTER CORP. (412) 836-2000
MENU PUBLISHER NUMBER 77006
SULCUS TOWER
41 N. MAIN ST.
GREENSBURG, PA 15601 USA

SUN REMARKETING (800) 821-3221
MENU PUBLISHER NUMBER 77034 *FAX:* (801) 563-3226
P.O. BOX 4059
LOGAN, UT 84321 USA

SUNCOM, INC. (312) 459-8000
MENU PUBLISHER NUMBER 95763 *TELEX:* 756588
290 PALATINE RD.
WHEELING, IL 60090 USA

SUNRISE SOFTWARE (415) 595-5255
MENU PUBLISHER NUMBER 77043
240 TWIN DOLPHIN DR.
SUITE E
REDWOOD CITY, CA 94065 USA

SUPERMAC SOFTWARE (408) 773-4457
MENU PUBLISHER NUMBER 77125
485 POTRERO AVE.
SUNNYVALE, CA 94086 USA

SURVIVOR SOFTWARE LTD. (213) 410-9527
MENU PUBLISHER NUMBER 77227 *FAX:* (213) 338-1406
11222 LA CIENEGA BLVD.
SUITE 450
INGLEWOOD, CA 90304 USA

SYMANTEC (408) 253-9600
MENU PUBLISHER NUMBER 77413 *TELEX:* 9103808778
10201 TORRE AVE. *FAX:* (408) 253-4092
CUPERTINO, CA 95014 USA

SYMMETRY CORP. (800) 624-2485
MENU PUBLISHER NUMBER 77437 *TELEX:* 6502614452
761 E. UNIVERSITY DR. *FAX:* (602) 890-2541
#C
MESA, AZ 85203 USA

SYNAPSE SOFTWARE (919) 895-6302
MENU PUBLISHER NUMBER 77487
110 MEDICAL CIRCLE DR.
ROCKINGHAM, NC 28379 USA

SYNEX (800) 44-SYNEX
MENU PUBLISHER NUMBER 77712
692 10TH ST.
BROOKLYN, NY 11215 USA

SYSCOM, INC. (516) 481-8201
MENU PUBLISHER NUMBER 77822 *FAX:* (516) 565-9042
217 HILTON AVE.
SUITE 217
HEMPSTEAD, NY 11550 USA

SYSTAT, INC. (312) 864-5670
MENU PUBLISHER NUMBER 77843
1800 SHERMAN AVE.
EVANSTON, IL 60201 USA

SYSTEC COMPUTER SERVICES (408) 723-2264
MENU PUBLISHER NUMBER 95775
P.O. BOX 7533
SAN JOSE, CA 951507533 USA

SYSTEMS SERVICES ENGINEERING (513) 253-3291
MENU PUBLISHER NUMBER 78968
P.O. BOX 32008
DAYTON, OH 45432 USA

T

T & M SYSTEMS, INC. (515) 493-2415
MENU PUBLISHER NUMBER 79401
3081 CANFIELD AVE.
RHODES, IA 50234 USA

T/MAKER CO. (415) 962-0195
MENU PUBLISHER NUMBER 79465 *TELEX:* 821 386 T MAKER
1390 VILLA ST. *FAX:* (415) 962-0201
MOUNTAIN VIEW, CA 94041 USA

TANGENT TECHNOLOGIES (404) 662-0366
MENU PUBLISHER NUMBER 79646
5720 PEACHTREE PKWY.
SUITE 100
NORCROSS, GA 30092 USA

TAXCALC SOFTWARE, INC. (817) 738-3122
MENU PUBLISHER NUMBER 79843
4210 W. VICKERY BLVD.
FORT WORTH, TX 76107 USA

TDI SOFTWARE (214) 340-4942
MENU PUBLISHER NUMBER 79965 *TELEX:* 888442
10355 BROCKWOOD RD.
DALLAS, TX 75238 USA

TEACH YOURSELF BY COMPUTER SOF- (716) 381-5450
TWARE, INC.
MENU PUBLISHER NUMBER 82981
349 W. COMMERCIAL ST.
SUITE 1000
E. ROCHESTER, NY 14445 USA

TECH 2000 SOFTWARE, INC. (407) 727-8815
MENU PUBLISHER NUMBER 80212
530 FRANKLYN AVE.
INDIALANTIC, FL 32903 USA

TECHALLIANCE (800) 245-8999
MENU PUBLISHER NUMBER 80216
290 S.W. 43RD ST.
RENTON, WA 98055 USA

TECHNOLOGY CONCEPTS (508) 443-7311
MENU PUBLISHER NUMBER 80569 FAX: (508) 443-7310
A BELL ATLANTIC CO.
40 TALL PINE DR.
SUDBURY, MA 01776 USA

TECHNOLOGY TRAINING ASSOCIATES (617) 497-5030
MENU PUBLISHER NUMBER 80612
50 WESTERN AVE.
CAMBRIDGE, MA 02139 USA

TECHWARE, INC. (KS) (913) 782-1249
MENU PUBLISHER NUMBER 04778
806 FOREST
OLATHE, KS 66061 USA

TELEROBOTICS INT'L., INC. (615) 690-5600
MENU PUBLISHER NUMBER 80981
8410 OAK RIDGE HWY.
KNOXVILLE, TN 37931 USA

TELETYPESETTING CO. (617) 266-6637
MENU PUBLISHER NUMBER 81055 FAX: (617) 266-3062
474 COMMONWEALTH AVE.
BOSTON, MA 02215 USA

TERRAPIN, INC. (617) 322-4800
MENU PUBLISHER NUMBER 81150
376 WASHINGTON ST.
MALDEN, MA 02148 USA

TESSERACT DISTRIBUTING, INC. (416) 641-0768
MENU PUBLISHER NUMBER 81204 FAX: (416) 641-1536
P.O. BOX 937
ST. CATHERINES, ONTARIO L2R 6Z4
CANADA

TESSERACT EDUCATIONAL SYSTEMS (713) 495-2292
MENU PUBLISHER NUMBER 81206
4010-I HWY. 6 S.
SUITE 187
HOUSTON, TX 77082 USA

TEXTCO (603) 643-1471
MENU PUBLISHER NUMBER 81277
27 GILSON RD.
R.R. 2, BOX 180
WEST LEBANON, NH 03784 USA

THINK EDUCATIONAL SOFTWARE (315) 265-5636
MENU PUBLISHER NUMBER 81375 TELEX: 797298
16 MARKET ST.
P.O. BOX 5077
POTSDAM, NY 13676 USA

THREE-SIXTY PACIFIC, INC. (408) 879-9144
MENU PUBLISHER NUMBER 81693 FAX: (408) 879-9739
2105 S. BASCOM AVE.
SUITE 290
CAMPBELL, CA 95008 USA

THUNDERWARE, INC. (415) 254-6581
MENU PUBLISHER NUMBER 81750 FAX: (415) 254-3047
21 ORINDA WAY
ORINDA, CA 94563 USA

TIME CYCLES RESEARCH (203) 444-6641
MENU PUBLISHER NUMBER 81875
27 DIMMOCK RD.
WATERFORD, CT 06385 USA

TIMELINE LTD. (313) 483-3939
MENU PUBLISHER NUMBER 81981
P.O. BOX 60
YPSILANTI, MI 48197 USA

TIMEWORKS, INC. (800) 535-9497
MENU PUBLISHER NUMBER 82000 TELEX: 754543 TIME UD
444 LAKE COOK RD. FAX: (312) 948-7626
DEERFIELD, IL 60015 USA

TISCHREDE SOFTWARE (508) 994-7907
MENU PUBLISHER NUMBER 82132
P.O. BOX 9594
NORTH DARTMOUTH, MA 02747
USA

TML SYSTEMS, INC. (904) 636-8592
MENU PUBLISHER NUMBER 82182
4241 BAYMEADOWS RD.
SUITE 23
JACKSONVILLE, FL 32217 USA

TOOL MASTERS LTD./DIV OF INT'L. TE- (703) 478-9808
LESYSTEMS CORP. FAX: (703) 478-9808
MENU PUBLISHER NUMBER 82278
600 HERNDON PKWY.
HERNDON, VA 22070 USA

TOPS (415) 769-9669
MENU PUBLISHER NUMBER 11962 FAX: (415) 769-8772
950 MARINA VILLAGE PKWY.
ALAMEDA, CA 94501 USA

TOUCHSTONE SOFTWARE CORP. (213) 598-7746
MENU PUBLISHER NUMBER 82400 TELEX: 4995480
909 ELECTRIC AVE. FAX: (213) 430-3829
SEAL BEACH, CA 90740 USA

TPS ELECTRONICS (415) 856-6833
MENU PUBLISHER NUMBER 82421 APPLELINK: D0206
4047 TRANSPORT ST. FAX: (415) 856-3843
PALO ALTO, CA 94303 USA

TRAVELING SOFTWARE, INC. (206) 483-8088
MENU PUBLISHER NUMBER 82540 TELEX: 294898 TSI UR
18702 NORTHCREEK PKWY. FAX: (206) 487-1284
BOTHELL, WA 98011 USA

TRI DATA (408) 746-2900
MENU PUBLISHER NUMBER 82556 TELEX: 172282
1450 KIFER RD. FAX: (408) 746-2074
SUNNYVALE, CA 94086 USA

TRIO SYSTEMS (213) 394-0796
MENU PUBLISHER NUMBER 82712
2210 WILSHIRE BLVD.
SUITE 289
SANTA MONICA, CA 90403 USA

TRIPLE-D SOFTWARE (801) 547-9328
MENU PUBLISHER NUMBER 82737
823 NORTH 1340 EAST
LAYTON, UT 84041 USA

TRONSOFT, INC. (805) 564-3386
MENU PUBLISHER NUMBER 82788
133 W. DE LA GUERRA ST.
SANTA BARBARA, CA 93101 USA

TRUE BASIC, INC. (800) TR BASIC
MENU PUBLISHER NUMBER 82789 FAX: (603) 298-7015
12 COMMERCE AVE.
WEST LEBANON, NH 03784 USA

TURTLE CREEK SOFTWARE (607) 589-6858
MENU PUBLISHER NUMBER 82925
651 HALSEY VALLEY RD.
SPENCER, NY 14883 USA

TYMLABS CORP.
MENU PUBLISHER NUMBER 83125
811 BARTON SPRINGS RD.
AUSTIN, TX 78704 USA
(512) 478-0611
TELEX: 755820
FAX: (512) 479-0735

U

UNGERMANN-BASS
MENU PUBLISHER NUMBER 83481
3900 FREEDOM CIR.
SANTA CLARA, CA 950528030 USA
(408) 496-0111

UNICOM SOFTWARE DEVELOPMENT GROUP
MENU PUBLISHER NUMBER 83550
400 RESERVOIR AVE.
PROVIDENCE, RI 02907 USA
(401) 467-5600
FAX: (400) 467-5607

UNICORN SOFTWARE CO.
MENU PUBLISHER NUMBER 83562
2950 E. FLAMINGO RD.
GREENVIEW PARK, SUITE B
LAS VEGAS, NV 89121 USA
(702) 737-8862

UNIVERSITY OF BRITISH COLUMBIA
MENU PUBLISHER NUMBER 83987
DEPT. OF ECONOMICS
VANCOUVER, BC V6T 1Y2 CANADA
(604) 228-5062

UNIVERSITY OF MINNESOTA
MENU PUBLISHER NUMBER 84215
MEDIA DISTRIBUTION
BOX 734, MAYO BLDG.
MINNEAPOLIS, MN 55455 USA
(612) 624-7906

UNLIMITED SOFTWARE
MENU PUBLISHER NUMBER 96343
P.O. BOX 825
ACTON, MA 01720 USA
(617) 264-9739

UTOPIAN SOFTWARE
MENU PUBLISHER NUMBER 84675
P.O. BOX 40028
LONG BEACH, CA 90804 USA
(213) 597-2130

V

VALUE LINE SOFTWARE
MENU PUBLISHER NUMBER 84762
711 THIRD AVE.
NEW YORK, NY 10017 USA
(212) 687-3965

VAMP, INC.
MENU PUBLISHER NUMBER 84771
6753 SELMA AVE.
LOS ANGELES, CA 90028 USA
(213) 466-5533
FAX: (213) 466-8564

VANO ASSOCIATES, INC.
MENU PUBLISHER NUMBER 84878
P.O. BOX 12730
NEW BRIGHTON, MN 55112 USA
(612) 788-9546

VAR ECONOMETRICS, INC.
MENU PUBLISHER NUMBER 84879
P.O. BOX 1818
EVANSTON, IL 602041818 USA
(312) 864-8772

VENTURA EDUCATIONAL SYSTEMS
MENU PUBLISHER NUMBER 84911
3440 BROKENHILL ST.
NEWBURY PARK, CA 91320 USA
(805) 499-1407

VERSACAD CORP.
MENU PUBLISHER NUMBER 79543
2124 MAIN ST.
HUNTINGTON BEACH, CA 92648
USA
(714) 960-7720
TELEX: 5101011 759TWINC
FAX: (714) 960-5826

VIDEX, INC.
MENU PUBLISHER NUMBER 85150
1105 N.E. CIRCLE BLVD.
CORVALLIS, OR 97330 USA
(503) 758-0521
TELEX: 469570
FAX: (503) 752-5285

VIKING TECHNOLOGIES
MENU PUBLISHER NUMBER 85231
174 BELLEVUE AVE.
NEWPORT, RI 02840 USA
(401) 849-4925

VIRGINIA SYSTEMS SOFTWARE
MENU PUBLISHER NUMBER 85284
5509 W. BAY CT.
MIDLOTHIAN, VA 23112 USA
(804) 739-3200

VISATEX CORP.
MENU PUBLISHER NUMBER 85340
1745 DELL AVE.
CAMPBELL, CA 95008 USA
(408) 866-6562
TELEX: 9102507725
FAX: (408) 866-6598

VISUAL INFORMATION, INC.
MENU PUBLISHER NUMBER 85412
16309 DOUBLEGROVE
LA PUENTE, CA 91744 USA
(818) 918-8834

VOYAGER CO.
MENU PUBLISHER NUMBER 96647
1351 PACIFIC COAST HWY.
THIRD FLOOR
SANTA MONICA, CA 90401 USA
(800) 446-2001
FAX: (213) 394-2156

W

WABASH MEDICAL RESOURCES
MENU PUBLISHER NUMBER 81175
6865 PARKDALE PL.
SUITE A
INDIANAPOLIS, IN 46254 USA
(317) 299-7800

WALKER, RICHER & QUINN, INC.
MENU PUBLISHER NUMBER 96905
2825 EASTLAKE AVE. E.
SEATTLE, WA 98102 USA
(206) 324-0350
TELEX: 311743 WRQ
FAX: (206) 322-8151

WATCOM PRODUCTS, INC.
MENU PUBLISHER NUMBER 85718
415 PHILLIP ST.
WATERLOO, ONTARIO N2L 3X2
CANADA
(519) 886-3700
TELEX: 06-955 458
FAX: (519) 747-4971

WESTERN SOFTWARE ASSOCIATES
MENU PUBLISHER NUMBER 86131
110 EL DORADO RD.
WALNUT CREEK, CA 94595 USA
(415) 932-3999

WESTERN UNION CORP.
MENU PUBLISHER NUMBER 86146
ONE LAKE ST.
UPPER SADDLE RIVER, NJ 07458
USA
(800) 527-5184
TELEX: 12452
FAX: (201) 825-3360

WHITE PINE SOFTWARE, INC.
MENU PUBLISHER NUMBER 86315
94 ROUTE 101A
P.O. BOX 1108
AMHERST, NH 03031 USA
(603) 886-9050

WILLIAMS AG PRODUCTS
MENU PUBLISHER NUMBER 86503
9191 TOWNE CENTRE DR.
SUITE 178
SAN DIEGO, CA 92122 USA
(619) 558-9193
FAX: (619) 458-1518

WILLIAMS AND MACIAS
MENU PUBLISHER NUMBER 86506
S. 3707 GODFREY BLVD.
SPOKANE, WA 99204 USA
(509) 458-6312
FAX: (509) 624-7581

WOLFRAM RESEARCH, INC.
MENU PUBLISHER NUMBER 86956
P.O. BOX 6059
CHAMPAIGN, IL 61821 USA
(800) 441-6284

WORDPERFECT CORP.
MENU PUBLISHER NUMBER 68012
1555 N. TECHNOLOGY WAY
OREM, UT 84057 USA
(801) 225-5000
TELEX: 820618
FAX: (801) 222-4477

WORKING COMPUTER
MENU PUBLISHER NUMBER 96949
P.O. BOX 87
SAN LUIS REY, CA 92068 USA
(619) 721-0501

WORKING SOFTWARE, INC.
MENU PUBLISHER NUMBER 92154
BOX 1844
SANTA CRUZ, CA 950611844 USA
(408) 423-5696
FAX: (408) 423-5699

WOS DATA SYSTEMS, INC.
MENU PUBLISHER NUMBER 96946
1321 WAHARUSA DR.
SUITE 2010
LAWRENCE, KS 66044 USA
(913) 843-8101
FAX: (913) 843-2103

WRITE HAND, INC.
MENU PUBLISHER NUMBER 87006
100 ELWORTHY AVE.
LONDON, ONTARIO N6C 2M4
CANADA
(519) 672-9271

WU CORP.
MENU PUBLISHER NUMBER 87029
P.O. BOX 699
AVON, CT 06001 USA
(203) 677-1528
TELEX: 91025 08065

X

X-10 (USA), INC.
MENU PUBLISHER NUMBER 87034
185A LEGRAND AVE.
NORTHVALE, NJ 07467 USA
(800) 526-0027
TELEX: 275593
FAX: (201) 784-9464

XOR CORP.
MENU PUBLISHER NUMBER 87125
7607 BUSH LAKE RD.
MINNEAPOLIS, MN 55435 USA
(800) 635-2425
FAX: (612) 831-0450

Y

YARDI SYSTEMS, INC.
MENU PUBLISHER NUMBER 87225
930 LAGUNA ST.
SANTA BARBARA, CA 931011405
USA
(805) 966-3666

Z

ZEDCOR, INC.
MENU PUBLISHER NUMBER 70625
4500 E. SPEEDWAY BLVD.
SUITE 22
TUCSON, AZ 85712 USA
(602) 795-3996
FAX: (602) 881-1841

ZIHUA
MENU PUBLISHER NUMBER 87412
P.O. BOX 51601
PACIFIC GROVE, CA 93950 USA
(408) 372-0155

ZONE1, INC.
MENU PUBLISHER NUMBER 87459
382 NALLEY DR.
SUITE 101
STONE MOUNTAIN, GA 30087 USA
(404) 381-8659

FOR MORE DETAILED INFORMATION, CALL (412) 746-MENU

OTHER MENU® PUBLICATIONS

Special-Interest Books from MENU® Publishing

ex•plore
Personal interest software for the IBM® PC & Compatibles
for under $100.

ex•plore helps you locate the software package specific to your area
of personal interest — everything from eating right and staying fit to
researching your family tree. ex•plore includes objective, comprehensive information about more than 600 software listings in these
application categories: Astrology and Divination, Cooking and Diet,
Gambling, Genealogy/Family History, Health/Self-Improvement,
Hobbies, Household Management, Miscellaneous Personal, Music,
Sports, and Travel. All packages priced under $100.

$9.95 U.S. ($12.95 Canada)
ISBN: 0-942821-27-0 February 1989

cre•ate
Word processing and graphics software for the IBM® PC &
Compatibles for under $200.

Whether writing and designing is your job or your hobby, **cre•ate**
will help you locate the word processing and graphics packages for
your skill and interest levels. **cre•ate** is the one source you need for
objective information about more than 600 software listings in these
application categories: Fonts/Images, Graphics, Graphics Support,
Word Processing, and Word Processing Support. All packages are
priced under $200.

$9.95 U.S. ($12.95 Canada)
ISBN: 0-942821-26-2 February 1989

learn
Educational software for the IBM® PC & Compatibles for under $50.

Now, using your PC to help your children with their ABCs is easy
— when you find just the right software package in **learn**. Comprehensive and objective, **learn** is a directory of more than 600 software
listings in these application categories: Addition/Subtraction,
Composition/Grammar, Decimals/Fractions/Percents/Ratios, Math
(Basic, General), Multiplication/Division, Reading/Vocabulary, and
Spelling. All packages are priced under $50. Some packages are
suitable for adults.

$9.95 U.S. ($12.95 Canada)
ISBN: 0-942821-25-4 February 1989

play
Entertainment software for the IBM® PC & Compatibles
for under $50.

If you want to have fun with your PC or compatible, take a look at
play. With **play**, you've got a single source for objective, comprehensive information about more than 600 software listings in these
application categories: Adult, Adventure, Arcade/Simulation,
Animation/Drawing/Movie Making, Miscellaneous Entertainment,
Sports, Games, and Strategy. All packages are priced under $50.

$9.95 U.S. ($12.95 Canada)
ISBN: 0-942821-28-9 February 1989

System-specific Software Directories from MENU® Publishing

A MENU® Information Directory for the IBM® PC & Compatibles
You can search the world over — looking for the right piece of
software. Or you can look in **A MENU® Information Directory for
the IBM® PC & Compatibles**. This directory lists more than 15,500
software packages for the PC/XT™, AT™, OS/2™, and compatible
PCs. Each listing includes a description, operating requirements, and
the publisher's name and address.

$29.95 U.S. ($35.95 Canada)
ISBN: 0-942821-11-4 Vol. 5, No. 2, 1989.

A MENU® Information Directory for COMMODORE® Computers
The home companion for owners of COMMODORE® computers. It's
an easy-to-use collection of software information that will fit nicely
next to your AMIGA®, COMMODORE 64®, COMMODORE 128™,
VIC 20®, or PET®. Over 5,000 listings of software especially for
COMMODORE® computers.

$12.95 U.S. ($16.95 Canada)
ISBN: 0-942821-14-9 Vol. 5, No. 2, 1989

A MENU® Information Directory for Apple® II Computers
An Apple® for the teacher. An Apple® for the student. And software
for everyone with an Apple® II — when you consult **A MENU®
Information Directory for Apple® II Computers.** It includes more
than 12,000 listings of software for the Apple® II. IIc. IIe. II+. and
IIGS — in 135 categories.

$19.95 U.S. ($24.95 Canada)
ISBN: 0-942821-12-2 Vol. 5, No. 2, 1989.

A MENU® Information Directory for LANs (Local Area Networks)
Not all software runs on a LAN. And not all LAN software runs on
every type of LAN. But some software comes in versions that will
run on several different LANs. Get all the facts straight — with **A
MENU® Information Directory for LANs (Local Area Networks).**
You'll get detailed product descriptions and cross-listings for over
1500 titles — 4000 listings in all.

$19.95 U.S. ($24.95 Canada)
ISBN: 0-942821-13-0 Vol. 5, No. 2, 1989.